New to This Second Edition

- Complete coverage of OEM Service Release 2 (which includes Service Pack 1) version of Windows 95 throughout (see Quick Reference on inside covers)
- Why, when, and how to install FAT 32 support on hard disks larger than 528MB, along with alerts on possible incompatibilities and pitfalls (Chapter 9)
- Entire chapter, now enhanced with the command-line version of RegEdit, devoted to tweaking the Windows 95 Registry (Chapter 7)
- Rev up the Performance page to attain warp-speed games and multimedia with DirectX, OpenGL and ActiveMovie (Chapter 17)
- Maximize on connectivity with the Universal Serial Bus, NetportExpress, CD-ROM recorders, and Dial-Up Networking with scripting (Chapter 19)
- Improved laptop support: trackball configuration (Chapter 16), power management (Chapter 11), PCMCIA Cardbus, infrared file transfer, and printing (Chapter 18)
- Diagnose hardware and firmware problems with updated utilities: CheckIt 4 (SysTest), and WINCheckIt (Chapter 26)
- Troubleshoot TCP/IP, Windows NT Server, and Novell NetWare connections on the network (Chapter 23 and Chapter 27).
- Review our checklist of the types of Internet service providers available, before you sign up (Appendix B)
- Become a seasoned surfer: Launch Internet Explorer 3.x, understand the nuances of the search engines that bring the world to your cursor (Chapter 21)
- Set up Internet security on your network before you venture further (Chapter 24)
- Frequent the best sites for Windows 95 support on the Internet, and discover in the process the Microsoft presence on the Internet (Appendix A)
- Jump directly to the Internet addresses (URLs) provided throughout the book to find additional information or to download a utility
- Create your own Web pages with scripted ActiveX controls, and deploy them with Personal Web Server (Chapter 22)
- Liven up your communications with voice modems (Chapter 20), animated .GIFs, and NetMeeting (Chapter 21)
- Learn about the various upgraded utility programs, such as Imaging for scanning, (Chapter 2) and scripting for Dial-Up Networking (Chapter 19)

Peter Norton's® Complete Guide to Windows® 95

Second Edition

Peter Norton
and
John Mueller

SAMS PUBLISHING 201 West 103rd Street
Indianapolis Indiana 46290

For Chuck and Ginny—rainy day friends to clear the clouds away.

International Standard Book Number: 0-672-31040-6

Library of Congress Catalog Card Number: 96-71999

2000 99 98 4

Interpretation of the printing code: the rightmost double-digit number is the year of the book's printing; the rightmost single-digit number, the number of the book's printing. For example, a printing code of 97-1 shows that the first printing of the book occurred in 1997.

Composed in Goudy, Helvetica, and MCPdigital by Macmillan Computer Publishing

Printed in the United States of America

Trademarks

All terms mentioned in this book that are known to be trademarks or service marks have been appropriately capitalized. Sams Publishing cannot attest to the accuracy of this information. Use of a term in this book should not be regarded as affecting the validity of any trademark or service mark. Peter Norton® is a registered trademark of Peter Norton. Windows® is a registered trademark of Microsoft Corp.

Publisher *Richard K. Swadley*

Publishing Manager *Dean Miller*

Director of Editorial Services *Cindy Morrow*

Assistant Marketing Manager *Rachel Wolfe*

Acquisitions Editor
Sunthar Visuvalingam

Production Editor
Robin Drake

Copy Editor
Judy Ohm

Indexer
Johnna Van Hoose

Technical Reviewer
Dennis Teague

Editorial Coordinator
Katie Wise

Technical Edit Coordinator
Lynette Quinn

Resource Coordinator
Deborah Frisby

Editorial Assistants
Carol Ackerman
Andi Richter
Rhonda Tinch-Mize

Cover Designer
Tim Amrhein

Book Designer
Alyssa Yesh

Copy Writer
Peter Fuller

Production Team Supervisors
Brad Chinn
Charlotte Clapp

Production
Jeanne Clark
Carl Pierce
Deirdre Smith
Ian A. Smith

Overview

Contents

Quick Reference

Peter Norton's Complete Guide to Windows 95, Second Edition makes it easy to find everything you need to make Windows 95 work for you, including Architecture, Compatibility, DOS, Windows 3.x, Windows NT, Accessibility, Printing, Networking, Communications, Standards, Peter's Principles, Performance, Troubleshooting, Warnings, Tips, and Notes. Entries are grouped under alphabetized categories under the different main topics, and are often repeated both within and across topics for quick reference. When you turn to the corresponding chapters, you'll immediately find the information marked by one or more icons. You can use these lists either for hasty lookups or to explore a particular aspect of Windows 95 from every possible angle.

Architecture

Compatibility

DOS

Windows 3.x

Windows NT

Accessibility

Printing

Networking

Communications

Standards

Peter's Principle

Performance

Troubleshooting

Warning

Tip

Note

Acknowledgments

Thanks to my wife, Rebecca, for working with me to get this book completed. I really don't know what I would have done without her help in researching and compiling some of the information that appears in this book. She also did a fine job of proofreading my rough draft.

Don Doherty deserves special thanks for his invaluable input, especially in Chapter 28.

Dennis Teague deserves thanks for his technical edit of this book. He greatly added to the accuracy and depth of the material you see here.

Readers don't often appear in the acknowledgments sections of a book, but I think they should. I'd like to thank all of you who took the time to write me an e-mail message. Some people told me what I was doing right, others what they would like to see changed. Both groups helped shape this new edition of the book and make it more reader-oriented than before.

I would like to thank Scott Clark for his help and direction. His input was instrumental in helping this book achieve the depth of information it required.

Matt Wagner, my agent, deserves credit for helping me get the contract in the first place and taking care of all the details that most authors don't really think about.

The technical support staff at Microsoft deserves credit for answering the questions that helped fill in the blanks and make the Windows 95 learning experience go faster.

Finally, I would like to thank Sunthar Visuvalingam of Sams, along with Robin Drake, Judy Ohm, and Deborah Frisby (and anyone else who worked on the book that I failed to mention), for their assistance in bringing this book to print.

About the Author

John Mueller is a freelance author and technical editor. He has writing in his blood, having produced 30 books and almost 200 articles to date. The topics range from networking to artificial intelligence and from database management to heads-down programming. Some of his current books include a Delphi programmers guide and a Windows NT advanced user tutorial. His technical editing skills have helped more than 22 authors refine the content of their manuscripts. In addition to book projects, John has provided technical editing services to both *Data Based Advisor* and *Coast Compute* magazines.

When John isn't working at the computer, you can find him in his workshop. He's an avid woodworker and candlemaker. On any given afternoon you can find him working at a lathe or putting the finishing touches on a bookcase. One of his favorite projects is making candlesticks and the candles to go with them. You can reach John on CompuServe at 71570,641 or on the Internet at JMueller@pacbell.net.

Tell Us What You Think!

As a reader, you are the most important critic and commentator of our books. We value your opinion and want to know what we're doing right, what we could do better, what areas you'd like to see us publish in, and any other words of wisdom you're willing to pass our way. You can help us make strong books that meet your needs and give you the computer guidance you require.

Do you have access to the World Wide Web? Check out our site at `http://www.mcp.com`.

Note: If you have a technical question about this book, call the technical support line at (317) 581-3833.

As the publishing manager of the group that created this book, I welcome your comments. You can fax, e-mail, or write me directly to let me know what you did or didn't like about this book—as well as what we can do to make our books stronger. Here's the information:

FAX: 317/581-4669

E-mail: `opsys_mgr@mcp.com`

Mail: Dean Miller
Sams Publishing
201 W. 103rd Street
Indianapolis, IN 46290

Introduction

Windows 95 represents a major leap in technology from the Windows 3.x days. It provides many of the features that DOS and Windows users have been asking for. You'll find new features such as long filenames and better utilities for maintaining your system. The new Explorer interface will make a lot of people happy as well.

When I was writing this book, I took the opportunity to really look at Windows 95. Not only did I look at the user interface, but also at the architectural changes that Microsoft made. I appreciated the differences you can't readily see. The 32-bit components really speed things along. Windows 95 handles many tasks differently as well. You'll find that it's a lot more stable than Windows 3.x.

Whether you like the changes that you can see or those that you can't, everyone will agree that Windows 95 is a superior operating system for the user. That's right—I said the user. If you're looking for a server, you're in the wrong place. Windows NT is the superior operating system for a server.

As you read this book, you'll learn about all the new things that Windows 95 has to offer. I'll also spend some time telling you about the features that haven't changed, those that need a bit more work, and some of the unexpected ways that you can use the new features that do work well.

Who Should Read This Book?

This book's intended audience is intermediate-to-advanced Windows 95 users who need to get the last ounce of computing power from their machines. I provide you with tips and techniques to make Windows 95 easier to use, enhance overall system performance, and improve system stability. Of course, every Windows 95 user can gain something from this book, even if only a better understanding of how Windows 95 works. We'll also spend some time looking at the internal workings of Windows 95. Not only will you learn about where Windows 95 is today, but I also help you understand how Windows 95 differs from its predecessor and how these differences can help you become more productive. If you want the most detailed description of Windows 95 available, this is the book for you.

What You'll Learn

Here are some of the more important topics I cover in this book:

- Installation tips that everyone can use
- Architectural details—how things work under the hood
- Exploiting the new utilities that Windows 95 provides

- Taking advantage of the Accessibility features
- The purpose of the files in the SYSTEM folder
- Windows 95 fonts and ways to make them easier to use
- Creating your own setup script files
- MSDOS.SYS features that can make your system harder to break into
- The truth about the DOS–Windows connection
- Performance tips to turn your machine into a speed demon
- Using Microsoft Exchange for all your communications needs
- OLE architecture and how to use OLE in your applications
- Navigating the new Explorer interface
- The new object-oriented approach to using resources on your machine
- How plug and play makes it easier to install new devices
- Compatibility tips about what works and what doesn't under Windows 95
- The objects available on the context menu and how you can modify the menu to meet your needs
- Modifying your system setup to fully meet your needs
- Workarounds for potential Windows 95 problems
- Internet usage techniques—including those needed to create your own Web page
- All the new OSR2 version features that everyone is talking about

We'll also spend some time learning about some of the fun parts of computing. For example, Appendix A deals exclusively with the features provided by the Microsoft Network (MSN), the Internet, and CompuServe. I even provide a few tips that should help you decide which one to subscribe to. This appendix also includes some important information about WUGNET (Windows Users Group Network)—an organization that every Windows user needs to know about.

Appendix B can help you find an Internet service provider (ISP). In today's computing environment, Internet access is becoming less of a nice-to-have option and more of a must-have tool. Getting in contact with the right ISP to fulfill your computing needs is absolutely essential.

I spend a great deal of time talking about the Windows 95 architecture in various chapters. There are two reasons for this extensive exposure. First, you, as a user, really do need to know how the operating system works—or at least get an overview—so that you can maximize the way you use its features. Second, you need to know what Windows 95 provides that Windows 3.x didn't. Exploring the architecture is one of the best ways to meet this goal.

How This Book Is Organized

This book divides Windows 95 into functional and task-oriented areas. These parts of the book break each piece of Windows 95 apart to see how it ticks and what you can use it for. Of course, many chapters also help you understand what's going on under the hood. Without this information, it would be difficult at best to make full use of the new features that Windows 95 offers.

I'd like to offer one final piece of advice. Windows 95 is a very user- and data-oriented operating system. It's probably the most user-tuned product available right now for the PC. This doesn't mean that Windows 95 is perfect, nor does it mean that everything is as it seems. Sometimes you'll find something that's so difficult to use that you'll wonder why Microsoft did it that way. For example, I found the Registry really difficult to work with until I discovered all the tools that Microsoft provides to make the job easier. You should take the time to really explore this product and figure out which techniques work best for you. Windows 95 offers more than one way to do every task. You need to find the one that's best for you.

Part I: Next Stop—Windows 95!

Before you start a journey, it always helps to know where you are and where you're going. Chapter 1 tells you where we are now. It also gives you a little history on why we're here. Chapter 2 tells you where we're going. These chapters work together to help you put Windows 95 into context. We'll look at important issues such as how Windows 95 compares to past versions of Windows and what you can expect from it. I also spend a little time predicting where we might go in the future.

Part II: Power Primers

This section of the book has three chapters. The first deals with tuning tips. Getting the best performance and highest reliability is the concern of everyone who's just starting to use a new operating system. Windows 95 offers many ways to tune your system. It would seem that all these controls could help you get a tuned system with a very minimal amount of effort. Actually, the exact opposite is true. All these controls interact—and you have to take these interactions into account as you change settings. Optimizing one area usually means de-tuning another area by an equal amount.

This section of the book helps you to determine what type of tuning you need to perform and how that tuning will affect your system. A little turn here and a bump there can really make a big difference in how your system performs. The idea is to tune each area of Windows 95 in moderation. You also need to take your special needs into account. Even the type of network you use affects the way in which you tune your system.

One thing is certain: Windows 95 offers more in the way of reliability and performance features than Windows 3.x did. Your job now is to decide how to use those features to your benefit. Getting that high-performance system together is the first goal you'll want to achieve under Windows 95. After that, the data-centric approach to managing your system should make operating it a breeze.

The second and third chapters of this section include setup tips (in Chapter 4) and startup shortcuts (in Chapter 5). There are a number of ways to set up Windows 95. The Microsoft documentation tells you most of the mechanical information you need but provides very little in the way of tradeoffs. What do you have to give up in order to use a server setup? How does a floppy setup differ from a CD-ROM? These are some of the questions I look at in this section.

Of course, I also offer a few tips on actually getting the installation done, based on real-world experience rather than what should theoretically happen. Sometimes you'll want to do the opposite of what the Microsoft documentation says to do, just to get a more efficient setup. This section of the book looks at some of the tips and techniques I've accumulated over months of beta testing Windows 95.

Windows 95 Anatomy

Learning how to use an operating system often means learning a bit about how it works inside. For some people, a quick overview of the Windows 95 internals will be enough, especially if you plan to use Windows 95 only in a single-user mode and really don't need to get every ounce of power from your machine.

But if you do have to manage a large number of machines or need to really get inside and learn how things work from a programmer's point of view, you'll really appreciate this section of the book. I don't go into a bits-and-bytes, blow-by-blow description, but this section blows the lid off all the architectural aspects of Windows 95. We'll examine every major component of Windows 95, from the file system to the API.

Understanding and Using Windows 95

Some people learn how to use a computer but never learn how to use it well. The problem, in many cases, is that they lack knowledge of some of the hidden features that a product provides. In other cases, a lack of system optimization is to blame. Still other people have problems understanding the documentation that comes with the product.

This section of the book is filled with tips and techniques that are so often missing from the vendor documentation. There's a big difference between the way things should work and the way they really do. Use this section of the book to gain the real-world information you'll need to really use Windows 95 to its full potential.

Surfing the Net

Getting online doesn't have to be difficult. I begin this section by looking at how Windows helps you get online in a variety of ways, not just the Internet. You'll be amazed at just what kind of tools Microsoft provides as part of Windows 95 and which tools are free for the asking from the Internet. I tell you about all kinds of interesting Web sites to visit and where to download the software you'll need to make your Internet experience truly rewarding. I also talk to you about Web-based tools. For example, we'll look at a few different solutions to finding what you need—both Microsoft-supported and those provided by third parties.

Once you get past the basics of using the Internet, you may decide to create your own Web site. I don't cover the heavy-duty server-based solutions in this book, because Windows 95 doesn't really lend itself to that environment. What I do cover is creating your own Web page. You can publish your new Web page on the company intranet or on the Internet, if your ISP provides this feature. (That's right, some ISPs allow you to create your own Web page and upload it to their server.) We'll also take the opportunity to visit some exciting new Internet strategies such as ActiveX in this section of the book.

Networking with Windows 95

Very few companies do without the benefits provided by networks these days. The smallest office usually has a network setup of some kind if for no other reason than simple e-mail and file sharing. The surprising thing is how many home networks are popping up. Not only are these networks used for obvious applications such as allowing a child to access some of the files on a parents' machine, but new applications such as game playing as well. It's surprising to see just how many new games allow two or more people to play a game, using a simple network setup.

Suffice it to say that, with all these new applications for home and small business networks, the need for network-specific information becomes greater every day. While this section can't fully explore every networking solution available to you, it does fully explore the solutions supported by Windows 95.

Given the networking environments in which you'll use Windows 95, security may not seem that big of an issue. However, even a small company has to protect its data. Needless to say, I spend some time looking at security issues in this section of the book as well.

Troubleshooting Windows 95

Have you ever installed something and gotten it to work right the first time? That's what I thought. I usually have some problems too. Unlike the Macintosh, the PC is made up of parts that come from a myriad of vendors. All these parts are supposed to work together, but sometimes they don't.

A lot of hardware and software installation-related problems have nothing to do with hidden agendas or vendor ineptitude. Some problems occur because of a poorly written specification. One vendor interprets a specification one way, and another uses a very different interpretation. The result is hardware and software that really don't work together. Each one follows the "standard," and each one follows it differently.

Other times, a user will shoot himself in the foot. How many times have you thought that you did something according to the instructions, only to find out that you really didn't? It happens to everyone. Even one bad keystroke can kill an installation. Take the Windows Registry. It's all too easy to take a misstep when editing it and end up with an operating system that won't boot.

Even if you do manage to get a fully-functional system the first time through and you keep from shooting yourself in the foot, what are the chances that the installation will stay stable forever? It's pretty unlikely. Your system configuration changes on a daily basis as you optimize applications and perform various tasks.

As you can see, the typical computer has a lot of failure points, so it's no wonder that things fall apart from time to time. This section of the book helps you quickly diagnose and fix most of the major problems you'll run into with Windows 95. I even cover a few undocumented ways to determine what's going on and how to interpret the information you get.

Microsoft Plus!

Sometimes it's nice to end a book on a fun note. Chapter 28 does just that. Sure, Microsoft Plus! provides some important aids, such as advanced disk compression and Dial-Up Networking, but it also provides some fun things, such as Desktop Themes. I take a look at everything you can expect from this Windows 95 add-on package. Once you get a good look at what it offers, you can decide whether or not this package will enhance your system.

What's New in This Book?

I placed my e-mail address in the initial release of this book for a specific reason—to make it easy for you to contact me. You certainly didn't disappoint me. I received numerous e-mail messages from readers. Every one of those messages was read at the time I received them and again while I wrote this edition of the book. The effects are pretty plain to see.

You told me that the book needed some organizational changes and I did my best to meet your every need in this area. Chapter 7 is the result of one organizational change request. All of the Registry information now appears in this separate chapter. I've also enhanced the content of this chapter and made it easier to read.

Another reader-requested change was the addition of a new network troubleshooting chapter. Take a look at the contents of Chapter 27—I think you'll like what you see. Not only have I covered troubleshooting techniques for Windows 95 itself, but those you'll need when using Windows 95 with other operating systems such as NetWare and Windows NT.

Still other users felt that I didn't give laptop computers their just due in the first edition of the book. That's all changed in this edition. Not only have I improved the coverage in every area, but I address laptop user concerns in many areas of the book.

Some of the changes in this book are the result of changes in the computer industry as a whole. One of the most drastic changes that has taken place is the use of the Internet as more than a means to communicate with others. This is a new must-have tool for anyone who is serious about computer use. Take a look at Part V, "Surfing the Net" for more information on the Internet.

Finally, you're going to see a lot of new material in the book that was brought on by changes made to Windows 95 by Microsoft. The first set of changes occurred when Microsoft released Service Pack 1. This release fixed many of the bugs that users reported after Windows 95 first was released. The more extensive changes, though, come from the latest OEM Service Release 2 version of Windows 95. This version includes all kinds of new features, such as FAT 32 support and a personal Web server. You'll also find some upgraded utility programs such as imaging and the scripting capability of Dial-Up Networking. I discuss all these new features in the book.

Conventions Used in This Book

I use the following conventions in this book:

File | Open	Menus and the selections on them are separated by a vertical bar. "File | Open" means "Access the File menu and choose Open."
Program Files\Plus!\Themes	The names of folders are separated by a backslash.
`monospace`	It's important to differentiate the text that you use in a macro or that you type at the command line from the text that explains it. I've used monospace type to make this differentiation. Whenever you see something in monospace, you'll know that this information will appear in a macro, within a system file such as CONFIG.SYS or AUTOEXEC.BAT, or as something you'll type at the command line. You'll even see the switches used with Windows commands in monospace.

italic monospace — Sometimes you need to supply a value for a Windows or DOS command. For example, when you use the DIR command, you might need to supply a filename. It's convenient to use a variable name—essentially a placeholder—to describe the kind of value you need to supply. The same holds true for any other kind of entry, from macro commands to dialog box fields. Whenever you see a word in italic monospace, you know that the word is a placeholder that you need to replace with a value. The placeholder simply tells you what kind of value you need to provide.

<*filename*> — A variable name between angle brackets is a value that you need to replace with something else. The variable name I use usually provides a clue as to what kind of information you need to supply. In this case, I'm asking for a filename. Never type the angle brackets when you type the value.

[<*filename*>] — When you see square brackets around a value, switch, or command, it means that this is an optional component. You don't have to include it as part of the command line or dialog box field unless you want the additional functionality that the value, switch, or command provides.

italic — I use italic wherever the actual value of something is unknown. I also use italic where more than one value might be correct. For example, you might see FILE*xxxx* in text. This means that the value could be anywhere between FILE0000 and FILE9999.

ALL CAPS — Commands use capital letters. Some Registry entries also use caps, even though they aren't commands. Normally you'll type a command at the DOS prompt, within a .PIF file field, or within the Run dialog box field. If you see all caps somewhere else, it's safe to assume that the item is a case-sensitive Registry entry or some other value. Some filenames also appear in caps.

➥ — The code-continuation character is used when one line of code is too long to fit on one line of the book. Here's an example:

```
{DDE-EXECUTE "[InsertObject .IconNumber = 0, .FileName = ""D:\WIN95\LEAVES.BMP"",
➥.Link = 1, .DisplayIcon = 0, .Tab = ""1"", .Class = ""Paint.Picture"",
➥.IconFilename = """", .Caption = ""LEAVES.BMP""]"}
```

When typing these lines, you would type them as one long line without the code-continuation character.

Icons

This book contains many icons that help you identify certain types of information. The following paragraphs describe the purpose of each icon.

Note: Notes tell you about interesting facts that don't necessarily affect your ability to use the other information in the book. I use note boxes to give you bits of information that I've picked up while using Windows 95.

Tip: Everyone likes tips, because they tell you new ways of doing things that you might not have thought about before. Tip boxes also provide an alternative way of doing something that you might like better than the first approach I provided.

Warning: This means watch out! Warnings almost always tell you about some kind of system or data damage that will occur if you perform a certain action (or fail to perform others). Make sure that you understand a warning thoroughly before you follow any instructions that come after it.

Peter's Principle: I usually include a Peter's Principle to tell you how to manage your Windows environment more efficiently. Boxes with this icon might also include ideas on where to find additional information or even telephone numbers that you can call. You'll also find the names of shareware and freeware utility programs here.

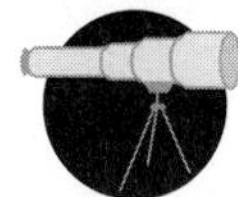

Looking Ahead: It's always good to know what you'll find along the road. Whenever you see a Looking Ahead box, I'm providing a road sign that tells you where we're headed. That way, you can follow the path of a particular subject as I provide more detailed information throughout the book.

Gaining good access to the features provided by Windows 95 is important for everyone—especially to those who are physically challenged. I applaud Microsoft's efforts in taking this first step toward making Windows 95 the operating system that everyone can use. You'll see the Accessibility icon wherever I talk about these special features. Don't be surprised at how many of them you can use to get your work done faster or more efficiently, even if you're not physically challenged.

Knowing how something works inside is important to some people but not so important to others. Whenever you see the Architecture icon, I'm talking about the internal workings of Windows 95. Knowing how Windows 95 performs its job can help you determine why things don't work as they should.

You can't survive in the modern business world without spending some time talking to other people. Whether you spend that time on the phone or with an online service such as CompuServe or the Microsoft Network, the result is the same. It's the exchange of information that drives business—at least in part. Whenever you see the Communications icon, you know that I'm describing some way of using Windows 95 to better communicate with those around you.

Whenever you change something as important as your operating system, there will be problems with older devices and applications that were designed for the older version. The Compatibility icon clues you in to tips, techniques, and notes that will help you get over the compatibility hurdle.

DOS is still with us and will continue to be for the foreseeable future. Microsoft at least provides better support for DOS applications under Windows 95. Whenever you see the DOS icon, I provide you with a tip, technique, or note about a way to make DOS applications and Windows coexist.

Even home users need to worry about networking these days. It's no surprise, then, that this book provides a wealth of networking tips and techniques that everyone can use. Expect to find one of these tidbits of knowledge wherever you see the Networking icon.

Microsoft recently released an updated version of Windows 95 that includes new features such as FAT 32 support. Whenever you see this icon, you know that you're reading about this latest update of the operating system. Unfortunate as it may seem, this update was released only to original equipment manufacturers (OEMs). Unless you buy a new machine with the OSR2 version of Windows 95 loaded, you'll receive only limited support for new Windows 95 features. However, many OSR2 features are downloadable and hence the new info is relevant to those who got Windows 95 with older hardware.

I use the Performance icon to designate a performance-related tip. There are many throughout this book, and they cover a variety of optimization techniques. You'll need to read them carefully and decide which ones suit your needs. Not every performance tip is for everyone. Most of them require a tradeoff of some kind, which I mention.

Before Windows 95 even appeared on the market, Microsoft was working on a way to enhance it. Microsoft Plus! is an add-on package for Windows 95 that enhances its built-in capabilities. Whenever you see the Microsoft Plus! icon, I'm talking about some enhancement that Microsoft Plus! provides to the standard Windows 95 environment. Of course, this product is covered in detail in Chapter 28.

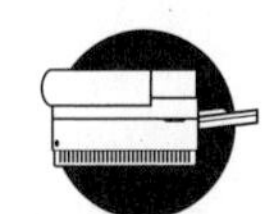

Your printer is probably the most used yet most frustrating part of your computer. I include the Printer icon to tell you when a tip or technique will help you keep your printer under control and make it work more efficiently.

Square pegs that had to fit in round holes—that's what some products were in the past. Recent standards efforts have helped reduce the number of square pegs on the market. I think it's important to know what these standards are so that you can make the best buying decisions possible. Getting a square peg at a discount rate isn't such a good deal if you end up spending hours making it round. Every time you see the Standards icon, you know that I'm talking about some standard that defines a product that will fit into that round hole with relative ease.

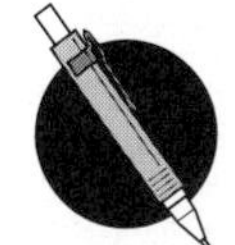

Technical details can really help you localize a problem or decide precisely what you need in order to get a job done. They can also help improve your overall knowledge of a product. Sometimes they're just fun to learn. However, sometimes you just need an overview of how something works; learning the details would slow you down. I use the Technical Note icon to tell you when a piece of information is a detail. You can bypass this information if you need only an overview of a Windows 95 process or feature. This icon also gives you clues as to where you can look for additional information.

Everyone encounters problems from time to time. It doesn't matter whether the problem is hardware- or software-related if it's keeping you from getting your work done. Every time you see the Troubleshooting icon, I'm providing you with a tool you need to find a problem.

The predecessor of Windows 95 left a lot of people wondering whether Windows would ever completely meet their needs. The Windows 3.1x icon tells you about a note that compares Windows 95 and Windows 3.1x. These notes help you understand what you can expect to gain (and, in some cases, lose) by using Windows 95 rather than its predecessor.

It's helpful to compare the benefits of using one operating system over another. I already gave you some tips in this regard earlier. You'll find a lot of other notes throughout this book. Every time I provide some insight into a comparison of Windows NT versus Windows 95, I use the Windows NT icon.

I

Next Stop—Windows 95!

1

A Decade Spent with Windows

The last 10 years have marked a major change in the way we view computing. PCs started out as mere playthings that had character-mode screens, a little memory, a few small applications, and not much more. Today we use computer systems crammed with megabytes of RAM, huge hard drives, impressive displays, and applications that provide an ease of use that early computer users wouldn't have dreamed possible. All this new activity centers around the graphical user interface (GUI) rather than the text-mode interface of yesterday. At least part of the reason for that change is Microsoft Windows. Of course, Microsoft would have you believe that Windows is the entire reason, but frankly, it isn't. Windows is only part of the GUI picture—albeit a large one.

If someone had told me 10 years ago that today I would be spending the majority of my time using Windows, I would have thought him crazy. The Windows of 10 years ago hardly merited a first look, much less a second. When Windows was first developed, it was competing with an entrenched GUI environment—the Macintosh—and the first few releases of Windows simply weren't designed as well as the operating system that came with Apple computers. Besides, not many applications made use of the Windows interface. You could run programs in Windows, but there was little benefit. I could do everything I needed to do faster, and with a lot less effort, under DOS. My favorite quote back then was "I don't do Windows."

Ever since Windows 3.0 hit the streets in late spring of 1990, many software vendors have announced products to support this GUI. The release of Windows 3.1, which included many enhancements, further fueled the growth of Windows-based applications. Windows for Workgroups and Windows NT added networking and other refinements to the Windows environment, further increasing its appeal to corporate America. (An interim release of Windows for Workgroups, version 3.11, took care of some reliability and speed problems found in earlier versions.) Unfortunately, some people viewed Windows for Workgroups as too little because it didn't provide a robust multitasking environment for some tasks, and Windows NT as too much because of its stringent hardware requirements. Enter Windows 95, Microsoft's latest entry in the Windows market. Now there are windowing environments for beginning, intermediate, and advanced users from the same source, and with much the same interface.

Why has Windows become so popular? Windows-based programs simply are easier—*much* easier—to learn and use than conventional DOS applications. And, as most mainstream products (the ones most PC users already know and love) have joined the Windows ranks, the real power of computing is being made available to people who couldn't use it before. In fact, some Windows versions of products such as WordPerfect are so popular that their vendors don't plan to release a new DOS version of the product, except to fix bugs.

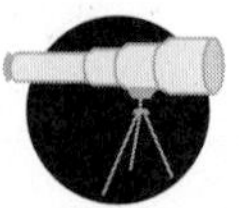

Looking Ahead: This chapter presents a historical view of Windows: What did we start with, and where did Windows go from there? It's always important to examine where you've been in order to fully appreciate where you are now. Windows 95 is far from perfect. In fact, it really wasn't ready for prime time when Microsoft released it in August 1995.

Hidden bugs in the release version of Windows 95 will certainly appear and provide lots of gossip for the industry. For example, there were problems with some device drivers, and many older DOS programs—especially games—caused some beta testers more than a few problems. The important thing to remember with this release is how much Windows really has improved over the years. This chapter gives you that historical view and helps you understand how Windows 95 adds to the Windows legacy.

Fortunately, Microsoft has released Service Pack 1 in the interim. It fixes some really nasty bugs—especially one in Explorer that could cause you to lose files under rare circumstances. Service Pack 1 also included a shell update for Explorer that lets you see NetWare Directory Service objects such as printers. The OLE32 update took care of a problem where data you thought you had deleted could remain in some types of documents. Take a look at the detailed information link at `http://www.microsoft.com/windows/common/aa2717.htm` if you want full details on the contents of Service Pack 1. You can download this patch from the Internet at `http://www.microsoft.com/windows95/default.asp` (look for the Product Updates option under the Free Software activity) or buy it directly from Microsoft.

The latest release of Windows 95 is Original Equipment Manufacturer Service Release 2 (OSR2). Unfortunately, many of the best features of this release aren't available for the general public. I discuss this release and what it means for users of new machines in the later section "OEM Service Release 2—The Complete Story." Look for other discussion points spread throughout the remainder of the book.

I'll also take a quick look at some of the new Windows 95 features that differentiate it from the previous versions of Windows. I won't really take a detailed look at them until later. The sole purpose of this chapter is to help you see the big picture. Future chapters take a detailed look at each feature.

A Historical View of Windows

The history of Windows is dotted with a number of successes and an equal number of failures. First we'll discuss the failures. Windows started out as little more than a task-switching environment. The initial 1985 release of version 1.0 left a lot to be desired, and its reception by the industry as a whole was, frankly, rather dismal.

There were many problems with the initial Windows release. Many of these problems stemmed from the hardware available at the time. An underpowered Intel processor, low-resolution graphics adapters, and a lack of memory made the PC a graphics-hostile computer. Other problems occurred because of a lack of support from software vendors. However, I believe one of the biggest hurdles was the user. The earliest computer users were technical types who understood hardware and software design. They took to cryptic procedures and arcane commands easily.

As computer power became available to a wider audience, however, users struggled with "computerese" and sought ways to ease access to applications. The Apple Macintosh, introduced in 1984, was the first successful business-oriented product to provide a natural, picture-oriented interface for the computer. (Everyone remembers the ill-fated Lisa, the predecessor to the Macintosh; even though the Macintosh eventually included many of the Lisa's features, the Lisa was a total failure before Apple even started.) The Macintosh operating system and other features were designed with this GUI in mind. Microsoft recognized the Macintosh as the wave of the future, and Windows was the result of its development efforts.

The following sections look at the four major Windows releases that preceded Windows 95. (We'll skip version 1.0, which was a total failure.) Hopefully, you'll see the progress that each version made toward the product we use today. Equally important is that you note which failures are still with us as Microsoft strives to provide backward compatibility as it moves forward. Should we give up some compatibility in order to get an improved operating system? Corporate America says no, but the typical user says yes. To whom do you think Microsoft will listen?

Windows 2.x

Microsoft's second attempt at a GUI wasn't much better than its first. Windows 2.0, which appeared in 1987, didn't offer the Program Manager interface that people associate with Windows today. In fact, it didn't even use the icons that most people associate with a GUI. This version of Windows provided a list of applications in text, and not much more. In fact, it didn't offer much more than a menuing system. This was due in part to the memory restrictions and lack of horsepower provided by the 8088 processor. However, it still made DOS easier to use and enabled the user to start more than one task at a time—as long as the multiple tasks would fit in available memory. Windows 2.0 was a small but important step away from DOS. This version, like its predecessor, did poorly in the marketplace.

Intel introduced two new chips prior to the release of Windows 2.0. The 80286 appeared on the scene in 1983, and the 80386 appeared in 1985. Both processors offered features that made them far superior to the 8088. You might wonder why Microsoft even bothered to introduce a version of Windows for the 8088. The answer is simple—marketing. The majority of PC owners still owned 8088 machines when Windows 2.0 became available, so that's the market they developed for.

Microsoft introduced two other versions of Windows that allowed people to use the power of Intel's newer chips. 80286 users could use all of their extended memory for applications by getting the Windows/286 version. Like its counterpart, this version offered task switching, not multitasking. Task switching allows you to run several applications, but not simultaneously. Only the foreground application does any work. The background applications are suspended until you bring them to the foreground. Multitasking allows both foreground and background applications to execute. The Windows/386 version, released in 1988, at least allowed the user to multitask applications. This wasn't the preemptive multitasking that provides a smooth transition from application to application that most people think about, but a cooperative multitasking that allowed one application to grab all the system resources if it wanted to do so. Think of cooperative multitasking as an honor-system method of managing applications (and we all know how well the honor system works). Preemptive multitasking leaves Windows in charge, ensuring that all the applications work together fairly. In other words, this version of Windows was a step in the right direction, but it was still a far cry from what Windows is today.

Here's the short take on Windows 2.0: None of its incarnations was very successful. All three versions suffered from the same problem. They didn't deliver the type of interface that people needed and wanted. A GUI without graphics isn't really a GUI at all. Reliability was also a problem, but people really never got past the interface to find this out. (We'll look at some of the reliability problems of previous versions of Windows throughout this book, and how Windows 95 fixes some but not all of them.)

Windows 3.x

Windows 3.0, introduced on May 22, 1990, really got the ball rolling. This was the first version that offered users a real reason for switching from DOS-based applications. Not only did Windows 3.0 offer enhanced memory support so that applications could do more, but it also offered an attractive interface. (See Figure 1.1.) This was the first version to make extensive use of icons. It also offered the Program Manager interface that most people associate with Windows. Most important, you could run more than one task simultaneously under Windows 3.0—a feat impossible with DOS alone. Of course, Microsoft had to make a few concessions to gain the support that version 3.0 enjoyed. For example, version 3.0 was the last version you could use on an 8088.

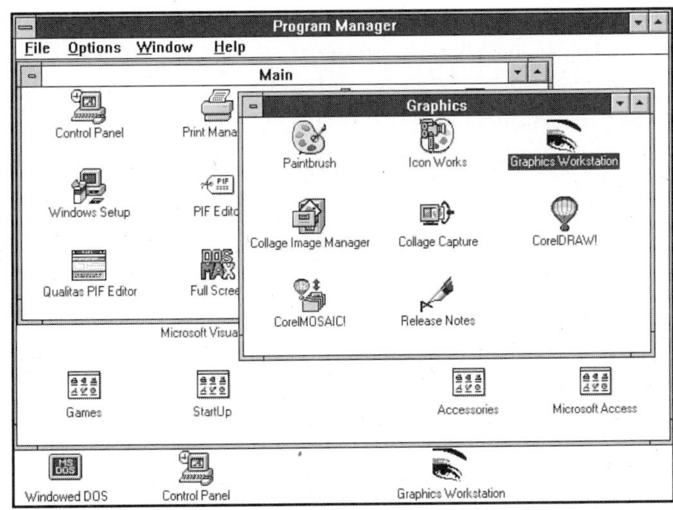

Figure 1.1.
Windows versions 3.0 and above offer one of the things that users need to use a computer efficiently: a graphical user interface (GUI).

Even though the marketplace welcomed Windows 3.0 with open arms, users soon discovered problems. Most of the negative aspects of version 3.0 revolved around the concessions Microsoft had to make for backward compatibility. For one thing, running Windows 3.0 in real mode meant that Microsoft couldn't make the system as reliable as they wanted it to be. (We look at what real mode is and its impact on the system in Chapter 6.) An operating system that runs in protected mode can intercept and deal with maverick applications that cause the system to crash. Using real-mode drivers in some areas meant that the Windows 3.0 safety net was pretty thin—or nonexistent. One faulty application could cause a data-killing system crash. The biggest complaint that people had about this version, however, was its own inherent instability.

Another problem was the infamous UAE (unrecoverable application error). Although Windows itself was responsible for some of these errors, they often had nothing to do with Windows itself, but with the applications it ran. An application could try to grab a file handle to a nonexistent file—or some other system resource—and crash the system as a result.

Undaunted by these problems, Microsoft introduced yet another version of Windows. Version 3.1 offered the user even more, but it was the hidden details that set this version apart from version 3.0. The UAE disappeared in this version because Microsoft added methods for validating system requests. Every time an application wanted to look at a disk file or perform some other task, Windows made sure that that task could succeed before it gave the go-ahead. This strategy forced a lot of vendors to rewrite their software to look for potential problems before the software requested a system service. Unfortunately, even with all these checks, some applications still violated system integrity. The result was a general protection fault (GPF). From a user point of view, the GPF didn't look much different from the UAE; both could cause the machine to freeze. However, Windows usually recovered better from a GPF. In addition, users saw fewer GPFs than UAEs. The GPF also showed that Windows at least recognized an error before the machine froze; the UAE always resulted from a failure to recognize a symptom. This difference meant that Windows could now provide more information to a vendor in an effort to find and fix the source of a GPF. (This is why Windows 3.1 included the Dr. Watson utility, which recorded the set of conditions that Windows detected just before a system failure.) Suffice it to say that version 3.1 added a lot under the hood and forced developers to rethink their Windows programming strategy.

Microsoft also decided to provide a fully enhanced memory environment for Windows 3.1. For example, no longer did the user have to pay as much attention to the amount of actual system memory available for running applications. Windows 3.1 could use virtual memory, a method of using part of the hard drive to simulate RAM. (I discuss this in detail later in this chapter.) Microsoft used part of this additional memory to provide enhanced driver support. A user could no longer run Windows on an 8088 by starting it in real mode, because the 16-bit drivers needed to run in protected mode. In addition, the extra memory allowed Microsoft to improve driver performance and the overall reliability of Windows. (We look at real versus protected mode in Chapter 6.) Needless to say, running everything in protected mode enabled you to utilize all that memory sitting above the 1MB conventional memory boundary. Using protected mode also made Windows 3.1 a little more stable than its predecessor. However, this version still had to call on DOS to perform some tasks.

Windows for Workgroups 3.x

Now that Windows was entrenched in the corporate environment, certain failings came to light. The biggest failure was the lack of good network support. I'm not talking about the big-mainframe-to-PC connection, but the small, intimate, local area network (LAN) connections required for workgroup computing. These small groups of users didn't have the monetary resources required to create a big network. What they really needed was something that allowed them to share a few devices and some files. Windows for Workgroups solved this problem. A user could now create very inexpensive connections for a small group of people by installing a network card and some cable. This version of Windows also provided some simple network-related utilities such as a meeting scheduler and an e-mail system. A peer-to-peer network that used Windows for Workgroups might not provide the robust environment needed for enterprise computing, but it would work for a small organization.

This version of Windows also provided better reliability than its predecessor. For one thing, Microsoft provided many bug fixes. As a result of these bug fixes and the enhanced support provided by Windows for Workgroups, many pundits in the trade presses recommended that people switch to Windows for Workgroups, even on stand-alone machines. Other than that, Windows for Workgroups provided essentially the same feature set as Windows 3.1.

Windows NT

Some people use Windows for mission-critical applications. They want more reliability from Windows than either the 3.1 or Workgroups versions can offer. For example, the reliability problems presented by the current Windows setup make it unfeasible as a database server. What if the server went down in the middle of a transaction? The results could be devastating, even in a workgroup setting. Windows NT solves this problem by getting rid of DOS altogether. It provides a totally new Windows environment that looks like the old one but runs completely in protected mode. Windows NT provides many other features as well. For one thing, it isn't restricted to the Intel family of processors. The initial version of Windows NT came out with support for the Hewlett-Packard Alpha processor as well.

Unfortunately, this new and improved version of Windows comes with a big price tag. Microsoft really designed NT as a server-based operating system. As a result, there's no way to run Windows NT with less than 8MB of RAM and a fast processor. Many users complain that the high hardware price tag just isn't worth the additional security that Windows NT provides. Enter Windows 95. This version of Windows doesn't rely on DOS for Windows application needs; all the Windows .DLLs and supporting code run in protected mode. (Windows 95 does rely on DOS to run DOS applications, to provide some low-level BIOS support on non-plug and play machines, and to support antiquated devices that use real-mode drivers.) It also uses a subset of the Windows NT 32-bit programming interface and runs completely in protected mode (except for real-mode drivers).

Not only does Windows 95 perform better, faster, and more reliably, but it also sports a new interface. (See Figure 1.2.) Windows 95 represents a halfway point between Windows for Workgroups and Windows NT. It also represents the future of Windows. For example, Windows 95 is the first version of Windows to include plug and play as an integral part of the operating system.

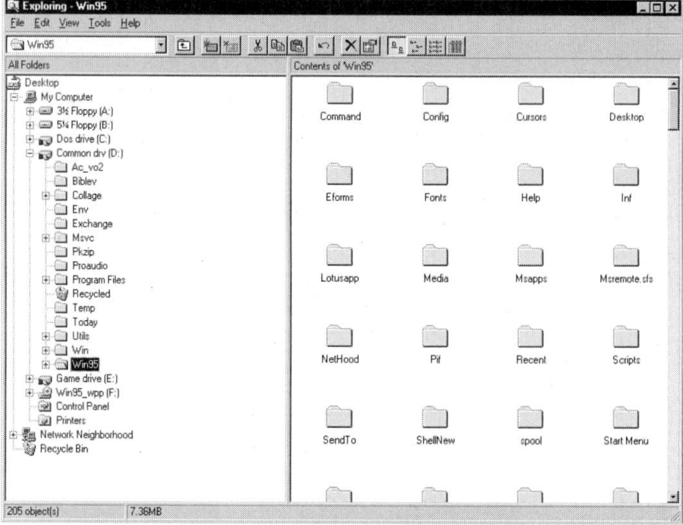

Figure 1.2.
Windows 95 sports a new interface that should make life a lot easier for the novice user.

Note: With the introduction of Windows NT 4.0, you can now get the Explorer interface in the kind of operating system package you need. Windows 95 is still the operating system of choice for laptop and portable users—especially with the improved level of support in OSR2. It's also the platform of choice for the user who needs to run older DOS applications or game programs. However, Windows NT provides the stable platform that many business users prefer. With the addition of the Explorer interface, it's also easier to use.

Windows 95 Improvements

Now that we have some idea of where we've been, let's get an overview of where we are. Windows 95 is the new version of Windows that Microsoft hopes will appear on every workstation sometime in the near future. Not only is it less expensive than Windows NT, but it's also more robust than Windows 3.1. The new interface and other design considerations make Windows 95 a lot better than any of its predecessors.

Tip: Even though Windows 95 provides a vast improvement in speed, reliability, and interface over Windows 3.x and Windows for Workgroups 3.x, it isn't the platform to use as a server. If you need a server, you'll need the additional reliability provided by Windows NT. On the other hand, if you want an inexpensive replacement for your current workstation operating system that provides a lot of added functionality, Windows 95 is the product you've been looking for.

Improvements Over Windows 3.11

There's no doubt that Windows 3.11 made a lot of headway in the bug department. Remember the GPFs I told you about? Some of them were Microsoft's fault (even though Microsoft would have you believe that Windows is the perfect product and that the third-party vendors are really to blame). There were situations in which Windows simply didn't work as advertised. Windows 3.11 fixed many of these problem areas, especially the crippling memory allocation problems that plagued earlier versions. Of course, Windows 3.11 still wasn't perfect, or we'd be using it in place of Windows 95. Some of the memory problems weren't in the code, but in the architecture. Microsoft didn't deal with any memory-related architectural issues in the 3.11 release.

Many people noticed that Windows 3.11 still had many problems. For one thing, GPFs were still common, although less common than before. Even though Windows 3.11 fixed a few architectural problems by providing features such as 32-bit disk access, it didn't—*couldn't*—fix all of them. Some of the problems in Windows 3.x—such as disk-related failures—were a result of using DOS for disk access. When you base your protected-mode, multitasking operating environment on a real-mode, single-tasking operating system, it's not too difficult to understand why there are problems. Any real-mode access leaves Windows open for attack from any application. As a result, even though Windows 3.11 offered 32-bit disk access and other reliability additions, it wasn't enough. Microsoft had to get rid of the underlying problem—DOS. Windows 95 does just that. (We'll see later that DOS isn't completely gone, but it's far enough away now that its impact is minimal.)

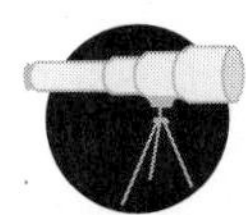

Looking Ahead: Chapter 6 provides the details of the Windows 95 architecture. It will help you understand not only why Windows 95 is more robust than Windows 3.x, but also why it's less robust than Windows NT. Read Chapter 6 if you want to find out more about the specific improvements that Microsoft has made to enhance Windows 95 reliability. If you want to know more about the Windows 95 file system and how it compares to previous versions of Windows, read Chapter 9, which compares the various forms of disk access used by previous versions. (This chapter also covers the new FAT 32 file system provided by the OSR2 version of Windows 95.)

Other problems occur when application writers misuse or misunderstand the Windows API (application programming interface). Anyone who has tried to figure out the Windows API in order to write an application knows what I mean. The problems aren't even limited to C programmers, as you might think. Microsoft Visual Basic, Microsoft Access, CA-Visual Objects, Borland Delphi, and a wealth of other "high-end" application development languages give the programmer access to Windows functionality through the API. In fact, you might be surprised at the level of access provided by some application programs, such as Microsoft Word for Windows, through its Word Basic "macro" language. Many API functions are so counterintuitive that Houdini himself couldn't untie the knot. Combining these counterintuitive commands with a programmer who might have very limited programming skills is a recipe for application disaster.

Windows 95 can't fix these API-related problems for you—at least, it can't fix the 16-bit API problems. However, Microsoft did take the opportunity to change the API and make it more intuitive when it developed WIN32s. Since programmers will probably use this 32-bit API in place of the old one to develop new applications, they should reap the benefit of using an API that is at least a little easier to understand. With understanding should come some level of enhanced stability.

Some users shot themselves in the foot while installing previous versions of Windows. You had to know quite a bit about DOS and Windows to get a decent installation on some machines. This meant looking up every IRQ and port address that your system was using. Windows 95 eliminates this problem to a certain degree. It includes dialog boxes that tell you what resources each device in your system is using. In addition, it tells you which resources you can't use when it's time to reconfigure a device. Is the Windows 95 installation foolproof? No. You can still shoot yourself in the foot in certain circumstances. However, the new installation features in Windows 95 can greatly reduce your chances of getting a bad installation due to device configuration conflicts.

Improvements Over Windows for Workgroups 3.11

One of the biggest reasons that people use Windows for Workgroups is the networking features it provides. Not only does it include the network operating system, but it also provides several utility programs. A small workgroup can easily get by using the features provided by Microsoft Mail for e-mail and Schedule+ to manage everyone's appointments. It's also easy to use WfW, as long as you already know how to use the stand-alone product. You can build a small peer-to-peer network for your local workgroup in a matter of hours.

Just like everything else with Windows, getting everything right the first time is nearly impossible. For example, what if you want a small workgroup setup and still have access to your NetWare or NT file server? WfW is ill-equipped to provide this level of functionality. The problem is twofold. Not only do you have to battle Windows 3.x-specific networking problems, but you also have to deal with the local peer-to-peer network. Many a network administrator spends sleepless nights trying to get everything to work together.

Windows 95, on the other hand, comes with dual-network protocol support built right in. Theoretically, all you need to do is select both networks in the Network Configuration dialog box. After doing a few additional setups, you should have a local peer-to-peer network that also connects to the company's main network on the file server.

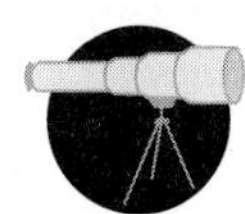

Looking Ahead: The networking support that Windows 95 provides might sound like a dream come true, but reality is a bit different. Although Windows 95 does make dual networks a reality and does reduce the amount of work required by an order of magnitude, it doesn't work completely. Chapter 23 helps you understand what Windows 95 does and does not do for networking.

We can all be thankful that Microsoft took a first step by offering the user WfW for simple networking needs. However, most people will leave WfW behind and never look back once they see the networking capabilities provided by Windows 95. These features might not be perfect, but they do go a long way toward providing the user with the capabilities needed to build an efficient networking solution.

Along with the better networking features that Windows 95 provides, it's also faster than WfW. Using 32-bit code to perform much of the work, coupled with preemptive multitasking, makes Windows 95 run much faster, using the same hardware as a WfW machine. However, faster isn't always better. Inefficient use of speed can rob a system of the power it should have. For example, if you spend time waiting for a print job to spool to the hard drive, you aren't efficiently using the speed your system can provide. Another example is when two applications require system resources and one ends up grabbing the entire resource. Windows 95 comes out ahead in this regard as well. The Windows 3.x tasking system just isn't as efficient as the one used by Windows 95. The use of threads for 32-bit applications under Windows 95 only serves to increase the efficiency of an already improved system. As with everything else, though, Windows 95 will probably need a little tweaking before all these new performance-enhancing features really do the job they're supposed to do.

Improvements Over Windows NT

No one should ever confuse Windows NT with a workstation operating system. It requires too many resources. Can you really justify a 486 or Pentium baseline machine with a minimum of 16MB just to start the operating system as a word processing workstation? Windows NT needs a lot of resources to perform well—there's just no way around it. The strange thing is that some people upgraded their workstations just so that they could gain the additional reliability that Windows NT provides.

There are many problems with using Windows NT as a workstation. For one thing, anyone who has ever tried to run certain older DOS applications, such as games, has been very disappointed with NT. The reason is simple: Windows NT is designed without any flexibility in mind. The only thing it knows is that the application you're trying to run just violated system integrity. As a result, the application gets squashed. Microsoft wrote this operating system to run as reliably as possible, which means that it can't bend to the needs of an application that thinks it needs to run alone.

Windows 95 will never be as stable as Windows NT. It will bend as much as possible to allow that old application to run. Because of this added flexibility, Windows 95 will run most if not all of your DOS applications with a little tinkering. Microsoft even provided a special startup mode for applications that don't run well in either a full-screen or windowed DOS session. With all this additional assistance, you might even find that these old applications run better under Windows 95 than from the DOS prompt. The tradeoff is that you don't get the same level of reliability.

The one new feature that Windows 95 provides is its interface. Windows NT still uses Program Manager (the 4.0 version uses the new Explorer interface). Right now, you might be wondering how you'll ever get used to the new interface. The longer you've used Program Manager, the more likely it is that you'll ask this question. You might even insist on hanging on to that old interface.

It's okay. Microsoft still provides Program Manager for those who are leery of trying something new. I took advantage of this alternative during the first few months I used Windows 95. I think it made the transition a bit easier, since I didn't need to worry about learning a new interface and new operating system features at the same time. However, after a few months, I did try the new interface, and now I don't think I'll ever go back. Using the Explorer interface is so much faster than Program Manager that you'll wonder how you ever got work done using it.

An Overview of Major Features in Windows 95

Stability, speed, and better networking aren't the only ways in which Windows 95 distinguishes itself from its predecessors. This new version of Windows is packed with so many new features that you might think Microsoft started from scratch. Actually, they didn't. They took some of Windows 3.x, added a bit of Windows NT, mixed them together, and added some new features. It's all there if you look hard.

Note: This section covers the features that are available to all users of Windows 95. We'll look at the special features provided by the latest OSR2 version of Windows 95 in the later section "OEM Service Release 2—The Complete Story." Users of Service Pack 1 will have essentially the same feature set as the initial version of Windows 95.

The bottom line is that the combination of a new 32-bit environment and new features gives Windows 95 that new operating system look-and-feel. The fact that it borrows some of the time-tested code from previous versions means that it should be more stable than a completely new operating system. Here are the major new features:

- A new interface: Explorer
- Configuration management: the Registry
- Distributed applications: remote procedure calls
- Printer support
- DDE/OLE support
- Connectivity: going online
- Special-needs support: accessibility options
- File system update: long filenames

In the next few sections we'll look at the new features that Windows 95 provides. You'll get an overview of just how much these features will help you in your day-to-day work. You'll see more details of these features as the book goes on. Right now, just sit back and think about the big picture. Windows 95 provides a new panorama of welcome changes that you're sure to like.

Tip: Unlike with previous versions of Windows, it's easy to add features to and remove features from Windows 95. If you really want to fully explore the capabilities of this new operating system, perform a full installation. Check out all the new applications and see which ones work well for you. Once you have time to really check things out, remove the applications you don't need. We go into the specifics of how to do this in Chapter 4.

Explorer

Explorer is the new Windows 95 interface that replaces both Program Manager and File Manager. It provides the functionality of both, but in one package. Of course, if that's all Explorer had to offer, you might be well advised to keep your current programs in place. After all, you already know how to use them, so why bother to learn something new?

Several features make Explorer an interface that you will want to learn how to use. Figure 1.3 shows one of the myriad of reasons that you'll want to switch to this product. It shows what appear to be two completely different utility windows, yet both are Explorer. This utility allows you to configure the Windows interface to suit your needs; it doesn't force you into a certain way of thinking.

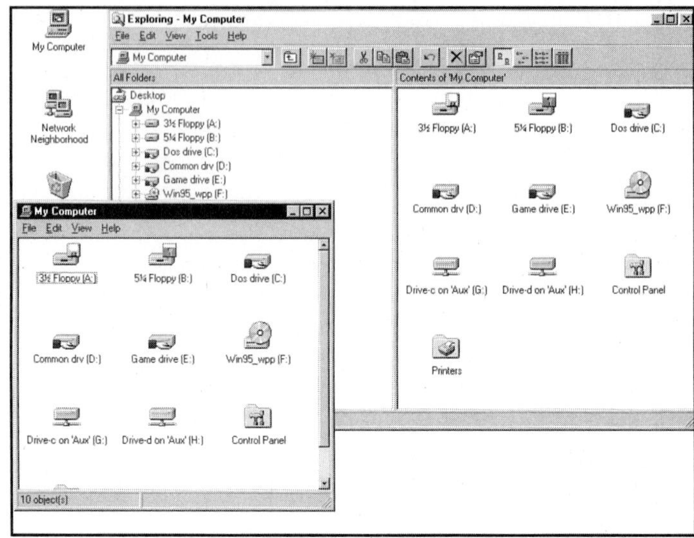

Figure 1.3.
Explorer offers both a one-pane and a two-pane interface that you can use to look at your hard drive. It doesn't require you to conform to one way of seeing the information you have available on your system.

Note: Windows 95 provides you with a new term—*folder*. It uses this term to describe any kind of container. A folder can hold files, applications, or other folders. Even the desktop is a folder. Whenever you see the term *folder*, you'll probably think of a directory. A folder isn't exactly the same as a directory, however. Think of it as a directory (real or imagined) with intelligence. We look at this concept in detail in Chapter 9.

The one- and two-pane look isn't the only way in which Explorer differentiates itself. Figure 1.4 shows another reason you'll want to make the change. There are four different ways to display the information on your hard drive: large icon, small icon, list, and details. I find that I'm most comfortable with the details view when I really need to know everything there is to know about a file, and the large icon view when I'm just working with some data. You'll likely find your own set of preferences. You might switch from view to view as I do. This is an important leap. Windows 3.x tended to stifle any kind of creative environment management. Windows 95 does everything it can to encourage this process.

There's actually a third form of Explorer, but you'll see only one copy of it installed on the system. It's better known as the Taskbar. You'll probably see it at the bottom of the Windows 95 display unless you specifically asked Windows 95 to move it. Figure 1.5 shows a typical Taskbar with some open applications.

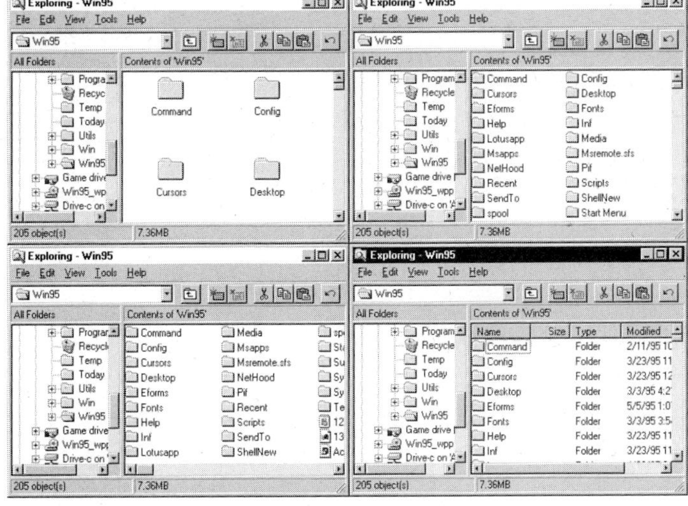

Figure 1.4.
Explorer provides a variety of ways to display the information on your system. You can choose from large icons, small icons, list, or details displays.

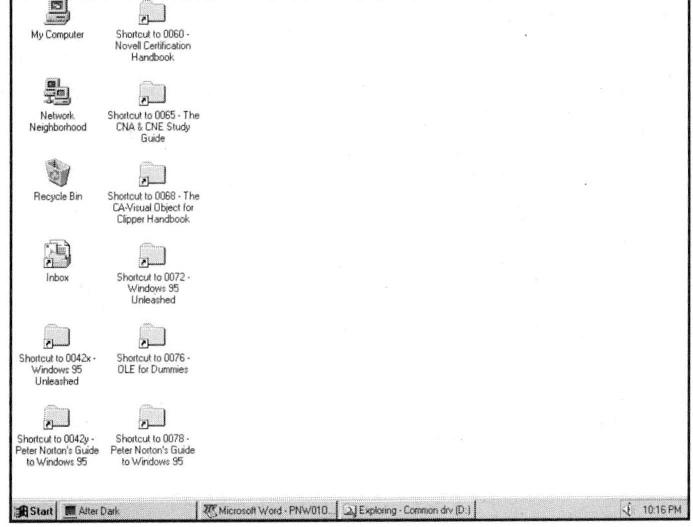

Figure 1.5.
The Taskbar is really just another form of Explorer. It allows you to keep track of any open applications and start new ones.

The Taskbar is probably one of the most versatile ways of keeping your system in check. Not only does it maintain a list of all your applications, but it helps you manage the open ones too. Ever try to find an application buried beneath all the other windows you have open? It's a real pain trying to figure out which window is which. The Taskbar displays all your applications in an easy-to-reach format. To select an open application, just click its button.

Starting a new application is easy, too. All you need to do is click the Start button and select from the menu the application you want to use. The Taskbar uses what is known as *sticky menus*. A sticky menu doesn't go away right away; it stays in place until you get done using it. You have to actually tell Windows 95 to get rid of the menu if you decide not to select something from it after all. This means that you don't have to work very hard to find something. Just point your way through the menu to find what you need.

At the right end of the Taskbar, you'll see one or more icons. In most cases, you'll see a clock. If your system has some type of sound board, the volume icon will appear there as well. Notebook computers usually display a battery icon in this area. International users might see an international icon at the end of the Taskbar. We cover all these features in detail in Chapter 5.

The Registry

The Windows 3.x Registry was so simple that most people never gave it a second thought. About the only thing it contained were some file associations and a few OLE settings. You might have found a few bits and pieces of other information in there as well, but for the most part, even Windows ignored the Registry.

Along came Windows NT. This product contains a Registry that's so complex that you need a four-year degree just to figure out the basics. The Windows NT Registry contains every piece of information about everything that the operating system needs to know. This includes equipment settings, software configuration, network setup, and all the .DLLs it needs to run applications.

Windows 95 uses a Windows NT-style Registry. However, because Windows 95 is designed for workstation use and not as a file server, its Registry is a bit less complex. You'll still see all the file associations that you had with Windows 3.x. The Windows 95 Registry also contains all your equipment settings, software configuration information, and a list of .DLLs to load. In essence, the Registry has become the central repository of information for the Windows 95 operating system.

The Windows 95 Registry also replaces two files that had bad reputations under Windows 3.x. Anyone who spent time working with Windows 3.x knows about the fun of working with the SYSTEM.INI and WIN.INI files. The WIN.INI file holds Windows environment settings; it changes the way Windows interacts with the user. The SYSTEM.INI file contains hardware and device-driver configuration information; it changes the way Windows configures itself during startup. Of course, the distinction between these two files is somewhat blurred. For example, WIN.INI holds the serial port and printer configuration information.

These two poorly organized, cryptic files hold the vast majority of configuration information for the Windows 3.1 system. Every time the user adds an application to Windows 3.1, the application adds yet another heading or two and some additional entries to both files. On the other hand, when the user gets rid of an application, the entries don't go with it. They just sort of hang around and slow system performance. Some entries can even cause error messages or, in extreme circumstances, a system crash. Windows 95 still supports these rather archaic and difficult-to-understand files, but it prefers that applications use the new Registry.

Note: Windows 95 copies the contents of SYSTEM.INI and WIN.INI into the Registry whenever possible. The only reason that these two files exist is to meet the needs of Windows 3.x applications. You could remove both files from your hard drive if you didn't have any older applications to run. Of course, in reality, it'll be quite a while before you can get rid of either file.

You use the RegEdit utility to view and change the contents of the Registry. It displays the Registry in the format shown in Figure 1.6. Windows 95 uses two hidden files, USER.DAT and SYSTEM.DAT, to store the Registry information, but RegEdit displays them as one contiguous file. Even though the RegEdit display might seem a bit difficult to understand at first, it's really not. The big difference between the Registry and the Windows 3.1 alternative of SYSTEM.INI and WIN.INI is that the Registry uses a hierarchical organization and plain English descriptions that you'll find easy to edit and maintain. Every application you add will add entries to this file, but the file's organization makes it easy for an application to remove the entries when you uninstall it. Even if you install an older application that doesn't understand the Registry, you can still remove its entries with ease.

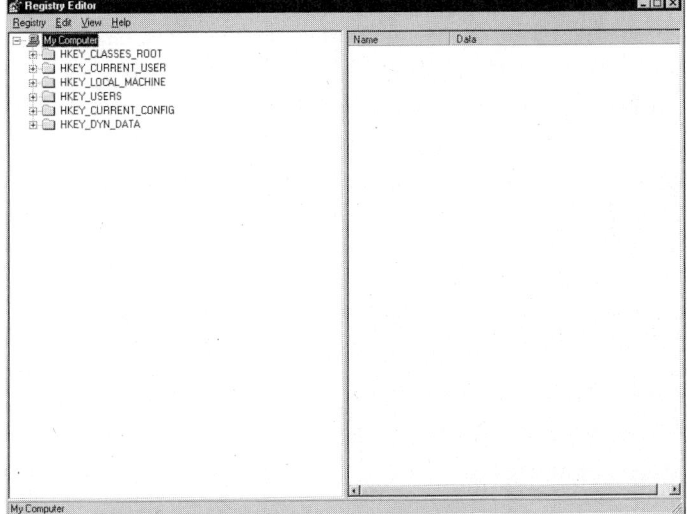

Figure 1.6.
A typical RegEdit opening screen. Each HKEY *key controls a different part of the Windows setup.*

The Windows 95 Registry uses two types of entries to maintain its organization: keys and values. Keys are a RegEdit topic. Think of a key as the heading that tells you what a particular section contains. Looking at all the keys provides an outline for a particular topic. The topics could range from the setup of each drive in the system to the file associations needed to configure the machine. The key at the top of the hierarchy usually contains generic information. Each subkey provides a little more detail about that particular topic. Keys always appear in the left side of the RegEdit window.

Values are the definition of a RegEdit topic; they describe the key in some way. Think of a value as the text that fills out the heading provided by a key. Values are like the text in this book, while keys are the headings that organize the text. A value can contain just about anything. For example, the value for a file association key can tell you which application Windows 95 will start when you double-click a file that has that extension in Explorer. A value could tell you which interrupt and I/O port settings a piece of hardware uses. Suffice it to say that you'll find the value you need by using the keys, but you'll find the actual information you need by reading the values.

There are three types of values: binary, string, and DWORD. Usually, only applications use the binary and DWORD value types. Values usually store configuration data in a format that can't be understood by humans. Some applications use DWORD or binary values to store data. For example, you might find the score from your last game of FreeCell here. String values provide a lot of information about the application and how it's configured. Hardware usually uses string values as well for interrupt and port information. Values always appear in the right side of the RegEdit window.

Key entries also have a superset. I differentiate these particular keys from the rest because they are the major headings in the Registry. During the rest of this discussion I refer to these special keys as *categories*. Think of categories as the chapter titles in a book. You need to go to the right chapter before you can find the right type of information. Information in one category might appear in the same order and at the same level in another category. The difference between the two is when Windows 95 uses the entries in one category versus another.

Categories are the six main keys under the `My Computer` key. Categories divide the Registry into six main areas:

- `HKEY_CLASSES_ROOT`
- `HKEY_CURRENT_USER`
- `HKEY_LOCAL_MACHINE`
- `HKEY_USERS`
- `HKEY_CURRENT_CONFIG`
- `HKEY_DYN_DATA`

Each category contains a specific type of information. As you can see, the Windows 95 Registry is much enhanced from its Windows 3.1 counterpart. Even though Windows 95 still has to use the infamous SYSTEM.INI and WIN.INI files for antiquated applications, the use of the Registry for all other purposes does reduce the user's workload. Eventually, all applications will use the Registry to store their configuration data.

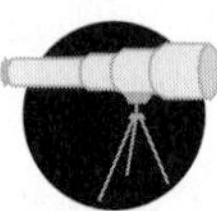

Looking Ahead: This part of the book provides you with a quick overview of the Registry. Chapter 7 provides an in-depth view of this very important aspect of Windows 95. The Registry allows you to mold Windows 95 into the configuration you need. As a result, learning everything you can about the Registry and how to modify it allows you to configure your system for optimum results. In addition, troubleshooting the Registry can often help you find problem areas that other tools might miss.

Remote Procedure Calls (RPCs)

Imagine, if you will, that your machine is part of a vast network of interconnected machines. Everyone on the network uses the same set of applications, including one fairly complex database program. In the old days, management would have simply gone out and bought a jumbo economy-sized mainframe to take care of the job. However, we're living in the days of distributed processing, where LANs abound and mainframes are somewhat passé. How do you make this big clunker of a database application work?

Remote procedure calls (RPCs) provide at least part of the answer to this puzzle. Everyone knows that Windows uses something called a .DLL (dynamic link library). What you might not realize is that these are mini-applications of a sort. Your application might need the functions contained in a .DLL. It asks Windows 95 to load that .DLL, and then it loads and executes the required code that the .DLL contains.

Old versions of Windows required that .DLLs appear on your machine. You couldn't use a .DLL that appeared on someone else's machine. Windows 95 changes all that. It allows you to call a .DLL on someone else's machine.

RPCs are a lot more than just a better way to find code that an application might need to run, though. They provide an extra bit of functionality that will literally change the way people compute. What would you do if you could install a second processor in your machine at a moment's notice, and then get rid of it when it was no longer needed? This is the second part of an RPC. The code that you ask it to execute actually does so on the machine where the .DLL resides. In effect, you get to load a second processor for a while, and you can get rid of it when it's no longer needed.

This is a very brief description of a complex process. The level of support you can expect from Windows 95 for RPCs varies as a factor of the network protocol you use. There are other environmental factors that you need to consider as well. Of course, your application has to make use of RPCs before you will see any benefit from them. In most cases, this means writing a custom application.

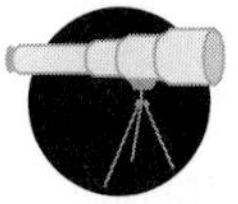

Looking Ahead: Chapters 12 and 23 help you understand what kind of RPC support you can expect from Windows 95. In most cases, it's a lot less than you might think, because this technology is still in its infancy.

Printer Support

How often have you heard people say that they disabled Print Manager under Windows 3.x for one reason or another? It's all too common, I'm afraid. There are several reasons that people do it. First and foremost, people feel that Print Manager is too slow to meet their needs. Lack of adequate DOS and interprocess support is another reason that people cite. Even the Print Manager interface receives its share of criticism.

Windows 95 fixes all these problems and more. Not only is the Printer dialog box easier to use in Windows 95, but it also provides far more options in the way you configure your printer. Figure 1.7 shows a typical display. Your dialog box might differ due to differences in printer capabilities. Network printing receives special emphasis in Windows 95 as well. Finally, you can now print from multiple applications—you can even mix a few DOS applications in for good measure—and never fear that the output from your printer will be a confused mess.

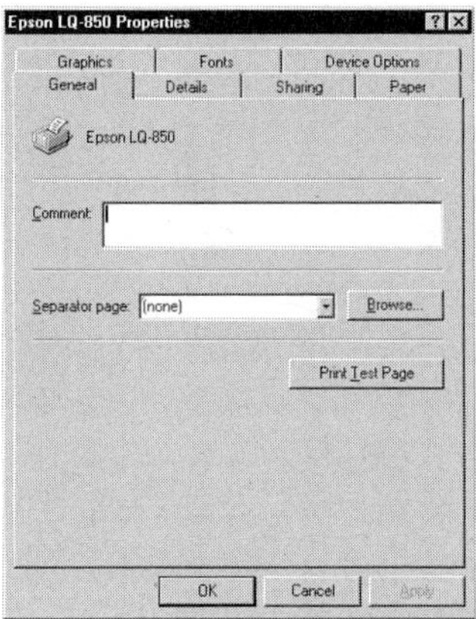

Figure 1.7.
Printing under Windows 95 is a lot easier and more flexible than it was under Windows 3.x.

Note: Be sure to get the Service Pack 1 update if you need access to NetWare NDS printer-related services. The shell update portion of the Service Pack will make it possible for you to use the Add Printer Wizard. This release also updates some of the printer drivers—most important of which are the PSCRIPT.DRV and UNIDRV.DLL drivers. Another printer-related issue is the security hole found in the initial release of Windows 95. Users of Samba's SMBCLIENT could gain unauthorized access to printers and network drives—Service Pack 1 clears up this problem. Finally, Service Pack 1 updates the LPT.VXD file to add support for ECP (Enhanced Communication Parallel) port bidirectional communications. ECP ports are used with certain printers like the Hewlett-Packard LaserJet 4/5 and the Lexmark LaserPrinters.

Looking Ahead: Chapter 14 contains the majority of the printer-specific information for this book. However, you'll find little nuggets of printer information throughout the book. For example, Chapter 9 describes printer configuration for the desktop. Chapter 13 gives you some ideas on how to fully exploit your printer hardware, and Chapter 17 looks at printer connections in general. Finally, Chapter 19 talks about some of the choices you need to make when using a printer in a network setting.

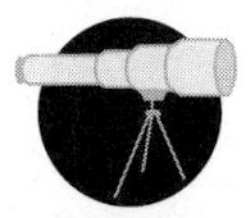

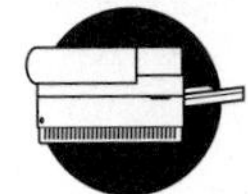

DDE/OLE Support

Windows 95 provides several new features, especially in the area of OLE (object linking and embedding) support. One of the biggest aids that Windows 95 provides is installed support for OLE 2. Windows 3.x came with OLE 1 support. If you've installed an application that provides OLE 2 support, you're in luck.

The differences between OLE 2 and OLE 1 are significant. For example, OLE 2 provides the means to embed objects within objects. It also provides methods of allowing the server application to change the menus and toolbar of the client application. As far as the user is concerned, he's using the same application. The window doesn't change; only the tools change to meet the current requirements.

Windows 95 provides a few additional features as well. For example, OLE now use 32-bit drivers whenever possible. This change will dramatically increase the speed of either linking or embedding objects in applications. It also helps reduce the memory burden of using OLE.

DDE support under Windows 95 hasn't changed much in theory from Windows 3.x. However, we'll look at some of the ways that Windows 95 does make it easier to use DDE.

Looking Ahead: Chapter 12 concentrates on both OLE and DDE support under Windows 95. Not only will we examine some of the architectural requirements for both, but we'll also spend some hands-on time with these two important features. Have you ever been able to figure out the Object Packager? This chapter will tell you how to use it to your advantage. I've also added updated information in this chapter for ActiveX. You'll want to find out how this updated technology can help you on the Internet and your local network as well.

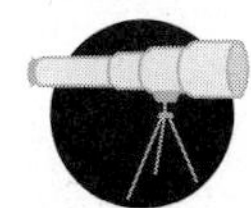

Going Online

Connectivity is the name of the game under Windows 95. Older versions of Windows provided only the most rudimentary communications facilities. Windows 95 provides Microsoft Exchange—a centralized location for all your communications needs. It doesn't really matter where a message needs to go—online or network. All you need to do is specify a recipient, and Microsoft Exchange will make sure it gets to where it needs to go.

Figure 1.8 shows Microsoft Exchange. As you can see, it consists of an inbox, outbox, and sent messages box. A fourth box allows you to recover messages deleted by accident. Overall, this represents one of the easiest ways to manage all your e-mail if you get it from more than one source. It also represents an efficient method of sharing that information with other people, even if they aren't connected to the same services you are.

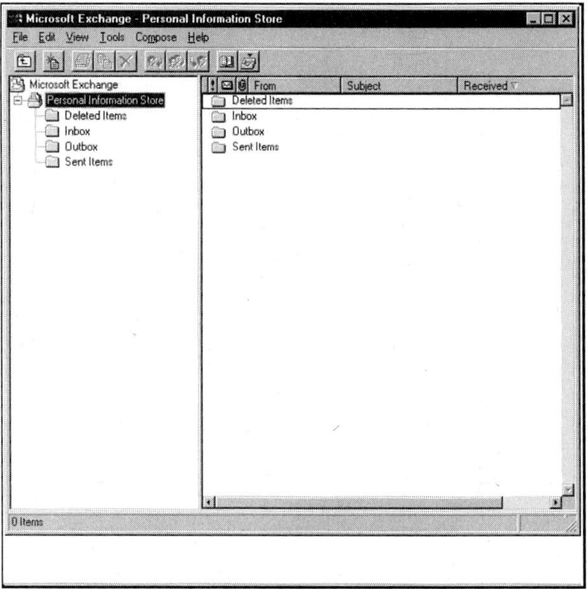

Figure 1.8.
Windows 95 provides extensive connectivity features using Microsoft Exchange. This centralized approach to managing all your e-mail presents some very definite advantages.

Of course, there are always a few problems with something as complex as this. We might eventually have a single package that provides every bit of support you'll need to access all your e-mail, but you won't see it today. Microsoft Exchange currently provides limited support for only some of the online services. In addition, you'll still need a separate communications program if you plan to "explore" these online services much. Even though Microsoft Exchange provides a platform for total coverage, it doesn't provide all the modules needed to do so today. Microsoft Exchange is excellent at managing your e-mail, but not much more.

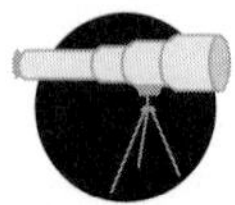

Looking Ahead: Chapter 19 helps you understand some of the hardware requirements for using the communications features that Windows 95 provides. Once you get the hardware working, look at Chapter 20 for full details on using the software. Connectivity has become a major need for most users. It doesn't matter what line of work you're in or precisely how you use your computer. Somewhere along the way, you'll need to communicate with someone.

Accessibility

Windows 95 addresses the needs of people who have special computing requirements. The Accessibility dialog box, shown in Figure 1.9, provides everyone with features that make the computer easier to use. Features such as sticky keys and the ability of the computer to ignore too many repeated keystrokes really help those who can't easily use a computer.

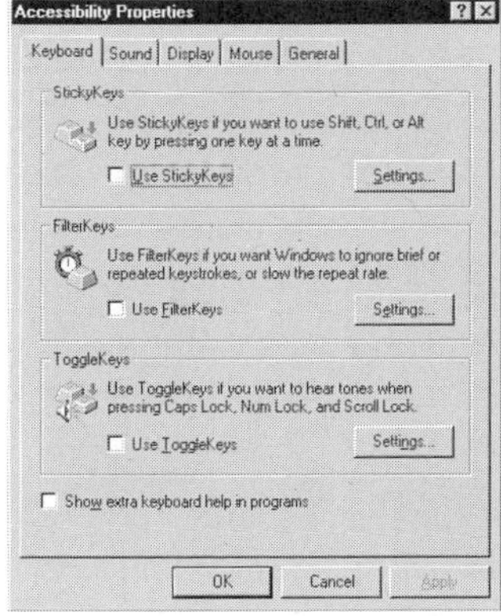

Figure 1.9.
The Accessibility features provided by Windows 95 are for everyone, not just those with special needs.

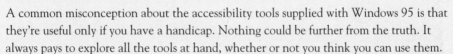

Peter's Principle: Always Check the Tools at Hand

A common misconception about the accessibility tools supplied with Windows 95 is that they're useful only if you have a handicap. Nothing could be further from the truth. It always pays to explore all the tools at hand, whether or not you think you can use them.

Many people turn on the ToggleKeys feature on the Keyboard tab of the Accessibility dialog box. This feature makes an audible noise when you press the Caps Lock, Num Lock, or Scroll Lock keys. It's a really handy feature for touch typists who might be paying more attention to the paper they're typing from than the screen they're typing to.

I personally find the MouseKeys feature a bonus. It allows you to use the arrow keys to move the mouse cursor. This is a real bonus when you're using a drawing program and need a little extra control over the size and position of drawing elements.

Still other people find that the High Contrast display feature is a nice way to give their eyes a break after a difficult day. You don't have to leave it on all the time—just when your eyes get tired.

Windows 95 is filled with little hidden tools. I discuss the majority of them in this book, but only you can decide to use them. Always use the tools at hand whenever possible to improve your productivity—especially when that tool is provided free of charge.

There are four major tabs within the Accessibility Options dialog box (plus one general tab that configures the dialog box itself):

- **Mouse:** MouseKeys lets you use the arrow keys to move the mouse pointer. Of course, any peripheral device that acts the same way that the arrow keys do will also move the mouse pointer, so you have a variety of options at your disposal. For example, some people use an external keypad that acts like the arrow keys. Using MouseKeys would allow you to use this external keypad instead of the mouse.
- **Keyboard:** There are actually three aids in this area. StickyKeys lets you send a Ctrl, Shift, or Alt key in combination with a second key to the computer. The FilterKeys option prevents Windows 95 from misinterpreting mistaken keystrokes. Essentially, it delays the repeating keystroke feature of most keyboards. The keyboard still sends the repeating keystrokes, but Windows 95 ignores them for a specific period of time—the additional keystrokes end up in the bit bucket instead of on your display. Finally, ToggleKeys causes Windows 95 to output a sound whenever you press the Caps Lock, Num Lock, or Scroll Lock keys.
- **Display:** The Use High Contrast option provided on this tab is fairly self-explanatory. It causes Windows 95 to use colors and fonts that are easily seen. This high-contrast display feature makes it very easy to see everything on the display without eyestrain.
- **Sound:** The SoundSentry feature displays a visual cue every time your computer makes a sound. The ShowSounds feature displays a dialog box with every sound. The caption tells you what sound the computer made.

Each of these features helps people who have special considerations when using a computer. The solutions aren't perfect, but they're a step in the right direction.

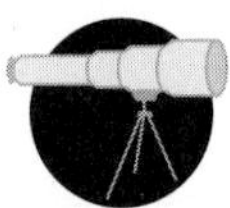

Looking Ahead: Chapter 15 takes a look at two of the most important aspects of the Accessibility dialog box—mice and keyboards. These two components represent a major challenge to a lot of people out there, but Windows 95 does a good job of making them more user-friendly. You'll find some additional information about the accessibility options in Chapter 16. This chapter shows how you can use the display adapter features to reduce eyestrain by making the display much more readable. Finally, Chapter 13 will help you understand some of the limited sound options provided by the Accessibility dialog box.

Long Filenames

Macintosh users have long thumbed their noses at PC users for a variety of reasons. Some of these reasons are right on the mark. Take long filenames, for example. Macintosh users have long had this very valuable resource at their disposal, while PC users have been stuck with filenames that are limited to eight characters and a three-character extension.

Trying to think of descriptive filenames while limiting yourself to eight characters is pretty difficult. You can end up with some very strange combinations if you're not careful. Also, these filenames almost always fail to help you much when it's time to figure out what the file contains. For example, consider a spreadsheet that contains the fourth quarter report on southeastern sales for 1996. How do you condense this idea into eight short characters? You'd probably end up with something like 4QSES96.WKS. Isn't that easy to remember?

Windows 95 fixes this problem. Filenames can now be up to 255 characters long. This means that you should be able to get as descriptive as necessary and that no one will ever again spend days searching through your files looking for the annual report.

Peter's Principle: Sometimes Long Is Too Long

Windows 95 finally provides one feature that Macintosh folks have had for a long time—long filenames. You could create a filename that contained 255 characters if you so desired, but that would be counterproductive for three reasons. First, a long filename should be descriptive, but making a filename too descriptive mires the meaning in a cloud of details. Second, making a filename too long makes it difficult to type from the command line if you need to do so. Third, extremely long filenames consume a great amount of space on-screen and reward you with very little additional information.

Use a simple but descriptive filename such as Letter to Sally at Accounting. You might even want to include a little more detail, such as Letter to Sally at Accounting About Pay Raise. The point where you cross the line between a filename that's descriptive and one that's too long is when you use one such as Letter to Sally Jones at the Accounting Department That Asks About the Pay Raise I Requested in 1996 But Got Turned Down by the Boss for Reasons Unknown. See my point? (This example uses only 125 characters—can you imagine what it would have looked like with 255?)

Microsoft did have to make a concession with long filenames. A lot of old applications on the market can read only 8.3 filenames. Microsoft had to come up with some way to allow these old applications to work with the new file system. Suppose you have a file with the name Fourth Quarter Report on Southeastern Sales for 1996.WKS. Windows 95 will display this as FOURTH~1.WKS to a DOS application. It takes the first six letters of the filename as a starting point. Then it looks to see if any other files start with the same six letters. If not, it adds ~1 to the filename. If so, it adds a tilde (~) with the next number in line. Assuming that there are three other FOURTH files in that directory, Windows 95 would name the fourth file FOURTH~4.WKS. It's not a perfect solution, but it works.

Tip: You won't always work with people who have access to Windows 95 long filename support. Therefore, it almost always pays to begin your long filename in a way that translates well into the old 8.3 file naming technique. Remember that because of the way Windows 95 creates an 8.3 filename, you'll get only six characters for the name itself.

Use a name such as FY 96 Accounting Support Data to name a spreadsheet file. This will translate to FY96AC~1.WKS or something similar. (Windows 95 automatically removes spaces from the long filename when creating a short filename equivalent.) You get the convenience of using a long filename without inconveniencing your coworkers.

I was a little amazed by something else Microsoft decided to do. The new file system used by Windows 95 isn't compatible with Windows NT. This means that anyone using Windows NT will still see the 8.3 filenames of yesterday when looking at your machine, even though Windows NT supports long filenames. You'd think that people could have gotten together to ensure compatibility across product lines for something as simple as a filename.

OEM Service Release 2—The Complete Story

Microsoft recently released a new version of Windows 95 that has users talking—this new release offers features that many of you have been asking for since day one. A good number of those users are upset that Microsoft only made the update available to original equipment manufacturers (OEMs) and not to the public at large. Microsoft's reasoning is that most of the features provided by OSR2 (OEM Service Release 2) are really useful only if you have a new machine. I agree that some of the features, such as the power management improvements, do fall into that category. However, there's nothing stopping someone from using the new FAT 32 file system or updating their machine to use the CDFS enhancements that OSR2 provides. Fortunately, after a lot of user complaints, Microsoft made a significant number of the non-hardware-related update pieces available for separate download. You might spend a lot of time getting all the updates you want, but at least you can get them. As far as the new hardware updates go, you'll just have to wait until Windows 97 becomes available or you get a new machine.

Let's begin by looking at what OSR2 has to offer. Table 1.1 tells you about the updated support that the OSR2 version of Windows 95 provides. It also tells you which updates you can download and from where. (You'll need an Internet account to get any of the updates unless you happen to know of a BBS that has them, or can get them from a WUGNET site like the ones on CompuServe.) All the Internet site names in the table begin with `http://www.microsoft.com/`. Simply append the rest of the URL listed in the Download column. For example, if you want to download Internet Explorer 3.0, look at `http://www.microsoft.com/ie/download/`. (The only exception to this rule is the MSN 1.3 update.) If you see an N/A for a particular feature, you can't download it.

Table 1.1. OSR2 update information.

Feature	*Download*	*Description*
32-bit DLC	`/windows/software/dlc.htm`	Data Link Control (DLC) support for SNA host connectivity.
ActiveMovie	`ie/download/ieadd.htm`	See high-quality QuickTime and MPEG-1 format videos, even over an Internet connection.
Automatic ScanDisk	N/A	Windows 95 now detects abnormal exits and automatically tests your hard drive before the next startup. This allows you to fix all errors on the hard drive, even if the files are normally used by Windows.
CDFS	N/A	The CD File System (CDFS) will now support ISO 9660 disks up to 4GB in size and CD-I (CD-Interactive) format CD-ROMs.
Desktop management	Available soon	Allows a desktop management application to monitor devices on your PC. (This feature currently supports the Desktop Management Interface standard 1.1.)
Dial-up networking	`windows/software.htm`	The big news with this release is scripting capability. You also get a number of user interface updates.
DirectX 2.0	`ie/download/ieadd.htm`	Get high-performance 2-D and 3-D graphics. It also enhances your system's sound capabilities. Games are about the only application that use this support right now, but expect other applications to use it in the future.
Display	Available soon	You can now dynamically change screen resolution and color depth (the resolution change was available in previous versions for certain displays). This update also allows you to change the refresh rate for most of the newer display adapter chipsets.

continues

Table 1.1. continued

Feature	*Download*	*Description*
DriveSpace	N/A	This update allows DriveSpace to support drives up to 2GB in size. Unfortunately, you can't use this update and FAT 32 at the same time.
FAT 32	N/A	As hard disks increase in size, more and more users are complaining about lost disk space. FAT 32 represents one way to get rid of this problem. It supports drives up to 2TB in size and uses a 4KB cluster size.
Fixes and updates	`/windows/software/updates.htm`	There are a variety of minor fixes and updates that you can download from this site. The most important updates are to the OLE components. You can also download an updated Windows Messaging client and fixes to Microsoft Fax.
Fonts	Available soon	Updated support for the new Hewlett-Packard LaserJet 4 gray scale fonts.
Infrared support	`/windows/software/irda.htm`	Need a non-wire connection for your laptop? This new infrared data support fits the bill. Your infrared port must support the Infrared Data Association (IrDA) 2.0 standard to use this support.
Intel MMX Support	N/A	Intel's multimedia extensions (MMX) support is available for applications that want to use it. Consider this future technology, for the moment.
Internet Connection Wizard	`ie/download/`	A new utility that helps you configure a connection for your ISP. It can also help in the sign-up process.
Internet Explorer 3.0	`ie/download/`	This new version of Internet Explorer includes support for ActiveX, HTML style sheets, frames, Java, and a lot more.

Feature	*Download*	*Description*
Internet mail and news	`ie/download/ieadd.htm`	Unlike many browsers, the mail and news reader for Internet Explorer 3.0 comes as a separate product. I find this the most inconvenient feature of Internet Explorer. This product does support both SMTP and POP3 mail clients.
IRQ routing	N/A	Along with enhanced PCI device support, this update includes support for PCI interrupt routers.
MSN 1.3	`http://www.msn.com/default.asp`	The biggest improvement here is speed.
NDIS 4.0	N/A	Supports NDIS 4.0 network interface card (NIC) drivers.
NetMeeting	`ie/download/ieadd.htm`	You can use this handy utility to make phone calls over the Internet. It supports conference calling. You also get a whiteboard, chat, and file transfer capability.
NetWare NDS Service	`/windows/software/msnds.htm`	You'll get a better level of NDS support with this release, but the Novell version is still more capable.
Online Services folder	N/A	Microsoft now provides client software for America Online, CompuServe, CompuServe WOW!, and AT&T WorldNet. Expect to see additional clients in the future. (Even though you can't download this support from a Microsoft site, you should be able to download it from the vendor-specific sites.)
OpenGL	Available soon	This graphics API has been available to Windows NT users for quite some time—now Windows 95 users have it, too. The OSR2 version of Windows 95 ships with screen savers that can use this support.
PCI docking/ bridging	N/A	You can now use PCI devices in PCI docking stations.

continues

Table 1.1. continued

Feature	*Download*	*Description*
PCMCIA	N/A	This update adds support for PC Card 32 (Cardbus) bridges, PCMCIA cards that operate on 3.3 volts rather than 5 volts, multifunction PCMCIA network and modem cards, and PCMCIA Global Positioning Satellite (GPS) devices.
Personal Web Server	`ie/download/ieadd.htm`	While this product won't allow you to build a full-sized Internet site, you can use it for testing and small-sized intranet purposes.
Power management	N/A	Advanced Power Management (APM) features on computers get more complex all the time. This update adds support for APM BIOS 1.2, wake-on-ring modems, multi-battery PCs, drive spin down, and powering down of inactive PCMCIA modems.
Storage devices	N/A	New storage support includes IDE Bus Mastering, 120MB floptical drives, removable IDE media, Zip drives, and CD changers. You'll also get better diagnostics through the use of the SMART predictive disk failure APIs.
Voice modem	`/windows/software/drivers/unimodem.htm`	Voice modems are the wave of the future. With these API enhancements, you can use one device to accept faxes, transfer files, and record your voice mail.
Wang imaging	`/windows/software/img_us.htm`	This utility allows you to view graphics in the JPG, XIF, TIFF, BMP, and FAX formats. You can also scan and annotate images, using the built-in TWAIN scanner support.

As you can see, OSR2 almost qualifies as a minor revision to the operating system rather than a patch. Some changes, such as FAT 32, are so significant that they really affect the way you work with Windows as a whole. This table should begin to whet your appetite for the information that follows. Throughout the book we'll look at how the OSR2 version of Windows 95 can benefit you as a user. Just look for the OSR2 icon if you want to find the update information quickly. We'll also look at some of the pitfalls of these new features. In the long run, you'll develop a better understanding of why Microsoft might have decided to make this a new-machine-only update rather than release it to the general public. Hopefully, they'll decide to make more of the pieces available by the time you read this. (They could at least provide a single place to download the update.)

On Your Own

Practice creating long filenames that a DOS or Windows 3.x user can understand. Use Explorer to create a new file in a temporary folder, and give it a long filename. Then open the DOS prompt and view that same filename. Does the name make sense in both contexts? If not, you'll need to spend a little more time working on this. Remember that you're effectively reduced to six characters for the filename because of the way that Windows 95 differentiates between different files with similar long filenames.

Install Service Pack 1 if you have an older version of Windows 95 installed on your machine. This patch file will help you get past some of the problem areas in the initial release of Windows 95. (Don't use Service Pack 1 on a new machine with OSR2 installed—that release already contains all the Service Pack 1 updates.)

Go through the list of Windows 95 improvements discussed in the "Windows 95 Improvements" section and see which of them will help you the most. Be sure to spend extra time considering the accessibility options.

If you don't already own OSR2, you may want to spend some time looking at Table 1.1 to see which updates you want to download. Laptop users will want to pay special attention to some of the laptop-specific features such as infrared port support. Users who already own OSR2 will want to take a look at Table 1.1 as well to ensure that they're getting the best use out of this updated version of Windows 95.

2

Introducing Windows 95

Learning to use a new product almost always involves some painful decisions on the part of the user. You always need to decide what to keep and what to throw away. For example, when I started making the move from DOS to Windows, I had to make a painful decision about my word processor. I was still using DOS enough that it would've been nice to have a word processor available there. Yet trying to make my DOS word processor work from within Windows was an exercise in frustration. In addition to the problems of using my old word processor, making the move also meant converting all those files to the new format. Talk about a nightmare! I eventually decided to use the Windows version exclusively and rely on a small text editor for taking notes while working in DOS. It actually worked out to my advantage, because the text editor was a TSR that allowed me to take all my notes without ever leaving the main application I was working with.

Moving from Windows 3.x to Windows 95 involves similar decisions on the part of the user—albeit for different reasons. My current word processor works just fine under Windows 95. I won't have to replace it anytime soon to make it do what I need it to. However, it's a pain having to translate any long filenames that I run across before I know which file to load. In other words, I might have several chapters for a book with a long filename such as Chapter 1 - Introducing a New Topic. This title ends up looking like CHAPTE~3.DOC when I go to open it under the Windows 3.x version of Word for Windows. Of course, using the file naming technique I introduced in Chapter 1 helps, but it doesn't do much in situations where people send me files with filenames that aren't recognizable in the 8.3 format.

You need to consider other things when making the move as well. For example, will that old Windows 3.x version of a product give you the same performance as a new Windows 95 version? In many respects it will, but checking out the differences between Word for Windows (a 16-bit application) and Word for Windows NT (a 32-bit application) shows that the NT version will always perform some tasks better. (Even though Microsoft has released Word for Windows 95 7.x—a product specifically designed for Windows 95—some vendors haven't followed suit. If you can't find a Windows 95-specific version of your application, a Windows NT version of a product may work better than its 16-bit counterpart.) For example, I send a lot of long documents to the printer. NT actually returns control to me a lot faster than its Windows 3.x counterpart, and I seldom notice any slowing while the print cycle proceeds. The reason for this improved performance is simple: Windows 95 allows you to use applications that provide 32-bit support. In addition, these applications normally hand off tasks such as printing and background pagination to a lower-priority thread. The application doesn't worry about the task again until it's complete. I discuss threads later. For now, all you need to know is that they enhance your system's performance in a variety of ways by organizing its use of resources better.

Tip: You don't have to wait until vendors get around to writing Windows 95-specific applications. Many Windows NT applications run just fine under Windows 95. For example, products such as the Windows NT version of Texam Project work just fine under Windows 95. In most cases, mainstream vendors such as Microsoft and Corel have already

come out with Windows 95 versions of their product. You should use the Windows 95 version whenever possible because it will provide better performance. Don't try to use Windows NT disk utilities under Windows 95, though; you could damage your system. The only other criterion that you need to worry about is whether the product supports the WIN32s standard. Even if an application doesn't use the full Windows NT API, it will likely run under Windows 95. Of course, it always pays to check the return policy of the software you buy—especially when you're not 100 percent certain that it will work. Using Windows NT applications today means that you won't have to wait for a vendor to release a new version of their product tomorrow.

Some of your decisions will even affect the Microsoft-supplied utilities that you use. For example, the version of Microsoft Paintbrush supplied with Windows 3.x provides support for both .BMP and .PCX files. This is a very handy feature to have available, because you can use this program to make quick transitions from the Windows format to the more common .PCX format that many applications support. The version of Microsoft Paint provided with Windows 95 supports only .BMP files. You no longer have the option of using .PCX files. This is a real loss in some situations. Unfortunately, the differences don't end here. Paintbrush provides only OLE 1 support, while Paint provides OLE 2 support (and 32-bit support at that). It's a no-win situation unless you keep both utilities handy, which really doesn't make sense either. The bottom line is that every transition involves compromise. You'll likely find this true for the transition from Windows 3.x to Windows 95 as well.

Note: Microsoft didn't fix the problems associated with using the OLE 2 features of Paint in the initial version of the product. Currently, you can't use the Copy and Paste Special method of inserting an object into a compound document by using Paint. You must use the newer "Insert Object" method of inserting the object from the client application. (Chapter 12 covers the differences between these two methods.) This could seriously affect how people use this handy utility. I often grabbed a piece of a .PCX file and used it in another document. Paint doesn't allow me to do this very easily. Both the Service Pack 1 and OSR2 versions of the product appear to fix the problem, though you still can't create a link to the picture.

This chapter continues where Chapter 1 left off. It gives you a bird's-eye view of what you can expect from Windows 95. This includes the new utilities as well as a quick look at the internal workings of Windows 95. Of course, I cover more specific details of some of these items in later chapters. Right now, just sit back and enjoy the view of a new operating system.

Explorer: The New Interface

The first thing that every Windows 95 user will notice is the new interface. Windows 95 has a new and cleaner look that every user will come to enjoy using. In fact, I'm often surprised at just how cumbersome Windows 3.x feels when I need to use someone else's machine. Explorer is the replacement for Program Manager that just about every user wanted from the very beginning. (The fact that Program Manager was a poorly designed interface was highlighted by the proliferation of alternative desktop products on the market.) It offers something for everyone, and in a way that makes it simultaneously powerful and easy to use.

Note: You can probably use your current Windows 3.x alternative interface under Windows 95, but you'll want to update it when a Windows 95-specific version becomes available (most vendors have made them available as of this writing). Most Windows 3.x interfaces can't offer the full support that they provided under the old version because they don't know how to work with Windows 95. In addition, you won't receive Windows 95-specific benefits such as long filenames.

Chapter 1 took a quick look at Explorer and some of the data views that it offers. Viewing information is only the tip of the interface iceberg. To really use an interface, you need to get inside and work with it. Your data has to be accessible at all times and yet not get in the way.

Let's begin our tour of Explorer by examining how it's organized. Figure 2.1 shows the two-pane configuration of Explorer and the large icons view. On the left side of the display is the directory tree. You need to make note of several features of this directory tree for future reference. The first thing you'll notice is that the tree doesn't represent a single drive or even the contents of all the drives; it's more of a "machine tree" than anything else. This "machine tree" is divided into three elements:

- **The drive section:** This is the area where the contents of all your data drives are displayed. This includes any network drives that you're connected to.
- **The configuration section:** This area contains two icons in our sample display. (You might also see other icons here, such as Dial-Up Networking.) Control Panel provides access to every machine configuration component that Windows 95 has to offer. It includes both hardware and software configuration. I take a much more detailed look at this particular component later in the book. Windows 95 also provides a Printers icon. You could access this icon from within Control Panel, but putting it here makes access a lot more convenient.
- **The ancillary section:** The ancillary section could contain any number of icons. The sample in Figure 2.1 contains several, including the Recycle Bin icon. The Recycle Bin is where any documents end up that you erase in Explorer. I cover this feature in greater detail later. This is the only icon that always appears. It performs the same function as the

Recycle Bin on your desktop. The Network Neighborhood icon appears when you have a network installed on your machine. It allows you to attach to network resources and view network data. The Network Neighborhood is a very handy way to discover what types of information you have at your fingertips.

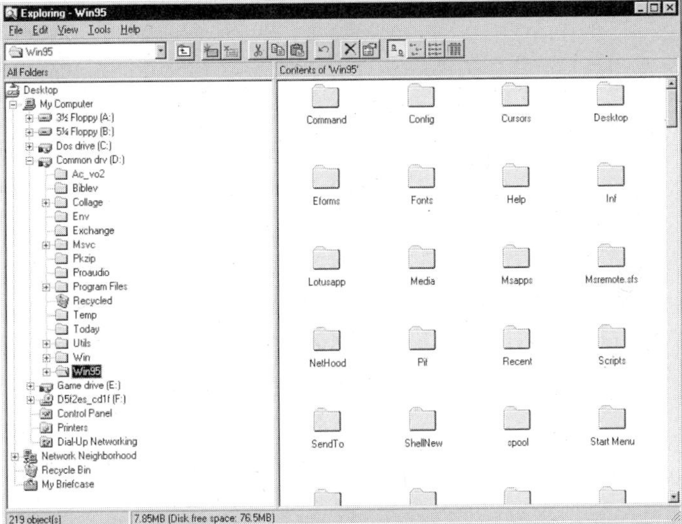

Figure 2.1.
The Explorer display is easier to understand when you break it into its components.

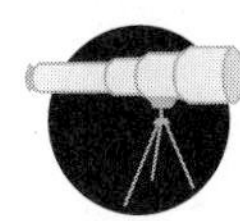

Looking Ahead: Future chapters look at other aspects of Explorer. Read Chapter 5 if you want some additional tips on optimizing your work environment using Explorer. I also talk about some advanced tips on ways to configure Explorer in the sections that follow.

Now that you have some idea of what the left pane contains, let's look at the right pane. Clicking any of the objects in the left pane displays its contents in the right pane. If you click a drive icon, you see the folders and files that the drive contains in the right pane. Click Network Neighborhood and you get a view of all the machines attached to the network. You can also use the icons in the right pane to open a file or folder. Double-click a folder and you see what it contains. Double-click a file and you perform the default action associated with that file.

There are a number of ways to use Explorer to organize your data. Each tool provides a different method of viewing and working with your data. Let's begin with one of the first tools that you'll need to use under Windows 95—the context menu.

Every object you use in Windows 95 provides a context menu. If you have a doubt as to what something is, how to configure it, or just about anything else you can do with that object, a simple right-click will answer your question. Figure 2.2 shows a typical context menu. Don't let its simplicity fool you. There's a lot more here than meets the eye.

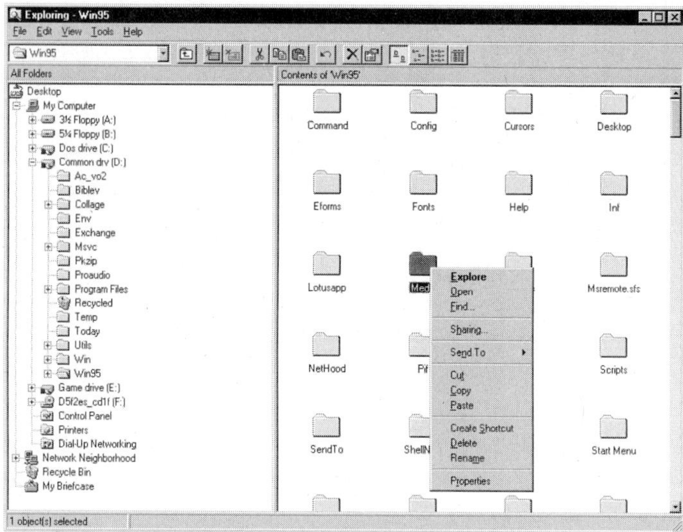

Figure 2.2.
The context menu is one way to discover exactly what you can do with an object. In most cases it also tells you enough about the object that you can determine its purpose.

Every context menu for a file or folder contains five or six major sections. Each section tells you something about the object associated with that menu. The following paragraphs outline each section and its purpose.

- **Actions:** The very first section of the context menu tells you what kinds of actions you can perform with the object. The default action—normally Open—appears in bold print. Chapter 5 shows how you can change the default action to meet your needs. In addition to the Open action, you'll likely see a Print data file action. Folders normally include an Explore and a Find action. One new feature of Windows 95 is the ability to view specific file types. This action appears on the context menu when available. Using a viewer allows you to see what a file contains without actually opening it for editing. A viewer also consumes less memory. We explore how View works a little later in this chapter. You'll see one other type of entry in the context menu. If the file extension doesn't appear in the Registry, Windows 95 won't know what to do with it. In this case, you'll see an Open With... entry in place of the usual ones.

- **Network:** This is an optional section that normally contains a single entry—Sharing. Some objects support sharing and others don't. It all depends on how you have your network set up. Normally, peer-to-peer networks enable this option only for folders. Larger networks—such as those from Novell—provide this entry for both files and folders.
- **Send To:** Use this special entry if you want to send the folder or file to a floppy drive or other location. We'll see later that you can modify the destinations listed in this entry to include just about anything you might need. Windows 95 comes installed to support the Briefcase and any floppies connected to your system as destinations. Chapter 18 describes the Briefcase in detail.

Tip: It's often handy to create additional destinations such as the desktop, project folders, and network drives for this section of the context menu. Always make these destinations practical. In other words, don't add another directory listing to this rather important list. All you need to do is add destinations that you use on a daily basis.

- **Editing:** Believe it or not, you can edit an object just like everything else under Windows 95. This section contains entries for Cut, Copy, and Paste. You can place a copy of the object on the Clipboard, and then paste as many copies as needed onto other objects. These are full-fledged copies, not the shortcuts (object links) that we examine in the next section. If you cut an object, Windows 95 doesn't remove the icon from the display. It grays the icon and waits until you paste the object somewhere else before removing it permanently. This prevents you from accidentally erasing objects. Cutting a new object before you paste the first one leaves the first object in its original location.
- **Manipulation:** This section usually contains three entries, but it can contain more. The Create Shortcut option allows you to place a link to a file or folder somewhere else. Chapter 5 shows how you can use this feature to make your desktop a friendlier place. The Delete option sends the file to the Recycle Bin. You can still recover it later, if necessary. The Rename option allows you to change the long filename associated with the file. Remember that Windows 95 automatically determines the 8.3 filename based on the specific formula we looked at in Chapter 1.

Tip: You don't have to send objects to the Recycle Bin if you don't want to. Simply select the object you want to delete, and then press Shift-Delete to erase it permanently (as far as Windows is concerned). Even if an object does get erased by accident, you can usually unerase it by using the Norton Utilities, for some length of time after you permanently erase it. (The time interval varies by the amount of empty space on your drive and the amount of use that drive gets.) Because the Recycle Bin's space is limited, you'll always want to reserve it for objects that you might need later.

- **Properties:** Every object—it doesn't matter what—contains a Properties entry on its context menu. Clicking this entry always displays a dialog box that allows you to view and configure the properties of that particular object. Figure 2.3 shows the Properties dialog box for a file. As you can see, the Properties dialog box for a file shows the full filename, any attributes associated with the file, and some statistical information. Folders usually contain about the same information as files but provide some additional statistics as well. Disks, on the other hand, contain a wealth of information about the drive as a whole. This Properties dialog box even provides access to the three maintenance tools that Windows 95 provides to manage disk drives. You'll find that the Properties dialog box for other objects, such as the desktop, contains a wealth of information too. For example, the Desktop Properties dialog box allows you to change the system colors and display resolution. You can even use it to change your wallpaper.

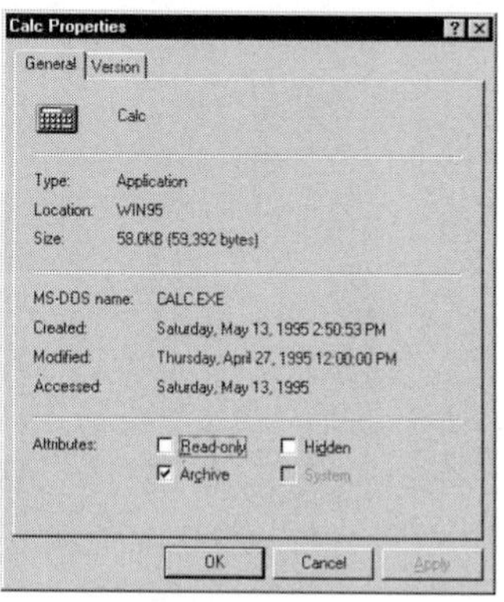

Figure 2.3.
Every object in Windows 95 has a Properties dialog box. The contents of this dialog box vary by object. This dialog box shows the properties of a file.

Peter's Principle: Learning by Doing: A Fun Way to Increase Your Windows 95 Knowledge

You'll want to spend some time right-clicking various objects on your system to see what type of context menu options they provide. It also pays to spend a little time looking at the Properties dialog boxes for various objects, even if you don't use certain objects very much. Windows 95 provides a variety of methods to access each of the configuration dialog boxes on your system, and most of them appear in these context menus or within the Properties dialog box. If you think—as I do—that changing common configuration items using Control Panel is a waste of time, see whether Windows 95 provides a faster method.

There are two things to remember when you experiment with your system. First, always click Cancel instead of OK when backing out of a Properties dialog box, to avoid making inadvertent changes to your system. Second, clicking outside of a context menu closes it without performing any action. In most cases, the safest place to click is the desktop.

Some objects on your system include some very specialized context menu entries. For example, if you right-click the Recycle Bin, you'll see an option to empty it. Right-clicking the desktop provides a New option that you can use to create new files. (You see the same menu option if you right-click a blank area of Explorer.)

The context menu isn't the only new tool that Windows 95 provides. You'll also enjoy the capabilities provided by other parts of this application. The toolbar, shown in Figure 2.4, is one feature that I use quite a bit. With a single click, it allows me to change the view I get.

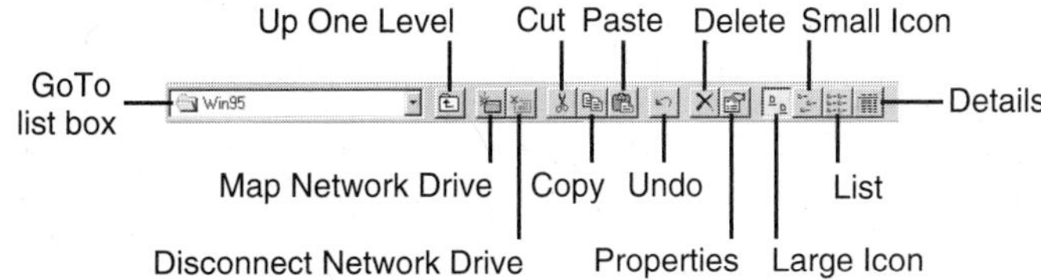

Figure 2.4.
The Explorer toolbar contains controls that perform a variety of tasks.

The following paragraphs describe the various toolbar features:

- **Go to a Different Folder list box:** The Go to a Different Folder list box contains a list of drives and other upper-level objects. It also contains the tree used to access the current folder, as shown in Figure 2.5. You can use this list box to quickly move from one area of your machine to another.

Figure 2.5.
The Go to a Different Folder list box allows you to quickly move between major areas of your machine. It also shows the directory tree leading to the currently selected object.

- **Up One Level:** Use this tool to move up one level in the directory tree. This tool isn't quite as handy in this view of Explorer as it is in others. The Up One Level tool is especially helpful when you're moving between levels in the single-pane view of Explorer.
- **Map Network Drive:** Explorer displays this tool only if you're connected to a network. It displays a dialog box that allows you to map one of your drives to a network drive (see Figure 2.6). Of course, you can still access the drive by using Network Neighborhood, even if you don't map it.

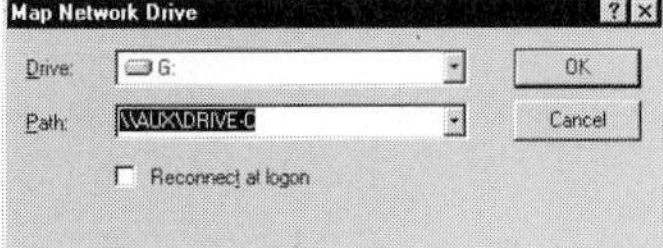

Figure 2.6.
The Map Network Drive dialog box allows you to map a local drive to a network location. Note the Reconnect at Logon box, which remaps the drives automatically each time you log onto the system.

- **Disconnect Network Drive:** This tool becomes active only when you install a network and map some network drives to your local drives. Clicking this tool displays the dialog box shown in Figure 2.7. You can use it to disconnect from any network drive. Of course, the drives remain accessible by using Network Neighborhood, even after you disconnect.

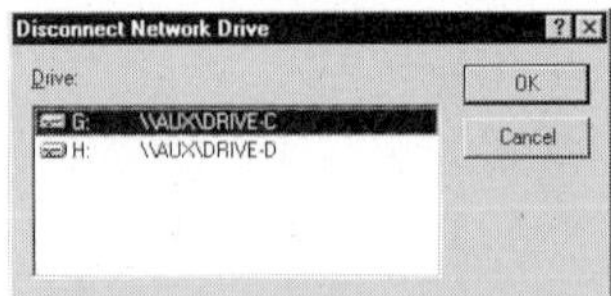

Figure 2.7.
Use the Disconnect Network Drive tool to remove one or more drive maps.

- **Cut:** Allows you to cut one or more objects.
- **Copy:** Allows you to copy one or more objects.
- **Paste:** This tool allows you to paste any object in the Clipboard to the currently selected object in Explorer.
- **Undo:** The Undo tool allows you to undo your previous action. This comes in handy if you send a file to the Recycle Bin and discover that you really intended to delete something else. The Undo tool doesn't work for some types of actions. For example, you can't undo a permanent erase.
- **Delete:** The Delete tool sends the currently selected objects to the Recycle Bin. It doesn't delete them permanently. You need to perform the second step of emptying the Recycle Bin to remove things permanently.
- **Properties:** This tool displays the Properties dialog box for the currently selected object. Nothing happens if you don't select an object.
- **Large Icon:** Displays the objects in the right pane in the large icon format.
- **Small Icon:** Displays the objects in the right pane in the small icon format.
- **List:** Uses the list format to display objects in the right pane. This doesn't include any details about these objects.
- **Details:** This tool displays the objects in a list format and includes all the details about that object, including file size, type, and date last modified.
- **Update All:** Used with Briefcase to update all the links it contains. See the "Briefcase" section of Chapter 18 for more details.
- **Update Selection:** Used with Briefcase to update just the link for the selected (highlighted) files. See the "Briefcase" section of Chapter 18 for more details.

This gives you a quick overview of using Explorer. Now it's time to take a more detailed look. The following paragraphs talk about various ways that you can use Explorer. Once you finish these sections, you'll start to see why I call Explorer the Swiss army knife that you need in order to learn how to use Windows 95 efficiently. Of course, once you know how to use that tool well, everything else will fall into place. Suffice it to say that you'll probably find more things you can do with Explorer as you become more proficient in working with Windows 95.

Tip: One of the keys to fully using Explorer's capabilities is to learn the Registry. Some changes to Windows 95 have to be made inside the Registry; Explorer can't make them. For example, if you want to change the name of the Recycle Bin, you must do it within the Registry. Some people have actually made a game of digging out all the Registry's secrets. The Registry and Explorer go hand-in-hand. See Chapter 7 if you want more detailed information about the Registry and what it contains.

An Information Center

The most common way to look at Explorer is as your information center. It can tell you everything you need to know about your computing environment, if you know where to look. Figure 2.8 shows a typical Explorer display. It's probably one of the first displays you see when working with Windows 95, and it will definitely become a constant companion. Notice that this display shows My Computer. The right pane contains all the things you'd normally see if you double-clicked on the desktop's My Computer icon. You should note something else as well. My Computer isn't the entire universe in Explorer. Quite a few icons fall outside the My Computer purview, just like they do in the real world, where my computer is only part of the network. An information center has to provide you with complete information, both inside and out. Explorer does just that.

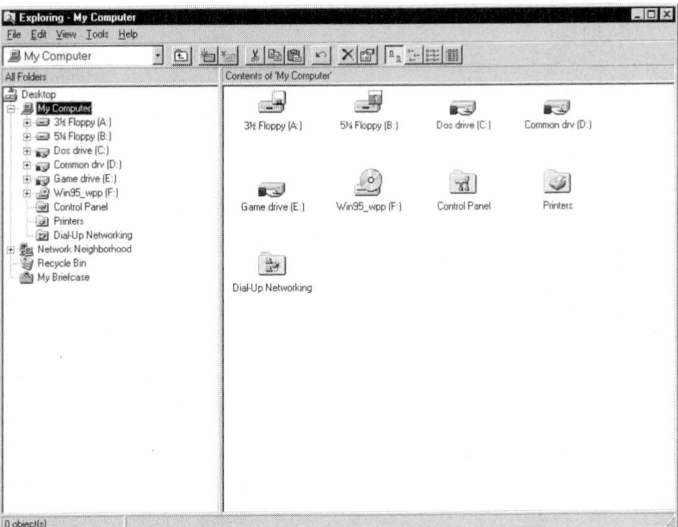

Figure 2.8.
The now-familiar Explorer interface in dual-pane view with large icons.

Chapter 1 talks about the various ways to display data when using Explorer and includes some of the elements associated with the Explorer display, such as the dual-pane display. Earlier in this chapter, you got an overview of how Explorer organizes information. For example, we looked at the way in which your machine is divided into drive, control, and ancillary sections. This section of the chapter also looked at the context menu and showed what you could do with a standard setup. Chapter 5 shows you how to add new file extensions to Explorer and make it more powerful in the process. It shows you two methods for adding extensions: DDE macros and command-line interfaces.

Once you have all the pieces of Explorer and understand how to use them, you can put them together so that you can use Explorer as your information center. Each of the following sections describes a major element of your information center. Remember that each element is a drive, control, or ancillary unit. If you've forgotten some of the material on Explorer that you've already read, you might want to review the chapters just mentioned.

Note: You probably won't see every one of the entries I discuss in your Explorer display. It depends on what options you have installed and the type of equipment your machine supports. I installed the maximum number of standard desktop computer features so that I could show you what they look like. I didn't install any specialty software that could change the appearance of Explorer. You'll also find some very minor differences in the entries automatically installed by the OSR2 version of Windows 95 and its predecessors. Finally, you'll likely find that laptop computers add a few default specialty icons that help you manage the laptop environment. In most cases, you need to read the documentation that comes with your laptop to understand how these specialty icons can help you.

Drives

Chapter 1 covers drives somewhat. (We also look at them again in Chapters 9 and 27.) However, I didn't show you everything. Windows 95 provides three different tools that you can use to manage your drives. You can start them from the Start menu as you would under Windows 3.x, or you can use the new Windows 95 method of managing your drives.

Let's look at what the drive icons have to offer. Right-click any of your hard drives. (Floppy and CD-ROM drives provide the same type of properties, but the hard drives are easier to use for purposes of this description.) You should see a dialog box similar to the one in Figure 2.9. This is the General page of the Drive Properties dialog box.

Note: Users of the OSR2 version of Windows 95 will see some minor differences on the General page of the Drive Properties dialog box. These changes reflect the use of the FAT 32 file system. Chapter 9 tells you more about these differences and how they affect the computing environment. You'll also notice some differences in the number of property pages on a network drive if you use Novell Client 32 in place of Microsoft's NDS client. Chapter 27 talks about these differences.

Figure 2.9.
The General page of the Drive Properties dialog box tells you quite a bit about the current status of an individual drive.

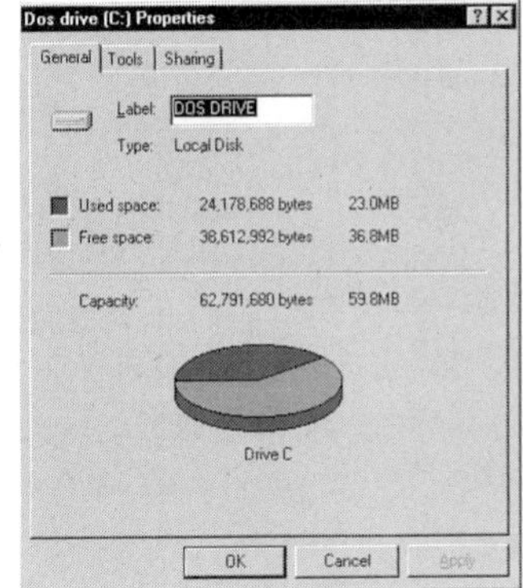

There are three noteworthy items on this page. First is the drive label. Labels aren't as important for hard drives, but I do use them on my floppy disks to identify projects that I'm working on.

The second item of interest is the Free Space indicator. It tells the amount of drive space remaining. It appears in magenta on most machines. Likewise, the Used Space indicator tells you how much space is used on the drive. In most cases, this value appears in blue. The pie chart helps you to determine the current drive status at a glance.

The third item is the drive location. In this particular case, you can see that this is a local drive. You can pull up pages for network drives as well. However, you might not be able to do much, because your access rights to that drive affect what Windows 95 will allow.

Warning: The OSR2 version of Windows 95 comes with the new FAT 32 file system. Never use a third-party diagnostic or defragmenting utility on a FAT 32 drive unless that utility is specifically designed to work with the FAT 32 file system. As of this writing, there aren't any third-party products that fall into this category. This means that you must rely on the Microsoft-supplied utilities to maintain a FAT 32 drive.

The Tools page of the Drive Properties dialog box, shown in Figure 2.10, can help you maintain your system. (You'll see a Tools page only for local drives.) Remember the three tools I told you about before? Well, here they are. Not only are these tools present, but Windows 95 keeps track of the last time you used them. This can be a big help to folks who have trouble remembering the last time they maintained their machine.

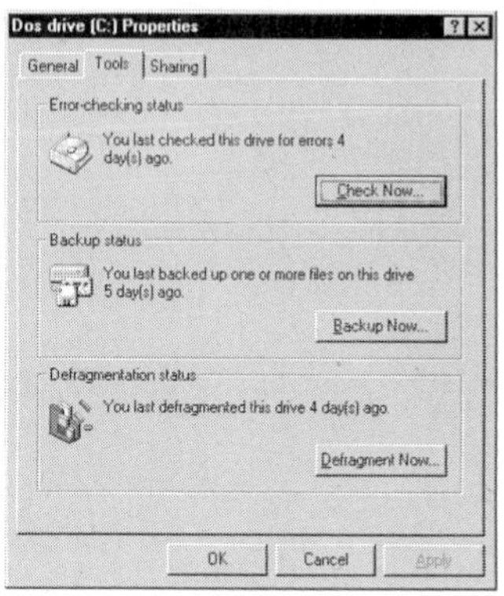

Figure 2.10.
The Tools page of the Drive Properties dialog box allows you to keep your drive in peak condition.

Peter's Principle: Disk Maintenance: A Necessity, Not an Option

Trying to perform any kind of diagnostic on your machine was a major headache in the days of DOS. I had several diagnostic utilities on my machine because none of them did everything. It was also very inconvenient to drop what I was doing and start a diagnostic cycle.

Windows 95 makes diagnostics a lot easier to perform—at least the ones on your drive system that are very important for maintaining data integrity. Even though the diagnostics are easier to access, a lot of people still don't use them because they really don't know how often they need to do so.

Chapter 9 delves into the details of creating backups on your machine. It even helps you understand the need for tape rotation and provides some ideas on how to set up your own backup schedule. However, simply backing up the data on your machine isn't enough. Your drives require more care than that if you plan to keep them in peak condition and your data error-free.

Every day, I start my machine and perform a standard disk scan in the background. That way, I can catch major structural problems before they eat an important file. (The OSR2 version of Windows 95 automatically performs a disk scan for you if it determines that you shut Windows 95 down abnormally. It performs this check before Windows 95 even gets started, so no files are open.) Once a week, I set aside some time to perform a thorough disk scan. I make sure that every other application is closed, including the screen saver, when I do this. ScanDisk can't really vouch for the status of any files you have open, so closing all your applications is a good idea.

Defragmenting your drive isn't a big deal from a data-security standpoint. If you don't defragment your drive, the worst thing that will happen is that the drive won't work as efficiently as it could. That said, do you really want to give up any performance due to a lack of maintenance? I usually defragment my drive once a week. In fact, I usually follow a routine of scanning the drive for errors, backing it up, and defragmenting. This is the same routine I recommend for you. The disk scan will ensure that you get the best possible error-free backup. The backup itself will ensure that your data is safe if a disk failure occurs while you defragment it, and the defragmenting program will improve overall system efficiency.

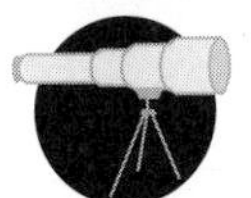

Note: Would you like to tell your computer to scan your disks, defragment your drives, back up your programs on a regular, preset schedule, and do your maintenance chores? Microsoft Plus! comes with a program scheduler, System Agent, that can do all these things. In fact, when you install Microsoft Plus!, it automatically sets up System Agent to perform a regular disk scan every weekday with ScanDisk for Windows. It also runs Disk Defragmenter four times a week and scans your disks thoroughly once a week. The Microsoft Plus! setup asks you whether you'd like to run these maintenance programs at night while you're sleeping or during the day in the background or while you're away from your computer. To learn more about automating maintenance routines, read Chapter 28.

The Check Now button opens ScanDisk, shown in Figure 2.11. This is the Windows form of the DOS utility you probably used sometime in the past. In essence, this utility works about the same. The difference is that you now gain the benefits of a GUI rather than a text-mode interface. (You might remember that ScanDisk replaced the old `CHKDSK` utility.)

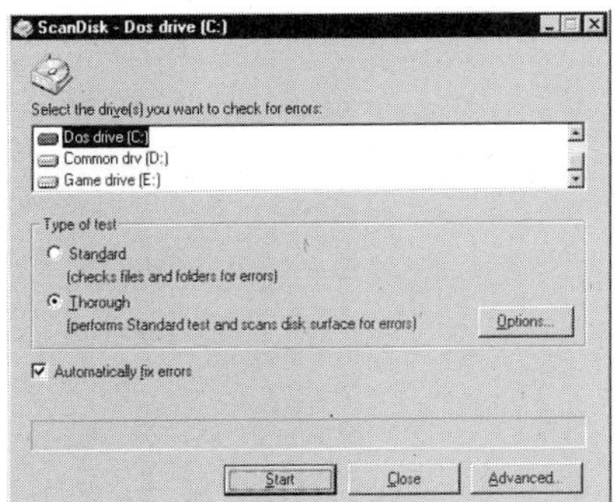

Figure 2.11.
ScanDisk allows you to check the current condition of your disk drive.

Tip: None of the three utility programs described in this section limits you to one drive. I usually check all the drives on my system at once instead of opening the Properties dialog box for each drive separately. Choosing to maintain your drives this way ensures that you don't miss any of them and also adds a certain level of automation to the process.

You can run two types of tests with this utility. The standard test simply checks the condition of your files and folders. All it does is check for major errors in the directory structure and the FAT. It also looks for cross-linked files and other structural problems. This test doesn't guarantee that the files are readable or that there isn't any damage to the drive media.

Use the thorough test when you want to check for more than just structural integrity. The Options button takes you to the dialog box shown in Figure 2.12, where you can modify the way that ScanDisk performs the thorough disk scan of your drive. The first group of options controls where ScanDisk looks for damaged media. Sometimes you might want to simply check the directory area for damage when troubleshooting your system. In most cases, you'll want to check both the system and data areas of your drive. Some people get queasy just thinking about an application writing to their drive to see whether it works. Other people don't want to take the time. The write test provides an added layer of testing integrity to your system. It actually tests to see whether the media is secure by writing to it and then reading back the results. This test will help you find certain types of drive failures that a read test won't find. The write test doesn't write to every data area on your drive; that would take an enormous amount of time. It simply checks a few unused areas of the drive. Some types of system and hidden file damage can't be repaired very easily. You can check this option if you think that a section of your drive contains such damage and you don't want to risk making the problem worse by "fixing" it. In most cases, though, you'll leave this check box unchecked because ScanDisk can handle the vast majority of hard-drive errors.

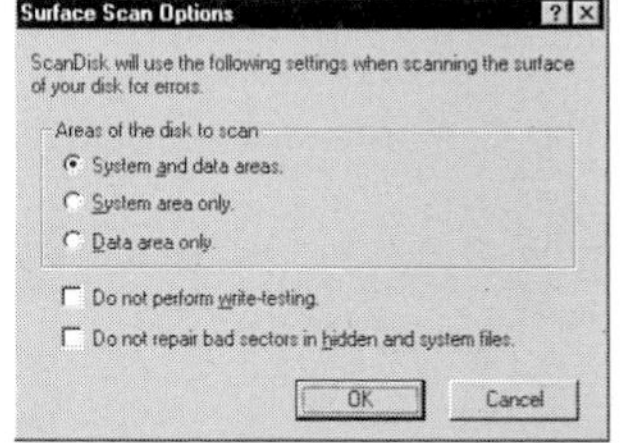

Figure 2.12.
Use the Surface Scan Options dialog box to modify the way ScanDisk performs a thorough test of your hard drive.

The Automatically Fix Errors check box lets you tell ScanDisk to fix the problems without notifying you about each one in advance. This is the option I use most of the time. It doesn't matter too much what the error was, just that it's fixed now. However, sometimes I uncheck this box because I want to see whether ScanDisk fixed a particular hard-disk error. For example, maybe I tried to access a file on the drive but couldn't for some reason. I would probably run ScanDisk to see whether a drive error was getting in the way. Because I would be looking for a specific problem, I'd want to know exactly what it was and how ScanDisk planned to fix it.

Clicking the Advanced button at the bottom of the ScanDisk dialog box displays the ScanDisk Advanced Options dialog box shown in Figure 2.13. Most of these options are self-explanatory and correspond to features provided by the DOS counterpart of this utility. I usually keep the Display Summary radio button set to Only If Errors Found, so that I can check all my drives at once. If ScanDisk doesn't find any errors, it checks all the drives without disturbing me. Using this option means that I can run ScanDisk unattended in most cases.

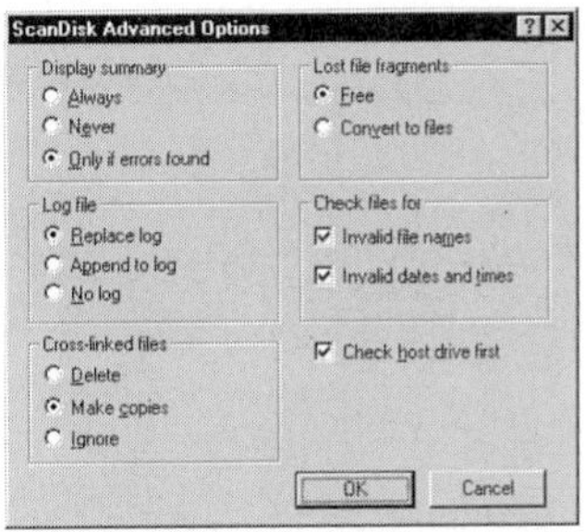

Figure 2.13.
The ScanDisk Advanced Options dialog box contains some user interface and other automatic settings.

There are two options in this dialog box that you might find interesting. Both check files for invalid data in the directory area. Unchecking these two boxes might save you a modicum of time during the disk scan but could lead to disaster somewhere along the way. The first entry checks for invalid filenames. Under the old 8.3 file naming strategy, the name you could give a file was pretty straightforward. Under Windows 95, naming files is more complex, so scanning filenames requires a little more time. The second entry checks files for date and time data. These are the extended dates and times that the new VFAT system provides. Under DOS, the only date you got was the last date a file was changed. Windows 95 provides the date on which someone created the file, as well as the date it was last accessed (but not necessarily changed or saved).

Clicking the Backup Now button of the Drive Properties dialog box brings up the standard Backup utility described in Chapter 9. Since we look at this utility in detail elsewhere, I won't describe it here.

The Defragment Now button brings up the Disk Defragmenter utility. However, it acts differently when you bring it up here as opposed to simply starting it from the Start menu. Disk Defragmenter displays the current status of your drive before it offers to defragment it for you. Figure 2.14 shows this dialog box.

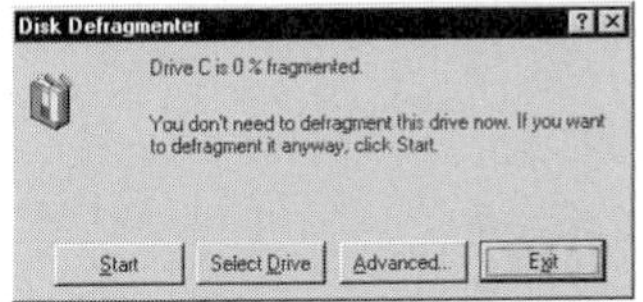

Figure 2.14.
Disk Defragmenter displays the status of your drive if you select it from the Tools page of the Drive Properties dialog box.

There are several buttons at the bottom of this dialog box. Clicking the Select Drive button lets you select which drive you want to defragment. There's also an option to defragment all your hard drives; this is the option I normally select. The Advanced button displays the dialog box shown in Figure 2.15, which allows you to change the way that Disk Defragmenter performs its work. You may also choose whether to use these options once or to save them for every defragmenting session.

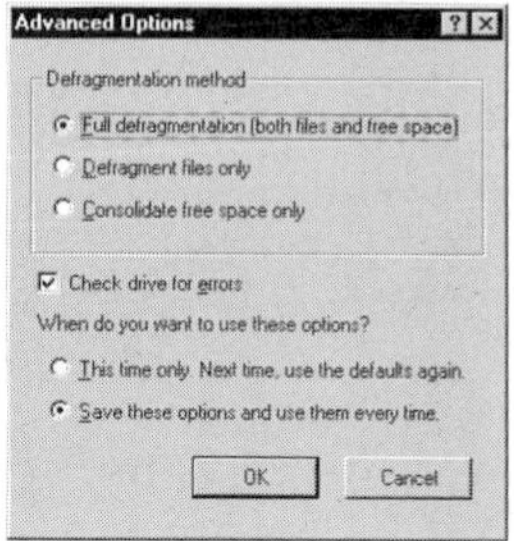

Figure 2.15.
Disk Defragmenter's Advanced Options dialog box allows you to select the method used to defragment your drive.

On to the third page of the Drive Properties dialog box—Sharing (see Figure 2.16). You'll normally see this page with systems that use a fully supported peer-to-peer network. Real-mode networks such as older versions of LANtastic don't add a page to this dialog box because they provide their own management programs. (LANtastic has released a Windows 95-specific version of their product since the initial release of Windows 95, but there are more than a few real-mode copies still around.)

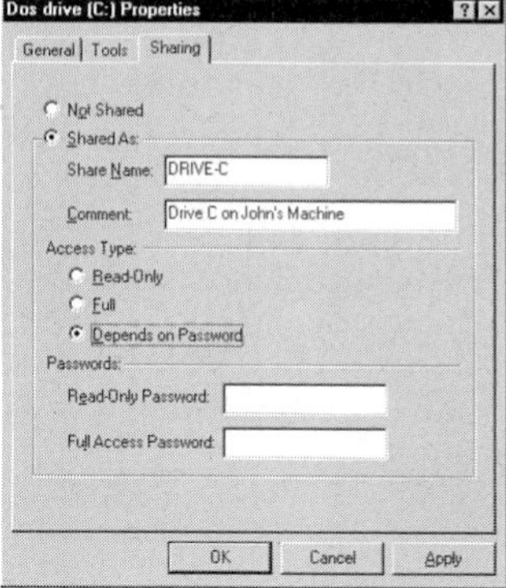

Figure 2.16.
The Sharing page of the Drive Properties dialog box allows you to share resources with other machines.

Note: Some people won't see the Sharing page because they don't have a network installed. This page appears only under specific conditions when you're using certain types of networks.

This dialog box allows you to share resources with another machine. Turning on the Not Shared radio button prevents other people from looking at your drive. If you turn on the Shared As radio button, Windows 95 enables the other fields and buttons displayed here. The first field, Share Name, tells other machines what name to use when they access your drive. The second field, Comment, is a plain-language description of the drive that other users will see.

Tip: It's never a good idea to give someone more access to your machine than he needs. Remember that you can provide access to individual files and folders. In most cases, you'll want to reserve drive-level access to common data drives on a server rather than the entire drive on a workstation. You can always give someone more access if he needs it. Taking back access after someone compromises your network is meaningless, because the damage is already done.

After you decide on a name for your drive, you need to determine what kind of access to it other people will have. In some cases, read-only access is all that the other person will need. This means that a person can see the file and read it but can't modify it in any way. (Of course, he can copy the file to his drive and modify it there.) You could use this for drives with informational databases that you want the other person to use but not modify. Full access allows the other person to read from and write to your drive. This is the level of access most people will require if you want to share data with them. A third possibility allows you to determine the level of access the other person gets to your system by the password he enters. This option provides the most secure access and flexibility. The two fields below these radio buttons will be enabled if the access option you select enables them. You can type any standard password here to grant access to your machine to a select group of people.

Peter's Principle: Disk Access and Workgroup Activities

There are two schools of thought about the way a workgroup should use the Windows 95 security features to enforce a specific way of modifying files. I find that they're both good, but for different reasons and in different circumstances.

The first method is to allow the people in the group read-only access to the master files on the leader's disk. This allows them to copy the file and make any required changes on their local drive. It also preserves the integrity of the master copy. Once a person finishes his edit, he moves the file to a temporary directory on the leader's drive. You could also create a home directory for each person and have them place the modified files there. The leader can then choose which additions and comments to incorporate into the master document. If you use a common temporary directory, each person should change the file extension or some part of the filename to include a distinctive signature. This prevents their files from accidentally overwriting the modified files that other people submit.

As an alternative to this first method, each person could keep his individual files to use as a basis for group discussion. Each member of the group would come to the meeting with a modified copy of the original document. This allows the leader to pick and choose which comments to incorporate, based on the results of any group discussion. Of course, this is also the least efficient method, because you have to schedule specific meeting times, and the comments might or might not appear in electronic form.

The second method allows full access to the master document. Each member of the group uses the revision marks feature provided by the application to make changes to the document in his designated color. The advantage to this method is that everyone gets to discuss the document "online" in an interactive fashion. The group leader doesn't have to schedule a specific meeting to modify the document; changes are made on an ongoing basis. Of course, to implement this method your application must support a revision marks feature that uses a different color of text for each member's modifications.

When you allow other people access to a drive on your machine, Windows 95 adds a hand to the drive icon, as shown in Figure 9.1. This visual signal appears wherever the drive icon appears. It doesn't tell you what level of access the drive provides, however. Microsoft could have used slightly different symbols or perhaps colors to differentiate between access levels, but at least this symbol tells you to look for more information.

Note: A Compression tab appears in the drive's Properties dialog box when you install Microsoft Plus!. (Never use this feature on a FAT 32 formatted drive—it will destroy the contents of the hard drive.) The Compression tab contains different information, depending on whether the drive is compressed. If the drive isn't compressed, the Compression tab shows you the amount of used and free space currently on your drive and how much you would have of each if you compressed the drive. It also tells the approximate size of a new drive that could be built by compressing your drive's remaining free space. This is the perfect option if you want to compress files on your boot drive, but you don't want to risk having your whole boot drive compressed. Buttons on this tab allow you to compress the drive or make a new compressed drive. If your drive is compressed, the Compression tab is filled with statistics on the percentage of files compressed, with various compression types and the amount of disk space you've gained. These and other Microsoft Plus! disk compression enhancements are discussed in detail in Chapter 28.

Control Panel

A lot of people are still used to the way they accessed Control Panel under Windows 3.x. It was a pain, because you had to minimize your applications and open a specific folder to access the various configuration programs. I was surprised to see just how many different ways you can access Control Panel or its components under Windows 95. Even Explorer provides a method of access, as shown in Figure 2.17.

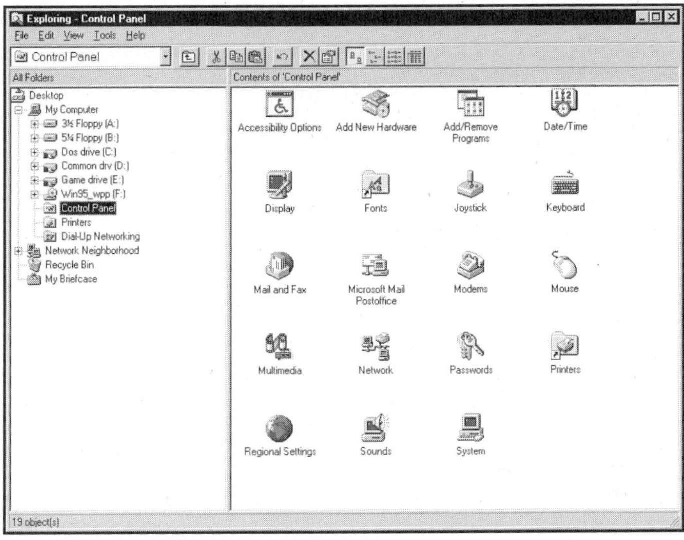

Figure 2.17.
You can access Control Panel or its components from many places in Windows 95, including Explorer.

The number and types of icons (now called *applets*) you'll find here vary with the applications and equipment you've installed. Items such as the Printer folder always appear in your Control Panel. On the other hand, you won't always see an ODBC folder or some of the other specialty items that Control Panel provides.

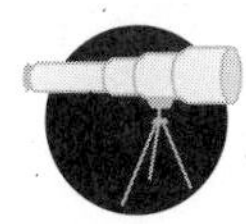

Looking Ahead: We won't look at the individual Control Panel applets (Microsoft just *had* to change the name) here. Chapter 11 provides a full description of all the applets and what they mean to you as a user and takes a look at some of the ways in which you can manipulate the Windows 95 Control Panel.

Printers

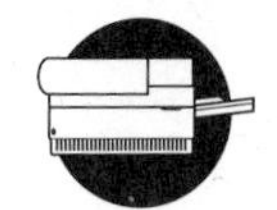

Using a printer under Windows 95 is a lot easier than with previous versions of Windows, even though the actual controls look about the same (many printers have a few additional controls). The good news is that Windows 95 provides what I call "quality modes" for many older printers, and the printing speed in the standard modes is a lot faster. You'll also notice less of an impact on other applications while processing print requests in the background—a nice change from Windows 3.x, where my foreground application would actually stop at times if I got decent print speed.

I have an older Epson LQ-850. This printer is capable of 360 × 360 graphics printing. I could get, at most, half of that resolution from previous versions of Windows. It was pretty frustrating when I needed the capability of a dot matrix to print through multipart forms and had to give up some quality to do it. Imagine my surprise when Windows 95 offered the higher-quality print mode. The 360 × 360 resolution really makes a big difference in the appearance of graphics output from this printer.

Tip: Service Pack 1 for Windows 95 offers some updated print drivers along with a few new ones for older printers that didn't ship with the initial version. If you have an older printer that didn't get the level of support you expected when Windows 95 first came out, download Service Pack 1. OSR2 users will be pleased to find out that their version of Windows 95 also offers some speed enhancements in addition to updated print drivers. Chapter 15 discusses the impact of both of these releases.

As with just about everything else, you can control your printers from Explorer by accessing the Printer folder. It usually appears right below the Control Panel folder in the system hierarchy. Figure 2.18 shows how the Printers folder looks when accessed from Explorer.

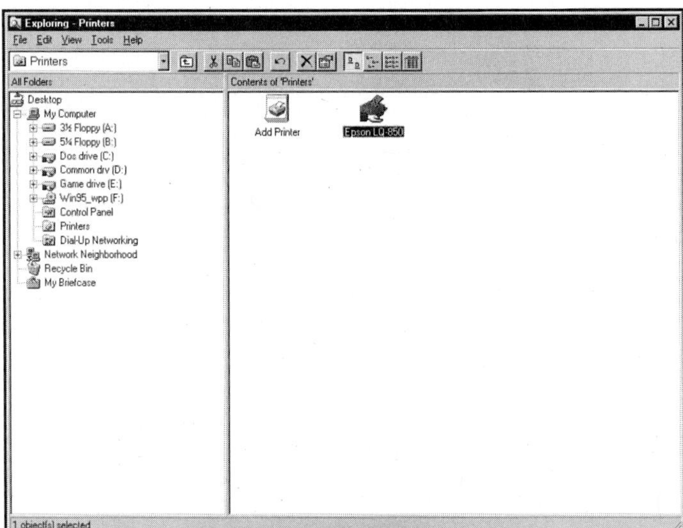

Figure 2.18.
The Printer folder offers a way to control print jobs, configure your printer, and add new printers, all in one location.

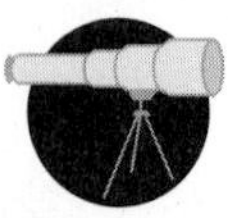

Looking Ahead: Chapter 15 covers all the details of managing your printers. It also looks at the process of adding a new printer to your system. The second half of this chapter looks at the details of using fonts to dress up your output.

This folder shows two icons, the minimum you should see if you have any printers installed. You'll always see one icon for each printer installed on your machine. Double-clicking that folder (or right-clicking and selecting Open) shows you any print jobs that the printer is currently processing. See Figure 2.19.

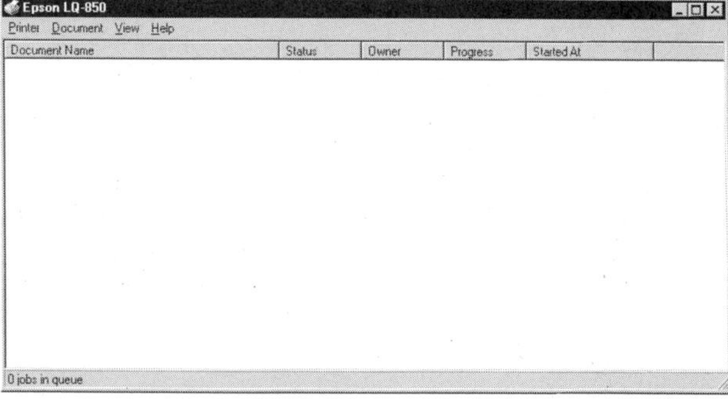

Figure 2.19.
Opening a printer icon shows the jobs that it's currently processing.

You can also configure your existing printers in this dialog box. All you need to do is right-click and select the Properties option to display the dialog box shown in Figure 2.20. Chapter 15 covers this dialog box in detail. Suffice it to say that Windows 95 provides a lot more in the way of printer control than in previous versions of Windows.

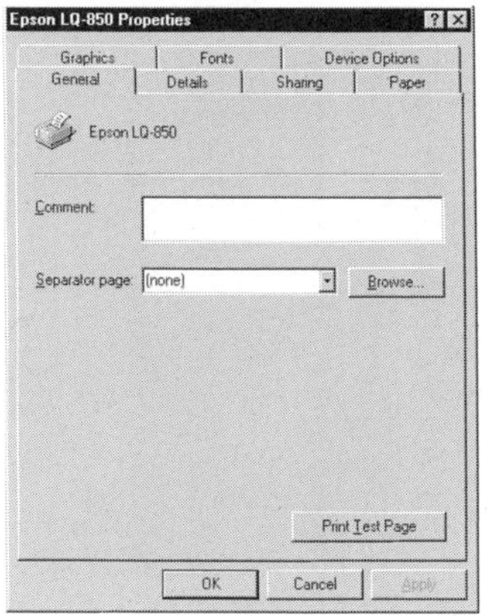

Figure 2.20.
The printer Properties dialog box contains everything needed to configure your printer.

The only non-printer icon in this folder is the one that you use to add a new printer. Windows 95 makes this process a lot easier than its predecessors did. Microsoft has gone to great … this process easier than ever before. The Printer Wizard will dazzle you with its … cially if you went through any nightmare configuration sessions with previous … Chapter 15 explores the process of adding a new printer.

Dial-Up Networking

Microsoft included a handy new utility in this version of Windows. I… to connect to another machine in much the same way as pcAnywhere… dial-in client, but at least it provides the functionality that many use… The bad news is that this is only a client version. Microsoft plan…

employed by Gillette: They'll give away the razors (client software) and sell everyone the blades (the host). The software that turns Windows 95 into a dial-up server is included in the add-on package Microsoft Plus!. You'll also be able to access Windows NT's dial-up server.

Note: Users of the OSR2 version of Windows 95 will like the new scripting capability provided by this version. You can learn all about Dial-Up Networking scripting in the "Using Dial-Up Networking" section of Chapter 19.

The Dial-Up Networking folder appears under the Printers folder if you installed the service. Figure 2.21 shows a typical Dial-Up Networking folder view from Explorer. Notice that this folder, like the Printers folder, contains two types of icons. The first provides access to a wizard for creating new connections. The second type is the actual connections.

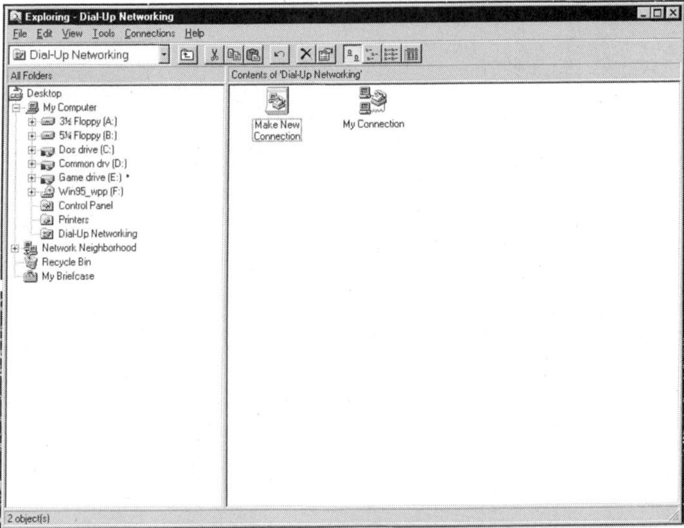

Figure 2.21.
A typical Dial-Up Networking folder contains one or more connection icons and access to a wizard for creating more.

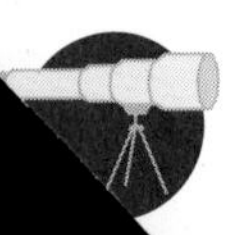

Looking Ahead: We take another look at Dial-Up Networking in several places. Chapter 19 shows you how to use this feature of Windows 95. Chapter 18 covers the implications of using Dial-Up Networking for the mobile user.

ing the Dial-Up Networking client is easy. You double-click a connection to open it. The
m dials the phone and tries to make a connection to the host. Right-clicking and selecting
displays the dialog box shown in Figure 2.22, which allows you to change the connection
nd other things. Chapter 19 takes a more in-depth look at the entire process.

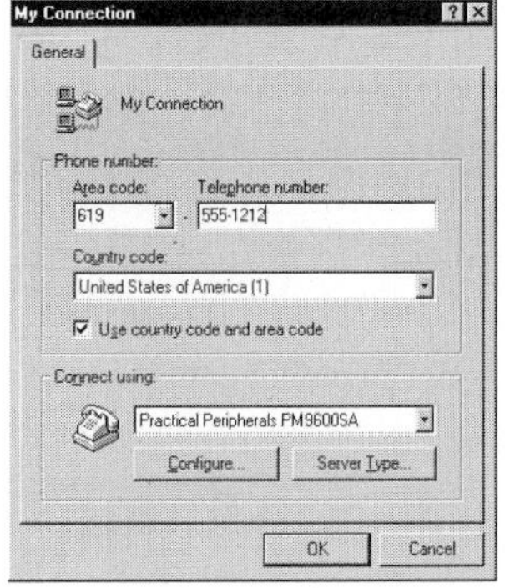

Figure 2.22.
The My Connection dialog box allows you to change the Dial-Up Networking properties of each connection you create.

Network Neighborhood

Think of Network Neighborhood as a dynamic extension of Explorer for a network. Figure 2.23 shows a typical Network Neighborhood folder. As you can see, My Computer gets replaced by the Entire Network icon. No longer are we looking at the local machine, but at all the resources that you can access on the network as a whole.

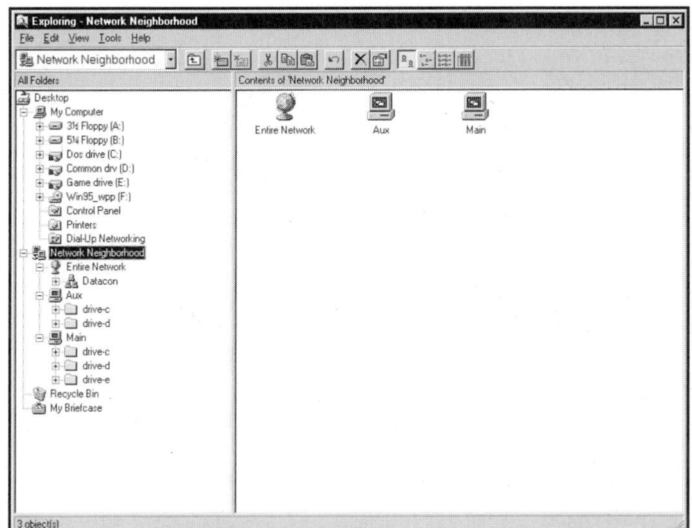

Figure 2.23.
Network Neighborhood provides a hierarchical view of the entire network and all the resources you can access on it.

Note: Novell Client 32 handles Network Neighborhood entries differently than its Microsoft NDS client counterpart. I cover Novell Client 32 differences in the "Using Novell Client 32" section of Chapter 27. Fortunately, the idea behind using the entries is the same, so you can still follow along in this section and learn what Network Neighborhood can do for you.

You might also see other entries at the same level as the Entire Network. These are machines that you can access on peer-to-peer networks. You can always access your own resources, so you'll always see your machine listed here. In this case, there are two machines on the network. Notice that you can see only the shared drives for the machines—not any drive that's local. I also found it interesting that not every shared resource appears on the tree. You have to actually select the drive to see any resources beyond drives. Figure 2.24 shows a printer resource on the AUX machine in addition to the two shared drives that show up in the tree listing.

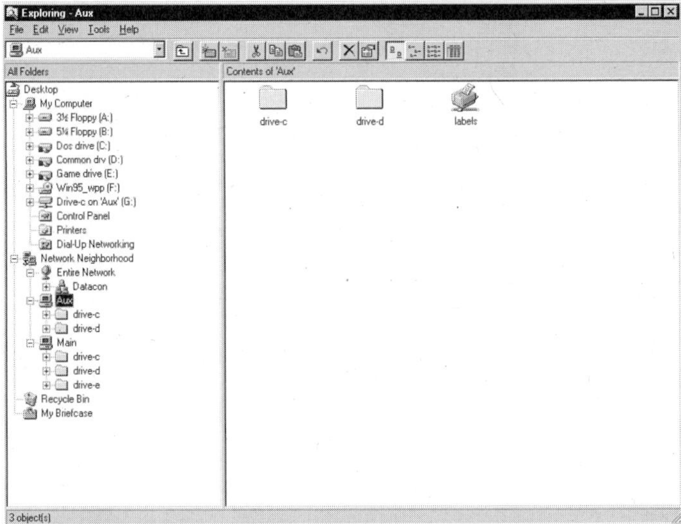

Figure 2.24.
Always check the machine in question if you want to see all the resources; the directory tree shows only shared drives.

Tip: At first glance, it might seem like a waste of effort to list your machine along with everything else in Network Neighborhood. However, there's one good reason to do so. Here you can see at a glance every resource you're sharing with the rest of the network. Instead of forcing you to look through the directory tree for these elements, Microsoft thoughtfully placed them here.

You need to know a few interesting things about Network Neighborhood that make it different from the rest of Explorer. First, you can't access the properties for the Entire Network. Unfortunately, this means that you can't disable the war and poverty settings. All joking aside, the Entire Network is simply a placeholder for Network Neighborhood; it doesn't exist as a concrete object.

Below the Entire Network are entries for each network you're currently connected to. In most cases, you'll see the actual workgroup or domain name, not the name of the network vendor or product. This list will change as your connections change. Looking here will tell you whether a problem is application- or network-related. An application error, such as the inability to open a file, might look like a network error for a variety of reasons. However, if you look in the Entire Network folder and see the connection, it's very unlikely that the connection is the problem. Chapters 25 and 26 contain tips that will help you locate and fix other problems with the hardware or software on your machine. Chapter 27 will help you find network-specific problems—especially those that you'll encounter using NetWare.

If you attach to a peer-to-peer network, the machine names will appear before each network entry in the Network Neighborhood hierarchy. Beneath the machine entries you'll see a list of the drives that you can access.

Network Neighborhood works the same as the rest of Explorer from a user perspective. Of course, you can't change the properties of network resources in most cases. All the Properties dialog box will tell you is the name of the resource and what type of network it's connected to.

Recycle Bin

The Recycle Bin works the same in Explorer as it does on the desktop. You can drop things into it, examine its contents, empty it, or restore a file that it holds to its original (or another) location. The Explorer copy of the Recycle Bin comes in handy if you see a file that you want to erase and the desktop copy is covered by another application. We partially examined this topic earlier in this chapter, but let's take a complete look now. Figure 2.25 shows the Recycle Bin. As you can see, it looks just like any other folder in Windows 95.

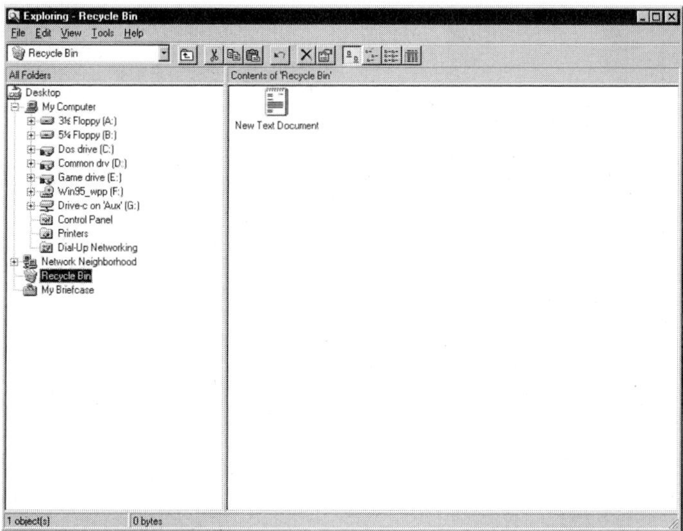

Figure 2.25.
Items in the Recycle Bin look just like they would anywhere else.

Tip: Files in the Recycle Bin continue to take up space on the drive. Windows 95 moves deleted files to the Recycle Bin—a special folder—until you erase them for good. (The short filenames or old DOS filenames are changed to allow multiple files of the same name in the Recycle Bin.) If you find that you're short on hard-drive space, you might want to see whether there's anything in the Recycle Bin you can get rid of.

In most cases, your bin won't contain anything. Files in the Recycle Bin look just like files anywhere else. You can move objects in the Recycle Bin to other areas of Explorer to "unerase" them. Until you do unerase them, the Properties dialog box won't tell you much except the file's name and the date you deleted it.

The context menu for objects in the Recycle Bin looks a little different, as shown in Figure 2.26. One of the really handy items I found on this list was Restore. You can select one or more files and then restore them by selecting this entry. Another handy option is Delete. This allows you to select just one or two Recycle Bin entries and delete them for good without disturbing the rest of the entries.

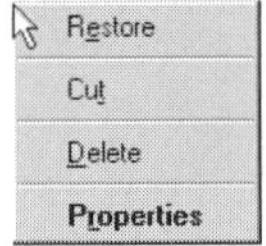

Figure 2.26.
The context menu for files in the Recycle Bin might look different, but it does contain some handy entries for managing erased files.

Briefcase

The Briefcase is one of the best Windows 95 features for mobile users. It allows you to pack everything you need for a project into one folder and then move that folder around, just like the briefcase you carry to and from work. Chapter 1 looks at some of the specifics of this particular part of Windows 95. Figure 2.27 shows the Explorer view of the Briefcase.

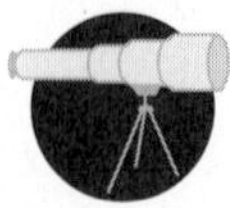

Looking Ahead: Chapter 18 takes a look at how you can use Briefcase. You might want to read through this material even if you aren't a mobile computer user, because I discuss a few techniques for using Briefcase that everyone will want to know about.

Briefcase adds one option to the context menu of items it holds. The Update option allows you to update a file from its original copy on your hard drive. This is one of the steps you need to take before packing your briefcase to go on the road. I cover this topic in greater depth in Chapter 18.

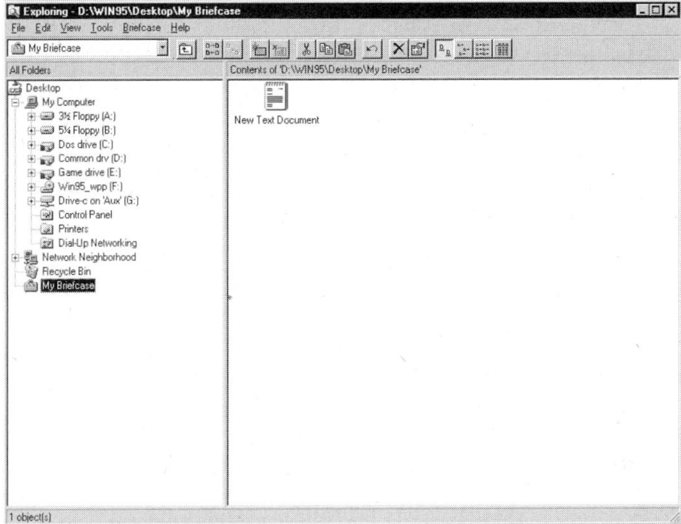

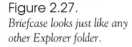

Figure 2.27.
Briefcase looks just like any other Explorer folder.

The Startup Folder

Windows 3.1 originated the idea of a Startup folder. It's a good idea, too. Instead of filling WIN.INI with `LOAD=` and `RUN=` entries that become a confused, tangled mess, the Startup folder allows you to maintain a certain level of order. (Of course, some applications still insist on using the antiquated method of automatically starting an application, so Windows 95 has to support it.)

Think of the Startup folder as a sort of AUTOEXEC.BAT file for your Windows applications. Windows automatically looks in this file during the boot process and launches anything it finds there. Under Windows 3.x, some types of files didn't work very well. For example, I found it difficult to automatically open any kind of data file, even when it was associated with an application. Under Windows 95, you can stick just about anything in the Startup folder and expect it to work properly.

Peter's Principle: Getting a Great Start in the Morning

A lot of people are under the impression that the Startup folder is only for loading applications. Other people feel that you should place only certain classes of applications there, such as screen savers. Although putting your screen saver in the Startup folder is a good idea, using the Startup folder for this purpose alone doesn't really make full use of this resource.

Because I was used to the Windows 3.x way of doing things, it never occurred to me how useful this particular folder was until I started setting up my desktop. Placing a shortcut to the Startup folder on your desktop is a great idea, because you can put things in there that you'll need the next morning. (Microsoft buried this folder so far in the directory tree that you'll quickly tire of trying to use it if you don't take this step.) For example, if I'm working on a proposal over the course of a few days, I'll stick a shortcut to the master file in Startup. That way, it automatically opens when I start my machine the next day.

Adding objects to the Startup folder can really boost your productivity. Instead of spending the first 15 minutes of the morning getting set up, you can start your machine, get a cup of coffee, and be ready to work when you return. Making Windows 95 more efficient is largely up to the user now. Most of the tools are there; all you need to do is use them.

Like everything else in Windows 95, you'll find the Startup folder in Explorer. Unfortunately, it's buried deep in the directory tree. If you look in the \WIN95\Start Menu\Programs folder, you'll see the Startup folder, shown in Figure 2.28. Another, faster way to access the folder is to right-click the Start menu icon on the Taskbar and select the Explore option. This will display a two-pane version of Explorer that you can use to get to the Startup folder faster.

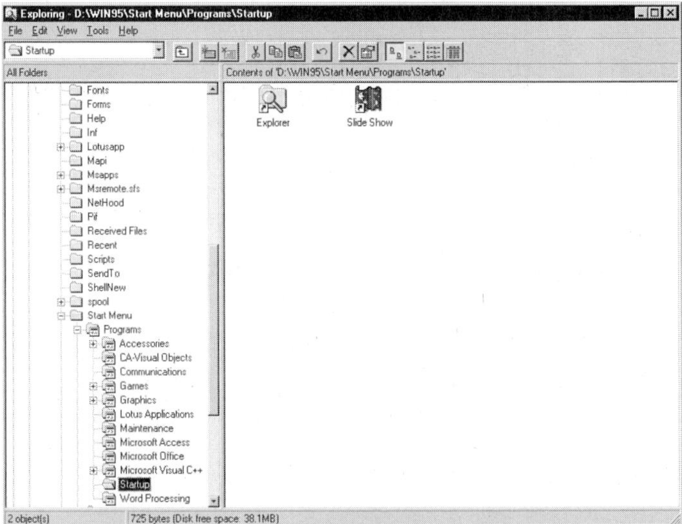

Figure 2.28.
The Startup folder is buried in the Windows 95 hierarchy under the Start menu.

Standard Windows 95 Applications

Windows 95 has a lot more to offer than just Explorer. A whole new group of utility programs is available to make life a lot easier for the user. In the past, most of these applications were supplied by third parties, but today you get them as part of the operating system package.

The next few paragraphs highlight these new utility programs. We take a close look at them in future chapters, but the information that follows should provide you with what you need to get started.

Looking Ahead: The following paragraphs provide only highlights of the new utilities. They all appear in other, product-specific areas of this book. For example, you'll find out more about the remote access utilities in Chapter 23. Microsoft Exchange also appears in several other chapters, including Chapter 20. You'll want to visit Chapter 11 to find out more about all the Windows 95 applets.

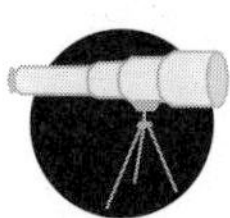

Microsoft Exchange

In days past, you had to use one program to access your company e-mail and another to get your online e-mail. In fact, depending on your online services, you might have ended up working with three or four applications just to maintain contact. Once you got past the contact hurdle, you had to figure out how to get everything to work together.

Microsoft Exchange, shown in Figure 2.29, acts as a central repository for all your e-mail, no matter where it comes from. Of course, this product has its limitations. For one thing, it supports only Microsoft Mail, Microsoft Network, and CompuServe right now. You can access the Internet through Microsoft Network, so that's not too much of a problem. However, you do start running into problems if you use online services other than these.

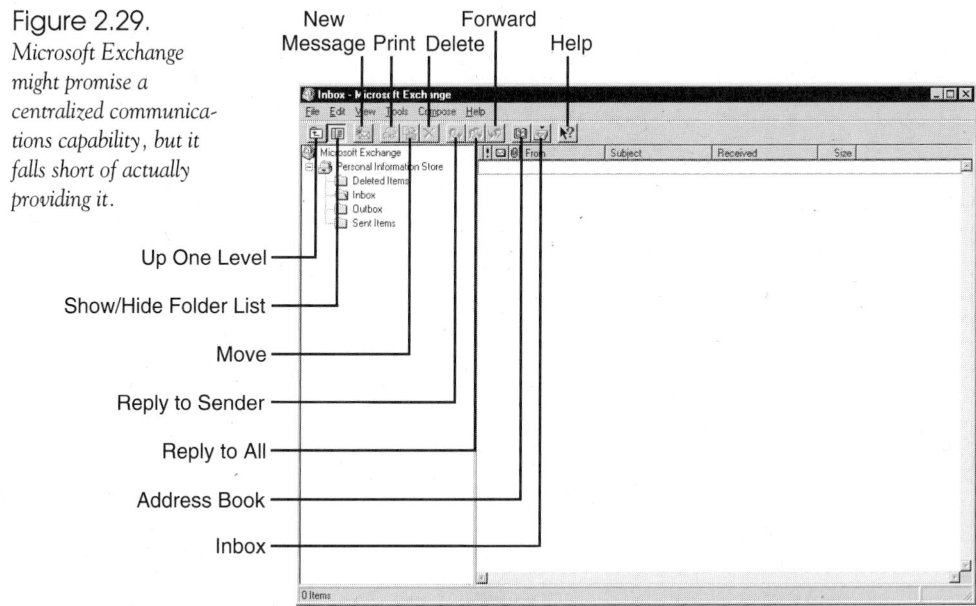

Figure 2.29.
Microsoft Exchange might promise a centralized communications capability, but it falls short of actually providing it.

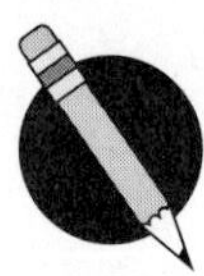

Note: Users of the OSR2 version of Windows 95 will notice a new name for Microsoft Exchange—Windows Messaging. This new name is designed to help people make the transition from local networks to the Internet. For purposes of this section, you won't notice any difference in the product, even with the name change.

The Exchange interface is fairly simple. It looks a bit like the Explorer interface (as do a great many things under Windows 95). You access Exchange by using the Inbox icon on the desktop. The left panel contains what looks like a directory tree. However, this tree uses the Microsoft Exchange icon as the root object. Below this object is the Personal Information Store folder, which contains four folders. These four folders include Deleted Items, Inbox, Outbox, and Sent Items. Their purposes are fairly straightforward.

The toolbar contains all the tools you'll need in most circumstances. It includes the following tools:

- **Up One Level:** Use this tool to move up one level in the directory tree. This serves the same purpose as the equivalent tool in Explorer.
- **Show/Hide Folder List:** Some people might find the dual-pane look of Microsoft Exchange less useful than the single-pane view. You can use this button to turn off the directory tree shown in the left pane.
- **New Message:** This button always creates a new message. It doesn't matter where you are in the directory tree. The new message can go to your company e-mail or an online service. Microsoft Exchange always uses the address to determine where a message gets sent. In fact, you can send a single message to a combination of local and online addresses if you want.
- **Print:** Select this tool to print one or more messages.
- **Move Item:** Use this tool to move the selected messages from one folder to another. I find this particular tool handy for resending messages that never got to the intended person.
- **Delete:** Moves the selected messages to the Deleted Items folder. If you delete messages in the Deleted Items folder, Exchange removes them completely. Exchange doesn't send messages to the Recycle Bin, so if you remove them from the Deleted folder, you can't undelete them later.
- **Reply to Sender:** This feature allows you to send a reply to the originator of a message.
- **Reply to All:** Use this feature if you want to send a reply to the originator of a message and all the other recipients. This works well in group-discussion-type e-mails.
- **Forward:** Allows you to send to a third party a copy of the message plus any comments you might want to make.
- **Address Book:** Select this tool to gain access to your personal address book or any other accessible address book. You can use this tool when you need to add a new address or edit an existing one.

- **Inbox:** Clicking this tool takes you to your inbox without going through the directory tree.
- **Help:** Provides online help for Exchange.

Besides the toolbar, you might notice that the individual column headings provide some functionality. If you move the mouse pointer between two headings, it turns into a double-headed arrow. This allows you to resize the column heading as needed. Right-clicking a column heading displays a context menu. The context menu allows you to sort the list of messages in either ascending or descending order by that column. For example, you would right-click the Sent column to sort your e-mail by date. Exchange places an up or down arrow in the column you select for sorting.

Remote Access

There are two tools you can use for remote access. The first is Dial-Up-Networking, shown in Figure 2.30. Interestingly, the interface for this application looks very similar to the single-pane Explorer interface that appears when you open a folder. Most of the controls operate the same way as well, so I won't discuss them here.

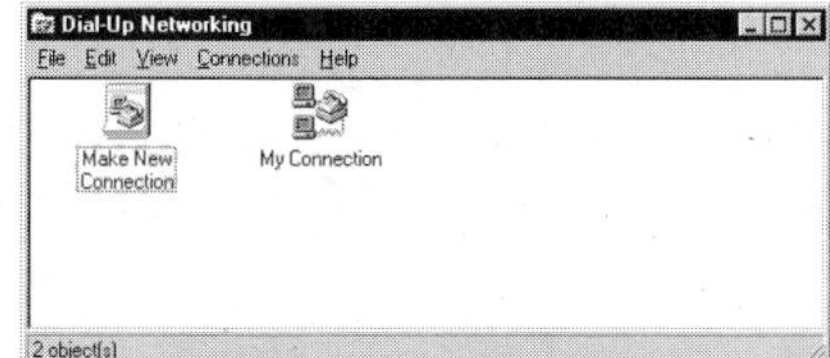

Figure 2.30.
Dial-Up Networking allows you to connect your machine to another machine through a modem.

Networking allows you to connect to another computer much as you would with any peer-to-peer connection. The big difference is that you use a modem instead of a NIC (network interface card) to make the connection. You could use this application to dial into a terminal connected to the company network, using your notebook. It would also come in handy for off-site employees who needed to check in for their e-mail.

The second utility is Direct Cable Connection. Figure 2.31 shows the host dialog box. Essentially, this utility replaces the Interserver application provided with DOS 6.x. It allows the client machine to access the host machine's drives and other resources. I find that I normally use it to move data from my notebook computer to the desktop machine. As you can see, there are no controls to worry about with this application.

Figure 2.31.
The Direct Cable Connection interface shows that its only purpose is to allow temporary data transfer between two machines.

Tip: Always use a parallel connection if at all possible when using the Direct Cable Connection utility. Doing so will greatly increase throughput. You can at least triple the amount of information moved per second by using a parallel cable. A machine-to-machine parallel cable might prove a little difficult to find. If so, you can modify a standard 25-pin serial cable by adding a gender changer to each end. Most electronics stores carry both serial cables and gender changers. The one advantage to this approach is that you can use the same cable for both serial and parallel connections.

Accessories

Windows 95 doesn't add very much when it comes to accessory applications. The multimedia offerings are much the same as you got with Windows 3.x. They consist of a multimedia player (media player), (sound) recorder, mixer (volume control), and CD player.

Windows 95 also includes some of the other familiar utilities from previous versions of Windows, including the calculator and WinPopUp. Conspicuously absent, though, are Cardfile and Calendar. Early beta releases of Windows 95 contained a replacement named WinPad, but it disappeared in later releases. Unfortunately, Microsoft never did replace the lost functionality.

You'll like two of the new utilities. The first one allows you to configure the various international settings. The second allows you to monitor system resources. Windows 95 doesn't automatically install either one of these features; you need to install them separately by using the Add/Remove Programs utility. Icons for both applications appear on the Taskbar, as shown in Figure 2.32.

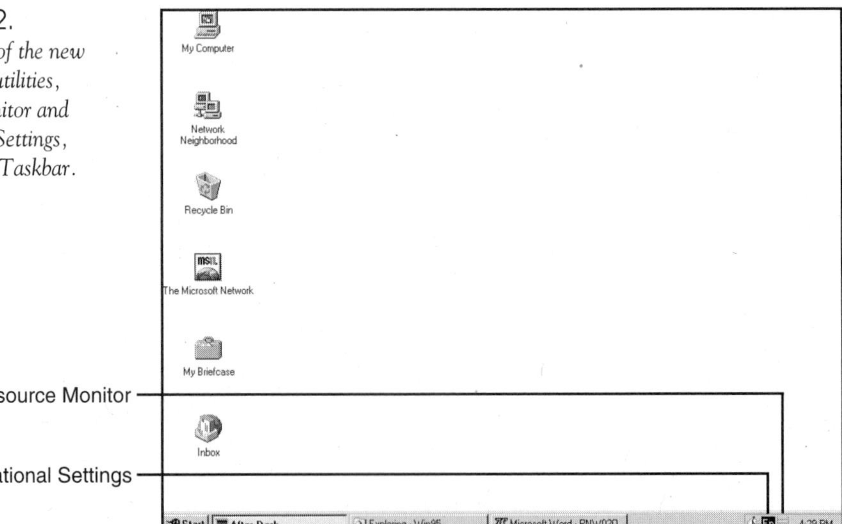

Figure 2.32.
Icons for two of the new Windows 95 utilities, Resource Monitor and International Settings, appear on the Taskbar.

Figure 2.33 shows the Resource Meter dialog box. You can display it by double-clicking the Resource Meter icon. Placing the mouse cursor over the icon for a few seconds displays a quick readout of all the various levels. All this display tells you is the status of the three memory-related areas of the system:

- **System resources:** This tells you the amount of memory you have left in the smaller of the two 64KB memory pools used for windows, icons, dialog boxes, and other system objects.
- **User resources:** This level tells you how much memory Windows 95 is using for interface-related objects such as windows and dialog boxes.
- **GDI resources:** All icon and other object memory usage associated with the graphical device interface appears in this level. This level always pertains to graphic system elements rather than an interface element such as a button or window.

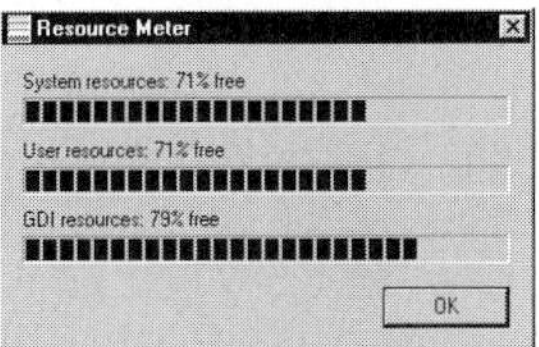

Figure 2.33.
The Resource Monitor helps you keep track of system memory usage.

There are a number of ways to use the International Settings utility. The first way is to click the Taskbar icon to display a list of installed languages. You can select which language you want to use from the list. This makes it easy to switch from language to language as needed.

The second way to use the International Settings utility is to right-click the International icon and select the Properties option. This displays the Keyboard Properties dialog box shown in Figure 2.34. As you can see, this dialog box allows you to change the currently selected language. It also allows you to add support for additional languages.

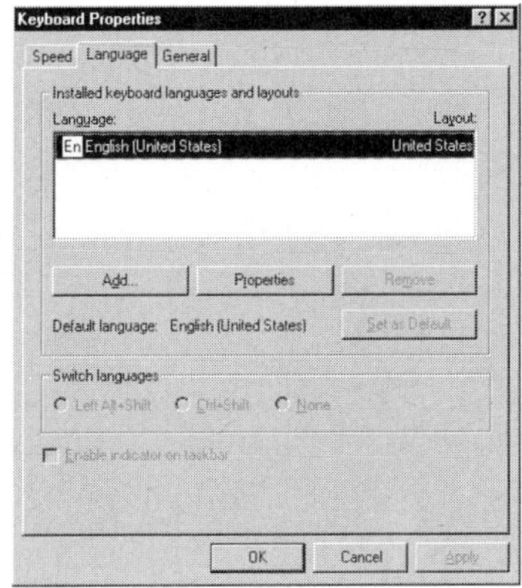

Figure 2.34.
Use the International Settings properties option to gain quick access to the Keyboard Properties dialog box.

Tip: Even if you don't use more than one language, adding the International Settings utility to your Startup folder can make you more productive. I use it to gain quick access to the Keyboard Properties dialog box without going through the Control Panel. The Speed tab of this dialog box contains settings that I can change as needed to make the system more comfortable to use.

New Windows 95 Applications for OSR2 Users

Normally people view a service release version of a product as something that fixes bugs. The OSR2 version of Windows 95 includes more than bug fixes—it contains several interesting new applications as well. Some of these applications, such as Windows Messaging, were added as a natural result of improving technology. A few of the new applications, such as the ActiveMovie control, are Internet-specific. The rapid pace of Internet technology has everyone issuing updates, so it's no surprise to see them here as well. Finally, a few of these updates are related to advances in hardware. For example, the Wang Imaging utility allows you to use a TWAIN scanner. As recently as a year ago, scanners were the domain of artists. Now they're appearing everywhere as people learn how to better use them in everyday situations.

We won't cover some advances in OSR2 here that some people may consider application updates. For example, the new level of infrared support appears in the "Working with an Infrared Data Port" section of Chapter 18. The "PCMCIA Devices on Your Notebook Computer" section of that same chapter also covers the new PCMCIA device support. We cover things like the scripting enhancements to Dial-Up Networking in the "Scripting Enhancements Provided by OSR2" section of Chapter 19. In short, this chapter concentrates on stand-alone applications.

Tip: This section isn't exclusive to OSR2 users, although they get all these applications by default. Users of older versions of Windows 95 can download and use these applications as well. Table 1.1 in Chapter 1 tells you where to find them. (In some cases the application isn't available as of this writing, but Microsoft promises to make them available to the general public soon.)

Be sure to spend some time learning what OSR2 can do for you as a whole before you get too involved with individual applications. I provide a very brief overview of the applications in Table 1.1 in Chapter 1. In this section of the chapter, we explore the stand-alone applications in greater depth. (We explore some of the applications such as Internet Explorer in the Internet-specific chapters of the book—most notably Chapters 21 and 22.)

Tip: Trying to get a handle on all of the issues surrounding the OSR2 version of Windows 95, such as FAT 32 support, could be a little difficult when you consider that Microsoft has spread this information all over the Internet. In addition, they've made it nearly impossible to get any support unless you're willing to pay for it (there isn't any free support for the OSR2 release). Look at the Support Boundaries section of the Description of Windows 95 OEM Service Release 2 Knowledge Base article at `http://www.microsoft.com/kb/articles/q155/0/03.htm` if you want more information about support. Part of the problem is that a lot of information appears in the Microsoft Knowledge Base and they don't provide an index that outlines all of the articles it contains. Fortunately, you can obtain a list of Microsoft Knowledge Base articles for OSR2-related issues from `http://ling.ucsd.edu/~erwin/kb.html`.

ActiveMovie Control

The easiest way to look at the ActiveMovie Control is as a replacement for the Media Player utility, but that really wouldn't look at the intended use for this utility program. There are three different applications that you can use to play multimedia files on your machine—each has a different forté. Double-click any .WAV file displayed in an Explorer window and you'll see a copy of the Sound Recorder appear. You'll also see this application appear if you right-click the file and choose Play or Open from the context menu. The reason that Sound Recorder appears is that you can use it to modify the .WAV (audio) file if so desired. ActiveMovie does the same thing for video files like the .AVI files provided as part of the Windows 95 installation disk—provided that you retain the default configuration (I'll show you how to modify the files associated with the ActiveMovie Control in the later section "ActiveMovie File Types"). The reason that we call on the ActiveMovie Control is that it's lightweight—you don't have to have a lot of memory to run it. The ActiveMovie Control is designed for Internet use. It doesn't provide all the bells and whistles that the Media Player does. However, the Media Player still is used the majority of the time when you insert any kind of multimedia file into an OLE client (such as a Word for Windows document). That's because the Media Player provides better capabilities—it's designed to work with all the devices on your machine. The Media Player also provides a standard user interface in the form of a menu.

Now that you have a better appreciation for the role that the ActiveMovie Control plays in the world of Windows 95, let's take a look at how it works. As I mentioned earlier, you only need to double-click a movie file to open this application. You can use the context menu options for any video file. Finally, you can open a copy of the ActiveMovie Control by using the ActiveMovie Control shortcut found in the Multimedia folder of your Start menu. If you open the ActiveMovie Control this way, you'll see a File Open dialog box. One shortcoming of the ActiveMovie Control is that it doesn't provide a menu for opening files. Figure 2.35 shows a copy of the ActiveMovie Control with a file loaded (the GOODTIME.AVI file from the Windows 95 installation disk).

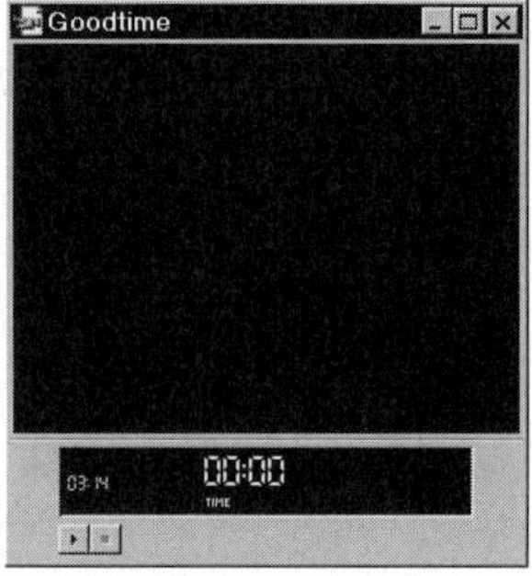

Figure 2.35.
The ActiveMovie Control is designed as a very small and lightweight video player.

Tip: The ActiveMovie Control isn't limited to video files—you can also use it to play audio and filter graph files. Unfortunately, you have to either open the ActiveMovie control manually (using the Start menu entry) or pass the filenames on the command line to get it to play non-video file types. You could also change the file associations for audio files to use the ActiveMovie Control instead of the Sound Recorder for a more permanent setup. I show you how to do this in the "Using Explorer to Get the Job Done" section of Chapter 5.

As you can see, there isn't much in the way of a user interface when you use the ActiveMovie Control as originally configured. However, like everything else in Windows 95, there's a context menu associated with this utility. Right-click the gray area below the display window and you'll see a context menu like the one shown in Figure 2.36. This context menu contains entries for playing, stopping, and pausing the current file, along with the usual Properties entry. You can also use this menu to change the amount of information displayed by the utility. Checking the Display entry displays the VCR-like time window shown in Figure 2.36. The Controls entry displays the Run and Stop buttons shown in the figure.

Let's look at what the Properties entry on the context menu will do for us. Select it and you'll see the ActiveMovie Control Properties dialog box shown in Figure 2.37. As you can see, the Playback page of this dialog box allows you to change the volume and balance settings of the playback. You use the Start and Stop fields in the Timing section of the page to control where the playback begins and ends within the file. This is a handy feature to use if you only want to see part of the file. The Play Count field tells the control how many times to play the video for you. If you select Auto Repeat, the video will play continuously until you tell it to stop. Finally, the Auto Rewind check box controls whether the ActiveMovie control repositions the position indicator at the beginning of the file when it's done playing.

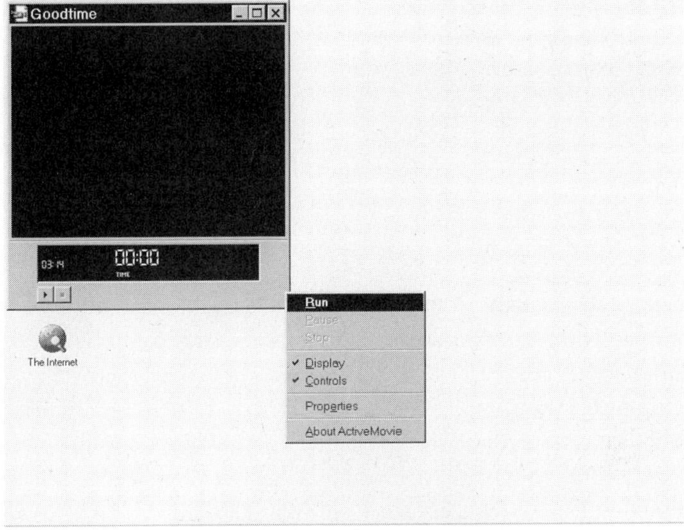

Figure 2.36.
You never know what you'll find by right-clicking things in Windows 95—a context menu for the ActiveMovie control in this case.

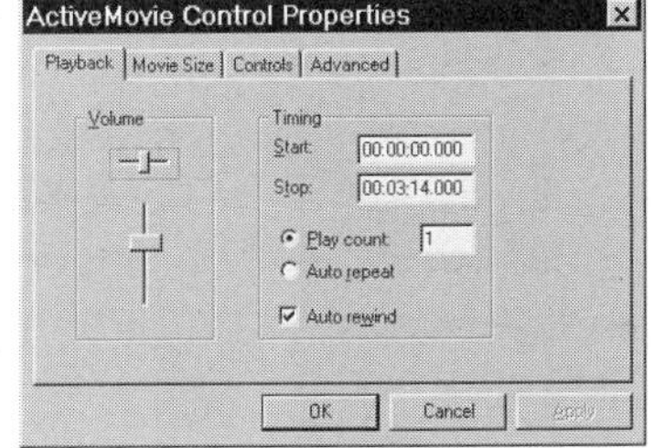

Figure 2.37.
The Playback page of the ActiveMovie Control Properties dialog box allows you to change the way your file is played.

The Movie Size page of the ActiveMovie Control Properties dialog box comes next (see Figure 2.38). You use the entries here to control how much of the screen the ActiveMovie Control uses to display a video file. It might be tempting to simply check the Full Screen check box. However, unless you have a very fast machine, you'll notice that you start seeing the picture jump when it's displayed this large. The reason is simple: You're using a lot of Windows resources to display the image—the ActiveMovie Control no longer has time to display the entire image before the next one is ready to read. As a result, you start dropping frames—losing parts of the image so that the movie can continue playing at full speed. Unfortunately, there isn't any speed control, so you don't have the option of playing the movie more slowly in an effort to get a larger picture. Fortunately, the Select the Movie Size drop-down list box allows you to choose a more convenient size. There's an option for playing the movie maximized or double the normal size. If you notice that your machine can't even play the movie at full size, you might need to select one of the fractional sizes provided instead. I'll show you later in this section how to determine whether the display is dropping frames.

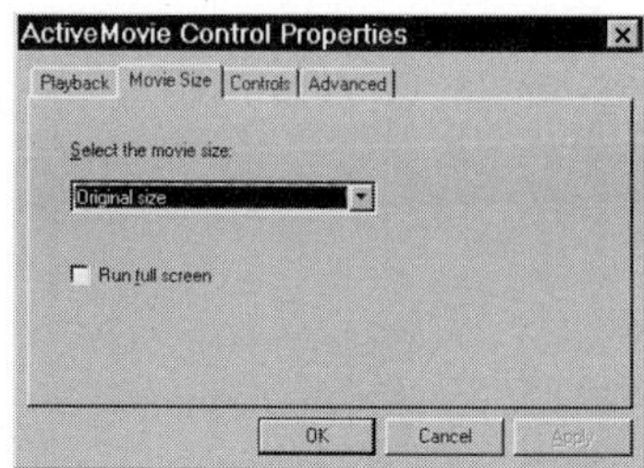

Figure 2.38.
The Movie Size page allows you to control how much of the screen is used for video playback.

Figure 2.39 shows the Controls page of the ActiveMovie Control Properties dialog box. Notice that you don't have to simply accept the minimal level of controls that we saw in Figure 2.35. This page allows you to add one of several control groups to the display. There are actually four settings. You must enable the Control Panel to use any of the settings at all. This automatically displays the Run and Stop controls discussed previously. The Position Controls option displays a set of controls for changing the current position within a file. For example, you can use these controls to change to the next or previous track. They're the Skip, Forward, and Reverse controls found on a normal VCR or CD player. The Selection Controls option displays the buttons needed to select specific areas of the file to play without opening the Playback page shown in Figure 2.37. Finally, the Trackbar option displays an indicator that shows your position within the current track (it doesn't show your position within the file for a multi-track file). Notice that this dialog box also contains an option for turning the display panel on or off. The two buttons in the Color section of the dialog box allow you to choose the foreground and background colors of the display. The default setting displays white letters on a black background.

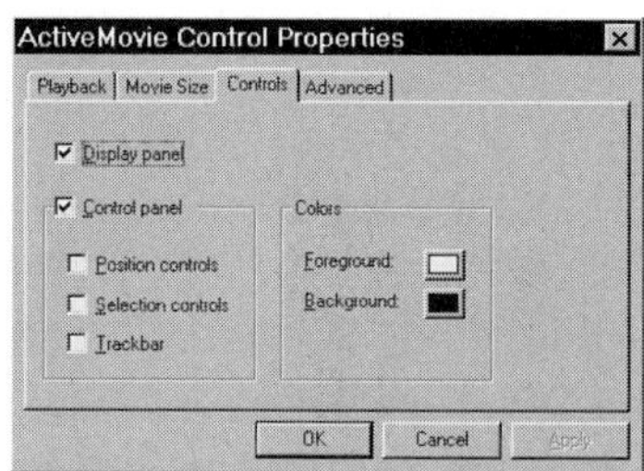

Figure 2.39.
You'll need the options on the Controls page to enable or disable controls provided by the ActiveMovie Control.

Remember that I told you earlier in this section that we'd look at a way for determining how well your computer is playing a file? That's what you'll find on the Advanced page shown in Figure 2.40. At first it doesn't look like much—all it displays is a list of filters used to play back this particular file. However, if you select one of the filter entries and then click the Properties button, you'll see a display like the one shown in Figure 2.41. Notice that this dialog box provides statistics for the video filter. The important statistic is the Frames Dropped in Renderer entry. If you start seeing a value higher than 0, you know that your computer isn't keeping up with the movie. Normally you can get rid of this problem by using a smaller screen for playback.

Figure 2.40.
The Advanced page doesn't appear to provide much more than a list of filters.

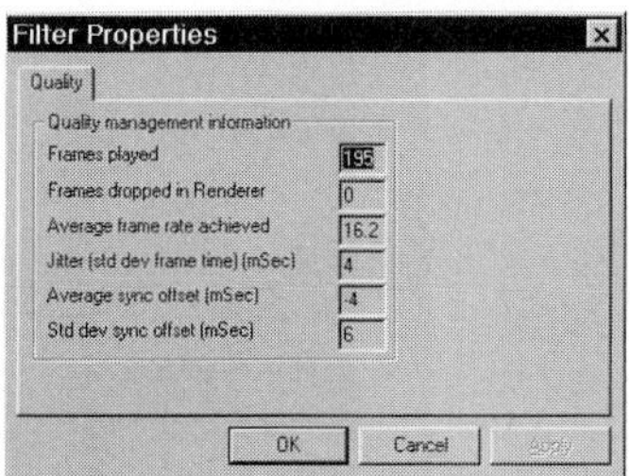

Figure 2.41.
Clicking the Properties button displays statistics for the selected filter on the Advanced page.

Tip: Tests on several machines and conversations with other users showed that most video files will play fine in full screen mode on a 200 MHz Pentium machine with at least 16MB of RAM. If you've got a lower-speed machine, you'll want to use something other than full-screen mode in most cases.

ActiveMovie File Types

The ActiveMovie Control has a counterpart in the Multimedia folder (located within the Accessories folder) on your Start menu. Clicking the ActiveMovie File Types icon displays a dialog box similar to the one shown in Figure 2.42. Right now you can do only one thing on the File Types page and that's to tell the ActiveMovie File Types utility that you want it to check all your file associations every time Windows 95 starts. This particular feature is really nice because of the number of applications that use the same file extensions. You may suddenly find that another application has taken over the file association and that your Internet connections no longer work as anticipated.

Let's say you install a program that changes one of the file associations. When you start Windows 95 the next time you'll see a dialog box similar to the one shown in Figure 2.43. All you need to do is click Yes to restore your file associations to the condition they were in prior to installing the application. Of course, now the new application won't be able to open the file automatically unless you add some new entries to the file association using the techniques in the "Using Explorer to Get the Job Done" section of Chapter 5. If you click the Advanced button, you'll see a new version of the ActiveMovie Settings dialog box like the one shown in Figure 2.44. As you can see, the dialog box now offers you three choices. You can restore all of the settings, part of the settings, or none of the settings that were changed. There are three levels of conditional change: MPEG video, Windows video, and all audio files.

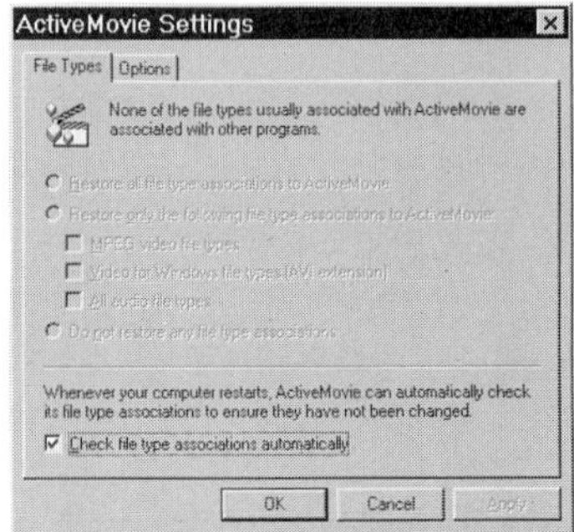

Figure 2.42.
The File Types page of the ActiveMovie Settings dialog box allows you to determine whether ActiveMovie automatically checks its file associations when you start Windows 95.

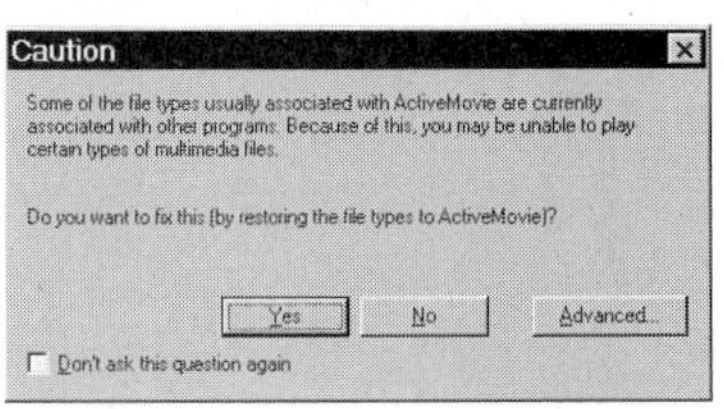

Figure 2.43.
ActiveMovie will warn you when its file associations are tampered with.

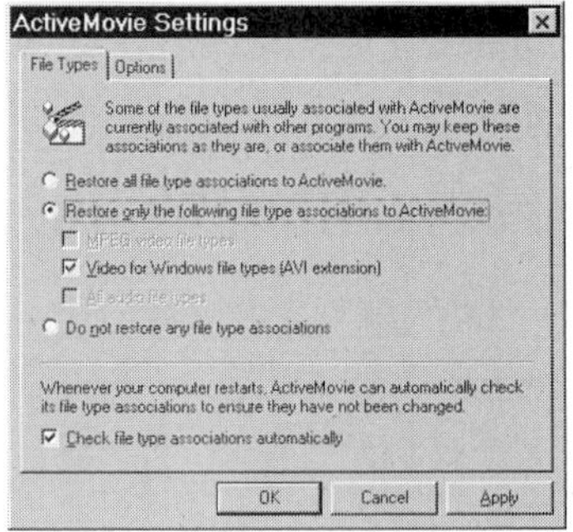

Figure 2.44.
You can use this version of the ActiveMovie Settings dialog box to restore only part of the file associations that got changed.

Let's take a look at the Option page shown in Figure 2.45. This is where you define which kinds of files the ActiveMovie Control will support. Currently you can chose from three options (though Microsoft will likely add more): MPEG video files, video CD (.DAT files), and QuickTime (.MOV and .QT files).

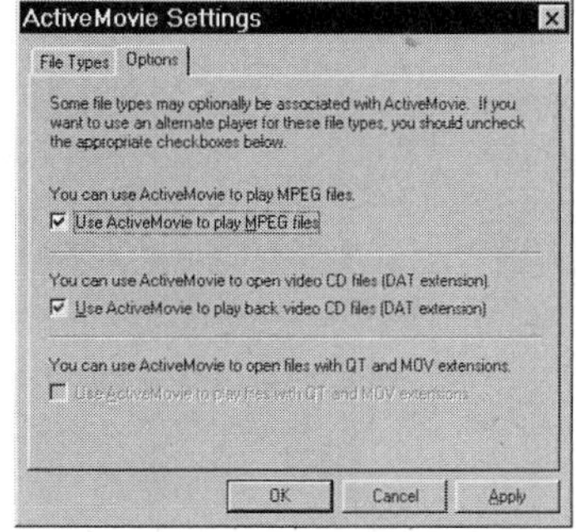

Figure 2.45.
The Options page allows you to decide which kinds of files the ActiveMovie Control will support.

Internet Explorer

The OSR2 version of Windows 95 comes with Internet Explorer 3.0. Figure 2.46 shows what this version looks like. The big news for this version of the product is support for ActiveX controls. The use of these controls can greatly enhance the usability of a Web site by allowing the Webmaster to do things that HTML code normally wouldn't support. For example, you can use an ActiveX control to figure out the total owed on a purchase before sending the page to the Web server. A control can also change the appearance of the Web page on-the-fly and perform other tricks unavailable when using straight HTML. (I talk more about designing your own Web page in Chapter 22.)

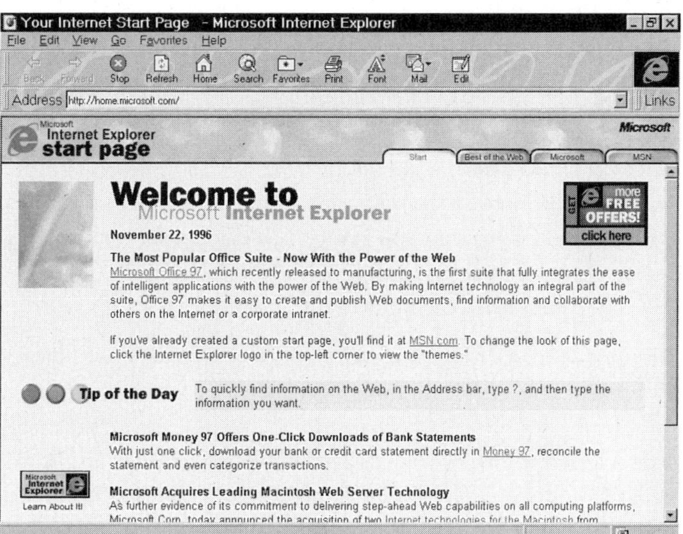

Figure 2.46.
Internet Explorer 3.0 offers many new features, including support for ActiveX controls.

In addition to the ActiveX control support, Internet Explorer 3.0 offers support for HTML-style sheets, frames, Java applets, JavaScript, VBScript, and an improved user interface. Let's talk about HTML style sheets (also called cascading style sheets) for a second. Using a style sheet (also known as a template) with a word processor allows you to create consistent documents with little effort.

They provide this same capability when used on a Web page. Instead of designing every page element, you can create a style sheet that dictates certain things like the use of icons and so forth. All that's left to the user is the placement of content. You can find out more about cascading style sheets at `http://www.w3.org/pub/WWW/Style/`. The actual specification is at `http://www.w3.org/pub/WWW/TR/WD-css1`.

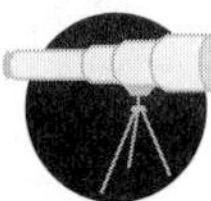

Looking Ahead: This section provides only an overview of Internet Explorer. We look at all the usage details for this product in the "Working with Internet Explorer" section of Chapter 21. All of Chapter 22 looks at the process of designing your own Web page. However, I pay special attention to ActiveX support in the "Using ActiveX Control Pad" section of that chapter. Finally, when it comes time to test out the new Web page you've designed, nothing's handier than your own Web server. Look at the "Personal Web Server" section of Chapter 23 for details.

Frames are another common method for reducing the amount of work required to create a Web page. In essence, a frame divides the browser windows into sections. Each frame used to fill the browser window contains HTML from a separate file (location on the Web server). You can then update one section of the window without disturbing anything else. Web sites that offer side bars of links or use a heading of some kind, like those provided by Microsoft, usually do so by adding frames to their Web page design. Not only do frames make it faster for a Webmaster to create a Web page, but they reduce network traffic and the time required to download a Web page update.

A lot of people are betting their futures on the success of Java applets. The short story on Java applets is that they're platform-independent applications that you can view in your browser. These applications are interpreted by a special Java virtual machine that runs on your computer—that's how a programmer can make them platform-independent. Because the Java virtual machine on a Macintosh speaks the same language as the Java virtual machine on your IBM, both machines can use the same applet. You'll likely see Java applets used a lot more as HPCs (hand-held personal computers) and Web televisions make their way to the market.

Scripting is another big issue today. Internet Explorer provides support for both JavaScript and VBScript. Like ActiveX, scripting can help reduce the amount of network traffic by performing some tasks locally instead of on the Web server. Unlike ActiveX, you usually can't access the system hardware or perform any low-level tasks by using scripts. Some people think that this makes scripts a lot safer than using ActiveX. In some ways they're right. However, there have been more than a few reports of holes in script security, which makes scripts something less than a 100 percent solution to the security problem that you face when surfing the Net. I talk more about scripting in the "Simple Scripting with VBScript" and "Simple Scripting with JavaScript" sections of Chapter 22. Be sure to read the "Internet Security" section of Chapter 24 for more details on what to look out for on the Internet.

In addition to all these built-in features, Internet Explorer also provides connections to a lot of other applications. The most important application from an Internet user point of view is the Internet Mail and Internet News viewers that come with Internet Explorer 3.0. I examine these products in detail when I look at Internet Explorer usage in Chapter 21.

Microsoft NetMeeting

NetMeeting is a new technology-type utility. It provides you with the capability of holding meetings over the Internet. Figure 2.47 shows the main window for NetMeeting. Immediately obvious are the voice capabilities of this product. There are separate controls for sending and receiving voice from other people. Because this is a duplex connection, you won't get the irritating "speaker phone" effect that's present in a conference call setup.

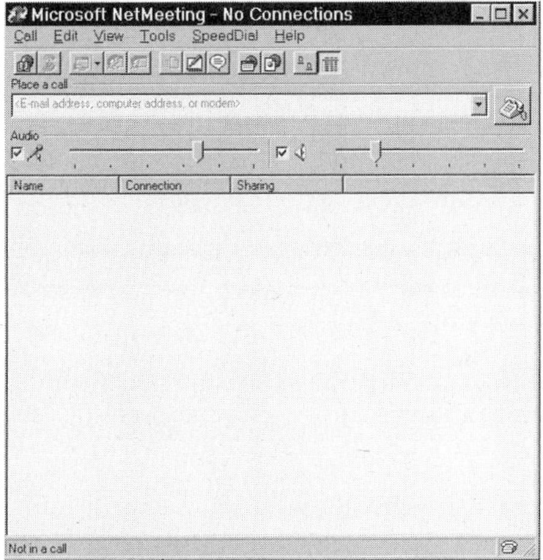

Figure 2.47.
NetMeeting provides the means to hold meetings with other people over the Internet.

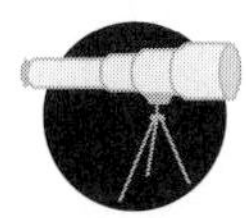

Looking Ahead: We cover this utility in a lot more detail in the "Working with Microsoft NetMeeting" section of Chapter 21. This includes sections on getting NetMeeting setup for use.

NetMeeting allows you to perform all the standard functions that you normally associate with an Internet connection. For example, you can send a copy of a file to one or more meeting attendees. You can also use NetMeeting to remotely control an application and perform other computer-related tasks.

One of the features I like best is the whiteboard. You can use it to give other people a visual representation of your idea. However, unlike the whiteboard in a meeting room, other people can draw on this one and help you expand your ideas. Overall, NetMeeting provides all the features of a physical meeting room without any of the inconvenience. In fact, there are some ways in which this utility provides a superior virtual meeting room to the physical rooms we're accustomed to using.

Windows Messaging

I put this particular entry in not because Windows Messaging is such a great new feature, but because of the confusion factor it provides. I don't know why Microsoft chose to rename Microsoft Exchange, but these two products are the same. You'll notice a couple of changes, albeit minor ones. From a user interface perspective, you'll notice that Windows Messaging comes installed with a shared folder area. It allows you to share information with coworkers right out of the box. The other change is under the surface. Microsoft has improved the performance of the messaging client—making Windows Messaging a bit faster than Microsoft Exchange. From every other perspective, though, the two products are identical. I talk about Microsoft Exchange and Windows Messaging in the "Using Microsoft Exchange" section of Chapter 20.

Imaging

Imaging is an entirely new product for the OSR2 version of Windows 95. It was designed by Wang, not Microsoft (even the About box states this fact). So, what precisely is this product? It's something that you'll wonder how you did without, once you use it. Imaging is a graphics manipulation program. You really can't draw with it (there is a set of tools designed to annotate images), but you can use it for a variety of other purposes such as scanning images. You can also use it for viewing existing graphics and preparing documents for FAX or e-mail transmission. Figure 2.48 shows the main window for the Imaging application.

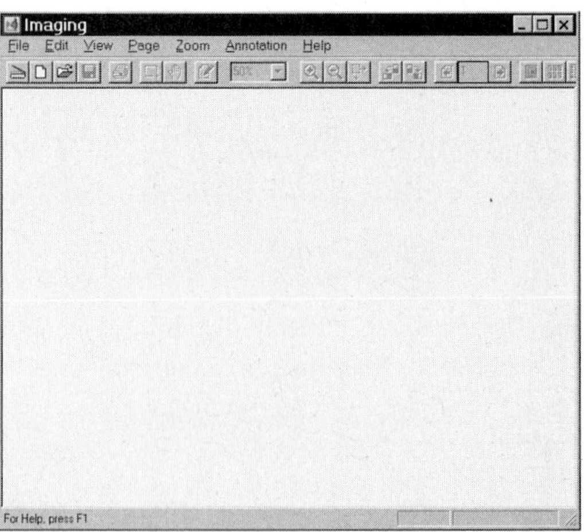

Figure 2.48.
The Imaging utility allows you to scan, annotate, and transmit graphic images.

Let's begin by looking at the toolbar from left to right. The following list explains the purpose of each control.

- **Scan New:** If you have a TWAIN scanner connected to your machine, you can use this button to start scanning an image. The image appears in the window as it scans (at least in most cases). The quality of the image depends on the capabilities of your scanner and the settings you've used.
- **New Blank Document:** Allows you to create a new document. I cover this option further in the "Creating a New Document" section that follows.
- **Open:** Displays a standard File Open dialog box that you can use to open an existing graphics file. Imaging supports more graphics than any of the previous Windows utilities have. The formats you can use include TIFF Document (.TIF), FAX Document (.AWD), Bitmap Image (.BMP), JPEG File (.JPG), PCX/DCX Document (.PCX/.DCX), and XIF Document (.XIF). I was surprised to see some of the more common choices missing, such as CompuServe graphics information format (.GIF) and Windows metafile (.WMF), but at least the support is better than what you've had in the past.
- **Save:** Displays a standard File Save or File Save As dialog box. You get only the TIFF Document (.TIF), FAX Document (.AWD), and Bitmap Image (.BMP) options when saving a file.
- **Print:** Displays a standard Print dialog box that you can use to send the document to a printer.
- **Select:** This tool allows you to select a specific area of the document for closer inspection or modification. Later I show how you can use this option to enhance the graphics environment.
- **Drag:** The name of this tool may be a little deceiving at first. It allows you to drag the image around within the display window (if you can't see the entire image at once). The advantage of using this option versus the scroll bars is that you can get more precise movement of the page.
- **Annotation Toolbox:** Clicking this button displays the only set of drawing tools you get with this application. I talk about this feature in the later section "Annotating Your Drawing."
- **Zoom/Zoom In/Zoom Out/Zoom To Selection:** There are four areas of the toolbar devoted to zooming. The first is a drop-down list box where you can select a specific level of zoom: 25%, 50%, 75%, 100%, 200%, and 400%. The Zoom In and Zoom Out buttons move you in and out from the drawing in double or half increments. For example, if you're currently at 100% zoom and you click the Zoom In button, the display will move to 50% zoom. Likewise, if you click Zoom Out, you'll be at 200% zoom. This doubling (halving) effect occurs whether you're at even increments or not. The Zoom To Selection allows you to zoom into the area that you've selected with the Select tool.

- **Rotate Left/Rotate Right:** These buttons allow you to perform some minor manipulation of the drawing. You can rotate it left or right in 90-degree increments.
- **Previous Page/Page/Next Page:** Use these three buttons to move to the previous, next, or a specific page on a multi-page document.
- **One Page View/Thumbnail View/Page and Thumbnail View:** You can select from one of three views for your drawing. Figure 2.49 shows all three views: one page, thumbnail, and page and thumbnail. The page view uses the current level of zoom to show you as much of the document as will fit in the current window. The thumbnail view allows you to see a small version of the entire document.

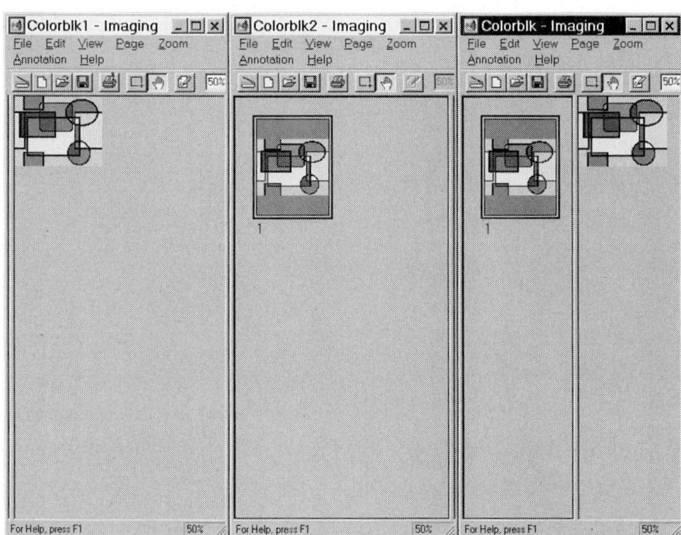

Figure 2.49.
You can view your data in one of three ways when using the Imaging utility.

Before we go much further, let's look at a few of the options that you can change. The first thing you need to know how to do is set up the scanner by using the Scan Preferences dialog box shown in Figure 2.50. You access this dialog box by using the File | Scan Preferences command. As you can see, the only settings available change the method used to store the image. You can select the best image quality, a mix between good quality image and small file size, or the smallest available file size. You can also choose the custom setting. We'll see how to use the custom settings as part of the "Creating a New Document" section that follows.

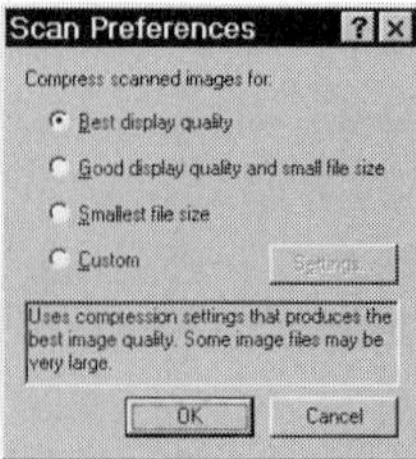

Figure 2.50.
The Scan Preferences dialog box allows you to configure your scanner.

There are some general settings that affect the Imaging utility as a whole. The first set of settings appears in the General dialog box shown in Figure 2.51. You access this dialog box by using the View | Options | General command. The Open Document Zoomed To field of this dialog box sets the default zoom value. Normally the 50% setting works fine for the majority of images. However, if you work with a lot of very small or very large images, you may want to select a different default zoom value. The Toolbar group includes two check boxes. The first check box allows you to select color icons on the Toolbar (it's set by default). The second check box, Large Buttons, changes the size of the Toolbar buttons—a real eye-saver on small screens. The Show Scroll Bars option is pretty self-explanatory. If you decide to hide the scroll bars, you can still use the Drag tool to move the picture around in the window. In addition, hiding the scroll bars gives you just that much more window area to work with your drawing. The final option, Show Full Screen Toolbar, actually hides the Toolbar when unchecked. Because the Toolbar provides so many conveniences, you'll probably want to leave this option checked.

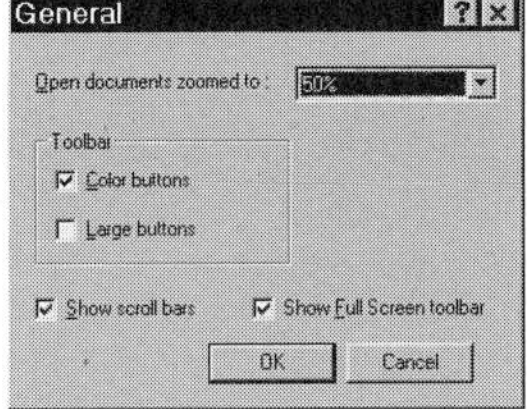

Figure 2.51.
The General dialog box allows you to change the appearance of the Imaging utility.

The second set of general options that you can change appears in the Thumbnail Size dialog box shown in Figure 2.52. You access this dialog box by using the View | Options | Thumbnail command. This dialog box affects the size of the thumbnail drawings. Every thumbnail in thumbnail view is the same size—regardless of the image size. If you get in a lot of faxes, you'll probably want to retain the Letter size shown. However, there are also legal and A4 sizes available. You can also choose to make the default thumbnail a square or an unconstrained size based on the largest image (all of the thumbnails are still the same size, but the size of the thumbnail grows or shrinks to accommodate the largest image).

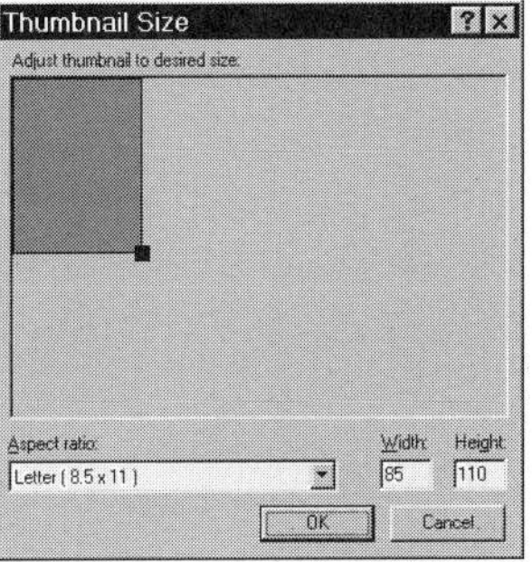

Figure 2.52.
The Thumbnail Size dialog box allows you to choose the drawing size used in thumbnail view.

Now that you have some of the basics down, let's look at some techniques for working with this utility. The following sections show how to perform the three most important tasks you can perform with Imaging. We'll begin by creating a new document. Then we'll add some annotations to it. Finally, we'll send the image to someone else, using Windows Messaging.

Creating a New Document

Creating a new document allows you to combine images into a cohesive whole, convert images to use the same format, or even annotate an image before you send it to someone else. Obviously, creating a new document always begins in the same place. You can either click the New Blank Document button on the Toolbar or use the File | New command. Figure 2.53 shows the New Blank Document dialog box that appears next.

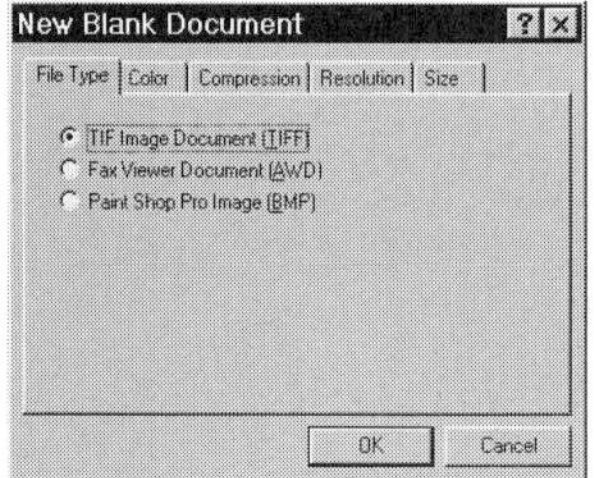

Figure 2.53.
The File Type page of the New Blank Document dialog box allows you to select what kind of document to create.

Once you select a file type, you need to define the number of colors the image will support. Figure 2.54 shows the Color page that you'll use to adjust this setting. Using more colors usually means a higher-quality image (though this depends on the images you have as source material). You also have to take the capabilities of the destination into account. It hardly pays to send a color image if the destination can handle only black and white or gray scale. Fortunately, Imaging automatically sets the color settings based on the file type you choose. For example, black-and-white is the only choice available if you choose to create a FAX file. The TIFF document setting provides the greatest number of color choices.

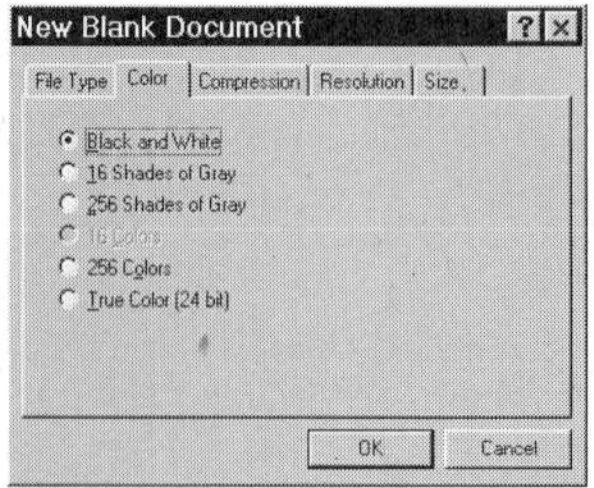

Figure 2.54.
The Color page is self-adjusting, but you still need to consider the destination for the resulting image file.

The Compression page shown in Figure 2.55 has a lot to offer as long as you use TIFF Document as the file type. It doesn't offer any settings if you use the other two file types. You have a choice between No Compress, CCITT Group 3 (1d) FAX, CCITT Group 3 (1d) Modified Huffman, Packed Bits, and CCITT Group 4 (2d) FAX compression settings. The actual amount of compression you get depends as much on the image as it does on the compression algorithm. Some images compress better using one method over another. Interestingly, the default setup for Imaging doesn't use the JPEG settings shown in the figure.

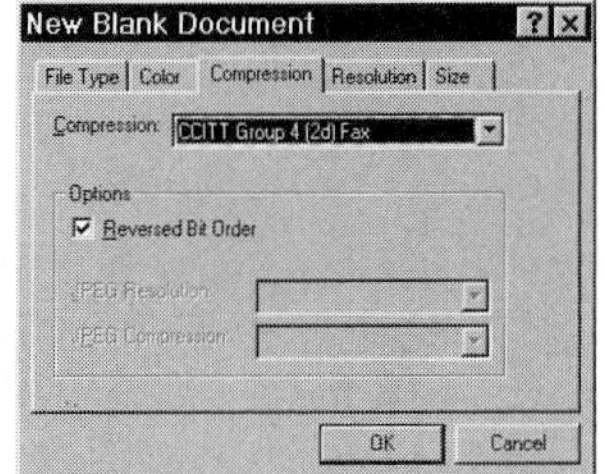

Figure 2.55.
The Compression page is accessible only when creating a TIFF Document.

There are two other factors that affect the final size of your image, and resolution is one of them. (Image size is the other factor, which we look at next.) The Resolution page appears in Figure 2.56. There are three standard resolutions supported by the Imaging utility: 100 dpi, 200 dpi, and 300 dpi. You can also use a custom setting, but I've gotten some strange results when using it. There are situations where you can create a custom resolution that the destination can't support. Sticking with the default resolutions is probably the best idea unless you know that the destination machine provides some custom capabilities.

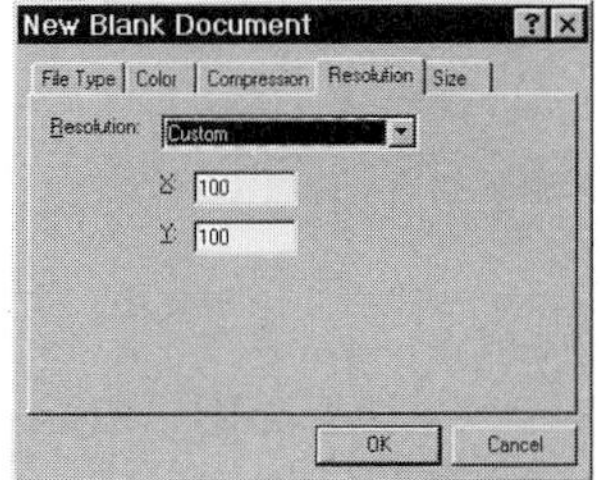

Figure 2.56.
Using a lower resolution can significantly reduce the size of the file you need to send to someone else.

Now we come to the final page of the New Blank Document dialog box, Size, shown in Figure 2.57. This page allows you to set the default size of the image you create. There are a lot of default sizes such as Letter and A4. However, as shown in the figure, you can also create a custom size for your image. I've found that the standard sizes are best if you want the recipient to print the page (or if you plan to send it by fax). Otherwise, you can usually get a bit of a file size reduction by using a custom image size designed specifically to accommodate the image you want to send.

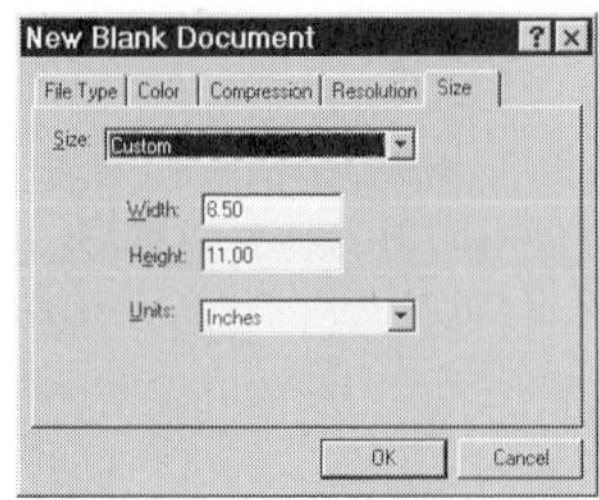

Figure 2.57.
The Size page allows you to select the final size of the image you want to create.

Once you finish setting up your new document, click OK to create it. The actual creation process may take a while, depending on the setting you choose. The New Blank Document dialog box disappears once the Imaging utility completes the creation process. You can now use the Edit menu option to paste existing images and text into the document. You can also use the annotation tools that I describe in the next section to add notes to the image.

There are two other commands you need to know about when it comes to the Imaging utility. You can create multi-page documents, but there aren't any Toolbar options for doing so. The Page | Insert | Scan Page and Page | Insert | Existing Page commands insert a new page at the current page position. Likewise, the Page | Append | Scan Page and Page | Append | Existing Page commands append a new page to the end of the document. Both of the Scan Page commands get their data from your scanner; both of the Existing Page commands open a standard File Open dialog box.

Annotating Your Drawing

The Imaging utility supports several kinds of annotation and they all appear in the Annotation Toolbox shown in Figure 2.58. You display this floating toolbox by clicking the Annotation Toolbox button on the Toolbox (you can also use the Annotation | Show Annotation Toolbox command).

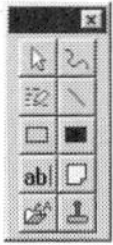

Figure 2.58.
The Annotation Toolbox contains all the tools you'll need to add comments your image.

The following list tells you about the function of each annotation tool:

- **Selection Pointer:** This tool allows you to select and move annotations around. Selecting an annotation also allows you to delete it.
- **Freehand Line:** Use this tool if you want to draw a freehand line. Hold the left mouse button down and drag the mouse cursor wherever you want to draw the line. Right-clicking this tool and selecting Properties from the context menu displays a Freehand Line Properties dialog box like the one shown in Figure 2.59. The Width (Pixels) field allows you to change the width of the line you draw. There's also a selection of colors below this field. Clicking the Palette button displays another dialog box like the one shown in Figure 2.60.

Using this dialog box is a little counterintuitive. The first thing you'll notice is that the colors in the Custom Colors area are the same as the colors in the Color field of the Freehand Line Properties dialog box. To change a color in the Color field, you must change a custom color. Simply click the Define Custom Color button in the Freehand Line Color dialog box and you'll see the dialog box extend (just as it would when used in any other situation). Click the custom color you want to change, select a new color for it, and then click the Add to Custom Colors button to change it.

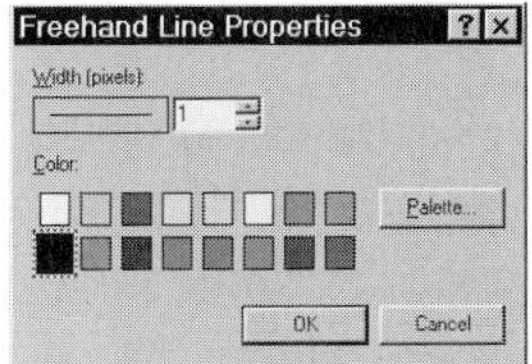

Figure 2.59.
The Freehand Line Properties dialog box allows you to change the kind of line you'll draw with the Freehand Line tool.

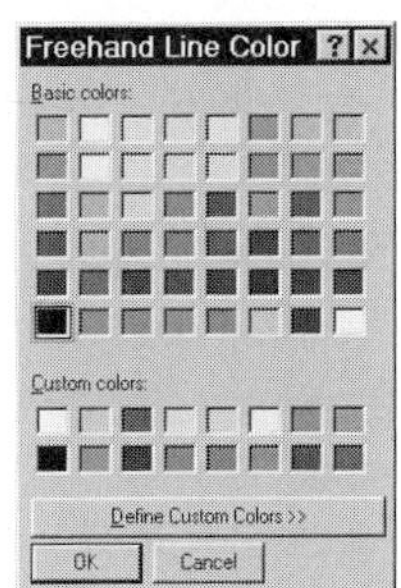

Figure 2.60.
You can change the default color palette by using the Freehand Line Color dialog box.

- **Highlighter:** You use this tool just as you would the real thing. It draws a transparent line in the color you choose. As with the Freehand Line tool, right-clicking the Highlighter tool and selecting Properties from the context menu displays a dialog box like the one shown in Figure 2.61. However, the only setting in this dialog box is a choice of colors. The Palette button in this dialog box works the same as the one for the Freehand Line tool.

Figure 2.61.
The Highlighter Properties dialog box offers only a choice of colors.

- **Straight Line:** Use this tool to draw a straight line. Left-click to start the line, drag the mouse until you reach the end of the line, and then release the mouse button to complete it. The Properties dialog box for this tool looks just like the one for the Freehand Line tool shown earlier in Figure 2.59.

- **Hollow Rectangle:** This tool allows you to draw a hollow rectangle. You can choose whether to make the inside of the rectangle transparent or not, using a check box in the Properties dialog box. In all other ways, the Properties dialog box for this tool looks like the one for the Freehand Line tool shown earlier in Figure 2.59.
- **Filled Rectangle:** The Filled Rectangle tool allows you to create a solid square. You can't make the interior transparent as with the Hollow Rectangle tool. The Properties dialog box for this tool looks like the one for the Highlighter tool (refer to Figure 2.61).
- **Typed Text:** This is one of two text tools. It allows you to place standard text on the drawing for annotation purposes. Click where you want to put the text and you'll see a Text Edit dialog box like the one shown in Figure 2.62. Right-clicking the Typed Text tool and selecting Properties from the context menu shows a Text Properties dialog box like the one shown in Figure 2.63. This is a standard Font dialog box like the one you'd use with a word processing application.

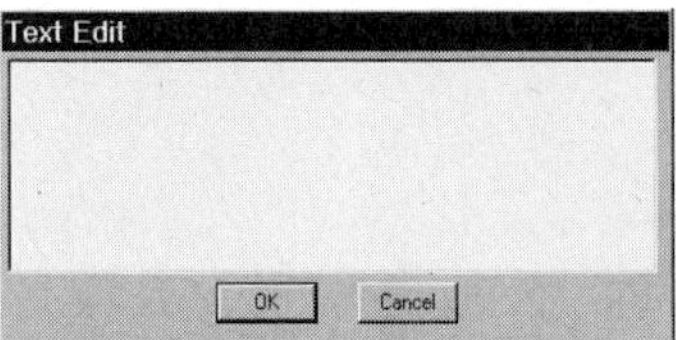

Figure 2.62.
The Text Edit dialog box allows you to add text to a drawing.

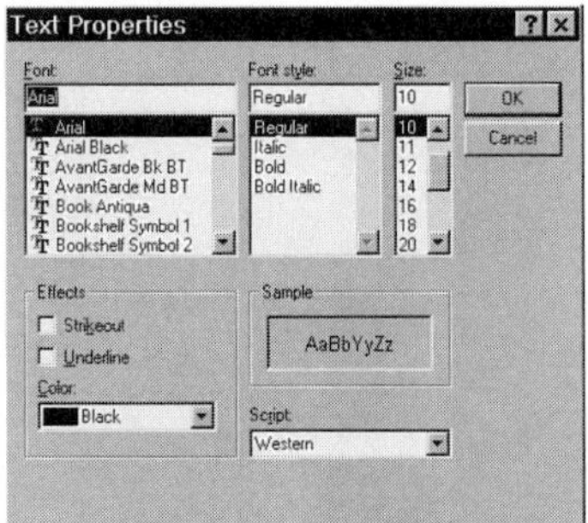

Figure 2.63.
The Text Properties dialog box works like any Font dialog box that you've used with a word processing application.

- **Attach-a-Note:** This tool is kind of interesting from a few perspectives. It works much like a Post-It note. You draw it just like you would a rectangle. After you finish drawing it, you see a Text Edit dialog box like the one shown in Figure 2.62. Unlike the text created by using the Typed Text tool, you can resize the square that the Attach-a-Note text is drawn in. The Properties dialog box for this tool looks just like the one for the Highlighter shown earlier in Figure 2.61. It includes an extra Font button that displays the Text Properties dialog box shown in Figure 2.63.
- **Text from File:** Got a text file that you want to place in your image? Use the Text from File tool to place it where you want. Just click and you'll see a standard File Open dialog box. Unfortunately, this tool supports only plain ASCII text—you can't insert formatted

text by using it. The Properties dialog box for this tool looks like the Text Properties dialog box shown in Figure 2.63.

- **Rubber Stamps:** The Imaging utility even includes the equivalent of a rubber stamp. You can use it to stamp one of the four common stamps provided with the utility: Approved, DRAFT, Received, and Reject. The Properties dialog box shown in Figure 2.64 allows you to create new stamps as needed. Fortunately you can use either text (Create Text button) or graphics (Create Image button) to create a stamp. You can't mix text and graphics in one stamp.

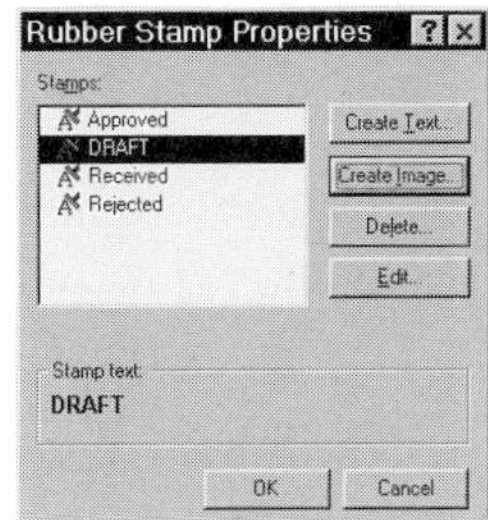

Figure 2.64.
The Rubber Stamp Properties dialog box allows you to create new rubber stamps as needed to annotate images.

Sending an Image to Someone Else

The whole purpose of going through all this work is to create an image that you can send to someone. The following procedure shows you how to send a document to someone else.

1. Use the File | Send command to display the Choose Profile dialog box shown in Figure 2.65. (You may be asked if you want to save the current file before you send it—always choose to save it.) The Profile Name will usually default to the profile created for your mailbox. You may have other profiles as well, depending on the services you have installed for Windows Messaging (Microsoft Exchange). The Options button displays two check boxes. The first allows you to set the current profile as the default. The second forces Windows Messaging to display the logon screens for all information services used to transmit the image. You can also create a new profile by clicking the New button and following the prompts. (In most cases you won't need to do this unless you want to add a new profile to Windows Messaging. Look at the "Using Microsoft Exchange" section of Chapter 20 for more details.)

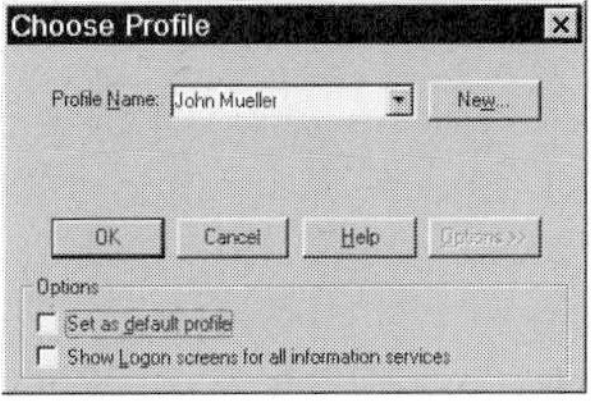

Figure 2.65.
The Choose Profile dialog box allows you to choose the communications service used to transmit your image.

2. Select a profile from the drop-down list box, and then click OK. You'll see a New Message dialog box like the one shown in Figure 2.66. The message includes the image file that you've created. Fill out the message by using the procedures in the "Using Microsoft Exchange" section of Chapter 20.

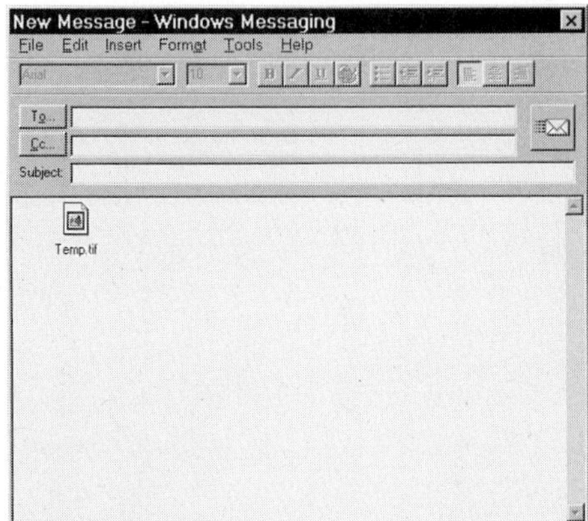

Figure 2.66.
The figure you want to send as a message will appear at the top of the message area in Windows Messaging.

3. Click the Send button in the New Message dialog box. The dialog box disappears as soon as Windows Messaging gets it sent. At this point you can quit the Imaging utility.

What's Next?

Windows is a moving target. Looking through Chapter 1 will tell you that. What you see today is only a shadow of what you'll get tomorrow. It's always fun to look back a bit and then see what you have today and use it as a basis for what you could have tomorrow. That's what most science fiction writers have to do to ply their trade.

I'm often reminded of *Star Trek*. Back when the series was first designed, Gene Roddenberry did his best to think about the future. Not the far-off future, but a realistic near future (as the timeline of history goes, anyway). When *Star Trek* was still a gleam in his eye, the computers and other futuristic machinery of the Enterprise seemed like a faraway dream. What seemed so far away then was in reality very close. I was struck by a recent article that showed that much of the technology that seemed so futuristic in 1966 is almost a reality today. In fact, I often look at those shows with just a little awe and a tad of amusement when I think that what was the future yesterday is the present now.

It's little wonder that science fiction writers have a difficult time coming up with ideas futuristic enough that they won't become reality until at least tomorrow. This is especially true of computers. Just think about how far we've traveled with the PC since its introduction. A few short years ago we were using machines that would be considered nonfunctional today. Text-based displays and 64KB of RAM today wouldn't even make it in most embedded equipment (discussed later), much less a personal computer. Take with me a step into the future of Windows—at least the way I see it.

Windows at Work

Reading the trade papers a few days ago turned out to be a worthwhile venture. Microsoft had released some new information about the future direction of OLE and how it will affect computers. Just yesterday, OLE was a simple method of connecting two applications. Today, a server application can actually make a client application change its appearance to meet a user's needs. Tomorrow, that same application will allow you to connect to anything on a network without really knowing where the connection leads. All you'll really need to know is what you want. The computer will find the information for you.

Connectivity isn't the only way that Windows will change the way you work. Consider the business trip. How many of us really like to get up early on a Sunday, trudge down to the airport, spend the day traveling, and then sleep in a bed not our own? It's a pain, but also a necessity of modern business. Windows might change all that. An article in the same trade paper talked about modems that allow both voice and data transfer using one telephone wire. Think about it: This technology is available right now. It's not in the future; you can have it today. How will this new technology affect business travel? I think we'll all spend a lot less time traveling. It doesn't take a college education to figure out that a telephone call, even a five- or six-hour telephone call, is a lot less expensive than sending someone halfway around the country.

Windows 95 also presents some new technology that I think will become the future of all communication. You can use Microsoft Exchange to manage your company and online e-mail. In fact, you don't even have to pay much attention to the source of the e-mail; Exchange will route it to the right place automatically. What does this mean to the user? It means that you can spend less time worrying about the details of communicating and more time worrying about the substance.

This idea of spending less time worrying about your environment relates to the general design of Windows 95. How much time did you spend under Windows 3.x worrying about which application to use and what types of data that application supports? Configuration details were a matter of a computer user's daily existence in that old environment. Windows 95 isn't perfect by a long shot, but the new data-centric approach that it provides takes users and places them in the driver's seat. Windows 95 enforces the idea that it's the data, not the application, that is your main concern. For example, I just stick all the files related to a particular project in a folder on my desktop and let Windows 95 worry about which application to start when I double-click one of them. You'll find that this approach allows you to organize and use your data just like its paper equivalent—a feature that Windows 3.x lacked.

As you can see, Windows 95 is not the future. It's today. Tomorrow will provide much more in the way of a user-friendly environment. Tomorrow's version of Windows will still have bugs—those won't go away—but you should be able to get a lot more work done in a lot less time, despite the problems with whatever direction Windows takes.

Embedded APIs

There's been a lot of talk about sticking Windows into embedded-systems technology. What are embedded systems? Think of the computer in your car or the alarm that protects your house. A computer in your television set provides automatic channel programming and other features. Of course, this is a personal view of embedded systems.

The industry view of embedded systems takes a slightly different route. Have you ever seen the robotic arms that put your car together? They contain embedded systems. What about the device that automatically machines the flywheel for that car? The number of embedded systems in industry is amazing.

Now, what do most of these embedded systems have in common? They almost always have size constraints that make it nearly impossible for them to contain what we would call a modern computer. Up to a few years ago, it wasn't uncommon to find embedded-systems programmers using hexadecimal to program older systems. Some of the newer systems actually allowed them to use assembler or perhaps C.

All that's changing. Embedded systems are slowly coming up to the level of modern computers, thanks to the constant miniaturization taking place. The same technology that put a Pentium in your notebook is putting it into embedded systems as well.

It's not unlikely that we might see a form of Windows in embedded systems tomorrow. This won't be the Windows that you use today. It will be something slightly different, something designed to provide for the special needs of embedded systems.

How will Microsoft enable you to use Windows for both your car and your work? Through the use of embedded APIs. We currently use several different APIs to make various parts of Windows work. (I discuss these APIs in detail elsewhere.) It's not too much of a leap to add some additional APIs that will work with nonstandard computers such as those used in embedded systems.

Windows APIs in Your Toaster?

What these embedded APIs mean to you as a user is that you'll eventually be able to control many household appliances with your computer. Your VCR will no longer be a challenge to program because it won't use an archaic text interface. It will probably use an interface that looks very familiar, perhaps even as familiar as the version of Windows running on your computer.

Have you ever watched futuristic movies and envied the person who walked into his house and talked to it? All of a sudden, the house began doing some of the more mundane tasks of living while the person worked on something creative. It's not too unrealistic to think that this technology is just around the corner.

Voice technology is already becoming a reality. Even though Windows 95 currently doesn't implement what I would consider a viable voice technology, it is on the drawing boards now. Sound-card vendors such as Creative Technologies and Media Vision are marketing Windows-compatible voice systems that can execute commands for you. If Windows becomes a part of embedded systems, it's only one more step before the emerging voice technology actually lets you talk to your house.

At Work Fax

Let's get back to reality. One of the things that Windows 95 should allow you to do today is share a fax. It doesn't sound like a big deal until you start to think about the logistics of people sharing one fax connected to a communications server. Outgoing faxes don't present much of a problem. It's the incoming faxes that you have to worry about.

How do you determine where to send an incoming fax? That's one of the things that this new version of Windows should help you resolve (but doesn't). Another problem is what format to provide for the incoming fax. Does the person receiving it want a text or graphic format? Text format would allow him to import the fax into a word processor. A graphic format would allow him to print faxes containing pictures and other non-text information. You need to choose that part of the equation almost immediately to make the fax software work properly.

Even though Windows 95 does come with fax software, it needs a lot of help before it will be truly useful. For one thing, a lot of people are having trouble making it work at all on a network. Routing is only one part of the problem that they seem to have. Another problem is getting the fax software to spool properly. I think it will be a while before Microsoft will get this one worked out.

At least the fax software provided with Windows 95 works well on a local machine. Of course, you need a standard fax/modem, or you'll run into other problems. Remember the fax/modems of about three years ago? I've yet to see one of them work with Windows 95. The problem is simple. Most of the faxes use nonstandard port assignments and might not even work properly with the attached modem.

At Work Photocopying

Because fax and scanner software are here today, it's not too surprising to think that we might be looking at Windows-controlled copy machines in the future. However, these won't be ordinary copy machines. What would happen if you could make copies of a company memo and distribute it through the company e-mail, through the Internet, or over CompuServe with equal ease? Not only would the recipient receive a copy faster, but she would receive it without wasting paper or postage. Sure, it costs a little bit to send some types of information over the online services; but in most cases that cost is far less than using the postal system.

There aren't any Windows-controlled copy machines today, but it's only a matter of time. More and more office equipment comes with a built-in Ethernet connection, and recent events would seem to point to an eventual connection to every piece of office equipment, including the copy machine. Just think, a few years ago an Ethernet-equipped printer was an unheard-of luxury. Today it's standard equipment.

On Your Own

Explorer is one of the cornerstones of the new Windows 95 interface. It allows you to move around your machine—and the network, for that matter—in a way that was impossible under Windows 3.x. Spend some time getting used to the interface and trying out the various display modes. Click the column headings in the Detail view to see how Explorer rearranges the filenames.

Context menus are also an important part of Windows 95. Try right-clicking all the objects you see. See how the context menus vary from object to object. Don't forget that even the desktop is an object with a context menu. Make sure that you click the desktop to close its context menu without selecting anything.

Thinking about the future can be a lot of fun. What kinds of future applications do you see for Windows based on the material in this chapter? It might be fun to make a list and see which items are actually available five or 10 years from now.

If you're currently using the original version of Windows 95, download the new applications we've discussed for OSR2 users in this chapter and try them on your machine. You'll never know what kinds of new capabilities the applications will provide until you actually try them. Remember that all the download sites for these new applications are listed in Chapter 1 (Table 1.1).

Power Primers

3

Performance Primer

Tuning or optimizing a machine for optimum performance is one of the first things that many people think about when they install a new operating system. After they get all their applications installed and check out some of the new utilities, they want to see just how much they can get out of their new toy. The first thing you need to consider when reading this chapter is what tuning means. Getting every last ounce of power out of a system to perform a specific task represents one type of tuning. Allowing a system to perform a variety of specific tasks simultaneously (multitasking) is another. General tuning to provide the best performance in a variety of situations is yet another. I could go on. The fact of the matter is that there's no default configuration and no standard machine. Everyone has different needs and different hardware that he or she needs to use to get the job done. Any form of worthwhile optimization will take your specific needs into account.

I won't tell you how to tune your specific machine in this chapter. There's no way I can provide step-by-step tuning instructions for anyone without knowing his or her situation. What I will provide are some guidelines and tips you can use to create your own solution. You'll need to decide which tips you should implement and which you should ignore. I plan to provide tips for a variety of machine configurations, and your machine will appear somewhere in the list.

So, do you start reading right this second and hope to find the tips you need the first time through? You probably won't. It takes a bit of time and patience to really tune a system for optimum performance. To get some idea of what I'm talking about, consider race car drivers. A race car gets tuned to fit its particular "personality." The mechanic and driver work together to come up with the best configuration for that particular car. In addition, the car gets tuned to fit the track that it will race on and even the weather conditions. Tuning the car is probably the easy part of the process. Planning how to tune it requires a bit more effort.

You won't need to worry about the weather when tuning your system, but many other principles do apply. Planning how you need to tune your system is always a good idea. Just like any other worthwhile endeavor, tuning your system requires that you create a few goals and take a few potholes into account. Your machine contains hardware from a variety of sources. It probably contains a combination of components that are unique within your company. You need to consider how that hardware will react. Your applications are unique. Even if your job isn't unique, your way of doing that job probably is. A system that's perfectly tuned for the way I work probably won't do a lot for you.

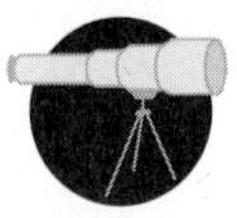

Looking Ahead: This chapter takes a look at the physical tuning of your system. We'll look at other aspects—such as tuning your desktop—in other chapters. Physically tuning your system is an important first step. Once you complete it, read the rest of this book (especially Chapter 10) for additional ideas on ways in which you can improve your efficiency in using your computer.

Keeping these personal needs in mind, let's look at some of the things you should consider before you start tuning up for the big race. The following list provides criteria you must consider before you start to tune your system. Of course, the time and effort you expend in this effort is directly proportional to the amount of performance you can expect to receive.

- **Memory:** The amount of real memory your system contains is a big factor in how well Windows 95 will operate. You shouldn't consider starting to tune until you have a minimum of 8MB of real RAM. You'll need to tailor this number to meet the demands of the applications you plan to run. For example, a spreadsheet requires a lot of memory, a database even more, but a word processor is relatively light when it comes to memory consumption. You might find that a graphics application requires a moderate amount of memory but takes a heavy toll on both the processor and graphics adapter. The number of simultaneous applications you plan to run also affects the point at which you should start to tune your system. I equipped my system with 24MB of RAM because I often run a word processor, spreadsheet, and communications program simultaneously. Virtual memory helps take up the slack between real memory and what you need, but you can't count on it to assume the full burden.
- **Hard disk size:** Windows 95 runs best when you give it a large swap area to work with. In addition, you need space for the application itself and some space for data files. The one factor many people underestimate is the size of their data files. I was quite surprised the other day when I translated a small Word for Windows file from 1.0 format to 6.0. The file consumed almost twice as much space even though the amount of data hadn't changed one iota. Of course, the 6.0 format file provides many features the 1.0 file doesn't. The extra space used by the 6.0 format bought me added functionality—an important tradeoff to consider. The general rule of thumb I use for figuring out the amount of hard disk space I need is to add up the space required for installed configurations of my applications and triple it. This is a very coarse calculation, but it works for me.
- **Hard disk speed:** Older operating systems were a lot less disk-intensive than Windows 95 is. Not only do you have the swap file that Windows 95 creates, but applications also make greater use of the hard drive today for temporary storage. To see what I mean, open just about any application and check for the number of .TMP files on your drive. You might be surprised by what you see. All this disk access means just one thing: You need a fast drive to make Windows 95 jump through the hoops that you want it to. Drive speed isn't the cure-all for every problem, but it has become a much bigger part of the overall picture.
- **Processor speed:** Your processor speed affects the way your computer runs. No other factor so greatly affects your system once you meet the basic storage requirements. Herein lies the rub. Many people opt for a high-speed processor, then choke it with limited memory and hard drive space. Remember, the processor makes a big impact on system throughput only after you meet the basic storage requirements. A thrashing hard drive can eat up every bit of extra speed you might add to a system.

- **Motherboard features:** Items such as the size of the motherboard's SRAM cache might seem a bit on the technical side, but these features aren't just for technicians. An optimized system starts with an optimized motherboard. Get a motherboard that offers plenty of room to grow and the ability to tune. For example, I just upgraded one of my systems from a 486-33 to a 486-66 with a simple processor change that took just 15 minutes from start to finish.
- **Peripheral devices:** I/O has always been a bottleneck in the PC. That was true yesterday, and it's true today. The two peripherals you need to concentrate on the most are your disk controller and display adapter. Think for a second about the way Windows is designed, and you'll understand why. Windows is a GUI; it consumes huge amounts of time simply drawing all those pretty images you see on the display. A display adapter that uses processor cycles efficiently (or even unloads some processing tasks) can greatly affect the perceived speed of your system. The less time Windows spends drawing icons and other graphics, the more time it will have to service your application. Likewise, a slow controller will make even a fast hard disk look slow. It's the controller that becomes a bottleneck with many systems today. The short take on peripherals? Always get 32-bit peripherals whenever possible and make certain that they are fully compatible with Windows 95. (Using real mode or 16-bit Windows device drivers is also a major source of speed and reliability problems on many systems.)
- **Bus speed:** You might not think very much about the little connectors that you stick cards into, but the system does. The system bus has been a source of major concern for a great number of years, and I don't see this changing anytime soon. What good is a fast peripheral if you can't access it at full speed? There are a slew of 32-bit bus architectures on the market. Everything from EISA to VL and the MCA bus has been used to try to solve the problem with bottlenecks. Suffice it to say that the speed of your bus is yet another factor in how your system will perform.
- **Network interface card (NIC):** If you spend a lot of time working on the network, you'll most certainly want a high-capacity NIC. The minimum you should settle for is a 16-bit Ethernet card. Anything less is a waste of perfectly good network bandwidth. People who share graphics or other very large files across the system should consider getting 32-bit NICs for their machines. Some NICs also come equipped with an expandable cache. Using a larger cache can buy you some additional network speed in some cases, especially under Windows 95.

Peter's Principle: Stretching Your Hard Drive

Making your hard drive hold more has become a major issue in the wake of today's mega applications. (Doesn't it always seem to come down to the size of your hard drive and/or system memory?) Talk to just about anyone, and the first way they'll suggest making your hard drive hold more information is disk compression. That's a good idea in some circumstances, but in others it could prove problematic. Some systems just don't compress all that well because of conflicts with the hard drive or controller. Other people worry about the reliability of disk compression, so they don't use it. Still another problem is the type of data your machine contains; application code doesn't compress all that well. If you store your data on the network, your machine probably won't make the best candidate for compression.

Several other ways you can extend your hard drive cost a bit but provide long-term benefits. The first is to buy a good CD-ROM. I'm not talking about an older double-speed model, but a high-end 8X (or even a 12X) drive. (NEC just introduced its new 12X drive; other vendors are sure to follow.) Make sure it gets connected to a good controller and that you have a separate hard drive extension. A few controllers actually limit throughput to the speed of the slowest device in the chain. Placing the CD-ROM on a separate chain ensures that you won't adversely affect the speed of higher-speed devices. Many vendors such as Corel Systems and Microsoft are making their applications so that you can copy a few files to the hard drive but run the application from the CD-ROM. Not only does this save hard drive space, but it also allows you to install the full capabilities of a product. You'll pay a performance penalty for using this type of installation, so you'll want to reserve it for applications you don't use on a daily basis.

Another disk space saver is to use compressed file formats whenever possible. This is especially true in the multimedia and graphics areas. For example, a CorelDRAW! file that consumes a mere 60KB in its native format could consume 1MB or more in .AI (Adobe Illustrator) format. Another example is the .PCX format. Storing a 1024 × 768 16-color image requires 90KB. That same image requires 200KB if you increase the number of colors to 256. Storing the same 256-color image in .TIF format (using LZW compression) uses 136KB, and only 124KB in .GIF format. As you can see, something as simple as a file format can make a big impact on the amount of space available on your hard drive.

Once you get your hardware configuration out of the way, it's time to consider your software configuration. Windows 95 does a much better job of managing resources than Windows 3.x did, but it's by no means perfect. The infamous system resources problem of Windows 3.x is still with us. You still have the same problem with the 64KB USER and GDI areas. Filling these areas with icons, windows, and other graphical elements still results in a system that runs out of memory before physical memory is exhausted. However, the way Microsoft configures and uses memory now really reduces the drag you will see as system requirements increase. (We'll see later that there's a lot more than meets the eye to the whole topic of system resources under Windows 95. Microsoft has tuned this operating system to make many of the problems you suffered under Windows 3.x disappear.)

Under Windows 3.x, I'd start to run out of resources after loading my word processor, spreadsheet, communications program, and one or two small utility programs such as a screen saver or Notepad. I usually consider closing an application or two when I get to the 35 percent system resources level, which is about where I was with this configuration. Windows 95 still has 78 percent of its resources free when using the same configuration. This means that I can usually open two or three more applications on top of my usual configuration.

Of course, system resources are only one memory factor. There's also the actual level of RAM to take into consideration. Under Windows 3.x, you would start to notice a fairly large performance penalty when you got to the point where the swap file was as large as real memory. Under Windows 95, this doesn't seem to be as much of a problem, but it's still very noticeable. The bottom line is that if your swap file starts approaching the size of your installed memory, it's time for an upgrade.

You need to take into consideration the combination of system resources and system memory when thinking about your software situation. A memory-constrained system always lacks enough memory to perform the job you need it to do. It's a subjective type of measurement based on how you actually use your system. You should load the Resource Monitor (discussed in Chapter 2) and, over a few days, track both the size of your swap file and the number of resources you have available. If you start to see a pattern of low memory, read the next section. You might even find that the problem isn't the amount of installed memory on your machine, but the way you use that memory.

By now you can see where all this preliminary checking is leading. A mechanic would never consider tuning a car before checking it over first. Likewise, you should never consider tuning your system before you know what type of system you have and how you use it. It's not enough to say that you have 24MB of RAM installed. The way you use that RAM determines whether it's sufficient. A 2GB hard drive might sound impressive—unless you're trying to create a lot of multimedia presentations with it. Then this will sound like a rather paltry amount. (I've seen some multimedia systems that have 4GB of storage, although that's by no means standard.)

Top Performance Tips for Memory-Constrained Systems

Memory would seem to be the biggest problem most people face on a system, but it really shouldn't be. I recently looked at memory prices at my local parts store and found that I could buy an 8MB SIMM for a mere $320. I'm almost positive that isn't the cheapest price in town, either. Although memory isn't free, it certainly isn't the most expensive upgrade you can make to your system. Few new items can provide as much potential for a noticeable increase in system performance as memory.

Microsoft will try to tell you that you can get by with as little as 4MB of RAM when running Windows 95. I wouldn't believe this if I were you. The minimum I recommend is 8MB, and that's if you intend to run only one application at a time. A more reasonable system will contain 16MB of RAM. Even with 24MB of RAM, I find my system a tad constraining at times. Of course, the opposite extreme exists as well. Few people I've talked to report any noticeable improvement in system performance after they exceed 32MB. At the present time, a system with 32MB would probably be the maximum you would need.

But let's say for the moment that your boss absolutely won't buy any additional memory for your machine and you're stuck at that 8MB level. What can you do to improve the situation? How can you stretch 8MB of RAM enough to make your single-tasking system (from a memory perspective) work as a multitasking system?

Tip: The generic optimization techniques in this section work equally well with Windows NT, WfW 3.x, and Windows 3.x workstations. If you're using Windows 95 in a peer-to-peer LAN environment, it's very likely that you'll use a Windows NT workstation as your file server. You also might have some older machines that still use WfW 3.x connected to the network. Whatever your setup, these generic tips can help just about any workstation make better use of the memory it contains.

General Tuning Tips for Windows

There are a few quick and easy methods that I recommend you start with. Anyone can use these methods, but using them always involves some level of compromise that you might or might not be willing to make. The following list shows my quick fixes to memory problems:

- **Wallpaper:** Did you know it costs you a little memory and some processing time to keep wallpaper on your system? If you have a memory-constrained system and can do without some bells and whistles, here's one item to get rid of. Don't think you'll save much by using smaller wallpaper or restricting yourself to patterns. Both items chew up some memory.
- **Colors:** The number of colors you use for your display directly affects the amount of memory it uses. A 16-color display uses roughly half the memory of a 256-color display. Although a 16-color display doesn't look as appealing as its 256-color or 32K color counterpart, using 16 colors does help you save memory. You probably won't notice that much of a difference in appearance if the programs on your machine are word processing and spreadsheets.
- **Screen resolution:** The resolution at which you set your display affects processing speed and, to a much smaller degree, memory. Of course, the problem with changing your display resolution is fairly simple to figure out. You can probably get by with fewer colors, but fewer pixels is a different matter. You'll probably want to save changing the screen resolution as a last-ditch effort to get that last bit of needed performance.
- **Doodads:** I put a whole realm of utility programs into the "doodad" category. For example, if you run one of the fancier screen savers rather than the built-in Windows counterpart, you're wasting memory. The new screen saver might look pretty, but it'll really cost you in terms of performance. Some people also keep a small game program such as Solitaire running. These small applications might provide a few seconds of pleasure here and there, but you really don't need to keep them active all the time. If you insist on using that screen saver, run it right before you leave the room for a while and then exit it when you return. The same holds true with a game program—keep it open when you play it, and then close it before you get back to work.
- **Icons and other graphics:** Every icon displayed on your desktop consumes memory. The same holds true for any other form of graphic image or window. At least Windows 95 doesn't penalize you for opening a folder like Windows 3.x did. You can actually recover the memory by closing the folder. The simple way of looking at this is to organize your data into folders and open only the folders that you need at any given time.
- **Leaky applications:** Some programs leak when it comes to memory. They allocate memory from Windows but never give it back, even after they terminate. After a while you might find that you don't have enough memory to run programs, even though you should. This problem was severe under Windows 3.x. It's less so under Windows 95 and Windows NT. However, the Windows 95 data-centric interface tends to accelerate the rate at which memory seems to dissipate if you open and close an application for each data file you want to edit. You can alleviate this situation somewhat by keeping leaky applications open until you know for certain that you won't need them again later. You can find a leaky application by checking system resources and memory before you open it, opening and closing the application a few times (make sure you also open some documents while inside), and then

checking the amount of memory again after you close it the last time. If you find you have less memory—I mean a measurable amount, not a few bytes—the application is leaky.

- **Extra drivers:** Windows 95 and Windows NT do a fairly good job of cleaning old drivers out of the Registry. Windows 3.x, on the other hand, doesn't do any cleaning at all. No matter which version of Windows you use, you'll want to take the time to see whether all the drivers were removed from the system after you remove an application. This isn't such a big deal for newer applications that are specifically designed for Windows 95 or Windows NT. Both of these newer operating systems provide a special installation utility that removes newer applications from the system—including the files they stick in the SYSTEM directory and any references to them in the system files. What I'm talking about are those old Windows 3.x applications that don't remove anything.
- **DOS applications:** Nothing grabs memory and holds it like a DOS application under Windows. Unlike other applications, Windows normally can't move the memory used by a DOS application around to free space. This means that you might have a lot of memory on your system, but Windows won't be able to use it because it's all too fragmented. If your system is so constricted on memory that it can't tolerate even the smallest amount of memory fragmentation, avoid using DOS applications.

Windows 95-Specific Tuning Tips

Now that we've gotten past the generic tips, let's look at a few Windows 95-specific ways to enhance overall system performance and the amount of memory you have available. Unfortunately, none of these tips will work for Windows 3.x systems. Even though a few might work with Windows NT, you'll want to give them a long test before making them permanent.

- **386 versus 486 or Pentium processors:** Windows 3.x didn't care about the processor you used, only the processing speed. The facts are plain: Windows 3.x used 16-bit code that ran equally well on any processor 386 or above. But there's a big difference in performance when using different processor types under Windows 95, because it uses 32-bit code. A 486 processor is better optimized to take advantage of 32-bit code. The Pentium is better still. Theoretically, you should notice a fairly substantial improvement in processing capability between a machine equipped with a 486 versus a 386 machine of the same processor speed. In reality, the difference is noticeable, but not that noticeable. You'll want to get the extra performance if possible, but don't worry about it until you take care of other problems, such as upgrading your memory.
- **CONFIG.SYS and AUTOEXEC.BAT:** In most cases, you're better off without any form of AUTOEXEC.BAT or CONFIG.SYS. If all you have in your CONFIG.SYS is a memory manager, get rid of it, because Windows 95 supplies its own. Adding a memory manager to CONFIG.SYS will reduce the amount of flexibility Windows 95 has in configuring your

system. The only time you should keep CONFIG.SYS around is if you have to load real-mode drivers. It's also a good idea to get rid of AUTOEXEC.BAT in most circumstances, but it isn't always possible. There's a problem with old 16-bit Windows applications under Windows 95—they need some of the entries in AUTOEXEC.BAT. The most common requirement is the addition of entries to the PATH statement. You can open a DOS window and add a PATH statement to a batch file to set the path. However, you don't have the same privilege for Windows applications. You have to set the path before you enter Windows for the application to work right.

- **Real-mode drivers:** There are all kinds of penalties for using real-mode drivers under Windows 95. The penalties are so severe that you should consider getting rid of real-mode drivers at all costs. As far as optimizing your system is concerned, real-mode drivers cost you in both performance and system reliability. We examine this topic in greater detail in Chapter 6, but suffice it to say that the penalty is very real. The short explanation is that real-mode drivers force Windows 95 to make a transition between protected and real mode every time an application requires access to the device. Not only does this transition waste precious processor time, it also makes it possible for a maverick application to cause system failure. Real-mode drivers might also reduce the amount of memory available in some circumstances, but this really isn't the major consideration.
- **16-bit drivers and .DLLs:** Windows 95 is essentially a 32-bit operating system with some 16-bit compatibility components and a few items left over from Windows 3.x. It runs every 32-bit application in a separate session. Doing this allows Windows 95 to perform some very intense memory management on the resources needed by that application. 16-bit applications all share one session. The amount of management Windows 95 can perform on this one session is a lot less than what it can do for the individual 32-bit sessions because it can't make certain assumptions about how that memory is being used. In addition, the 32-bit memory space is flat (every call is a near call), reducing the number of clock cycles required to make a function call or look at something in memory. On the other hand, the segmented address space used by 16-bit components requires two to three times the number of clock cycles to process because every call is a far call.
- **Using Explorer in place of folders:** Folders are more efficient to use than Explorer. This might seem like a contradiction in terms, because folders use the Explorer interface, but it's not. Opening a copy of Explorer will eat a lot more system resources than opening a folder. Actually, you might think this is a foregone conclusion—opening any application will eat system resources. Here's the memory saver for you. Place all your data in folders, and then place a shortcut to those folders on the desktop. You can still get to all your important files without opening a copy of Explorer. The cost in memory will be a lot less than keeping Explorer running all the time. Use Explorer to actually explore your system, not as a substitute for File Manager.

- **Use context menus in place of the Control Panel:** I find I occasionally need to adjust the properties of various system elements during a session. Windows 3.x always forced me to open the Control Panel to make these adjustments. Old habits die hard. It took me a while to adjust to the new Windows 95 way of dealing with this situation. Chapter 2 talks a lot about the context menu attached to every object. Using that context menu is not only more efficient from a keystroke perspective, but it uses less memory as well. This is something to consider if you need to keep a Properties dialog box open for any length of time.
- **Reset your printer for RAW printing:** Windows 95 automatically installs support for Enhanced Metafile Format (EMF) printing on systems it thinks will support it. This feature allows Windows 95 to print faster by translating the output to generic commands in the foreground, and then creating printer-specific output in the background. Creating generic commands requires a lot less processing time than writing printer-specific output. Changing the setting of the Spool Data Format field of the Spool Settings dialog box to RAW forces Windows 95 to create a printer-specific output in the first pass. (You can access this dialog box by opening the Details tab of the Printer Properties dialog box and clicking the Spool Settings button.) Using the RAW setting means that less operating system code is maintained in memory during the print process. Some memory-constrained systems receive a large benefit by using this print mode. Of course, the tradeoff is longer foreground print times.
- **Keep your disk defragmented:** Older versions of Windows allowed you to create a permanent swap file. Using a permanent swap file improved performance by reducing hard disk head movement to read swap file data. It didn't matter how fragmented your drive got after you set up the swap file, because the swap file always resided in the same contiguous disk sectors. Windows 95 doesn't provide the permanent swap file option. It always uses a temporary file. However, Microsoft has improved the access algorithms and reduced the penalty for using a temporary swap file. Of course, the system doesn't work perfectly. You can still get a highly fragmented drive that reduces system performance as Windows moves from area to area in an attempt to read the swap file. Defragmenting your drive will reduce the possibility that the swap file will become too fragmented. Most people find that a weekly maintenance session takes care of this requirement.

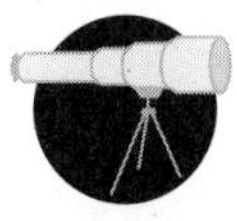

Looking Ahead: System Agent, a scheduling program supplied with Microsoft Plus!, can automatically run Disk Defragmenter and help maintain your system in the background while you work or sleep. See Chapter 28 for details on how to use this and other tools that allow you to automate much of the system maintenance drudgery.

- **Place your swap file on the fastest drive:** Windows 95 usually chooses the drive with the largest amount of available memory for the swap file. (There are other occasions in which the exact criteria Windows used to select a swap-file location eludes me—it seems to use hit-and-miss tactics from time to time.) In most cases, the drive it chooses doesn't make that big of a difference. However, if you have a system with one large, slow drive and a second small, fast drive, you'll probably want to change the virtual memory settings. See the later section "Using Windows 95 Automatic Tuning Features" for details.

- **Get rid of nonessentials:** You'll find that some parts of Windows 95 will make you slightly more efficient, but at a fairly large cost in memory. For example, enabling the International Settings feature (described in Chapter 2) will make you more efficient if you work with several languages, but that enhancement will cost you some memory. Unfortunately, once you activate this feature, you can't get rid of it until you reboot the machine—the memory is gone for good. The same holds true for the Resource Monitor and many of the other icons that appear on the Taskbar near the clock. All these features are nice to have, but not essential. For example, the Accessibility options are a nice enhancement to have, but you might want to get rid of them on a memory-constrained system unless you actually use them. Even though it doesn't display an icon on the Taskbar, installing Accessibility options feature consumes some memory every time you start Windows 95.

Peter's Principle: Efficiency of Actions Versus Memory Usage

Something I'm discovering under Windows 95 is that efficiency of action is sometimes accompanied by some decrease in memory usage. The Windows 95 interface seems to be designed to make every movement as easy as possible (although some users still find it difficult to use).

Using features such as a context menu might not seem like a very big deal—you save only two or three mouse clicks in most cases—but they also result in memory savings. Windows 95 provides other speed-enhancing features that save memory. For example, using the automatic settings for most of the system parameters such as virtual memory will improve performance and enhance memory usage.

Some Windows 95 features are not only extremely efficient, but also save you a considerable amount of time. For example, you'll find that using Explorer costs you a lot less memory compared to using Program Manager. (A comparison on my machine shows system resources at 98 percent when using Explorer, but only 87 percent when using Program Manager in the same configuration.) You can check this out on your machine by changing the `shell=Explorer.exe` line in SYSTEM.INI to `shell=Progman.exe` and then shutting down and rebooting your system. Using the Explorer interface is so much more efficient that I would think twice about going back to Program Manager.

Using Windows 95 Automatic Tuning Features

Besides user-related activities, Windows 95 provides some additional features for making automated changes to your configuration. In most cases, you can determine at a glance whether all these automated features are in effect. All you need to do is display the Performance tab of the System Properties dialog box. Simply right-click the My Computer icon and select Properties from the context menu to display it. You should see a display similar to the one in Figure 3.1 if your system is completely tuned. Windows 95 will provide some suggestions on things you can do to improve system performance. In most cases, this means enabling an automatic feature to provide additional memory, reduce the system's reliance on out-of-date drivers, or allow some additional flexibility. If your system isn't completely tuned, Windows 95 will provide tips on what you can do to make the automatic tuning features work properly.

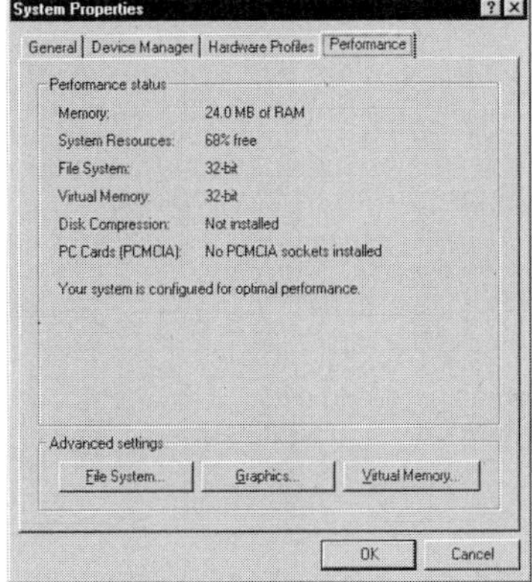

Figure 3.1.
The Performance tab of the System Properties dialog box.

Notice the three buttons near the bottom. Clicking the first one displays a dialog box similar to the one shown in Figure 3.2.

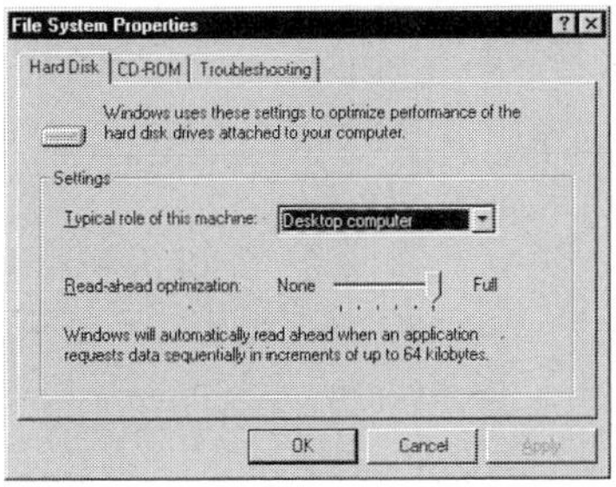

Figure 3.2.
The File System Properties dialog box.

The Hard Disk and CD-ROM tabs of the File System Properties dialog box allow you to change the way Windows 95 reacts to certain requests for information and allocates memory for the file system without really changing its overall management strategy:

- **Typical Role of This Machine:** This field has three settings. The way you should use this field is pretty self-explanatory: Select the role that best describes your computer. In most cases, you'll select either Desktop Computer or Mobile or Docking System. If your machine acts as a file server on a peer-to-peer network, select the Network Server setting. There's one way in which you can use this setting to improve performance. I found that the Network Server setting actually seems to speed some tasks that perform small data reads, such as database managers. It also seems to enhance performance in a multitasking environment.
- **Supplemental Cache Size:** This is one field where you can save about 1MB on a memory-starved system. Of course, you'll trade performance for that savings. Because this setting affects only the CD-ROM cache, you might not notice much of a difference if you use your CD-ROM on an occasional basis. Don't shortchange this area if you regularly use your CD-ROM to run applications, though, because the loss in cache size will become very noticeable after a while. Using a large cache means that you set aside 1238KB of RAM for a cache. The small cache uses a mere 214KB.
- **Optimize Access Pattern For:** Set this field to reflect the speed of your CD-ROM drive. Windows 95 uses a different timing formula for each drive type. You can play with this field to see whether there's any performance benefit to changing it from the default. I actually found one double-speed Toshiba CD-ROM drive that worked better at the triple-speed setting. It's pretty rare to get any kind of increase by doing this, but you never know.

The Troubleshooting tab (see Figure 3.3) is where you can really help or really damage your system's memory management strategy. The key term here is *troubleshooting*. Microsoft originally included this tab for the sole purpose of troubleshooting. However, on certain rare occasions you can use these items as part of your tuning strategy. Each of the check boxes allows you to change a part of the Windows 95 file system management strategy. Be careful when changing these settings, or you might find yourself troubleshooting a nonfunctional system.

The following list describes each of these options in detail:

- **Disable New File Sharing and Locking Semantics:** Windows 95 uses new drivers to maintain file locks for networks. The new setup uses a 32-bit protected-mode driver. The old setup uses a 16-bit driver similar to the VSHARE.386 driver provided by WfW 3.x. The only reason to check this box is if you experience network-related file-locking problems. In some cases, file locking will work either way, but checking this box will reduce the number of failed attempts. The time differential is quite noticeable with applications such as database managers that require many locks during any given session.

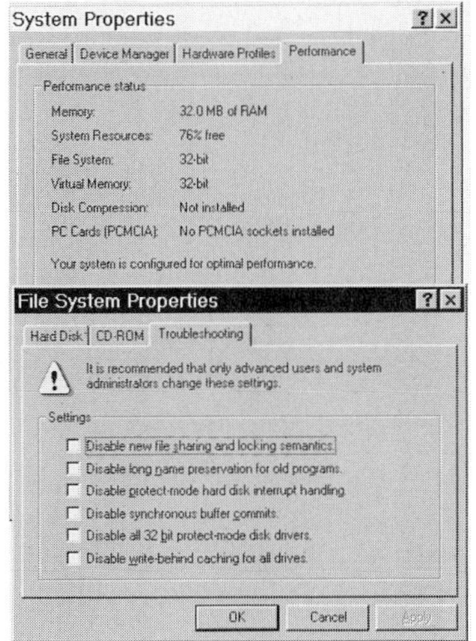

Figure 3.3.
The Troubleshooting tab of the File System Properties dialog box.

- **Disable Long Name Preservation for Old Programs:** Checking this box helps you maintain compatibility with existing DOS machines. It forces Windows 95 to use the 8.3 file-naming scheme everyone has used from the earliest days of DOS. Of course, you lose the benefits of long filenames, and you won't garner even one byte of additional RAM for your system. Companies that use a mixed group of workstations on the network, however, will gain a benefit from consistent file naming. In most cases, you'll want to leave this box unchecked.
- **Disable Protect-Mode Hard Disk Interrupt Handling:** Some applications won't work properly using the new Windows 95 interrupt handlers. You can check this box in order to install the old real-mode handlers. One word of caution: Make sure that you don't use non–Windows 95 disk defragmenters or other low-level file management utility programs, because they don't support long filenames and other Windows 95 features. These old programs probably will require you to disable the protected-mode handlers.
- **Disable All 32 Bit Protect-Mode Disk Drivers:** A few hard drives and controllers won't work properly with the Windows 32-bit drivers. Chapter 6 takes a detailed look at the architectural aspects of these drivers. The important consideration right now is that these drivers might not cause a total drive failure; they might simply cause the drive to slow down. If you notice that your drive's performance isn't what it used to be, you might want to see whether disabling 32-bit support brings it back to normal.
- **Disable Write-Behind Caching for All Drives:** Data loss on network drives is a major headache for most administrators at one time or another. Windows 95 uses a write-behind caching scheme to improve workstation performance. This same feature can actually cause data loss, especially with networked database managers. If you find you have records that don't get written or other forms of data loss, you might want to check this box. Even though checking this box will most certainly reduce local workstation performance, it

might improve overall network performance by forcing the workstation to write shared data faster. This is especially true in situations where many people share relatively few records in the database—for example, a reservation or scheduling system.

Clicking the Graphics button in the System Properties dialog box displays the Advanced Graphics Settings dialog box, shown in Figure 3.4. The new protected-mode drivers provided with Windows 95 accelerate writes to the display adapter. The slider controls the amount of acceleration you receive. Most adapters work fine at the highest setting. However, if you find that your adapter performs only partial screen writes, or if you see other types of corruption, you might need to use a lower setting.

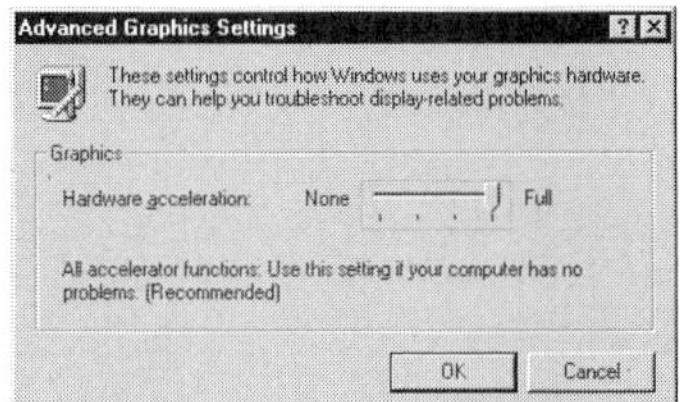

Figure 3.4.
The Advanced Graphics Settings dialog box.

Figure 3.5 shows the Virtual Memory dialog box, which provides one way to enhance system performance when the automatic method selects the wrong drive for your swap file. (Click the Virtual Memory button in the System Properties dialog box to get here.) In most cases, it pays to let Windows manage the virtual memory settings. However, there are a few cases where you'll want to manually adjust the virtual memory settings. Windows 95 normally selects the drive with the largest amount of free disk space as the virtual memory drive. However, this might not be the fastest drive on your system. In this case, it would make sense to manually adjust the virtual memory drive to use the fastest one on your machine.

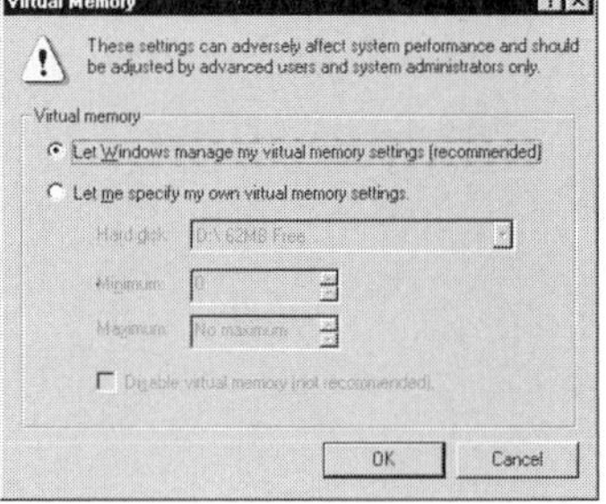

Figure 3.5.
The Virtual Memory dialog box.

Warning: Never disable virtual memory. The Virtual Memory dialog box provides this setting for troubleshooting purposes only. Disabling virtual memory can (and probably will) result in some type of system failure. Such a failure could prevent Windows 95 from writing everything in disk cache to the drive. This could corrupt the Registry or other system files and prevent you from rebooting the operating system.

There are other ways to configure the swap file. For example, what if the fastest drive on your machine doesn't contain enough space for the size of swap file you need? Windows 95 allows you to individually configure the swap file for each drive on your system. If you don't want a swap file on a particular drive, set its minimum and maximum sizes to 0.

You also can create a pseudo-permanent drive using the manual parameters. Setting the minimum size for a drive to something other than 0 always reserves that amount of disk space for the swap file. If you defragment the drive on a regular basis, you could end up with what will look like a permanent swap file. Of course, if Windows needs to increase the file beyond this minimal setting, the new data could end up in a fragmented area of the drive.

Finding Unneeded Hidden Drivers

Sometimes Windows 95 does a less-than-perfect job of setting up your machine. Earlier I mentioned that you should remove any unneeded drivers. What would happen if you had some "hidden" drivers you really didn't need installed on your system? Figure 3.6 shows a dialog box that illustrates this point perfectly. I installed Windows on a machine in a peer-to-peer networking environment. The installation program even asked about the level of support I wanted when I got to that point in the installation. However, it assumes that not everyone knows what they're talking about, so it installed both Microsoft and Novell support on my system. The Novell support goes to waste because this is a peer-to-peer network that doesn't connect to a NetWare file server. I have a Windows NT server, a Windows 95 workstation, and a WfW 3.x machine all connected and sharing resources.

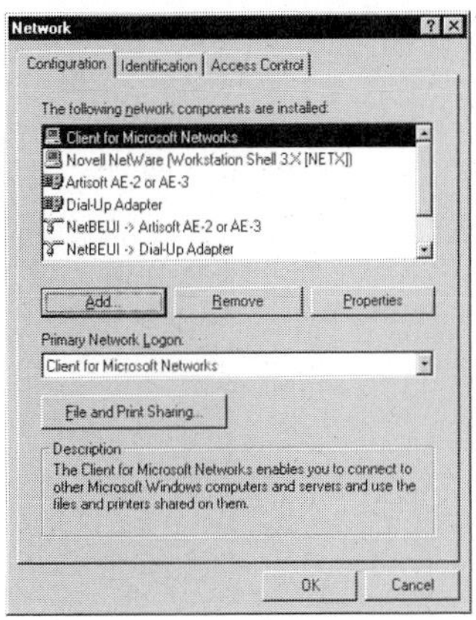

Figure 3.6.
Sometimes Windows 95 installs too much support. You can reduce your memory footprint and improve performance by getting rid of this additional support.

There are three things you need to look at in this particular situation. First, eliminate additional network support. You need to install support for only one network if you're using a peer-to-peer setup. In most cases, this means that you'll retain the Microsoft network and discard NetWare support. Likewise, if you don't plan to set up a peer-to-peer network, remove the Microsoft network support in a NetWare environment.

Tip: LANtastic users will want to consider moving to a Microsoft network for three reasons. First, LANtastic currently requires you to load real-mode drivers that introduce a certain level of instability into your system. Second, Windows 95 doesn't provide all the services that a LANtastic network requires. For example, the network drives won't show up in Network Neighborhood. Finally, you can't run a dual-network environment when using LANtastic. This means that you can't run a peer-to-peer network and connect to a NetWare file server at the same time.

If you do decide to use an older, non-Windows 95-specific LANtastic network, don't install either a network adapter or a protocol. Installing either of these items will produce some very strange results. In some cases, your network won't work at all. You'll also want to install version 5.x or above. Older LANtastic versions won't run properly under Windows 95. Finally, you won't be able to use Artisoft Exchange unless you have the Windows 95-specific version.

You'll also want to reduce the number of protocols you have installed. I typically maintain NetBEUI support for a peer-to-peer setup if at all possible. Of course, the protocol you choose must reflect the capabilities of the network you install.

Tip: If you remove one of the protocols from your workstation and find that you can't connect to the other workstations, make sure that all of the workstations are using the same protocol. Many people find that working networks suddenly fail when they try to optimize their setup. This simple fix repairs the vast majority of "broken" installations.

Installing the fewest possible network services is the third step I take. For example, installing sharing support for a floppy drive is a waste of memory because it's unlikely that anyone will need it. If someone does need it, you can always add the support later. Try starting out with the lowest level of support possible. You'll also want to think about which workstation printers you really want to share. If a workstation has an older printer attached, you probably won't want to install print sharing support for it.

Top Performance Tips for DOS Applications

DOS applications represent a big challenge under Windows 3.x. I'd love to say that Windows 95 will run every DOS application you ever owned without any major configuration problems, but that wouldn't be accurate. You'll encounter problems when running certain DOS applications, and you need to tune your system to avoid them.

The good news is that you can make all the required changes using the application's Properties dialog box. Windows 95 supports all the old configuration features provided by Windows 3.x and adds quite a few of its own. (You'll find that Windows 95 provides support for DOS applications that's far superior even to Windows NT. Microsoft made some design decisions to make this level of support possible; we'll explore them in Chapter 6.) This means that you can make the required changes by right-clicking the object and selecting Properties from the context menu. Say you wanted to change some of the settings for the DISKCOPY.EXE file. You'd just right-click the DISKCOPY icon in Explorer, and then select Properties from the context menu. The first thing you'd see is a Diskcopy Properties dialog box similar to the one shown in Figure 3.7. (The Properties dialog box always includes the application filename in the title bar—I'll use the Diskcopy Properties dialog box throughout this section for explanation purposes.) Everything you need to run DOS applications efficiently under Windows 95 appears in this dialog box, which replaces the PIF editor used in previous versions of Windows.

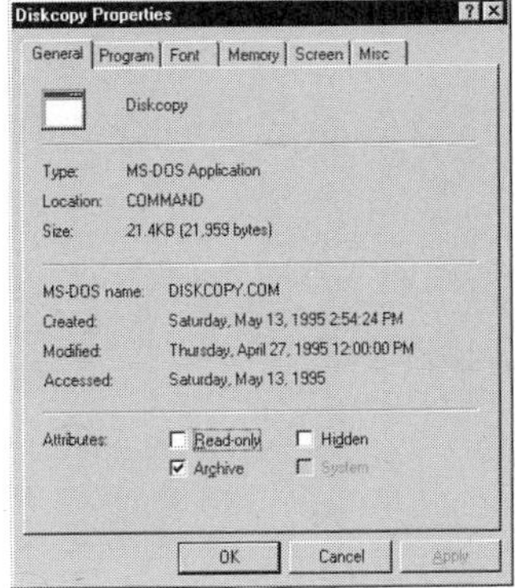

Figure 3.7.
The Diskcopy Properties dialog box.

There are many similarities between the entries in the Properties dialog box and those in the PIF files of previous versions of Windows. Don't be fooled. Windows 95 provides much the same functionality as those previous versions; it just makes it a bit easier to change the settings. Fortunately, the Properties dialog box does add some much-needed fields and a new mode or two.

Tip: Some Windows 95 users will find it very easy to set all their DOS applications to run in MS-DOS mode, because this mode provides the most familiar configuration options. However, running your applications in this mode means that you have to forego any DOS-to-Windows interaction. It also means that you won't be able to use any Windows 95 features. Finally, because running an application in MS-DOS mode unloads all the Windows 95 drivers, you lose the benefits of 32-bit driver support. The application might run slower than if you ran it under Windows 95 directly.

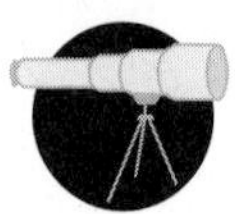

Looking Ahead: This chapter looks at the Properties dialog box settings that affect DOS application performance. I cover the rest of the settings in Chapter 12.

Several tabs directly affect the way a DOS application behaves under Windows 95. The first one we'll look at appears in Figure 3.8. The visible part of the Program tab contains some fields that tell Windows 95 what application to run and where to run it. This includes the application name and its working directory. The area of concern for this chapter is the Advanced button near the bottom of the dialog box. Clicking that button displays the Advanced Program Settings dialog box, shown in Figure 3.9, which contains some of the DOS-specific settings that affect how Windows 95 will react.

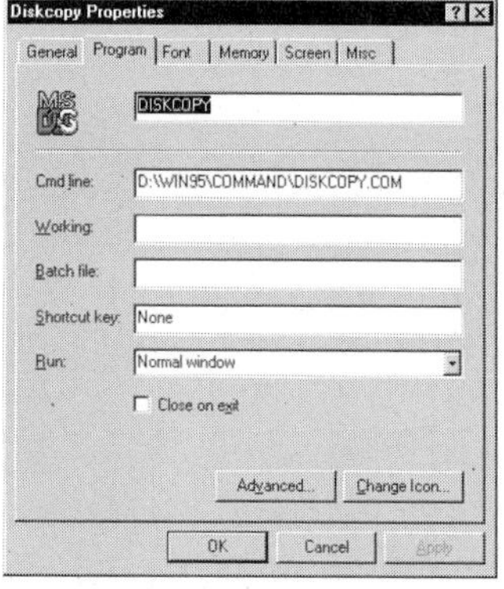

Figure 3.8.
The Program tab of the Diskcopy Properties dialog box.

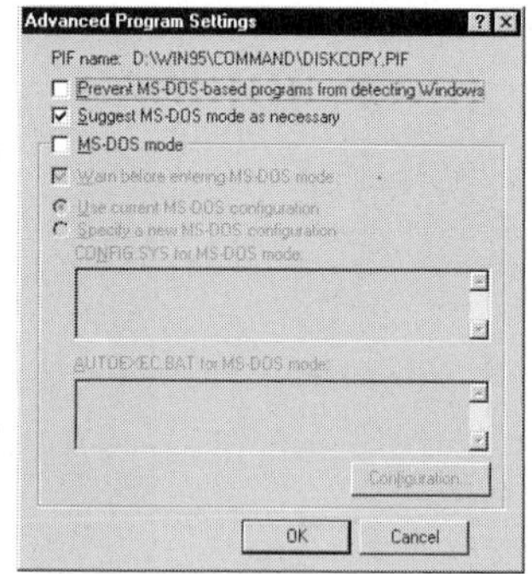

Figure 3.9.
The Advanced Program Settings dialog box.

The check box I like the most in this dialog box is Prevent MS-DOS-Based Programs from Detecting Windows. I had several applications that wouldn't work under Windows 3.x simply because the application looked for the Windows signature before it ran. Even if the application could run, it wouldn't. This check box allows you to fool those applications into thinking that they're all alone on the machine. In many cases, this is all you need to do to get an application to cooperate with Windows.

Many applications still will experience problems when running under Windows 95. The next check box provides a diagnostic mode of sorts. The Suggest MS-DOS Mode as Necessary option is another automatic tuning aid that you can turn on. If you use an application that really has to be run in MS-DOS mode, Windows 95 displays a dialog box that suggests you do so. Unfortunately, Windows doesn't check this box for you automatically, so you need to check it yourself.

The final check box is a real performance-buster in every situation, according to Microsoft. The fact is that using MS-DOS mode will slow the majority of your applications at least a little. I'd be a lot more concerned about the loss in functionality you'll experience when using this mode. However, there are at least two categories of applications in which you'll probably experience a performance gain, not a loss. The first one is game programs. Many of these applications run correctly under Windows 95; many more don't. Your only choice in this case is to run the program in MS-DOS mode.

The other category—strangely enough—is older graphics applications. For some reason, they actually perform better in MS-DOS mode. For example, the old copy of Harvard Graphics I had lying around performed almost twice as fast in MS-DOS mode as it did under Windows 95. After a bit of research, I concluded that it was a combination of factors such as direct-screen writing and other rule-breaking behaviors that make these applications run faster in MS-DOS mode. I'd still say this is the exception to the rule. The best idea is to check out an application both ways and see which way it runs faster. Better yet, replace it with a Windows 95-specific product if at all possible.

After you place a check in the MS-DOS Mode check box, you get several more options. The first check box asks whether you want Windows 95 to warn you before it enters MS-DOS mode. Keep this one checked as a precaution. You wouldn't want to accidentally leave some other application in an uncertain state. This check box provides a sort of safety valve to ensure that you don't start something you'll regret later.

The two radio buttons allow you to choose between the default DOS setup and a custom setup for this particular application. Since Windows 95 gives you the choice, I'd recommend a custom configuration whenever possible. If the application you want to run is having problems with Windows 95, it probably will also have special needs when running in MS-DOS mode. I have several custom configurations on my hard drive right now. One works fine for games that need expanded memory but don't use the CD-ROM drive. Another helps my old copy of Harvard Graphics squeeze that last ounce of performance out of the system. You don't necessarily need a separate CONFIG.SYS and AUTOEXEC.BAT for each application, but it does help to have separate configurations for each group of applications.

Tip: An easy way to take care of the various configuration needs you might have for MS-DOS mode applications is to specify the CONFIG.DOS and AUTOEXEC.DOS files as special configuration files. If the application worked with your old DOS setup, there's no reason why the same configuration won't work under Windows 95.

The Memory tab, shown in Figure 3.10, can also help you to obtain the best possible setup for your application. In most cases, you'll want to stick to the Auto setting. However, I have several applications that require more environment space than the Auto setting provides. All you need to do is adjust the setting in the list box as required. The same thing holds true for any other memory settings you might need to adjust.

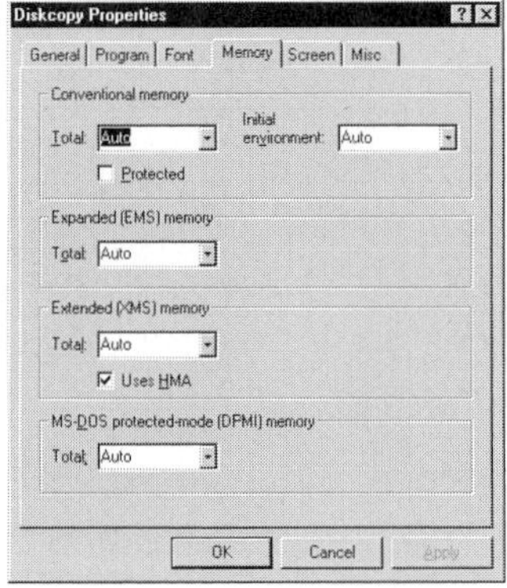

Figure 3.10.
The Memory tab allows you to customize the DOS application's memory settings.

There's one thing you should always keep in mind with this tab. Setting any memory entries you don't need to None will save system memory and allow Windows 95 to provide better services to the rest of the applications on your machine. Windows 95 always assumes a worst-case scenario with DOS applications; setting the various memory options gives it a little more information to work with.

The Protected check box in the Conventional memory group is a two-edged sword. Setting it allows some applications to run; it also prevents Windows 95 from moving applications around in memory. Some applications that access memory directly need this kind of protection. The downside of checking this box is that a fixed session in memory always increases memory fragmentation and the chance that you'll artificially run out of memory.

The last tab we'll look at from a performance perspective is the Screen tab, shown in Figure 3.11. We'll talk about only two of these check boxes in this chapter—the rest will be covered in Chapter 13. Not surprisingly, both appear in the Performance group near the bottom of the dialog box.

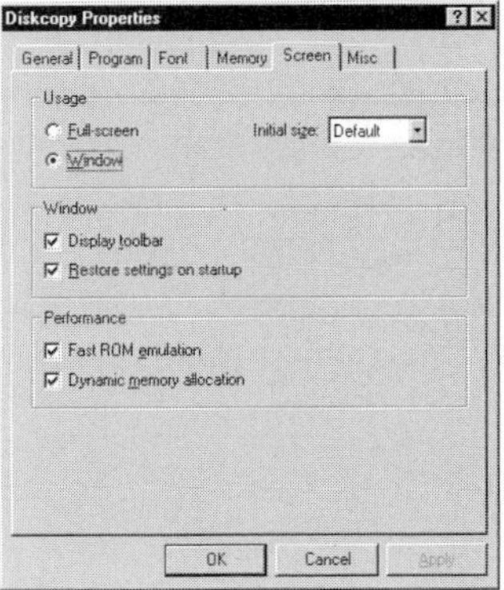

Figure 3.11.
The Screen tab provides two performance settings.

The Dynamic Memory Allocation check box is the important one here. As with the Protected check box in the Memory tab, this check box determines whether Windows 95 can move memory around. Here's the problem. Many graphics applications resort to using direct screen writes to get the performance they need. Those same graphics applications won't work under Windows 95 if you keep this box checked, because Windows might move the "virtual" screen that the application is writing to somewhere else. The warning sign you need to look for on a graphics application is some type of distortion. Most applications display vertical bars or some type of striation. You might see part of the display shift or what appear to be cursor trails on-screen. All these types of distortion tell you that you need to uncheck the Dynamic Memory Allocation check box.

Another group of applications somewhere (I've yet to find it in my office) needs to directly access the ROM routines. The Fast ROM Emulation check box tells Windows 95 to emulate the display ROM in fast protected-mode RAM. However, if your application is looking for the system ROM in conventional memory, it won't find the emulated version. One way to tell that your application needs to have this box unchecked is that you get unexplainable system crashes that you can't pinpoint to another cause. These crashes could be caused when the application looks for ROM code at a certain address and doesn't find it.

Top Performance Tips for Multitasking Systems

Getting more than one application to run on a system at the same time usually involves making some compromises. You can tune a single-tasking system to provide the best performance for that one application. For example, you could tune your system in such a way that a disk-intensive application gets everything it needs in order to get the job done quickly. But what happens if you run one application that's disk-intensive and another that's CPU-intensive? Do you starve the resources of one to get better performance from the other?

We've already looked at most of the generic ways to provide additional memory. This is one area where you need to concentrate if you plan to multitask. Running more than one application at once always consumes a lot of memory. What you might not realize is that your performance levels might become artificially low because of the way Windows 95 handles memory management.

Disk swapping, the same feature that provides so much virtual memory for your applications, can wreak havoc in a multitasking environment. Two big clues tell you that disk swapping has become a problem and not a cure:

- First, you'll notice a dramatic increase in your system's disk activity. This isn't always a bad thing under Windows 95, but it is an indicator. Windows 95 uses a very aggressive disk-writing algorithm to make the most of system idle time. You might see what seems like a lot of disk activity, when all Windows 95 is doing is writing some of the data from memory to disk.
- The second clue will tell you just how bad the memory situation is. Look at the size of your swap file. If your swap file is about the same size as your real memory, your system is memory-starved, and you really can't run the number of applications you're trying to run. Windows 95 will try its best to provide a satisfactory level of performance, but the truth is that you just won't see it.

There are far more scientific ways to measure system performance precisely, and we look at them in the next section. The two clues just discussed provide you with a very quick idea of what your system performance is like right this minute, without wasting a lot of your time trying to define it completely. Of course, using System Monitor to display your actual system performance for your boss could get you the memory upgrade you've been wanting.

You'll also want to take into account the needs of the LAN as a whole if your system doubles as a file server. A peer-to-peer network depends on the resources of one or more workstations to act as file and print servers. This doubling of tasks is really another form of multitasking. You might run only one or two tasks on your machine, but it will run very slowly if you don't take into account the needs of other people who use your system. In this case, however, a simple look at the swap file and disk activity probably won't provide you with enough information. You'll have to monitor the network statistics, using the System Monitor program.

Windows 95 also provides another utility that will come in handy here. The Net Watcher utility (described in Chapter 19) provides information about who is logged in and what type of resources they're using. You can combine this information with that obtained from System Monitor to create a clear picture of how your machine is being used in the network environment. Figure 3.12 shows a typical example of the type of information you can expect. Making a correlation between who is using which resource and the level of activity might seem like a difficult task, but after a while you'll notice certain patterns emerging. You can use those patterns as a basis for tuning your system.

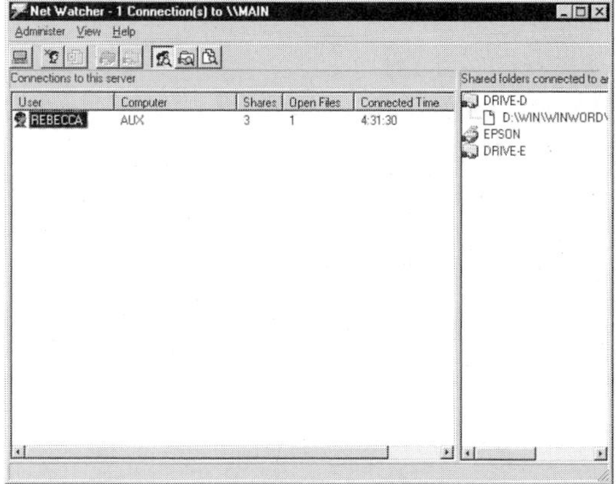

Figure 3.12.
Net Watcher allows you to monitor who is sharing your computer and which resources they're using.

Load balancing was a term I thought I'd never have to apply to a PC, but here it is. You can get better performance out of your system if you balance the types of tasks it performs. Scheduling all your disk-intensive tasks to run at the same time is one sure way to bring your system to its knees. Likewise, scheduling all your CPU-intensive tasks at the same time will garner the same results—only faster. If you're working on a spreadsheet in the foreground, that might be a good time to compile an application or perform some database-related task in the background. Of course, the opposite is true as well. You can always perform that really intensive spreadsheet recalculation in the background while performing data entry in the foreground.

Tip: Unlike previous versions of Windows, Windows 95 actually does a reasonable job of downloading files and performing other forms of online communication in the background. I recently spent almost eight hours downloading a new copy of Windows 95 from the Internet at 9600 baud while working on articles and my spreadsheet in the foreground. I never did miss a file or experience any form of corruption. Under Windows 3.x, I would've had to give up my system for the day in similar circumstances. One rule of thumb you need to follow is to keep resource-hogging 16-bit applications to a minimum. Windows 95 does a good job of handling short delays without losing characters. However, some older applications grab the system for so long that background communications are impossible, even with the improved features that Windows 95 provides.

There's one final issue you need to consider when you want to get the most out of your multitasking environment. Using 16-bit applications under Windows 95 means that you must suffer the consequences of cooperative multitasking. In essence, a program can be a bad sport and grab the system for however long it wants. 32-bit applications don't get this kind of treatment. Ready or not, they have to return control of the system to Windows 95 at specific intervals. The difference between multitasking 16-bit and 32-bit applications will absolutely amaze you. If multitasking is the name of the game, 32-bit applications are what you need to make it work smoothly.

Monitoring the Results of Performance Enhancements

There are three ways I monitor the results of any optimization changes I make. The first is by looking at the Resource Monitor. Checking how much system resource memory you have left after an optimization is one way to see whether the change was effective. I also monitor the size of the swap file. Even though this isn't a precise measure of the state of system memory, it provides an overall indicator of system memory. Windows 95 increases the size of the swap file as it needs more memory, so checking the size of the swap file is one way to see how much memory Windows 95 needs over the physical memory available on the system.

The third method is an actual monitoring tool. System Monitor is an optional utility that you can install—and it's a very worthwhile tool. It allows you to track a variety of system statistics, including CPU usage and actual memory allocation. Monitoring these statistics tells you whether a certain optimization strategy was successful. System Monitor also provides a means of detecting performance-robbing hardware and software errors on the system. Figure 3.13 shows a typical System Monitor display.

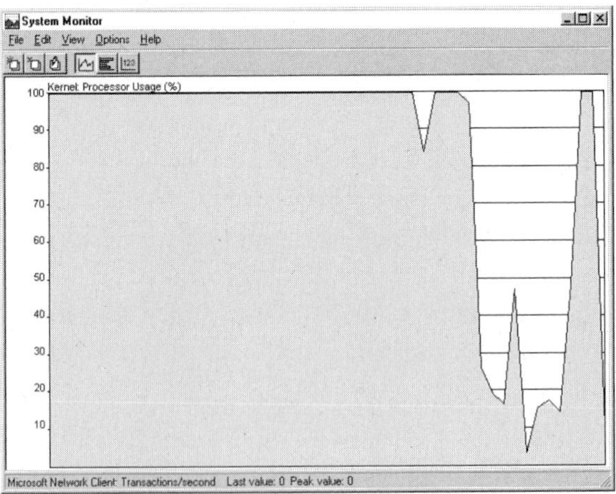

Figure 3.13.
System Monitor.

When you start System Monitor, it always displays the current Kernel Processor Usage. Figure 3.13 shows one way to display this information. You can use the View | Bar Chart or the View | Numeric Chart command to change the presentation. I find that the bar chart presentation (see Figure 3.14) is the most helpful when I need to monitor system performance over a long interval, and the numeric chart (see Figure 3.15) is handy when I need to troubleshoot a particular problem area. Notice the line displayed somewhere along the length of the bar. This line tells you the maximum usage level for that particular statistic. Of course, the bar itself shows the current usage level. You can also select any of the three chart types by clicking the correct toolbar icon.

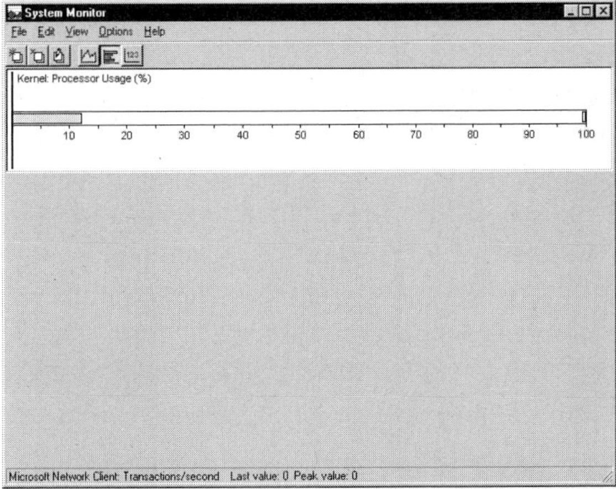

Figure 3.14.
The bar graph presentation allows you to easily monitor events over the long term.

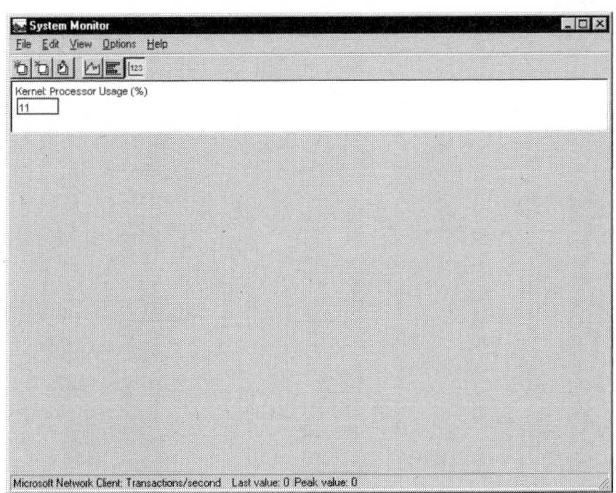

Figure 3.15.
You can use the numeric chart presentation to get a quick look at the current machine statistics.

System Monitor uses a default monitoring period of five seconds. This might not be fast enough in certain situations. If you're troubleshooting a bad NIC or you want instant feedback on a configuration change, you'll want to change this setting to a lower value. Likewise, if you're performing long-term monitoring, you might want to set it high. Use the Options | Chart command to change this setting. Figure 3.16 shows the dialog box that changes the interval.

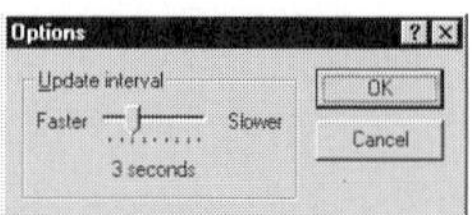

Figure 3.16.
Short intervals aid troubleshooting efforts; long intervals help you monitor your machine's performance more accurately.

The first three toolbar buttons allow you to change the items that System Monitor displays. Use the Add button to add new items to the list. Use the Edit button to change the way System Monitor displays a particular value. For example, you might want to display something in green rather than blue. You can also change the upper limit of some values to provide a consistent range of values for particular items. Finally, the Remove button allows you to remove an item from the monitoring list. Remember that the more items you display on-screen, the less screen area each item will receive. This in turn limits the accuracy of the readings you'll take. Make sure that you monitor only the essentials. For that matter, you might want to break the items into groups and monitor a single group at a time.

What types of things will System Monitor track for you? Tables 3.1 through 3.7 provide a complete list grouped by functional area. Of course, there's no limit to the ways in which you can arrange the items you want to track.

Table 3.1. File system items.

Item	*Function*
Bytes Read per Second	This item tells you how many bytes the file system reads each second. It helps you understand how much data the file system is reading.
Bytes Written per Second	This item tells you how many bytes the file system writes each second. It helps you understand how much data the file system is writing to disk.
Dirty Data	This number tells you how much data is stored in memory instead of on disk. A high level can indicate that a system is overloaded, because Windows 95 usually waits until system idle time to write data to disk.

Item	Function
Reads per Second	Use this number to determine how many reads the system makes per second. If you divide the Bytes Read per Second value by this value, you'll get the average read size. This value can help you tune your system for either large or small reads.
Writes per Second	Use this number to determine how many writes the system makes per second. If you divide the Bytes Written per Second value by this value, you'll get the average write size. This value can help you tune your system for either large or small writes.

Table 3.2. IPX/SPX-compatible protocol items.

Item	Function
IPX Packets Lost per Second	This number tells you how many IPX packets the workstation ignored due to a lack of resources or other problems. A high number here indicates an overloaded system in some cases.
IPX Packets Received per Second	Use this number to determine the total number of IPX packets the workstation received. This includes the packets the workstation ignored.
IPX Packets Sent per Second	This item records how many IPX packets the workstation sends per second. A high value tells you that the workstation makes heavy use of the network and that you might want to concentrate on optimizing network resources.
Open Sockets	The number of free sockets.
Routing Table Entries	Use this entry to determine the number of internetworking routes the workstation knows about. It can help you find some types of network communication problems.
SAP Table Entries	Use this entry to determine the number of service advertisements the workstation knows about. It can help you find some types of network communications problems.
SPX Packets Received per Second	This item records how many SPX packets the workstation receives per second.

continues

Table 3.2. continued

Item	Function
SPX Packets Sent per Second	This item records how many SPX packets the workstation sends per second. A high value tells you that the workstation makes heavy use of the network and that you might want to concentrate on optimizing network resources.

Table 3.3. Kernel items.

Item	Function
Processor Usage (%)	Use this number to determine how much of the time the processor is busy. A high number doesn't necessarily mean you need a better processor. Check to make sure that you have enough memory and that the other system settings are correct before you get a new processor.
Threads	Each 32-bit application under Windows 95 can create a thread (subprogram). For example, a word processor might create a print thread to output a document to the printer in the background. This item monitors the number of active threads.
Virtual Machines	This item allows you to track the number of virtual machines that are currently active on your system. It's one way to measure the amount of multitasking you're performing. Remember that this number includes system virtual machines as well as those used by any applications.

Table 3.4. Memory manager (VMM32) items.

Item	Function
Allocated Memory	Use this item to determine the total amount of memory allocated in the system. This includes all your application needs as well as any memory used by the operating system itself. You can check this entry to see the effect of any memory conservation steps you take.
Discards	This item tells you how much page swapping Windows has to do to provide enough resources for all your applications. This is the number of pages Windows can remove from memory without writing them to the swap file. In most

Item	*Function*
	cases, this is application code that's no longer needed. A high value indicates that you don't have enough RAM in your system and really should upgrade.
Disk Cache Size	The current size of the disk cache in bytes. This item tells you how much memory Windows has set aside to speed disk access.
Free Memory	If you add physical memory and swap file memory together, and then subtract the amount of memory in use for a variety of purposes, you'll arrive at this value. Essentially, this item tells you how much memory is left over after Windows satisfies every system need.
Instance Faults	This item tells you how many instance faults Windows experiences. In most cases, you really don't need to worry about this value.
Locked Memory	An application locks memory when it needs to maintain access to it and keep Windows from moving the block around. There's no cut-and-dried answer as to how much locked memory is too much. However, a high percentage of locked memory when compared to the overall allocated memory might indicate that your application is hogging system resources. It also means that Windows can't do as good a job of maintaining large blocks of accessible memory. (In other words, the memory is still available, but it might be fragmented.)
Maximum Disk Cache Size	This number tells you the largest disk cache that Windows will allocate to speed disk access.
Minimum Disk Cache Size	This number tells you the smallest disk cache that Windows will allocate to speed disk access.
Other Memory	Use this entry to determine the amount of allocated memory that's not stored in the swap file. For example, memory-mapped files, non-pageable memory, and disk cache pages all provide specific types of non-swap-file memory used by your application.
Page Faults	This item tells you how much page swapping Windows has to do to provide enough resources for all your applications. This is the number of pages Windows writes to the swap file.

continues

Table 3.4. continued

Item	Function
	A high value indicates that you don't have enough RAM in your system and that you really should upgrade.
Page-Ins	This item tells you how much page swapping Windows has to do to provide enough resources for all your applications. This is the number of pages that Windows reads from the swap file. A high value indicates that you don't have enough RAM in your system and that you really should upgrade.
Page-Outs	This item tells you how much page swapping Windows has to do to provide enough resources for all your applications. This is the number of pages Windows discards per second by either writing them to disk or simply overwriting them with new data. A high value indicates that you don't have enough RAM in your system and that you really should upgrade.
Swapfile Defective	You'll want to monitor this number carefully, because it indicates the number of bytes in the swap file that are bad due to media defects. What this really tells you is that there's a bad spot on the hard drive and that you need to maintain the hard drive. Windows allocates page frame file segments in 4000-byte blocks, so even a small media defect can look huge.
Swapfile In Use	Windows normally makes the swap file a lot bigger than necessary. This value tells you just how much of the current swap file is in use. It gives you a more accurate picture of the memory situation than the swap file size would.
Swapfile Size	Use this item to monitor the size of the swap file on your hard drive.
Swappable Memory	This item tells you how much of the swap file memory is actually allocated for some purpose. This includes all allocation types, including locked memory.

Table 3.5. Microsoft client for NetWare networks items.

Item	Function
Burst Packets Dropped	This entry tells you the number of burst packets lost in transit. A high number could indicate an overloaded system, an

Item	*Function*
	inoperative NIC, or bad cabling. In some cases, it also reflects a lack of memory needed to process requests.
Burst Receive Gap Time	This item tells you how long Windows will wait between packets (in microseconds) before it sends another packet. This wait allows the previous packet to circulate throughout the network.
Burst Send Gap Time	This item tells you how long Windows must wait between packets (in microseconds) before it can receive another packet. The wait represents the time it takes for Windows to recover from processing the previous packet.
Bytes in Cache	The redirector acts as a buffer (container) to hold incoming data until Windows can process it. It also holds data waiting for transmission to other machines. This value represents how much information the buffer contains.
Bytes Read per Second	This item tells you how much data Windows reads from the redirector per second.
Bytes Written per Second	This item tells you how much data Windows writes to the redirector per second.
Dirty Bytes in Cache	Use this item with the Bytes in Cache value. It contains the amount of data in the redirector that Windows needs to write. A high value here indicates an overloaded system. This isn't a memory-related problem. It usually indicates some type of throughput restriction such as a bus or an underpowered processor.
NCP Packets Dropped	This entry tells you the number of NCP packets lost in transit. A high number could indicate an overloaded system, an inoperative NIC, or bad cabling. In some cases, it also reflects a lack of memory needed to process requests.
Requests Pending	This value tells you how many requests the server needs to fulfill. A high number normally indicates an overloaded system or a lack of system resources. If additional memory doesn't bring this value down, you probably need to upgrade the server or not allow anyone to use it as a workstation. (If the server is currently a workstation and you need to dedicate it as a server, you might want to upgrade it to Windows NT as well.)

Table 3.6. Microsoft network client (client for Microsoft networks) items.

Item	*Function*
Bytes Read per Second	This item tells you how much data Windows reads from the redirector per second.
Bytes Written per Second	This item tells you how much data Windows writes to the redirector per second.
Number of Nets	This value tells you how many networks are running. In most cases, you'll see a value ranging from 1 to 3. A dial-up network counts as a separate network in this category.
Open Files	Use this value to determine how many files are open on the network. This value could help you determine how users are actually using the network.
Resources	This item tells you the number of resources in use.
Sessions	Use this number to determine how many people are logged into your machine. Each login counts as one. (If the same person logs in from multiple locations, Windows updates the number to reflect each login separately.)
Transactions per Second	This value indicates the level of redirector activity as the number of SMB transactions per second.

Table 3.7. Microsoft network server (file and printer sharing for Microsoft networks) items.

Item	*Function*
Buffers	A buffer stores one unit of data. DOS uses buffers to hold data read from the disk. A Windows server does essentially the same thing: It uses buffers to hold the data it receives from the local hard drive. This value tells you how many buffers the system needed to allocate in order to handle network data requests. A high number might indicate an overloaded system. It could just as easily reflect a network with a high usage rate, so you will need to verify this number, using other sources.
Bytes Read	This item tells you how many bytes the server reads from disk in a given period of time.
Bytes/Second	This value tells you how many bytes the server is writing to and reading from the local hard drive per second. A high value indicates a large amount of network activity. It doesn't necessarily reflect any type of resource problem.

Item	*Function*
Bytes Written	This item tells you how many bytes the server writes to disk in a given period of time.
Memory	Use this item to determine the amount of memory used by the server. It doesn't include any memory used by the workstation. This means you can determine the memory cost of using a workstation as a server.
NBs	Like the Buffers item, this item tells you about the server's data storage requirements. This value tells you how many buffers the system needed to allocate in order to handle network requests. A high number might indicate an overloaded system. It could just as easily reflect a network with a high usage rate, so you'll need to verify this number, using other sources.
Server Threads	Like applications, the server can offload some tasks as separate "mini-applications" called threads. This item indicates the current number of threads used by the server.

As you can see from the tables, the System Monitor utility can provide a wealth of information. The trick is to leverage that information in a way that you can really use. For example, you'd want to look at all server-related items as a group. In addition, you wouldn't want to look at the current number of server threads if resource allocation was your major concern. There's no hard-and-fast rule as to what you should and shouldn't monitor in a given circumstance. However, you should strive to keep the number of items to a minimum so that the load on your system is minimal and you can see the statistics without squinting.

On Your Own

Survey your hardware to see whether any components might be holding back your system performance. Consider replacing that old CD-ROM drive or adding more memory if necessary to enhance system throughput. A whole new machine might be in your future if the current one is completely out-of-date—don't waste a lot of money replacing all the components in your machine one at a time.

Check out the "General Tuning Tips for Windows" section of this chapter to see whether you can get rid of any memory- or performance-wasting features. For example, consider spending a week without wallpaper. The performance improvement you get might be worth the sacrifice. Look at some of the doodads you have loaded as well. I'm often surprised at how many of these little utility programs are loaded on my machine, and then never used.

Look at the Performance tab of the System Properties dialog box (refer to Figure 3.1) to see whether your system is using all the automatic tuning features that Windows provides. Make sure that all the automatic tuning features are working *for* you, rather than *against* you. For example, you may want to change the drive used for the virtual memory swap file to a faster drive on your machine.

Hunt for any unneeded drivers on your machine (if you suspect there are any—new machines usually don't have unneeded drivers lurking around). Be sure to look for some of the non-obvious sources of wasted device drivers, such as network protocols that you don't use.

Start monitoring your machine once you get it optimized. Make sure that all the changes you made actually improved system performance, rather than hindering it. If you find that some change reduced system performance, try to figure out why. A good knowledge of how changes affect your machine will make it easier to tune in the future.

4

Setup Primer

I'm often surprised at just how little emphasis some people put on the installation of their software. Many people—including me—got the idea somewhere along the way that you should be able to stick a floppy in the drive, type a command (or double-click an icon), and then forget about anything other than shuffling the rest of the floppies in the stack. This is the way software installation should work for the most part, but it doesn't.

Reality is somewhat different from the theory of software installation. I recently spent half an hour configuring a piece of software for installation and another 15 minutes installing it from the CD. The amount of time that it took to configure this piece of software was staggering when compared to the relatively short time required to actually install it. Software now comes with many different configuration options because some people want bells and whistles and others don't. (Of course, the fact that vendors are trying to create applications that are all things to all people doesn't help matters much. What happened to the good old days when you got a word processor to perform just word processing?)

Today's software often reminds me of the proverbial Chinese menu in which you have to select one from Column A and two from Column B. I don't mind having a few choices, but some software has become ridiculous. You could easily get lost in the sea of choices that some software offers.

Imagine you're a network administrator (perhaps you don't need to try too hard, because you are one). How many weeks would you spend installing the same piece of software I did on the company network of about 100 machines (assuming, of course, that the installation on each machine went perfectly)? You're looking at a minimum of two and a half weeks—just for one application! Now imagine that you have to install all the applications required by each machine in addition to a copy of Windows 95. This is one of the major reasons that many people think the move from Windows 3.x to Windows 95 will be a very slow one. To its credit, Windows 95 does provide some methods to automate the installation process, but the transition will still take a lot of time for most network administrators. (We'll talk about automation methods later in this chapter.)

If Windows did free us in any way, it was from having to tell every one of our applications what hardware has been installed every time we install it. That's one of my pet peeves with DOS software: You have to know everything about your machine to get any and every application installed. Of course, this ease of installation didn't extend to Windows 3.x itself. To install the operating system, you still had to know a lot about the machine where you were installing it. For most people, this meant dragging out every piece of paperwork you could find about the machine to answer the myriad of questions Windows 3.x presented.

My previous installation experience was still fresh in my mind as I tore open my copy of Windows 95. Would the installation cost me as many hours as OS/2 did the first few times I tried it? Worse still, would I have to spend endless hours trying to configure the software after installation, as I did with Windows NT? Thankfully, the answer to both questions was no. Windows 95 is about as easy to install as Windows 3.x in most cases, and perhaps a tad easier in others.

Before we go much further, let's get a few important items out of the way. If you're installing the upgrade version of Windows 95 on your system, you'll need to install one of the following operating systems first. Windows 95 looks for these operating systems as a prerequisite to starting the installation process:

- MS-DOS version 3.2 or higher, or an equivalent OEM version that supports partitions larger than 32MB
- Windows 3.x
- Windows for Workgroups 3.1x
- Dual-boot OS/2 (with MS-DOS)
- Dual-boot Windows NT (with MS-DOS)

You'll also need to do a quick check on your hardware. Microsoft has one set of hardware specifications, but I don't think you'll want to use them. (Microsoft played the same game when creating the system requirements for Windows NT.) The problem is that the "minimum" system that the specifications describe is too minimal to get any kind of performance. If you want a system that will really work with Windows 95, use the following parameters:

- **80486SX or higher processor:** You can try to use one of the faster 80386 systems, but the performance you receive won't be all that useful.

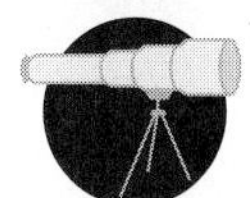

Note: You must have an 80486SX or higher to use Microsoft Plus!. It simply won't run on anything less. You really should have a fast 80486DX, preferably the 100 MHz or better Pentium machine, to use it. See Chapter 28 to learn more about Microsoft Plus!. In addition to the requirements for Microsoft Plus!, using a machine that contains the latest upgrades from Microsoft OEM Service Release 2 (OSR2) will require a lot more horsepower. If you want to use advanced features like 32-bit FAT, a Pentium machine with lots of memory is the only way to go.

- **8MB memory minimum:** I would really think about increasing your memory to 16MB as soon as possible, but an 8MB system will perform adequately using standard Windows 95 or Windows 95 with Service Pack 1. If you're using a machine that has OEM Service Release 2 (OSR2), you'll definitely want 16MB or higher. Service Release 2 is available only to OEMs (original equipment manufacturers), so you won't have it installed on your machine unless you've bought a new one since October 1996.
- **80MB of free hard disk space:** The Microsoft minimum of 30MB just isn't realistic unless you want to install a stripped version of Windows 95 with no room to run any applications. If you plan to upgrade from Windows 3.x, you can decrease this amount by 10MB. Likewise, a Windows for Workgroups (WfW) 3.x upgrader can reduce this requirement by 20MB.

Note: If you're squeezed for disk space, you probably shouldn't install Microsoft Plus!. Much of it is for desktop beautification, a luxury you might not be able to afford. On the other hand, you could take advantage of its very useful tools, such as System Agent, the program scheduler, and its enhanced disk compression tools. See Chapter 28 for more details on Microsoft Plus!.

- **High-density 3½-inch floppy drive:** Everyone who installs Windows 95 will want to create an emergency boot disk. You need a high-density floppy to store the emergency files. Windows 95 can create this disk for you automatically during installation. You can also create or update the disk later from the Startup Disk page of the Add/Remove Programs Properties dialog box.
- **SVGA (800 × 600) or higher display adapter:** You can get by using a VGA display with Windows 95, but that doesn't really provide enough space to get any work done. The Explorer interface does clear a lot more room than you had under Windows 3.x. But let's face it, was a VGA display really adequate under Windows 3.x?

Note: If you're using Microsoft Plus!, you'll want to consider your display adapter's ability to display colors along with its resolution. Most modern adapters display at least 256 colors at all resolutions. However, you might have an adapter that displays only 16 colors, especially at higher resolutions. Most of Microsoft Plus! demands at least 256 colors. If you stick to maintenance utility programs, you don't need to worry about the number of colors you can display with your adapter. However, if you want to use Desktop Themes to make your desktop interesting, exciting, or at least attractive, you'll want a display adapter that can handle at least 256 colors at the resolution you plan to use. Ideally, your adapter should be able to handle high color.

- **Mouse (pointing device):** Someone will try to tell you that you can work efficiently under Windows 95 using the keyboard. You can get around; there's no doubt about it. But a mouse makes Windows 95 so much more efficient that I can't understand why anyone would want to go without one.
- **Optional devices:** You can also install any number of optional peripheral devices. I strongly recommend that you install a modem and a CD-ROM drive as a minimum. Windows 95 provides much better multimedia capabilities as well. You'll probably want to install a sound board somewhere along the way. Now is as good a time as any.

Note: You must have a CD-ROM drive in order to install Microsoft Plus!. As of this writing, there are no plans to make it available on floppy disk. Also, although it's not required, you should have a sound board to fully appreciate the Desktop Themes and 3D Pinball.

Note: Windows 95 won't install at all on machines that use the B-step 80386 processor. Intel introduced the B-step processor early in the 80386 production cycle to fix some minor problems. Think of it as a .1 revision of an application software package and you'll have the right idea. This processor has an ID of 0303. If you have any doubt as to whether you have a B-step processor, contact the hardware vendor before you start the Windows 95 installation.

The one feature that will stick out in your mind is the way Windows 95 automatically detects the majority of your hardware. I installed the product on a variety of machines using all the methods mentioned here and met with a variety of successes in that regard, but at least Windows 95 provides a starting point for future efforts. I also like the way that the software led me by the hand in getting things configured. Again, there were choices to make, but the way they were laid out made it a lot easier to figure out what I wanted to do. In addition, unlike previous versions of Windows, the online help for this installation routine actually told me a little bit about what I was installing.

Is the new installation for Windows 95 perfect? Not by a long shot. I experienced some truly weird problems during installation—from hardware that was detected fine during one installation but not during another to utility programs that installed even when I asked Windows 95 not to install them (more about that later). Some of the worst failings of the installation routine in one way were the highlights in another. For example, during one installation I found it nearly impossible to get through the installation procedure and end up with the correct sound card installed in my machine. (I finally figured out a surefire method for getting an accurate detection from Windows 95. I'll explain it later in this chapter.)

Installing Windows 95

You might want to spend a little time preparing for your Windows 95 installation, especially if you're the ill-fated network administrator who will spend the next few weeks getting it installed on all 100 network workstations. Of course, the first piece of preparation is to make a complete backup of each system before you start the installation. Trying to back out of a failed installation can prove to be quite a problem in some situations. In fact, if you have the upgrade version of Windows 95, you might find recovering from a failed installation quite impossible without reinstalling your old software first.

Peter's Principle: Boot Disks: The Cheap Form of Insurance

You just started an installation and it goes south for the winter. The machine is frozen and you can't get back to the DOS prompt. What do you do?

If you're like me, you stick your boot disk into the A drive and reboot the machine. I never start anything as involved as an operating system installation without making a boot disk first. In fact, I usually make a boot disk for all my installations, even if I think the software will install without a hitch.

Just what does a boot disk contain? It has to contain the operating system; otherwise, you can't use it to boot the system. I usually include renamed copies of my CONFIG.SYS and AUTOEXEC.BAT files as well. You don't want to use the original files to boot the machine because they contain entries that you probably won't need. If I'm performing some type of Windows installation, I always include copies of my WIN.INI and SYSTEM.INI files as well. In fact, for shaky installations, I make a copy of all my .INI files on a separate disk.

A boot disk really needs some utility programs too. I usually include FDISK and FORMAT. DEBUG normally makes an appearance also. The disk has to include any files required to activate your disk compression, if the drive is compressed. A disk editor usually comes in handy, as does a small text editor. You'll probably want to include a disk scanning program such as CHKDSK or its equivalent as well, because a disk crash will require the services of such a diagnostic program.

You'll also need a DOS backup program that can read the backup of the workstation you created. There are two fatal assumptions that some people make when they make a workstation backup. First, you can't assume that you'll have network access after a failed workstation installation. That's why I make a local backup of the machine instead of using network resources. Second, because you're booting DOS, you need a DOS application that can read your backup. I once ran into someone who thoughtfully made a backup of his hard drive but used a Windows program to do it. His only choice after the system failed was to reinstall Windows and all the software required to gain access to the tape drive. It cost him almost three hours to restore the drive. Using a DOS backup program means nearly instantaneous access to the data you need to restore after a failed installation attempt.

Don't be afraid to make up a two- or three-disk package to ensure that you'll have everything you need in order to diagnose problems with the machine. Just because this is a software installation, you can't assume that the hard drive will be accessible. Those trips back and forth to the office to pick up this utility or that can get to be time-consuming. A little preparation goes a long way toward making what looks like a difficult problem easier to fix.

Tip: When you partition your hard drive, it's always a good idea to keep this principle in mind: Don't compress your boot drive. The reason is simple: You can't access a compressed drive very easily in an emergency. I always set aside a 30MB to 40MB partition that I won't compress. A partition this large is just big enough to accommodate my copy of DOS, any files required to boot the machine in its normal configuration, a few utility programs, and some diagnostic aids. Compressing your boot drive is just another way to play Russian roulette. Somewhere along the line you'll shoot yourself, and it won't be in the foot.

Getting all the required equipment together to perform the installation is only the first step. You need to do other things before you perform the installation. The following sections give you the inside scoop on all the pre-installation steps you should take. Then you'll see several different installation methods.

Check Your Hardware

Remember that stack of hardware manuals and pamphlets I talked about earlier? You can probably put some of them away, but not until you've checked a few details. Windows 95 automatically detects the vast majority of hardware out there. It even includes information files (discussed near the end of this chapter) that allow it to detect older hardware. However, the detection capabilities that Windows 95 currently provides are less than perfect, so you'll want to spend a little time checking your system hardware for potential problems.

Tip: Service Pack 1 for Windows 95 fixes many of the hardware detection problems you'll face. A simple download could save you quite a bit of trouble when detecting new hardware. You can find the Service Pack at `http://www.microsoft.com/WindowsSupport/`. The Service Pack is also available on CompuServe (at least as of this writing) or you can buy it directly from Microsoft on CD.

Microsoft groups all Windows 95 autodetection capabilities under plug-and-play. Even if your hardware isn't plug and play-compatible, Windows 95 will try to treat it as such for installation purposes. We'll look at plug and play from an installation perspective later in this chapter. Suffice it to say right now that Windows 95 won't do a perfect job of installing your hardware if you don't have a 100 percent plug and play-compatible machine.

Certain types of hardware almost guarantee problems under Windows 95. If you have hardware with the following characteristics, you might want to take a second look at it before you install Windows 95.

Of course, you can always try to install it, but I've run into more than my share of problems with these hardware types:

- **Older disk controllers that don't provide their own BIOS:** A lot of old MFM controllers fall into this category. Windows 95 depends on the contents of the peripheral BIOS as one of the means to detect it. Every vendor writes its company name (or at least someone else's name) into the BIOS. Looking for this company name is one way to determine who made the device. The first step in reducing the number of checks required to detect a piece of hardware is knowing the vendor. If you have a peripheral that lacks a BIOS and other characteristic "electronic" signatures, Windows 95 won't be able to detect it. Because Windows 95 requires a working disk controller and display adapter to get the installation started, you can see what would happen if it couldn't detect your disk controller.
- **Machines that use a clone BIOS:** Some older machines use what I call a "clone BIOS." These are the machines that boot with some strange logo from a company you've never heard of. A machine containing a BIOS from one of the mainstream companies such as AMI or Phoenix is almost always a better bet than a clone BIOS machine. Of course, machines containing an IBM or other major hardware vendor BIOS are the safest bet. You might be able to replace the BIOS on a motherboard containing a clone BIOS, but replacing that dinosaur is probably the easiest way to fix the problem.
- **Nonstandard peripheral devices:** Developers who latch onto new technology early in the game are often applauded by everyone when they first introduce an item. Later, the same people who applauded these developers wonder why they would ever buy such a non-standard piece of equipment. Standards evolve as users and companies gain knowledge about a particular area of technology. Unfortunate as it might seem, some of the hardware that appeared before the standard was introduced just isn't compatible with that standard. Without a standard way to access the hardware, it's very difficult to talk to it and determine what capabilities it provides. Windows 95 easily detects standard devices, but it might have problems with older peripherals that don't adhere to the standards.
- **Peripherals that almost emulate something else:** IBM and other vendors are to blame for this problem. They started placing their company name in the BIOS of some types of hardware. When someone would try to use some piece of generic software developed by these companies, the first thing the software would do is check the BIOS for the correct company name. Clone makers aren't stupid, so they started putting the IBM (or other) company name where needed in their BIOS chips too. That isn't a problem as long as the device in question completely emulates the hardware it replaces. The problems begin when the clone vendor adds some additional "features" that render this emulation incompatible with the original. Because Windows 95 has no way to recognize the clone from the real McCoy, you could end up installing the wrong kind of support during installation.

There's also some marginal hardware out there that you can fix after the initial installation is over. Sound boards are one big item that falls into this category. Windows 95 does a pretty good job of detecting them, considering that one sound board is designed to emulate the qualities of another. Just about every sound board out there claims some sort of Sound Blaster emulation mode. Trying to detect this hardware is a nightmare. In some cases, you'll just have to manually install the hardware later. You'll see the procedure for performing a manual installation later in this chapter.

A final "difficult to install" hardware category is the older stuff that depends on a real-mode driver for support. I had an old Hitachi 1503S CD-ROM drive that fell into this category. Believe it or not, it worked just fine under Windows 95, even though I had to use real-mode drivers. The downside is that I couldn't seem to share it on the network, and the stability and performance problems it introduced into the system just weren't worth the effort of keeping it around. I finally replaced the drive with something a little less archaic and haven't looked back since.

Peter's Principle: Replacing Old Hardware to Save Money

Sometimes you'll actually save money right now by spending a little on new hardware. Whenever you choose to keep an old piece of hardware to save money, but introduce some type of instability into your system as a result, you're actually wasting more money than you're saving.

Windows 95 provides an opportunity to rid your system of all the old hardware that makes it inefficient. Not only will you get your work done faster, but you'll get it done with fewer problems. Think about the last time you spent days trying to find a problem with your system, only to discover that it was a bad driver or some other hardware-related problem. The hardware still works, so it's very difficult to give it up. But doing so when you upgrade might mean that you spend a few less hours trying to find those mysterious problems related to the real-mode drivers that the hardware requires to work.

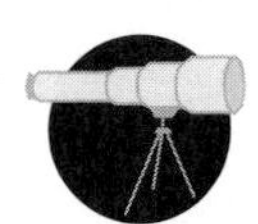

Looking Ahead: Just because you have a few pieces of older or incompatible hardware in your system is no reason to roll over and give up any idea of installing Windows 95. Chapter 26 takes a detailed look at hardware troubleshooting techniques—especially tough-to-install hardware. You'll also want to take a look at Chapter 27 for network-related problems—including hardware. In some cases, you might find that Windows 95 even provides protected-mode drivers that you can use with the old stuff.

When you figure out whether you're going to have any potential problems with your hardware, you'll want to create an inventory of what you have. Some hardware, such as the newer sound boards, uses a real-mode driver that accepts configuration parameters as part of the device-driver command line. If Windows supports the device, you can normally `REM` the driver out of CONFIG.SYS before you start your Windows 95 installation. (Make sure that you also take care of any AUTOEXEC.BAT entries when you do this.) There are exceptions to this rule. You wouldn't want to get rid of any drivers needed for your CD-ROM drive (if you plan to use it for installation purposes) or your hard drive controller. Any essential drivers should stay in place; any nonessential drivers should be REMed out.

Some hardware still uses jumpers for configuration purposes. The one big item that just about everyone will need to consider is NICs (network interface cards). NICs usually have one or more address settings and an IRQ setting. You need to write down the settings of any boards that use jumpers before you start your Windows 95 installation. This list will come in handy later as you try to resolve any IRQ or address conflicts that arise during installation. Changing a "soft" setting is easy; changing jumpers is a lot more difficult.

When you get to this point, you have just about every piece of hardware information you need. It doesn't seem like such a big deal to take care of this step prior to installation if you're doing it on your personal machine. Gathering all this information before you leave the office to work on a remote machine is essential if you want to do it with any level of efficiency.

There's one final piece of information that you should check for machines that use file compression. Windows 95 will supposedly work with the following list of drive compression software:

- Microsoft DriveSpace and DoubleSpace
- Stacker versions 3.0 and 4.x
- AddStor SuperStor

A few people I've talked with say they had problems getting Windows 95 to work properly with their disk compression software. In most cases, it turned out to be some kind of interaction between the compression software, the drive controller, and Windows 95. Almost everyone will use their disk compression software without any problem under Windows 95. However, if you want to make absolutely certain that there aren't any problems, decompress the drive prior to installation and recompress it using Windows 95-specific disk compression software.

Inside Setup Information Files

Network administrators will really like one of the new features of Windows 95. There's a method for automating the responses required during setup. The rest of this section looks at the script-writing program provided with the CD-ROM version of Windows 95. The floppy disk version doesn't include this utility.

Look on your CD-ROM in the \ADMIN95\NETTOOLS\NETSETUP directory. You should see a utility named NetSetup. Even if you installed Windows using the Complete installation option, you won't see that utility on your hard drive. (For that matter, all of the network-related tools require a separate installation.)

The following procedure takes you through the automated portion of creating a network setup directory and a batch file. It's pretty easy to do, and creating a network installation directory will make that 100-user setup a lot easier to complete, in most cases. The next section of this chapter shows you how to edit the default batch file to meet your special requirements.

1. Double-click the NetSetup icon. You'll see a display similar to the one in Figure 4.1, with options for installing a server version of Windows 95, creating a home directory for users who use the server to start Windows 95, and automated script writing.

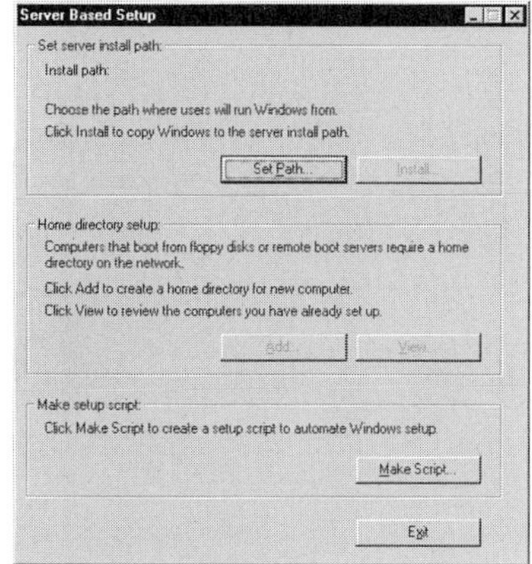

Figure 4.1.
The main NetSetup dialog box.

2. Click the Set Path button. You'll see the dialog box shown in Figure 4.2. Type the drive and path you want to use to install the server software. It's important to choose a drive with a lot of space because you'll need to create home directories for each user later.

Figure 4.2.
One of the first server installation steps is to select the destination path all users will use to install Windows 95.

3. Click OK. If the path doesn't exist, NetSetup asks whether you want to create it.
4. Click the Install button. NetSetup displays the Source Path dialog box shown in Figure 4.3. The Server setting creates an installation script that leaves most of the files on the file server. The installation program places a limited number of files on the user's local hard drive. This option optimizes hard disk usage. The Local Hard Drive option places all the files on the user's hard drive. It provides the best performance on machines that provide enough space. The final option, User's Choice, gives the user the option of where to install the files.

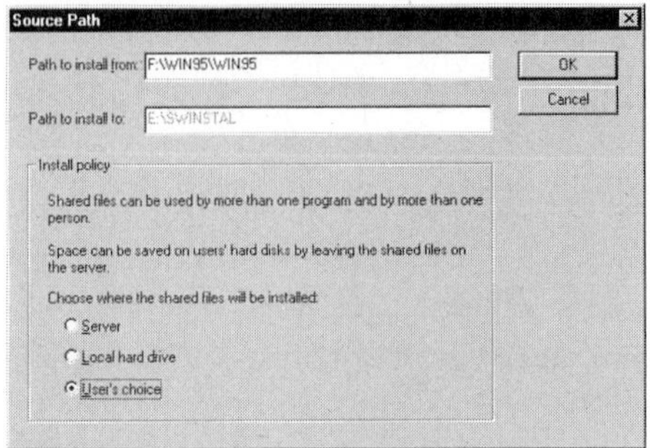

Figure 4.3.
The Source Path dialog box allows you to select the method used to install Windows 95 on the workstations.

5. Fill in the source and destination path fields (if required). Select the desired installation choice and click OK to start the installation. NetSetup displays the Create Default dialog box shown in Figure 4.4.

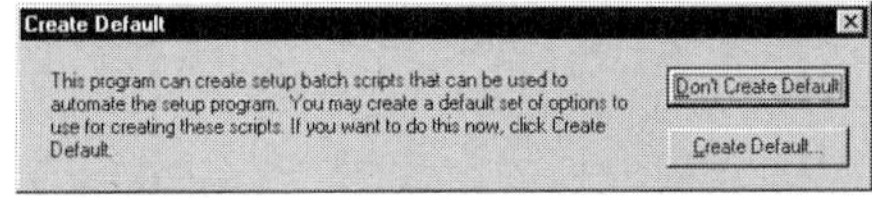

Figure 4.4.
The Create Default dialog box provides one method for creating the installation script that Setup will use later to install the software on the workstations.

6. Click the Create Default button. NetSetup displays the Default Properties dialog box shown in Figure 4.5. Notice that this dialog box looks like the Policy Editor display. It uses the same interface. Table 4.1 outlines all the options you can modify within the display. The dialog box uses a hierarchical format; just keep clicking plus (+) signs until you reach the option that you want to modify.

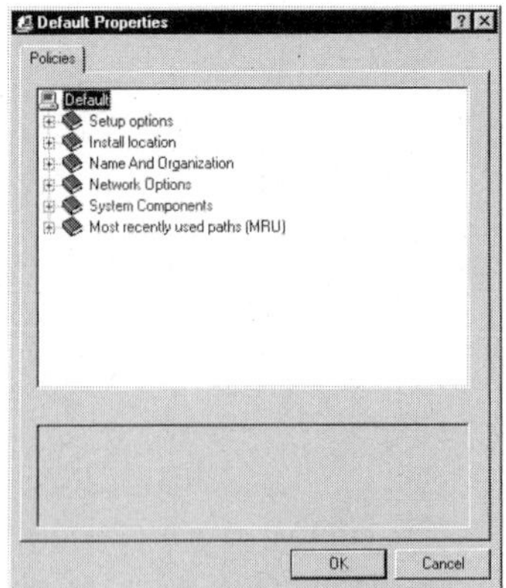

Figure 4.5.
The Default Properties dialog box is a powerful tool. It allows you to define the majority of the installation options that the user will have.

7. When you finish modifying all the options in the Default Properties dialog box, click OK. NetSetup displays the Copying Files dialog box, shown in Figure 4.6, until it completes the copying process.

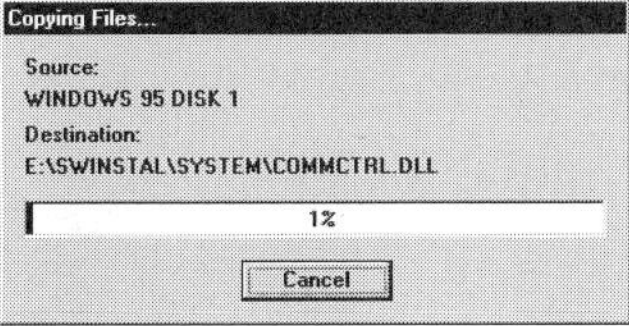

Figure 4.6.
You can use the Copying Files dialog box to monitor the server software installation process.

8. Follow the remaining prompts until you get the Server Setup dialog box saying that Windows 95 completed the installation successfully.

This procedure takes you through the process of creating a server installation and an automatic script. You use the script by entering **SETUP** ***<script name>*** at the Run prompt within Windows or at the DOS prompt. You can define many options using this automated script capability. Table 4.1 describes all the options, leaving them in hierarchical format to make it easier to figure out which ones you actually need. Words that appear within angle brackets describe a value that you should supply. Don't add the angle brackets when you type the entry in the script file. Likewise, values that appear within square brackets provide you with a list of entries from which you can select. Don't type other values or the square brackets when adding this entry to a script file. The headings contains the heading name as you see it in NetSetup (first column) and the name of the heading it affects within the script file (second column).

Table 4.1. Server-based setup options for custom scripts.

Option	*Script Parameter*	*Meaning*
Setup Options:	`[Setup]`	
Automated Install	`Express=[0 ¦ 1]`	A setting of `1` allows you to bypass the Safe Setup screen after a failed install. It also forces Setup to use only the values in MSBATCH.INF (or another batch file). Because this option disables a significant portion of the user interface, you'll need to test the batch file before enabling it.

continues

Table 4.1. continued

Option	Script Parameter	Meaning
Setup Options:	`[Setup]`	
Setup Mode	`InstallType=` `[0 ¦ 1 ¦ 2 ¦ 3]`	Selects the installation type: compact (`0`), typical (`1`), portable (`2`), or custom (`3`).
Create an Emergency Boot Disk	`EBD=[0 ¦ 1]`	Determines whether Setup creates an emergency boot disk (`0` means no).
Install Verification	`Verify=[0 ¦ 1]`	Setting this value to `0` bypasses install verification. This setting allows Setup to check the integrity of the files already installed in the system directory.
Enable Pen Windows Warning	`PenWinWarning=[0 ¦ 1]`	Setting this value to `0` bypasses the Pen Windows Warning dialog box. This dialog box tells the user if there's an unknown version of Pen Windows installed in the destination directory.
Installation Location:	`[Setup]`	
Install Directory	`InstallDir=<path>`	This setting allows you to install Windows 95 in a directory other than the default.
Server-Based Setup	`[Network]`	Checking this option creates the `[Network]` header entry in the script file. It doesn't actually select an option.
Name and Organization:	`[NameAndOrg]`	
Display Name and Organization Page	`Display=[0 ¦ 1]`	A value of `0` in this entry bypasses the Name and Organization dialog box.
Name	`Name=<name>`	You can use this entry to enter the user name automatically.
Organization	`Organization=` `<organization>`	You can use this entry to enter the organization name automatically.

Option	Script Parameter	Meaning
Network Options:	`[Network]`	
Display Network Screens During Custom Setup	`Display=[0 ¦ 1]`	A value of `0` here bypasses the network dialog box when using a custom installation.
Clients to Install	`Clients=<client list>`	The NETCLI.INF and NETCLI3.INF files contain the values you can enter here. The default setting is in NETDEF.INF. This entry allows you to define which network clients get installed.
Hard Disk Boot (for Shared Installations)	`HDBoot=[0 ¦ 1]`	Setting this value to `1` allows the user to boot from a local hard drive. Setting this value to `0` and `RPLSetup` to `0` forces the user to boot from a local floppy.
Remoteboot (RPL) Setup	`RPLSetup=[0 ¦ 1]`	Setting this value allows the user to boot from a server drive. (You must set up the appropriate boot image to make this feature work.)
Workstation Setup	`WorkstationSetup= [0 ¦ 1]`	Setting this value to `0` forces the user to install Windows 95 on his or her local hard drive rather than use the server copy. Setting this value to `1` and Display Workstation Setup to `1` allows the user to choose between a local or file server setup.
Display Workstation Setup	`DisplayWorkstationSetup =[0 ¦ 1]`	Setting this value to `0` bypasses the Workstation Setup dialog box (which gives the user a choice of where to install Windows 95).
Client for Microsoft Networks:	`[Vredir]`	
Validated Logon	`ValidatedLogon=[0 ¦ 1]`	Setting this value to `1` forces the user to provide a password.

continues

Table 4.1. continued

Option	*Script Parameter*	*Meaning*
Client for Microsoft Networks:	[Vredir]	
Logon Domain	LogonDomain= *<domain name>*	This entry contains a string that automatically defines the workstation domain.
Client for NetWare Networks:	[Nwredir]	
Preferred Server	PreferredServer= *<server name>*	Use this entry to define a default server name.
First Network Drive	FirstNetDrive= *<drive letter>*	This entry allows you to define the first network drive letter (usually F).
Search Mode	SearchMode=[0 - 7]	This entry contains one of the search mode values that appear in NET.CFG.
Protocols:	[Network]	
Protocols to Install	Protocols= *<protocol list>*	This entry tells Setup which network protocol to install. See the NETTRANS.INF file for a list of appropriate numbers. The NETDEF.INF file contains the default settings.
IPX/SPX-Compatible Protocol:	[Nwlink]	
Frame Type	FrameType=[0 ¦ 1 ¦ 2 ¦ 3 ¦ 4 ¦ 5 ¦ 6]	This entry allows you to select from one of the following frame types: 0 = 802.3 1 = 802.2 2 = Ethernet II 3 = SNAP 4 = Auto 5 = Token Ring

Option	*Script Parameter*	*Meaning*
		6 = Token Ring SNAP The default setting is 4.
NetBIOS Support	NetBIOS=[0 ¦ 1]	Setting this value to 1 installs IPX/SPX NetBIOS support.
Microsoft TCP/IP:	[Mstcp]	
DHCP	DHCP=[0 ¦ 1]	A value of 1 tells Setup that TCP/IP is configured to use DHCP for dynamic TCP/IP configuration.
IP Address	IPAddress=*<IP address>*	Sets the computer's IP address if you don't enable DHCP.
Subnet Mask	SubnetMask=*<IP address>*	Sets the computer's subnet IP address if you don't enable DHCP.
WINS	WINS=[0 ¦ 1 ¦ DHCP]	Setting this entry to 1 enables WINS resolution. Setting it to DHCP enables WINS but gets the parameters from the DHCP server.
Primary WINS	PrimaryWINS= *<IP address>*	Use this entry to set the address of the primary WINS name server.
Secondary WINS	SecondaryWINS= *<IP address>*	Use this entry to set the address of the secondary WINS name server.
Scope ID	ScopeID= *<scope ID string>*	This entry contains the scope ID.
Enable DNS	DNS=[0 ¦ 1]	You can enable DNS name resolution by setting this value to 1.
Hostname	Hostname= *<hostname string>*	Contains the DNS host name for this computer. (Usually the same value as the computer name.)
Domain	Domain=*<domain string>*	Use this entry to specify the DNS domain name for this computer.
DNS Server Search Order	DNSServers= *<list of servers>*	This entry contains a list of comma-delimited DNS server names.

continues

Table 4.1. continued

Option	Script Parameter	Meaning
Microsoft TCP/IP:	`[Mstcp]`	
Domain Search Order	`DomainOrder=` *`<list of domains>`*	This entry contains a list of command-delimited domain names used for host name resolution.
LMHOST Path	`LMHostPath=` *`<LMHOST file path>`*	Sets the path for the LMHost file.
Gateways	`Gateways=` *`<IP address list>`*	Use this entry to specify a list of IP gateway (router) addresses. Enter them in the same order that you want them to be used.
Network Adapters:		
Network Adapters to Install	`Netcards=` *`<list of adapters>`*	This entry contains the ID number of the NIC you want to install. See the appropriate vendor-specific .INF file for the correct number.
Services:		
Services to Install	`Services=` *`<list of services>`*	Use this entry to define which file, print, and other network-related services to install. See the appropriate vendor-specific .INF file for a list of identifiers.
File and Printer Sharing for NetWare Networks:	`[Nwserver]`	
SAP Browsing	`SAPBrowse=[0 ¦ 1]`	This entry contains `1` if a computer that provides file and print sharing for NetWare uses Server Advertising Protocol (SAP) browsing. A SAP-enabled computer doesn't appear in Network Neighborhood, but any NetWare client can see it.

Option	*Script Parameter*	*Meaning*
Browse Master	`BrowseMaster= [0 ¦ 1 ¦ 2]`	This entry determines whether a computer that provides file and print sharing is the preferred browse master (`2`), can be a browse master (`1`), or is ineligible to be the browse master (`0`).
File and Printer Sharing for Microsoft Networks:	`[VServer]`	
LMAnnounce	`Announce=[0 ¦ 1]`	A setting of `1` announces VSERVER to the network.
Browse Master	`BrowseMaster=[0 ¦ 1]`	A setting of `1` allows the computer to become the browse master.
Identification:	`[Network]`	
Computer Name	`ComputerName=` <*name string*>	Contains the name of the computer for network purposes. The default setting uses the first eight characters of the user name minus any spaces.
Workgroup	`Workgroup=` <*workgroup string*>	Contains the name of the workgroup to which this computer belongs. The default setting uses the first 15 characters of the organization name minus any spaces.
Description	`Description=` <*description string*>	Contains a string that provides a plain English description of the computer for other users. The default setting is the user name.
Access Control	`[Network]`	Checking this option creates the `[Network]` header entry in the script file. It doesn't actually select an option.

continues

Table 4.1. continued

Option	Script Parameter	Meaning
Identification:	`[Network]`	
Security Type	`UserSecurity=[share ¦ domain ¦ msserver ¦ nwserver]`	Defines the types of security used. `share` is share-level security, `domain` is user-level security passing to a Windows NT domain, `msserver` is user-level security passing to a Windows NT server, and `nwserver` is user-level security passing to a NetWare server.
Pass-through Agent	`PassThroughAgent=` <*server*> `or` <*domain*>	This entry defines the passthrough agent used for security purposes. It's ignored if you specify share-level security. NetWare servers always use the preferred server as a passthrough agent.
System Components:	`[System]`	***This section contains references to the default drivers you want to use. The device must already exist as a class entry in the specified .INF file section.***
Power Management	`Power=` <*.INF section name*>	Determines the .INF file section used to install this feature.
Locale	`Locale=` <*.INF section name*>	Determines the .INF file section used to install this feature.
Machine	`Machine=` <*.INF section name*>	Determines the .INF file section used to install this feature.
Pen Windows	`PenWindows=` <*.INF section name*>	Determines the .INF file section used to install this feature.
Tablet	`Tablet=` <*.INF section name*>	Determines the .INF file section used to install this feature.
Keyboard	`Keyboard=` <*.INF section name*>	Determines the .INF file section used to install this feature.
Monitor	`Monitor=` <*.INF section name*>	Determines the .INF file section used to install this feature.

Option	Script Parameter	Meaning
Display	`Display=` `<.INF section name>`	Determines the .INF file section used to install this feature.
Mouse	`Mouse=` `<.INF section name>`	Determines the .INF file section used to install this feature.
Most Recently Used Paths:	`[InstallLocationsMRU]`	
UNC Name for Path to Windows 95 Source File	`MRU1=<install path>`	This entry is a string containing the installation file path. You can provide more than one default path for the user to choose by adding `MRU<number>=` entries on separate lines. Each MRU is numbered in order of preference.

The initial installation doesn't represent the only time you can modify the script. At the bottom of the Server Based Setup dialog box (refer to Figure 4.1) is a button called Make Script. You can also use this button to modify an existing script. Clicking this button presents a dialog box that asks for an .INF filename. All you need to do is select an existing script or type the name of a new one. After you accept the new filename, NetSetup displays a dialog box exactly like the one shown in Figure 4.5. When you accept the options you selected, NetSetup creates a new script for you.

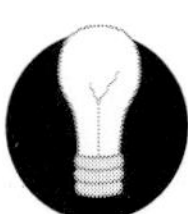

Peter's Principle: Keeping Your .INF Files Straight

You might think all .INF files are the same, but they aren't. At least three different kinds of .INF files are used under Windows 95, and they're all incompatible. The first type is the OEMSETUP.INF file Windows 3.x used to configure devices. This file might work under Window 95, but in most cases it won't work correctly. You'll probably want to get Windows 95-specific drivers from the vendor anyway, so don't take a chance on using this old file. The second type is the MSBATCH.INF we just created as a script file for Setup. Table 4.1 shows you that its format varies from the third type of .INF file, which we'll explore later. The third type of .INF file contains hardware and software configuration information for Windows 95. It's a superset of the OEMSETUP.INF file.

The best thing you can do to avoid confusing one .INF file with another is to keep them totally separate. This is actually very easy to do with only a little work from you. The Windows 95 hardware and software configuration .INF files always appear in the \WIN95\INF folder. If you only use that folder to hold those files (and nothing else), you already have part of the problem solved. I always see the OEMSETUP.INF files in my

\WIN95\SETUP folder or on a floppy disk, but some vendor probably stuck them in other places as well. If you see any .INF files in the SYSTEM folder, it's a good bet that they're leftovers from Windows 3.x. I always keep my setup scripts in a separate folder. If you place them in the \WIN95\SCRIPTS folder on the server, you have a pretty good chance of keeping them separate as well.

Of course, the problem with finding an .INF file anywhere else on your system is that you'll never be sure just what kind of an .INF it is. I always begin by checking the date. If it's older than sometime in 1995, you know that the file is probably something left over from Windows 3.x. The Windows 95 hardware and software configuration files follow a very specific format that you can see by just looking at them with a text editor. I usually check for this kind of file next. Finally, if I just can't figure out where that .INF is supposed to go, I move it to a special directory and keep it there until an application asks for it. If it sits there very long, it's probably time to recycle it.

The very last item you need to look at is creating a home directory for any users who will use the server files instead of placing Windows 95 on their local hard drive. The following procedure helps you through this process. It assumes that you've already started NetSetup.

1. Click the Add button in the Server Based Setup dialog box (refer to Figure 4.1). NetSetup displays the Set Up Machine dialog box shown in Figure 4.7. Notice that there are two different ways to tackle the task of creating home directories. In most cases, setting up one machine is less error-prone and provides more flexibility. Use the multiple-machine method only if you have a lot of machines to set up and after you gain some experience using Windows 95.

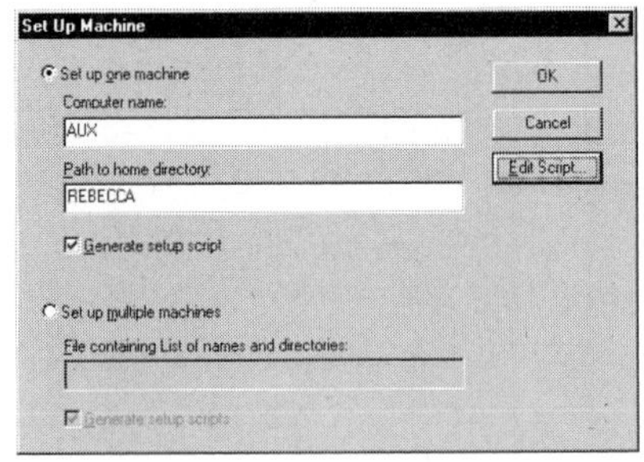

Figure 4.7.
The Set Up Machine dialog box allows you to create the home directory required by users who will use the server copy of Windows 95 instead of running it from a local hard drive.

2. Click OK to add the new user. NetSetup returns you to the main screen.

You might have noticed that a script was automatically generated for the new user. This script will help set up Windows 95 for file server use (if the user chooses that option or you selected it as a forced option). You can modify the default script by entering the same machine and user name in the Set Up Machine dialog box, and then clicking the Edit Script button.

Customizing Setup

Creating a default installation for Windows 95 is relatively easy. The preceding section showed you how to do it in eight easy steps. You can use the information contained in Table 4.1 to further customize the setup file. Simply make a copy of MSBATCH.INF (the default installation script) and make any required changes, using a text editor.

There are several advantages to this approach. The biggest advantage is that a properly configured script allows you to add the setup routine to the network login script. The next time the user logs into the network, he'll automatically install Windows 95 on his machine. Of course, a successful installation requires a bit of work on your part to get the script just right. In addition, you should still expect the occasional glitch that will keep the automated installation from working. In theory, automated installations sound wonderful. In practice, they require a lot of work, a little luck, and a very thorough understanding of the network on the part of the administrator. The problem is very simple: You need to set up each user's script to take into account the quirks of his or her machine, or the setup will fail.

Manually editing the setup script allows you to modify or add some parameters not supported by the automatic script-creation utility. Some of these items fall into the "nice to have" category, but others are essential if you plan to create a script that will allow the users on your network to install Windows 95 automatically. In fact, some of them will come in handy even if you perform all the installations using the network by yourself. Table 4.2 contains a complete list of these items. Assume that all the values appear under the `[Setup]` heading of the file unless the comments tell you otherwise.

Table 4.2. Custom setup script options.

Option	*Comment*
`ChangeDir=[0 ¦ 1]`	A value of `0` allows you to bypass the Change Directory dialog box that appears if you decide to install Windows 95 into a directory other than the default. Using the automatic script generator automatically inserts this value.
`Customize=[0 ¦ 1]`	Use this option to specify whether the user can customize the setup process.
`Detection=[0 ¦ 1]`	This entry allows you to skip all or part of the hardware detection process. A value of `0` bypasses the entire detection process.

continues

Table 4.2. continued

Option	Comment
`Devicepath=[0 ¦ 1]`	Contains `0` if you want to use the normal method for installing new device support. A value of `1` allows the network administrator to place updated .INF files in one location. The user configuration is updated automatically the next time the user checks into the network. This parameter works only for server installations.
`IgnoreDetectedNetCards=[0 ¦ 1]`	Use this entry to tell Setup whether you want to detect any installed network adapters. A problem exists if you decide to install a network that doesn't provide protected-mode support for the NIC—LANtastic 6.x, for example. (You may want to consider updating your NOS if you're still using the real-mode version. For example, LANtastic now provides full Windows 95 support.) If you don't provide this entry, Windows 95 automatically assumes that you want to install a Microsoft network, in many cases. Installing two sets of NIC drivers (one Windows 95 and other real-mode) will cause conflicts with your installed real-mode network. This setting appears under the `[Network]` heading.
`LogonDomain=`*`<string>`*	This setting appears under the `[VReDir]` heading. It allows you to specify a Windows NT logon domain to use for password validation. You can set this value even if you set `ValidatedLogon` to `0`.
`Network=0`	Adding this entry allows you to define which network components are selected (see Table 4.1 for a complete description of the `[Network]` section entries). A value of `0` bypasses the entire network-installation process.
`[`*`optional components`*`]`	This is an actual section within the batch file. You create the header as shown and then add entries below it—one for each optional component you want to install or not install. The entries take the format `"`*`<optional component>`*`"=[0 ¦ 1]`, where *`<optional component>`* is the name of an option enclosed in quotes. A value of `1` installs that option. Windows 95 provides

Option	*Comment*
	a default installation status for each optional component based on the type of installation you perform (see Table 4.4 for details). Here's a list of the optional components that you can install:
	Accessories options include Accessories, Accessibility Options, Briefcase, Calculator, Character Map, Clipboard Viewer, Desktop Wallpaper, Document Templates, Extra Cursors, Games, Multi-Language Support, Net Watcher, Object Packager, Online User's Guide, Paint, Quick View, Screen Savers, Scrolling Marquee, Blank Screen, Curves and Colors, Mystify Your Mind, Flying Through Space, System Monitor, Windows 95 Tour, and WordPad.
	Communications options include Communications, Dial-Up Networking, Direct Cable Connection, HyperTerminal, and Phone Dialer.
	Disk Tools options include Disk Tools, Backup, Defrag (disk defragmenter), and Disk Compression Tools.
	Microsoft Exchange options include Microsoft Exchange, CompuServe Mail Services, Internet Mail, and Microsoft Fax.
	Multimedia options include Multimedia, Audio Compression, CD Player, Media Player, Musica Sound Scheme, Nature Sound Scheme, Robotz Sound Scheme, Sound and Video Clips, Sound Recorder, Utopia Sound Scheme, Video Compression, and Volume Control.
	The Microsoft Network options include the Microsoft Network.
`ProductID=`*`<string>`*	This entry allows you to add the product identification found on the Windows 95 installation disks. In most cases, you'll want to use the default setting.
`RemoveBinding=`*`<DevID>`*`,`*`<DevID>`*	This option allows you to unbind one device from another. You can use it to tune bindings in a setup script. This setting appears under the `[Network]` heading.

continues

Table 4.2. continued

Option	*Comment*
`ValidateNetCardResources=[0 ¦ 1]`	Setting this entry to `1` displays a configuration wizard if Setup detects a network card IRQ or address conflict with another device. This setting appears under the `[Network]` heading.
`ValidatedLogon=[0 ¦ 1]`	This setting appears under the `[VReDir]` heading. A setting of `1` forces a validation of the user password when logging into a Windows NT domain.

In addition to all the installation parameters you can place in a script file, you can add an `[Install]` heading. This heading allows you to install optional programs or even Windows components such as the network administrator's tools. It's especially handy for automatically entering all the "run once" installation routines such as setting the time zone. The key to making the `[Install]` section work is adding the proper macro instructions. We explore this process for hardware and software configuration later in this chapter. You can also use the files in the \WIN95\INF directory on your machine. In most cases, the files follow the same general format, but there are subtle differences you need to observe. Be sure to look at a file that installs a component just like the one you want to install. That way, you can get all the details correct the first time. The run-once install entries consist of a combination of `DelReg=` and `AddReg=` macro commands. You delete the old Registry entry using the `DelReg=` command, and then add the new entry using the `AddReg=` command.

Getting Ready to Install

When you get to this point in the chapter, you should have created a boot disk and inventoried your hardware. Network administrators will have created an MSBATCH.INF file to make installation easier. You also should have removed many of the device drivers from CONFIG.SYS and AUTOEXEC.BAT. Before you begin the setup process, you might want to make a few additional changes to these two files. It might seem like a pain to have to preset your machine to provide the best possible environment for an operating system installation, but you really will get better results this way.

The first thing you'll want to do is `REM` out any unnecessary TSRs from your AUTOEXEC.BAT. I even took out the little utility programs such as DOSKey. You'll also want to `REM` out ANSI.SYS (or a vendor-specific alternative) because you won't need it under Windows 95. If you use a real-mode network such as LANtastic, disable it for the time being—at least as a server. Windows 95 has problems with LANtastic (and other peer-to-peer real-mode network software) when you try to install it with the server running. In addition, disable any drive mappings, or Setup will run into problems trying to identify your boot drive.

Tip: The Windows 95 Setup program will overwrite or replace some of the files in your DOS directory. If you have any intention of uninstalling Windows 95 later, it's a good idea to make a copy of this directory before you start the installation. That way, you can easily restore it later.

After you complete these final modifications, reboot your system. You should now have a completely clean environment in which to install Windows 95. One last check using the `MEM /C` command to verify that memory is as clean as possible is always a good idea.

Tip: When you start the setup process, the first thing Windows 95 does is scan your drives for errors. You might want to save yourself a bit of time by doing this check in advance. That way, you can fix any errors and prevent the Windows 95 Setup program from stopping before it even gets started.

Let's look at some of the Setup command-line switches. They'll help you get around any problems you might experience while installing Windows 95. For example, some computers might freeze when Setup tries to perform a disk scan, so you can use the `/IQ` or `/IS` switch to get around the problem. The following is a complete list of these switches. There's one thing you need to know about the way I present this information. When you see something between angle brackets (< >), it means that you have to supply a value of some kind. The description will tell you what to provide. Don't type the angle brackets when you type the switch.

- `/?`: Use this switch to display a list of currently documented command-line switches. As of this writing there are two: `/T:`*`<temporary directory>`* and *`<batch>`*.
- `/D`: The `/D` switch helps you get around situations in which one or more of your Windows 3.x or WfW 3.1x support files are missing or corrupted and Setup won't run properly. It tells Setup not to use the existing copy of Windows for the initial phase of the setup. As soon as the new Windows 95 support files are copied to your drive, Setup switches back to a Windows interface.

- `/ID`: Setup doesn't check for the required disk space when you use this switch. I can't think of any time when you'd want to use it. If your system is that short on hard disk space, you should consider clearing additional space before you try to install Windows 95.
- `/IQ`: Use this switch to bypass ScanDisk as the first step of the installation process when performing the installation from DOS. It's not a good idea to skip this step unless your system experiences some kind of problem running ScanDisk with Setup running. Be sure to do a separate scan of your drives if you use this switch.
- `/IS`: Use this switch to bypass ScanDisk as the first step of the installation process when performing the installation from Windows. It's not a good idea to skip this step unless your

system experiences some kind of problem running ScanDisk with Setup running. Be sure to do a separate scan of your drives if you use this switch.

- `/NOSTART`: The `/NOSTART` switch allows you to copy to the hard drive the minimum number of Windows 3.x .DLLs that the Windows 95 Setup program requires to start. Setup then exits to the DOS prompt. You can use this feature to replace or repair any missing or damaged Windows 3.x or WfW 3.1x support files prior to starting an installation.
- `/T:<temporary directory>`: This switch allows you to tell Windows 95 which drive to use as a temporary directory. It normally tries to use the drive you're using for installation. However, if the drive you chose is a little short on space, you can use this switch to redirect installation-specific items to another drive.
- `<batch>`: This option was discussed in detail in the preceding two sections. The MSBATCH.INF or other batch file contains custom installation instructions.

Believe it or not, you're finally ready to install Windows 95. The very last thing you need to do before you start Setup is to choose what type of installation you want. (My personal choice is the Custom Setup option, because it gives you the most control over the final appearance of the installation.) You can perform four types of installations:

- **Typical Setup:** This is the default setup that Windows 95 provides. It allows you to install a standard set of options for your machine (the table that follows shows the features this method includes). Because this is the default setting, the only questions Setup will ask are where you want to put the Windows 95 files and whether you want to create an emergency disk.
- **Portable Setup:** Use this setup if you're using a portable computer. It installs a minimal set of standard utility programs—the same set included with the Compact Setup option. This installation also includes all the special utilities that Windows 95 provides for portable computers, such as the Briefcase and Direct Cable Connection features.
- **Compact Setup:** This is the option to use if you're really tight on hard disk space. It installs only the bare essentials—perhaps a little too bare for many users. The nice thing about using this particular option is that you can get a minimal system started and then add other features as you need them. That way, you never end up with more than you'll actually use on your computer. Of course, this option also presents very little opportunity for the user who wants to explore what Windows 95 has to offer.
- **Custom Setup:** The custom option provides the most flexibility of all the Setup options. It also requires the greatest amount of time to set up. This is the perfect option for those who already have a good idea of what they do and don't want out of Windows 95. It's also a good option for a network administrator who uses a batch file to install Windows 95 on workstations. The administrator gets the maximum flexibility, yet the batch file hides any details from the user.

Note: As of this writing, you must use the Portable installation option if you want the installation program to place the power management utilities on your system. You can manually install these utilities by using the Expand utility later. However, Microsoft (for whatever strange reason) decided not to include this option on the Windows Setup page of the Add/Remove Programs Properties dialog box.

The decision on which installation route you want to use is based partly on which files you need to use. The one thing you'll want to remember is that you can always add or remove features later on. A mistake right now doesn't mean that you'll have to start the installation from scratch later. With that in mind, Table 4.3 contains a list of the various files that Windows 95 installs using the four installation options. (All four options obviously install the entire core system.)

Table 4.3. Optional features installed by various setup options.

Feature	*Typical*	*Portable*	*Compact*	*Custom*
Accessories	✓			✓
Audio Compression	✓	✓		✓
Codecs				
Backup	✓			✓
Briefcase		✓		
Desktop bitmaps	✓	✓		✓
Dial-Up Networking	✓	✓		✓
Direct Cable Connection	✓	✓		✓
Disk compression tools	✓	✓	✓	✓
Disk maintenance and repair	✓	✓	✓	✓
Tools				
Document templates	✓			✓
Games	✓			✓
HyperTerminal	✓	✓		✓
Internet mail service				
Microsoft Exchange				
Microsoft Fax				
Multimedia applications	✓	✓		✓
Multimedia sound and video	✓	✓		✓

continues

Table 4.3. continued

Feature	*Typical*	*Portable*	*Compact*	*Custom*
Clips				
Musica sound scheme	✓	✓		✓
Network administration tools				
Online user's guide				
Paint	✓			✓
Quick View	✓	✓		✓
Screen savers	✓	✓		✓
The Microsoft Network				
Video compression Codecs	✓	✓		✓
Windows 95 tour	✓			✓
WordPad	✓			✓

Installing Windows 95 from Floppy Disks

Installing Windows 95 from a floppy is just as simple as the same installation was for Windows 3.x. All you need to do is start DOS or Windows and type **`Setup`**. Microsoft suggests that you install Windows 95 from an existing copy of Windows 3.x, and it's true that this particular installation provides you with a better interface. However, beyond the interface issue, both installation methods (character-mode and GUI) are the same. The following steps walk you through the installation procedure:

1. Type **`Setup`** at the Run prompt and press Enter. You should see a display similar to the one in Figure 4.8.

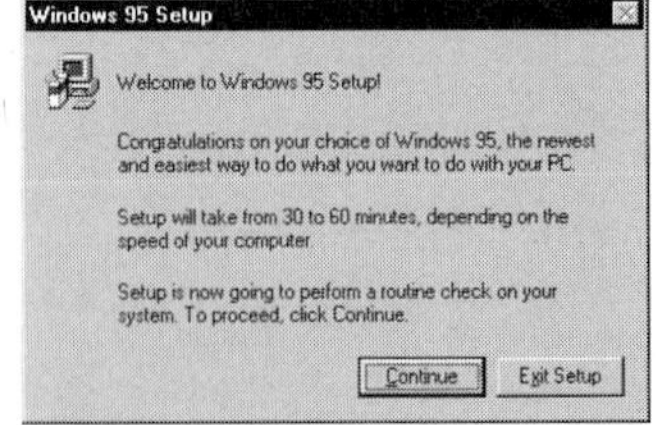

Figure 4.8.
The initial Windows 95 screen starts like most Microsoft installation programs.

2. Click Continue. You'll see a dialog box similar to the one in Figure 4.9. Windows 95 checks your hard drive for errors before it starts the install. When it gets past this point,

Setup displays a message saying that it's installing the Windows 95 Setup Wizard. About halfway through this process, it asks you to insert disk 2.

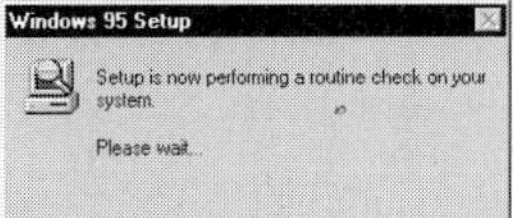

Figure 4.9.
The Windows 95 Setup program scans your drive before it starts the installation.

3. Insert disk 2 and click OK. When the Setup Wizard installation is complete, Setup displays the licensing agreement shown in Figure 4.10 and asks you to agree to the terms of the licensing agreement. If you decide that you don't like the terms, Setup exits.

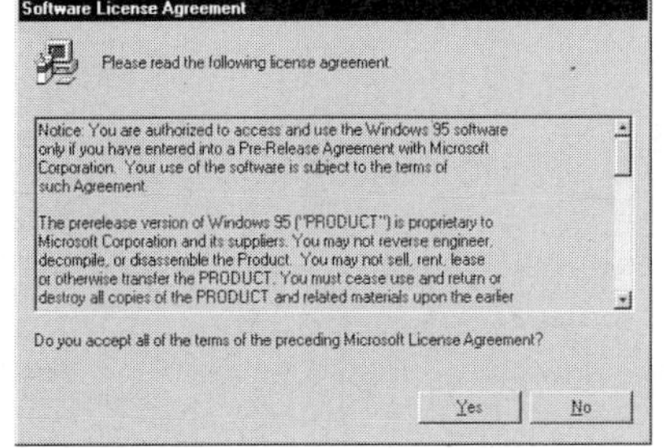

Figure 4.10.
When the Setup Wizard installation is complete, Setup asks you to agree to the terms of the licensing agreement.

4. Signal your agreement to the licensing terms by clicking Yes. Setup makes some checks at this point. For one thing, it checks to make sure that it's the only application running. If it finds any other applications running, Setup displays a dialog box telling you to use Alt+Tab to access the applications and exit them. It provides similar dialog boxes for any other problems that it finds. You should see a Setup Wizard dialog box similar to the one shown in Figure 4.11 at this point. This is the entry point for the main part of the Windows 95 installation.

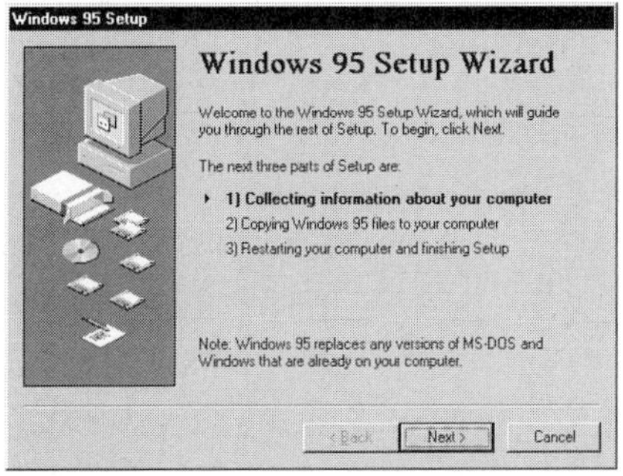

Figure 4.11.
The Setup Wizard helps you get the rest of the operating system configured and installed on your machine.

5. Click the Next button to get to the next dialog box. At this point, Setup asks where you want to install Windows 95, as shown in Figure 4.12. It suggests a default directory, or you can choose another location. Setup always suggests your current Windows directory if it detects a prior installation. If you plan to keep Windows 95 on your machine, this is the right way to go, because you'll preserve all your current settings and application configurations. However, if you think you might want to return to your previous setup, select a new directory. You'll have to reinstall all your applications, but at least it will be easy to return your system to its previous condition.

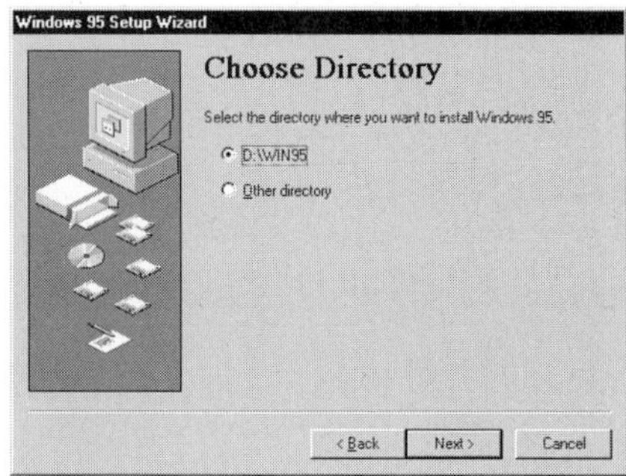

Figure 4.12.
This dialog box allows you to choose a location for Windows 95.

6. Select a directory option and click Next. If you chose a new directory, Windows 95 asks you to enter it in the next screen and click Next. Setup then displays a message saying that you'll have to reinstall your applications if you install Windows 95 in a new directory. Click OK to get past this dialog box. Either directory selection will take you to the dialog box shown in Figure 4.13. If you don't have enough disk space, Setup provides some additional dialog boxes to help you find enough space on the hard drive, or recommends some other corrective action. When Setup finishes checking for installed components and the amount of required disk space, it presents the dialog box shown in Figure 4.14.

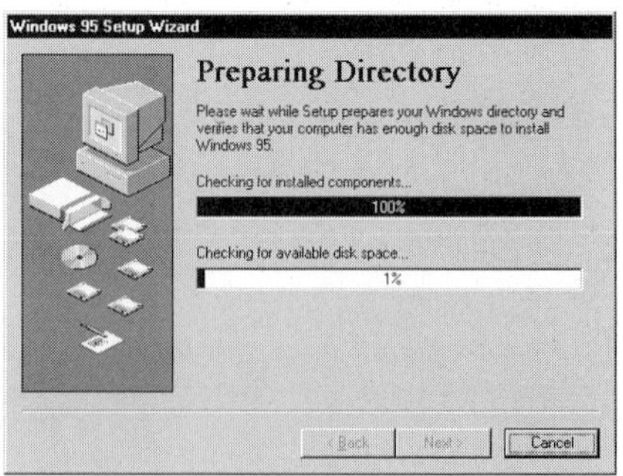

Figure 4.13.
Windows 95 begins the installation by checking for installed components and the correct amount of disk space.

7. Select one of the four installation types. These options are discussed at length in the preceding section. Most users should select either the Typical or Custom installation type.

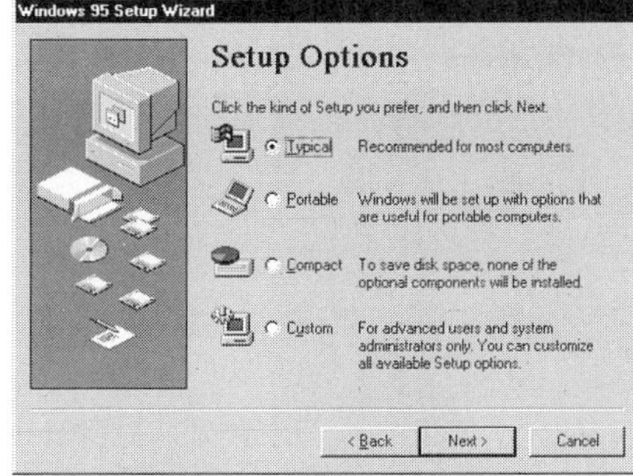

Figure 4.14.
Now that Setup is ready to go, you must select an installation type.

8. After you select an installation type, click Next to get to the display shown in Figure 4.15.

Figure 4.15.
Setup assumes that you want all your hardware detected automatically, except for a few special devices such as the CD-ROM.

Note: If you select the Custom installation, Windows 95 asks whether you want it to autodetect the devices installed on your machine. The other configurations don't get this option. If you choose to modify the hardware configuration list, Windows 95 displays a dialog box containing all the various types of hardware available on your machine. You need to select which types you want to detect automatically.

Tip: Users of LANtastic and other real-mode peer-to-peer networking systems should select the Custom installation option. This allows you to tell Windows 95 not to automatically detect your network adapter. Automatic detection assumes that you want to install a Microsoft network when using these networks.

9. Click Next to start the hardware detection phase. Setup displays a dialog box similar to the one shown in Figure 4.16. When Setup finishes this process, it displays the Get Connected dialog box shown in Figure 4.17.

Note: The hardware detection phase can take quite a while—especially on older machines. The one constant I've noticed is that when disk activity stops for more than five minutes, it's a pretty safe bet that the machine is frozen. As long as you hear disk activity during this phase, you can assume that hardware detection is still taking place. (The hardware detection indicator doesn't move at a steady pace. It appears to take more time as it nears the end.)

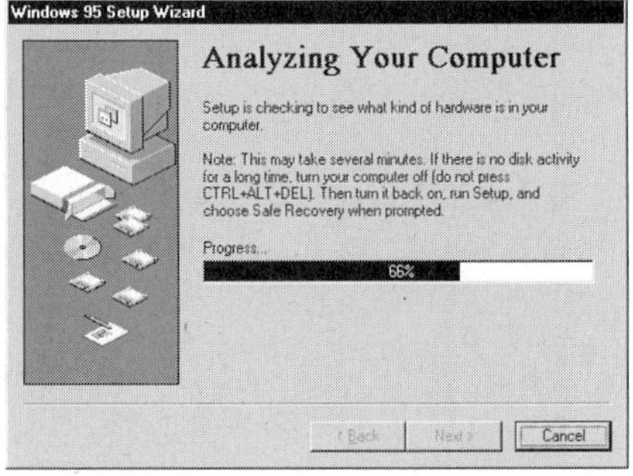

Figure 4.16.
The hardware detection phase is one of the few areas where Setup could freeze.

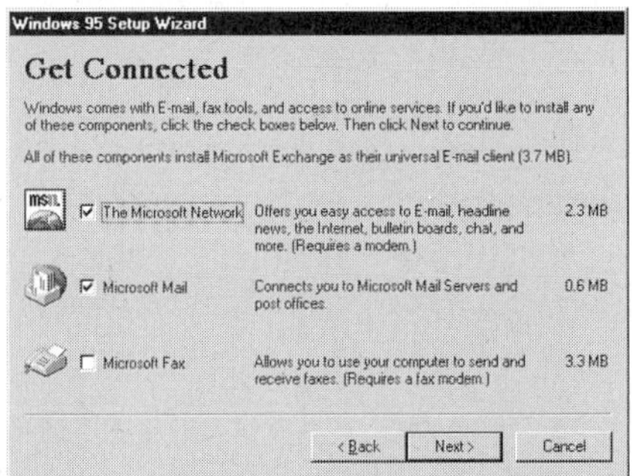

Figure 4.17.
The Get Connected dialog box is where you select your connection options.

10. Check the connection options you think you'll need and then click Next to continue. Windows 95 presents one of two dialog boxes at this point. The Custom option allows you to select individual components, using the dialog box shown in Figure 4.18. The other three installation methods only allow you to select between no optional components or the most common components for that installation type. See Table 4.3 for a list of common components. (I also provide an overview of these accessories in Chapter 2.)
11. If you're using the Custom installation feature, use the dialog box to select the components you want to install. If you're using one of the other three installation options, select either No Optional Components or the Common Components radio button. Click Next to display the Network Configuration dialog box, shown in Figure 4.19, which is the most

confusing step for new users. Most network administrators will want to provide a script to get users through this part of the installation automatically.

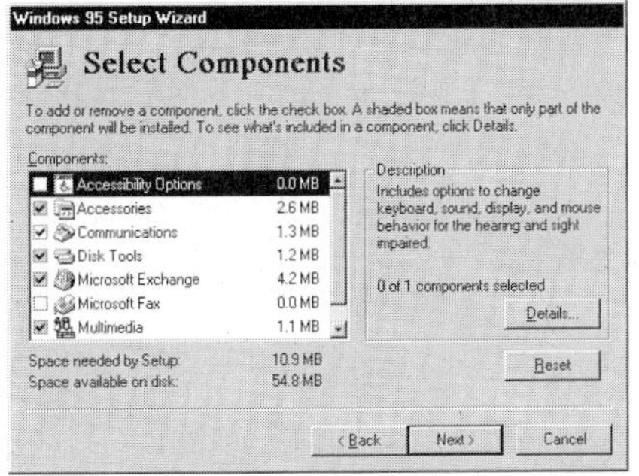

Figure 4.18.
Using the Custom installation option gives you the most flexibility when it comes time to select Windows 95 features to install.

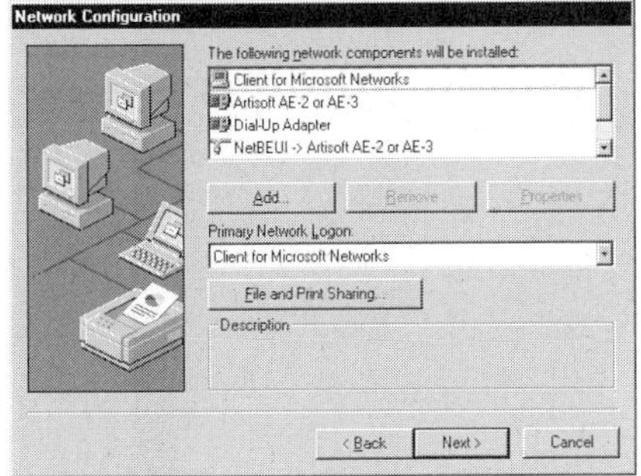

Figure 4.19.
The Network Configuration dialog box is the most confusing step for new users.

12. After you select the network installation options, Setup takes you through a series of screens to configure that network. Each network has different requirements, so the installation screens will vary. You'll see various network options later in this book. If you find that you can't answer the questions here, you might want to skip ahead to those networking chapters for a few answers. It's also important that you read the manuals that come with your networking software. In many cases, they provide the answers you need.
13. Complete the network configuration dialog boxes one at a time. Click Next to move from screen to screen. Some networks, such as Microsoft networks, require a single screen. Others might require more screens, depending on the options you select. The last time you click Next, Setup displays a dialog box similar to the one in Figure 4.20. This dialog box contains all the settings for your machine.
14. Check all your hardware settings completely by scrolling through the list. Sometimes the Setup Wizard fails to detect a piece of hardware. Worse still, it might detect a piece of hardware incorrectly. There are techniques you can use to make this process a little less error-prone. These techniques are discussed in the plug and play section that follows. If this list doesn't reflect your computer, change the settings in this dialog box, using the Change button.

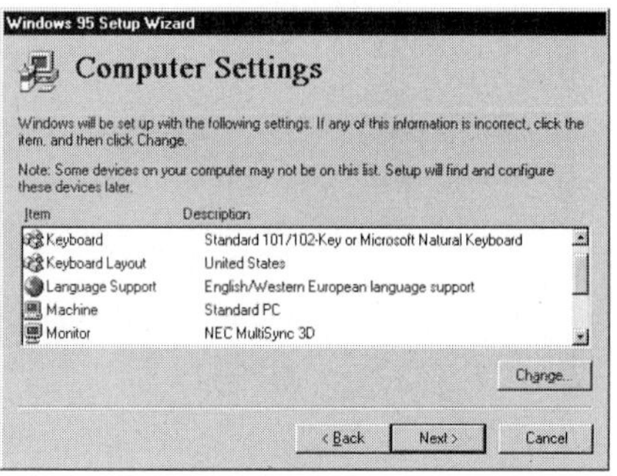

Figure 4.20.
You need to check the Computer Settings dialog box thoroughly to be certain that the Setup Wizard detected all your hardware correctly.

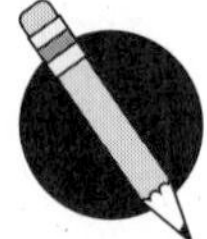

Note: This dialog box doesn't display every hardware and software installation choice that the Setup Wizard made. You have to check all the settings for your hardware after Setup completes. See Chapter 26 for tips and techniques that you can use to troubleshoot hardware-related problems. Network hardware appears in Chapter 27.

15. After you complete any required changes to your hardware setup, click Next. The Setup Wizard will ask whether you want to create a startup disk (see Figure 4.21).

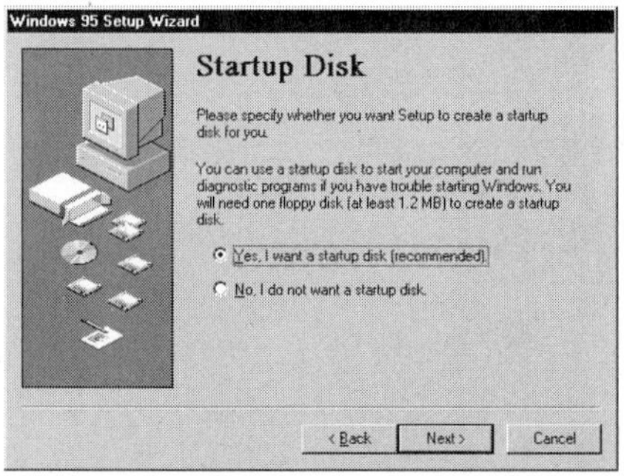

Figure 4.21.
The Startup Disk dialog box is one place where you shouldn't take the quick way out. Always create a startup disk for your machine.

Tip: There's never a good reason to avoid making a startup disk. This is the most automatic method at your disposal for ensuring that you'll always have a way to boot your machine. In fact, you can run this procedure from within the Add/Remove Programs Properties dialog box. You should keep the startup disk up-to-date by creating a new one whenever your system configuration changes (even a little).

16. Always select Yes and click Next. The next display tells you that the configuration portion of the installation is complete. Remember that disk-swapping exercise I talked about at the beginning of this chapter? You're about to start doing just that. Setup now starts to copy

files to the hard drive. All you need to do is click Next and follow the prompts. Sometime during the copying phase, Setup will ask you to provide a blank formatted floppy for the startup disk.

As you can see, Windows 95 requires a lot more configuration than its predecessors. I think it makes this process much easier, though, by organizing the configuration dialog boxes better and asking for the information in a more logical sequence. Of course, a higher quality of online help doesn't hurt either.

Installing Windows 95 from a CD-ROM

The only difference between installing Windows 95 from floppy disks and from a CD-ROM is that you use a different drive. The CD-ROM installation doesn't require you to change disks, either. It automatically knows that all the information required to install Windows 95 is on that one disk.

Note: You need to retain any drivers and TSRs required to access your CD-ROM drive in the DOS startup files to install Windows 95 from a CD. Remember to `REM` out any unneeded drivers once the Windows 95 installation is complete.

The CD-ROM version of the installation program contains some added features. First, it includes all the network administrator tools and help files. The floppy disk version doesn't provide these tools because it's designed for the single-user machine. The CD-ROM also contains a copy of the Windows Resource Kit in Windows Help format. The CD-ROM contains a few additional goodies as well. You'll find an additional game—Hoover—and a few video demonstrations in the FUNSTUFF folder. The PRODUCTS folder contains a summary of many Microsoft products that you can access from the Autoplay dialog box that comes up when you insert the CD in the drive. There are other features as well—all of which I cover throughout the rest of the book.

Installing Windows 95 from a Server

A server installation can differ from the floppy disk version in quite a few ways. You could install the entire operating system without telling the user much, if anything, about what you're doing (believe me when I say that this isn't a good idea). You might not choose to provide any automation at all, in which case the user would see the same thing you did for the floppy disk installation in the preceding section. Reality will probably fit somewhere between these two extremes. As a network administrator, you should provide some level of automation to protect the user from the ambiguities of installing network support. However, whether you install Windows 95 from a server, a CD-ROM, or a floppy, the same sequence of events must take place. The only factor is the way you choose to smooth the way for the users on the system.

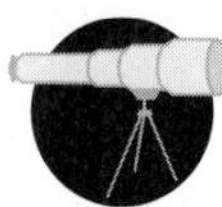

Looking Ahead: Part of getting a network installation to work is maintaining good communication with the server. If you find that the installation isn't going as well as you'd hoped, it could be a sign of trouble with your network as a whole. Even a slow installation may be a sign that something is going wrong. I cover network troubleshooting issues in Chapter 27.

Earlier we looked at all the automation you could provide using an MSBATCH.INF file. The level of automation that you provide as a network administrator is the one random element in the server installation. As I said earlier, as a minimum you should hide the network installation details from the user. My personal preference, though, is to allow the user as much freedom as possible when it comes to installing optional components. I can't really give you a play-by-play look at a server installation. Each server installation differs, because each network and company has different needs. You determine how the install program looks to the user.

The one other thing you need to determine for a server installation is the location of the operating system. Forcing users to use Windows 95 from the server is certainly more secure than allowing them to install it on a local workstation. It also allows you to maintain a firmer grip on the licenses. Finally, keeping the files on the server reduces the amount of hard disk space that Windows 95 consumes across the network. (You have to provide room for just one copy of the operating system on the network and a home directory for user-specific files.)

The advantages of a local hard disk install are few but very important. A local install definitely increases performance. That's going to be a big factor for many people who are already looking for ways to get the last ounce of performance out of a machine. Using the local install option also reduces network activity. Some networks suffer from a lack of bandwidth, and installing Windows 95 on the server makes a bad situation worse. Finally, a local hard disk installation allows you to keep the server clear of user files and open for data files. The distinction is important. A user configuration file helps only that particular user, while a data file helps the company as a whole. Keeping user data on the file server might add a lot of clutter and make it more difficult for people to find the data files that they need.

Plug and Play Installation Tips

I am a great fan of automation that works. Anything that will make my job easier or faster is a good idea, in my book. Using plug and play to automatically install the hardware it recognizes is one form of that kind of automation. It makes sense that a computer could figure out a set of port and interrupt settings faster and with greater accuracy than the average human. Windows 3.x didn't provide any form of plug and play. Even if it did, it couldn't have dealt with the problems of supporting older, non-plug and play hardware. One reason that this is possible under Windows 95 is that the computer has all the statistics it needs to do the job. The majority of this information is contained in the onboard BIOS that plug and play hardware uses to communicate with the rest of the machine.

Of course, the BIOS takes care of only one part of the equation. Plug and play is an example of a good idea—but one whose time hasn't yet come. Windows 95 does a fairly good job of detecting non-plug and play hardware, even when it gets mixed with plug and play-compatible hardware. All the configuration information for the hardware that Windows 95 supports is stored on the hard disk. In fact, if you look in the \WIN95\INF directory, you'll see some of these files (they all have an .INF extension). Besides storing the required configuration information on disk, Windows 95 gives older hardware first choice of ports and interrupts. This allows older hardware to work most of the time.

Problems start to arise when the system doesn't or can't recognize one or more components in your system. The problem is so bad on some systems that I've heard people refer to the new Windows 95 hardware detection scheme as "plug and pray." Usually, the unrecognized hardware refuses to work properly, if at all. The second this happens, Windows 95 has the unfortunate tendency of either going to pieces or ignoring the problem. Unrecognized hardware falls into two categories. There's the difficult-to-recognize piece of hardware, which emulates something else so well that the computer has a hard time telling exactly what it is. The second category is older hardware that lacks Windows 95-specific drivers.

So now that you have some idea of what the problem is, let's take a quick look at ways you can fix it. This list isn't exhaustive, but it will help you with the majority of the problems you're likely to run into:

- Avoid interrupt and port address conflicts whenever possible. This is probably the number one reason that Windows 95 fails to recognize the board. If two devices use the same address, there's no way that Windows 95 can test for the presence of the second board.
- Plug all your older boards into the slots next to the power supply whenever possible. The BIOS checks the slots in order during POST. Placing these older boards first, followed by the plug and play boards, ensures that the BIOS will see the older ones first.
- Try different board configurations to see whether Windows 95 recognizes one of them. There are situations in which the .INF files that Windows 95 uses to check for the older boards contain only the default board settings. A good rule of thumb is to try the best setting first and then the default setting if that doesn't work.
- Check the .INF files to see whether they contain all the settings for your boards. There's an .INF directory directly below the main Windows 95 directory. It contains ASCII text files that Windows 95 uses to search for these older boards. Modifying these files is a tricky proposition, but it could help Windows 95 find the peripherals in your machine.

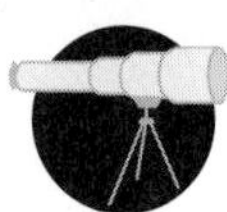

Looking Ahead: If you didn't find a technique that helped you here, take a look at the end of this book. Chapter 26 takes a detailed look at hardware troubleshooting techniques—especially tough-to-install hardware. (Network-specific hardware appears in Chapter 27.) In some cases, you might find that Windows 95 even provides protected-mode drivers that you can use with the old stuff.

Installation with Real-Mode Drivers Intact

If the quick help in the preceding section didn't help much, you can always try some backdoor techniques that I've discovered. Some devices—especially those that rely on software configuration instead of jumpers—don't provide enough information for autodetection until you turn them on. Normally, this means that the user has to install any required real-mode drivers in CONFIG.SYS. These drivers perform the setups required to make the device visible to Windows 95. The following procedure helps Windows 95 "discover" these hidden boards in most cases:

1. After you install these drivers, reboot the machine. When Windows 95 starts, use the Start | Settings | Control Panel command to open the Control Panel.
2. Double-click the Add New Hardware icon. You should see the dialog box shown in Figure 4.22.

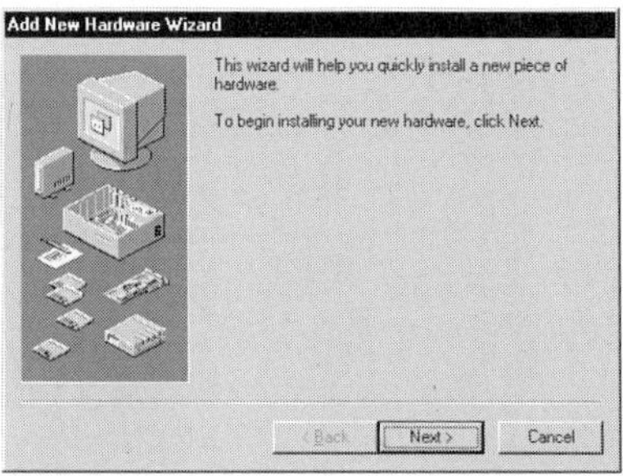

Figure 4.22.
The Add New Hardware Wizard allows you to install new hardware with a minimum of effort.

3. Click the Next button. You should see the dialog box shown in Figure 4.23. Using automatic hardware detection reduces the amount of work that the user needs to perform, and it can reduce the possibility of hardware conflicts because Windows 95 performs some additional detection steps. Notice that the Yes (Recommended) radio button is selected. Selecting this radio button tells Windows to detect your hardware automatically.
4. Click the Next button in this dialog box and again in the next dialog box. Windows 95 displays the dialog box shown in Figure 4.24 during the detection process.

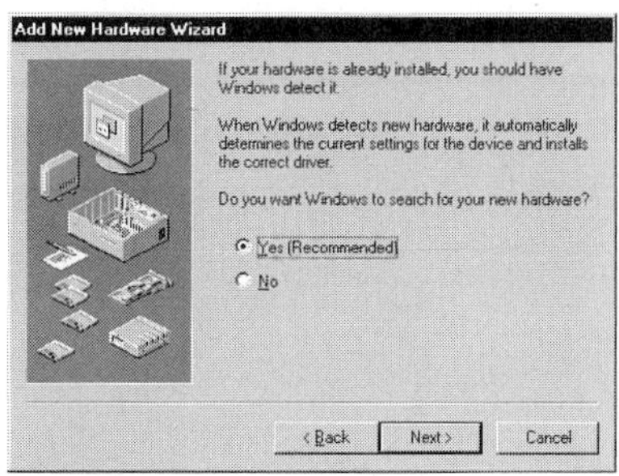

Figure 4.23.
Using automatic hardware detection reduces the amount of work that the user needs to perform.

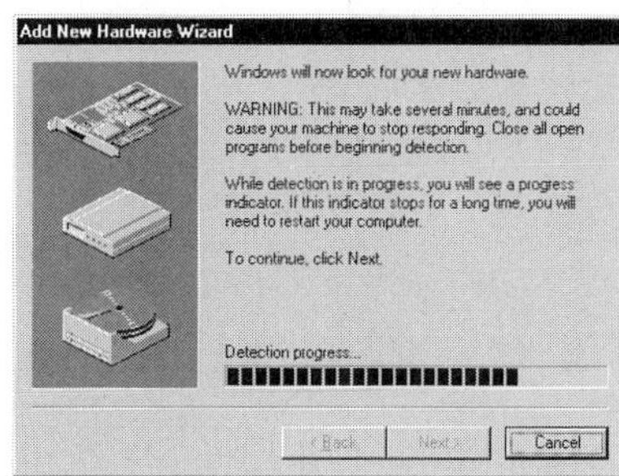

Figure 4.24.
Windows 95 displays this detection progress indicator while it searches the machine for new devices.

Note: The hardware detection phase can take quite a while—especially on older machines. The one constant I noticed is that when disk activity stops for more than five minutes, it's a pretty safe bet that the machine is frozen. As long as you hear disk activity during this phase, you can assume that hardware detection is still taking place. (The hardware detection indicator doesn't move at a steady pace; it appears to take more time as it nears the end.)

5. Click the Details button to determine whether Windows 95 successfully detected the new hardware, as shown in Figure 4.25.

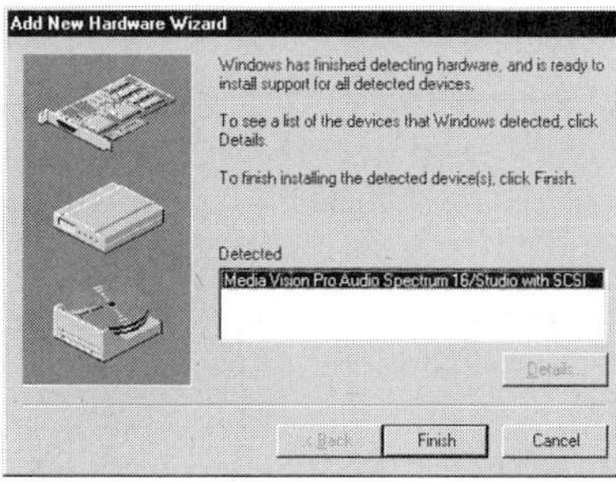

Figure 4.25.
The Detected field of the final Add New Hardware Wizard dialog box tells you whether Windows 95 detected the new hardware correctly.

6. If Windows 95 detected the new hardware successfully, click the Finish button to complete the installation process. Windows 95 might ask you to supply some setting information if this is a non-plug and play device. In most cases, it provides default settings that match your current real-mode setup. Windows 95 copies all the required drivers to disk. It also displays some messages about the new hardware it found, and perhaps a "driver database building" message. In some cases, Windows 95 asks you to reboot when you complete this step. Even if it doesn't ask you to reboot, you must do so to make this procedure work properly. The real-mode drivers that you installed to aid in detection will destabilize the system if you leave them in place.
7. Be sure to remove the real-mode drivers from CONFIG.SYS before you shut down and reboot the machine. If Windows 95 didn't detect the new hardware, remove the real-mode drivers from CONFIG.SYS, shut down and reboot the system, and then perform the manual installation procedure in the next section.

Manual Installation

It always seems to come down to the same old procedure. You finally get everything working using the automated procedures, except that old CD-ROM drive or an especially difficult sound card. There are a few situations in which you'll have to help Windows 95 install an older device in your machine. Usually, something else you installed—probably a plug and play device—is using some resource that the older device needs. The following example shows how to install a CD-ROM drive; the same principles apply to any manual installation. However, let me warn you ahead of time that simply installing the device might not make it work. You might have to perform some troubleshooting to get this older device to work (see Chapter 26). At the very least, you'll have to shuffle some IRQ and address settings around.

1. Use the Start | Settings | Control Panel command to open the Control Panel. Double-click the Add New Hardware icon (refer to Figure 4.22). Click the Next button (refer to Figure 4.23).
2. Click the No radio button and then click Next. Highlight the CD-ROM Controller entry of the Install Specific Hardware field and then click the Next button. You should see the dialog box shown in Figure 4.26. The Manufacturers and Models lists in this dialog box allow you to scroll with ease through the list of devices supported by Windows 95. If the device installed on the current machine doesn't appear in the list, the dialog box also affords the opportunity to use a third-party disk.

   This dialog box appears every time you select a device from the previous dialog box. The Manufacturers list changes to match the selected device type.
3. Normally, you would select the device connected to your machine. In this case, however, leave the default device highlighted and click the Next button.

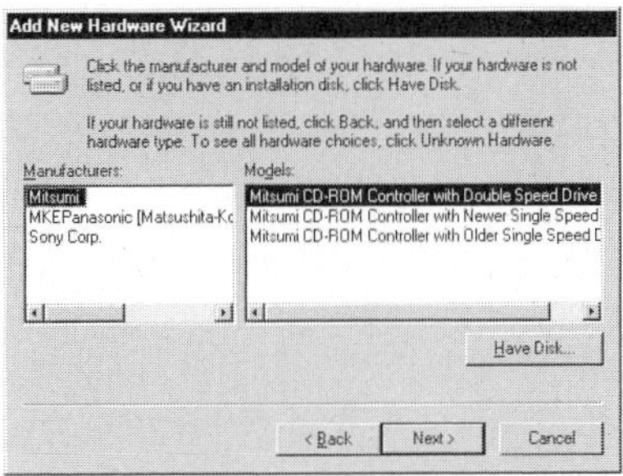

Figure 4.26.
Use the lists in this dialog box to scroll through devices supported by Windows 95.

4. Click the Details button. Windows 95 displays a dialog box containing the interrupt and address settings for this particular device, as shown in Figure 4.27. Windows 95 chooses a device setting based on all available information; it chooses the best setting that won't interfere with other devices in the system (if possible).

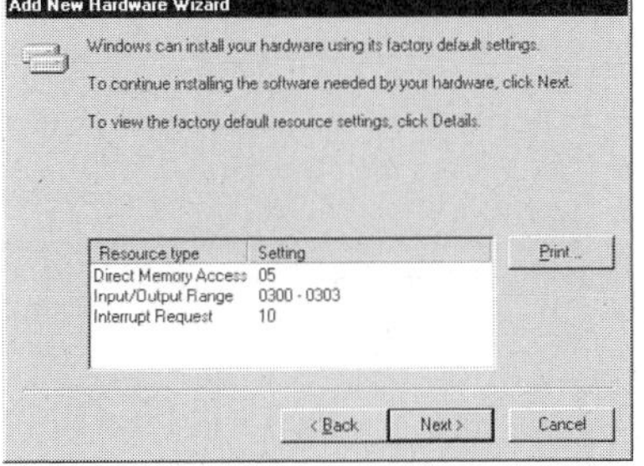

Figure 4.27.
Windows 95 always tells the user what interrupts and addresses it uses for the devices it installs.

Tip: A special "Unknown hardware" device type allows you to view all the devices supported by Windows 95 on one screen. This comes in handy for two purposes. First, Microsoft doesn't always place devices in the category where you expect them to be. Searching through this list provides one final check if you don't find a device where you expect to see it. Second, you can use this list when researching a new product. It allows you to choose a device that Windows 95 will definitely support. I'm not saying that other products are incompatible—just that these products received a little more attention than some of the others you might find.

5. Clicking the Next button again installs the device drivers required for this device. Normally, you would take this action. Windows 95 might prompt you for a disk if the driver didn't appear on the hard drive and the appropriate disk didn't appear in the CD-ROM drive. It would display a dialog box showing the progress of the file copy process. However, because you don't want to install this particular device, click the Cancel button. Windows 95 exits the Add New Hardware Wizard without installing the new device.

Adding Your Own Devices

Now that you have Windows 95 installed, let's take some of the magic out of the new Windows 95 detection capability. If you take a look in your \WIN95\INF directory, you'll see a new type of file there. The .INF file is part of the database of information that Windows 95 uses to recognize hardware that isn't plug and play-compatible. These files are enhanced versions of the OEMSETUP.INF files that used to appear on the vendor-supplied installation disks under Windows 3.x. They contain a description of the hardware—the same type of information that the plug and play BIOS would normally provide when Windows 95 scanned it.

There are two main differences between these .INF files and the Windows 3.x version. First, the Windows 95 version contains a lot more information. It provides detailed configuration and detection information to the system. Under Windows 3.x, the same file would provide only general operating parameters. Second, Windows 95 has constant access to these .INF files. It can scan them anytime you install new hardware or reconfigure the existing hardware. Under Windows 3.x, this file tended to stay on the OEM disk that you got with your display adapter or other hardware. Even if the vendor did write this file to the \WIN\SYSTEM directory, the next vendor installing a product would overwrite the file. Under Windows 3.x, every setup disk contained an OEMSETUP.INF file. Using the same filename prevented you from saving these settings for future use (or at least it prevented you from doing so in a convenient way).

As good as these new .INF files are, there might be times when you want to modify them. For example, what if you have a piece of hardware that provides interrupt and port address settings in addition to those found in the .INF file? Modifying the .INF file to reflect these additional capabilities could help you install a piece of hardware in some cases.

Tip: Microsoft is devoted to making the .INF file format a standard way to configure future versions of Windows to support non-plug and play hardware. However, the contents of that file are a moving target at the moment, because Microsoft is still trying to work out bugs in the detection scheme. You can obtain your own copy of the .INF file specification from the CompuServe Plug and Play forum (GO PLUGPLAY). Just download INFWHITE1.DOC or INFWHT.ZIP. You also get a copy with the Windows 95 DDK (Driver Development Kit). This file contains a lot more information than the average user will need; however, it can help a system administrator find a way to incorporate some devices into the Windows 95 environment.

Let's look at some of the general characteristics that every .INF file shares. You might find all or only some of these sections in the file; it really depends on what kind of hardware the .INF file is trying to define. An .INF file needs to contain only the information required to fully define the characteristics of the hardware. For example, a display adapter would need to define the resolutions that it supports. A multiscanning monitor, such as the NEC MultiSync series, would need to define the precise frequency ranges that it supports. This includes the refresh rate, an important specification for the new ergonomic display adapters. Table 4.4 shows these generic sections and tells you what they mean. You might even want to open one of the .INF files and see whether you can identify each section. (Just make certain that you don't save the file or change its contents in any way.)

Table 4.4. .INF file generic sections.

Heading	*Description*
`Version`	This section provides version-specific information such as the operating system, vendor name, and the device class supported by the .INF file. It also provides the name of the general setup file. The general setup file contains the definitions common to all the devices of that type. You might see some additional entries in this section. One special entry allows the vendor to link a new .INF file into the list of files for a specific device type. Never change the contents of this section.
`Manufacturer`	The `Manufacturer` section contains a list of all the manufacturers for devices of this class. Not every .INF file contains this section. For example, this section appears in the MONITOR.INF file but not the MSPORTS.INF file. The only time you need to change this section is when you want to add a new vendor. The list might seem incomplete if there's more than one .INF file required to describe a specific class of device. There are four monitor files, and each one contains only the vendors that appear in that particular file. You need to check all of the .INF files for a particular device class before you resort to adding a new vendor. Make sure that you add the new vendor in alphabetical order, in the correct .INF file (you see an example later in this chapter). There's a subsection after this one that provides specifics about each device supported by that vendor. If the vendor already appears in the manufacturer list, adding a new device consists of adding an entry here, in the `Install` section, and in the `Strings` section.
`Install`	This is the most important section of the file. It describes all the characteristics of the hardware and the device drivers needed to activate it. It also contains macro commands that perform the installation of support in the Registry. Follow the example of other entries in this section when adding a new device. When modifying an existing entry, change only physical characteristics such as port address and interrupt.

continues

Table 4.4. continued

Heading	*Description*
`Miscellaneous Control`	A vendor can use this section to describe how a device works with the Windows 95 interface. If you see this section, you need to use other entries as an example for creating your own entries. Most .INF files don't contain this section.
`Strings`	Later in this chapter, you learn how to add a new device to Windows 95 by using the Add New Hardware dialog box. When you use this dialog box, you see some descriptive strings that tell you about the hardware. This is the section that contains those user-friendly strings. It identifies the device in human-readable form.

I was looking through my list of available displays the other day and noticed that one of my displays—a Samsung CQ-4551 VGA monitor—wasn't supported. It's a fairly easy matter to add support for this new device to the .INF file, so I made a copy and placed it in a backup folder right below the .INF folder. That way I wouldn't erase the original file by accident. We can go through this exercise together to make the process for adding a new device a little clearer. Before we begin, though, I'll outline a few guidelines that I used during the modification process.

- Always print a copy of the original .INF file. This way, you can scan through the listing quickly as you make a new entry. Some entries depend on the contents of other entries in the file. A mistyped or misinterpreted entry will make the .INF file useless.
- Use the other entries in the file as a guideline for your new entries. Windows 95 performs a very strict interpretation of the contents of the .INF file. Adding your own "enhancements" to what seems like an inadequate entry might make the .INF file unusable. Remember, some of the .INF file entries appear in one or more generic files that appear in the `Version` section of the file.
- Follow punctuation marks, spelling, and capitalization carefully when making a new entry. Windows 95 is extremely sensitive when it comes to how you format the entries in an .INF file.
- Never change the `Version` section of the file. Yes, it's very tempting to fiddle with what looks like an interesting file section, but don't do it in this case.
- Make your entries to an existing file. You might be tempted to create your own unique .INF file. Don't do it! Always add new devices to existing files. That way you can be absolutely sure that your entries look like the other entries in the file.

Warning: Always modify the original copy of an .INF file after making a backup. Place the copy in a backup directory, using a different extension from the original file. Your modified version of the original file must appear in the .INF directory for Windows 95 to recognize it. Keeping a copy of the original version in a temporary directory allows you to restore the file later.

Now that you have a better idea of what an .INF file contains, let's go through the procedure for modifying one. You can use the same set of steps to modify any of the files in the .INF folder. The only thing that changes from file to file is the precise format of the entries and the sections that the file supports.

Note: This procedure is based on the released version of Windows 95 without any service packs or service releases installed. The filename you need to find may differ from the one I listed in the procedure. For example, Service Pack 1 places the Samsung information in MONITOR4.INF, rather than MONITOR2.INF as stated in the procedure. You can use the Find utility provided with Explorer to locate the exact MONITORxx.INF file that you need to use on your machine.

1. Use WordPad to open MONITOR2.INF. There are four sections in the .INF file that you need to change (refer to Table 4.4). The first section we'll modify contains the manufacturer information. Because I wanted to add an entry for a Samsung monitor, I used WordPad's Find command to see whether I could find the vendor name. Samsung is already in the vendor list, so I didn't need to add it. However, if you decide to add a new vendor, all you need to do is follow the format of the other vendor entries in the first `Manufacturer` section. After I found the vendor name entry, I searched for the device subsection that would contain the list of devices from that vendor that Windows 95 supports. I added the following text (shown in bold) to this section so that Windows 95 would know to add a new device.

   ```
   [Samsung]
   %CQ-4551%=CQ-4551.Install
   %CT-4581%=CT-4581.Install
   ```

   As you can see, I formatted my entry to look exactly like the existing entry. This is a very important part of the process for adding an unsupported device to Windows 95. This entry tells Windows 95 that Samsung produces a model CQ-4551 monitor and that it can find further details about that monitor in the `CQ-4551.Install` section of the .INF file.

2. Now use the Find command to locate the second `CT-4581` entry (it's the Samsung model that appears directly below our new entry). This entry appears in the `Install` section of the .INF file. I added the following bold text to tell Windows 95 how to install this new monitor. Notice that these instructions look a lot like the macros you might have created with applications in the past—which they should, because that's exactly what this section contains.

```
[KDM-2066.Install]
DelReg=DEL_CURRENT_REG
AddReg=KDM-2066.AddReg, 1280
[CQ-4551.Install]
DelReg=DEL_CURRENT_REG
AddReg=CQ-4551.AddReg, 640
[CT-4581.Install]
DelReg=DEL_CURRENT_REG
AddReg=CT-4581.AddReg, 800
```

I started by adding a heading that identifies the macro code that follows as the Samsung model CQ-4551 installation procedure. An .INF file always encloses its headings between a left and right bracket, just like WIN.INI and SYSTEM.INI do for their headers. I also added two macro entries to the section. The first one tells Windows 95 to delete the current Registry entry. You need to delete the old entry so that Windows 95 won't get confused when it tries to configure the display adapter to match the monitor. The second entry tells Windows 95 to add a new Registry entry following the instructions located in the `CQ-4551.AddReg` section of the .INF file. Notice the `640` after the `AddReg` command. This tells Windows 95 to use the 640 display mode as a default.

3. Use the Find command to find the `CT-4581` entry in the next section of the file. I added the following bold text to tell Windows 95 how to modify the Registry to support this new monitor. We're still in the `Install` section of the file.

```
[KDM-2066.AddReg]
HKR,"MODES\1280,1024",Mode1,,"30.0-67.0,40.0-120.0,+,+"
[CQ-4551.AddReg]
HKR,"MODES\640,480",Mode1,,"31.5,60.0-70.0,-,-"
[CT-4581.AddReg]
HKR,"MODES\800,600",Mode1,,"15.0-38.0,47.0-73.0,+,+"
```

The Registry entry section of any .INF file requires some detective work on your part. I always look at the Registry itself as a starting point (see Chapter 7 for a complete description of the Registry). Knowing how the existing device modified the Registry can help you to determine how to add support for a new device. You should also check the specification sheet that comes with the device for "common" characteristics. Any change you make to an .INF file will ultimately require this type of detective work. In this case, the first important component is `"MODES\640,480"`. This describes the operational resolution for that monitor mode. The second component, `Mode1`, tells Windows 95 that this is the first mode supported by the monitor.

Looking at other entries in this .INF file shows that some monitors support multiple modes. The final component, `"31.5,60.0-70.0,-,-"`, looks a bit mysterious until you check a monitor manual. The first number, `31.5`, is the horizontal scanning frequency. You could supply a numeric range here as well. The second numeric range, `60.0-70.0`, is the vertical scanning frequency. The two minus signs tell you that this isn't a multiscanning monitor. I figured this out by checking the other entries in the file. After looking at a few monitor models that I recognized, it was pretty evident that the ones with multiscanning capabilities used plus signs in place of the minus signs.

4. Let's get to the final section of the .INF file—the `Strings` section. This is where you'll describe the monitor in terms that the user can understand. To do this, use the Find command to search for the next (and last) occurrence of the `CT-4581` string. When I found this entry, I added this bold text:

```
CQ-4551="Samsung, Inc. CQ-4551"
CT-4581="Samsung, Inc. CT-4581"
```

Well, that's all there is to it. When you get the hang of it, you can add support for just about any unsupported device to Windows 95. Of course, that won't solve some problems such as the lack of protected-mode drivers and some of the incompatibilities you'll experience with some older devices. But it makes it easier to install an older device. If you want to see how the new entry looks, save the MONITOR2.INF file and close WordPad. Right-click the desktop and select Properties from the context menu to display the Display Properties dialog box shown in Figure 4.28.

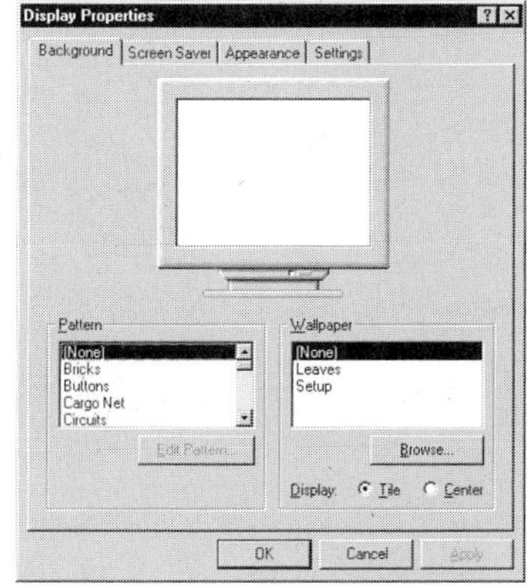

Figure 4.28.
Right-clicking the desktop and selecting Properties from the context menu displays the Display Properties dialog box.

You can use this quick procedure to display the monitor entries:

1. Click the Settings tab to display the settings (see Figure 4.29).
2. Click the Change Display Type button to open the Change Display Type dialog box (see Figure 4.30).
3. Click the Change command in the Monitor Type group to display the Select Device dialog box. Windows 95 displays an update message while it adds the new monitor to the list.

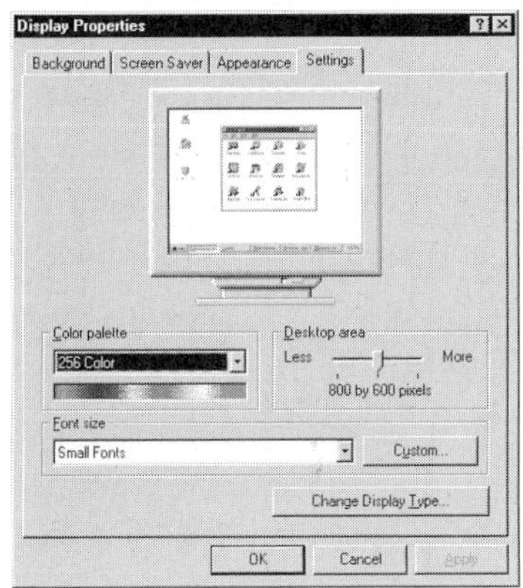

Figure 4.29.
You can change the current monitor settings on the Settings page of the Display Properties dialog box.

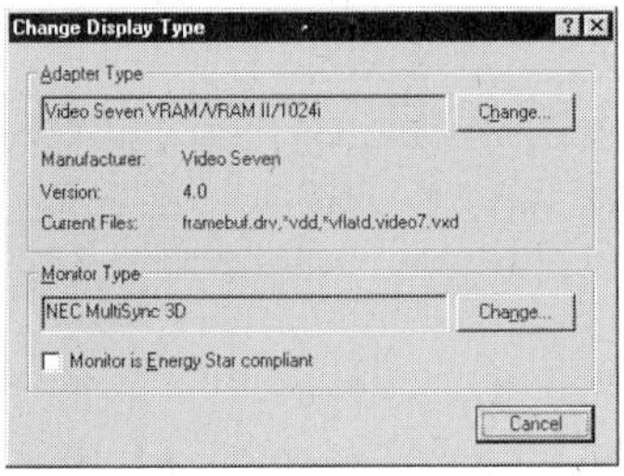

Figure 4.30.
The Change Display Type dialog box allows you to modify either the display adapter or monitor settings.

4. Scroll through the list of vendors until you find Samsung, Inc. (there might be a Samsung entry right before this one). You should see the new monitor selection, as shown in Figure 4.31.

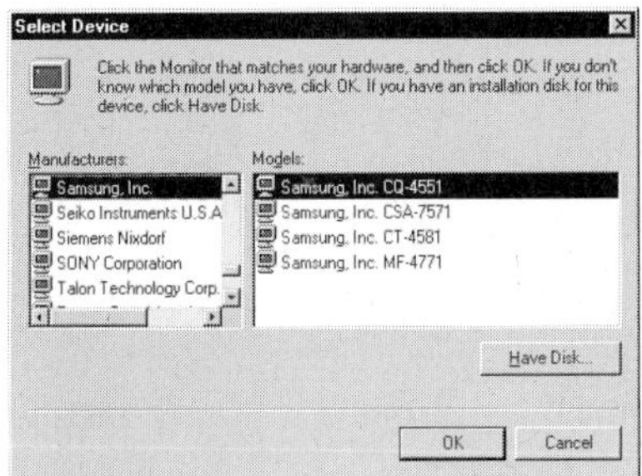

Figure 4.31.
Modifications to the MONITOR2.INF file appear in the Select Device dialog box.

5. Click Cancel three times to exit the Display Properties dialog box without changing the monitor type.

Adding a new device to an .INF file can prove time-consuming and even frustrating at times. However, the benefits in reduced maintenance time are well worth the effort.

This has been a quick tour of adding new devices to Windows 95. You might find that some devices are so complex that you'll end up downloading the full .INF file specification (see the tip earlier in this chapter) to really understand how to make the change. The worst thing you can do is try to tackle a complex device addition as your first project. Look for something fairly easy as your first project, such as a monitor, so that you can get a better idea of what the modification will require.

Uninstalling Windows 95

As of this writing, Microsoft hasn't included an uninstall feature with Windows 95. You can install it on your system, but you won't get it back off very easily—that is, unless you took my advice earlier in this chapter.

It wasn't too difficult to figure out that there wasn't going to be an easy way to get rid of Windows 95 once I installed it, if it overwrote all my system files and changed quite a few others. Even if I did manage to get my old operating system to boot, I'd have to spend a lot of time reinstalling all my applications.

There's an easier way. The following procedure assumes that you did three things. First, it assumes that you made a boot disk like the one I mentioned at the beginning of this chapter. Second, it assumes that you made a copy of your DOS directory. Finally, it assumes that you installed Windows 95 in a clean directory. If you didn't follow one of those three steps, you won't have the resources to put your system back together.

1. The first step in this process is to get DOS to boot again. Use your boot disk to reboot your machine from the floppy. (First shut down Windows 95 properly.)
2. Use the `SYS` command to restore the system files. Then copy COMMAND.COM and an original copy of AUTOEXEC.BAT and CONFIG.SYS from your floppy to the hard drive.
3. Copy the contents of your DOS directory backup to the DOS directory.
4. Take the floppy out of the drive and reboot your system. You should now get a DOS prompt.
5. Carefully erase all the Windows 95-specific files. Make absolutely certain that you look for all the hidden files that Microsoft thoughtfully stored in your root directory. You can find them by using the `DIR /AH /S` command. The `/AH` switch displays every file with a hidden attribute. The `/S` command tells `DIR` to look in any subdirectories as well as the root directory. Don't erase any DOS-specific files such as IO.SYS and MSDOS.SYS. The date stamp on the file should give you a clue about which files belong to DOS and which ones belong to Windows 95. If in doubt, leave the file in place, rather than remove it and make your system non-operational. It's going to take a little effort to find all the entries. In fact, this is where a good disk editor will come into play.
6. Reboot your machine one more time to make sure that everything works correctly.

That's it. This isn't the fanciest uninstall method in the world, but it works. You'll probably find bits and pieces of Windows 95 lying around on your system for a few weeks. If you were careful when you installed it, the pieces should appear in the root directory of all your drives. Of course, the first directory you'll erase is the \WIN95 directory. Be sure to get all the Recycle Bin directories (one on each drive) and the program directory that contained Microsoft Network and other accessory applications.

On Your Own

Create your own boot disk that contains the items I mentioned earlier in this chapter. Be sure to test it before you install Windows 95. You'll also want to create a Windows 95-specific startup disk during installation. Label both disks and keep them until you're certain that your Windows 95 installation is stable. When it's stable, create a new startup disk, using the Startup Disk page of the Add/Remove Programs Properties dialog box.

Make a list of all the equipment you think you might have problems with. Include all the items for which Windows 95 doesn't provide entries in the existing .INF files. Do you see any entries that you can fix by using the procedures provided in this chapter? Are there any ways to eliminate some of the real-mode drivers that you might need to use to keep older equipment running? Develop a comprehensive strategy for handling any problem areas before you begin the installation process.

5

Startup Shortcuts

An efficient machine is only as fast as the operator using it. If you can't use all the speed your machine provides, part of that speed is lost, and you might as well not look for anything faster. I've found that Windows 3.x users—like me—have developed some terrible habits because of that operating system's inefficiencies. For example, do you automatically assume that the machine is going to be tied up every time you use the modem? I know that's what I thought when I started using Windows 95.

As an experiment, awhile back I tried performing a background download with one additional task running—my word processor. The download completed in the background at 9600 baud without a single missed character while I worked in the foreground. The next day I decided to add another task. This time I compiled a program in one background session, downloaded a few files in another, and typed away in a third. I was ecstatic, to say the least. Everything went perfectly. So, I tried a third task, but Windows 95 just wasn't up to it. Everything bombed.

So what's the moral of this story? I don't think any operating system will ever be able to perform every task there is to perform and simultaneously communicate in the background. You need to have the required resources if you want to get the job done. In my case, two tasks in addition to the background download are about all my machine can handle.

I did learn something important, though. Using Windows 95 allowed me to get three times the amount of work done that I would have under Windows 3.x, in this particular instance. I want to emphasize that point because the new and exciting methods that Windows 95 introduces can become very inefficient, too.

Peter's Principle: Discovering Your Maximum Load—Without the Pain of Failure

Windows 3.x provided so many visual cues, I almost always knew when it was time to stop adding tasks by the way it acted. That "old shoe" feel doesn't come with Windows 95, because you really haven't had a chance to break it in yet. Until you do start learning the little quirks that tell you when it's time to stop adding new tasks, you can do a few things to keep your system from crashing.

Unlike Windows 3.x, Windows 95 actually comes with some easy-to-use tools that keep track of your system resources. For example, I keep a copy of Resource Meter loaded all the time. (This isn't the Resource Monitor application that I describe elsewhere; Resource Meter is a small utility designed to track system resources.) A quick check of the Taskbar tells me just how low I'm getting on system resources. (For more information about this utility, see the Accessories section of Chapter 2.) I also run Resource Monitor as needed to keep track of how certain tasks load the processor and disk subsystems. As a result, I'm learning how to use the Windows 95 capabilities more efficiently.

Now that we have a user-friendly operating system that can actually run more than a couple of tasks at a time without dying, we need to learn how to use it efficiently. Task loading is a new technique that all of us old hands will have to learn.

This chapter looks at some of the ways you can make yourself a little more efficient so that you can get the full benefits of using Windows 95 as an operating system. This means everything from the way you start your applications to the way you arrange your desktop. Windows 95 provides many new tools that you can use to make each step a little faster.

Windows 95 Shortcuts and OLE

Chapter 12 spends a lot of time discussing OLE from a user's perspective. The programmer's point of view appears in Chapter 7. Let's take some time now to look at one unique way that Windows 95 uses OLE.

Every shortcut you create is a form of OLE. It's an actual link to another object on your machine. Windows 95 provides some special handling for these objects.

Unlike an application that can create compound documents to hold all the linking information, Windows 95 has to store that information someplace on the drive. After all, the drive is the container that Windows 95 uses to store information. The .LNK file is the Windows 95 answer to this problem. It contains all the linking information needed to keep the shortcuts on your desktop current with the real object.

You can easily test this by creating a shortcut of a folder on your desktop. Every change you make to the real folder will appear in the linked copy. Likewise, every change you make in the linked copy will appear in the real thing. OLE and the desktop are part of Windows 95—a new part that will take time to get used to.

Faster Startups

Starting an application might not seem like a big deal. It wasn't a big deal under Windows 3.x. After all, how many ways can you double-click an application icon sitting in a folder in Program Manager? Windows 95 provides more than just one or two ways to start your applications. In fact, here's a whole list of ways:

- Right-click the application's icon while in Explorer, and then click Open in the context menu.
- Double-click the application's icon while in Explorer or File Manager.
- Double-click a data file associated with the application while in Explorer. (This requires that you create a file association or that the application create it for you.)
- Choose Start | Run and then type the application's path and filename. Click OK to start the application.

- Choose Start | Run and then drag-and-drop the application's icon into the Run dialog box. Click OK to start the application.
- Select the application's entry from the Start menu.
- Create a shortcut icon on the desktop. You can start the application by right-clicking or double-clicking the icon.
- Assign a shortcut key to the application, and then start it by using the keyboard shortcut. (You must create a .LNK file to do this. We look at the process for doing this later.)
- Use the Windows 3.x Program Manager (provided in the \WIN95 directory) to run the application.
- Place the application's icon or associated data file in the Startup folder in the Start menu to run it automatically the next time you start Windows. Placing a data file in the Startup folder automatically opens it for you.
- Use the Find dialog box to find your application, and then right-click or double-click it.
- Embed or link the application's data in an OLE compound document. The user can start the application by double-clicking the object embedded in the document. (The application must support OLE for this to work.)

Because I grew up using DOS, I really hated having to use the mouse just to start an application, so I didn't. Few users really understood this, but you can make Windows 3.x somewhat keyboard-friendly by installing shortcut keys. Windows 95 provides this same feature.

If all Windows 95 provided were this particular shortcut, I could stop right here and let you read some text on Windows 3.x. Even though Windows 95 uses the same type of shortcut method, the implementation is a lot better. We'll also look at some "undocumented" ways of using the keyboard.

There are times where you really do need to use the mouse—if for no other reason than the fact that your hand is resting on it at that particular moment. Like many people, I spend my share of time mousing around. CorelDRAW! and other drawing programs come in handy for some of the work I do. Using the mouse is nothing new for most people.

Windows 95 provides a lot of neat ways to use the mouse with your applications. You'll find that you can do a lot of things you couldn't do before with a simple mouse click. We look at some of these mouse techniques in this section.

Startups from the Keyboard

Nothing beat the keyboard if DOS was your home before you moved to Windows 95. But a quick look at the Windows 95 GUI tells you that most of your keyboard techniques won't work here. Some people figure that there's no way to use any of the old techniques. But nothing could be further from the truth.

Some shortcut keys come installed with Windows 95. I find that many of them are attached to the Accessibility options, but you can change all that with a just a little effort (we look at this later in this section). Table 5.1 provides a list of keystrokes and the actions they perform. You're probably familiar with most of them, but others are new to Windows 95.

Note: Windows 95 doesn't provide any way to get to the Control (system) menu by using just the keyboard. This means that you'll have to use the MouseKeys feature of the Accessibility options to move windows and perform other Control-menu-related functions when using the keyboard instead of the mouse.

Table 5.1. Windows 95 shortcut keys.

Key or Key Combination	*Purpose*
Alt+F4	Ends the current application. You can also use this key combination to end Windows if you're at the desktop.
Alt+Shift+Tab	Switches to the previous window.
Alt+Tab	Switches to the next window.
Ctrl+Esc	Opens the Start menu on the Taskbar. You can then use the arrow keys to select an application. Pressing Enter starts the application you selected.
Esc	Cancels the last action in most cases. However, you can't back out of some actions.
F1	Displays online help. In most cases, this help is general in nature but is application-specific.
F2	Pressing this while an icon is highlighted allows you to change the object name.
F3	Unless your application uses this key for something else, you can press it to access the Find dialog box. In most cases, you'll get better results if you press F3 while at the desktop. You can also use this key at the Taskbar and the Start menu.
Left Alt+Left Shift+ Num Lock	Holding these three keys down turns on the MouseKeys feature of the Accessibility options.
Left Alt+Left Shift+ Print Screen	Holding these three keys down turns on the High Contrast feature of the Accessibility options.
Num Lock	Holding the Num Lock key down for five seconds turns on the ToggleKeys feature of the Accessibility options.

continues

Table 5.1. continued

Key or Key Combination	*Purpose*
Right Shift	Holding the right Shift key down for eight seconds turns on the FilterKeys feature of the Accessibility options.
Shift five times	Pressing the Shift key five times turns on the StickyKeys feature of the Accessibility options.
Shift+F1	Displays context-sensitive help when the application supports it. The Windows 95 desktop doesn't appear to support this option.
Shift+F10	You must select an object before you use this key combination. It displays the context menu. Considering the number of options on the context menu, this key combination allows you to do almost anything with the object.
Tab	Use this key while at the desktop to switch between the desktop, Taskbar, and Start menu. You also can use Ctrl+Esc to bring up the Start menu and then press Tab to switch between applications.

Tip: Combining the various keystrokes makes them much more powerful. For example, what if you have a lot of applications open and need to get to the desktop quickly? Use Ctrl+Esc to display the Start menu, Esc to close the menu itself, Tab to get to the Taskbar, and Shift+F10 to display the context menu. All you need to do now is select Minimize All Windows and press Enter. Pressing Tab one more time takes you to the desktop.

Windows 95 provides two additional methods of using the keyboard to start applications. You can use the Windows 3.x method of assigning a shortcut key to the application. There are also automated methods of starting some applications.

Tip: Some keyboards, such as the Microsoft Natural Keyboard, come with a Windows key. Pressing this key opens the Start menu when using Windows 95. (The Windows key used to open the Task Manager under Windows 3.1x.)

Undocumented Parameters

The first program you need to learn about in order to use this section of the book is START. It's a new program that you'll find in your \WIN95\COMMAND directory. At first, I couldn't figure out what use this program would really be. Then I started playing with it and figured out a few ways you could use this program if you learned about the undocumented parameters that most Windows applications provide. First, though, let's look at some documented parameters that START provides:

- /MAX: Use this to run a maximized application in the background.
- /M: This switch allows you to run the application minimized in the background.
- /R: The default setting for START is to run the program in the foreground. You can still switch back to the DOS prompt, but you'll take a quick trip to Windows first.
- /W: Use this switch if you want to start a Windows application, work with it for a while, and return to the DOS prompt when you're done.
- *<program name>*: This is the name of the program you want to run and any parameters it needs in order to execute.

All this is fine if you want to run a Windows application from DOS. However, this information doesn't really become useful until you can get some work done in Windows without leaving the DOS prompt. What would happen if you wanted to gain the advantage of Windows background printing while performing other work at the DOS prompt? You could switch back to Windows, start Notepad or some other appropriate application, load your file, and print, but that would disrupt what you were doing. The following line shows an easier, faster, and much better method:

```
START /M NOTEPAD /P SOMEFILE.TXT
```

There are a few things here you really need to take a look at. The first is the /P parameter right after NOTEPAD. Where did I get it? It isn't documented anywhere. All you have to do is look in Explorer.

Let's take a look at this now. Open Explorer. It doesn't matter what directory you're looking at or how it's configured. Use the View | Options command to display the Options dialog box. Click the File Types tab. Scroll through the file types until you come across an entry for Text Document. Highlight it and click Edit. Click Print and then Edit. You should see a display similar to the one in Figure 5.1.

Now you can see where I came up with the /P parameter. Press Cancel three times to get back to the main Explorer display. Every other registered application will provide the same types of information. Some of them will be a little too complex to use from the DOS prompt, but you could use them if you wanted to do so. The whole idea of this shortcut is that you get to stay at the DOS prompt and still use the new features that Windows provides.

Tip: Just about every Windows application provides undocumented command-line switches. Even though you can only guess at what those switches are in most cases, you can usually count on them supporting one or two switches. The /P parameter almost always allows you to print by using that application. Some applications also provide a /W parameter that suppresses the display of any opening screens. Looking through the Explorer file listings will provide you with additional ideas.

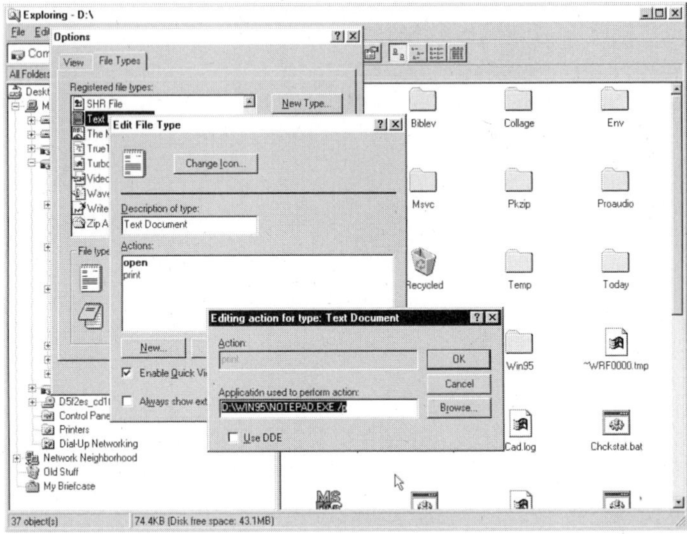

Figure 5.1.
Windows 95 hides a wealth of information. Explorer is just one of the gold mines. It's a treasure hunt; make sure you spend enough time digging.

There are a few other caveats you need to consider. Notice how I formatted my command line. You have to place the START program command-line switches first, and then the application name, the application switches, and any filenames. If you change this order, the application usually will start, but will report some type of error in opening your file. I've even had some applications insist that the file isn't present on my drive.

Shortcut Keys

After you spend some time with Windows 95, you'll discover that it's a lot more user-friendly than Windows 3.x. I find that I spend a lot less time at the DOS prompt now because I can get just about everything accomplished without it. However, that still doesn't make me happy about moving my hand from the keyboard to the mouse to start a new application.

Remember in the first section of this chapter, where I talked about the desktop and OLE? This is one of those times when that fact comes into play. To really make use of the shortcuts that Windows 95 provides, you have to create a shortcut. It doesn't matter where the shortcut is, but it does matter that it's a shortcut.

Tip: Every entry on the Start menu is a shortcut. If your application appears on the Start menu, you already have a shortcut to use. If it doesn't appear on the Start menu, you'll want to add it there or on the desktop.

To get the ball rolling, let's look at the Notepad shortcut on the Start menu. All you need to do is open the Start menu (press Ctrl+Esc, then Esc), open the context menu (Shift+F10), and select Explore. Use a combination of the arrow keys and Enter to get to the Notepad shortcut. Press Shift+F10 to display Notepad's context menu. Select Properties and press Enter. You'll need to select the Shortcut tab. You should see a display similar to the one in Figure 5.2.

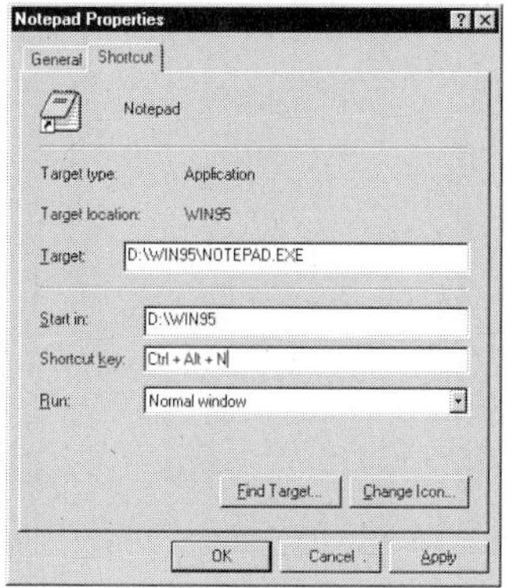

Figure 5.2.
The Shortcut tab in the Properties dialog box allows you to add a shortcut key to an application or to another shortcut.

The Shortcut Key field of this dialog box is where you enter the shortcut key combination you want to use. To save the setting, just close the dialog box as normal. The next time you press that key combination, Windows 95 will open the application for you.

Startups from the Desktop

Windows 95 comes installed with several applications already on the desktop. If you decide to install Exchange, you'll find it there. The Microsoft Network icon is also connected to an application. Just like the Start menu, none of these icons represents the actual application. You create a shortcut to the application, just like you would for the Start menu.

Of course, the big question is why you would even consider adding an application shortcut to the desktop. The big reason is convenience: It's faster to grab an application on the desktop than to burrow through several layers of menus to find it. Of course, your desktop has only so much space, so placing all your applications here would lead to a cluttered environment very quickly. In addition, remember from Chapter 3 that each icon uses memory, so you need to consider whether the efficiency you'll gain is worth the memory you'll use by adding an icon.

However, placing on the desktop the one or two applications that you use regularly could mean an increase in efficiency. Just think how nice it would be if your word processor and communications program were just a double-click away. You could open them as needed and close them immediately after you finished using them. This would mean that the applications you used most would still be handy, but they would be out of the way and wouldn't use up precious memory.

Tip: Keyboard users will probably get the same response time by using shortcut keys instead of placing their applications on the desktop. Not only will this give you a neater-looking desktop, but it will reduce the number of redundant links your computer has to maintain.

Placing a shortcut to your application on the desktop might provide an increase in efficiency, but double-clicking isn't the only way to open an application. The next few sections describe other ways you can access your applications faster by placing shortcuts to them on the desktop. The later section "The Data-Oriented Approach to Applications" also looks at something new for Windows 95. You really owe it to yourself to get out of the application-centric mode and take the new data-centric approach.

Click Starts

Right-clicking is new to Windows 95. Previous chapters took a quick look at the context menu. However, it's such an important concept that I felt we needed to take a special look at right-clicking for applications. Figure 5.3 shows the context menu for an application.

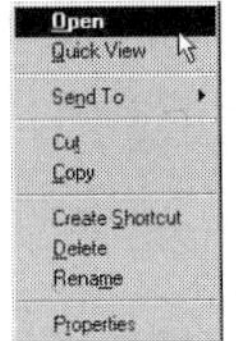

Figure 5.3.
Right-clicking an application shortcut produces this context menu.

To start an application this way, all you need to do is select the Open option. This has the same effect as double-clicking, but it might be more convenient if you have slower fingers. Some people really do have a hard time getting the double-click to work. This new method of starting an application has the advantage of requiring only a single click.

I was kind of curious about the Quick View option on this menu. If you select it, you'll see a dialog box similar to the one in Figure 5.4. The majority of the information here is stuff that only a programmer could love. At first glance, you do see some useful information, such as the name of the program and the version of Windows that it expects to find on your machine. You might even be able to use some of the information here to determine the amount of memory that your application needs to run.

In reality, this isn't the information you want to see, because you can determine most of it by using other methods. However, this view provides some special information that makes it easier for you to figure out which files to remove the next time you need to get rid of an old application. If you scroll down a bit, you'll notice a heading that says Imported-Name Table (Link-Time Imports), as shown in Figure 5.5.

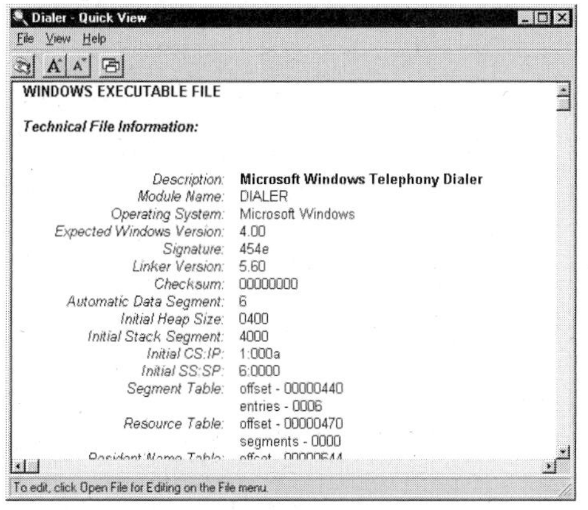

Figure 5.4.
The Quick View option for executable files provides some interesting information that you can use to learn more about how the application works.

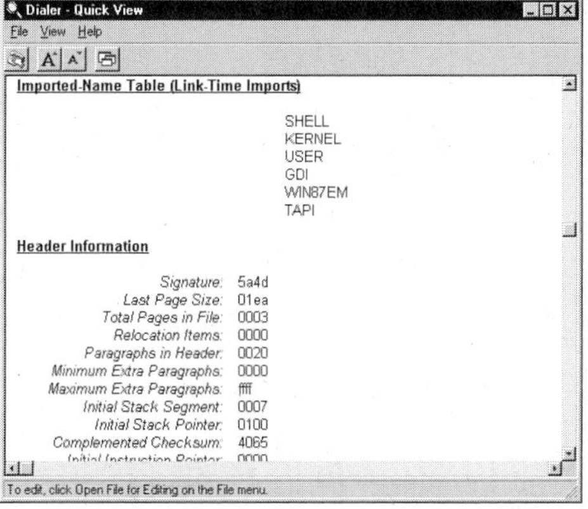

Figure 5.5.
The Imported-Name Table heading is the one you really want to look at in this view.

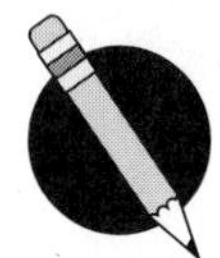

Note: Unfortunately, there are a number of ways to defeat the Quick View utility, and programmers use them all. The most common method is to mangle the names of the files used by the program in such a way that you can't read them but Windows can. The safest method for ensuring that you can remove a program you no longer need is to get those that are specially designed for Windows 95 and that include the requisite uninstall capabilities. That way, you can simply remove the program by using the Add/Remove Programs applet in the Control Panel. Chapter 11 covers the standard program-removal procedure.

Look at the list of files underneath this heading. All of them are somewhere on your drive—usually in the application folder or the \WIN95\SYSTEM folder. Unlike Windows 3.1, where it took some major tinkering to discover the files you needed to run an application, Windows 95 makes this information easy to find.

Use this information when the time comes to remove an application from your system. This view will help you come up with a list of files you need to delete. Of course, you don't want to delete any files that another application needs; prune this list carefully, so that it reflects only the files that are unique to a particular application. There's another problem with this list as well: It provides only one level of import file support. If one of the support files calls yet another group of files, you won't see that file here. Fortunately, you can also get to this view using other types of Windows executables. Be sure to look through the entire hierarchy before you consider your list of files complete.

This isn't the end of the story. There's another way to use this information to your advantage. Have you ever had an application that refused to start? It gave you some really cryptic message that looked like it was written in Klingon, and then killed itself and perhaps a few other applications. Once you got past this point, Windows displayed that really helpful message about not finding one of the components needed to run the application. The Quick View dialog box can help you get past this situation. Coming up with a list of .DLLs and other support files needed by the application is the first step in getting it to run. Next, check the application and the \WIN95\SYSTEM directory. As soon as you find which one of the files is missing, replace it and, voilà, no more mystery message.

Auto Starts

If you used Windows 3.x, you probably used the Startup folder to run specific applications every time you started your machine. Windows 95 provides the same feature. All you need to do is add an application to the Startup folder to allow it to run automatically. I always start a copy of Explorer this way so that my machine is ready for use the instant Windows completes the boot process.

Windows 95 can do something that Windows 3.x couldn't. I usually drag the data files I'm going to be working on for the next few days into my Startup folder. The reason is simple: Not only do I automatically start the application associated with that data file, but I also automatically load the file itself. This makes morning startups extremely efficient. When I get back to Windows after starting it, my machine is completely set up for use. Every application I need is already loaded with the files I want to edit.

Peter's Principle: Becoming Too Efficient for Your Own Good

Have you ever seen the "ransom note" effect produced by someone who has just discovered the joy of using multiple fonts in a document? To that person, it looks like the most incredible document he has ever produced. The rest of us think the document is pretty incredible too, but not for the same reason.

You can get into the same kind of habit with Windows 95 and its advanced features. Consider the Startup folder. It would be very easy for people to load every document they think they'll use for the entire week in there so that the documents would be ready when they booted the machine the next morning.

The best way to use this feature is to think about what you plan to do first thing the next morning or perhaps for the majority of the day. Don't open more than two or perhaps three documents unless they all use the same application. Someone who works on the same document, such as a writer, can really benefit from this feature. People who create presentations or work on other documents for long periods of time can also benefit. However, if you work a little bit on one document and then a little bit on another one, you might be better off starting the main application you use and letting it go at that.

So how do you add entries to the Startup folder? Just as you would with any other folder. The following procedure shows you a quick way to do it, using some of the new features that Windows 95 provides:

1. Right-click the Taskbar to display the context menu. Select the Properties option. Click the Start Menu Programs tab. You should see the Taskbar Properties dialog box shown in Figure 5.6.

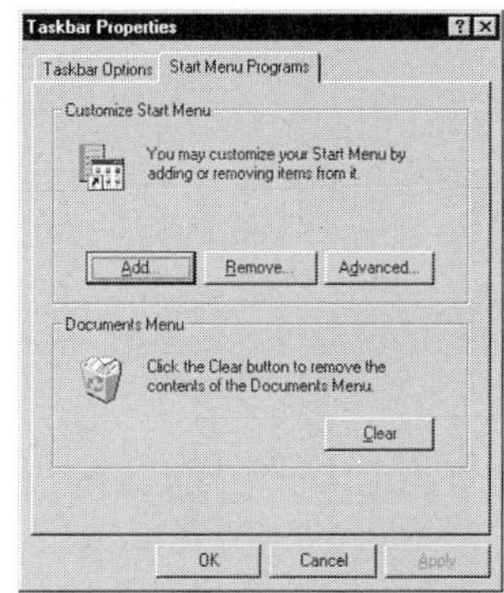

Figure 5.6.
The Taskbar Properties dialog box allows you to add new programs to the Start menu, using a menu-driven interface.

2. Click the Add button to open the Create Shortcut dialog box shown in Figure 5.7.

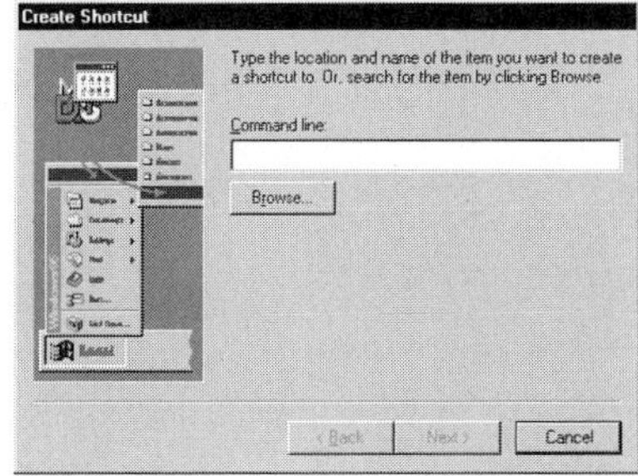

Figure 5.7.
The Create Shortcut dialog box is where you provide the name of the application or file that you want to add to the Startup folder (or another folder).

3. Click the Browse button to look for the file you want to add. As an alternative, you can type the full path and filename in the Command Line field of this dialog box. Click Next. You should see the Select Program Folder dialog box shown in Figure 5.8. This dialog box allows you to select the location of the shortcut in the Start menu. In this case, we'll select the Startup folder, but you could just as easily select something else. Notice that you can add a new folder as well.

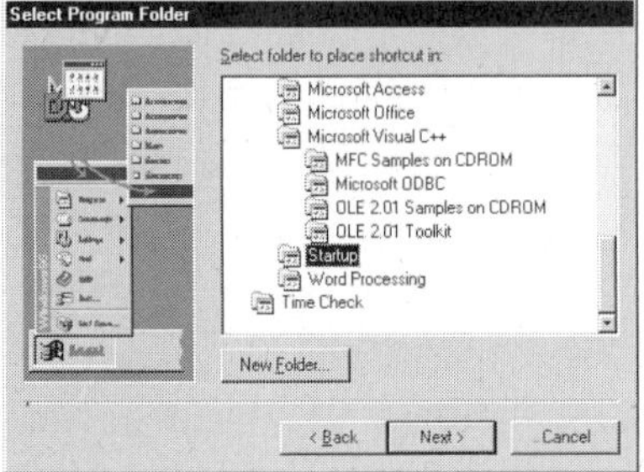

Figure 5.8.
The Select Program Folder dialog box.

4. Scroll through the list of folders and highlight the Startup folder. Click Next. You should see the Select a Title for the Program dialog box, as shown in Figure 5.9. This is the final dialog box of the process. It allows you to change the name of the shortcut.

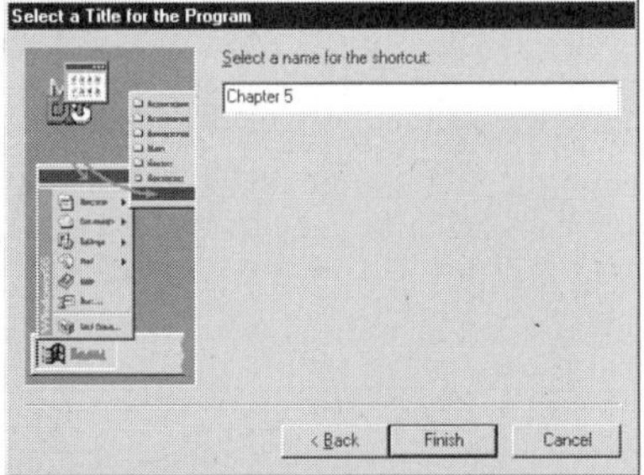

Figure 5.9.
The Select a Title for the Program dialog box.

5. Type the name you want associated with this file. Using a name you can remember is the best idea. Changing the name here won't change the name of the file, only the shortcut—this is the entry as it will appear in the Startup folder.
6. Click Finish to complete the task, and then click OK to close the Taskbar Properties dialog box.

Once you complete this task, the application or data file you added to the Startup folder will load automatically each time you start Windows 95. Getting your system set up efficiently means that you can do a little extra reading or perform some other task while you wait for everything to load. Of course, adding a file to the load sequence won't make it load faster, but it will give you a bigger block of time.

Controlled Starts

We won't spend a lot of time on this category of starting your application because you're already familiar with most of what you can do here. Everyone is familiar with double-clicking an application to start it. The fact that Windows 95 provides so many places to double-click doesn't really change the mechanics one iota. It might be useful, though, to take a quick look at the number of ways you can double-click to start an application. The following list does just that:

- **Explorer:** You can double-click an application or its associated data file. This interface also supports DDE, something I had trouble with when using File Manager. Of course, Program Manager didn't support DDE at all.
- **Program Manager:** As in Explorer, you can double-click any application.
- **File Manager:** As in Explorer, you can double-click any application or its associated data file. However, the interface isn't quite as flexible as that provided by Explorer. You'll find that DDE is hard to implement.
- **Find:** The Find dialog box comes in very handy. You can look for a data file and then double-click it to bring up the application associated with it. I've also used this dialog box as a quick method of finding the program I need.
- **Desktop:** Any data file or application sitting on the desktop follows the same rules as Explorer.
- **Network Neighborhood:** You can double-click any application or file sitting on someone else's machine to which you're connected.

Tip: Double-clicking under Windows 3.x always meant that you started the application. There's no such limitation under Windows 95. You can assign other default actions to an application or its data folder. For example, instead of unzipping when I double-click a .ZIP file, I view its contents instead. You could make opening and printing the default action for a word processing file instead of just opening. The actual number of ways you can use this feature is fairly unlimited.

Well, that's the long and short of double-clicking. You can always use the old controlled start method we all know and love to start an application. I hope this section provided some food for thought on other—perhaps better—ways of using the Windows 95 interface.

The Data-Oriented Approach to Applications

Windows 95 really shines when it comes to data. In fact, the whole interface is oriented toward data-centric access. You can force it to work the older Windows 3.x way, but Windows 95 will give you a lot less grief and a lot more efficiency if you start thinking about your data first and your application second. The next few sections discuss some of the tools that Windows 95 provides to make a data-oriented approach a lot easier.

Using Explorer to Get the Job Done

We've taken a long, hard look at Explorer in several sections of this book already. However, we haven't really taken a good look at one important feature. No longer are you tied to one specific action when it comes to data on your machine. If you've looked at the various context menus presented in this and other sections, you've noticed that there's always more than one thing you can do to a particular file. What you might not have realized is that the actions you saw are all under your control. You don't have to do things the Windows 95 way; you can do them any way that feels comfortable and allows you to get your work done faster. This is a nice change from the rather rigid tools that Windows 3.x provided.

Tip: The first time you double-click a file that lacks a file association, Windows 95 will ask which application you want to use to open it. You can choose an application that's already on the list or use the Browse feature to find a new one. Windows 95 defines only one action for this new association—open. Always take the time to modify that file association to add options for all the ways you plan to work with it. That way, the context menu associated with it will be completely set up the next time you right-click the file or any others like it.

Let's take a look at how you can add a new file extension and then define a set of actions associated with that file:

1. Open a copy of Explorer.
2. Use the View | Options command to open the Options dialog box. Click the File Types tab. You should see a dialog box similar to the one shown in Figure 5.10.
3. Click New Type to display the New Type dialog box.
4. Fill in the first two fields as shown in Figure 5.11. The first field describes what kind of file it is. This is the text you'll see in various list boxes. The second field contains the exact file extension.

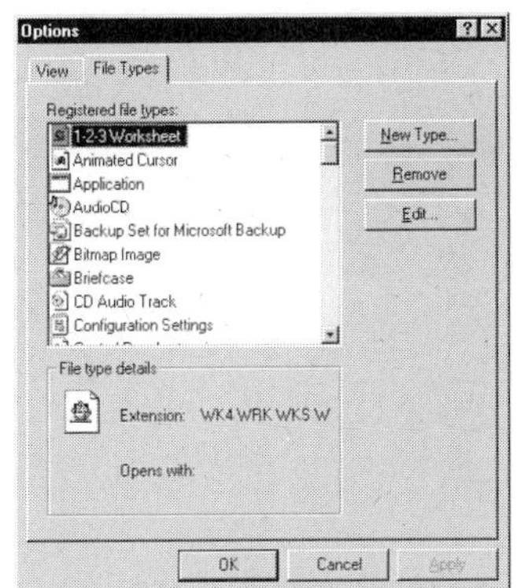

Figure 5.10.
The File Types tab of the Options dialog box allows you to add, remove, and modify file associations.

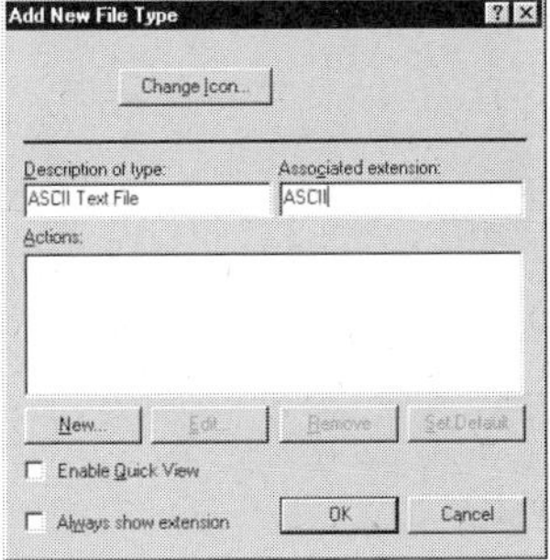

Figure 5.11.
The Add New File Type dialog box contains several fields that you use to describe a file's association to an application.

Tip: One problem you might run into is thinking about file extensions in the familiar 8.3 DOS/Windows 3.x format. Remember that Windows 95 supports long filenames, including long file extensions, as shown in Figure 5.11. You can define new file extensions that are more than three characters long. Windows 95 even allows some alternative characters in this format. For example, you could have a file extension of `Word_Document` if you wanted to. One character you need to avoid is the period (for obvious reasons).

5. Now we need to define some actions for this association. Click the New button. Fill out the information as shown in Figure 5.12. This is just one way to fill out this dialog box. WordPad uses a command-line interface, so all you need to do is fill out the Application Used to Perform Action section of the dialog box. Click OK.

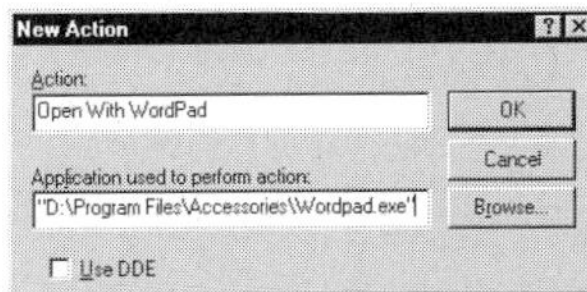

Figure 5.12.
This dialog box shows one type of file association entry. It uses command-line parameters.

6. Create the same kind of entry for Notepad. Be sure to substitute NOTEPAD.EXE for the location and change the path as necessary. Also change the Action to read Open with Notepad.
7. Click the New button. Fill out the information as shown in Figure 5.13. This second type of association might look overly complicated, but it really isn't. It's the DDE format of a file association and an extremely powerful way to manage your data files. The DDE instructions form what equates to macros. They actually force the application to perform the same types of tasks that you would accomplish by using a menu or the product's built-in macro capability. Chapter 12 discusses this topic at greater length. Right now, suffice it to say that if your application provides DDE support, you really owe it to yourself to use it. Click OK.

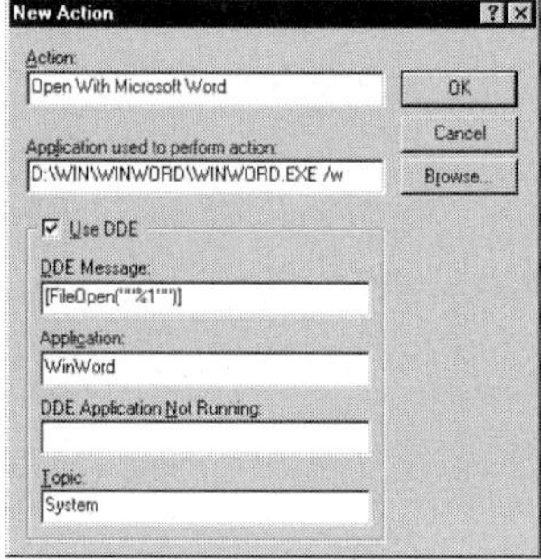

Figure 5.13.
This dialog box shows the second type of association you can create. This DDE entry allows you to include macro-like instructions that control the way the application opens or works with the file.

8. Create the DDE entry shown in Figure 5.14 to add some extra support for this new file association. This DDE macro allows you to print the file by using Microsoft Word.

Note: The DDE Application Not Running field is incomplete in the figure because it was too long to fit in the area provided. Here's the complete entry:

```
[FileOpen(""%1"")][FilePrint .Background = 0][FileExit(2)]
```

9. After you finish this entry, click OK. Your Add New File Type dialog box should now look like the one shown in Figure 5.15. Notice the two check boxes near the bottom of the dialog box. The second allows you to display the file extension at all times. Normally you would leave this off to make it easier to rename files in Explorer without accidentally changing their extensions. Because this is an ASCII file, you probably would turn on the first check box, Enable Quick View. This will allow you to use the Quick View utility provided with Windows 95.

Figure 5.14.
The previous example showed you how to open the file. This one shows you how to print it, using the same type of macro commands.

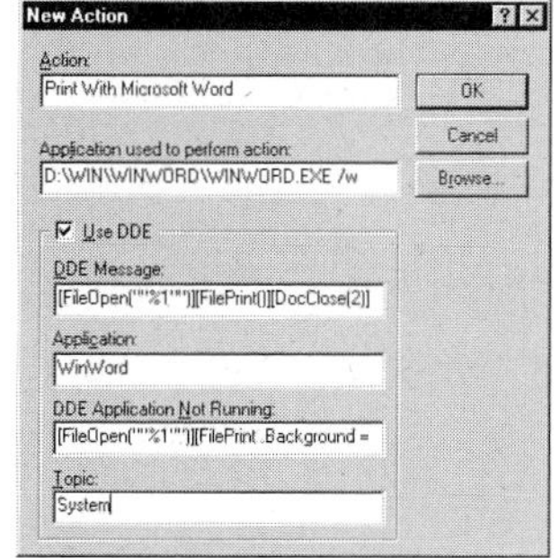

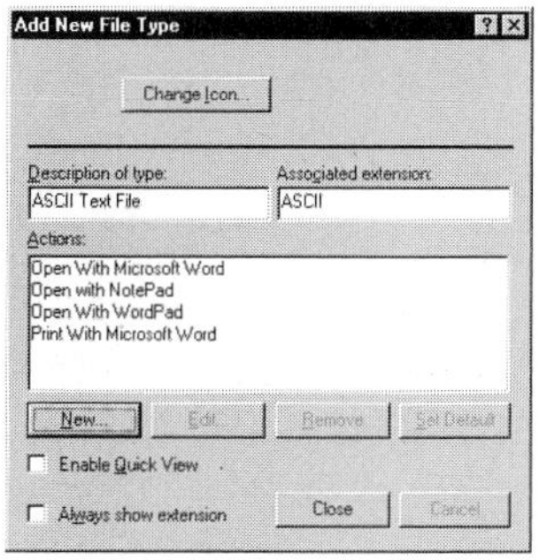

Figure 5.15.
Here are the completed entries for this Add New File Type dialog box.

Add New File Type
Change Icon...
Description of type: ASCII Text File
Associated extension: ASCII
Actions:
Open With Microsoft Word
Open with NotePad
Open With WordPad
Print With Microsoft Word
New... Edit... Remove Set Default
Enable Quick View
Always show extension
Close Cancel

10. Highlight Open with Notepad and click Set Default. This sets the double-click action for the file type. You can right-click to display the full context menu and use a different application to open the file, but this is the default action. You might also want to change the icon. I used the Notepad icon, but you could use any of those provided by the applications in this group or within an icon file. Click Close to complete the process. Click Close to close the Options dialog box.
11. Create a new file with an extension of .ASCII. I placed my copy on the desktop for sample purposes, but you could put your copy anywhere.
12. Right-click the file. You should see a list of opening options similar to the ones shown in Figure 5.16. Notice that Open with Notepad is highlighted, indicating that this entry is the default setting.

Figure 5.16.
The final result of the new file association is an extended context menu that allows any of three applications to open the file.

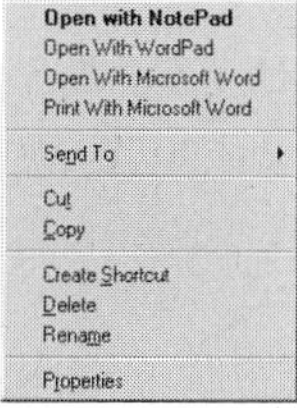

You could do a few additional things to really extend this new file association. Chapter 7 tells all about the Registry and the file association entries there. Pay special attention to the section "Special Extension Subkeys." Because we just added a new text-file entry to the list of file associations, you could use the Registry to add a ShellX entry to it as well. That way, when you right-click the desktop or within Explorer, you would see the new file extension as one of the files you could create by using the New option of the context menu. In most cases, there won't be a convenient method to add this support, but you should use it whenever possible.

This example also shows you something else. Productivity under Windows 95 is as much a matter of how you configure the desktop and the file associations as it is anything else. Being able to really use your machine's speed is what this data-centric approach to computing is all about.

Folders: A Real Organizational Tool

I really hate it when someone creates a new name for something I've been using for a long time. It's like throwing out a perfectly usable set of clothes because fashion has changed, or giving someone a new title in order to be politically correct. That's how I used to feel about the use of the term *folder* under Windows 95. As far as I was concerned, it was a new name for directories.

Nothing could be further from the truth. Folders aren't directories. They might look similar and provide about the same functionality when viewed from a certain perspective, but folders really do provide some features that directories don't. I'm still not as happy as I could be about the name switch, but at least it makes sense.

So how do folders help you work efficiently? Figure 5.17 shows one way. Folders support a context menu. Like most of the objects in Windows 95, you can open and explore folders. This isn't really all that surprising by now. I *was* a little surprised, however, when I saw that you could copy and paste folders just like any other object. Putting a group of files in a folder allows you to move an entire project from place to place or make a copy of the data for someone else to use. It's actually faster to use folders than it is to type the required commands at the DOS prompt—something I thought I would never see.

The Sharing option of the context menu allows you to share the folder with other folks on your network. Chapter 23 covers this feature in greater detail.

You'll find the Send To option very useful. This option allows you to place the folder somewhere else. Default locations include the floppy drives and your Briefcase. You can even send the folder to Microsoft Exchange. Imagine using e-mail to send the folder to a partner or coworker who needs to see the information you've put together so far. Unlike past experiences in which I had to get all the files together and zip them up, this option is fairly convenient and really makes the workflow smoother.

I use the Create Shortcut option to create a link to the existing file. Then I move the shortcut to my desktop or some other convenient place. Each shortcut uses 1KB of memory, a small price to pay for the convenience shortcuts provide.

Chapters 10 and 23 cover the Properties option in greater detail. For right now, suffice it to say that files and folders share many of the same characteristics. The Properties dialog box reflects this fact.

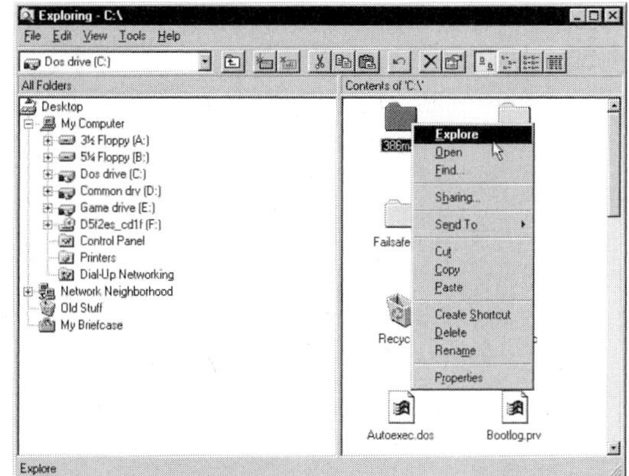

Figure 5.17.
The Folder context menu tells it all when it comes to the intelligence that this new form of directory possesses.

Desktop Tips and Techniques

I've gone to a totally data-centric approach on my desktop when it comes to projects. All I do is create a folder, give it a project name, and then gather shortcuts to everything I need for that project in that folder. It doesn't matter anymore where the data resides or what application I need to use to open the file. The only important element is that I have a data file that needs editing, so I open the project folder and double-click its icon.

This data-centric approach is very important for managers. Think about the time you'll save by putting one folder together, and then mailing that folder to all the people who have to work on it. You control the location of the data and the type of access these people have to it. They need to know only that the data exists and that they access it as needed. All the other information that you needed when working under DOS or Windows 3.x is no longer important.

Of course, like everything else under Windows 95, all is not perfect with the total data-centric approach. Even Microsoft agrees with me on this issue. They placed your Inbox, Recycle Bin, My Computer, and Network Neighborhood on the desktop for a reason. There are times when you need to open an application instead of a piece of data.

I keep my communications program handy on the desktop. I can't really access any of its data from outside the application. My database manager sits on the desktop too, but that's for a different reason. I use Access to design databases more often than I use it for data entry, so, for me, it's really more important to work with the application.

You'll probably run into situations in which the application is more important than the data. The bottom line is that you should try to work with the data first. If this proves to be an inconvenient solution, the data-centric approach probably isn't correct for that situation. The following is a list of some of the types of data I work with, using the project folder approach I just described. You'll probably have some of these applications, too:

- **Word processing:** Every word processor is designed to work primarily with data, so it makes a perfect candidate for the data-centric approach. Microsoft Word even appears on the New submenu of the context menu, so there isn't any problem with creating new files without entering the word processor first. There's one minor inconvenience here: Word always creates a new document using the Normal template. This means that if I use the context menu to create a new file, I'll probably have to change the template after I open the file. It's a minor flaw, but an irritating one all the same.
- **Spreadsheet:** I very seldom open just one spreadsheet. If I open one at all, I'm in there for hours. Therefore, I stick all my major files into a folder and place it on my desktop. That way, I can at least open a data file that will stay open throughout most of the editing session. I usually end up opening the other files I need in the usual way—using File | Open.
- **Graphics:** I work with quite a few different types of graphics, each of which requires its own application. Keeping the graphic files in a folder and opening them that way makes perfect sense. In fact, it's actually one of the application types that really made me see the value of a data-centric approach. By the way, this is one place where you'll really want to enable the Quick View option, if you haven't done so already. Most graphics files are time-consuming to load. Having Quick View handy for the files that it supports can really save time.

On Your Own

Try adding a shortcut to the Startup folder on your desktop. Tonight, place in that folder any work that you'll need to do tomorrow. Watch what happens when you start your machine tomorrow morning. You should get a desktop that has all the work you need to do loaded automatically.

Start separating your work into projects, if possible. Place each project in a separate folder on the desktop. Use separate folders, if necessary, to make it easier to find a particular kind of data. For example, you might need to place your graphics files in one subfolder to keep them from crowding the text files.

Look through your drives for data files that Windows 95 can't associate with a particular application. In Explorer, add any new file extensions that you might need, using the procedure discussed earlier. Check out each new association as you add it. Does the new addition work as anticipated? Evaluate the results you get after a few weeks, to see if you need to add more options to the data file's context menu.

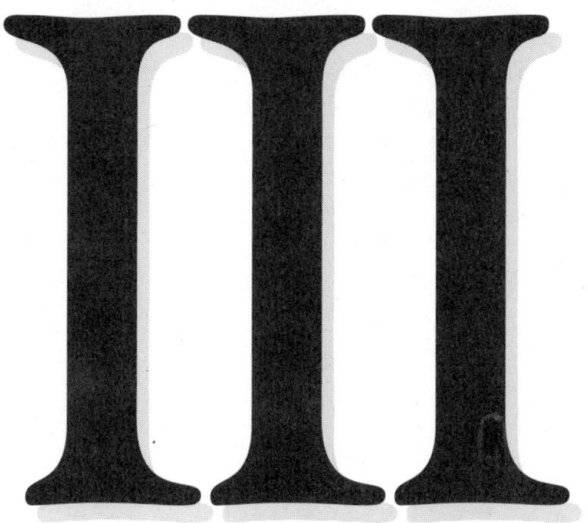

III Windows 95 Anatomy

6

The Windows 95 Architecture

Windows 95 uses an architecture that borrows from the past while embracing the future. Many of the components you've come to know and hate in Windows 3.x are still present in Windows 95. Some people think DOS has gone completely away, but it's still there under the covers. The 16-bit interface that gave us so much grief under Windows 3.x is still there, too.

That's the bad news. The good news is that the problems that plagued users in the past are a lot less noticeable under Windows 95. DOS isn't present at every turn—Windows 95 actually uses it very little once you start it up (depending on some very specific conditions that I explain later). The 16-bit interface is augmented by new 32-bit underpinnings. You can actually get some decent performance from Windows 95 and a moderate level of application protection as well. All these new features make Windows 95 better than Windows 3.x, but it's still far from the perfect operating system if reliability is your main concern.

Windows NT is the operating system that provides an entirely new way of doing things—few people would say that it shares the same stability problems that have made Windows 3.x almost unusable in mission-critical situations—but it falls short on one count. It just isn't as compatible as the average user needs it to be. Just try to play a DOS game using Windows NT, and you'll see what I mean. The types of security required to make Windows NT or any other operating system stable also prevent it from running some types of ill-behaved applications. Windows 95 represents a halfway point—you get some added stability and a new 32-bit capability, and still keep the compatibility that most people need to make Windows really work on a workstation.

The following sections examine the details of all these architectural wonders. I'll show you the great and the not-so-great components that make Windows 95 better than Windows 3.x ever thought of being, but a lot less than it could be. This chapter also provides a few additional glimpses of what Windows could become in the future. It's important to realize that, even with all its flaws, Windows 95 is a step in the right direction. It really does show how workstation operating systems will evolve in the future.

A Quick Look Inside

Learning about a new operating system usually includes knowing a bit about the components that comprise it. You don't start learning about DOS by knowing that there are two hidden files (MSDOS.SYS and IO.SYS) and one visible file (COMMAND.COM) that make up its core, but you do learn about them later. It doesn't take very long for most people to figure out some of the things that take place under DOS as well. An in-depth knowledge of interrupts and vector tables isn't required, but a basic knowledge of what takes place is needed. Just about every user spends some time learning about ancillary system files as well. Everyone knows about the DOS configuration files—AUTOEXEC.BAT and CONFIG.SYS—because you can't do much without them.

With this in mind, let's take a look at the Windows 95 architecture and some of the components that comprise it. We won't go into bits and bytes during this discussion. In fact, in this section, we barely scratch the surface of what Windows 95 contains. Still, you'll gain an appreciation of what goes on under the hood of this operating system. Having that knowledge can make it a lot easier to both configure and use Windows 95 effectively.

Peter's Principle: Nailing Down an Architecture

When you begin to look at the very first version of any operating system, it's fairly easy to nail down the precise set of components that make it up. That's what a study of operating system architecture is all about. It's for people who want to know what the various pieces are and how they work together to make up the operating system as a whole. Learning how the pieces go together can help in a variety of ways, such as when troubleshooting problems.

As companies begin to add various pieces to an operating system, the architecture gets a little harder to nail down in precise terms. Changing a device driver or enhancing the way Explorer works might be a good idea, but adding the update involves changing the way things work. Once the architectural changes begin to stack up, you can say that the operating system generally works in a certain way or provides an overview of the architecture as a whole, but providing precise details becomes very difficult. That's the situation Windows 95 is in now. It has been over a year since Microsoft released the first version and the architecture has changed. We look at the general architecture and some precise details in this book, but you may find that various components on your system work differently from what you see here.

For example, consider the network client used to access your Novell network. If you use the Microsoft client, you get one specific set of features; the Novell client works just a bit differently. (Chapter 27 discusses the pros and cons of using these two drivers.) Other major pieces of the architecture have the same problem: They work in a certain way based on which patches, drivers, and other components you've installed. As part of discussing various architectural elements, the following chapters look at the major architectural differences that you see when you install various options.

Drivers and enhancements aren't all that you face as you study the architecture. Another source of potential problems is all the upgrades that Microsoft has provided. There's the kernel upgrade that you can download as a separate file. It fixes a problem with using Internet Explorer. Service Pack 1 fixes problems to Windows 95 as a whole and adds a few feature updates. Service Release 2 adds new features to Windows 95, such as 32-bit FAT (file allocation table) support. Microsoft has also provided DirectX technology to game vendors, and a wealth of other patches almost too numerous to mention. All of these fixes to the operating system change its architecture—albeit only slightly. (To read more about the Service Pack and Service Release updates, check out the appropriate section in Chapter 1.)

What architectural changes don't you find in this book? I don't discuss many vendor-specific changes to Windows 95. To get an idea why, let's look at a simple example. I have a display adapter with no less than four different sets of drivers. If you were to extend this out to all of the hardware that's out there, you'd quickly figure out that we could be looking at literally hundreds of minor changes to the architecture. Obviously, I can't cover that many permutations in this book. Just as obviously, all these minor differences don't change the way that Windows 95 works as a whole—the graphics subsystem doesn't radically change when you update your display driver. What's the bottom line? It's important to remember what kind of setup you have and how those differences affect what you read here. While reading this book, you'll find out how Windows 95 works in a very specific way. However, when you look at any description of an operating system's architecture, you have to maintain a perspective of what that description tells you in a general sense, versus the realities of your specific hardware and software configuration.

Architecture

Several elements make up the Windows 95 architecture, as shown in Figure 6.1. Each element takes care of one part of the Windows environment. For example, the Windows API (Application Programming Interface) layer lets applications communicate with Windows internals such as the file management system. You couldn't write a Windows application without the API layer. I describe each of these main components in detail in the following sections.

The System Virtual Machine (VM) component of Windows 95 contains three main elements: 32-bit Windows applications, the shell, and 16-bit Windows applications. Essentially, the System VM component provides most of the Windows 95 user-specific functionality. Without it, you couldn't run any applications. Notice that I don't include DOS applications here; Windows uses an entirely different set of capabilities to run DOS applications. It even runs them in a different processor mode.

Two Windows APIs are included with Windows 95. The first API is exactly like the old one supplied with Windows 3.1. It provides all the 16-bit services that the old Windows had to provide for applications. An older 16-bit application will use this API when it runs. The other API is the new Win32 API used by Windows NT. It provides a subset of the features that all 32-bit applications running under Windows NT can access. The 32-bit API provides about the same feature set as the 16-bit API, but it's more robust. The next section explores both of these APIs as part of the system file discussion.

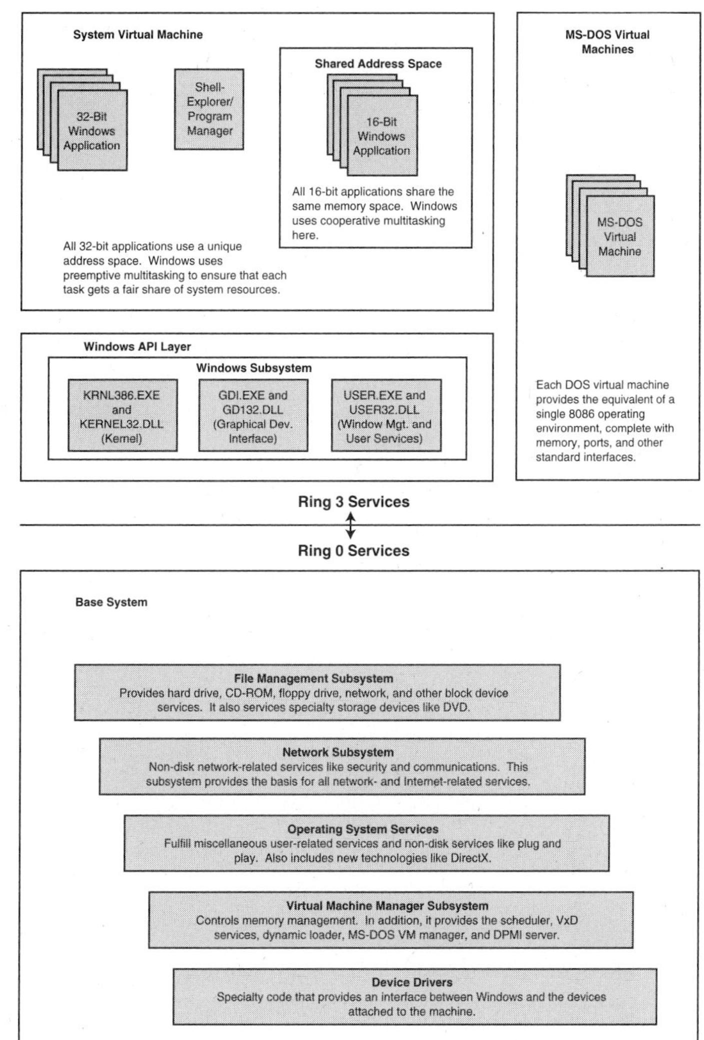

Figure 6.1.
Windows contains several major elements. Each element provides a different service to the user and to other applications running under Windows.

The Base System component of Windows 95 contains all the operating-system-specific services. This is the core of Windows 95, the part that has to be operating in order for Windows to perform its work. The following paragraphs describe each part of the Base System in detail:

- **File Management Subsystem:** This particular part of Windows 95 is examined in detail in the section "A Historical View of Windows" in Chapter 1. (Take a look at Chapter 9 as well, as it contains everything you need to know about the file system.) Essentially, this part of the Base System provides an interface to all the block devices connected to your machine. It doesn't matter how the connection is made—physically or through a network. All that matters is that your machine can access the device. The big thing to remember about the File Management Subsystem is that Windows 95 no longer relies on DOS to manage files.

- **Network Subsystem:** Windows for Workgroups was the first version of Windows to address the networking needs of the workgroup. It even incorporated networking as part of the operating system rather than as a third-party add-on product. Windows 95 extends this capability. Not only can you run a Microsoft peer-to-peer network, but Windows 95 provides protected-mode hooks for most major LAN products as well. In fact, you can keep more than one network active at a time. The modular nature of the Network Subsystem enables other vendors to add to Windows 95-inherent capabilities through the use of VxDs (look at the "Windows in 386 Enhanced Mode" section of Chapter 8 for an explanation of VxDs).
- **Operating System Services:** This is the part of the operating system that deals with features such as plug and play. Here you'll also find new Windows 95 capabilities such as DirectX (the new technology used by games and other programs requiring high-speed access to the hardware). The Operating System Services section also fulfills miscellaneous user and operating system requests. For example, every time the user asks Windows 95 for the time of day, he's requesting a service from this Windows 95 component.

Tip: The Operating System Services part of the Windows 95 base system is one area that has changed rapidly since its introduction. You might find that some applications refuse to run correctly until you install updates such as Service Pack 2 or the latest device driver. Other programs may require specialized updates such as the new DirectX 2.0 drivers. You can find all of these updates at `http://www.microsoft.com/kb/softlib/windows95.htm`. Be sure to check out the Miscellaneous Files and Utilities link at the bottom of the page. The page where it points contains some files that you won't find in other places. For example, one of the entries will help you update the OLE capabilities of Windows 95.

- **Virtual Machine Manager:** Ever wonder where the exact center of Windows 95 is? This is it; this is the component that holds everything else together. The Virtual Machine Manager takes care of task scheduling, and it starts and stops every application on the system (including any DOS applications that you might run). This operating system component manages virtual memory on your machine as well. Of course, your application uses the Windows API to make the request instead of talking directly with this part of the system. Because the Virtual Machine Manager handles all memory allocations, it also has to act as a DPMI (DOS protected-mode interface) server for DOS applications that run in protected mode. When a DOS application makes a memory request, it's actually calling routines in this component of Windows. As with Windows applications, DOS applications can't directly access this component of Windows. The DOS application uses a DOS extender API to make its call. Finally, the Virtual Machine Manager is responsible for intertask communication. All this means is that all DDE and OLE requests filter through this section of the operating system.

- **Device Drivers:** Windows would never know what to do with your system if not for the lowly device driver. This bit of specialty code acts as an interpreter. It takes Windows requests and provides them to the device in a format it can understand. Windows 95 supports two forms of device driver. The first type is the real-mode device driver that you used with Windows 3.1. The problem with using this type of driver is that Windows has to keep switching between real and protected mode to use it. Windows 95 also provides the VxD (virtual device driver), which lets Windows talk to the devices on your system without switching to real mode. There are three reasons to use VxDs over standard real-mode device drivers: Your system remains more stable, runs faster, and recovers from errors better.

I've separated the DOS Virtual Machine component of Windows from the other components for several reasons. DOS applications have formed the basis for using the PC for a long time. In fact, for many years, nothing else was available. Yet most of these applications were written at a time when the standard PC ran one application and one application only. That one application had total control of the entire machine.

Windows 95 deals with DOS applications differently than it deals with the Windows-specific applications on your machine. Each DOS application runs on what Intel terms a *virtual machine*. Essentially, the processor fools the application into thinking that it's the only application running on your machine at the moment. Each virtual machine has its own memory space and access to devices on the system. The amazing thing is that you can have many virtual machines running on your one physical machine at a time. We'll take a more detailed look at the DOS Virtual Machine later. Suffice it to say that Windows 95 has to literally perform backflips to make this whole concept work properly, especially when you consider Windows-hostile applications such as games.

This section gives you just a brief overview of the Windows 95 architecture. If you want a more in-depth view of the internal structure of Windows 95, look at the later section "Windows 95 Internals." It gives you a much more detailed look at how Windows 95 works as a whole.

The System Files

DOS programmers know you're supposed to gain access to the operating system using an interrupt service routine. These interrupts ask the operating system to perform a specific task. All the code for the interrupt routines appears in the system files. This old method worked well in the DOS single-tasking environment, where the application was in control. Under Windows, the user is in control, and the old system won't work properly. Every Windows application gains access to the operating system by using an API. Essentially, an API call does the same thing as an interrupt: It asks the operating system to perform a task. The code for the API appears in the system files, just as it does for DOS. Of course, this is a very simplified view of the API. An API is written using protected-mode code—unlike DOS, which is written in real-mode code. In addition, API code is reentrant; DOS code isn't. A reentrant piece of code allows Windows 95 to process more than one call at a time. Under DOS you couldn't reenter a piece of code—you had to complete one call at a time.

There are other differences, but the only people who really need to know about them are programmers. As discussed in the preceding section, Windows 95 actually uses two APIs—one 16-bit and one 32-bit.

DirectX—A Middle Road for Programmers

Anyone who plays games on the computer with any regularity understands the need for high-speed hardware. The entire gaming experience is built around fancy graphics and multimedia presentations. This kind of environment isn't very forgiving when it comes to processor cycles and definitely doesn't allow much room for the programmer to work. It isn't any wonder then that Microsoft had a problem trying to convince game programmers to take Windows seriously. After all, direct hardware access provides a much faster interface than using the Windows API.

Unfortunately, direct hardware access is out of the question when using Windows. Unless the operating system knows exactly what's going on with all the hardware all the time, there isn't any way for it to provide access to more than one application. As far as game vendors were concerned, there wasn't any way for Windows to support games of any complexity under these conditions.

DirectX is a middle ground. It gives a game programmer (or anyone else, for that matter) a higher-speed interface than Windows normally provides, without taking Windows itself out of the loop. Windows still monitors the events taking place when using DirectX, but it provides a lot less in the way of support. DirectX technology provides the means for a programmer to access the hardware, without damaging the Windows multitasking environment.

It may sound like DirectX is a perfect solution. After all, both sides of the equation get what they want. There are a few problems, though, and you need to decide whether you want to live with them. The biggest problem right now is that DirectX is evolving. That means that you might get a piece of software that doesn't work even if you have DirectX installed, because the software is written to a newer standard. DirectX also causes compatibility problems on some machines when used in certain ways. In other words, there isn't any guarantee that a DirectX application will work all the time if the game vendor didn't follow the specifications to the letter (and even then there isn't the best guarantee).

At best, DirectX represents a partial solution to a problem that people have had with Windows. It allows the programmer direct access to the hardware with a minimum of interference from Windows. Before installing it on your machine, obviously, you need to carefully weigh the pros and cons of using DirectX. More importantly, you need to find out whether the software you're installing uses DirectX in the first place. When troubleshooting graphics problems with a particular piece of software, ask yourself whether DirectX might be the source of your problem.

The big news under Windows 95 is the 32-bit API. Not only are 32-bit system calls a lot more logical from a programmer's point of view (Windows 3.x was a programmer's nightmare; Windows 95 is merely an inconvenience), but they also provide many more features. In addition, a 32-bit application enjoys the benefits that this environment provides. Of course, the biggest benefit that you'll hear most programmers talk about is the flat memory address space. Every application running under Windows—until now—has had to spend time working with Intel's segmented address scheme. A 32-bit application doesn't need to worry about segmentation any more. Every call is a near call; every call is in a single segment.

No matter which API you use, your application will address three basic components. The 16-bit versions of these files are GDI.EXE, USER.EXE, and KRNL386.EXE. The 32-bit versions of these files are GDI32.DLL, USER32.DLL, and KERNEL32.DLL. The following list describes these three components in detail:

- **Windows kernel (KRNL386.EXE or KERNEL32.DLL):** This is the part of Windows 95 that provides support for the lower-level functions that an application needs to run. For example, every time your application needs memory, it runs to the Windows kernel to get it. This component doesn't deal with either the interface or devices; it interacts only with Windows itself.
- **Graphical Device Interface (GDI.EXE or GDI32.DLL):** Every time an application writes to the screen, it's using a GDI service. This Windows component takes care of fonts, printer services, the display, color management, and every other artistic aspect of Windows that users can see as they use your application.
- **User (USER.EXE or USER32.DLL):** Windows is all about just that—windows. It needs a manager to keep track of all the windows that applications create to display various types of information. However, User only begins there. Every time your application displays an icon or button, it's using some type of User component function. It's easier to think of the User component of the Windows API as a work manager; it helps you organize things and keep them straight.

There's actually one more piece to the Windows API, but it's a small piece that your application will never use. Windows 95 still starts out as a 16-bit application so that it can implement plug and play. The plug and play BIOS contains separate sections for real-mode and 16-bit protected-mode calls. If Windows 95 started out in 32-bit mode, it couldn't call the plug and play BIOS to set up all your devices without a lot of overhead (to understand why, see the later section "Getting 16-Bit and 32-Bit Applications to Work Together"). All device configuration has to occur before Windows actually starts the GUI.

However, 16-bit mode operations end very soon after you start Windows 95. The user shell is a 32-bit application. When the 16-bit kernel sees the call for the shell, it loads an application called VWIN32.386. This little program loads the three 32-bit DLLs that form the Win32 API. Once it completes this task, VWIN32.386 returns control to the 16-bit kernel, which in turn calls the 32-bit kernel. Windows runs in 32-bit mode from that point on.

The Plug and Play BIOS

Plug and play (PNP) is big news for Windows 95. The first misconception that I want to clear up is that this is some new piece of "magic" that Microsoft pulled from its bag of tricks. PNP isn't magic, nor is it even all that new. The only thing that Windows 95 does differently is actually use the capabilities provided by PNP hardware.

Let's go back a bit. The very first MCA (microchannel architecture) machine produced by IBM contained everything needed by PNP except one thing—an operating system. The same can be said of many EISA machines.

The problem wasn't simply a matter of adding some capabilities to an operating system. You have to build this feature into every aspect of the operating system; it can't be added on. You also need routines that will handle problems between the various pieces of hardware vying for a particular port address or interrupt. Finally, the BIOS itself has to provide a standardized interface, and these earlier offerings were anything but standard.

PNP is actually the work of three system components: hardware, BIOS, and operating system. The BIOS queries all the system components during startup. It activates essential system components such as the disk drive and display adapter. Everything else waits on the sidelines until the operating system boots. During the boot process, the operating system finishes the task of assigning interrupts and port addresses to every system component. It also asks the BIOS to provide a list of previous assignments so that it won't use them again.

The EISA and MCA BIOS weren't prepared for this kind of interaction with the operating system. Enter the PNP BIOS. This isn't the work of Microsoft, but of Compaq Computer Corporation, Phoenix Technologies Ltd., and Intel Corporation.

In addition to cooperating with the operating system, the PNP BIOS provides something very important that the EISA and MCA BIOS don't—protected-mode routines. The current BIOS specification only requires vendors to provide 16-bit protected-mode routines. That's why Windows 95 still starts in 16-bit mode instead of 32-bit mode. In addition, that's one of the reasons why a real-mode DOS stub (a functional subset of the DOS that you're familiar with) is part of the picture. (The version of real-mode DOS provided with Windows 95 also executes AUTOEXEC.BAT and CONFIG.SYS, but we'll look into that aspect later.) You can't use the protected-mode routines without first gathering the information that the BIOS needs in real mode. The real-mode DOS stub performs this function for the BIOS.

Tip: A few "used car salesman" type of people out there will try to convince you that their systems are fully PNP-compatible. If you look inside, you'll see shiny new components, all of which are indeed PNP-compatible. But, unbeknownst to you, something is missing. A lot of folks find out too late that their system lacks a PNP BIOS. So how can you avoid the same fate?

Intel, inspired by the PNP BIOS problems, created a test utility to check your PNP BIOS. You can download a copy of this BIOS test program from the plug and play forum (GO PLUGPLAY) on CompuServe. Look in Library 6 for BIOTST.ZIP. You might want to check out BIO10A.DOC (BIO1A.ZIP) while you're at it. This specification talks about the capabilities of the plug and play BIOS. It also provides some information about the peripheral board setup.

When looking at a PNP-compatible system, you should see a lot more than just three different entities cooperating to provide automatic system configuration. PNP wouldn't be worth all the hubbub if that's all it provided. The following paragraphs provide a list of additional features that you get as part of a PNP system.

- **Identify installed devices:** Windows 95 automatically detects all the plug and play components attached to your system. This means that you need to provide a minimum of information during installation and nothing at all during subsequent reboots. Contrast this with the almost continuous flow of information needed under Windows 3.1.
- **Determine device resource needs:** Every device on your computer needs resources in the form of processor cycles, input/output ports, DMA channels, memory, and interrupts. Windows 95 works with the BIOS and peripheral devices to meet these needs without any intervention.
- **Automatic system configuration updates and resource conflict detection:** All this communication between peripheral devices, the BIOS, and the operating system allows Windows 95 to create a system configuration without any user intervention. The Device Manager configuration blocks are grayed out because the user doesn't need to supply this information anymore. The enhanced level of communication also allows Windows 95 to poll the peripherals for alternative port and interrupt settings when a conflict with another device occurs.
- **Device driver loading and unloading:** CONFIG.SYS and AUTOEXEC.BAT used to contain line after line of device driver and TSR statements, because the system had to bring these devices online before it loaded the command processor and Windows 3.1. Windows 95 can actually maintain or even enhance the performance of a plug and play-compatible system without using an AUTOEXEC.BAT or CONFIG.SYS. Plug and play compatibility allows Windows 95 to dynamically load and unload any device drivers that your system needs.
- **Configuration change notification:** Plug and play might make system configuration changes automatic, but that doesn't mean that Windows 95 leaves you in the dark. Every time the system configuration changes, Windows 95 notifies you by displaying a dialog box on-screen. Essentially, this dialog box tells you what changed. This capability provides an

additional side benefit. Windows 95 also notifies you whenever your equipment experiences some kind of failure. When a piece of equipment fails, Windows 95 notices that it's no longer online. Plug and play requires three-way communication, and a defective device usually fails to communicate. Instead of your finding out that you no longer have access to a drive or other device when you need it most, Windows 95 notifies you of the change immediately after it takes place.

Windows 95 Compatibility Configuration Files

There's no doubt about it: Windows 95 starts by booting DOS. You can even gain access to this "raw" DOS (as Microsoft calls it) using a variety of methods—some sanctioned, some not. Microsoft had to provide the four compatibility files that older applications need in order to run. Some of these files are easy to bypass; others won't go away until you get rid of all those applications. Part of the reason DOS is still hanging around is because of these compatibility files. Windows 95 has to boot using real mode so that it can read and process both CONFIG.SYS and AUTOEXEC.BAT. There are other reasons that Windows 95 boots into real mode, examined later in this chapter.

The following sections take an in-depth look at the four compatibility files: AUTOEXEC.BAT, CONFIG.SYS, SYSTEM.INI, and WIN.INI. I'll show you that even though Microsoft doesn't want to admit it, Windows 95 still needs at least one of these files to work properly. Fortunately, you really only need this one compatibility file—SYSTEM.INI—to run Windows 95. The other files are there for compatibility purposes only.

Note: You could probably boot Windows 95 without keeping any of the four compatibility files and expect it to work sometimes. The majority of your 16-bit applications wouldn't run, because they couldn't find the information stored in the compatibility files. A lot of Windows applications also require that the PATH statement contain an entry that points to their files. Even if you avoid running any 16-bit applications, it's unlikely that you'll keep Windows 95 running for very long without SYSTEM.INI. For reasons I don't understand, there are still system settings that Microsoft chose to store there. These system settings are important to Windows 95, no matter which applications you decide to run.

AUTOEXEC.BAT

This is the one file you could get rid of if you didn't have any 16-bit Windows applications that required a PATH statement. Windows 95 provides the means for defining a path and a prompt and loading any TSRs that a DOS application might require to run. The most efficient way to use Windows 95 is not to load anything a DOS application would need here.

Use AUTOEXEC.BAT only for settings you need on a global basis or as part of the requirement for running an older Windows application. Some 16-bit Windows applications require `SET` and `PATH` entries to run. This is especially true of compilers and advanced applications.

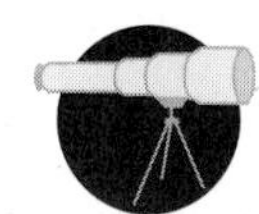

Looking Ahead: Chapter 13 looks at how you can replace both CONFIG.SYS and AUTOEXEC.BAT for DOS applications. If your only reason for keeping these two files around is so you can run DOS applications, consider the faster alternative presented here.

The following list contains a few things you should never run from AUTOEXEC.BAT. Most of these items consume memory before you load Windows—memory you can't retrieve later. Using this technique might cost you a little conventional memory for your DOS applications, but you'll still have about the same or perhaps even more than you had available under Windows 3.x. The reason for this is simple: You don't have to load a bunch of drivers in CONFIG.SYS to make Windows 95 run.

- **TSRs:** Try to avoid running any TSRs from AUTOEXEC.BAT. A small utility such as DOSKey might not appear to consume much memory, but why run it from AUTOEXEC.BAT at all? You can easily customize the settings for your DOS applications. Those that will never use DOSKey don't need to give up the memory required to install it. In essence, loading a TSR in AUTOEXEC.BAT penalizes the applications that can't use it.
- **DOS application environment variables:** If you have a DOS application that requires a `PATH` entry or other environmental variables, load them as part of its special configuration rather than as part of AUTOEXEC.BAT. You can individually adjust the size of the environment for each DOS application you run.
- **DOS applications with Windows counterparts:** I used to run `CHKDSK` as part of every startup cycle. A lot of other people do the same thing. Running some DOS applications before you enter Windows doesn't harm the amount of memory you have available one iota. Running other applications can consume memory. For example, if you run `MODE` to change your screen size to 43 lines before you enter Windows, every DOS program you load will consume 43 lines worth of memory (more if you ask for a larger screen in the custom settings). You can reduce the memory required for each DOS session by using the application's custom screen settings.
- **Disk- or printer-caching software:** You'll find that the Windows 95 disk- and print-caching services are far superior to those provided with Windows 3.x. The memory allocated to these services is dynamic—Windows 95 can increase and decrease the amount of memory used as needed—as long as you use the Windows 95-specific capability. When you load disk- or print-caching software in AUTOEXEC.BAT, you lose the ability to

control the size of that cache within Windows (in most cases). Even if you could change the size of the cache, it's unlikely that Windows 95 could use it, unless the caching program is specially designed to communicate with Windows.

CONFIG.SYS

Unless you're still playing Russian roulette with those real-mode drivers on your system, you can get rid of CONFIG.SYS. Windows 95 provides its own extended memory manager (EMM), so it doesn't need one loaded like Windows 3.x did. Windows 95 also takes care of the `BUFFERS`, `LASTDRIVE`, and `STACKS` entries for you. In other words, CONFIG.SYS is out of a job unless you give it one.

I recently threw caution to the wind and tried booting my system for several days with a pared-down AUTOEXEC.BAT and no CONFIG.SYS. Not only did I notice a speed increase when loading Windows, but I also had far greater control over the settings for each individual DOS setting. Windows also could provide much better memory control than before. (I used the System Monitor utility described in Chapter 3 to check all this out.)

I had to deal with a few negatives, however. Getting rid of CONFIG.SYS lost me about 5KB of conventional memory. I still have 600KB of RAM available in a DOS window, though, so the memory loss is pretty minimal. I could probably get even more available memory by decreasing the environment size and not loading DOSKey as part of my custom settings. It also cost me some time to set up each of my DOS applications. The greater flexibility and better memory management came at the cost of increased complexity. Even though there were negative elements, I'd still say it was worth the effort.

Tip: In the past, users with large hard drives usually resorted to using special drivers like those from OnTrack Systems to access their entire drive, using one partition. You can still do this under Windows 95 with relatively good success. However, such an action will destabilize your system. The reason is clear: Every time Windows needs to access the drive, it has to switch to real mode to access the real-mode driver. It's probably a better idea to partition your drive into more manageable partition sizes and get rid of the real-mode drivers if at all possible.

WIN.INI

Windows 95 can get along just fine without WIN.INI. However, before you get rid of your file, you might want to check it out first. A few applications, especially screen savers, load themselves by using the `LOAD=` or `RUN=` lines of this file. You can get around this limitation by adding the filenames to your Startup folder and changing the application settings as needed.

Many applications also store their file association information here. Windows 95 applications don't need these entries, because they already appear in the Registry. Any new 32-bit applications will know to look in the Registry for file association information, but some older 16-bit applications won't. You might want to check for problems by saving a copy of WIN.INI under a different name and then editing out the `[Extensions]` section. If all your applications seem to work properly, you might be able to remove this section for good.

Note: Windows 95 always checks for new entries in both WIN.INI and SYSTEM.INI. It automatically adds any new entries that it finds to the appropriate section of the Registry. This is why you can get rid of these two files if you have a stable system and none of the 16-bit applications that you use relies on them. Of course, that's a big if, and you still have the mysterious Windows 95 problem with SYSTEM.INI to deal with. In reality, you probably need to wait until you've gotten rid of all your 16-bit applications before you can get rid of these two files.

If you look through the Windows 95 version of WIN.INI, you'll notice that it's a lot slimmer. Microsoft moved all the Windows-specific information that this file contained into the Registry. Windows 95 doesn't use it at all. In fact, if you compare the contents of the Registry to a Windows 3.x version of WIN.INI, you'll find every entry that the old file contained.

SYSTEM.INI

Getting rid of SYSTEM.INI will take a major miracle. Just about every application on my machine sticks something in there. Even Microsoft still uses this file—though Microsoft swears otherwise. Most of these settings have become so standard that other applications read the file in anticipation of finding out about the environment.

Of course, this is one source of the problem. Getting rid of SYSTEM.INI or even excluding some of the settings would break a lot of applications out there. Part of the goal of Windows 95 is to provide the compatibility people need out of a workstation. Windows NT is the place to go if you need reliability and stability. Microsoft probably made the right call by keeping SYSTEM.INI in place and up-to-date.

Note: Microsoft is spending a great deal of time telling programmers not to place anything in SYSTEM.INI anymore. The Registry is the new way to store all these settings. A quick look at SYSTEM.INI, though, shows some Windows 95-specific information there. For example, look near the bottom of the file and you'll see entries for passwords and VCache. These two entries don't appear in Windows 3.x-specific versions of the file.

A Look at the Windows 95 Boot Sequence

Getting your machine up and running after you turn on the power is called the *boot process*. It includes everything from the time that the power-on startup test (POST) routines begin until the time you can start to use the machine. Under DOS, this boot process was relatively straightforward. Windows 95 requires something a bit more exotic, because we expect it to do more.

The next few sections look at the boot process from a user's perspective. This means that you won't get a blow-by-blow "this bit does this and that byte does that" explanation. We just look at the highlights of the boot process.

Tip: If you ever want to see a blow-by-blow description of the entire boot process, look at BOOTLOG.TXT in the root directory of your boot drive. This file records every action that Windows 95 performs during the boot process. However, it doesn't include a few of the initial actions such as loading IO.SYS. At most, three or four actions take place before the log starts, though, so your chances of missing anything important are almost nonexistent.

Starting at the DOS Prompt

Windows 95 doesn't (as some people think) start the boot process in protected mode. It actually starts up a copy of DOS. The difference is that the copy of DOS it uses isn't the same as the one you used in the past. Even the system files are different.

The whole reason for starting DOS (at least the one that Microsoft sort of admits to) is for compatibility purposes. All those machines with older hardware still need to run device drivers and the like from CONFIG.SYS and AUTOEXEC.BAT. Something has to read those files and act on their contents in a way that the drivers can understand.

Your system starts just like it always has. Installing Windows 95 doesn't stop the system from performing POST. Once the ROM BIOS determines that your machine is working correctly, it takes care of any required hardware initialization and builds a vector table in lower memory. The vector table contains pointers to all the BIOS routines so that DOS can use them later as part of its boot process. Once this initialization phase is over, the BIOS looks for a bootable drive. A bootable drive contains an operating system loader. In the case of both DOS and Windows 95, that loader will look for a file called IO.SYS.

Up to this point, the workings of DOS and Windows 95 are precisely the same. However, unlike the old version of DOS, everything that the new version needs in the way of code appears in the IO.SYS file. The old MSDOS.SYS file is no longer required. Microsoft combined the contents of the two files that used to appear in your root directory into one.

By now you're looking at your drive and noticing that there's still an MSDOS.SYS file. The MSDOS.SYS file now contains important boot configuration information. You can include a lot of different configuration switches here. Most of them aren't essential, but some are. Figure 6.2 shows the shortest MSDOS.SYS that most people can get by with. Notice that there's a special section that contains what looks like junk. Actually, it *is* junk. MSDOS.SYS must contain more than 1,024 bytes for compatibility reasons.

Figure 6.2.
MSDOS.SYS doesn't have to contain a lot of information, but what it does contain is very important. These "switches" help configure Windows 95 during the DOS portion of the boot process.

Note: MSDOS.SYS is a hidden, read-only file on your boot drive. You can use the `ATTRIB` command to remove these attributes and edit the file from the DOS prompt. An easier way is to right-click the file in Explorer, use the Properties dialog box to remove the file attributes, and edit it using Notepad.

Figuring out what these entries mean is pretty straightforward in most cases. The main thing to remember is that they all affect how your system boots. If you remember this, you won't have too many problems. The minimalistic MSDOS.SYS shown in Figure 6.2 doesn't give you any idea of the types of things you do with it, though. Table 6.1 provides a complete description of all the entries you can put in it.

Table 6.1. Configuration switches for MSDOS.SYS.

Switch	*Description*
	`[Paths]` *Section*
`HostWinBootDrv=C`	This switch tells Windows 95 where to find the host (Windows 95) boot drive. This isn't the same as the physical boot drive; it's the drive that contains the Windows 95 files. The default is drive C.
`WinBootDir=C:\WIN95`	All the Windows 95 executable files appear in the directory you provide here. Setup automatically places the installation drive here. If you ever move Windows 95 to a different directory, you'll need to change this setting.
`WinDir=C:\WIN95`	Use this switch to define the Windows 95 directory. It should be the same as the `WinBootDir` setting.
	`[Options]` *Section*
`BootDelay=2`	Windows 95 provides a dual-boot capability that allows you to use your old setup if you want to do so. All you need to do is press F4 when you see that POST is finished. Pressing F8 during this time displays the Safe Boot options. (I examine this feature later.) This setting changes the delay that Windows 95 provides for pressing either of these two function keys. The default setting is 2 seconds. Add an entry of `0` if you want to disable the delay.
`BootFailSafe=0`	This switch allows you to bypass the Save Boot option screen unless you really need it after a failed boot. Normally you'll want to boot Windows in a regular mode. However, if you write software or for some reason need to fully control how Windows loads, set this value to `1`.
`BootGUI=1`	If you'd rather boot to DOS 7.0 (or raw DOS, as Microsoft calls it), set this switch to `0`. You can still start Windows by typing `WIN` as before.
`BootKeys=1`	System administrators will really like this switch. Setting it to `0` disables all the startup keys, such as F8, that a user could use to bypass your security measures. However, this isn't a perfect solution. The user can still get past security with a boot disk and an editor, but at least this adds a little extra protection.
`BootMenu=0`	Set this switch to `1` if you want to see the Windows 95 boot menu. Essentially, this is the same menu you get when you press F8.
`BootMenuDefault=1` or `3`	This switch changes the default boot menu option. It normally defaults to `1`. If your system experienced a failure of some kind, the boot menu defaults to `3`.

Switch	*Description*
`BootMenuDelay=30`	Use this switch to change the number of seconds that Windows 95 displays the boot menu before it executes the default option. The default setting is `30`.
`BootMulti=0`	Setup normally doesn't include this switch in MSDOS.SYS. It allows you to add dual-boot capabilities to your system. Pressing F4 at the `Starting Windows` prompt (right after POST is finished) allows you to boot your previous version of DOS if it's still intact.
`BootWarn=1`	This switch enables the Safe Mode startup warning and menu.
`BootWin=1`	If you use DOS 5 or 6 as your primary operating system and you want to use Windows 95 only on an experimental basis for now, this switch is a must. It allows you to boot your old operating system as a default, instead of Windows 95.
`DblSpace=1`	You can disable automatic loading of DBLSPACE.BIN by setting this switch to `0`.
`DoubleBuffer=0`	This switch tells Windows 95 whether a SCSI controller needs a double-buffering driver loaded. Setting this value to `1` enables double buffering.
`DrvSpace=1`	You can disable automatic loading of DRVSPACE.BIN by setting this switch to `0`.
`LoadTop=1`	Use this switch to tell Windows 95 whether you want to load COMMAND.COM or DRVSPACE.BIN at the top of 640KB memory. The default setting does load these items at the top of memory. However, you might need to set the switch to `0` if you experience network-related problems. This is especially true for Novell NetWare.
`Logo=1`	If you aren't all that thrilled with the logo that Windows 95 displays during the boot process, you can set this switch to `0`. This also keeps Windows 95 from grabbing some interrupts that might cause conflicts with some memory managers.
`Network=0`	Setting this switch to `0` tells Windows 95 not to install any network components. Use a value of `1` to enable the Safe Mode with Networking menu option.

IO.SYS reads the contents of MSDOS.SYS as part of the pre-booting cycle. Think of MSDOS.SYS as a configuration file for the boot process, because that's exactly what it is. After IO.SYS configures itself, using the contents of MSDOS.SYS, it reads the contents of CONFIG.SYS (if there is one).

There's no longer a need for CONFIG.SYS, because IO.SYS has several features added to it. The following list tells you everything you need to know about these new settings:

- `DOS=HIGH,UMB`: IO.SYS always loads DOS high unless you override this setting in CONFIG.SYS.
- `HIMEM.SYS`: IO.SYS always loads a copy of the real-mode memory manager. It doesn't load EMM386.EXE. You need to load this from CONFIG.SYS if you plan to run an application that requires expanded memory without going into Windows first.
- `IFSHLP.SYS` (installable file system helper): Loading this device driver also loads several others. It gives you full access to the file system.
- `SETVER.EXE`: Some of your older applications might require a specific version of DOS. This program fools them into thinking that the version of DOS provided with Windows 95 is the one they need.
- `FILES=60`: Windows 95 doesn't require this setting. It's provided for any MS-DOS applications that you might run. Some older applications require more than 60 file handles, but this setting should work for the majority of installations.
- `LASTDRIVE=Z`: This sets the last drive letter you can use for your DOS applications. As with the `FILES` setting, Windows 95 doesn't require a `LASTDRIVE` setting.
- `BUFFERS=30`: The `BUFFERS` setting affects the number of file buffers that IO.SYS provides. Windows 95 uses its own file management system and is unaffected by this setting.
- `STACKS=9,256`: IO.SYS sets up a specific number of stack frames, using this entry. Each stack frame is the same size.
- `SHELL=COMMAND.COM /P`: If you don't specify another command processor in CONFIG.SYS, IO.SYS defaults to using COMMAND.COM, just as it always has. The `/P` parameter makes the command processor permanent.
- `FCBS=4`: Ancient programs used file control blocks. These programs are so old that I really can't believe anyone would still have them lying around. You can provide additional FCBs by overriding this setting in CONFIG.SYS.

As you can see, IO.SYS comes with a fairly complete CONFIG.SYS built in. Once IO.SYS loads the command processor, its job is finished for the time being. The command processor takes over and reads the contents of AUTOEXEC.BAT. At this point, you're running DOS. You might not see a DOS prompt, but that's because Microsoft hides it behind a logo.

Loading the 16-Bit Core

After the command processor completes its work, a new phase in the boot process begins. You might wonder why Windows 95, a 32-bit operating system, would even think about starting in 16-bit mode. There are several interesting reasons.

One reason has to do with the way the plug and play BIOS specification is written. The current specification requires a vendor to provide a 16-bit protected-mode interface. This allows an operating system vendor such as Microsoft to check the plug and play hardware without switching to real mode. The result is a much more stable operating system that (supposedly) always runs in protected mode.

The first thing Windows has to do once you start it is to check the status of all the hardware. It calls on the plug and play BIOS to provide it with a list of all the installed equipment. Windows uses this information to configure the system. Of course, it also has to take any non-plug and play peripherals into account as well. Once it comes up with a configuration list, Windows 95 starts to load all the 16-bit VxDs required to support that hardware.

What precisely is a VxD? It's a virtual device driver, the protected-mode version of the device drivers you used under DOS. However, it's more than that, because a device can be a lot more than just a piece of hardware under Windows 95. To avoid getting into the bits and bytes of device management, let's just say that Windows uses virtual device drivers to manage all its low-level functions.

Once it completes this step, Windows initializes all those drivers. It starts with the system drivers—all the drivers required to make the low-level functions in Windows work (such as the file system drivers). The device drivers come next.

At this point, Windows 95 loads the three 16-bit shell components: USER.EXE, GDI.EXE, and KRNL386.EXE. It also loads some additional drivers and a few other components, such as fonts. Now Windows 95 is completely up and running in 16-bit mode. It doesn't have an interface yet, but every other component is present.

Loading the 32-Bit Core

The preceding section ended with a copy of Windows running in 16-bit mode without any form of user interface. 16-bit mode operations end very soon after you start Windows 95. The user shell, Explorer, is a 32-bit application. As soon as the 16-bit kernel sees the call for the shell, it loads an application called VWIN32.386. This little program loads the three 32-bit DLLs that form the Win32 API: USER32.DLL, GDI32.DLL, and KERNEL32.DLL. Once it completes this task, VWIN32.386 returns control to the 16-bit kernel, which in turn calls the 32-bit kernel. Windows runs in 32-bit mode from that point on.

Now that it's operating in 32-bit mode, the operating system loads and initializes all the 32-bit drivers. This is the same process that the 16-bit part of the operating system performed, so I won't discuss it again here.

Somewhere in all this, Windows 95 asks the user to provide some input in the form of a name and password (if you've enabled this feature). It checks this against the contents of the appropriate .PWL file. If the password checks out, Windows 95 completes the boot process.

Finally, Windows gets the Explorer interface up and running (it was loaded before but wasn't running). It displays all the required objects on the desktop and initializes the Taskbar. This is the point where it also looks at your Startup folder to see which applications you want to start automatically. You're set up and ready to compute.

Cooperative Versus Preemptive Multitasking

Multitasking is one of those nebulous words that everyone uses but no one takes the time to define. The first thing you need to do before you can understand multitasking is to define the word *task*. A task is essentially an application that's running. When you start Windows, you might think that nothing is running, but there are already several applications getting work done on your machine. For example, Explorer (or Program Manager) is considered a task. Any network connections or print spoolers are considered tasks. A screen saver is yet another task. There are numerous system-related tasks as well. The Windows kernel is considered a task. The industry uses two terms to refer to a running application or thread: process and task. I prefer *task* because it's a little less nebulous than *process*. However, you'll probably see a mixture of both in the documentation you read.

When talking about Windows 3.1, you can associate every task with a single application. The definition of *task* doesn't really stop here for Windows 95 and Windows NT. Some 32-bit applications use a technique called *multithreading*, which enables them to perform more than one task at a time. For example, you could recalculate your spreadsheet and print at the same time if the application supports multithreading. What happens is that the spreadsheet starts a task (called a *thread*) to take care of printing. It might even start a second thread to do the recalculation, so that you can continue to enter data. One way to look at threads is as a subtask under the application that's running.

Now that you understand what a task is, it's time to look at the definition of multitasking. Everyone assumes that multitasking is just that—several tasks (or processes) running simultaneously on one machine. This is a good start for a definition, but it doesn't end there. An important consideration is how the operating system allocates time between tasks. When talking about Windows, it becomes very important to define the method used to manage tasks and to differentiate between different kinds of multitasking. Windows 95 supports two kinds of multitasking: cooperative and preemptive.

Windows 3.0 introduced a feature called *cooperative multitasking*. This is how it was supposed to work: Application A would run for a little while, just long enough to get one component of a task finished. It would then turn control of the system back over to Windows so that Windows could take care of any housekeeping chores and allow application B to run for a while. This cycle continued in a round-robin fashion between all the tasks running at any given time.

What really happened is that some applications followed the rules but others didn't. Under cooperative multitasking, the operating system gave up too much control; an application could hog all the system resources if it wanted to do so. Some applications do just that. The result is that cooperative multitasking doesn't really work all that well. Most of the time that the user spends looking at the hourglass is really time in which Windows has temporarily lost control of the system to an application that doesn't want to share with anyone else.

All the legacy applications that run under Windows 95—the 16-bit applications that you moved from Windows 3.x—still have to run in a cooperative multitasking mode. However, Windows 95 minimizes the impact of these applications by running them in one shared address space. All the 16-bit applications have to cooperate with each other, but they don't affect any 32-bit applications running on your machine. This includes Explorer and any other Windows 95-specific tools. (And, of course, you will upgrade most of your commonly-used 16-bit applications, such as your word processor and spreadsheet, to Windows 95 versions. Right?)

In designing Windows NT, Microsoft wanted something better than cooperative multitasking, and designed an operating system that uses preemptive multitasking. Windows 95 supports preemptive multitasking for any 32-bit application you run. Think of it this way: Preemptive multitasking works like a traffic light. Traffic goes one way for a while, but then the light changes and traffic goes the other way. The amount of time each task gets is weighed by the user and the operating system to meet some criteria, but this access is supposed to be fair. Every application is supposed to get its fair share of processor time, and preemptive multitasking enforces this principle. Windows 95 monitors each application and interrupts it when its time is up. It doesn't matter whether the application wants to give up control over the system. Windows 95 doesn't give it a choice.

There's another, more important difference in the way the system reacts under preemptive multitasking. Under Windows 3.1, an hourglass means that the system is tied up. You can't do anything else until the hourglass goes away. On the other hand, an hourglass under Windows 95 means only that the current task is tied up. You can always start another task or switch to an existing task. If that task isn't busy, you can perform some work with it while you wait for the initial task to complete its work. You know when the original application has finished because the hourglass goes away when you place your cursor over the task's window. The bottom line? Preemptive multitasking means that the user doesn't have to wait for the system.

Finally, cooperative multitasking has a serious flaw. Because Windows lost control when some applications took over, there was no way to clear that application if the machine froze. Because Windows 95 maintains constant control of the machine, you no longer need to worry about the machine freezing in the middle of a task. Even if one application hangs, you only need to end that task, not reboot the machine. As with Windows 3.1, pressing Ctrl+Alt+Delete doesn't automatically reboot the machine. However, unlike Windows 3.1, Windows 95 displays a list of applications, and you get to choose which one to terminate (see Figure 6.3).

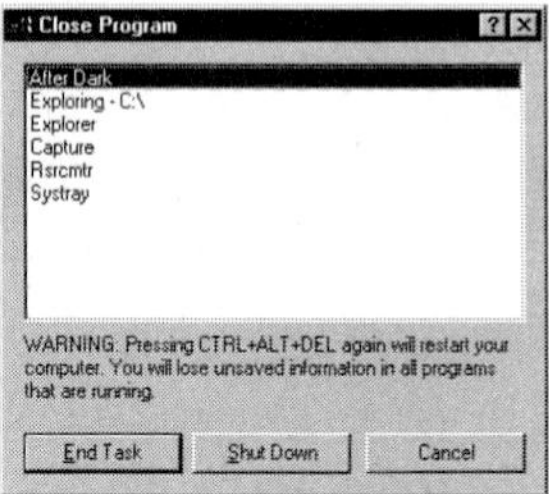

Figure 6.3.
Preemptive multitasking means that Windows 95 never loses control of the machine. It also means that you can recover from an application error with ease.

You might wonder why Microsoft (or any other vendor) would use cooperative multitasking if preemptive multitasking is so much better. There are a few good reasons. First, DOS is non-reentrant. This means that you have to allow DOS to complete one task before you give it another one. If you disturb DOS in the middle of a task, the entire system could (and will) freeze. Because Windows 3.x runs on top of DOS, it can't use preemptive multitasking for any services that interact with DOS. Unfortunately, one of those services is the disk subsystem. Do you see now why it would be fairly difficult to use preemptive multitasking on any system that runs on top of DOS?

The second problem with preemptive multitasking is really a two-part scenario. Both relate to ease of designing the operating system. When an operating system provides preemptive multitasking, it also has to include some kind of method for monitoring devices. What if two applications decided that they needed to use the COM port at the same time? With cooperative multitasking, the application that started to use the COM port would gain control of it and lock out the other application. In a preemptive multitasking situation, the first application could get halfway through the allocation process and be stopped, and then the second application could start the allocation process. What happens if the first application is reactivated by the system? You have two applications that think they have access to one device. In reality, both applications have access, and you have a mess. Windows 95 handles this problem by using a programming construct called a *critical section*. (I discuss this feature more in a moment.)

Preemptive multitasking also needs some type of priority system to ensure that critical tasks get a larger share of the processor's time than noncritical tasks. Remember, a task can no longer dictate how long it needs system resources; that's all in the hands of the operating system. Theoretically, you should be able to rely on the users to tell the operating system how they want their applications prioritized, and then allow the operating system to take care of the rest. What really happens is that a low-priority task could run into a fault situation and need system resources immediately to resolve it. A static priority system can't handle that situation. In addition, that low-priority task could end up getting little or no system resources when a group of high-priority tasks starts to run. The priority system Windows 95 uses provides a dynamic means of changing a task's priority. When a high-priority task runs, Windows 95 lowers its priority. When a low-priority task gets passed over in favor of a high-priority task, Windows 95 increases its priority. As you can see, the dynamic priority system enforces the idea that some tasks should get more system resources than others, yet ensures that every task gets at least some system resources.

There's a final consideration when looking at preemptive multitasking. Even if you use the best dynamic priority system in the world and every piece of the operating system works just the way it should, you'll run into situations where a task has to complete a sequence of events without being disturbed. For example, the application might need to make certain that a database transaction is written to disk before it hands control of the system back to the operating system. If another task tried to do something related to that transaction before the first task completed, you could end up with invalid or damaged data in the database. Programmers call a piece of code that performs this task a *critical section*. Normally, a critical section occurs with system-related tasks such as memory allocation, but it also can happen with application-related tasks such as writing information to a file. Cooperative multitasking systems don't have to worry as much about critical sections, because the task decides when the operating system regains control of the system. On the other hand, a preemptive multitasking system needs some way for a task to communicate the need to complete a critical section of code. Under Windows 95, a task tells the operating system that it needs to perform a critical section of code by using a semaphore (a flag). If a hardware interrupt or some other application were to ask to perform a task that didn't interfere with any part of the critical section, Windows 95 could allow it to proceed. All that a critical section guarantees is that the task and its environment will remain undisturbed until the task completes its work.

Windows 95 Internals

The earlier section "Architecture" provides an overview of Windows 95's internal architecture. This section of the chapter assumes that you've read that overview and are ready to move on to bigger and better things. The following paragraphs start where that discussion leaves off, and show you some of the deeper and darker secrets of Windows 95.

Before I begin a discussion of individual Windows architectural components, I'd like to direct your attention to the "rings" of protection provided by the 80386 (and above) processor. There are four security rings within the Intel protection scheme, but most operating systems use only two of them (or sometimes three). The inner security ring is ring 0. This is where the operating system proper is. The outermost ring is 3. That's where the applications reside. Sometimes an operating system gives device drivers better access to some operating system features than an application gets by running them at ring 1 or 2. Windows doesn't make any concessions; device drivers run at ring 0 or 3, depending on their purpose.

Windows uses these protection rings to make certain that only operating system components can access the inner workings of Windows—that an application can't change settings that might cause the entire system to crash. For example, Windows reserves the right to allocate memory from the global pool; therefore, the capabilities needed to perform this task rest at ring 0. On the other hand, applications need to access memory assigned to them. That's why Windows assigns local memory a protection value of 3.

Think of each ring as a security perimeter. Before you can enter that perimeter, you have to know the secret password. Windows gives the password only to applications that it knows it can trust; everyone else has to stay out. Whenever an application tries to circumvent security, the processor raises an exception. Think of an exception as a security alarm. The exception sends the Windows police (better known as an *exception handler*) after the offending application. After its arrest and trial, Windows calmly terminates the offending application. Of course, it notifies the user before performing this task, but the user usually doesn't have much of a choice in the matter.

Figure 6.1 gives you a pretty good idea of exactly whom Windows trusts. Applications and device drivers running at ring 3 have very few capabilities outside their own resources. In fact, Windows even curtails these capabilities somewhat. Some of the activities that a DOS application could get by with, such as directly manipulating video memory, aren't allowed here. The reason is simple: Video memory is a shared resource. Whenever another application would need to share something, you can be certain that your application won't be able to access it directly.

Now, on to the various components that actually make up Windows. The following sections break the Windows components into main areas. Each of these general groups contains descriptions of the individual components and what tasks they perform. Remember that this is only a general discussion. Windows is much more complex than it might first appear. The deeper you get as a programmer, the more you'll see the actual complexity of this operating system.

System Virtual Machine

The System Virtual Machine (VM) component of Windows 95 contains three main elements: 32-bit Windows applications, the shell, and 16-bit Windows applications. Essentially, the System VM component provides most of the Windows 95 user-specific functionality. Without it, you couldn't run any applications. Notice that I don't include DOS applications here. This is because Windows uses an entirely different set of capabilities to run DOS applications. It even runs them in a different processor mode.

Theoretically, the System VM also provides support for the various Windows API layer components. However, because these components provide a different sort of service, I chose to discuss them in a separate area. Even though applications use the API and users interact with applications, you really don't think about the API until the time comes to write an application. Therefore, I always think of the API as a programmer-specific service rather than something that the user really needs to worry about. The following list describes the System VM components in detail:

- **32-bit Windows applications:** These are the new Win32-specific applications that use a subset of the Windows NT API. In fact, many Windows NT applications, such as Word for Windows NT, will run just fine under Windows 95. A 32-bit application usually provides better multitasking capabilities than its 16-bit counterpart. In addition, many 32-bit applications support new Windows features such as long filenames, while most 16-bit applications don't. 32-bit applications provide two additional features. The more important one is the use of preemptive versus cooperative multitasking. This makes your work flow more smoothly and forces the system to wait for you as necessary, rather than the other way around. The second one is the use of a flat memory address space. This feature really makes a difference in how much memory an application gets and how well it uses it. In addition, an application that uses a flat address space should run slightly faster, because it no longer has to spend time working with Intel's memory segmentation scheme.

- **The shell:** Three shells are supplied with Windows 95, and you can choose any of them. The standard shell, Explorer, provides full 32-bit capabilities. Explorer combines all the features you used to find in Program Manager, Print Manager, and File Manager. You can also use the older Program Manager interface with Windows 95. It doesn't provide all the bells and whistles that Explorer does, but it certainly eases the transition for some users who learned the Program Manager interface. The third interface is the result of using Internet Explorer 4.0. It allows you to maintain your local and remote resources in one place. Obviously you have to purchase or download this shell before you can use it; Microsoft doesn't provide Internet Explorer 4.0 as part of the Windows 95 package. (This interface will become standard with the next update of Windows 95.)

  Switching between shells is easy. All you need to do is change the `Shell=` entry in the `[Boot]` section of SYSTEM.INI. Of course, Windows 95 also lets you choose which shell you want to use when you install it.

- **16-bit Windows applications:** All your older applications—the ones you own right now—are 16-bit applications, unless you bought them for use with Windows 95 or Windows NT. Windows 95 runs all these applications in one shared address space. Essentially, Windows 95 groups all these 16-bit applications into one area and treats them as if they were one task. You really won't notice any performance hit as a result, but it does make it easier for Windows 95 to recover from application errors. With it, Windows 95 can mix 16-bit and 32-bit applications on one system.

The Windows API Layer

Two Windows APIs are included with Windows 95. The first is exactly like the one supplied with Windows 3.1. It provides all the 16-bit services that the old Windows had to provide for applications. This is the API that an older application will use when it runs.

The other API is the new Win32 API used by Windows NT. It provides a subset of the features that all 32-bit applications running under Windows NT can access. The 32-bit API provides about the same feature set as the 16-bit API, but it's more robust. In addition, a 32-bit application enjoys the benefits that this environment provides. Check out the earlier section "The System Files" for more details about the system files and the Windows 95 API.

Getting 16-Bit and 32-Bit Applications to Work Together

Windows 95 consists of a combination of 16-bit and 32-bit applications. All those older applications and device drivers you use now have to work within the same environment as the new 32-bit drivers and applications that Windows 95 provides. You already know how Windows takes care of separating the two by using different memory schemes. The 16-bit applications work within their own virtual machine area. It would be nice if things ended there, but they can't.

There are times when 16-bit and 32-bit applications have to talk to each other. This doesn't just apply to programs that the user uses to perform work, but to device drivers and other types of Windows applications as well. Most Windows applications use a memory structure called the *stack* to transfer information from one application to another. Think of the stack as a database of variables. Each record in this database is a fixed length so that every application knows how to grab information from it. Here's where the problems start. The stack for 32-bit applications is 32 bits wide. That makes sense. It makes equal sense that the stack for 16-bit applications should be 16 bits wide. See the problem?

Of course, the problems are only beginning. What happens when you need to send a 32-bit value from a 16-bit application to a 32-bit application? The 32-bit application will expect to see the whole value in the EAX register. On the other hand, the 16-bit application expects to see the value in a combination of the DX and AX registers. This same problem translates to pointers as well. A 32-bit application, for example, will use the SS:ESP register pair to point to the stack.

But wait, there's more! Remember that 16-bit applications use a segmented address space. An address consists of a selector and an offset. A 16-bit application combines these two pieces to form a complete address. On the other hand, 32-bit applications use a flat address space. They wouldn't know what to do with a selector if you gave them one. All they want is the actual address within the total realm of available memory. So how do you send the address of a string from a 16-bit to a 32-bit application?

By now you're probably wondering how Windows keeps 16-bit and 32-bit applications working together. After all, there are a number of inconsistencies and incompatibilities to deal with. The stack is only the tip of the incompatibility iceberg. It's easy to envision a method of converting 16-bit data to a 32-bit format. All you really need to do is pad the front end of the variable with zeros. But how does a 32-bit application send data to a 16-bit application? If the 32-bit application just dumps a wide variable onto the stack, the 16-bit application will never know what to do with the information it receives. Clearly, the data needs to go through some type of conversion. Windows uses the thunk layer to allow 16-bit and 32-bit applications to communicate. Figure 6.4 shows the interaction of 16-bit and 32-bit applications through the thunk layer.

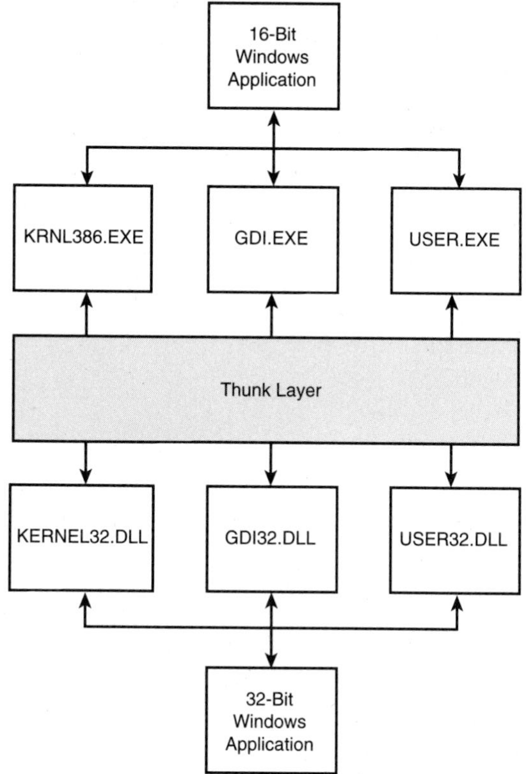

Figure 6.4.
The thunk layer makes it possible for 16-bit and 32-bit applications to coexist peacefully under Windows.

As you can see, the three components of the API layer also provide translation services in addition to the other services they perform. Each API component translates the data and addresses within its area of expertise. For example, the two GDI components translate all graphics data between 16-bit and 32-bit applications.

Most thunking is pretty straightforward. For example, Windows simply moves register data to the appropriate register. The thunk layer builds a new stack to meet the needs of the application receiving it. Address translation takes a little more work. In addition, address translation is very expensive, time-wise. Every time Windows has to translate an address, it must perform several selector loads. The processor has to verify every selector load, so these translations can get cumbersome. Fortunately, you, as an application programmer, won't have to worry too much about the actual thunk process. What you do need to worry about is making certain that the process actually takes place when calling a piece of code that needs it.

Windows and .DLLs

Under DOS, an application must contain every component it needs in order to execute. The programmer links library support for graphics, low-level utilities, and a variety of other needs. Of course, this whole scenario is based on the fact that the application is the only thing running under DOS.

Windows is a different kind of environment. There's always more than one task running under Windows. Somewhere along the way, someone figured out that if you have multiple applications running, there might be some duplicate code out there as well. For example, the display routines used by one application are probably the same as the display routines used by another application at some particular level. The same person probably figured out that you could reduce the overall memory requirements of a system if you allowed all the applications to share these redundant pieces of code instead of loading them from scratch for each application.

The .DLL (dynamic link library) is the culmination of just such an idea. There are two forms of linking under Windows (or OS/2 or UNIX, for that matter). The first link combines all the object modules required to create a unique application. That link cycle happens right after the programmer finishes compiling the code. The second link cycle happens when the user goes to load the application. This is where the .DLL comes in.

Every Windows application has unresolved references to functions. Microsoft calls them *import library calls*. What these calls do is load a .DLL containing the code required to satisfy that function call. If the .DLL happens to be in memory when Windows calls it, Windows increments the .DLL's usage level to indicate that more than one application is using the .DLL. When an application stops using a .DLL, Windows decrements its usage level. When the .DLL's usage count goes to 0, Windows can unload it from memory. In effect, using .DLLs can save quite a bit of memory when you're loading multiple applications.

So what does this have to do with the API? The Windows API starts with three files, as just described. However, these three files call other files—.DLLs, to be exact. Rather than create three huge files, Microsoft chose to reduce the size of the Windows kernel by using .DLLs.

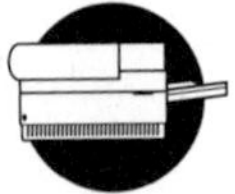

This capability also makes Windows more flexible. Consider printer support. All you need to do to add printer support for a new printer is copy some files to disk. At least one of those files will be a .DLL. Every printer .DLL contains the same entry points (function names), so Windows doesn't need to learn anything new to support the printer. The only thing it has to do is install a new .DLL. Your application performs the same task when you tell it to print. It looks at the .DLLs currently installed for the system. The application doesn't have to care whether the printer is a dot matrix or a laser. All it needs to know how to do is tell the printer to print; the .DLL takes care of the rest.

The Base System

Windows 95 uses the base system component to take care of any system-specific services. The earlier "Architecture" section covers this particular component in detail. Please refer to that discussion if you want to know the details of the base system.

The DOS Virtual Machine

The word *virtual* gets severely overused in the Windows environment. We have virtual memory, virtual system machines, and every other kind of virtual device you can think of. I want to make sure that you understand that the DOS virtual machine is a different kind of virtual than all these other virtuals on the system. A virtual DOS machine runs in the virtual 8086 mode of the processor. All the other virtual machines in Windows run in protected mode. Virtual 8086 mode creates multiple 1MB 8086 machines in protected memory. Each machine has its own copy of DOS, device drivers, I/O space, and everything else that an 8086 would have. About the only thing missing is the hardware itself, and that's why this machine is known as a virtual machine. You can't touch it, but it does exist. As far as the application is concerned, there's no difference between this machine and any real machine it could run on.

The virtual machine hasn't changed much since the days when Quarterdeck first introduced QEMM. Except for a few new features designed to enhance the performance of applications running under the Windows virtual machine, this aspect of Windows hasn't really changed much from version 3.1. However, there's one exception to this rule. Some DOS applications use DPMI-compatible extenders that allow them to run in protected mode. Under Windows 3.1, these applications would still run under the processor's virtual 8086 mode. Windows 95 improves system performance by allowing these applications to run in protected mode.

On Your Own

Open MSDOS.SYS, using Notepad or another text editor. Identify all the switches in your current configuration, using Table 6.1. Are there any switches you could add to this file to improve system performance? If so, follow this procedure to modify MSDOS.SYS:

1. Right-click MSDOS.SYS and select Properties from the context menu.
2. Uncheck the Hidden and Read-Only attributes on the General page. Close the Properties dialog box by clicking OK.
3. Use an editor, such as Notepad, to make the required changes. Save the changes and exit the editor.
4. Open the MSDOS.SYS Properties dialog box again. This time, check both the Read-Only and Hidden attributes. Click OK to close the dialog box.

Spend some time looking through the SYSTEM directory on your machine. Can you identify the various operating system files discussed in this chapter? Go through the architecture overview again to make sure that you fully understand it before going on to the subsystem-specific sections in the rest of the book.

Download a copy of BIOTST.ZIP from CompuServe if you own a plug and play-compatible machine. See whether your BIOS really does support plug and play features by running this test program.

7

The Windows 95 Registry

Anyone working with Windows 95 for long enough will figure out that a working knowledge of the Registry is always welcome. Just about any discussion of compatibility problems or software configuration issues will eventually end up at the Registry if standard resolution techniques don't work. All you need to do to verify all this is to take a look at any Internet newsgroup or CompuServe forum discussing Windows 95 issues. On any given day, you'll find several Registry-related questions and answers on a fairly active forum.

The fact that the Registry is complex becomes apparent when you begin to look at all the ways that Microsoft uses it to fix current problems with Windows 95. Appendix A talks about online resources—one of which is the Microsoft Knowledge Base. Many of the articles in the Knowledge Base contain Registry-related solutions to problems that you may be experiencing with Windows 95.

This chapter tells you all about the Registry. We'll start with a simple overview for those of you who don't want to get mired in detail. As the chapter progresses, I take a much deeper look at what the Registry has to offer and how you can use it to your benefit. It won't take long for you to figure out that the Registry is more than just a configuration aid—it can help with a variety of troubleshooting and research needs. For example, you can use the Registry to find the hidden capabilities of applications on your machine.

The Registry: The New Method of Configuration

When Microsoft started work on Windows NT, they looked for a better configuration tool than the .INI file. Users were ending up with loads of these files in their Windows directory, not to mention the .INI files floating around in application directories. Trying to find the right file to correct a problem when using Windows 3.x could be daunting, to say the least.

File bloat wasn't the only problem facing Microsoft. .INI files also encouraged vendors to come up with distinct ways of configuring their software. No one could figure out one .INI file from the other, because they all used different formatting techniques. Obviously, this made life even more difficult for the user, not to mention the support staff at the various software companies.

The Registry is a complex piece of software—it has to be to get the job done. Windows 95 can't boot without a clean Registry. Any corruption in this file will cause a host of problems, even if Windows 95 does manage to boot. Of course, the fact that you can't edit this file at the DOS prompt is another potential problem. It's important to realize these problems up front. While the Registry is a lot easier to maintain than the .INI files of old and does provide a central repository of information, it also presents unique problems of its own.

Tip: Windows 95 stores the previous copy of your Registry in the USER.DA0 and SYSTEM.DA0 files. If you make a mistake in editing the Registry, exit immediately, shut down Windows 95, and boot into DOS mode. Change directories to your Windows 95 main directory. Use the `ATTRIB` utility to make the SYSTEM.DA0, SYSTEM.DAT, USER.DA0, and USER.DAT files visible by using the `-R`, `-H`, and `-S` switches. Now copy the backup of your Registry to the two original files (that is, SYSTEM.DA0 to SYSTEM.DAT and USER.DA0 to USER.DAT). This will restore your Registry to its pre-edit state. Be sure to restore the previous file attribute state by using the `+R`, `+H`, and `+S` switches of the `ATTRIB` utility.

Chapter 1 presents a brief overview of the Registry, but I never really say anything there about what the Registry can do for you. When you look at the Registry, you're seeing a complete definition of Windows 95 as it relates to your specific machine. Not only does the Registry contain hardware and application settings, but it also contains every other piece of information you can imagine about your machine. You can learn a lot about Windows simply by looking at the information presented by this application. For example, did you know that you can use multiple desktops in Windows 95? Of course, that leads to another problem—maintaining those separate desktops. The hierarchical format presented by the Registry Editor helps the administrator compare the differences between the various desktops. It also allows the administrator to configure them with ease. Best of all, editing the Registry doesn't involve a session with a text editor. Windows provides a GUI editor that the administrator can use to change the settings in the Registry.

Knowing that the Registry contains a lot of information and is easy to edit still doesn't tell you what it can do for you. When was the last time you used Explorer to check out your hard drive? I use it a lot because it provides an easy way to find what I need. The Registry can help you make Explorer easier to use. One of my favorite ways to use it for Explorer modifications is to create multiple associations for the same file type. Suppose that you want to associate a graphics editor with .PCX and .BMP files. This isn't very difficult. However, what if each file type requires a different set of command-line switches? Now you get into an area where using the Registry can really help. Using the Registry to edit these entries can help you customize file access.

Note: Before proceeding, you should add the Registry editor, RegEdit, to your Start menu. It helps to look at the Registry entries as you read about them. I'll also present some exercises that will help you better understand the inner workings of the Registry. See Chapter 10 if you need information about adding new applications to the Start menu.

A Centralized Database of Setup Information

It's time to take a look at how the Registry is organized. To start the Registry editor, simply open RegEdit as you would any other application on the Start menu. You'll probably get a lot more out of the detailed discussion that follows if you actually open the Registry editor now. Using the Registry editor to see how Windows 95 arranges the various entries can make using it in an emergency a lot easier.

I always step lightly when it comes to the Registry. You might want to follow the same procedure I use to back up the Registry before you go much further. The big advantage to this method is that it produces a text file that you can view with any text editor. (The file is huge, so Notepad won't handle it, but WordPad will.) You can use this backup file to restore the Registry later, if you run into difficulty. Unfortunately, this method won't help much if you permanently destroy the Registry and reboot the machine. Windows 95 needs a clean Registry to boot. To preserve a clean, bootable copy of the Registry, you need to copy the USER.DAT and SYSTEM.DAT files to a safe location. (Later I'll cover a technique for importing a text copy of the Registry by using RegEdit at the DOS prompt, but this technique isn't guaranteed by anyone to work. The bottom line is that a good backup is always worth the effort.)

Warning: RegEdit is an application designed to assist experienced users in changing Windows 95 and associated application behavior. Although it will allow you to enhance system performance and make applications easier to use, it can cause unexpected results when misused. Never edit an entry unless you know what that entry is for. Failure to observe this precaution can result in data loss and even prevent your system from booting the next time you start Windows 95.

1. Highlight the `My Computer` entry of the Registry. Choose Registry | Export Registry File, as shown in Figure 7.1.

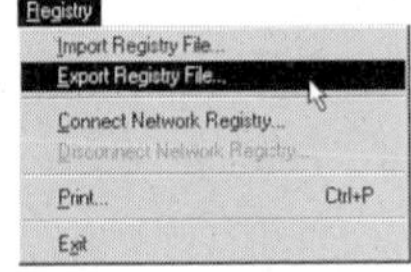

Figure 7.1.
The Registry menu allows you to import and export Registry settings.

2. You should see an Export Registry File dialog box similar to the one shown in Figure 7.2. Notice that the File Name field already contains a name. You can use any name you want. I selected OLDENTRY to designate a pre-edited Registry. Notice that the All radio button is selected in the Export Range group.

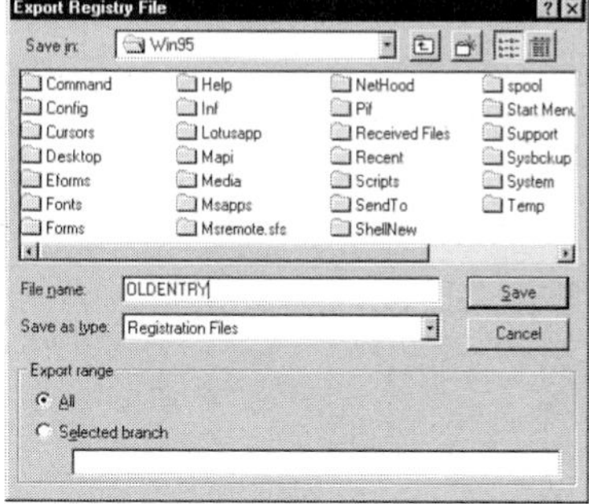

Figure 7.2.
The Export Registry File dialog box allows you to save your current Registry settings.

3. Click the Save button to place a copy of the Registry on disk. The OLDENTRY.REG file in your main Windows 95 directory now contains a complete copy of your original Registry.

Now that you have a copy of the Registry, let's take that brief overview that I talked about previously. The next few sections acquaint you with the contents of the Registry as a whole. I won't go into much detail, but at least you'll know the general location for specific types of information. If you intend to actually edit the Registry at some time, you'll want to read the rest of the chapter.

HKEY_CLASSES_ROOT

There are two types of entries in the `HKEY_CLASSES_ROOT` category. The first key type (remember, a key is a RegEdit topic) is a file extension. Think of all the three-letter extensions you've used, such as .DOC and .TXT. Windows 95 still uses them to differentiate one file type from another. (Because Windows 95 also provides long filename support, you can use the Registry to create associations for extensions longer than three letters.) The Registry also uses extensions to associate that file type with a specific action. For example, even though you can't do anything with a file that uses the .DLL extension, it appears in this list because Windows 95 needs to associate .DLLs with an executable file type. The second entry type is the association itself. The file extension entries normally associate a data file with an application or an executable file with a specific Windows 95 function. Below the association key are entries for the menus that you see when you right-click an entry in Explorer. The association also contains keys that determine what type of icon to display and other parameters associated with a particular file type. Figure 7.3 shows the typical `HKEY_CLASSES_ROOT` organization.

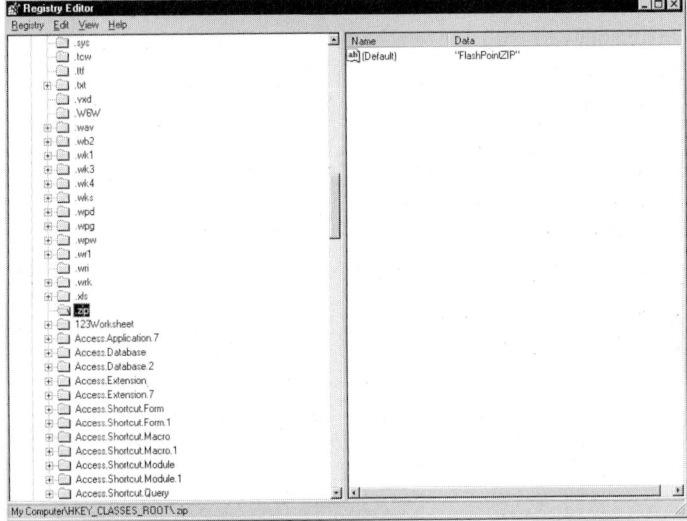

Figure 7.3.
A typical HKEY_CLASSES_ROOT *display. Notice the distinct difference between file extension and file association keys.*

HKEY_CURRENT_USER

The HKEY_CURRENT_USER category contains a lot of "soft" settings for your machine. These soft settings tell how to configure the desktop and the keyboard. This category also contains color settings and the configuration of the Start menu. All user-specific settings appear in this category.

The HKEY_CURRENT_USER category is slaved to the settings for the current user, the one who is logged into the machine at this time. This is differentiated from all the user configuration entries in other parts of the Registry. This is a dynamic setting category; the other user-related categories contain static information. The Registry copies the contents of one of the user entries in the HKEY_USERS category into this category and updates HKEY_USERS when you shut down.

This is the area where Windows 95 obtains new setting information and places any changes you make. As you can see from Figure 7.4, the keys within the HKEY_CURRENT_USER category are pretty self-explanatory in most cases. All the entries adjust some type of user-specific setting—nothing that affects a global element such as a device driver.

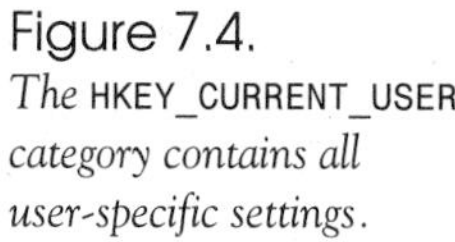

Figure 7.4.
The HKEY_CURRENT_USER *category contains all user-specific settings.*

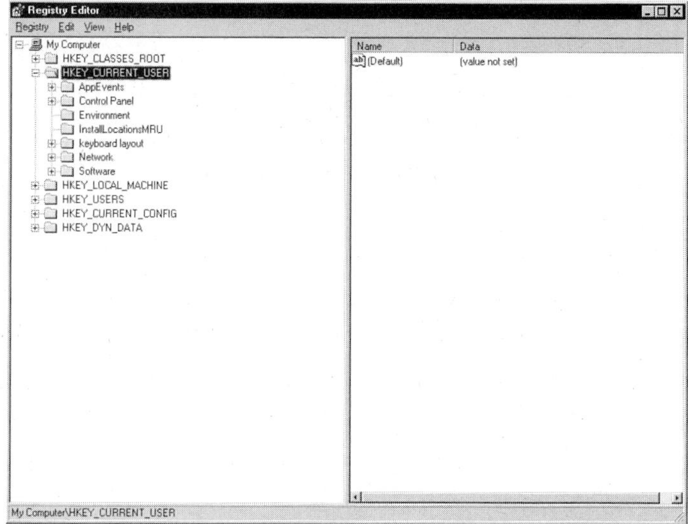

HKEY_LOCAL_MACHINE

The HKEY_LOCAL_MACHINE category centers its attention on the machine hardware. This includes the drivers and configuration information required to run the hardware. Every piece of hardware appears somewhere in this section of the Registry, even if that hardware uses real-mode drivers. If a piece of hardware doesn't appear here, Windows 95 can't use it.

A lot of subtle information about your hardware is stored in this category. For example, this category contains all the plug and play information about your machine. It also provides a complete listing of the device drivers and their revision levels. This section might even contain the revision information for the hardware itself. For example, there's a distinct difference between a Pro Audio Spectrum 16+ Revision C sound board and a Revision D version of that same board. Windows 95 stores that difference in the Registry.

This category does contain some software-specific information of a global nature. For example, a 32-bit application will store the location of its Setup and Format Table (SFT) here. This is a file that the application uses during installation. Some applications also use it during a setup modification. Applications such as Word for Windows NT store all their setup information in SFT tables. The only application information that appears here is global-configuration-specific like the SFT. Figure 7.5 shows a typical HKEY_LOCAL_MACHINE category setup.

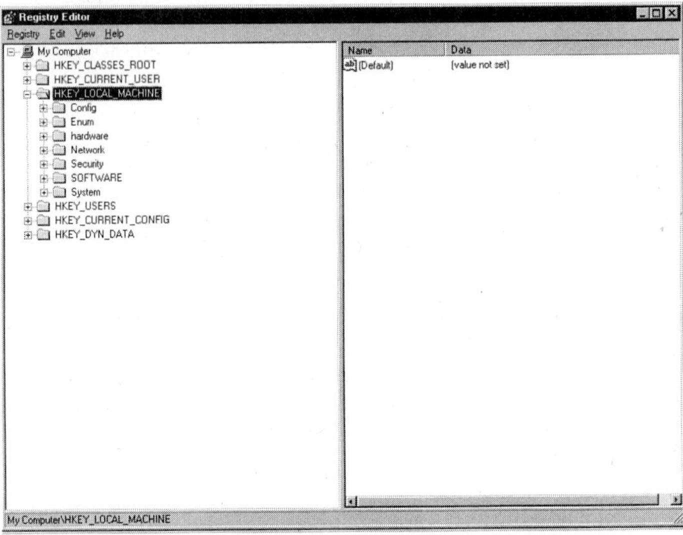

Figure 7.5.
The HKEY_LOCAL_MACHINE *category contains all the hardware- and device-driver-specific information about your machine. It also contains the global application setup information.*

HKEY_USERS

The HKEY_USERS category contains a static listing of all the users of this particular Registry file. It never pays to edit any of the information you find in this category. However, you can use this category for reference purposes. The reason for this hands-off policy is simple: None of the entries here takes effect until the next time the user logs into Windows 95, so you really don't know what effect they'll have until you reboot the machine. In addition, changing the settings for the current user is a waste of time, because Windows 95 overwrites the new data with the data contained in HKEY_CURRENT_USER during logout or shutdown.

There's one other problem associated with using this category as your sole source of information. Windows 95 actually maintains multiple Registries in a multiuser configuration—in some cases, one for each user who logs into the system. Because of this, you never quite know where you'll find the information for a particular user. Windows 95 tracks this information, but it's really a pain for the administrator to have to do it as well. Besides, Microsoft thoughtfully provided a utility that helps network administrators maintain static user information with ease. Using the Policy Editor lets the network administrator bridge the various Registry files on the system when each user provides his or her own desktop configuration.

Figure 7.6 shows a setup that includes the default key. If this system were set up for multiple desktops, each user would have a separate entry in this section. Each entry would contain precisely the same keys, but the values might differ from user to user. When a user logs into the network, Windows 95 copies all the information in his profile to the HKEY_CURRENT_USER area of the Registry. When he logs out or shuts down, Windows 95 updates the information in his specific section from the HKEY_CURRENT_USER category.

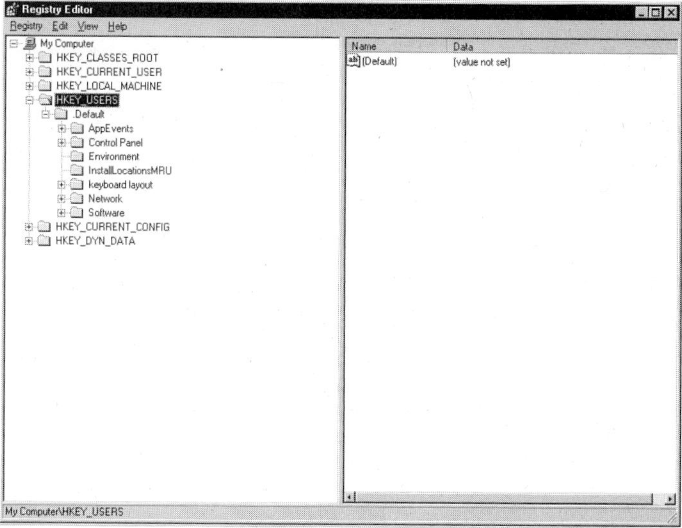

Figure 7.6.
Windows 95 creates one entry in the HKEY_USERS *category for each user who logs into the machine.*

HKEY_CURRENT_CONFIG

The HKEY_CURRENT_CONFIG category is the simplest part of the Registry. It contains two major keys: Display and System. Essentially, these entries are used by the GDI API (described in Chapters 15 and 17) to configure the display and printer.

The Display key provides two subkeys: Fonts and Settings. The Fonts subkey determines which fonts Windows 95 uses for general display purposes. These are the raster (non-TrueType) fonts that it displays when you get a choice of which font to use for icons or other purposes. Raster fonts are essentially bitmaps or pictures of the characters. Chapter 15 takes a more detailed look at fonts.

The Settings subkey contains the current display resolution and number of bits per pixel. The bits per pixel value determines the number of colors available. For example, 4 bits per pixel provides 16 colors, and 8 bits per pixel provides 256 colors. The three fonts listed as values under this key are the default fonts used for icons and application menus. You can change all the settings under this key by using the Settings tab of the Display Properties dialog box.

The System key looks like a convoluted mess. However, only one of the subkeys under this key has any meaning for the user. The Printers subkey contains a list of the printers attached to the machine. It doesn't include printers accessed through a network connection. Figure 7.7 shows the major keys in this category.

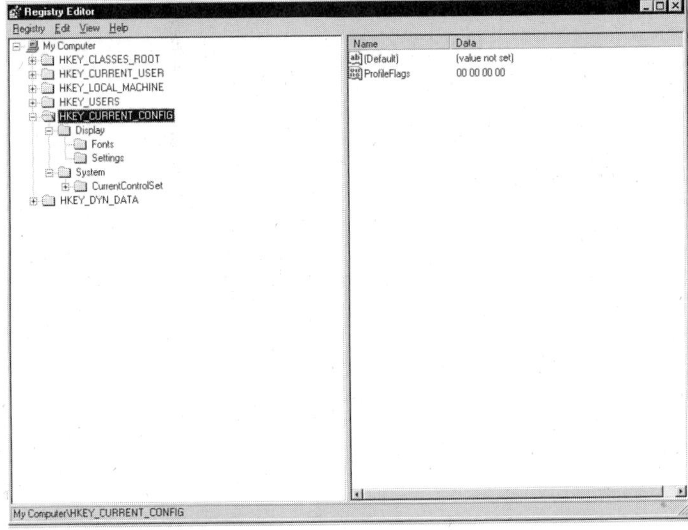

Figure 7.7.
The `HKEY_CURRENT_CONFIG` *category echoes the settings under the* `Config` *key of the* `HKEY_LOCAL_MACHINE` *category.*

HKEY_DYN_DATA

The final category, `HKEY_DYN_DATA`, contains two subkeys: `Config Manager` and `PerfStats`. You can monitor the status of the `Config Manager` key by using the Device Manager. The `PerfStats` key values appear as statistics in the System Monitor utility display. Figure 7.8 shows these two main keys and their subkeys.

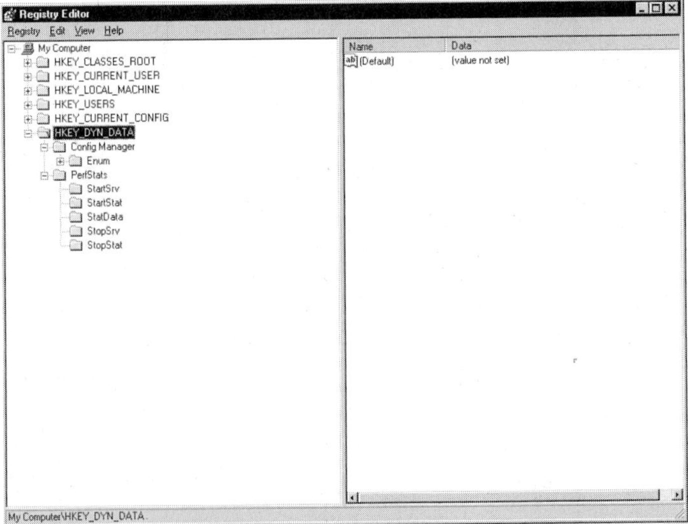

Figure 7.8.
`HKEY_DYN_DATA` *contains Registry entries for current events. The values in these keys reflect the current (dynamic) state of the computer.*

HKEY_CLASSES_ROOT

The preceding sections introduced you to the Registry. Now it's time to take a more detailed look. The `HKEY_CLASSES_ROOT` category is the first and most important category (from a user perspective) in the Registry. It's the one you'll probably change the most often. This is also the category that affects your ability to use applications the most. Don't let the deceptively simple appearance of this category fool you. As previously stated, there are two key types in this category: file extensions and file associations. These are the two obvious key types. We'll explore a third key type a bit later.

Tip: You should always change your application file entries to make your working environment as efficient as possible. However, you should never change an executable file association. Changing an executable file extension such as .DLL could make it hard for Windows 95 to start your applications or could even crash the system. The later section "Modifying File Associations" looks at the procedure for changing an application file association.

Special Extension Subkeys

Some file extensions, such as .TXT, provide a `ShellX` subkey (see Figure 7.9). In the case of .TXT and .DOC, the standard subkey is `ShellNew` (the most common key). The term `ShellX` means "shell extension." I like to think of it as an automated method of extending the functionality of Windows 95 as a whole. When you right-click the desktop and look at the New option on the context menu, all the types of files you can create are the result of shell extensions. Even though `ShellNew` is the most common type of shell extension, a variety of other shell extensions are available. The actual number is limited only by your application vendor. For example, Microsoft Excel provides no less than three shell extension entries for the .XLS file extension.

A shell extension is an OLE hook into Windows 95. Only an application that supports OLE 2 extensions can place a `ShellX` key into the Registry; don't add one of these keys on your own unless you know that the application provides OLE 2 support and that it makes sense to create blank files with it. When you see this key, you know that the application provides some type of extended OLE-related functionality—normally the ability to create blank or standard files. For example, if you double-click a shortcut to a data file that no longer exists, an application with the `ShellNew` shell extension will ask whether you want to create a new file of the same type. You'll also see any file extensions that provide a `ShellNew` key under the New entry of the context menu you see when you right-click the desktop or within Explorer. For example, because the .TXT extension has a `ShellNew` entry, you'll see a Text File entry under the New menu item of the desktop context menu. Obviously, even if a program supports OLE 2, it doesn't always make sense to add a `ShellNew` entry. For example, what good is a blank graphics file in most cases? (In the values associated with `ShellNew`, there's always a `NullFile` entry that tells the shell extension what type of file to create.)

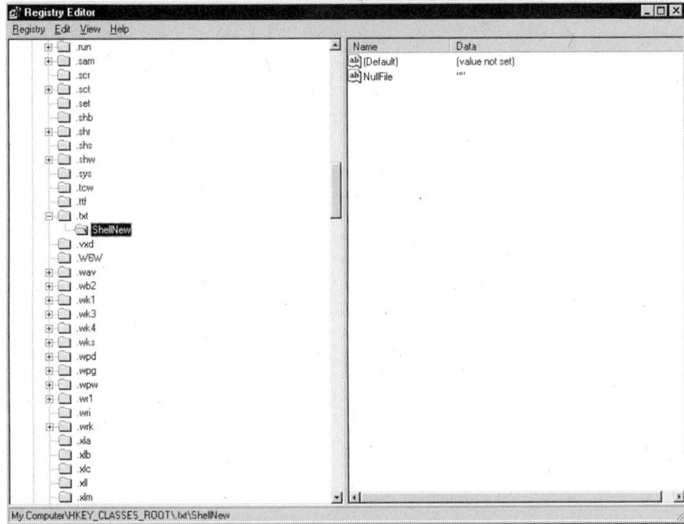

Figure 7.9.
The shell extension is a powerful OLE 2 feature that few applications implement.

Tip: Sometimes a file type won't appear on the context menu, even though the application provides support for it. Most of the time it happens with 16-bit applications that don't install correctly. You can use the shell extension behavior to create new files as if the context menu entry did exist. All you need to do is create a temporary file, place a shortcut to it on your desktop, and erase the temporary file. (Make certain that the application provides a `ShellNew` shell extension before you do this.) Whenever you double-click the shortcut, your application will create a new file for you. This behavior also works if you place the file shortcut in the Start menu folder.

There are also more generic shell extensions. For example, the `*` extension has one or more generic `ShellX` subkeys that affect all files equally. Below this you'll see a `PropertySheetHandlers` key (at a minimum) and in some cases a `ContextMenuHandlers` key. The `PropertySheetHandlers` key contains subkeys that affect the Properties dialog box that you see when you right-click a file or folder and then select Properties from the context menu. The `ContextMenuHandlers` subkey adds new items to the context menu. For example, the WinZip entry in Figure 7.10 adds a context menu that allows you to compress the file and then add it to a .ZIP file. Under each of these keys you'll see either a plain text entry or a 128-digit key that looks like some kind of secret code. Figure 7.10 shows a typical `*` extension with several kinds of shell extensions added.

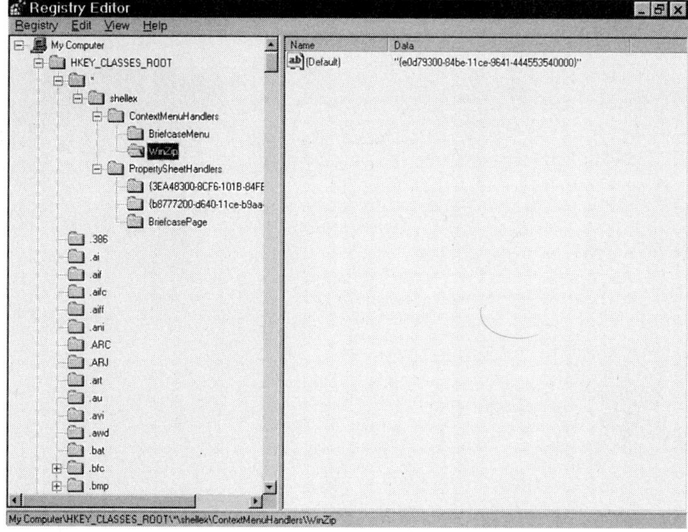

Figure 7.10.
*The * extension provides special shell extensions that affect all files equally.*

Note: Don't get the `PropertySheetHandlers` and `ContextMenuHandlers` `ShellX` entries confused with those that appear with specific file types as a `ShellNew` entry. These `ShellX` entries provide a different kind of functionality than those provided by the file-specific `ShellX` entries. In this case, you'll almost never get a new file; you'll get some kind of special feature instead. For example, WinZip provides a `ShellNew` entry under the .ZIP file extension that creates blank .ZIP files. The WinZip entry under `ContextMenuHandlers` allows you to compress a file and then add it to a .ZIP file. Even though WinZip provides two different `ShellX` entries, they perform entirely different tasks as well.

Notice that Figure 7.10 shows the WinZip entry highlighted. The value for this key is a 128-digit secret value. If you were to look at one of the 128-digit values, you would see that they don't have any value defined. Actually, the 128-digit value *is* a secret code. It's a reference identifier for the .DLL (a type of application) that takes care of the * extension. As you can see, Windows 95 allows any number of programmers to define .DLLs that will service all file types (the * extension) equally. You'll find the description for the 128-digit key under the `CLSID` key. (`CLSID` stands for "class identifier.")

Let's take a look at one of these secret codes. The first one under the `PropertySheetHandlers` key is `3EA48300-8CF6-101B-84FB-666CCB9BCD32`. This secret code is for the `"OLE Docfile Property Page"`. Looking at the value of the `InProcServer32` subkey will tell you that the program for handling a standard property page exists in DOCPROP.DLL, as shown in Figure 7.11. This .DLL also provides the dialog box that asks which application you want to use to open a file when no Registry entry is associated with that extension. If you look at Figure 7.10 again, you'll notice that there are two other kinds of property sheet handlers listed. The first is for NetWare drives (it was installed by the Novell client). The second, as shown by the plain text description, handles the Briefcase.

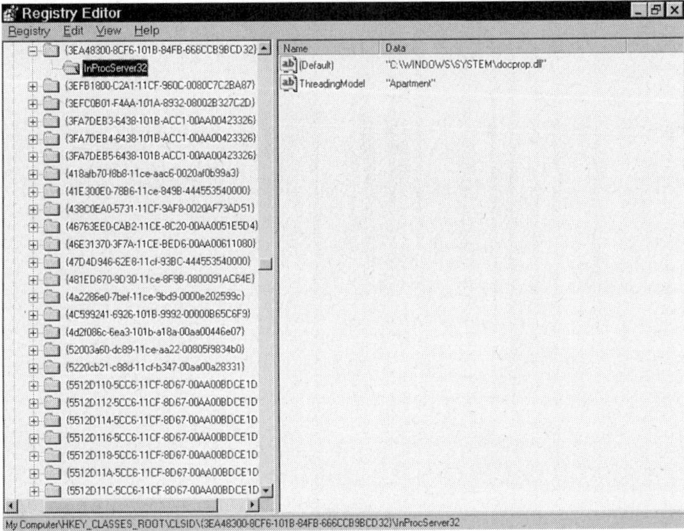

Figure 7.11.
You can trace the 128-digit class identifier to a .DLL or other application file.

As you can see, shell extensions are a powerful addition to the Windows 95 Registry. Suffice it to say that you shouldn't change or delete shell extensions; let the application take care of them for you.

OLE 1 Registry Entries

Windows 95 provides both OLE 1 and OLE 2 support; so do many of the applications. To show you just how organized the Registry is, the OLE 1 and OLE 2 entries appear in different areas. You can always tell what kind of OLE support an application provides by checking its Registry entries. If you see Registry entries in one area of the Registry, you'll know that the application provides OLE 1 support. Registry entries in a second area of the Registry show that the application provides OLE 2 support. In fact, the Registry will often tell you more than the application's documentation does. You might find by looking at the Registry that the application supports certain verbs. Think about a verb in OLE just like you would in a sentence; it represents some type of action that you can perform using the OLE capabilities of the application. I'll tell you a little more about verbs later on. Windows 95 always places OLE 1 support information in the file association area. (I'll show you where the OLE 2 support appears in the Registry after we look at OLE 1.) Figure 7.12 shows a typical setup, but the actual setup varies between applications. Table 7.1 describes the various entries in this area (plus a few not supported by this particular application). The OLE support provided by each application on your machine will probably differ from the one shown in the figure; this is only a sample for you to look at right now. Table 7.1 talks about all the potential OLE 1 entries you might find. I don't think any application uses them all.

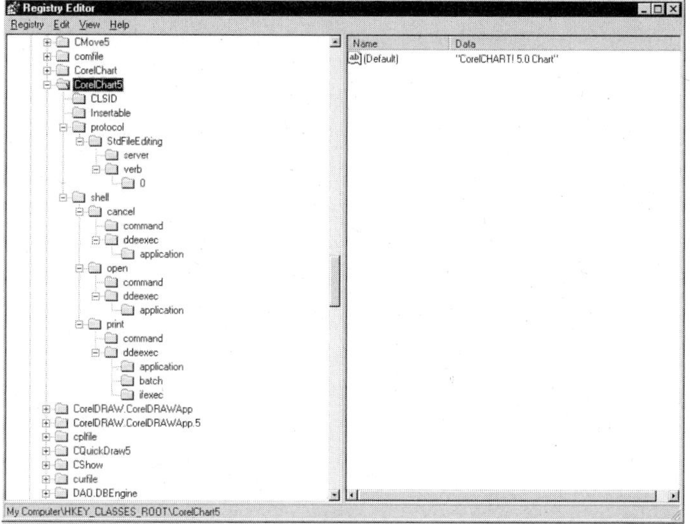

Figure 7.12.
Windows 95 places OLE 1 support in the file association area of the Registry.

Table 7.1. OLE 1 entries in the Windows 95 Registry.

Entry	*Description*
`CLSID`	This is actually part of the OLE 2 entry, even though it appears in the OLE 1 section. It's a pointer to an entry in the `CLSID` section of the category. C programmers use a special application to generate this 128-digit "magic number." If you look for this number under the `My Computer | HKEY_CLASSES_ROOT | CLSID` key (as we'll do in just a bit), you'll find the OLE 2 entries for this file association.
`Insertable`	Normally you won't see any value associated with this key. A blank value means that Windows can place this file association in the Insert Object (or equivalent) dialog box provided by many applications, such as Word for Windows. Some OLE 1 objects aren't insertable, for a variety of reasons.
`Protocol`	This is a header key (think of it as a heading in a book—a means to group like information in one place). Underneath it you'll find all the standard actions that this OLE 1 application can perform. The only supported function in most cases is a standard file edit.
`StdFileEditing`	This key is another header. In this case, it's the heading for all the keys that define a particular action—standard file editing.
`Server`	For this file association, you'll find the name of the application that Windows will call to service any OLE 1 calls. The string always includes the application's name, extension, and path. If you ever run into a situation in which your OLE links worked yesterday but won't work today, check this value to make certain that the path matches the actual application location.

continues

Table 7.1. continued

Entry	*Description*	
`Verb`	Several verbs are associated with an OLE 1 object. Each verb defines a specific action that the server will perform. This key doesn't have a value associated with it; its sole purpose is to organize actual verb entries. A client application can use only the verbs that are defined for a specific server.	
	`-3 = Hide, 0, 1`	This verb allows the client application to hide the server window. The first number following the verb is a menu flag. The second number is the verb flag. As a user, you don't need to worry about either value as long as you supply the values shown here (or use the settings provided by the vendor).
	`-2 = Open, 0, 1`	This verb allows the client to open the server in a separate window rather than allow it to take over the client window.
	`-1 = Show, 0, 1`	A client would use this verb to display the server window in its preferred state. The whole idea of a *state* can get to be quite complex. Think of it as the way the window looks, and you'll have a pretty good idea of what to expect from a user's point of view.
	`0 = &Edit, 0, 2`	Every server provides this verb. It allows the client to call the server to edit the object.
	`1 = &Play, 0, 3`	The only time you'll see this verb is when you're looking at some form of multimedia object.
`RequestDataFormats`	This entry allows the server to define the data formats that it supports for retrieval purposes.	
`SetDataFormats`	This entry allows the server to define the data formats that it supports for storage purposes.	

While you're still looking at this OLE 1 entry, you'll notice that I didn't cover anything under the `Shell` key. Each of these entries defines an action that you can perform on the file, using Explorer. The `Shell` key is a refinement of the same entry used for file associations by File Manager. The entries defined here appear on the context menu for each file of that type. Chapter 5 looks at the process of defining a file association with Explorer in the section "Using Explorer to Get the Job Done." We'll also cover a Registry-specific technique later in this chapter.

OLE 2 Registry Entries

Now it's time to look at the OLE 2 part of the Registry. You'll find these entries under the `HKEY_CLASSES_ROOT | CLSID` key. Each of the 128-digit numbers here represent a specific *class* (a programmer's term for a specific type of object) of information. Not all of entries under the `HKEY_CLASSES_ROOT | CLSID` key are OLE 2 entries, but some of them are. You'll also find that not every application supports OLE 2. Your first clue that CorelCHART! supports it is the `CLSID` entry in the OLE 1 section. (Table 7.1 talked about the `HKEY_CLASSES_ROOT | CorelChart5 | CLSID` key, and you saw it in Figure 7.12.) The `HKEY_CLASSES_ROOT | CorelChart5 | CLSID` entry is a pointer to the OLE 2 entry under the `HKEY_CLASSES_ROOT | CLSID` key. Figure 7.13 shows this key for CorelCHART!—the same application I used to describe an OLE 1 Registry entry. Table 7.2 describes these entries in detail. An application doesn't necessarily need to provide every entry in the Registry that I describe in Table 7.2. It depends on what OLE 2 features the application vendor decided to support. You can use these Registry entries to determine the capabilities of your application, just like you can with OLE 1.

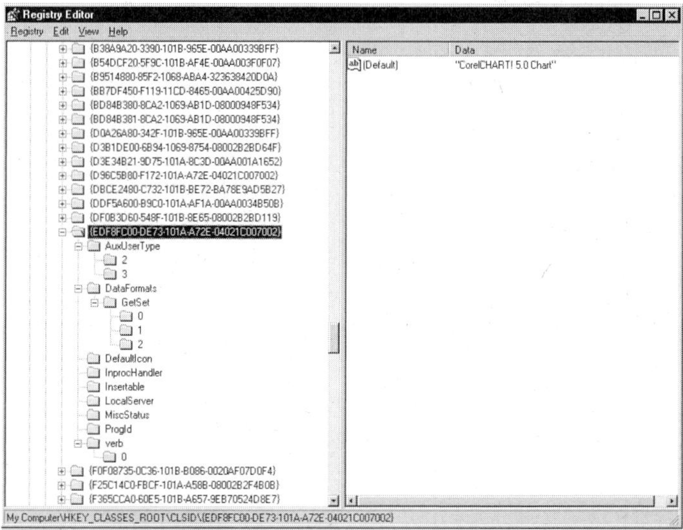

Figure 7.13.
Windows places OLE 2 support in the file association area of the Registry.

Table 7.2. OLE 2 entries in the Windows 95 Registry.

Entry	*Description*
`AuxUserType`	This key is a heading for all the user type keys that follow: `2` The `2 AuxUserType` always contains the short name for the application. A client can use this name in a list box to identify the object's owner. `3` This key contains the full name of the application that created the object. Like the `2` key, a client could use the `3` key value to provide an English application name for the object.
`DataFormats`	This key is a heading for all the data format keys that follow.
`GetSet`	This key is a subheading for all the data formats that the server can store and retrieve. For example, an OLE server such as Word for Windows would support a .DOC, .RTF, and standard text format. Its OLE 2 entries would reflect this fact. Each entry below this one defines a specific format type. `n = format, aspect, medium, flag` Each of the sequentially numbered keys contains a different format. `format` contains the type of format as a string. You might find some as easy to read here as `"Rich Text Format"` or as cryptic as `"Embed_Source"`. In every case, this string tells you the name of the format that the application supports. The client displays this string (for `get` formats) in the dialog box where you select the format you want to use when performing a Paste Special command. `aspect` tells the client what display orientation the object supports. This usually means portrait and/or landscape. You'll usually find a value of `1` here for portrait. `medium` contains the supported format as a computer-readable number. `flag` tells the client whether this is a `get`, `set`, or both format—a value of `1` is `get`, a value of `2` is `set`, and a value of `3` is both.
`DefaultFile`	This entry works much like `GetSet`, except that it identifies the default file format for this particular object.
`DefaultIcon`	The value of this key tells the client which application icon to use when displaying the object as an icon.
`InProcHandler`	This key contains the name of the in-process handler. In most cases, this is OLE2.DLL, unless the application provides its own OLE 2 handler. (A handler is a special program that helps two programs communicate.)

Entry	*Description*
`Insertable`	Normally you won't see any value associated with this key. A blank value means that Windows can place this file association in the Insert Object (or equivalent) dialog box provided by many applications such as Word for Windows. Some OLE 1 objects aren't insertable, for a variety of reasons.
`LocalServer`	Every OLE 2 object must have a server. This key contains the name of the server on the local machine. Because OLE 2 doesn't support RPCs (remote procedure calls), you'll always need a local server.
`MiscStatus`	This key contains the default value for all data format aspects.
`ProgID`	The program identifier is a pointer back to the file association to which this class identifier belongs. The file association is always a character string of some sort. It's the same string that you look for when you try to find the file association that goes with a file extension in the `HKEY_CLASSES_ROOT` category. For example, if you looked at the `ProgID` value for CorelCHART!, you'd see `CorelChart5`. That's the same value shown in Figure 7.12 as the first key for the file association.
`Verb`	Several verbs are associated with an OLE 2 object. Each verb defines a specific action that the server will perform. This key doesn't have a value associated with it; its sole purpose is to organize actual verb entries. A client application can use only the verbs that are defined for a specific server. See Table 7.1 for a list of verbs and their meanings.
`InProcServer`	This is a special form of OLE server. Instead of calling the application that created the object, the client calls a .DLL to handle any necessary display or editing functions. This has the advantage of speed; a .DLL is faster than calling the executable. However, the programmer has to do a lot more coding to make this kind of interface work.
`TreatAs`	When this key is present, it contains the `CLSID` for another file format. The client can treat the current file format like the specified file format. For example, if you looked at the Paintbrush `Picture` OLE 2 entry, you'd find a `TreatAs` value with the same 128-digit value as a `Bitmap Image`. This tells you that Windows 95 uses the same application to service Paintbrush picture files as it does for bitmap image files. A little more research would tell you that the OLE 2 server for Paintbrush pictures is Microsoft Paint.

continues

Table 7.2. continued

Entry	*Description*
`AutoTreatAs`	This key forces the client to treat the current file format the same way it would treat the file format specified by the `CLSID`. From a user perspective, it works just like the `TreatAs` entry described previously.
`AutoConvert`	Some objects' context menus contain a Convert option. This key allows you to automatically convert the current file format to the one identified by `CLSID`. For example, Word for Windows allows you to convert many types of data to a format that it specifically supports. This conversion process changes the embedded or linked object into a Word for Windows object. In other words, it changes the data into something that Word might have created itself.
`Convertible`	There are two levels of subkeys below this one. The first level contains two keys, `Readable` and `Writeable`. Below them are keys that contain a list of readable or writeable file formats to which you can convert this file format. For example, you'll find that Word for Windows supports several formats, including Word Document. The number of entries in this area usually varies by the number of file filters you install for the application. For example, if you install WordPerfect file support for Word for Windows, you'll likely find an entry for it here. Remember, though, that these are OLE 2 entries. Even if an application supports another application's file format as part of a Save As option, it still might not support it for OLE purposes.
`Interfaces`	This key contains a list of interfaces supported by the server. The value for this key will eventually contain the names of other ways of accessing the OLE server (other than from the local machine), but there aren't any applications that support it right now. For example, this entry could contain the types of network protocols that the application supports.

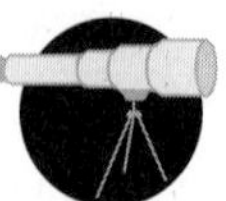

Looking Ahead: This chapter tells you about only the Registry portion of the OLE picture. Chapter 12 provides detailed information about OLE from a user level.

HKEY_CURRENT_USER

The earlier discussion of the HKEY_CURRENT_USER category centered on the fact that it's slaved to the current user settings. These settings are copied to the HKEY_USERS category when you shut down. In other words, this particular category is a scratch pad of sorts. It's very useful to remember this fact. If you make a mistake, you can always use the settings in HKEY_USERS to reset the values to their previous settings. The following sections describe each of the HKEY_CURRENT_USER keys in detail.

Note: Using a common setup for all users means that HKEY_CURRENT_USER settings automatically reflect the default setting in HKEY_USERS. (Click the first radio button in the User Profiles tab of the Passwords applet in Control Panel.) See the "HKEY_USERS" section for more details on these settings.

AppEvents

Everyone likes to add a few sounds to their system to make it through the day. This key defines these sounds in a number of ways. Take a look at Figure 7.14 to see what the AppEvents subkeys look like. There are two subkeys under this one: EventLabels and Schemes. The EventLabels key holds a list of events. Each event key contains the long name of a sound event. For example, the EmptyRecycleBin event uses "Empty Recycle Bin" as a long name. This is what Windows displays in the dialog box you use to set the sound value.

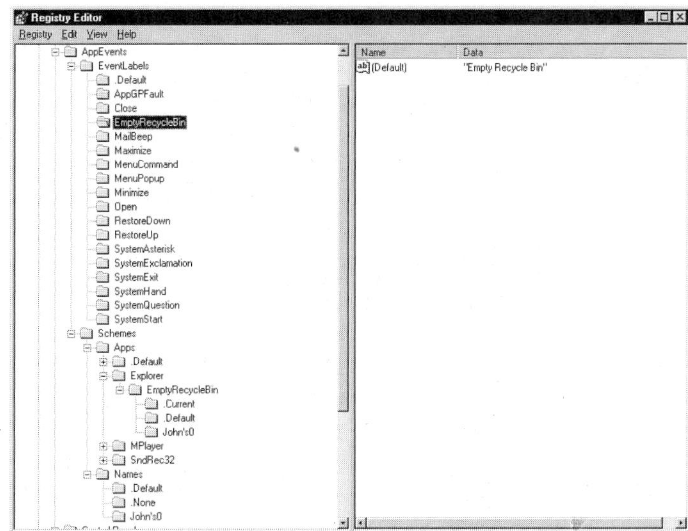

Figure 7.14.
The AppEvents *key controls the sounds you hear for various system events. It also contains the strings used to display these event names in the Sounds Properties dialog box.*

Tip: This Registry key provides the only way you can change the strings displayed in the Sounds Properties dialog box. You might want to use this option after changing the name of the Recycle Bin or other Windows components.

The `Schemes` key is the one you'll probably want to explore. There are two subkeys below this one. The first one we'll look at is the `Names` key. The subkeys hold the full names of the various sound schemes you might have defined. The `Apps` key contains subkeys for each kind of application that defines special sounds. For example, the `MPlayer` (media player) subkey has two sound subkeys: `Close` and `Open`. You could define a sound for each event. There's also a default sounds subkey that defines the beeps and other general Windows noises you hear on a daily basis. If you looked at the values for each of the application sound subkeys such as `Close` and `Open`, you'd see one or more sound profile subkeys. Each of these sound profile subkeys contains the name of a sound file as a value. So let's put all this into perspective. Say you wanted to look at the sound associated with the Start Windows event in the current profile. You'd look at the value for the key `HKEY_CURRENT_USER | AppEvents | Schemes | Apps | .Default | SystemStart | .Current`.

Control Panel

This is probably the most familiar Registry key. Figure 7.15 shows all the subkeys that this key contains. As you can see, the `Control Panel` key doesn't contain subkeys for each icon in the Control Panel, but it does contain keys for all the icons that control user-specific settings.

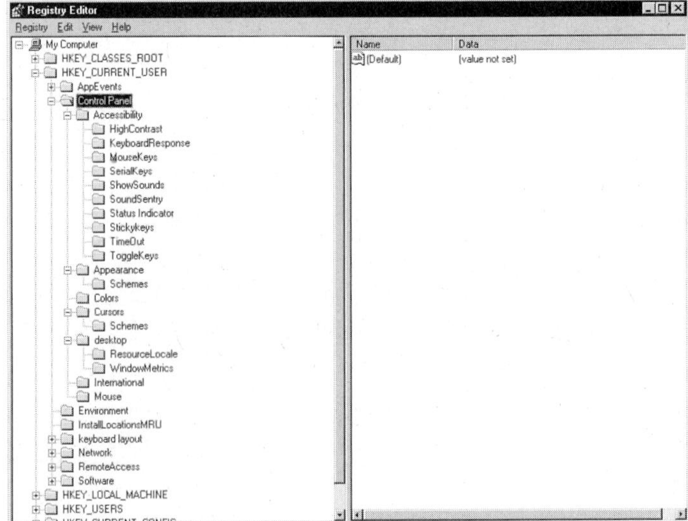

Figure 7.15.
The `Control Panel` key contains subkeys for every user-specific feature in the Control Panel.

The following list describes these subkeys in more detail:

- `Accessibility`: This subkey contains all the settings for the Accessibility features, such as StickyKeys and high-contrast monitor. You can find a complete description of these features in Chapter 1.
- `Appearance`: The `Appearance` key contains the current display's color settings. It includes both a text description and the custom colors. This value doesn't include the actual color values. Below this key is the `Schemes` subkey. It contains the text description and color value for all the color schemes you've defined.

Tip: If you want to share your color schemes with someone else, you can export this key by using the same procedure used to save the Registry. Instead of saving the entire Registry, save just the `Schemes` branch. When the other person imports your .REG file, she'll have the same color schemes you do.

- `Colors`: This subkey contains a list of object types and their associated colors. Windows 95 uses these settings to present everything on your display.

Tip: The `Colors` key settings provide a level of flexibility that you can't get using the standard Display Properties dialog box. For example, clicking the button displays the 3D object settings. These settings don't provide the same precise control as the `Button` values in this key.

- `Cursors`: This subkey contains a list of cursor types and their associated cursor files. Below this key is the `Schemes` subkey. It contains a list of all the cursor schemes you've defined and their associated settings.
- `desktop`: All your desktop settings appear in the values of this key. It includes the current wallpaper, background, and screen saver settings. Below this key is the `ResourceLocale` subkey, which contains the current country code. The `WindowMetrics` subkey defines all the icon spacing and other graphic specifications for the desktop.
- `International`: The `International` key contains the current country code.
- `Mouse`: This key contains the standard mouse settings, not the Accessibility mouse settings. It determines how the mouse reacts when you're using a standard setup.

Environment

This key contains the DOS environment settings. Windows stores them in hexadecimal instead of plain English. It uses these values when you start a DOS session. Windows applications can request this information as well.

InstallLocationsMRU

This Registry key contains the most-recently-used locations of installation files. This doesn't pertain to the location of software installation files, but to device or service-related installation files. For example, installing a new set of network drivers would place an entry here, but installing a new word processor wouldn't. Notice that there's a special value called `MRUList`. This value controls the order in which Windows displays the filenames that appear in the list. If you add an entry to the list, you also have to add it to the `MRUList` value.

Keyboard Layout

This Registry key provides information about the keyboard currently attached to the machine. It doesn't really change from user to user unless one user needs to use a different language or keyboard layout. The `Preload` key under the `Keyboard` section reflects the different languages in use. The `Substitutes` key reflects the keyboard layout. For example, you could use English (United States) as a language and English (Dvorak) as a layout. The `Toggle` key tells you which control-key combination you can use to switch between languages.

Peter's Principle: Using Two Keyboard Layouts

I ran into an interesting situation the other day. Two friends were using the same machine. One uses the Dvorak layout, and the other uses the standard layout. Windows 95 will allow you to install multiple languages and switch between them using the International icon on the Taskbar, but not different layouts of the same language. So how do you get around this?

Start by installing two languages, using the standard Keyboard Properties dialog box. Make certain that the languages are at least compatible. To make life simple, I installed English (United States) using the standard layout and English (British) using the Dvorak layout. If you look at the `HKEY_CURRENT_USER | Keyboard Layout | Preload` key, you'll notice two subkeys. The value for one is `00000409 (United States)`, and the value for the other is `00000809 (British)`.

Look at the `Substitutes` key. You'll see a subkey for `00000809`. The value in this key says `00020409`. If you look up this value in the `HKEY_LOCAL_MACHINE | System | CurrentControlSet | Control | Keyboard Layouts | 00020409` key, you'll see that we're using the standard Dvorak keyboard KBD driver. Our language is English, and the keyboard layout matches what the second person needs.

The only thing left to do is change the International icon list so that it matches what the machine actually has installed. If you look at it right now, it says that you have an English (United States) and an English (British) keyboard setup installed. What you really have is an English (Dvorak) keyboard installed. Look at the `HKEY_LOCAL_MACHINE | System | CurrentControlSet | Control | NLS | Locale` key. Find the `00000809` value and change it from `British` to `Dvorak`. Close the Registry Editor to make sure the change is recorded. Now open the Keyboard Properties dialog box in the Control Panel. Make a simple change and then change it back. Click Apply. The International icon will now show a United States and a Dvorak keyboard, making it simple for you to switch back and forth.

Network

Unfortunately, most of this key's contents are network-specific. Essentially, it provides the user-specific network information that your machine needs. One key remains constant across networks—the `Recent` key. This key contains one subkey for each of the network drives you've recently accessed. Windows 95 updates it only on a session basis, so you probably won't find current information here if you maintain your network connection for a long time between sessions. Each subkey uses the full network access path for a drive. For example, if you have a Microsoft network installed and you connect to drive C on a machine named AUX, one of the subkeys might look like this: `//AUX/DRIVE-C`.

RemoteAccess

You may or may not find this key in your Registry. It depends on what features you choose to install. Within the key itself is an area code value and a DWORD configuration value for the Make New Connection Wizard.

Below this key you'll find one subkey that holds the addresses you define. There's one binary value for each address you define. These values include all the configuration information for that address. Obviously, you won't want to edit this value outside the Dial-Up Networking application.

Software

This Registry key should contain plenty of configuration information for your software. However, until you upgrade to 32-bit versions of your applications, it will probably contain a few default entries for Windows 95-specific applications. The `SSC` section contains information related to the viewers. The `Microsoft` section contains keys for a variety of applications, whether you have them installed or not.

The Registry provides this section to replace all those entries you used to have in WIN.INI and SYSTEM.INI. The hierarchical structure of this key makes it very easy to remove application-specific information from your Windows 95 installation. There's one subkey of particular interest. The `MS Setup (ACME) | User Info` key shown in Figure 7.16 contains the user's name and company information. Applications look at this entry during installation. This is the only place where you can change this information in Windows 95. If you need to change the user name for software installation purposes, this is the place to do it.

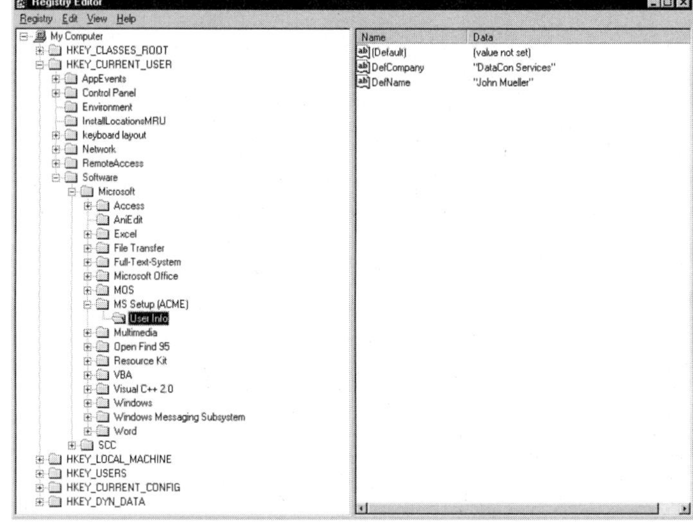

Figure 7.16.
Many 32-bit programs use the information in the `User Info` *key as a default during installation for burning the user information into the application.*

HKEY_LOCAL_MACHINE

The `HKEY_LOCAL_MACHINE` category centers its attention on the machine hardware. This includes the drivers and configuration information required to run the hardware. A lot of subtle information about your hardware is stored under this category. For example, it contains all the plug and play information about your machine. It also provides a complete listing of the device drivers and their revision level.

This category contains some software-specific information. For example, a 32-bit application will store the location of its setup table here. The application uses this table during installation. Some applications also use it during a setup modification. Applications such as Word for Windows NT store all their setup information in SFT tables. Figure 7.17 shows a typical `HKEY_LOCAL_MACHINE` category setup. The following sections describe each key in detail.

Config

The `Config` key provides specific information needed to set up the machine during boot. The two main references are the display and the printer. The printer settings appear under the `System` key. In most cases, the only printer configuration information you'll see is the specific name of the printer attached to the current machine. This key doesn't provide any network-specific information.

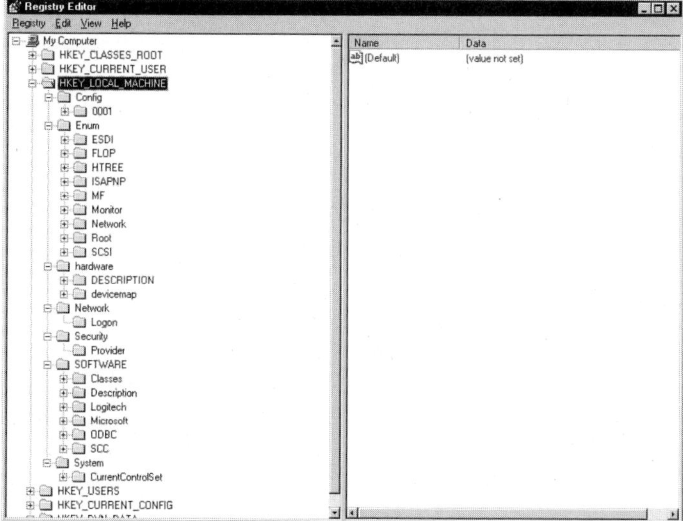

Figure 7.17.
The HKEY_LOCAL_MACHINE *category contains all the hardware- and device-driver-specific information about your machine, as well as the global application setup information.*

Note: Windows 95 copies the contents of the Config key to the HKEY_CURRENT_CONFIG category. It overwrites any changes you make to the values in this key during logout or shutdown. Make any required changes to the HKEY_CURRENT_CONFIG values. Fortunately, having a backup copy of the configuration under the HKEY_LOCAL_MACHINE | Config key means that you can easily correct editing mistakes in the HKEY_CURRENT_CONFIG key values.

The Display settings include the resolution and fonts. It's a lot more detailed than the printer settings. There are two subkeys under the main Display key. The Fonts key provides a list of default font requirements and the name of the font file that satisfies that need. In most cases, you can change these settings by using the Display utility in the Control Panel. The Settings key provides information on the current number of colors (as bits per pixel) and the display resolution. It also provides the names of the default display fonts.

Enum

This Registry key enumerates the hardware connected to your machine. Figure 7.17 shows a typical installation. Some hardware receives special attention through the use of separate keys. For example, an IDE hard drive and the floppy drives fall into this category. Other hardware falls into the plug and play category. The actual plug and play hardware listing appears under the Root key. The subkeys under the Root key also appear in the Device Manager listing. Figure 7.18 shows a typical set of values for the COM ports.

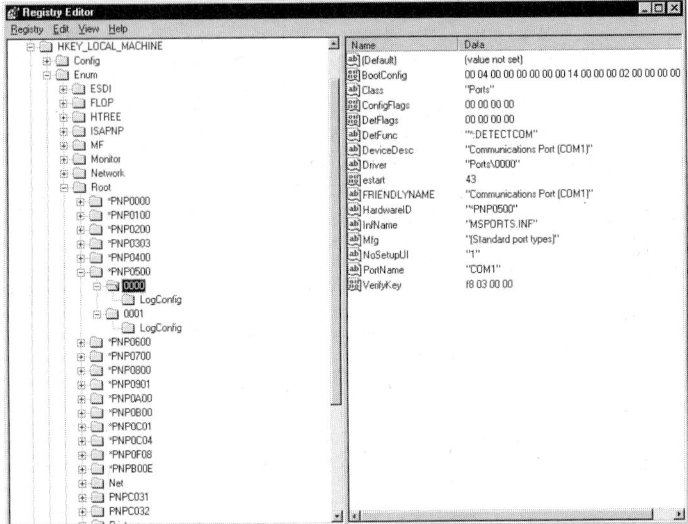

Figure 7.18. *A typical plug and play Registry entry doesn't provide much information. However, it does provide important clues for the network troubleshooter. One of the most important pieces of information is the location of the .INF file associated with the device.*

As you can see, the Device Manager display is much easier to read. However, the Registry display provides one important piece of troubleshooting information: the name of the .INF file that holds the COM port configuration information (MSPORTS.INF). These .INF files provide a wealth of information about the default port interrupts. They also provide information about the .DLLs and VxDs used to support them. You can also modify the .INF files for any device, to provide support for nonstandard devices or additional port/interrupt configurations. Think of an .INF file as an .INI file for devices.

hardware

In most cases, you can ignore the `hardware` Registry key. Its only function is to list the communication ports and any floating-point processors attached to the machine. This key doesn't contain any actual configuration information.

Network

This key contains some network-specific security information. The only entry most users will find here is what parameters—their user and machine name—they use to log onto a network. This key also contains some configuration information, such as whether Windows needs to process a login script.

Security

This Registry key is network-specific. Refer to your network manuals for additional information. As a general rule, it contains pointers to files holding account and other network-security-specific information. In some cases (usually with peer-to-peer networks), you won't see anything here, even if you have a network connected to your machine. It's also interesting to see some information placed here when you enable multiple desktop configurations.

SOFTWARE

The `SOFTWARE` Registry key contains device driver and global-application information. Most applications store their specific configuration information under the `Application` key and any global information under another (common) key. Refer to Figure 7.17 to see a typical setup. Notice that the subkeys include a variety of vendor-specific information.

One of the interesting subkeys is `Classes`. Opening this key reveals a list of file extensions and associations just like the one in `HKEY_CLASSES_ROOT`. The purpose behind this set of keys is totally different, though. Windows 95 uses this list to locate application-specific or device-driver-specific files instead of creating links for Explorer or providing OLE configuration information. Changing these keys won't affect your Explorer display. Unfortunately, it might affect how some of your applications work. The bottom line is, don't change any of these settings unless you have a good reason to do so and know exactly how the change will affect your setup.

The `Description` key also provides some interesting information. A default setup always contains the Microsoft remote procedure call (`RPC`) listing. However, a network could use this section to describe other links between machines as well. An RPC allows your machine to use the resources found on another machine. This is an automatic feature. The application and operating system have to support RPCs. In addition, the resource has to be available—you can't steal someone's resource if he's already using it. RPCs can include all kinds of resources, but they normally refer to code. For example, you could borrow someone else's .DLL if that .DLL didn't appear on your machine. The unique aspect of RPCs is that the code for that .DLL would execute on the other person's machine, not your machine. In effect, you would borrow not only his code, but his processor. Notice that this section doesn't define any light remote procedure call (LRPC) information. An LRPC is the same as an RPC except that it deals with very specific types of resources, and it always deals with code. You could borrow another person's .DLL, but the code for that .DLL would execute on your machine, not his machine. The LRPC statistics always appear as part of the OLE configuration information or within the `RPC` keys.

Unless you have a Microsoft mouse, there's a good chance that you'll have a mouse-specific entry—even if your mouse doesn't provide Windows 95-specific software. The `Logitech` key shown earlier in Figure 7.17 provides mouse setup information as well as the driver version. For example, under the `MouseMan | 0000` key are values that determine which buttons are assigned to various mouse functions.

Tip: Using the Registry to edit a hardware configuration setting is almost always more flexible than using the Control Panel settings. For example, what if you wanted to gain some additional control over your three-button Logitech mouse? The default setup program allows you to assign a left- or a right-handed setup to the mouse. What if you wanted to exchange the right and middle button functions, essentially creating a two-button mouse? You could do so by transposing the `MappingButton2` and `MappingButton3` Registry values, even though the configuration utility doesn't provide the means to do so.

The `Microsoft` section of the `SOFTWARE` key provides some useful information as well. One of these keys is the `New Users Settings` key. Most 32-bit applications and some 16-bit applications can provide an entry in this area. A new user inherits these settings when you set up a new login on her machine. In essence, this key contains the global settings that everyone uses with this application (at least until she customizes her setup). This key also provides the location of shared tools and any global network settings required to make the application work.

If you install any applications that support open database connectivity (ODBC), all those settings appear under this key. ODBC is Microsoft's method of allowing you to access information in foreign data formats. Its main purpose is to allow access to mainframe databases, but you'll find it used to access other sources of information, including those commonly found on a PC. You'll also see the 32-bit ODBC settings here. The strange thing is that they aren't identified using separate keys, even though the 32-bit settings appear as a separate icon in the Control Panel. Every ODBC connection and its configuration appears under the `ODBC | ODBCINST.INI` key. The two important values are the name of the ODBC driver and its version. Most 32-bit drivers include a `32` somewhere in the filename. This fact allows you to separate the 32-bit drivers from the 16-bit drivers in this area.

The `SCC` key contains information about the viewers (if you installed them). At first glance, you might not think that there's anything worthwhile to look at. There are two keys at the bottom of the hierarchy, and both use descriptive value entry names such as `Element 1`. However, if you double-click one of these entries, you'll find the name of the .DLL that controls it embedded in the binary data that each value contains.

System

The last Registry key in this category is also the most destructive when edited incorrectly. A bad entry in any value under this key can kill your installation. Figure 7.19 shows the subkeys associated with the `System` key.

Microsoft split these keys into two categories: control and services. The `Control` key contains all the subkeys that change the way the user reacts to the system.

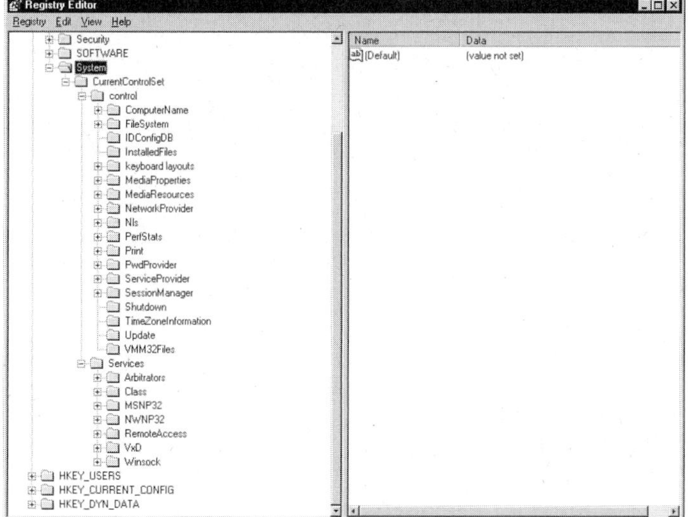

Figure 7.19.
The `System` *key provides much information and many opportunities for system optimization.*

Warning: Exploring this part of the Registry is somewhat risky. Some settings won't harm your system much—they might just change the text in a list box or under an icon. However, other settings will damage your Windows 95 installation beyond repair, and still others will prevent access to your system. Wandering through this section and seeing what will happen when you change a setting is one sure way to make your system unusable. Always make a backup of your Registry before you make any change to this section.

One of the keys you'll see here is the `NLS` (national language support) key. Remember the keyboard setting discussed earlier? This is where all the language settings come from. If you had the correct driver, you could add support for Martian by changing the value of one of these keys. The network-administration-specific keys appear here as well. One of the first keys you'll see is the computer name used to log onto the network.

Several subkeys give the advanced user an opportunity to tune system performance. One of the most interesting keys to look at is the `Known16DLLs` key under the `SessionManager` key. The values in this key tell you where you can optimize the system. A 16-bit .DLL doesn't perform as well as its 32-bit counterpart. Finding 32-bit .DLLs to replace the 16-bit .DLLs in this section can improve your system performance without requiring you to buy any new hardware.

Tip: Not every 16-bit .DLL is bad. You pay a price in program size when you use a 32-bit .DLL. This translates to larger code size and actually means a decrease in performance. However, most 32-bit .DLLs offset this performance hit by offering more efficient code. In addition, 32-bit .DLLs are more stable because of how Windows manages them. You should always base the decision to try and get rid of a specific 16-bit .DLL on known performance improvement. Hoping you'll get something in return is like gambling: You never quite know if you'll win.

One of the more dangerous keys in this section is the `PwdProvider` key. It tells Windows 95 the location of any password or user account files. This key also contains the name of any .DLLs or VxDs required to implement system security. You can't log into the network if this key is deleted. The problem is that you can't get into Windows because the key doesn't exist, and you can't add it back in because you can't use the Registry editor without Windows. You can't even access the Registry from another machine, because Windows must be online to enable remote Registry support. The bottom line is that you should get those backup disks out and hope you have a DOS-based backup program that can read them. You're going to need a good copy of the Registry to get back into Windows.

The System Monitor utility (installed during network installation) gets some of its input here as well. Look under the `System | CurrentControlSet | control | PerfStats | Enum` key. Here are all the statistics that you can choose from in the System Monitor utility. Each subkey in this section contains a description, a differentiate flag, and a name. Theoretically, you could add a Performance Monitor statistic here and it would show up in the System Monitor utility. Of course, you wouldn't get any useful information out of it, unless you happened to find an undocumented statistic. Other Registry entries are required, and you'd need to write the supporting software. However, you could remove statistics from here to prevent network users from monitoring areas that you don't want them to touch. You could also change the name or description of a statistic to meet your needs.

On to the second part of the `System` key, `Services`. This group of keys does just the opposite of what the `Control` key section does: It allows the user to change the way the system reacts.

Warning: There are a few subkeys under the `Services` key that you should never touch. They include `Arbitrators`, `Unknown`, and `Nodriver`.

The majority of the `Class` key subkeys provide useful information. For example, the `CDROM` key can tell you about the drivers associated with the CD-ROM drive. In some cases, it might provide clues about why the CD-ROM drive fails to play music or interface with the system in some other way.

The `Display` key contains several subkeys related to the display adapter. This includes specifics about resolution and color combinations that the driver supports. (In one case, I was actually able to change this entry and provide 256-color support at 1024×768 resolution on one machine, even though the driver originally showed that it didn't support this combination.) Of course, as with any other keys in this group, editing the values for these keys can result in a boot failure or other unforeseen occurrences.

In addition to these keys, you might find some network-related information in this section. For example, anyone using the Microsoft Network support provided with Windows 95 will see an `MSNP32` key. The values under this key contain information about the user setup and logon information.

HKEY_USERS

The earlier section "A Centralized Database of Setup Information" discusses the major aspects of this category. All this category contains is one profile for each user who logs into a particular workstation when you enable multiple desktops by using the User Profiles tab of the Password Properties dialog box.

So where does the original information for each user come from? The Registry contains one entry called `.Default`. (Notice the period in front of the key name; `Default` without a period is a user name.) Windows 95 takes the information in this key and copies it to a user-specific key when the user logs in for the first time. Each profile looks precisely the same as the one provided for the `.Default` key. The user can't add new keys for his configuration.

Each subkey and value under the `.Default` key is echoed in the `HKEY_CURRENT_USER` category, so I won't go into the settings again here. (The initial login does more work than create a simple Registry entry, but I won't cover that in this chapter.) You should follow a few Registry-related tips when setting up your network:

- Always configure the workstation for the minimum possible access rights for the `.Default` user. This allows you to create new users without the risk of circumventing network security.
- Consider renaming the `.Default` user entry so that other people can't log in without a password. (Windows 95 will come to a screeching halt if it can't find the default user.)
- Use the System Policy Editor instead of the Registry Editor whenever possible to make changes to the network setup.
- Make a backup of both the USER.DAT and SYSTEM.DAT files before you set up the network. Failure to take this step means that you'll have to reinstall Windows 95 from scratch if the network setup fails.

Tip: By using the same profile for all users, you can save at least 100KB for each user who logs onto a particular machine (each user profile on my machine ate 300KB). Unless you need the security or desktop setup flexibility that such a setup provides, the additional hard disk space is wasted. Never enable multiple desktops for a single user setup; instead, use the shortcuts discussed in Chapter 5.

HKEY_CURRENT_CONFIG

The HKEY_CURRENT_CONFIG category is the simplest part of the Registry. It's so simple that I covered it completely earlier in this chapter (see "A Centralized Database of Setup Information"). There aren't any hidden secrets here—nothing for you to exploit. Overall, it's probably the most boring part of the Registry.

HKEY_DYN_DATA

The final category, HKEY_DYN_DATA, contains two subkeys, Config Manager and PerfStats. The earlier section "A Centralized Database of Setup Information" takes a generic look at this key, but let's take a more detailed look now. Figure 7.20 shows a detailed view of this particular category.

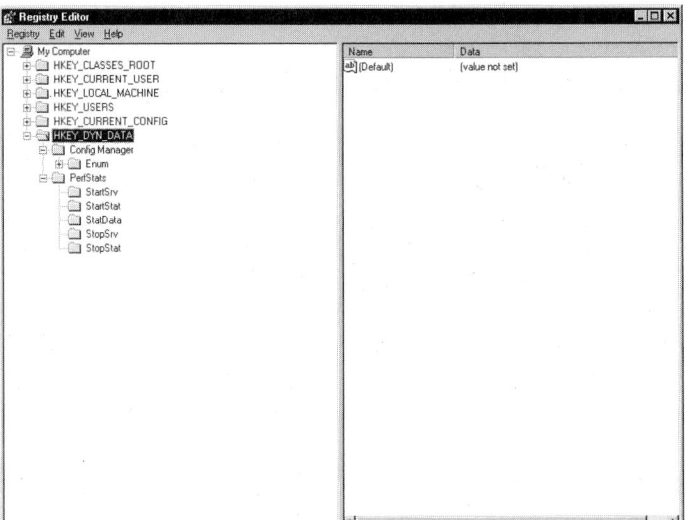

Figure 7.20. *You'll always find the current (dynamic) state of the computer under the* HKEY_DYN_DATA *key*.

The Enum key contains subkeys for every device attached to the computer. Each of the subkeys contains the same four values. The Allocation value shows which process has control of the device. The HardwareKey value contains an entry that matches the plug and play values discussed earlier for the HKEY_LOCAL_MACHINE | Enum | Root key. Essentially, this value identifies the device. For example, a plug and play value of 0500 matches the first serial port. The Problem value should equal 0 in most cases (unless the hardware experiences a fault). This value always contains an error number during a hardware failure. The final key, Status, contains a value of 4F 4A 00 00 when the hardware is error-free.

The PerfStats key contains five subkeys. The first two subkeys control the starting time for gathering server and statistical data. The last two control the stopping time. These four keys probably won't tell you too much about your machine or how to improve its performance. The only interesting key in this group is the `StatData` key. It contains the current usage level data for each of the categories that the System Monitor utility tracks. In fact, if you press F5 to refresh the Registry data, you can watch the data values change. (You must start the System Monitor utility to see any change, because this utility tracks the data values and places them in the Registry.) Keeping the System Monitor utility window and the Registry Editor window on-screen at the same time will show you how these numbers track the information you see in the utility.

Getting the Most from RegEdit

I've spent a lot of time talking about the Registry in this chapter, and almost no time at all talking about the tool you need to use to actually see the Registry. RegEdit is the simple utility program that you use to modify the Registry. There are some very specific tasks that you can perform with RegEdit, besides just viewing your setup. The following sections show you how to use RegEdit for a variety of task-oriented purposes. I even take a quick look at the command-line usage of RegEdit. Remember that text version of the Registry that you saved at the very beginning of this chapter? You can use the command-line version of RegEdit to restore your Registry, using a text file. I would recommend caution when doing this, though—a binary backup is still much better insurance against accidental editing mistakes and other potential problems with the Registry.

Modifying File Associations

Explorer is the Windows 95 alternative to the Windows 3.x File Manager. It goes a long way toward making Windows 95 truly usable. However, as with any other tool, you'll probably want to customize this one to meet your needs. One of the first things you'll want to do is change the file associations.

The problem with Explorer is that you can't add new extensions to an existing file type. This means that if you want to extend the ability of Word for Windows to open file types other than the default types, you can't do it with the tools that Explorer provides. However, you can still get the job done using the Registry Editor. This simple procedure allows you to add new extensions to an existing entry. (I'll approach it from an exercise point of view to make the illustration clearer. Just substitute the values you need in place of the ones I provide here.)

Tip: Always use the right tool for the job. You might be tempted to use the Registry Editor to make all your file association changes, after reading about the flexibility in editing that it provides in this section. However, the Explorer interface is a lot faster, simpler, and less error-prone than making the modifications by hand. The only time you should need to use the Registry Editor on a file extension is when you need to extend an existing association.

1. Open a copy of the Registry Editor.
2. Click the plus (+) sign next to the `HKEY_CLASSES_ROOT` key. Click the `.DOC` entry. You should see `"Word.Document.6"` or something similar as a value for this key. We'll use this value as the basis for adding a new value to Word. Notice the use of periods. Formatting is very important in the Registry, as are punctuation marks.
3. Click the `HKEY_CLASSES_ROOT` key. Use the Edit | New | Key command to add a new key named `.ASC`. (Be sure to type a period before `ASC`.)

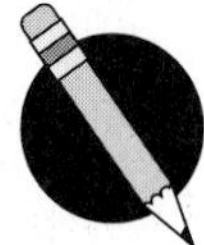

Note: If you already have an `.ASC` extension in your Registry, choose another extension for right now.

4. Double-click the `Default` value and type `Word.Document.6` as a value. You should see a display similar to the one shown in Figure 7.21.

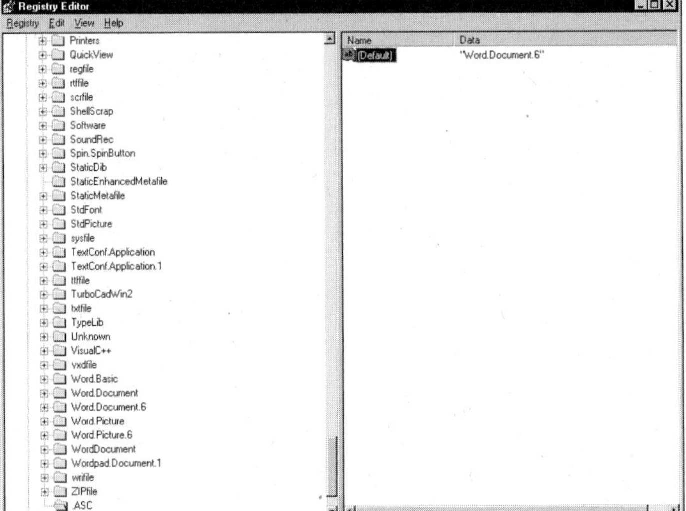

Figure 7.21.
Adding a new key to extend the linkages supported by an application is relatively easy when using the Registry Editor.

5. Close the Registry Editor.
6. Open a copy of Explorer.
7. Use the View | Options command to display the Options dialog box. Click the File Types tab. Highlight the Microsoft Word 6.0 Document entry. You'll see the new Word file association shown in Figure 7.22.

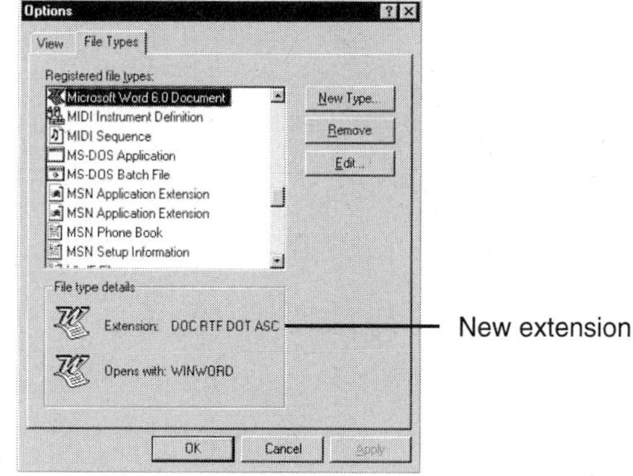

Figure 7.22.
Word used to provide just three file associations. It now provides four, including the new .ASC extension.

Using Find to Change Strings

One of the things that really annoyed me when I started using Windows 95 was that Microsoft prevented me from changing some names—and for no real reason. One of these was the name of the Recycle Bin. I'd prefer just about any name to that (and so would a lot of other people I've talked to).

You don't have to live with any names you really don't want under Windows 95. The vast majority of the titles that appear under icons and, in some cases, even the items you'll see in a list box, are all in the Registry. This simple procedure uses the Find command to help you locate the offending string and change it.

Warning: Windows 95 relies on the contents of some strings to perform specific work. For example, you might change your network name, and it will work fine. Then again, in other cases it won't, because your network embedded that name in a file. Changing a string without knowing how it will affect your computer is never a good idea. Change only the strings that contain names you can see. Icons and some list boxes are good candidates.

As with the preceding section, I'll approach this task from an exercise perspective. I've kept things as simple as possible so that you can use this procedure to modify other names you might not like.

1. Open a copy of the Registry Editor.
2. Use the Edit | Find command to open the Find dialog box. Type **`Recycle Bin`** in the Find What text box. Click Find Next. Be patient; the Registry might take a little while to find the first occurrence of `"Recycle Bin"`. There's very little chance your machine will freeze during the search.
3. Double-click the value that holds the words `"Recycle Bin"` (usually `Default`). You should see the Edit String dialog box. Type anything you want (within reason, of course). This will be the new name of your Recycle Bin. Your new entry should look similar to the one shown in Figure 7.23.

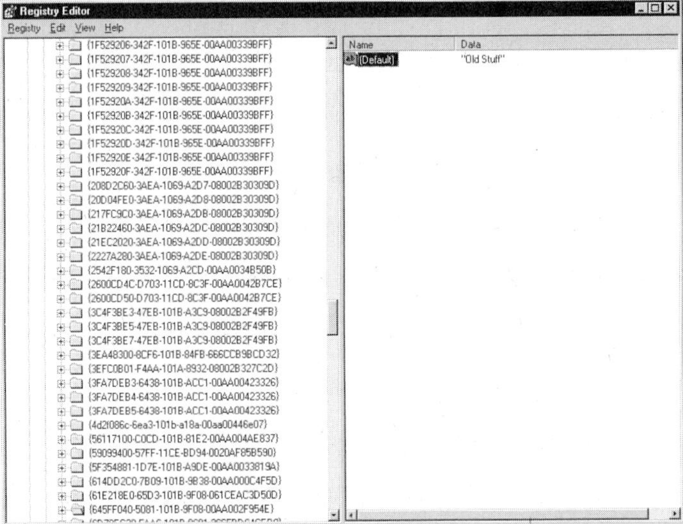

Figure 7.23. *Changing the name of the Recycle Bin consists of changing the value of the strings that define it.*

4. Press F3 to find the next occurrence of the string.
5. Repeat steps 3 and 4 for every occurrence of the string. Make sure that you find every occurrence and replace it with exactly the same value in every instance. Otherwise, you could end up confusing Windows 95 when it looks for that value later.
6. Close the Registry Editor and reboot the machine. This will allow the change to take effect.

That's all there is to it. You can use this procedure for a variety of tasks, including changing names you don't like. The same word of caution applies here as everywhere else. If you decide to change the Registry, be sure to make a backup first. Trying to restore a failed Registry is pretty much impossible under Windows 95.

Importing and Exporting Registry Data

One of the problems with using a Registry for everything is that you have to put the configuration data into a form that the Registry can accept. But quite a few mainstream applications create a .REG file that you can import into the Registry. Even the .REG files created with 16-bit applications are compatible with the Windows 95 Registry.

Importing Data

You can use several techniques to import your current Registry information into the Registry. First, you can open a copy of Explorer and find the Registry file you want to import. Figure 7.24 shows a typical example.

Figure 7.24.
A typical Registry file entry. This one is for Word for Windows 6.0.

All you need to do is double-click the .REG icon (shown as `Winword6.reg` in Figure 7.24), and RegEdit automatically enters it into the Registry. Notice that the .REG file icon looks like the Registry Editor icon with a document behind it. After the Registry enters the new configuration information for your application, it displays the dialog box shown in Figure 7.25.

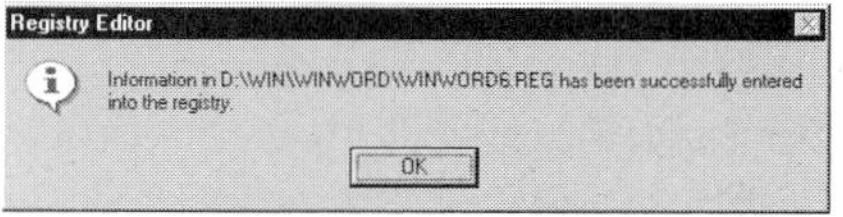

Figure 7.25.
The Registry signals a successful configuration data entry for Word for Windows 6.0.

A second technique comes in handy when you have the Registry Editor open. Simply choose Registry | Import Registry File. The Registry Editor displays a dialog box similar to the one shown in Figure 7.26.

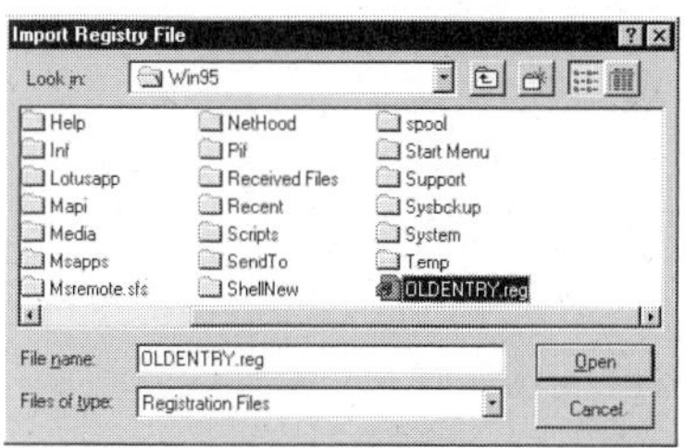

Figure 7.26.
You can use menu commands to import a configuration into the Registry when RegEdit is open.

Click the Open button to complete the task. You should see the dialog box shown earlier in Figure 7.25 when RegEdit completes the task.

Exporting Data

What happens when you want to save some configuration changes you made in the past? For example, what if you added a new file extension to the Registry and want to save those entries for future use? How about the custom color combinations that you create—wouldn't it be nice to save them before installing a new version of Windows 95? You can export either all or part of the Registry by using the Registry | Export Registry File command in the Registry Editor. Figure 7.27 shows the Export Registry File dialog box.

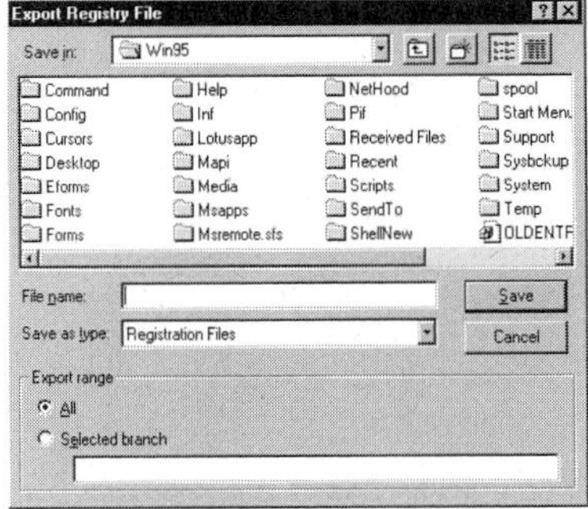

Figure 7.27.
The Registry provides the means to export configuration data into a pure ASCII text file. You can edit this data by using a standard text editor such as Notepad.

Notice that this dialog box has the All radio button selected. This option saves the entire Registry to a text file. Use this option when you want to save the Registry before you start editing it. It's also easy to save a branch (or section) of the Registry, using one of two techniques. The first technique is to highlight the branch you want to save, open the Export Registry File dialog box, and click the Selected Branch radio button. The second technique is to open the Export Registry File dialog box, click the Selected Branch radio button, and then type the fully qualified name of the branch you want to save.

All you need to do to complete the process is click the Save button. RegEdit doesn't provide any kind of feedback once it exports the Registry to disk. You'll probably want to view the saved file before you make any changes to the Registry.

Viewing the Contents of an Exported Registry Entry

Exported Registry data files contain pure ASCII text. They don't contain any control characters that you need to worry about. You normally need to use WordPad to view a saved version of the entire Registry. (A full Registry export file normally takes between 400KB and 500KB of storage.) Notepad will probably do the job if you just want to look at a saved branch.

Figure 7.28 shows a typical saved Registry branch. Notice that this file has three lines. The first line contains `REGEDIT4`, which identifies the version of the Registry Editor that created the file. It also prevents you from importing the file into an older version of the Registry. Application .REG files normally don't contain any version numbers as part of the `REGEDIT` entry. This allows you to import them using any version of RegEdit.

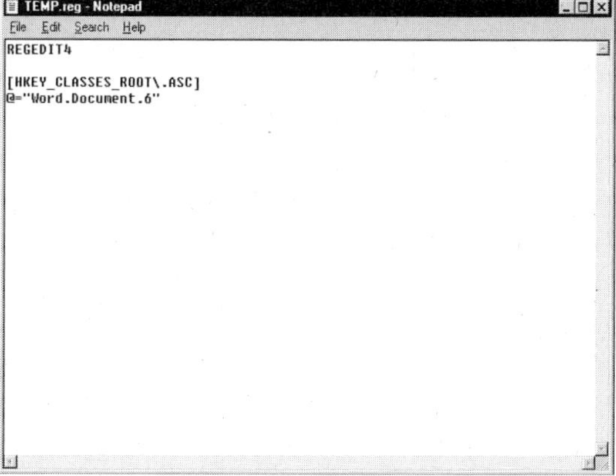

```
REGEDIT4

[HKEY_CLASSES_ROOT\.ASC]
@="Word.Document.6"
```

Figure 7.28.
This saved Registry branch contains a mere four lines of data. Each line serves a specific purpose during the import process.

The real second line of the file contains a blank. RegEdit uses this blank line as a delimiter between Registry key entries. The second line of text (the third line of the file) contains the Registry key. Notice that it looks like a hard disk directory listing. Each backslash tells RegEdit to create a new key level.

The final line of text contains the actual key value. The `@` symbol at the beginning of the line tells RegEdit that this is the default entry. Any other value begins with a value name. The double quotes around the value itself tell RegEdit that this is a string value. Binary values begin with the word `hex` followed by a colon, and DWORD values begin with the word `dword` followed by a colon.

Tip: You might find that you need to add the keys from one branch to another branch in the Registry. For example, you might want to use some of the OLE information from one file association when creating a new one. It seems that RegEdit should provide some type of cut-and-paste capability to take care of this task, but it doesn't. The fastest, most efficient way to add the contents of one branch to another is to export the Registry, use a text editor to cut-and-paste the values you need, and import the modified Registry file. Of course, by using this method you could find yourself with a machine that won't boot. Be sure to keep an unmodified copy of the Registry handy, just in case.

Importing and Exporting at the Command Line

Microsoft thoughtfully provides a command-line interface for RegEdit. This means that if you can't boot your machine and you just happen to have a recent text version of your Registry handy, you can restore it. After the file is restored, you should be able to boot Windows 95 normally, or at least close enough to normal to repair whatever damage your installation may have suffered.

Warning: There's no guarantee that Microsoft will maintain a command-line interface for RegEdit. For example, the Windows NT version of RegEdit doesn't support the command-line interface (at least not the most current version). It's always better to have a backup of the binary version of your Registry than to try and fix a problem by using the command-line interface. Even with these potential problems, however, using the command-line version of RegEdit to fix Registry damage is still better than not having any kind of resource at all.

The command-line switches for RegEdit aren't very complex. Table 7.3 shows the command-line switches for the release version of Windows 95 with Service Pack 1 installed. It doesn't take any Service Release differences into account.

Table 7.3. RegEdit command-line switches.

Switch	*Description*
`/L:<system>`	Provides the location of the SYSTEM.DAT file.
`/R:<user>`	Provides the location of the USER.DAT file.
`<filename>`	The name of the file that you want to import into the Registry. It must be an ASCII text file that uses the format shown in Figure 7.28. A filename by itself will always add information to the Registry.
`/C <filename>`	Creates an entirely new Registry. `filename` contains the name of the file you want to use. The file must contain a complete Registry, because you're going to replace the existing Registry with a new one. This is the option you'd use to restore the Registry by using a text copy that you exported previously. The Registry file must follow standard formatting like the example shown in Figure 7.28.
`/E <filename>`	Exports the Registry to a file. You can't use this option to export part of the Registry—it always exports everything. Use RegEdit from within Windows if you want to export a single Registry branch. (If you absolutely must export a branch from DOS, then use the `<registry path>` option defined next.)

Switch	Description
`<registry path>`	Specifies the Registry branch that you want to export to a file. This is an extremely risky option to use, because it relies on your knowledge of the Registry in choosing a unique branch. Always use RegEdit from Windows to export a branch, if at all possible.

As you can see, using RegEdit from the command line isn't too hard. There are three basic operations you can perform. You can import a new branch. For example, if you wanted to import the data for Word for Windows, you could simply type **REGEDIT WORD.REG** (or something similar) at the command line. Another operation is the complete replacement of the Registry with the contents of a previously saved Registry text file. This is a troubleshooting aid of last resort, but it does work. Finally, you can export all or part of the Registry to a text file. All you need to type at the command line is **REGEDIT /E MyReg.TXT**. If RegEdit complains that it can't find your Registry files, use the /L and /R command-line switches.

Tip: If Windows 95 won't boot, one damage control method would be to export the entire Registry to a text file, use a text editor to repair any damage, and then create a new Registry from the edited text file. You can try to start Windows 95 to see whether the repair does everything that it needs to do. Make absolutely certain to copy the damaged Registry text file and binary files (USER.DAT and SYSTEM.DAT) before making any changes. This way, someone else can help you resolve any problems by using a fresh copy of the Registry files.

On Your Own

Use the Registry Editor to create a copy of your Registry, using the procedure in this chapter. Be sure to store this text copy of the Registry in a safe place.

The Registry is a central part of Windows 95. You can't do anything without it. Explore the Registry by using RegEdit. What do the values associated with each of the keys tell you about your system's configuration? Be sure to exit RegEdit without making any changes to any of the keys.

Go into MS-DOS mode. Export a copy of your Registry to a text file, using the command-line version of RegEdit. Store away this copy of your Registry for future use. Make sure that you also store a copy of USER.DAT and SYSTEM.DAT.

8

Windows 95 Memory Management: A New Model

I hear so much about managing this and that today that I often wonder how anyone gets any work done. Management tools abound to help people perform the complex task of making the most out of the resources they have available, whether it's people, equipment, or even components of that equipment. In this respect, using Windows 95 is no different from any other aspect of life. You have to manage your resources carefully to get the biggest payback from your investment. However, if you spend all your time managing your resources, you won't get any return, because you'll have spent everything before you start. Therein lies the challenge of managing time without wasting it.

So what are the resources you have to be so careful about? Memory and hard disk space are the two major concerns that come to mind. Of course, processor cycles are in there somewhere as well. However, you might not think about some resources right away. For example, how valuable is your time? Trading some memory or processor cycles for a big increase in your personal productivity can mean having more resources available for other people to use in the long run. For right now, let's take a close look at managing memory. We'll pursue the other topics later.

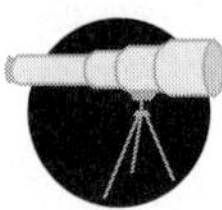

Looking Ahead: Chapter 9 looks at managing your hard drive. Personal time management appears in Chapter 10. We'll look at things like arranging your desktop for optimal access to your data. Reading the "An Information Center" section of Chapter 2 will help you learn how to use Explorer in the most efficient manner possible. Learning to use Explorer well is just one of the time management principles you'll learn about in this chapter. Chapter 2 also presents some other time management aids, such as how to use the Startup folder (see the section "The Startup Folder") to reduce the time you spend configuring your machine by hand. Looking at Chapters 2, 8, 9, and 10 together will give you the total management picture for Windows 95. The trick is to balance them as needed.

Managing memory was always a problem under Windows 3.x. The problem wasn't so much a matter of lack of memory, but a lack of the tools required to adequately manage memory. The first thing you need to understand is that there are two different kinds of memory to worry about when you're working with Windows applications. You need enough system memory to load the application and any data files. Windows also needs enough system resources to load things such as the windows, dialog boxes, and icons that your application uses.

System memory is very difficult to pin down under Windows 3.x. For example, when you look at the About box in Program Manager and see that you have 15MB of RAM and 55 percent system resources left, what does that really tell you? There are a few problems here. First, Windows 3.x always includes the amount of virtual memory it creates on disk in the number it provides for RAM. This means that you could have almost no physical memory left, and all your RAM is really on disk. A lack of physical memory under Windows 3.x always leads to disk thrashing—Windows spends more time swapping things to disk than it does taking care of your application's needs. This is just one example of an improperly managed system.

What about the system resources number? Does it really tell you what kind of system resource? Windows 3.x actually has two system resources to worry about: user and GDI (graphics device interface). The first one contains all your windows and other user presentation elements. The second one contains all the graphic elements that make Windows a joy to use. A lack of one resource means closing some applications. A lack of the other might be cured by removing your wallpaper for a while. The difference is important. Wallpaper isn't a productivity enhancer; you can get by without it for a while. The same can't be said of an important application you might need to run.

Here's the problem: Windows 3.x never gives you enough information to manage those system resources. The About box tells you about the system resource with the least amount of memory left. Of course, this doesn't tell you which resource the number refers to or what's left of the other resource. So now what do you do? I usually got rid of my wallpaper long enough to see whether I had enough system resources to get the job done. If that didn't work, one of my applications had to bite the dust. This productive way of managing system resources usually cost me a lot more than it saved. With such wonderful tools available to the average user, it's no wonder that no one could manage system resources under Windows 3.x without buying a third-party product.

Windows 95 doesn't follow the example of its predecessor. It provides a lot of tools to manage your system resources. Chapter 3 looks at some of these new tools. The short view of this is that Microsoft has finally provided at least a minimal set of tools to manage your memory (and other system resources). Those tools aren't automatic by any definition, and they don't provide the most detailed information, but at least they're available and they can get the job done. It's definitely a step in the right direction.

Peter's Principle: Management Versus Micromanagement

A good manager will often provide a little input and see what happens. If more input is required, fine. Otherwise, the manager leaves his employees alone to get their jobs done in whatever way works for them. This is the kind of person everyone likes to work for, and he still manages to amaze his superiors with the amount of work he can accomplish. There isn't much of a secret to his success. Spending your time getting your work done instead of doing someone else's work is always more productive.

There's another kind of manager: the micromanager. He's the one you see following behind an employee at every step of every task. There's only one way to get the job done: his way. It might not be efficient—it might even be counterproductive for that particular employee—but at least the micromanager can always tell his superiors what the people under him are doing. This fellow will always fail to impress everyone.

You might become a micromanager under Windows 95 if you're not careful. There are a lot of tools at your disposal, and it's easy to suppose that they're there for a reason. The truth of the matter is that even though you have more tools when using Windows 95, the operating system is actually better at managing its memory without any help from you. The tools are there so that you can better determine what kind of "little input" Windows 95 needs.

When working with Windows 95, the best principle is to provide a little input and see what happens. If more input is required, fine. If not, you've got a fully tuned system that gets the job done for you. Let the system do the work it's designed to do until you see a good reason to provide that little bit of input.

The problems with Windows 3.x don't stop at a lack of tools. I find myself constantly fighting to get enough of the type of memory I need at any given time. If I manage to get enough memory together to run a program that requires expanded memory and a page frame in a DOS window, I don't have enough conventional memory because my device drivers won't load high. (A page frame consumes a memory-killing 64KB of upper memory, more than enough to load one or two drivers.) It always seems that Windows 3.x can't provide the kinds of memory that I need.

The bottom-line reason for all these memory problems under Windows 3.x is all the real-mode drivers and TSRs you have to load just to get your system running. My CONFIG.SYS and AUTOEXEC.BAT are filled with all kinds of entries, many of which are essential to configuring the machine the way I need it. For example, there's no way I can get by without loading the drivers for my CD-ROM, yet these drivers consume about 62KB of RAM. My sound card consumes another memory-clogging 37KB—and don't forget about all those handy utilities that most people load. All these drivers mean that I need some form of advanced memory management to load some of it high. The alternative is to give up running some of my DOS applications—all of which assume that I have at least 512KB of conventional memory free.

You can force Windows 95 to have this same kind of problem. Installing a memory manager is about the worst thing you can do if you don't have real-mode drivers to load. Letting Windows 95 manage memory for you will provide better—or at least more consistent—results. Before we get into a heavy-duty discussion of specific memory-tuning techniques, let's look at the types of memory that Windows 95 provides and how it affects you from a user standpoint. We'll also take a quick look at the various Windows operating modes and how they affect memory.

Memory Types

Windows uses a variety of memory types to accomplish a variety of tasks. Some of them relate to Windows itself; others relate to the applications that Windows supports. The following paragraphs help you understand these memory types:

- **Conventional:** This is the original 640KB of memory that IBM set aside for DOS applications. Every DOS application needs conventional memory in order to run. Windows always uses a small piece of conventional memory as well, even if there's enough upper memory for it to load. Even though the processor can access that upper memory, DOS can't. For Windows to activate itself, it has to load a section of itself where DOS can call it. Chapter 9 provides a series of diagrams that show how Windows and DOS interact for file transfers (Figures 9.1 though 9.3). This is the reason why Windows has to load part of itself low. DOS calls this "stub" to get Windows to pay attention.

- **Upper:** IBM set aside 384KB of the 8086 address space for ROMs and video memory. In most cases, a system never uses all of that memory. A memory manager can fill this area with RAM, allowing you to load some of your device drivers high and free conventional memory for applications. Part of Windows 3.x has to load in either conventional or upper memory to support the file system and other DOS-related functions. The more upper memory Windows has to use, the more conventional memory you'll have free to run DOS applications.
- **High:** This is a magic 64KB block that actually appears above the 1024KB address limit. Special segmentation techniques make it possible for the processor to address this memory in real mode. The later section "Addressing Memory" looks at the topic of segmentation. Most users place DOS in this area to free more conventional memory.
- **Extended:** This is where Windows spends most of its time. A machine has to run in protected mode to access extended memory. This is the area beyond the addressing capability of the 8086.
- **Expanded:** Many game and some older business applications require expanded memory. At one time, you needed a special EMS card to create expanded memory. Now memory managers can convert extended memory to expanded memory on-the-fly. There are a number of ways to convert extended memory to expanded memory under Windows. The easiest way, of course, is simply to specify the amount of expanded memory you need in a PIF file.

Conventional Memory

Let's talk for a few minutes about conventional memory and Windows 95. Except for a few system calls, Windows 95 never even moves to real mode anymore, so you don't really need any conventional memory to run it. However, just about everyone has some DOS applications to run, and every DOS application needs conventional memory. You could easily get mired in a lot of details when running DOS applications under Windows 95, but here's the short view: Don't use a memory manager to increase the amount of conventional memory you have, unless you really need to clear some space to get an important application to run.

Tip: A lot of people think that MS-DOS mode is a "bad" way to run your applications. In reality, there's nothing bad about using MS-DOS mode at all. If you find that you have one application that requires more conventional memory than your standard setup will support, running it in MS-DOS mode might be the way to go. The whole idea of MS-DOS mode is to provide the flexibility you need in order to run demanding applications without giving up the overall efficiency of a hands-off setup. This doesn't just apply to applications that won't cooperate with Windows 95; it applies to applications with special needs, too. If you have an application with special conventional memory needs, MS-DOS mode might be the way to go.

As I prepared to write this chapter, I decided it might be fun to run a few different setups to see what kind of memory configurations I could get on my machine. Figure 8.1 shows the results I got. The goal was to see how much conventional memory I could get without seriously impairing my machine. After several attempts, I finally got 386MAX to install. (The product has some significant problems with this particular memory manager.) The 386MAX configuration netted me a machine with 613KB at the DOS prompt. Of course, my system crashed more often after the installation because the real-mode memory manager kept fighting against Windows 95, but this setup did give me the biggest conventional memory boost.

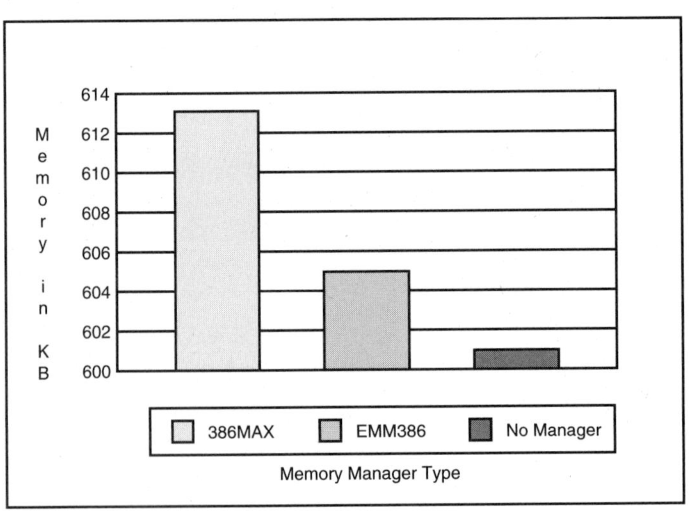

Figure 8.1.
Using no memory manager costs you some conventional memory, but results in a flexible setup with greater stability.

Next, I tried to use EMM386. It worked fine, and I didn't suffer as many debilitating crashes as I did when using 386MAX. Unfortunately, I was now down to 605KB, using the same DOS prompt setup as before. Still, a loss of 8KB isn't very significant. I don't have any applications that require that much conventional memory, anyway; all of them require 600KB or less (including my games). The big difference between the two setups seems to be the way that 386MAX loads DOS high. I noticed that it had a smaller footprint than the EMM386 setup seemed to have.

Finally, I tried getting rid of CONFIG.SYS altogether. None of my peripherals require a real-mode device driver, so getting rid of CONFIG.SYS made sense because I didn't plan to use a memory manager. The same DOS prompt I had used for the previous two tests now showed 601KB. That's a total loss of 12KB from my 386MAX setup. I admit that some applications could really use that 12KB to run, but how many do you own that fall into that category? A hands-off approach to memory management won't give you the ultimate conventional memory setup. Any set of tests will tell you that. However, I consider the gain in stability and flexibility well worth the loss of 12KB of conventional memory.

Note: It's extremely important to remember that Windows 95 provides its own memory manager. The only reason to load an additional driver is if you have a lot of real-mode device drivers or TSRs to load. Otherwise, all your DOS applications will work fine from a window or by using MS-DOS mode.

I cover the use of the Program Properties dialog box later in this chapter; this is where you should work on creating the perfect environment for your application. In most cases, the 600+KB of conventional memory that you can achieve using the automatic Windows 95 settings will provide more than sufficient memory for your applications.

Upper Memory

The first thing you need to know about upper memory is what it is. There are six 64KB segments between 640KB and 1MB. Originally, IBM called this area "reserved memory." They had reserved it for add-on peripherals and BIOS extensions. The current term for this area of real-mode addressable memory is the *upper memory block* (UMB). Microsoft invented the term UMB when programmers learned how to circumvent IBM's original plan. Faced with a demand for more conventional memory, programmers from Quarterdeck Office Systems figured out how to use the "reserved" area as additional space for user programs. Microsoft eventually incorporated some of these techniques into the DOS operating system (starting with version 5.0).

You have to use a memory manager if you need UMBs under Windows 95. Of course, you can only access these UMBs before you run the operating system to load device drivers or TSRs high. (You can also use them within an MS-DOS session, but this is the same as working without Windows loaded.) The problem with using UMBs under Windows 95 is the real-mode memory manager. Using the built-in Windows 95 capabilities is always the best solution. You get the most flexibility and the least number of stability problems.

Tip: Never run a TSR before you load Windows 95 unless you have to do so. For example, I used to run DOSKey before I got into Windows, so that every DOS box would contain a copy of this very handy TSR. To save memory, I now run all my utility commands from a batch file when I open the DOS box. The same holds true for environment settings. Use the smallest environment possible, and then set the size of your environment as needed when you open the DOS box. Optimizing each DOS box to meet the needs of the application you're running is the best way to use the flexibility that Windows 95 provides. This type of optimization also reduces your need to rely on UMBs.

There are situations in which UMBs do come in handy. For example, what if you have a device that uses a real-mode driver, and it's unlikely that the vendor will produce a Windows 95-specific version? Suppose you have a data-collection device that uses a DOS data manager, and the manager needs every bit of conventional memory it can get. This is one situation in which you need the UMB to load the device driver. Loading the device driver high frees the conventional memory you need to load the data manager that uses it. I follow one of three routes in such situations. The following list shows them in order of preference from a system reliability point of view. You'll have to choose the route you want to use based on personal needs and system requirements.

- **MS-DOS mode:** If you can get by with using the driver by itself, run it in MS-DOS mode. (Later I show you how to create custom setups for applications and devices that need it.) This solution has the advantage of allowing you to load a device driver and run its associated application whenever you need to do so. The downside is that you can't access any of your Windows applications while using the device.
- **Multiple-boot configuration:** When interaction between the device, a real-mode application, and Windows is absolutely essential, you can still reduce the effect by using a multiple-boot configuration. All you do is set up the boot menu the way you used to do under DOS. Use the memory manager setup when you need to load the device driver. Otherwise, boot into an empty configuration that doesn't do anything. The benefit of this setup is obvious: You don't lose access to Windows while running the real-mode device driver and its associated application. The downside is that you have to reboot every time you want to restore your configuration to a default state.

- **Use a memory manager:** This is the setup that I'd encourage you to avoid. You'll definitely run into problems using a real-mode memory manager under Windows 95. If you have to go this route, try to use the copy of EMM386 that comes with Windows 95 as your memory manager—at least until reliable Windows 95-specific versions of any third-party memory managers arrive on the scene. (There are a few Windows 95-specific memory managers on the market now, but they've proven problematic at best, fatal at worst.) The downside of this setup is that you'll have stability problems. The benefit of this solution is that you'll always have access to the device and its associated application.

Expanded Memory

Anyone who has been computing very long will run into the need for expanded memory (EMS) at some point. EMS first appeared in 1985 as a means to bypass the DOS address limitations. Spreadsheet users were complaining that they didn't have enough memory to run those gargantuan worksheets anymore. These were the same folks who kept expanding the memory envelope throughout most of the PC's early history. This initial version allowed you to place data in the expanded memory area, but not code. The spreadsheet users and, to a larger degree, database users were happy for a while, but not forever.

In 1985, the buying public put considerable pressure on software vendors to find more memory for spreadsheet and database applications. This meant running code in the expanded memory area. Remember, there wasn't any extended memory yet for most users. The 80386 had just appeared on the scene, and the 80286 wasn't what you would call a good extended-memory candidate. The alternative was to handle large files by swapping information to the hard disk, a slow and unwieldy procedure. If the user paged down in a spreadsheet or address list, the application would pause to read the next page from disk.

Adding to this already-bad situation was the proliferation of TSR utilities that popped up over the user's display. Every one of these programs had to load in conventional memory because UMBs didn't exist yet. It's hard to remember sometimes just how crunched memory could get under those old versions of DOS. Let's take a quick stroll down memory lane and look at the history of EMS before we get into the Windows 95 specifics.

EMS Version 3.0

Lotus and Intel announced EMS version 3.0 at the spring Comdex convention in 1985. This specification was designed to head off the rapid demise of 8088/8086 machines. However, this specification was short-lived because Microsoft almost immediately announced it would support EMS in the fall of 1985. Microsoft further promised to enhance Windows to use the memory made available by EMS hardware and software.

LIM EMS Version 3.2

The LIM expanded-memory standard, version 3.2, was a joint effort of three companies: Lotus, Intel, and Microsoft. LIM 3.2 memory allowed 1-2-3, Symphony, dBASE III, and Framework to keep relatively large data files in memory. Before expanded memory was introduced, the only way to manipulate large spreadsheets was to swap portions to and from disk. Under LIM 3.2, the user could add memory cards containing from 64KB to 8MB of RAM, using expansion slots on the PC's bus. Only the expanded memory manager (EMM) could address all the memory; DOS looked at a 64KB window (called a *page frame*) supplied by the EMM in the upper memory area. The page frame was placed in reserved memory between 640KB and 1MB. Normally this page frame appeared at segment D000h, but other page frame segments were used as well. All PCs (including 8088 machines) could use LIM 3.2 memory to ferry information to applications from the expanded memory card.

Note: As out-of-date as this specification might seem, many applications still use it because this is the version of EMS many programmers understand best. If you have ever tried to run an application that requires EMS under Windows 3.x and have received the message that it couldn't find any (even though you know that the memory is present), you've seen the effect of this old specification. The newer 4.0 specification doesn't require a page frame. An old application that's looking for a page frame under 4.0 might not find it. As a result, you can run the DOS `MEM` program and see that EMS is available, but you won't be able to use it with some applications unless you allocate a page frame. Herein lies the rub. If you use an external memory manager with Windows 95 and don't allocate an EMS page frame, you won't be able to allocate one after Windows 95 starts (Windows 3.x had the same limitation). This is just one more area in which not using an external memory manager with Windows 95 provides greater flexibility. The built-in Windows 95 EMM automatically allocates a page frame for every application that needs it.

The LIM 3.2 EMM could tag and stash 16KB chunks of data, shipping them to the "warehouse" of extra RAM on the expanded memory card. When an application claimed the data, the EMM placed it back into the page frame 16KB at a time. Storing data in expanded memory was similar to storing it on a RAM disk: Applications could retrieve the information without time-consuming hard-disk access. Figure 8.2 illustrates how the LIM 3.2 EMM ferries data between expanded memory and DOS, using the EMS page frame.

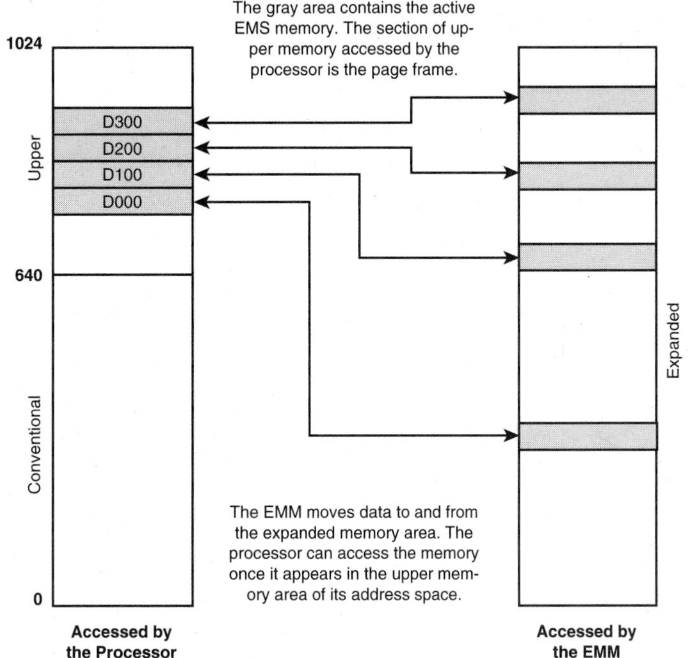
The gray area contains the active EMS memory. The section of upper memory accessed by the processor is the page frame.
1024
D300
D200
D100
D000
Upper
640
Conventional
0
Expanded
The EMM moves data to and from the expanded memory area. The processor can access the memory once it appears in the upper memory area of its address space.
Accessed by the Processor
Accessed by the EMM

Figure 8.2.
LIM EMS 3.2 used 4KB to 16KB pages to store data required by any application running under DOS.

EEMS

The LIM EMS 3.2 standard was fine for storing data such as spreadsheets, but PC users wanted even more power from their machines. Utilities that performed background processing, such as Print and Sidekick, whetted the PC user's appetite for multitasking. However, even the most sophisticated TSR left a lot to be desired when compared to the features of a full-fledged application. Users wanted memory to multitask DOS applications.

Unfortunately, LIM EMS 3.2 provided neither the hardware basis nor the software interface to multitask applications. An application couldn't use LIM EMS 3.2 memory to run program code. This annoying limitation of LIM EMS 3.2 was tied to the fact that DOS couldn't directly access the expanded memory hardware; only the EMM was allowed to do that. In addition, the memory-mapping hardware limited the size and location of each page in the page frame.

In 1986, AST Research Corporation, QUADRAM Corporation, and Ashton-Tate added some enhancements to the Lotus-Intel-Microsoft specification. Their improved standard, Enhanced Expanded Memory Specification, was a breakthrough in the PC industry.

EEMS revised the hardware functions of memory cards to improve the software standard. With EEMS, areas larger than 64KB could be used as a page frame. The page frame could be mapped below 640KB as well as between 640KB and 1MB. This permitted entire programs to run in enhanced expanded memory.

When the AST Research EEMS cards were combined with Quarterdeck's DESQview, PCs had the capability to multitask a number of applications exceeding 640KB. A communications program could download files while a spreadsheet was recalculated. The user could type a document in a word processor and format a floppy disk concurrently.

LIM EMS Version 4.0

Lotus, Intel, and Microsoft eventually recognized the superiority of EEMS to LIM 3.2. In 1987, the LIM partners collaborated with AST Research, QUADRAM, and Ashton-Tate to define a new joint standard called LIM EMS version 4.0. EMS 4.0 superseded AST's EEMS by allowing the memory manager to control 32MB of expanded memory instead of 8MB. It incorporated many but not all of the features provided by EEMS. Improvements of EMS 4.0 over EMS 3.2 included the following:

- The capability to hold larger spreadsheets and databases in memory
- The capability to address more than 64KB at a time (although the page frame was still 64KB)
- The capability to map memory both above and below 640KB

How EMS 4.0 Works

There are many differences between EMS 4.0 and its predecessors. Under EMS 4.0, allocated expanded memory can be mapped as conventional memory. The memory is usually divided into 16KB segments called *standard pages*. However, a program may use pages other than the standard 16KB size. These pages are called *raw pages*. Obviously, determining the number of pages of memory available is no longer a matter of simply knowing how many 16KB segments are installed, so EMS 4.0 also provides methods of determining the number of raw and standard pages.

Instead of only providing access to expanded memory through the page frame (as LIM 3.2 memory does), any number of standard or raw pages can be mapped between conventional memory and the RAM set aside for EMS. In addition, EMS 4.0 provides methods of moving memory regions between conventional and expanded memory. This makes it possible to execute multiple programs up to the full 640KB address range. The same EMM addresses both the conventional and expanded memory-storage areas. To perform this task, the EMM marks a block of EMS memory for each program and assigns it an EMS handle. An EMS handle works and acts much like a DOS file handle, so programmers can easily make the transition in terms of understanding how the process works.

Other, more subtle differences include handle management. Under EMS 3.2, there was no standard technique for managing handles. EMS 4.0 provides the means to get, set, and search for handle names. This enables an application to determine not only what memory is in use, but also who owns it.

Even with these changes, however, it would be impossible to run specific types of programs without another capability added to EMS 4.0. Some programs perform direct memory access (DMA) transfers. For example, many backup programs and some telecommunications programs do this.

Transferring information one byte at a time through the processor would take too long, so the program creates a direct link between one storage device and another. Unlike EMS 3.2, EMS 4.0 allows specific types of DMA transfers to occur. This is made possible through the use of alternative register sets, part of the hardware (or hardware emulation). Alternative register sets also allow a whole range of other unique and powerful software-management routines, many of which are at the operating-system level.

One of the most unique differences between the two versions is that EMS 4.0 provides the means to allow the contents of expanded memory to survive a warm boot. DESQview uses this capability to allow you to reboot a hung window without affecting any other windows. Of course, should the errant application affect the memory containing the EMM, your only recourse is the big red switch. Figure 8.3 depicts some of the differences between EMS 3.2 and EMS 4.0.

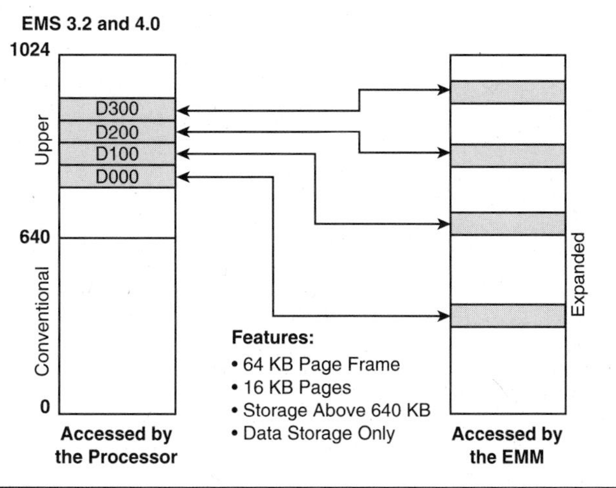

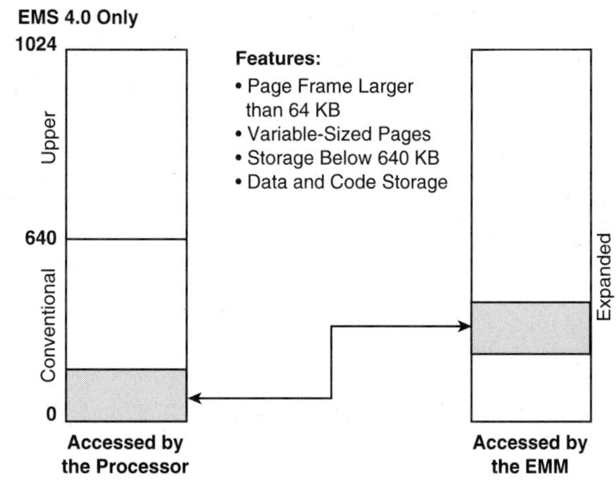

Figure 8.3.
Differences in the way that LIM EMS 3.2 and 4.0 get the job done.

VCPI Versus DPMI

You might be tempted to say that everything DOS needs to multitask is provided by EMS 4.0. Nothing could be further from the truth. The Extended Memory Specification (XMS) doesn't really do the job, either. Both of these specifications talk about the availability of memory, not necessarily how to control it. Think about the memory provided by EMS or XMS as city streets. Your application is a car traveling on that street. It needs the road to get from point A to point B. If you started running more than one application, then there would be one car for each application and the street would begin to fill with traffic. What would happen if there were no traffic lights? Cars could still move around on the streets, but they would crash into each other because there wouldn't be any way to control their movements.

Applications need traffic lights to multitask successfully. An 80386 multitasks DOS applications in virtual 8086 mode. DOS extenders operate in protected mode. To avoid conflicts between programs using virtual 8086 mode and programs running in protected mode, a standard was devised by Quarterdeck, Rational Systems, Phar Lap, and other companies. The Virtual Control Program Interface (VCPI) is the standard that allows DOS extended programs to coexist in an 80386 multitasking environment. In other words, VCPI adds traffic lights to our city streets and keeps applications from crashing into each other. Under VCPI, users of DESQview can run protected-mode AutoCAD, 1-2-3, or Paradox side by side with other DOS applications.

Curiously, IBM and Microsoft didn't choose to actively support VCPI. Perhaps in 1988 and 1989 they expected that OS/2 would soon replace DOS, so it wasn't worth the trouble. In 1990, Microsoft premiered its own independent protected-mode standard called the DOS Protected-Mode Interface (DPMI). This is the function of the `HIMEM.SYS` entry in CONFIG.SYS. Microsoft developed DPMI specifically for Windows version 3.0, and we've been using it ever since (even Windows 95 automatically loads it as part of IO.SYS). Like VCPI, DPMI provides mode-switching and extended-memory management to client programs.

Unfortunately, Microsoft's DPMI standard for Windows is incompatible with the VCPI DOS extender software. In most cases, users can't run the old 386 versions of Paradox, AutoCAD, and so on as DOS tasks under Windows. Microsoft eventually agreed to participate in a committee that included representatives from Quarterdeck, Intel, Lotus, Phar Lap, and Rational Systems. The committee's goal was to develop a more generic version of DPMI. The resultant standard, DPMI version 1.0, is fully VCPI-compatible, but to date Microsoft hasn't implemented DPMI version 1.0 in Windows. Version 3.x of Windows still uses Microsoft's older DPMI version 0.9, the version that's incompatible with VCPI DOS extenders.

The thinking in 1991 was that if Microsoft wouldn't go to the mountain, other companies would accommodate Microsoft. In July of 1991, Rational Systems introduced a series of 32-bit DOS extenders designed to be Windows 3.x-compatible, even under the older standard. However, even these extenders failed to make the grade. The result, of course, was that the world is using DPMI now. Programs that use VCPI are probably sitting on a shelf somewhere. Of course, now that no one is using VCPI, Microsoft graciously decided to add VCPI support to EMM386. There's probably a profound moral to this entire story, but I've yet to see it. Suffice it to say that you can run those old moth-eaten VCPI applications if you really want to, but a new Windows version of the application would probably give you a lot more in the way of features and stability.

Using EMS with Windows 95

The simple way to get expanded memory under Windows 95 is to load Windows without a memory manager and select the appropriate settings in the program's Properties dialog box. Chapter 13 looks at this dialog box in detail. For right now, the important thing to remember is that Windows 95 requires a different EMS strategy than previous versions.

Tip: Many TSRs provide some method of loading into either expanded or extended memory. The TSR normally leaves a small 1KB to 2KB footprint in conventional memory but loads the rest of itself where your DOS application can't see it. I always create DOS boxes with the automatic maximum amount of both expanded and extended memory. That way, both types are available whenever I need them to load a TSR out of reach. Using this method allows you to load the TSR high without killing your conventional memory settings or loading the TSR before you start Windows 95.

You can also load an EMM prior to running Windows 95. To do this, follow the instructions provided with your EMM. (Use the copy of EMM386 provided with Windows 95, if possible.) There are several very limiting problems with using an EMM under Windows 95:

- The real-mode EMM will limit the amount of EMS available to your applications to the amount of memory you set aside in the CONFIG.SYS entry. Of course, this amount of memory will always be less than the total amount available on your machine, because there's no way that you can run Windows 95 without setting some extended memory aside. Each of my DOS windows under Windows 95 has a total of 24MB of EMS (16MB of which is available), because I don't use an external EMM. This is the same amount of memory I have installed on the machine.
- The real-mode device driver will affect your machine's stability. Even the copy of EMM386 produces a noticeable result on my machine. I invariably have to reboot more often whenever there's any real-mode driver around to trash the system memory.
- If you don't allocate enough memory when you boot the machine, you can't adjust it later on. The same holds true if you allocate too much EMS. The extra memory will go to waste. You can adjust the amount set aside in CONFIG.SYS and then reboot, but this runs counter to the other ease-of-use features provided by Windows 95.

Extended Memory

Microsoft's Extended Memory Specification (XMS) got its start from the discovery of a Quarterdeck programmer in 1986. At the time, Quarterdeck was looking for any means possible to reduce the conventional memory overhead of DESQview, its multitasking product. Here's a quick view of what they discovered.

A standard PC breaks the first megabyte of memory into sixteen 64KB address segments. To produce an address, the processor combines this 16-bit segment with a 16-bit offset. The result of combining these two numbers is a 20-bit address. Each of these 20 bits controls an address-line gate circuit. The address lines are numbered A0 through A19. Each address line can contain a 1 or a 0, resulting in 2^{20}, or 1,048,576 memory locations (1MB).

The A20 gate circuit (the 21st address line) isn't present in the original 8088 version of the PC. Therefore, when an address exceeds the amount addressable by 20 address lines, it simply wraps to low memory. For example, if you have segment FFFFh and offset 0010h, the resulting address is 100000h. However, the original PC simply lops the 1 off the left and ends up with address 00000h. Instead of ending up near the very end of memory, you're at the very beginning.

What the Quarterdeck programmer discovered was that turning on the A20 gate of an 80286/80386/80486 chip also turned off the wraparound. Because these chips have a 21st address line (actually, the 80286 has 24 and the 80386 and 80486 have 32), you can address the additional memory as if it were conventional memory. If a program were instructed to load code between 960KB and 1024KB, up to 64KB of code could spill over into the first segment beyond 1024KB. DOS could actually address code placed in the first segment of extended memory. Because the last segment of DOS memory isn't normally contiguous with conventional memory, programs can't use it automatically. But the last segment of DOS memory can be specially programmed to hold up to 64KB of a single device driver or application program.

This bug (or feature) of the 80286-and-above architecture prompted Quarterdeck to develop its QEXT.SYS device driver to reduce the conventional memory overhead of DESQview. In 1987, Microsoft formalized this quirk by issuing its own driver, HIMEM.SYS, and by naming the first segment above 1MB the High Memory Area (HMA). By publishing instructions on how to use the HMA, Microsoft allowed third-party vendors to reduce the conventional overhead of their programs. Xerox was one of the first to recognize the HMA, with Ventura Publisher. Microsoft's popularization of the HMA with HIMEM.SYS was the beginning of its Extended Memory Specification.

In 1990, Microsoft revised its HIMEM.SYS driver with the release of Windows version 3.0. The scope of XMS memory was increased to include all of extended memory. The new release of Windows could use all of extended memory to multitask Windows applications. Disk caches, print spoolers, and RAM disks could now access extended memory through Microsoft's device driver.

Formerly, any driver using extended memory had to provide its own scheme for switching in and out of protected mode. Microsoft established new terminology for all memory above 640KB:

- **UMB (Upper Memory Blocks):** This became the term for the memory area above the 640KB boundary and below the 1MB boundary.
- **HMA (High Memory Area):** This term refers to the 64KB block of memory starting at the 1MB boundary (1024KB). This is the beginning of extended memory on 80286 and 80386 systems.
- **EMB (Extended Memory Blocks):** This term refers to the remaining extended memory (above the HMA) available to an XMS driver.

Tip: TSRs almost always run faster in expanded memory than they do in extended memory. Try the TSR both ways to see which works best for you. For example, I found that Collage (a screen-capture program) actually works faster when you load it into extended memory.

As with expanded memory, Windows 95 provides the means to precisely control how much extended memory you give to an application. Of course, you can always give it as much as it could possibly want, by using the automatic settings. My system currently offers 23MB of extended memory to each DOS application if I use the automatic settings and the Windows 95 memory manager. There's absolutely no reason to load an external XMS driver if an application needs it. IO.SYS automatically loads HIMEM.SYS as part of the boot process.

Virtual Memory

The "Addressing Memory" section of this chapter looks at the actual process of addressing memory. This includes a detailed description of how virtual memory works under Windows 95, so I won't address that issue right now. However, knowing the theory behind how something works, and actually using that theory to do something useful, are two different things.

I've spent a lot of time in this chapter telling you how great the automated features of Windows 95 are and how they'll make your life a lot easier and provide much more flexibility. I've even gone so far as to say that you'd be better off leaving them completely alone. Of course, you knew that wasn't going to last, didn't you? Yes, it's true that Windows 95 does provide all those things, but we're still talking about a piece of software that can't think independently the way you and I can. The problem with Windows 95 is it looks only for a "convenient" drive when it creates your swap file. It doesn't look at the speed of that drive or how you use it. The latter kind of thought process is something only you and I can accomplish. It's also the reason why you might want to manually adjust your machine's virtual memory settings, in some cases.

Let's take my machine as a case in point. I have a small, fast drive and a larger, slow drive. The small drive contains some boot information, my DOS files, and a few other things I need to get my machine up and running or to figure out why it won't work. There's more than enough space left on that drive for a swap file. The faster speed of this drive and the fact that I very seldom change anything on it makes this drive the perfect location for a swap file. Of course, Windows 95 is absolutely determined to use the slower, fragmented drive.

Tip: In some cases, you can get a speed boost from your machine by hand-tuning the virtual memory setup. Generally, you'll want to allow Windows 95 to choose the drive and the size of the swap files. However, there are times when Windows 95 will choose the slowest drive on your machine. You can override this selection and choose the fastest drive. This means that you'll trade some extra speed for a little bit of flexibility. As soon as you turn off the automatic settings, you become responsible for adjusting the size of the swap file as required. (Of course, if Windows 95 runs out of swap file space before you adjust it, you could experience a system crash. At the very minimum, you'll get an error message when you try to run another application.)

Let's take a look at the process for changing your virtual memory setup. If you cut your teeth on Windows 3.x, you'll recognize this dialog box, even though it looks a bit different under Windows 95.

1. Right-click My Computer and select the Properties option.
2. Click the Performance tab. You should see the System Properties dialog box shown in Figure 8.4.

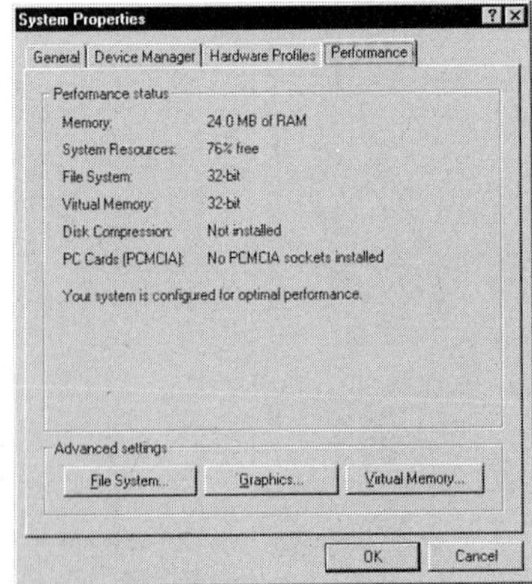

Figure 8.4.
The Performance page of the System Properties dialog box provides access to the virtual memory settings for your machine.

3. Click the Virtual Memory button. You should see the dialog box shown in Figure 8.5.

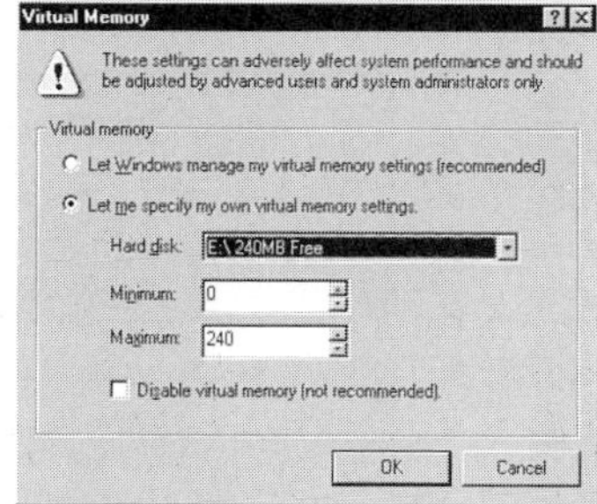

Figure 8.5.
The Virtual Memory dialog box allows you to hand-tune your machine's virtual memory settings.

4. Select the drive you want to use, and then the amount you want to allocate for virtual memory.

Tip: Another way to get a little bit of a speed boost out of your virtual memory setup is to create a pseudo-permanent swap file. Under Windows 3.x, you could defragment your drive and then allocate a permanent swap file. Using this arrangement would provide a noticeable speed boost, because Windows could read from contiguous disk sectors instead of looking all over the drive for various pieces of the swap file. Microsoft claims that this is no longer necessary, but you can still get a speed boost by optimizing your drive and manually changing the virtual memory settings. All you need to do is select your fastest drive and set the minimum virtual memory setting to something other than 0. If you set the minimum and maximum size to the same value, you'll experience a lot less disk fragmentation and get a slight speed boost. Of course, you'll give up some flexibility to get this boost.

I would be remiss in my duty to you as a writer if I didn't mention the Disable Virtual Memory check box near the bottom of the dialog box. When Microsoft recommends that you not check it, they really mean it. I used to run Windows 3.x without any virtual memory management (VMM) because my system was actually faster without it. Under Windows 95, this has all changed. Microsoft really did tune the VMM algorithms, to a certain extent. You can't run Windows 95 safely without a swap file. It depends on that swap file a lot more than Windows 3.x ever did, and it uses that swap file much more efficiently. Unless someone at Microsoft tells you to turn off the VMM for some type of maintenance check, leave it on.

Well, that's about all there is to the VMM. It's not like Windows 3.x, where you could spend weeks just trying to figure out the best settings for a particular task. The only thing you need to worry about with Windows 95 is choosing the fastest drive and making sure that it has enough space for the swap file. Making sure that the drive stays defragmented is one way to ensure that you always get the best performance. I also included a couple of tips in this section that you can use to get the optimum performance from your setup. VMM still isn't perfect under Windows 95, but it's a lot closer. The amount of tuning you'll need to do is a lot less under this new operating system. Of course, it would be nicer if you didn't have to tune the system at all. Maybe the next version of Windows will take us there.

Addressing Memory

Previous sections of this chapter concentrated on telling you what kinds of memory are available. They didn't tell you how Windows accesses that memory or how it manages memory once it has access. If you think memory management under Windows 95 is a simple matter, think again. Windows has many ways of looking at this critical resource, and it's important to understand how they differ. This section looks at the two different memory models that Windows must use to manage the memory on your system: segmented and flat. Of the two, flat is more efficient, but Windows needs to maintain both for compatibility reasons. The following paragraphs explain why.

The Windows 3.1 Segmented Memory Model

The preceding sections briefly presented the two Windows memory models and explained how they differ. I told you that the segmented memory model is a lot harder for a programmer to use than the flat memory model used with Windows NT. Of course, the first question that comes to mind is why Microsoft would even bother using the segmented memory model for enhanced-mode Windows 3.1. After all, enhanced mode is designed for the 80386, and we already know that it supports the flat memory model. There are two good reasons. First, the 80286 processor doesn't provide flat memory model support. If Microsoft had decided to use the flat memory model, they would have had to include a double set of files for every aspect of Windows 3.1. The second reason is equally simple: Windows 3.1 rides on top of DOS, and DOS uses 16-bit code. Windows 3.x already performs quite a juggling act in talking with DOS, and keeping a 32-bit ball up in the air as well would have been a little too much. So we ended up with a 16-bit operating environment called Windows 3.1.

Now that you have a feel for why segmentation is still around, let's look at how it works. A segmented memory model uses two 16-bit registers to hold an address. In real mode, the processor uses a segment and an offset. Think of the segment as the street number and the offset as a specific house on that street. The processor combines the segment with the offset to create a 20-bit address for the 8086 or a 24-bit address for the 80286. Just how does it do this? The processor shifts the segment register's contents 4 bits to the right to make the transition. A 20-bit address yields the 1MB of address space that you've come to know and love when using DOS. Of course, the bottom line for the application is that the application, not the operating system, has control over the memory it uses.

Windows doesn't operate in real mode; it uses protected mode. The theory behind the protected-mode segmented memory model is slightly different than with real mode. Look at Figure 8.6, which shows a simplified version of the protected-mode segmented memory model. Notice that we no longer use a segment:offset pair, but a selector:offset pair. There's a big difference between a segment and a selector. A segment represents an actual location in memory, and a selector represents a position in a descriptor table. The table contains the actual location in memory. (It also contains a variety of other information that I won't cover here.)

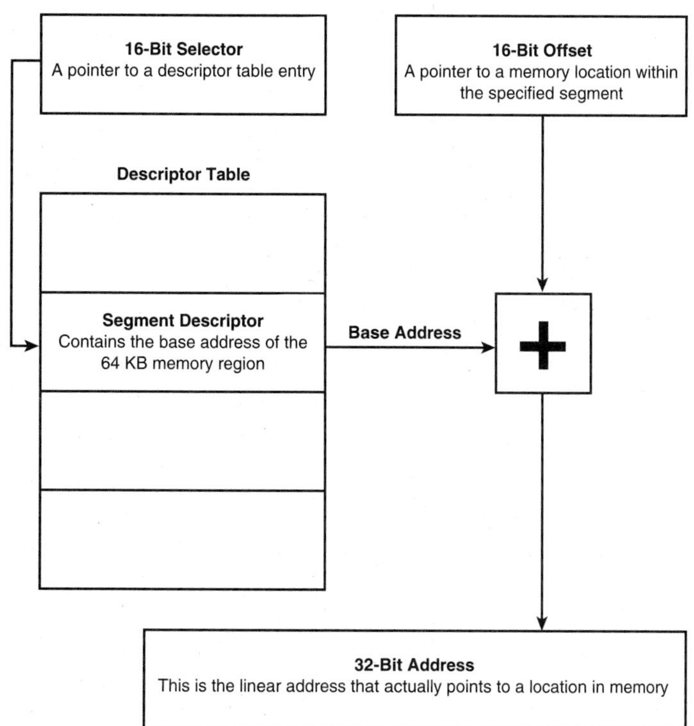

Figure 8.6.
Windows 3.x uses the segmented memory model shown here. Windows 95 also uses this model for 16-bit applications.

So how does this lookup table work? When Windows grants an application access to a specific range of memory, it gives that application a key to that range. The key is the selector. The application sends two values to the processor when it needs to access memory. The first value is the key (selector) that the processor needs to unlock the memory. The second value is the exact location (offset) within that range. Using selectors gives the operating system control over the entire range of memory on the system. Because an application must use a key to unlock its memory, and only the processor knows the physical location of that memory, the system should be fairly secure.

In fact, the selector does provide some security information to the operating system. Bits 0 and 1 of the selector tell the operating system its privilege level. This equates to the rings of protection that I discuss later. Suffice it to say that 0 (00b) provides the most privileged access and 3 (11b) provides the least privileged. All applications run at privilege level 3 under Windows; only the operating system runs at privilege level 0. Bit 2 contains the number of the table that Windows should use to access the memory. There are two descriptor tables: the global descriptor table (GDT) and the local descriptor table (LDT). A value of 1 selects the LDT. Windows uses the GDT for all common data. There is only one GDT for the entire system. Each application also has its own LDT for private data. Finally, bits 3 through 15 contain the actual index into the table.

Rather than get mired in a wealth of bits at this point, let's just say that Windows verifies that the application's security level is high enough to access the data it wants to see. It then takes the base address value (the protected-mode version of a segment) that it finds at the specified location in the descriptor table and combines it with the offset to find the physical location of the requested data in memory.

The segmented memory model has several problems. The biggest one (if you're a programmer) is that you can allocate memory only in 64KB chunks. Remember, the address is made of a selector and an offset. Because the offset register is only 16 bits, it can handle only 64KB of memory. This means that the programmer has to write an application that manages a bunch of selectors, each pointing to a different 64KB chunk of memory. The chance of corrupting one of these selectors increases as the application uses more and more memory. It isn't too difficult to understand why a 16-bit Windows application could get confused and end up writing to the wrong section of memory. The results are usually catastrophic and end in a frozen machine.

Of course, there's a limitation here for the user as well. Have you ever wondered where all those "out of memory" messages come from? Many users have experienced the problem of Windows reporting that it has all kinds of memory available, and then seemingly deciding for no reason that it doesn't. Well, here's one culprit. Every icon, every dialog box, every menu, and every other resource you can imagine has to go somewhere in memory for Windows to use it. When Microsoft originally designed Windows 3.0, they decided that all those resources had to go into what programmers call the *near heap*—a 64KB chunk of global memory that Windows 3.0 sets aside for resources. Using the near heap increases execution speed, especially for time-consuming screen redraws, because the operating system isn't constantly manipulating selectors to access multiple 64KB chunks of memory. Needless to say, when you consider that just one icon is 766 bytes, it doesn't take too many of them to fill that 64KB heap.

After many user complaints about strange memory problems, Microsoft set aside two heaps in Windows 3.1. The first heap, the GDI heap, contains icons and other graphic resources. The other heap, the USER heap, contains nongraphic resources such as dialog boxes. Even with two 64KB heaps, Windows 3.1 users still ran out of memory. There's an easy way to determine whether you're about to run out of space in one of these two heaps. If you look at Program Manager's About dialog box, you'll notice a value that tells you the percentage of system resources—the amount of that 64KB chunk of memory that's left in the smallest heap. In other words, if the GDI heap has 20 percent of its space left and the USER heap has 30 percent, Windows will report a value of 20 percent (12.8KB) for system resources.

The Windows NT Flat Memory Model

When Microsoft designed Windows NT, they decided to use a different memory model supported by 80386 and above processors—the flat memory model. When the operating system places the processor in this mode, it essentially says that everything will use the same segment. The processor hasn't done away with segmentation, but the operating system chooses to ignore this capability. Eliminating segmentation greatly simplifies life for the programmer. No longer does the programmer need to worry about the segment registers—only the address is important.

Finding an Address

You might wonder how the operating system maintains control of memory using the flat addressing scheme. Under the segmented scheme, the processor maintained control through a table of selectors. The application used a selector as a key to open up to a 64KB chunk of memory. The flat addressing mode has a protection scheme as well. In fact, this scheme provides even more flexibility than the segmented model. Figure 8.7 shows the flat memory model.

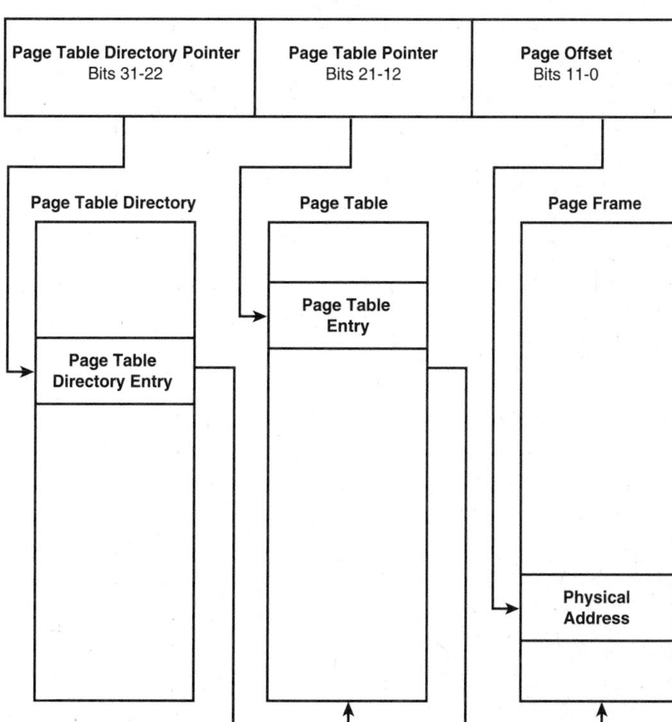

Figure 8.7.
The flat address model doesn't use a selector:offset pair to address memory. Each register contains a 32-bit address that's split into three fields.

Each 32-bit address has three fields. Each field corresponds to one level of protection enforced by the processor under the flat memory model. Even though the programmer doesn't have to worry about these fields when writing an application, the operating system and processor do. The first field resides in bits 31 through 22 of the address. It points to an entry in the page table directory. Just like the segmented memory model, the flat model gives the application a key to a specific piece of memory, not its actual location. Locating the right page table is the first step in finding the address.

Let's take a moment to look at what a page table really is. Remember that in the segmented memory model, an application would have to allocate memory in 64KB chunks. If it needed a larger allocation, the application would have to ask for multiple chunks. A page table gets rid of this problem; the application simply asks for the total amount of memory it needs, and Windows provides it. The number of pages in this table corresponds to the number of 4KB pages that the application allocates. If an application asked for 400KB of RAM, the table would contain 100 entries. As you can see, the flat address model is already more flexible than the segmented model.

Once Windows finds a specific page table, it uses the value in bits 21 through 12 of the address to find a specific page. Think back to what I told you about an application's memory limit. Every application can use up to 4GB of memory. Now look at the number of bits set aside for pages under Windows. There are 10. There are also 10 bits set aside for page table directory entries. If you take 2^{10} page table directory entries × 2^{10} page table entries × 4KB pages, you get 4GB.

After Windows finds a specific page within a specific page table, it takes the address it finds there and adds it to the offset in bits 11 through 0 of the address. These 12 bits allow an application to select any byte within the 4KB page.

Sleight-of-Hand Memory Management

Using 4KB pages provides a number of benefits when it comes to memory management. Remember in the preceding section when I talked about the page table directory and the page table? Each entry in these tables contains 32 bits of data, yet the actual pointers consume a lot less than that. So what does the processor use the additional space for? I don't want to go into a blow-by-blow description of 80386 memory management. However, it might be useful to look at what some of these extra entries do. Fortunately, both tables use the same format, so I'll cover them at the same time.

Of course, the main purpose of using these tables in the first place is to point to something. That's what bits 31 through 12 do. In the page table directory, they point to a page table. In the page table, they contain the physical address that's combined with the offset in the original address. Bit 6 contains the D (dirty) bit. Whenever an application changes the contents of a page of memory, Windows changes the dirty bit. This reminds the processor that it hasn't written the change to disk. If the processor wants to use this page of physical memory for some other purpose, it needs to write the existing page to the Windows swap file.

Bit 5 contains the A (accessed) bit. Whenever an application reads, writes, or executes a 4KB page of memory, Windows changes the status of this bit. Windows can use this bit to determine whether it should remove the page from memory to make room for something else.

Bit 2 contains the U/S (user/supervisor) bit. This is part of the 80386 protection scheme. If the bit is set to 0, it contains a supervisor page. Applications can never access supervisor pages, because they belong to the operating system. On the other hand, setting the bit to 1 means that it's a user page. Applications can access any user page that belongs to them.

Bit 1 contains the R/W (read/write) bit. You wouldn't want an application to overwrite the code in a page. Setting this bit to 0 prevents an application from doing so. Data pages are set to 1; code pages are set to 0.

Bit 0 contains the P (present) bit. Windows needs to know whether a page is in physical memory. The application can't use a page of memory that's sitting on disk in the swap file. The page must reside in physical memory. If the application asks for access to a page of memory that's on disk, the processor raises an exception (basically an alarm). This exception tells Windows that it needs to retrieve the page from its swap file on disk so that the application can access it.

As you can see, these table entries help Windows perform memory management sleight-of-hand. It can move 4KB pages from physical memory to disk as needed. Other bits protect operating-system-specific memory from prying application eyes. Still other bits help protect your application from itself by preventing it from overwriting precious application code.

Virtual 86 Mode

DOS

Up to this point, you've seen how Windows manages memory for its own applications. What happens when you open a DOS box and run an application? The first thing you need to realize is that Windows takes a snapshot of your DOS environment before it completely boots. It creates a "phantom" DOS environment and holds on to it until needed. When you open a DOS box, Windows creates what's known as a virtual machine. This isn't a physical machine that you can touch, but it has all the capabilities of a standard 8086. After Windows creates this virtual machine, it copies the phantom DOS environment to it, and you have a DOS box. This DOS box has all the same device drivers and TSRs as the DOS environment you left when booting Windows.

But what differentiates a virtual DOS machine from the rest of the Windows environment? The 80386 processor introduced a new mode called Virtual 86 mode (V86 for short) in which Windows can create multiple 8086s. Each of these virtual machines thinks it's the only machine running. On the other hand, Windows applications run in protected mode. Windows has to switch between protected mode (to run Windows applications) and V86 mode (to run DOS applications). I won't go into the intricacies of how the processor switches between protected and V86; only a heavy-duty chip designer would enjoy that conversation. Suffice it to say that each machine is totally separate and that V86 mode is a third mode that emulates real mode but doesn't actually run there.

Windows Modes and Memory

Any discussion of Windows and its evolution has to include the modes of operation that Windows supports. Previous versions of Windows supported three modes: real, standard, and 386-enhanced. Real mode went out with the 8088 and Windows 3.0. It's just too limited to perform any useful work, so I won't waste time talking about it here. Suffice it to say that real mode is limited to a mere 1MB of memory, hardly enough to load Windows, much less applications. The following sections provide an overview of the other two modes of operation.

Windows Applications in Standard Mode

The only reason for the existence of standard mode is the 80286. This mode enables Windows to run on a chip that provides access to only 16MB of RAM as a maximum and doesn't provide all the features that the 80386 does. The important feature that the 80286 lacks is the capability to create virtual machines. Think of a virtual machine as a way of separating tasks so that they can't interfere with each other. Every application thinks it's running on its own machine, but each virtual machine is really part of the "real" machine you can see.

Standard mode has some important limitations. For one thing, you can't multitask. Windows only task-switches in this mode. Essentially, this means that you can open as many applications as memory will permit, but only the foreground task will actually do anything.

Another important limitation of standard mode is the lack of virtual memory support. Without this support, the user is limited to the physical memory provided by the machine. Because 80286 machines were never known for their surplus of memory, most users will run out of memory long before they run out of applications to run.

Note: The only version of Windows that still supports standard mode is Windows 3.1. You access it by using the `/S` switch at the command line. Newer versions of Windows—including Windows for Workgroups 3.11—support only 386-enhanced mode.

DOS Applications in Standard Mode

I'm not going to beat around the bush with this topic: Standard mode is dead, and for good reason, if you need to run DOS applications under Windows. Like their Windows application counterparts, you can task-switch between DOS and Windows applications only in standard mode. There's no multitasking in standard mode. The big surprise is that you can have only one active DOS application running at a time in this mode. That's one of the reasons that this mode is such a waste of time.

Most people who used it opened a DOS window and started one application at a time, just like they would at the command prompt. The thing I wonder about is why they even bothered.

Windows also provides very limited memory in this mode, because you can't create a virtual machine. What you got at the DOS prompt was what you had before you entered Windows, minus a lot of memory for Windows itself. Often, the amount of memory left just wouldn't do the job. Many people who used standard mode did so only for their Windows applications, because memory was at such a premium at the DOS prompt.

The combination of a lack of memory and the inability to multitask is a significant problem if you need to run more than one application at a time. Just think—even though it used to be difficult to run a communications program in the background under Windows 3.x in enhanced mode, you couldn't do it at all in standard mode. Suffice it to say that since Windows 95 no longer supports this mode of operation, you can always multitask as many DOS applications as you need to.

Windows in 386-Enhanced Mode

You need to have an 80386 or above processor to use 386-enhanced mode. This is the default mode that Windows 3.1 and above use to get the most out of your machine. It offers all the features people normally associate with Windows now. Even though someone out there might be trying to run Windows in standard mode, most people switched to 80386 machines long ago. Several important features differentiate 386-enhanced mode from standard mode:

- **Multitasking:** Using 386-enhanced mode enables Windows to perform more than one task simultaneously. There are various forms of multitasking. I cover them in the section "Cooperative Versus Preemptive Multitasking" in Chapter 6.
- **Virtual Memory:** Have you ever used a machine that has enough memory? Most of us haven't. Applications always seem to require 1MB more RAM than you have installed. Virtual memory enables Windows to get past this problem so that you don't have to worry about whether your application will run.
- **VxD Support:** Virtual device drivers make Windows a much safer environment to work in. (VxD stands for "Virtual Anything Driver.") Not only are VxDs safer, but they're faster as well. Standard mode never supported the 32-bit enhanced disk services or any of the extended functionality that 386 enhanced mode can.

It's not too difficult to imagine why 386 enhanced mode is the way to go if you have an 80386 machine to run Windows on. In fact, I often wonder how people could expect to run Windows on an 80286 in the first place. Frankly, as I said in a column I wrote for *PC Week* many years ago, I wonder why anyone ever *bought* an 80286, but that's another story entirely. It's one of those "hindsight is 20-20" situations, I guess.

DOS Applications on Virtual Machines

Enhanced mode is the name of the game if you want to multitask DOS applications under Windows. As I stated earlier, this is the only mode you get with Windows versions 3.11 and above (including Windows 95). The underlying reason that you can run more than one application is that they no longer load on the physical machine, but on a virtual machine instead. You may have only one physical machine, so if you use it to run an application, there's nothing left to run something else. (A lot of people have two machines these days—one at home and one at work.) Virtual machines are different. Windows can continue to create new virtual machines as long as it has the memory to do so. Each virtual machine can run one DOS application. The capability to create multiple virtual machines means that you can always run more than one application.

What exactly is a virtual machine? Chapter 6 looks at many of the ramifications from an architectural point of view. Essentially, a virtual machine is a memory structure that acts like a physical machine. There used to be big gaps in this technology under Windows 3.x, but Microsoft has greatly improved the virtual machine under Windows 95. Of course, Windows 95 is still far from perfect. In fact, there will be situations in which Windows 95 just can't cope. Thankfully, Microsoft includes the ability to run your DOS application on the physical machine under Windows 95 using DOS mode. Of course, this means that you lose the ability to use the machine for any other purpose.

From a memory standpoint, Windows 95 creates each virtual machine from extended memory. Once it sets the memory aside, it loads a copy of DOS from the phantom copy Windows 95 keeps around just for this purpose. It then loads and runs your DOS application. As far as the DOS application is concerned, it's running on its own 8088 machine. Of course, this application can still request expanded and extended memory. It can even use Windows DPMI services to switch to protected mode and run itself as a protected-mode application.

Warning: DOS applications that use DPMI services to load themselves into protected memory can cause a lot of problems under Windows 95. These applications essentially reside outside the watchful eye of the Windows 95 memory manager. The fact that they switch back and forth between protected mode and real mode only complicates matters. You can—and probably will—experience memory corruption from time to time if you load an application of this type. Checking the Protected check box (located on the Memory page of the Application Properties dialog box) will slow the application slightly, but will help Windows catch some errant applications before any memory corruption occurs. The best way to prevent this problem, though, is to update to 32-bit applications as quickly as possible.

Once you exit from your DOS application, Windows destroys the virtual machine it used. It returns the memory used by the virtual machine to the system memory pool. Windows might or might not decrease the size of your swap file (depending on your virtual memory settings and the current system load). Each DOS application you load gets a new virtual machine to operate in. Windows simply creates and destroys them as needed.

Which Mode Do You Need?

There's only one mode for any modern user of Windows—enhanced mode. A standard-mode machine is so limited and the cost for upgrading so small in comparison to the speed you'll gain that I really don't think anyone has an excuse for running one of these dinosaurs. The 80286 was brain-dead before it even appeared in the first PC. It's time to bury this relic for good. If you aren't using 386-enhanced mode, you really need to ask yourself why you use Windows at all.

Memory Tuning and Optimization

I've gone through most of the following material in other chapters. However, this is a good place to summarize the various tips and techniques that I present in Chapter 13. Here are my top 10 tips and techniques for tuning your system to make the best use of memory.

Note: You might ask yourself how much memory you need to obtain optimum performance. An operating system such as Windows 95 doesn't have any theoretical limits as far as memory goes—at least, none that any of the current crop of desktop machines can achieve. However, from a practical point of view, you'll see performance top off at 32MB of RAM for most installations, because everything should be loaded in memory at that point. Depending on your processor, you might actually see a performance drop-off starting at 64MB, as Windows 95 spends more time managing memory than using it. Your performance curve will vary depending on a lot of factors, including processor type and the number and size of applications you run.

1. Always use the built-in memory manager if possible. This chapter has looked at quite a few of the ways you can use the extra flexibility. I present a few more in future chapters.
2. Use your fastest drive for the swap file, but don't starve Windows in the process. A fast drive will improve performance in one respect. A small swap file could kill that performance gain by reducing system stability and introducing some memory thrashing. Always choose the fastest drive that contains enough memory to hold the entire swap file.

3. Manage your system, but don't micromanage it. This will be a major problem area for some users. Tune the individual files for the performance you need. Tell Windows what you need to do, but don't worry too much about how it gets the job done. I wouldn't have said this under Windows 3.x, but leaving Windows 95 alone to do its work is about the best performance enhancement you can provide. (Of course, a little monitoring from time to time as your computing habits change wouldn't hurt, either.)
4. Never load real-mode device drivers or TSRs you don't need. The old approach of loading everything before you start Windows is a dead end under Windows 95. Make each environment unique—custom-made to perform the job you need it to do.
5. Use the automatic memory settings whenever possible. There are times when you'll have to step in and adjust them manually if you have an application that starts by grabbing everything available. In most cases, though, you'll get ahead if you let Windows manage the memory for you. Letting Windows manage your memory provides a much greater degree of flexibility for you in the long run. That flexibility usually translates into increased efficiency and performance.

6. Avoid MS-DOS mode, but use it if you must. Windows 95 has come a long way in providing the level of support that Microsoft has promised for years. It still isn't perfect, but neither are the applications that run under it. If you find an application that simply won't run using the default Windows memory setup, try creating an optimized environment for it in MS-DOS mode. (I show the procedure for doing this in Chapter 13.)
7. Enhance your memory usage by getting rid of the frills. Wallpaper, excess icons, screen savers, and other doodads consume memory without giving you much in return. Entertainment is always nice, but not at the cost of efficiency. The question you should always ask yourself is whether something relieves fatigue or merely consumes resources.
8. Increase your level of physical RAM as needed. Windows 95 can literally make as much RAM as you need from your hard drive, but there's a limit to how much performance you can get by doing this. I always follow a simple rule: When the size of my swap file consistently equals the amount of RAM in my machine, it's time to buy more RAM.
9. Get a faster hard drive. Swap files are a fact of life under Windows 95, and that means you're at least partially dependent on its speed for overall system performance—even when it comes to memory. I find that a drive with a higher level of throughput is a better choice than one with faster access time when it comes to memory management. Windows tends to read from the swap file in small, contiguous blocks. A drive with a higher throughput can deliver that data faster.

10. Kill those old applications. If you're still using a lot of DOS applications, it's time to upgrade. Get rid of those old moth-eaten remnants. The only thing that old DOS applications will do for you is slow the system down and cause reliability problems. Of course, 16-bit Windows applications aren't much better, for the most part. Upgrading to the newer 32-bit applications will help you use memory efficiently and usually will provide a speed benefit as well. Remember that you can use many Windows NT applications under Windows 95 until the official Windows 95 version of your product hits the streets. (Be sure to check with the vendor; most have Windows 95 versions of their products available as of this writing.)

On Your Own

Open a DOS box and use the MEM command to see what kinds of memory you have available. Also note the amount of each type of memory you have available. If you don't see that both expanded and extended memory are available, try to discover the reason that one or the other is absent.

If you're using a memory manager, try booting your machine without it. What differences do you see in the amount of Windows 95 memory available? What about the memory available in a DOS box? You'll want to use the information you get as part of your criteria for determining whether to get rid of the memory manager.

Explore the list of memory-tuning techniques in the preceding section. Can you use any of these tips to improve your machine's performance? Try different ways of implementing these changes to see what works best with your configuration. Windows 95 is a new operating system, so you need to explore its weaknesses and strengths to see what you can do to improve your machine's capabilities. I think you'll find that many of the old techniques you once used no longer work properly.

9

The Windows 95 File System

One of the biggest news items for Windows 95 is its use of long filenames. From a user's perspective, it's one of the more noticeable changes in the operating system (besides the interface and a few new utilities). Although many of the inner changes will go unnoticed—mainly because they work—this is one feature that you're fairly certain not to miss.

Long filename support also ends one of the main criticisms that really irked me when talking with a Macintosh user. Flat memory address space and long filenames were two things the Macintosh had that the PC just couldn't seem to get a grip on. Now that it has those two items, I am prepared for every Mac user who comes toward me at a convention.

Those of you lucky enough to have OEM Service Release 2 (OSR2) installed on your machine will see another very important feature. FAT 32 is an upgrade of the venerable FAT 16 all of us know and love. I'll discuss this new technology as the chapter progresses. In short, it reduces the cluster size of large hard disks—improving storage efficiency and also providing a small increase in speed.

Of course, every time you change the file system, you must change the utilities to manage that file system. Fortunately, most Windows 95 installations still use the 16-bit version of the FAT (file allocation table) file system. This means that a lot of your old utilities will still work, albeit a little less than they did before. (You can't use any of those old disk utilities on a FAT 32 drive. As of this writing, you must use Microsoft-specific products to perform any kind of drive maintenance.) Actually, the new and improved file system looks and works a lot like the old one. Microsoft merely used some of the space in the directory table that it didn't use in the past.

Warning: Using an old disk management utility with Windows 95 might mean a loss of your long filenames, because these old utilities don't know to move everything needed to support them. Windows 95 actually provides support for two filenames—an older DOS version and a newer, long filename. They are stored in separate areas and require different DOS and Windows operating system calls for you to use them. These old utilities know how to use the DOS 8.3 filename, but they know nothing about long filenames and invariably destroy them. The next time you try to view a long filename with Windows 95, there is nothing to view, because the long filename was destroyed by the old utility. This might seem like only an inconvenience until you realize that loss of the long filenames also means a loss of the Start menu and other Windows 95-specific long filenames. Windows 95 might not even restart if you lose the long filenames it requires. Use the LFNBACK utility (on the CD-ROM in the \ADMIN\APPTOOLS\LFNBACK folder) to create a backup of all your long filenames prior to using any utility you're not absolutely certain about. Unfortunately, the Add/Remove Programs dialog box doesn't provide an entry for this useful utility, so you'll need to install it manually. I'll go into more detail later in this chapter. (Machines with OSR2 installed may not have access to the LFNBACK utility.)

This chapter takes you on a tour of the Windows 95 file system from a user perspective. We'll even take a brief look at the architecture and put on our programmer's hat for a while. The Windows 95 VFAT (virtual file allocation table) file system might look and act like an enhanced version of the old system, but I think you'll be surprised at all the new features under the hood.

Note: From this point on, unless I specifically mention the FAT 32 file system, assume that all conversation about the FAT file system refers to the older FAT 16 file system. The new file system presents many issues that we'll discuss in the "What Is 32-Bit VFAT?" section of this chapter. Any discussion of VFAT-specific issues refers to the FAT 32 and FAT 16 file systems equally.

File Structures

There's a proliferation of file systems on my hard drives. Right now I can boot Windows 3.x, Windows 95, Windows NT, and OS/2. Each of these operating systems supports the FAT file system. The last three also support their own file systems. Of the three, only the VFAT file system used by Windows 95 looks familiar. The other two are enhanced file systems that started from scratch, because no one thought that the FAT file system could ever be repaired. The following paragraphs take a look at a few of the remaining problems with VFAT.

So what do you do with a system that's literally bogged down with incompatible file systems? You could take the easy way out—the way I originally took when I started working with OS/2. If you stick with the FAT file system, you'll certainly get everybody talking to each other and run into a minimum of problems.

There's only one problem with this solution: If you stick with the FAT file system, you'll have compatibility, but you'll also miss out on the special features each of the other file systems has to offer. Both NTFS (Windows NT file system) and HPFS (high-performance file system) offer improved reliability and a higher access speed than the old FAT file system. The battle's still raging over which one is better—HPFS or NTFS. My personal favorite is NTFS, but that's another story.

Note: Even though older versions of Windows NT do provide support for HPFS, Windows NT 4.0 doesn't provide support for it right out of the package. Some people have reported that you can install Windows NT 4.0 over an existing Windows NT installation to gain HPFS support, if it's important to you.

Peter's Principle: A Method of Dealing with Multiple File Systems

After a lot of thought, I finally came up with a middle-ground solution to the problem of dealing with multiple file systems on one computer. It offers the maximum in compatibility, yet lets me make the most out of what the other file systems have to offer.

The first thing I did was partition my drives. I set aside one partition for each of the operating systems installed on my machine. I had to do that anyway to have everything boot correctly. Each operating system's specific partition uses the special file format that it provides. This way, the operating system and its utility programs can benefit from the improved performance and reliability that the new file system has to offer. I also stick any operating-system-specific applications in these partitions.

Once I figured out where each operating system would go, I installed them. Each installation required a bit of time and patience, but I got through it. It's important to test the ability to boot each operating system after you install a new one. Both Windows NT and Windows 95 like to overwrite the bootable partition marker. This means that whatever boot manager you have installed won't boot until you use a disk editor to set the active partition back to its original position.

After I installed the operating systems and tested the boot sequence, I had one large partition left (actually, I set the whole second drive aside). I labeled the partition on this drive COMMON and placed all my data and common applications there. It uses the FAT file system so everyone can access it. In some cases, I had to install each application once for each operating system. However, if you're careful, you can determine which files to copy from your Windows SYSTEM directory into each of the other SYSTEM directories. (.DLLs and VxDs need to appear in the SYSTEM directory in most cases or Windows won't be able to find them.) Is this a perfect solution? Not by a long shot. However, it's a solution that works.

So why did I go through this entire rundown of my system configuration? I think that you might find yourself in the same dilemma that I was in. You must test all (or at least many) of the solutions available today, which means keeping multiple operating systems on your machine. This solution might be just what the doctor ordered when the time comes to test an OS/2 or a Windows NT solution that the entire company might adopt. If you don't test the advanced file system that comes with the operating system, can you really say that you tested everything when the time comes to make a decision?

FAT Versus VFAT

Now that we have some preliminaries out of the way, let's look at the new VFAT file system provided with Windows 95. As I said in an earlier chapter, one of the reasons for the success of Windows 3.0 is the capability to upgrade DOS to use it. In other words, the user could make the transition slowly, without having to give up a comfortable environment. Windows 95 continues this line of reasoning, even to maintaining a level of compatibility with the old FAT file system. However, people weren't satisfied with the old 8.3 filenames. They wanted long filenames, and the FAT file system can't provide this feature. The VFAT file system represents an effort on the part of Microsoft to give people what they want and still maintain a level of compatibility with previous versions of DOS (and more importantly, the applications that ran under it).

The following paragraphs provide a bit of history and then a current look at the way Windows handles file access. It's important to start at the beginning to see what you've gained with various versions of Windows. Even more important, this historical view will help you understand certain constraints that faced Microsoft programmers when they designed Windows 95. It's easy to start out with a new product and design all the features that people want today, but it's another story to start with something that was fine yesterday and redesign it to meet today's needs. Windows 95 isn't a completely new operating system; it's the next generation of Windows 3.x, from a compatibility point of view. In other words, even though much of Windows 3.x is gone, Windows 95 still has to work as if Windows 3.x were still present.

A Look at Windows Under DOS

Everyone who has worked with DOS and Windows 3.x knows that they have at least one thing in common: the FAT file system. That relationship between DOS and Windows 3.x also caused some problems for the user. Consider the speed issue many people bring up when you talk about using Windows. Because this older version of Windows rode on top of DOS, it used some DOS services to access the hardware. The hard disk drive falls into this category. DOS provided all the file services that Windows 3.x used. In fact, this was about the only DOS service that Windows 3.1 did use.

What using DOS to provide file services means to the user is that the system has to slow down every time Windows wants to access the hard drive. To see what I mean, look at Figure 9.1. Every time Windows wants to access the hard drive, it must create a request in a format that DOS understands, switch over to real mode so that it can access DOS, and then wait for DOS to get the job done. Meanwhile, all those applications that are supposed to do something in the background are suspended. Remember, the Intel processor can't multitask in real mode; it can do that only in protected mode. Once DOS finds the bit of information that Windows needs, Windows has to copy that information out of the conventional memory space into an area that it can reach in protected mode. It must then switch the processor from real mode back into protected mode.

This is only where the problem starts, not where it ends. Every time Windows has to make the switch from protected mode to real mode, it becomes vulnerable to attack from a maverick application. When the processor is in real mode, the operating system can no longer track system activity. Because the processor won't alert the operating system when an application creates a memory fault, an application could crash the system before Windows 3.x even knows what is going on.

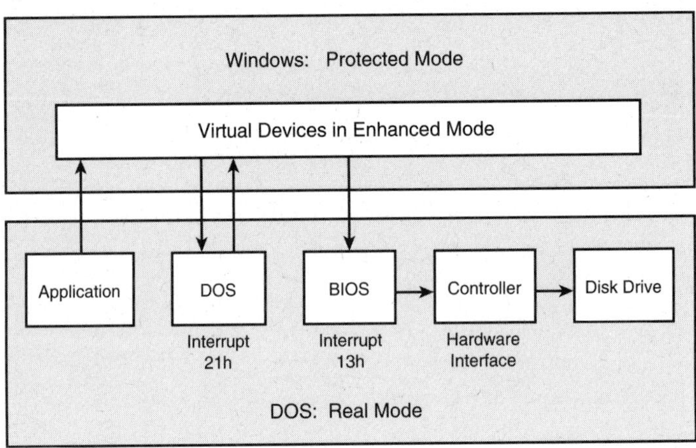

Figure 9.1.
Windows 3.1 needs to switch from protected mode to real mode to access the hard drive through DOS. Not only does this waste time, but it also opens the door for a system crash if a rampant application decides to do something unexpected.

32-Bit Access Under Windows 3.1

Windows 3.1 provided a new feature called 32-bit access. This feature reduced the opportunity for system crashes and enhanced overall system speed. However, before I talk about how 32-bit access affects your computing environment, you need to understand what it is.

If you tried to figure out what 32-bit access is by its name, you might suspect that it's some new technique for accessing the data on your drive 32 bits at a time. What 32-bit access actually provides is a little more complex.

Every time an application requests data from the hard drive, Windows intercepts the request to see whether it can be fulfilled using data in protected memory. Usually this request asks to open a file or to read specific byte ranges of data. Once Windows determines that it can't fulfill the request, it switches to real mode and passes the request to the DOS interrupt 21h handler. This handler looks at the request and starts to take care of it by issuing interrupt 13h requests. You can look at interrupt 21h as the manager and interrupt 13h as the worker. Interrupt 21h receives the whole problem in one big chunk. It then breaks up the problem into small pieces that interrupt 13h can handle. As a result, each interrupt 21h call can result in many interrupt 13h calls.

Because Windows is monitoring everything, the system doesn't just stay in real mode and take care of the entire disk request at one time. Windows intercepts each interrupt 13h call that the DOS interrupt 21h handler makes, and sees whether it can fulfill the request using data in protected memory. If not, Windows switches back to real mode and the call is handled by the BIOS. The BIOS performs the work required to fulfill the call and passes the information back to Windows, which passes it back to DOS, which passes it back to Windows, which finally passes it back to the application. This might seem like a lot of work just to read a few bytes of data from the disk, and it is.

Figure 9.2 shows the new 32-bit access method used by Windows 3.1x. Notice that the BIOS is completely cut out of the picture. That's because FastDisk (a 32-bit protected-mode driver) emulates the BIOS, using protected-mode code. This means that Windows can eliminate two mode

transitions for every interrupt 13h call as well as effectively multitask during more of the disk access cycle. You lose only the DOS processing time instead of both DOS and BIOS processing time. This improvement accounts for part of the noticeable speed-up in Windows 3.1. It also accounts for some of the improved stability that people experience.

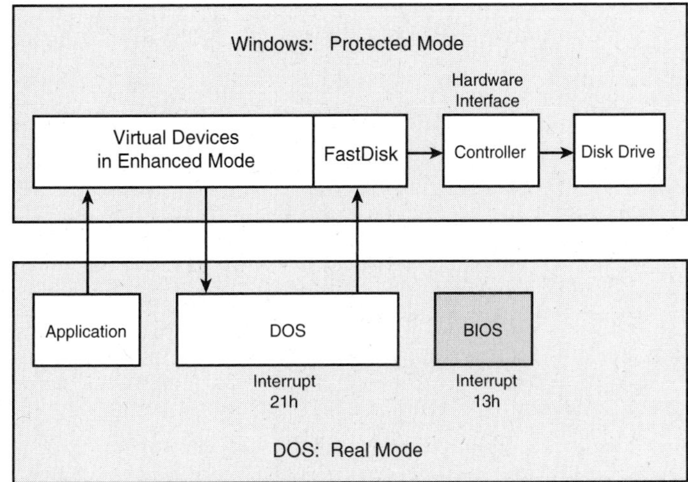

Figure 9.2.
Windows 3.11 provides a 32-bit access feature that reduces the opportunities for a system crash and enhances system throughput.

Windows 3.11 and Windows for Workgroups 3.11 added even more 32-bit file access. These versions of Windows use the DOS file access features to search for files and to perform other file-specific activities. (This differentiates a file access from a disk access, which deals with reading and writing sections of data.) This means even fewer transitions to DOS, because the file system no longer keeps the BIOS in the picture. The result is an overall improvement in system speed and reliability.

The Windows 95 Alternative to 32-Bit Access

Windows 95 gets around the entire real-mode access problem by incorporating all operating system functions into a 32-bit architecture. Microsoft named this technique the VFAT interface. Its full name is the Protected-Mode FAT File System. Figure 9.3 shows how this disk management system differs from the one used under Windows 3.x. Using protected-mode drivers means that there's less chance that a random application will cause a system failure, because Windows 95 is never unprotected for a long enough time—it always runs in protected mode. (The only exception to this rule is if you install real-mode drivers in CONFIG.SYS to support an antiquated device such as a CD-ROM drive. Windows 95 does switch to Virtual 86 mode when accessing a device that uses a real-mode driver.) Using protected mode means that the operating system constantly monitors every event taking place on the machine. It has the final say before a particular event takes place. This new system runs totally in protected memory and reduces the chance of system crashes (due to disk-related problems) to nearly zero, and greatly enhances disk access speed.

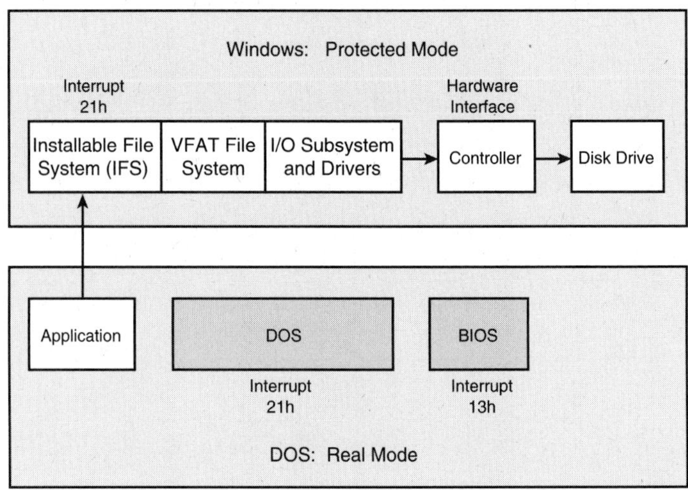

Figure 9.3.
Windows 95 uses a totally different system than its predecessors to access this disk.

As Figure 9.3 shows, there are several discrete components in the Windows 95 file system. Actually, Microsoft refers to these components as layers. There are 32 possible layers in the Windows 95 file system, starting at the I/O subsystem. (The current configuration doesn't use all 32 layers.) Layer 0 is closest to the I/O subsystem, whereas layer 31 is closest to the hardware. The current version of Windows 95 requires only a few of these layers (normally 12) to do the job. The other layers are placeholders for future use. Each layer provides hooks for third-party software used to support custom file systems and devices. For example, adding a network driver to the file system layer enables you to access drives on other machines. Unlike previous versions of Windows, a vendor can retrofit the Windows 95 file system to provide additional capabilities with relative ease. Each of these components performs a different task:

- **Installable File System (IFS) manager:** This is the highest layer in the file system. The IFS is a VxD that provides the interface to applications. It doesn't matter whether the application uses the interrupt 21h interface or either the 16- or 32-bit Windows interface, this is the component that receives application requests. It's the responsibility of the IFS to transfer control to the appropriate file system driver (FSD). The VFAT FSD component appears in Figure 9.3, but Windows 95 also includes network and CD FSDs.
- **File System Driver (FSD) layer:** The most common file system driver layer component is the VFAT FSD. This is the VxD that takes care of all local hard drive requests. It provides the long filename support and protected-mode stability that makes Windows 95 better than its predecessors. Your machine might have several other FSDs, depending on the type of equipment you've installed. For example, Windows 95 installs a network file system handler if you install any form of a LAN. All of the FSDs talk with the IFS manager and send requests to the layers that directly communicate with the hardware.

- **I/O Subsystem (IOS) layer:** This is the highest level of the block device layer. A block device is any device that sends information in blocks. A hard drive usually uses some multiple of 512 bytes as its block size, but other devices might use a different block size. Network devices, tape drives, and CD-ROM drives all fall into the block device category. The IOS provides general device services to the FSDs. For example, it routes requests from the FSDs to various device-specific drivers. It also sends status information from the device-specific drivers to the FSDs.
- **Volume Tracking Driver (VTD) layer:** Windows 95 may or may not install this driver. It handles any removable devices attached to your system; for example, if you have a floppy or CD-ROM drive, Windows 95 will install this component. On the other hand, if you use a diskless workstation or rely on local and network hard drives alone, Windows 95 won't need to install this component. The VTD performs one, and only one, basic function. It monitors the status of all removable media drives and reports any change in media. This is the component that will complain if you remove a floppy prematurely (usually in the middle of a write).
- **Type-Specific Driver (TSD) layer:** Every type of device needs a driver that understands its peculiar needs. For example, the hard disk drive driver wouldn't understand the needs of a floppy drive very well. This layer deals with logical device types rather than specific devices. For example, one TSD handles all the hard drives on your system, another TSD handles all the floppy drives, while a third TSD handles all network drives.
- **Vendor-Supplied Driver (VSD) layer:** This is where a vendor would install support for a proprietary bus CD-ROM or a removable media device, such as a floptical drive. Every specific device type needs a driver that can translate its requests for Windows. This is the layer that performs those services. The VSD knows things such as the number of heads a disk has or the amount of time it needs to wait for a floppy to get up to speed.
- **Port Driver (PD) layer:** The PD performs the actual task of communicating with the device through an adapter. It's the last stage before a message leaves Windows and the first stage when a message arrives from the device. The PD is usually adapter-specific. For example, you would have one VSD for each hard drive and one PD for each hard drive adapter. If your system uses an IDE hard drive, Windows would load the IDE PD to talk to the IDE adapter.
- **SCSIzer:** Don't let the strange-looking name for this layer fool you. It deals with SCSI command language. Think of the command language as the method the computer uses to tell a SCSI device to perform a task. It isn't the data the SCSI device handles; rather, it's the act the SCSI device will perform. Windows 95 has one SCSIzer for each SCSI device.
- **SCSI Manager:** Windows NT introduced something called the miniport driver. With Windows 95, you can use the Windows NT miniport binaries. However, before you can actually do this, Windows 95 must translate its commands to a format that the miniport driver understands. The SCSI Manager performs this service.

- **Miniport Driver:** This is a device driver that provides support for a specific SCSI device. No other device uses the miniport driver. The miniport driver works with the SCSI manager to perform the same task as a PD. Windows NT and Windows 95 use the same miniport drivers.
- **Protected-Mode Mapper:** This layer performs a very special task. It enables you to use your DOS drivers under Windows 95. Without the support of this VxD, Windows 95 couldn't support legacy devices that lack drivers specific to Windows 95. Essentially, the protected-mode mapper disguises a real-mode driver to look like a Windows 95 protected-mode driver.
- **Real-Mode Driver:** It's almost certain that some vendors won't supply drivers for every device they ever made, and in reality, they have no reason to do so. The older device that still does the job for you is probably so far out-of-date that you're the only one still using it. Still, like a really comfortable pair of shoes, you hate to give up that old device. (I personally have a proprietary bus Hitachi CD-ROM hanging around; it still does the job, so I'm not going to give it up just yet.) One of the goals of the Windows 95 development team was to allow you to keep that old legacy device hanging around until you're ready to give it up. It's going to cost some system speed to keep it, but that real-mode driver will work just fine under Windows 95.

OEM Service Release 2 (OSR2) Updates to the I/O Subsystem (IOS)

The previous section talked about the purpose of the IOS as part of the Windows 95 file system. OSR2 provides some updates to this very important part of the operating system, and these updates are in addition to the FAT 32 support that we'll talk about later. The following list provides a brief description of each feature:

- **Drive spin-down support enabled:** Previous versions of Windows 95 would use the power-saving features of your display adapter and monitor if they provided them. My monitor shuts down after 20 minutes because of this feature. However, even if you had a drive that would power itself down, Windows 95 would keep it running. This new feature will power your hard disk drives down after a period of inactivity.
- **120MB floptical support:** Just like everything else, the amount of data that you can store on a floptical is on the rise. The OSR2 version of Windows 95 enables you to use 120MB flopticals natively.
- **IDE (Integrated Development Environment) busmaster support:** A busmaster setup can greatly improve system performance by reducing or completely eliminating the need for processor calls when servicing a hard disk drive. Obviously, this calls for some level of

support by the operating system. It needs to issue calls that make use of this special disk controller feature instead of using the old calls that use the processor instead. IDE busmasters are a fairly recent innovation, but using one can really improve system throughput. Unfortunately, you won't see this performance boost unless your machine has the OSR2 version of Windows 95 installed.

- **Smart predictive disk failure API:** RAID (redundant array of inexpensive disks) and other disk technologies take a reactive approach to disk failure. In other words, they help you recover after a problem has already occurred. Sometime in the future, drives will accurately predict when they're going to fail and send that information to the operating system. By having this information, you could back up your drive and replace it before it actually fails.
- **Removable IDE Media Support:** Removable media is an important element in data management strategies today. For example, a floptical or SyQuest drive can provide high-speed, intermediate storage for files that you don't use every day, but often enough that tape storage would prove inconvenient. Your vendor previously had to provide special support software to manage removable IDE media under Windows 95. OSR2 corrects that oversight by providing removable IDE media support within the IOS.

As you can see, OSR2 is much more than a simple update of the file system. Some of these features won't work with older hardware. This is one of the reasons that Microsoft chose not to make OSR2 publicly available. Trying to provide a reasonable level of support with so many new features thrown into the file system would have been very difficult indeed. (We'll examine other compatibility issues as the chapter progresses.)

Gaining Access to VFAT from DOS

You can access the VFAT interface in a DOS application. Microsoft incorporated a new set of services into the interrupt 21h handler. Table 9.1 shows the various calls you can make to this new interface. Notice that the AL part of the service call corresponds to the current disk service call numbers. The contents of the other registers also correspond to the old DOS register setups. If you know how to use the current set of interrupt 21h disk routines, using the new ones only requires a simple change in the contents of the AX register. Microsoft recommends that you use the Get Volume Information (71A0h) to detect whether the current system supports long filenames. Set the carry flag before making the call. If the machine doesn't support long filenames, the carry flag will be unchanged on return, and DOS will clear the AL register. Never use the long filename calls on a system that doesn't support them. Remember that all these service numbers go into the AX register and that the values are in hexadecimal.

Table 9.1. VFAT interface interrupt 21h functions.

AX Code	*Function Name*
7139h	Create Directory
713Ah	Remove Directory
713Bh	Set Current Directory
7141h	Delete File
7143h	Get/Set File Attributes
7147h	Get Current Directory
714Eh	Find First File
714Fh	Find Next File
7156h	Move or Rename File
716Ch	Extended Open/Create File
71A0h	Get Volume Information
71A1h	Find Close

VCache

Did you ever play with the size of the cache you provided for SmartDrive under Windows 3.x? If you ever spent as much time doing it as I did, you became pretty frustrated with the results. The problem was simple: If you allocated enough memory to cover every situation that the cache might encounter, you didn't have enough left to run all those applications you needed.

You also may have encountered other problems. Until the latest release of DOS, SmartDrive didn't support CD-ROM drives. This wasn't a problem a few years ago when CD-ROM drives were still not in common use. Today, however, CD-ROM drives are very common, and it won't be very long before a CD-ROM drive is standard equipment on every machine sold. It makes sense, then, that later versions of the drive cache support a CD-ROM drive.

One thing SmartDrive still doesn't support is network access, even when that access is through a Microsoft network. How many PCs in your company are still used in stand-alone mode? In a few more years, I doubt that many stand-alone machines will be found in corporate America or even small companies. I know of some home users who network their machines. If you fall into the "networked" category in any way, you know the frustration of waiting for your machine to load data from the server. A cache that could keep track of some of the most-recently-used data would be a big help in speeding network access.

The VCache VxD found in Windows 95 is a 32-bit protected-mode replacement for SmartDrive that does all the things I just mentioned, and more. It automatically supports the standard local hard drive, the network, and CD-ROM drives.

VCache creates a separate cache for each type of drive. It also balances the total cache size with the memory requirements of your system. The result is a dynamically sized cache that's optimized to meet the needs of the particular kind of access you're performing most often. If you're loading a lot of data from the network, VCache increases the size of your network cache. Loading a new application from the CD-ROM drive allocates more space for the CD-ROM cache. Likewise, local drive access will change the size of that cache.

When I say that VCache does all this work, I don't mean that it does the work by itself. The CDFS (compact disc file system) part of the miniport driver comes into play for CD-ROM drives. The OSR2 version of Windows 95 also adds support for CDI (CD-ROM Interactive) to the CDFS support. CDFS cooperates with VCache to create a part of the drive cache picture. Likewise, the network redirector (depending on which network you install) works with VCache. Windows 95 automatically changes the configuration of both drivers as the configuration of your system changes. For example, it won't add network redirector support on systems that don't have access to a network. The same holds true for CD-ROM drive support on non-CD-equipped systems.

Peter's Principle: Real Mode and 16-Bit Windows Drivers: Just Say No

Everything that VCache provides will work as I just described if you use 32-bit drivers for all your drives. However, if you use an older CD-ROM that needs a real-mode or 16-bit driver, you'll lose part of the dynamic caching that VCache provides. MSCDEX uses a static cache that VCache won't override and it needs the cooperation of CDFS to provide support for CD-ROM drives.

Likewise, if your network uses real-mode drivers (as the current version of LANtastic does), VCache can't provide network drive cache support. The network will run just as sluggishly as it did before. You won't see any of the anticipated speed boost, because Windows 95 can't override those real-mode drivers. It has to have a 32-bit substitute before it can remove the old drivers.

The entire Windows 95 drive system relies on the new 32-bit drivers to provide a complete package. If you replace an element with a real-mode or 16-bit Windows driver, you remove a piece of the picture. Getting the most out of VCache means that your network and CD-ROM have to use the 32-bit drivers.

What's the bottom line? If you want maximum reliability and performance, don't use old drivers. A piece of equipment that requires a real-mode or 16-bit Windows driver is a disaster waiting to happen. Do you really want to play Russian roulette with your data? If the answer is no, replace that old equipment.

We looked at how you could change the way that VCache looks at the CD-ROM drive in Chapter 3, when we discussed the supplemental drive cache and other CD-ROM drive caches. Essentially, this is all the tuning you need to do; everything else is optimized dynamically to meet system file access and memory requirements.

VCache also supports a feature that you might not want to use. Lazy writes enable Windows 95 to write data to the cache and then write the data from the cache to your hard drive during idle time. A lazy write is an industry term for a cache—especially a hard drive cache—that delays writing data from the cache to the drive until a time of low disk activity. Because writing to the cache is faster, you get a speed boost by using this feature. I keep it enabled on my system because I haven't experienced too many lockups or GPFs since I installed Windows 95. However, if you fall into the select group that does experience problems, turning off lazy writes may save your database. Here's the way to disable lazy writes.

Right-click the My Computer icon and select Properties. Click the Performance page and then the File System button. Select the Troubleshooting page. You should see a display similar to the one shown in Figure 9.4. (I describe the other features of this tab in the "Using Windows 95 Automatic Tuning Features" section of Chapter 3.) This dialog box enables you to disable lazy writes for all drives by checking the Disable Write-Behind Caching for All Drives option. All you need to do now is click OK twice to save your changes. Windows then tells you to reboot your machine (in most cases) to allow the change to take effect.

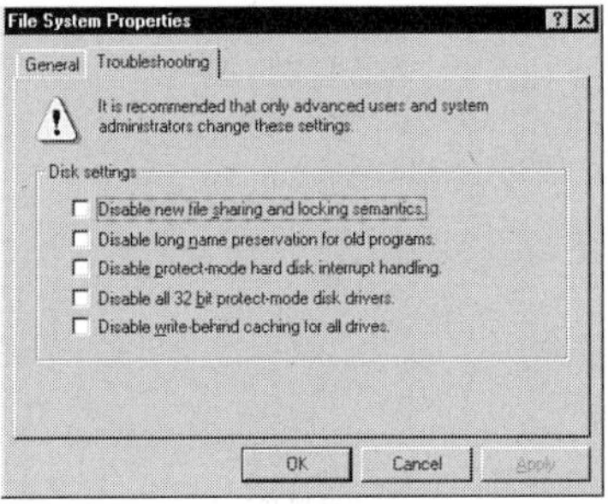

Figure 9.4.
The Troubleshooting page of the File System Properties dialog box enables you to turn off lazy writes for all drives.

The positive side of this change is that all writes go directly to the drive instead of the cache. This might actually help you resolve some database problems where the program displays old or incorrect data on another user's display after the first user changes it. The negative aspect is that you'll lose a lot of performance by going this route. In other words, lazy writes offer a big plus in the way of a speed boost for your system, especially for network drive access.

The main reason to disable lazy writes is to avoid losing data due to a system crash. If Windows 95 writes some data to the cache and the machine freezes before Windows has a chance to write that data to disk, you'll experience a data loss. It's unlikely that you'll recover the data if Windows can't move it to disk. Fortunately, this is a rare event under Windows 95, barring any major problems with drivers, DOS applications, or older 16-bit Windows applications. Many applications provide an autosave feature that you may want to set to a shorter interval on systems that experience many problems with machine freezes.

Tip: Occasionally, Windows 95 may freeze to the point where pressing Ctrl+Alt+Delete won't allow you to regain control of the system. Under Windows 3.x, this would mean instant data loss. Windows 95 seems to recover better than its predecessor in some cases. You can usually reduce data loss under Windows 95 if you allow the system to go idle before performing a reboot after a system freeze. Wait for all data to be written to disk before you reboot the system. When the disk access light goes out and stays out for at least 30 seconds, you can reboot the system with a minimum of data loss.

HPFS and NTFS Compatibility

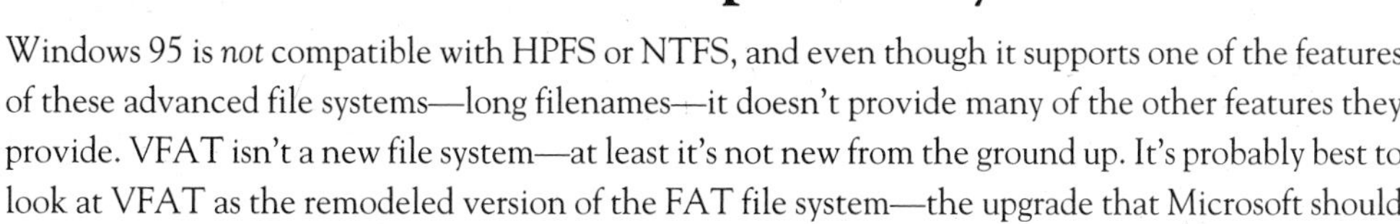

Windows 95 is *not* compatible with HPFS or NTFS, and even though it supports one of the features of these advanced file systems—long filenames—it doesn't provide many of the other features they provide. VFAT isn't a new file system—at least it's not new from the ground up. It's probably best to look at VFAT as the remodeled version of the FAT file system—the upgrade that Microsoft should have done long ago.

VFAT can't provide two important features that these other new file systems can: Reliability and improved access speed. If either one is of higher importance than compatibility with old applications, you may want to look at Windows NT or OS/2 instead of Windows 95. The one thing Windows 95 provides is a higher level of compatibility, but you will lose these two features.

I could go into all the gory details of these two advanced file systems here, but the important part of this discussion is what you will miss. OS/2 definitely provides a higher level of throughput with HPFS. This file system is redesigned to eliminate one of the major flaws of the FAT file system. Every time you need to access a file under FAT, you must go to the very beginning of the disk, look up the filename, and get the location of the first cluster of data. You then have to move the head to the data location and read the cluster before you find out whether it contains the data you need. Every access requires another trip to the directory or file allocation table (FAT). The drive head moves back and forth from one extreme to another like a pendulum. All that head movement is very time-intensive and could potentially wear out the drive sooner. HPFS takes care of this problem by moving the directory and file allocation table to the middle of the drive where you can access them with much less head movement.

NTFS has the reliability part of the equation down pat. Not only does it support a much-enhanced file storage system, but you can also use it directly with some of the modern data safeguard techniques such as RAID (redundant array of inexpensive disks) and data mirroring. NTFS is an advanced file system for people who can't afford to lose any data. Of course, fully using those data features is more expensive in drive purchase cost than the old FAT system.

In this day and age of huge drives, NTFS takes into account another problem with the old FAT file system—large cluster sizes. Buy anything larger than a 1GB drive when using FAT and you'll pay with 32KB cluster sizes. To put this problem into perspective, think about large cluster sizes in this way. Even a 1-byte file consumes 32KB on a large drive, and that's not very efficient. Drive capacity is also a problem. The old FAT file system can only support 2GB partitions (still a huge amount of space, but not all that uncommon). So what is the price of using FAT versus NTFS or HPFS when it comes to wasted drive space? Table 9.2 gives you the information you need to make an intelligent decision.

Table 9.2. File system statistics comparison.

Statistic	*FAT 16*	*FAT 32*	*HPFS*	*NTFS*
Maximum partition size	2^{16}	2^{32}	2^{32}	2^{64}
Maximum file size	2^{16}	2^{32}	2^{24}	2^{64}
Cluster size	512+ bytes	4KB	512 bytes	512 bytes–4KB
Maximum volume size	2GB	2TB	1TB	8,589,934,592TB
Maximum file size	2GB	2TB	4GB	8,589,934,592

Just in case you haven't noticed, Table 9.2 contains an entry for a new file system type called FAT 32. We'll talk about it in the next section. You'll also notice that while HPFS and FAT 32 both provide 2^{32} partition size, HPFS can only address up to 1TB of disk space. That's because HPFS uses a signed integer (one that can be both positive and negative) to address the disk space, which reduces the potential disk address range by half. For now, the table says it all. If you want to create some truly huge files, NTFS is the way to go.

What Is 32-bit VFAT?

FAT 32, or more precisely 32-bit VFAT, is a new file system supported by the OSR2 release of Windows 95. You're going to see more than just a little discussion about this file system, because it's extremely controversial. The most basic question people will ask is why Microsoft didn't simply add NTFS to Windows 95 rather than come up with yet another file system. This is actually a fairly easy question to answer. To begin with, Microsoft would have had to come up with many more drivers and an enhanced file system setup for Windows 95 to support NTFS. The time required to do this would have delayed this much-needed update. Creating FAT 32 involved some changes, but they weren't nearly as extensive as NTFS would have required. At a very basic level, FAT 32 is still the file allocation table method of storing data. True, it does use 32 bits instead of 16 bits, but that really isn't such a big issue when compared to the file system design as a whole. In addition, while FAT file system users do need a more efficient way to store data, NTFS is one of the differentiating factors between Windows 95 and Windows NT. The marketing department at Microsoft wouldn't have been happy if one of the reasons for buying Windows NT suddenly went away.

So why use FAT 32? Storage efficiency is the big plus. In fact, you can boil the whole thing down to one disk parameter—cluster size. A 1GB or larger drive that uses the FAT 16 file storage system requires 32KB clusters. This means that even a 1-byte file requires 32KB of disk storage space. If you have a lot of small files on your drive, the waste of storage space begins to mount quickly. FAT 32 allows a cluster size of 4KB. That's still a lot of wasted space for a 1-byte file, but a lot less than FAT 16 would waste. Okay, so what should you expect in the real world as far as space savings go? I tried out several different installations and the range of space savings was anywhere between 20 percent and 50 percent disk storage space savings, all without compressing your drive. (Microsoft guarantees a space savings of at least 10 to 15 percent, but actual experience shows even better results in most cases.) A typical installation that included Windows 95, Microsoft Office, CorelDRAW!, and a couple of game programs went from a whopping 870MB of disk storage to 650MB. That's a savings of 220MB on the hard drive, which is pretty significant, in my book. Obviously, your results will vary depending on how many small files (4KB or less in size) you store.

Less well known, but very important, are the reliability features of using FAT 32. Unlike FAT 16, the root directory of a FAT 32 volume can be located anywhere on the drive. Drive utility software will now be able to relocate root directory information as needed to repair drive problems. The relocatable root directory also means that FAT 32 doesn't suffer from the old root directory limitations, such as the number of files that you can store there. FAT 32 uses the copy and the default copy of the FAT. This means that FAT problems that used to stop your machine cold won't even appear to the user. (Even though FAT 16 maintains two copies of the FAT, it can only use the default copy.) The ability to use more than one FAT will also allow for dynamic partition resizing in the future. (Even though the capability exists to do so now, Microsoft won't implement this feature until a future version of Windows.) Another feature is that FAT 32 keeps a copy of critical drive structures in the boot record now. Unlike FAT 16, there aren't any single point-of-failure errors that can kill your hard drive.

Warning: If you choose to use FAT 32 on your machine, it's an all-or-nothing decision for the drive you use it on. FAT 32 is incompatible with FAT 16. This means that any old disk utilities (including disk compression) have to go out the door—you can't use them on a FAT 32 drive. In addition, you must consider some of the problems of using FAT 32. For instance, you can't create a dual-boot system, since neither Windows NT nor OS/2 knows anything about FAT 32.

OSR2 also ships with four FAT 32-specific utility programs: FDisk, Format, ScanDisk, and Defrag. All four of these utilities can be used in either real (MS-DOS) or protected (from within Windows) modes. Other than these four utilities, you'll probably start using FAT 32 without any other utility support. In fact, this is one of the sources of concern for people using FAT 32. Even though the Microsoft utilities are adequate, they aren't the tools of choice for many people. It won't be long, though, until most other utility vendors will support FAT 32.

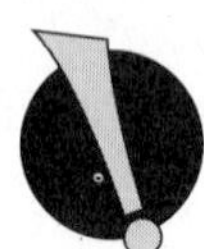

Any software that writes directly to the disk is suspect when it comes to using FAT 32. Most of us know not to use disk utilities that would allow you to edit the disk directly, but this problem could also affect other kinds of utility programs. For example, many utility programs check the format of your drive before they'll do anything to it, just to make sure that you don't lose data. One user of a FAT 32 drive reported that the CD-ROM writing software wouldn't work with FAT 32 installed. That's because the CD-ROM writing software checked the drive configuration before doing anything—even on the drives that it wasn't writing to. FAT 32 confused the utility program. The user finally ended up reinstalling Windows 95 without FAT 32 support, just to get the CD-ROM drive writing software to work.

Despite the growing pains that some people will experience when using the FAT 32 support provided by OSR2, there are some other file-system-related benefits to look at. We talked about one of them already—CDI support. Another benefit is a little difficult to see at first, but I think you'll find it very helpful along the way. Figure 9.5 shows what I'm talking about. This is the Drive Properties dialog box that you open by right-clicking the drive and selecting Properties from the context menu. Notice that instead of simply telling you that the drive is local or remote, Windows 95 now tells you what file system it's using, in the Type field. In this case, I'm showing several kinds of drives so you can see what they look like. Notice that the NetWare drive in this example says that it's actually a Network Connection (OS/2) HPFS drive. That's because of the way you need to enable long filename support when using NetWare—you actually load the OS/2 name space module instead of something Windows 95-specific. A Network Connection NTFS drive and a Network Connection FAT 16-(shown simply as FAT) formatted drive is also shown with the local disk FAT 32 drive.

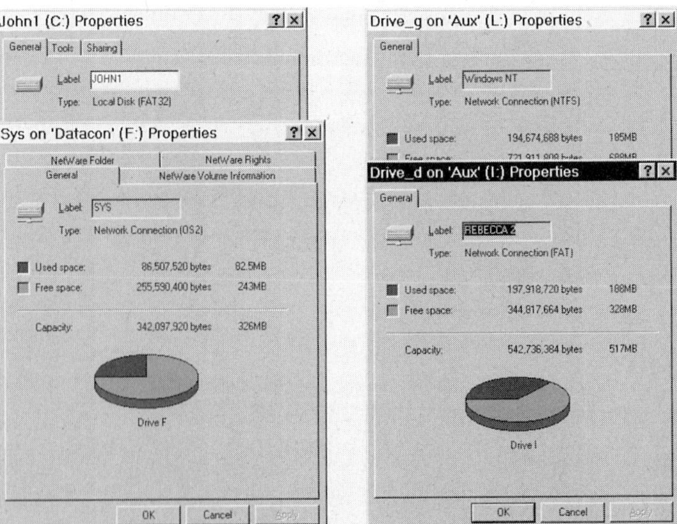

Figure 9.5.
OSR2 provides one nice new feature—the ability to determine what kind of drive you're using without checking drivers.

Note: A lot of applications won't report the correct size of your drive if it's 2GB or over. The reason is pretty simple: Microsoft artificially limited drive size reported by the `GetDiskFreeSpace()` function to 2GB for compatibility reasons. If a programmer wants to find out the true size of large drives, the `GetDiskFreeSpace()` function must be used. Because this function was only recently made available, it's very likely that install programs and the like won't use it for a while. When in doubt, always check the space remaining on your drive by using Explorer.

Warning: There are some additional considerations you need to make before switching to FAT 32. The big one is that you can't easily move from FAT 16 to FAT 32 (or back). If you choose to install FAT 32, the only way to eliminate it is to partition and format your drive from scratch. It also means that you must reinstall all of your software from scratch. Obviously, we aren't talking about a small undertaking, if you find that installing FAT 32 was a mistake for you.

Another consideration is that some of the disk-enhancing utilities you've used in the past won't work. We've already talked about utilities that you might use to repair a failure, but this class of utility performs another function. For example, Microsoft's DriveSpace 3 won't work with FAT 32. You must make a decision up front about the value of using disk compression on your machine. It could be that FAT 32 will provide everything you need without using disk compression, but you'd better be certain before making the change.

Fortunately, one of the considerations you won't have to take into account is old software. You can still boot a FAT 32 machine into MS-DOS mode and use it to play games. However, you absolutely can't use a boot disk formatted using previous versions of DOS or Windows 95. You must format any boot disks with FAT 32 to access a FAT 32 drive on your machine. (There isn't any actual difference in the formatting process; you just have to format the disk on a machine running FAT 32.)

So how do you create a FAT 32 drive? Even though the OEM who puts your machine together will probably do all the work for you, it's a good idea to know how to create the drive yourself. The first thing you need is a disk drive 512MB or larger, because it doesn't pay to use FAT 32 below that level. The new FDisk utility does all the work. When you enter **`FDISK`**, you'll see a dialog box similar to the one shown in Figure 9.6. All you need to do is answer Y when asked whether you want to enable FAT 32 (large disk) support. The partition you create if you answer Y will be marked as FAT 32. You won't actually see any difference until after you format the drive. Only then will FDisk show that the drive is formatted for FAT 32. Of course, you can also check the drive's format by using the Properties dialog box, as shown in Figure 9.5. Remember that FAT 32 is an all-or-nothing proposition. You won't be able to create a FAT 16 primary DOS partition and then use FAT 32 on an extended partition.

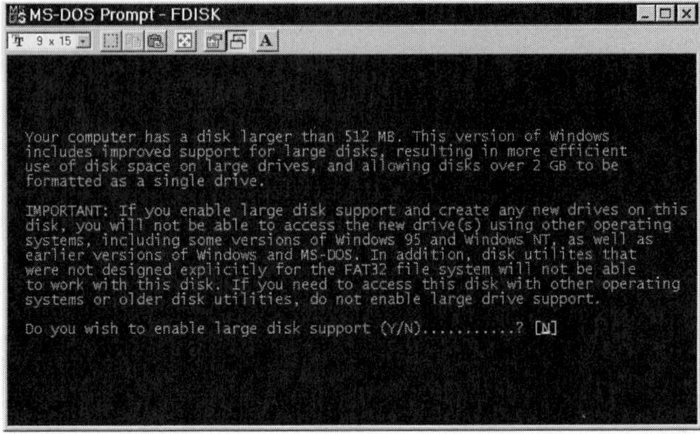

Figure 9.6.
Creating a FAT 32 partition is easy; just answer Y when asked if you want to enable FAT 32 support.

Using .LNK Files

Pointers is a term familiar to programmers when used as a computer term, or familiar to everyone when talking about a directional finder. Think about .LNK files in Windows 95 as a pointer to something. They enable you to create an image of any Windows 95 object somewhere else. In most cases, the object is a file or folder.

So what good are .LNK files? Say that you're a manager and you need to combine a bunch of files for a group that will eventually put a project together. A graphics illustrator has been creating drawings for the last few weeks. A second group has worked up all the figures and statistics with Lotus 1-2-3. Still another group has worked on some text and charts to go with the other elements of the project. You're ready to gather everything together for a full-fledged presentation.

You could copy all the files to one directory and print them. After a lot of redlining during your meeting, each group could go back and make the required changes. What a time-consuming way to spend your week! This is actually the way a lot of companies work right now, but I can't think of anything more inefficient.

Of course, some groups have become more modern. They place all these files in a directory on the network so the group can work on them without making redlines. This is a bit better, but it's still not optimal, because you have two copies of the files lying around. This allows too many chances to make a mistake. What happens if Mary finds another change later? Does she try to find the correct file and make the change (or worse still, try to find the correct person to make the change for her)? Using double files is okay, but it's still not the right way to go.

Windows 95 offers a new alternative. The manager can now make up a project folder containing links (or pointers) to all the project files. The folder is easy to distribute to everyone who is working on the project, even if they aren't in the same building. The links (.LNK files) make it easy for the person using the folder to access a single copy of the real file. No duplicates are needed. There's no chance for mislaid files, everyone can work on all the files as needed, and no one but the manager needs to know the physical location of the files. This is what a .LNK file can do for you. (The only downside of using .LNK files, and therefore a common data file, is that your application must be set up for file sharing.)

Of course, using .LNK files can help a single user manage his or her work just as easily. In fact, we'll look at some of these methods in the "Working with Desktop Objects" section of Chapter 10. I have found that I can manage all my work as projects and not really worry about applications or the actual location of the data anymore. Let's take a look at some of the details of .LNK files—a small idea with big implications.

Your Start Menu folder contains a ton of .LNK files. If you think that any of your applications actually appear in the Start menu, you're wrong. Only the pointers to those files appear there. If you erase a Start menu entry, you erase only a .LNK file, not the application itself.

Right-click the Start menu icon on the Taskbar and select the Explore option. What you should see now is a dual-pane Explorer view of your Start menu entries. You can easily recognize the .LNK files because they look like shortcuts (the icons with the arrow in the lower-left corner). Right-click any of the .LNK files and you'll see a display similar to the one in Figure 9.7. (I chose the Microsoft Exchange .LNK file, but any choice is acceptable for this discussion.)

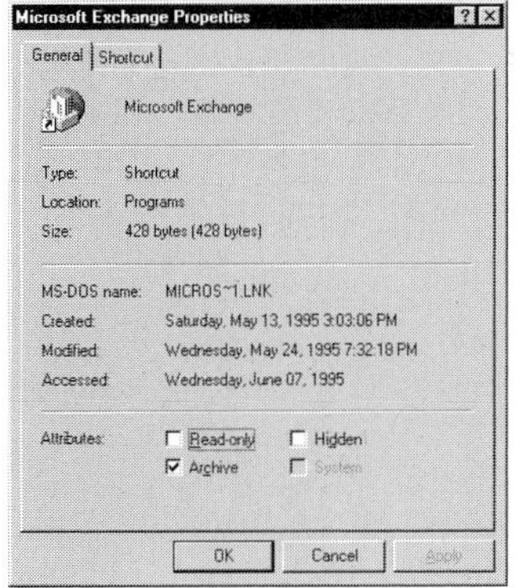

Figure 9.7.
A .LNK file's Properties dialog box provides a General page similar to that provided by other file types.

As with the General page of any file Properties dialog box, you can set the file attributes: Hidden, Archive, and Read-Only. This page also tells you the short and long filename and other statistics, such as when someone last modified the file. This is all interesting information, but you'll probably bypass this page in most cases to get to the Shortcut page. Figure 9.8 shows what this page looks like.

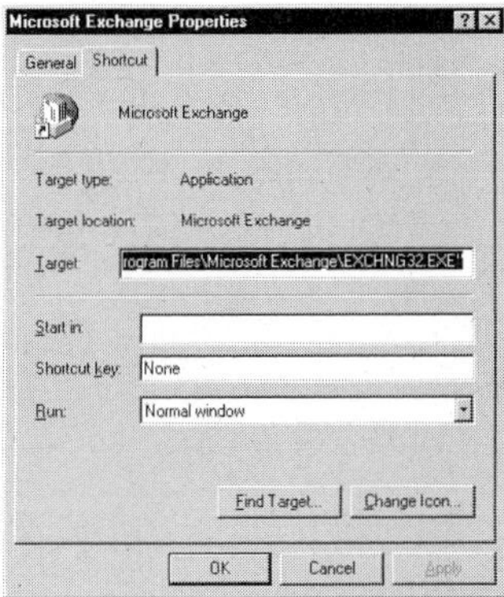

Figure 9.8.
The Shortcut page contains all the .LNK file setup information.

The four major fields on this page are listed in the following bullets, along with the function of each entry. The two you'll use most often are the Target and Run fields. I personally never use the Start In field, but you're likely to need it in some places.

- **Target:** This is the name of the program you want to run. Notice that this dialog box doesn't provide any way to change the settings for that file. You must change the original file instead of the link. This makes sense when you think about it, because each file could have multiple links pointing to it.
- **Start In:** Windows 95 always assumes that everything the file will need appears in its target directory. This is probably true for data files. However, you might find that some applications need to use a different "working directory" than the one they start in. The term *working directory* should be familiar if you've moved from Windows 3.x. It's the directory that Windows tells the application to look in for data files, and it's the same field you used in a .PIF file to control where a program started. This field does the same thing for Windows 95.
- **Shortcut Key:** I cover this topic in Chapter 3. It enables you to assign a shortcut key combination to this particular .LNK file. Using a shortcut key can dramatically speed access to your favorite applications or data files. We'll see some other methods of speeding access to your data in the "Customizing Your Desktop" section of Chapter 10.
- **Run:** Windows provides three run modes for applications. You can run them in a window, minimized, or maximized. I find that the default setting of the window mode works for most of my applications. (In most cases, this is a normal window.) I start data files maximized for certain jobs. This is especially true of my word processing files, because I like to see a full screen of them. How you set this field is determined solely by the way you work.

That's all there is to .LNK files. Chapter 5 gives you some usage tips for .LNK (or shortcut) files. You'll want to read about the various methods you can use to create shortcuts to your data files and applications. We'll revisit this topic from a desktop point of view in the "Working with Desktop Objects" section of Chapter 10. The desktop is where you can really benefit from using these productivity enhancers.

VxDs and DLLs

Modular programming is the way to go these days. Programmers will tell you that modular programming is easier to maintain and understand. Those are perfectly good reasons, but they don't really tell you much as a user. The user's view of modular programming is this: It takes a lot of code to tell your machine how to get anything done when using a GUI, such as Windows 95. More code always translates into more memory. If you replicated the common code that Windows needs for tasks, such as displaying a dialog box for every application you ran, the memory shortage you would experience would dwarf the current problems.

Windows 3.x started the .DLL (dynamic link library) and VxD (virtual anything device) craze for a good reason. Creating a Windows program is a complex undertaking, and programmers needed tools to finish the job quickly. A modular approach also ensures that things such as dialog boxes look the same, no matter which application you use. However, the important reason for our current discussion is memory. People were already starting to complain about the huge memory footprint of Windows. Even when applications could share some code or data, it still took a lot of memory to get anything done. A GUI will always require more memory than a character-based operating system. If Microsoft had taken a DOS view of programming when designing Windows, we would all be using OS/2 today.

A program calls a .DLL or VxD to perform specific tasks. Essentially, both files contain executable code—similar to a mini-application. When Windows sees the request, it loads the program (.DLL or VxD) into memory. Of course, this sounds similar to what DOS does with external files called overlays. In theory, .DLLs and VxDs do act somewhat as overlays from a code use point of view, but that's where the similarities end.

Like overlays, both file types contain entry points. Unlike overlays, any number of applications can simultaneously access the program file and use whatever parts are needed. For example, you might have noticed that the File | Open command in most applications produces the same dialog box. That dialog box is actually part of the COMMDLG.DLL file located in your SYSTEM directory. An application makes a call to the COMMDLG.DLL to display a File Open dialog box. Windows loads the .DLL, looks for a specific function number, and then lets the .DLL do its work.

Let's take a look at that file. Open Explorer and then the Windows SYSTEM folder. Right-click the COMMDLG.DLL file to display the context menu and select Quick View. Page down until you see the Exported Functions entry. It should look similar to the one in Figure 9.9.

If you look at this table, you'll notice two columns. I won't take the programmer's view of this information (that could fill a book of its own), but we can take a quick look at it. The first column tells you the function number. The second column (the one that we're interested in) tells you the function name. Notice the kinds of things that a programmer can do with the COMMDLG.DLL. Especially important are function `1`, which allows you to open a file; function `2`, which enables you to save a file; and function `20`, which displays the Print dialog box.

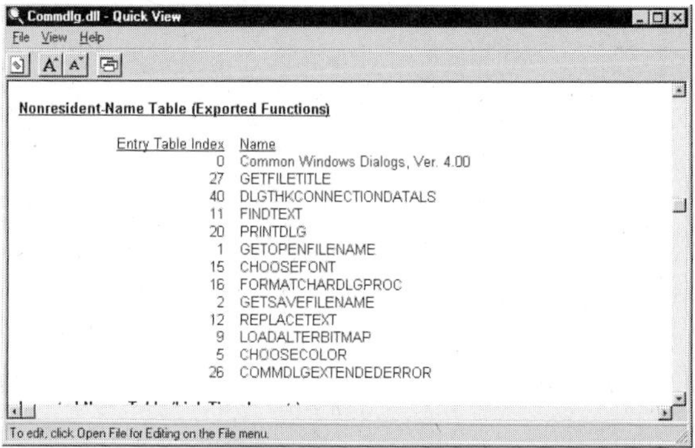

Figure 9.9.
The Quick View display of COMMDLG.DLL can tell you a lot about the way Windows works.

You can check out some of the other .DLLs in the SYSTEM directory by using this same method. Learning what the .DLLs do for you can help when something doesn't work the way it should. For example, what would you do if the File Open dialog box suddenly stopped working? It might seem to be a very unlikely prospect, but data corruption can affect any file on your system. (If you were a Windows 3.x user, you may have found out about your system files the hard way when your system stopped working unexpectedly. .DLL and other system file corruption was a fairly common problem for some people.) Knowing that the File Open dialog box appears in the COMMDLG.DLL file could help you fix the system with just a few minutes of work. All you would need to do is restore a good copy of this file from your backup. (We'll cover backups later in this chapter.)

What .DLLs do for software, VxDs do for hardware. When part of your system needs to access a piece of hardware, it normally calls a VxD. Of course, drivers can also work with software components, but from a different perspective than .DLLs. Drivers always provide some type of interface to a system component. For example, some types of memory allocation are performed with a VxD. This isn't a function most users would worry about, but one that's very important to the proper functioning of your system. One of the most-used VxDs on your drive is the VMM32.VXD. It combines the functionality of many older files you found under Windows 3.x into one file. (Most of these entries appeared in the 386ENH section of SYSTEM.INI.)

Tip: If you right-click a VxD file, you'll notice that it offers no quick view option. To view the file, make a copy and give it a .DLL extension. You can now use Quick View to see the header of this file. This same technique also works with other executable file types. Unfortunately, about the only things the file header tells you are the amount of memory that the VxD requires to load, and some programmer-specific information such as the size of the stack that the VxD creates. In most cases, it isn't worth your while to look at the file heading unless you're low on memory and are looking for a peripheral to unload from your system. Unloading a peripheral device can free memory that you can use for applications. (Be sure to make a backup of any drivers that you unload, using the procedures near the end of this chapter.)

Viewing File Contents

We've already taken a long look at the process of viewing files in quite a few of the chapters in this book, so I won't bore you with a lot of details here. It's important to realize that Windows 95 does come with some file viewing support built in. Most of the major applications you'll use are already entered in the Registry. Other levels of file support come from Registry entries made by your applications during installation. Even if your applications aren't successful during installation, you can always import the .REG files they create to add support to Windows 95. We talk about all of these types of file viewing supports in Chapter 6.

You can also add support to the Registry for your own file extensions. We look at one way to add it for existing files in Chapter 6. Chapter 10 will show you still other ways to add support for viewing files. The method you use to add file support isn't important. The important thing to consider here is how efficient the new support makes you. Customizing Windows 95 to the way you work is the best way to use all the added speed that this product can provide. Using your old work methods means that you'll actually ignore those new features—a major problem with some people who have tried Windows 95 and have been disappointed in its performance.

Tip: OLE is a real memory hog when it comes to moving data from one major application to another. You can usually accomplish the same thing by using a small application such as Notepad, WordPad, or Microsoft Paint as the server, in place of the major application you normally use. Adding multiple-application support could make OLE practical on machines that normally don't have enough memory to support it. (DDE and OLE are covered in detail in Chapter 12.)

Here's a practical example of another type of file support you can add to Windows 95. I found that the level of Explorer support for .DOC files didn't meet my needs, so I changed it. That's one of the first rules you'll need to learn about Windows 95. Nothing is cast in concrete as long as you have some idea of what to look for in Explorer or the Registry. In this case, I simply modified an Explorer entry to suit my needs.

Figure 9.10 shows the context menu I designed for .DOC files. Of course, you could just as easily do the same thing for .PCX, or any other file extension, for that matter. Windows 95 doesn't care how you customize your system—all it cares about is interacting with you and your applications after you're done.

Notice that I can open .DOC files with Word for Windows or WordPad. I can also use the quick viewer to display the files when necessary. Another entry allows me to use Word for Windows to print the file without opening it first.

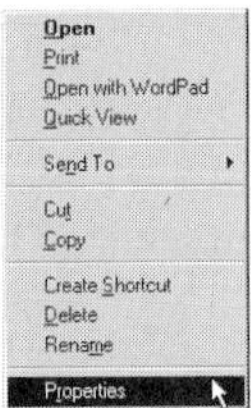

Figure 9.10.
There's no specific way to view data in Windows 95. Everything is configurable if you know how to use the Registry, and are creative.

Now that you've seen the results, let's look at the implementation. Figure 9.10 shows the Explorer entries I made to create this context menu. You can use it as a basis for making your own changes. All I did was open the Options dialog box using the View | Options command in Explorer and select the File Types page and Microsoft Word 6.0 Document. Clicking Edit displays the dialog box shown in Figure 9.11.

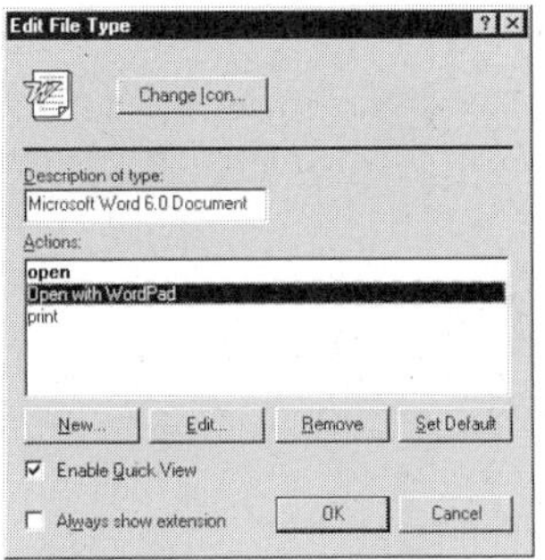

Figure 9.11.
Creating your own context menus for viewing files under Windows 95 is as simple as a few Registry entries.

Tip: It usually pays to associate more than one application with the files you use most often, because memory limitations will sometimes prevent you from opening the full-fledged application you normally use to view or print the file. Adding a second application with a smaller footprint ensures that you'll always have access to your data files.

Adding the Quick View option is simple. Mark the Enable Quick View check box. Windows will allow you to mark this check box even if Quick View doesn't support your application. You'll need to check the Windows 95 documentation and any Windows 95 application documentation for application support before you check this box.

The WordPad entry is almost as simple to make. Click New to add a new entry to the list of actions. Type the information shown in Figure 9.12. That's all there is to it. Click OK three times to save your new entries, and you'll have a custom context menu for .DOC files.

Viewing files under Windows 95 doesn't have to be the painful experience it was under Windows 3.x. I won't say that customizing your system is easy; it certainly isn't as easy as it could be. However, at least Windows 95 provides the means to do it. Maybe the next release of Windows will allow you to perform these tricks without resorting to using RegEdit.

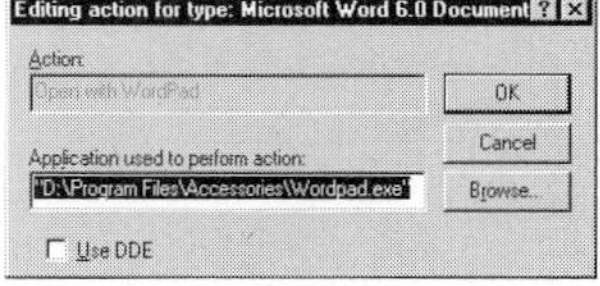

Figure 9.12.
Adding new options to the context menu for a file extension is as simple as adding a new option to this dialog box.

Formatting Disks

Formatting floppy disks is one of those tasks that everyone must perform from time to time, such as taking out the garbage or doing the laundry—something you'd rather not do but end up doing anyway. I found the old File Manager interface under Windows 3.x to be difficult to use for any length of time, because the interface just wasn't all that usable, formatting floppies in Windows 3.x was slow, and I could never get it to work right in the background. It was just faster and easier from the DOS prompt.

I took another look at formatting floppies when I got Windows 95 installed. Windows 95 does improve on the interface problem. All you need to do is right-click the drive you want to format from within Explorer, as shown in Figure 9.13.

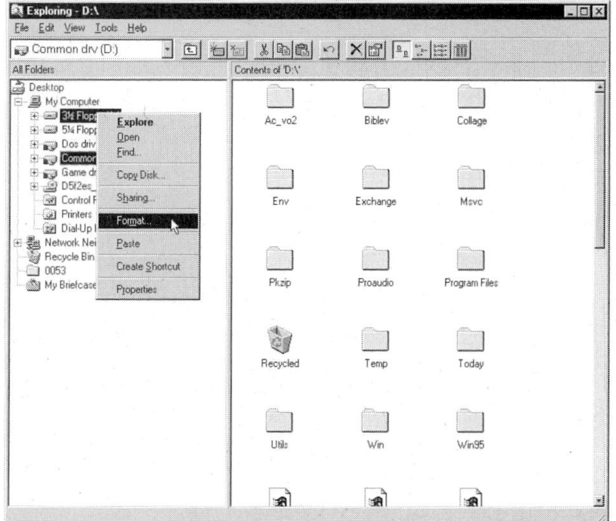

Figure 9.13.
Windows 95 always displays a Format option for any drive that supports formatting.

Select the Format option and you'll see the dialog box shown in Figure 9.14. This dialog box should look somewhat familiar, because it's actually an improved version of the same dialog box that you used under Windows 3.x. I say "improved" because every field is self-explanatory now, so there's no guessing about what this check box or that list box might do.

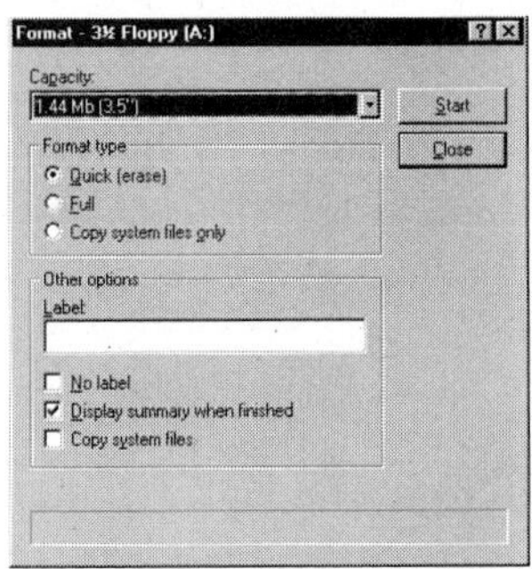

Figure 9.14.
The Windows 95 Format dialog box is an enhanced version of the File Manager dialog box used with Windows 3.x.

Tip: Always use the Quick Erase option to format floppies that you know are good. This option will format the floppy in a little over a tenth of the time that a full format takes.

Now you need to select the options you want and click OK. Windows 95 did offer a few nice surprises. For one thing, it works very well in the background. I didn't experience a single problem with working on something else while the floppy took its time formatting. Of course, Microsoft didn't fix everything—formatting under Windows 95 is just as slow as it was under 3.x.

Tip: You can double or even triple your formatting capacity by selecting network floppies to format under Windows 95. A peer-to-peer connection enables you to use the floppy on another machine if you have access. Two machines in close proximity in one office doubles the number of disks that you can format at once.

Backup

Backing up your data is an exercise everyone hates to do. It always seems to take a long time and wastes perfectly good man-hours you could use for some other purpose. Of course, the day will come when your system will take a nose-dive (usually after you've decided that backing up takes too much time), and you really will need that backup. Making a backup of your system is like buying insurance: No one ever sees a good reason to do it until disaster strikes, and then it's too late to do anything if you didn't prepare in advance.

Some people will try to make a backup of their system by using floppy disks. That worked in the days of 33MB hard drives, but with today's 300MB to 1GB systems it just won't work. If you're going to back up your system, you need to invest in a tape drive of some type.

Now, here's where someone at Microsoft really wasn't thinking. Backup supports only one tape drive format—QIC. Of course, you have a nifty new DAT drive, so it won't work with the Microsoft product. Hopefully the next version of Windows 95 will include a decent level of support. Until that happens, though, you'd better go out and purchase a third-party product if your drive isn't of the Colorado Jumbo variety. If you do have one of those SCSI or IDE drives, read the sections on maintaining your drive and rotating tapes.

Note: I won't cover the process of performing a floppy backup in this chapter, for two reasons. First, a floppy backup really isn't all that practical except for the smallest backup sessions. Second, the procedure for a floppy backup is so similar to the tape backup that you won't experience any problems going from one to the other.

Now, if you really can use Microsoft Backup, let's take a quick tour of the product. The first time you start Backup, it creates a default backup set for you that includes all the files on your drive. In most cases, you can use this backup set as a starting point to create your own custom setups. Go ahead and start Backup if it's installed, so you can take a look at this utility with me.

Once you're past the initial screen, it might take Backup a few seconds to complete the hardware detection process. Backup automatically detects your tape drive in most cases. You can always tell whether the detection was successful by the status of the Tools menu. If you see that all the tools are available, Backup successfully detected your drive. Be sure to perform the detection with a tape installed. Backup can't detect some tapes correctly if the tape isn't in place. Now you're ready to perform any of the three actions outlined in the following sections: back up, restore, or compare.

Creating a Backup

The first activity you'll perform with Backup is creating your first backup tape. Figure 9.15 shows the initial Backup window. As you can see, there are boxes next to each drive and folder on the left side of the display, and next to each folder and file on the right side of the page. (The interface works much like Explorer, in which the right pane shows a detailed view of whatever you select in the left pane.) You select the items you want to back up by clicking the boxes. An empty box means that Backup won't send that item to tape. A gray box with a check mark appears next to a folder or drive that you intend to partially back up. A check mark appears next to a file, folder, or drive that you intend to completely back up.

You'll probably see a dialog box during the file selection process. Windows 95 continues to peel blank pages from a stack and add a check mark to them as long as it's selecting files. (The machine froze on me several times during the selection process.) You can usually detect a problem if the pages continue to peel after the disk activity stops. Make sure that you check the client machines as well as the local machine when backing up more than one machine on a peer-to-peer network.

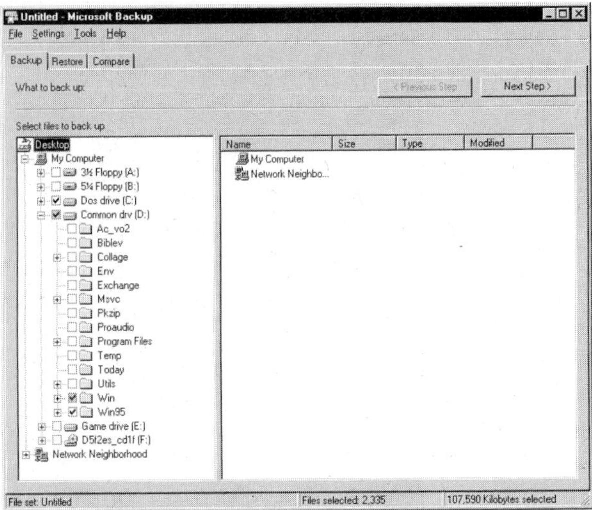

Figure 9.15.
The initial Backup dialog box enables you to select the files you want to store on tape.

Tip: The first time you back up your system, Backup might find some files that it can't verify. Always check the ERROR.LOG file in the folder \PROGRAM FILES \ACCESSORIES\LOG. This file tells you which files Backup couldn't verify. In most cases, you'll want to exclude these files unless you have a good reason to keep them in the backup set. I've found that most of these files end up being system-specific—files I would normally need to install manually before a restore.

Once you complete the selection process, it's time to select a target for the backup. Figure 9.16 shows a typical selection window. As you can see, Backup allows you to select any drive or the tape as a storage location.

Now is the time to save your backup set. If you try to save it before this point in the process, Backup displays an error message. Notice that a target is part of the file set information. You need this information to conduct automatic backups by double-clicking a file set icon in Explorer.

After you save the file set, click Start Backup to begin the actual backup process. Backup will ask you to provide a set label for this particular session. A tape can contain more than one session—I usually store an entire week's worth of backups on one tape. The amount that you can store depends largely on how much storage space the tape contains and how much you need. This dialog box also enables you to password-protect the backup. Adding a password isn't required for on-site storage. However, if you plan to use off-site storage, a password will protect your valuable data.

Click OK in the Backup Set Label dialog box and you'll see Backup start storing the data on your machine to tape. Using this application is fairly simple—even more so once the backup sets that you want to perform are configured and stored on disk. All you need to do then is double-click the set you want to use for that particular session.

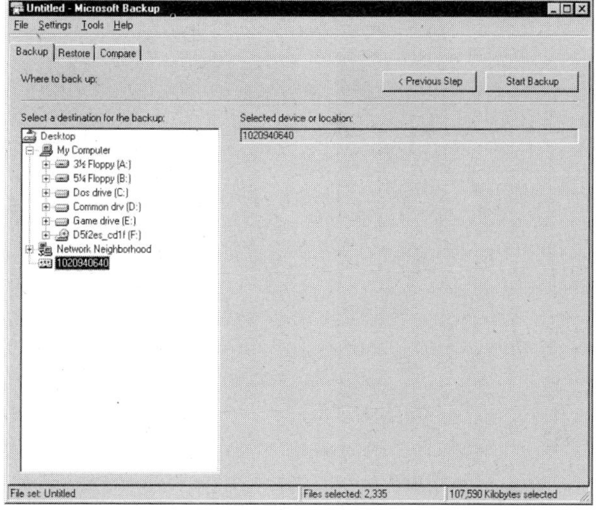

Figure 9.16.
This is the window where you select the backup target. You also use it to save the backup set.

I did skip past a few of Microsoft Backup's features during this quick look. Let's take a look at some of them now. All the feature dialog boxes appear under the Settings menu. They include File Filtering, Drag and Drop, and Options.

The File Filtering dialog box appears in Figure 9.17. This dialog box looks complicated but contains only two settings. The first enables you to exclude files by date range. Suppose that you want to back up only files from this week. Using this entry allows you to do that. The second enables you to select files by type. Here's another quirk of Microsoft Backup: You can exclude only registered file types. Most people don't register the file types they don't plan to use. For example, the .BAK extension rarely appears in the Registry naturally. Yet, if you want to exclude that file type from your backups, you'll need to register it. Hopefully, Microsoft will fix this shortcoming. All the file types you can select for exclusion appear in the upper list box. The file types that will be excluded from this backup appear in the lower list box.

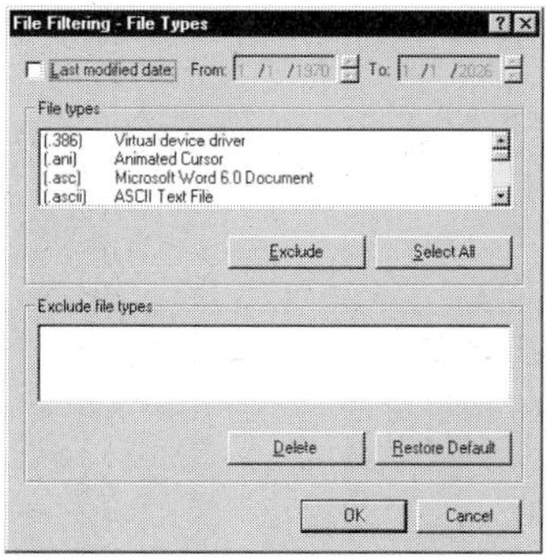

Figure 9.17.
The File Filtering dialog box enables you to select which files appear in the backup set.

You control the exclusion and inclusion of file types by using four buttons. Select All highlights all the files in the File Types list box. Exclude places any highlighted file types in the Exclude File Types list box. You can remove a file type from the Exclude File Types list box by using Delete. Finally, the Restore Default button removes all the file types from the Exclude File Types list box.

The Drag and Drop dialog box appears in Figure 9.18. Notice that this dialog box contains only three entries. The first automatically keeps Microsoft Backup minimized when it starts. The second forces it to display a dialog box asking your permission to start the backup. The third automatically ends the application once it completes the backup. Microsoft Backup defaults to checking all three entries. It's a good idea to leave them this way unless you have a reason for changing one or more of them. (I usually uncheck the second check box—Confirm Operation Before Beginning—if I plan to be away from my desk when the backup starts.)

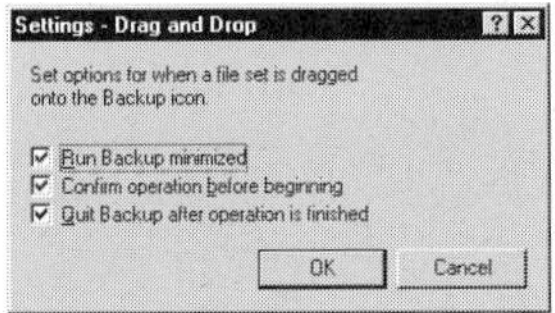

Figure 9.18.
The Drag and Drop dialog box enables you to set the automatic settings for Microsoft Backup.

We'll look at two pages of the Options dialog box in this section. The first page, General, contains two check boxes, as shown in Figure 9.19. The first check box tells Backup to prompt you with a beep at the end of an operation. For example, if it completely fills one tape, Backup beeps and asks you to supply another. The Overwrite Old Status Log Files option, the second check box, prevents Backup from saving old information. This keeps your drive relatively free from extra clutter and still allows you to retain the status of the previous backup.

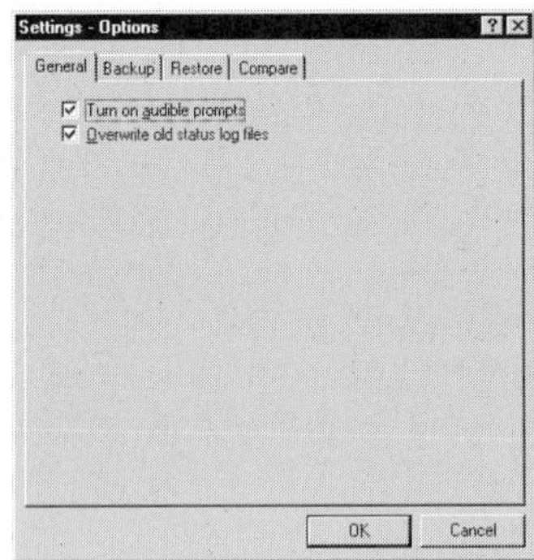

Figure 9.19.
The General page of the Options dialog box enables you to select the notification and log settings.

The second page we'll look at is the Backup page, shown in Figure 9.20, which has three main sections. The first entry, a check box, tells Backup to exit as soon as the backup is completed.

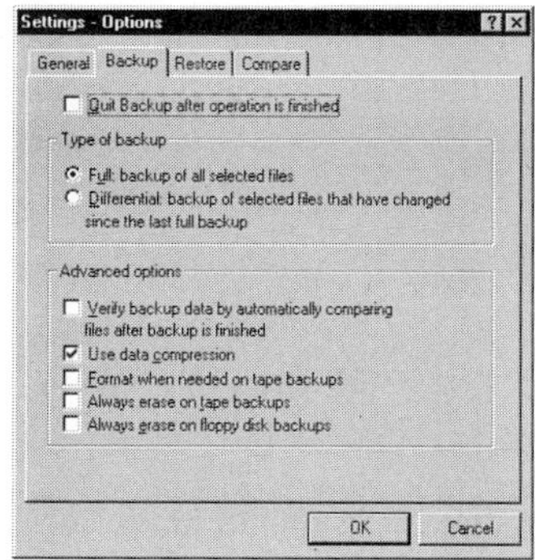

Figure 9.20.
The Backup Page of the Options dialog box contains all the parameters that affect how Microsoft performs the backup.

The second section of the Backup page contains two radio buttons. Select the first radio button if you want Backup to perform a full backup of the selected files on the drive. The second option enables you to perform a differential backup. The only files that Backup selects from the backup set are those with the archive bit set. Backup resets this bit each time it backs up your files. Whenever you change the file, Windows sets the archive bit. The status of this bit tells Backup whether you changed the file since the last time you archived it to disk. (You can see whether the archive attribute of a file is set by right-clicking it in Explorer and selecting the Properties option. The file attributes appear on the General page of the file Properties dialog box. A check in the Archive checkbox tells you that the file will be backed up.)

The third section of this dialog box contains some special settings. I always check the first check box. Making a backup without performing a compare afterward is one sure way to end up with something unusable. I've run into several situations where the network administrator thought he had a perfect backup, only to find out that the tape wasn't any good. If you don't perform a compare, you won't know whether the backup is any good. The other options in this group are fairly self-explanatory. You can usually count on a 2:1 ratio for a normal backup if you turn on data compression. I've gotten as high as 15:1 for graphic and sound file backups. An all-data backup usually nets a 4:1 ratio with compression turned on. You'll probably want to use the 2:1 figure for your first few backups. Once you figure out the compression ratio, use it to determine how many tapes you'll need to complete a backup.

Restoring a Backup

Restoring a backup follows a process that reverses the one you used for creating the backup in the first place. You start by specifying the original target device and the backup set that you want to use. In most cases, this will be a hard drive or a tape drive. Then select the files from that backup set that you want to restore. Finally, you start the restore process.

Just as with the backup process, you can also access settings for the restore process by using the Settings | Options command. Figure 9.21 shows a sample of this dialog box. As you can see, it has three groups of controls, similar to the Backup dialog box. The first control tells Backup to automatically exit when it completes the restore, if checked.

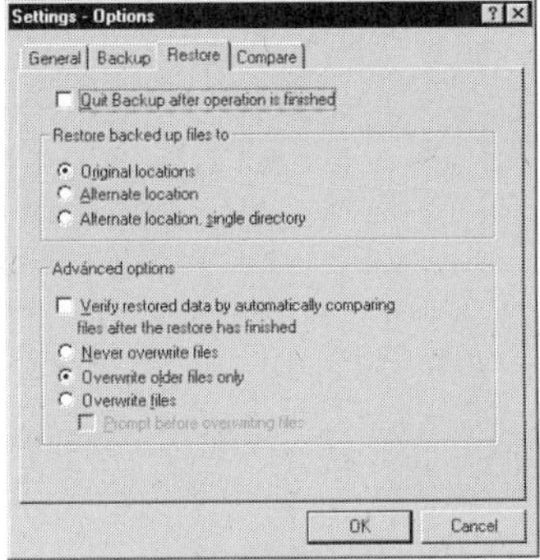

Figure 9.21.
The Restore page of the Options dialog box enables you to set all the restore options.

The second group of controls is fairly straightforward. These options enable you to select a restore location. Normally, you would choose the same directory from which Backup originally copied the files. However, you can choose the second option to restore the file to an alternate location. This particular option retains any directory structure. If you want to place all the files in a single directory, no matter where they originally appeared in the directory tree, select the third option.

The final group of controls enables you to change the way that Backup restores the files. As with the Backup page, I always select the compare option. If you don't compare the restored file with what appears on tape, you can't be sure that you got a good restore. A momentary system glitch has corrupted more than a few files as they were restored to the hard drive from tape, even though the file was actually good. I also use an overwrite option so I can replace corrupted files with good ones. Checking the Prompt Before Overwriting Files option gives you the option to keep the original file. Of course, using these two options together means that you'll have to sit in front of the machine during the restore to answer any questions it might have about overwriting files. Select one of the other two overwrite options if you want to perform an automatic restore.

Performing a Compare

The Compare feature of Backup works much like Restore. You begin by selecting the backup device. In most cases, this will be the tape drive. As usual, you select the files, folders, and directories you want to compare. Once you make your selections, Backup compares the contents of the selected files with the files that exist on the hard drive in the same location. I find that a compare is useful when I want to check the status of a master backup. It lets me know how out-of-date the material really is.

Figure 9.22 shows the Compare page of the Options dialog box. Notice that it contains the same first and second group of controls as Restore. I won't go through them again here.

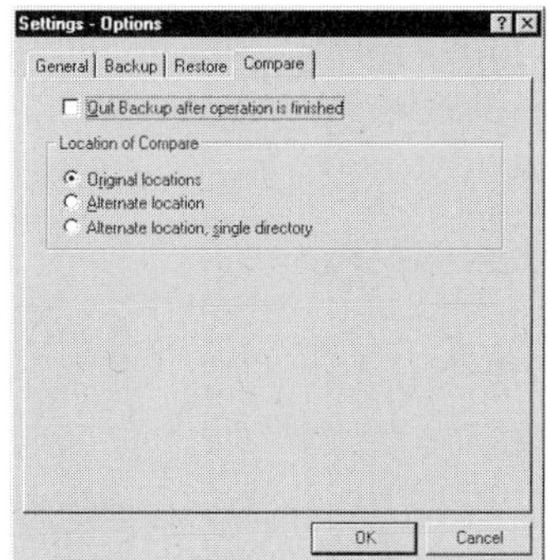

Figure 9.22.
The Compare page of the Options dialog box looks very similar to the Restore page. The options let you compare the contents of the original file to your backup.

Testing and Maintaining the Backup System

I'm almost never satisfied with the thin brochures that tape vendors call manuals. A quick look inside usually provides one or perhaps two pages of installation instructions. If you're lucky, you'll also have a page or two of troubleshooting instructions. Because these rather short instructions leave too much to the imagination, I came up with a few time-tested techniques for getting the most out of your backup system.

The first step is to select some hardware and software. I go by three simple rules:

- To compute the minimum tape size you need, multiply your hard drive size (including any client machines that you plan to back up) by 1.5 for weekly backups or 3 for daily backups using the differential method I describe later in this chapter.
- Determine the cost of the fastest tape backup system you can afford to buy. A slow backup system makes it more difficult for you to perform the required level of maintenance. After all, who wants to hang around waiting for the tape backup to finish right before the weekend starts?
- Add the cost of at least three backup tapes to the purchase price of your tape drive to determine the final cost. What good is a tape drive without tapes? Make sure that you have enough tapes. I outline several backup scheduling methods near the end of this chapter. You may want to look through them before deciding how many tapes to buy.

I always shop around for my tape drives, because the prices tend to vary for common items such as memory. You never know—you may get the deal of a lifetime from one of the stores that you frequent less often. Once you select the hardware and software that you intend to use to back up your system, it's important to test and maintain it. I find it hard to believe that some people just throw the tape drive into their system and expect it to work. Testing ensures that the data you back up today will actually work when an emergency arises. Maintenance increases the longevity of the equipment you use.

It's important to take a two-phase approach to testing your new backup system—a full test today and a maintenance test tomorrow. After the initial equipment installation, you should completely test your system to make certain that it works. You need to test the hardware, software, automated procedures, macros, and anything else that might stop you from getting a good backup. Test your system in stages, using the procedures contained in the following section, and be sure to use techniques that fully test the hardware and software combination as well as the individual components.

Once things are up and running, you need to continue testing your system from time to time to confirm that the software and hardware are still working. Remember, this is your life's work in data we're talking about, so even a little failure is of concern to you. Some breakdowns aren't as obvious as smoking tapes or tape drives and remain undetected by the backup software.

I still remember one shop that called me in as a consultant to solve a mystery. Someone at the shop installed a tape backup system and checked to make sure that it worked. After that, they performed a backup of their system every day. The backup software always told them that they received a good backup and they had no reason not to believe it. Eventually, they needed to use the backup they made to restore some data. To their horror, the previous day's tape contained absolutely nothing. One by one they checked every other tape they had made; the network administrator discovered that these were also blank. The culprit of this gruesome scene? The write head had fallen off inside the tape drive with the wires still connected. As a result, the tape drive never sensed that the head was dysfunctional. In fact, the tape head worked just fine. The data it wrote simply didn't get onto the tape. Because the backup software didn't compare the contents of the tape to the contents of the drive after the backup, everything appeared to work fine. The moral of this story? Test your system or you can become a casualty of hardware or software errors. Hardware tests aren't a convenience; they're a necessity for anyone who wants to get the most out of their system.

Let's talk about another issue that most people fail to consider—tape drive maintenance. Many network administrators delay their tape drive maintenance until it's too late. After all, who will ever see the tape drive sitting in his office? It's much better to keep the print server clean, which the boss can see. In the preceding example, the network administrator would have found the fallen write head if he had maintained his tape drive. Every drive on the market requires cleaning and physical head inspection. You can use either a cotton swab and alcohol (much like the maintenance you perform on your tape system at home), or a specially designed tape cartridge to clean the drive. In addition, the vendor manual that comes with your tape drive should include some detailed maintenance procedures. (Most don't include complete instructions, so I've included the set that I use in the following sections.)

Initial Installation

I always perform a visual check of any equipment I buy before I install it. The more pieces I have to install, the closer I look before I begin. You can use the same procedure I do to make sure that you obtain the best installation possible. First, if the vendor supplies a checklist or picture of the equipment, use it to make sure that you have everything. It's not unheard of to have a package that doesn't contain everything you need. Perform the same check for your software. Perform a virus check on any disks, and make sure that you have the right licenses and that the disks aren't corrupted. Check your tape supply to be sure that you have enough on hand to perform a full backup cycle. (I talk about this topic in the next section.) Once you have all the components required to install your tape drive, it's time to do the actual work.

Now that the easy part is out of the way, it's time to start a staged installation/test of your system. This process begins with a test of the base installation and then tests each addition you make to it. As a result, you spend a lot less time troubleshooting installation problems, and you know exactly where weak areas in the system may occur. The following paragraphs provide you with the six easy steps to a great tape drive installation. These are generic instructions, so you'll need to make some modifications of this procedure to reflect your hardware and software setup. Some companies also have a set of policies in place, so be sure to follow any company-specific regulations.

1. Install the hardware using any vendor-supplied instructions. Make sure that you observe the proper static safeguards by grounding yourself before you begin. A standard installation usually includes attaching slides to the drive (if required) and mounting it in the system. Once you complete that step, attach any required cables, including a power cable. Many people skip the extra step of attaching a grounding cable to the drive. Don't do it, because the ground cable can prevent transient signals from trashing your backup.
2. Test your initial hardware installation. This usually involves an initial test of the hardware using vendor-supplied diagnostic software. Some drives, such as the Jumbo series from Colorado, don't provide any diagnostic software, so you can skip this step and move on to step 3. If your hardware fails the diagnostic test, check for interrupt conflicts, jumpers in the wrong place, or other configuration problems. Reread the diagnostic program manual to make sure that you set it up correctly. If you can't correct the problem yourself, call the vendor and tell them about the symptoms you notice. Be sure to provide them with complete information about your machine. This includes the BIOS revision number and vendor, the model and vendor of all your peripheral devices and motherboard, and all the jumper settings for peripheral cards that use them. Also include the diagnostic software version number, a listing of unusual noises or odors, the failure number displayed by the diagnostic program, and any steps you took to correct the problem.
3. Check for hardware and software interaction. Once you have the hardware working, it's time to test the software. I usually begin by performing any software tests that the vendor supplies. For example, most backup software provides a speed test to make sure that your hardware can perform at a given backup speed.
4. Once you complete the vendor-specific check, perform a check of your own. Back up a directory containing nonessential data and then do a compare of the tape's contents to the drive's contents (if your software supports this feature). If possible, restore your data to another directory. Use the DOS `COMPARE` utility (or any other utility that performs a detailed comparison) to compare the files in the original directory to the new directory. If you can't restore to a different directory, try restoring the files to a different drive. You

could also copy your existing data to a temporary directory and restore the old data to the default directory. If either of these steps fails, check the setup of your software to make sure that all the settings are correct for your machine, tape drive controller, hard disk controller, and tape drive. Check your machine's environment to see whether you have enough buffers and files allocated, and check any network driver settings to make sure that you have them set up correctly. If you still can't get a good backup from the software, call the vendor and describe the symptoms. Be sure to tell them that you ran a complete diagnostic on the hardware so they don't try to place the blame on that. Provide the vendor with the version of your software as well as all the hardware specifications.

5. Create any required macros and setup files. Check each of these setups manually to make sure that you set them up correctly. You'll want to verify that the backup software works, by carefully executing the macros using simulated conditions. Resolve any problem areas by reviewing the procedures for setting up the macros and setup files in the vendor-supplied file. Asking a coworker to look at a printout of any handwritten macro procedures might help locate problem areas. Everyone tends to overlook obvious errors after they look at the same piece of code for more than an hour. If the procedures still don't work correctly, call the vendor. Some vendors provide a BBS that you can use to upload your setup files. This might provide faster response times than just a call, because the vendor can test the files you've created, using its software.
6. Perform any required setups for the scheduling software. Be sure to take power failures and other contingencies into account. Check the scheduling software by resetting the backup workstation's system clock and seeing whether the software starts at the proper time, to make sure that it will trigger properly. Double-check the backup by restoring a single directory on the tape to another directory or drive, and then use the DOS `COMPARE` utility to compare the contents of the original directory with the new directory.

This six-step procedure should help you get up and running quickly. The most time-consuming part of the process should be writing and testing the macros required by your backup system. In most cases, you should be able to get a tape drive installed and running in less than a day. It's always a good idea to prepare for the worst, just in case it happens.

Routine Maintenance

Every piece of equipment on the network requires maintenance, and the tape drive is no exception. Maintenance includes both cleaning and physical examination, and could include replacing filters and belts. Your vendor manual should include a set of procedures for maintaining your tape drive. Remarkably, some vendor manuals don't include these vital instructions. Somewhere along the way, a few vendors got the idea that they should sell maintenance instructions as a separate item. You may want to give your vendor a call, just to be sure that they don't fall into this category. If you can't seem to find any vendor instructions, feel free to use the same set I do for generic tape drive maintenance. Make sure that you have a flashlight, cotton swabs (the type used to clean tape drives), methyl or isopropyl alcohol, and any required filters.

1. Carefully open the tape drive door, using a nonconductive material. The plastic screwdrivers included with some computer maintenance tool kits are very useful for this purpose. Use a flashlight to examine the interior of the tape drive. Penlights usually work the best.
2. You need to examine several things in the drive. Figure 9.23 provides a basic tape drive diagram as it would appear when you open the drive door. To obtain specific details about your drive, refer to the tape diagram in the vendor manual, if the vendor supplied one. The first thing you should look at is the black rubber wheel (idler wheel) on one side of the drive carriage. If this looks shiny and has a brownish cast to it, you need to clean it using alcohol and a cotton swab. It might take a little time to get the wheel clean, but it's essential to do so.

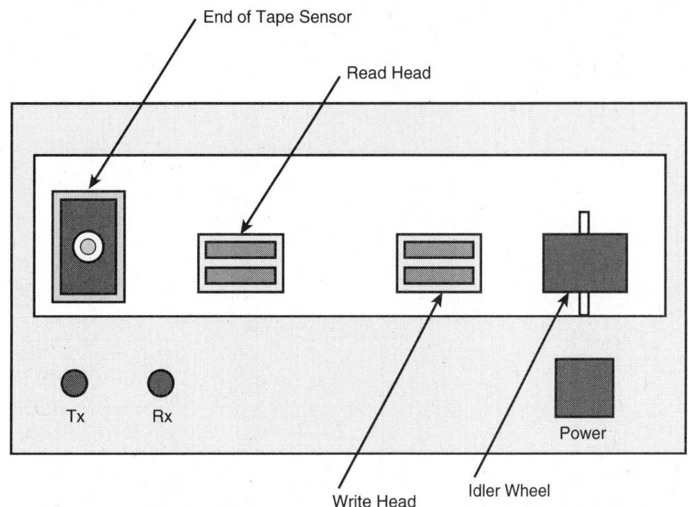

Figure 9.23.
Anatomy of a tape drive, showing the parts you need to pay particular attention to.

3. Check the read and write heads next. (Some tape drives use a combination read/write head, so you might see only one head.) Clean them with a fresh cotton swab and some alcohol. Be careful not to apply a lot of pressure; otherwise, you might scratch the head surface. Polish the heads with a dry cotton swab, using gentle pressure. Check the heads for damage, such as scratches. Both heads should appear brightly polished.
4. Clean the end of the tape sensor if your tape drive has one. This usually looks like a square or rectangular black plastic box with a tiny round light in it. The light is actually a photo sensor. You must clean the plastic covering the photo sensor so light can get through and tell the tape drive when it reaches the end of the tape. Simply moisten a cotton swab with alcohol and use a rotating motion to clean the sensor. The sensor is usually recessed into the black plastic case, so rubbing back and forth only forces dirt further into the recess.

5. Close the tape drive door. If this is an internal tape drive, complete the cleaning sequence by opening your computer and vacuuming any dirt out of the inside of the case, and then proceed to step 9.
6. External tape drive units often come with filters. Look at the back of the tape drive unit to see whether it uses a filter. If there's a filter, carefully remove the old one. The filter is usually held in place using a holder and some screws. Refer to the manual supplied with your tape drive for further details.
7. Replace the old filter with a new one, if possible. Some vendors might not supply replacement filters for their systems. If this is the case, carefully wash the filter, using clear water. Don't use soap, because this will actually clog the filter. Let the filter dry thoroughly. Replace the filter on the back of the tape drive unit.
8. If the tape drive provides some form of external access, open the case and carefully vacuum the inside. Never force the case open. In most cases, the vendor manual will indicate whether the case is designed to allow user access.
9. Now that you've fully cleaned your tape unit, place a blank tape in the drive and test it. Make sure that this is a test tape and not one of the tapes in your backup set. Format the tape if necessary.
10. Test your tape drive, using the diagnostic program supplied by the vendor. Follow the procedures I supplied in the installation section if the tape drive doesn't work for some reason. In most cases, you'll find that you nudged a jumper or cable, so that should be the first thing you check. Also make sure that you have everything back together properly.
11. Check for hardware and software interaction. Once the hardware is working, it's time to test the software. I usually begin by performing any software tests that the vendor supplies. For example, most backup software provides a speed test to make sure that your hardware performs at a given backup speed.
12. Once you complete the vendor-specific check, perform a check of your own. Back up a directory containing nonessential data and then do a compare of the tape's contents to the drive's contents (if your software supports this feature). If possible, restore your data to another directory. Use the DOS `COMPARE` utility (or any other utility that performs a detailed comparison) to compare the files in the original directory to the new directory. If you can't restore to a different directory, try restoring the files to a different drive. You could also copy your existing data to a temporary directory and restore the old data to the default directory. If either of these steps fails, check the setup of your software to make sure that all the settings are correct for your machine, tape drive controller, hard disk controller, and tape drive. Check your machine's environment to see whether you have enough buffers and files allocated and check any network driver settings to make sure that you have them set up correctly. If you still can't get a good backup from the software, call the vendor and describe the symptoms. Be sure to tell them that you ran a complete diagnostic on the hardware so they don't try to place the blame on that. Provide the vendor with the version of your software as well as all the hardware specifications.

I find that maintaining the tape drive attached to my system is a lot easier than the alternative. Never buy faulty insurance. A tape drive that isn't maintained is worse than no tape backup at all. At least if you don't have a tape backup, you won't have any unexpected surprises when a hard drive fails. It's a good idea to perform this maintenance at least once every three months unless the vendor specifies a different maintenance cycle. You might want to perform maintenance more often if the tape drive is located in a dirty or hazardous area.

You may want to take this opportunity to check your tapes. Tapes become old and wear out, like anything else in your system. You can use three quick steps to check a tape:

1. Look for any physical damage, such as a cracked case. Damage of this type may have damaged the tape drive.
2. Look at how the tape is wound on the spool (also known as the tape pack). Does it appear wavy instead of smooth? Can you see individual wraps sticking above the level of the other wraps on the spool? If so, try to re-tension the tape (unless the manufacturer doesn't recommend doing this). If re-tensioning doesn't give the tape a smoother appearance, the tape might contain stretched areas.
3. Finally, remember that tape life is limited. DAT tapes last about five years, whereas others last about two years. If your tape is more than five years old, consider replacing it, even if it looks good. You might want to consider replacing heavily used tapes more often. If you use a tape every day, you should consider replacing it every two years.

Tip: Some tape vendors suggest placing a label on the tape and making a hash mark every time you use it. Once you reach 40 uses, discard the tape and use a new one. Tapes will last much longer (remember, the people who sell tapes are the same people who tell you to buy new ones), but if you store your tapes in a warm or dirty environment, increased tape turnover might give you an added level of security.

Tape Rotation

I actually walked into a business once that had a state-of-the-art file server, up-to-date workstations, and a tape backup system to boot. The only problem was that they had only one tape. A one-tape shop always runs into problems. Even if you assume that every backup will work exactly as expected, other things could go wrong. For example, a fire could strike at any moment. A one-tape shop would come in the next morning and find its tape safely stored in the safe. Of course, it would be a ball of melted plastic, but it would still be there. Floods and theft aren't out of the question, either. A lot of things can happen to your data, and if you keep it all in one place, it takes only one accident to turn your business into a disaster. Hopefully, this makes my point about the need for rotating your tapes.

You can rotate tapes in many different ways. The technique you use depends on the requirements of your company, the value of your data, the types of applications you use, and the number of tapes you have on hand. Every tape rotation method shares three things in common:

- Always store at least one tape off-site. An off-site tape has a better chance of surviving the smaller disasters of life.
- Use at least three tapes to implement what the industry terms as a "grandfather" backup strategy. A grandfather strategy ensures that at least three generations of tape are available at all times. Using this strategy usually reduces the probability of virus infection or other forms of data loss.
- Include some plan for retiring old tapes and integrating new ones.

I usually use a three-tape strategy for small businesses. My own setup uses a six-tape strategy. The following paragraphs examine some common backup-rotation techniques. Although none of these methods might exactly fit your needs, they do provide you with enough information to come up with a reliable rotation scheme of your own.

Tip: Tapes are cheap when compared to the cost of the data they hold. Buying a few more tapes might rescue your data from disaster. Never let the cost of the tapes you buy interfere with a good backup strategy.

The Three-Tape Full Backup Technique

This is the method I recommend for small businesses on a very tight budget, because it represents the very least you can get by with and still maintain a safe backup strategy. Use this method for less complex installations that use the network primarily for word processing and small spreadsheet files. For example, this technique usually meets the needs of a small four- or five-person company that doesn't use a complex accounting package or rely on a database management system. You may not want to use it for applications that rely heavily on shared files. The reliability of this technique greatly diminishes as the number of files you want to protect increases. Figure 9.24 illustrates this technique.

The nice thing about this tape storage method is that you still maintain an off-site storage capability. This method easily expands to four, five, or even six tapes. Because the tapes rotate at a fairly high rate, you'll need to replace them more often.

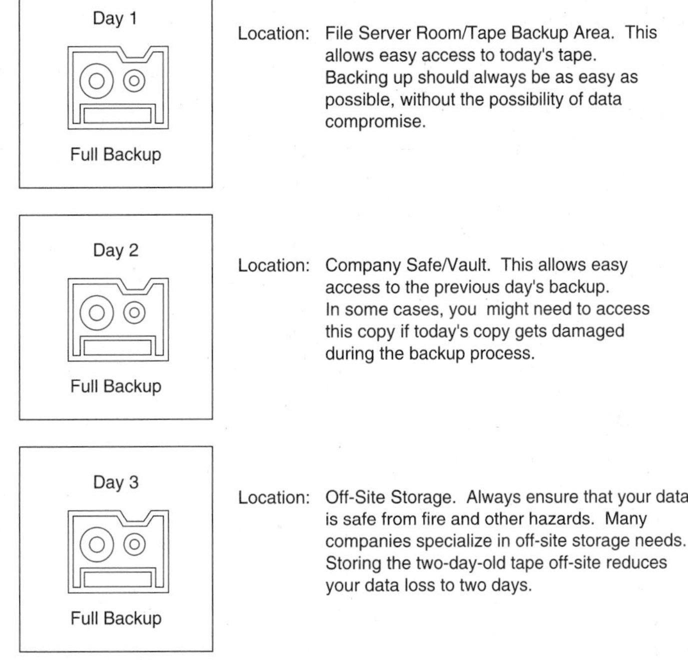

Day 1
Full Backup
Location: File Server Room/Tape Backup Area. This allows easy access to today's tape. Backing up should always be as easy as possible, without the possibility of data compromise.
Day 2
Full Backup
Location: Company Safe/Vault. This allows easy access to the previous day's backup. In some cases, you might need to access this copy if today's copy gets damaged during the backup process.
Day 3
Full Backup
Location: Off-Site Storage. Always ensure that your data is safe from fire and other hazards. Many companies specialize in off-site storage needs. Storing the two-day-old tape off-site reduces your data loss to two days.

Figure 9.24.
The three-tape full backup technique works well for small businesses.

The Six-Tape Full/Incremental Backup Technique

This technique uses one dedicated tape for each day of the week and reduces the probability of virus infection or other damage that can occur when you use one tape for both full and incremental backups. Monday and Friday are full backup days, while Tuesday through Thursday requires only incremental backups. The Friday tape alternates between off-site storage and on-site storage. Use this technique for moderately complex setups that rely mainly on word processing and spreadsheet applications in a nonshared environment. You can also use this technique for installations with small accounting systems or moderately complex database management systems. Figure 9.25 illustrates this technique.

The advantage to using this system is that it's more reliable than the three-tape system, yet requires less maintenance time than creating full backups each day of the week. The only disadvantage of this system is that the Monday backup represents a weak link in the backup chain. If the Monday backup becomes corrupted, the incremental backups you make from Tuesday through Thursday also become worthless. You could conceivably lose four days of work using this method. Of course, this assumes that a network crash occurs on Thursday afternoon or Friday and that you have a corrupted Monday backup. Although this sequence of events is unlikely, it could happen.

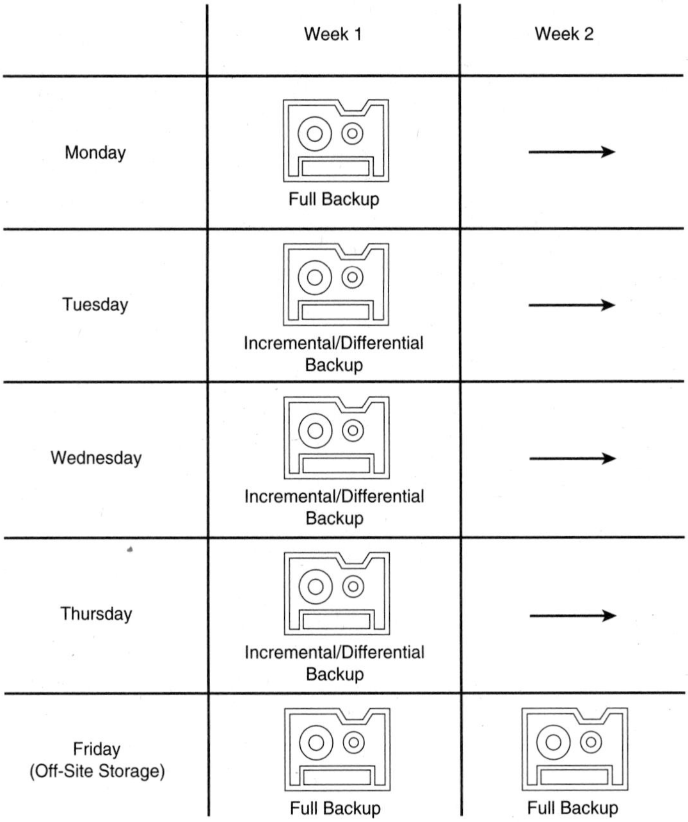

Figure 9.25.
This six-tape method works well for moderately complex setups.

	Week 1	Week 2
Monday	Full Backup	→
Tuesday	Incremental/Differential Backup	→
Wednesday	Incremental/Differential Backup	→
Thursday	Incremental/Differential Backup	→
Friday (Off-Site Storage)	Full Backup	Full Backup

One way to expand this particular backup technique is to add additional Friday tapes to the sequence. For example, you could easily make this a nine-tape sequence, which would allow one Friday tape for each week of the month. Expandability is one of the things that I try to keep in mind when setting up a tape rotation scheme. It's always easy to use fewer tapes, but finding a good way to use more can be a challenge.

The Six-Tape Full Backup Technique

I find that this particular rotation scheme works best with medium-sized businesses that have very robust data storage needs (see Figure 9.26). For example, if you rely heavily on a data entry or an order entry system, this is the rotation scheme you need to look at. This technique uses one dedicated tape for each day of the week. The Friday tape alternates between off-site storage and on-site storage.

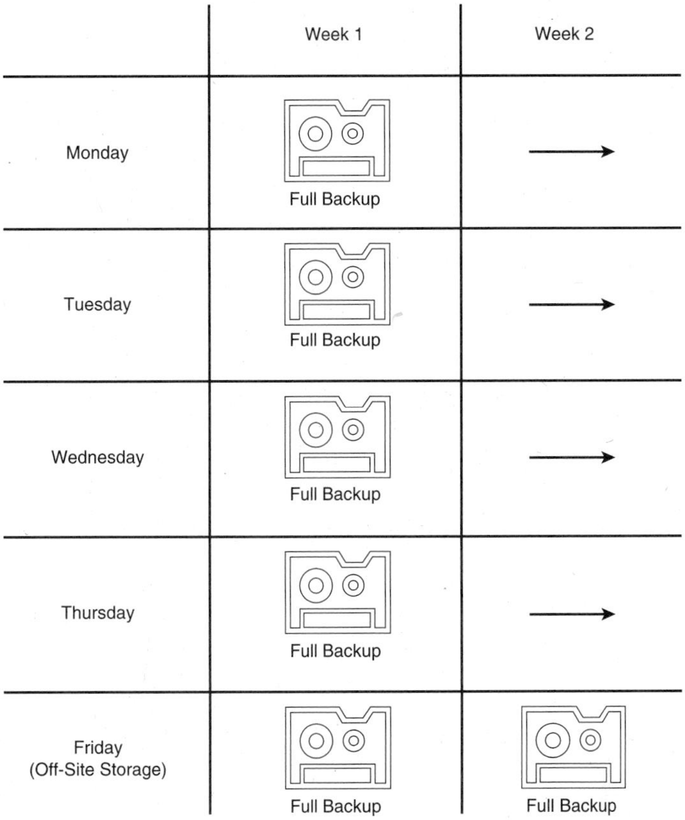

Figure 9.26.
This six-tape method works well for moderately complex setups that rely on data entry systems.

	Week 1	Week 2
Monday	Full Backup	→
Tuesday	Full Backup	→
Wednesday	Full Backup	→
Thursday	Full Backup	→
Friday (Off-Site Storage)	Full Backup	Full Backup

This rotation scheme overcomes the weakness of the six-tape full/incremental rotation described in the preceding section, by using a full backup each day of the week. This means that maintenance time increases in proportion to the total size of your network rather than the size of the files that you change each day. On larger networks, it might also mean an increase in the total number of tapes, if you need more than one tape to make a full backup of the network. Unfortunately, your tapes will wear out faster because they'll receive a higher level of use with this method.

The best way to expand this rotation scheme is to double the number of tapes so that you alternate sets between odd and even weeks. This will improve security and reduce tape wear. It also would allow you to maintain more tapes off-site and further reduce the chances that one tape failure would prove disastrous.

The 14-Tape Full Backup Technique

Large businesses require a more complex rotation scheme to ensure that their data remains safe. Not only is it unlikely that you'll use a single application or perhaps a simple group of applications, but it's also very unlikely that the network administrator will have as firm a grip on the inner workings of the company. (It's not that the administrator is incompetent, but administering a large setup leaves little time to understand how everyone else uses the computer.) The larger and more complex your network, the more desirable it is to provide several stages of network backup.

Added to these other complexities are the problems of local storage. It's improbable that all your data will appear on the network, because managers will probably keep some of it on their local hard drives. Proposals and other sensitive information are likely candidates for local storage. Unfortunately, the manager could lose that data during an emergency unless you back it up. The 14-tape full backup technique combines the best features of the six-tape method with workstation backup. Figure 9.27 illustrates this technique.

Figure 9.27.
The 14-tape rotation scheme adds workstation backup to the mix of features.

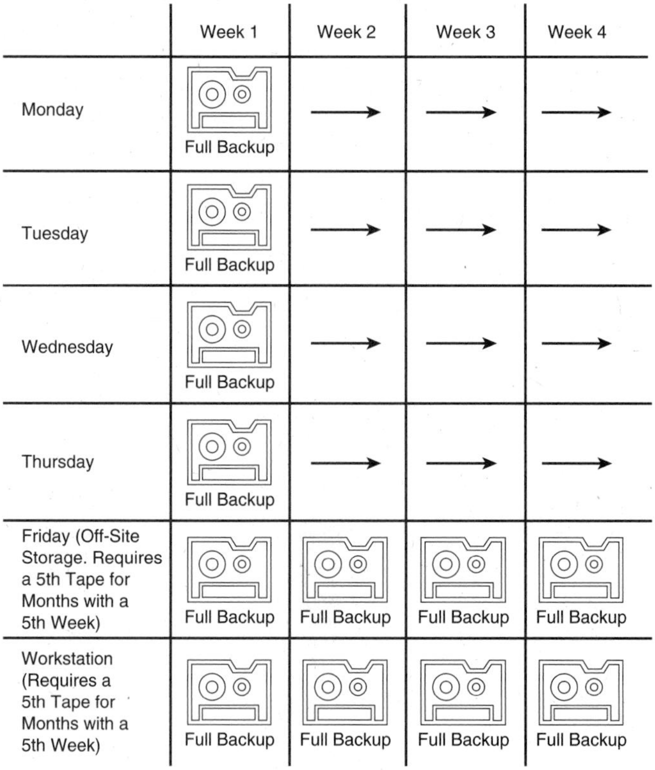

	Week 1	Week 2	Week 3	Week 4
Monday	Full Backup	→	→	→
Tuesday	Full Backup	→	→	→
Wednesday	Full Backup	→	→	→
Thursday	Full Backup	→	→	→
Friday (Off-Site Storage. Requires a 5th Tape for Months with a 5th Week)	Full Backup	Full Backup	Full Backup	Full Backup
Workstation (Requires a 5th Tape for Months with a 5th Week)	Full Backup	Full Backup	Full Backup	Full Backup

As you can see, this technique provides one backup per week for all workstations on the network along with one tape per week for file server off-site storage. You could further expand the backup scenario to make daily full or incremental backups of the workstations. However, in most cases you should find the Friday workstation backup sufficient. You can look at this backup method in two distinct ways.

The first way is a 4- or 5-tape rotation. Instead of looking at tape backup on a monthly basis, keep the Friday backup and workstation backup tapes in constant rotation. To implement this strategy, mark a calendar with the numbers one through five (or one through four) on each Friday of the year. The first Friday you use tape one; the second, tape two; and so on. On the sixth Friday of the year, you start over with tape one. Of the two methods, this is the easiest way to implement a 14-tape strategy.

The second way to look at this backup method keeps the needs of accounting firms and other month-oriented organizations in mind. Some applications perform special processing at the end of the month and the end of the quarter. They summarize the previous month's data and then delete the information used to create the summary. Making a backup before you do this processing ensures that you keep the old data in case a problem occurs during processing but doesn't become apparent until sometime later. To implement this method, always use Friday and Workstation tape number one on the first Friday of the month. Likewise, use the second tape on the second Friday of the month. Using five tapes ensures that you have enough tapes for months with five Fridays.

Off-Site Storage

You should never consider off-site storage an *option*. It's a *mandatory* part of the backup process. Disasters strike when and where you least expect them. An unexpected electrical fire could totally wipe out your company tomorrow. Floods, earthquakes, broken pipes, and other disasters can strike at any moment.

Protecting your company's data is the main reason to create a backup. It's unlikely that a disaster will annihilate two places simultaneously, especially if those places are some distance apart. Placing your data in more than one location helps reduce the probability of tape destruction by a disaster.

Two types of off-site storage are available. The more expensive solution is to use the services of a company that specializes in providing off-site storage. These companies usually provide a fireproof vault for storage purposes. It's very unlikely that tapes stored in such a facility will be damaged in the event of an emergency. You'll want to examine the cost factor and types of service offered by the company. Some companies offer 24-hour service, but this costs significantly more than those that offer only daytime service. Although you might save money using the latter, it's also unlikely that you could retrieve a tape on the weekend or after working hours when using this type of service. In some cases, this might prove inconvenient, but it shouldn't sway you from using these services.

The second solution is to select one or two people from management to use their homes as off-site storage sites. Be sure to obtain the approval of management to do this. Unless management really trusts this person, you could end up handing company secrets to someone who might try to sell them elsewhere. When using this technique, the person stores the tape at home and brings it in when it's time to replace it on-site. Although this form of off-site storage is less secure than using a professional service, it's a lot less expensive. The downside to using this method is that the same disaster that destroys the on-site tape could also destroy the off-site tape. The off-site tapes are also subject to theft and vandalism. Of course, one advantage of using this technique is that you'll have a good chance of retrieving a tape on the weekend or after hours.

You can also combine both techniques. Storing one tape in a vault and another at a manager's house provides you with the advantages of both systems. In addition, you reduce at least one of the problems with using either technique alone. By storing one tape in a vault, you no longer need to worry about the same disaster destroying a tape in both the on-site and off-site storage location. In addition, you can count on reaching the manager after hours or on the weekend to retrieve a backup tape.

Using the LFNBACK Utility

All kinds of utilities are out there, and they are all waiting to destroy the long filenames on your hard drive. Whenever you use a disk utility to perform some kind of task on your drive—whether it's a file recovery, a disk optimization, or a backup—that utility could destroy the long filenames that Windows 95 needs in order to operate correctly. You don't have to let it happen, of course. Windows 95 comes with a utility called LFNBACK that can save your long filenames to a file and restore them later. You can find it in the \WIN95\OTHER\LFNBACK folder of the Windows 95 installation CD-ROM.

Note: Users of the OSR2 release of Windows 95 probably won't have this utility on their machine. I would recommend not using a copy taken from any other Windows 95 machine, since the new FAT 32 file format is incompatible with that used by FAT 16. Not only is the actual structure different, but FAT 32 includes features like a relocatable root directory, which will render the older version of the LFNBACK utility useless. The bottom line if you're using FAT 32 is to use only the Microsoft-provided FAT 32 utilities with it (at least until third-party vendors start providing FAT 32-compatible products).

This isn't a very fancy utility, and it doesn't even sport a GUI. You need to use it from the DOS prompt without having Windows 95 loaded. I just boot into MS-DOS mode, perform it from the DOS prompt, and type `exit`, and I go right back into Windows 95.

Warning: Never use LFNBACK from within Windows, because you don't know which files are open. If Windows has a file with a long filename open, that filename won't appear in the LFNBK.DAT file. This means that you'll lose the filename if you perform a restore on the drive. Always use LFNBACK from the DOS prompt. Using MS-DOS mode is fine, but using the Windows 95 DOS prompt is probably even safer. (To go to the MS-DOS prompt, press F8 at the boot message and select that mode from the menu.)

I use LFNBACK about once a week to create a backup of the long filenames on each hard drive. It's easy to do—just type **LFNBACK /B *<drive>*** at the DOS prompt. You need to do this once for each drive on your machine. The result is a file called LFNBK.DAT that contains all the long filename information for that particular drive.

Peter's Principle: LFNBACK as a Maintenance Tool

Backing up your long filenames should be a regular part of your maintenance cycle. I usually back them up right before I perform a full backup of the machine. That way, the long filename backup ends up on the tape that I'm using. This double backup provides an extra measure of security when it comes to your long filenames. Remember, you could have a perfectly functional machine that won't boot because the long filenames on your drive got corrupted. Restoring them using LFNBACK could make a bad situation right again in a matter of minutes.

To restore a drive after some utility decides to eat it for lunch, follow the reverse procedure. Be sure to run LFNBACK on a drive that has the LFNBK.DAT file on it. To perform the restoration, type **LFNBACK /R *<drive>*** at the DOS prompt.

On Your Own

Spend some time looking at the file-system-related files in the Windows SYSTEM folder. Look especially at the exported functions for .DLLs such as COMMDLG.DLL. What do these entries tell you about the .DLL and its purpose?

If you have a CD-ROM drive, spend some time optimizing the VCache, now that you know a little more about how it works. What size of CD-ROM cache seems to use memory the most efficiently? How much of a speed difference do you notice between a large and a small cache when using applications directly from the CD-ROM drive?

Determine whether you have FAT 32 installed on your machine, using the various clues we've talked about in this chapter. For example, when you look at the drive Properties dialog box, does it match the view shown in Figure 9.5 or does it use the older Windows 95 dialog box? Make certain that you also know what kind of installation you're getting on a new machine, so that you don't inadvertently corrupt your hard drive by using old utilities on a FAT 32-formatted drive.

Try using the LFNBACK utility to create a backup of the long filenames on your drive. Make sure that you don't erase the LFNBK.DAT file; it contains all the long filename information. Keep this file handy, just in case one of your older applications removes the long filename information from your drive. Update the LFNBK.DAT file on a weekly basis to keep it current.

Write your own tape rotation plan based on the examples in this chapter. Be sure to weigh the cost of the time involved in creating the backup versus the cost of replacing lost data after a system crash. Also add times to the schedule for replacing your tapes, and don't let an old tape lull you into a false sense of security.

Determine what kind of an effect disabling lazy writes has on your system from a performance perspective. Use the following procedure to disable it. (If the performance penalty is too great, you can always use this same procedure to enable lazy writes again later.)

1. Right-click the My Computer icon and select Properties.
2. Click the Performance page and then the File System button.
3. Select the Troubleshooting page. Click the option Disable Write-Behind Caching for All Drives.
4. Click OK twice to save your changes. Windows will tell you to reboot your machine in most cases, to allow the change to take effect.

IV

Understanding and Using Windows 95

10

The Windows 95 Desktop

In the previous edition of this book, I predicted that the Windows 95 desktop would be the most misunderstood part of the Windows 95 interface. I was right. Except for the Registry and networking (neither of which are interface elements), more people wrote messages concerning the desktop than anything else that I saw on both CompuServe and various Internet newsgroups. Because of the continued evolution of this particular Windows 95 feature, people will continue to write books and articles about optimizing it, and others will decry the lack of some feature that they thought essential. Adding Internet Explorer 4.0 into the mix only complicates matters (refer to Chapters 1 and 2 for an overview of this new product). Now you have three interfaces to choose from: Program Manager (Windows 3.x), Explorer (Windows 95), and Internet Explorer 4.0. Even with all this complexity, one fact is still clear: The desktop is the plain face of the Windows 95 interface, and it's up to you to dress it up.

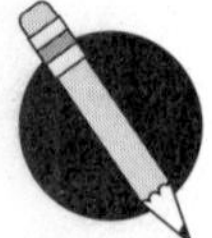

Note: You aren't even limited to the selections that Microsoft provides, because there are any number of Windows 95 shells available on the market. For that matter, you can choose to run a specific application instead of using Explorer by changing the `Shell=` statement in SYSTEM.INI. There are limits to what you can choose to use in place of Explorer, because any limitations in the shell you choose translate into lost capability within the Windows 95 environment. For example, I was able to use Netscape Navigator as my shell. It enabled me to get on the Internet, download files, and do anything else that that product normally allows you to do. Of course, I couldn't use it to open any other application or edit any files without special programming of HTML pages, but it's an interesting way to see just how far you can go.

This chapter isn't going to tell you anything about the Program Manager interface of old—there are plenty of other books on the market that tell you about this interface. I also won't cover the new Internet Explorer interface in this chapter. Refer to Chapters 1 and 2 for an overview of Internet Explorer. Chapter 21 fills you in on the details specific to Internet Explorer. What I cover in this chapter is the standard Windows 95 Explorer interface. Most of the information you read here will also work with Internet Explorer 4.0, though you'll be able to extend the techniques I'll talk about to the Internet environment as well.

Windows 95 makes heavy use of Explorer. You've already seen that in many ways in earlier chapters. Believe it or not, there's still more to learn about this particular utility. It's a lot more flexible and provides more features than most people will ever use. That's the beauty of the Explorer interface—it allows you to do things your way. Windows 95 doesn't force you to do things a certain way, like its predecessor did.

Once you figure out how Explorer can help you, giving your desktop a face you can really use becomes a much simpler matter. It's no longer a bothersome task you're embarking on; rather, it's a voyage of discovery. You see, very few people really know how to make something work the way that they do. Most of us are accustomed to simply following someone else's advice. Explorer and the Windows 95 desktop will change all that.

The following sections will help you see how to use the Windows 95 desktop and Explorer together to create an environment that truly reflects the way that you work. It might take a little time for you to adjust to this new level of freedom, but once you do you'll find that you work more efficiently, and you'll never view Windows the same way again.

Tip: More than the centerpiece tool of Windows 95, Explorer is your gateway to freedom. As such, it really pays to take the time to learn how to use this key. Make sure you spend the time to fully optimize Explorer to your needs first, and then concentrate on the rest of Windows 95. The decisions you make in Explorer tend to snowball into other areas of Windows 95. For example, Chapter 9 shows how the choices you make in Explorer (actually, the choices Microsoft makes for you) change the way Backup works. A fully optimized Explorer interface includes all the objects you normally work with, including such things as backup files. Unless Windows 95 knows how to work with a particular object, you might find yourself fighting against Windows 95 instead of working with it. Optimizing Explorer is your first real step in optimizing Windows 95 from the user perspective.

Customizing Your Desktop

At work, you probably don't have a "formal" desktop. In fact, I'll bet it's customized to meet every need you have. It's a sure thing that your desk reflects the way you work. No one, for example, forced you to place the stapler in the far right corner.

Windows used to tell people how to set things up. It had a very formal way of arranging things that made some people feel extremely uncomfortable. In fact, it's this formality that made some people go out and purchase a third-party replacement for Program Manager, the old "desktop" in Windows 3.x.

Windows 95 doesn't force you to do things its way. Someone at Microsoft must have followed Burger King's lead by allowing people to have it their way. The Explorer interface is so flexible that I doubt any two people will ever have the same desktop under Windows again. The desktop is the area where everything else in Windows goes. It's not like the background you used to have under Windows 3.x. The Windows 95 desktop is an object, just like everything else in Windows 95.

The Windows 95 desktop has some changes that you might not think about right away. For example, remember in Chapter 1 when I told you to start right-clicking everything? You can right-click the desktop. It has a context menu (shown in Figure 10.1), just like everything else in Windows 95. I won't go into detail about the contents of the context menu right now—all that information appears in the "Working with Desktop Objects" section of this chapter. Suffice it to say that there are plenty of nice surprises when it comes to arranging things under Windows 95.

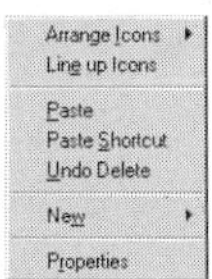

Figure 10.1.
The Windows 95 desktop has its own context menu and is an object, just like everything else.

Two entries I'd like to briefly mention are Arrange Icons and Line Up Icons. Arrange Icons allows you to rearrange your desktop in a specific order. It works just like the same entry under Explorer. (See how everything seems to have a bit of Explorer in it?) You can rearrange your icons by name, type, size, or date. Personally, I find the type and name orders the most convenient.

Some people detest all the standard arrangements, so they just stick the icons in the order they want them. If you're not one of these people, you might find that the Line Up Icons option is custom-tailored for you. It allows you to keep the icons in the order you want them but rearranges them into neat rows and columns. This option provides a grid effect that allows you to keep your desktop neat, yet arranged in the order in which you want to see it.

The following sections look at the desktop as a whole. They are meant as a guide to things you can do to make your desktop more usable, but I probably won't stop there. Think of this section as the most common tricks that people use to optimize their Windows 95 environment. This is the "must do" check list you should look at when trying to get the most out of your setup.

Taskbar

A major part of the new look in Windows 95 is the Taskbar. This is the gray bar at the bottom of Figure 10.2. You might think of the Taskbar in Windows 95 as a replacement for Program Manager. The Taskbar can do a lot more for you than that. The Taskbar is the central control area for most of the things you'll do under Windows 95. It contains three major elements: a Start menu, a task list, and a settings area.

Before giving you a full description of each of the major elements, I want to show you a few ways you can configure the Taskbar itself. The Taskbar starts out at the bottom of the display, but you don't have to leave it there. With Windows 95, you can always change your desktop to suit your needs. Figure 10.3 shows what happens when you grab the Taskbar with the mouse pointer and move it toward the right side of the display. Windows 95 lets you place the Taskbar on any of the four sides.

Like the other objects under Windows 95, the Taskbar also provides a Properties dialog box (simply right-click the Taskbar and select the Properties option to display it). This dialog box has two pages. One controls the Start menu setup, and the other controls the Taskbar itself. The four settings on the Taskbar tab enable you to change how it reacts. For example, you can remove the Taskbar from view by removing the check mark from the Always on Top field. The Show Clock field enables you to clear more space for applications on the Taskbar by removing the clock from view. My personal favorite is the Auto Hide field. Figure 10.4 shows what happens when you select this option. The Taskbar appears as a thin gray line at the bottom of the display. As soon as the mouse cursor approaches it, the Taskbar resumes its normal size. This enables you to delete the Taskbar to clear space for application windows, yet keep it handy for when you need it.

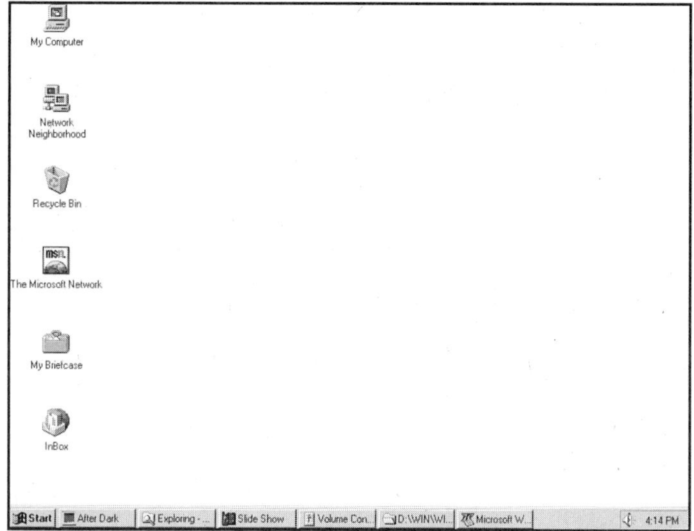

Figure 10.2.
This is a typical Taskbar, but don't be fooled—it can take a variety of forms.

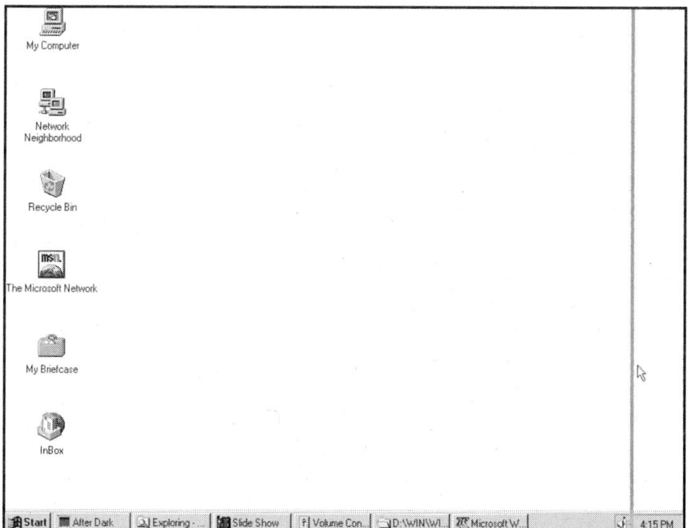

Figure 10.3.
You can move the Taskbar. The gray box shows where the Taskbar will appear when you let go of the left mouse button.

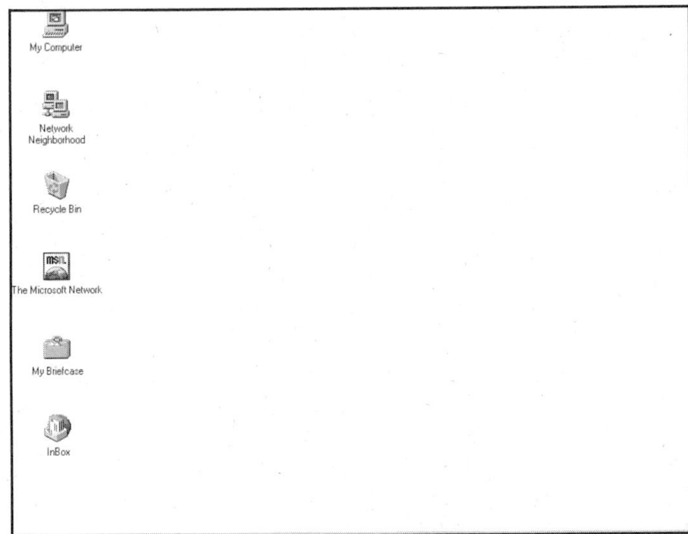

Figure 10.4.
The Auto Hide feature of the Taskbar Properties dialog box makes it possible for you to remove the Taskbar from sight until you need it.

Right-clicking the Taskbar displays a few other object-specific options. All of them affect the way in which Windows 95 organizes the applications that appear on the Taskbar:

- **Cascade:** When you select this option, all the application windows are resized to the same size. Windows 95 arranges them diagonally, much like the display you'd normally see in a spreadsheet program when opening more than one file. You can select any application out of the entire list by clicking its title bar (the area at the top of the application window that contains the application's name).
- **Tile Horizontally and Tile Vertically:** Use either of these options if you want to see the window areas of all your applications at once. Windows 95 uses every available inch of desktop space to place the applications side by side. Each application receives about the same amount of space.
- **Minimize All Windows:** If you ever arrive at the point where your screen is so cluttered that you can't tell what's opened and what's not, use this option to clean up the mess. The Minimize All Windows option minimizes every application you have running on the desktop.

The Start Menu

The Start menu normally appears on the far-left side of the Taskbar. It contains a complete listing of all your applications, access to some system settings, and a few other things thrown in for good measure. Figure 10.5 shows how the Start menu looks. Notice that it has seven main entries. The following paragraphs describe each entry in detail.

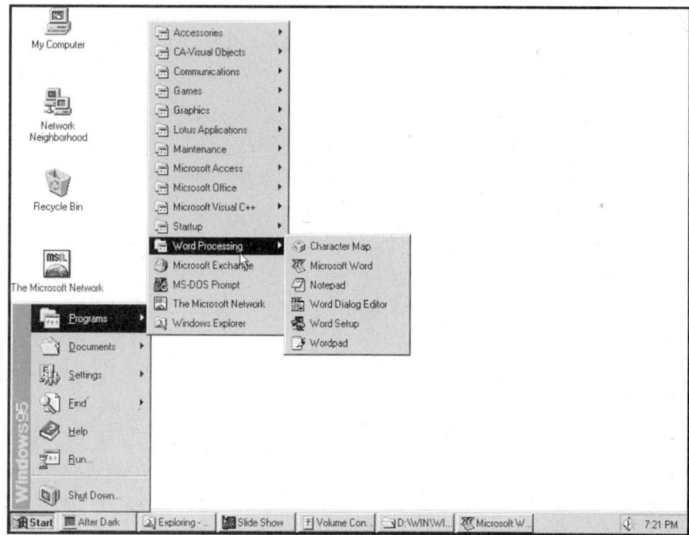

Figure 10.5.
The Start menu replaces Program Manager as the means to start applications installed on your machine.

- **Programs:** This is the list of applications installed on your machine. Unlike Windows 3.x, the Explorer interface enables you to place folders within folders (programmers call this *nesting*). As Figure 10.5 shows, you can place applications several levels deep within the menu tree.
- **Documents:** Use this option to select a document you previously opened using Explorer. This list doesn't store the names of documents you open using your application's File | Open command. The list can contain up to 15 document names.
- **Settings:** Windows 95 provides you with a number of ways to change your environment. The Settings menu is just one centralized location for this information. It provides access to the Control Panel, the Printers configuration dialog box, and the Taskbar configuration dialog box.
- **Find:** This option opens the same dialog box you see when you use the Tools | Find command within Explorer. It enables you to find any file on your hard drive or on a network drive, using a variety of search criteria. You can select a file by name, location, and modification date. The Advanced tab of this dialog box even enables you to look for a file based on its contents or size.
- **Help:** The Help option opens the main Windows 95 Help file. You can use this file to search for just about any information you need to run Windows 95. Microsoft has come a long way in improving the Help files in this version of Windows. Instead of providing you with dry facts, these files actually provide procedures that you can use to do the job. As if that weren't enough, some of the Help screens provide angled arrows, as shown in Figure 10.6. When you click an angled arrow, Windows 95 starts the application related to the Help topic. For example, I opened the Date/Time Properties dialog box by clicking the angled arrow shown in this figure.

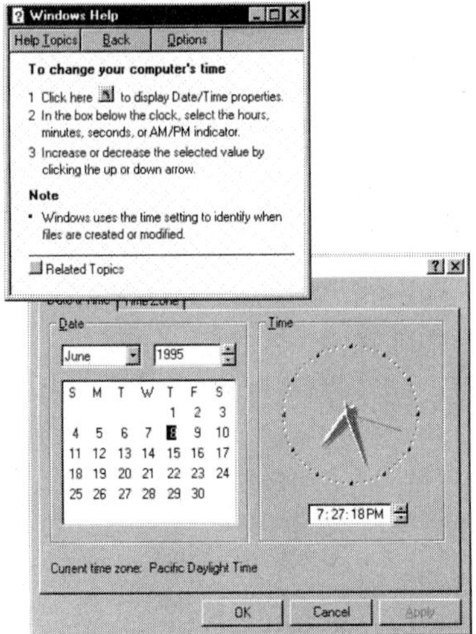

Figure 10.6.
The Windows 95 Help screens provide procedures that you can use to get the job done, and the ability to automatically start the applications required to do it.

- **Run:** Remember the File | Run command under Program Manager? You can still use it under Windows 95. The Run menu option opens a dialog box that enables you to start an application by typing its path and name, and you can also include any appropriate parameters.
- **Suspend:** This option isn't shown in Figure 10.5. In fact, the only time you'll normally see it is on a laptop that supports this feature. The Suspend option allows you to shut down the laptop without actually leaving Windows. It's a productivity option that allows you to stop and start your work quickly without wasting power. The next time you power up your laptop, you'll return to Windows exactly the way you left it. There are two potential problems with this particular feature. First, it circumvents the security provided by the initial login screen. Anyone who starts up the machine will be logged in under your name and will have the same access rights that you do. The second potential problem is that any applications or files that are open when you suspend Windows will remain that way. The potential for data damage is greatly increased when you suspend rather than shut down the machine. Figure 10.7 shows the Suspend option on a laptop.
- **Shut Down:** This option enables you to perform an orderly shutdown of Windows 95. This includes things such as making sure that all the data is written to disk and that the Registry information is saved.

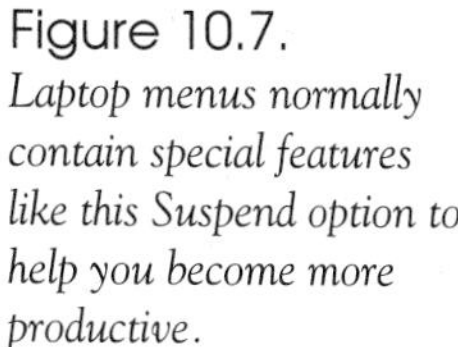

Figure 10.7.
Laptop menus normally contain special features like this Suspend option to help you become more productive.

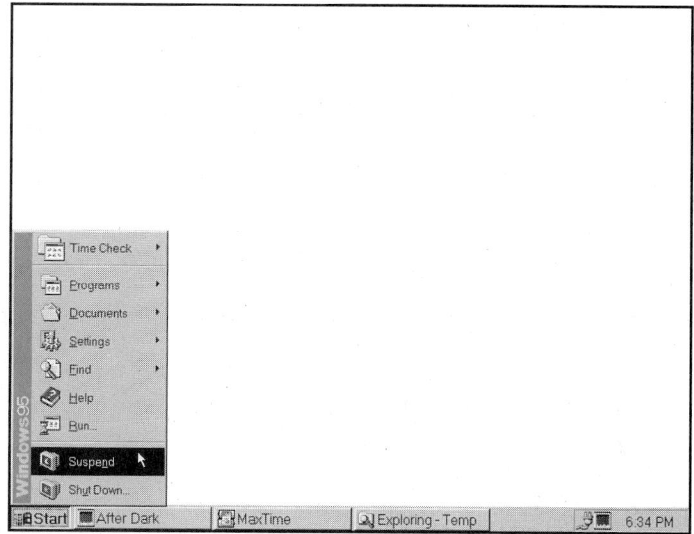

The Taskbar Buttons

The Taskbar proper contains one icon for each application currently running on the machine. This group of buttons replaces the Task Manager found in Windows 3.x. Instead of using the Alt+Tab key combination to switch from application to application, you can now choose an application much as you would select a television station using a remote control. All you need to do is press the appropriate button.

You should be aware of a few features. For one thing, the buttons shrink in size as needed to accommodate all the running applications. You can increase the size of the Taskbar to hold two, three, or even more rows of buttons if you so desire. Placing the mouse cursor near the edge of the Taskbar produces the same double arrow that you use to resize other objects under Windows 95. Of course, there is a limit to the size the buttons can attain.

Another feature is the ability to obtain more information about the application by simply placing the mouse cursor over its button. After a few seconds, Windows 95 displays a long title for the application and the foreground data file. The same principle holds true for other items on the Taskbar. For example, holding the mouse cursor over the time indicator shows today's date. In some cases, the information you receive is very minimal; for example, the Volume icon displays a single word—Volume.

The Settings Area

The Settings area (also called a toolbox) of the Taskbar usually contains two or more icons. Normally, these icons are hardware-related, but there isn't any reason that they couldn't be applications or utility programs. Each icon can serve multiple purposes, depending on what piece of hardware it's supposed to control. The two most common entries in this area are the Clock and Volume icons. In the preceding section, I explained how each of them reacts when you position the mouse cursor over their respective icons.

The Volume icon does a couple of things, depending on the action you take. A single click produces a master volume slider. You can use this to adjust the volume of all sounds produced by the sound board. Double-clicking the same icon displays the Volume Control dialog box, which provides detailed control of each input to your sound board. It also includes a master volume slider. Right-clicking the icon displays the context menu. In this case, it displays only two entries. The first takes you to the Volume Control dialog box; the second displays the Audio Properties dialog box. I take a better look at the volume controls in other sections of this book. For example, you'll find an overall description of the Volume control in the "Accessories" section of Chapter 2.

A double-click on the Clock icon displays the Date/Time Properties dialog box. A right-click shows the context menu. Detailed information about the clock appears later in this chapter.

Note: Several other interesting icons can appear in the Settings area. One of them enables international users to adjust their settings with ease. A special icon for PCMCIA-equipped machines displays the current bus status and the type of card plugged into the bus. Portable users will appreciate the battery indicator that appears in this area. With a quick click of the mouse, you can check your battery status before it becomes critical. If you see a plug (like the one shown in Figure 10.7) in place of the normal battery indicator, you know that the laptop is plugged into the wall socket.

Note: Installing Microsoft Plus! usually results in adding the System Agent icon to the Taskbar's Settings area. Double-click the icon to open System Agent, a program scheduler discussed in Chapter 28.

Passwords

Windows 95 provides an added measure of security through passwords. You can initiate password protection in several ways. The most automatic method is to install a Microsoft (or any other) network.

You'll also see a password screen if you allow users to configure their own desktops. No matter which way you install password protection, you'll need to manage it from time to time, and that's the purpose of this section.

The Passwords Properties dialog box is displayed by opening the Control Panel and double-clicking the Password applet. The first page contains two options, as shown in Figure 10.8. You use the Change Windows Password option to change the password you see when you initially log into the system. The same password is in effect whether you enable passwords through multiple user configurations or by using a Microsoft network.

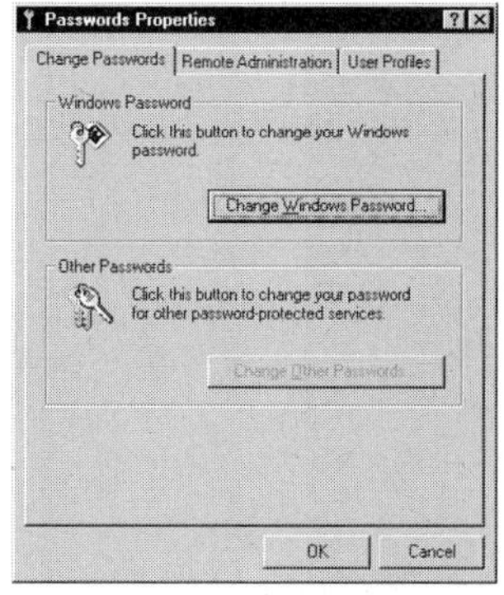

Figure 10.8.
Use the Change Passwords page of the Passwords Properties dialog box to manage your passwords.

Tip: There's a fatal flaw in the password protection provided by Windows 95. The way that Windows checks the user password is to "unlock" a decrypted file that contains the password. The filename usually corresponds to the user name and has an extension of .PWL. Windows 95 stores the .PWL file either in the main Windows folder or in the user's profile folder. Erasing this file effectively erases the security for that particular person. A person without a .PWL file can enter Windows 95 without a password.

The positive side of this is that if a user forgets his password, you can always regain access for him by erasing his security file. However, the negative side is that a user could actually circumvent security, given the right set of circumstances. All he would need to do is to boot the computer from a floppy and erase the proper file. This change could allow him to gain access to the administrator's account so that he could change the restrictions on his own account. The bottom line is that no system is 100 percent effective; someone will always find a way to circumvent it.

The second option on the Change Passwords page allows you to change any passwords that you might have for other resources or networks. If you have access to a NetWare installation in addition to a peer-to-peer network, for example, you could use this option to change the password.

The process of changing your password doesn't vary much. Select the password you want to change and Windows will display a dialog box containing three fields. (Clicking the option to change your Windows password bypasses the Password Selection dialog box.) The first field contains your original password. This ensures that someone else won't come along and change your password without your permission. Type the new password into the second field and then again into the third field so that Windows can verify it.

The Remote Administration page of the Passwords Properties dialog box appears in Figure 10.9. Enabling this feature allows someone else to manage your machine from a remote location. With this option, a network administrator could make changes to every machine on a peer-to-peer network without ever leaving his desk. We'll explore exactly how this works in Chapter 23. Fortunately, you can also password-protect remote administration. Type the access password into the first password field and again in the second field for verification purposes.

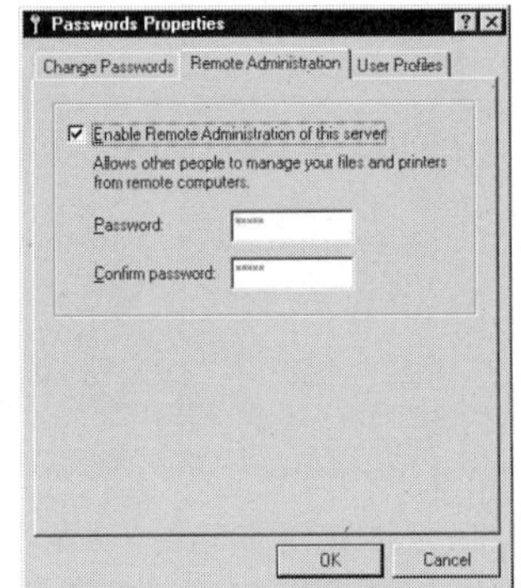

Figure 10.9.
Remote administration is a time-saving feature for peer-to-peer network administrators with multiple servers to configure.

Windows 95 allows you to select from two different desktop configuration methods. You can either force every user of a single machine to use the same desktop, or you can allow multiple desktops by selecting the correct option on the User Profiles page shown in Figure 10.10. A single desktop is a lot easier to maintain, reduces training costs, and enhances security. Multiple desktops keep users happier, provide much more flexibility, and could make users more efficient. The selection you make depends largely on the needs of the people using the machine. If they all perform about the same type of work and have similar needs, a single desktop is probably the right answer.

Tip: Multiple desktops aren't limited to more than one user. A single user can use multiple desktops to work more efficiently. If your current desktop is too cluttered, it might be time to build a second one. You could keep one desktop for each major task you perform. As an alternative, you could create a special desktop for each project you administer. This might not be the best way to separate your work into manageable pieces, but it's one way to do so.

Figure 10.10.
A single desktop is easy to maintain, but multiple desktops are more flexible.

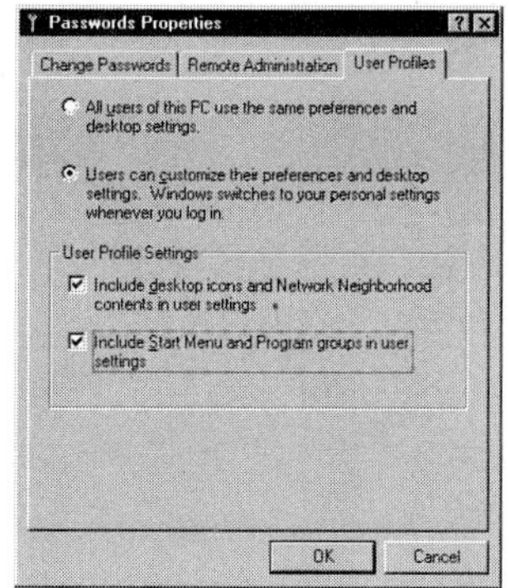

Once you decide to use multiple desktops, Windows 95 gives you two additional options that determine the level of flexibility this feature offers. The first check box in the User Profile Settings group allows the user to configure desktop icons and Network Neighborhood. These user-specific settings are saved in that user's profile folder. The second check box allows the user to create a specialized Start menu and program groups. These settings also appear in that user's profile folder.

Enabling multiple desktops also allows password protection. Windows 95 must know which user is using the computer so that it can open the correct profile. To do so, it displays the same password dialog box as the Microsoft network.

Desktop Settings

Everyone looks at desktop settings in one way—as improving the appearance of their computer. For the most part, they're right. Just changing the color of something under Windows won't make it work better—at least most of the time. Configuring your desktop for a pleasing appearance might not provide much in the way of a direct efficiency increase, but it will affect the way in which you view your system. A new piece of wallpaper or a change of colors can greatly affect the way you view your machine. Any positive change in attitude usually translates into improved efficiency. I find that changing my wallpaper and my display colors from time to time gives my computer that "new" feel that everyone needs occasionally.

Other reasons call for a change of configuration. Chapter 3 explains that wallpaper, while attractive to the eye, chews up valuable memory. You might run into a situation where memory is at a premium. Giving up your wallpaper is one way to increase memory in order to complete a specific task.

Eyestrain is also a common problem among computer users. Sitting eight hours in front of what amounts to a television at close range won't do anyone's eyes much good. However, if you're like me, you probably spend more than eight hours a day staring at that screen. Somewhere along the way, you'll want to make your icons and text bigger to reduce eye fatigue. Changing your desktop settings to improve readability is a very practical use of this feature.

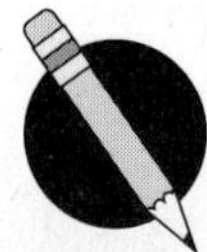

Note: Microsoft Plus! gives you increased control over your desktop environment by making it easier to change all the settings discussed here, and more. For more information on how to use Microsoft Plus! features such as Desktop Themes to enhance your desktop environment, see Chapter 28.

Selecting Wallpaper

Wallpaper is one of those personal items that every computer user wants to customize. Windows 95 makes changing your wallpaper even easier than it was under Windows 3.x. Right-click the Desktop icon and choose Properties. You should see the dialog box shown in Figure 10.11.

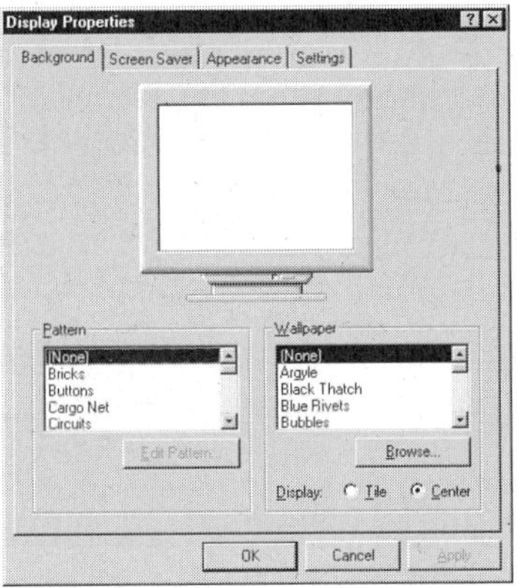

Figure 10.11.
The Background page of the Display Properties dialog box allows you to change your wallpaper.

This dialog box has three major sections. The first contains an image of a monitor. Changing any of the wallpaper or pattern settings immediately affects the contents of this display. The monitor gives you a thumbnail sketch of how your background will appear.

The next section contains a listing of available patterns. You can choose one of the existing patterns or create your own. To change a pattern, click the Edit Pattern button to display a bitmap editor similar in function to those used by most paint programs.

Tip: Patterns are a memory-efficient way to dress up a system. Because a pattern uses only two colors, it's a lot faster to draw and doesn't consume many system resources. If your system is short on memory but you'd still like an interesting background, consider using patterns instead of wallpaper.

The Wallpaper listing defaults to the files found in your main Windows folder. Of course, you don't have to use these files. Click the Browse option if you want to look in other folders on your drive. To display wallpaper, center it on the background, the best choice for pictures; or tile it, the best choice for patterns.

Note: Microsoft Plus! features a wallpapering enhancement that stretches desktop wallpaper to fit your screen. This feature is available on the Plus! page of the Display Properties dialog box. The Plus! page is available only if you've installed Microsoft Plus!. For more information, see Chapter 28.

Screen Saver

There is a very healthy third-party market for screen savers. Some Windows users buy screen savers in bulk. You can find them in stores and on just about every BBS in existence. Unless you own an older system, using a screen saver probably isn't necessary, just fun. I own a *Star Trek* screen saver for the "fun" element, even though it isn't necessary.

Tip: You don't have to spend a lot of money to get some really interesting screen savers. For example, at Screen Savers A2Z (`http://www.sirius.com/~ratloaf/`), you'll find a screen saver for displaying your favorite JPEG, PIC, and KQP files. If you happened to be a gardener, this same site will allow you to build your own virtual garden on-screen. Obviously, I can't even begin to tell you about all the screen savers on this site; you'll just have to look for yourself.

Windows 95 also provides a screen saver feature. It isn't as fun as some of the screen savers on the market, but it does the job. You'll find it on the Screen Saver page of the Display Properties dialog box, shown in Figure 10.12.

Note: Microsoft Plus! has fun screen savers that include animation and sound. They also include advanced settings that let you set Now and Never spots on the screen. In other words, if you put your mouse pointer in one corner of the screen, the screen saver will turn on, but if you put your mouse pointer in another corner, the screen saver will never turn on.

Just like the Wallpaper selection, this dialog box contains a miniature view of your monitor. You can use it as a thumbnail sketch of what the display will look like when you configure the screen saver. The Screen Saver field allows you to choose from one of the screen savers in the SYSTEM folder. If you decide to use a third-party screen saver that uses the Windows format, you need to place the file in the same directory as the others, or Windows won't see it.

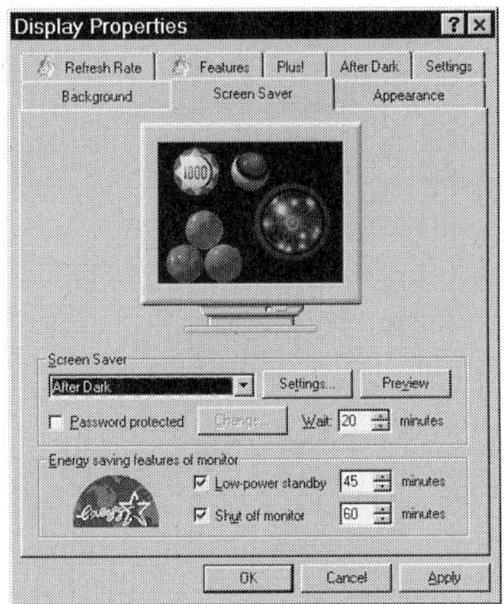

Figure 10.12.
The Screen Saver page of the Display Properties dialog box allows you to change your screen saver and its settings.

Once you select a screen saver, you can use the Settings button to change its settings. In most cases, the settings affect how Windows 95 displays the screen saver. For example, it might change the number of lines you see, or the number of colors.

The Wait field allows you to change the number of minutes Windows 95 waits before it activates the screen saver. To turn the screen saver off, move the mouse cursor or press a key.

You can also password-protect your screen saver. This allows you to leave the room without any fear that someone will use your machine while you're gone, because a password is required to turn the screen saver off. I like the third-party screen savers that automatically restore their current condition even if you turn the machine off and reboot. Unfortunately, the Windows 95 screen saver doesn't provide this feature, so you can circumvent password protection by rebooting the machine. This does have the advantage of resetting the display so that no one knows what you were working on before they rebooted the machine. Some people might be thwarted if you also have passwords enabled on the opening Windows screen.

The final option, Preview, allows you to see what the display will look like when Windows 95 turns the screen saver on. I've used this as a quick way to hide my display when someone walks into my office and I don't want them to see what's on my display. It's a quick solution to a potential problem. Of course, you'll want to be very careful around the mouse and keyboard if you use this method. Unless you enable the password option, your display clears if you bump the mouse or tap a key on the keyboard.

You'll notice that this dialog box also contains some settings for an energy saving monitor. These fields appear only if you have a monitor and display adapter that support automatic display shutdown. One check box tells Windows that you want to place the monitor in low power standby. This mode reduces the energy requirements of the monitor but allows it to come back online quickly after shutting down. Another check box tells Windows that you want to shut the monitor down completely. This has the same effect as turning off the power. The only difference is that the monitor will turn itself back on when you move the mouse. It will take the usual amount of time for the monitor to display color as it does normally. The two remaining fields set the amount of time that Windows waits before performing each action.

So how would you use the energy-efficient features? You might run the screen saver after 15 minutes of inactivity. That way, when you go to lunch or on a break, your monitor won't suffer the effects of burn in. (I usually set my display for 20 minutes because I spend a bit more time thinking about what I want to write down. Obviously you'll need to set the various times as needed for your occupation.) After 45 minutes of inactivity, you might want to put your monitor in low power standby mode. That way, it won't waste power while you're at a short meeting, yet you'll be able to return to work quickly. After 60 minutes, you'll probably want to shut the monitor off. This is a good interval to wait if you attend longer meetings. In fact, you may not even be able to return to your office, so turning the monitor off will save the company a lot of money if you go to several meetings in a week. Even if you do shut your monitor off, you'll have the satisfaction of not having to set everything back up when you return. Move the mouse, wait for the monitor to warm up again, and you're back to work. It's a lot faster than turning your machine completely off and starting everything up from scratch.

Palette

The Appearance page of the Display Properties dialog box, shown in Figure 10.13, allows you to change the appearance of your display, not just the desktop. I find that this particular dialog box is a lot easier to use than its Windows 3.x counterpart, even though the two dialog boxes look similar. Click the picture of the display to select an item.

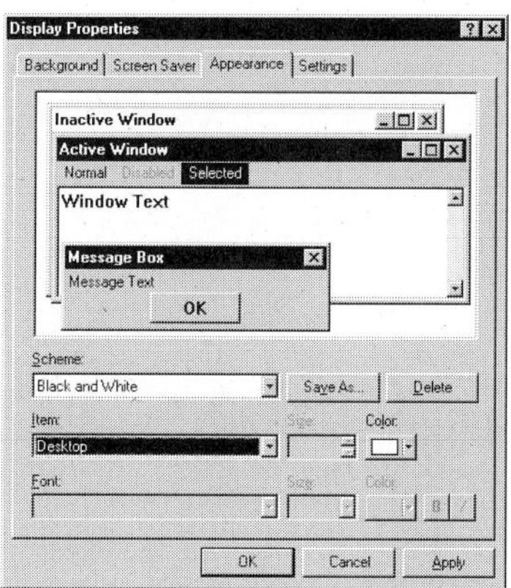

Figure 10.13.
You can change the colors and fonts used by your display with the settings on the Appearance page.

Windows 95 does provide a feature unavailable in Windows 3.x. The older versions of Windows enabled you to change the font used to display text only with a great amount of fiddling with the WIN.INI file. Windows 95 moves all this information into this dialog box and also gives you more flexibility. I have several configurations with "tired eye"-sized text settings. You can individually change the size of the menu and title bar text. Everything that has text also has a setting here for the font and type size.

Changing an entry consists of making list box selections. This dialog box has six of them. The first three affect the contents of the item itself and include the item name, size, and color. The size in this case is the size of the window or another display element. For example, you could change the width of a menu bar by using this option. The second three control the text used within that display element. These settings include font style, size, and color. You can select any installed font as your display font, but most people find that the MS Serif and MS Sans Serif fonts work best on displays. They were specially designed for this purpose. I occasionally use Arial and find that it works quite well.

This dialog box also contains a list box for selecting from existing color schemes, a Delete button for removing the schemes you no longer want, and a Save As button for adding new schemes.

Resolution

Changing your display resolution under Windows 3.x was a nightmare. You first had to escape out of Windows, use the Setup program to make the change, and then reboot and hope that you hadn't accidentally overwritten anything important. In some cases, you even had to dig up a copy of your installation disks to supply the font that Windows needed.

The Settings page of the Display Properties dialog box, shown in Figure 10.14, allows you to change your display resolution, the number of colors, and the standard font with ease. Except for the system font setting, you can usually change the settings without rebooting your machine. Non-plug and play systems require a reboot if you change the system font.

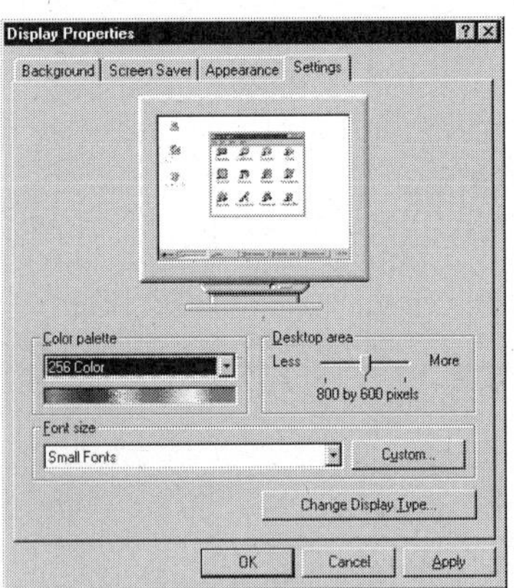

Figure 10.14.
You can change your display resolution by using the controls on the Settings page.

Windows 95 provides another new feature that you should look at if the fonts provided by Microsoft don't quite fit the bill. You can click the Custom button to display the dialog box shown in Figure 10.15. This dialog box enables you to create a custom-size system font. This is a very handy feature to have if you need a font that's either very large or very small. Normally, you'll want to use the standard sizes that come with Windows.

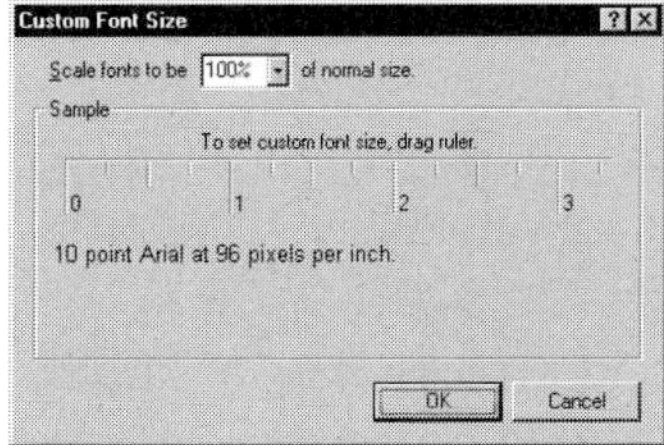

Figure 10.15.
Windows 95 enables you to use custom font sizes to optimize your display's appearance.

Another button, familiar from Chapter 4, can be used to check the results of adding a new monitor to your system. I won't go through this particular part of this display settings again here, because they only change the monitor and display adapter type.

Refresh Rate

This isn't a standard page, but it's one that you'll see often enough that I wanted to describe it for you. Ergonomics has taken the world by storm and it's not difficult to figure out why. Repetitive stress injuries and eye damage are major cause for concern. The Refresh Rate page (see Figure 10.16) shows one way that you can protect your eyes. It enables you to set the refresh rate of your display adapter higher. A high refresh rate is easier on the eyes than a low one.

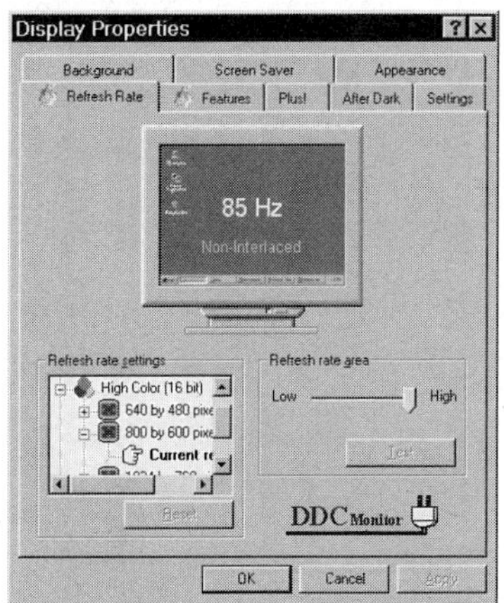

Figure 10.16.
The Refresh Rate page is fairly common today, although it's still a specialty feature of your display adapter.

Of course, this page begs the question of why you shouldn't just set your display adapter to the highest refresh rate all the time. There are three good reasons for adding a control. The first is heat. A high refresh rate creates more heat within the computer chassis. On a hot summer day you may decide to give your computer a break and turn the refresh rate down. Another problem is lighting—especially fluorescent lighting. You may actually find that the highest refresh rate available is also the one that interacts with the lighting the most. The resulting strobe effect can cause all kinds of problems, not the least of which is a severe headache. Multiple refresh rates allow you to choose something that works with your environment. Some monitors also won't work with the highest refresh rate available from your display adapter. Having a switch means that you might not have to upgrade your system as quickly as before.

System Setup

You can quickly access the System Properties dialog box from the desktop by right-clicking My Computer and selecting the Properties option. I discuss this particular dialog box in detail in Chapters 2 and 3, so I won't go into its features again. You learn some ways to use this particular dialog box to assist in fixing hardware-related problems in Chapter 26.

Clock

We took a quick look at the clock earlier when talking about the Taskbar. Unlike the clock utility provided with Windows 3.x, this clock affects the way in which the system reacts. You can actually use it to affect the CMOS setting and, therefore, the time stamp on all your files. Of course, it will also affect any events that you might schedule and anything else that relies on the clock.

The clock properties consist of a single check box in the Taskbar Properties dialog box named Show Clock. The only thing this entry does is either display or not display the clock on the Taskbar. In most cases, you'll want to display the clock because there's nothing to be gained from shutting it off.

Tip: When you display the clock, it shows only the current time. You can use the mouse cursor to also display the date. Move the mouse cursor over the clock icon for a few seconds and the clock will display the current date.

Double-clicking the clock icon displays the dialog box shown in Figure 10.6. This is the same dialog box that the Help button activates. It contains a calendar and a clock. You use them to change the system settings.

The second page of this dialog box, Time Zone, allows you to change the current area of the world (see Figure 10.17). It's the same dialog box you saw when you completed the installation of Windows 95. Setting this dialog box is self-explanatory. The daylight savings time check box allows the computer to automatically adjust the time for you.

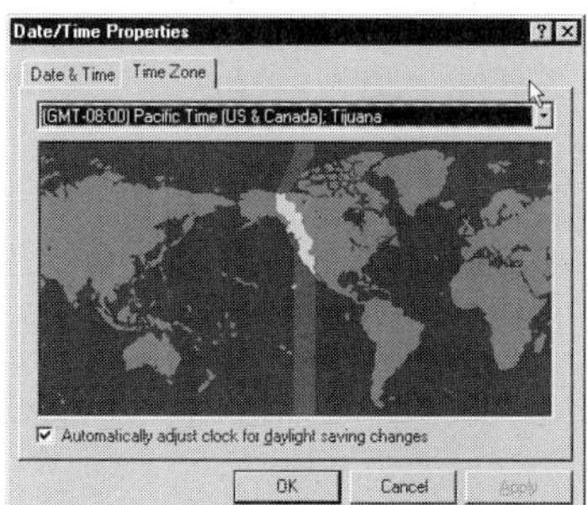

Figure 10.17.
The Time Zone page of the Date/Time Properties dialog box enables you to indicate the area of the world that you're located in.

Warning: The current version of Windows 95 has a minor bug in the way that it adjusts for daylight savings time. If you just happen to be awake at 2:00 a.m., Windows 95 will ask whether you want to reset your computer clock. Obviously, you'll want to do so, and the clock then resets to 1:00 a.m. The problem only occurs if you shut down the machine between 1:00 a.m. and 2:00 a.m. When it reaches 2:00 a.m. again, Windows 95 will reset itself. As soon as you turn on your machine the next morning, Windows 95 will ask again whether you want to reset your clock, and you'll end up being an hour behind instead of setting the clock to standard time. The bottom line is that you should make sure that you don't reset the clock before 3:01 a.m. to avoid this particular problem (or simply leave it up all night). Even though this isn't a major problem, Microsoft should still consider fixing it.

Working with Desktop Objects

Making your desktop efficient is very easy under Windows 95. The first thing you need to do is throw away those outdated application-centered ideas that Windows 3.x encouraged. You need to learn to work with data—the way you should have learned to work in the first place. After all, what's more important—the tool that creates an object or the object itself? The end result is the most important goal in working with Windows.

The following sections provide some ideas on how to arrange your desktop to make maximum use of the new Windows data-centric approach. This is not the only way to pursue the problem, but it's the way that many people are starting to work with this new product. Try this approach and then modify it to meet your needs.

We'll start by looking at the methods of moving data around. Remember that Windows 95 uses objects. Everything is an object of some sort and objects are easy to copy, cut, and paste. You can move them around just like any object in the physical world. Once we are finished looking at data movement techniques, we'll review some methods to organize that data on your desktop.

Making Copies

Many people use cutting-and-pasting to move data around. You cut the data from the place where you no longer need it and then paste it to a new location. Windows 95 also supports cut-and-paste for objects. To move a file from one location to another, cut and then paste it. The beauty of this approach is that the copy of the file is now on the Clipboard. This means that you can make as many copies of it as you want. Of course, anything you can cut, you can copy. Copying the object means that you leave the original in place and create copies where needed. Figure 10.18 shows the context menu for a folder. Notice the Copy, Cut, and Paste entries.

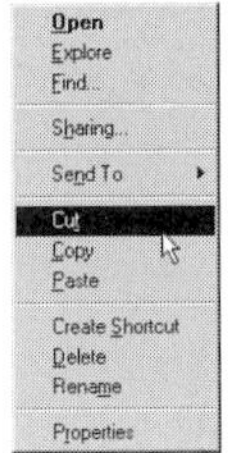

Figure 10.18.
Every object that you can copy, cut, or paste has entries for these tasks on its context menu.

Obviously, you can't paste a file on top of another file. You can, however, paste a copy of a file on the desktop or within a folder. If you take a logical, real-world approach to moving objects under Windows 95, you'll never run into problems getting objects to work.

Creating New Objects

Everywhere you can paste an existing object, you can also create a new object. The desktop, Explorer, and most Windows 95 folders have a New option on the context menu, as shown in Figure 10.19. This menu option displays a list of file types that Windows 95 can produce automatically.

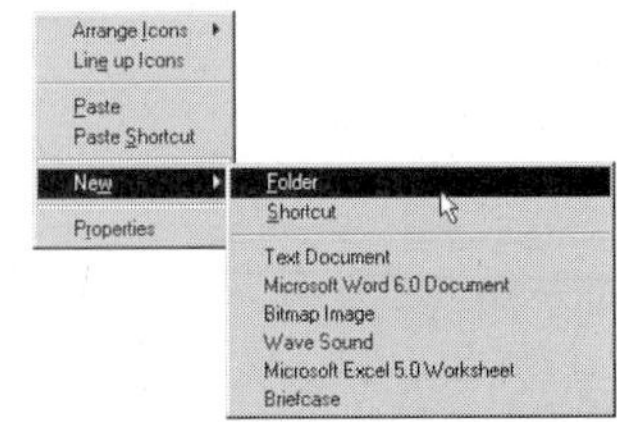

Figure 10.19.
The desktop and other storage objects enable you to create new objects by selecting the object from a list of choices on the New menu.

Notice that one of the entries is Folder. You can always place a folder within another object normally used for storage (even another folder). Using folders helps you organize your data into more efficient units. We'll see later how you can combine these elements to make your desktop an efficient place to work.

Using a Template

One of the problems with the New submenu of the context menu is that it always creates objects of a default type. Take Word for Windows. If you create a new Word for Windows object by using the selection on the context menu, that new object will use the Normal style sheet. What you really wanted was the Accounts style sheet, but there isn't a fast way to create a document by using the current system.

I got around this problem by placing a folder named "Templates" on my desktop. Inside are copies of each of the sample files that I use to create new documents. For example, if you write a lot of letters that use the same format, you might want to use your word processor to create a document that contains everything that normally appears in a letter. You then place a copy of the letter template in your Templates folder; every time you need to write another letter, right-click the template in your Templates folder and drag the template to a new destination, such as a project folder. When the context menu appears, select Copy to create a copy of your template. This template approach to creating new documents can greatly reduce the time you need to start a task. In a few seconds, you can create enough copies of a template to satisfy project needs. Using the template also means that all your settings are correct when you enter the document for the first time.

There are several ways you can use a template document. You can right-click, select Copy, right-click your project folder, and select Paste from the context menu. Another method is to drag the template with the mouse key pressed. When Windows asks what you would like to do, select Copy from the menu.

Creating Work Areas

Now that you have some idea of how to move and copy data, let's look at a more efficient way to work with it. I've started using a new method of organizing information because of the way that Windows 95 works. You can follow several easy steps to start a project:

1. Create a main project folder on the desktop.
2. Open the folder and place one folder inside for each type of data that you plan to work with. For example, when writing this chapter, I created one folder for the word-processed document, another for the electronic research information, and a third for the graphics files.

3. Open the first data folder, create a copy of your template, and then make as many copies as you'll need of that template within the data folder.
4. Rename the data files to match what they'll contain.
5. Close this data folder and repeat steps 3 and 4 for each of your other data folders.
6. Complete your project by filling each data folder.

Tip: Using a particular method of creating new data files for all your data might not work because of the way the application is designed. In other cases, as with the screen shots in this book, the data file is created in a different way. My screen shots are all captured from a display buffer. I don't need to create a blank file to hold them because the screen capture program does this for me. Always use the data-creation technique that works best with the applications you use.

Figure 10.20 shows one way to arrange your projects. It contains a main folder, a few data folders, and some notes about the project. This is still only one approach to managing your data. The trick is to find the method that works best for you—one that reflects the way in which you work.

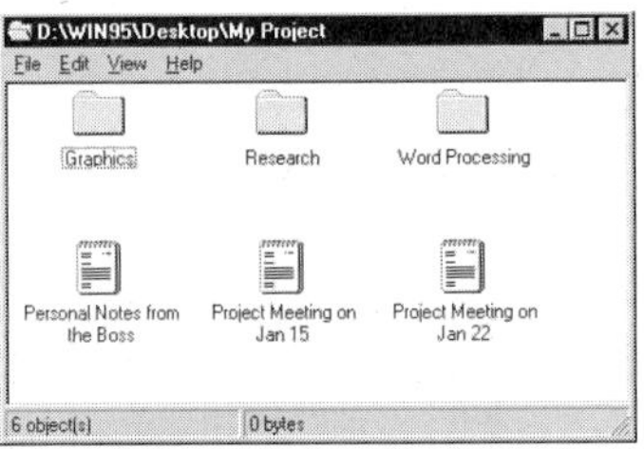

Figure 10.20.
One way to arrange your data for easy access. Windows 95 provides almost unlimited possibilities.

By now, you're wondering why you should go this route. After all, the old method of managing your data seemed to provide just about the same results as the method I've outlined. This new technique offers several advantages that you just can't obtain by using the application-centered approach:

- **Data transmittal:** Giving someone else access to a group project means sending him a folder, not a bunch of individual files. How often have you thought you had all the files for a project together, only to find that you didn't send an important file? This method of organizing data prevents such problems.
- **Application independence:** It doesn't matter which application you need to use to modify a file. If everyone in your office uses the same applications, modifying a file means double-clicking it and nothing else. You no longer need to worry about which application to open or where that application is located. All that matters is the data.
- **Location:** Where is your data? Do you ever find yourself searching for hours to find that small file you thought you lost somewhere? This method enables you to place all the data

related to a project in one place. Its physical location no longer matters once the pieces are together. You still need to know, of course, where the data is when you organize the project folder. However, would you rather look for a file once or a hundred times? Using desktop folders means that you find the data once and never worry about it again.

- **Ease of storage:** When I finish a project under Windows 95, I don't worry about putting all the bits and pieces together. I send one folder to storage. When I need to work on the project again, I know I only need to load that one folder back onto my local drive.

On Your Own

Open Explorer and check out each of the special sections talked about in this chapter. Try to identify each section and its purpose without referring to the discussion. Also, look at some of the unique capabilities provided by your machine. For example, see if there are any special applets in the Control Panel. You'll also want to check out your machine's network capabilities.

Spend some time customizing your desktop for optimum efficiency. See which wallpapers or other aesthetics you can change. Remove any features that might slow performance if you're using a memory-constrained system, and try out the screen saver and password options.

11

The Windows 95 Applets

It seems like we're always being inundated with yet another set of new words to describe something old and familiar. I was reminded of that when I started working on this chapter. What do you call the conglomeration of small utility programs and configuration utilities that an operating system needs in order to function? I've heard a variety of names, but it appears that Microsoft finally settled on *applet* as the term of choice. It makes sense when you think about it—an applet is a small application.

I cover the vast majority of the utility applets in other chapters of this book. For example, I devote quite a bit of space to the Backup applet in Chapter 9. Each of these utility applets helps you maintain, troubleshoot, or otherwise improve the system. A few even provide new features that you can use to make life easier. Because I covered most of them, I won't bore you with another rendition of the utility applets.

There's a second group of applets: Those that help you configure your computer. I also covered some of them in previous chapters, but I haven't combined them in an overview format. That's what this chapter is all about. I cover the mundane applets that you'll only use from time to time. Most of these applets are a one-shot deal. You'll generally use them when you install the operating system or change a piece of hardware.

What I'd like to do in this chapter is to provide a few ideas that could expand the potential uses for this underused resource. For example, did you know that several of these applets provide full-fledged troubleshooting modules? Few people do, because they don't really take the time to see what's available in this resource.

Configuring Windows 95 Applets

One topic I haven't covered yet is the process of installing and removing applets on your system. Part of the installation process always involves configuring the applet before you use it. For example, when you install Dial-Up Networking, Windows 95 automatically asks you for information regarding your computer setup. You can't network without a telephone number, so it makes sense that Windows 95 would ask about this information before it completes the installation process. The same reasoning holds true the first time you start Backup. Even though Windows 95 automatically takes care of the configuration, it displays a dialog box telling you that it completed the job (in this case, created a backup set of files for you). You can use the sample file as the basis for your own configuration sets. That's one of the reasons why Backup creates it for you. The other reason is that you can't perform a backup without at least some idea of what to do. This sample file can form the basis for someone to learn how Backup works.

Tip: Every applet that appears in the Control Panel has a corresponding file with a .CPL extension in the SYSTEM folder. There are times when a user may think that a particular applet disappeared, but in most cases the .CPL file became corrupted or was deleted. Administrators could simply move the .CPL files that they don't want the user to access to another directory. No .CPL file means that the user won't be able to access a particular Windows 95 configuration feature. Finally, you can double-click most .CPL files to open them. This allows you to determine the exact identity of any .CPL files on your system.

The following sections outline four different methods of installing applets on your system. The standard method that I cover initially is the one you're probably most familiar with, because it allows you to install or remove standard Windows 95 features. The "Special Utility Installation" section tells you how to install some of the extra utilities that Windows 95 provides. For example, you'll use this procedure to install the Policy Editor and other utilities that the standard user probably shouldn't know about. Be sure to read any text files provided with the utilities, because it's unlikely that you'll find sufficient documentation elsewhere. Windows 95 also provides printer utilities that help you manage this resource better when using certain types of printers. I tell you how to install them in the "Special Printer Installation" section. You'll also find that Windows 95 provides a wealth of network management tools. The installation procedure is covered in the "Special Network Installation" section. A few of the applets you can install are so specialized that Microsoft provides a special installation method for them. I was a little surprised when I finally figured out how this works. Although I can understand Microsoft's willingness to hide a nonstandard utility from a user who might not know how to use it properly, it seems to me that there should be a better way to do it. Part of the reasoning behind this four-layered approach to installation is the nature of the applets themselves. They aren't all necessarily applets in the full sense of the word, because you can't really execute them and expect something useful to happen. Some of them are halfway between a driver and an applet, whereas other types of applets work almost as TSRs, helping Windows 95 to monitor specific items of information in the background.

Make sure that you scan the Windows 95 CD-ROM. The first method we will cover installs all the floppy disk utilities. The special programs appear on the CD-ROM version of Windows in a variety of folders that don't appear on the floppy version. If you want these utilities, you need the CD-ROM version of Windows, or you can download them from their Internet site at `http://www.microsoft.com/windows95/default.asp`. Most of these specialized programs appear in the ADMIN folder. Beneath this folder are three subfolders that categorize the type of applet and make it easy to tell which of the following methods you should use to install a specific applet.

Tip: Keeping average users on your network away from some of the utilities that might damage the system could prove difficult if you give them the CD-ROM version of Windows. It doesn't take a rocket scientist to read a few text files and do some experimentation. If you really want to keep those utilities away from prying eyes, purchase the floppy disk version of Windows 95 for your network users. You don't actually have to use the floppies for an installation; you can use the network-based installation covered in Chapter 4 instead. Using a script file keeps the installation easy, but floppies will keep the installation from becoming corrupted—at least by a stray applet.

Standard Installation and Removal

You start the standard installation in the Control Panel. Double-click the Add/Remove Programs applet and select the Windows Setup page, as shown in Figure 11.1. Looking through the list of applications you can install, you'll see all the familiar utility programs that Windows provides. This list has no network administration tools, but we'll take care of that deficiency a little later.

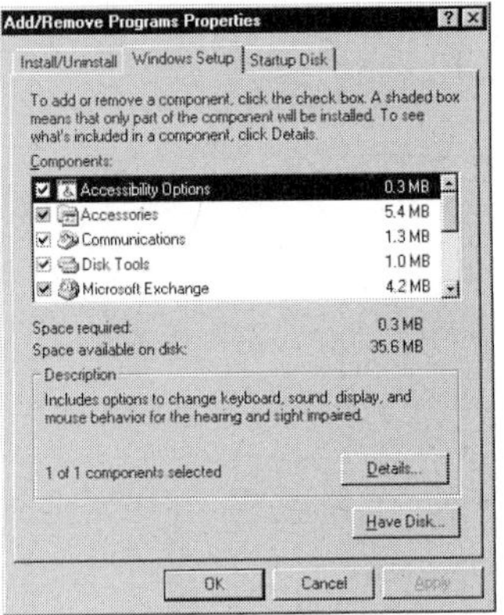

Figure 11.1.
The Add/Remove Programs applet enables you to install the standard Windows user applications.

Completing this particular installation process is easy. Simply check the items you want to install and click OK; the Add/Remove Programs applet will take care of the rest. You might need to supply a disk or two if you aren't using the CD-ROM installation; otherwise, the rest of the process should be fairly automated.

Note: Make sure that you don't accidentally uncheck any item you want to keep. The Add/Remove Programs applet will automatically uninstall any applet you uncheck. Accidentally removing something could cause problems as you frantically try to figure out what went wrong with your system.

Most of the Windows 95 applets wait until you run them the first time to either automatically detect the required configuration information or ask you to supply it. However, some of them immediately ask, because they provide a system service. For example, installing modem support requires an immediate answer because the system never knows when it will need that information.

Special Utility Installation

The CD-ROM contains some utilities that don't appear in the Add/Remove Programs dialog box. You learn that they exist by reading about them in one of the files located on the CD-ROM, or by doing a little exploring, like I did. It's surprising to see how many different utilities the CD-ROM contains. To check your CD-ROM, use Explorer's Find tool to look for .INF files. You won't find any of the installation .INF files, because they're in compressed format. It's usually safe to assume that any .INF files you see on the CD-ROM have something to do with an applet's installation routine. Figure 11.2 shows the results of my search.

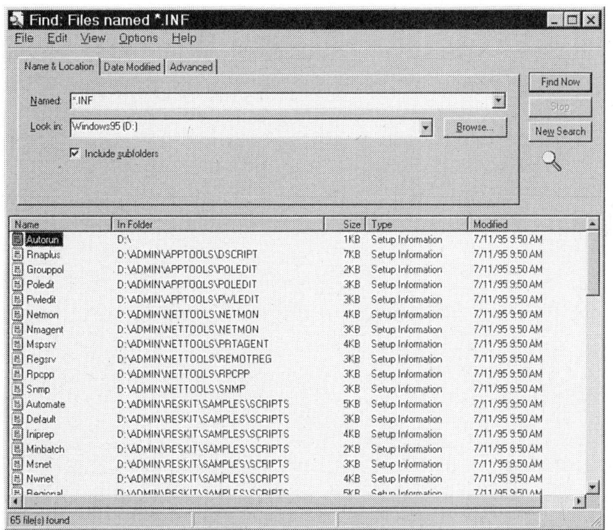

Figure 11.2.
On your CD-ROM, .INF files usually provide support for some type of applet installation routine.

Tip: Many of these applets appear in the Windows 95 Resource Kit provided in the \ADMIN\RESKIT\HELPFILE folder on your CD-ROM. Searching for the utility name by using the Explorer Find tool, especially the Containing Text field of the Advanced page, helps you find the needed information quickly. Don't be surprised if you don't see the applet listed in the online help. Some of these applets are for network administrators only, so you'll need to look at the documentation provided in the applet folder instead. Using the Resource Kit and applet documentation together should help reduce any confusion over the applet's intended use.

As you can see from Figure 11.2, my list is extensive. The CD-ROM has lots of .INF files, and it's pretty difficult to tell which ones you'd like to have installed on your machine. However, knowing that the file exists does provide some information. Many .INF files contain notes about the application they're supposed to work with. The folder that holds the .INF file and the application might also provide a README file.

Note: Hopefully, Microsoft provides better documentation for these utilities in the future. At the time of this writing, the documentation hadn't changed, so some of these utilities are only described in a single line in the Resource Kit (provided as part of the CD-ROM). You may need to do a little detective work before using any of the other utility programs.

After you decide that an applet meets your needs, you need to decide what type of installation to perform. You'll find that some of these applets are general-purpose utilities. Use the procedure described in the following steps to install them. Other applets require special installation. For example, use the section "Special Printer Installation" later in this chapter to install printer-specific applets. Likewise, use the "Special Network Installation" section for any network-related applets. Using the correct installation procedure ensures that you have a usable utility when you finish. When in doubt, use this general-purpose installation and test the application to see whether it works:

1. To perform a special utility installation, open the Control Panel and double-click the Add/Remove Programs applet. Select the Windows Setup tab.
2. Instead of choosing an applet from the list, click the Have Disk button. You should see a dialog box similar to the one in Figure 11.3.

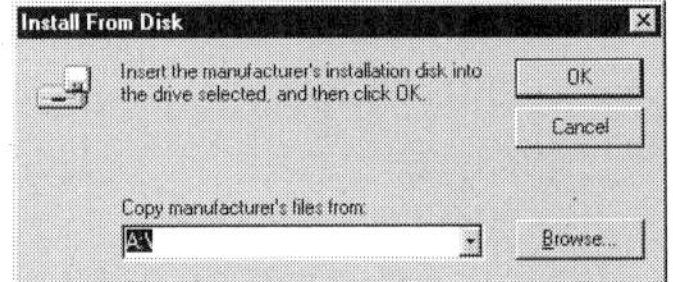

Figure 11.3.
The Install From Disk dialog box enables you to install an applet that normally doesn't appear in the Add/Remove Programs Properties dialog box.

3. Click the Browse button and use the Open dialog box to find the applet's .INF file. Double-click this file to add its name to the Copy Manufacturer's Files From field of the Install From Disk dialog box. Click OK to complete the selection process. Windows 95 will display a dialog box similar to the one shown in Figure 11.4.

Figure 11.4.
The Have Disk dialog box displays a list of any special applets that the .INF file contains.

4. Use the Have Disk dialog box to select the applets you want to install. Notice that you make the selections by using a check box.

Tip: If you find an .INF file that doesn't contain a list of applets, cancel the installation process immediately. Some .INF files on the CD-ROM don't contain applet-specific information. Fortunately, the installation won't proceed unless there are some boxes to check in the Have Disk dialog box.

5. Click the Install button to complete the installation. Windows 95 copies the required files from the CD-ROM and returns you to the Add/Remove Programs Properties dialog box. Scrolling through the list of installed components should reveal the new applets you installed. Figure 11.5 shows an example of the applets I installed using this procedure. Unchecking a box next to one of these utilities will uninstall it. This process works exactly the same as for the standard applets. Notice that these special applets use a diamond-shaped icon to differentiate them from the standard applets in the list. Any special applets that appear in the list will have this indicator.

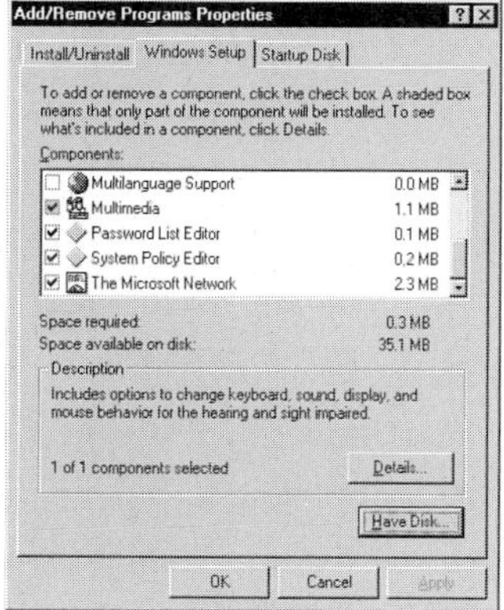

Figure 11.5.
Any new applets you install appear in the Add/Remove Programs Properties dialog box.

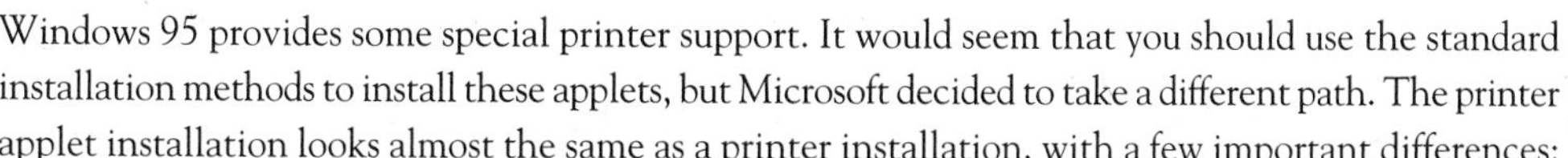

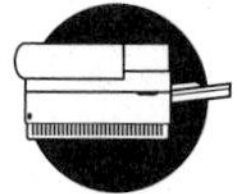

Special Printer Installation

Windows 95 provides some special printer support. It would seem that you should use the standard installation methods to install these applets, but Microsoft decided to take a different path. The printer applet installation looks almost the same as a printer installation, with a few important differences:

1. To begin the installation process, open the Printers folder and double-click the Add Printer icon. You should see the Print Wizard opening display. Click Next to go to the next screen.
2. Select Local Printer and click Next to go to the next screen. You should see the Add Printer Wizard dialog box shown in Figure 11.6.

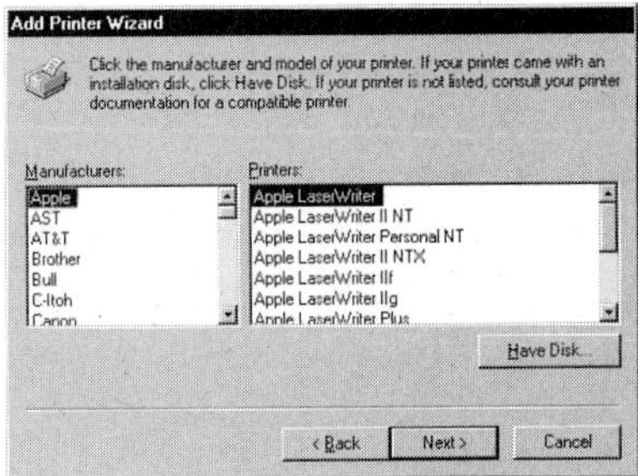

Figure 11.6.
The Add Printer Wizard dialog box enables you to add a new printer or applet.

3. Click the Have Disk button. You should see a dialog box similar to the one shown in Figure 11.3.
4. Click the Browse button and use the Open dialog box to find the applet's .INF file. Double-click this file to add its name to the Copy Manufacturer's Files From field of the Install From Disk dialog box. Click OK to complete the selection process. Windows 95 will display a dialog box similar to the one shown in Figure 11.7.

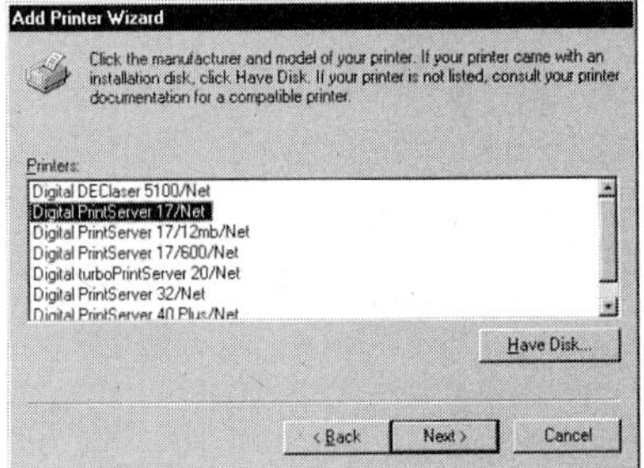

Figure 11.7.
Adding a printer resource using a disk is fairly easy under Windows 95.

5. Use the Add Printer Wizard dialog box to select the applets you want to install. Notice that the method of listing the potential resources has changed.
6. Windows 95 will copy some files to disk and then ask some additional questions based on the type of resource you want to install. Following the prompts is fairly easy and should resemble the process of adding a printer.

Special Network Installation

There are some special network administration tools on your CD-ROM. As with the printer-specific resources, you don't use the standard installation routine to add these applets to your system. The following procedure helps you perform a special network installation:

1. Open the Control Panel and double-click the Network icon. Click the Add button, select Service, and click the Add button. You should see a dialog box similar to the one in Figure 11.8.

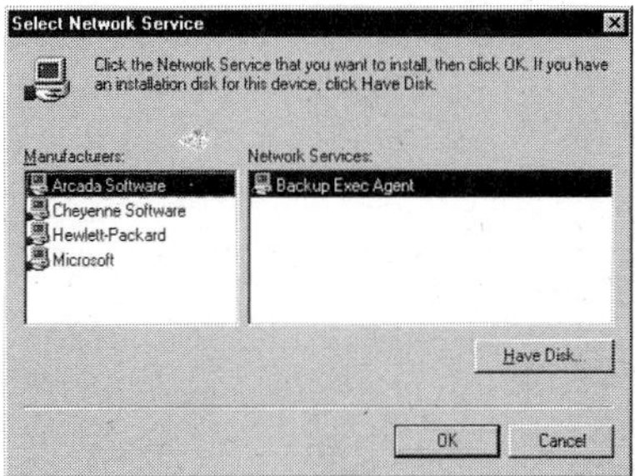

Figure 11.8.
The Select Network Service dialog box enables you to install a new network resource.

2. Click the Have Disk button. You should see a dialog box similar to the one shown in Figure 11.3.
3. Click the Browse button and use the Open dialog box to find the applet's .INF file. Double-click this file to add its name to the Copy Manufacturer's Files From field of the Install From Disk dialog box. Click OK to complete the selection process. Windows 95 will display a dialog box similar to the one shown in Figure 11.9.

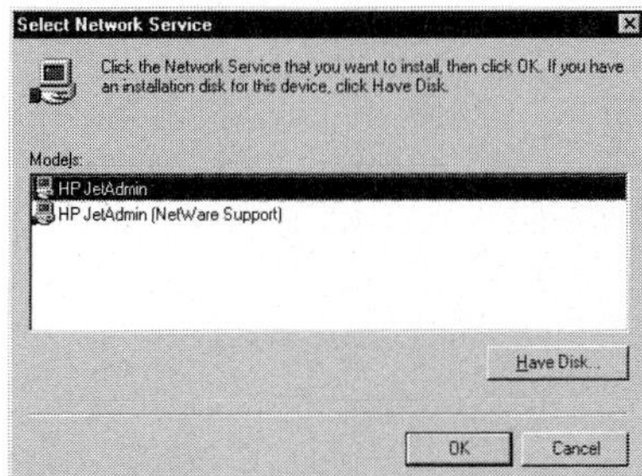

Figure 11.9.
Use this dialog box to select a special network-related resource.

4. Use the Select Network Service dialog box to select the applets you want to install. Notice that the method of listing the potential resources has changed.
5. Click OK. Windows 95 will copy some files to disk and then display the Network dialog box with a new entry added. In this case, we have added an HP LaserJet administration tool. Figure 11.10 shows the new addition.

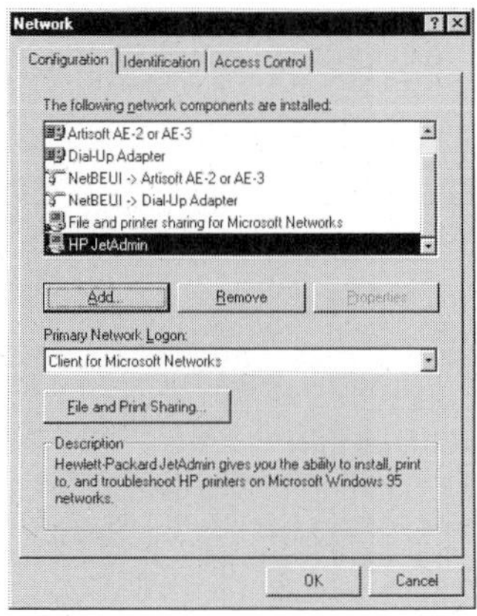

Figure 11.10.
Adding this new applet helps an administrator manage an HP LaserJet on the network.

The Control Panel

Few people become comfortable with the Control Panel. You access it to change a major hardware or software configuration item and then leave. You don't come back to it until your system needs adjustment again, and of course you don't visit the Control Panel on a daily basis.

The reason I brought up this point at the beginning of this discussion is simple: This lack of contact with the Control Panel is probably the reason why people almost forget that it's there. I've personally spent hours trying to figure out how to change some setting in there. It's not just that the Control Panel is difficult to use or illogically laid out, but too few people have experience with it.

Figure 11.11 shows a typical Control Panel setup. However, no two Control Panel setups are alike. The Control Panel usually contains a set of default icons, along with icons related to your particular system configuration. I still remember the purple Logitech Mouse icon in Windows 3.x. I didn't need it with Windows 95, so you don't see it installed.

Figure 11.11.
The Control Panel is a deep, dark secret to some people, and not very familiar to everyone else.

Now might be a good time to check out some of the applets in the Control Panel. Some of them will seem familiar because I've already talked about them elsewhere in the book, whereas others haven't been covered yet. The following list provides an overview of the Control Panel's contents:

- **Accessibility Options:** I've visited this particular applet several times. It allows you to change some Windows 95 features to make them easier to use. For example, this applet allows you to enable the StickyKeys option for the keyboard.
- **Add New Hardware:** This applet allows you to install new hardware on your system. You can choose one of two installation methods—manual or automatic. Microsoft recommends the automatic method in most cases, because it's the least error-prone (assuming that the detection program works properly).
- **Add/Remove Programs:** Adding and removing applications is easier in Windows 95, but probably not as easy as it could be. We looked at some of the difficulties of using this particular applet earlier in this chapter.
- **Date/Time:** Keeping the date and time current on your machine will become more important as your machine makes more connections to other resources. Older installations had to worry about the date and time only when it came to time-stamping files. New users rely on the clock to schedule automated tasks, keep track of appointments, and a host of other responsibilities.
- **Display:** I use this applet the most. Not only does it allow me to change my display resolution and colors with ease, but I can use it to enlarge the display fonts and change the wallpaper on the desktop. All these features add up to an incredibly flexible and easy-to-modify display system. The big surprise is that you no longer have to reboot your machine to see the effect of a change.
- **Fonts:** When I started out computing with PCs, the only font available was the one that you got in the character ROM of your printer or display adapter. Now you can quickly overwhelm your system with fonts that you'll never use. One drawing package I purchased recently included more than 500 fonts. It's no wonder that people need an applet like this one to manage their font libraries.
- **Joystick:** Few action games would be complete without joystick support, yet older versions of Windows failed to provide this feature. Windows 95 corrects this error by providing full joystick support. Not only does Windows 95 support the joystick, but this applet includes both a calibration and a testing module. It even supports advanced joysticks such as the Thrustmaster Flight Control System.
- **Keyboard:** If you've ever had to do strange things such as write entire sentences using the Character Map utility under Windows 3.x, you'll really appreciate the keyboard support under Windows 95. Now you can have more than one language available as needed. The International icon on the Taskbar allows you to choose between any of the installed keyboard layouts. This applet not only installs support for these languages, but it also provides other forms of keyboard support, such as repeat rate adjustment.

- **Mail and Fax:** If a network is installed, you probably have some type of mail module in the Control Panel. This particular applet is Microsoft-network-specific, but I'm sure that you'll find similar applets for NetWare and Banyan. Noticeably absent right now are any applets from real-mode networks such as LANtastic. Hopefully, these vendors will provide 32-bit protected-mode drivers in the near future. The Mail and Fax applet helps you configure your online connections and even the location of your address books. It's the configuration utility for Microsoft Exchange.

- **Microsoft Mail Postoffice:** The difference between this applet and the preceding one is that the Microsoft Mail Postoffice is specific to the local e-mail setup. While the Mail and Fax applet helps you make the right connections, this applet deals with the intricacies of managing a post office. You can change security levels and add new users when using this applet. Minor conflicts with Windows for Workgroups might keep you on your toes for a while (and keep you visiting this particular applet a little more than you really wanted to).

- **Modems:** Online communication is a very serious business these days. It includes services such as CompuServe and America Online, dial-up networking, and a host of other forms of communication. The Modems applet allows you to configure your modem settings for optimum performance under Windows 95. It also includes a diagnostic so that you can troubleshoot any problems that the modem might experience.
- **Mouse:** In some respects, I miss the old purple Logitech mouse sitting in my Control Panel. Not only did the Logitech applet allow me to do a few things that even the Windows 95 applet wouldn't, but it looked kind of neat, too. The purpose of this applet is to help you configure the mouse. This includes the double-click speed, other mouse-specific features, the pointers that the mouse uses, and whether Windows 95 displays mouse trails. I find the addition of pointers to Windows 95 a welcome change. The animated icons might prove bothersome on some displays, but they show up very well on the LCDs I've checked out.
- **Multimedia:** This applet controls everything related to the new sound and video features supported by Windows 95. It not only controls the drivers and their settings, but it helps you configure the interface as well. One thing you won't find here is a way to control the system sounds. Other than that, this applet is the one to check out whether there is a sound or video problem.

- **Network:** We've viewed this particular applet several times in this book so far. It's the one that allows you to install new network components or delete old ones. It's also where you set your network's password policy and how the network controls access to your resources. TCP/IP users will use this applet to configure the various addresses needed to make their network functional. This is the one place you need to go to see the overall picture of your network's current setup.

- **ODBC and ODBC32:** Anyone who deals with database management systems for very long understands the importance of this applet. It allows you to create new table connections and modify old ones. You also can see which drivers your system has available. Each ODBC applet is separate. There's one applet to manage 16-bit applications and a second applet for 32-bit applications. Unfortunately, I see this as another source of confusion. Be sure to use the correct applet for your application when changing its setup. I was surprised to see some of the 32-bit drivers listed in my 16-bit applet and vice versa. If I hadn't looked carefully, I could have made the changes using the wrong applet. Whenever you start creating configuration errors, there's a chance of data loss.

- **Passwords:** We viewed the contents of this applet at length earlier in this book. Chapter 24 provides yet another opportunity to revisit network security. Suffice it to say that this applet provides one of the ways you can control access to the network and its resources.

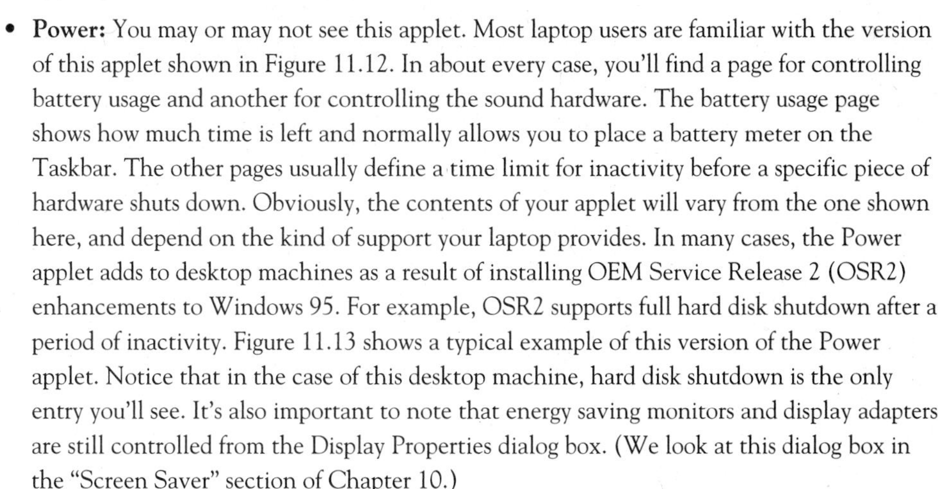

- **Power:** You may or may not see this applet. Most laptop users are familiar with the version of this applet shown in Figure 11.12. In about every case, you'll find a page for controlling battery usage and another for controlling the sound hardware. The battery usage page shows how much time is left and normally allows you to place a battery meter on the Taskbar. The other pages usually define a time limit for inactivity before a specific piece of hardware shuts down. Obviously, the contents of your applet will vary from the one shown here, and depend on the kind of support your laptop provides. In many cases, the Power applet adds to desktop machines as a result of installing OEM Service Release 2 (OSR2) enhancements to Windows 95. For example, OSR2 supports full hard disk shutdown after a period of inactivity. Figure 11.13 shows a typical example of this version of the Power applet. Notice that in the case of this desktop machine, hard disk shutdown is the only entry you'll see. It's also important to note that energy saving monitors and display adapters are still controlled from the Display Properties dialog box. (We look at this dialog box in the "Screen Saver" section of Chapter 10.)

Tip: Because OSR2 enables you to shut down both the display and the hard drive, it becomes feasible for you to leave your machine on all the time. A machine that's totally powered down will use around 20 watts—not much more power consumption than keeping a night light on all night. The positive side of this arrangement is that you reduce the amount of time it takes to get started in the morning. You also reduce wear and tear on your machine from turning it on and off. The negative side is that you may create a security hole by using this feature. Because your machine is already on and set up for use, a hacker need only figure out your screen saver password (assuming that you use one). Of course, another problem is that the disk shutdown feature may not work in some cases. For example, if you use a screen saver that accesses the hard drive, you may find that the drive won't shut down. The Power applet will keep the drive active because it thinks you're using it.

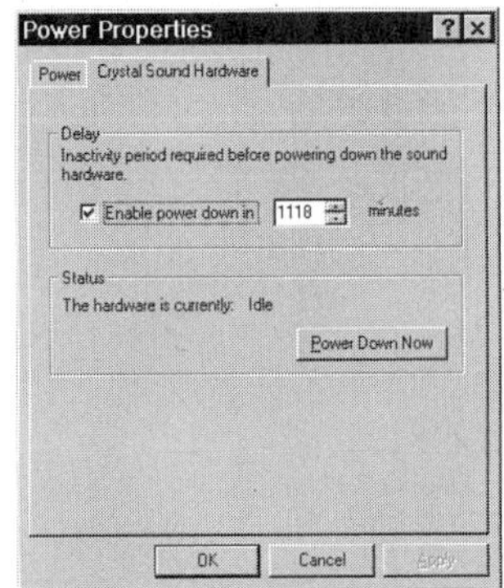

Figure 11.12.
About every laptop computer on the market sports some type of Power Properties dialog box.

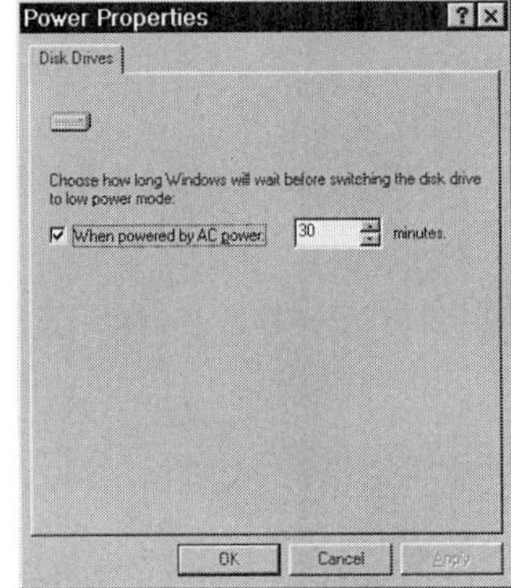

Figure 11.13.
Desktop computers recently added the Power applet to the repertoire as a result of OSR2 installation.

- **Printers:** A printer is the one item no one can do without. If you don't have a printer connected directly to your machine, there's a good chance you maintain a network connection to one. The Printers applet allows you to configure existing printers or add new ones. It also allows you to maintain control over any print jobs that the printer is processing.
- **Regional Settings:** This applet manages all of the text-formatting information required to make the output of an application correct. It includes the time zone, and you can use this applet to change the numeric, currency, time, date, and regional settings.
- **Sounds:** This is one of my favorite applets. It allows you to add a sound to almost any Windows event, and I really like the fact that Windows 95 is no longer limited in the number of events that it can monitor. The list of events will definitely change as you install and remove applications from your system.

- **System:** This applet allows you to maintain your computer as a whole; it provides access to the Device Manager. Not only is this an invaluable tool for configuring your system, but it also acts as a troubleshooting aid. Even though you don't receive specific feedback, Device Manager at least lets you know which card is bad. This applet also enables you to enhance system performance and displays a list of things that you can do to enhance it.

Your setup might have more or fewer applets than mine did, but this list should give you a good idea of what the common applets do. If you have a few additional icons, the vendor documentation should tell you what types of configuration tasks you can use them for. Returning to the Logitech mouse example, the applet associated with this device allows you to change the way the mouse behaves. More specifically, you could assign a macro to an unused key. I always used my middle mouse button for pasting and my right mouse button for cutting. Fortunately, Windows 95 has removed some of the need for this additional applet.

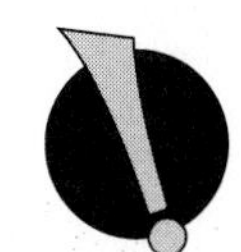

Warning: Some applications insist on installing a custom applet in the Control Panel. In most cases, Windows 95 ignores any incompatible applets that it doesn't need to work with the hardware or software you installed. If you have a situation where the old driver loads and affects system stability, call the vendor and see whether there's an easy way to remove the applet. In most cases, you can eliminate the problem by deleting a few lines of text from SYSTEM.INI.

What other kinds of applets can you expect to see in the Control Panel? This is limited only by the types of applications and hardware you install. A few examples include a digitizer pad, CAS-compliant fax, and data-capture boards. You'll probably see special applets for certain types of network connections. Most mail packages require an entry here. It's surprising to note that applications such as Lotus 1-2-3 might place an applet here to manage their data connections. (Most applications use ODBC now, so you'll see more options in the ODBC applet, rather than more applets.)

Customizing Icon Displays

Some people fail to realize that the Control Panel is another form of Explorer—albeit a somewhat specialized form. You saw how to access the Control Panel from Explorer in Chapter 10. The display even looked the same as the other displays, and there was nothing strange about Explorer's ability to interact with the Control Panel.

What that chapter really showed you was all the similarities. There are also a few differences between a standard Explorer interface and the Control Panel. I think the most obvious difference is that you can't manipulate Control Panel objects the same way you can other objects. The context menu shown in Figure 11.14 reveals this fact. Notice that about the only thing you can do with a Control Panel object is open it or create a shortcut; even the Properties option is grayed out.

There are other display differences, too. A standard Explorer display and the Control Panel provide four different methods of displaying objects. However, when it comes to arranging these objects, you have only two choices, as shown in Figure 11.15. In actuality, you'll probably never even rearrange these icons. There are so few to look at that most people leave them the way they are.

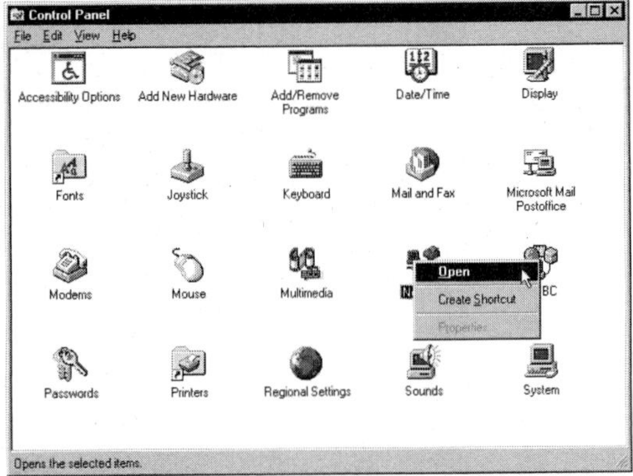

Figure 11.14.
Objects in the Control Panel don't provide much flexibility through the context menu.

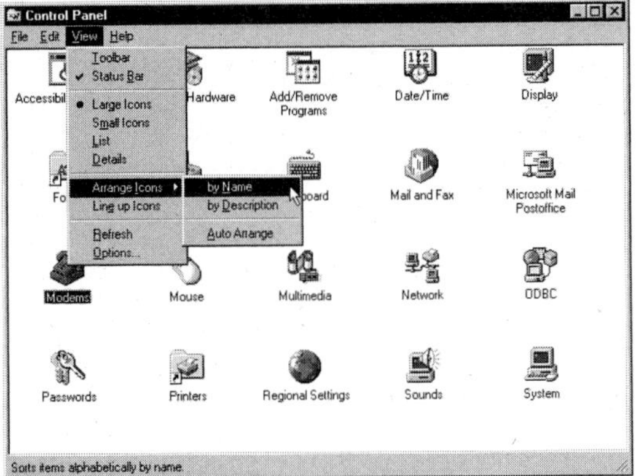

Figure 11.15.
The methods that you can use to arrange Control Panel objects are fairly limited.

Refer again to Figure 11.15. Did you notice the Refresh option? Every time you add a new application or piece of hardware and want to see whether it added a new Control Panel icon, you can use this command to refresh the display. Unlike Explorer, closing the Control Panel might not force it to display any new icons you add, so using this command ensures that you receive an accurate picture.

If you leave the Control Panel alone, you might never see some of the nice features it provides. Use the View | Details command to change the way in which the Control Panel icons are displayed. Normally, you would see a list of files, their date of last modification, size, and so forth. Figure 11.16 tells a completely different story. As you can see, the Control Panel displays a description of each of the applets instead of simply showing their statistics. This is a very handy feature if you ever see an applet that you can't figure out.

I never thought I'd use the Control Panel's shortcut option either, but I did. After reading the past few pages, you've probably figured out that there's no fast method to access all the applets in the Control Panel. You can right-click the desktop and change your display settings. Right-clicking the My Computer icon grabs the System applet for you, but what if you want to change your system sounds? You must go to the Start menu or use some other means to bring up the Control Panel and then the applet.

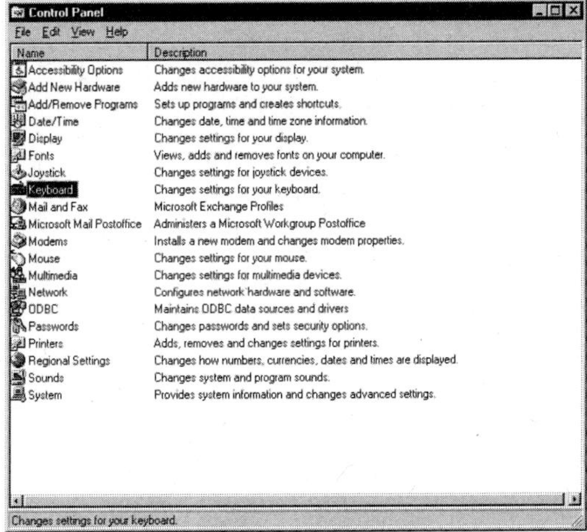

Figure 11.16.
Descriptive information about each applet is about the last thing you'd expect to see in a Details view, yet here it is.

Placing a shortcut to the applet on the desktop is one of the best ways to optimize your setup. Just think: Anytime you needed to change your system sounds (or any other configuration item), you'd only need to double-click the icon on the desktop. The problem is in how to create the shortcut. If you use the context menu entry, Windows will either ignore you or display an error message saying that it can't create the shortcut.

To make this task a little easier, right-click the applet and drag it to wherever you want the shortcut to appear. When you release the mouse button, Windows displays the context menu for you to select the Create Shortcut Here option.

Tip: Don't become icon-happy. Crowding your desktop with unneeded icons is one sure way to decrease efficiency. Instead of spending your time working, you'll spend it looking for the icon you need. Try to keep the number of icons on your desktop to 5 or 10. Any more than that and you'll start crowding yourself out.

Accessing the Control Panel from the Command Line

Trying to access the Control Panel from the command line might seem like a pretty strange idea. How would you do it? The process of opening the Control Panel from the command line is fairly easy. Type **`START CONTROL`** at the command prompt (you could also type **`CONTROL`**, but that seems to destabilize the system for some reason). Microsoft provided the `START` command to regulate access to Windows applications from DOS.

Of course, once you arrive at the Control Panel, you can do anything you normally would and then exit to DOS. The whole idea behind this command-line access is to promote continuous work flow. Have you ever had someone come into your office and disturb you right in the middle of a thought? Trying to retrieve that thought can be pretty frustrating. Interruptions come in all sizes. It doesn't have to be a person who interrupts you; it could be the interface that you use. When you need to stop what you're doing, think about another task, and then resume the first task later, you've experienced an interruption. Using this new technique means that you can move from one task to another without interruption. I think you'll find this new method a lot faster.

On Your Own

Open the Control Panel and check its contents against the list of standard applets in this chapter. Does your Control Panel contain additional applets? Open any additional applets to see whether you can figure out what purpose they serve. If there's a Help or About button, click it to see what kind of information it provides.

Try using the START command to open the Control Panel from the DOS prompt. Do you notice any differences in the Control Panel's contents? Exit the Control Panel and reopen the DOS session. Try using the various switches that we talked about in Chapter 5 to open the Control Panel. What effect do they have?

If OSR2 is installed on your machine, see whether there is a drive shutdown page in the Power applet. Set the drive shutdown time to match that for the Shut Off Monitor field on the Screen Saver page of the Display Properties dialog box. Make sure that you also disable any screen saver that requires access to the hard drive.

12 DDE, OLE, and ActiveX

Dynamic data exchange (DDE) and object linking and embedding (OLE) are both methods for sharing data between documents. In most cases (unless you have special software), the documents have to be accessible from the local machine. Of the two, DDE is older. There are actually two versions of OLE. Windows 95 supports the newer OLE 2 standard, but that doesn't mean that your applications will. A lot of people know what the acronym means—perhaps they even use OLE from time to time—but they can't understand what all the hubbub is about. After all, it's just another form of cut-and-paste—or is it? The first thing you need to understand about OLE is that it's not just cut-and-paste. In most of the chapters in this book, I talk about the objects that Windows 95 uses to make life simpler for the user. Would it surprise you too much to learn that these objects are a form of OLE support?

A problem with OLE is that it's pretty much limited to documents that you can access from the local machine. In addition, you have to rely on the local hardware to perform any required object processing. That brings us to the third entry in the title of this chapter, ActiveX. It relies on a new kind of OLE technology called DCOM (distributed component object model). OLE 2 uses COM (component object model) as the basis for creating compound documents—ones that contain other objects. When you embed or link an object by using OLE, COM is the underlying technology that makes this possible. As the DCOM acronym implies, this is a form of object that resides not only on the local machine, but anywhere on the network. In other words, a compound document could consist of objects created in a variety of places.

So why is DCOM important? It's the basis for new Internet-based technologies such as the ActiveX controls used with Internet Explorer 3.0. It's also the technology that allows people to create Internet Information Server add-ons that execute only on the server. The most common use for DCOM today is on the Internet, where people want to share data over the World Wide Web. Tomorrow you'll see DCOM embedded into Windows 95 itself and used for a variety of purposes, even data sharing on your local network. However, the most important contribution that DCOM can make is distributed processing of data.

Let's talk a little more about objects in the OLE and ActiveX sense of the word. Objects (not object orientations) can really make your documents easier to use and maintain, if you use them correctly. At first it will seem as if there are a lot of rules to follow, but once you learn the rules of the road you'll find that you can create very complex documents in a lot less time, and with far better results than before. (The benefits that you'll receive vary widely, so I'll cover those in the information-specific sections of the chapter.)

Let's get one of the ground rules out of the way. OLE isn't the technology to use on a simple document. If the only thing you plan to do is create a word-processed memo or some other small document, you're probably right in thinking that OLE is a waste of time. However, the more complex the document becomes, the greater the benefit of using OLE. Likewise, you won't want to use the vast capabilities of ActiveX unless Internet support or at least intranet support is important to you.

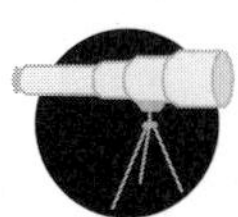

Looking Ahead: We look at the Internet in quite a bit of depth in this book. Check out Chapter 21 if you want to know about getting online. Chapter 22 will help you design a Web page. Finally, Chapter 23 looks at the ways in which you can use Personal Web Server. Be sure to take a close look at the section "What Is an Intranet?" for a better understanding of what this term means.

Compound Documents: The Microsoft Strategy

Let's look at a bit of terminology before going much further. You need to speak the language of OLE to really understand it. The following list defines some of the terms you'll see in this chapter (and those that follow):

- **Client:** This term refers to the application that holds the linked or embedded object. For example, if you place a spreadsheet object in your word-processed document, the word processor becomes the client. The differentiation between client and server used to be pretty easy to figure out. We'll see later on that ActiveX technology has created some subtle changes in the way that clients appear. With the advent of Active Document, the application you see as a client may actually be just a frame for another application beneath. The idea of a container within a container isn't new, but ActiveX makes it easier to see.
- **Server:** The server is the application that the client calls to manipulate an object. Embedded or linked objects are still in the native format of the application that created them. A client must call on the originating application to make any required changes to the object's content. What you really have is two applications working together to create a cohesive document. When using OLE, it's usually assumed that the server resides on the local machine. For example, when you embed an Excel spreadsheet into a Word document, you need to have both applications on your machine. When using ActiveX, the server need not exist on the local machine (though it does help improve response time, in some cases). For example, if a programmer develops an ActiveX extension for Internet Information Server, the actual processing occurs on the server, not your local machine. The server always returns data in a form that the local application can accept.
- **Compound document:** This is a document that contains one or more objects. Every OLE document is considered a compound document. We take a better look at what this means a little later in this chapter.
- **Object:** An object is a piece of data that you move from one application to another in its native format. You can create objects from any data if the originating application supports OLE. This is the big difference between an object and cutting-and-pasting. You can do a lot more with an object because it contains intelligence that a simple piece of text doesn't.

- **Object menu:** We'll take another look at how to use this particular OLE menu later. Suffice it to say that this is the menu you use to change the contents of an OLE document, convert it, or perform any other operations that the object allows.
- **Container:** An object that holds other objects. Visualizing a folder like the ones used by Explorer will give you a good idea of what a container represents. However, instead of simply holding files like a folder, an OLE container can hold any kind of object.

Now that you have some idea of what these OLE terms mean, we can take a look at some examples. I cover ActiveX examples in the later section "ActiveX—An Internet Strategy." In this section, we look at OLE. I used Microsoft Paint and WordPad for my example so that you could follow along if you want. It isn't really necessary to do so; the important thing is that you understand the process.

The first thing I did was double-click a .BMP file—Honeycomb—in the main Windows folder. Then I opened a copy of WordPad. You should see something similar to Figure 12.1. There isn't anything particularly special about these two applications, but they do both support OLE 2. This will allow me to show you some of the things you can look forward to.

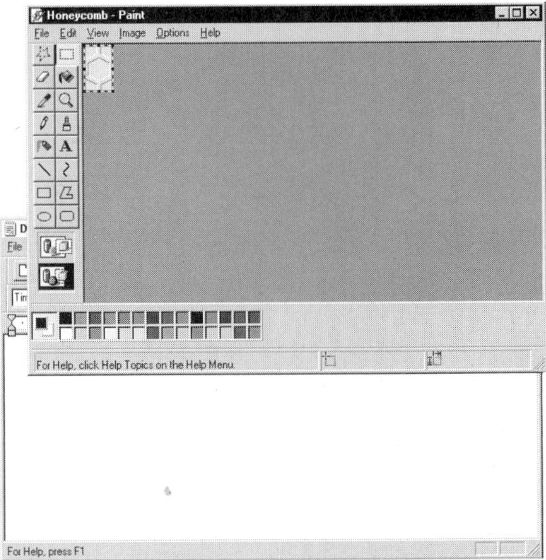

Figure 12.1.
Using OLE starts with something as simple as opening two applications.

Use the Edit | Select All command in Paint to select the entire image, and then right-click it. You should see the object menu shown in Figure 12.2. Notice that you can't drag and drop this image because Paint doesn't support that particular OLE 2 feature. If it did support drag and drop, you could simply right-click the object and drag it where you wanted it to go in WordPad. We'll need to take a somewhat longer route.

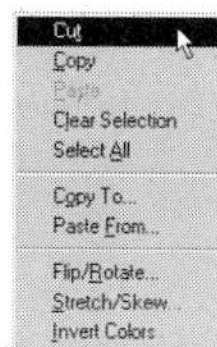

Figure 12.2.
This object menu contains options that allow you to place the object on the Clipboard.

The object menu allows you to cut or copy the image. Notice the number of other editing options this menu contains. You might want to make note of what's available and compare it to the object menu after copying the image to WordPad. For right now, select the Copy option to place a copy of the object on the Clipboard.

Note: You could use the Edit | Paste Special command in place of the object menu when working with WordPad (or another application that provides this feature). In fact, some applications don't provide an object menu, so you have to resort to using the Edit menu. I demonstrate this method of linking or embedding an object later in this book.

Click WordPad to bring it forward. Right-click anywhere within the window. You should see an object menu similar to the one in Figure 12.3. Notice how this menu differs from the one in Paint. Each object menu has features that are unique to that application. A graphics application needs menu entries to help it manipulate graphic images. A word processor needs a different set of options to manipulate text.

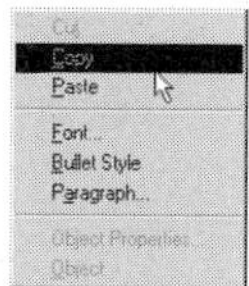

Figure 12.3.
The WordPad object menu differs from the one found in Paint because it needs to perform different work.

Select the Paste option from WordPad's object menu. You should see a copy of the graphic image in WordPad, as shown in Figure 12.4. The first thing you should notice is the sizing handles around the image. These handles allow you to enlarge or shrink the object as needed. This feature is really handy in some cases. For example, when I need to draw a logo, I usually draw it very large. That way, I can get it done quickly without worrying too much about detail. When I paste the logo into a document, I shrink it to the size I need it to be. Voilà—instant detail. As you shrink the graphic, it actually gains some amount of detail that you normally wouldn't get if you drew the image that size.

Now that the image is stored in WordPad, go ahead and close Paint. We can always open it back up if we need it later. If you right-click the graphic object, you'll see a menu similar to the WordPad object menu that you saw earlier. Notice the two bottom options, Bitmap Image Object and Object Properties. Highlight Bitmap Image Object to display a submenu.

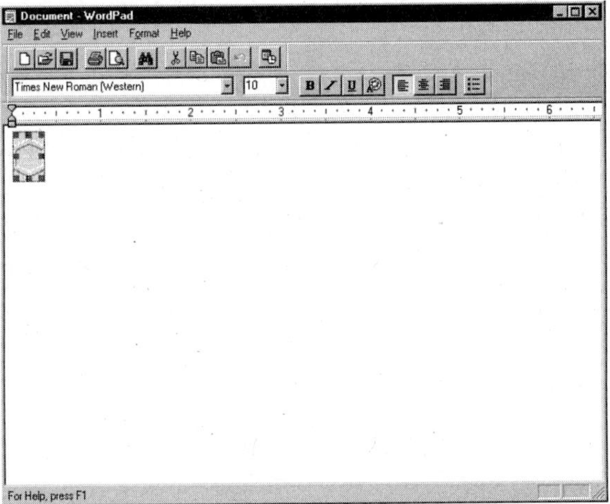

Figure 12.4.
The pasted object always provides sizing handles when you select it.

There are two options: Edit and Open. The difference between them is distinct. You select Edit if you want to perform in-place editing. The Open option actually opens a copy of Paint with which you can edit the graphic. To see what I mean, select Edit now. You should see a display similar to the one in Figure 12.5. You should notice quite a few changes. For one thing, there's a hatched box around the object. This is an OLE 2 way of telling you which object you're currently editing. Also notice that the toolbar and menus changed to match those of Paint. This is what I mean by in-place editing. The window didn't change, but the tools did, to meet the editing needs of the object.

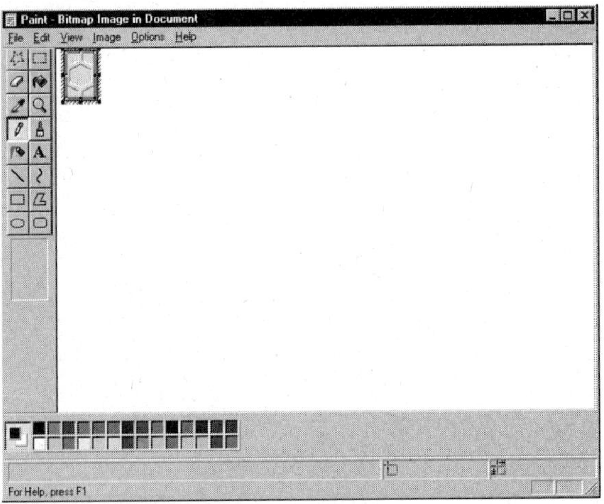

Figure 12.5.
In-place editing is one of the OLE 2 features.

You can click anywhere outside the object to restore the original WordPad menu and toolbar. This time, select the Open option to see what happens. You should see a display similar to the one in Figure 12.6. This figure provides you with some visual cues. The most obvious is the fact that you're editing the graphic object outside WordPad, using the originating application. The method you use is largely dependent on personal taste, because the end result of using either method is the same. The advantage of using the in-place method is that you remain in the same window all the time. This tends to increase efficiency and reduce the chance of losing your train of thought. The Open method has the advantage of returning you to the native editing environment. If I chose to edit one of my logos instead of opening it, I would have to perform in-place editing on a much smaller version of my original picture. Of course, I could always resize it to its original state, but that would be as inefficient as any other method—perhaps more so. Notice also that the object is hatched over in WordPad. This is another visual cue telling you which object you're editing externally.

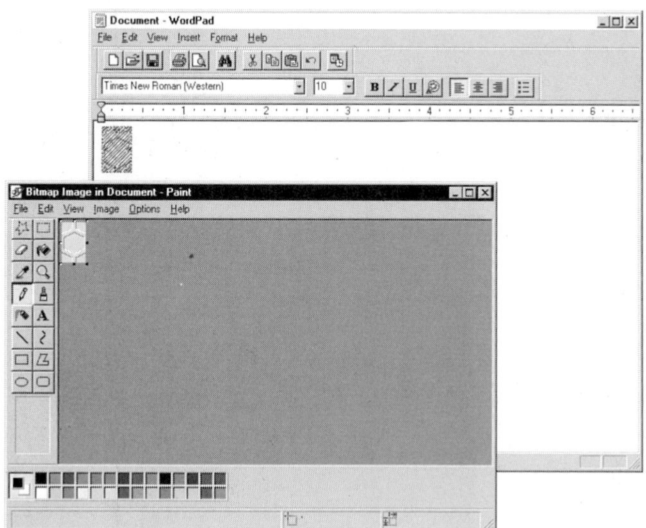

Figure 12.6.
The Open option produces an entirely different result than Edit does.

The Open method does require one extra step. You need to tell Paint to update the copy of the graphic that's still in WordPad. Choose File | Update Document, as shown in Figure 12.7. Notice how this option replaces Save. In essence, the update process does save the graphic. The only difference is where the graphic is saved.

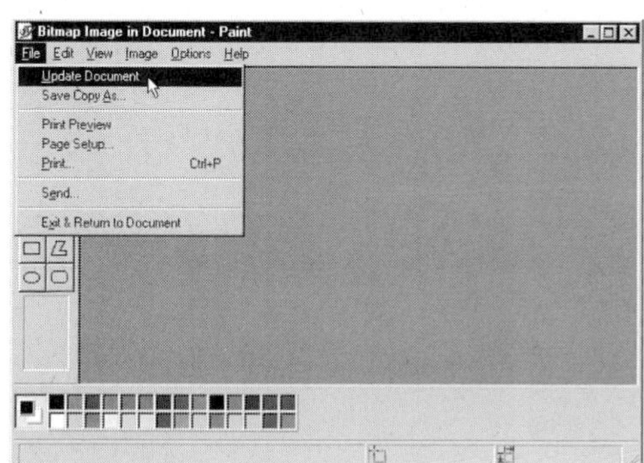

Figure 12.7.
Be sure to update your document before you leave the server application.

Exit Paint and return to WordPad. Notice that the Exit entry on the File menu now says Return to Document. Now it's time to see what that other object menu entry contains. Right-click the graphics object and select the Object Properties option. You should see the Bitmap Image Properties dialog box shown in Figure 12.8. About the only interesting entry on the General page is the Convert button. Clicking this displays another dialog box with a list of conversion options. In essence, this option allows you to convert the graphic object from one file type to another. This page also displays the file size and type.

Figure 12.8.
The General page of the Bitmap Image Properties dialog box provides access to the Convert dialog box.

Note: Each object type provides a unique set of pages in the object dialog box. It's important to remember that each dialog box reflects a combination of the capabilities of the server applications and the needs of the data file format. Some file formats can't support some application features. As a result, some options might appear grayed out.

Click the View tab. You'll see the View page of the Bitmap Image Properties dialog box, shown in Figure 12.9. This page has several interesting entries. The first is the radio button that determines whether the image is displayed as a graphic or an icon. You can make your machine run faster and use less memory if you select the icon option. Using an icon means that Windows doesn't need to load the actual image or the application required to support it unless you decide to edit the image. Windows will suggest a default icon, but you can use the Change Icon button to select another.

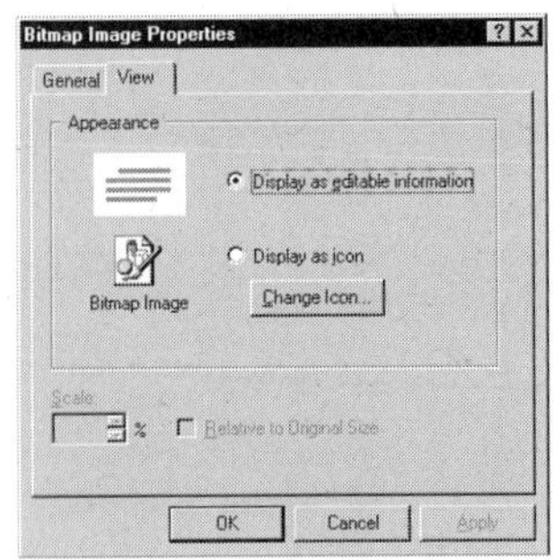

Figure 12.9.
The View page of the Bitmap Image Properties dialog box allows you to change the appearance of the object.

The bottom part of this dialog box is fairly interesting too, even if you can't select it at the moment. It allows you to select a precise scale to use when displaying your graphic. The .BMP format and application used to display it don't support the scaling option in this particular case. Close WordPad; we don't need it anymore, for now. You don't have to save the image unless you want to.

This was a whirlwind tour of some of the things you can look forward to with OLE 2. Of course, we haven't even come close to exercising every feature yet. Now it's time to take a step back into the past to examine some of OLE's roots. The next section talks a bit about DDE before we go on with our discussion of OLE.

Data Exchange: A Static Solution

"The King is dead; long live the King!" I just had to say that. A lot of people have the mistaken idea that DDE is dead. Oh, it used to be the way to transfer data between applications, but OLE is the way to go today. There's only one thing I want to say. If DDE is so dead, why does it keep popping up in the Registry? Even Explorer, an application designed for Windows 95, provides DDE capability. The fact is that every OLE application uses a little DDE to make it run. I use the term *uses* here instead of *used* because OLE 2 might actually make DDE a thing of the past, but we'll look at that later.

Now that I have your attention, let's look at DDE a bit. There are some significant problems with using DDE. The most significant of these is that it creates a static link, much like the one you get using cut-and-paste. The fact that it provides a stable macro language that you can use to open files and perform other fancy maneuvers from the command line doesn't change much.

DDE is a messaging protocol. It sends a message from one application to another and asks it to do something. Originally, DDE was supposed to provide the means to open another application and copy some data to the Clipboard. You could also get it to do other chores such as printing files. A DDE macro contains part DDE and part application macro language. This is another problem with using it. Not only do you need to learn the native language of the application you're using and DDE itself, but you also have to learn the macro language for the server application. Needless to say, DDE didn't get the kind of reception that Microsoft originally hoped it would. DDE is simply too hard for the average user to consider using. In fact, even some programmers find it difficult to use (unless they use it on a regular basis).

Just to give you an idea of how difficult DDE can be to understand, here's a short macro that I created for Lotus 1-2-3. DDE is anything but user-friendly. I've seen low-level languages that provide more information than this. All this application does is place a copy of LEAVES.BMP into a Word document. The amazing thing is that I actually got this to work. In essence, Lotus 1-2-3 is controlling Word.

```
{LAUNCH "D:\WIN\WINWORD\WINWORD"}
{DDE-OPEN "WINWORD","SYSTEM"}
{DDE-EXECUTE "[InsertObject .IconNumber = 0, .FileName = ""D:\WIN95\LEAVES.BMP"",
➥.Link = 1, .DisplayIcon = 0, .Tab = ""1"", .Class = ""Paint.Picture"",
```

```
➥.IconFilename = """", .Caption = ""LEAVES.BMP""]"}
{DDE-EXECUTE "[CharLeft 1, 1]"}
{DDE-EXECUTE "[EditBookmark .Name = ""DDE_LINK1"", .SortBy = 0, .Add]"}
{SELECT A1}
{LINK-CREATE "LINK1";"Word.Document.6";"Document1";"DDE_LINK1";"Picture";"Automatic"}
{LINK-ASSIGN "LINK1";"A:A1"}
```

The first line of this mini-application launches Word for Windows. DDE sends a message to Explorer, telling it to start Word. Once Explorer completes this task, it sends a completion message back to the DDE server. The next line opens Word as a DDE server. Even though Word is running, the DDE server won't know it exists until it gets a message from your application. The third, fourth, and fifth lines are the most difficult to understand. The short version is that they tell Word to insert a copy of LEAVES.BMP into the current document. The sixth line tells Word to highlight the image, just as you would by clicking it with the mouse. The seventh line creates a bookmark. Now, you might wonder why we would do all this just to assign a bookmark to an object embedded in Word, but you'll find out in a second. The eighth line places the Lotus 1-2-3 cursor in the upper-left corner. The next line is very important. It assigns the object we created in Word to a link in Lotus 1-2-3. The final line makes that link a reality.

By now you're asking yourself why I would go through all that trouble just to link a .BMP file to a Lotus 1-2-3 worksheet. To answer that question, you'll have to experiment a little. I think you'll find it pretty tough to create the same kind of link that the DDE procedure performs, without performing this procedure manually. Just try it sometime. OLE doesn't provide all the features necessary to create every type of link you'll need, and it certainly doesn't allow you to create those links as part of a macro or program. (OLE automation should change that in the future, but it isn't here today.) The automatic method allows me to place logos in my worksheets with a minimum of effort. As you can see, learning DDE is a requirement if you plan to create automated links in macros and other types of programs.

You normally don't need to worry about the vagaries of DDE programming when using OLE. In fact, the first example in this chapter showed what a typical OLE session is like. The DDE section showed you what goes on in the background—the part of OLE you don't normally see. I don't want to get into all the fine points of OLE programming here. However, if you really do want to get started in OLE programming, you'll need a copy of the OLE SDK from Microsoft. The package you'll get includes a heavy-duty CD and a rather large and cumbersome book. The fine points of OLE programming are so esoteric that I really doubt that anyone understands all of them completely.

Linking Versus Embedding

We saw the object part of Object Linking and Embedding earlier. There was no doubt that what we were working with was an object, not merely a cut-and-paste example of the graphic. Now it's time to take a look at the linking and embedding part of the picture.

Peter's Principle: A Time to Link and a Time to Embed

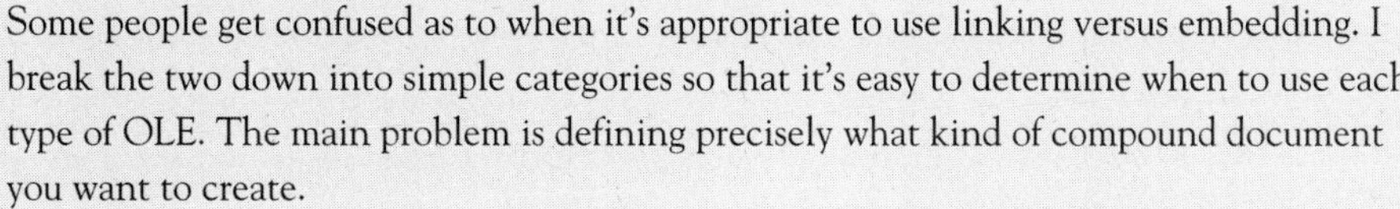

Some people get confused as to when it's appropriate to use linking versus embedding. I break the two down into simple categories so that it's easy to determine when to use each type of OLE. The main problem is defining precisely what kind of compound document you want to create.

Embedding works best when you need to share a file with a lot of people. If the compound document is going to move around, you'll want to package it in such a way that nothing gets lost. An embedded object meets this criterion. Even though embedding is less subject to data loss, it does have a disadvantage: You can't easily share with other people the data embedded within your document.

On the other hand, linking does work well in this instance. If you plan to use the same file in more than one place, linking is the route to go. I almost always use this technique instead of embedding when working with logos.

When you link a document, you are, in essence, creating a pointer to that file on disk. Think of a link as a road sign pointing to your house. As long as you don't move the house, everyone will be able to find it, because the road sign will point them there. But what happens if you do move the house? The sign still points to where it thinks your house is, but anyone who follows the sign will find nothing but an empty foundation.

The same principle holds true for links in compound documents. The link works fine as long as you don't move the document. The second you do move the document, you break the links. Of course, you can always reestablish the links, but that's a waste of time when not moving the file in the first place would require a lot less work.

OLE 1 had a significant problem in this regard because it noted the location of the linked file in precise terms. It would be the same as using your complete address to tell someone how to get to your house. Again, if you moved, the address information would do them little good. OLE 2 takes a different approach. Instead of using a precise location, it uses a relative direction. For example, what if you told your friends that you lived two blocks south of Joe? As long as you and Joe always lived two blocks apart, people would be able to find your house. (Of course, they would need to know the location of Joe's house.)

Embedding is a different process from linking. Instead of creating a pointer to your data, embedding actually places the data object within the compound document. This means that wherever the compound document goes, the data will follow. This sounds like a great fix for the problems with linking. However, embedding comes with several price tags attached. First, you'll find it very difficult to update multiple compound documents at once. For example, suppose that your company just decided to go to a different logo and they want all the letters updated to reflect that change. If you had linked the logo file to the letters, the change would be simple. You would need to change just one file. The first person who opened each document after that would see the new logo. With embedding, you'd have to change each document on an individual basis.

You'll also use a lot more disk space to store an embedded file. A link takes only a few bytes to create a pointer. An embedded object is complete. If the object is 4KB, your compound document will grow by 4KB to accommodate it. Unfortunately, you won't get off that easily. In addition to the size of the object, some "housekeeping" data is included as well. The server needs this information to help you maintain the object.

Now that you know the difference between linking and embedding, let's take a look at how you would implement them. Begin by opening a copy of WordPad. We're going to explore another route you can take to link and embed objects in your documents. Use the Insert | Object command to display the dialog box shown in Figure 12.10. Notice that you can go two routes at this point. You can insert either a new object or an existing one.

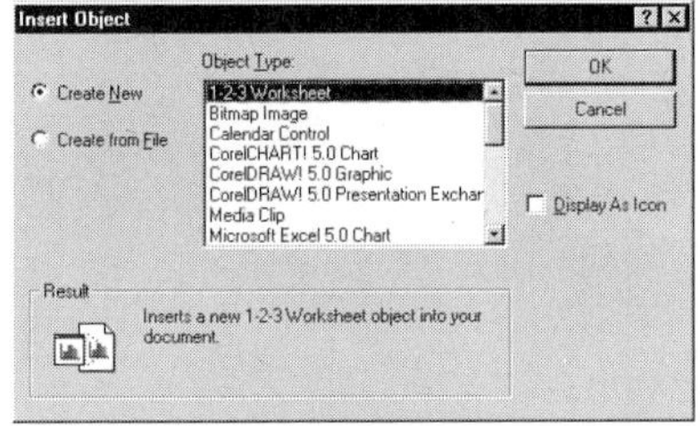

Figure 12.10.
Use the Insert Object dialog box to embed or link a new or existing object into your document.

Click the Create from File radio button. The dialog box will change to the one shown in Figure 12.11. This will allow you to embed or link an existing file. Click the Browse button and find any .BMP file that you like. Double-click to select it. Select the Link check box. If you don't check this box, Windows will automatically embed the object instead of linking it. Notice the Display As Icon check box in Figure 12.11. Clicking this option would display the object as an icon rather than as a full image. Displaying the image as an icon significantly increases performance.

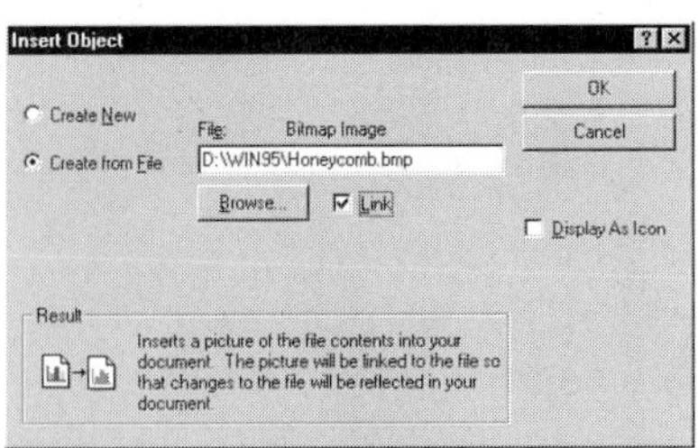

Figure 12.11.
You can also use the Insert Object dialog box to embed or link an existing file into your document.

Click OK to place a link to the object in the current document. A quick glance at this object doesn't show anything different from the last time you created a compound document. However, when you right-click the object, you'll notice that the menu entries are slightly different. The big difference comes when you try to edit the file. Instead of the in-place editing you could do after embedding the object, linking always opens the server application. You must edit the object in a separate window when using linked objects rather than embedded ones. If you really dislike seeing the other application start, you might want to use embedded rather than linked objects.

I hope you now completely understand the differences between linking and embedding. These differences are important for a lot of reasons. Where there's a little overlap in functionality and it's acceptable to use either linking or embedding, select the method that appeals to you most. My favorite is embedding, because I prefer to use in-place editing when I can.

Clients and Servers

Every application that supports OLE provides one or more services. You might have noticed in all the previous examples that I used Paint as the server and WordPad as the client. The reason is simple: Paint can't function as a client; it offers itself only as an OLE server.

This distinction is important because it affects the way you use an application. More than that, limitations of OLE support necessarily limit an application's value for creating a finished product. Consider what would happen if you tried to use a graphics program to create a poster, but it didn't support OLE as a client. Would you simply settle for cut-and-paste if you might need to modify the chart frequently? If Paint supported OLE as a client, you could create a chart for your poster in one application, the text in another, and the graphic elements in a third, and then link them all together within Paint. The lack of client support would mean that you would have to copy the text to the Clipboard. When you pasted it into Paint, the text would become a graphic element, part of the Paint graphic image. The text wouldn't be an OLE object that you could easily manipulate later using a word processor; it would be a graphic element that you would have to erase and redo from scratch. This makes changes as small as using a different type style or font size a lot more difficult than they need to be.

Whether your application is a client or a server is an important consideration. You might find that it's less expensive from a time-investment perspective to get rid of an application with limited OLE support. You can follow some general guidelines when it comes to applications.

Any application that will serve as a central location for all the objects in a project must support OLE. In most cases, you'll want to use a word processor or presentation graphics program for this purpose. They provide the greatest amount of flexibility when it comes to formatting your data. Charts and graphs might need the services of a graphics program. Unfortunately, most low-end packages won't work as clients, so you'll need to invest in a high-end package such as CorelDRAW!. You'll definitely want a package of this sort to provide both client and server capabilities, because you'll need to use both.

You can do quick-and-dirty edits with low-end packages. They usually have just enough features to get the job done and don't waste a lot of precious memory. Programs of this sort usually support OLE as a server but not as a client. No one would want the output from these programs; it just doesn't look professional. Microsoft Paint and other low-end graphics packages commonly fall into this category. You might also see some note-takers here. In some cases, all you need is the text. A note-taker (such as the Notepad utility provided with Windows 95) works fine for this purpose.

Finally, you'll never use some packages as servers because they just don't generate enough data on their own to make it worth your while to use them in that capacity. Some presentation graphics programs fall into this category. Since their output looks nice, you can use them as OLE clients without worrying about their server capabilities.

Differences Between OLE 1 and OLE 2

Microsoft introduced OLE 1 as part of Windows 3.x. It provided a basic set of linking and embedding features that users soon outgrew. One of the biggest problems was the huge amount of memory that OLE required to create more than one or two links with other applications. The lack of speed was also a major concern.

OLE 2 is supposed to remedy some of these problems and provide much more functionality to boot. The following list gives you an idea of all the improvements Microsoft made in OLE 2. Some of them are programmer-specific, but everyone benefits from something that makes a programmer's life even a little easier.

Tip: Most of these new features require that both applications support OLE 2. At the very minimum, the client must support OLE 2 to make any of the features work. Some vendors give you an idea of how to use OLE but don't really tell you how they support it. Looking in the Registry can provide important clues as to the type and level of OLE support that an application provides. (Chapter 7 looks at the Registry.)

- **Visual editing:** One of the problems with OLE 1 was that the user's train of thought got disrupted every time he needed to make a change to an object. The reason is simple: OLE 1 loaded a copy of the server and displayed the object in the originating application's window for editing. OLE 2 allows visual (in-place) editing. Instead of opening a new window, the host merely overlays its toolbar, menu structure, and controls with those of the client. The user simply sees a change in tools, not a change in applications. As a result, the transition between documents is less noticeable.
- **Nested objects:** OLE 1 allowed you to place one object at a time in the container document. An object couldn't become a container; all the objects existed as a single layer

within the container. OLE 2 treats every potential container as just that—a container. It doesn't matter how many containers you place inside a container or how many ways you stack them. To get a better idea of how nesting will help you, look at the way Windows 95 implements folders. You can treat OLE 2 container objects the same way.

- **Drag and drop:** You used to cut or copy an object in the server application and then place it in the client by using the Paste Special command. This option still works. However, OLE 2 provides a new method of creating links to other documents. You can simply grab the object and move it wherever you want. It becomes linked wherever you decide to drop it.
- **Storage-independent links:** OLE 2 allows you to create links to other documents, even if they aren't physically located on the local drive. It implements this using an LRPC (light remote procedure call) mechanism. Unfortunately, this linking mechanism has limitations. For example, you'll find that it works fine with some peer-to-peer networks, but it works only marginally with other network types. The next revision of OLE is supposed to fix this problem by supporting RPCs (remote procedure calls).
- **Adaptable links:** Many users screamed for this feature. If you moved any of the files required to create a compound document under OLE 1, all the links were destroyed, and you had to re-create them. This older version stored the full path, including drive, to the linked data. OLE 2 stores only enough path information to maintain the link. If you create links between two files in the same directory, you can move these two files anywhere on the drive, and OLE 2 can maintain the link. The only criterion for maintaining a link under OLE 2 is that the relative path remain the same.
- **OLE automation:** Everyone knows about Visual Basic for Applications (VBA), right? This is the programming language that Microsoft is trying to get everyone to support. OLE automation is part of VBA. VBA defines a standard interface for talking with the server application. This allows the client application to send commands to the server that will change the contents of an object indirectly. OLE automation is the direct descendent of the DDE macro language that many applications still use. The big difference from the user's perspective is that DDE macros were difficult to write and very prone to error. VBA is the native language of the application and is consistent across platforms. The surprising thing is that even though many applications support the VBA interface right now, none of them support it as a programming language. In essence, no one has fully implemented this feature yet. This whole picture is supposed to change when the new versions of Visual Basic and Access appear. Rumor has it that the new Microsoft Office products still won't provide VBA programming support. However, the next versions of Access and Visual Basic will provide this programming capability.
- **Version management:** Have you ever received a document from someone only to find that part of it wouldn't work with your software? OLE 2 can store the application name and version number as part of the link. If an application developer implements this feature correctly, a server (or client, for that matter) will detect an old version of a file and ask

whether you want to update it. This means that you'll never have an old file sitting around just waiting to make life difficult. Unfortunately, except for a few Microsoft applications and one or two other vendors, this feature is largely unimplemented right now. Hopefully, future versions of 32-bit Windows products will incorporate it; most don't right now.

- **Object conversion:** Your friend uses Excel and you use Lotus 1-2-3, yet you need to share OLE documents containing spreadsheets. One of you could go through the inconvenience and expense of changing to the other person's application and document format, but OLE 2 can probably solve this problem without such a change. Object conversion allows Excel to act as a server for a compound document containing a Lotus 1-2-3 object. All you do is select the Convert option from the object menu. At least, that's how it's supposed to work. Real life is a bit different. Conversion works only if the other application already supports that data format. Of course, when you think about it, this restriction makes sense.

- **Optimized object storage:** Remember the memory problem I told you about at the beginning of this section? This feature is part of the cure. It allows the linked documents to stay on disk until needed. That way, Windows doesn't need to load every application and data file required to support the compound document. In most cases, Windows uses a buffer-zone technique. A word processor might keep the applications and objects required for the preceding, current, and next page in memory. The rest of the objects stay on disk, greatly reducing the memory footprint of a compound document in some cases.
- **Component object model:** This is the programmer issue I was telling you about. Essentially, it means that Microsoft simplified the application programming interface (API) for OLE 2. An API is a set of tools that programmers use to create applications. Simpler tools mean programs with fewer bugs. This also means that the programmer can write at least that part of the application faster.

With all the changes to OLE 2, you might think that there would be compatibility problems. OLE 1 and OLE 2 can mix freely on your machine. Remember the two separate sets of Registry entries in Chapter 7? Each application had a set of OLE 1 and OLE 2 entries in the Registry. This is the reason for the dual set. The important thing to remember here is that OLE takes a least-common-denominator approach. Everything is tied to the application that has the fewest capabilities. This means that if you had four OLE 2 applications and one OLE 1 application, everything would be tied to the level of support provided by the OLE 1 application.

Application Interoperability

Getting two applications to work together might not always be as easy as it seems. We've already seen a lot of different ways that two applications can differ in their implementation of OLE, and this barely scratches the surface. For the most part, we've looked at the standard ways that two applications can deviate. The following list gives you some ideas of what to look for when you can't get your objects to work properly:

- **Neither application is a server.** Remember that you must have a server and a client to make OLE work. One application must communicate needed changes to the other. The server then makes any required changes to the object and hands it back. The whole purpose of OLE is to maintain this kind of communication.
- **Data corruption has ruined one or more OLE files.** This isn't very common, but it does happen. One of the reasons for this particular kind of corruption is old data files. I've seen applications overwrite newer versions of OLE files with old ones. Even though the overwriting application can use the older files, other applications might not be able to use them. It's usually a good idea to record the time and date stamps on your OLE files. That way, you can always check for this special form of data corruption.
- **One program provides 32-bit services and the other 16-bit.** This problem isn't supposed to happen. I've seen it only once or twice, and when it did occur, I couldn't get the problem to repeat after I rebooted my machine. What exactly happened is debatable. If you find that two programs that normally talk to each other with ease are suddenly hostile toward each other, it might be time to reboot the machine and see whether clearing memory helps.
- **Corrupted entries in the Registry prevent the application from working correctly.** Chapter 7 covers the Registry entries in detail. The bottom line is that if you have so much as a punctuation mark wrong, the Registry will balk and your OLE connection won't work.
- **Old entries in the Registry are confusing the application.** Remember the discussion of the WIN.INI and SYSTEM.INI files in Chapter 6? (In the "Windows 95 Compatibility Configuration Files" section—other chapters contain hints and tips about these files as well.) The Registry is a lot better organized, and you'll definitely find it easier to maintain, but there are still times when you might have to remove an entry manually. Some applications get confused when they run across these old OLE entries and end up trying to use the wrong files or settings.
- **Your network doesn't fully support OLE links.** Some networks require the use of special software when creating OLE 2 links. LANtastic falls into this category. As long as you use Artisoft's procedures, you should maintain good OLE connections. Other networks, such as the Microsoft network supplied with Windows 95, use OLE without any additional software. A third category of network software seems to have trouble maintaining links. Banyan falls into this category. Unfortunately, all this assumes that you create exactly the same drive mappings every time you log onto the network. As an experiment, I tried a setup in which the user needed to use her old CD-ROM only occasionally. She didn't want to load the real-mode drivers every day because the driver lowered system stability. On the days she didn't have the CD-ROM connected, all her OLE links worked fine. On the days it was connected, none of the OLE links would work. We finally traced the problem to changes in the drive mapping when the CD-ROM drive was active.

This is just a sample of the types of problems you could encounter with a common setup. Add to these problems a vendor that doesn't fully support the OLE 1 or OLE 2 standard. I actually ran into one piece of software that ended up providing some strange cross of support between the two standards (and I don't think this vendor was alone). These support problems only make the situation worse. If every application supported OLE perfectly, you could probably get past the other problems I listed in this section. The combination of faulty support and less-than-adequate linking mechanisms paints a grim picture for the user. It would be easy to point a finger and say that the vendor was totally at fault. Yet anyone who has tried to read the OLE standards, much less follow them, will attest to the level of difficulty involved.

Note: Just in case curiosity has gripped you, the OLE SDK disk weighs in at 129MB. That doesn't include all the documentation or even a compiler. (Documentation includes some white papers, a copy of the OLE 2 specification, and the complete text on OLE automation.) I also received another book with the kit that consumed another 975 pages and came with two additional floppies' worth of sample programs. Talk about a lot of information to learn! When you consider that OLE isn't the entire application—it's only a small piece of an application—would you be willing to spend the time required to go through all this material?

Before you get the idea that all is lost with OLE, let me inject a dose of reality. I wanted you to be aware of all the problems you might find. In most cases, I don't have any substantial problems with OLE that I didn't cause myself. Sure, there are times when I would like to be able to do more than the applications I'm using will allow, but these are inconveniences; they don't make OLE unusable. The best thing you can do when using OLE is to thoroughly check everything before you make a huge commitment in time and energy to a specific solution. It always pays to check for potential pitfalls, but this is especially true of a technology as new and complex as OLE.

Packaging OLE Objects

OLE wasn't the smashing success Microsoft hoped it would be, and I've already discussed some of the reasons why. Part of Microsoft's answer to the problem of a lack of OLE support was Object Packager, which comes with Windows. You can still find this utility in your main Windows directory, but you won't see it on your Start menu. I added my copy to the Start menu to make it easier to access.

Object Packager is good for only one thing: It allows you to create a package that you can insert into a document. The result is similar to an object you create using the native capabilities that many programs provide today. It's still a good utility to keep around for those older applications that don't directly support OLE.

Rather than bore you with a lot of details about this particular product, let's put a package together. In fact, we'll use the same two applications we've used throughout this chapter, along with the same data file. This will allow you to see the difference between an object package and an object.

The first thing you need to do is create the object package. Open Object Packager. You should see the display shown in Figure 12.12. A lot of people claim this utility is difficult to use. Actually, they're only half right. This utility isn't all that hard to use; it's the documentation that makes using it seem difficult.

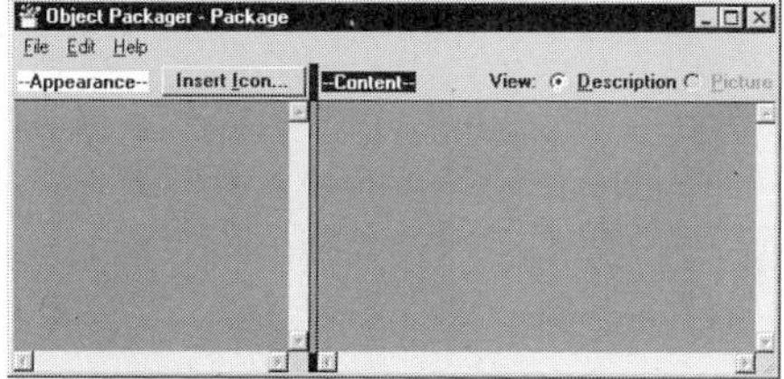

Figure 12.12.
Object Packager looks simple, and it really is once you get the hang of it.

Click the Insert Icon button. Object Packager automatically assumes that you want to use one of the icons out of Program Manager, because it was designed for that interface. You can choose another icon by using the Browse button, but we'll use one of the icons listed here for now. After you select an icon, click OK to complete the task.

Use the Edit | Label command to add a label to the icon. This will identify the file you plan to use. I typed `HONEYCOMB.BMP`, but you could use any other identification you choose.

The Edit | Command option allows you to add the location of the file you want to edit, along with the application that will perform the editing. You need to know the command-line syntax for the application in order to do anything fancy here. In most cases, you won't use Object Packager directly with an application that registers itself, so you'll probably be limited to opening the file with the application. To do that, just type the name of the program followed by the filename, just like you would at the DOS prompt. I typed `MSPAINT D:\WIN95\HONEYCOMB.BMP` in this case. You can modify the contents of your command to meet the needs of a particular situation. Figure 12.13 shows the results of all the edits so far. Your display might look slightly different, depending on the choices you made.

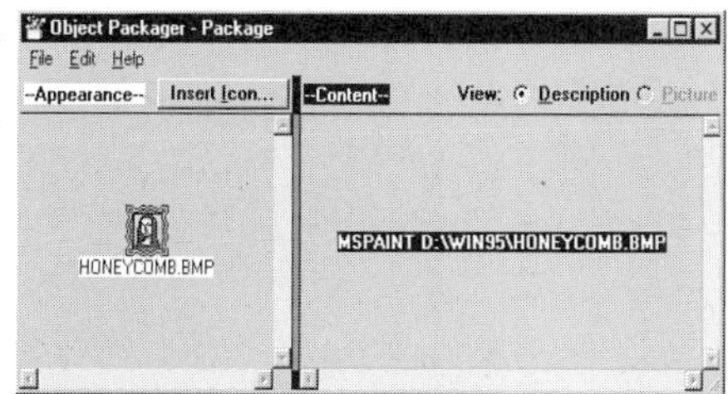

Figure 12.13.
This is the simplest form of a completed package.

Now that we have a completed package, it's time to do something with it. Use the Edit | Copy Package command to place the package on the Clipboard. Open WordPad or Word for Windows. Right-click the edit area and select Paste from the object menu. You should see a display similar to the one in Figure 12.14.

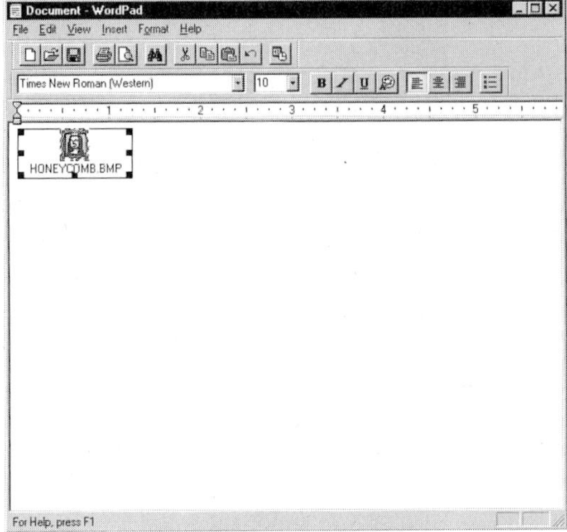

Figure 12.14.
An object package looks and acts a lot different from its object counterpart.

There are several differences between this object package and the object we worked with before. The first difference is pretty obvious: There's no way to determine what the object looks like. This isn't the icon form of the package; it's what the package actually looks like. You can double-click the package to bring up Paint, so at least that part of the package works satisfactorily. However, as you can see from Figure 12.15, Object Packager doesn't support in-place editing.

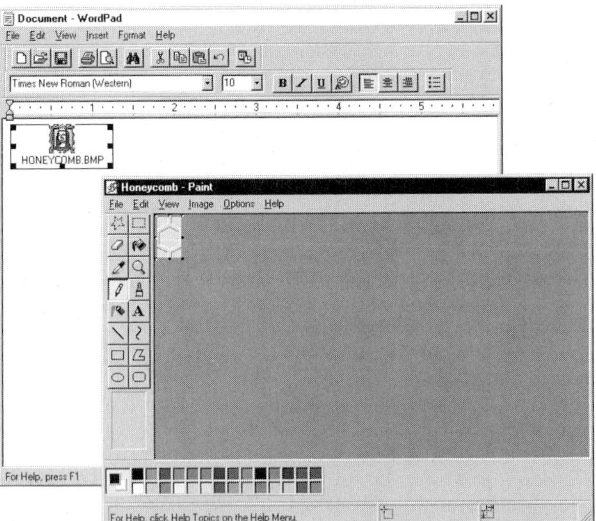

Figure 12.15.
Even though this object package is embedded, it acts as if it were linked.

You don't have to use Object Packager this way. It supports other methods of creating an object package. Some of them work with certain kinds of software. This first method works with any kind of application, even if it doesn't support OLE. The only requirement is that the application support a command-line interface.

The preceding example left a little to be desired as far as capability goes. Let's try one more time to make a better package. Open HONEYCOMB.BMP (or any other .BMP file), using Paint. Use the Edit | Select All command to select the graphic, and then copy it to the Clipboard using Edit | Copy.

Open Object Packager. Use the Edit | Paste command to copy the contents of the Clipboard into the package area. Figure 12.16 shows the results. Notice how different this package appears from the first one. The problem with this method is that the originating application must support OLE as a client. Fortunately, it doesn't have to provide a specific level of support.

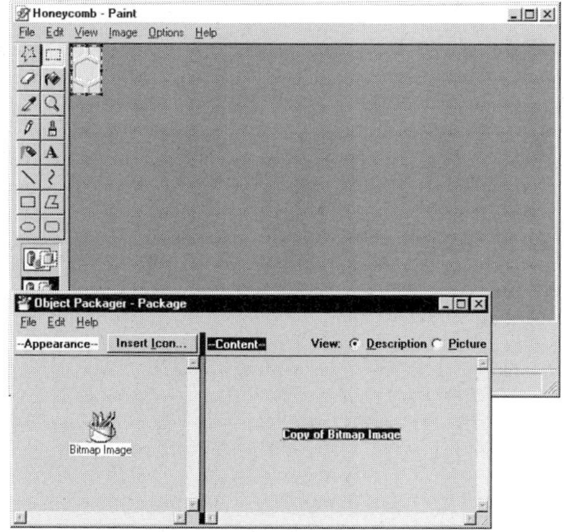

Figure 12.16.
This method of creating an object package produces a different result from the previous method.

It's time to check the results of this second attempt at creating an object package. Use the Edit | Copy Package command to place the package on the Clipboard. Open WordPad or Word for Windows. Right-click the edit area and select Paste from the object menu. You should see a display similar to the one in Figure 12.17.

Notice that this object looks and acts the same as the previous object. Even though the package looked like it would support in-place editing while it was in the Object Packager, it won't support it now. I wanted to point this out because it's a limitation of Object Packager rather than Paint or WordPad. It's a factor that you need to remember whenever you resort to using Object Packager. Any objects that you create using this method go from the client through Object Packager and to the originating application. If you want features such as in-place editing, you must use an application that supports this feature directly, rather than resorting to Object Packager. Remember that Object Packager was designed to help people gain some of the benefits of OLE, even when using applications that didn't support it. In most cases, you'll want to leave this dusty tool where it belongs. However, it's still nice to know that it's there when you need it.

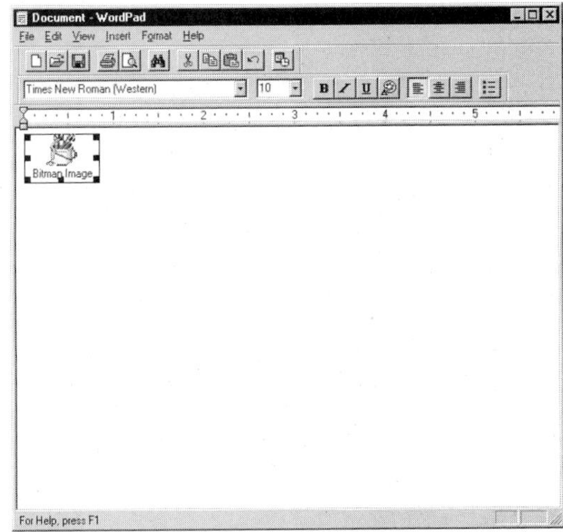

Figure 12.17.
The new object package seems to produce the same results as before—an obvious limitation of Object Packager.

OLE Components

You'll probably see a whole group of files in your SYSTEM directory that provide support for OLE. The following list provides some details on the tasks each file performs. You can use this list if you ever run into a problem with corruption or if you would simply like to know what level of support you can expect from a certain application. The presence or absence of these files might indicate problems with your installation as well. Missing OLE files means that you won't get the kind of support needed to make your system work efficiently.

- OLE2.DLL: If you see this file, you know that some part of the Windows installation on your machine supports the OLE 2 standard. Windows 95 always installs this file. This dynamic link library (.DLL) provides some "foundation" functions. (A.DLL is a special Windows program.)
- OLECLI.DLL: This file contains all the basic client code your application needs. Your application uses this file as a base for building its own client features.
- OLESRV.DLL: This file contains all the basic server code your application needs. Like the client code, this .DLL won't provide everything. Your application uses it as a basis for building its own set of features.
- OLE2CONV.DLL: This file provides the generic routines a program needs to convert an object to the client program's native format.
- OLE2DISP.DLL: Every OLE client application uses this program to help it display the objects it contains.

- OLE2NLS.DLL: Most versions of Windows provide National Language Support (NLS). This program helps OLE keep pace with the rest of Windows in providing support for other languages.
- OLE2.REG: You can import this Registry file into your Registry to install OLE 2 support. In most cases, your application will do this automatically, so you don't need to worry about it. The only time you'll need to use it is when you can't get OLE 2 to work and you discover that the Registry doesn't contain the correct entries.
- MCIOLE.DLL: Sounds require special handling under Windows. Unlike with most objects, you don't display a sound. This special .DLL provides the support that an application needs to handle a sound object.
- OLE32.DLL: A whole group of OLE files in the SYSTEM directory has "32" somewhere in the name. These files provide the same services as their 16-bit counterparts to 32-bit applications.
- MFCOLEUI.DLL: C programmers need every bit of help they can get. They use something called *Microsoft Foundation Classes* to make their workload a little lighter. This file (and any with similar names) provides the C interface to OLE. If you see a file with "MFC" in its name, you know one of your applications uses the Microsoft Foundation Classes.

Note: The first World Wide Web browser that's also an OLE server is included in Microsoft Plus!. Microsoft's Internet Explorer allows full integration between the Internet and your desktop, using OLE. Read Chapter 28 to learn more about Internet Explorer.

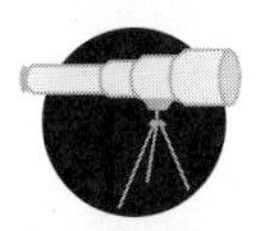

These are all the files you'll need for OLE2. There are also a wealth of files required for ActiveX. Precisely what files you'll need to perform a specific activity depends on the needs of the ActiveX control itself. At a minimum, each ActiveX control requires the use of an .OCX file, but there isn't any limitation on the number of files that a vendor could use. You'll normally find permanent ActiveX controls in the SYSTEM folder. Your Internet browser may place some ActiveX controls on your hard drive as well when you visit Web pages that use those controls. The precise location depends on your browser (to some extent). Internet Explorer places these files in the OCCACHE folder (normally located within the main Windows folder), unless the Web site specifies a different location. Because Netscape Navigator doesn't support ActiveX directly (at least not as of this writing), the default location for ActiveX controls is up to the plug-in that you use.

ActiveX controls are fairly easy to spot. They always have an extension of .OCX (OLE Control eXtension). This file contains a combination of executable code and data. So where's the OLE connection? The connection comes from the way that data is managed by the control. Think of an ActiveX control as a very specialized form of OLE client and/or server, and you'll have a pretty good idea of how things work. The Microsoft ActiveX section of Chapter 22 looks at some specifics on using ActiveX controls. The next section of this chapter, "ActiveX—An Internet Strategy," gives you a pretty good idea of what the controls look like from the user perspective.

Unlike other kinds of files on your machine, simply erasing an ActiveX control to remove it isn't a good idea. ActiveX controls make their presence known to Windows by "registering" themselves. In fact, there's a special program in the SYSTEM folder, RegSvr32, that gets called to register the control within the Registry. You can register a control that Windows loses by typing **`RegSvr32 <OCX name>`** at the command line. Likewise, if your OCCACHE folder starts getting too full from visiting numerous Internet sites, you can unregister an ActiveX control by typing **`RegSvr32 /U <OCX name>`** at the command line. Always unregister the control before you erase it. How do you know whether you were successful? Windows always displays a dialog box like the one shown in Figure 12.18 when you successfully unregister an ActiveX control. RegSvr32 displays a similar dialog box when you register an ActiveX control.

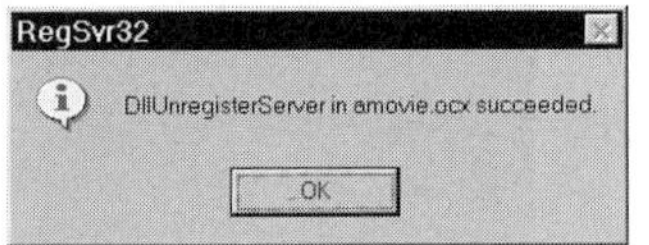

Figure 12.18.
Unregistering your ActiveX control is an important step before removing it.

Warning: Never remove ActiveX controls that appear in the SYSTEM folder (under your main Windows directory). Doing so may disable one or more of your applications. Most applications clean up any ActiveX controls they've installed when you remove the application from your machine. In addition, use the greatest care when removing ActiveX controls that appear in other folders. An ActiveX control that appears in an application directory usually belongs to that application. Fortunately, you can always assume that the controls that appear in the OCCACHE folder are safe to remove.

ActiveX—An Internet Strategy

ActiveX has actually been around in one form or another for quite a while. The ActiveX technology is an extension of a technology that appeared with the first 32-bit compilers from Microsoft. Originally programmers called ActiveX controls *OLE Control eXtensions*. Unfortunately, that name wasn't officially endorsed by Microsoft, even though it appeared in a number of books and magazine articles. The official name now is ActiveX—though you'll more than likely find the old name in more than a few places (even Microsoft's documentation).

OCXs (ActiveX controls) originally provided a component capability for products such as Visual Basic. You build an application by placing various components on a form and then setting their properties. The control doesn't actually exist within the application; it exists in a separate file. The application and the control talk to each other. A programmer monitors the communication by looking at the contents of the properties and by asking the application to react to certain events. Rather than get into bits and bytes here, though, let's take a look at ActiveX in action.

Figure 12.19 shows a Web page that contains some ActiveX controls. In this case, we're looking at a button and a set of radio buttons that control its properties. Any Webmaster will tell you that standard HTML (hypertext markup language) supports only three kinds of buttons: submit, reset, and cancel. The use of ActiveX in this case allows us to define any kind of button needed. The dialog box shows the result value of the button, which changes to reflect the kind of button you select by using the radio buttons. Chapter 22 looks at a specific example of how to do this kind of ActiveX work.

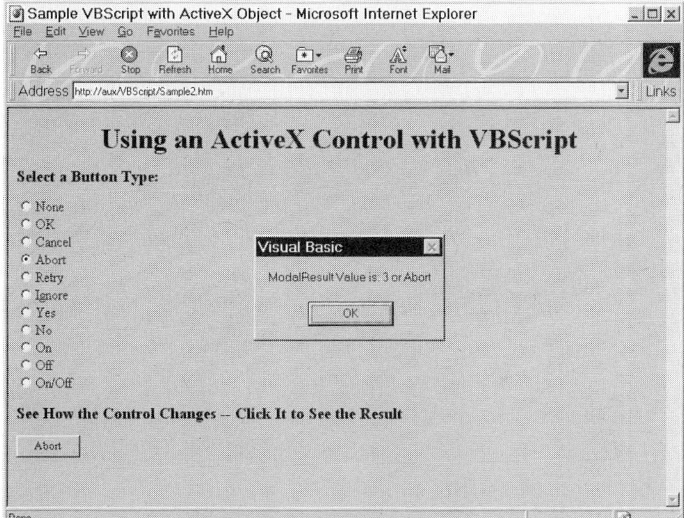

Figure 12.19.
ActiveX works on Web pages like it does within an application—it allows a programmer to build the page by using components.

Okay, you're a little underwhelmed by a Web page containing some radio buttons and a command button. ActiveX has a lot more to offer than components. Take a look at Figure 12.20. What you're seeing is another kind of ActiveX application, called Active Document. In this case, we're looking at a Word for Windows document displayed within a browser window. Unlike other kinds of Web documents, you can edit this one and save the changes locally. If the Web server allows you to do it, you can also publish the changed document on the Web server.

There are a lot of ways to use Active Document, but the way that I see most people using it is as a method for exchanging information without resorting to groupware. Think about the advantage of allowing four people—one in New York, another in Delhi, another in London, and still another in Tokyo—to collaborate on a document located on the company's Web server in Los Angeles (all without a single long-distance phone call). That's the beauty of using Active Document. You can create connections through the Internet that were difficult or even impossible in the past.

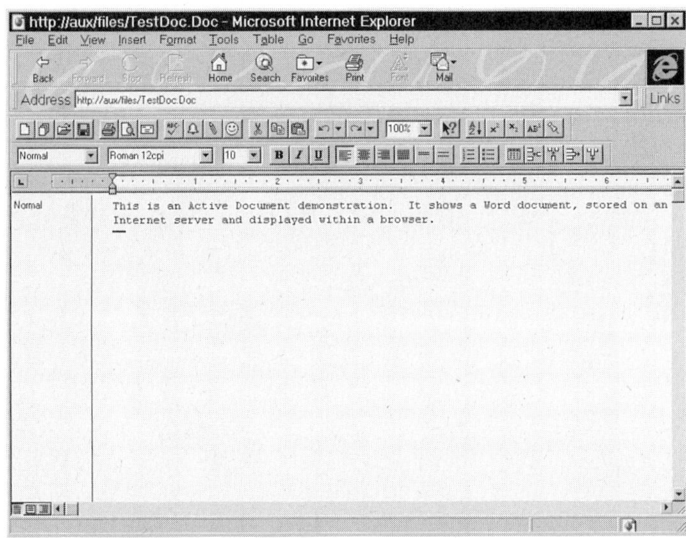

Figure 12.20.
Active Document, a special form of ActiveX, allows you to interact with a link on an Internet site.

Still not very impressed? ActiveX is used for a variety of other technologies as well. For example, Active Movie allows you to play multimedia over a Web connection. That's not so spectacular until you consider that a single player located on your machine will allow you to play most multimedia file types. Figure 12.21 shows an example of Active Movie in action.

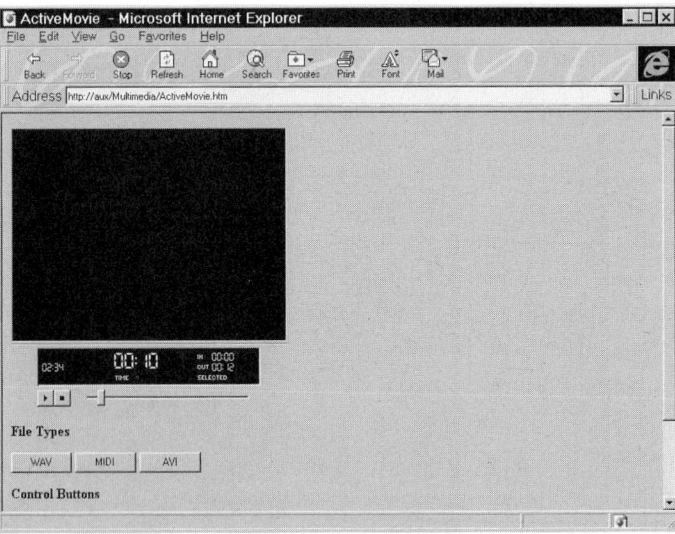

Figure 12.21.
Active Movie provides the means to work with multimedia over the Internet.

I really haven't covered everything there is to know about ActiveX, even from a user perspective. Suffice it to say that this is a vast new technology that you really need to know about. Don't think that you're limited to using Internet Explorer, either. There are several good plug-ins for Netscape Navigator that will allow you full access to everything that the Internet provides.

Tip: NCompass Labs produces a selection of plug-ins for Netscape Navigator that allow you to work with ActiveX-enabled Web pages. The first is ScriptActive. It allows you to download and use ActiveX controls. The second plug is called DocActive. It allows you to work with Active Documents such as the one shown in Figure 12.20. The only problem with this solution is that the Webmaster at the Web site you want to visit has to cooperate. ScriptActive provides a conversion tool that implements every `<OBJECT>` tag that ActiveX normally uses as an `<EMBED>` tag that Navigator can understand. In some cases, you'll run into an Internet site that you still can't access with Navigator simply because it wasn't converted to work with a plug-in. You can contact NCompass at the following address: `http://www.ncompasslabs.com`.

On Your Own

Test the OLE capabilities of the various applications on your machine. Which ones support OLE as a client? Which ones support it as a server? Do you see any difference between the applications that support OLE 1 and OLE 2?

Use the various techniques for inserting an object into a container that I covered in this chapter. Which methods do you find easiest to use? Why do you think that some applications support one technique and others another technique?

Try making an OLE link in a large document using an OLE 1 application. Make the same link using an OLE 2 application such as WordPad. Do you see a difference in the load time of the two documents? What additional features does WordPad provide that the OLE 1 application doesn't?

Open a copy of Explorer and use it to search your SYSTEM folder. Can you find all of the OLE-specific files installed on your system? What does the name of each of the various files tell you about that file's purpose?

Use an ActiveX-capable Internet browser to find one or more ActiveX-enabled Web sites. Microsoft provides a gallery that you can use for ideas at `http://www.microsoft.com/gallery/`. If you can't find one immediately, try the NCompass Labs ActiveX Showcase at `http://www.ncompasslabs.com/showcase.htm`. It contains examples of the most common ActiveX technologies. Another good place to look is Stroud's CWSApps List—Windows 95/NT Apps—ActiveX Controls at `http://www.caboose.com/cwsapps/95activx.html`. This site features vendors that write ActiveX controls. Be sure to take the time to interact with the site and see how these technologies work. Try to think of ways that your company could use ActiveX to improve its Web site (if your company has a Web site).

13

Exploiting Your Software

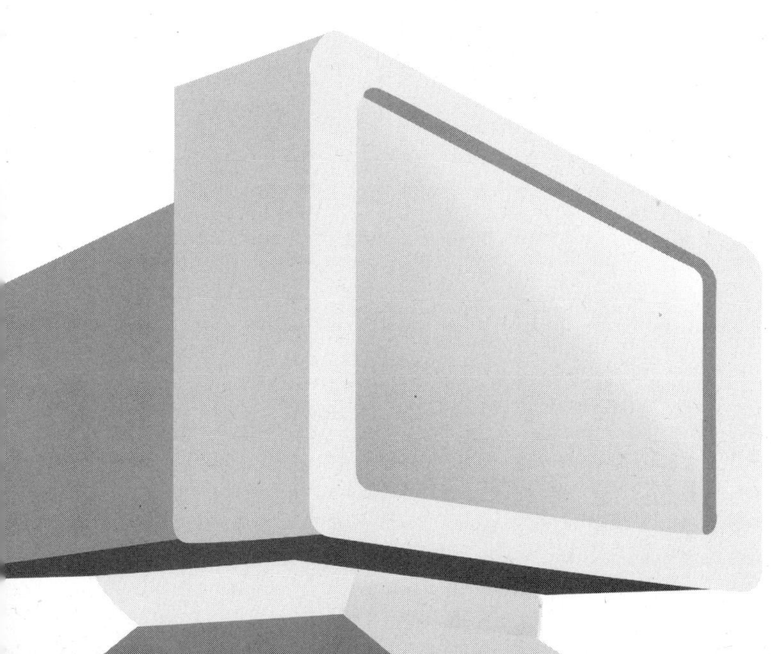

I played with a lot of titles for this chapter before I finally decided to use this one. It expresses the entire thought behind the way some people manage their systems today. In fact, it should express the way that you use your system. Of course, exploiting your software could mean a lot of things, so let's take a few minutes to define what I mean.

Exploiting every possible feature of some of today's software products would be impossible for the average user. The fact that some power users have a problem doing it really says something about software bloat. Take CorelDRAW! as an example. I recently installed the latest version of this product on my system. Even if I decided not to install all the fonts, I'd still have access to a drawing program, a presentation graphics program, and a desktop publisher—and that only scratches the surface. The folks at Corel thoughtfully provided me with three CD-ROMs full of valuable information, most of which I'll never use. Obviously, exploiting your software doesn't necessarily involve using every feature it has to offer.

Note: Don't get the idea that I'm bashing anyone by saying that there's a certain level of software bloat in most packages today. The computing environment has become so complex and the tasks we perform so varied that you need to expect a certain level of bloat. Even if you don't use a particular feature, some users would feel that the package wasn't complete unless the vendor provided it. Combining the requests made by the majority of customers is the reason that most vendors produce the bloated packages we see on the market today. A product feature that I don't need to get my work finished might make all the difference in the world to someone else.

What I mean by exploiting your software is exercising every feature you do use to its fullest potential. I use four basic criteria to measure my level of software exploitation. They're all interactive, so you'll find that changing one element will, of necessity, affect all the other elements. For me, it's kind of a game to see just how well I can get all these elements to work together. So what are these four criteria? A fully exploited piece of software will do the following things:

- **Accomplish the job at hand with a minimum of effort.** Everyone knows that learning how to use a computer is both expensive and time-consuming. Add to that the cost of buying the equipment itself and you have a major investment before you see any kind of return. A fully exploited piece of software allows you to accomplish the same job as before, but with a lot less effort. Concentrating on the task rather than the means of performing it means that you can be a lot more creative in your work. I've always felt that computers should provide a way of removing the burden of work and leaving the "fun" parts for us to accomplish. A fully exploited piece of software can do just that.
- **Produce results in a modicum of time.** It wasn't too long ago that people wondered why it was faster to do something by hand than to use a computer. I personally saw this problem often. What these people were forgetting was that if you were going to use that older software to its fullest potential, you needed to set up the application only once. The

computer could then automate the task for you, so it would take you less time to perform the task the second time you did it. If you didn't set up your computer for rapid duplication of rote work, you weren't exploiting it. Fortunately, the old problem of spending more time to create your original document just isn't there anymore. I can use a variety of packages to write an application in a fraction of the time it used to take. Templates and other software add-ons make it faster to produce the first copy of a document, in addition to variations of that document later. The "wizards" provided with a lot of software packages give you a built-in ease of use that was unheard of only five years ago. In many cases, a fully exploited piece of software today will allow you to produce results faster than you could by hand.

- **Produce output that requires the least amount of system resources.** The amount of system resources you have is relative. Much of it has to do with the technology you have at your disposal. There are other considerations as well, such as the money you have to spend on upgrades, but let's concentrate on the relative aspect of this picture. A fully exploited piece of software is optimized so that it uses a minimum of system resources. As shown in Chapter 12, there are a number of ways to embed or link an object into your document. Other chapters in this book show various aspects of other forms of optimization. A fully exploited piece of software uses the least memory-intensive yet fastest way to accomplish a task. Optimizing the way you use the software's features will almost always result in reduced system resource requirements.
- **Produce the best results possible.** Optimizing your software to reduce system requirements, improving your techniques to reduce the time it takes to get the job done, and reducing the effort required to complete the task are all fine goals. However, it's the result of all this effort that everyone will see. The boss won't care that it took you half the time to get something done if the final result isn't up to par. That's a problem for many people: They look for a quick fix to a problem, and that often isn't the route they really need to pursue. The test of whether you've successfully exploited your software is in the results you produce. Using the software and hardware available today should allow you to produce an end product that's superior in every way to what you could do yesterday. If you aren't getting that result, it's time to take another look at how you're exploiting your software.

Exploiting your software also means that you use the right tool for the task you're trying to accomplish. Sure, you can use a spreadsheet as a word processor (a lot of people do), but is that really exploiting your software, or is the software exploiting you? Of course, no one can afford to buy every application on the market. There are limitations to what you can realistically use. If an inexpensive tool will do the job, that's the one you should select. It's a matter of defining the parameters of the job. Just how much work do you need to do? If I need to dig a small hole, I get a spade. A really big hole requires a backhoe.

To summarize, exploiting your software means that you get an application that's the right size and type for the job. You optimize its operation and environment. Then you sit back and watch the application do its job in the most efficient manner possible.

If this sounds impossible, read on. A lot of things seem impossible until you take the time to analyze the situation, break it into its component parts, and solve the small problems. Trying to take an entire project and solve it with one answer isn't going to do much, if anything, to make you efficient. Of course, you probably do all this with your current business. Most successful businesses take the time to get the most out of their employees and the resources they have available. Now what you need to do is apply these same principles to your computer.

Peter's Principle: Operating-System Flexibility Is the Key

Windows 3.x was very inflexible in some regards. Even if you could get around some of its limitations, there were enough times when you couldn't that a total system solution was impractical. I have a lot of books and other resources sitting on my shelf that claim to provide the answer for Windows 3.x optimization or the inner secret that will unlock all its power. Even with all this help, I could seldom run more than three tasks at a time or fully exploit the software installed on my machine.

Using Windows 95 has shown me that it still has bugs and other limitations. This product is still inflexible in some areas. Earlier chapters even look at some of the strange decisions Microsoft made when putting this operating system together. However, even with all these little "gotchas," Windows 95 provides a level of flexibility that will allow you to circumvent the problem areas and (finally) use the system to its full potential. You can really exploit Windows 95. A fully optimized operating system does several things for you as the user. Besides all the obvious answers you'll probably come up with, such as improved stability, an optimized operating system allows you to fully exploit the software packages sitting on your shelf.

A flexible environment such as Windows 95 provides you with the space you need to maneuver that application into the best possible setup for use. Of course, with added flexibility comes some additional responsibility for the user. Microsoft still provides you with a default setup for your Windows installation. However, if you want to fully exploit your software, you need to fully exploit the operating system as well.

Tip: Exploiting your system means that you need to tune it, too. Have you ever seen a race car driver who paid more attention to his paint job than his engine? Optimizing your applications doesn't really make sense until you spend a little time under the hood optimizing Windows. Read Chapter 3 if you need some ideas on how to do this.

Using the Add/Remove Programs Utility

Have you seen the immense size of some applications today? I'm often appalled at how fast the applications I install can eat up a major piece of the 1GB drive on my machine. Most people don't have a drive this size, so sometimes they need to remove one or more applications they don't use much to make room for the applications they use often. If you ever tried to do this under Windows 3.x, you know how difficult it can be to perform this task. You'll also be pleasantly surprised by a new Windows 95 capability. It allows you to install and remove your Windows 95 applications with ease.

Note: The Windows 95 Install/Uninstall capability doesn't extend to non-Windows 95 products. This includes both Windows 3.x and Windows NT products. To install and then later uninstall these products, you still need to use a third-party option. Unfortunately, there's a problem with this method as well. The Windows 95 utility ensures that the proper Registry entries are made. You need to decide between the ability to easily remove the application later and performing a little more work to get the application installed correctly, or getting the best possible installation up front and doing a lot of work later to remove it. Using the correct installation utility will help you get rid of those old applications fast.

Tip: Many of the newer applications on the market provide their own uninstall programs. Chances are that the custom uninstall program will work better than most third-party products, because the vendor can hand-tune its uninstall program. Unfortunately, this isn't always the case. I've had uninstall programs remove too many files or not enough. In some cases, they've even trashed the Registry to the point where I had to reinstall some of my applications. When these native uninstall programs work, they work well. When they don't, watch out.

So what's involved in removing an application after you've installed it? Every uninstall program needs to take five things into consideration. Uninstall programs handle each criterion to a different degree.

- **Application directory:** Every uninstall program handles this one the same way. For that matter, it would probably take you even less time to remove the application directory when no longer needed. The problem is the application's data. Some uninstall programs leave it in place so that you can recover it later; others simply remove the entire directory without giving much thought to the data it contains. I prefer the first approach because it keeps me from shooting myself in the foot. The second approach is a little too thorough, in my opinion.

- **Windows directory:** Most applications place an .INI file in the Windows directory so that they can find it easily. Some applications place two or even three files there. For example, when I installed LANtastic, it placed three different .INI files there. Each managed a different aspect of the product. I was surprised by the number of uninstall programs that don't take these files into account.
- **Windows system-file modification:** It's a sure bet that Windows 95 will have the same problem that previous versions of Windows did when it comes to spurious entries in WIN.INI and SYSTEM.INI. Even though it only provides compatibility support for these files, it reads them when you boot. Suffice it to say that some of the same problems you had in the past will still crop up when you install 16-bit applications.
- **SYSTEM directory:** There are a ton of files in your SYSTEM directory, and there's no way of knowing which ones belong to your application. Even if an uninstall program tracks these files, it has no way of knowing how many applications use a particular file. This is especially true of .DLLs. For example, an application might install a copy of the file VBRUN300.DLL in your SYSTEM directory. When you install another application that requires that same file, the second application might not add the file because it sees that the file is already present. If the uninstall program removed VBRUN300.DLL along with all the other files for the first application, the second application would also cease to work. So how do you handle this situation? I don't know, and neither does your uninstall program. Some programs make a valiant effort to remove the less common files. But when it comes to removing one, you're on your own—deleting files from the SYSTEM directory by hand.

Tip: Chapter 6 contains a procedure for viewing the contents of .DLLs and other system files. You can use this procedure to view the files that you suspect an application uses, in order to decide whether or not to delete them. Making a list of the .DL_ and .DLL files on the distribution disk is also very helpful. Comparing this list to the contents of the SYSTEM directory will at least provide clues on what you can remove. Be careful, though, not to remove any "common" files that your SYSTEM directory might contain. Reading the heading information for the .DLL will also give you clues in this regard, because common files are normally written by a compiler vendor and not the vendor of the application you're removing. (Unfortunately, this doesn't help much when it comes to Borland and Microsoft applications.)

- **Common application directories:** Many applications try to reduce the number of files on your hard drive by placing files that more than one application could use in a separate directory. For example, you'll find an MSAPPS directory on your machine if you use Microsoft applications. The positive side of such directories is that they do indeed reduce the load on your hard drive. The negative aspect is you really don't know which files to remove if you use multiple products from the same vendor and you want to remove only one product. In fact, I found that this common directory can actually confuse your uninstall program. Some of them remove the entire directory, whether or not more than one application is using those files.

As you can see, trying to remove a Windows application from your machine isn't the easy task that it was under DOS. A Windows application spreads files all over the place and makes entries in system files that you might need even if you remove the application. (Multiple applications might need the same entry to run.) It's not too surprising that Windows uninstall programs normally do a partial rather than a complete job of removing old programs from your system. Of course, a partial removal is better than nothing.

Tip: Windows won't let you remove a file that's in use. Even if you close an application, Windows might not unload all its associated .DLLs right away. Whenever you want to remove an application from your drive, shut everything down, reboot, and perform the uninstall routine with all applications closed. This will ensure that the uninstall program can actually remove all the files it identifies as part of the application.

A Windows 95 application gives the operating system much more information about what it installs and why than previous versions of Windows. That's why you can uninstall only Windows 95-specific applications with the new Install/Uninstall capability. Newer applications actually make Registry entries that tell the operating system what to remove later. This also allows Windows 95 to look for common files and perform other types of analysis. When you can finally upgrade every application on your machine to a Windows 95-specific version, the Windows 95 Install/Uninstall program should work perfectly—theoretically, at least.

Adding an Application

Now that we have all the preliminaries out of the way, let's take a look at the future. Remember that we're looking at a less-than-optimal setup here because I don't have Windows 95 applications to replace all my current applications (and neither will you, for the foreseeable future). Because of this problem, you might get slightly different results than I did. The following steps tell you how to use the Install/Uninstall program.

1. Open Control Panel by using the Start menu or Explorer.
2. Double-click Add/Remove Programs. You should see a dialog box like the one shown in Figure 13.1.

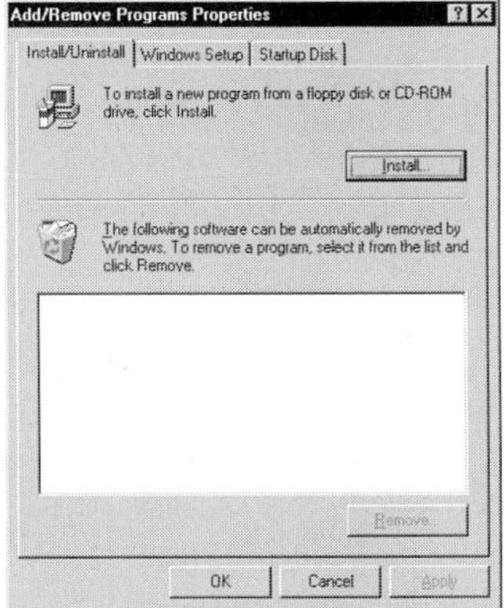

Figure 13.1.
The Install/Uninstall page of the Add/Remove Programs Properties dialog box lets you install any application. It will uninstall only Windows 95-specific applications.

3. Click Install. You'll see a dialog box similar to the one shown in Figure 13.2. Notice that this dialog box tells you to place a floppy in one of the floppy drives or a CD-ROM in the CD-ROM drive. You don't have to do this. The Install/Uninstall program lets you search for applications on a hard drive. However, to use the automatic search features, you need to place a disk in the appropriate drive.

Figure 13.2.
Don't believe everything you read in this Install Program dialog box.

4. Click Next. The Install Wizard searches drives A and B and the CD-ROM drive for SETUP.EXE. If you're installing a program from the hard drive, or if the setup program uses a different name, the wizard won't find it. You need to enter the value by hand or use the Browse dialog box.
5. If the Install Wizard finds a setup program, it enters the name here for you. If not, you see a dialog box like the one shown in Figure 13.3. Type the name of the application you want to install or use the Browse dialog box to find it. To use the Browse dialog box, simply click the Browse button.

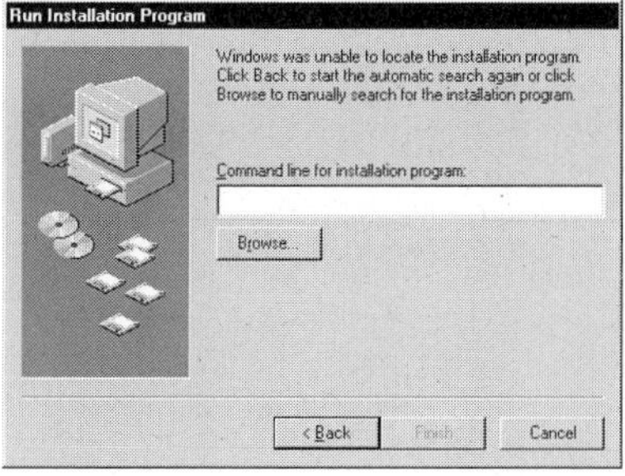

Figure 13.3.
The Run Installation Program dialog box is the last time you'll see the Install Wizard.

6. As soon as you complete step 5, Windows 95 launches the setup application. Follow the vendor instructions for installing it. You won't come back to the Install Wizard when you get done. However, you might want to open the Add/Remove Programs Properties dialog box again to make sure that the application name appears in the list of products you can remove. Figure 13.4 shows a typical entry.

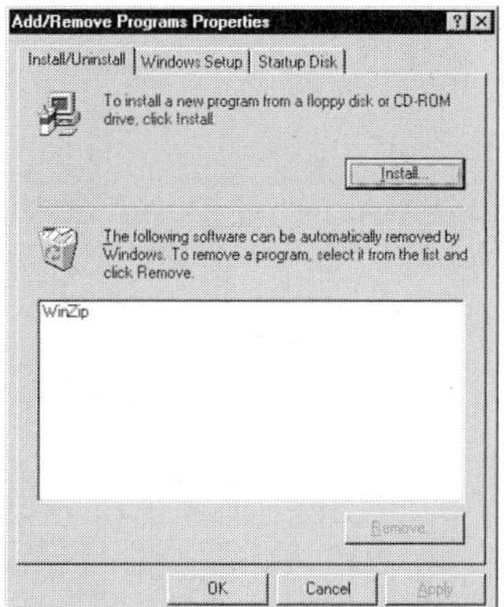

Figure 13.4.
The Install/Uninstall page, containing an entry from an installed application.

Removing an Application

Uninstalling an application with the Install Wizard is as easy as if not easier than installing it. The following procedure shows you the steps you'll follow in most cases. Remember that you also have the option of using the application's uninstall utility to get this done. Of course, the tradeoff is that the application might not remove all the Registry entries that Windows 95 made when you installed it.

1. Open Control Panel by using the Start menu or Explorer.
2. Double-click Add/Remove Programs. You should see a dialog box like the one shown earlier in Figure 13.1.
3. Select the application you want to uninstall and click Remove. The Install Wizard will ask whether you want to remove the application, as shown in Figure 13.5.

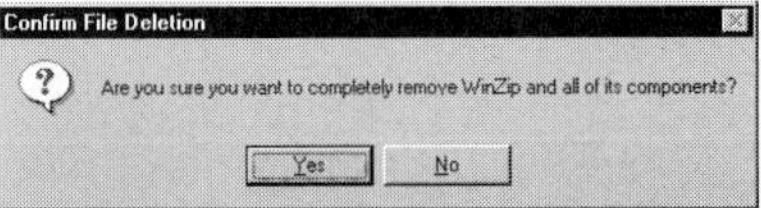

Figure 13.5.
Windows 95 always asks permission before it removes an application.

4. Click Yes. The Install Wizard usually displays a list of everything it will remove, as shown in Figure 13.6. Notice that this list includes items such as .INI files.

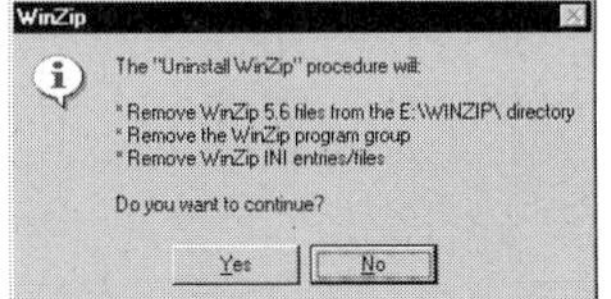

Figure 13.6.
You always get to see which files Windows 95 will remove before it removes them.

5. Click Yes. Just to make sure that you really want to remove the application, Windows 95 displays yet another screen asking if you're sure. This might seem a bit extreme until you consider how many people remove applications from their machines by mistake and regret it later.
6. Click Yes one last time. Windows 95 attempts to remove all the application components. If successful, it displays a success message. Otherwise, it displays the dialog box shown in Figure 13.7. You can use the contents of this dialog box to complete the uninstall process.

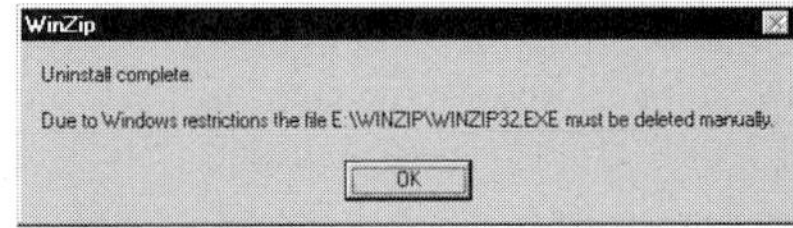

Figure 13.7.
The Install Wizard displays an error message if it can't complete the uninstall.

7. Click OK to exit the Install Wizard.

Optimizing Windows Applications

Once you get a new application installed, you need to optimize it for your use. Notice that I said "for your use." The difference between an optimized and an exploited application is simple: The optimized application might run fast, but the exploited application is more efficient. Windows applications provide a wealth of settings that allow you to tune the way they work. Not only do these tuning steps affect the application's speed and memory requirements, but they also affect the user interface. I'll look at both elements in the following sections, because they're both important for fully exploiting your applications. Be sure to read the entire section before you start tuning your applications. Some elements are a tradeoff: You need to select one over the other. I cover the most common ones, but you might need to make some decisions based on your application's specific setup.

Installation Options

Installing your new application is a very important part of the tuning process. The decisions you make here affect the way you view the application in the future, as well as determine how the application performs. The following list should help you make some of the hard decisions that come up during installation:

- **Hard disk space:** If hard disk space is at a premium, you might need to limit the number of installation features you provide. For example, very few applications come without a fully functional tutorial. Generally, the tutorial makes use of the Windows multimedia features to reduce the time it takes to learn the product. However, all these features come at a price. Learning how to use the product from the manual might not seem as efficient as using the interactive tutorial—in fact, I'll tell you right out that it isn't—but the disk space you save could make room for another option you'll use long after the need for the tutorial is gone. Theoretically you could install the tutorial and remove it later, but some people invariably forget to do this, and the result is permanent loss of disk space. If you install the tutorial, be sure to remove it once it's no longer needed.
- **Uninstall capability:** You'll find that a lot of applications now provide an uninstall capability. More than that, they provide a feature-dependent capability. What you do is select which features you want to install by checking them off on a menu. Changing the check box selections installs or uninstalls that particular feature. Not every application provides this feature, but you can make good use of it with the ones that do. Even if your application provides only a stock uninstall capability, you could install it fully once to learn how to use the product, uninstall it, and then install it partially a second time to get your running installation together.
- **Memory:** This particular selection applies to graphics programs, for the most part, because they're the biggest users of memory in this regard—but other applications are equally guilty. Have you ever noticed that some applications seem to gobble every spare bit of memory on your system? The problem might be your installation choices—not the way the application works. Graphics programs (and, to a smaller degree, other categories) often ask what types of filters and other "utility" elements you want to install. A graphics application might include a laundry list of application files that it will import from and export to. A database manager might include an autodial feature, and spreadsheets are rife with background problem solvers. It might seem like a good idea to select them all. After all, you might need them sometime. From a memory standpoint, this decision could be fatal. Some applications load all those fancy utilities and filters whenever you start the application. Each filter and other add-on costs you memory that you could use for some other purpose. If you need that product element, fine, but why pay for something you don't need? The bottom line is that you should install only the filters and utilities that you'll actually use later.

- **Interapplication communication:** I used to absolutely hate packaged applications. These suites of products normally contained things that no one wanted—mini word processors with limited capabilities and a spreadsheet that could barely track your checkbook. Bundled applications suffer a lot less from this problem now and have improved in one other area as well. If you install a suite of products (such as Microsoft Office) instead of separate applications, there's a much better chance that they'll communicate seamlessly. I used to use products from different companies to get the best that each category had to provide. With today's bloated applications, features are no longer a consideration, for the most part. Unless there's a very good reason to do so, you'll probably want to go with a "one-stop shop" solution to fulfill the better part of your application needs.
- **Other support options:** Some applications provide features that don't relate directly to how that product works, but how it reacts in a given situation. I just installed a new utility that gives me a thumbnail-sketch view of several files on my system. One of the installation options was to add that utility to my Startup folder. I had the memory required, so I said yes. It seems like a straightforward decision, but you still need to make it. Some of the other decisions aren't quite so straightforward. For example, one application provided the capability to track my OLE links across the network. To do this, it had to load a rather large piece of code and allow it to remain resident. Since I very seldom even think about using such a capability, I didn't install it. These other support decisions affect the way you work, as well as the amount of memory that the application uses.

The installation process that used to seem so straightforward is no longer so simple. You need to make some hard decisions before you embark on the actual installation process. The tips that I just mentioned will help you make these generic decisions, but you'll find others more difficult to resolve. For example, how do you balance workgroup and individual needs? For some products, such as Lotus Notes, this is a major concern. Using products such as these requires the administrator to make some decisions for the benefit of the group as a whole. Some users will definitely view the decisions as arbitrary and overly confining. When working with workgroup-specific applications, you'll probably need to consider some additional problems:

- **Installation location:** Deciding where to put a workgroup application is a major decision. Placing all the installation files on the network makes it a lot easier for the administrator to manage and maintain the application. It also reduces the chance that someone will attempt to pirate the application, because the network usually provides better security for the server than it does for the workstation. A server installation also makes it easier to add new users and reduces overall application size, because not every workstation needs a copy of the common files, such as .DLLs. The negative aspects of using a server installation are fairly substantial, on the other hand. The network has to handle a lot more traffic as the application requests .DLLs and other support files from the server. In many cases, the users don't get as many configuration options as they would using a workstation installation.

- **Gateway options:** Many network-specific applications include gateway support. The decision of which gateways to support is fairly obvious unless your network is in a state of transition. If you're in a state of transition, it might be a good idea to wait and install the new application when the network is stable.
- **Local support for network features:** Many network products secretly invade the user's system and steal workstation statistics on a regular basis. This covert form of monitoring probably has its uses, and I don't mean to start spreading a "Big Brother" rumor. However, unless you're the sole administrator for a very large network, you have to weigh the importance of such a feature against the memory it will take from each workstation. Windows 95 is fairly memory-hungry to begin with. Adding a burden of unneeded drivers will only make things worse.

Now that we've looked at some of the things you need to consider when installing an application under Windows 95, the need to plan that installation becomes a lot clearer. Add to the installation problems the need to upgrade each user's machine and the cost of administrator time in doing so, and you'll begin to understand why some companies don't like software updates. Overall, a planned installation should provide you with a solid foundation on which to build your fully exploited application later.

Getting Application Settings Right

Very few applications use the same settings. You'll find that applications of a particular kind (such as word processors) might share a few of the same settings, but for the most part you need to spend some time reading the user manual to figure them out. We won't discuss the actual process of changing your application's settings in this section; you'll need to read the vendor manuals later. We'll look at some general principles you can use to make life easier. These are areas where you can start looking for potential speed, memory, or efficiency gains.

Tip: Everyone's first inclination is to get into the application and complete this part of the setup immediately. That would probably be the worst mistake you could make. Software settings change as you learn how to use the application more efficiently. As your knowledge about the application increases, the feature that seemed important yesterday will appear almost foolish today. The settings I use for my applications are in an almost continuous state of flux. A little change here or a little tweak there can make a big difference in how well the application works for me. Take the time required to go through the tutorial first, and then make any settings changes you think will help. I usually keep Notepad handy to record any ideas I come up with while running the tutorial.

Changing your settings is largely a matter of personal preference. However, even a small change can make a big difference in the way you use an application. For example, you can do something as small as customize a toolbar and reap a fairly large increase in efficiency. Not using an application's autocorrect feature might allow you to run background tasks more efficiently. It's not the major changes you'll notice the most, but the little extras that you add to your computing environment. The following tips can help you get the most out of your applications:

- **Toolbars:** A toolbar represents one way that you can greatly increase your efficiency for a very small increase in memory usage. Remember, every icon you allocate uses some additional system resources, so you'll want to maintain the minimum number required to get the job done. On the other hand, the amount of memory an icon uses is very small—usually less than 1KB. When setting up my toolbar, I don't assume that the vendor provided something even close to optimal, so I try to track which commands I use the most. The commands that get used a lot should appear on the toolbar. It takes less time to access a command from the toolbar than from a menu, so placing common commands here is one way to improve your efficiency. Seven icons should appear on every toolbar: Open, Close, New, Print, Cut, Copy, and Paste. You might want to add Print Preview to this list as well. People who use OLE a lot might want to stick Paste Special here to make inserting objects faster. Be certain to remove any standard toolbar buttons that you don't use. For example, Microsoft Word usually adds links to Microsoft's other products to the toolbar. I usually remove these icons, because I don't use the links that way.

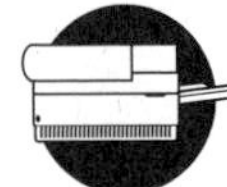

- **Printer settings:** Every application I own (with the exception of a few small utilities) allows me to set the printer configuration separately from the Windows general configuration. I usually set my printer configuration to match my use of that application. For example, I use my word processor for final output, in most cases, so I use the best letter-quality resolution available. On the other hand, I never use one of my graphics programs for final output, so I select draft quality there. A draft printout might not seem very acceptable, and it isn't if you plan to send the document to someone, but it's a lot more efficient than letter quality when you just want a quick look at your document. (A minor benefit of using draft output whenever possible is that you'll use less ink, making those expensive toner cartridges last longer.) You can also vary the print resolution. A low-resolution letter-quality printout might work fine for workgroup presentations, but you'll want to use the highest available quality when making the same presentation to a larger audience. The resolution you use will affect the amount of memory and time required to complete the printout.
- **Macros:** The first thing you need to know is what a macro is. I always look at a macro as "canned keystrokes." Think about the steps you take to create a letter. Every time you do it, you probably add a heading with the company name and other information. Wouldn't it be nice if you could tell the program to do this for you automatically? That's what a macro does. It replays the keystrokes you would normally make by hand, by recording them in a separate area of memory. A macro recorder works just like a tape recorder. It records your keystrokes and allows you to play them back later.

Macros are one area where you might find it difficult to come up with a concrete rule for settings. I almost always create macros for every repetitive task I perform with my main applications. The investment in time required to create the macro always gets paid back in improved efficiency. (Let me quickly define two terms. If I perform a task manually nearly every time I use the application, that's *repetitive*. I really don't need to perform that task if the computer can do it equally well and in a lot less time. A *main application* is one that I use at least eight hours a week. Any shorter time than that, and you have to wonder when you'd have time to use the macro.) Some tasks work better as macros. For example, I always set up my word processing files using a macro. It makes more sense for the computer to do the work than for me to do it. In fact, I use this macro so often that I attached it to my toolbar as an icon. (This is another decision you'll need to make. Attaching a macro to a toolbar button is always a good idea if you use the macro a lot.) Other tasks don't work well as macros. For example, I always thought that changing the format of a document from one form to another would make a great macro, but implementing it proved frustrating. It takes a human mind to perform some tasks.

Note: Windows 3.x provided a macro recorder that allowed you to record various Windows-related tasks and replay them later. The problem was that the macro recorder's implementation was flawed, and people complained about it. Many bugs in the macro recorder caused GPFs. It was also a little on the limited side as far as capabilities were concerned. Instead of fixing the problem, Microsoft decided to eliminate it. Windows 95 doesn't provide a macro recorder.

- **Style sheets and templates:** One thing you can never have too many of is custom style sheets and templates. I always use a style sheet for my documents if the application supports them. The reason is simple: A style sheet doesn't take more than a few minutes to create, but it can save a lot of time later. Templates are the same. They take only a short time to create, but they definitely reduce the time needed to create useful output later. Templates and style sheets also provide one other benefit: They tend to enforce uniformity in the format of your document. This is important whether you're part of a group or working as an individual. I view consistent output as one of the marks of a professional, and most other people do, too. In addition, if you spend less time worrying about how to format your document, you'll have a lot more time to work on its contents.
- **Autocorrect:** The autocorrect features provided by many applications are a source of much consternation for me. On the one hand, they provide a valuable aid: autocorrecting misspelled words or other types of user input. The problem is that most of them chew up valuable memory and processor cycles—resources that you could use to run a task in the background. I normally turn off my autocorrect features and rely on my spelling checker (or other tools) to find all those mistakes at one time. Whether this approach is efficient for you is a personal decision, based on how you work.

Tip: There's an another way to use autocorrect. You can use it to substitute short phrases for long ones. For example, suppose you have to type your company name a lot—Jackson Consolidated Freight Company. You could add an acronym such as JCFC to your autocorrect dictionary. Then, every time you needed to type your company name, you could type JCFC, and your application would substitute the long name in its place.

- **Autoload:** This goes back to those utility and filter programs mentioned earlier, in the "Installation Options" section. Some programs, such as Microsoft Access and Lotus 1-2-3, let you autoload some of your utilities or filters. This allows you to access them faster. There's a tradeoff for the convenience of instant access, however: You have to give up some memory and perhaps a few processor cycles to do it. The middle ground is to autoload the features that you know you'll use every time. It takes only a few seconds to load the other features, so you'll want to do that manually, in most cases.

Peter's Principle: My Settings Won't Work on Your Machine

We're all individuals. Nowhere is this more apparent than in the way we use software. I might think that the way you do something is absurd, but if it works for you, it's probably the right way to go (at least until you learn better).

There are some constants in the world of applications, and a wealth of tip and technique books to prove it. You can probably buy any number of tip and technique books that will help you get your application set up in a very short time with a minimum of effort. On the other hand, you need to make just as many, if not more, personal decisions. For example, I usually include the Insert Annotation command for Word for Windows on my toolbar because I use this feature a lot. I suggested the same thing to a colleague and he found it a waste of time, because he used a different technique for making annotations.

I find that the same thing holds true for just about every type of user setting, but that you might have to give up some autonomy in workgroup situations. For example, I usually use three different user dictionaries: common, computer, and jargon. This allows me to keep some words separate so that they don't contaminate my general-purpose dictionary. In a workgroup situation, you might find that everyone needs to use the same dictionary to ensure consistent results for a project. The same thing holds true for other user settings, such as templates and style sheets. A group project usually requires the individual to defer to the group's needs to enforce a certain level of consistency.

The point is that you need to work with an application long enough to build a rapport with it. Once you figure out how you want to work with the application, you can start changing some of those personal settings to meet your specific requirements. In fact, you might find that some of your settings end up working for the group as well. Experimentation is a prime ingredient in finding the settings that work best for you.

Setting up an application is a continual process. Exploiting your software is often as much a matter of using the software in the best way you know how as it is a matter of optimizing memory and speed settings. Don't give up too much personal comfort for a perceived memory or speed benefit. You have to weigh the time that a specific feature will save against what it will cost. That's what you do in other business decisions; evaluating your software is no different.

Running 16-Bit Windows Applications

Chapter 6 looks at how 16-bit applications run. That discussion should clue you in to some of the problems you'll encounter running them. The fact that all 16-bit applications share one address space is part of the problem. This means they have to share the system resources required to display windows, icons, and graphic elements of all sorts. A 16-bit application also faces other problems, such as cooperative multitasking, which I talked about earlier. That particular problem only gets worse under Windows 95, because 32-bit applications run in their own session.

Tip: Some older Windows applications display an invalid dynalink call error message when you try to run them. This means that they're incompatible with a new Windows 95 version of a .DLL. You have two choices. Upgrading the application is the best alternative, because you'll replace that old product with something that will work better with Windows 95—hopefully, a 32-bit version of what you used in the past. If upgrading isn't an option, reinstall the application, reboot Windows 95, and try it again. You have to reboot in order to reload the .DLL into memory. Otherwise, you'll see the same error message, because the Windows 95 version is still in place. If you still get an invalid dynalink call message, there's some incompatibility between the application and a basic Windows 95 system file. You absolutely must upgrade in this case, because you can't replace those common files to meet the needs of one program. One or more Windows 95 applications might cease to function if you do (including the operating system itself). Windows 95 always maintains a copy of its system files in the SYSBCKUP folder under the main Windows folder. You can use this copy of the file to replace the old .DLL if necessary.

The same types of optimization techniques you used under Windows 3.x will probably work here as well. You'll still need to keep the cooperative multitasking aspect of 16-bit applications in mind when running certain types of applications in the background. For example, you'll probably find it difficult to run your 16-bit database and your communications program at the same time at high speed. The cooperative nature of these applications means that the database will probably take control of the system for that one second longer than the communications program can hold data in the buffer. The result is lost data. Windows 95 is a lot better in this regard than Window 3.x was, but it still isn't perfect, because the applications it runs aren't perfect.

Chapter 3 looks at many ways in which you can tune the Windows environment, by getting rid of excess icons and the like. These same tips apply to applications, for the most part. Be sure to spend some time reviewing that chapter for some additional hints.

Tip: Some 16-bit applications give you a choice between storing .DLL files locally or in the Windows SYSTEM directory. Choose the local option to make it easier to remove the application later. This also reduces the chance that the application's setup routine will accidentally overwrite a Windows 95 version of a file.

You should ignore a few of those old Windows 3.x optimization techniques when using Windows 95. The one I tell most people about is the use of virtual memory. If your system contained enough memory under Windows 3.x, you could get a performance boost by disabling virtual memory. Of course, this meant that you were effectively limited in the amount of system memory you could expect, but the performance gain was worth it. Don't disable virtual memory under Windows 95.

Using the Print Manager was something else that a lot of people avoided when they needed to get their output fast. Windows 95 uses a much-improved form of Print Manager that you'll want to use for optimum performance. I'll stop short of saying that the output will arrive at the same speed, though. If you have a heavy system load when you start the print job, you'll definitely see a decrease in print speed. However, you gain increased system performance and regain control of your application faster as a result. It's another tradeoff, but I think it's a good one in this case.

Running 32-Bit Windows Applications

I tested a lot of 32-bit applications and found a few interesting facts. Overall, a 32-bit application is larger and just a tad slower (when you view a single section of code) than its 16-bit counterpart. It's larger because you're using 32 bits for everything, even structures that might not require 32 bits. In addition, 32-bit code is typically larger than its 16-bit counterpart. Does this mean that 32-bit applications are memory hogs that you shouldn't use? Not by a long shot.

Let me explain the slower part of 32-bit application performance a little better. A 32-bit application starts out a tad slower than its 16-bit equivalent but ends up faster for a number of reasons. Most of these have to do with the use of a flat address space and other architectural benefits of using a 32-bit format. Yes, it takes more time to process 32-bit code than the equivalent sections of 16-bit code, because the 32-bit code is larger. However, there's still a big speed benefit in the long run, due to the way that a 32-bit application executes.

There are definite benefits in the way of speed when it comes to running a 32-bit application. For one thing, it supports true multitasking. I found that background repagination in the 16-bit version of Word usually meant that I had to wait until the application finished the task anyway. Under the 32-bit version, Word spawns a task that really does run in the background. I very seldom even notice that anything is going on anymore; the document just gets repaginated without my thinking about it. This is how multitasking should work, from a user perspective.

Multitasking also helps you to perform some tasks, such as printing, a lot faster than you could by using a 16-bit application. For one thing, Windows can make better use of idle time with a 32-bit application. But this isn't the big feature that users will notice. You'll notice that you regain control of the system faster. After a 32-bit application spawns a print task, it can return control of the computer immediately. It doesn't even need to slow you down as it checks on the status of the "background" print job, like a 16-bit application does.

Warning: Every time a 32-bit application spawns a new task (called a *thread*), it uses some system resources. Some applications can create so many threads that your system begins to slow to a crawl and Windows runs out of resources. The second you run completely out of resources, the machine usually freezes. Although Microsoft increased the size of some memory areas and moved others to the 32-bit area, Windows 95 still isn't perfect when it comes to managing 32-bit resources. The best thing to do is to avoid the situation altogether. Don't try to run every feature that a 32-bit application can provide at one time. Limit the number of tasks you ask an application to perform in the background to a reasonable level. Finally, run the Resource Monitor from time to time just to see how you're doing on system resources. You might find that you need to adjust some of your techniques to compensate for limitations in the Windows 95 design.

The big performance-tuning tip for Windows 95 and 32-bit applications is to use as many automatic settings as possible. The more room you give Windows 95 to compensate for changing system conditions, the better. Chapter 3 contains quite a few tips that you can follow to optimize the environment. For example, it looks at the need to monitor the swap file size to ensure that you don't end up wasting processor cycles in thrashing. Once you optimize the environment for a 32-bit application, you've essentially optimized the application itself. All you need to do is check out the earlier section called "Getting Application Settings Right" to make the application as efficient as possible during use.

Optimizing DOS Applications

It will be a long time before we see the demise of all DOS applications. It's true that very few commercial application vendors are updating their DOS products anymore, but that isn't the total picture. There's more to the DOS scene than just commercial applications.

One of the biggest areas where DOS will remain king for the foreseeable future is games. Why are games such a hot DOS item? Because the DOS environment gives the programmer access to more of the hardware and allows him to write a fast and visually stimulating program. Windows is notorious for grabbing too many system resources and running games at almost a snail's pace when compared to a DOS version of the same program. Microsoft is working on several strategies, including WinG and DirectX, that will make Windows more attractive to game vendors, but they aren't there yet. (Microsoft is getting closer every day, though—a lot more games are coming out with dual DOS and Windows 95 versions.) I can usually find Windows versions of many games if I look hard enough, but the DOS versions are still selling like hotcakes. Even if these new technologies were to mature by tomorrow, though, it's unlikely that users will give up their old games immediately. Some games have an amazing shelf life when you consider the technology they use. For example, I still know people who like to play the original ZORK series—a text-based DOS game with a great plot but no graphics at all.

Fortunately, change is in the air: Game vendors are actually starting to produce a reasonable number of Windows games now that DirectX is in its third release. The only caveat when using a Windows game that supports DirectX is to make certain that you have the latest version of that product. You'll also want to check with your video and audio card vendor to make sure that you have the latest drivers—some vendors are coming out with DirectX-specific drivers. Right now you can download the current version of DirectX at `http://www.microsoft.com/mediadev/download/isdk.htm`. Fortunately for OSR2 users, the current version of DirectX comes as part of the package (as of this writing, at least). Make absolutely certain that you have a complete copy of your current video drivers. Some users have complained of severe compatibility problems when using DirectX with certain display adapters. You'll want a copy of your current drivers just in case you need to remove DirectX from your machine. (DirectX 3 does provide an option for restoring your original video and audio drivers, but it doesn't always work properly, according to some people that I've talked with.)

Tip: Microsoft's efforts in creating its own line of game programs have netted some valuable tools for game vendors as well. Most noticeable of these are all the DirectX technologies that Microsoft has made available. DirectX allows a game program direct access to the hardware from within Windows 95, yet keeps the operating system informed as well. While this means that Windows games still aren't quite as fast as their DOS counterparts, they do come a lot closer. Expect to see a lot more Windows games in the near future, as game vendors tire of supporting DOS games through boot disks and other kludges.

Custom applications are another area where people are still using DOS. This time it's for a different reason. A custom application can cost thousands of dollars. The consultant who writes the program has to charge that much because the chances of his selling more than a few hundred copies are slim at best. Because custom applications usually manipulate very sensitive company data that's hard to move to another application, people are going to think twice before attempting to move that data somewhere else. Fortunately, I see this particular class of DOS application coming to an end as Windows tools become easier and faster to use. A consultant can be a lot more productive now, so the cost is less for creating a new application, in some cases.

Also, old habits die hard. Some people are used to using DOS utility programs, so that's what they'll continue to use. There are perfectly acceptable substitutes for these applications in most cases—substitutes that are easier to use and that run faster—but some people just won't use them. This is the third group of people who will make at least some use of DOS under Windows 95.

The following sections explore a variety of DOS options. In most cases, I show you the best methods first and later add a few marginal methods you can use in a pinch. Of course, my advice is to move to a 32-bit Windows 95 or Windows NT application as soon as possible. DOS isn't dead, strictly speaking, but it does have one foot in the grave. Very few application vendors even support DOS anymore. It won't be long before other vendors follow as well. You'll end up with a hard disk full of old applications that no one will support.

MS-DOS Emulation

You use MS-DOS under Windows 95 through the MS-DOS emulation mode. What actually happens is that Windows makes a copy of the phantom DOS session stored in memory, spawns a new V86 session, and places the copy it made in the new session. What you see is either a windowed or full-screen DOS session. All you need to do to open a DOS session is select MS-DOS Prompt from the Start | Programs menu option. You'll also start a DOS session whenever you select a DOS application from either Explorer or the Start menu. Figure 13.8 shows a windowed session.

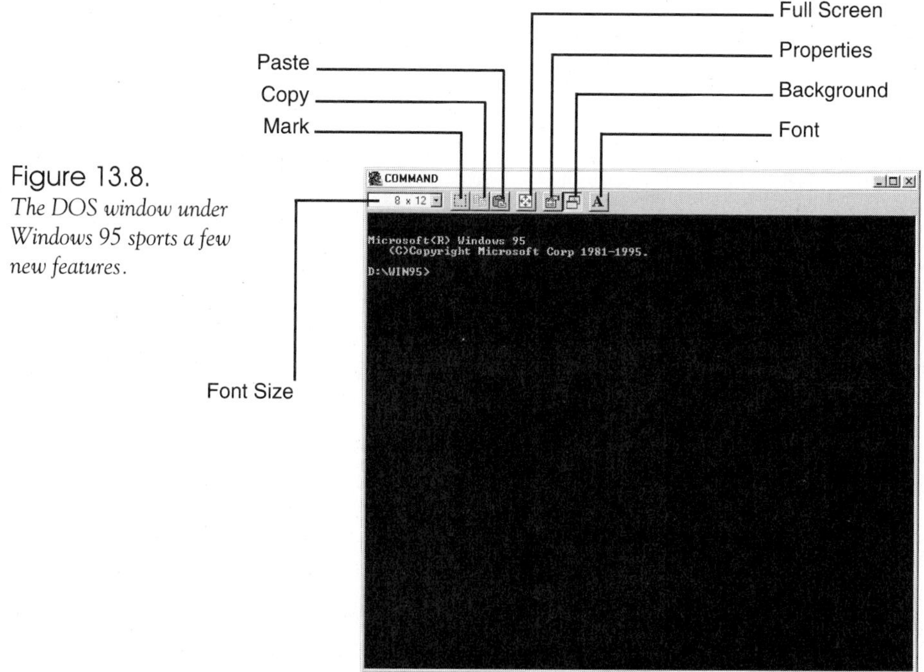

Figure 13.8.
The DOS window under Windows 95 sports a few new features.

It isn't too difficult to see that this DOS window doesn't even come close to matching what you used in the past. Windows 95 provides about the same features, but it makes the window a lot easier to use and configure. All the controls you need immediately are displayed as part of a toolbar on the window. There are also many hidden configuration options, which we'll discuss later. Here's the list of new controls:

- **Font Size:** This list box allows you to choose the size of the font used to display information in the DOS window. It defines the number of horizontal and vertical pixels used for each character. You need to find a balance between readability and the ability to view the entire screen at once. I usually use the font size shown in Figure 13.8 because it offers the best of both worlds. Of course, the font size you choose is partially determined by the resolution of your display. A DOS window normally defaults to the Auto setting. What this means is that Windows 95 will attempt to find the proper font size based on the number of lines of text in the DOS box and the resolution of your display. For example, if you choose an 80-character × 25-line display mode and your screen provides 640×480 resolution, Windows 95 will select the font nearest to 8×19.2 pixels. To get these numbers, I divided the horizontal resolution by the number of characters (640/80) and the vertical resolution by the number of lines (480/25). In this case, Windows 95 would probably default to the 8×16 font listed in the Font Size list box. I usually find that the Windows 95 setting makes maximum use of the display but isn't usually the best setting for my needs. Optimizing the setting to meet your particular needs is the best way to go.
- **Mark:** Use this control to select an area of the screen for copying. Windows 95 places the selected area on the Clipboard when you select the Copy command, so that you can use the selection in other applications. The selected area is highlighted, as shown in Figure 13.9. You can use either the cursor keys or the mouse to select the desired area.

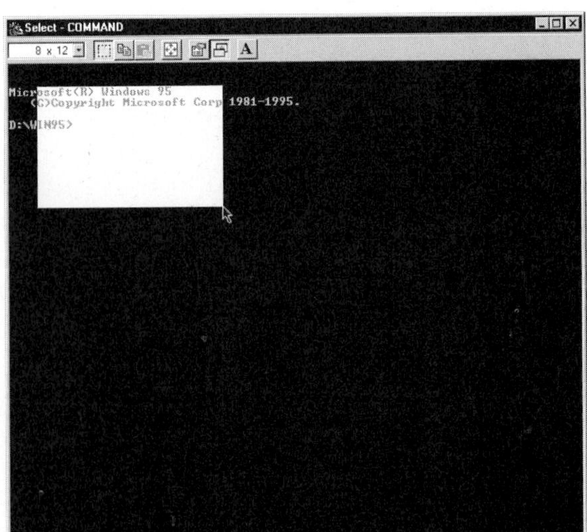

Figure 13.9.
You can use the Mark button to copy part of the DOS screen to the Windows Clipboard.

- **Copy:** The Copy button places on the Clipboard the area you highlighted by using the Mark button.
- **Paste:** You can also paste information from a Windows application into the DOS box. Obviously, you can't paste anything other than text unless the display is in graphics mode. Even then, your ability might be limited by the DOS application running at the time.
- **Full Screen:** Clicking this button changes the windowed DOS prompt into a full-screen version.
- **Properties:** Every DOS application has a number of properties that you can set (discussed later in this chapter). Clicking this button displays the Properties dialog box for the current application.
- **Background:** Click this button to run the current DOS application in the background. This comes in handy for situations in which you want to monitor the application but don't really need to interact with it.
- **Font:** This button performs about the same task as the Font Size list box mentioned earlier. However, instead of merely displaying a list of font sizes, it displays the Font page of the program's Properties dialog box.

Once you get past the fancy new display, you'll see that DOS is unchanged. It doesn't really provide anything more than you had in the past. One feature that it does provide is long filename support. Use the `DIR` command if you want to see what I mean. Figure 13.10 shows the results of using it to display all the .BMP files in the \WIN95 directory.

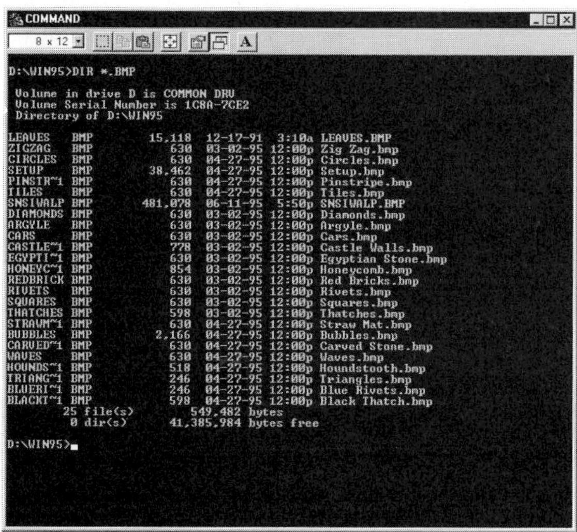

Figure 13.10.
DOS reacts differently when you use the `DIR` *command under Windows 95.*

Note: Long filename support is available only under Windows 95. Once you leave that environment to work in MS-DOS mode, the `DIR` command operates exactly as it did before. The MS-DOS mode of operation is also known as raw DOS mode. None of the Windows 95 drivers are loaded when you use this mode, including long filename support. Obviously, you must be very careful about corrupting your long filenames when in this mode.

Tip: You can also use long filenames when typing commands. The only requirement is that you use quotes to enclose the long filename or directory, like this:

```
DIR "Some Long Directory Name"
```

In addition to long filename support, there are a few new utility programs and changes to some old utilities. For example, you no longer need to run a copy of QBasic to use Edit. In addition, Edit now provides the capability to modify more than one file at once. The next section covers the specific changes in DOS utility support.

DOS Versus Windows 95 Commands

Microsoft must have expected people to use the DOS prompt for a while longer, or they wouldn't have improved some of the utilities that come with Windows 95. We looked at one of those utilities earlier, so I won't describe it here again. The `START` utility (described in the "Undocumented Parameters" section of Chapter 5) is one new feature most people will really like. It allows you to start a Windows application from a full-screen DOS session. We really don't have room here to explore all the DOS commands, so I'm going to give you the highlights. The following list shows the changes that MS-DOS (running under Windows 95) provides:

- All the disk-scanning utilities from previous versions of DOS are upgraded to support long filenames. Windows 95 also replaces many of these files with batch file substitutes, in case you decide to maintain a dual-boot capability. The renamed files include DBLSPACE.BAT, DRVSPACE.BAT, DEFRAG.BAT, and SCANDISK.BAT on my machine.
- `EDIT` is a stand-alone command now. It also provides the means for editing more than one file.
- Some applications, such as ScanDisk, start the Windows version of the program even when executed at the DOS prompt. There's no longer a true DOS version of the program.

- Windows 95 includes a new NET command. You can use it to determine a wealth of information about your network from the DOS prompt. For example, typing **NET VIEW** displays a list of computers and other resources currently available on the network. To learn more about this command, type **NET?** at the DOS prompt.

The OSR2 release of Windows 95 also provides new MS-DOS versions of FDISK, FORMAT, SCANDISK, and DEFRAG. These new utilities are FAT 32-enabled—they're designed to work with Microsoft's new file system for Windows 95. The "What Is 32-Bit VFAT?" section of Chapter 9 describes this new file system in detail.

Along with the new features that the Windows 95 version of MS-DOS provides, there are a few features that you won't find. For example, the Windows 95 version of MS-DOS doesn't include any of the following commands (although you can use them in raw DOS mode if your old DOS directory is still available):

APPEND	INTERLINK	RAMDRIVE.SYS
ASSIGN	INTERSVR	RECOVER
BACKUP	JOIN	REPLACE
COMP	MEMCARD	RESTORE
DOSSHELL	MEMMAKER	ROMDRIVE.SYS
EDLIN	MIRROR	SHARE
EGA.SYS	MSAV	SMARTMON
FASTHELP	MSBACKUP	TREE
FASTOPEN	POWER	UNDELETE
GRAFTABL	PRINT	UNFORMAT
GRAPHICS	PRINTER.SYS	VSAFE
HELP	QBASIC	

Warning: Users who have the OSR2 version of Windows 95 installed on their machines absolutely must not use any of these old utility programs. Doing so will definitely cause problems with your FAT 32-formatted drive. At a minimum, you'll lose a few files—but you could lose everything on your drive. Use only Windows 95 utilities on an OSR2 machine. The way to tell which version of Windows 95 you have installed is to right-click the My Computer icon, select Properties from the context menu, and look at the version number. If the version number is 4.00.950B, you have the OSR2 version of Windows 95 installed on your machine.

Microsoft's reason for removing the majority of these commands is that they aren't compatible with long filenames. Other programs were removed because Windows 95 supposedly makes them obsolete. I still would have liked to see Microsoft retain some of the commands. For example, an enhanced version of MEMMAKER could help a user tune a setup for an MS-DOS session. Needless to say, some users will be very unhappy about the absence of these commands and utilities.

Creating a DOS Session

You can create a DOS session by using a variety of methods. Double-clicking a DOS application from Explorer creates a DOS session. The session ends as soon as you end the application.

Like previous versions of Windows, Windows 95 includes a DOS prompt. All you need to do is click the MS-DOS Prompt option found in the Programs section of the Start menu. You'll need to type **`exit`** and press Enter to end this session.

Another way to start a DOS session is to select the Restart the Computer in MS-DOS Mode entry of the Shutdown dialog box. This will take you to a full-screen raw DOS session. You can perform any required tasks and then type **`exit`** and press Enter to leave. Windows 95 will automatically reload itself.

DOS Objects

As with any other object under Windows 95, right-clicking a DOS object displays a context menu like the one shown in Figure 13.11. You can cut, copy, and paste a DOS object, like any other object that Windows 95 supports. The Properties option takes you to the Properties dialog box, described in the next section. This is one major area where DOS applications are treated differently from Windows applications.

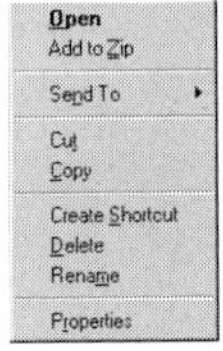

Figure 13.11.
A DOS object's context menu looks much like any other context menu under Windows 95.

Settings

A DOS application's Properties dialog box contains a lot more than the same dialog box for a Windows application. In fact, if you were looking for the PIF (program information file) Editor, here it is. The Properties dialog box shown in Figure 13.12 allows you to change every setting that the PIF Editor provided—and more. In fact, Windows 95 provides several new features for DOS applications that make running them a snap. The following paragraphs describe each section of the Properties dialog box in detail.

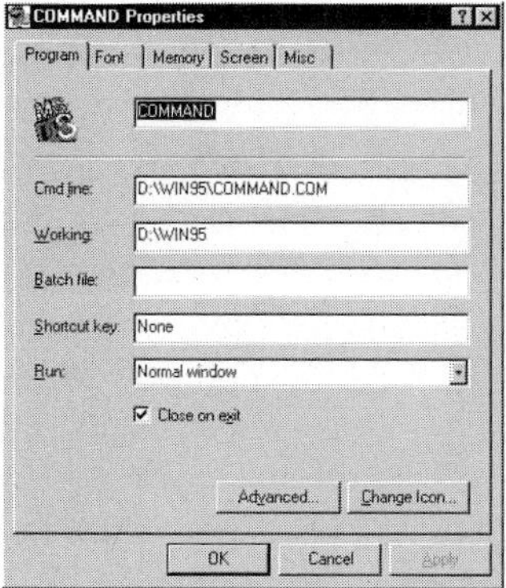

Figure 13.12.
The Properties dialog box replaces the old PIF Editor that you used under Windows 3.x.

Tip: Editing the Properties dialog box doesn't perform some mysterious trick with your DOS application. It saves the settings in a .PIF file, just as it used to under Windows 3.x. In fact, Windows 3.x .PIF files work just fine under Windows 95. However, you won't want to try to move the .PIF files the other way. Windows 95 adds a lot of information to the .PIF file, making it incompatible with older versions of Windows.

Program

The Program page (refer to Figure 13.12) allows you to change the way Windows executes the program. At the very top of the page are an icon and a field containing the application's name. This is the name you'll see within Explorer.

The next three fields determine which application to run. The Cmd Line field contains the name of the application you want to run. It must end with an .EXE, .COM, or .BAT extension. In this case, we're running a copy of the command processor. The Working field tells Windows 95 what directory to start the application from. In most cases, you'll start the application from either its home or its data directory. The choice depends on what kind of information the application requires to start. We'll run the command processor from the \WIN95 directory. The third field, Batch File, is new to Windows 95. It allows you to designate a batch file that runs with the application. For example, in the case of the command processor, you could include a batch file that would set up the path and prompt and load any TSRs you might need.

The Shortcut Key field allows you to assign a shortcut key to the program. Chapter 5 covers this, so I won't cover it again here.

Use the Run field to determine how Windows 95 runs the application. There are three choices: Normal Window, Minimized, and Maximized. The first two choices affect both windowed and full-screen sessions. The third choice starts windowed sessions maximized.

It's normally a good idea to close the DOS session as soon as you get done. Checking the Close on Exit field does just that.

Clicking the Change Icon button displays the dialog box shown in Figure 13.13. It allows you to select the icon used to identify the application within Explorer and the Start menu. Windows 95 provides the same default choices as other versions of Windows. You can also choose from custom icon sets by clicking the Browse button.

Figure 13.13.
This dialog box allows you to change the icon used to identify the DOS application.

MS-DOS Mode

There's one more button left on the Program page, and I wanted to give it special attention. If you click the Advanced button, you'll see the dialog box shown in Figure 13.14.

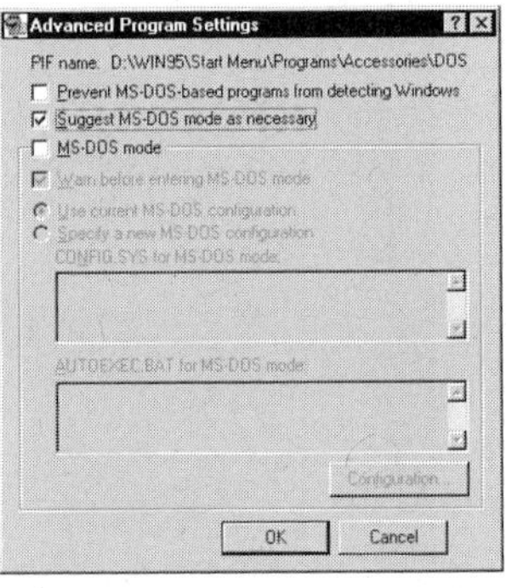

Figure 13.14.
The Advanced Program Settings dialog box is where you make the selections that enable MS-DOS mode for an application.

The first three check boxes in this dialog box control the actual implementation of MS-DOS mode. Some applications run fine under Windows, but they look for specific Windows files when you run them. If they see Windows 95, they quit. Checking the first check box prevents the application from detecting Windows 95, in most cases. The problem with using this particular feature is that less conventional memory will be available to the application, and the application will run more slowly as Windows works to keep itself hidden.

The second check box in this group keeps a detection program running with the DOS application. You can use this as a diagnostic aid when the application won't run properly under Windows 95. However, keeping this box checked after you're reasonably sure that the application doesn't require MS-DOS mode just wastes processor cycles and memory. Unfortunately, Windows 95 automatically defaults to checking this box. This means that you'll have to remember to uncheck it to gain optimum performance from your application.

The MS-DOS Mode check box is third in this dialog box. Checking it means that the application won't run under Windows 95. It also changes the options you have available, as shown in Figure 13.15. If you double-click an application to start it, Windows 95 shuts down all running applications, shuts itself down and unloads from memory, and executes the application. You use this option as a last-ditch effort to get an application to run under Windows 95. Unfortunately, many game programs fall into this category.

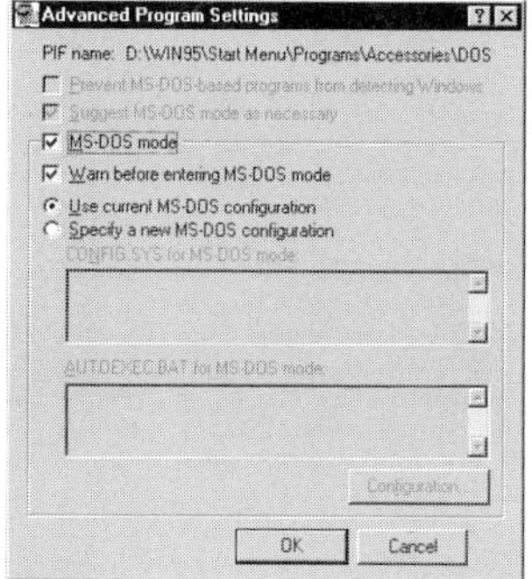

Figure 13.15.
Checking the MS-DOS Mode box makes some new options available but disables others.

I recommend that you always have Windows 95 warn you about entering MS-DOS mode by checking the first new check box in this dialog box, Warn Before Entering MS-DOS Mode. This action will prevent you from entering the mode accidentally. It could prevent data loss in some rare cases, where an application doesn't react properly to the Windows shutdown message.

Windows 95 usually provides default CONFIG.SYS and AUTOEXEC.BAT files for your application. I recommend against using them, for one very good reason: The whole purpose of MS-DOS mode is to get your application to run. Using a set of configuration files specifically designed for MS-DOS mode is a good first step in ensuring that you not only get the application to run, but run efficiently. I usually check the second radio button to enable the configuration entries, as shown in Figure 13.16.

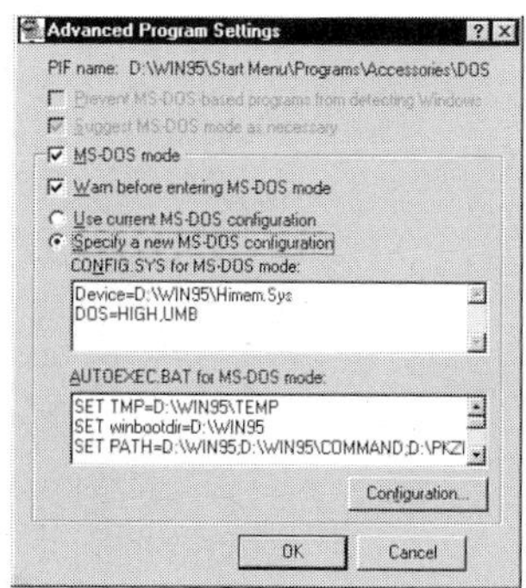

Figure 13.16.
Always use custom configuration files if your application requires MS-DOS mode to run.

There are a number of ways to create a configuration for your application. You can even use the automated configuration method that Microsoft provides, by using the Configuration button. However, I usually copy the appropriate sections of the CONFIG.DOS and AUTOEXEC.DOS files to these screens. (You can paste by using Ctrl+V; Microsoft didn't add a Paste button to this dialog box.) These files contain the old configuration that ran the application. I usually modify the entries as appropriate for this particular situation, but you won't need to do too much tuning.

As you can see, setting up an application for MS-DOS mode doesn't have to be difficult. It's very inconvenient, though, because you can't run any other applications while an MS-DOS-mode application runs. Your hard drive (and associated long filenames) are also susceptible to damage from an MS-DOS-mode application. Make certain that the application is relatively well-behaved in regard to writing to disk before you trust it with your setup.

Font

The Font page, shown in Figure 13.17, allows you to change the appearance of the fonts used to display data in a windowed DOS application. These settings don't affect a full-screen session.

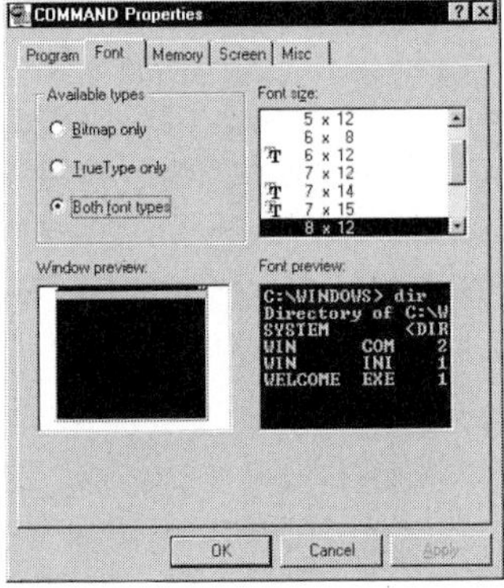

Figure 13.17.
The Font page allows you to control the way a DOS application is displayed in windowed mode.

This dialog box contains four main sections. The first section controls the type of fonts you get to see in the Font Size list box. You'll normally want to use the fullest set of fonts available, by selecting Both Font Types. The only time you might want to switch to one font type or another is when your display has problems displaying one type of font.

The Font Size list box in the second section lists the font sizes you have available for the DOS window. The numbers represent the number of pixels used for each character. A higher number of pixels makes the display more readable. A smaller number of pixels makes the window smaller.

The Window Preview section of this dialog box shows how big the window will appear on the display. The Font Preview section shows the size of the print. You should combine the output from these two displays to determine how large a font to use. It's important to reach a setting that balances the need to see what you're doing with the need to display the entire DOS box at once.

Memory

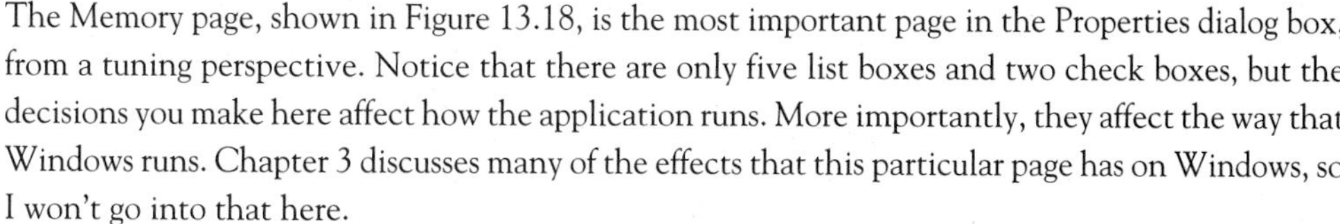

The Memory page, shown in Figure 13.18, is the most important page in the Properties dialog box, from a tuning perspective. Notice that there are only five list boxes and two check boxes, but the decisions you make here affect how the application runs. More importantly, they affect the way that Windows runs. Chapter 3 discusses many of the effects that this particular page has on Windows, so I won't go into that here.

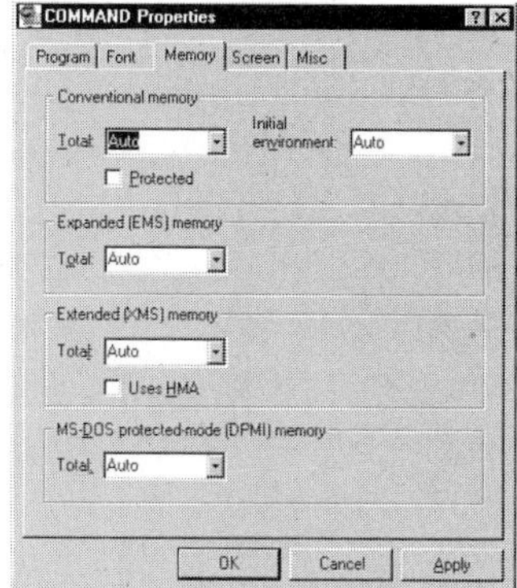

Figure 13.18.
The Memory page allows you to modify the way Windows allocates and manages memory for your DOS application.

Tip: In most cases, you'll want to keep all the list boxes set to Auto and both check boxes unmarked on the Memory page. Windows normally performs better if you allow it to manage memory. The default settings might include checking the Protected check box; unchecking the Protected check box will result in better application performance.

The first group of settings affects conventional memory. The Total field allows you to select any value up to 640KB. You absolutely won't get more than 615KB of conventional memory, so don't try to set the conventional memory any higher than that. Windows normally allocates a 1024-byte environment for your DOS application. This is enough to handle most situations. However, I usually set mine to 4096 to provide space for all those environment strings required by real-mode compilers. The Protected check box is another diagnostic aid. Checking it tells Windows 95 to monitor the application for memory protection errors. The only problem is that you'll suffer a performance loss when using it. If your application tends to corrupt memory, then by all means check this box to keep your environment stable. Otherwise, consider leaving it unchecked for better performance.

The second group of settings contains a single list box that controls how much expanded memory Windows 95 allocates for your application. If you leave it on Auto, MEM reports expanded memory up to the amount of memory your machine has installed. Windows 95 will make only 16MB of it usable if you have more RAM than that installed. The only time you should change this setting is when the application grabs every bit of expanded memory it can find. Some older DOS applications get a little greedy, so you need to provide some controls for that greed.

Note: Unlike other versions of Windows 95, the OSR2 version assumes that you don't want expanded memory support. Instead of the Expanded (EMS) Memory field shown in Figure 13.18, you see a message saying that this computer isn't configured for expanded memory. All you need to do to get expanded memory support is add a `DEVICE=EMM386.EXE` line to your CONFIG.SYS. Make sure that you absolutely must have expanded memory support before you add it, though. The performance gain of not using expanded memory is small, but noticeable.

The third group of settings controls the amount of extended memory available to your application. The default setting allocates the full amount of RAM installed on your system. This isn't an unlimited amount of memory, but it could be fairly high—much higher than the automatic expanded memory setting. As with the expanded memory setting, I usually change this setting from Auto to some specific number if the application gets greedy or if it has problems coping with the full amount of extended memory available on my machine. I usually leave the Uses HMA check box blank, because I normally load DOS in the high memory area. However, if you don't use the HMA, you can always choose to load all or part of an application there by checking this box.

The final group of settings allows you to determine the amount of DPMI memory available to applications. Windows 95 normally sets this to a value that reflects the current system conditions. There's little reason to change this setting from the default.

Screen

The Screen page, shown in Figure 13.19, allows you to configure the screen settings. The first group of settings, Usage, determines the screen mode and number of display lines. You should set the number of display lines here before you set the options on the Font page of this dialog box. Otherwise, a setting that worked well at 25 lines might not work at 50.

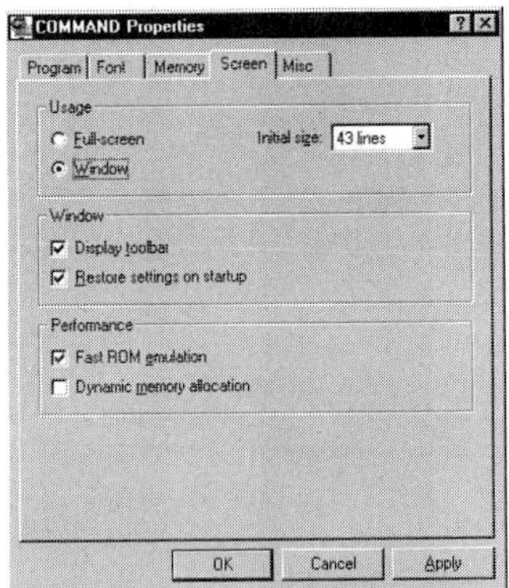

Figure 13.19.
The Screen page allows you to adjust the size and type of display, as well as the method that Windows uses to display it.

The second group of settings lets you change the window settings. It doesn't come into play if you use full-screen mode. I always turn on the toolbar. This is the toolbar I described earlier in this section. It allows you to modify the font size and perform many other tasks with your application without opening the Properties dialog box. The second check box tells Windows 95 to update the .PIF to reflect any changes you made while using the toolbar. Normally the entries are good only for that session. I prefer that Windows remember my settings from session to session, so I check this box.

The third group of settings on this page affects your application's performance. I was a little surprised that this is the only section Microsoft chose to label as Performance, considering the number of other settings that affect the way your application runs. The first setting, Fast ROM Emulation, acts just like shadow RAM. It allows your application to use a RAM version of your display ROM. If an application had trouble with shadow RAM under DOS, it will also have trouble with this setting. Otherwise, you'll want to leave this option checked to get maximum performance from your application.

The second setting in the Performance group helps Windows more than it helps the application. This setting allows Windows to retrieve some of the memory that the DOS application uses for graphics mode, when it goes into character mode. This modicum of memory isn't much, but it could add up if you run a lot of DOS sessions. As with so many other settings, giving Windows the flexibility it needs to fully control the memory on your system is usually a good idea. The only time you'd want to remove the check mark from this setting is when your application spends all or most of its time in graphics mode.

Misc

The Misc (miscellaneous) page mainly provides settings that determine how Windows interacts with your application from a functional point of view. Figure 13.20 shows the settings you'll find here.

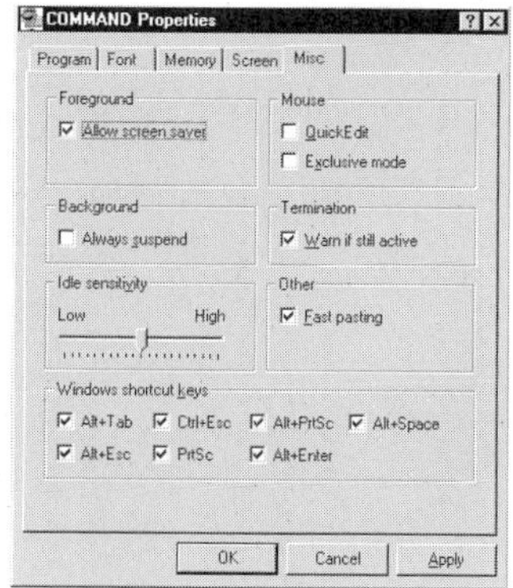

Figure 13.20.
The Misc page allows you to control a variety of settings that don't fit into the other categories explored earlier.

The Allow Screen Saver setting doesn't really have much of an effect when you're using windowed applications. It determines whether Windows can interrupt a full-screen session to run a screen saver. Some full-screen applications really get confused if you allow the screen saver to operate. This is especially true of graphics applications and those that use RAM fonts. (A RAM font provides the check box and radio button controls that you see in some character-mode applications.)

The Mouse group contains two settings. The QuickEdit check box allows you to use a mouse within a DOS window, just as you would with any Windows application. This means that you can select, copy, and paste with a lot less trouble than you could before. The Exclusive Mode check box gives a windowed application exclusive control over the mouse. The consequences of doing this on a permanent basis are pretty severe. This means that you can't use the mouse with your regular Windows applications as long as this application is active. It would probably be a better idea to run this application in a full-screen session if it has this much trouble sharing the mouse.

Some of the settings on this page can provide subtle performance control over your application. The Background and Idle Sensitivity controls fall into this category. Checking the Always Suspend check box does more than suspend the application when it's in the background. It frees resources for Windows 95 to use with other applications. If you're using a DOS application for data entry or some other task that requires continuous input, it pays to check this box and use those resources for other applications. The Idle Sensitivity setting also controls how Windows allocates resources. Normally, Windows tracks the amount of activity from an application. It if determines that the application is sitting there doing nothing while waiting for input from you, Windows 95 reduces the application's CPU resources. This is fine in most cases, but sometimes Windows doesn't give the application enough resources to complete the task it's performing. If this is the case, lowering the Idle Sensitivity setting gives the application the resources it needs, at the expense of other applications that are running on the system at the time.

The Warn If Still Active check box in the Termination group displays a message if you try to terminate the DOS application window without ending the program first. Normally you'll want to keep this checked to prevent potential data loss from a premature application termination.

Another performance enhancement, albeit a small one, is the Fast Pasting check box. You should normally keep this box checked so that Windows can use a high-speed method of pasting information into your DOS application. The only time you should change this is when data gets damaged during transition if you using the fast-paste mode.

The final group on the page controls the use of control-key combinations under Windows 95. Checking a box in the Windows Shortcut Keys group allows Windows to use that key combination. Unchecking it allows the application to use the key combination. Obviously, you'll want to keep as many key combinations checked as possible. The only time you really need to change these settings is when the application needs them for some purpose and you can't change the application's settings.

On Your Own

Find a .DLL for one of the smaller applications installed on your machine. Use the procedure described in Chapter 6 for viewing the contents of files, to determine which .DLLs and other system files this application needs in order to work. Once you make up the list, see whether other applications require the same files. You might be surprised by what you find. Windows 95 reuses a lot of files.

Use the procedures outlined in this chapter to create an MS-DOS-mode session for one of your ill-behaved applications. Does the application run any better in MS-DOS mode? Try this with an application that seems to work fine under Windows 95. Does the application run any faster in MS-DOS mode than under Windows 95? Can you see any difference in the way it runs?

14

Exploiting Your Hardware

Chapter 13 looked at some of the things you could do to exploit your software. Getting the most out of your software is really only part of the process, however. You have a large investment in hardware as well, so it pays to get the most you can out of it. A combination of optimum hardware and software usage will enable you to get your work done quickly, yet use the least number of resources. I use the same criteria in this chapter as in Chapter 13 to define exploiting your hardware. In short, this chapter provides the information you need to get the job done fast and with few resources, without sacrificing any quality.

One of the problems with trying to come up with a set of definitive hardware guidelines is that not everyone has the same equipment. Your equipment is probably different from just about everyone else's. Unlike software, which must at least standardize to the hardware and follow the interface rules used by all Windows software in general, each piece of hardware seems to need a unique set of drivers. Sure, two SVGA display adapters use some of the same access methods, but hardware vendors differentiate their products by the things they *don't* do the same way.

Another problem with hardware is variances within the same model. My Pro Audio Spectrum 16+ Revision D has some subtle differences from Revision C that cause problems under Windows in some cases. In fact, I can't use the Revision C drivers with my Revision D device; they simply won't work. Obviously you can't provide a driver for every little variation that a piece of hardware might have; that would require literally hundreds of drivers for each vendor. However, you can provide a driver that uses the common features of each variation and hope that the subtle differences won't cause any problems.

Problems aside, you'll find that Windows 95 provides good support for most of the hardware on your machine and even takes a few quirks into account so you don't have to. The following sections look at all the classes of hardware you can install. I provide general tips for optimizing your setup and give you some guidelines that you can use to implement an effective strategy for nonstandard hardware.

Installing and Deleting Devices

Windows 95 normally detects all the hardware on your machine during setup. It goes through a checklist to see whether it can figure out what kinds of devices you have and then loads the appropriate drivers for you. Chapter 4 covers this entire process. That chapter also covers some of the things you can do if Windows 95 doesn't detect your hardware, so we won't cover any of that ground again here. However, what happens if you install a new piece of hardware after installing Windows 95? What do you do with old devices that are no longer installed? These are the topics we cover in this section of the chapter. We also look at troubleshooting procedures that you can follow if Windows doesn't act as expected.

Installing Hardware

Windows 95 normally conducts a check of your system during startup. It automatically searches for each device you're supposed to have installed and loads the appropriate drivers. Normally it also looks for new devices you don't have listed anywhere. If Windows 95 finds a new device, it performs the same kind of .INF file search that it did during initial installation to detect the kind of new device.

At least, this is the way things are supposed to work. Reality is very different. I tried installing and removing a variety of devices from several types of machines just to see how Windows 95 would react. It does a superb job on plug and play-compatible machines. The better the manufacturer followed the plug and play guidelines, the better Windows 95 detects the new hardware.

The problem starts with older systems. Windows 95 can't always detect a new device with a non-plug and play system because the device might not even turn on until you load the device driver. Chapter 4 covers most of the reasons behind this, so I won't bore you with the details again. Suffice it to say that, without help, Windows 95 won't detect every device installed in those older systems.

I did find a correlation between device type and the capacity of Windows 95 to detect it. For example, I didn't experience too many problems getting Windows 95 to detect network adapters or name-brand hard drive controllers. It had a little more trouble detecting display adapters. Windows 95 normally could tell me that the display adapter was present, but it couldn't always accurately detect the type. The worst card on this list was the sound board. I found that even if Windows 95 did detect the sound board, it was usually wrong about the vendor. For example, it kept insisting that my Pro Audio Spectrum was an older Sound Blaster. I wasn't too surprised about the outcome of my tests. Without getting any real information from the device itself, Windows 95 does a good job of detecting the devices in your machine.

Automatic Installation

Now that you understand the problems, what do you do to get around them? I usually try to get Windows 95 to detect the device automatically, using the following procedure. Always try this method first:

1. Open the Control Panel and double-click the Add New Hardware applet. You should see the Add New Hardware Wizard shown in Figure 14.1.
2. Click Next. You should see the dialog box shown in Figure 14.2. Notice that this dialog box has two options. The first allows Windows 95 to automatically detect the hardware for you. Use this method first, because it involves the least amount of effort on your part and reduces the chance that you'll install the wrong driver.

Figure 14.1.
The initial screen of the Add New Hardware Wizard.

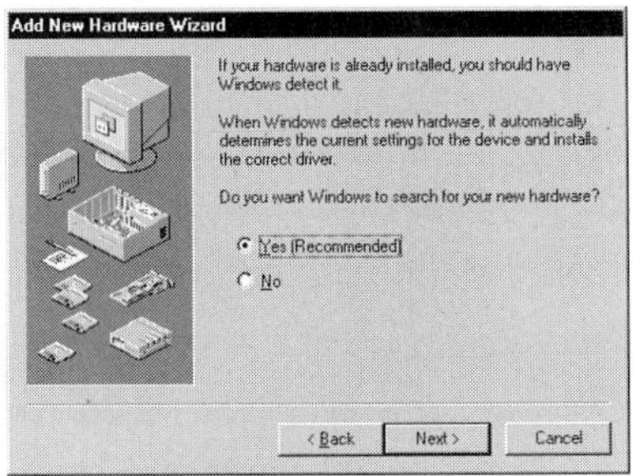

Figure 14.2.
Use this dialog box to select the automatic or manual hardware installation method.

3. After you've clicked the Yes radio button, click Next. Windows displays a dialog box telling you what the program will do. Essentially, it performs the same type of hardware search as when you first installed Windows 95.

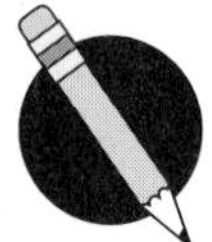

Note: The hardware-detection phase can take quite a while, especially on older machines. The one constant I noticed is that when disk activity stops for more than five minutes, it's a pretty safe bet that the machine is frozen. As long as you hear disk activity during this phase, you're fairly safe in assuming that hardware detection is still taking place. (The hardware detection indicator doesn't move at a steady pace. It appears to take more time as it nears the end.)

4. Click Next. Windows 95 displays a dialog box showing you its hardware-detection progress, as shown in Figure 14.3.

   Once Windows 95 completes the hardware detection phase, it displays a dialog box similar to the one shown in Figure 14.4 if it finds something new.

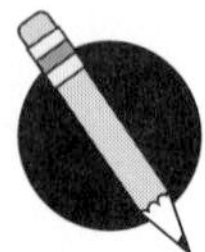

Note: If Windows 95 doesn't detect any new hardware, it displays a dialog box telling you so. You'll then have the opportunity to perform the manual installation that I outline next. All you need to do is click Next to start the process.

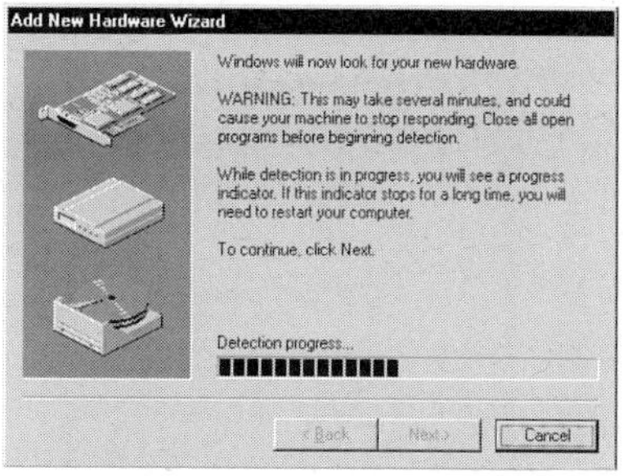

Figure 14.3.
The Add New Hardware Wizard keeps you informed of its progress, using this dialog box.

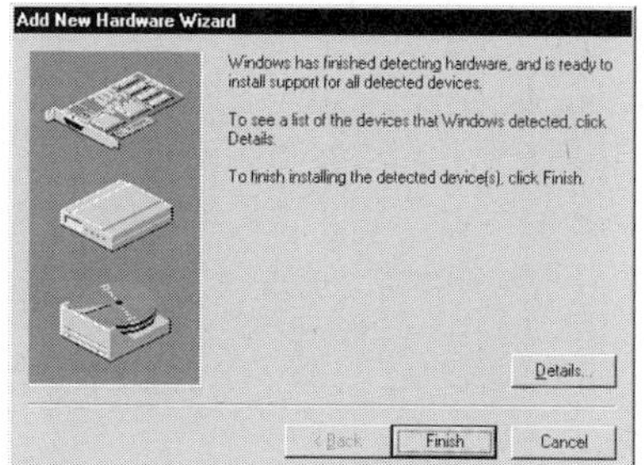

Figure 14.4.
Use this dialog box to determine whether Windows 95 detected your hardware correctly.

5. Click the Details button to determine whether Windows 95 successfully detected the new hardware (see Figure 14.5).

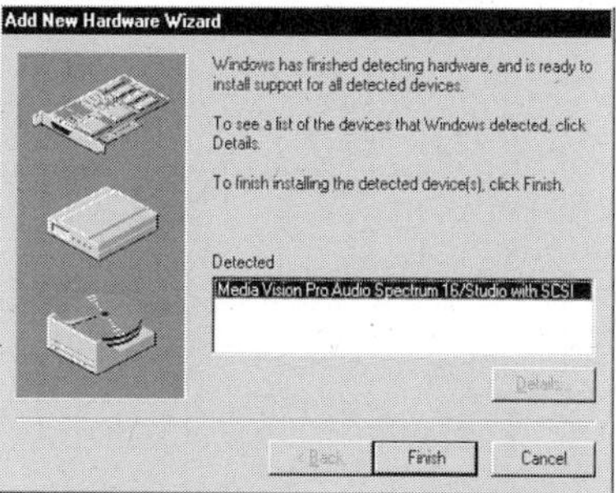

Figure 14.5.
The Add New Hardware Wizard tells you exactly what hardware it detected.

6. If Windows 95 successfully detected the new hardware, click the Finish button to complete the installation process. Windows 95 might ask you to supply some setting information if this is a non-plug and play device. In most cases, it provides default settings that match your current real-mode setup. Windows 95 copies all the required drivers to disk. It also displays some messages about the new hardware it found and perhaps a message about building a driver database. In some cases, Windows 95 will ask you to reboot after you complete this step. If it doesn't ask you to reboot, you should do so anyway, to make certain that all new drivers are loaded properly.

Note: If the Add New Hardware Wizard didn't correctly detect your device, click Cancel. Check your hardware's settings to make sure that they won't conflict with any other devices, using the initial steps of the manual process outlined next. If the hardware settings do conflict with something else, change them to an unused setting and try the automatic installation procedure again. Otherwise, proceed with the manual installation.

Manual Installation

Windows 95 might not detect some of your hardware when using the Add New Hardware Wizard's automatic-detection method. For example, some sound boards don't provide any kind of useful information until you install a device driver to turn them on. These devices rely on the older real-mode drivers you used under DOS. The vendor assumed that you'd load the device drivers before using the device, so there's no reason to turn on the device before then. It was a good assumption in the days of DOS, but a real problem when using Windows 95. Now, instead of being a feature (devices that didn't turn themselves on until needed could actually prevent conflicts under DOS), it's a hindrance to installation.

Another problem could get in your way as well. What happens if two devices are currently set to use the same I/O (input/output) port address, DMA (direct memory access) address, or IRQ (interrupt request) setting? The active device would mask the inactive one. (We'll see in Chapter 26 what happens when both devices are active.) If an active device is masking the device you want to detect, there's no way for the automatic procedure to succeed. You need to correct the settings first. Of course, this applies only to hardware that uses jumpers for configuration purposes. Windows 95 automatically reconfigures hardware that uses software configuration settings, as well as plug and play-compatible hardware.

The following procedure starts by showing you where to look for the settings that your machine is currently using. Determining this information in advance will allow you to set the jumpers correctly the first time. If you're using this section to continue from an automatic installation, proceed to step 6. You can also proceed to step 6 if you've already installed your adapter and don't need to find a set of nonconflicting IRQ and I/O settings. Otherwise, be sure to check your hardware settings before you start the manual installation.

1. Right-click the My Computer icon and select the Properties option.
2. Select the Device Manager page. You should see a dialog box similar to the one shown in Figure 14.6. (The dialog box for your machine will look slightly different from mine, because your machine contains different equipment.) Notice that this dialog box displays a complete list of each category of equipment installed on your machine.

Figure 14.6.
The Device Manager shows you a list of all the equipment installed on your system.

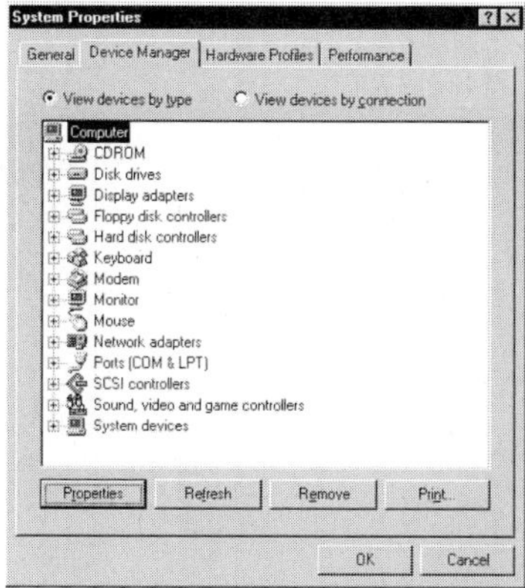

3. Select the Computer entry, as shown in Figure 14.6, and click the Properties button. Click the View Resources tab and the Interrupt Request (IRQ) radio button on that page. You should see a dialog box similar to the one shown in Figure 14.7. This is a complete list of all the interrupts that are in use on your machine. What you'll need to do is select an interrupt for your new device that doesn't conflict with any of these current settings. If all 16 interrupts are in use and your new device requires one, you'll need to remove an old device before you can install the new one.

Figure 14.7.
The IRQ section of the Computer Properties dialog box shows you all the interrupts that are in use on your machine.

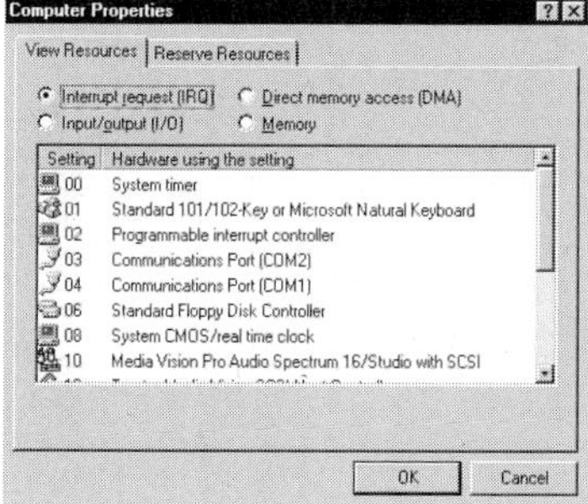

Note: Some people used to place more than one device on an interrupt if needed. For example, if they had four serial ports, ports 1 and 3 would share one interrupt and ports 2 and 4 another. Although this setup might have worked if the user didn't accidentally try to access both devices at once, it was a source of conflict. Using one interrupt for two devices won't work under Windows 95. It will simply deactivate one of the conflicting devices.

4. Click the Input/Output (I/O) radio button. You'll see a dialog box similar to the one shown in Figure 14.8. These are the port addresses mentioned earlier. You'll need to select an unused port address range for your new card. Some adapters won't let you select a port

address, which means that you might have to change the settings for another card to make this one fit. Fortunately, this is pretty rare.

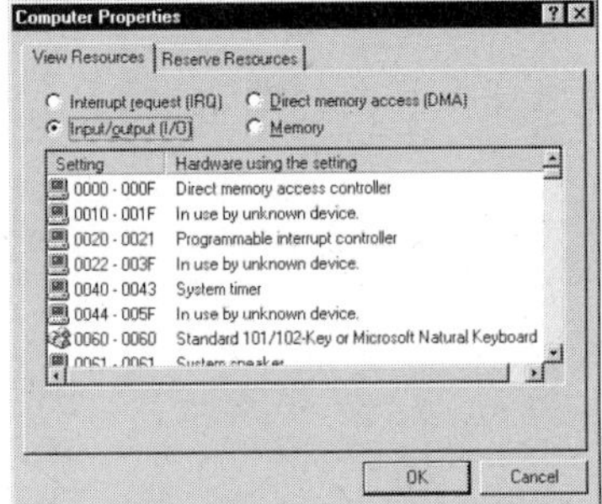

Figure 14.8.
The I/O section of the Computer Properties dialog box shows you all the port addresses that are in use on your machine.

5. You'll need to follow the same steps to find a DMA setting if your card uses one. Once you get all the required settings, close the dialog box by clicking Cancel twice. Shut down the machine and install your adapter according to manufacturer instructions. Restart Windows.
6. Use the Start | Settings | Control Panel command to open the Control Panel. Double-click the Add New Hardware applet and click the Next button.
7. Click the No radio button and then click Next. Highlight the CD-ROM Controller entry in the Install Specific Hardware field and then click the Next button. You should see the dialog box shown in Figure 14.9.

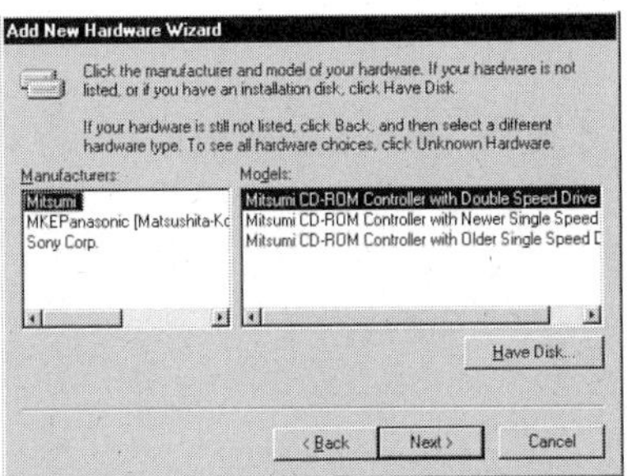

Figure 14.9.
The Manufacturers and Models lists in this dialog box allow you to scroll with ease through the list of devices supported by Windows 95.

8. This dialog box will appear every time you select a device from the previous dialog box. The Manufacturers list will change to match the particular device type. If the device installed on the current machine doesn't appear in the list, the dialog box gives you the opportunity to use a third-party disk. Normally you'd select the device connected to your machine. In this case, leave the default device highlighted and click the Next button.
9. Click the Details button. Windows 95 displays a dialog box containing the interrupt and address settings for this particular device, as shown in Figure 14.10. Windows 95 chooses a device setting based on all available information. It chooses the best setting that won't interfere with other devices in the system (if possible).

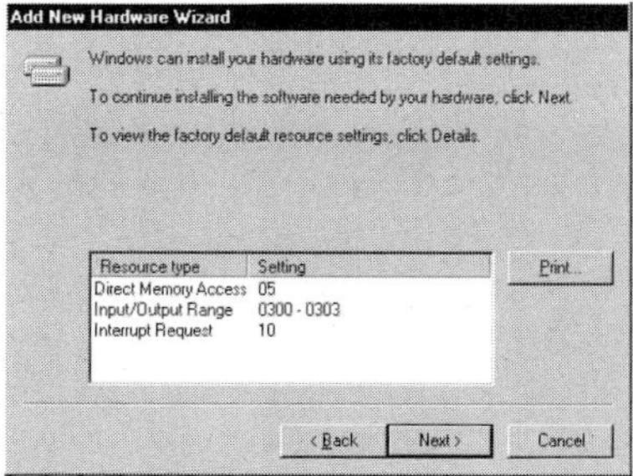

Figure 14.10.
Windows 95 always tells the user what interrupts and addresses it uses for the devices it installs.

Tip: A special "unknown hardware" device type allows you to view on one screen all the devices supported by Windows 95. This comes in handy for two purposes. First, Microsoft doesn't always place devices in the category where you expect them to be. Searching through this list will provide one final check if you don't find a device where you expect to see it. Second, you can use this list when researching a new product. It will allow you to choose a device that Windows 95 will definitely support. I'm not saying that other products are incompatible, just that these products received a little more attention than some of the others you might find.

10. Clicking the Next button again installs the device drivers required for this device. You will normally take this action. Windows 95 might prompt you for a disk if the driver didn't appear on the hard drive and the appropriate disk didn't appear in the CD-ROM drive (or whatever other location you're using for storage of the Windows 95 CAB files). It would display a dialog box showing the progress of the file copy process. However, since we don't want to install this particular device, click the Cancel button. Windows 95 exits the Add New Hardware Wizard without installing the new device.

Removing Hardware

It's interesting to note that removing hardware—at least the driver—is easier than installing it. In most cases, you'll want to remove the drivers for a device first and then remove the device. Reversing the process could prevent Windows 95 from booting properly. Fortunately, Windows 95 will at least boot in safe mode (unlike Windows 3.x, which could cause significant problems in this regard). However, I always like to take the safest route possible when it comes to my machine's configuration. Removing the driver first is the safest route. The following procedure shows you the method for removing a driver from your machine:

Note: You might want to use the Device Manager to obtain a list of the drivers for the device you plan to remove. Windows 95 usually does a good job of removing all the unneeded files from your system, but sometimes it doesn't. Making a list of drivers will help you find them in the SYSTEM directory later.

1. Right-click My Computer and select the Properties option. Click the Device Manager tab. Select the device category you want to remove and click the plus (+) sign next to it. You should see a dialog box similar to the one shown in Figure 14.11.

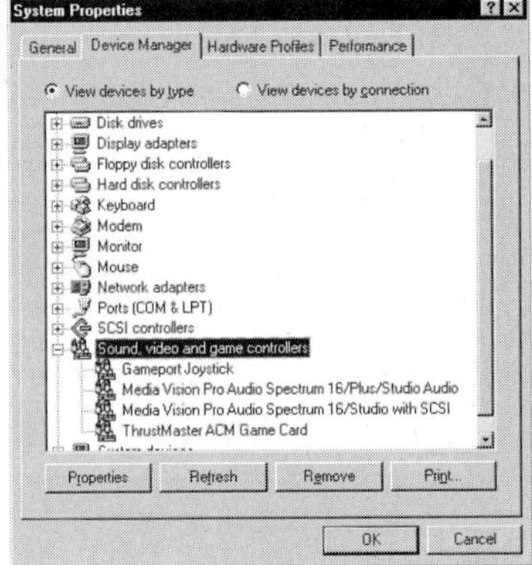

Figure 14.11.
Clicking a device category shows you a list of installed devices.

2. Click the device you want to remove. Click the Properties button and select the Driver tab. You should see a dialog box similar to the one shown in Figure 14.12. Make a copy of the driver list so that you can later verify that Windows 95 removed them. (You don't necessarily have to copy this list of drivers by hand—simply use Shift+Print Screen to copy it to the Clipboard, paste the list into your favorite graphics editor, and then print a copy.) Otherwise, you'll end up with a lot of additional disk clutter after installing and removing a few devices.

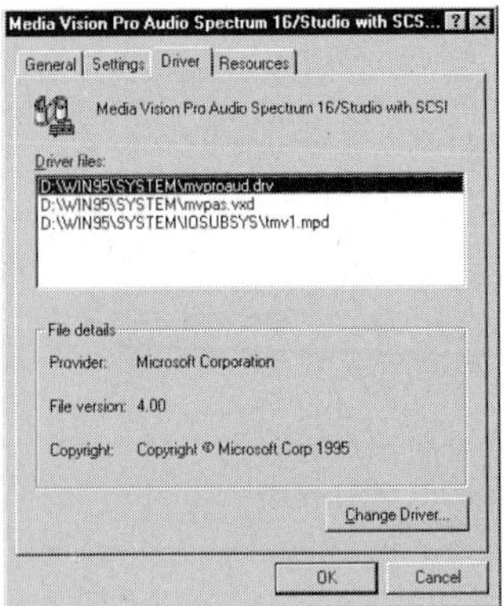

Figure 14.12.
Making a list of the drivers needed by this device is always a good idea.

Note: Some adapters contain more than one real device. For example, the Pro Audio Spectrum adapter in my machine contains a sound board, a joystick controller, and a SCSI adapter. Each device requires a separate entry in the Device Manager. To remove the device, you must find the main entry and remove it. Windows 95 will automatically remove all of the supporting entries. Make sure that you record the drivers used by each entry, because the main entry won't provide you with a master list.

3. Once you finish recording the driver names, click Cancel.
4. With the device that you want to remove highlighted, click the Remove button. Windows 95 removes the device and all supporting entries.
5. Shut down Windows and reboot your machine to allow the changes to take effect.

Tip: For some strange reason, Windows 95 occasionally forgets to remove all the required entries from the Registry. If you get a message saying that Windows 95 can't find a specific device when you start the computer, there's a good chance that it didn't delete all the required entries. You might need to use the procedure in the "Using Find to Change Strings" section of Chapter 7 to locate any entries for the device or its associated device drivers. Simply remove the unneeded keys by using the Delete command. Be sure to make a copy of the Registry before you delete any entries.

Configuring Ports

Ports provide the means for the processor and other devices to communicate with the peripheral hardware on your machine. Any data that a device requires to work goes through the port. Think of the port as a mailbox and the data as the mail. If everyone had the same address, the mail carrier would never know where to put the mail. The same idea holds true in your computer. If two devices were to use the same address, the computer wouldn't know where to send the data.

A port conflict does more than just annoy the user; it can cause system instability or a malfunction of some type. The user might not be able to use part of the system or might experience "the slows" as the system tries to figure out which device it's supposed to use. A system with fully exploited hardware lacks any kind of port conflict. Each device has its own port to use.

Fortunately, there's an easy way to get rid of port conflicts. Windows 95 provides three port configuration methods, depending on the type of hardware you want to configure. Most hardware uses the first method, which I present in the next section. The second and third methods apply to your parallel and serial ports. The last two configuration methods provide more of a performance boost than a means of conflict resolution. They tune your ports for maximum application and network compatibility.

Standard Port Configuration

Communication is the name of the game in your computer. For communication to occur, there must be some way to exchange information. In the PC, the physical part of the communication path is called an I/O (input/output) port. If you want to send data from one area of the machine to another, your application must first tell the computer what I/O port (or address) to send it to. We looked at part of this process earlier in this chapter when we examined hardware installation. The Computer Properties dialog box tells you the address of every port on your machine. Normally you'll never need to change these settings, but sometimes you will. For example, if you have a board in your system that allows more than one setting and it happens to occupy the same address as a board that doesn't, you can change the address of the flexible board as needed. The following procedure takes you through the process of changing an I/O port on your machine:

Note: This procedure changes the settings of the device driver. It won't change the settings of your adapter if it depends on jumpers. Be sure to change any required jumpers after you make changes to the driver configuration. Failure to do so will prevent the hardware from responding.

1. Right-click My Computer and select the Properties option.
2. Select one of the device classes—such as Sound, Video and Game Controllers—and click the plus (+) sign to display the list of devices it contains.
3. Select one of the devices and click the Properties button. Click the Resources tab. You should see a dialog box similar to the one shown in Figure 14.13. Notice that this dialog box has the Use Automatic Settings check box checked. Letting Windows 95 manage the settings for your equipment is always a good idea.

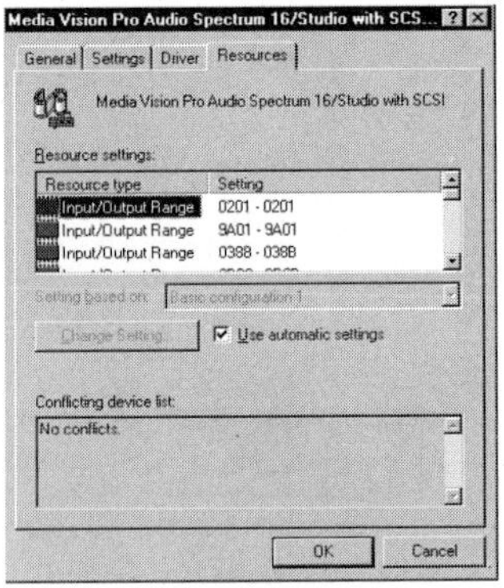

Figure 14.13.
The Resources tab of the device's Properties dialog box makes it easy to see what settings each peripheral uses.

Looking Ahead: This particular dialog box also contains some diagnostic information covered in Chapter 26.

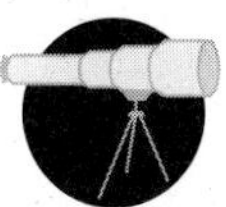

4. Uncheck the Use Automatic Settings check box. This should enable the Change Setting button and the Setting Based On list box.
5. Click the Setting Based On list box. You'll see a list of basic configurations, as shown in Figure 14.14.

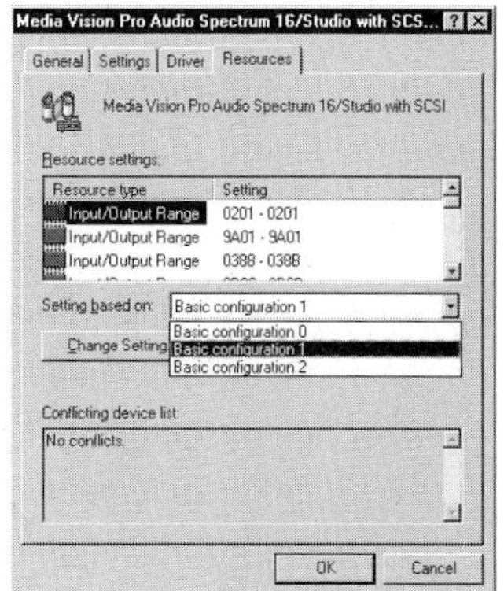

Figure 14.14.
The Setting Based On list box displays the standard configurations that Windows 95 provides for a particular device.

6. Try each setting in turn to see whether one of the other settings will allow you to resolve the port conflict. Windows 95 alerts you to any conflicts with registered devices, as shown in Figure 14.15. Notice that the error message tells you exactly which device you're conflicting with. This allows you to change that device's settings, if necessary, to resolve the conflict. Obviously, you'll want to keep the number of changes to the absolute minimum. The more you change the Windows 95 setup, the greater your chances of introducing unforeseen conflicts.

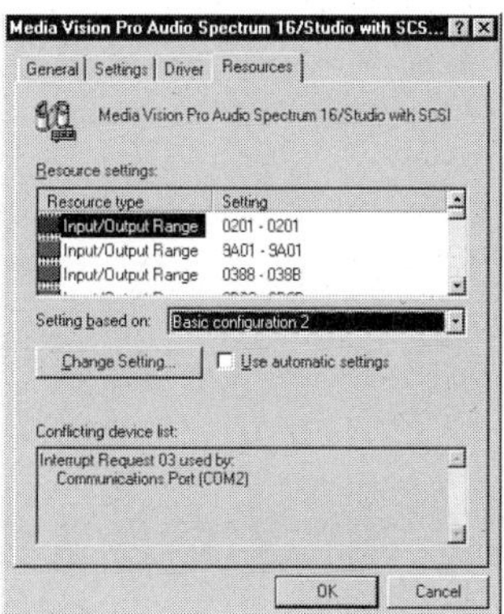

Figure 14.15.
Windows 95 instantly alerts you to any problems in the settings you choose.

7. If you try all the basic configurations offered and none of them work, reset the Setting Based On list box to its original setting. Otherwise, click OK twice to save the setting, and then shut down and reboot the machine to make the setting active.
8. To change a single port address, highlight it and click the Change Setting button. You should see the dialog box shown in Figure 14.16.

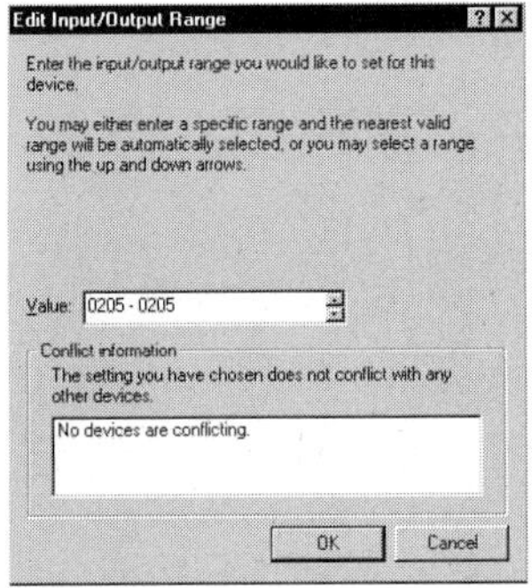

Figure 14.16.
This dialog box allows you to change the setting of a single port.

Tip: Some revisions of a specific piece of hardware provide more settings than Windows 95 will recognize. Modifying the .INF file by using the procedure in Chapter 4 will often resolve this problem. All you need to do is add the settings that Windows 95 doesn't recognize and then shut down and reboot the machine. Be sure not to add unsupported settings to the .INF file, or you'll get unpredictable results.

9. Scroll through the list of acceptable settings. As before, Windows 95 tells you if you select a conflicting setting, by displaying a message in the Conflict Information field.
10. Once you select a new port address, make it permanent by clicking OK three times. Shut down your machine and reboot.

This procedure isn't limited to just port settings. You can use it to configure any hardware setting. Windows 95 won't allow you to change some settings. If you try to change one of these settings, Windows 95 displays the appropriate error message. In most cases, a hardware limitation rather than a problem with the driver will prevent you from changing a setting.

Serial Port Configuration

The serial port offers a variety of configuration options that go beyond address conflict resolution. Several options control both the speed of the port and its compatibility with software. Figure 14.17 shows the Port Settings page, where you would make changes of this nature. You access it through the System Properties dialog box (refer to Figure 14.6). Notice that this page controls the actual port parameters such as communication speed and number of data bits. Normally you set a port's parameters to match those of your modem and any online service you want to access.

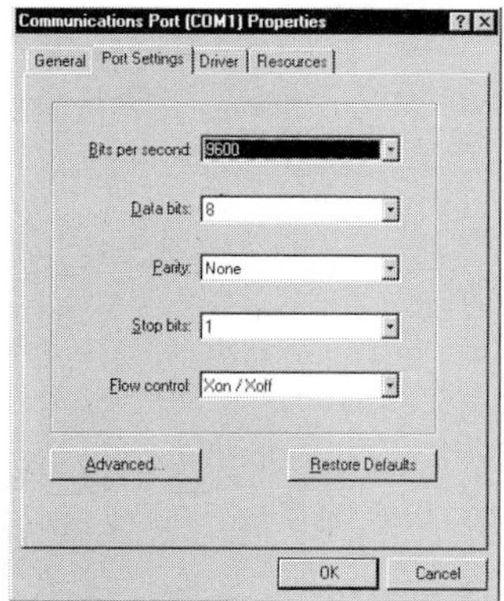

Figure 14.17.
The Port Settings page of the Communications Port Properties dialog box allows you to change some of the port's speed-enhancing features.

There's another way to set these parameters. When you're using the Direct Cable Connection program provided with Windows 95, you'll want to reset these settings to maximum. Some users will miss this particular bit of irony, because the utility never asks you to set the port settings. They just assume that the Direct Cable Connection program uses the maximum settings available. However, experience says otherwise. You can actually slow data transfers from your notebook to a crawl by failing to observe this little "gotcha."

Windows 3.x provides all these settings, as do most DOS applications. The one area where Windows 95 rises above its predecessors is in the way that it handles advanced UART (universal asynchronous receiver transmitter) chips. A UART contains the intelligence of the serial port, and some of the newer models contain features that allow better performance in a multitasking environment. It's this support that lets Windows 95 provide a higher level of support for background communications than you might expect.

Clicking the Advanced button displays the dialog box shown in Figure 14.18. Notice that it contains only one check box and two sliders. Windows 95 automatically checks the Use FIFO Buffers check box if it detects the proper port. This option is available only on the 16550 UART. Attempting to use it with an older 8250 UART will result in lost data.

Figure 14.18.
The Advanced Port Settings dialog box is one place where you can tweak the performance of your communications program.

Note: MSD (Microsoft Diagnostics) can't reliably determine your UART type. In many cases, it will tell you that you have an 8250 UART even if your system contains the newer model. Microsoft claims that this is due to a bug in the UART that makes it difficult to detect, yet many third-party diagnostic programs can make the determination. If you're uncertain what kind of UART is installed in your system, either check the documentation that came with your machine or use one of the better third-party diagnostic aids to check your port type. You can also check the part number on the UART itself (it's placed rather conspicuously on most motherboard configurations) or ask your local computer store or direct-sale manufacturer to verify the type for you.

Tip: Some motherboards come equipped with emulations of the 16550. Unfortunately, some of these emulations work better than others. If the motherboard vendor states that the communications port supports the full 16550 capability, but Windows 95 doesn't automatically check the Use FIFO Buffers option, you might want to test this capability anyway. In some cases, the option works even if Windows 95 doesn't detect the port properly. I usually check the box and then test the port by downloading a large file in the background while using a single application in the foreground. Something like a word processor or data-entry program works best, but you should test the port by using the same application you'd normally use while downloading a file. If the background transfer works without any data errors, you'll know that the port at least marginally supports the FIFO capability.

Before we go much further, let's talk about the differences between certain UARTs. Older UARTs could store only one character at a time. This meant that the CPU had to retrieve that character immediately, or the next character the UART received would overwrite it. This is what people mean when they say that their port "dropped" a character. It means that the CPU couldn't respond fast enough and the UART overwrote a character in its buffer as a result. Forcing the CPU to attend to the needs of the UART is fine in a single-tasking system like DOS, but it isn't all that efficient in a multitasking environment like Windows. Once UART vendors realized that the older UARTs were a bottleneck when used in a multitasking environment, they started making new UARTs with a FIFO (first in, first out) buffer. The FIFO buffer can store up to 16 characters, giving the CPU time to complete whatever it was doing and then respond to the needs of the UART.

Once you select the Use FIFO Buffers option in the Advanced Port Settings dialog box, Windows 95 will enable the two sliders, which control the FIFO buffer. There are actually two buffers: one for data you want to send and another for data you receive. The setting affects the number of buffer slots that the CPU can use. Setting a high number allows a longer time between CPU checks, making your system more efficient. However, using a large number also reduces the margin of error. You might find that your application no longer transmits or receives data accurately. The way to fix this is to reduce the number of buffers, giving the CPU a wider margin of error. Tuning your buffer for maximum performance will involve some experimentation, but it's well worth the effort.

Tip: Your modem's transmission speed affects the buffer slider setting. A high-speed data transfer leaves less time between characters in which the CPU can respond. As a result, you might have to set the buffer setting lower. On the other hand, a high-speed CPU partially compensates for this problem. You might find that a Pentium can handle the load of a 9600 baud transfer better than an 80486 in some cases. Hand-tuning this setting is about the only way you can ensure optimum performance. The biggest mistake you can make, though, is tuning it in the foreground. Always test your settings with the communications program as a background application.

Parallel Port Configuration

The parallel port offers fewer, yet more customized opportunities for tuning than the serial port does. You need to consider a few things when making changes to the printer port settings that you didn't need to consider with the serial port. The most important is that a device attaches to the serial port. In other words, the device must abide by the settings that the serial port provides. This is why you have one centralized dialog box for tuning a serial port. On the other hand, the parallel port attaches to the device. You can hand-tune the parallel port settings for each device that will connect to it. When you think about it, this arrangement makes a lot of sense. Seldom will you see more than one device attached to a serial port, yet AB switches for parallel ports abound. People are always attaching multiple devices to their parallel ports.

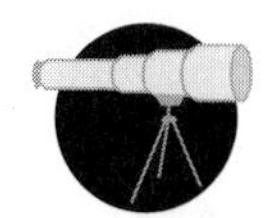

Looking Ahead: Chapter 15 provides complete details of the Printer Properties dialog box. I provide only an overview of it in this section.

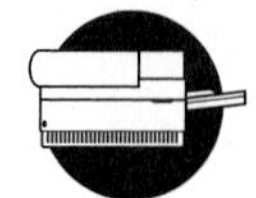

With this first difference in mind, you'll probably figure out that we don't change the printer port settings in Device Manager. You use a simple four-step approach to opening the dialog box shown in Figure 14.19: Open the Control Panel, double-click the Printers folder, right-click the printer, and select Properties from the context menu. All the port settings appear on the Details page of the Properties dialog box, as shown in Figure 14.19.

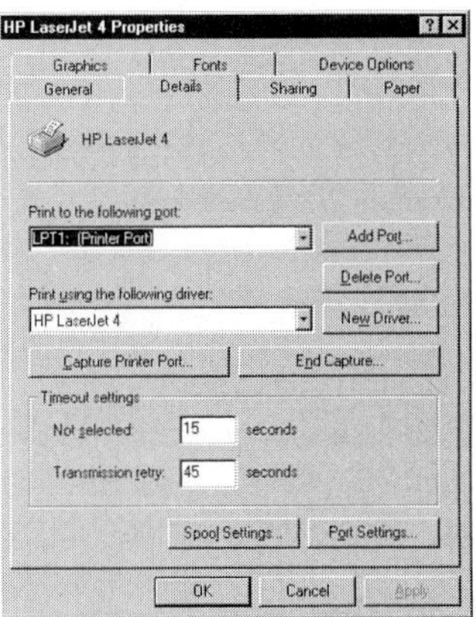

Figure 14.19.
A parallel port's configuration settings are attached to a particular printer.

Two different settings affect the efficiency of your printer connection to varying degrees: port and spool. The Port Settings button displays the dialog box shown in Figure 14.20. The first check box, Spool MS-DOS Print Jobs, tells Windows 95 to place a copy of any DOS print jobs in the spooler so that they can print in the background. Using this setting will return control of the machine to you faster. The tradeoff is that you'll experience reduced machine efficiency until the print job completes. The Check Port State Before Printing option tells Windows to check the printer's status before it starts the print job. If the printer is offline or otherwise unable to print, Windows displays an error message. You'll get a chance to fix the problem and then retry the print job.

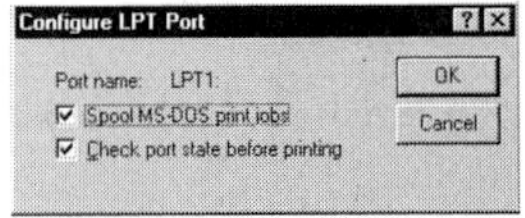

Figure 14.20.
This dialog box allows you to set the method used to handle DOS print jobs.

The Spool Settings button opens the dialog box shown in Figure 14.21. Of all the radio groups shown, only the first is always available. Spooling print jobs is a requirement if you use the printer as a network printer. Selecting the first suboption in this group tells the spooler to send data to the printer after it spools the last page of the print job. This will return machine control to you a lot faster. I normally use it for long print jobs, because the machine will be tied up printing for a while anyway. At least I can get back to work quickly, at a slightly reduced level of efficiency. The second suboption, Start Printing After First Page Is Spooled, allows the spooler to start printing immediately. If you normally print short jobs, this option makes more sense because it completes the overall print job faster.

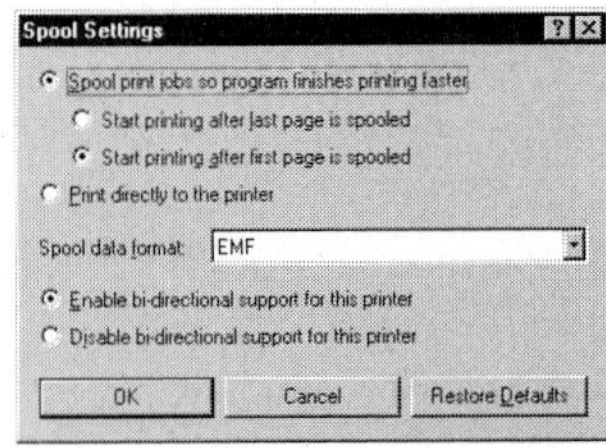

Figure 14.21.
Use this dialog box to change the way your printer handles spooling.

The Spool Settings dialog box also includes a list box with two entries: RAW and EMF. EMF (enhanced metafile) is a new way of sending information to the printer in Windows 95. It uses a data-independent method that's much smaller than the RAW option and frees your program up faster. The downside to this format is that it takes longer for the print job to complete in the background, because Windows 95 still has to convert the metafile format to something printer-specific. The RAW format sends the data to the printer in a format it already understands. It will take your application longer to produce this output, but this could save substantially on the amount of time the spooler spends working in the background. Combining the EMF spool data format with the Start Printing After Last Page Is Spooled setting provides the fastest method of sending data to your printer.

If this isn't a shared printer, you can choose to print directly to the printer. The advantage of this method is that you don't waste time spooling the job and then sending it to the printer. When the machine returns control to you, it's at full efficiency because the print job is finished. This particular feature comes in handy when I have one or two pages and I don't want to wait very long for them to print.

Peter's Principle: A Printer for Every Task

No law states that you can't create multiple copies of the same printer connected to the same port but configured in different ways. I do it to improve the flexibility of the Windows environment. I have one printer with spooling disabled, and I don't share it with anyone. It allows me to print small jobs very quickly.

A second copy of the same printer is shared with everyone on the network. I enable spooling with it and allow it to start printing after the first page. This way, my machine doesn't get a lot of heavy jolts as someone else uses the printer attached to it. There's a constant but barely noticeable load. I also use this strategy for my medium-sized print jobs. It reduces the overall time that I wait for the print job to complete.

A third copy of the same printer isn't shared with anyone, but it does use spooling. I set this one up to wait until the last page of the print job appears in the spooler. This allows me to regain control of my machine in the minimum amount of time. I use this particular setting when I have a long print job that's going to reduce overall machine efficiency for a long time anyway.

There are numerous ways you can set a single printer on your machine to look like more special-purpose printers. Doing this might take a little time and thought, but it will enhance your overall efficiency and improve printer throughput. You can also use this same idea for control. For example, what if you don't want a particular group to use the font cartridge attached to the machine? You could create a special setup for them that allows full printer access but doesn't provide access to the fonts. (All you have to do is choose "none" when asked for fonts on the Font page.)

Normally you'll want to enable bidirectional printer support. This allows your printer to communicate with the computer when the printer needs maintenance. Bidirectional support also allows the computer to get better information about printer failures. However, bidirectional support also exacts a toll in speed. This isn't a problem with the printer or the computer, but with the amount of traffic flowing through the parallel port. The port has to support a lot more traffic in bidirectional mode than it does regularly. As a result, you might notice slightly better printer performance when you turn off bidirectional support. The speed gain is minimal, though, so think twice before you actually take this step. The loss of information could make a big difference in the computer's ability to help you diagnose problems.

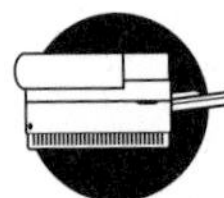

Fonts and Printers

There are a number of ways to look at fonts under Windows 95. Some people look at them the wrong way and end up thrilling us all with "ransom note" presentations and letters. Aesthetics aside, fonts can create problems in a number of efficiency-related ways as well. For example, every font you load consumes disk space. If you have a lot of disk space, this isn't a problem. However, at an average size of 60KB, each TrueType font you load can quickly start to consume space that your hard drive can't afford to provide.

Space considerations aside, too many fonts in your application list boxes can also present a dilemma. Which font do you choose for a given job? I find that using style sheets helps a lot, but there are still times when I must choose a font manually.

When you get right down to it, just how many fonts does the average person really need? I find that I can usually get by just fine with roman, bold, bold italic, and italic versions of three or four fonts. After a lot of fumbling around with a bunch of fonts I would never use, I decided on one serif, one sans serif, a fancy font, and a symbol font. These four fonts handle all my business correspondence and personal needs.

Of course, I'm not a graphic artist or someone who creates presentations on a daily basis. If you're in one of those lines of work, you'll need a wealth of fonts loaded on your machine. I'm equally certain that you'll have the real estate to deal with them as well. Still, sometimes even I need a special font to make that dramatic presentation. Windows 95 makes it easy to load and unload fonts as necessary. Chapter 15 covers all of this.

What do fonts and printers have to do with efficiency? Once you get past the font-management issues, you encounter several speed-related issues. The following list provides some of the tips I've gathered while working with Windows 95:

- A laser printer can usually print with a native font much faster than it can with a downloaded font. Not only that, but the memory that you'll save using the built-in fonts will usually allow you to print larger pages.

- Dot-matrix printers also benefit from the use of internal fonts. In this case, it's the difference between printing in character or graphics mode. You need to print using graphics mode when you select a Windows TrueType font, which slows things down. A native printer font allows you to print in character mode—the speed differential is quite noticeable.
- More fonts usually means longer print times. On a dot-matrix printer, you have to wait for the machine to render each font. A laser printer needs to download each font before you can use it. Either way, using more fonts takes longer. Discreet use of fonts normally produces a better effect and is more efficient from a printing perspective as well.
- Using raster fonts is usually faster but less flexible than using TrueType fonts. The computer doesn't have to create a raster font; it's already in pixel format. Unfortunately, this also means that the computer can't resize the font without a loss in resolution. Overall, using TrueType fonts to gain the benefits of flexibility is a better idea. I cover the exact differences between raster and vector fonts in Chapter 15.
- Avoid using non-TrueType fonts if possible. Alternatives to TrueType were a good idea at one time. They allowed you to gain access to fonts you might never be able to use otherwise. However, the extra memory and system incompatibilities that the managers of these fonts introduce into Windows 95 make them relics.
- Printing at a lower resolution is faster than printing at a higher resolution. The printer needs more time to output text or graphics at a higher resolution. However, using a lower resolution reduces the quality of the font output. Many fonts include a special form of high-resolution and size control known as hinting, which can help reduce the disparity between low and high resolution, but not remove it completely.

Depending on the printer you use, there might be even more ways to use fonts efficiently. Always match your font requirements to the job at hand. Never use more than you need, but always use enough to get your point across.

Miniport Driver Support

What exactly is a miniport driver? This was the first question that came to my mind. Chapter 9 touches on this particular topic when looking at the file system architecture. A miniport driver is a device-independent way of moving data. It doesn't matter what form that data takes—it could be graphics, sound, or text. Windows 95 uses the miniport driver concept for every subsystem on your machine. The benefit of using the miniport driver for your applications is improved speed. The application only needs to worry about the data it wants to output, not the format that the data takes.

Not only does miniport driver support mean a better and easier-to-use interface for the user, it also means a lot to software vendors. Under DOS, you have to write code for every little function. If you want to provide a File menu, you have to write all the code that the File menu requires. The same thing holds true for every other function a program might perform. Windows 3.x started a process in which the programmer didn't have to write so much code. Using the common dialog boxes is just one example. You no longer have to write a File menu, because Microsoft provides one as part of the common dialog box .DLL.

Windows 95 takes this concept even further with the miniport driver support it provides. If you develop communications programs, you used to worry about the differences in control sequences for each modem type. Using Windows 95 Unimodem support (a miniport driver), the programmer opens each modem and writes to it like a file. The miniport driver takes care of details such as control codes.

There are other significant advantages to this approach. For one thing, you no longer need to worry as much about how well an application will handle the details. Because each vendor is writing to the same interface, any changes to that interface will come from Microsoft. Using a common interface also means that every application will provide the same level of support for the various devices on your system. If one application supports a device, they all do, and to the same level.

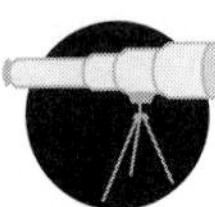

Looking Ahead: We'll look at the specifics of miniport driver support as we visit each subsystem. Chapter 9 covers the miniport driver concept from the file system point of view. I also mention this form of support in the earlier "Fonts and Printers" section of this chapter. Chapter 15 covers printer support in much more detail. Look in Chapter 16 for information about mouse miniport driver support and in Chapter 17 for the same information on the video subsystem. Details on network miniport driver support appear in Chapter 23. You'll get your last bit of miniport driver support information in Chapter 18, when we cover the mobile computing environment. In most cases, I've shortened "miniport driver" to "driver" in the rest of this book because a miniport driver is simply a special form of driver.

Faxes and Modems

Communication is a major part of the job these days. It used to be that you could take care of everything with the office fax and a few phone calls. Today, a lot of people can't take the time to use the office fax; they need one close by to take care of their needs. The amount of electronic "paper" passing hands these days is amazing. A lot of people are busier in other ways, too. Playing telephone tag isn't fun, especially when you can leave a message for the person on e-mail and expect a response later that day. Online services are becoming a major source of information for many people. Sometimes I can actually get an answer to a networking or application-related question faster by getting online than I could if I called a vendor support line. The difference is the vast amount of knowledge that these online services represent.

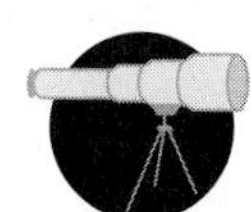

Looking Ahead: Chapter 20 takes a closer look at using your fax and modem under Windows 95. Chapter 18 looks at the mobile computer user's point of view.

It's no wonder that people are always looking for better ways to use the communications features that their computers offer. Under Windows 3.x, it was a foregone conclusion that you would find it difficult, if not impossible, to communicate in the background. Windows 95 is a totally different story. Communication isn't only possible, it's also easy.

Configuring your machine for optimum performance when using background communication isn't difficult; it just takes time. You need to try a setting, communicate a little to see its effect, and then tune a little more as necessary. Unlike other tuning tips I've presented in this chapter, there's no easy way to tune your communications programs. The problem is that every machine is slightly different, as is every modem and every communications program that uses the modem.

Tuning Your Modem

To tune your modem settings, open the Control Panel and double-click the Modems applet. Select your modem and click the Properties button. Select the Connection page. You'll see a dialog box similar to the one shown earlier in this chapter for the serial port (refer to Figure 14.17). Figure 14.22 shows that this dialog box contains those settings plus a few related to modem communications.

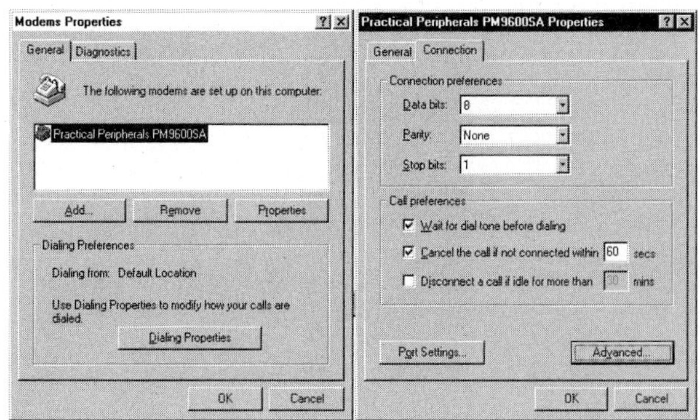

Figure 14.22.
The modem's Properties dialog box looks similar to the serial port configuration dialog box, but it has some modem-specific additions.

Note: These settings affect your communications program only if it uses the Windows 95 miniport driver setup. Older 16-bit communications programs will maintain their own settings. Check the software vendor's manual for the procedure to tune these applications.

Click the Advanced button. You'll see a dialog box similar to the one in Figure 14.23. This is where you can modify your connection settings for added efficiency. The settings look straightforward, and they are. If your modem supports error correction, it's normally a good idea to select it. The same holds true for data compression, which boosts your effective transfer rate by as many as four times.

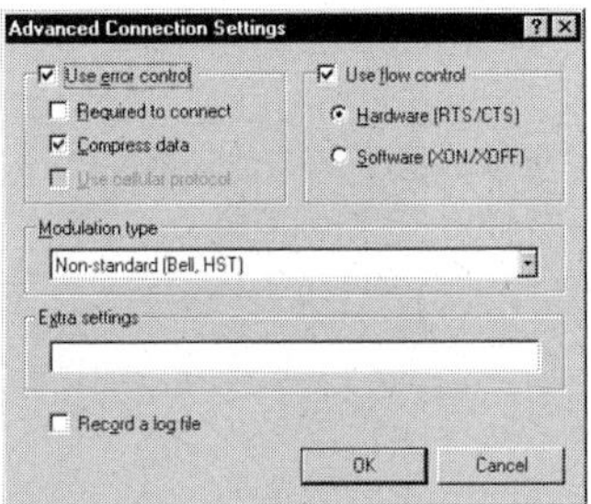

Figure 14.23.
The Advanced Connection Settings dialog box allows you to configure your modem for maximum efficiency.

Tip: Sometimes, using error correction and data compression can actually hurt the efficiency of your transmission. Certain types of Telnet connections fall into this category, as do some BBS calls in which the host modem doesn't quite support your modem's protocols. If you're having trouble maintaining the connection, or the data transfer rate isn't as high as you expected, try turning off data compression first, then error correction, to see if there's any improvement.

I've found an interesting use for the Required to Connect check box. Some BBSs have more than one connection. They use a switch to move you to the nearest unused connection when you call in. If this is a local call, the fact that you can't use error correction and data compression might not be a big deal. On the other hand, the cost of using such a connection during a long-distance call can add up quickly. I use this check box when I don't want to make a connection that will disable the advanced features of my modem—the ones that will reduce my overall telephone bill.

The Modulation Type list box allows you to select from the various forms of signal modulation that the modem provides. Using the standard modulation is usually more efficient than the alternatives. However, using the modulation that gives you the best connection is always the route to follow. I always try the standard connection first. If it proves reliable, I use that mode. I switch modes only when the connection doesn't work properly.

Some modems provide additional control sequences that you can use in specific situations for added speed. The Extra Settings field allows you to enter these control sequences. You'll need to consult your modem manual for details.

Tuning Your Fax

The number of fax settings that Windows 95 provides is fairly minimal. To access them, you need to open the MS Exchange Settings Properties dialog box. I usually do this by right-clicking the Inbox applet and selecting Properties. You can also access it by double-clicking the Mail and Fax applet in the Control Panel. After you open this dialog box, select Microsoft Fax, click the Properties button, and select the Modem tab. You'll see a dialog box similar to the one shown in Figure 14.24.

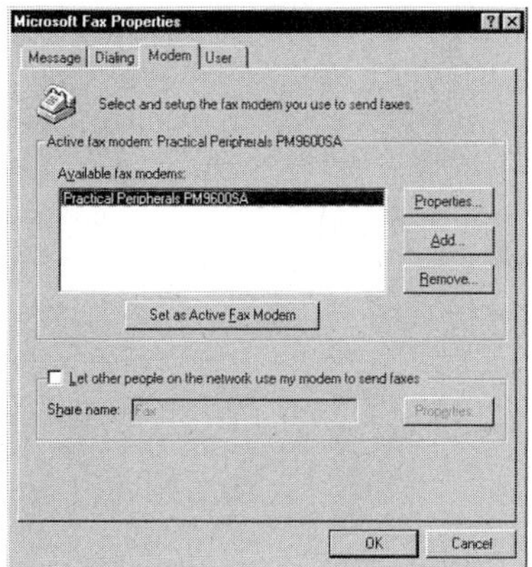

Figure 14.24.
The Modem page of the Microsoft Fax Properties dialog box allows you to configure your modem for optimum performance.

I cover the user-specific fields in this dialog box later. For now, select the modem you'll use to transmit faxes, and then click the Properties button. Once you see the Fax Modem Properties dialog box, click the Advanced button. You'll see the dialog box shown in Figure 14.25.

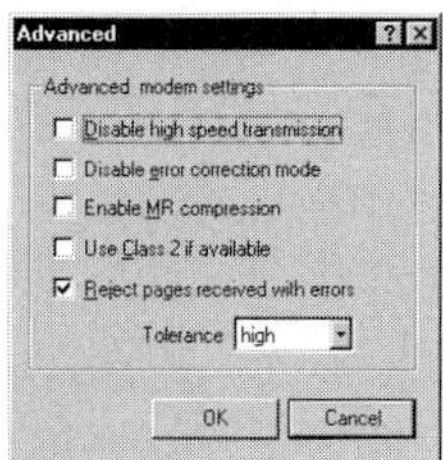

Figure 14.25.
This dialog box allows you to select the advanced properties for your fax modem.

The settings in this dialog box allow you to change the way the modem works. In most cases, you can improve either usability or efficiency, but not both at the same time. Checking the first setting, Disable High Speed Transmission, will keep you from transmitting or receiving faxes above

9600 baud. This can actually improve your machine's multitasking capability. Receiving high-speed faxes in the background might improve transmission speed, but it also costs you processor cycles. Microsoft also mentions that you can check this box if you can't receive faxes without error. Normally, errors occur when the serial port starts dropping characters due to high traffic. (Incidentally, this situation has much more to do with the other background and foreground tasks that you're running than with which UART you have. If your CPU is heavily bogged down with other tasks, the CPU itself—not the UART—becomes the bottleneck, and you open yourself up to the danger of degraded performance or lost data.)

The Disable Error Correction Mode setting also affects efficiency. In one way, working without error correction is faster. The additional processing time required for error correction slows down transmission speeds. However, without error correction, you might find yourself resending faxes. You'll normally want to leave error correction turned on, unless the receiving modem uses a different protocol.

I can understand why Microsoft didn't default to checking the first two options. Using them does improve foreground fax transmission speeds. However, disabling data compression doesn't make a lot of sense unless you have a very noisy line. In most cases, you'll want to enable data compression to gain the additional transmission speed that it offers.

The Enable MR Compression option allows you to use one of two advanced fax data compression techniques: MR and MMR. The actual technique used depends on the capabilities of the fax you call. Each of these techniques provides data compression as follows:

- Modified Huffman (MH): This is the standard compression technique used by all fax machines today. It can just about double the transmission speed of most fax machines. A fax scans each line of your original document and converts it into a series of 1s (black) and 0s (white). One line is equal to 1/200 of an inch. (Fax machines normally transmit data at 200 dpi.) The Huffman coding technique takes these long strings and breaks them into characters of 8 bits. It then uses a "code word" to represent each character. Common characters use short code words, and rare characters use longer code words. For example, an *e* might be represented as a single-bit 1, while a *z* might require 16 bits. The end result is that the overall data stream requires less space. You might want to refer to a book that deals specifically with encoding techniques if you're interested in how this coding technique works. Chapter 19 also provides a list of the fax standards that tell exactly how a fax transmission works.
- Modified read (MR): Some of the newer fax modems provide this option. The first line of fax data is compressed using the MH technique just described. The second line begins with only the changed data. In other words, if at a specific point in the data stream the first line contains a 0 and the second line contains a 1, the fax would record the bit's location and difference. It then compresses this change data, using MH. The third line is a full line of MH data, just like the first line, while the fourth line contains only change data. The fax

machine alternates between sending full lines of data and changed lines of data until it has sent the entire page. This method of data compression provides an inherent level of protection. Even if you do lose a line of data during transmission, the next full line will restore the fax data stream to its original state. That way, even if you do lose one line of data, it will affect at most two lines of fax output. You will see a 15 to 20 percent increase in data transmission rate, using this method of compression.

- Minimized modified read (MMR): Using this option gives up some of the security of MR and trades it for speed. The fax transmits only the first line of the fax as a full line of data. All remaining lines are transmitted as change data only. This means that an error anytime during transmission has the potential for destroying the rest of the fax. Of course, this means that you can use MMR only on a very clean (non-noisy) telephone line. MMR may include its own error-correction method along with the transmission, but this will reduce some of the benefit of using the compression technique in the first place. Normally, you can expect a near doubling of transmission speed when using this method.

The next option, Use Class 2 If Available, prevents you from receiving Class 1 faxes. The only time you'll want to check this box is if the software you're using won't let you receive Class 1 faxes. Class 2 faxes are the standard graphic type. Class 1 faxes are editable and therefore easier to manipulate.

Finally, the Reject Pages Received with Errors list box/check box combination lets you do a couple of things. Removing the check from this box tells Windows that you don't want to receive any pages a second time, even if they're totally garbled. This usually isn't the best route to pursue. On the other hand, checking the box and selecting Very Low in the Tolerance list box virtually guarantees you'll get at least one resend of each page. (Tolerance is the level of tolerance that Windows has for errors on a fax page.) I usually use the high setting unless I need better fax quality for some reason. For example, if I wanted to use the information in the fax for a presentation, I might select the low or medium setting. The only time I would select very low is if I needed to use the pages as is, without any changes at all, for some type of presentation or formal document.

TAPI and MAPI Support

Application programming interfaces (APIs) allow programmers to accomplish a lot of work with only a little effort. That's the first goal of every API. The second goal is to ensure a standardized form of access to specific system resources and capabilities. Using a standard interface allows the operating system vendor to change the implementation details without "breaking" too much code. Finally, an API also standardizes the results of using specific system resources and capabilities. For example, using the Windows API ensures that the user will see some of the standard types of interface components that we take for granted.

Windows 95 provides two new APIs. The Telephony API (TAPI) provides a standardized method of handling telephone services. The Messaging API (MAPI) provides a standardized method of handling online services and other forms of messaging. Both APIs provide standardized methods for utilizing your modem more efficiently to conduct business. I examine both APIs in depth later in this book. Right now, the important thing to remember is that both APIs exist under Windows 95 in the form of new utilities.

You'll see the effects of TAPI directly in the Modems applet in the Control Panel. It allows you to configure your modem in one place. Any application that supports TAPI will use those settings. This includes Microsoft Exchange and Microsoft Network as native Windows 95 applications. It doesn't include older 16-bit Windows applications. If you want the benefits of TAPI, you'll need to upgrade those applications as the vendors come out with new versions.

Microsoft Exchange is an example of a MAPI application. It allows you to access Microsoft Mail by using a MAPI driver. A different MAPI driver provides access to CompuServe. Still another driver allows you to send a fax. In fact, you could have a MAPI driver to access each online service you subscribe to. The presence of these drivers would allow you to access them all by using one application. The result is reduced training costs and the ability to move information from one service to another with the click of a button.

MAPI and TAPI aren't limited to Windows 95-specific applications. For example, Microsoft Word provides a Send option on the File menu. This option allows you to send all or part of a document using MAPI anywhere you can communicate. Using the native capabilities of Windows 95, this means that you could send it as a fax or an e-mail or to an online service—all without leaving Word.

Multimedia

Multimedia is another big area of improvement under Windows 95. The CD-ROM ships with several samples of multimedia presentations. They don't fully exploit the potential of multimedia, but they do give you an idea of what's possible. I can foresee a lot of people using this media for interactive training. The instructor could appear in a corner of the screen and provide you with interactive instructions as you perform a task.

Multimedia will change the way we conduct business in other ways. Instead of flying a group of people to one place to see a presentation, you could send the presentation to the group of people, using a CD-ROM. This same group could meet using conferencing software and discuss the presentation's impact and viability. Air travel might not become a thing of the past, but using the multimedia capabilities that Windows 95 is starting to provide will help reduce the need to travel.

Notice that I said Windows 95 is only starting to provide this capability. The cost of building a multimedia machine that will really do the job is still fairly high. Using something less than optimum almost always results in a presentation that lacks the pizzazz of a live presentation. We also have a long way to go before interactive training is a real option. It's getting closer, and the Windows 95 demonstration programs show this, but it's still not perfect. Multimedia still needs improvement in some areas before anyone can say that it's ready.

Warts aside, multimedia under Windows 95 is greatly improved. The sections that follow give you an overview of multimedia under Windows 95 and how it allows you to better exploit your hardware. Right now, it's hard to say who's ahead in the game—hardware or software. Neither is to the level where I'd say that it gives you the kind of presentation you're looking for, but I'll leave it for you to decide just how far we need to go.

MPEG Support

Motion pictures revolutionized the world, and now they'll revolutionize your PC. MPEG (Motion Pictures Experts Group) is a method of compressing VHS video into a very small format that will fit on a CD-ROM. VHS is the same format that your VCR uses.

The technical term for the type of functionality that MPEG provides is a codec (coder/decoder). Think of a codec in the same way you would think of a modem. It allows you to send and receive video data using a standard medium. Instead of a telephone wire, you're using a CD-ROM drive. In place of digital data, you're receiving video images.

Windows 95 currently provides the capability to display VHS-quality images in a 640 × 480 window at 30 frames per second. That's about the same rate that you see on television. You're supposed to get this level of performance from a double-speed CD-ROM drive, but I have a quadruple-speed unit connected to my system and just barely get what I would call acceptable performance. I'm sure part of Microsoft's assumption is that you won't be running anything else when using the multimedia capabilities, but that probably isn't valid. Most people will want to use this capability for training, which means that they'll probably have another application open.

Suffice it to say that if you want to fully exploit your machine's hardware capabilities to perform training, this is one way to do it. Make sure that you get more than a minimal system if you plan to use the multimedia capabilities Windows 95 provides on more than an occasional basis, though. Otherwise, you'll probably be disappointed with the acceptable performance that low-end hardware will provide.

Sound Boards

I've had sound for so long that I can't imagine using Windows without it. In fact, you've probably had it that long, too. So why even mention it here? What does Windows 95 provide that Windows 3.x didn't?

There are all kinds of sound. You don't have to settle for the mediocre level of sound that Windows 3.x provided. Windows 95 provides the controls required to fully exploit the expanded capabilities that modern sound boards provide. All you need to do to start using these capabilities is to adjust the settings found in the Audio Properties dialog box. To access this dialog box, right-click the Speaker icon on the Taskbar and select Adjust Audio Properties. You should see a dialog box similar to the one shown in Figure 14.26.

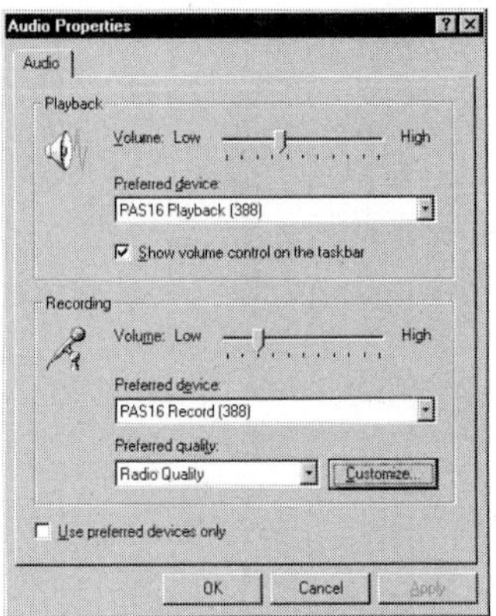

Figure 14.26.
The Audio Properties dialog box allows you to make full use of the audio capabilities your system provides.

Windows 95 will always play back any audio using the full capability of the sound board you select. However, there's a lot of room to customize the recording of sound. Microsoft thoughtfully provided three default recording selections. Each selection reflects the kind of sound recording quality these settings will give you: CD, radio, or telephone.

The actual level of quality you get has to do with the frequency, or the number of samples of sound that Windows takes per second. The more samples it takes, the better the quality of your sample. Using stereo and 16-bit samples also improves the sound quality, as does the recording format. Before we go much further, let's define a few terms.

- **Sample rate:** The number of times per second that Windows samples the microphone input line. A higher setting means that you get more samples. More samples always provide a better playback.
- **Sample size:** Windows supports two sample sizes: 8-bit and 16-bit. A 16-bit sample allows you to record a broader range of values. This means that you can better differentiate between various sounds, resulting in a higher-quality recording.
- **Format:** There are many ways to store a sound, just as there are many ways to store graphics. Some formats take more space but preserve image quality better. Likewise, some audio formats are better than others at preserving sounds. You'll have to experiment to see which one sounds the best to you. Most recordings use the PCM (pulse-code modulation) format. Because this is the most common format, you'll probably want to use it when you need to exchange the recording with someone else, unless there's an overriding reason to do otherwise.
- **Number of channels (mono or stereo):** You probably already know the implication of this setting. A stereo recording uses two microphones to record the sound from different perspectives. During playback, a stereo recording has much greater depth than a mono recording of the same quality.

Now that you have some ideas of the ways you can customize sound under Windows 95, let's look at the dialog box you use to do it. Click the Customize button to see the Customize dialog box, shown in Figure 14.27.

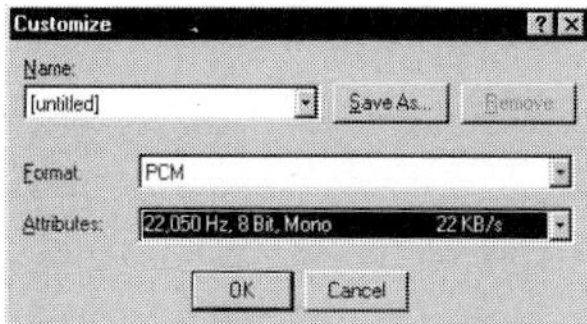

Figure 14.27.
Use the Customize dialog box to change the way you record sound under Windows 95.

Notice that there are two list boxes. One determines the recording format, and the other allows you to select from a variety of options, including the sample rate, sample size, and number of channels. Notice that this list box also tells you the storage requirements for the sample in kilobytes per second. This is the number of kilobytes that the sample would consume for each second you recorded. Obviously, some formats can eat a lot of storage space quickly.

You can save any custom settings that you create, using the Save As button. Windows stores the settings and presents them later in the Preferred Quality list box of the Audio Properties dialog box.

So what's the best way to customize these settings? Remember that the better the quality, the higher the storage requirements. I tend to prefer stereo over mono recordings because the depth of sound can make up for a host of other problems. The trouble comes when you have only one microphone. In that case, selecting stereo is a waste of disk space, because you can record only one channel of information. Selecting 16-bit sound improves quality a great deal for a very small increase in storage size. You get a sample 2^{16} (65,536 possible combinations) versus 2^{8} (256 possible combinations) for a mere doubling of disk space. Unless you're recording music, the highest sampling rate you need is 22,050 Hz. In fact, using 11,025 for simple voice recordings usually proves sufficient.

Virtualizing Your Hardware

To make the best use of your hardware under Windows 95, you must be able to access it. There are three ways to do this, and I've mentioned them all before. If absolutely necessary, you can use a real-mode driver to access an older device. .DLLs allow you to access devices that provide Windows 16-bit support but don't provide a Windows 95-specific driver. This is better than using a real-mode driver but shy of the real goal you want to achieve. The best driver to use is a Windows 95-specific virtual "anything" driver (VxD). The following sections cover all three types of support from an efficiency and ease-of-use standpoint.

Real-Mode Drivers for Older Devices

There are a lot of problems with using real-mode drivers under Windows 95. Other areas of this book cover just about every problem you can experience. Suffice it to say that a real-mode driver isn't the best choice you could make.

The first decision you'll need to make is whether the device is even needed all the time. You had to load a device you intended to use at boot up in the DOS and Windows 3.x environments because there was no way to load it later. If you need a device for a very special purpose under Windows 95, you can always load it later in an MS-DOS mode session. Simply set up a copy of the command processor with the CONFIG.SYS and AUTOEXEC.BAT settings required to load the device in its optimum environment. Of course, you won't be able to load Windows 95 when using MS-DOS mode—or access other applications, for that matter. It's a problem of balancing convenience with overall system performance and stability.

You'll need to make a few decisions when using such a driver under Windows 95. The first choice is the amount of DOS space you need in comparison to the flexibility you want to give Windows when it comes to managing your memory. Loading all your device drivers low will affect the amount of conventional memory you need. However, this choice also means that you won't have to load a memory manager and that Windows will be able to provide the maximum flexibility possible.

If you find that you have to load the driver high, you'll also have to load something other than the Windows 95 memory manager. Try to optimize both the driver and memory manager settings to reduce their impact on the Windows environment. For example, use the least amount of memory possible for buffers.

Using 16-Bit Drivers

Using an older 16-bit Windows driver is a little bit better than using a real-mode driver. At least Windows still controls the memory environment. Unfortunately, using these older drivers will still have an effect on overall system efficiency. Remember that all 16-bit applications, including drivers, run in a single session. Using that session's resources for a driver doesn't seem like the best way to go.

The 32-bit drivers that come with Windows 95 also provide built-in safeguards to help protect your system environment. The older 16-bit drivers provide no such protection. They're more likely than a newer driver to crash or at least destabilize the system.

Finally, a 16-bit driver won't know how to interact with the miniport driver architecture used by Windows 95. This means that you'll lose all the user and programmer benefits of such an architecture for that specific device. I provided an overview of those benefits earlier in this chapter. We'll take a detailed look at them in the architecture-specific chapters. I provided a list of these chapters earlier.

Default 32-Bit Drivers

Using 32-bit Windows 95 drivers is the best solution if you want to get the most out of your hardware. Windows 95 isn't a perfect operating system, but it does provide enough advanced features that updating your hardware to use the new drivers is the best way to go. Exploiting your hardware always means getting the most out of it. Using old drivers is just another way to introduce inefficiencies and stability problems into your system.

On Your Own

Use the automatic installation technique in this chapter to determine whether your machine has any undetected devices. Normally, Windows 95 will report that it didn't find anything. If so, click Cancel to exit the detection routine.

Try changing the configuration settings of various devices listed on the Device page of the System Properties dialog box. Be sure to save the settings in case you can't get Windows 95 back to its original configuration. Use settings that conflict with another device to see how Windows reacts. Be sure to change the setting back so that you can use the device again.

15

Fonts and Printing

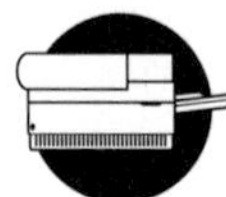

Printing and fonts go hand in hand. You can't have one without the other. From the very first day that Gutenberg used movable type to print a document, we've looked for ways to improve the process. It would be inaccurate to say that Gutenberg had much to worry about from early computers. Those green screens with monospaced type that you could barely read were an exercise in frustration for most people. Today we can put together a document that would've made Gutenberg green with envy in a fraction of the time that it would have taken him just to lay out the type.

Windows 95 improves on the process of printing a great deal from what most people were used to seeing with Windows 3.x. Even the simple act of installing a printer is easier now. Removing one is easier still. Managing your fonts has also taken a turn for the better. For one thing, you no longer have to dig through your \SYSTEM directory looking for them. Windows 95 places them in a separate directory and provides a utility that you can use to manage them.

The following sections take you on a tour of the complex world of printers. Windows 95 has taken some of the pain out of managing your printer; now there are more choices and more features than ever before. I'll show you how to use these features to your benefit and explain some of the more intriguing aspects of the new environment that Windows 95 provides.

Installing a Printer

Before you can use a printer, you have to install and configure it. I used to hate doing this under Windows 3.x because it seemed as if every printer was just different enough to make life difficult. It was a nice surprise to see how easy things are under Windows 95. Chapters 11 and 14 briefly look at the topics of installing and configuring your printer. Chapter 11 tells you how to perform a special file installation. Chapter 14 looks at a few of the most efficient ways to use your printer's capabilities. This section provides the details required to install a printer. It also includes some productivity tips.

The Printer Folder

Even if you don't have any printers installed on your system, you'll have a Printer folder in the Control Panel. At a minimum, this folder will contain an applet that allows you to install a new printer. This is the applet you use to add a new printer to your system. The following procedure takes you through a generic installation session and takes a look at some configuration details:

1. Use the Start | Settings | Printers command to open the Printers folder. You might see one or more printers already installed in the folder, along with the Add Printer applet.
2. Double-click the Add Printer applet. You'll see the dialog box shown in Figure 15.1.

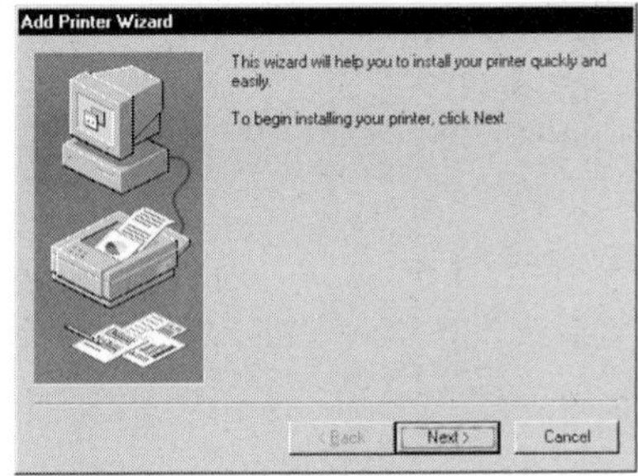

Figure 15.1.
The Add Printer Wizard provides an easy method of adding a new printer to your system.

Note: You might not see the dialog box shown in Figure 15.2 if your machine doesn't have network support installed. If you don't see Figure 15.2, simply bypass step 3 and the first sentence of step 4. You should see the dialog box shown in Figure 15.3, which allows you to select a printer type.

3. Click Next. The dialog box shown in Figure 15.2 will appear. This is where you determine whether this will be a network or local printer. Selecting the Network Printer option allows you to share the printer with other people. Selecting the Local Printer option doesn't allow sharing, but it provides some advantages when it comes to the spooler. (See Chapter 14 for more details on this topic.)

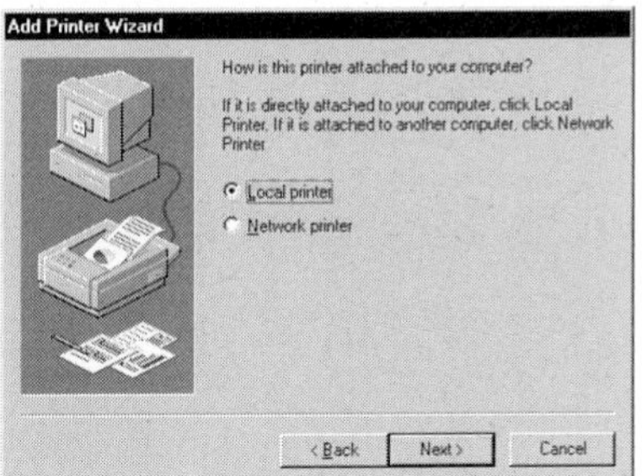

Figure 15.2.
This dialog box allows you to choose between a local and a network printer setup.

Tip: Windows doesn't restrict you from creating multiple installations for the same printer. In fact, doing so allows you to create multiple setups that are optimized for specific types of jobs. Chapter 14 covers this topic in detail.

4. Choose either Network Printer or Local Printer and click Next. The Add Printer Wizard asks you to select a printer, using the dialog box shown in Figure 15.3. Notice that there are two lists. The one on the left contains a list of printer manufacturers. Selecting a vendor changes the list on the right to display printers manufactured by that vendor. Windows also allows you to install an unsupported printer by clicking the Have Disk button. Chapter 11 covers this procedure, so I won't talk about it again here.

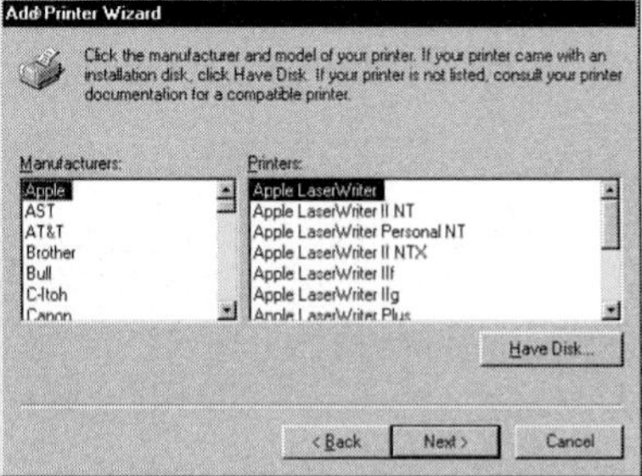

Figure 15.3.
Use the entries in this dialog box to select a printer vendor and model.

5. After you've selected a printer vendor and model, click Next. The next dialog box (see Figure 15.4) asks you to select a printer port. In most cases, you'll see only the local ports if you haven't used a network printer port. The later section "Configuration" shows you how to add a network printer port. That section also looks at a problem with using network ports in Windows 95.

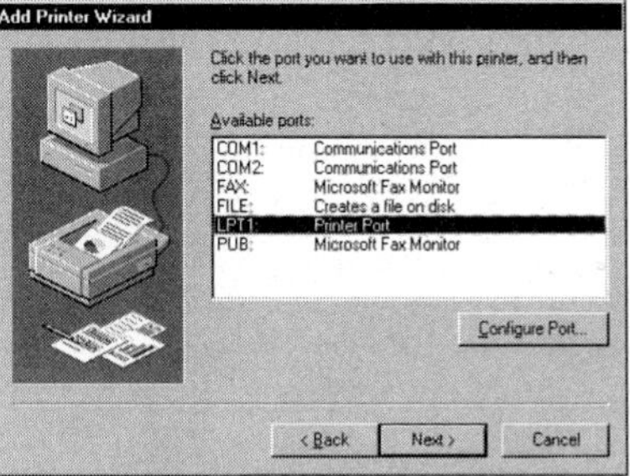

Figure 15.4.
The port selection list might not include any network connections if you haven't used them previously.

Tip: You can create multiple connections for one printer. I normally add a file connection as a minimum, so that I can delay printing until later. A fax connection is also a good idea to support applications that don't provide a fax connection.

6. Select a port. You can configure the DOS options for the port by clicking the Configure Port button. Chapter 14 covers these options. Click Next to continue. You'll see the dialog box shown in Figure 15.5.

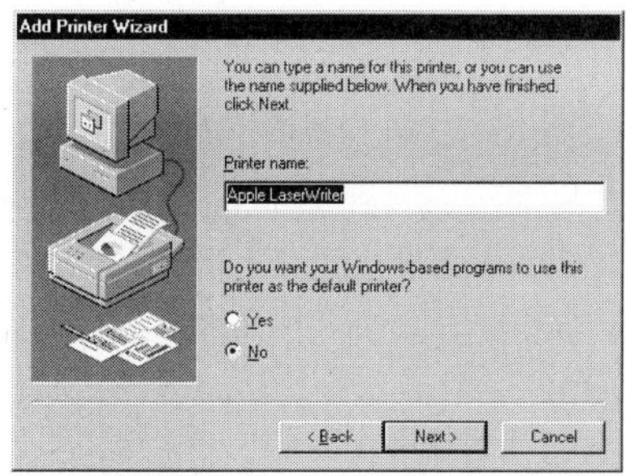

Figure 15.5.
This dialog box allows you to select a printer name and specify whether it's the default printer.

7. You have two important decisions to make in this dialog box. The first is what to name the printer. The Add Printer Wizard will suggest something appropriate, and you can accept this name if you intend to create only one copy of the printer. However, you might want to use a more descriptive name if you plan to install multiple configurations of the same printer. The second decision is whether to make this the default printer. Windows applications use the default printer unless you specifically select something else. You should make the default printer the one you'll use the most often.
8. Click Next to continue. You should see the dialog box shown in Figure 15.6. I always send a test page to a local printer connected to an actual port. It makes little sense to print a test page for a file connection. Unless you already have your network connections configured, you'll need to test them later. Choose whether you want to print a test page and click Next to complete the installation.

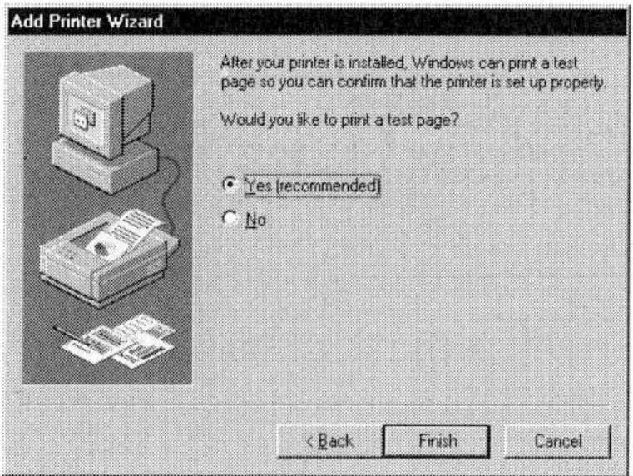

Figure 15.6.
The final step in the configuration process is to print a test page to test your printer connection and configuration.

9. Windows 95 displays a status dialog box as it copies all the needed files to your drive. Once it completes this task, you'll see the appropriate icon in the Printers folder. Double-clicking this icon allows you to view the current print jobs. Right-clicking allows you to see the context menu.

As you can see, installing a printer isn't difficult. The next section takes you through the process of adding a port. Then we'll look at the overall configuration procedure.

Note: You'll probably need to configure the printer for your specific needs. I've found that Windows doesn't always choose the optimum settings for some items. For example, it chose the 180 × 180 resolution for my dot-matrix printer instead of the higher-resolution 360 × 360 mode.

Adding a Port

Adding a network port is very easy under Windows 95. All you need to do is right-click the Printer icon, select Properties, and click the Details tab. You should see a dialog box similar to the one shown in Figure 15.7. Windows 95 allows you to perform a variety of tasks in this dialog box, including changing the printer by changing the driver you're using. The port-specific buttons allow you to add a new port or delete an existing one.

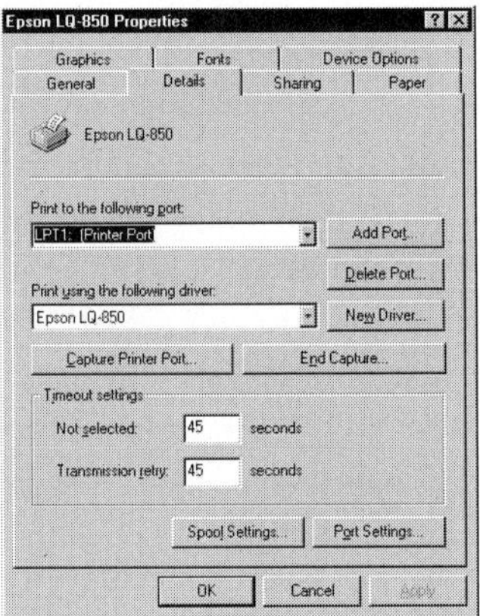

Figure 15.7.
The Details page of the Printer Properties dialog box allows you to add, delete, and configure the ports where your printer attaches.

Clicking the Add Port button displays the dialog box shown in Figure 15.8. You can choose between two types of ports: local and network. The local (Other) options vary according to the utilities you have installed. They'll include a local port, as a minimum. The options could include Fax and Microsoft Network, if you have them installed. The network connections depend on the type of network you have installed and the devices shared on the network. You can use the Browse button to find a particular device. If you're using one of the networks that Windows 95 supports directly, a copy of Network Neighborhood will pop up.

Note: If your network isn't directly supported by Windows 95, its connections won't appear in Network Neighborhood. This means that you have to type the precise network connection information by hand. Don't use any mapped names. Always use the fully qualified network path in this dialog box.

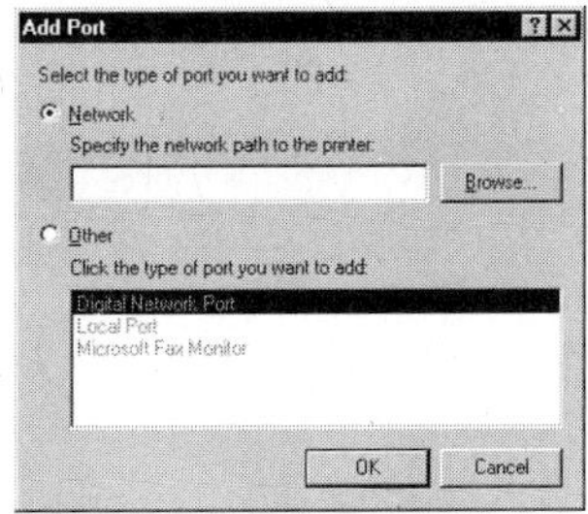

Figure 15.8.
You can select from a variety of port connections in this dialog box.

Clicking OK at this point stores the new connection name and returns you to the Details page. Windows 95 automatically selects the port as a destination. There's a problem with network connections, though: You can't configure them. You must capture the port first before you configure it. Capturing a port assigns it to a local connection. To capture a port, all you need to do is highlight it and click the Capture Printer Port button on the Details page. You'll see the dialog box shown in Figure 15.9. Notice that it consists of three entries: a local port name, the network connection path, and a check box that asks whether you want to reconnect to the port after each logon. I've noticed that Windows 95 still looks for the printer connection at each logon, even if you choose not to reconnect. The only difference that the reconnect check box makes is whether the connection is actually available for use.

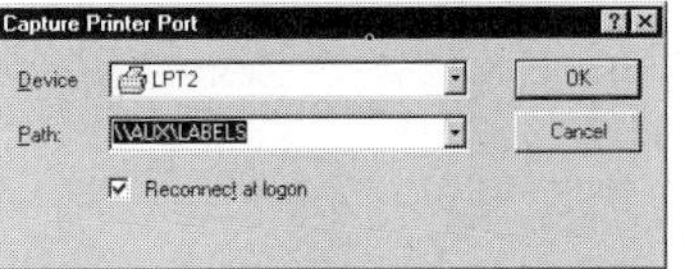

Figure 15.9.
The Capture Printer Port dialog box allows you to assign a network connection to a local port.

Tip: If you don't plan to use the network connection on a daily basis, use the End Capture button on the Detail page of the Properties dialog box to remove the connection. This saves system resources and reduces boot time. It also keeps Windows 95 from displaying an error message if the connection isn't available the next time you boot the machine.

There's a final configuration issue for the ports you create on your machine: You need to decide what timeout settings to use. The first Timeout Settings field on the Details page, Not Selected, determines how long Windows 95 will wait for a printer-ready signal. The only time the printer provides this signal is when it's online and ready to go. The default value normally provides sufficient time. However, some specialty printers might require additional time if they perform some type of paper cycling or other maintenance procedure. The second setting, Transmission Retry, determines how long Windows will try to send data to the printer. In some cases, the printer is online but is unable to print for some reason. Normally, the default value works fine here as well. However, you might need to increase the value for network printers, especially on networks with print servers such as NetWare. Sometimes the print server is slow to respond because it's serving another request.

Now we come to one of the problem areas associated with Windows 95 and ports. What happens when the network connection that you just created becomes invalid? Logic would dictate that you should be able to remove the network connection by using the Delete Port dialog box. However, doing so will only net you an error message in some cases (see Figure 15.10). Windows 95 will refuse to delete the port.

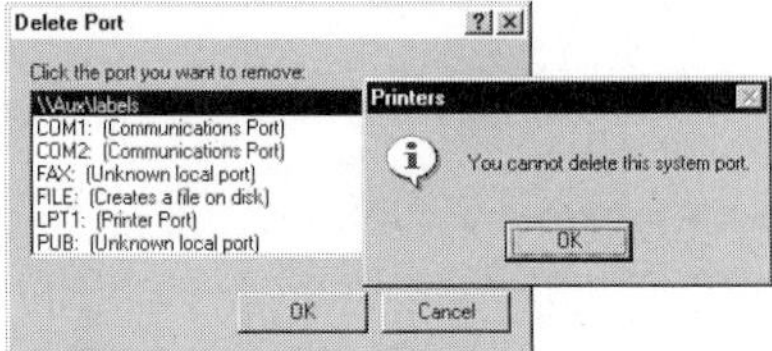

Figure 15.10.
One of the potential problems that you'll face with a network connection is the inability to get rid of it.

There's a way around this problem. Simply open the Registry to the key shown in Figure 15.11. Notice that this key contains subkeys—each one a network connection. In this particular case, LPT2 is assigned to the \\AUX\LABELS connection. You can delete the LPT2 key and remove the old network connection from your system. This technique is also more selective than simply deleting the old connection by using the Delete Port dialog box. In some situations, Windows will decide to delete *all* the network connections when you use the Delete Port method. Directly editing the Registry is risky, but it can provide more control for the savvy network administrator.

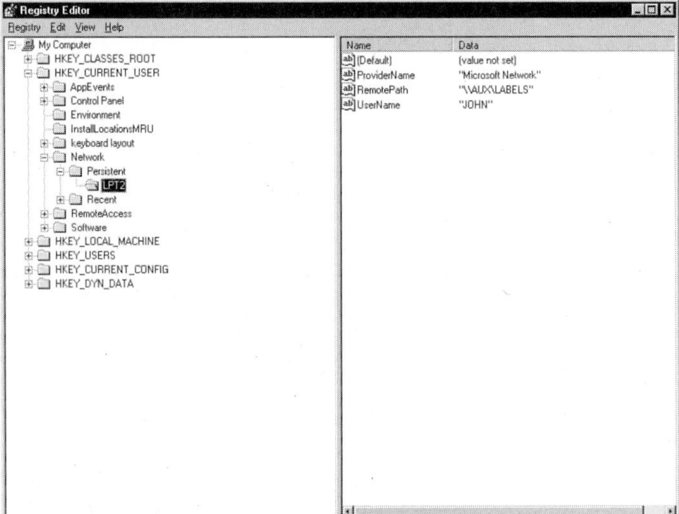

Figure 15.11.
When Windows won't let you delete a port, use the Registry Editor to delete it instead.

Configuration

Configuring your printer should be the next step after you assign it to a port. Most of the settings control the appearance of the output and the features that the printer provides to the user. In some cases, a configuration option also affects the speed of printing. I'll let you know what kind of choices you'll be making as we go along.

Opening the Printer Properties dialog box is as simple as right-clicking the Printer icon and selecting the Properties option from the context menu. The first page you'll always see is the General page shown in Figure 15.12. This page contains only the printer name, a comment that other users can use to identify the printer, and a separator page entry. The comment can contain any information you want it to, such as the days and times that the printer is available for use. You shouldn't make any temporary comments, because this field is copied only once to other machines that need to use the printer. In other words, the comment is permanent and won't change as you change the comment on your machine. The Separator Page option is useful when more than one person uses the printer. It sends a page containing your name and other identifying information to the printer before it prints your document. Using a separator page wastes a piece of paper for each print job, but it does make sorting through the printouts a lot easier. There's also a Print Test Page button at the bottom of the screen. You can use this to test the capabilities of your printer at any time.

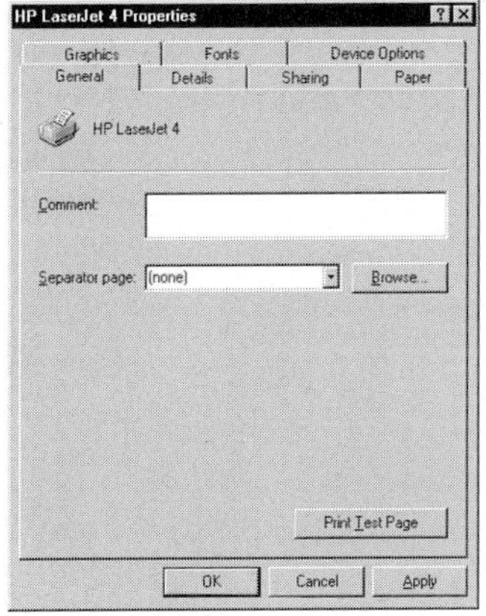

Figure 15.12.
The General page of the Printer Properties dialog box allows you to change the basic identification of the printer.

If you make a connection to a network printer (one attached to a file or print server), you'll see a Printer Settings page like the one shown in Figure 15.13. There are three main sections to this page: Output Settings, Banner Settings, and Other Settings. The Output Settings section defines how you want the print server to handle specific page elements such as form feeds and tabs. You can also tell the print server to always output a specific number of copies. For example, you could tell it that you always need three copies: one for you, another for your boss, and a third for the file. The banner settings are very important for home network users. You'll want to uncheck the Enable Banner check box as shown in the figure to avoid wasting a lot of paper. Business users, especially those in large offices, will want to enable this feature to help keep print jobs separate. There are two banner-specific text boxes if you do enable the banner feature. Both are normally 12 characters long. The first text box tells what will appear in the upper half of the banner. The second text box tells what will appear in the lower half of the banner. A banner page is always one full page long. The final section, Other Settings, allows you to define three print characteristics. The Hold check box tells the print server to place this job in the print queue, but not to print it until you tell it to do so. The Keep check box tells the print server to print the job as usual, but to retain a copy of the print job in the print queue afterward. Finally, the Notify check box tells the print server to notify you when the print job is complete—an especially handy feature on large networks or when you're printing a large number of pages.

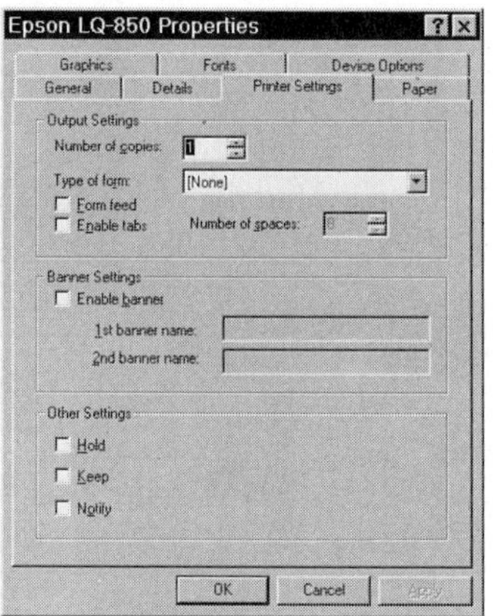

Figure 15.13.
The Printer Settings page of the Printer Properties dialog box allows you to change the basic identification of the printer.

The Sharing page, shown in Figure 15.14, allows you to share the printer with other people. (You'll see it only when looking at a local printer.) It contains two radio buttons. Selecting the Shared As button allows other people to use the printer. You must provide a share name. The comment and password are optional. I always recommend including a comment so that other people will know whether this printer is the one they're looking for. Doing so will reduce the number of inadvertent connections to your machine. Once you share a printer, Windows 95 adds a hand to the printer's icon. This shows that the printer is shared and helps prevent any confusion over local and network resources.

Tip: Sharing reduces your spooling options. In addition, using a shared printer imposes other speed penalties on the local user. I always create a second printer for myself that isn't shared. This way, I get the best of both worlds: a shared printer for other people to use, and a nonshared printer that's configured specifically for my needs.

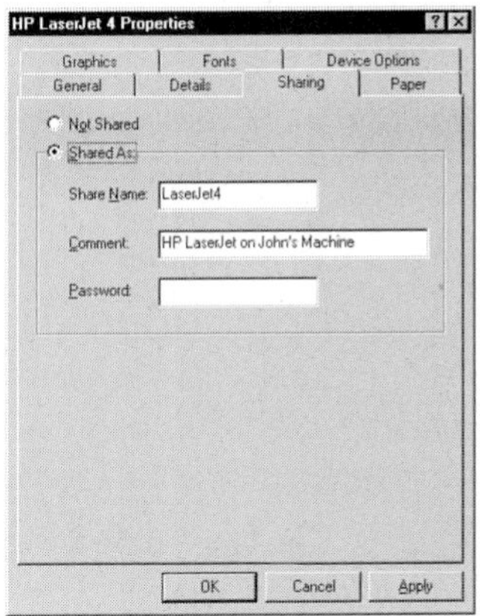

Figure 15.14.
Use the Sharing page to allow other people to use your printer.

The Paper page, shown in Figure 15.15, allows you to select the paper you want to use. Windows 95 supports a much broader range of paper types than Windows 3.x did. I especially like all the envelope options. Although I don't use this particular feature, you might want to configure an envelope printer if you print envelopes a lot. The Orientation section allows you to choose the direction of printing—landscape or portrait. The Paper Source list box allows you to choose from the various bin options that the printer provides. The Copies field tells Windows how many copies of the printout to make. I usually find it easier to select the number of copies from within the application than to specify it here.

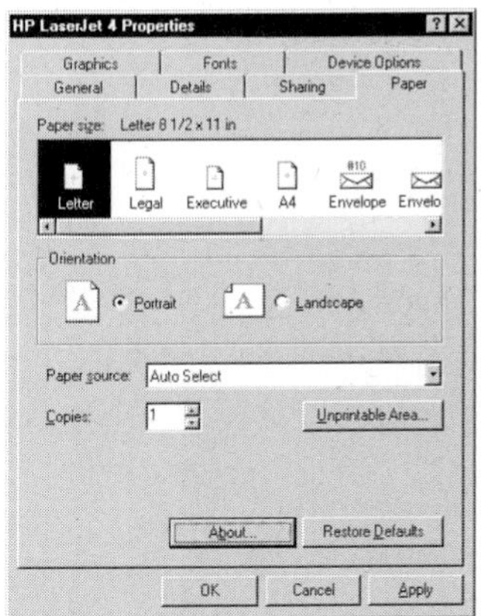

Figure 15.15.
The Paper page contains all the entries required to select your paper type and print orientation.

Clicking the Unprintable Area button on the Paper page displays the dialog box shown in Figure 15.16. This dialog box is especially important for laser printers, because they have a "dead zone" where the toner can't reach. The default settings are usually adequate unless you run into a special printing situation. For example, sometimes with my dot matrix I want to run the print almost to the edge of the page. The default settings won't allow me to do this, so I change them as required for the work I'm doing.

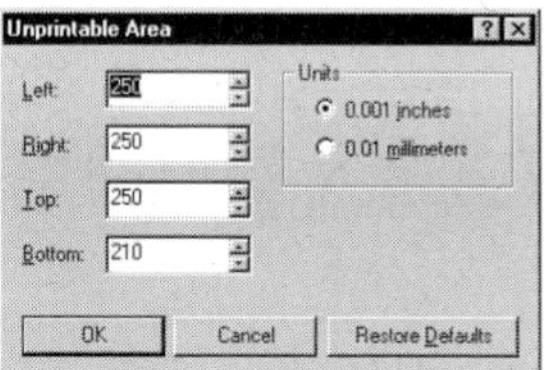

Figure 15.16.
You might need to change the defaults in the Unprintable Area dialog box when printing to the edge of the page.

Tip: Some applications, such as Netscape Navigator, rely on the settings in the Unprintable Area dialog box to determine where to stop printing. If you have fanfold paper installed in a dot-matrix printer and set the Top and Bottom fields to 0, these programs will continue to print without observing any margins at all. (This despite any margins you set using the Printer Setup option of the program.) At a minimum, they'll place any headers or footers you create in strange places. If you run into a situation where an application doesn't seem to observe any margin settings that you request, try changing the settings in the Unprintable Area dialog box.

The name of the Graphics page is somewhat misleading. It also determines the print quality of the text you output using TrueType or other nonresident fonts, when using some types of printers. For example, the settings on this page will affect a dot-matrix or inkjet-type printer, but not a laser printer. The laser printer downloads its fonts, so the printer determines their quality level within the limitations of the resolution you set for it. Figure 15.17 shows the Graphics page.

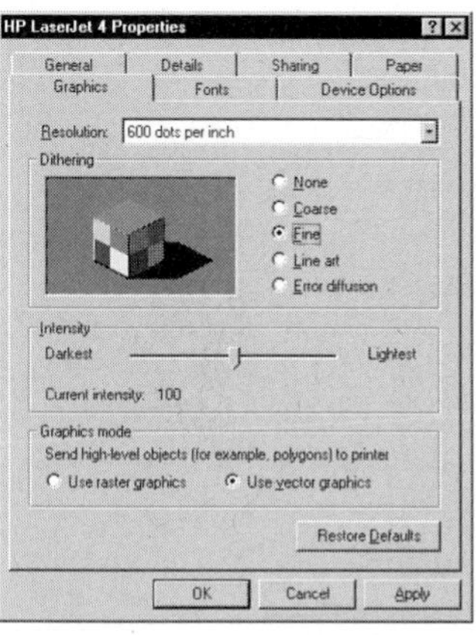

Figure 15.17.
The Graphics page might affect more than just graphics, depending on the type of printer you use.

The Resolution field on this page has a significant effect on the output quality of your document. It also has an effect on print speed and could affect system memory. High-resolution printouts require more time, especially from a dot-matrix printer, in which the output speed could drop to as little as one-tenth the normal level. In addition, managing these printouts requires more system resources, such as CPU cycles and memory. Finally, any high-resolution printout that uses the spooler will need more temporary disk storage as well. Always consider all the factors before choosing a particular course of action with your printer. A lower-resolution printout might not look as appealing, but it will reduce the drain on system resources.

The various Dithering options allow you to determine how Windows represents color on your printer output. It's especially important to use the correct settings for black-and-white printers, because Windows has fewer methods to provide aesthetically-pleasing color differentiation. The following list describes the most common dithering options that you'll see.

- **None:** This option forces Windows to use the printer's built-in capabilities rather than dither the image. It usually doesn't work very well with non-color printers.
- **Course:** This option takes less time to process but produces less pleasing results. Coarse dithering normally provides one-fourth the number of color combinations that the Fine option produces.
- **Fine:** I use this option for final print output. It provides the best color differentiation your printer can support.
- **Line Art:** Use this option if you want to remove the colors and print only the lines used to create a graphic. It comes in handy when you need to print an outlined graphic and don't want the colors to interfere with the quality of the output.
- **Error Diffusion:** Windows 95 provides this option to take care of special color dithering problems. Have you ever seen a pattern in the dithering scheme used by some printers? This is called a *moiré pattern*. Most artists consider it a nuisance. The Error Diffusion option trades a little additional processing time for a random dithering scheme. It reduces the chance that you'll see patterns in your printed output.

The Intensity slider allows you to change the darkness of your printout. It works like the slider on your toaster. The default value of 100 usually produces the crispest printout when you're using a new ribbon or cartridge.

Tip: The Intensity slider can actually save you money. Simply set it lower when you first install a ribbon or cartridge. This will reduce the amount of ink or toner that you use per page. Of course, the quality of the printout will suffer slightly. Increasing the darkness as you near the end of the ribbon or cartridge's life will allow you to use it longer. Doing so might cause some graphics to look "muddy," but this setting won't adversely affect text.

Some printers include an additional setting like the one shown at the bottom of the Graphics page. In this case, the Printer Properties dialog box is asking whether you want to output graphics in vector or raster mode. (I describe the difference between vector and raster graphics later, in the "Font Types" section.) Using vector graphics might provide a little more flexibility. This will also reduce the processing load on the machine at the expense of the printer. In addition, vector graphics require more printer memory, because you need to store both a vector graphic and its raster counterpart. Using raster graphics means a slower printout, but this could allow you to print pages that wouldn't otherwise fit in printer memory.

The Fonts page, shown in Figure 15.18, allows you to control how the printer handles fonts. Because the font capabilities of a printer vary from machine to machine, it's very likely that your Font page will differ from mine. However, there are some standard capabilities, and we'll cover them here.

Figure 15.18.
The contents of the Fonts page can vary greatly from machine to machine.

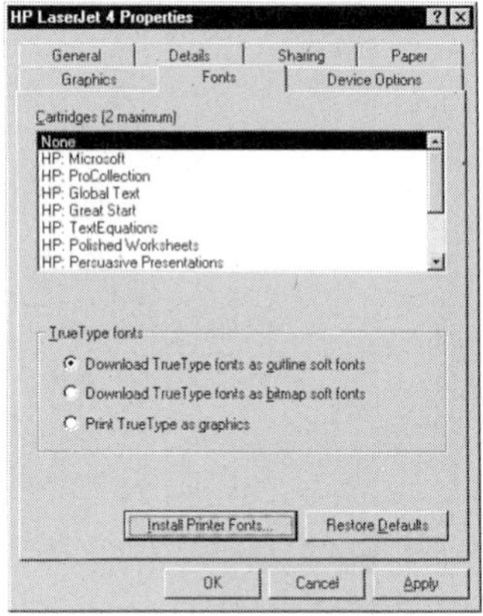

Most printers support cartridges these days. Even the lowliest dot-matrix printer usually provides some type of cartridge support. The Cartridges list box in this dialog box allows you to tell Windows which cartridges the printer contains.

Note: Windows 95 still doesn't provide complete cartridge support for all printers. For example, Epson has sold a master cartridge for its LQ series printer for a number of years. This cartridge contains all the fonts that the printer will support. Unfortunately, Windows 95 doesn't list this option in the Cartridges list box, so you can't use the full potential of this feature. Always check the Cartridges list box to determine which fonts Windows 95 supports before you make an investment.

Most laser printers provide the capacity to manage TrueType fonts. There are three options in this case, but your printer might support only one or two of them. The first option allows you to download the fonts as an outline. This is the most flexible option and the one that I generally recommend. The advantage of this method is that the printer can create the full range of type sizes that TrueType allows. This method also saves memory, because the TrueType font will probably take less room than the bitmap equivalents. The negative side to this selection is that it will cost you some print time. The printer will have to render all the fonts that it needs for a print job rather than just use them. The second option allows you to download the fonts as bitmaps. You would use this option if you intend to use only a few fonts for your print jobs and speed is a critical factor. This option will probably use more memory, but it really depends on how many bitmaps you download and their size. The third option is for people who don't have much printer memory to spare. It keeps the TrueType fonts loaded on the local machine. The advantage is greatly reduced printer memory requirements. The disadvantage is greatly increased print times. Sending output to a printer in graphics rather than text mode takes at least twice as long under the best circumstances. Think twice before committing to this particular option.

HP LaserJets (and other printers) come with a special utility that allows you to download fonts. You access the download utility by clicking the Install Printer Fonts button near the bottom of the dialog box. Figure 15.19 shows how the resulting dialog box looks. Essentially, you tell the utility which fonts you want to download to the printer, and it takes care of the rest. Since each download utility is different, I won't go into further detail here.

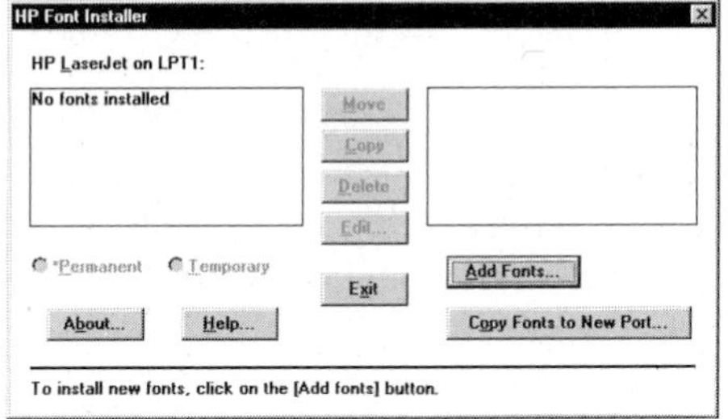

Figure 15.19.
Some laser printers include a font download utility that you access from the Fonts page of the Printer Properties dialog box.

The final page of the Printer Properties dialog box is Device Options (see Figure 15.20). As in so many other cases, the laser printer provides more options than other types of printers you might use. Just about every printer you use will include a Print Quality list box. This allows you to select from the various quality modes that the printer supplies. In most cases, the term is a little nebulous. A printer might provide a "letter quality" mode and a "draft" mode. Don't confuse this setting with resolution, because the two settings are completely different. The best course of action is to check out your printer manual to find out exactly what this term means to a particular vendor. In general, letter quality is always better than draft. However, as you can see from Figure 15.20, some vendors don't use easily recognized terms. In this case, there's nothing you can do but read the manual.

There are three other optional fields on this page. One that's common to most laser printers is the Printer Memory field. The printer normally knows how much memory it has, but the Windows 95 driver doesn't. The LaserJet 4 also includes special features such as page protection and a printer memory manager. Spend some time reading your printer manual to determine precisely what these settings will do for you.

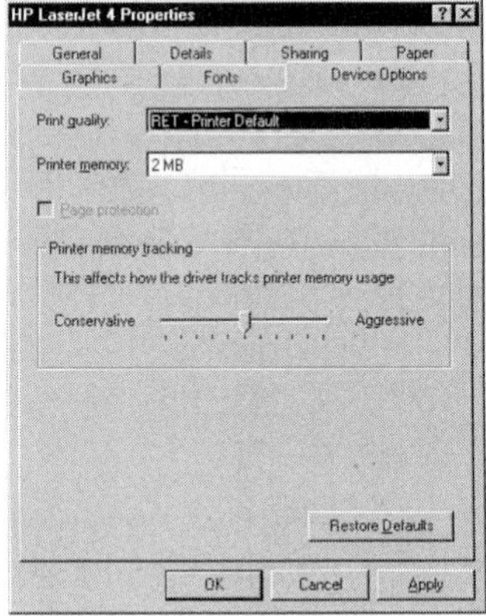

Figure 15.20.
The Device Options page can contain just about anything.

Point and Print

Point and print is a new Windows 95 feature. It allows you to do a few things you couldn't do with previous versions of Windows. The most significant thing it does is simplify remote printer installation. All you need to do to install a remote printer from a Windows 95, Windows NT, or NetWare network location is drag the icon from Network Neighborhood into the Printer folder. Windows 95 will take care of the rest. It might ask you to insert the CD-ROM so that it can load the proper drivers on your machine. Other than that, installation is as close to automatic as you can get.

Note: If you need access to a printer attached to a WfW workstation or a print server that doesn't support point and print, you can still load the printer driver by using the standard technique mentioned at the beginning of this chapter. Dragging any icon from Network Neighborhood to your Printer folder should at least start the installation utility. Double-clicking the Printer icon in Network Neighborhood will accomplish the same thing as Windows attempts to open the Printer Status dialog box. (Whether it's successful depends on the limitations of your network, the printer driver, and whether the remote workstation responds.)

Quick Printing Techniques

Remember the context menu I've been talking about throughout the book? Well, you won't escape it in this chapter, either. Windows 95 takes a proactive approach when it comes to printing. There are a lot of different ways you can get a document to the printer. I usually use the context menu shown in Figure 15.21, because most of my documents go to the same place if I don't have them open. Of course, you still have the usual Windows defaults for sending a document to the printer, including your application's Print menu.

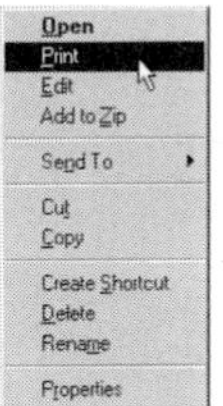

Figure 15.21.
The context menu for a document usually offers the choice of sending the document to the default printer.

Tip: We've viewed DDE in a variety of ways throughout this book. The most recent is in Chapter 12, which discusses some of the ways in which you can use DDE with a document. Chapter 5 looks at the way Explorer uses DDE. Here's one additional way to use DDE: Use Explorer to add another menu option to the context menu of your documents if you normally use more than one printer. This will allow you to select something other than the default printer with the context menu. Unfortunately, your application must support DDE for this option to work. Use the current Print entry as a basis for creating your advanced Print option.

Another method that people use to send documents to the printer is to place a shortcut to the printer on the desktop. Then all you need to do to print a document is drag it to the icon for the printer you want to use and drop it. Of course, this technique consumes some valuable desktop real estate, so use it only when required.

32-Bit Printing

Now that you have a printer configured and ready for use, it might be a good time to look at the way Windows 95 handles this task. An understanding of how printing works will often help you discover new optimization techniques or track down an equipment failure with ease. Figure 15.22 gives you an overview of the Windows 95 print architecture. I describe each component in the following list:

- **Graphics device interface (GDI):** I talk about this particular element of the printing picture elsewhere. The GDI is the API that an application uses to talk to the printer. An application doesn't directly access a printer like DOS did. It uses the Windows services. This allows for centralized scheduling and control of print jobs, a necessary requirement of a multitasking environment.
- **Device-independent bitmap (DIB) engine:** The DIB engine is normally associated with the display adapter. It works with the GDI to produce the bitmap you see on-screen. For example, when Windows displays wallpaper on the desktop, it's the DIB engine that produces the bitmap under the instruction of the GDI. I talk more about this topic in Chapter 17. As far as a printer is concerned, the DIB engine provides a convenient method of manipulating graphics. For example, if you choose to print a file in graphics mode instead of text mode, the DIB engine helps prepare the print job for you.

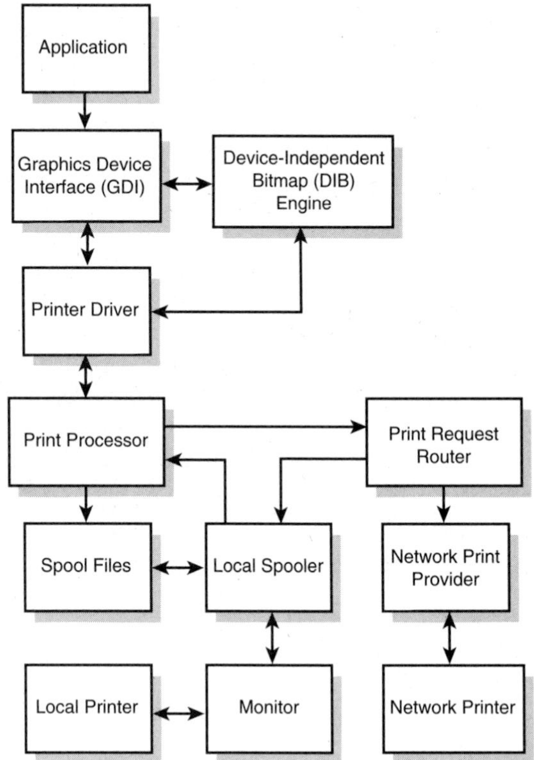

Figure 15.22.
Windows 95 uses an improved print architecture that depends on minidriver support.

- **Printer driver:** This is the third piece of the print page preparation. It interfaces with both the GDI and the DIB engine to produce printer-specific output in the form of journal records. Think of a journal record as the disassembled pieces of a puzzle. All the pieces will eventually be put together but, for right now, each record is just a piece of that puzzle. Just as with puzzle pieces, you can look at them individually and recognize what they will eventually become.
- **Print processor:** The print processor accepts the printer-ready data from the printer driver. Its only function at this point is to despool the data to the print request router. In other words, it sends the journal records out single file in an orderly manner. Later, the print processor takes care of spooling the data to the local hard drive (spool files), if this is a local print job. This means that it takes all the puzzle pieces (journal records) and connects them into a single document.
- **Print request router:** This component routes the formatted data to the appropriate location. It determines whether the job is for a local or remote printer. If it's for a remote printer, the print request router sends the data to the network print provider. Otherwise, it sends the data to the local spooler.

- **Network print provider:** The network print provider is network-specific. It's the interface between your machine and the beginning of the network data stream. Its job is to accept the journal records, connect them into a single document, convert the document into a network-specific format (if required), and transmit the converted data to the next component in the network data stream. If all goes according to plan, this data will eventually find its way to a network printer.
- **Local spooler:** The first job of this particular component is to hand off print jobs to the print processor. The print processor converts the journal records it receives into a document. The local spooler reads the data files that the print processor stores on disk and sends them to the monitor. It also accepts messages from the monitor regarding the status of the printer. I discuss the types of information it receives when I discuss the monitor.
- **Spool files:** These are the physical files that the print processor stores in the Spool folder under the main Windows folder. Each printer type has its own storage location in this folder.
- **Monitor:** The monitor handles all communication with the printer. It accepts data from the spooler and transmits it to the printer. The monitor is also responsible for providing the spooler with plug and play information about the printer. Finally, the monitor provides the spooler with printer error information. Instead of giving you a "printer not ready" message, printers that support a bidirectional port can supply an "out of paper" or "toner low" message.

This might look like a lot of work just to get your document from an application to the printer that's connected to your machine. You're right. If that's all the tasks that Windows 95 could handle, this architecture would be very inflated indeed. However, there's much more here than meets the eye. Using this kind of interface provides the user with a lot more freedom in regard to printer usage. It ensures that everyone gets equal access to the printer. Programmers benefit as well, because it's easier to write print drivers. The DIB engine improves the quality of your output. I could go on, but I think the point is made. The printing architecture might be complex, but it makes printing easier from a user perspective.

Managing Print Jobs

With so many new capabilities, it's small wonder that your ability to manage print jobs under Windows 95 is improved as well. Gaining access to the print jobs you have running is no problem. Whenever you print, Windows adds a Printer icon to the control area of the Taskbar. Resting your mouse pointer over the Printer icon will tell you how many print jobs are pending (see Figure 15.23). This provides a quick method of monitoring your printer status without opening any new windows.

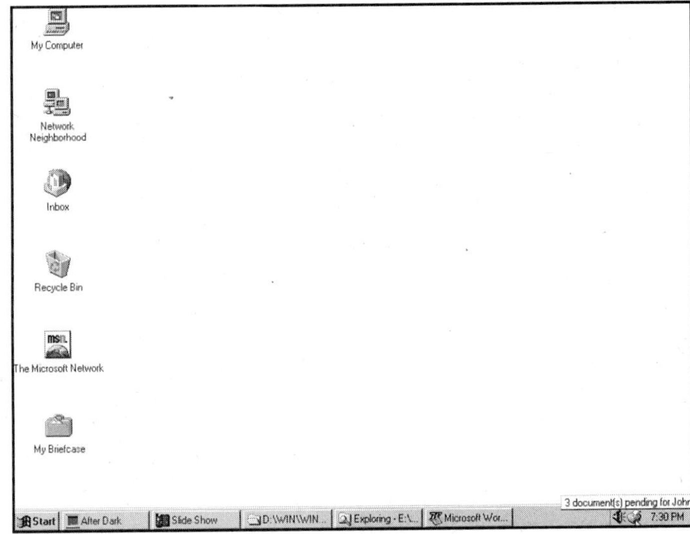

Figure 15.23.
The Printer icon tells you how many print jobs are pending. Right-clicking tells you which printer is being used.

If multiple printers are in use on your workstation at one time, right-clicking the Printer icon will display a menu of available printers (see Figure 15.24). You can choose to open one or all of them. The top menu item will open all active printers—those with print jobs. It doesn't matter whether the print job is paused.

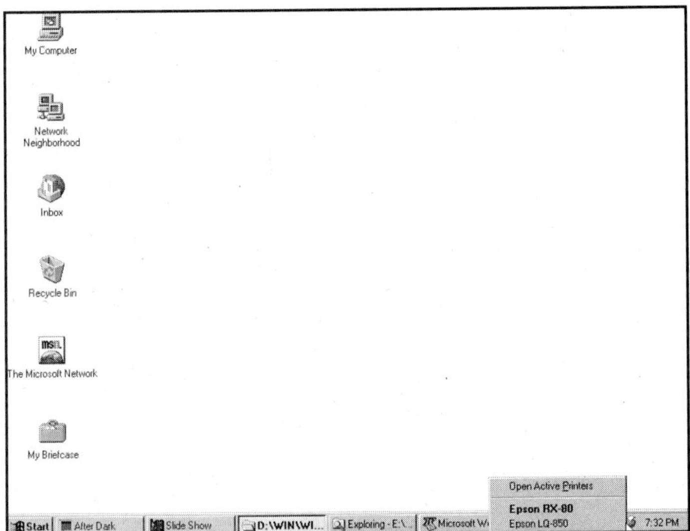

Figure 15.24.
Right-clicking the Printer icon on the Taskbar allows you to choose a new printer.

The following sections describe the management tools that Windows provides for printers, looking at both local and remote printers.

Local Printers

The first type of printer we'll look at is the local printer. All you need to do to open a printer is right-click the Printer icon and select it from the list. As an alternative, double-clicking this icon displays the current print jobs for the default printer. The printer management display is shown in Figure 15.25.

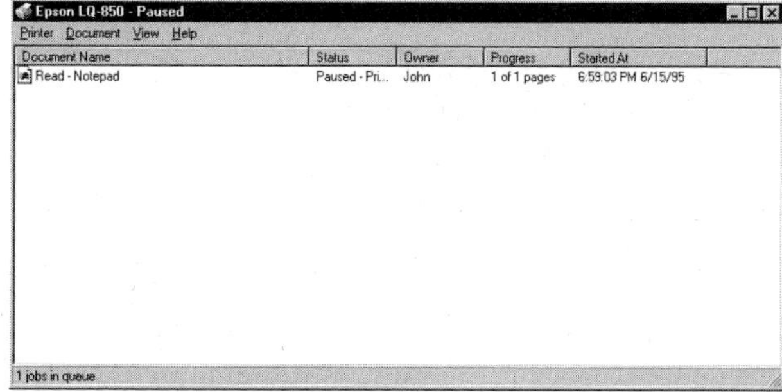

Figure 15.25.
Getting to the dialog box needed to manage your print jobs under Windows 95 is easily accomplished from the Taskbar.

Note: Windows 95 will always default to a printer with an error. If you're having a printing problem, double-clicking the Printer icon will display the problem printer. The Printer icon will also change in appearance to tell you that there's a failure. This allows you to track the status of all your print jobs, even if the printer isn't in the same room as you.

Managing jobs is fairly simple. Once you open the printer management display, you can access all the print jobs on an individual basis. The Printer menu contains two options that allow you to control the printer itself: Pause Printing and Purge Print Jobs. The Pause Printing option allows you to stop the printer momentarily and restart it later. You could use this option to stop the printer for a quick ribbon change or to correct a paper jam. Purge Print Jobs clears all the print jobs from the spooler. Use this option with care, because you might accidentally remove something you didn't want to remove.

This menu has several other options as well. The Save as Default option allows you to maintain any configuration changes you make as permanent settings. The Properties option opens the Printer Properties dialog box discussed earlier.

You can access the Document menu in one of two ways. The first method is to select a document and access the menu directly. The second method is faster: Just right-click the document you want to work with and select the option from the context menu. The Document menu has two options. You can pause print jobs by using the Pause Printing option. The Cancel Printing option removes the print job from the spooler.

Tip: One thing that isn't apparent when you look at this display is the fact that you can select a print job and move it somewhere else in the list. This allows you to change the priority of print jobs by simply moving them around as needed. You can move groups of print jobs with equal ease.

Remote Printers

Managing a remote printer under Windows 95 is nearly as easy as managing a local one. The only caveat is that the print server must be a Windows 95, Windows NT, NetWare, or other network that supports point and print. Otherwise, remote print jobs won't show up on your display. Once you establish a connection with the remote printer, you can exercise all the document-management capabilities you have with a local printer. (All this assumes that you have the access rights required to perform the task.)

Remote printing does offer one opportunity that local printing doesn't. You can perform what's called an *offline print*. Essentially, this is a form of pause. The Printer menu contains a special option for remote printers called Work Offline. Figure 15.26 shows a remote printer in the Work Offline mode. Checking the Work Offline selection pauses the printer and stores the print jobs on disk. When you uncheck this entry, all the print jobs are sent to the remote printer.

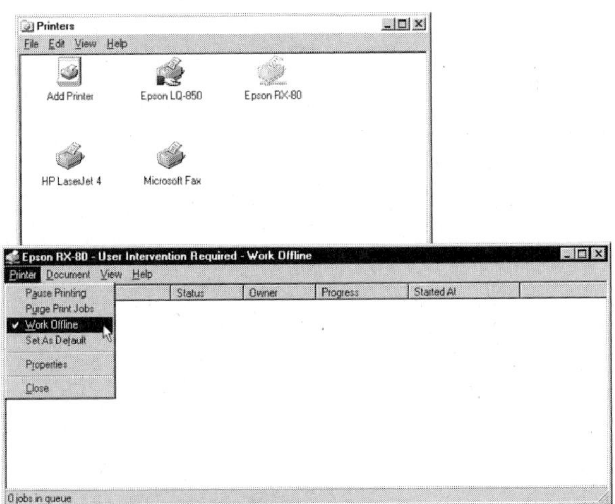

Figure 15.26.
The Work Offline option allows you to work with a printer even when it isn't connected.

Notice the Printer folder display in Figure 15.26. The printer that's in Work Offline mode is dimmed. Windows 95 provides this visual indicator to tell you that you can use the printer but that none of the print jobs will actually go anywhere. Another reminder is the Printer icon on the Taskbar. You'll see the Printer icon, but it will include the error indicator I mentioned earlier. Again, this tells you that one of the printers requires service. In this case, it isn't an unexpected error—merely a feature that Windows 95 provides.

Font Types

You'll need to learn about two different types of fonts when using Windows 95. The raster font provides you with a non-resizable bitmap form of font that's quick to use. The vector font comes in a variety of forms, but all of them share one common feature: They all represent the font as a series of math equations rather than a bitmap. This makes the vector font easy to resize. The following sections detail the use of both font types under Windows 95.

Raster Fonts

Most people don't use raster fonts for printing purposes anymore. The biggest reason is that they're inconvenient. You can't resize a raster font. That means that you have to keep on disk one copy of each font size you plan to use. In addition, you have to keep one copy of each style: roman, italic, bold italic, and bold. Because raster fonts represent each character as a bitmap, the size of the file used to hold them also increases in size as the point size of the font increases. A small 6-point font might consume only 4KB, but a 12-point font will consume 8KB or more. It doesn't take very many of these fonts to exceed the 60KB storage that most TrueType fonts require.

Problems aside, raster fonts don't require any additional work to use; they're already bitmaps. It's this factor that keeps some forms of raster font around. A raster font is easy to display, so you'll often see it used as a display font. This is especially true for areas in which you need only one or two font sizes at a time, such as the DOS window.

Another advantage to raster fonts is that they tend to produce a better display when used at their specific size than a vector font does. The reason is simple: The vendor can hand-tune the appearance of each raster font for a specific size. A vector font has no such ability. Unless the vendor that created the font includes hinting (which I'll describe later), a raster font will produce the better result in most cases.

Vector Fonts

Vector fonts are stored as mathematical formulas. These formulas specify how to draw each character in the font. A vector font doesn't contain a bitmap that a device can use as output, so it must render (draw) the font each time it's used. Windows 95 reduces the overhead of creating recently used fonts by storing them in the TTFCACHE file in your main Windows directory. However, this takes care of only one problem with using vector fonts.

A vector font's rigid mathematical representation of how the font should look also has problems. Many people have noticed that some vector fonts look good at one point size and others at a different point size. The problem is that even though the font is a perfect representation, the number of pixels used to represent it allows discrepancies to creep in. Normally, a font vendor would hand-tune this representation to get rid of the discrepancy or at least fool the eye into thinking that it was gone. Vector fonts have no such luxury.

TrueType and other font types introduced a new idea called *hinting*. A hint is a way to create an exact representation of the font and then modify that representation slightly to fool the human eye. What you see is a tuned version of the font. It's not as well-tuned in many cases as a raster equivalent would be, but it's close enough to create the right visual effect.

These problems aside, vector fonts have a great deal to recommend them. Their relatively small size allows you to keep many of them on your hard disk without filling it up. In addition, you can resize a vector font to just about any point size. It even allows you to create fractional-point-size fonts. You can't do this with a raster font.

Understanding TrueType

TrueType is a specific form of vector font. It comes with hinting and other features that mark an advanced font format. The important thing to remember is that TrueType is the native font format supplied with Windows 95 (and many previous versions of Windows, for that matter). To use other font formats, you need to install a third-party manager. In most cases, you won't want to expend the memory to use a third-party manager. All the vendors who used to support alternatives to TrueType have now dropped that support because of the problems with supporting more than one font manager under Windows.

Note: There's a big difference between printer fonts and third-party fonts. Laser printers usually include a number of specialized printer fonts that you can download to the printer. You can still use these fonts with ease under Windows 95. In fact, Windows has actually made the process of downloading easier. Contrast this with third-party products such as Adobe Type Manager, which must load as an application under Windows. Trying to use two different font managers at the same time not only wastes time and effort, but also seems more than a little counterproductive. Even though such measures were warranted before TrueType font support became widespread, they are no longer necessary under Windows 95.

How can you differentiate between a TrueType font and any other font on your system? We'll see later that Windows 95 provides different icons for the two types. Another way to detect the difference is by their extensions. Windows 95 provides a number of files with the .FON extension. These are either raster or vector fonts originally supplied with Windows 3.x. TrueType fonts are far superior to these fonts in capability and appearance.

Tip: Windows 3.x required that a TrueType font use two files. The first had a .FON extension and pointed to the second, which had a .TTF extension. Windows 95 no longer requires the first file. As a result, you can erase any .FON files on your hard drive without any loss of font data. Make certain, however, that the .FON file really is an older Windows 3.x font file. Normally these files appeared in the Windows \SYSTEM directory.

Hinting is one of the things that differentiates a TrueType font from a standard font. This normally affects the printed output by making characters appear "normal" to the human eye. As I explained in the discussion of vector fonts, storing fonts as a mathematical expression has the undesired effect of introducing small errors at some resolutions. The result is very unappealing. The fonts look normal, but your eye tells you that something isn't quite right.

Windows 95 also provides another font feature called *anti-aliasing*. This feature removes the jagged lines you normally see when a font becomes too large. It can also help small fonts become more readable. All this comes from the way that Windows 95 uses the hinting contained in TrueType fonts to display them.

The final benefit of using TrueType fonts is the fact that Windows uses the same font for both screen and printer. Older font technologies used one font for the screen and another for the printer. The reason is fairly obvious with raster fonts. The different resolutions of your display and printer would make the raster font appear much larger on one than the other. The same thing holds true for vector fonts, but to a much smaller degree. Using the same font for both screen and printer means that what you see on the screen is what you'll receive from the printer in the form of output.

Installing Fonts

Just about everyone needs a new font from time to time. Getting ready for a presentation, a new company policy, the need to differentiate your work from someone else's, or simply a need for change can all provide the motivation needed to install a new font. Under Windows 3.x it was fairly easy to install a font, but you were never quite sure what you were getting. In addition, you had to use a program that made the whole process seem a little more mysterious than it needed to be.

There are actually two ways to install a font in Windows 95. I'm going to show you both ways. The first method is the one that Microsoft recommends. The second method is the one that I use because it allows me to look before I leap.

Tip: The OSR2 version of Windows 95 supports HP LaserJet 4 gray scale fonts right out of the box. Microsoft also plans to make this support publicly available (the download site information wasn't available at the time of this writing). Be sure to download this new support feature if you own a LaserJet 4. The optimized gray scale fonts provide superior output to the more generic TrueType fonts supplied with Windows 95.

The Standard Font Installation Method

The standard method of installing a font is pretty straightforward, but it prevents you from really seeing the font before you install it. In this way, it shares some of the deficiencies of the older Windows 3.x method. On the other hand, it's safer, because it's guaranteed to work every time. With that in mind, let me show you the first method of font installation:

1. Open the Control Panel and double-click the Fonts icon. You should see the window shown in Figure 15.27.

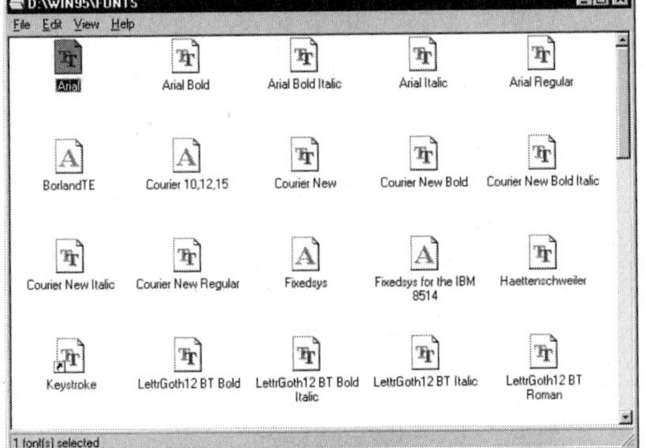

Figure 15.27.
This Explorer-style display allows you to view all the fonts installed on your machine.

2. Choose File | Install New Fonts to display the Add Fonts dialog box shown in Figure 15.28.

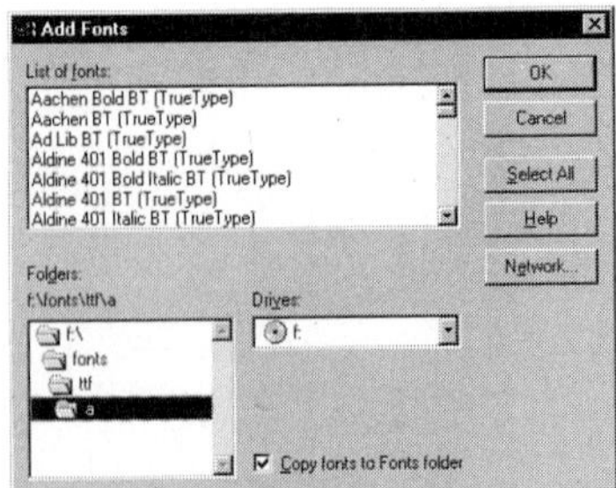

Figure 15.28.
The Add Fonts dialog box allows you to select fonts to add to your Windows installation.

3. Browse your hard disk, floppy disk, or CD-ROM drive until you find the fonts that you want to install. Highlight the desired fonts and click OK. You'll see the new fonts in your Fonts folder.

The Enhanced Font Installation Method

I prefer a little more control when I install fonts on my machine. For one thing, I like to have a good idea of what they look like. Installing a font so that you can view it seems a little counterintuitive to me, and it should to you as well. Windows 3.x didn't offer me much of a choice in this regard; I had to follow the Microsoft way of installing a font. Windows 95 does offer some choices. I found that this particular installation technique is both easy and flexible. Best of all, it allows me to view the fonts before I install them.

1. Open Explorer. Open the directory tree so that you can see the Fonts folder under the main Windows 95 directory, as shown in Figure 15.29.

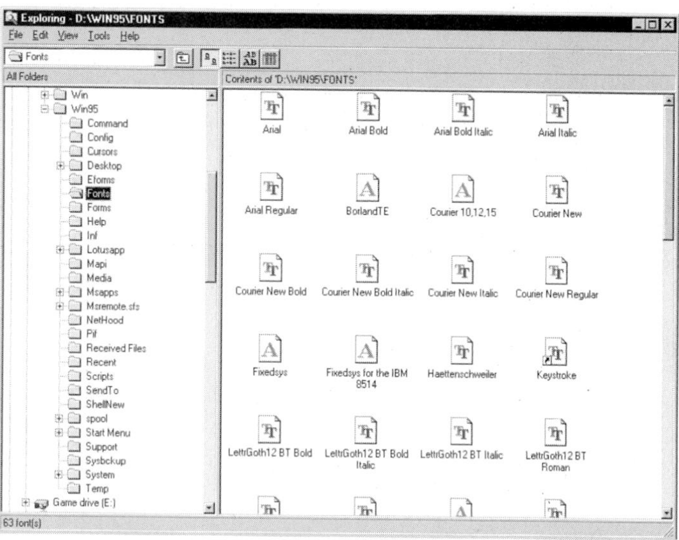

Figure 15.29.
You can see the Fonts folder by using Explorer; you just have to look in the right place.

2. Select the directory that contains the fonts you want to add. Double-click the first font to see what it looks like. You should see a dialog box similar to the one shown in Figure 15.30. Repeat this process until you find all the fonts you want to add to your Fonts directory.

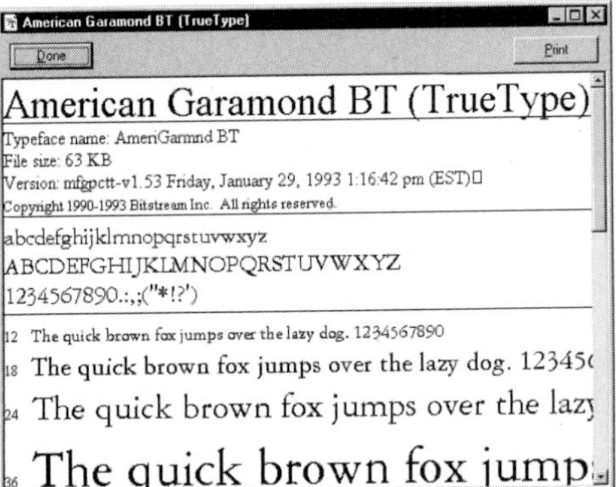

Figure 15.30.
Double-clicking a font allows you to see what it looks like.

3. Use the scroll bar to move the Fonts folder into view, but don't select it. Select all the fonts you want to move in the right window, and then simply move them to the Fonts folder, as shown in Figure 15.31.

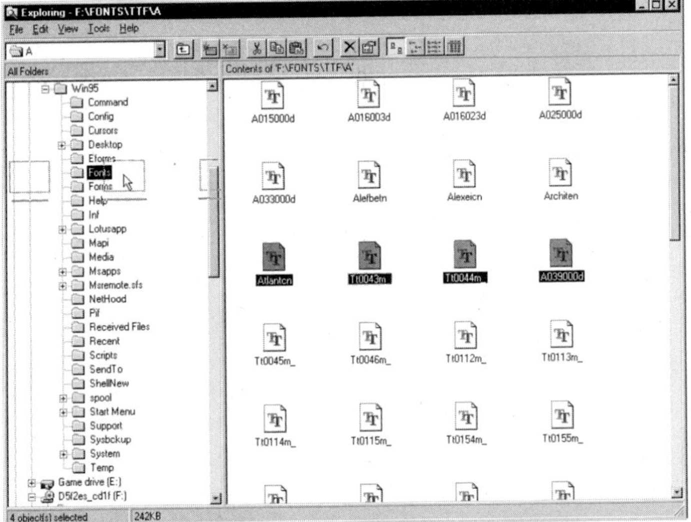

Figure 15.31.
Windows 95 allows you to simply move the fonts that you want into the Fonts folder.

That's all there is to it. See how easy that was? This technique works just as well as the more formal technique. I find that it's more flexible, it's faster, and I really know what I'm getting.

Removing Fonts

Removing fonts is very easy under Windows 95. All you do is open the Fonts folder (either through Explorer or by double-clicking the Fonts applet in Control Panel), select the fonts you want to remove, and press the Delete key. It's that easy.

You need to observe a few precautions. First and foremost, don't erase any font that you're not sure of. Windows 95 requires some fonts for system use, and erasing them could cause problems. Second, if you do erase a font, make sure that you don't need it anymore or that you have a copy stored somewhere.

Tip: Instead of deleting a font that you no longer require, archive it. All you need to do is move it from the Fonts folder to a floppy disk or a network drive. You can even use the Send To option on the context menu to do it. This technique will save you heartache later when you look for the font you deleted and it's no longer available.

Viewing and Printing Fonts

The interface in the Fonts folder might be Explorer, but the options are different. The View menu contains some unique features that you'll want to use to really see your fonts. I'm not talking about the files themselves, but the fonts. Let me show you what I mean.

Open the Control Panel and double-click the Fonts applet. (You can get to the same place by using the Explorer technique that I talked about earlier.) Open the View menu. You'll notice that Explorer now sports some new View options, as shown in Figure 15.32.

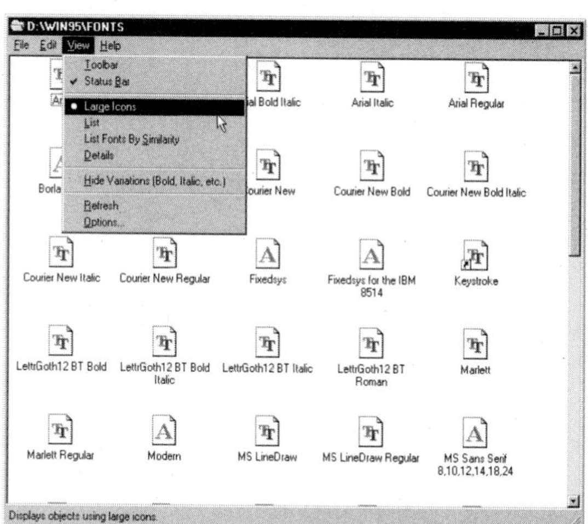

Figure 15.32.
The Fonts folder provides font-related view options that will come in handy as you learn how to use Windows 95.

The List Fonts By Similarity option is the one I like. It allows you to see which fonts you could use as a substitute for something else. For example, what if you really like the font you're using for a particular purpose but want a slightly different effect? You could use this option to find the closest match in your directory or on a CD-ROM full of fonts. Figure 15.33 shows this display. Notice the field at the top of the display. This is where you select the name of the font you want to use for comparison purposes.

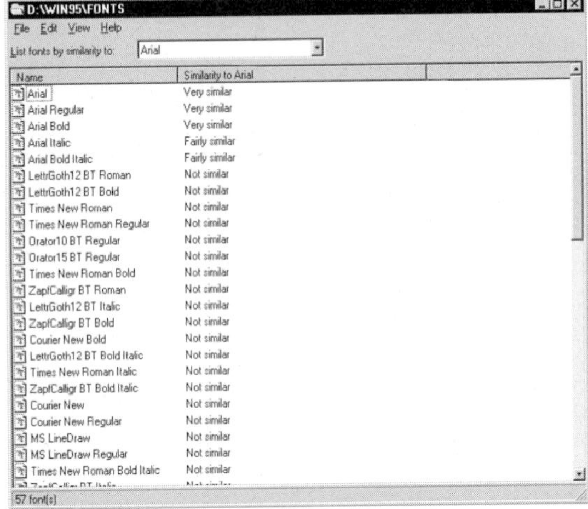

Figure 15.33.
You can quickly find font families on a disk full of fonts by using the List Fonts By Similarity option.

Another handy view selection is the Hide Variations option. You can use it with any of the display formats to hide the different files required to create a complete font family. For example, if you turn on this option, you'll see only one Arial font, even though there are four files in the directory. Variations typically include bold, italic, and bold italic versions of the font. Figure 15.34 shows how this display looks if you use the large icons format.

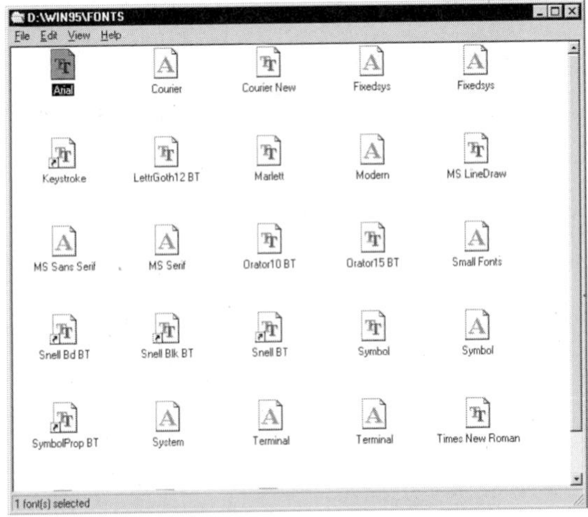

Figure 15.34.
Use the Hide Variations option to clear some of the clutter that might otherwise obscure a specific font that you want to see.

Unlike with Windows 3.x, it is very easy to print a sample of a font. All you need to do is right-click and select Print from the context menu. As an alternative, you can always click the Print button when viewing the font, or use the File | Print command. The printout you get will look similar to Figure 15.30.

How Windows Matches Fonts

Windows uses a specific set of criteria to find a replacement font if the one you request isn't available. To get an idea of how this works, use the List Fonts By Similarity option in the Fonts folder. The results will tell you a lot about how Windows 95 implements the rules in something called the *font-matching table*.

The font-matching table isn't actually a table; it's an algorithm that Windows 95 uses to match fonts. Windows uses the following criteria to find a matching font: the character set, variable versus fixed pitch, family, typeface name, height, width, weight, slant, underline, and strikethrough.

A TrueType font is always replaced with another TrueType font, even if a raster or vector font is a closer match. This enables your application to maintain the flexibility that TrueType provides. The negative aspect of this is that the output might not look even close to what you originally anticipated.

If the font you're trying to use is either a vector or raster font, Windows 95 will use some additional methods to obtain a good match. The following list shows, in order, the sources that Windows 95 will try to tap:

1. Printer ROM font
2. Printer cartridge slot font
3. Downloadable soft font
4. TrueType font

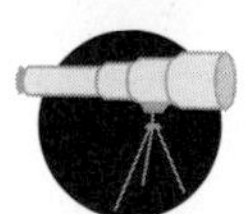

Microsoft Plus! adds font-smoothing to Windows 95 if you're running high-color video or better. Font-smoothing gets rid of jagged edges you might see when the fonts are very large. To turn on font-smoothing after installing Microsoft Plus!, right-click the Desktop icon in Explorer and select Properties from the context menu. On the Plus! page of the Display Properties dialog box, check the Smooth Edges of Screen Fonts check box. For more information on other Plus! features, see Chapter 28.

On Your Own

This chapter showed you two different ways to install fonts. Try both methods to see which works best for you. Many graphics programs include additional fonts. You can also download them from CompuServe and many BBSs. Use this exercise to install the set of fonts that will get the job done for you.

Look in your \FONTS folder to see whether you can identify the various types of fonts that Windows 95 supports. How can you tell them apart? What purpose does each kind of font serve?

Install several versions of your printer, each with different settings. Try this new installation for several weeks and see whether you notice the additional ease of use that several pseudo-printers can provide. Also try the various print settings to see whether you notice the variations in print speed and output quality that I mentioned earlier.

Place a shortcut to your printer on the desktop and try the drag-and-drop method of printing. Simply drag a file with your mouse pointer to the printer icon and drop it. This is the easy way of sending output to the printer, using the default setup. You might want to experiment to see which printer settings work best as a default setup for you.

16

Mice and Keyboards

The keyboard has been the mainstay of data input from the very beginning of computers. Even before people used displays—when everything was done using keypunch cards—they still sat at a keyboard to create input. It's somewhat amusing to see the strange arrangements of "ergonomically correct" keyboards on the market today. There was one keyboard, not too long ago, that looked like Chinese finger puzzles. You slipped the keyboard over your hands. Moving a finger forward would type one character, back another, right still another.

Some newer keyboard permutations have met with more success. For example, the Microsoft Natural Keyboard (and others like it) attempt to solve the problems people encounter with carpal tunnel syndrome and other types of repetitive stress injury. In some cases, I've heard about very good success using such keyboards when other forms of therapy failed. (If you really want to help your hands and eventually increase your typing speed as well, consider using the Dvorak keyboard layout. Using this layout will greatly reduce the distance your fingers travel to get text input into the computer.)

A little less strange are the permutations that the mouse has gone through. It started out looking like a bar of soap. Today's versions are all shaped to fit the palm of your hand. The fact that every vendor used a different human for measurement is reflected in the size and shape variations of this new breed of rodent. Every manufacturer seems to have at least settled on two or three mouse buttons. If you've been around long enough, you'll remember the multibutton monstrosities that some companies introduced. I still remember the 12-button mouse that one company tried to get everyone to buy. It allowed the user to basically replace the keyboard for command codes by using the mouse buttons. Unfortunately, it was nearly impossible to use, and the button combinations were even worse.

Aside from these physical manifestations, there are a variety of other ways that the keyboard and mouse have changed. Every mouse used to come with menuing software for your DOS applications; perhaps many of them still do. I haven't had to use my software for quite a while now; I might retire it permanently if things continue to go well with Windows 95. Still, this old software sits on my hard drive waiting to fulfill its destiny as an aid to DOS application enhancement.

Gone, too, are the keyboard enhancers that everyone bought into. They were well worth the money when introduced, but the benefits they provided seem a little weak in retrospect. Still, I don't know what I would have done without some of them when DOS was in its prime.

The more things change, the more they stay the same. My Logitech mouse came with some handy Windows utilities. For example, I can change the way that the buttons work within applications. I assigned one key combination to cut text and another to paste it. It's pretty handy to be able to grab some text, cut it, move the mouse, and then paste where needed. Of course, I don't even need this feature in applications such as Word, which provides full text-movement features.

Windows 95 has also gotten in on the new-and-improved input device bandwagon. Some of these changes are very worthwhile, and others are sort of ho-hum unless you really need them. The following sections give you a tour of the great and not-so-great mouse and keyboard improvements that Windows 95 has made.

Multilingual Support

I partially covered this feature in past chapters. More of the world is using Windows today, so it's not too surprising to see Windows come in a variety of language options. I was a little surprised by the fact that this language support is at least partially built into every copy of Windows. No longer do you have to perform strange rituals and hand-edit your system files to get the proper level of language support. Windows 95 has it built right in using the code pages that we all learned to hate under DOS.

Installing a New Language

The convenience factor of using multilingual support under Windows 95 is compounded by the fact that you don't have to memorize code page numbers. Installing a new keyboard language is as simple as a few clicks. Let's take a look at what you'll need to do to install a new language on your machine:

1. Open the Control Panel. Double-click the Keyboard applet and select the Language tab. You should see a dialog box similar to the one shown in Figure 16.1. Notice that English is the only language listed in the Language field. This field also provides other information that you can use to determine the installed language type. In this case, it tells you the type of English (United States) and the keyboard layout (United States).

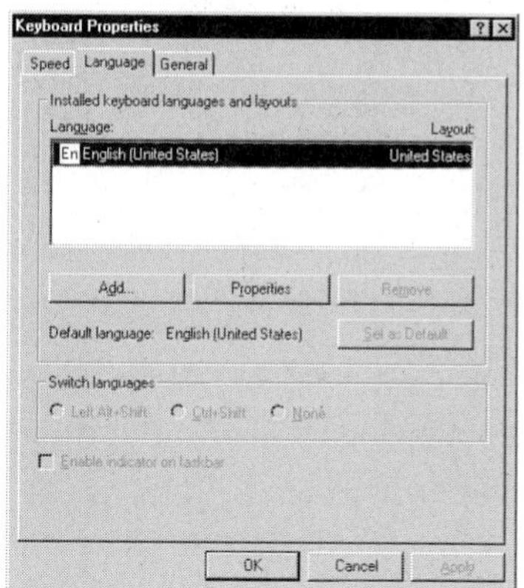

Figure 16.1.
The Language page of the Keyboard Properties dialog box allows you to select one or more languages for your computer.

Note: Users of the OSR2 version of Windows 95 will notice a few minor changes to the Language page of the Keyboard Properties dialog box. The most important change is that some of the layout settings have changed slightly. For example, the standard United States layout now says United States 101. You'll also notice a few new layouts. For example, there are Dvorak-LH (left hand) and Dvorak-RH (right hand) layouts now. You can still choose the standard Dvorak layout, if you want.

2. Click the Add button. You'll see the dialog box shown in Figure 16.2. It's important to consider which version of a language to choose. The English example is a good one. I currently have United States English installed. There's also a selection for other forms of English that might require a different keyboard layout. For example, pressing Shift+4 could produce a pound symbol (£) instead of a dollar sign ($). The choice of language also affects the way Windows makes assumptions about other setup needs. For example, it affects the default selection for monetary and numeric formats.

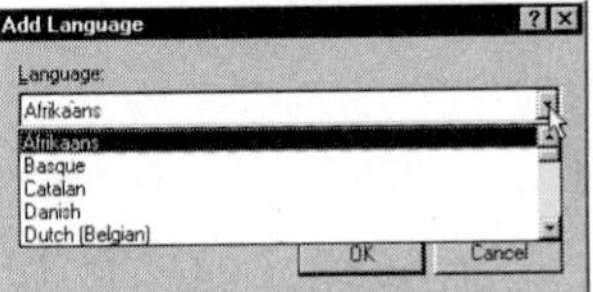

Figure 16.2.
Make your choice of language carefully, because there are several variations of some languages.

3. Click OK to complete the process. You should see a new language added to the Language field. Completing this process also enables several other fields. For example, you can now choose which Ctrl+*key* combination to use to switch between languages. You can also choose whether to display the International icon on the Taskbar (I'll you show how to use this icon in a little while).
4. Choose a default language by highlighting it and then clicking the Set as Default button. You'll see the new default displayed in the Default Language field.
5. You'll probably want to check the layout for your new language. Highlight the new language and click the Properties button. You should see the dialog box shown in Figure 16.3. (This dialog box also displays the other changes you've made.) The dialog box is a little deceptive. At first you might think that it's asking you to change the language again, but this isn't so. What it's asking you to change is your keyboard layout. Select a new layout to see for yourself.

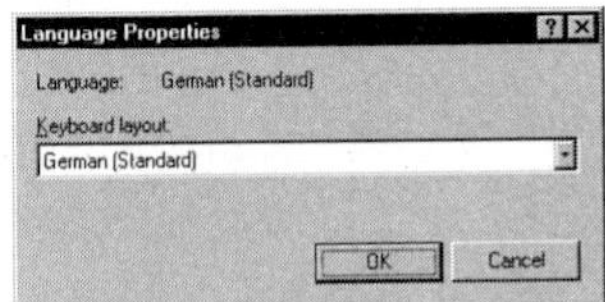

Figure 16.3.
This dialog box will change your keyboard layout, not the language you're using.

6. Click OK to complete the process. In this case, I chose the Dvorak layout. Figure 16.4 shows the results. Notice that the language remains the same; only the keyboard layout has changed. I'll use the Dvorak layout whenever I choose the German language from my list.

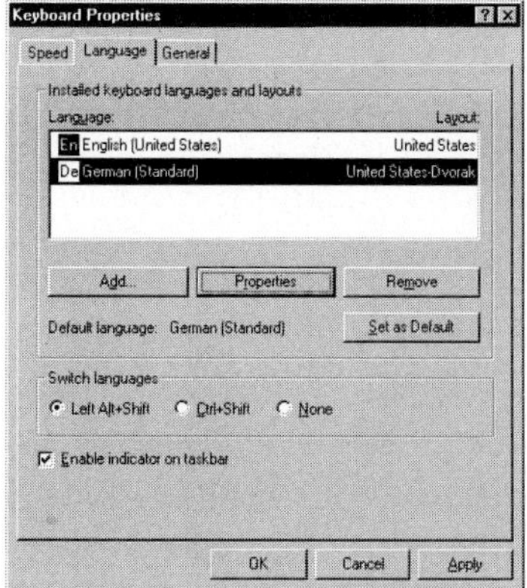

Figure 16.4.
This dialog box shows the results of choosing another layout, using the Properties button.

Note: You might have noticed that this combination of language and layout provides the means to create a very customized keyboard layout. The folks at Microsoft call this *localization*. I call it a good idea for those of us who lived through the DOS code page nightmare. This elegant solution provides far greater flexibility than the user ever had in the past. If you need multilingual support, try the various options to see which setup is most comfortable.

7. Close the Keyboard Properties dialog box to complete the process. (Windows might ask you to insert a disk containing any files that it requires.) You can accomplish the same thing by using the Apply key if you don't want to close the Keyboard Properties dialog box.
8. Close Windows and reboot your computer to make the change permanent.

Changing your keyboard layout and language won't display prompts in the language you select. It affects only the way your keyboard reacts and, to some extent, helps Windows 95 provide better input in regard to other configuration selections.

Removing a Language

You'll probably run into a situation in which you no longer require a specific keyboard layout. For example, you might have needed to use a German layout for a while to type letters to another office, but you don't need it any longer because that office closed. Whatever your reason for wanting to remove the language, Windows 95 makes it easy. The following procedure shows you how.

Tip: This would be a good time to use the procedures shown in Chapter 7 for checking the filenames of the drivers used to support the language you want to remove. Windows 95 won't remove these drivers, which means that they'll clutter your hard drive until you decide to install Windows from scratch—hopefully, a long time from now. Recording the filenames now, before you remove the name from the Language page, means that you'll be able to remove the driver files later on. Be sure to shut down and reboot your machine first, or Windows 95 will display an error message stating that the driver is in use.

1. Open the Control Panel. Double-click the Keyboard applet and select the Language page. You should see a dialog box similar to the one shown in Figure 16.1.
2. Highlight the entry for the language support you want to remove from your machine—in this case, the German language support.
3. Click the Remove button.
4. Close the Keyboard Properties dialog box to complete the process. You can accomplish the same thing by using the Apply key if you don't want to close the Keyboard Properties dialog box. Windows might get confused and think that another application is using the keyboard layout if you activated it at any time during this session. All you need to do is click OK to accept the error message. Windows will still remove the layout, but it won't do so until the next session.
5. Close Windows and reboot your computer to make the change permanent.

Note: Windows 95 will disable the Remove button if you have only one language installed. This makes sense, because you have to use a language in order to use the keyboard. It also removes the International icon from the Taskbar if you have only one language.

Accessing a Language from the Taskbar

Whenever you have more than one language installed on your machine, Windows gives you the opportunity to automatically add the International icon to your Taskbar. Figure 16.5 shows what this icon looks like.

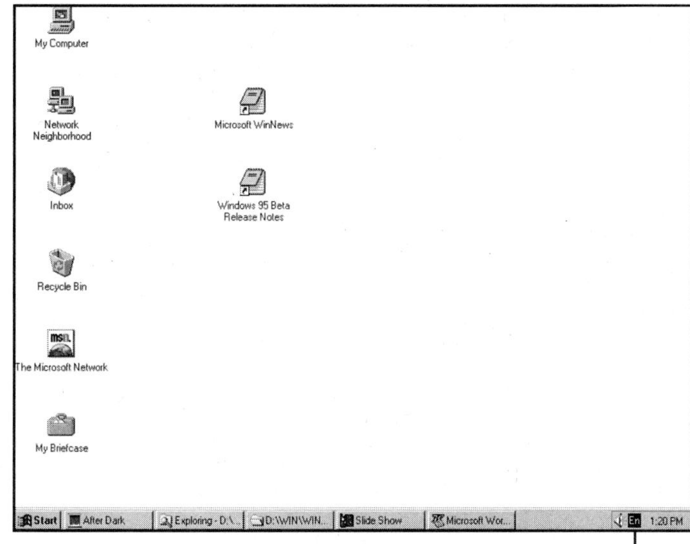

Figure 16.5.
The International icon provides quick access to multiple language selections.

Peter's Principle: Easy Keyboard Access

Adding the International icon to your Taskbar is more than just a convenience that comes in handy when you need to change layouts from time to time. It provides a quick way to change all your keyboard settings whenever you need to do so. Of course, the number of keyboard settings is rather limited, but they're important. So, the question remains, why would I want easy keyboard access?

If you're like me, long hours at the keyboard really take their toll on your hands. The keyboard settings that you used this morning could make for a lot of mistakes this afternoon as you find yourself repeating more keystrokes than you intended. It's a pain to go through the Control Panel every time you want to change something, so most people don't. That's where the trouble lies—in a lack of accessibility.

Having the International icon on your Taskbar provides quick access to the keyboard settings. However, it doesn't normally appear unless you install more than one language on your machine. You can manually add this icon to your Taskbar by adding the International Settings application—INTERNAT.EXE—to your Startup folder. You'll find it in the SYSTEM folder, under the main Windows folder for your machine. (I don't know why Microsoft is so fond of placing the really neat utilities there, but if you ever need something, this is a good place to start looking.) This will give you access to the keyboard settings, even if you have only one language installed.

There are several ways to use this icon. The first is to determine which language you're currently using. Each language has a two-character abbreviation (refer to the dialog box in Figure 16.4). The Taskbar is where this two-digit abbreviation is used. For example, the icon shown in Figure 16.5 tells me that I have the United States English configuration installed.

Clicking the International icon displays a list of languages currently installed on the machine, as shown in Figure 16.6. Notice that each entry is preceded by its two-digit abbreviation. This is one way to determine which language you're using if you forget what the abbreviation on the icon means. All you need to do to select a new language is click it, just as you would with any other menu.

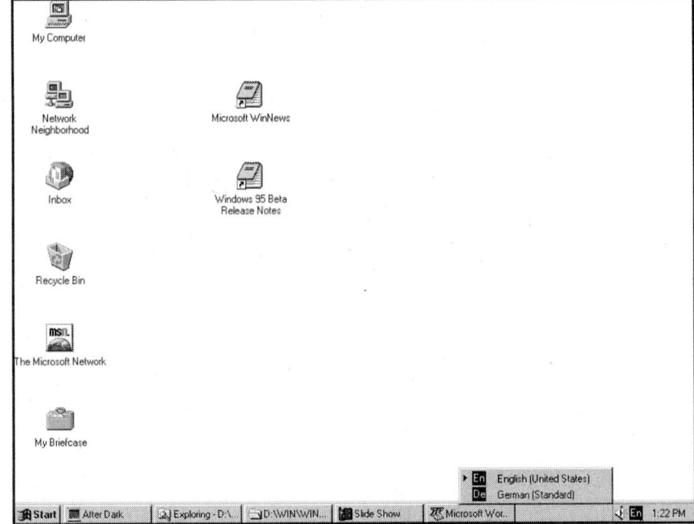

Figure 16.6.
Clicking the International icon allows you to switch quickly between installed languages.

A right-click brings up the context menu shown in Figure 16.7. I was especially taken by the What's This? entry. It's apparent that no one at Microsoft thought the user would be able to figure out this icon for himself. At least the associated help text is useful and could help someone who is just starting to learn how to use Windows 95. I just wonder why Microsoft didn't include this help with the other icons for the sake of consistency, if for no other reason.

The Properties option of the context menu acts as you would expect. It takes you to the Keyboard Properties dialog box that we looked at earlier. Even though it automatically displays the Language page, you can quickly switch to other pages as needed.

As with many of the other icons on the Taskbar, you can also momentarily hold your mouse cursor over the International icon to get more information. Doing so displays the full name of the language that you're currently using.

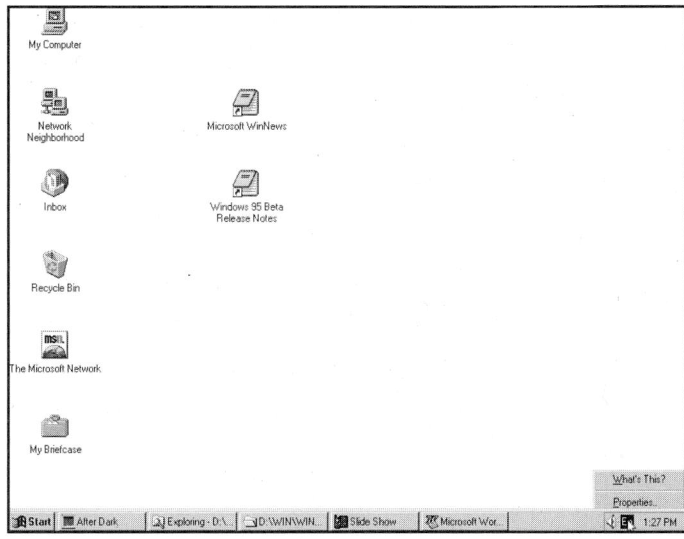

Figure 16.7.
The context menu for the International icon has a somewhat strange entry in it—What's This?

Configuring Your Keyboard

Languages aren't the only thing you can change about your keyboard. There are two more pages of selections that you can make regarding its setup. Figure 16.8 shows the first page. This is where you decide how the keyboard will react to your key presses.

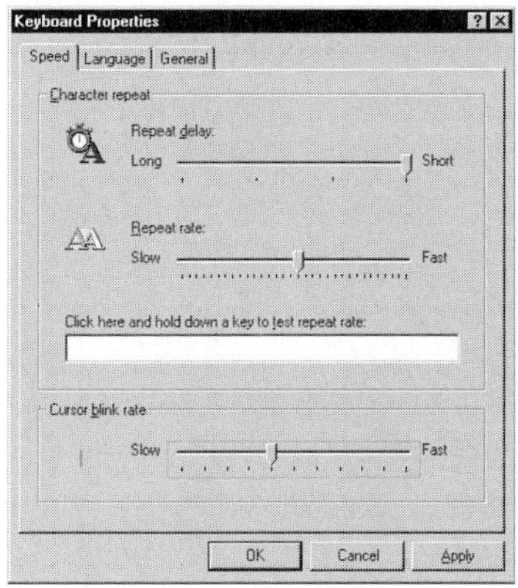

Figure 16.8.
The Speed page contains the settings required to adjust the keyboard to your typing habits.

The Repeat Delay setting adjusts how long the keyboard waits before it starts repeating keys. Setting this value too short could force you to undo a lot of excess keystrokes. You'll probably find this more of a problem at the end of the day. The Repeat Rate setting adjusts how fast the characters repeat across the screen. Setting a slightly lower rate enables you to control repeated keys better. Microsoft thoughtfully provided a test area that you can use to check the combination of settings.

Make sure that you actually try the keyboard settings for a while before you make big changes in the settings. I found that even small changes affect the way the keyboard reacts.

Use the Cursor Blink Rate setting to change how often the edit cursor blinks per second. Some people like a very fast rate, and other people like things a bit slower. You'll want to use a slower rate on portables than you would on your desktop machine, because it takes displays on these machines a little longer to react. A setting that works well on your desktop machine might make the cursor disappear on your laptop.

The General page, shown in Figure 16.9, contains only one entry—the type of keyboard you're using. If you decide to use a different keyboard, click the Change button to see a list of compatible devices. This list comes in handy when the driver you're currently using doesn't work as well as it should and you want to try a driver for a compatible device. In reality, you'll seldom if ever need this option, because the keyboard driver setting is pretty straightforward. Clicking the Show All Devices radio button displays a complete list of keyboards that Windows 95 supports.

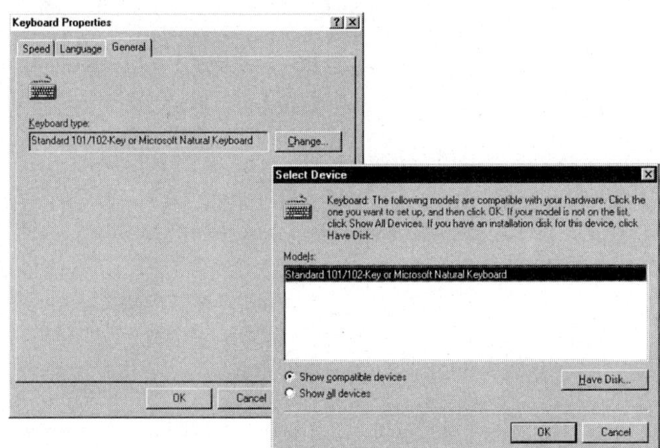

Figure 16.9.
Use the General page to view the name of the keyboard driver you're using or to select a new one.

Configuring Your Mouse

Using a mouse started out as a nice feature in DOS. You really didn't have to use one, but some people viewed it as a productivity enhancer. By the time I started using Windows, the mouse had gone from being a nice feature to being a should-have feature. Early versions of Windows allowed you to get around pretty well without a mouse. Today a mouse is a must-have. To really use Windows, you have to have a mouse. Some tasks are difficult or impossible to perform without one.

Standard Mouse Configuration

Just as you should configure your keyboard for optimum performance, you should configure your mouse as well. To do this, open the Mouse Properties dialog box by double-clicking the Mouse applet in the Control Panel. Figure 16.10 shows the first page, Buttons.

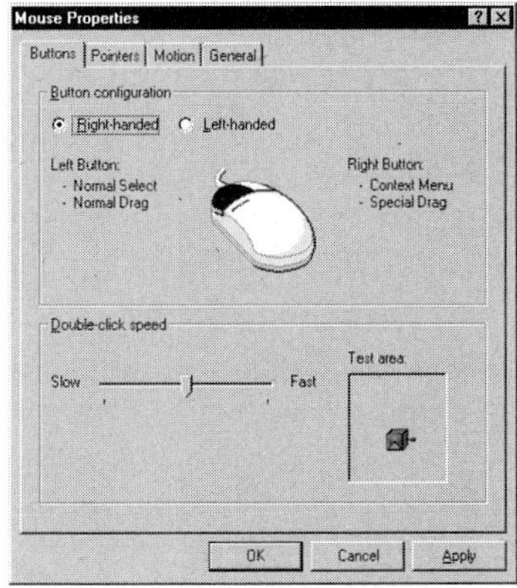

Figure 16.10.
The Buttons page of the Mouse Properties dialog box allows you to change the way the mouse is configured and reacts.

The first group of settings on this page allows you to reverse your mouse buttons for left-handed use. Windows 95 defaults to a right-handed installation. The second group allows you to change the double-click speed. I find that setting this during the middle of the workday seems to provide the best configuration for me. Your mouse's double-click speed is important. Setting it too low might mean that you'll double-click where you didn't intend to, especially in graphics programs, where you move the mouse and click a lot to select items. Setting this value too high is an exercise in frustration, because Windows won't wait long enough for you to double-click things. In some cases, this means that you'll get a menu in place of an action. In other cases it means that you won't get anything done at all. The test area allows you to test this setting. A jack-in-the-box alternately appears and disappears when you double-click.

The Pointers page, shown in Figure 16.11, allows you to change the mouse pointers used to indicate specific events. In addition to the standard cursors that Windows 3.x provided, Windows 95 provides a few "fancy" cursors, such as the 3-D versions displayed in the figure. In addition to the static cursors that you could use before, Windows 95 also provides some cursors that move. (Plus! pack users will have an even wider assortment of cursors to choose from.)

The upper section of this page allows you to save and load various mouse schemes. Think of a mouse scheme in the same way that you would a color scheme under Windows 3.x, and you'll have the right idea. Use the list box to select a previously saved scheme. Clicking the Save As button displays a dialog box that you can use to enter the name of a new scheme.

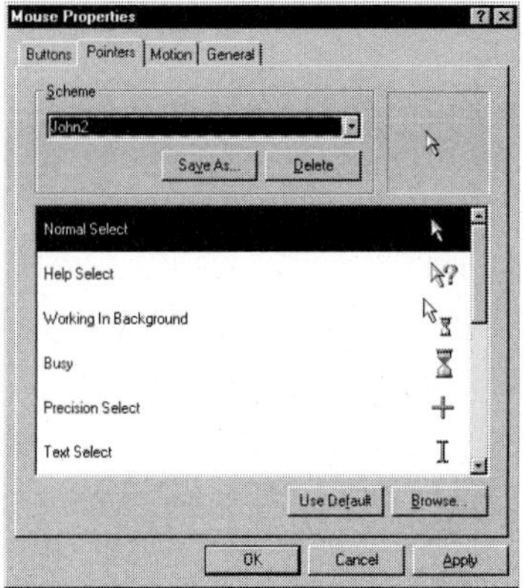

Figure 16.11.
This page of the Mouse Properties dialog box allows you to change the appearance of the mouse cursor.

Tip: Windows 95 provides a wealth of mouse pointers, including some extra-large ones. The extra-large pointers are actually designed for use with some of the Accessibility options. However, they also come in handy on laptops, where seeing the cursor can be a real chore, and presentations, where a larger-than-normal cursor helps you make your point.

The lower section of the Pointers page contains the actual mouse pointers. The purpose of each pointer is self-explanatory. To change a cursor, highlight it and click the Browse button. Windows will display a list of cursors in the CURSOR folder (found within the main Windows folder), as shown in Figure 16.12. All you need to do is double-click the cursor you want. Windows replaces the current cursor with the one you selected. Notice that this dialog box also displays a preview of the cursor. Any animated cursors will appear to move within the preview box. This is how they'll look when you use them in an application or another area of Windows. If you ever select a cursor by accident and want to return it to the default setting, click the Use Default button at the bottom of the Pointers page.

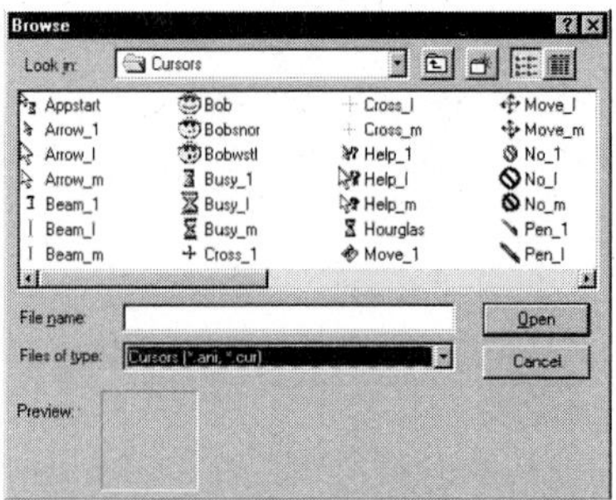

Figure 16.12.
Use the Browse dialog box to select from the list of currently available cursors.

The Motion page, shown in Figure 16.13, affects how the mouse cursor tracks your hand movements. This is the slider at the top of the page. Setting the speed too high can cause jerky cursor movement and make it difficult to control some operations, such as drawing. Set the speed too low and you'll need to make a large movement with the mouse to get a small movement on-screen. (Repetitive stress injury sufferers may want to talk with a physical therapist to see whether a particular range of mouse motion could help the condition.)

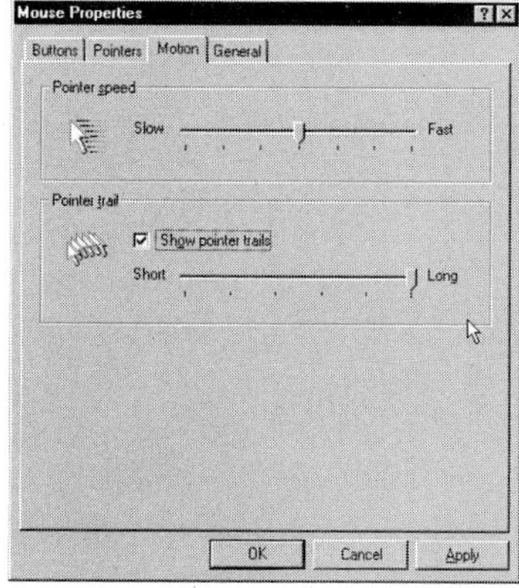

Figure 16.13.
The Motion page allows you to set the pointer speed and whether Windows provides pointer trails.

The bottom half of this page controls whether Windows provides pointer trails. A pointer trail really isn't what most people think. Windows produces many copies of the pointer that track the movements you make with the mouse. These additional pointers are the pointer trail. The slider controls the length of the trail, and the check box turns it on or off. This feature is specially designed to make it easier for portable users to track the mouse's position. However, kids really like to see extra pointers on their display. Adding pointer trails can also help the visually impaired or new user track the mouse.

The General page, shown in Figure 16.14, lets you change the type of mouse installed on your machine. The only time you would need to do this is if you replaced your mouse with a different type. Clicking the Change button displays a dialog box containing a list of supported mouse types. All you need to do is select the correct mouse type and click OK to change the mouse driver.

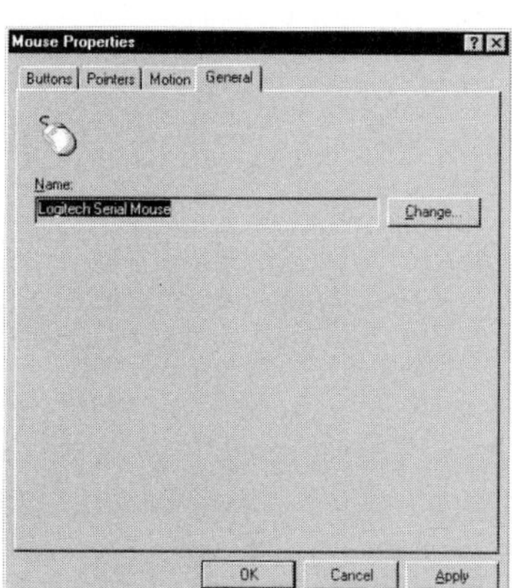

Figure 16.14.
You use the General page to select a different mouse driver for your machine.

Special Laptop Configuration Considerations

Laptop computers normally have special needs when it comes to a mouse. For example, there isn't any good place to put a mouse when using a laptop, especially when you're on a plane. Some laptop vendors take care of this problem by incorporating a special mouse right into the keyboard area. In other cases, you'll use a trackball that rides along the side of the case. Whatever mouse you use on the road, it more than likely requires some special form of configuration.

Let's take a look at some of the configuration pages you might see with a typical laptop. (The pages you'll actually see depend on the laptop vendor and the type of mouse you have installed.) As with a desktop machine, you access the Mouse Properties dialog box on a laptop by double-clicking the Mouse applet in the Control Panel. Figure 16.15 shows the first page you're likely to see—the Quick Setup page.

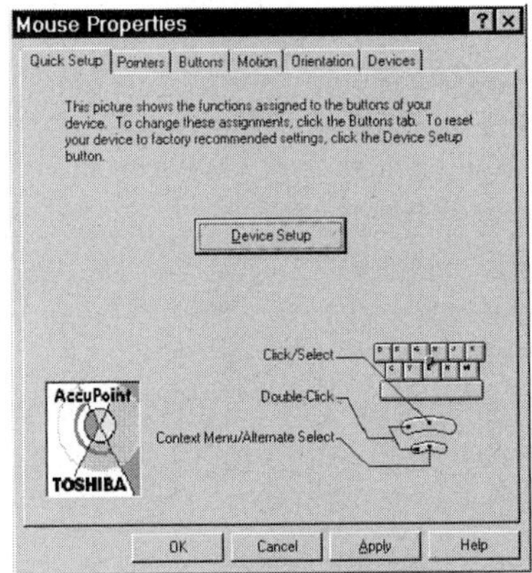

Figure 16.15.
The Quick Setup page allows you to change the configuration of your mouse.

Unlike when using a desktop machine, you can't rely on your laptop's environment staying the same. For that matter, you can't even be certain that you'll use the same mouse from session to session. You may prefer to use a standard mouse at the office, another type of standard mouse at home, and the built-in mouse on the road. Needless to say, configuring a laptop mouse isn't even close to the same as configuring a desktop mouse. (Because each mouse configuration is different, you'll need to rely on vendor documentation to actually set it up.)

Another problem with laptops is answered by the Orientation page shown in Figure 16.16. Think about trackball users for a second. They may need to place the trackball at the right side of the laptop for part of a trip, but move it to the left side for another part of the trip because their seat is next to the window and there isn't any room to move. For that matter, it wouldn't be all that impractical to place the mouse at the bottom of the laptop if you have room. These subtle changes in position could drive you crazy if you couldn't change the orientation of the mouse to match its position with respect to the laptop.

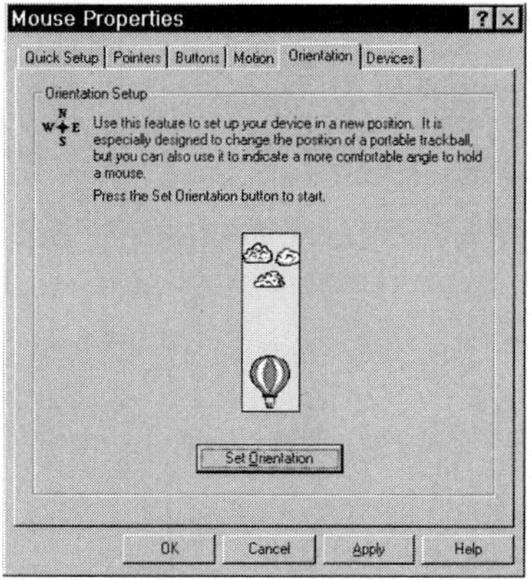

Figure 16.16.
Trackballs usually need some type of orientation setup, depending on where you place them on the laptop.

Using this feature is quite easy. Just click the Set Orientation button. Windows 95 asks you to move the balloon toward the clouds at the top of the screen. Moving the trackball adjusts the orientation as needed to keep mouse movement the same as it normally is when you use a standard mouse (in other words, moving the mouse up actually moves the cursor toward the top of the screen). If you don't move the mouse cursor in a straight line, Windows displays an error message telling you so. Simply choose to try again and Windows 95 will set the orientation for you.

I previously mentioned the fact that most people use more than one mouse with their laptops. Unlike other hardware components, Windows 95 won't automatically register a mouse change—especially if your laptop has a built-in mouse. That's what makes the Devices page shown in Figure 16.17 so important. It allows you to do two things: You can add a new mouse device to those that your laptop supports, or select an existing one.

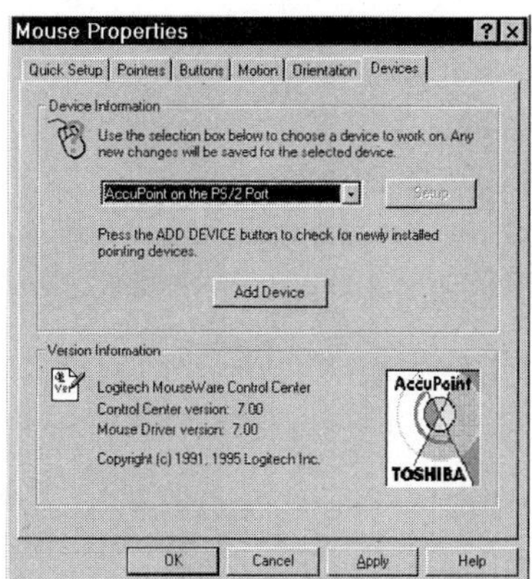

Figure 16.17.
The Devices page allows you select a specific mouse or install a new one.

Selecting an existing mouse device is easy. All you need to do is choose it from the drop-down list and then click Apply. Make sure that the mouse is plugged in before you do this or you may find yourself without a functional pointer device. (Most laptop software searches for the pointing device before switching over, but you can't be sure that it will.)

To add a new device, simply click the Add Device button. The first thing you'll see is a warning message. As stated by the message, you can normally plug in a serial mouse while the machine is running. If you try to plug in a PS/2 port mouse while the machine is running, there's a good chance that you'll damage it. Always shut the machine down first, and then plug in the PS/2 mouse. Once you see this warning message, you can click OK to start the search for a new pointing device. If Windows 95 finds a new mouse, it takes you through the setup and configuration process.

You'll likely find other extras included with a laptop mouse. For example, some laptops include a special feature for forcing the mouse to jump to a highlighted button on a dialog box. This saves you from having to move the mouse pointer yourself. You'll also find that the button assignment software for a laptop may differ from what you're used to on a desktop. How it differs (if at all) depends on the kind of mouse you're using.

Access for Users with Disabilities

Windows 95 provides special access features for people with disabilities. I give you an overview of these options in Chapter 1. We also look at some of the speed keys that the Accessibility options provide in Chapter 5. I won't go over these details again here. What we'll look at is the features themselves and how you can use them to enhance productivity. The first thing you'll need to do to look at these features is open the Control Panel and double-click the Accessibility Options applet.

Special Keyboard Features

Windows provides three special keyboard features: StickyKeys, FilterKeys, and ToggleKeys. You'll find them on the Keyboard page of the Accessibility Properties dialog box, as shown in Figure 16.18. You can turn on any of them by using the special key combinations that Microsoft provides.

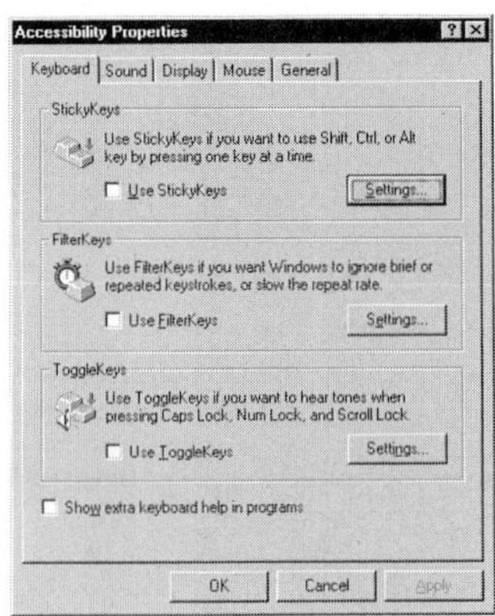

Figure 16.18.
You can turn on any of the keyboard accessibility-related functions from this page.

All these features have one thing in common: They change the way that the keyboard works, independently of the keyboard driver. You must install the Accessibility Options feature to make them work. The option that intrigued me was the Show Extra Keyboard Help in Programs check box at the bottom of the page. It adds help information to applications that support this feature. Unfortunately, none of the applications that I tested, including the new Windows 95 utilities, supports it. Hopefully, some vendors will pick up on this option later.

Using StickyKeys

The StickyKeys feature comes in handy for a variety of purposes. It makes the Shift, Ctrl, and Alt keys act as a toggle switch. Press the key once and it becomes active. Press it a second time and it's turned off. I don't really need this feature a lot, but it does come in handy sometimes.

One of the ways I use it is in graphics programs that require you to hold down the Ctrl key to select a group of items. It's kind of inconvenient to hold down the Ctrl key while you look around for objects to select. The StickyKeys feature alleviates this problem.

I also find that it's pretty handy when I want to type a lot of Alt+*key* combinations—for example, when I want to use the extended ASCII line-draw characters in a document. It's true that I could use the Character Map utility to do the same thing, but Character Map isn't always easy to access, and I might need only one or two characters.

Let's take a look at some of the options you can select. Click the Settings button to open the Settings for StickyKeys dialog box shown in Figure 16.19.

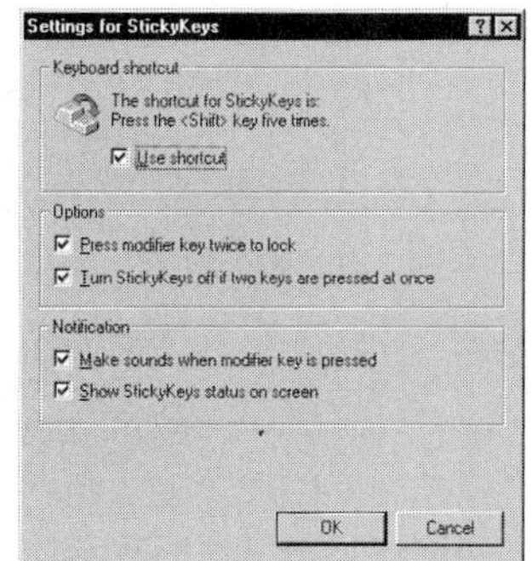

Figure 16.19.
The Settings for StickyKeys dialog box allows you to change how this feature works.

There are several groups of settings for StickyKeys. The first option, Use Shortcut, allows you to enable StickyKeys by using the shortcut key. There really isn't any good reason to turn this off, as it's very unlikely that any application would use the same control key sequence.

The Options group contains two settings. Normally, the StickyKeys option works like a toggle. Checking the first box tells Windows to wait until you press the same control key twice before making it active. The second check box is designed to allow two people to use the same keyboard. Pressing a control key and a non-control key at the same time turns StickyKeys off.

The Notification group also contains two settings. The first setting tells Windows to play a different sound for each unique control key that it makes active. This can keep you from activating a control key by accident. The second option displays an icon on the Taskbar so that you can control StickyKeys more easily. I normally select this option to make it easier for me to turn StickyKeys on and off.

Using FilterKeys

Do you ever find yourself making a lot of extra keystrokes at the end of a long day? I do. There are times where some words come out like "tthis" instead of "this." FilterKeys is a perfect solution to the problem of tired hands. I use it all the time near the end of the workday to filter out those extra keystrokes.

As with StickyKeys, you can adjust the way FilterKeys works by clicking the Settings button. The Settings for FilterKeys dialog box is shown in Figure 16.20. Notice that the first option in this dialog box allows you to turn the shortcut key on and off. It works just like the same feature in StickyKeys. The Notification group at the bottom of the page should look familiar. The only difference is that instead of playing a sound, FilterKeys beeps when you activate it.

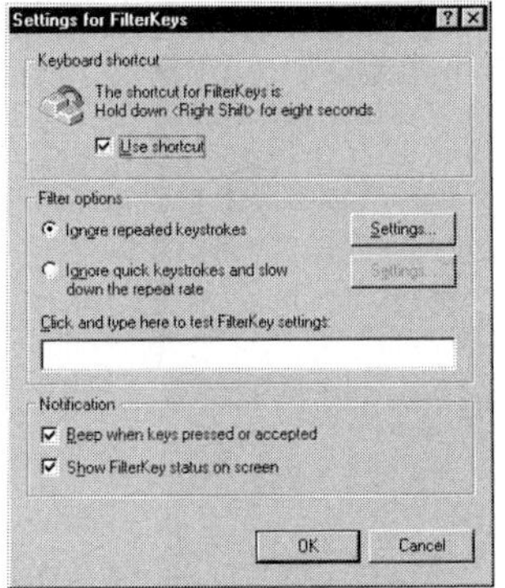

Figure 16.20.
The Settings for FilterKeys dialog box allows you to change how this feature works.

The Filter Options group allows you to select between two ways of filtering keystrokes. The first option filters keys that get pressed in rapid succession. For example, this feature would filter the rapid typing of the extra "t" in the example just mentioned. The Settings button displays a dialog box that allows you to select how long an interval must pass between the first and second times you press the same key. It also provides a field where you can test the setting. The second option in this group filters accidental key presses. You might press a key for a moment, not really meaning it. As with the StickyKeys option, the Settings button takes you to a dialog box where you select how long you have to press a key before Windows will accept it.

Using ToggleKeys

Ever start typing an e-mail message to someone, only to see later that you left the Caps Lock key on? It's time-consuming to fix such a mistake, but you have to do it for formal documents or memos. A better solution would be to be alerted each time you turned one of the Lock keys on or off. That's precisely what ToggleKeys does. It emits a tone every time you turn the Caps Lock, Scroll Lock, or Num Lock key on or off.

Figure 16.21 shows the Settings for ToggleKeys dialog box. Notice that it has only a single option. This option allows you to turn the shortcut key on or off.

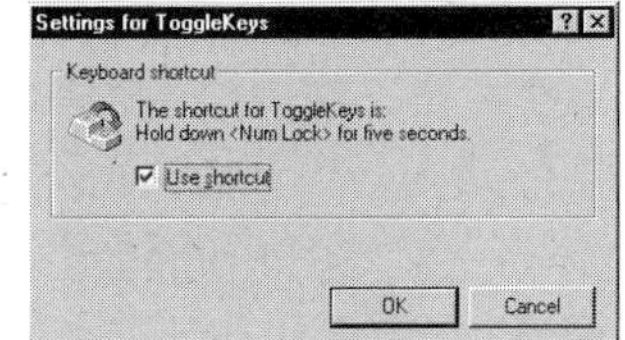

Figure 16.21.
The Settings for ToggleKeys dialog box allows you to change how this feature works.

Special Mouse Settings

Have you ever gotten to the point of screaming as you try to precisely position an object on a drawing screen by using the mouse? It's difficult to do after a full day of drawing—especially if you aren't a graphic artist with the training and tools required to get the job done right. That's one of the reasons why I really like the MouseKeys feature. It allows you to use the arrow keys as a mouse. Instead of moving the mouse cursor with the mouse, you can move it with the arrow keys. Of course, this doesn't disable your mouse; it merely augments it. Figure 16.22 shows the Mouse page of the Accessibility Properties dialog box.

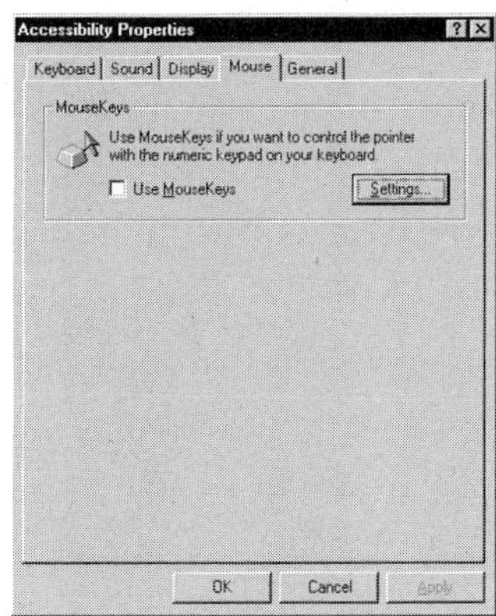

Figure 16.22.
MouseKeys can put the control back into your mouse cursor.

MouseKeys has only one dialog box of settings. You access it by clicking the Settings button on this page. Figure 16.23 shows the features that this dialog box provides. The first option, Use. Shortcut, allows you to enable MouseKeys by using the shortcut key. There really isn't any good reason to turn this off, because it's very unlikely that any application would use the same control key sequence.

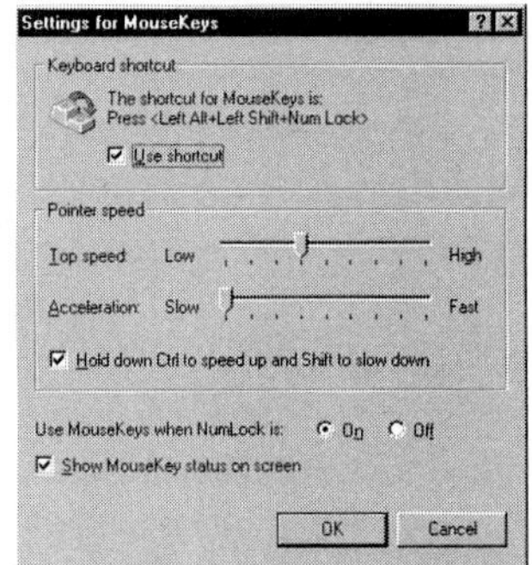

Figure 16.23.
The Settings for MouseKeys dialog box allows you to change how this feature works.

The second group, Pointer Speed, is where you can optimize the performance of this particular feature. The first option allows you to set the fastest speed at which you can move the mouse cursor by using the arrow keys. Set it to a slower speed to gain better control of the mouse cursor. Using a higher speed allows you to move around the display faster. The Acceleration setting determines how fast the cursor reaches full speed after you press it. Windows doesn't start the cursor off at full speed; it brings it there gradually. This allows you to make a small change without seeing the cursor take off for the other side of the screen if you set the speed fairly high. The combination of these two settings will determine just how much added control MouseKeys gives you over the cursor. Notice the check box in this group. Checking it gives you another option. Pressing the Ctrl key speeds up the mouse cursor; pressing the Shift key slows it down. You can use this option when you need a variety of speeds to get the job done.

The final group contains two settings. The radio button controls when MouseKeys is active. You must specify whether the Num Lock key should be on or off when you use MouseKeys. The choice you make depends on how you normally use the numeric keypad. The second option determines whether the MouseKeys icon appears on the Taskbar. As with most of the special features that Windows provides, I keep this icon on the Taskbar for quick access to this feature. It's a lot more efficient to do so.

On Your Own

Try all the different Accessibility options to see if any of them provide features you can use. I provided suggestions on how you could use each feature in this chapter.

Install and try using the Dvorak keyboard layout. Once you learn how to use this setup, you'll find that you can type faster and with a lot less fatigue. This particular setup can also help you fight repetitive stress injuries such as carpal tunnel syndrome. Of course, nothing will provide 100 percent protection. The Dvorak keyboard layout can't reverse years of abuse, but learning this new setup could help keep any problems you have now from getting worse.

Go back to earlier chapters—especially Chapter 5—and practice using the various shortcuts discussed with the Accessibility options turned on. Does using this feature with your standard shortcuts make a difference? Try a variety of combinations to create the fastest keyboard interface possible.

17

Video Configurations

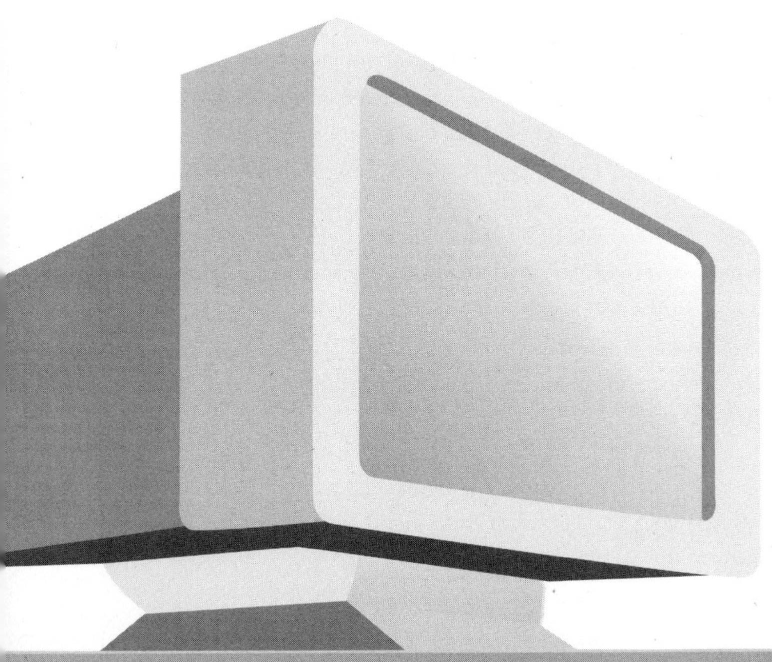

Video is the most noticeable architectural component of Windows 95. It's the underlying combination of hardware and software that allows you to see the graphics, dialog boxes, icons, and other elements that make Windows 95 worth using. It's little wonder, then, that this is also one of the more complex parts of the computing picture.

The problem isn't simply one of displaying a picture on-screen; that would be easy to manage. The problem is one of communication between the various elements that create and manage the picture in the first place. The following list illustrates some of Windows 95's communications problems:

- **Application level:** Three different kinds of applications use Windows 95. DOS applications normally think that they're alone in the world, so they violate just about every imaginable rule for displaying information. Game programs are the worst in this area. You can count on them to change the display adapter registers in unusual ways and write directly to video memory with nary a thought that anything else might be using the system. Although 16-bit Windows applications are a bit more conscientious than their DOS counterparts, they still use an older interface to draw to the display. Finally, newer 32-bit Windows applications might offer the ultimate in available features right now, but they're often hampered by other applications running on the machine.
- **Device driver:** I own an older display adapter that drives me crazy when I use Word for Windows. It's not really a problem with the adapter; it's a problem with the drivers that support the adapter. If the display driver doesn't correctly interpret the commands issued by applications running under Windows, or if those applications use undocumented command features, there's a good chance of miscommunication. In the case of my faulty setup, the adapter misinterpreted some of the commands that Word and a few other applications used, resulting in an unreadable screen.
- **Adapter:** In the beginning, IBM set the tone and the baseline for all display adapters. Its leadership was responsible for the somewhat standard way in which the CGA and EGA display adapters worked. By the time VGA came around, IBM was starting to lose its leadership position. Then came SVGA (super VGA), and there was no IBM standard to follow. For a while, there was a lack of any kind of standardization for the extended modes that vendors built into their display adapters. The result was total chaos. How do you build a set of standardized drivers for an operating system when there's no standard to follow? A little later in this chapter, we'll look at how this problem was finally resolved.
- **Monitor:** There's less of a standardization problem with monitors, but it's still present. This problem manifests itself in setups in which one monitor works fine but another doesn't. The problem is in the signals coming from the display adapter. With today's ergonomic concerns, such as the 70 Hz refresh rate needed to reduce eyestrain, frequency ranges have expanded dramatically. Some monitors just can't handle the increased frequency requirements. Add to that some level of ambiguity on the part of vendors. I'll never get over the fine-print problem with several monitors I looked at. A monitor supposedly supports 1024×768 mode. When you look at the fine print, though, it becomes obvious that this

support is good only in interlaced mode. This led to a problem with one monitor when I installed Windows NT. I got the upper half of the picture just fine, but the lower half disappeared. The problem was some combination of adapter, driver, and monitor. If the monitor had supported 1024×768 noninterlaced mode, there wouldn't have been a problem.

- **Operating system requirements:** Normally, the operating system itself is the least of your worries with the display. However, sometimes it can actually be the source of your problems. Take icons, for example. We all take them for granted because they generally work without any difficulty. But what happens if some file that the operating system needs gets changed by an application or gets corrupted somehow? On one machine, I had to completely install everything from scratch. One of the system files had suffered some type of damage, and all the icons disappeared. No amount of work would bring them back, so I finally ended up reinstalling everything from scratch to get them back.

Now that you have a better idea of the communications problems that Windows suffers from, you might wonder why it works at all. Windows uses something known as an *event loop* to talk with applications. Think of an event loop as a bulletin board where Windows and applications post messages. A message could ask for a service such as opening a file or telling an application that it needs to perform some maintenance task. Windows notifies the application that it has a message waiting. The application picks up its messages and acts on them. The event loop allows Windows to send "paint" messages to any application that might require them. The combination of an event loop and constant redrawing allows Windows to keep your display up-to-date, even if small amounts of miscommunication do occur.

You can usually tell when Windows is going through a repaint cycle. You can actually see each application quickly flash as it redraws itself. Of course, the cycle becomes a lot more prominent if each application uses a conflicting palette, because then you can also see the color changes.

This chapter talks about video under Windows 95. However, more than that, it talks about communication. Without the required level of communication between all the system elements, you would never see anything when using Windows 95. I'll refer to this idea of communication whenever necessary. Look for the communication requirements, though, as I discuss each of the following topics.

Graphics Standards

Many standards organizations help keep things running smoothly on your computer. Several competing standards affect how your modem works. One of these organizations, the CCITT, has become a major contributor as of late. Another organization, EIA, defines specifications for the various port connectors, serial and parallel, that attach your machine to the outside world and peripheral devices. The standards organization you want to keep your eye on for display adapters and monitors, though, is the Video Electronics Standards Association (VESA).

Tip: VESA can provide you with detailed specifications for a number of display adapter and monitor standards. You can usually get copies of these standards from online sources such as CompuServe. They also often appear in the manuals that come with your adapter or monitor. You can contact VESA directly using the following information:

Video Electronics Standards Association
2150 North First Street, Suite 440
San Jose, CA 95131-2029
Voice: (408) 435-0333
Fax: (408) 435-8225

I first ran into this organization in 1989, but they were probably around a while before that. IBM had dropped VGA in favor of its proprietary 8514/A display adapter. Without a leader in the field to dictate a standard, the entire display adapter arena fell into a state of disarray. At the time I first heard about VESA, they were working on a standard to fix the SVGA problem. Of course, the resolutions and number of colors were severely limited in comparison with what you can get today. They were also working on defining the 8514 ports that IBM wouldn't talk about at the time.

The main difficulty facing the graphics community was communications. Before this time, every display adapter used the same programming interface, in the form of a BIOS call, to change display settings and otherwise control the display adapter. All the old display methods worked, but vendors chose to differentiate their products by implementing the VGA "extended" modes differently. The resulting chaos made it impossible for any programmer to write an application that used SVGA modes without writing a different driver for each adapter.

VESA stepped in to make sense of all this chaos. The result of these initial efforts was several VESA standards and some additional software for each display adapter. That VESA driver that you load for some applications is actually a BIOS extension that allows display adapters to use a standardized SVGA interface. The extension translates VESA standard BIOS calls into something adapter-specific. As a result, an application can use one set of BIOS calls to configure and control the display adapter. Newer display adapters no longer require you to load a special driver; their BIOS chips come with VESA support installed. Table 17.1 shows many of the common standards that VESA has produced. There are also older standards that will shed some light on some issues that these newer standards don't cover. A representative at VESA will be more than happy to answer any questions you might have.

Table 17.1. VESA standards for display adapters and monitors.

Standard	*Title*	*Purpose*
VS911020	Super VGA protected-mode interface	This document provides information on a standardized method of accessing the BIOS routines from a protected-mode program.
VS911021	Video cursor interface	Use this standard to learn how to build an interface between a pointing device and the display adapter.
VS911022	Super VGA BIOS extension	This is the document you need to learn about VESA standard display modes for the SVGA.
VXE 1.0	XGA extensions standard	This document tells you about some of the standardization efforts underway for the XGA.
VS910810	Monitor timing standard for 1024×768 with 70 Hz refresh rate	This standard helped provide a consistent method of producing ergonomically correct displays. It allows a vendor to create a display adapter and monitor that will work together at the 70 Hz refresh rate, which greatly reduces eyestrain.
VS900601	Standard 8514/A register bit fields	A programmer needs to know the details of show a register works. This standard provides that information.
VS890803	Standard VGA passthrough connector	There was a lot of confusion as to how to get a high-resolution display adapter to work with a standard one. The passthrough connector seemed an ideal way to do it, but the connec tions for it weren't standardized. That's what this standard does: It defines the passthrough connector and allows you to use multiple adapters in one machine.
VS890804	Standard 8514/A registers	Before you can program a register, you need to know what to call it. This standard defines what registers an 8514/A contains. Remember that IBM didn't want to share this information with anyone, so VESA had to come up with their own naming scheme.

Of course, this selection of standards is by no means complete. VESA works on a whole array of other standardization efforts, such as industrial guidelines for the manufacture of computer components. Its most famous non-display-related standard is probably the VL bus. This was such an important standard at one time that, in 1993, Dell wanted to take VESA to court over the matter of who owned the standard.

The OEM Service Release 2 (OSR2) version of Windows 95 supports several new standards in addition to those that you'll find with the standard package. For one thing, it comes equipped with DirectX 2.0 support. This standard allows game vendors to write high-speed graphics routines, using a standard interface. In essence, DirectX provides the means to write directly to the hardware, yet keep Windows in the picture. Windows still tracks everything that the game program does, but without the interference that a normal application would encounter. The plus side of using DirectX is high speed and maximum flexibility. The minus side is that the vendor has to do more work to get an application up and running. In addition, many people have run into compatibility problems when using DirectX with substandard display adapters. Even though these adapters work fine when used with standard Windows applications, the DirectX interface causes significant problems. Fortunately, you can update existing Windows 95 systems to use DirectX by downloading an update from the Web site at `http://www.microsoft.com/ie/download/ieadd.htm`.

Tip: DirectX 2 isn't just for game programs. Unlike the previous version of the standard, DirectX 2 provides 3-D drawing support. Don't be surprised if you see one or more CAD packages come out with DirectX 2 support in the next year. Multimedia applications will probably use DirectX as well to provide the high-speed graphics displays that most people want when giving presentations.

OpenGL used to exist only for Windows NT users. Now you can use this standard on Windows 95 machines as well (OSR2 users get it as part of the Windows 95 package). Microsoft plans on releasing this update publicly, but the download site wasn't available at the time of this writing. Essentially, OpenGL is a set of graphics library routines. Using these routines will save a programmer a substantial amount of time. You can see the effects of OpenGL by installing the new screen savers that come with the OSR2 release of Windows 95. What you'll see is a set of high-speed 3-D graphics routines in action.

ActiveX technology is going to be the wave of the future—at least, according to Microsoft. There are a number of technologies grappling for control of the Internet now, so I'd rather wait and see what comes of them before saying that ActiveX is an absolute certainty. One thing is for certain, given Microsoft's track record in the past. You're going to see ActiveX technologies such as ActiveMovie become part of the Windows infrastructure. As a result, you should probably consider ActiveX a standard for Windows 95 machines.

Intel is also introducing somewhat of a standard for all kinds of multimedia, including video. The new MMX (multimedia extension) Pentium processors will greatly increase the speed at which applications can display multimedia on-screen. Unfortunately, the operating system you're using has to be written to take advantage of these new extensions. The good news is that the OSR2 release of Windows 95 contains this support (at least some level of support). Users of old versions of Windows 95 won't be able to use the capabilities of the MMX Pentium processors, because Microsoft hasn't made this particular update available for public download.

The Windows 95 Graphics Architecture

Now that you have some idea of the problems that Microsoft (and any other vendor) faces in providing something for you to look at, it's time to discuss how they do it. Display adapters and monitors have both moved beyond the simpler requirements of the time when IBM was at the helm. In the interim, we've seen the emergence of even higher resolutions and a new adapter called the XGA. The SVGA is also improving on an almost daily basis. It used to be that 640×480 resolution and 256 colors were something to whistle about. Today an adapter is considered almost inadequate at 1024×768 resolution and 24-bit (16.7 million) colors. Windows 95 endeavors to handle this wide range of capabilities by using the same centralized control mechanism that it uses for printing—a combination of the minidriver and DIB engine.

One of the main architectural components is the GDI. The GDI has been tuned and retuned throughout the various incarnations of Windows. It's no surprise that Microsoft has spent so much time in this area, because many benchmark tests focus on graphics performance. In fact, the thing that users notice most is the way that the graphics engine performs. Microsoft did more tuning of the GDI for Windows 95, but I would term this tuning more incremental than major. The following list provides details on some of the more significant changes:

- **DIB engine:** The new DIB engine is handcrafted assembly language. Not only is this area used heavily in rendering graphic images, but it's used for the printer as well. The GDI and DIB engine work together with the display device driver to produce the picture you eventually see on-screen. Unlike previous versions of Windows, though, Windows 95 doesn't force every graphics instruction to go through the DIB engine. If a display adapter provides a coprocessor that can handle the operation more efficiently, Windows uses it in place of the DIB engine.
- **TrueType rasterizer:** This is the component responsible for changing the font descriptions in your .TTF files to a bitmap that Windows can display on-screen. Microsoft moved the data for this part of the GDI out of the 64KB heap area to a 32-bit area. They also rewrote the rasterizer code in 32-bit format to improve overall performance.

- **GDI component duplication:** Chapter 6 talks about the use of a thunk to convert 16-bit data to 32-bit format. Thunks cost time. This isn't a big deal in most cases, because a thunk can be a lot less expensive than a transition to real mode to handle a device need. However, some operations are performed so often that Microsoft decided to provide both a 16-bit and a 32-bit version in Windows 95. This allows for a small but noticeable speed improvement over Windows NT.
- **Path support:** A Windows application used to create complex objects by using lots of standard objects such as squares, triangles, and circles. All these little calls could eat up a lot of processor time if the program needed to create something really complicated. Using paths allows a Windows 95 application to describe a complex shape in one function call. The GDI can then figure out the most efficient way to present it. The result is that the programmer spends less time describing the object, and the user sees a performance improvement.

- **Metafile support:** A metafile contains drawing commands that describe the drawing instead of actually providing a bitmap for it. Each command is called a *record*. The GDI processes records to reconstruct the image. The advantage of a metafile is that you can make it any size you want and adapt it to any device resolution. Windows 3.x didn't provide metafile support as part of the operating system. Windows 95 improves on this by providing partial metafile support. It doesn't include the full range of metafile commands that Windows NT does, but it does provide some. The result is that you gain the advantages of using a metafile, but Windows 95 won't completely understand some Windows NT metafiles. Fortunately, if the GDI doesn't understand a particular command, it ignores it and goes on to the next one.
- **Bézier curve drawing:** A Bézier curve is drawn using a set of points. A curved freeform line connects the points. The idea isn't necessarily to touch all the points, but to draw a line that most nearly defines a shape that flows from point to point. Many advanced graphics applications, such as CorelDRAW!, support this feature right out of the box. Windows 95 adds this feature so that an application can describe a curve by using points and allow the GDI to figure out how to draw it.
- **Image color matching (ICM):** It wasn't long ago that everyone used green screens and black-and-white printers. Today the cost of a color printer is dropping rapidly, and color displays are standard on every machine. There's a problem in trying to get the color on your screen to match the color on your printer, however. For one thing, the two devices use different methods to create colors. Another reason is that it's nearly impossible to create some colors on certain devices. The technical details of all this are keeping several standards groups talking right now, so it's impossible to say how the problem occurs or what to do about it. Still, the problem remains. With the emergence of color as a major new component of computing, Microsoft saw the need to provide color matching between devices. Although it's not a perfect solution, ICM is a good start for people who can't afford professional publishing equipment.

Improvements in the GDI aren't the only change in Windows 95. There are some pretty big architectural changes as well. Let's take a look at the overall architecture. I won't get into bits and bytes here, but I'll tell you about the basic components required to display something on-screen. Figure 17.1 is an overview of the Windows 95 graphics architecture.

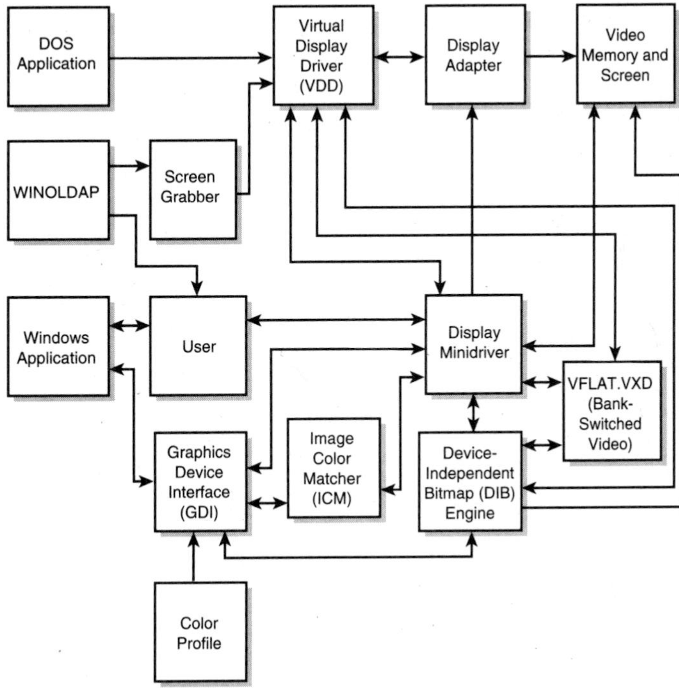

Figure 17.1.
An overview of the Windows 95 graphics architecture.

The following paragraphs tell you what task each of the components performs:

- **WINOLDAP:** This is a module that senses when a DOS application is about to take control of the display area. It notifies USER and the screen grabber so that they can preserve the graphics system status information. You'll find this module listed as WINOA386.MOD in your SYSTEM directory.

- **Screen grabber:** I always think of this as a camera. In essence, that's what it is. The screen grabber takes a picture of the screen and preserves it for later. This allows Windows to restore the screen to its former appearance after you exit a DOS session. Any file with a .2GR or .3GR extension in your SYSTEM directory is a screen grabber. You don't need the .2GR files for Windows 95, because it doesn't support standard mode. In addition, you need only one .3GR file—the one designed for your display adapter.
- **User:** I've already discussed the uses for this module extensively. This module tracks the state of all the display elements, such as icons and dialog boxes, in addition to drawing

them. That's why it needs to be informed before a DOS session comes to the foreground—so that it can take a snapshot of the current state of these components. As stated earlier, there are actually two User-related files on disk—a 16-bit and a 32-bit version.

- **GDI:** This is another module that I've spent a lot of time discussing. Like the User module, there are two physical files—one for 16-bit and another for 32-bit needs. The GDI module works with the display driver and the DIB engine to produce the graphic components of a Windows display.
- **Display minidriver:** With Windows 3.x, every video signal went through the Virtual Display Driver (VDD). The VDD would process the signal and send it to the display adapter. Windows 95 can use a combination of the display minidriver and the DIB engine for adapters that can support them. Using this driver combination results in a speed increase from 32-bit code. The name of this file varies, depending on the type of display you're using. On my system, it's named SUPERVGA.DRV. Unlike the VDD, which performs all video processing, the display minidriver takes care of only device-specific details. The DIB engine takes care of graphics rendering. A minidriver contains a lot less code than a full-fledged VDD, reducing the amount of code that a vendor must write.
- **Device-independent bitmap (DIB) engine:** The DIB engine takes the graphics instructions provided by the GDI and renders them into an image. Unlike printing, in which the DIB engine doesn't do the whole job, it actually draws the rendered image on the frame buffer. A frame buffer is a piece of system memory set aside to represent video memory. When the drawing on the buffer is complete, the entire buffer is sent to video memory at one time. Anything sent to video memory usually ends up on the display. This process is known as *virtualization*. The DIB engine itself is found in DIBENG.DLL. There's also a compatibility module for Windows 3.x applications called DISPDIB.DLL, which was the predecessor to the DIB engine. This second DLL allowed Windows 3.x to use a DIB for small objects instead of the entire display. You might also find several DIB*.DRV files in your SYSTEM directory. Each of these files provides some type of expanded display or memory management function for Windows 3.x DIBs. In almost all cases, these drivers are designed to work on individual objects rather than the entire display. The frame buffer management routines are found in FRAMEBUF.DRV.
- **Color profile:** This is a data file that contains the color capabilities for your output device. It doesn't matter whether the device is a printer or a display adapter; the type of information is the same. The purpose of a color profile is to provide the ICM with the information it needs to keep the display and other color devices in sync. That way, when you select dark red on the display, you get the same dark red on your printer. I talked about some of the problems with color matching earlier, so I won't go into them again here. You'll find all the color profile files in the COLOR folder in the SYSTEM folder. All these files have an .ICM extension. The Properties dialog box associated with each one will give you many more technical details about the profile.

- **Image color matcher (ICM):** The whole process of matching the output of your printer to what you see on the display is complex—much too complex to really cover here. Earlier in this chapter, I discussed the problem of color matching. The ICM is the module that performs the work. It subtly changes the output of your printer and display so that they match. The GDI, display minidriver, and ICM work together to compare the current color set and translate it into something that will work on both devices. It's not a perfect solution, but it works, for the most part. Let's just say that the results are very close, but not absolutely the same. Most of us wouldn't notice, but a professional artist might. Of course, this solution can't take into account the many details that a professional would, such as temperature, humidity, and other environmental aspects beyond the control of Windows. The files that contain the ICM include ICM32.DLL and ICMUI.DLL; both appear in the SYSTEM folder.
- **VFLATD.VXD:** This module is used only for bank-switched video adapters. Its main purpose is to manage the video memory window that these devices provide. The easiest way to think about this is using the explanation provided for expanded memory in Chapter 8. The display adapter on your machine could contain a very large amount of memory. Unfortunately, there's only a 64KB window set aside to access that memory. Depending on your adapter's configuration, Windows might not be able to get around this limitation. VFLATD.VXD can manage up to a 1MB frame buffer. It reads this buffer into video memory as required, in 64KB chunks.
- **Virtual display driver (VDD):** Windows 3.x used this module as its sole source of communication with the display adapter. Windows 95 provides it for compatibility purposes and for DOS applications. In most cases, the name of this file contains some part of the name of the display adapter vendor. For example, the name of the VxD for my system is VIDEO7.VXD. You'll find it in the SYSTEM folder. This driver converts drawing commands into signals that the display adapter can use. It also manages the display adapter and performs a variety of other tasks related to the way that all the applications on your machine share the display adapter. In essence, it's a 16-bit version of the display minidriver and DIB engine combination.
- **Display adapter:** This is the physical piece of hardware in your machine.
- **Video memory and screen:** Video memory is where the electronic form of the image that you see on-screen is stored.

Keep in mind that this was a quick tour of the video subsystem. The actual inner workings of this part of Windows are a lot more complex than you might think. To give you a better idea of the way things work, think of Windows as having three video paths (it's more complex than that, but let's not get mired in too much detail at this point): one 16-bit DOS, one 16-bit Windows, and one 32-bit Windows. The path that Windows uses depends on which applications you're using, the type of adapter you have, and the video performance settings you select in the System Properties dialog box.

The 16-bit DOS path consists of the VDD, display adapter, and video memory. It also might include VFLATD.VXD, if required. The 16-bit Windows path adds WINOLDAP, the screen grabber, User, and the GDI. The 32-bit path includes User, the GDI, the display minidriver, the DIB engine, and video memory. It also includes VFLATD.VXD if your display adapter uses bank-switched memory. Both Windows paths could include the ICM and the associated color profiles. It depends on your setup, the drivers that Microsoft eventually includes, and the capabilities of the devices you're using.

Video Boards

While I have your attention focused on the complexities of the video subsystem, let's take a quick look at video boards. You might have missed a few performance clues tucked away in the discussion of architecture. Did you notice that VFLATD.VXD supports only a 1MB address space? What happens if your display adapter contains 2MB or more of memory? Don't worry. Windows 95 will completely support the entire range of memory provided by your display adapter. However, it might have to rely more on the display minidriver to do it. This means a lot more calls and perhaps a few more thunks between various display components. The end result is a slight loss in performance, from a purely display-subsystem point of view.

It's not all bad news, of course. You'll gain from having more video memory in several ways. First, more memory means more colors. A higher number of colors could result in better font anti-aliasing and other aesthetic qualities of your display. Second, more memory means higher resolution. A higher level of resolution could help you position graphic elements more accurately and result in reduced eye fatigue.

No matter which way you look at it, though, more colors and high resolution spell decreased performance. Moving the video window around takes a little time; allowing the frame buffer to manage more than 1MB of video memory takes even more. Each layer of management you add to the video subsystem will chew up processor cycles. So how do you get around these problems?

- **Dual-ported video RAM (VRAM):** Many display adapters come with this feature, but some don't. VRAM is a Texas Instruments innovation. They first introduced it with their TMS340x0 series of processors, such as the one used in the Artist TI12 display adapter. The reason that it's called dual-ported is that it actually contains two ports. A serial buffer allows the display to read the contents of video memory. A parallel buffer allows Windows to simultaneously write to video memory. Dual-ported memory gets rid of one of the constraints that an application had with the display adapter: You could write to video memory only during part of the display cycle.
- **Display coprocessor:** Quite a few display adapters also come with a coprocessor. Windows 3.x didn't make use of this feature; it sort of ignored the fact that it was there. Windows 95, on the other hand, has coprocessor support built right in. It offloads as much of the display

processing as possible to the display coprocessor, instead of using the DIB engine. There are two ways that this speeds performance. First, because offloading part of the graphics processing responsibility frees processor cycles, you'll notice an overall improvement in system speed. Second, the display processor is usually a special-purpose-state machine. It processes the graphics instructions much faster than the DIB engine could. Think of it this way: The math coprocessor in your machine is a state machine. It can't replace the general processor for most purposes. However, it's incredibly fast when performing some types of math calculations.

- **32-bit display adapter:** Graphics routines process a lot of data. There's no way around it. To display an image, you have to move data, and that requires time. However, you can reduce the amount of time by using a wider data path. Some display adapters come with a 32-bit path. Just the increase in data width will improve graphics performance. Add to that the fact that the 32-bit bus on a computer normally operates at a higher clock speed than its 16-bit counterpart, and you have an opportunity for a significant increase in performance.
- **MMX Pentium processor:** A lot of the processing required to display an image on-screen is done within the processor. In most cases, the display functions use generic processor calls to get the job done. What if the processor was designed to provide special high-speed display routines? That's what the MMX version of the Pentium processor from Intel is all about. It's designed to process graphics and audio much faster than its predecessors. Unfortunately, unless your applications and the operating system both know how to use the new capabilities of the processor, you won't see much of a change in processing speed. To make this particular option work, you need the OSR2 version of Windows 95. Getting the full speed enhancement will require MMX-enabled applications as well. It's safe to say that you'll see a very noticeable difference when processor, operating system, and application all work together to give you the fastest graphics processing possible.

OSR2

Tip: Look through the list of devices that Windows 95 supports with native drivers before you buy a new display adapter. The hand-tuned Microsoft drivers almost always work better than those that you get from the vendor, because they're tested more extensively. They definitely work better than a 16-bit driver, which some older display adapters come with. Buying a new adapter that sports a Windows 95 logo will probably cost you more but won't buy you that much, other than a label. Looking through the supported hardware list will probably net you a great display adapter at lower prices, yet retain all the capabilities that Windows 95 provides.

There are other things that you need to look for in a Windows 95 display adapter. One of the biggest convenience items is plug and play. You gain a lot from having both a plug and play-compatible monitor and display adapter. Not only are these devices self-configuring, but they allow a greater level of flexibility. One of the ways that Windows 95 limits you with a non-plug and play device is color selection. I can change the resolution of my Video 7 display adapter without rebooting, but I can't change the number of colors.

Peter's Principle: More Than Enough Graphics

You'll probably be very tempted to go out and buy the first 24-bit display adapter that offers 16.7 million colors and 2048×2048 resolution. That might be a good way to build for the future, but it might be a little too much for today unless you're an artist or work in a graphics-oriented field. Go ahead and get the tomorrow solution today; that only makes sense from a financial perspective. However, once you do get a high-performance display, think about the way you'll actually use it. In many cases, a 256-color display provides more than enough color. A 17-inch monitor supports a resolution of 1024×768 just fine, too. Once you start going beyond this color and resolution level, your machine will take a performance hit because of the way Windows 95 handles video memory.

So when is it acceptable to go to a higher display level? You need to consider the tradeoff of performance versus need. For example, if you're using your computer more than eight hours a day for word processing, you might find that eye fatigue becomes a major factor. The font-smoothing capability provided by the Plus! pack may be the answer you're looking for, but it requires more than 256 colors. (Font smoothing often provides more comfort at a lower performance penalty than using a higher-resolution display.) Instead of going right to a 24-bit color display, consider using 16-bit color instead. You'll still take a performance hit, but it won't be as severe. 16-bit color often represents a viable middle ground between performance and comfort when using your computer.

Using the higher level of display capability is fine if you don't mind giving up performance as well. I'd rather squeeze every ounce of performance from my machine and use settings that are a little more in line with what I can actually use. Of course, that shouldn't stop you from getting a high-performance display adapter, but it should change the way you configure it. Always consider when you have "enough" graphics to meet the need.

Installing Video Display Adapters

Chapter 14 covers the physical process of installing your display adapter as part of the hardware installation process. The process for installing a new display adapter isn't all that much different. However, I'd like to show you an alternative to that process.

Of course, installing a new display adapter or monitor isn't the end of the process—it's the beginning. Chapter 10 contains a complete description of the four pages of configuration settings for the

Display Properties dialog box, so I won't go through them again here. Suffice it to say that Windows 95 provides all the settings you had under Windows 3.x, plus a few pleasant surprises.

Installing a Display Adapter

Installing a new display adapter can be very easy. You can use the standard hardware installation procedure, but the one I show you here is shorter and a little more straightforward. However, it skips the automatic detection method I describe in Chapter 14. You might want to use that procedure if you have a plug and play display adapter.

1. Right-click the desktop and choose the Properties option. You should see the Display Properties dialog box.

2. Select the Settings page. Click the Change Display Type button (OSR2 users will see an Advanced Properties button) to see the Change Display Type dialog box shown in Figure 17.2. (OSR2 users will see an Advanced Display Properties dialog box like the one shown in Figure 17.3.) Notice that this dialog box has two settings (settings pages for OSR2 users—the third page is performance-specific). You use the same dialog box (but different fields) to install a monitor or a display adapter. There are several other features that you should notice in this dialog box. First is the fact that it tells you which drivers the display adapter requires. Note that this is the adapter itself, not the video subsystem as a whole. The video subsystem also contains a number of files that are either generic or specific to certain conditions. Second, notice that this dialog box tells you the current display adapter type and its version number. This could provide important information when you're troubleshooting. OSR2 users will notice a third feature in their dialog box. The Refresh Rate field allows you to set the refresh rate of the display. Using a higher refresh rate usually results in less eye fatigue. Unfortunately, a high refresh rate will also produce more heat. In addition, there are situations where one refresh rate will interact with the lighting in your office and another won't. Always check this setting to make sure that what Windows thinks is right really does work in your situation.

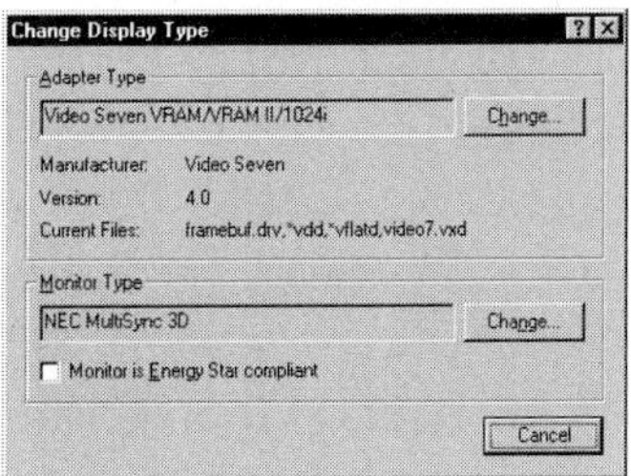

Figure 17.2.
The Change Display Type dialog box allows you to reconfigure your display adapter or monitor.

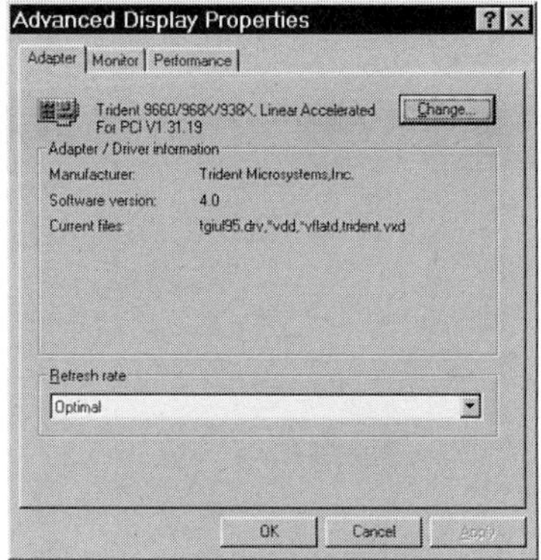

Figure 17.3.
The OSR2 version of Windows 95 provides an improved dialog box that allows you to change the hardware and its performance from one location.

3. Click the Change button in the Adapter Type group (Adapter page for OSR2 users). You'll see the dialog box shown in Figure 17.4. Notice that only one display adapter type is listed. If other display adapters were compatible with this one, this list box would contain those as well.

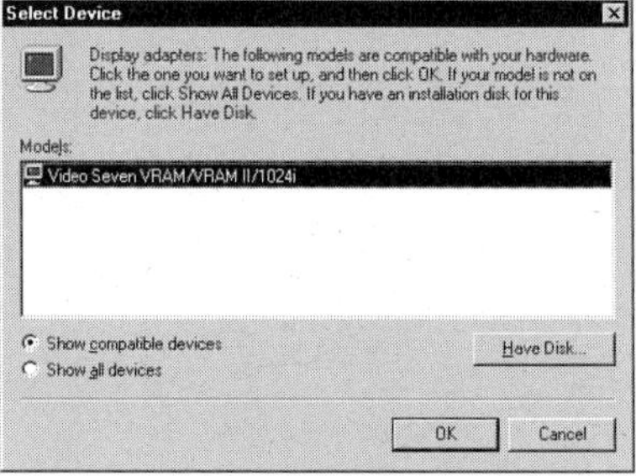

Figure 17.4.
The initial Select Device dialog box shows only compatible display adapters.

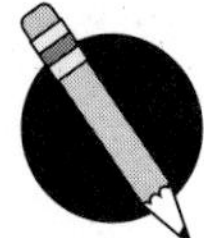

Note: If you have a vendor disk containing drivers for your display adapter, click the Have Disk button to look at it. The Have Disk dialog box works just like any other browsing dialog box under Windows 95.

4. Click the Show All Devices radio button. Windows changes the list to show all the display adapters it supports, in order by vendor (see Figure 17.5). You can use this screen when selecting a new display adapter. Clicking Cancel here takes you back to the initial screen without changing your display type.

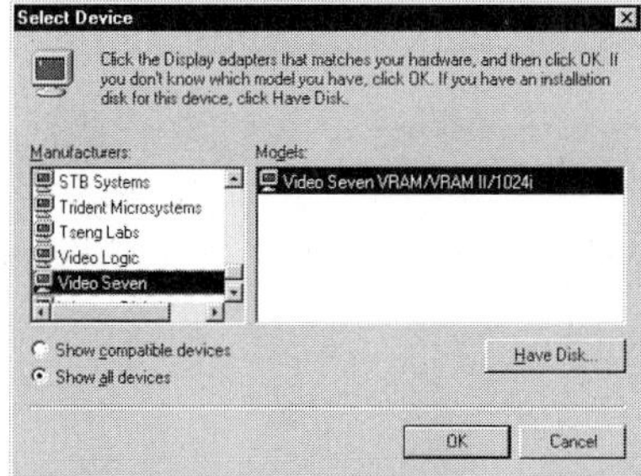

Figure 17.5.
Clicking the Show All Devices radio button shows every display adapter that Windows 95 supports.

Tip: If your display adapter vendor doesn't appear in the list and you don't have a special disk for it, you can always use the Standard Display Adapter category at the very beginning of the Manufacturers list. It might be a good idea to use this category anyway if your special driver disk contains only older 16-bit drivers. You won't get the same number of features that you might with the special disk, but using the standard drivers will provide a performance boost.

5. After you select the correct manufacturer and display adapter model from the list, click OK. Windows takes you back to the Change Display Type dialog box.
6. Click Cancel, and then click Apply. Windows might ask you to insert disks as it installs the new adapter. It also asks whether you want to restart your machine to make the changes permanent. Click Yes to restart your machine.

Installing a Monitor

It might not seem like a very big deal to tell Windows 95 which monitor you're using, especially if that monitor doesn't provide any special capabilities. However, the monitor you use determines which display adapter features you can use. Selecting the right monitor type helps Windows 95 provide you with better information regarding your display choices.

1. Right-click the desktop and choose the Properties option. You should see the Display Properties dialog box.
2. Select the Settings page. Click the Change Display Type button (Advanced Properties button for OSR2 users) to see the Change Display Type dialog box (refer to Figure 17.2). OSR2 users select the Monitor page of the Advanced Display Properties dialog box, as shown in Figure 17.6. Notice that this dialog box has two settings. You use the same dialog box to install a monitor or a display adapter. Monitors provide only one additional setting. You can check the Monitor Is Energy Star Compliant check box if this feature is provided. The Monitor Type group tells you which monitor you currently have installed. The OSR2

version of Windows 95 also allows you to set two other monitor features. Checking the Automatically Detect Plug & Play Monitors check box tells Windows 95 to use the plug and play features of both the display adapter and the monitor. You must have both installed on your machine to use this feature. A plug and play monitor tells Windows 95 about itself and reduces the amount of configuration you have to do. It can also tailor some of the options you have to choose from in the Display Properties dialog box. Some monitors offer both a suspend (standby) and a power-down mode. The power-down mode works about the same as shutting off the monitor. Some monitors have to go through a restart cycle to work properly after being powered down. The third check box, Reset Display on Suspend/Resume, tells Windows 95 to send the monitor a reset signal.

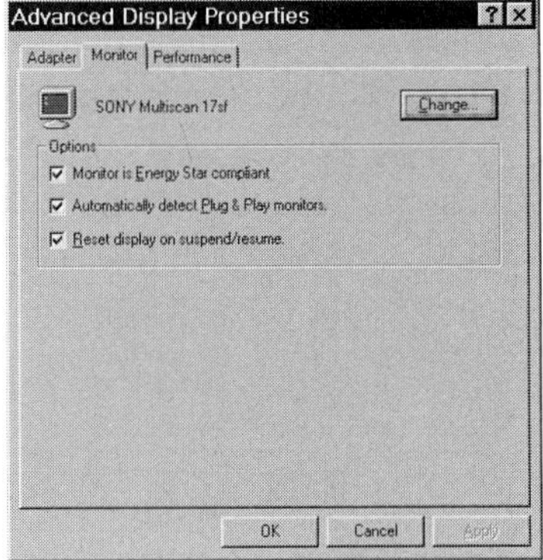

Figure 17.6.
The OSR2 version of Windows 95 provides more configuration features for monitors.

3. Click the Change button in the Monitor Type group. Click the Show All Devices radio button. You'll see the dialog box shown in Figure 17.7.

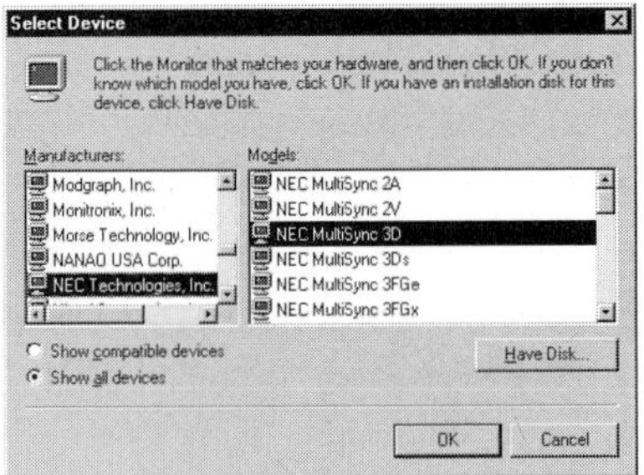

Figure 17.7.
The Select Device dialog box allows you to choose from a list of monitors.

4. After you select the correct manufacturer and monitor model from the list, click OK. Windows takes you back to the Change Display Type dialog box.
5. Click Cancel. Notice that Windows doesn't enable the Apply button this time. It doesn't ask whether you want to restart your machine, either. I usually restart the machine anyway,

just to make sure that the change is permanent and that every part of Windows knows about it. This is especially important when you're installing an Energy Star-compliant monitor.

6. Click OK to close the Display Properties dialog box. Use the Start | Shutdown command to restart Windows 95.

Using the Performance Page Provided by OSR2

The OSR2 version of Windows 95 provides an additional page in the Advanced Display Properties dialog box, as shown in Figure 17.8. This page provides the same features as the Advanced Graphics Settings dialog box shown in Figure 3.4 of Chapter 3. I won't go into the similar features here.

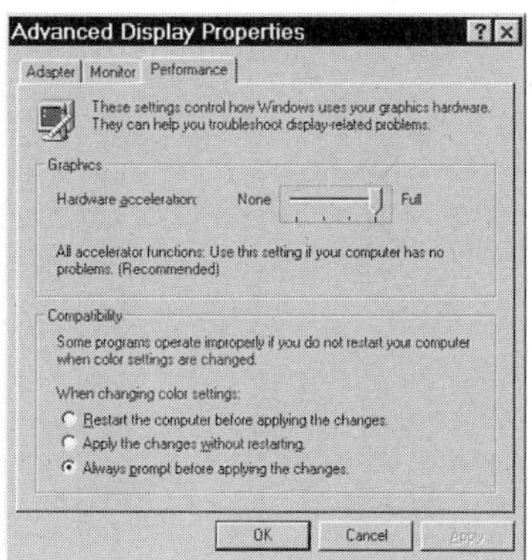

Figure 17.8.
The OSR2 version of Windows 95 allows you to set the performance features of your display adapter, using the same dialog box that you used to install it.

Notice, however, that there's an additional section provided in this dialog box. The first radio button tells Windows 95 to reboot any time you change the color settings for your machine. (This same setting seems to reboot the machine if you change the display resolution, when using some display adapters.) There are some situations where your machine will actually appear to freeze immediately after an application resets the display colors or resolution. Game programs certainly fall into this category. The solution is to automatically reboot the machine so that the new settings take hold. You'll obviously have to restart the offending program, but at least you'll be able to use it.

The second setting is for the truly brave. You may find that you can change your color and resolution settings at will without any negative results. Before selecting it, I'd make absolutely certain that this setting will work with every program you use. If you have any marginal applications installed, you'll want to use the third setting that I describe next.

Most programs are much better behaved. Even though they may not operate correctly, you can still see the display well enough to tell Windows 95 to reboot. The third option tells Windows to prompt you about rebooting the machine after a color change (and, in some cases, a resolution change). This is the default option, and I find it works just fine in most cases. If you make a color change without any problem, simply tell Windows that you don't want to reboot the machine.

On Your Own

Some people find that an underpowered machine might not provide all the speed they need to get their work done fast. Try a variety of display resolutions and color-level settings to find a compromise between system performance and the aesthetic value of the display. You'll find these settings on the Settings page of the Display Properties dialog box. Also try the various font-size settings. Perhaps a custom setting will provide that perfect balance between readability and the number of icons you can fit on the desktop or within an Explorer pane.

Check your SYSTEM folder and see whether you can find all the files that make up the video subsystem. Use the video subsystem discussion in this chapter as the basis for your search.

18

Mobile Computing

Few people who travel can get by without their constant companion, the notebook computer. In this chapter, I use the term *notebook* to refer to every kind of mobile computer. Of course, mobile computers actually range in size from the smallest PDA (personal digital assistant) to some of the luggable dinosaurs I still see from time to time.

Fortunately, most people use something that provides enough flexibility to get the job done, but without all the weight. It's the transition from klunky and archaic to sleek and feature-packed that has brought on another change that Windows 95 addresses. No longer does everyone regard notebooks as second computers. They contain most if not all of the features of desktop computers. The only difference is the display and keyboard, both of which are easily taken care of by a docking station.

Yet, before Windows 95 came along, many notebook computer users were still strapped to a desktop. The reason was simple: The operating system wasn't up to the task of working with a notebook. Consider the following scenario. You're working on a report and decide to take it home with you. Because you're in a car pool and not driving today, you figure that you can work on the report on the way home. To do that, you have to completely close all your applications, undock your machine, reboot your computer, and set everything up again. That's not too bad, but you have to go through the same process all over again when you get home.

The inconvenience of using a notebook can be illustrated in a number of ways. The "taking work home" scenario was just one example. What happens when you need to change a card in your machine? Say that you no longer need the modem card and want to replace it with a NIC to access the network. Unless you have some special setup software, you actually have to turn off the machine and reconfigure it to make the switch. It's time-wasting events like this that really frustrate people who use a notebook from time to time. Windows has a fix for this problem that you'll really like—I know I like it.

Before we go much further, let's define this "notebook" computer a little. First, Windows 95 won't take your PDA (personal digital assistant) and make it into a desktop equivalent. We're looking at machines that are really capable of running Windows 95. This means that they have to meet all the installation criteria discussed in earlier chapters. I'm also talking about something that's a bit newer than the Model T. A notebook has to provide a PCMCIA (Personal Computer Memory Card International Association) slot or its equivalent in order to use some of the features that Windows 95 provides. You'll also want a computer that can use a docking station. In other words, I really don't care how heavy or large the computer is, but it has to provide enough features to take the place of a desktop.

Tip: The OEM Service Release 2 (OSR2) version of Windows 95 contains infrared port support, but you must have an Infrared Data Association (IrDA) 2.0–compliant device to use this support. The current software also includes infrared LAN connectivity. Fortunately, you can download this update from `http://www.microsoft.com/windows/software/irda.htm`. This same site has several other interesting programs that you can download. For example, there's a file transfer program for moving files from one computer to another via an infrared data port. You'll also find the Windows 95 Fast Infrared DDK Beta 2 at this site.

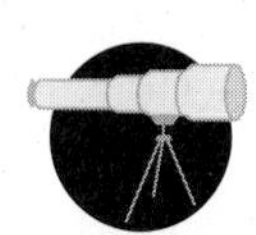

Looking Ahead: The OSR2 version of Windows 95 also provides voice modem support. The "Understanding Voice Communications" section of Chapter 20 covers this very important topic.

Chapter 2 took a look at how every computer can use plug and play (PNP). We revisit PNP in this chapter. There are some new capabilities that will really make a difference for notebook computer users. If you're at all intrigued, read on.

PCMCIA Devices on Your Notebook Computer

The first topic on our agenda is the PCMCIA bus. This is a "little" bus that's specially designed to meet the needs of the notebook computer market, but it's found in a growing number of desktop machines as well. The PCMCIA bus uses credit-card-sized cards that connect to external slots on the machine. This is perfect for a notebook, because notebooks are notorious for providing few, if any, expansion slots. A PCMCIA bus makes it very easy for the user to change a machine's hardware configuration without opening it up. For example, you could take out a memory card to make room for a modem card.

Note: The OSR2 version of Windows 95 provides additional levels of PCMCIA support. For example, it supports the new PC Card 32 (Cardbus) bridges. You can also use 3.3-volt cards in addition to the older 5-volt models. This latest version of Windows 95 also supports multifunction PCMCIA cards and specialty devices such as Global Positioning Satellite (GPS) cards. Unfortunately, you can't download the files required to update an existing system—you must get a new one with OSR2 installed.

This bus also supports solid-state disk drives in the form of flash ROM or SRAM boards. The flash ROM boards are especially interesting, because they provide the same access speeds as regular memory with the permanence of other long-term storage media such as hard drives. Unlike SRAM boards, flash ROM boards don't require battery backup. Many people use solid-state drives to store applications or databases that change infrequently. This frees up precious space on the internal hard disk for data and applications that the user needs to access on a continual basis.

Unfortunately, the PCMCIA bus also creates a problem for people who use it. Imagine, if you will, the reaction of Windows 3.x to the user taking a card out of the system and replacing it with another. The user will definitely see the difference right after rebooting the machine. Every time you plug in a new card type, you need to reconfigure your system to accept it. (Of course, this doesn't necessarily apply to exchanging one hard disk or a similar card for another.) Configuration programs make this really neat feature a real pain to implement under Windows 3.x. Of course, some vendors provide utility programs to make the change easier, but this still doesn't change the way that Windows itself operates. It also can't make up for deficiencies in DOS. The operating system must provide dynamic loading and unloading of device drivers to make the system as user-friendly as possible.

PNP changes all this. No longer do PCMCIA bus users need to reconfigure their systems when a component changes. Windows 95 is designed to detect system changes and make the appropriate modifications to its setup. However, this flexibility comes at a price. Users must disable their PCMCIA-specific utilities and allow Windows 95 to manage the bus. The bus vendor must also provide the 32-bit drivers needed under Windows 95 (unless your bus already appears in the Windows 95 support list). Doing this enables the PCMCIA enhanced mode. So what does enhanced support buy you? Figure 18.1 shows a typical PC Card (PCMCIA) Properties dialog box. (You access it by double-clicking the PC Card (PCMCIA) applet in the Control Panel.)

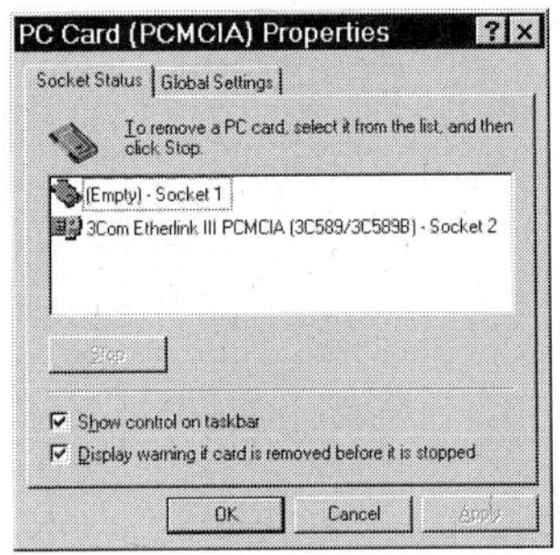

Figure 18.1.
The PC Card (PCMCIA) Properties dialog box gives you access to the PCMCIA cards installed on your machine.

The following list provides an overview of enhanced support features:

- **Friendly device names:** This feature provides users with device names that they can recognize. Instead of the more familiar XYZ.VXD, the user will see something like Flash ROM Driver. It also helps the user to determine which devices are actually present and which ones are disconnected.

- **Automatic installation:** The automatic installation feature allows the user to hot-swap various devices in and out of the PCMCIA slot without worrying about reconfiguring the machine.
- **Drive change detection:** In some situations, the user will have to unmount and then mount a PCMCIA drive before Windows 95 will recognize the change, if enhanced support is disabled.
- **Other device-specific mode and configuration information:** Each PCMCIA card vendor implements special features for their device. Check the documentation that comes with the device for further details.

As Figure 18.1 shows, there are a few options that you can use with PCMCIA cards. The first check box, Show Control on Taskbar, displays an icon in the Taskbar tray. You can use it to get a list of currently installed cards, stop one that's installed, or (by right-clicking) display a context menu containing the Properties option. The second check box tells Windows to display a message if you try to remove a card before you stop it.

Just what is stopping? Normally Windows 95 will detect changes in your PCMCIA setup. However, you can help things along by stopping the card before you remove it. Stopping the card tells Windows 95 to remove support for that feature. All you need to do is highlight the card you want to stop, and then click the Stop button shown in Figure 18.1 to stop the card.

Let's take a quick look at the Global Settings page of the PC Card (PCMCIA) Properties dialog box shown in Figure 18.2. Notice that there are only a few options on this page. Normally you'll want to keep the Automatic Selection check box checked, as shown in Figure 18.2. Unchecking this box allows you to set the card service memory area manually—a task that you'll normally need to perform for troubleshooting purposes only. The second check box, Disable PC Card Sound Effects, tells Windows that you don't want to hear a sound effect every time the status of the PCMCIA bus changes. This is a handy feature in an office where you don't want to disturb other people with sound effects from your computer.

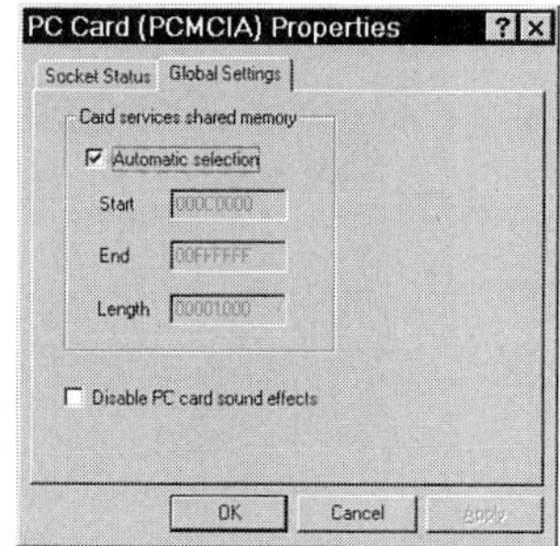

Figure 18.2.
The Global Settings page of the PC Card (PCMCIA) Properties dialog box contains a handy check box for silencing your machine during card changes.

In most cases, Windows 95 automatically enables enhanced mode, but it won't do so if you have any real-mode PCMCIA drivers loaded. Fortunately, it's very easy to see whether Windows 95 has enabled enhanced mode on your machine. Right-click My Computer and select the Properties option to open the System Properties dialog box. Click the Performance tab to display the dialog box shown in Figure 18.3.

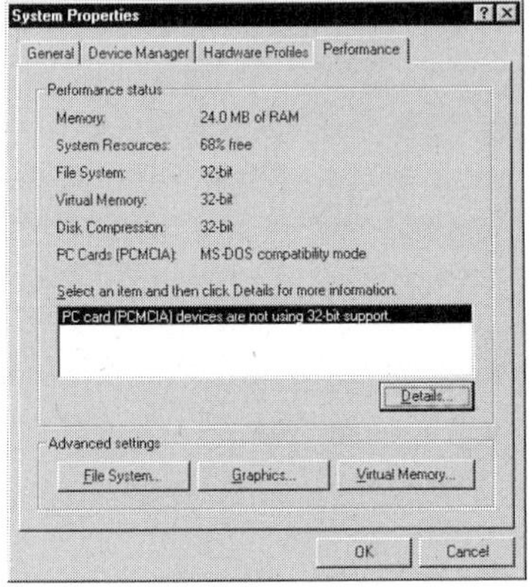

Figure 18.3.
The Performance tab helps you optimize system performance. It displays all performance bottlenecks, including PCMCIA status.

If your dialog box looks like the one in Figure 18.3, Windows 95 hasn't enabled enhanced support. The first method you should use to try to correct the problem is to click the Details button. This displays the Windows Help dialog box shown in Figure 18.4.

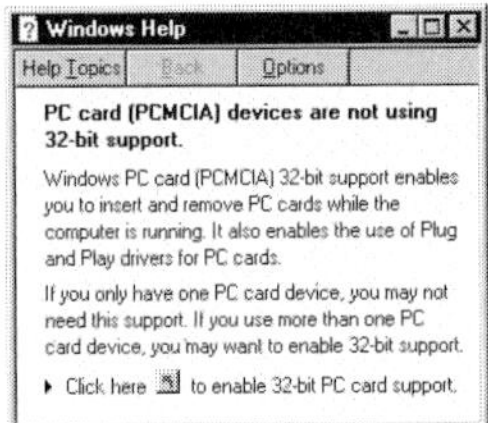

Figure 18.4.
This Help dialog box provides a button that enables PCMCIA 32-bit support.

Notice the button that enables 32-bit PCMCIA support. If you click it, you'll see the PCMCIA Wizard shown in Figure 18.5. Windows 95 will attempt to help you enable 32-bit support. All you need to do is follow the prompts to diagnose any problems that Windows can detect. However, sometimes this attempt will fail.

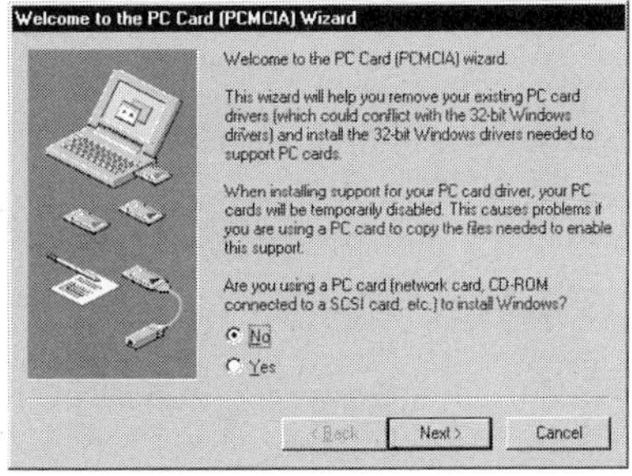

Figure 18.5.
Use the PCMCIA Wizard to help you diagnose problems with your installation or with the bus itself.

The following paragraphs provide some troubleshooting tips:

- The most common problem associated with enabling enhanced support is that there are PCMCIA device drivers in CONFIG.SYS or TSRs in AUTOEXEC.BAT. Removing these entries should fix the problem.
- Windows 95 normally tells you if there's an I/O port address or interrupt conflict, but you should check the settings under the Resources tab of the PCIC (peripheral connect interface card) or Compatible PCMCIA Controller Properties dialog box, as shown in Figure 18.6, to make sure. (To open this dialog box, simply right-click My Computer, select the Properties option from the context menu, and select the Device Manager tab of the System Properties dialog box.) Any conflicting devices appear in the Conflicting Device List field near the bottom of the dialog box.

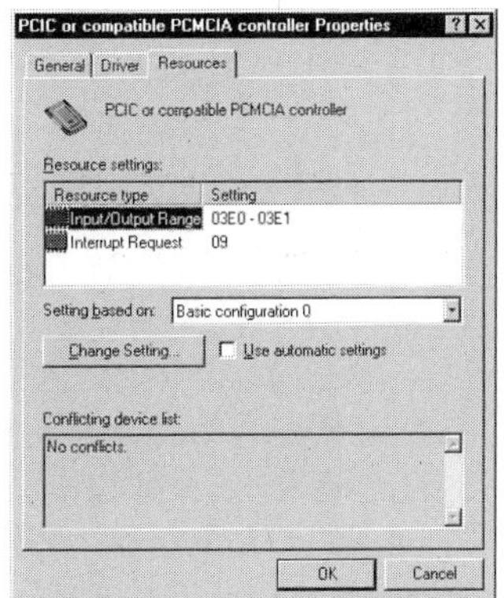

Figure 18.6.
The Resources tab of the PCIC or Compatible PCMCIA Controller Properties dialog box alerts you to any conflicting devices.

- Always install a card in the slot while booting. Failure to do so can prevent Windows 95 from detecting the PCMCIA card slot.
- Make sure that Windows 95 supports your card by checking it with the Hardware Installation Wizard in the Control Panel. (You can browse through the list of hardware presented on the second screen and then click Cancel to exit the utility without installing anything.)

Even if Windows 95 doesn't support your PCMCIA slot, you can still use it by installing real-mode drivers. Of course, using real-mode drivers means that you won't gain any benefit from the PNP features. It always makes sense to contact the bus vendor to see whether a 32-bit driver is available.

Hot Docking

Remember at the beginning of this chapter when I mentioned that Windows 95 had a solution to your docking problems? A PNP feature called *hot docking* allows you to remove a portable computer from its docking station without turning it off. The portable will automatically reconfigure itself to reflect the loss of docking station capability. Plug that portable back into the original docking station, or a new one somewhere else, and it will automatically reconfigure itself to take advantage of the new capabilities that the docking station provides.

Tip: It isn't always the best idea to move your computer with the power on. Sure, it can save you a little time when you perform a setup, but unless you're right in the middle of something that you spent hours setting up, it's usually better to shut down and turn the power off before you remove the computer from its docking station. By moving it with the power on, there are a number of ways that you could create surges or other electrical interference that could shorten the life of your machine. For example, you could accidentally short something out when removing the notebook from its docking station. Moving your machine from place to place without turning it off is OK—it's a supported feature—but you need to consider the cost of exercising that option.

Hot Swapping

Another problem that I talked about at the beginning of this chapter was the ability to take one card out of the PCMCIA slot and plug another into its place. PNP answers the call here as well. A PNP-compatible system reconfigures itself dynamically. You might have seen advertisements for portables that provide a capability called *hot swapping*. This is really a component of the PNP specification. Hot swapping allows you to remove components from a machine without rebooting it. For example, what if you had a modem card in your PCMCIA slot and needed to exchange it for a network card? Currently, you would need to turn off the machine, exchange the cards, and reboot. Of course, you'd also need to remove any modem-specific device drivers or TSRs and add the network card software.

Warning: Never touch the contacts of your PCMCIA cards when you remove them from the bus. Doing so could give the card a static electric shock that will damage it or shorten its life.

Hot swapping allows you to take the card out and put the new one in without turning the machine off. The computer automatically recognizes that it can no longer communicate with your favorite BBS, for example, but that the network lines are now open. The PNP component of Windows 95 even installs the required drivers and configures them for you in the background. This means that users no longer need to worry about how a device works; they only need to think about what work they need the device to perform. (The only exception to this rule is when Windows 95 can't find the required drivers on your hard disk. It will ask you to supply a disk containing the required drivers.)

Windows 95 Mobile Computing Services

Some of the new utility programs that come with Windows 95 take up where PCMCIA leaves off in making life easier for the user. Microsoft went a long way toward meeting the needs of notebook computer users with the release of Windows 95. I'd like to say that they went all the way, but that wouldn't be quite true. Windows 95 started out with a lot fuller feature set, but some features were dropped and others moved to the Microsoft Plus! offering. Still, Windows 95 is miles ahead of Windows 3.x. It provides what I would call the very basics needed to make Windows 95 notebook-computer-friendly. Communication is the key feature that Windows 95 provides for the notebook computer user. Chapter 19 discusses most of these features. However, you'll find other features equally impressive.

So what are these features I keep talking about? One of them is Briefcase, which I describe next. I wouldn't call this a feature exclusive to mobile computer users, though. I've even used it to send files to other people across the network. You don't always have to follow to the letter Microsoft's suggested uses for a utility; there's a lot of potential in a utility like Briefcase. Experiment to see where it will work best. Sometimes I use Briefcase in place of folders because of its ability to update files for you (something else that we'll look at later). Other times this feature gets in the way, so I use folders to move data around instead.

I'll also take a quick look at Dial-Up Networking in this section, from a notebook computer user's point of view. We'll take a look at some of the ways that you can get around potential problems by using this new feature to communicate on the road. Chapter 19 covers all the usage basics, so you can skip this section if you really don't foresee a need to use Dial-Up Networking on your next business trip.

Briefcase

Windows 95 includes a Briefcase. Like its physical counterpart, you use the Windows Briefcase to store files that you need to move from place to place. Of course, a physical briefcase uses paper as its storage media, while the Windows Briefcase uses electronic media. The Briefcase sits on the desktop, along with the Recycle Bin and My Computer.

Setting up your Briefcase is very easy. All you need to do is install the Briefcase software (it's optional), and a Briefcase icon will appear on the desktop. Stuff the Briefcase with files that you plan to move from place to place. What you should get is a centralized storage location for all the files you work on, even if those files appear in different areas of your hard drive. (For that matter, they could appear on a network drive.)

Working with Briefcase files is no different from working with any other file. Windows 95 monitors the status of the files and presents a display of their status when you open the Briefcase icon, as shown in Figure 18.7. Notice that it tells you when your Briefcase requires an update to keep it up-to-date with the files on your machine. All you need to do is select the Briefcase | Update All command if the files are out-of-date. Once the files are up-to-date, you can move the briefcase from your machine to a network drive or floppy.

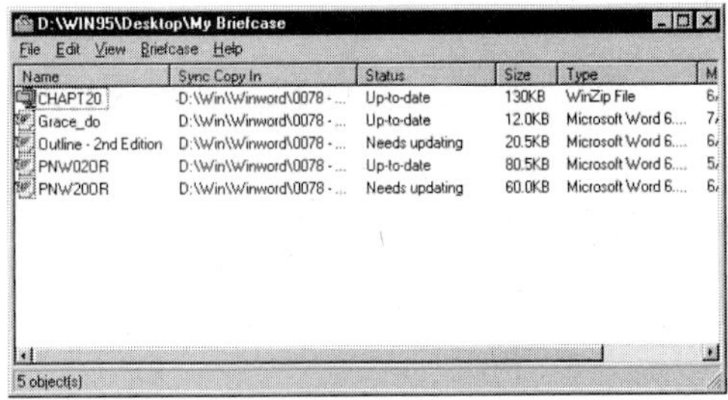

Figure 18.7.
Briefcase offers a fast and convenient method of centralizing your files. It also provides the means to move those files from work to home and back with a minimum of fuss.

Briefcase provides a context menu for each of its files, just like the context menus you're used to seeing in Explorer. It also provides a document Properties dialog box, shown in Figure 18.8. The General, Summary, and Statistics pages all look like the ones that you'd see in a standard document.

The one change you'll notice is the addition of an Update Status page (see Figure 18.9). This page provides quite a bit of information about the document in your Briefcase versus the one on your drive. It also provides some options that you wouldn't normally get from the menu. The middle of the page shows the current document status—which document has been updated and when you made the changes.

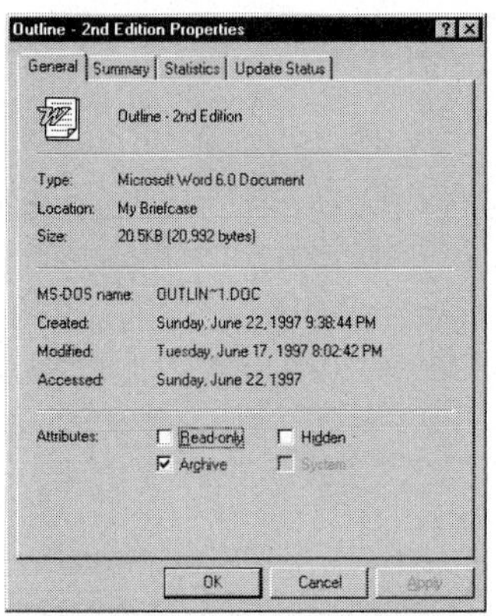

Figure 18.8.
A Briefcase file provides a standard document Properties dialog box that looks similar to the ones in Explorer.

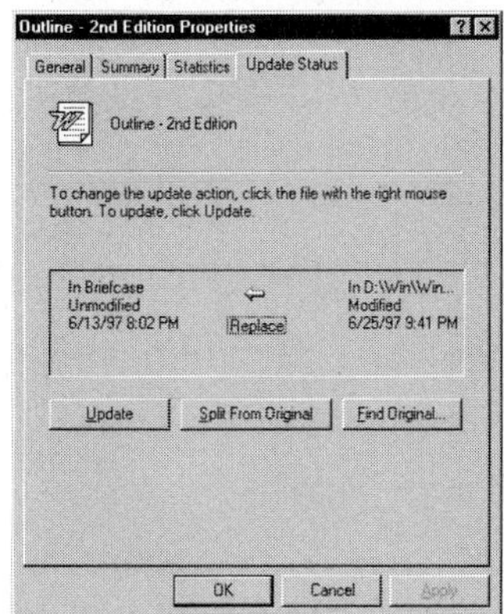

Figure 18.9.
The Update Status page shows you the current document status and gives you the ability to update the file.

There's an interesting feature in the information box. It looks like an ordinary information box. All it tells you is that the original document has a newer date than the one in the Briefcase. However, if you click the Replace icon in the middle of these two entries, you'll see the context menu shown in Figure 18.10. The interesting thing about this menu is that you can choose to replace your updated document with the original in your Briefcase.

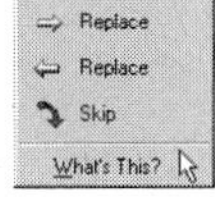

Figure 18.10.
The Replace context menu item is a hidden extra that Briefcase provides.

How many times have you wished that you had a copy of your original file when the changes you made didn't quite fit? Wouldn't it be nice if you could restore the document to its original form without resorting to a backup tape? Using this feature will help. If you keep your Briefcase up-to-date, you can always restore an original copy of a document after you change it. This safety feature comes in handy when a few hours of editing just don't turn out as you anticipated. Notice that this list has a third entry. You can choose to skip an update. Just select the Skip option and close the dialog box. This allows you to use automatic updating for all your other files and still retain the original version of this particular file.

Tip: You can use Briefcase as a rudimentary version control system. Here's how it works. Create a new Briefcase as you reach each new milestone in a project. Change the name of the Briefcase to match the milestone's name or date. Place a copy of all the files in the Briefcase, but never update it. What you should end up with is a bunch of Briefcases, each one representing a stage of your project. Even though this technique does consume a lot of hard drive space, it could also save you a lot of rework time later.

The three buttons in the document Properties dialog box allow you to manipulate the link you've created. The Update button updates your linked copy to match the original document (or just the opposite). The direction of the update depends on which way the Replace arrow is pointing in the information box. Briefcase uses a default of updating whichever document is older than the original. The Split From Original button allows you to separate the copy from the original. This comes in handy if you decide to make a new document out of the original in your briefcase. The Find Original button opens a copy of Explorer with the original document highlighted. You can use this button to quickly find a document in the Briefcase. I found it strange that this particular button doesn't appear on the context menu; you must access it using the Properties dialog box.

Moving your Briefcase from work to home is just as easy as using it. Just stick a floppy disk in one of your drives and right-click the Briefcase icon. You should see a display similar to the one in Figure 18.11. Notice that you can update the Briefcase from here as well; you don't have to open it if you don't want to. To move the Briefcase from your machine to a floppy, just select the Send To menu option and choose a location. The Briefcase icon will disappear from the desktop and reappear on the floppy. Moving it back to your desktop the next day is just as easy. Just select the floppy drive in Explorer so that you can see the Briefcase icon. Then right-click it and drag it to the desktop. When Windows displays a menu asking what you want to do, click Move. That's all there is to it! So what happens if you lose your Briefcase? You can create a new Briefcase by right-clicking the desktop and selecting New from the context menu. One of the new items you can create is the Briefcase.

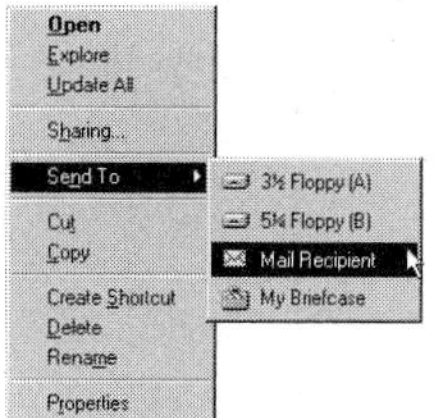

Figure 18.11.
The Briefcase context menu provides access to some but not all of the Briefcase features.

Tip: Here's a tip for you if you have a bulging Briefcase. You can compress the floppies used to transport information from one machine to another. Use the DriveSpace utility to do this. Compressing the floppy will nearly double its carrying capacity, especially when you consider that most people carry data files, not the executable files required to edit them. Data files normally contain a lot of empty space that compression programs can squeeze out.

Synchronizing Files

Keeping the files on your notebook computer in sync with your desktop system isn't just a nicety—it's a necessity. Taking work home is one thing, but making sure that those changes get into the final document is something else. The easiest way to keep your files in sync is to use the same machine as both notebook and desktop machine. Of course, that isn't always practical. Your desktop machine might provide features that you can't get from the notebook, or maybe you simply like using the Windows 95 desktop better.

Before Windows 95, the notebook user had only two choices when keeping the files on two or more machines in sync. One method was to keep all the mobile data on a floppy. All you needed to do was pass the floppy around as needed to keep the files in sync. This easy solution also had a pretty significant problem: A floppy's access speed isn't very good, and its storage capacity is very limited when compared to a hard drive. Suffice it to say that this wasn't the best way to go.

Another solution was to copy the files from your hard drive to a floppy and then back again. This had the advantage of using the best possible speed for opening and using the files. The big disadvantage was that it relied on the person's memory to make sure that the files were kept in sync.

Using the Briefcase option in Windows 95 is a big step forward for notebook users. It has one of the characteristics of floppy-based synchronization: You just move the Briefcase around as needed. It also provides the advantage of the file-copying method. Every application makes use of the hard drive's enhanced access speed when you open and edit files.

Is Briefcase the only Windows 95 solution? Probably not. I've also used the folder concept that I've talked about in various places in this book. It allows a group to keep one set of files on a central machine in sync. But how do you use this feature if you're working on a document at home? That's where Dial-Up Networking comes into play. Instead of simply moving a Briefcase around, you can use Dial-Up Networking to call into the network and edit the files remotely. That way, even though you're working on the file from another location, your team can continue updating it as well.

Tip: Using the combination of folders and Dial-Up Networking is ideal if you're a team supervisor. It allows you to continue your work on the documentation that the team is preparing while you're on the road, without resorting to the Briefcase. Even if you're currently working on the documents alone, there could be an occasion in which a team member needs them as well. Using the Briefcase means that the folks at home won't know whether they're using the current documents. There's never a good reason to slow the team's progress on a project because you need to work on it while on the road. Using this combination also allows you to monitor the team's progress. Checking in each day to see the work that they've accomplished will help you to keep an eye on things back home while you're on the road.

Remote Dial-Up (Dial-Up Networking)

Chapter 19 talks about the mechanics of using Dial-Up Networking, so I won't go through that process here. However, once you do get the software installed and configured, where do you go from there? If you're a notebook user, there are plenty of reasons to use this particular Windows 95 feature:

- **Document access:** I've already mentioned how you can use Dial-Up Networking to enable an entire group of people to work together. All you need to do is place a folder with shortcuts to the team's documents in a folder on the network. When a person calls into the network, he can open the folder and see all the pieces of the project without looking very hard for them. I often place this folder in the user's home directory on the network. That way, I can personalize each folder as required, and the user doesn't need to memorize yet another location on the network.
- **Application access:** You won't need to access applications such as word processors or spreadsheets from a remote location (at least, not very often). But what about the custom database that your company uses as a contact manager? Unless you plan to either print the entire database or create a copy of it on your notebook's hard drive, you'll need to access it remotely. In fact, this is probably the only way you could use this centralized application if it contains sales or inventory information that you'll need to update later.

- **E-mail:** It's surprising just how much a company depends on e-mail to keep employees apprised of events. Think about the e-mail messages that you receive that talk about marriages and new babies—as well as company-specific events such as getting a new access code for the security system or updating your W-2 form. Losing this communication means that you'll be out-of-touch when you return from your trip. A few minutes of online time could keep you up-to-date on current situations in your company and reduce that "vacation" syndrome that many people feel after a road trip.
- **Emergency decisions:** What if you're traveling in Europe and your company is in California? How do you find a good time to call them and make a decision that requires a 24-hour turnaround? The old way of doing things was waiting up until the wee hours of the morning and calling your company during normal business hours. Either that or waking someone up at home. Using the company or an online service e-mail to leave a message and then checking for responses later could give you those few extra hours of sleep at night. After all, who wants to fight politics and sleepiness at the same time?
- **Missing-file syndrome:** Notebooks almost always need at least twice as much hard disk space as they really have. How often have you cleared a bunch of files off your notebook only to find that you really needed them after all? If you're on the road, it's usually too late to regain access to those files, and you have to figure out a way to do without them. Or do you? A remote connection can let you grab some files that you didn't think you'd need. Placing a copy of your desktop machine's hard drive—or at least the data—where you can access it by using a remote connection will save you a lot of trouble later. Be sure to ask the network administrator's permission before you do this, though.

These are just some of the common ways in which you can use Dial-Up Networking with a notebook. You'll need to find the specialty technique that applies to your specific situation. For example, in my particular case, I find it handy to use Dial-Up Networking to grab presentations. I have room for only one or two on my notebook at a time, but I might need several during the time I'm on the road. Using this feature allows me to call in and grab the next presentation in line. The result is that each presentation is fresh and specifically designed for the group I'm talking with, yet I don't have to lug around a monster-sized hard drive or other storage.

Remote Network Users

Networking is an essential part of any business today. I've already talked about Dial-Up Networking to an extent, but let's take a look at some of the communication and other considerations you'll need to make. Using Dial-Up Networking is one thing; using it efficiently is another.

I'd like to begin by providing a little insight into one of the problems with using Dial-Up Networking. Most people know that the telephone company charges more for the first three minutes of a long-distance call than for the time that follows. People try to keep their long-distance calls short and to the point. The telephone company capitalizes on this by charging you more when you make several short calls instead of one long one.

Given this set of circumstances, imagine the cost differential of making one long computer call as compared to a whole bunch of short ones. It's very easy to get into the habit of dialing the company every time you need a bit of information. Consolidating all your information needs into one call is better than making several short ones. Chapter 20 covers the method of dialing after hours using Exchange. You can save a lot of money by delivering all your mail during off-peak hours.

There are still times when it's impossible to take care of all your communication needs at one time. You'll still find the need to make a few short calls during the day to gather information. However, you don't have to do that for message delivery. Delivering responses to e-mail and performing other chores can always wait for off-peak hours, especially when you're overseas and the people who wrote the message won't see it until after you're in bed anyway.

The following sections describe some of the other methods that you can use to reduce the cost of Dial-Up Networking. Although these techniques won't work when your need for data exchange with another party is immediate, they'll work in the majority of cases.

Local Communications

There are many forms of long-distance communication, and some of them are local. Here's one scenario. You're in Detroit and your company is in Los Angeles. It's important that you send a file containing some new information about your client to an assistant for processing. You also need some additional information about another client that's stored in your company database. You have access to both Dial-Up Networking and CompuServe (or some other online service such as the Internet). Which do you use? Some people would use Dial-Up Networking because it's faster and more convenient, but the low-cost solution would be CompuServe (or the Internet), in this case.

Note: Even though I talk specifically about CompuServe in this section, the same principle applies to other online services such as America Online (AOL). You can use many of them by making a local call and paying a small fee for transferring large files (the transfer fee is most noticeable if you're overseas, but can occur if you're in smaller towns in the United States as well). Be sure to compare the rates of the various online services, if you subscribe to more than one. Some services might charge less than others for specific types of file transfers. Make sure that you have a nationwide ISP (worldwide for overseas travelers) if you plan to use the Internet to transfer files. Some ISPs are local only and you could end up paying quite a bit in long-distance charges for a large file transfer.

Making a local phone call to CompuServe is just as fast as transferring that file over the company e-mail, and will cost you a lot less. CompuServe requires only a local call and perhaps a few cents for an upload charge. For example, I recently uploaded a 600KB file for about $1.80. That's a lot less than a long-distance call would have cost.

However, sometimes the obvious choice isn't the one you should use. For example, suppose that you need to transfer the same files and get the same information. The difference is that this time you're in another part of the state instead of another part of the country. It costs only about 40 cents to make the toll call to your company, so using Dial-Up Networking is the right choice. CompuServe adds a surcharge to some types of billing systems, but not to others. You should check the CompuServe rate against the toll charge to see which one is better.

Tip: Once you determine a local rate, write it down for future reference. Keeping a rate sheet for the places you frequent will save you from having to look up the information more than once. Most communications programs provide some method of determining your CompuServe rate. All you need to do is look at the long-distance rate versus the CompuServe rate.

If your company has its own Internet address, you might be able to use it to transfer information by using a local call. Of course, you'll need an account with a local provider to make this work. As with the other suggestions in this section, you'll want to check the cost of using an Internet solution against that of making a long-distance call.

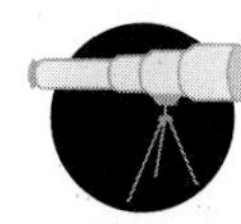

Looking Ahead: Appendix B will help you learn all the details of getting an Internet Service Provider (ISP). In most cases, the cost of using the Internet has declined drastically as Internet usage has gone up. A lot of ISPs now offer unlimited dial-up access hours for a small charge of $19.95 a month. Some ISPs even provide 800-number access for a small additional charge, in case you travel to rural areas in the United States a lot.

Dynamic Networking

Despite your best efforts, you'll run into times when you need to work "live" with the company database or other applications. You can't solve every problem with e-mail or a file upload. There are times when working with live applications or data is the only way to get the job done. You'll want to keep these times to a minimum, but keeping a local database management system (DBMS) current might override other cost considerations. Even if this is the situation your company is in, you don't need to pay through the nose to get the kind of service you need. Your notebook still has a few tricks up its sleeve to solve the problem. The following list provides some of the ideas I've come up with, but you can probably think of others based on your unique set of circumstances.

Tip: If you're using a custom DBMS, it might be possible to add batch-updating capability to it. This would allow you to use a smaller version of the application on the road, create new records, modify existing ones, and make all the changes in batch mode when you return from your trip or as part of an upload to the company database. In many cases, this is a less-expensive solution for inventory control or other types of sales databases than making the changes live. There are two criteria for using a batch system: You need a fairly large outside sales force to make the change cost-effective, and the company must be able to get by with daily or weekly database updates instead of real-time data. This would work in most situations, but you couldn't use it for something like an airline ticket database.

- **Internet access:** Using the Internet still might provide the best means of working with live data. You'll need to overcome two problems. The first is gaining access to a local server that allows live connections. The second is that you'll have to make a TCP/IP connection and use a special modem to make this work. Both problems can be solved given enough resources. In the past, this solution may have seemed more like a dream than reality. Today, intranets (the private version of the Internet) abound. Even small businesses can occasionally write off the cost of using an intranet solution because it's less expensive than anything else I've covered here.

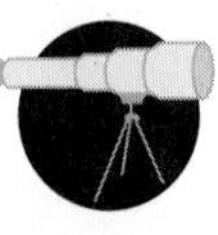

Looking Ahead: Be sure to take a close look at Chapters 21 and 22 for more ideas in this area. Chapter 21 tells you all about getting online. You'll learn the basics of creating a Web page in Chapter 22. The OSR2 version of Windows 95 comes with a special feature—Personal Web Server. You can use it to at least try out various intranet solutions before you invest the money in a full-sized solution. Chapter 23 covers Personal Web Server usage.

- **Using a local office's PBX connection:** Sometimes a local office will provide the long-distance call solution you need. It might mean a little wrangling with the local boss and perhaps a short drive, but this solution could save your company some money.
- **Keeping notes:** Even if your database doesn't support batch-mode processing, you could still keep notes and make all the updates at one time. This would allow you to make one phone call instead of many to record the required information. Of course, this solution still won't work with "live" data such as ticket sales and the like.
- **Off-hour calling:** This is probably the least likely solution. If your data needs are so time-critical that you can't afford to wait even a few minutes, off-hour calling won't work. However, you could combine this technique with batch mode or note-taking methods to work with live data on the network. You could even use this off-hour calling technique when using a local office's PBX connection. This would reduce the local boss' objection to tying up the line in order to service your needs.

Offline Printing

In Chapter 15, when I cover printing, I talk about two techniques that the notebook computer user will love. The first is the idea of creating a printer for every purpose. You can create printers for all the local offices that you'll visit during a trip. That way, you can print any notes or documents you need, without worrying about whether you have the proper print driver to get the job done. You can also use this technique to print at client sites that are amenable to your doing so.

However, that isn't the only way you can print. You can also print to your hard drive by using the offline printing technique discussed in Chapter 15. All you need to do is set the printer to work offline. Everything you send to disk will wait on the hard drive until you send it to the printer.

What I didn't include in that chapter was something notebook-specific. Whenever you disconnect your notebook from the network printer or docking station, Windows 95 detects the loss of printing capability and sets the printer to work offline automatically. Unfortunately, this doesn't work all the time. I experienced a few situations in which the printer disconnection wasn't detected. Either way, detection was consistent. Check your printer the first time, and you should be able to rely on the connection being consistent from that point on.

Working with an Infrared Data Port

Infrared data ports weren't very popular when Windows 95 was first released. Things have changed. As I mentioned at the beginning of this chapter, the OSR2 version of Windows 95 comes with infrared data-port support built in. You can also download from the Internet a copy of the files required to perform an update of an existing Windows 95 installation.

Let's look at what you get with the Windows 95 infrared support. Chapter 14 already covers standard hardware installation techniques, so I won't cover them here. Once you install the software for your infrared port, you'll see an Infrared applet in the Control Panel. Double-clicking this applet displays the Infrared Monitor dialog box shown in Figure 18.12.

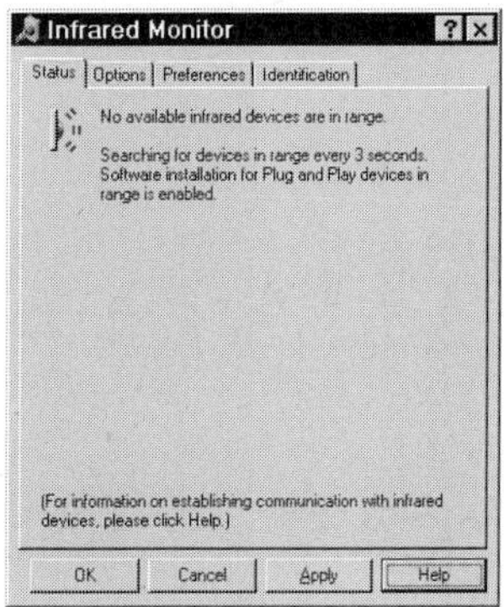

Figure 18.12.
The Status page of the Infrared Monitor dialog box tells you whether there are any other infrared ports in the area.

The Status page of the Infrared Monitor is where you look for connection information. If there aren't any ports to connect to, you'll see a display similar to the one in Figure 18.12. This page also tells you the status of any existing connections. You can find out how well the connection is working. This information comes in handy when you need to transfer a large amount of data and it seems to be taking too long. Sometimes you can improve the connection by moving your machine more in line with the other infrared data port.

Figure 18.13 shows the Options page. The first check box allows you to enable infrared communication using a specific serial port—in this case, COM3. Notice that the actual communication doesn't take place on COM3—we'll use COM4 for serial communication and LPT2 for parallel communication. It's important to keep this in mind as you set up your software to use the infrared port.

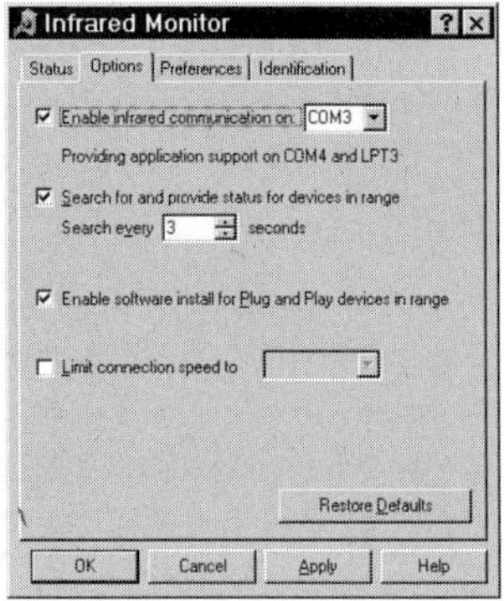

Figure 18.13.
The Options page of the Infrared Monitor dialog box contains all the configuration options.

The second check box on this page enables automatic search for other infrared ports. Scanning for other ports uses processor cycles that you may want to devote to other activities. Turning off the scan feature while you're on the road won't just make your computer run faster—it will save some power, too. Notice that there's also a field for defining how often you scan for another port. The default value of three seconds will work just fine in most cases. However, you may find that a smaller value will help you fine-tune a connection faster. A longer increment could save precious processing cycles once you have a connection established.

You'll find that the Enable Software Install for Plug and Play Devices in Range option of this dialog box is simultaneously helpful and annoying. I found that it was most helpful when I visited locations that I didn't visit on a regular basis. This option automatically configures your machine to use any plug and play infrared devices that happen to be in the area—making life a lot more automatic. On the other hand, I keep finding my machine getting configured for devices I really don't want. You'll probably want to keep this check box unchecked unless you're planning to visit a new location.

The fourth (and final) check box on this page serves an interesting purpose. It allows you to limit the connection speed. Now, that may not seem like such a good idea at first, but there are a few situations where you may find it helpful. The first is when the receiving device can't handle the full-speed connection. For example, you may want to establish a connection with some type of serial device and find that it doesn't work properly. Data overruns are the first symptom of this problem. The second situation occurs when you have a good connection, but keep getting data errors. For whatever reason, you're spending more time transmitting old data than new data. Slowing down the connection could reduce data errors and actually improve the data rate of the connection.

The Preferences page of the Infrared Monitor dialog box allows you to set the features of your infrared port. Figure 18.14 shows what this page looks like.

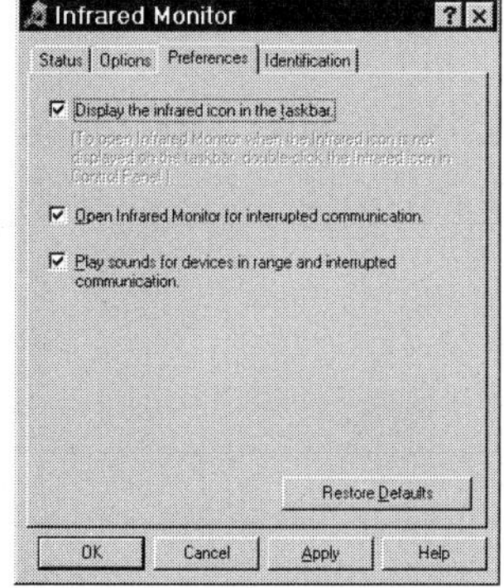

Figure 18.14.
The Preferences page of the Infrared Monitor dialog box allows you to place an Infrared icon on the Taskbar.

The first check box on this page allows you to display an Infrared icon on the Taskbar. As with most of the icons that you can display on the Taskbar, there are three actions that you can perform: Leaving the mouse over the icon gives you the current port status, a left-click performs a default action (opening the Infrared Monitor dialog box), and a right-click displays a context menu. The context menu contains four simple entries. The first opens the Infrared Monitor dialog box. The second enables infrared communications. The third option enables automatic searches for other devices in range. The fourth option enables automatic installation for plug and play devices.

The next two check boxes on this page work together. The second check box on the page allows you to open the infrared port for interrupted connections. This comes in handy when the line of sight to the other port could be interrupted by someone passing by. You'd also want to enable it when you have a less-than-ideal connection to the other device. The third check box on the page tells Windows 95 to sound an alarm whenever it finds a device in range or if it loses a connection to another device. It would have been nice if Microsoft had used two separate sounds for these events, but at least you'll get some kind of an alert. Obviously, you'll want to turn off this option in an office where you're sharing the same space with other people. Some people find the constant noise of sounds coming from the computer more than a little distracting.

We're down to the last page in this dialog box, Identification. Figure 18.15 shows this page. As you can see, it contains two edit fields. The first field tells who you are. The second field provides a description of your computer. In most cases, you'll want to come up with something pretty unique, yet generic, for a portable computer. There really isn't any way of knowing who will be using your computer, so a generic name is best. On the other hand, you don't want the name you chose to interfere with others on the network. Picking something really unique (as shown in the figure) should help you meet both criteria.

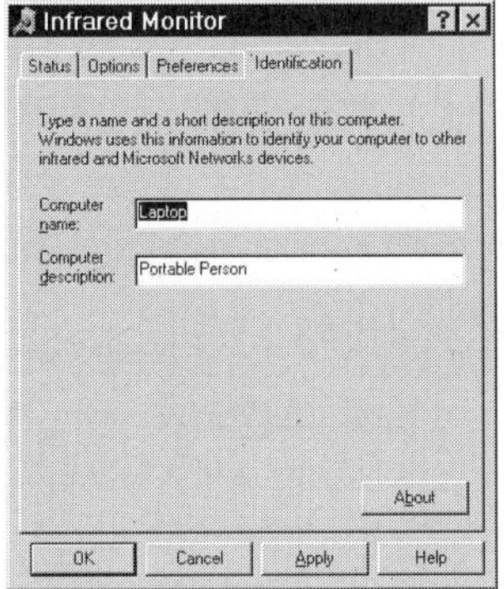

Figure 18.15.
The Identification page of the Infrared Monitor dialog box allows you to identify yourself to other users.

Power Management Strategies

Chapters 3 through 5 cover a lot of useful tips for getting the most out of your computer. You may want to review those chapters when setting up your laptop. However, once you get past these basic strategies for making your computer do more with fewer resources, you can start working with some special strategies for laptop computers. The following list provides ideas on what you can look for on your laptop. Not every laptop provides every feature listed here, and you could certainly find some that are unique to your system. The first tip, then, has to be to explore the vendor documentation that comes with your laptop. You'll be amazed at the little tips you'll find there.

- **Forget fancy software:** Screen savers probably eat more power on a laptop than most people imagine. Because most laptop computers come with a feature for turning off the monitor automatically, there isn't any reason for you even to install a fancy screen saver. In fact, because most laptops use flat-screen displays, you may actually cause more harm than good by using a screen saver. A screen saver could inadvertently interfere with the automatic shutdown software and end up reducing the life of your screen, not extending it. In addition to interfering with the normal way your laptop runs, some screen savers constantly access the hard disk, causing further drain on the battery. There are other culprits in this area as well. For instance, see whether you can get by with a subset of your word processing software. I installed the full version of my word processor the first time around and found that one of the features kept hard disk activity at a frantic pace. In an effort to provide me with the latest information on my files, the software was actually just eating power. I don't keep a lot of files on my laptop, so I always know exactly what I have available. Kill the fancy features of your software and you'll find that the battery that normally lasts 3 hours will probably last 3½.

- **Look for power-saving features:** A lot of laptops come equipped with a function key (FN on my system) that's poorly understood by the majority of users. In my case there's a faucet at the top of the screen. Pressing FN-Faucet reduces power consumption on my machine by a lot—yet I wouldn't have found this feature simply by looking at the documentation. The vendor hid it in the screen section of the text, not in the power management section where I expected to find it. If you're in doubt about one of those buttons sitting on your laptop, keep searching the documentation until you find it. Most laptops now come with a power saving mode that you can use while on the battery. In some cases you'll find that programs run a little slower and that the backlight doesn't seem to work as well, but you'll get a lot more life out of your battery.
- **Change power-wasting habits and software configurations:** I find that I occasionally develop a habit that's great in intent, but short on true usefulness. For example, when I start thinking about what I want to write, I'll save my document. It sounds like a good habit to get into. After all, if you save during think time, power outages and other types of hardware failure are less likely to affect you. However, consider for a second that it's fairly unlikely that you'll experience a power outage when working with a laptop unless you totally ignore the battery level. In addition, the ruggedized hardware used in laptop construction is a lot less prone to failure than hardware of days gone by. Consider looking at your software configuration as well. I used to set the automatic save for my word processor to 10 minutes. That was just enough time for the drive to start spinning down. As a result, I wasted a huge amount of power starting and stopping the drive. Setting the automatic save to 20 minutes proved a lot more efficient from a power perspective and I haven't lost a single bit of data as a result of the change.
- **Turn off your sound:** It's really nice having sound effects going at times. At least, I've always liked them, and I suspect a lot of other people do, too. Sound boards consume quite a bit of power, though, and you have to ask whether you really need to hear any sounds while working on a document at 30,000 feet. In most cases, you can turn off your sound board with a simple setting in the Control Panel. Making this very small change in configuration not only will save you power, it will make you more popular with the person sitting in the next seat. You'll also want to avoid playing your latest music CD while on battery. A CD will keep the disk running almost continuously, greatly reducing battery life.
- **Give it a break:** I've seen more than a few folks try to eat lunch and work on their laptop at the same time. In addition to the risk of spilling something on the keyboard, trying to work and do something else (such as eat) at the same time probably isn't the most efficient way to use laptop battery power. Simply suspend your laptop for the duration of your meal. Not only will you use battery power more efficiently, you'll also get to enjoy your food hot for once.

On Your Own

This chapter presented a lot of different ideas on how a notebook user can use the capabilities provided by Windows 95 to improve productivity. Of course, one of the big things covered was the use of the PCMCIA interface. If you have a PCMCIA bus on your notebook computer, right-click My Computer and select the Properties option. Click the Performance tab to see whether your system is fully optimized. Be sure to double-check the bus.

Another productivity enhancement is the combination of Briefcase and Dial-Up Networking. Try splitting your projects into two categories: those that you're working on alone, and those that you're working on with a group. Try using the Briefcase method with the projects that you're working on alone. Use the folder and Dial-Up Networking combination for projects that you're working on in a group.

Make a list of the ways in which you can use Dial-Up Networking to improve your productivity. I mentioned the most common ways in this chapter, but your company might have special needs that I didn't cover. It's important to use a little creativity when thinking about the ways that Windows 95 can help you. This is one way to do it. Keep the list handy for later and refer to it when you're looking for ways to solve a particular mobile computing problem.

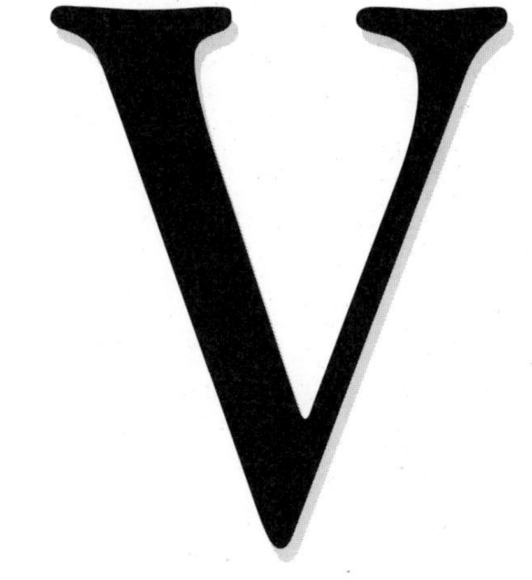

Surfing the Net

19 Connecting and Communicating

Connections and communications are what make using the computer worthwhile for some people. It's not being able to do something faster that drives these people; it's a matter of being able to obtain and present information. Exchanging information with others means that you'll have to spend a little more time thinking about how you'll do it. Windows 95 provides a lot of different types of connections, and each of them helps you communicate in some way.

I'm not going to tell you that every type of connection works well under Windows 95. You'll need to address some real problem areas in order to make things work properly. Communications aren't always as clear as they could be. You'll find that not only do you need to learn new computing skills, but you need to learn a new way of talking with other people as well. This chapter takes you through the pitfalls you could experience and helps you avoid them.

This chapter has two distinctly separate parts. Both of them build on information talked about in previous chapters. The first part spends some time with physical details I haven't covered yet. Hardware connections are a necessary step in getting your machine ready for information exchange of all types. I'm not going to spend any time talking about troubleshooting or network specifics here, but I will spend some time talking about common connections—the devices you use every day.

The second topic I talk about is software connections. Anyone who works out of his or her home knows the problems involved in keeping up with what's going on at the office. Sharing files and any other type of communication is a problem as well. Previous versions of Windows left the user out in the cold when it came to these very necessary concerns. Windows 95 takes care of that discrepancy by providing some very real assistance for the remote user.

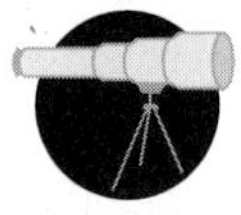

Looking Ahead: I don't cover the particulars of online communication here. I cover that issue in Chapter 20. Network connections begin in Chapter 23. Be sure to look there for the ins and outs of that type of connection. If you're a mobile computer user, be sure to read Chapter 18. I also cover troubleshooting in Chapters 26 and 27. Of course, these other chapters cover a lot more than just connections; they cover many user issues as well.

When you combine the software and hardware connections that Windows 95 provides, you find a somewhat complete level of coverage. However, I was appalled at some of the areas where Microsoft skimped when it came to this important subject. I was equally pleased at some of the new features that they decided to include. Overall, Windows 95 is an improvement, but perhaps not as big an improvement as you might expect. It's not time to throw away that third-party remote connection package yet, but perhaps in another few versions it will be.

Making Hardware Attachments

As advanced as some users are when it comes to software, they're handicapped when it comes to hardware. Perhaps you've heard the story of the guy who placed a floppy in the space between the two drives because his machine lacked a 5¼-inch floppy drive. It's funny to think about someone actually doing something that silly. Of course, there's also the joke about people who use correction fluid to cover up on-screen mistakes. Everyone has a favorite joke about someone who did something harebrained on his or her computer.

Making the wrong connection in real life is another story. Finding that your printer or modem doesn't work when there's a critical deadline isn't funny at all. Frantic workers trying to figure out why their external SCSI drive or another device won't work without a terminator is enough to send chills up anyone's spine. That's the kind of serious connection work we'll talk about here. I won't bore you with stories of the oddball; I'm going to tell you about real-life connection problems and how to avoid them.

Any Port in a Storm

The first thing we need to talk about is the external ports on your machine. The problem for many people is not knowing where these ports connect or what they do. Some very different ports even look alike. For example, there's the distinct possibility that you could confuse a game port with a thick Ethernet port, because they look exactly the same. Even though most ports are easy to identify given certain clues, just grabbing any port on the back of your machine isn't such a good idea. It's always better to mark the ports and know exactly what they do before you try to use them. You might end up costing yourself a lot of time if you don't. For example, what if you have two 9-pin serial ports on your machine? Which one is COM1? Just knowing what function the port serves might not be enough.

An End to Port Confusion—Universal Serial Bus (USB)

I've spent more than a little time trying to figure out foolproof ways to make sense of that web of confusion on the back of everyone's machine—it can't be done with today's technology. Obviously, we need some new technology that will clean up the mess sometime in the future. Just as obviously, any solution will make a big mess out of things for the interim.

Intel, Microsoft, and other companies are currently working on a new port standard called the *Universal Serial Bus* (USB). So what's this new standard all about? It's a standard single-sized peripheral port designed to meet the needs of every device connected to your machine. In addition, it allows you to daisychain up to 127 devices to one port (at least at the time of this writing), eliminating the need for separate interrupt and port settings for each of those devices within your machine. A user will also benefit from the 32-bit data path that this new standard offers, because it exceeds just about any connection offered right now.

A USB port works much like a LAN in some ways. You connect devices to a hub. The main computer chassis will have two hubs (at least in the current scheme of things). Other hubs will likely appear on the keyboard and the monitor. Unlike network hubs, a USB hub can also function as a device. The term *hub* in this case refers to a distribution point. A hub is different from a device because a device doesn't provide any plug-in points. Adding hub capabilities to the keyboard will allow you to plug in a mouse or light pen without the usual tangle of cords going to the main unit. Likewise, the hub associated with your monitor will support a microphone and speakers.

Using USB ports will allow users to do things that they couldn't do in the past. For one thing, you can add or remove USB devices with relative ease. The operating system will poll the USB ports every so often. Devices that answer the call will remain connected to the USB; devices that don't will be disconnected. Connecting new devices will be just as easy. In addition to these new capabilities, USB will support at least two different data transmission speeds for devices: 1.5 Mbps and 12 Mbps. This means that slow devices such as a mouse won't hamper faster multimedia devices on the bus. The hub will perform any data-rate translation required to make this multiple-speed capability work. USB will also support suspend and resume modes so that you can use power efficiently—which is a simple extension of the technology we use today to turn a monitor on and off as needed. Finally, USB guarantees on-time data delivery through the use of isochronous transfers. What this means is that you'll hear continuous music or see continuous video (assuming that your computer can deliver it).

Lest you think that all this new technology is mere vaporware, Intel actually demonstrated a desktop machine that included USB at the 1995 fall Comdex and released a version of the chip early in 1996. (Problems with the chip have kept it out of the mainstream, as of this writing.) More than a few notebook vendors have signed up for USB as well. The list includes companies such as Dell Computer Corporation, Hewlett-Packard, and Toshiba. We're supposed to see all these new goodies in the first half of 1997, but I wouldn't hold my breath. What you'll probably see is a reasonable version of the machine that you could buy early in 1997 at best. Microsoft will also need to provide the operating system drivers to support this new bus—something that will take a little time and effort to do. Even if you do buy the hardware early in 1997, it will take until the end of 1997 to get everything working right.

Are there other flies in the ointment? Sure. Just think about the vast stockpiles of printers and other peripheral devices sitting out there right now. Even if everyone gets a USB machine out sometime in the middle of 1997 that does provide full operating system support, it's going to take several years to integrate that new port into the current corporate environment. USB: It's a technology that's better than anything we have now, but it's definitely a future technology.

Fortunately, some types of ports are tough to confuse. For example, a 25-pin port with male pins is a serial port. Nothing else on your system uses that configuration. Some external SCSI ports are pretty difficult to confuse. They contain so many pins that they fill the entire width of the expansion slot. But those are the only really easy ports—the ones you can identify just by looking at them. The other ports require closer identification before you know what they do.

In particular, you must be careful not to confuse a printer port (which uses a 25-pin female connector) with a Macintosh-compatible SCSI port (which uses the same connector). Plugging a printer into a Mac-SCSI port can cause actual physical damage to the printer or the port card or both.

You can make several generalizations by looking at the back of your PC. Table 19.1 contains a partial list of the clues I used to identify the ports on the back of my machine. You, too, can use these clues if there's some reason that you can't open up your machine. (Some warranty policies don't let you open the machine because the vendor is concerned about user tampering. I strongly suggest that you not give your money to such companies. A lease is one thing; a purchase is another. No vendor should put you in the position of having to call them—or physically return your system to them—every time you want to insert or remove a card or some other device.)

Table 19.1. Adapters and their associated ports.

Adapter	*Port Description*
Ethernet	This adapter frequently has a 15-pin thick Ethernet port and a coaxial-cable thin Ethernet connector. The round coaxial connector is the same width as the slot and has two knobs on it for connecting the cable. The adapter might also provide DIP switches. Another version of an Ethernet card has the 15-pin connector and an RJ-45 jack (which looks like an oversized telephone jack). Similar-looking cards include ArcNet and token ring adapters. However, these always lack the 15-pin port. ArcNet adapters usually provide an active indicator LED as well. (You may find LEDs on other card types as well, but they're more prevalent on ArcNET cards.)
I/O port combo	The combination port card provides a 25-pin parallel port and a 9-pin serial port on the back of the adapter. The serial port is usually COM1 and the parallel port LPT1. Be warned that the installer could have changed these default settings by using the jumpers on the card or software setup. An I/O port combo adapter might also include a 9- or 25-pin serial port or a 15-pin game port that attaches through the back of the machine. If your case doesn't provide the extra cable connector holes, these ports might appear in one of the expansion slot openings. Some older multifunction cards such as the Intel Above Board used this port layout as well. Fortunately, the ports served the same purpose.

continues

Table 19.1. continued

Adapter	*Port Description*
SVGA display	Some older versions of these cards provide both a 9-pin digital and a 15-pin analog port. Note that this 15-pin port is the same size as the 9-pin port. The pins are arranged in three rows of five rather than the two-row arrangement used by the game port. They're also a little smaller than the ones used by the game port. The display adapter might include a mouse port for a PS/2-style mouse. Some adapters provide only the 15-pin port (a requirement for SVGA). Other features on the back of this card might include DIP switches or three high-frequency connectors to connect to a high-resolution monitor.
Game	This adapter usually contains two 15-pin game ports, although only one is present on some very popular models. The one nearest the top of the machine is usually the one you want to use. Game adapters sometimes include a submini plug used for a variable-speed controller. This controller matches the speed of the game port to the speed of the machine. If you see a connector with 15 pins in two rows plus an RJ-45 connector (similar to a telephone jack), you're probably looking at an Ethernet card. If you see a connector with 15 holes in three rows, it's for (S)VGA video output.
Sound board	You'll usually see a 15-pin game port that doubles as a MIDI port when you select the right jumper or software settings. This adapter also includes three submini jacks that look the same as the earphone jacks on a portable radio. The precise arrangement of these jacks varies by vendor, but they serve the following purposes: output, microphone, and line input from an external source, such as a CD-ROM drive. Some older sound boards also include a volume level thumbwheel.
External SCSI	You might also see a number of large connectors on the back of a machine. One type of external SCSI connector has 50 lines and looks like a larger version of the Centronics connector on your printer. Unlike the Macintosh-compatible version (which has only 25 pins and is exactly like a printer port connector), this type of external SCSI connector doesn't use the same type of pins as the more familiar serial or parallel connector. The newer SCSI-II connectors are miniaturized versions of the large 50-pin SCSI. Again, they're quite unlike anything else that you're likely to find on a PC.
External drive	A number of older CD-ROM drives used a 37-pin plug. It looks like a huge version of the parallel port. You might see this with other types of drives as well. It's never safe to assume anything about this plug. Always check it against the vendor documentation.

Adapter	*Port Description*
Fax/modem	A fax or modem card will usually provide two RJ-11 jacks (they look like the ones on your telephone). One jack allows you to connect the incoming cable, and the other jack is for your telephone. This adapter usually provides some DIP switches as well.

In addition to all these combinations, there are a multitude of third-party adapters that might look like one of the adapters described in Table 19.1 but won't provide the same functionality. Fortunately, you'll probably know that you have one of them installed, because you'll need it to perform some special task on your machine. The general rule to follow is this: If you see a port that you don't recognize and it isn't marked, open the machine to identify it. The second rule I always follow is that you shouldn't always believe the markings on the back of your machine. If you look back there and see that all the ports you recognize are correctly marked, you can probably assume that the rest are correct, too. However, if you see a serial port identified as a parallel port, you should question whether any of the markers are correct.

Tip: After identifying the ports, mark them. Also, don't simply write down that something is a serial port. Specify COM1 or COM2 as part of the marking. Performing this little extra step can save you a lot of time later. You might want to follow this same procedure with cables, especially if the machine is connected to a workstation setup in which the cable source might become hidden. Trying to identify the correct cable when there are several possibilities is never a welcome task. It's easier to mark everything at the outset.

Printers

Chapter 15 covers the topic of printers in great detail. I'd like to cover printer connections in this chapter. Some people think there's only one way to connect a printer—through a parallel port. And for some printers, that's correct. A few older printers used only a serial port connection. Some other, newer printers provide two or three connection types. These printers might have a serial port connector in addition to the standard Centronics parallel port connector, and they might have a network connector (AppleTalk or Ethernet) in addition to the serial and/or parallel port connectors.

Tip: Some printers don't provide a serial port as standard equipment; you have to buy it as a separate piece. Your vendor manual should provide details on buying the serial port option. Look to see whether the vendor also supports other connection options that might help in some situations. Many vendors now support a network connection as standard equipment; others support it as an optional module. If your printer doesn't provide a network connection, you may want to look at print server solutions such as Intel's NetportExpress. This small box connects to the side of your printer. It provides three printer connections (1 serial and 2 parallel) and connects to the network through an Ethernet port. The setup software allows you to install and manage the printer server from the administrator workstation.

Choosing between these two connections isn't always easy, even though it seems like a no-brainer. A parallel port delivers the data 8 bits at a time and at a faster rate than a serial port. Choosing the parallel port doesn't take too much thought if your machine has only one printer attached to it. But what if your machine acts as a print server for many different printers? You could easily run out of parallel ports in this situation. Just about everyone resorts to an A/B switch to increase the number of available connections, but there might be a better solution. Connecting your printer to the machine through an unused serial port will allow better access to it. No one will have to flip an A/B switch to use it. (Some electronic A/B switches provide an automatic switching scheme when you send certain commands through the printer cable, but this means training the user to send those commands and a lot of frustration when the user forgets to do so.) The problem is that the access is slower—a lot slower than with a parallel port.

Warning: If you're thinking about using a mechanical A/B switch with a laser printer, be sure its use won't void the printer's warranty. Check with the printer's manufacturer to be sure.

Categorizing how people will use the printers attached to your machine is the next step. Placing a printer that the user is less likely to use or a printer that normally experiences a lower level of activity on a serial port shouldn't cause any problems. Just make sure that you warn people that their print job could take a little longer in the new configuration. I find that this allows me to connect at least four different printers to most machines. Of course, when you get to this level, you need to question whether you should dedicate a machine to act as a print server instead of trying to get by using a workstation on a peer-to-peer network.

Tip: There's a point at which it becomes difficult to support too many printers on a peer-to-peer network. I usually start to look at other solutions once the number of workstations reaches 10 people or the number of printers exceeds 4. After that limit, the performance of a peer-to-peer setup diminishes to the point where it's doubtful that you can get any useful work accomplished. There are always exceptions to the rule, but observing these limits usually provides the best measure of when it's time to upgrade.

These days, some printers come with a built-in NIC. You can attach them directly to the network without using a workstation connection. The two most popular connection types are Ethernet and AppleTalk. Of course, the appropriate selection depends on the network you're running. Whether this solution will work for you depends not on the NIC so much as it depends on the software included with the printer. The printer actually boots as a workstation or a self-contained print server on the network. You see it just as you would see any other workstation. The only difference is that this workstation is dedicated to a single task—printing. You need to find out which networks the vendor supports. Unfortunately, the very nature of this type of connection excludes it from consideration until more vendors come out with Windows 95-specific products. This really is a great solution for a peer-to-peer network, because it allows you to use the printer without overloading the workstation. Adding a printer this way also preserves precious workstation resources such as interrupts and I/O port addresses.

Printers also support some of the more exotic network connections these days, but you might be hard-pressed to find them. One solution that I see gaining in popularity is the wireless LAN. Just think—using this type of connection, you could unwrap the printer, plug it in, and perform a few configuration steps to get it up and running. In the future, adding a printer to the network might be even easier than adding it to your local workstation.

Modems

There are two different kinds of modems: internal and external. I prefer an external modem for several reasons. The biggest reason is portability. I can move a modem in a matter of minutes by disconnecting it from the current machine, moving it, and reconnecting it to the new machine. It's a lot faster and easier than opening the machine to get at the modem. I also find that external modems provide better visual feedback, although some software is taking care of this now by displaying all the indicators that you normally see on the modem. An external modem still has the edge when it comes to troubleshooting, though, because the light indicators you get from your software might not always reflect reality. In addition, most of the software out there doesn't accurately report the modem's connection speed, an important piece of troubleshooting information.

Yet another advantage of the external modem is that you can turn it off without turning off your computer. This can come in handy when you must reset the modem manually and you don't want to reboot your computer. It also provides some people with added peace of mind, because when the modem is turned off, no one can call into their computer. (You can keep people from calling into a computer with an internal modem simply by setting up the modem so that it won't answer the phone line. Seeing the modem power light off is a way to know for sure that this has been done.)

Note: The old 8250 UART chip won't provide a good connection beyond 9600 bps. You must use a 16450 or 16550 UART with a 14.4 Kbps or above modem to ensure an error-free connection. Although there's nothing wrong with the UART itself, the lack of a buffer in the 8250 will cause data overflows. These overflows will in turn cause failures in the connection protocols.

Once you get past the physical location of a modem, you get to the connections. The first connection is the telephone cable required to contact the outside world. Most offices don't have the RJ-11 jacks that a modem uses as standard equipment. They might use a six-wire jack that looks like a larger version of the RJ-11. You can plug an RJ-11 jack into this plug, but I can guarantee that it won't work. Or they might use a long multipin connector that carries many phone lines to the instrument. Normally you have to get an office wired for a modem before you can actually use it. Some recent phone instruments in offices and, increasingly, in hotel rooms, sport a standard RJ-11 jack labeled a "data port." This is a fine place to plug in the cable from your modem. Of course, home users won't run into this problem because a modem uses a standard home telephone jack.

The second connection for a modem, if yours is external, is between the modem and the computer. This cable normally is a standard serial port cable (not a null modem cable) and might have either a 9- or 25-wire connector at each end. (A few external modems differ in this area; they're designed to connect to your computer's parallel port.)

Finally, there might be a second RJ-11 connector on your modem where you can plug in a standard single-line telephone. Doing so will enable you to make and receive voice calls on the same line that you use for modem calls at other times. It also lets you use the modem to dial outgoing voice calls. When the dialing is complete, you just pick up the handset and then press the Esc key to make the communications program let go of the line.

Modems are also rated by speed and capability. The speed at which a modem can communicate is increasing all the time. It seems that just a short time ago a 14.4 Kbps (kilobits per second) connection was considered the fastest around. Now 28.8 Kbps is a requirement and some vendors have introduced 33.6 Kbps modems. You'll soon reap the benefits of using cable modems as cable companies upgrade their transmission lines. There aren't any hard facts right now, but rumor has it that these lines will top out at 128 Mbps. What does this mean for those of you still using 9600 baud modems? It's time for an upgrade, of course. You'll find that a 33.6 Kbps modem is probably the smart buy now, even though some online services still top out at the lower 28.8 Kbps transfer rate, as do many BBSs. This will change with time. Some of the bigger online services, such as CompuServe, already offer 28.8 Kbps lines in the larger cities (and a very few 57.6 Kbps lines as well). You'll also find that more than a few Internet providers offer access at the 28.8 rate. Because a modem can usually communicate with any modem at its speed or lower, there's never a good reason to buy a low-speed modem unless the cost for a higher speed becomes prohibitive.

There are a ton of modem standards, most of which won't make a lot of difference to you as a user. However, there are some standards that you should know about. A lot of standardization has to do with the modem's speed, the way it corrects errors, or the method it uses to compress data. Knowing about these standards could mean the difference between getting a good buy on a modem or getting one that's almost useless. Table 19.2 provides a list of the more common modem standards, but you should also be aware of any new standards that develop around higher-speed modems.

Table 19.2. Common modem standards.

Standard	*Description*
Bell 103	The American standard for 300 baud communication. It's pretty much outdated now, but when PCs first arrived on the scene, it was the rate that everyone used.
Bell 212A	The 1200 baud modem included both this standard and the Bell 103 standard if you bought an American model. The European standards included just enough differences to require a separate modem in most cases. Fortunately, we're well beyond this requirement now.
CCITT V.21	Defines the European standard for 300 baud communications. Like its counterpart, this standard is very much out of date.
CCITT V.22	The European version of the 1200 baud modem standard. It also includes the V.21 standard.
CCITT V.22bis	You might wonder what the "bis" in this standard number means. Just think of it as revision B. In this case, it refers to the general standard for 2400 baud modems.
CCITT V.23	A specialty 1200/75 bps standard for the European market. The slash indicates that the modem sends at one speed and receives at another. Many modems don't support it unless they're specifically designed for overseas use. You might want to check your requirements before getting a modem that supports this standard.
CCITT V.25bis	Defines an alternative command set for modems. In most cases, you won't need these alternative commands unless your modem also supports an X.25 interface.
CCITT V.32	Defines the 4800 bps, 9600 bps, 14.4 Kbps, 19.2 Kbps, and 28.8 Kbps standards.
CCITT V.34	Defines the data compression specifics for the 28.8 Kbps standard. It also defines the 33.6 Kbps standard.
CCITT V.42	Defines a data compression method for modems. It allows the modem to transfer data at apparent rates of up to 19.2 Kbps. This standard also requires the modem to provide MNP levels 2 through 4.

continues

Table 19.2. continued

Standard	Description
CCITT V.42bis	The second revision of a standard that defines how data is compressed on a modem. It allows up to a four times compression factor or an apparent transfer rate of 38.4 Kbps from a 9600 bps modem. Of course, some of this speed is eaten up in control characters and the like.
CCITT V.FAST	This was a proprietary method of defining data compression for the 28.8 Kbps standard. It has been replaced by the CCITT V.34 standard, but some vendors still adhere to this older standard. Always look for a V.34-compatible modem for maximum compatibility.
CCITT X.25	Some asynchronous modems also support this synchronous data transfer standard. You won't need it if your only goal is to communicate with online services or to access your local BBS. It does come in handy if your company plans to send interoffice data via a leased line.
MNP 2-4, 5, 10	Microm Networking Protocol, a standard method of error-correcting for modems. The precise differences between levels aren't important from a user perspective. A higher level is generally better. Essentially, MNP provides a method of sending data in larger blocks, eliminating some of the control characters that usually impede data transmission.

Knowing about these standards should help you choose a modem. It's vitally important that your modem adhere to all the standards for speed and other capabilities. Otherwise, the modem might not be able to make a good connection at a lower speed. Also make sure that the modem manual outlines just how the modem adheres to the standards. It should include information on FCC rules Parts 15 and 68 or the equivalent for the country you're in. The manual should also state what kind of serial port it can connect to. The current standard is RS-232C. Some modems require that standard; others can use older ports. In most cases, you won't need to worry unless you have an older machine.

Here's the bottom line: You want a modem that will work with as many other modems as possible, over phone line connections that might be anything from superb to horrible. The more standards your modem supports, the more likely it is to work when you need it to. (Also look for support for fax/modem standards if you'd like to be able to send or receive faxes as well—a point discussed in more detail in the next section.)

Fax Boards

The preceding section introduced you to modem connections. Fax boards characteristically appear on the same board as the modem, or perhaps on a daughter card. They usually use the same telephone connector as the modem.

After looking at the section on modems, you might wonder what's in store for you in this section. You should follow some general rules of thumb when selecting a fax board. The most important of these is to make sure that your modem will communicate correctly with whatever is at the other end of the line. For normal faxing to standard fax machines, support for Group 3 faxes is sufficient. Supporting various error-correction protocols can help ensure that your faxes arrive ungarbled.

If you use an application that requires DCA/Intel CAS (communicating applications specification) compatibility, you must be sure to get a fax board that supports that standard. For example, many database applications require a fax board with this capability before they'll recognize it. You'll also want to make sure that the fax follows the same version of the standard that the application requires, because there are some variances between versions of the specification.

Some vendors decided to follow the CAS standard because it provided a simplified method of accessing the fax. Before this time, every fax used its own set of port addresses and usually required a special application to access it. Using the CAS standard still allows for that flexibility, but it provides an API that allows a program to determine what that interface is and how to use it.

The only problem with CAS is cost. It's very expensive to buy a CAS-compatible fax. Invariably, the modem part of the equation is an extra cost. Fortunately, Windows 95 appears to support a wide range of fax/modems, even those that don't support CAS. If all you plan to do is fax documents using Exchange, you might be able to do so without buying a lot of fancy hardware.

Every fax/modem transfer consists of five phases. The ITU (formerly CCITT) defines these phases in several standards, which we'll examine later. These five phases aren't cast in concrete, and each one could repeat during any given session. It all depends on the capabilities of your fax/modem, the software you're using, and the environment conditions at the time.

- **Phase 1, call establishment:** Your computer calls another computer or a standard fax machine.
- **Phase 2, pre-message procedure:** The sending and receiving machines select parameters that will allow them to transfer data at the fastest possible rate. These parameters also take into account the resolution, modulation, and other factors.
- **Phase 3, message transmission:** This is the phase in which the actual data transfer takes place. If the initial group of parameters set in Phase 2 end in less-than-optimal results, the fax/modem will perform Phase 2 and Phase 3 again as required.
- **Phase 4, post-message procedure:** Some software considers each page as a separate message. In fact, that's the way your fax machine works as well. Phase 4 allows the sending and receiving machines to evaluate the results of each message and then raise or lower the transmission speed as required. This is also the phase in which the sending machine transmits a page break marker. This is the same thing as a form feed on a printer, except that the fax might simply print a line across the page or might actually cut off the page at that point. Remember that faxes can be either long or short, depending on the message needs.

- **Phase 5, call clear down:** This is the easiest part of the conversion. The two machines hang up the phone after the sending machine transmits an end-of-transmission signal.

As with modems, there are several fax/modem specifications. You'll want a fax/modem that adheres to the following ITU standards. Table 19.3 lists these various standards.

Table 19.3. Common fax/modem standards.

Standard	*Description*
ITU T.4	Defines the image transfer portion of the session used in Phase 3.
ITU T.30	Defines the negotiation and interpage phases (2, 3, 4, and 5). A normal multipage transfer uses T.30 only at the beginning of the call, between pages, and after the last page.
CCITT V.17	Defines the specifications for the 4800/1200 bps speed. The slash shows that the fax receives at one speed and sends at another. If the fax portion of a fax/modem is the sender, the data is sent at 4800, but the fax receives acknowledgment at 1200. Some vendors reduce the complexity of this rating by giving only the first number (the higher of the two speeds), but this can be misleading.
CCITT V.27	Defines the specifications for the 9600/7200 bps speed.
CCITT V.29	Defines the specifications for the 14400/12000 bps speed.

Note: The ITU V.34 standard now defines the combined voice, FAX, and data standards for modems. This one standard includes both the 28.8 Kbps and 33.6 Kbps speeds. There are also rumors of a 56 Kbps specification in the works, but it hasn't appeared on the scene as of this writing.

Microsoft also provides for two different classes of fax communication between fax/modems. Here's the user view of what these different classes mean. Class 1 communications send an editable fax to the other party. This means that the fax appears as actual text that the other party can edit. Class 2 communications are more like the fax you usually receive. They're graphic representations of the text and graphics in the document. This is the same format as Group 3 faxes, like the one you're used to seeing in the office.

The real-world difference between Class 1 and Class 2 fax/modems is really quite distinct. A Class 1 fax performs both the T.4 and T.30 protocols in software. This allows the additional flexibility that Windows 95 needs to create editable faxes. All data translation is performed by Windows 95 drivers. A Class 2 fax performs the T.4 protocol in firmware—an EEPROM in the modem that does part of the work for the processor. This is a faster solution because it removes part of the processing burden from the processor. A Class 2 fax/modem should also be able to create editable faxes. However, this is where the plot thickens. Because the Class 2 standard isn't defined very well, Microsoft didn't have any dependable information on what to expect from a Class 2 fax/modem. They made the decision to restrict Class 2 faxes to the Group 3 graphics format.

Note: The Electronic Industries Association (EIA) recently approved a new Class 2 standard that stringently defines what vendors need to provide in firmware. As a result, you might see software that uses Class 2 fax/modems more efficiently in the next six months to a year. Look for software vendors to make a big deal out of the new "high-speed" fax transmission capabilities offered by their products sometime in the future. This fax/modem software will use this new Class 2 fax/modem specification.

CD-ROM Players

CD-ROMs usually have two connections that you need to worry about. The first is the bus connector that allows data transfer between the computer and the CD-ROM. Generally, this is a SCSI connector or an IDE or EIDE connection. The principle is the same; the data transfer rate might be a lot slower, depending on the method of connection. SCSI will always beat IDE hands down, but SCSI and EIDE offer comparable performance. The bus connector for a CD-ROM serves the same purpose as the equivalent connector for your hard drive. It allows you to transfer data from the CD-ROM to your machine.

Some people don't really think about the second connection. They'll try to use the CD-ROM with a game or another application that plays sound right off the CD—just as you would with a music CD—and discover that the game doesn't appear to work with their machine. The problem is that they don't have the RCA plugs in the back of the CD-ROM drive connected to anything. External CD-ROM drives use the RCA connectors (the ones that look like the speaker connectors on your stereo). Internal CD-ROM drives usually require some type of special connector for your sound card. This is a proprietary connector in some cases; in other cases, the vendor will try to make you believe that their common cable really is proprietary. Check with your local computer store to see whether they have an inexpensive alternative to the expensive cable that the vendors normally offer.

Peter's Principle: How Much Speed Do You Need?

Once you get the connectors in place, your CD-ROM drive is ready to go. However, the speed at which it goes is cause for concern for many people. Although a single-speed CD-ROM drive might be adequate for data transfer, it won't work for multimedia applications at all. I recently bought a CD game. The sound was great on my 4X (four-speed) CD-ROM drive, but the same CD sounded very jerky and hesitated a lot on my 1X drive.

There's a gray area when it comes to other drive speeds. A 2X drive will probably work for the majority of older games because game vendors try to get every ounce of speed from them that they can. Newer games may require 3X or even 4X drives to get the job done—be sure to check the game package before you buy. On the other hand, you'll probably get very poor results from most multimedia education products using a 2X drive. And don't even think about using a 2X drive for full-motion video. A 3X drive is marginal for full-motion video. Plan on missing some frames. It will work perfectly with the vast majority of educational multimedia applications and with just about every game out there.

Of course, there are other performance factors as well. The same factors that affect the performance of your hard drive also affect CDs. Things such as bus width and hardware caches can make a big difference in the actual performance you'll see. Even the controller you choose will make a big difference in the performance you get from your CD. It hardly pays to use a 16-bit controller with a 4X CD drive. You'll want to maximize performance by using a 32-bit controller instead.

Buying the best CD-ROM player available is probably a good idea when you consider the small price differential between them. The latest 8X and 10X drives cost only a small amount more than the price of a 4X drive (when you can still find them that slow). However, if you're on a tight budget and need to get the best value for your money, try to match the speed of your drive with the type of use it will get. A drive that's too slow for the job will only frustrate you and make it impossible to do the required work. Just imagine the effect of a multimedia presentation in which a slow drive, rather than your stunning graphics and sound, grabs the audience's attention.

In addition to the other connections on your CD-ROM drive, there's a headphone connector on the front of it. Imagine my surprise when I plugged some headphones in and heard sound out of my speakers and headset at the same time. Some vendors disable the speaker output when you plug in the headset; others don't. You'll want to check out this feature if this is an important consideration for your application.

CD-ROM recorders have also become a big item. You can get one of these devices for around $1,000, although most vendors bring them in at just below this price. (At least one person has told me that he has seen 2X CD-ROM recorders in the $500 range, but this seems to be a bargain-basement price for a lower-quality device.) Getting a CD-ROM recorder might seem like the way to go because you can make copies of all those CDs you've been collecting for archive purposes. The bottom line is that CD-ROM records exact a price in performance. The most you'll be able to get is a 4X drive—and that's when playing back. The maximum record speed is usually half the playback speed. If you plan on using your CD-ROM drive for multimedia, don't pay the extra amount for a slower drive with recording capabilities.

Tip: The price of CD-ROM recorders has dropped significantly in recent months. In the near future, you may be able to buy a CD-ROM recorder for about three times the price of a player. There are two advantages to buying a CD-ROM recorder instead of a player. First, you can use it to make archive copies of CDs. Despite popular folklore, CDs are resistant—not impervious—to damage. Considering the cost of some CDs and the less-than-thrilling replacement policy some vendors have, an archive copy could make a big difference when the inevitable does occur. Second, you could use a CD-ROM recorder in place of a backup tape. The permanent nature of the backup makes it a medium of choice in cases where long-term storage is desired, such as with law firms and the medical community. A CD-ROM backup is also faster than some types of tape backup, although I won't say that you can't get better performance out of some DAT tapes. One thing is certain: The random-access feature of a CD makes it a lot faster than a tape for data retrieval.

Making Software Attachments

Once you get your hardware up and running, you have to get some software to talk to it in order to do any useful work. That's where some of the utilities you get with Windows 95 come in. They don't necessarily provide the best capabilities, but they do provide enough for you to get going. In fact, you might be surprised at just how well they meet some of your needs.

Looking Ahead: The following sections describe several of the utilities that come with Windows 95. These utilities won't help you "surf the Net" or download the latest industry gossip. We'll cover some types of general online communication services (such as those provided in Microsoft Exchange) in the next chapter when we look at online services. Look at Chapter 21 if you want to learn how to surf the Net. These utilities help you make the necessary connections.

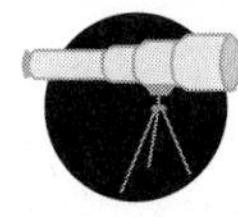

Peter's Principle: The Right Kind of Connection

It might be very tempting to use a single type of connection to meet all your computing needs, but that wouldn't be the most efficient way to do things. You might view a direct cable connection as the panacea for all your portable data-transfer woes, but the direct cable connection is really designed for occasional use rather than daily use. A direct cable connection (using either serial or parallel ports to link two computers in conjunction with the Windows 95 "Direct Connection" program, the roughly equivalent DOS Interlink program, or Laplink, or a similar third-party program) works fine for those quick transfers

from one machine to another when you have a fairly large amount of data to move. For example, it works very well when you initially set up the portable.

If you use a portable on a daily basis, using such an Interlink-style connection is a waste of time. You'll want to find some other method of creating your connection to the desktop. If you have a docking station that can accept a standard network card, or if you plug in a PCMCIA network card, you'll be able to use this much-faster Ethernet connection to make your data transfers. However, this works only if you have a network and a PCMCIA card. Alternatively, you could get an external Ethernet adapter that plugs into your portable's parallel port. This solution works fine, but it isn't quite as speedy as the standard network interface cards that plug into the computer's bus or the PCMCIA network adapters.

Chapter 2 briefly covers the Briefcase, and Chapter 18 covers it in more detail. This isn't a physical connection to your desktop machine, but it does do the job for smaller amounts of data. In fact, you'll find out that a Briefcase can hold a substantial amount of data if you use it correctly.

Okay, so the network and Briefcase options are out of the question because you're out of town. You can still make a connection to your desktop by using Dial-Up Networking. It won't be as fast as some of the other techniques, but it will allow you to get the data you require while on the road or when working from home.

Windows 95 provides a lot of different connections. You need to use the right one for the job, and that means taking the time to learn about the various options available to you. A connection that works well in one instance could be a time killer in another. Don't succumb to the one-connection way of computing; use every tool that Windows 95 provides.

Making a Direct Cable Connection

Portable users will love the direct cable-connection feature that Windows 95 provides. You can make a direct connection using the serial or the parallel port. Of course, the parallel port is a lot faster than the serial port, but either connection will net good results. Direct Cable Connection is a much better version of a similar utility offered with DOS version 5.0 and above. The older version tied up the host machine as the client looked around for the files it needed. This new version allows you to make the connection in the background, effectively freeing the host for use while the client makes the required transactions.

Windows 95 won't automatically install this utility as part of a default package. It isn't part of a standard application such as Dial-Up Networking, either. You need to load the separate Direct Cable Connection utility by using the Add/Remove Programs applet. I've visited this procedure elsewhere, so I won't go through it again here.

Once you get Direct Cable Connection installed, you have to get the host set up. This means that you'll define the port that your machine will use and its mode. Let's look at this procedure first.

Tip: You can create the required data-transfer serial cable by using a standard serial cable, a null modem, and a gender changer. This will provide all the components you need to make a data-transfer cable using a standard modem cable. Your local electronics or computer store can usually provide the null modem and gender changer.

1. Use a special serial or parallel cable to connect the two computers. You can normally get one of these at your local computer store. Be sure to tell them that you plan to connect two computers for the purpose of data transfer. The parallel cable uses a very special crossover wiring, and the serial cable must be wired with the required wires cross-connected, or else you'll need to use a null modem as well for the connection to work.
2. Open the Direct Cable Connection utility on the host computer. You should see a dialog box similar to the one shown in Figure 19.1. Notice the Listen button. This allows you to start listening for the client computer immediately after opening the program, if you already have it configured. The dialog box displays the current settings so that you can find out whether you can use them.

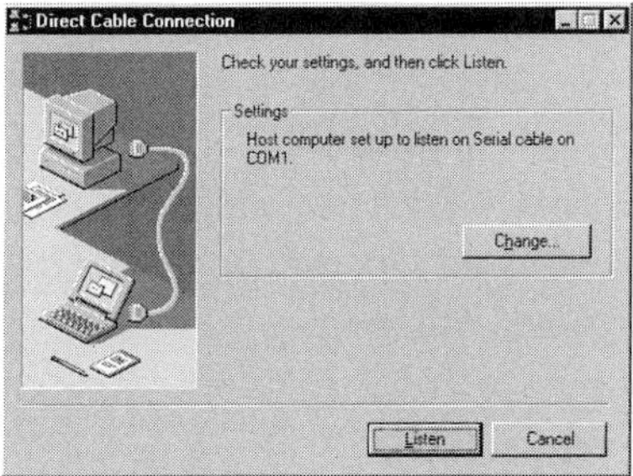

Figure 19.1.
The initial Direct Cable Connection dialog box allows you to go directly to listen mode.

3. Click Change to display the dialog box shown in Figure 19.2. Notice that there are two radio buttons—one for each mode of operation. One computer must provide host services; the other must act as a client. Normally, the computer supplying resources is the host. You can't create a dual connection by using Direct Cable Connection. In other words, you can't make it act as a pseudo-peer-to-peer network with both machines acting as servers.
4. Select the service type—in this case, Host—and click Next. You'll see a dialog box similar to the one shown in Figure 19.3. Notice that the local ports are listed automatically. You can add other ports by using the Install New Ports button.
5. Select the port you want. Be sure to use the same type of port on both machines. Click Next. You'll see the dialog box shown in Figure 19.4.

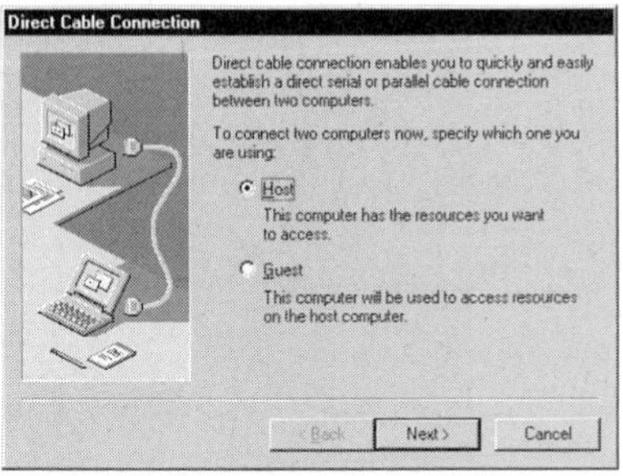

Figure 19.2.
This dialog box allows you to select the operating mode.

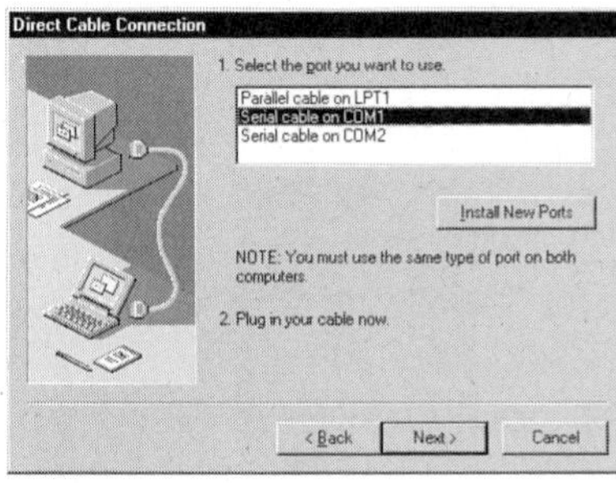

Figure 19.3.
This dialog box allows you to select the port used for data transfer.

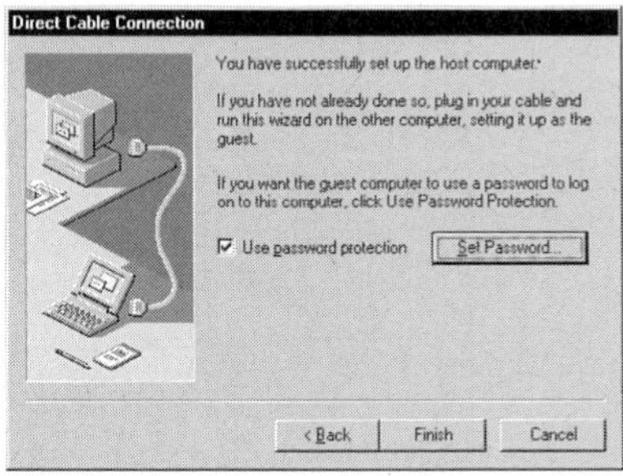

Figure 19.4.
Use this dialog box to set a password, if necessary.

Tip: The password option in this dialog box comes in handy when more than one person needs to use the direct cable connection to a machine. You could leave the host running in the background and then connect other machines as necessary—even remote machines. However, this feature is limited, especially when you consider that the Dial-Up Networking utility allows remote users to call into a machine using a better interface. Microsoft doesn't provide the Dial-Up Networking host software with Windows 95. Connecting your serial cable to a modem will allow you to use a desktop machine as a rudimentary remote server, but it would probably be better to invest in software designed for remote access if you make this type of connection very often.

6. Check the Use Password Protection check box if you want to password-protect your connection. If you select this option, use the Set Password button to change the password from a blank.
7. Click Finish. Direct Cable Connection will wait for the client machine to log in, as shown in Figure 19.5. If the client doesn't respond in about 30 seconds, Direct Cable Connection will ask whether it's properly connected. Ignore the message until you get the other machine running.

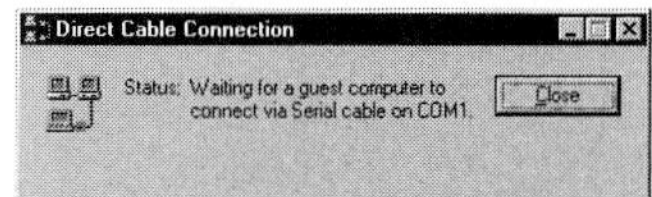

Figure 19.5.
Once you complete the Direct Cable Connection setup, it will wait in the background for a connection.

The procedure for setting up a guest computer is exactly the same as for a host computer. The only difference is that you don't need to set a password. Once the two computers establish a connection, the client computer will be able to use the resources of the host.

Using Dial-Up Networking

Dial-Up Networking under Windows 95 is limited to calling into a server. Microsoft decided not to provide the host software required to turn your Windows 95 workstation into a host. (Microsoft does include the host software as part of Microsoft Plus!, an add-on package for Windows 95 that's described in Chapter 28.) Most of the time, this means that you'll need to call into a Windows NT server—at least until third-party software vendors create solutions for other network servers.

Before you can use Dial-Up Networking, you'll need to install it using the Add/Remove Programs applet in Control Panel. I covered that procedure earlier in this book, so I won't discuss it again here. The following paragraphs assume that you've already installed Dial-Up Networking.

Creating a Connection

In most cases all you'll really want to do with Dial-Up Networking is create a simple connection. This section describes the minimum that you'll need to do to create a connection of any kind. As with the Printers folder visited earlier in this book, Dial-Up Networking has its own folder. You'll always see at least one component in that folder: the Make New Connection applet. Let's look at this part of the service first.

1. Open the Dial-Up Networking folder. Double-click the Make New Connection applet. You should see the dialog box shown in Figure 19.6. Note that the utility suggests a default name of My Connection. Be sure to provide a descriptive name here if you plan to create

more than one connection. Notice that this dialog box also provides a Configure button, which brings up the same set of dialog boxes for the Modems applet described in Chapter 14.

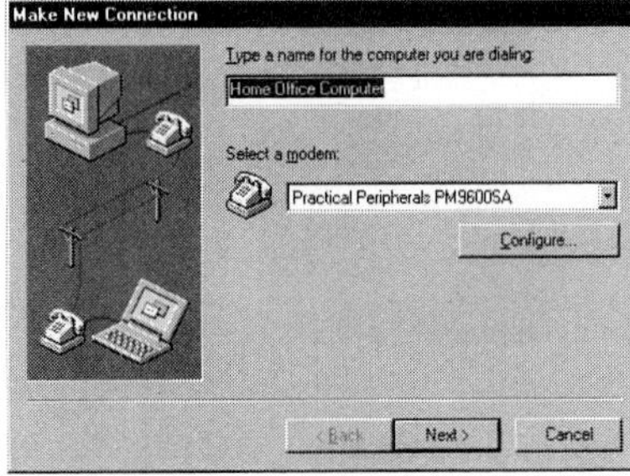

Figure 19.6.
The initial Make New Connection dialog box allows you to specify the name of the computer you're calling and the modem type.

2. Once you select a connection name, choose a modem model, configure the connection, and click Next. The next dialog box, shown in Figure 19.7, allows you to input the area code and telephone number for your connection. Notice the Country Code list box, which allows you to create connections even if you aren't currently at home.

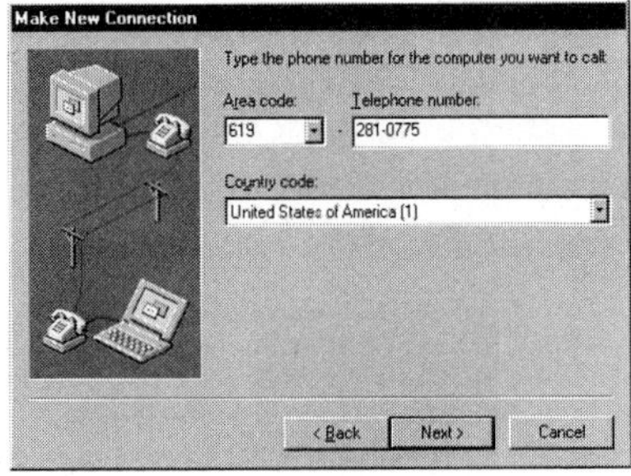

Figure 19.7.
At a minimum, you'll need to provide an area code and telephone number for the new connection.

3. Click Next to see the dialog box shown in Figure 19.8. This is the final screen. The Make New Connection applet gives you one more chance to change the connection name before it saves it. Of course, you can always change the name later if you need to.

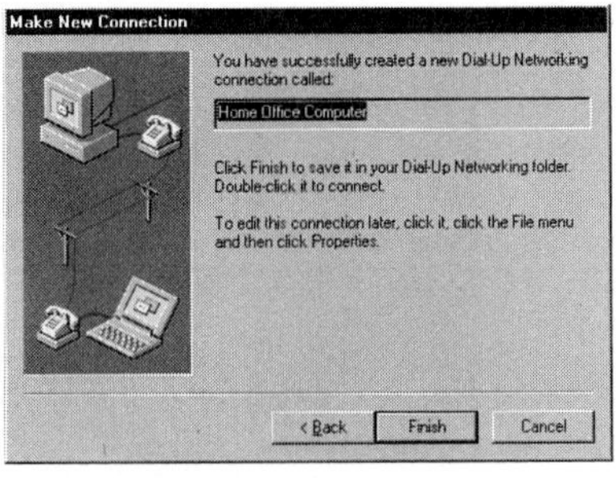

Figure 19.8.
The Make New Connection dialog box gives you one last chance to change the connection name before saving it.

Using the Connection

Creating a connection is the first part of the equation. Using the connection after you create it is simple. Just double-click the Connection icon to see the dialog box shown in Figure 19.9. Notice that your name and the telephone number you need to call are automatically added to the dialog box. The only thing you need to add is the password for the machine that you want to call.

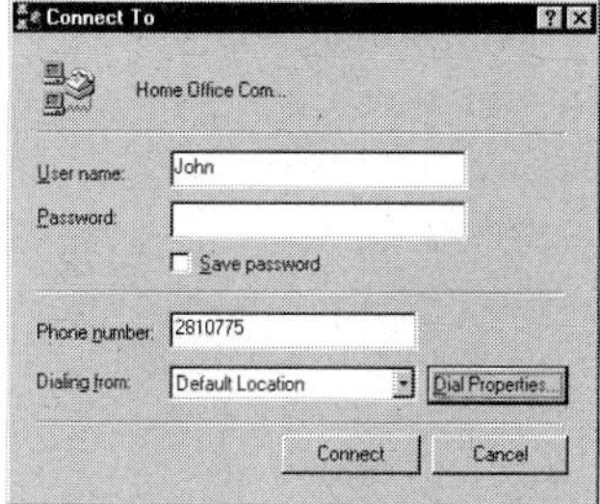

Figure 19.9.
Using a connection after you define it is easy. Just a double-click and a password are all you need.

If you use the same connection a lot and you have password protection enabled for getting into Windows 95, you may want to check the Save Password check box. Saving your password is probably a safe bet for an Internet connection, but you may want to refrain from saving passwords for a connection to the company network, where security is paramount. Now all you need to do to use the connection is double-click to open it, and then click the Connect button.

Tip: Some people have had problems getting Windows 95 to remember their passwords. They'll check the Save Password check box, but the password is still missing the next time they try to use a connection. There's a fairly simple fix for this problem that works in a majority of cases. In many cases the problem you're seeing is a corrupt password file. All you need to do is erase the PWL file that corresponds to your login name in the main Windows 95 directory. Of course, you'll have to enter all of your passwords from scratch again, but everything should work once you get this task accomplished.

Calling from Another Location

In most cases you'll find that once you create a connection, you never need to look at it again. What happens, though, if you need to call from another location? You can select any predefined location from the Dialing From list box. But let's say that you're dialing from another location, perhaps outside the country. The following procedure shows you how to quickly add a new location to the Dialing From list box by using the Dial Properties button. (Double-click your connection to display the Connect To dialog box.)

1. Click the Dial Properties button shown in Figure 19.9. You'll see the dialog box shown in Figure 19.10. Notice that this dialog box contains everything you need to define a local connection.

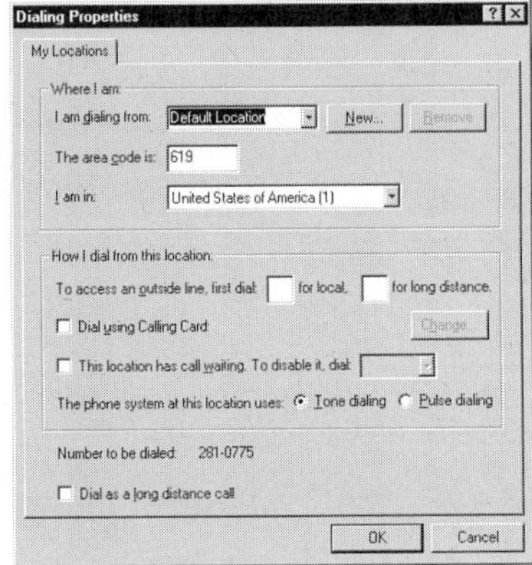

Figure 19.10.
The Dialing Properties dialog box contains a complete description of your current location.

2. Click the New button. You'll see the dialog box shown in Figure 19.11.
3. Type a descriptive location name and click OK. You'll see the Dialing Properties dialog box shown in Figure 19.10. Notice that it contains all the settings I described for the default location.

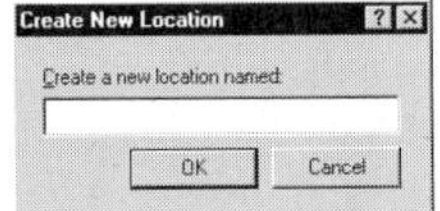

Figure 19.11.
The Create New Location dialog box allows you to specify a new location.

4. Change the area code and country fields to match your current location. Don't worry about any long-distance considerations. Windows 95 will take care of that for you automatically. All you need to know is your current location.
5. The How I Dial From This Location group contains settings that describe the telephone connection. Most of the fields are self-explanatory. The one field that might require a little explanation is the Calling Card field. You'll need to work with your local calling-card company to fill this out completely. Windows 95 presents the dialog box shown in Figure 19.12. You need to supply a calling card type and perhaps a calling card number.

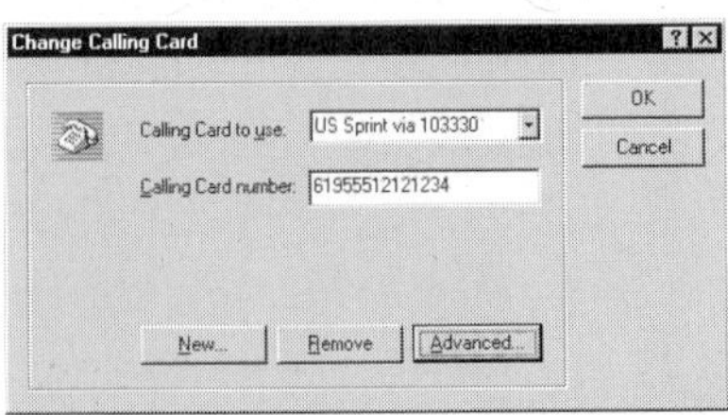

Figure 19.12.
Setting your calling card parameters correctly is very important.

6. Once you complete the Location dialog box, click OK to save it. Notice how the telephone number automatically changes to reflect your location. Figure 19.13 shows an example of dialing from another country instead of within your current country. Windows 95 automatically includes all the required codes for you.

Figure 19.13.
Windows 95 automatically tracks details such as the country code for you.

Of course, the last thing you need to do is click Connect to actually make the connection. When you do so, Windows 95 will send the server your name and password. It will also take care of details such as using your phone card if you supply that information. Configuring the connection the first time might take time, but once you get it done, everything is automatic from that point on.

Modifying a Connection

Note: Even though any Windows 95 user will be able to use most of the information in this section, a lot of new features and changes for the OSR2 version of Windows 95 are included. Don't worry, though—I'll always let you know when a change or feature is OSR2-specific. If you're using one of the other versions of Windows 95 on your machine, just ignore the OSR2-specific comments.

You'll likely run into a situation where you want to modify an existing connection. For example, you may change ISPs and need to change your Internet access number. This capability also comes in handy if you need to change your connection type or server type, troubleshoot a connection problem, or simply change your dialing country. It's important to remember that you can access all your connections from two places. Windows 95 always places a Dial-Up Networking folder in Explorer. You'll also find a Dial-Up Networking entry in the Accessories folder within the Start menu. Opening the Dial-Up Networking properties dialog box is easy. Just right-click the connection you want to modify, and select Properties from the context menu. You'll see a dialog box similar to the one shown in Figure 19.14. (OSR2 users will see the slightly different dialog box shown in Figure 19.15.)

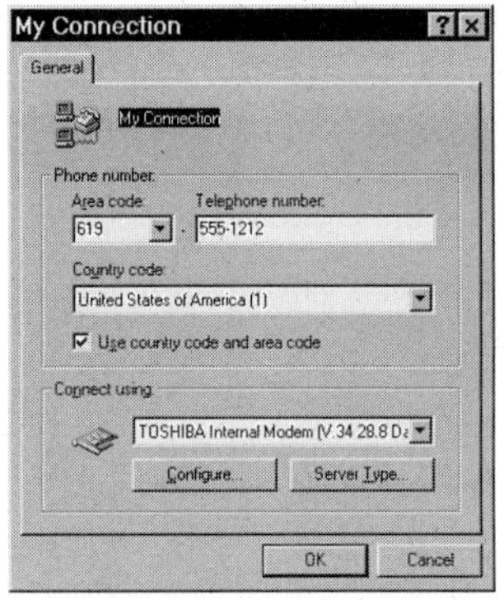

Figure 19.14.
The Dial-Up Networking properties dialog box always contains the name of your connection in the title bar.

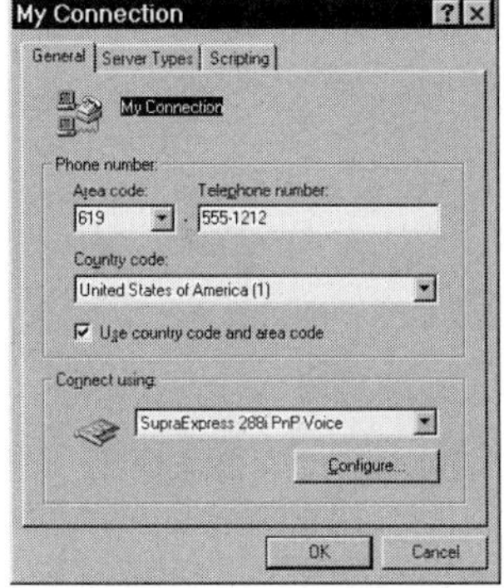

Figure 19.15.
OSR2 users will find some added capabilities in this version of the Dial-Up Networking properties dialog box.

Note: The OSR2 Dial-Up Networking properties dialog box contains an extra capability that the older versions of Windows 95 didn't contain; the next section of this chapter discusses this Scripting page. Even though the dialog box looks slightly different, you'll find all the capabilities of the older versions of Windows 95 here.

This dialog box contains most of the information you used to create the connection in the first place. You can use it to change the area code, telephone number, and country code, along with the modem you want to use. There isn't anything here that I haven't already discussed. To see some special settings, click the Server Type button (or select the Server Types page if you're using the OSR2 version of Windows 95).

Figure 19.16 shows some settings that you didn't get to change when you created the connection, because Windows 95 assumes certain defaults. Let's look at these entries. The first field contains a list of server types. Every Windows 95 installation supports at least three kinds of server: NPN (Novell NetWare networks), PPP (Windows NT, Windows 95, or Internet connection), and a special connection for Windows for Workgroups (Windows 3.x). The OSR2 version of Windows 95 supports two additional server types: CSLIP (UNIX connection with IP header compression) and SLIP (a standard UNIX connection).

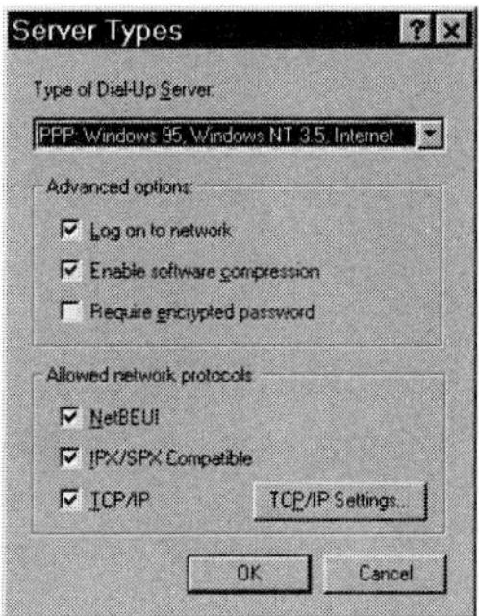

Figure 19.16.
The Server Types dialog box allows you to configure your connection in a variety of ways.

Right below the Type of Dial-Up Server field, you'll find a group of check boxes that control the advanced options for your connection. In most cases, you'll never have to modify these options. The Log On to Network check box tells Windows 95 that you want to log onto the server automatically. You can't use this option with callback systems—it works only with servers that allow automatic login, such as the Internet. The second check box, Enable Software Compression, sets up software compression to reduce the transfer time for any data you want to send to or receive from the server. You'll find that this option works in most cases, but you'll want to disable it for UNIX connections or older mainframe connections that don't support encryption. You'll also want to disable this option if you're using hardware compression on a dedicated connection. The Require Encrypted Password option enables software encryption of your user name and password. Obviously, the server has to support this option before you can use it. Normally your user name and password are sent using plain ASCII.

The final section of this dialog box contains a list of allowed protocols. Normally you'll see every protocol installed on your machine checked. In some cases, this causes problems. For example, if you have TCP/IP installed for a local intranet, use Novell NetWare for your file server, and also use a dial-up connection to the Internet, you'll want to disable all the protocols listed here except TCP/IP. Otherwise, you'll find that your connection conflicts with the NetWare connection and could even cause problems with your local intranet. Disabling the protocols you don't need also seems to speed up the connection, because Windows 95 doesn't have to spend as much time monitoring it.

You'll notice that there's also a TCP/IP button on this dialog box. It displays a TCP/IP Settings dialog box like the one shown in Figure 19.17. The "Configuring TCP/IP—The Short Form" section of Chapter 23 discusses the ins and outs of TCP/IP.

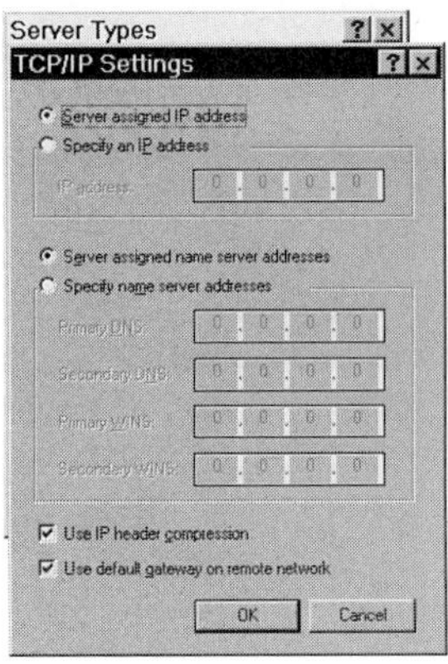

Figure 19.17.
You can configure the TCP/IP settings used on a connection-by-connection basis, using the TCP/IP Settings dialog box.

Scripting Enhancements Provided by OSR2

The connections provided by older version of Windows 95 worked fine if you had a straight connection. However, the connection feature could also become a bit cumbersome if you wanted to create a connection for something like a Windows NT server. Because a standard connection still works for the vast majority of users out there, Microsoft wisely chose to leave it alone. To supplement the standard connection, the OSR2 version of Windows 95 provides a scripting capability. If you create a script and then add it to a connection, Windows 95 uses the script instead of the standard connection setup to make your dial-up connection to a server work. Figure 19.18 shows the Scripting page of the Dial-Up Connection properties dialog box. As you can see, adding a script is quite easy (writing one may be a different story).

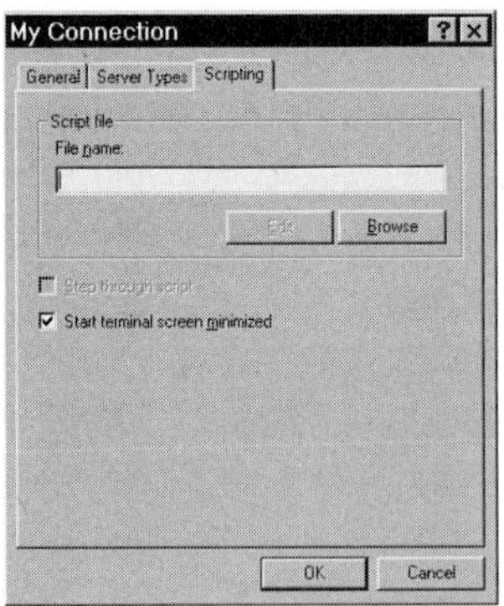

Figure 19.18.
The OSR2 version of Windows 95 provides a new scripting capability that greatly enhances the flexibility of Dial-Up Networking.

Note: This section assumes you have at least a modicum of programming experience. You need to know what a variable is and have a least a little experience creating macros. Obviously, the more programming experience you have, the faster you'll learn the material in this section.

Let's take a look at the dialog box first. Up at the top you'll see the File Name field that contains the name of the script file you want to use. Notice the two buttons directly below this field. The first, Edit, allows you to modify your script. The second, Browse, displays a File Open dialog box that you can use to find a script file. There are also two check boxes on this page. The Step Through Script option walks you through your script one line at a time when you use the connection. It's useful for troubleshooting a script when you first create it, but you'll want to disable this option later. The second option, Start Terminal Screen Minimized, is handy once you've debugged your script, because it keeps screen clutter to a minimum. However, you'll want to keep this option unchecked until you're certain that the script will work as intended.

Starting a Script

Now that we've looked at how you can incorporate scripts into your connection, let's look at scripting itself. You'll always create a script by using a text editor such as Notepad. A script can't contain any fancy formatting or other additions that you normally associate with a word processing document. Script files should also have an .SCP extension to make them easy to find.

So, now you have a blank text file with an .SCP extension. How do you start the scripting process? If you've programmed in C, some of what I'm going to tell you will sound familiar. Scripts use procedures. You'll enclose all your scripting code with a pair of statements: `Proc` and `endproc`. Every script has to have a main procedure, and you should add some comments to tell other people (or simply remind yourself) how it works. These are the first lines of text that you'll add to your script file:

```
; This is a comment telling about the script.
proc main
endproc
```

Okay, now that you have a main procedure, Windows 95 will actually recognize this file as a script. It still won't do anything, though, until you add some functional code to it. You may also want to use variables.

Using Variables

Let's talk about variables. You must declare all of the variables you use, and these declarations have to appear at the beginning of the procedure. A declaration always contains the variable type and the variable name; you can also assign the variable a value. Dial-Up Networking won't allow you to declare variables outside a procedure. Variable names always begin with a letter or an underscore—you can't use reserved names for a variable. The following lists shows what types of variables you can use within a script:

- **Integer:** Any number, either positive or negative.
- **String:** A collection of characters such as `"Hello World"`. You may also have strings that contain numbers.
- **Boolean:** Variables that are either true or false.

Now that you've seen what kinds of variables you can use, let's look at them in action. Here's a script with some variables. Some of them are declared incorrectly (or not at all) so you can see what to avoid:

```
; This script shows some variables.
proc main
    ; This is an integer variable.
    integer    iValue
    ; This is a string variable with an assigned value.
    string     sMyString = "Hello"
    ; This is a boolean variable.
    boolean    lAmICorrect
    ; This is the first line of code, so you can't declare any more variables.
    iValue = 5 * 5
    ; This variable doesn't exist, so the script will stop here.
    iValue2 = iValue
    ; All declarations must appear before the first line of code, so this won't work.
    integer    iValue2
endproc
```

You'll also find some predefined variables used with Dial-Up Networking scripts. Table 19.4 provides a list of these predefined variables and their purposes.

Table 19.4. Predefined script variables.

Name	*Type*	*Description*
`$USERID`	String	The name of the user as it appears in the User Name field of the Connect To dialog box (refer to Figure 19.9).
`$PASSWORD`	String	The user's password as it appears in the Password field of the Connect To dialog box (refer to Figure 19.9).
`$SUCCESS`	Boolean	A variable that's set by certain commands. You can use this variable to determine whether a command succeeded.
`$FAILURE`	Boolean	A variable that's set by certain commands. You can use this variable to determine whether a command failed.

Special Considerations for Strings

Trying to get a string to do everything you need it to do could prove frustrating if the scripting language didn't provide a few additional features. For example, how do you send a control character to the server? A lot of servers require you to send a Ctrl+Break character before they'll even respond. The caret translation feature takes care of this. You simply place a caret in front of one of the first 26 characters. For example, "^M" sends a carriage return and "^C" sends a Ctrl+Break. (Make sure that you always use quotes when defining a string in a script, even if that string represents a control character.)

There are some text substitutions for control characters as well. For example, `"<cr>"` is a carriage return and `"<lf>"` is a line feed. Using a `"<cr>"` in your code is a lot less cryptic than `"^M"`.

Finally, you'll find that Dial-Up Networking scripts support several escape character sequences that C programmers are familiar with. For example, using "\"" in your code produces a double quote. You also need a way to display the caret. You do it like this: "\^". Likewise, you need a way to display the backslash—"\\"—and the less-than sign—"\<".

Using Commands

The scripting language provided with Dial-Up Networking supports certain commands right out of the box. You can also create other commands (very simple ones) using the proc and endproc keywords to create a procedure. Let's take a look at the commands that you get as part of the product. Table 19.5 lists the built-in commands that you can use within a script.

Table 19.5. Built-in script commands.

Command	*Description*
delay <*iSeconds*>	Allows you to pause the script for *iSeconds*. You'd usually use this kind of a command when you need to wait for the hardware to complete a task. For example, when dialing out from the company PBX, you may have to wait for it to make a connection to an outside line.
getip [<*iIP*>]	Use this command to retrieve the IP from the host. If your ISP sends the IP in the string, you can use the optional *iIP* variable to specify which IP you want.
goto <*Label*>	Basic programmers should be familiar with this script command. It tells the script to go to the label you've defined. A label is a piece of stand-alone text followed by a colon. For example, MyLabel: is a label.
halt	This command tells the script to stop. You'd normally use it as part of your error control or in response to an unexpected event. This command doesn't remove the terminal window—which allows you to see what kind of error condition halted the script.
if <*lValue*> then	Every scripting language needs some kind of flow ... endif control. The if command checks for a specific condition (a Boolean value) specified by *lValue*. If the condition is true, the script commands between then and endif are executed. If not, program execution continues with the first command after then. Unlike more complex programming languages, you won't find an else clause in this script language.

continues

Table 19.5. continued

Command	*Description*
`set port databits <iValue>`	Use this command to set the number of data bits used for communication purposes. Essentially it allows you to set up the communications port automatically instead of relying on the user to do so manually. You have a choice of 5, 6, 7, or 8 data bits.
`set port parity <sValue>`	Like the `set port databits` command, this command allows you to set up the communications port. Choose between none, odd, even, mark, and space.
`set port stopbits <iValue>`	This is the final communications-port-specific command. Use it to set the number of stop bits to 1 or 2.
`set screen keyboard <lValue>`	You may not want the user to interact with the host computer. Using this command with a value of `Off` turns the keyboard off in the terminal window. You can turn the keyboard back on by using this command with a value of `On`.
`set ipaddr <sValue>`	Use this command to set the workstation's IP address for the session. `sValue` must contain a string in IP format, such as this one: `"200.100.100.1"`.
`transmit <sValue> [raw]`	One of the reasons for creating scripts in the first place is to send specialized information to the host computer. You use the `transmit` command to perform this task. `sValue` can contain any string of characters that you choose. Normally Dial-Up Networking interprets the string as shown in the earlier section "Special Considerations for Strings." You can send the actual string without any interpretation by adding the `raw` argument to this command. You'll also find the `raw` argument useful when sending predefined strings like those shown in Table 19.4.
`waitfor`	This is the most complex command provided by the script language. Its basic function is to receive input from the host and act on it. I discuss this command in the text that follows this table.
`while <lValue> do ... enddo`	Looping commands are a big part of writing any script or macro. The `while` loop tells Dial-Up Networking to continue performing the commands between `do` and `enddo` until `lValue` returns a value of `false`. You can use any conditional statement for `lValue`. The only criterion is that it return a value of `true` or `false`.

Now that we've looked at all of the available commands, let's take a close look at the `waitfor` command. The full command-line version looks like this:

```
waitfor <sValue> [, matchcase] [then <sLabel> {...}] [until <iTime>]
```

At first, this command line looks more than a little daunting, but it's not too complicated if you take it apart. Let's look at a simple example first:

```
waitfor "Login:"
```

All this command says is to wait until you get a `Login:` string from the host computer. Once you get it, start executing the statement immediately following this one. But what if you don't want to proceed with the very next statement? This form of the command shows what to do in that case:

```
waitfor "error" then FixError
```

In this case, we'll wait for a string containing error from the host, and then go to a label called `FixError`. Obviously, this form of the command is a bit limited, so you might want to add other labels to it as shown here:

```
waitfor
    "Go For It"     DoGoForIt
    "Logged In"     DoLogInStuff
    "Error"    FixError
```

This command waits until it sees one of three strings. It then goes to a specific label and carries out the instructions that the string requires. Of course, formatting the command like this could keep you waiting all day, and you may not have all day to wait. This form of the command tells Dial-Up Networking to wait 15 seconds and then proceed with the next command after the `until` argument:

```
waitfor
    "Go For It"     DoGoForIt
    "Logged In"     DoLogInStuff
    "Error"    FixError
until 15
```

As you can see, you can keep building on to this command until it directs every kind of traffic possible. Place this command within a `while do ... enddo` command and you have a program loop for handing the entire communications session. We still haven't looked at one argument, though. The `matchcase` argument forces Dial-Up Networking to perform a case-sensitive search for a specific string. For example, `"Login"` is different from `"LogIn"` when you use this argument. Because most online communication is case-insensitive, you'll want to use this argument with care.

Using Phone Dialer

I didn't think that Phone Dialer would come in very handy for me. After all, I have an autodialer built right into my phone. It's a pretty fancy autodialer, too. I press just one button to call my most common numbers.

Phone Dialer comes in handy not for your most common calls but for those that you make infrequently. Have you ever tried to call a government agency? I used to spend a lot of time just trying to get through, only to find that I had reached the wrong number. Phone Dialer might not fix the wrong number part of the equation, but I've found that it works very well for the first part. I can have it call in the background while I continue to work in the foreground—a very handy, time-saving feature.

Let's look at what Phone Dialer has to offer. Open Phone Dialer. You'll see a display similar to the one in Figure 19.19. Notice that there's a keypad on the left side of the dialog box, a list of speed dial numbers on the right, and the current number at the top.

Figure 19.19.
The Phone Dialer dialog box looks like a telephone keypad with an autodialer.

There are several ways to dial a number. You could just cut it out of your database manager and paste it into the blank at the top. This is one of the methods I use for infrequently called numbers. It has the advantage of allowing you to call a lot of numbers quickly without giving yourself a case of carpal tunnel syndrome in the process.

Before you make any real connections, you should look at the Tools menu to see what configuration options you have. This menu has three options; each one addresses a different need. If you select the Connect Using option, you'll see the dialog box shown in Figure 19.20. This dialog box has only three fields. The first field, Line, asks which modem you want to use. Only modems that you've set up using the Modems applet in Control Panel are listed. The second field, Address, asks which telephone line you want to use to dial out. It's active only if you have more than one line available. The Use Phone Dialer check box tells Windows 95 to use Phone Dialer for all application requests. Here's the real story on that one: It services only Windows 95 applications that know how to request outgoing phone services from the autodialer. It wasn't too surprising to see that even Access doesn't use this capability yet (the 97 version of Access may add this feature). Clicking the Line Properties button brings up the Modem Properties dialog box discussed in Chapter 14.

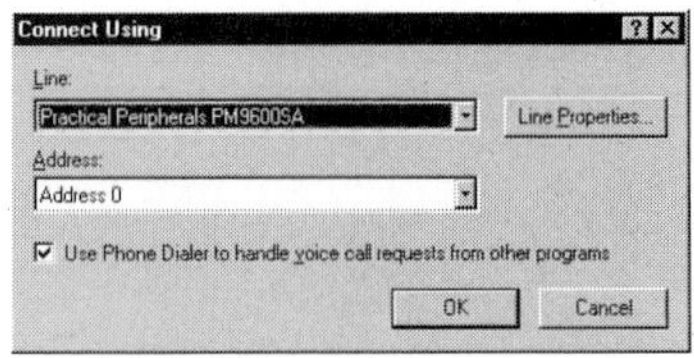

Figure 19.20.
The Connect Using dialog box allows you to select from more than one modem if you have more than one attached to your machine.

We saw how to use the Dialing Properties option of the Tools menu in the earlier section "Calling from Another Location" (refer to Figure 19.10). Essentially, it allows you to specify the location you're dialing from so that Phone Dialer can automatically compensate as needed for long distance calls.

The Show Log option of the Tools menu displays the Call Log dialog box shown in Figure 19.21. There isn't too much to say about this particular dialog box except that it maintains a record of the calls you make, including the number, the person's name, and how long you were on the phone. The nicest feature of this particular dialog box is that you can double-click an entry to call it again. With this feature, I can save some time when calling a number I don't have memorized, because I don't have to look it up.

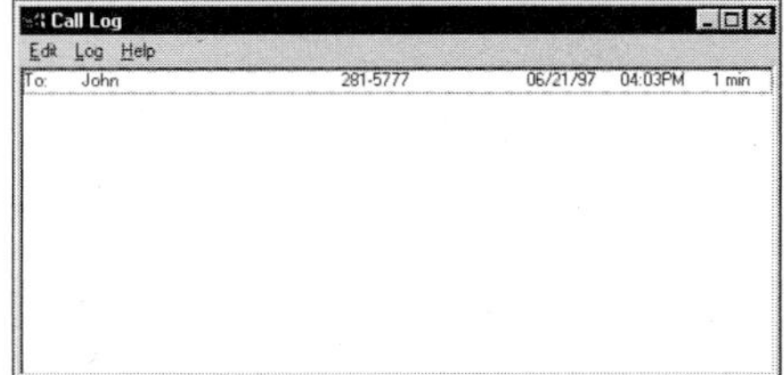

Figure 19.21.
The Call Log dialog box not only keeps track of the calls you make, but it also allows you to dial them again with ease.

There are two convenient methods for adding new numbers to your Speed Dial group. The first method is to simply click a blank spot. (The only problem with this technique is that it works only for blank buttons. Clicking a filled-in blank dials the number.) You'll see the dialog box shown in Figure 19.22. This dialog box contains only two entries: the name of the person you want to call and the number to reach him or her. The buttons on the side are self-explanatory.

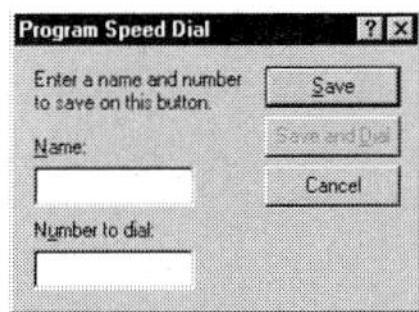

Figure 19.22.
Adding a new speed dial number is as easy as clicking a blank button.

You can also use the Edit | Speed Dial command to display the dialog box shown in Figure 19.23. This dialog box allows you to access any of the buttons. All you need to do is click the one you want to edit. Erasing the contents of both the name and number fields blanks that button for future use.

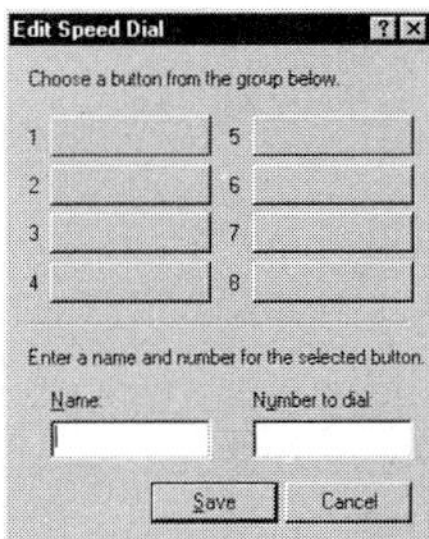

Figure 19.23.
The Edit Speed Dial dialog box allows you to change the single-button connections provided by the Phone Dialer.

On Your Own

Look through the vendor manual that came with your printer. See whether the vendor provides any accessories for your printer that might make it more flexible to use. Especially important is the availability of alternative port options. You also might want to check for third-party solutions for your printer. Some third-party vendors provide port accessories for some of the more prominent printers, such as the HP LaserJet.

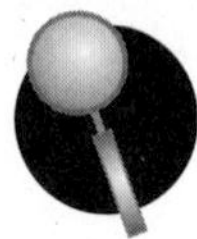

If you have a fax/modem attached to your machine, identify the five phases of a fax transaction. This is especially easy when using an external model. The lights on the front of the device help you detect when the various phases occur. Tracking this type of information can help you troubleshoot a faulty connection.

If you have a notebook computer, and both a network and a direct cable connection are available for it, try both methods of transferring a file. Most people have a serial connection available, so try that first. You should find that the network connection is a lot faster, but it's interesting to see how much faster. Try the same thing with a parallel connection (if possible).

Install and set up Phone Dialer. Try it out for a few days to see whether its additional features make phone calling a little easier for your harder-to-reach numbers. Also try the log feature to see how well it meets your needs.

If you're using the OSR2 version of Windows 95, try creating a script program for a Dial-Up Networking connection. You may want to try this with a local setup first to get a feel for the capabilities of the scripting language.

20

Talking to the Outside World

The preceding chapter looked at some of the intricacies of making connections within Windows 95. This chapter looks at some of the things that you can do with those connections after you make them. Unlike its predecessor, Windows 95 provides a combination of communications options that should meet the majority of your needs.

Microsoft doesn't include much in the way of support for any online services other than Microsoft Network (MSN) in the standard copy of Windows 95. Fortunately, this is changing as Microsoft becomes more involved with the Internet. OEM Service Release 2 (OSR2) users will be surprised at the number of new communications features they'll find. (Chapter 19 covers the new scripting feature for Dial-Up Networking users.) There's even an Online Services folder with setups for some of the larger communications providers. Chapter 21 looks at the contents of this folder. Fortunately, you can download many of the new communications features. I'll be sure to tell you where to get them as you go through this chapter and the next one. (For a complete look at the kinds of changes that you'll find on an OSR2 machine, look at the "OEM Service Release 2—The Complete Story" section of Chapter 1.)

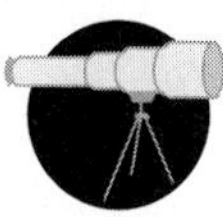

Looking Ahead: I cover standard communications in this chapter. All the Internet-specific communications features provided by Windows 95 are covered in Chapters 21 and 22. Chapter 21 covers new products such as Internet Explorer 3.0 and Internet Connection Wizard. Chapter 22 shows you how to create your own custom Web page. If you really want to get started with the Internet, look at Chapter 23 for coverage of Personal Web Server (a Windows 95 version of Internet Information Server).

An Overview of the Communications Architecture

Before we get into the communications packages, let's look at the communications subsystem architecture. We won't get the total picture in this chapter. Figure 20.1 reflects only the local part of the communications structure. Chapter 18 looks at the remote network architecture. However, if you look carefully, you'll see all three of the main connections discussed in Chapter 19: Dial-Up Networking, Phone Dialer, and Direct Cable Connection.

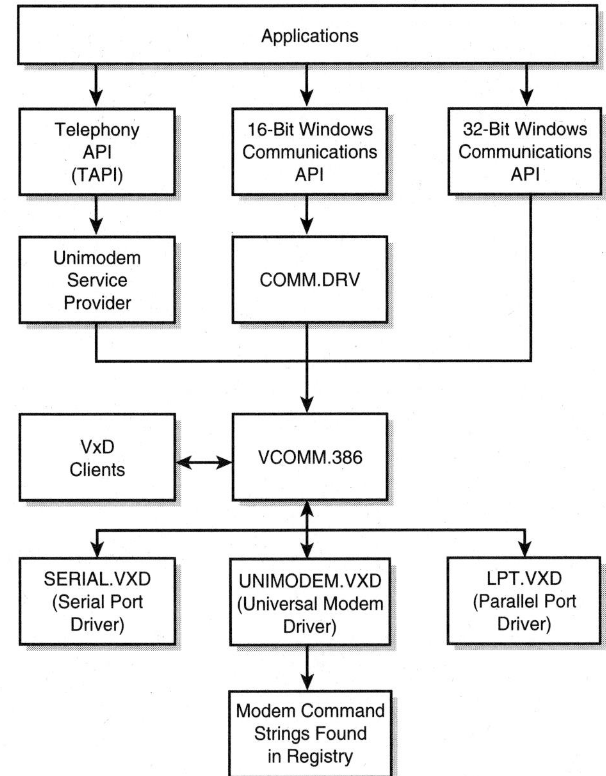

Figure 20.1.
An overview of the Windows 95 local communications architecture.

The following list provides details about all the components of the communications subsystem:

- **Telephony API (TAPI):** All the new modem-specific services are clustered under this API. It provides command translation for the new Windows 95 applications that make use of it. When an application asks about the modem setup or status, this module provides the information translation required for a seamless interface. TAPI might configure the modem from a virtual point of view, but VCOMM still manages the actual port. Modem commands flow through the port from TAPI. A good analogy of this arrangement is that VCOMM provides the pipe, but TAPI provides the water.
- **Windows 16-bit communications API:** The API is the module that accepts instructions from an application and translates them into something that Windows 95 can understand. One API instruction might actually require an entire module's worth of detailed instructions in order to perform. Windows 95 doesn't really use the 16-bit version of the Windows

communications instructions. The old instructions didn't provide the robust environment that the rest of Windows 95 provides. However, instead of writing a new 16-bit module, Microsoft provides access to the new 32-bit interface through these instructions and the COMM.DRV module that I'll describe in a moment.

- **Windows 32-bit communications API:** This is the enhanced 32-bit instruction set for Windows 95. Like its 16-bit counterpart, the 32-bit API translates application requests into commands that Windows can actually implement.
- **Unimodem service provider:** This is the specific driver for your modem. It takes the generic commands provided by the TAPI module and translates them into something that your modem will understand.

- **COMM.DRV:** Under Windows 3.x, this module carried out the communications tasks ordered by the API. The Windows 95 version is a thunk layer to the 32-bit instructions held in the 32-bit communications API and VCOMM.386. The positive aspect of this is that you'll see a definite boost in the speed of communications programs, even if you use an older 16-bit application. For example, I noticed that background downloads go well, even using my older copy of Procomm for Windows, which never worked in the background under Windows 3.x. This decision will probably solve more problems than it creates.
- **VxD clients:** VCOMM.386 provides services to more than just the communications subsystem. Every time any other Windows subsystem requires port access, it must go through VCOMM.386 as well. These requests are fielded through APIs that act as clients to this module. This is an internal Windows 95 function that you'll never really notice, but you should know that there are interactions between subsystems. A port failure might not always be the result of a communications- or print-specific problem; it could be related to some interaction from another, unrelated subsystem.
- **VCOMM.386:** Calling this a part of the communications subsystem is almost inaccurate. VCOMM.386 is a static device VxD that Windows 95 always loads during the boot process. Part of the job that VCOMM.386 performs is to load all the port drivers shown in Figure 20.1. Other parts of Windows also call VCOMM.386 through their respective APIs to perform a variety of port-specific services.
- **SERIAL.VXD:** This is the serial port driver. It's the actual serial port engine. Another driver is associated with the serial port as well: SERIALUI.DLL provides the interface that you use while setting up the serial ports.
- **UNIMODEM.VXD:** The modem setup is a little more complex than the other port drivers supported by VCOMM.386. This one actually works with either a serial or parallel port to provide modem services for the rest of Windows. It's also responsible for making any modem-specific Registry changes. Every time you change the modem strings, this

module records the strings in the Registry. As with the serial port driver, the VxD doesn't provide any interface elements. It relies on MODEMUI.DLL to provide these services. There's also a Control Panel element to worry about in this case. You'll find that MODEM.CPL manages this aspect of the interface.

- **LPT.VXD:** This is the parallel port driver. Unlike the serial port, the parallel port is usually managed by the printer subsystem. As a result, it relies on MSPRINT.DLL for user-interface services.
- **Modem command strings found in the Registry:** Actually, this is the completion of a circle. Many of the upper modules rely on the Registry entries to know how to interact with the modem. These strings provide those instructions. Each string defines some aspect of modem behavior. In most cases, it affects the modem's setup or the way that it communicates with another machine. You'll need to refer to your modem manual to get a better idea of exactly how these strings work.

Unlike many other subsystems, the communications subsystem looks fairly straightforward, and it is—to a point. There's a risk of underestimating the effect of this subsystem on the rest of Windows if you don't account for the number of ways in which it interacts with other subsystems. The centerpiece of this whole subsystem is VCOMM.386. This module loads the port drivers, provides access to them during system operation, and generally manages the way that Windows interacts with the outside world. It's an important role that you might take for granted until it stops working. Chapter 26 looks at some things that can go wrong with this subsystem.

Understanding Voice Communications

The latest rage in the world of modems is the voice modem. A voice modem allows you to exchange data and talk on the same line by using digitized voice signals. In other words, you don't need two telephone lines anymore to have an online discussion with a colleague. Having a voice/data/fax modem combination also means that you don't need a lot of messy wires hanging around the office. You can use one phone as a fax machine, network host, and answering machine. The only problem with voice modems up to this point is that each vendor has completely different drivers and even command sets. What you really need is two voice modems from the same vendor to create a voice connection. At this point, bells should be going off in your mind. The Windows telephone application programming interface (TAPI) was supposed to get rid of all of the compatibility problems between modems—it was supposed to provide a worry-free environment for the user. Fortunately, as technology changes, TAPI seems to change as well. The next few sections look at voice modems and how to use them within the Windows 95 environment.

Getting TAPI Support for Voice Modems

Native Windows 95 doesn't provide support for voice modems through TAPI—you need to download a special update file from the Internet at `FTP://ftp.microsoft.com/softlib/mslfiles/unimodv.exe`. This file installs Unimodem V support on your machine, which is the basis for standardized access to the voice capabilities of your modem. (In most cases, you'll get this update as part of any new modem purchase you make, if the vendor provides a Windows 95-specific installation program.) Chapter 14 talks about TAPI in the "TAPI and MAPI Support" section, so I won't go into that technology again here. However, I do want to quickly tell you what you'll get in your Unimodem V package when you download it.

Tip: If you really want to get the developer view on what's happening with TAPI, take a look at the FTP site at `ftp://ftp.microsoft.com/developr/tapi/`. The README file in the directory will tell you about the various files and what they can do for you. Most of this information is developer-related, but there are a few sample applications that may interest users. You'll also want to download a special developer-related README file regarding Unimodem and Unimodem V from `FTP://ftp.microsoft.com/developr/drg/modem/modemdev.exe`.

From a user perspective, the Unimodem V package (the self-extracting UNIMODV.EXE file) contains four items of interest. First are the drivers that you need to use your voice modem. The package includes a new UNIMODEM.VXD file along with several other support drivers. (I described this file in the earlier section "An Overview of the Communications Architecture.") Part of these driver updates includes a Telephony Service Provider (TSP). Its job is to handle program requests such as dialing and answering the phone line. The second item of interest is the Operator Agent. This is a special program that runs on your computer. It identifies whether an incoming call is voice, data, or fax, and directs it to the appropriate program for handling. If the Operator Agent can't determine what kind of call you're receiving, it asks the caller for information. Finally, if the Operator Agent can't get a response from the caller, it directs the call to a default application. The third item in this package is a series of .WAV file drivers that allow your telephony applications to record and play back messages. Finally, the fourth item is a series of .INF files used for installation and support of the Unimodem V package.

The Unimodem V update promises to bring order out of the chaos that originally reigned on machines with voice modems installed. However, your voice modem has to be one of the models supported by Microsoft's new Voice Modem Extensions for Windows 95 (the Unimodem V files). Following is a list of the modems with which you can use this support:

- Compaq Presario Models 520, 720, 820, and 920
- Creative Labs Phone Blaster
- Logicode 14.4 Data/Fax/Voice PCMCIA
- Diamond Multimedia TeleCommander 2500
- Cirrus Logic
- Aztech Systems
- Rockwell PCMCIA

Once you've downloaded the UNIMODV.EXE file and determined that you have a modem that works with the drivers supplied with the package, you can install the support. Installation couldn't be easier. The following procedure will help you get the job done:

1. Place the UNIMODV.EXE file in its own directory. Double-click the UNIMODV.EXE file to extract all the files it contains.
2. Right-click the UNIMODV.INF file. You'll see an Install option on the context menu. Select it and you'll see a Copying Files dialog box.
3. Once Windows 95 completes the file copying process, you need to restart your machine. At this point the support is installed, but you still need to get your modem set up to use it.
4. Right-click the My Computer icon and select Properties from the context menu. You'll see the System Properties dialog box.
5. Select the Device Manager page. Click the plus (+) sign next to the Modem entry. You should see one or more modems listed, as shown in Figure 20.2. Highlight the voice modem installed on your machine, and then click Remove to remove it.

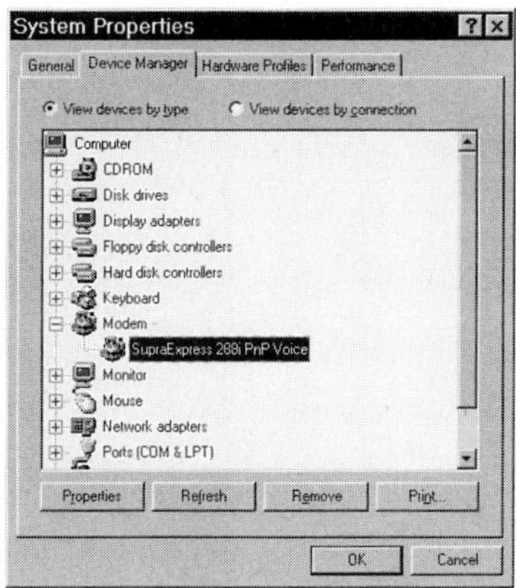

Figure 20.2.
The Device Manager page of the System Properties dialog box will contain one or more modem entries for your machine.

6. Click the Refresh button on the Device Manager page. Windows 95 will check for new devices and reinstall your modem. The whole purpose behind this is to install the new drivers you need.
7. At this point, I normally restart my machine again, just to make sure that everything is installed and registered correctly. You don't absolutely have to perform this step, but it's a good step to take.

Installing the Operating Agent

Installing Unimodem V support on your machine allows one or more applications to use the voice modem support that it provides. The Unimodem V package also comes with an Operating Agent. You can choose whether or not to install this support, but it's usually a good idea to do so if you plan to use Microsoft products. Remember that the Operating Agent is the software that allows Windows 95 to determine whether the incoming call is fax, data, or voice. The following procedure shows how to install the Operating Agent.

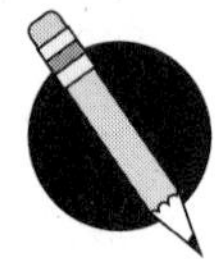

Note: The following procedure assumes that you've already installed Unimodem V support by using the procedure in the preceding section. If you haven't installed this support, do so now.

1. Select the Operator icon in the Start | Programs | Accessories folder. You'll see the Microsoft Operator Wizard shown in Figure 20.3.

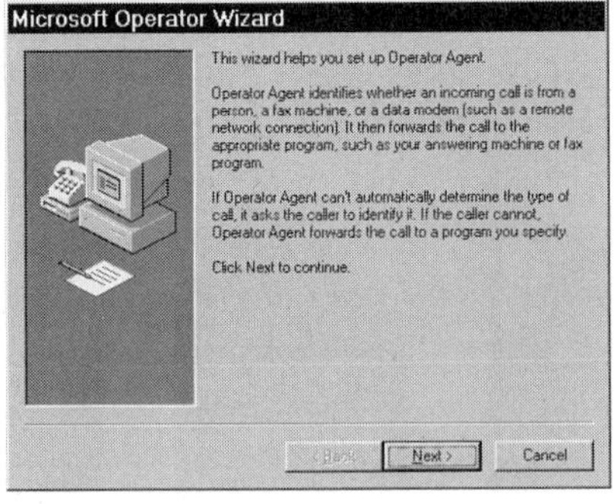

Figure 20.3.
The first page of the Microsoft Operator Wizard tells you about this product and what it can do for you.

2. Click Next. You'll see a second page of instructions; be sure to read through them. This page tells you what you'll be doing as you use the wizard to install Operator Agent support. At this point you need to perform three steps: Select a default message, select a default application, and select a message for those times when a particular application isn't running.
3. Click Next. You'll see the dialog box shown in Figure 20.4. This dialog box allows you to choose the message that a caller will hear if the Operator Agent can't determine what kind of call it's receiving. Click the Play button to hear the current message. If you want to change this message, select the Change the Greeting radio button. Otherwise, keep the second radio button selected as shown in the figure. If you choose to keep the current greeting, skip to step 6. Steps 4 and 5 will help you through the process of selecting or recording a new message.

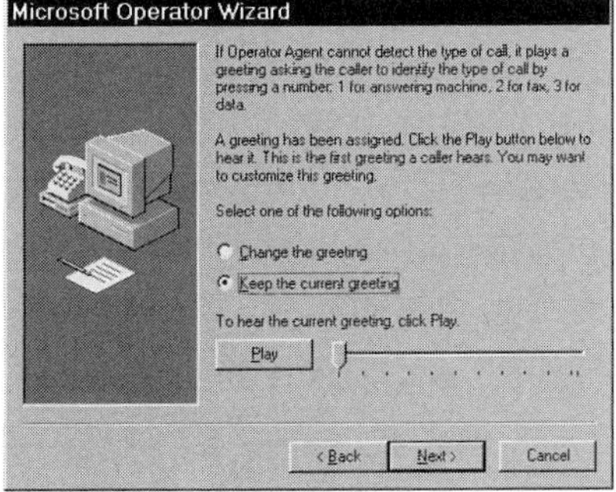

Figure 20.4.
This dialog box allows you to choose between the default message and your own custom message.

Tip: The Operator Agent comes complete with a male and a female version of the default message. The female version of the message is installed as a default. You can follow steps 4 and 5 to choose the default male version of the message in addition to recording your own message. Make sure that you have a microphone attached to your machine, if you choose to record a new message.

4. Click Next. If you selected the Change the Greeting radio button in the preceding step, you'll see the dialog box shown in Figure 20.5. This dialog box allows you to save the current message by clicking the Yes radio button and then the Save button. (Because we're using the default message in this example, you would select the No radio button.) After you click Save, you'll see a standard File Save dialog box.

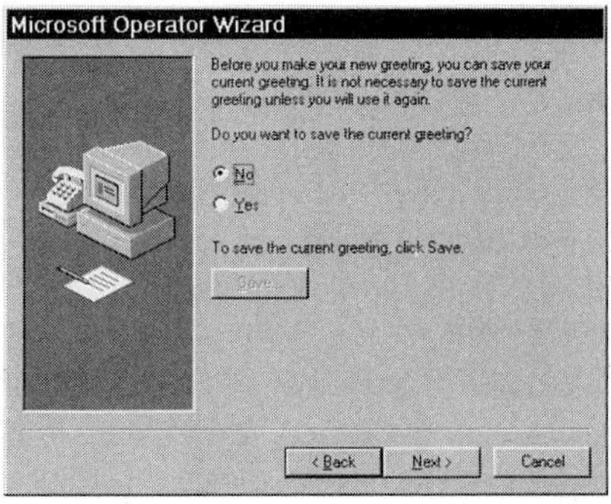

Figure 20.5.
The Microsoft Operator Wizard allows you to save your message before recording or selecting a new one.

5. Click Next. You'll see a dialog box like the one shown in Figure 20.6. This figure shows the default setup. Clicking the top radio button takes you to a recording dialog box where you can record a message, using a microphone or other media input device. This dialog box also allows you to play back the recorded message to make sure that it's correct. Clicking the second radio button in the dialog box shown in Figure 20.6 allows you to choose a prerecorded file. Theoretically you can choose any .WAV file, but you'll want to make sure that it tells your caller what to do. The drop-down list box shows the .WAV files in your Media folder. You can use the Browse button to explore your hard drive and find .WAV files located in other areas. As with the previous dialog box, the Play button allows you to hear the prerecorded .WAV file that you've selected.

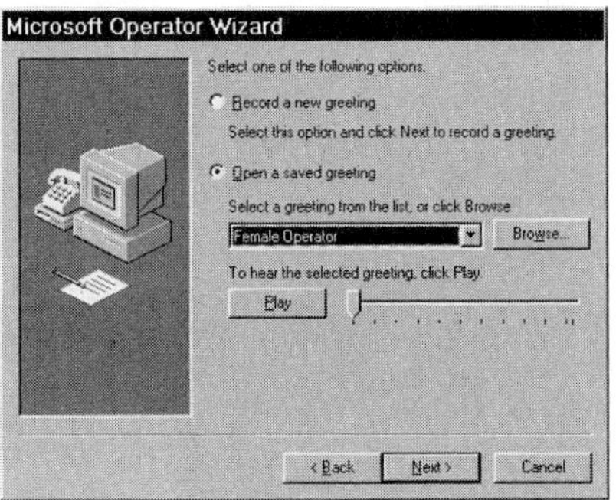

Figure 20.6.
In this dialog box, you can choose to use a prerecorded message or record your own.

6. Click Next. You'll see the dialog box shown in Figure 20.7. This dialog box allows you to choose the order in which the Operator Agent answers calls. In other words, if you expect to have a lot of voice messages, a few faxes, and almost no data uploads, then you would want to move the data entry to the very end.

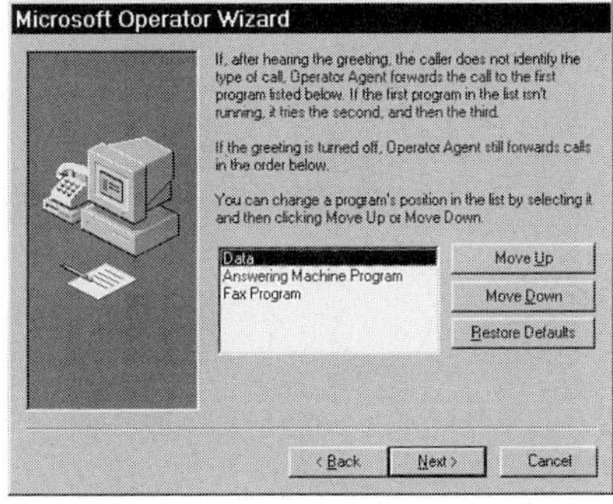

Figure 20.7.
Choosing in what order you want the Operator Agent to answer your calls makes using it more efficient for the caller.

7. Highlight any entries that you need to move, and then use the Move Up or Move Down button to change its position. If you decide that you want to go with the default setup, click the Restore Defaults button.
8. Click Next. You'll see the dialog box shown in Figure 20.8. This dialog box allows you to choose the message that the caller will hear if the Operator Agent can't complete a call. Setting up this dialog box is much the same as the default call-type selection message discussed in steps 3, 4, and 5, so I won't talk about it again here.

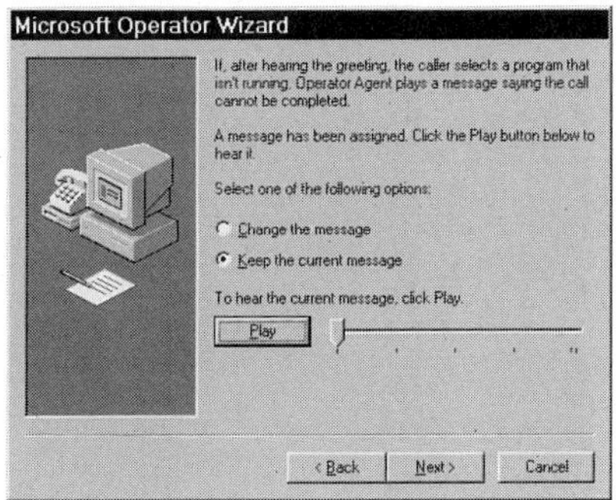

Figure 20.8.
The Microsoft Operator Agent allows you to choose a message for those calls that can't be completed.

9. Click Next. You'll see the dialog box shown in Figure 20.9. It tells you that you've completed the setup process. You'll also see some additional information concerning the Operator Agent—such as how to determine whether it's running.
10. Click Finish to complete the setup process. At this point the dialog box simply disappears. However, if you look at the Taskbar, you'll see a new icon for managing the Operator Agent.

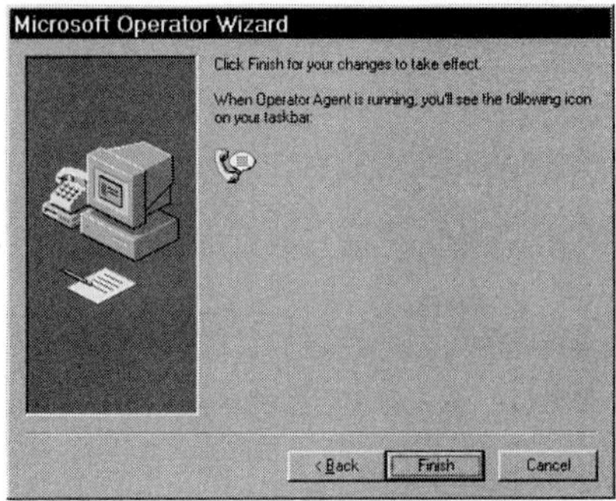

Figure 20.9.
The final Microsoft Operator Wizard dialog box tells you that you've completed the setup process successfully.

This procedure works fine the first time you set up the Operator Agent, but what if you need to change your message or another setting? As with everything else under Windows 95, you can right-click the Operator Agent icon on the Taskbar to see a context menu. There are three different options on this menu. The first opens the Microsoft Operator Agent dialog box shown in Figure 20.10. I'll cover the contents of this dialog box in a few seconds. The second option suspends the Operator Agent. The agent is still available; it just won't answer the phone. The third option, Stop Using Operator, actually removes the Operator Agent from the Taskbar. You'll use this option when you install a third-party product to handle your phone calls or simply don't need the capability any more.

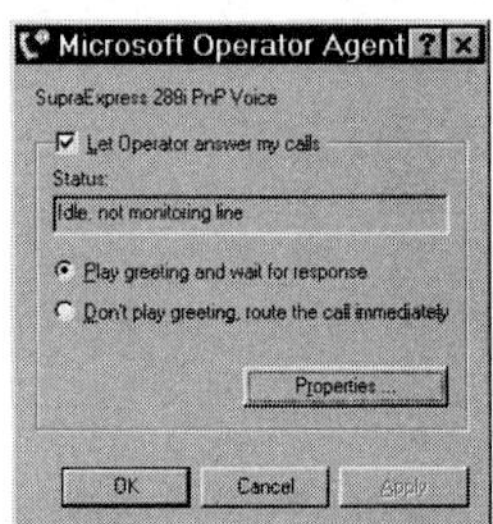

Figure 20.10.
You can change the Operator Agent properties by using this dialog box.

Let's talk about the dialog box shown in Figure 20.10. The first check box enables or suspends the Operator Agent. Unchecking this box is the same as selecting the Suspend Operator option on the context menu. It keeps the Operator Agent installed, but prevents it from managing your phone line. Notice the edit box directly below the check box. It contains the current status of the Operator Agent. In this case it's idle because there aren't any active applications on the test machine. An idle message doesn't necessarily mean that the Operator Agent is malfunctioning, even if you have applications installed for recording messages and so forth. An idle message also appears if none of the applications have placed the modem in answer mode. (See the documentation for the application to see how to do this.) The two radio buttons you see in this dialog box determine whether the caller will hear a message. Select the first radio button if you plan on getting a lot of voice calls and want to give the caller an opportunity to choose a course of action. On the other hand, you may want to select the second radio button if you plan on getting a lot of fax or data calls so that the caller doesn't think that your machine is broken. (A lot of people want an instant response from a fax or data line and hang up if they don't get it.)

Figure 20.10 also shows a Properties button. Clicking this button displays the dialog box shown in Figure 20.11. This is where you can change either of the two messages and set the order in which the Operator Agent directs calls. All you need to do is click the button corresponding to the configuration item you want to change. You'll actually see that part of the Microsoft Operator Wizard come up and help you set the configuration. Because I already covered the wizard as part of the initial installation procedure, I won't cover it again here.

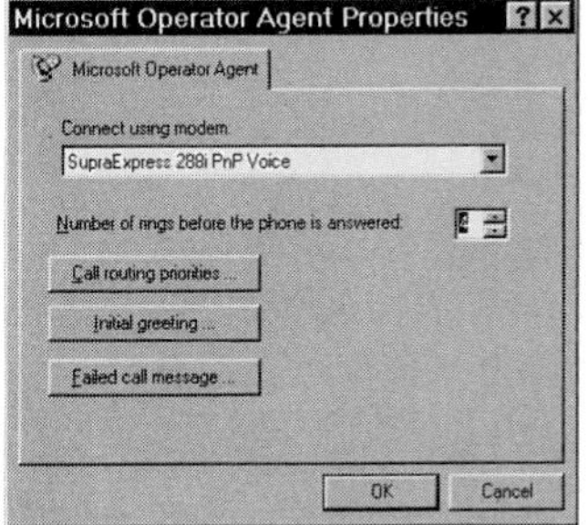

Figure 20.11.
You can change any of the configuration settings for the Operator Agent by using the Microsoft Operator Agent Properties dialog box.

The Inner Workings of Unimodem V

Okay, so you've got Unimodem V support and the Operator Agent installed on your machine. Does that mean you're ready to go? Just having a few drivers and the right modem won't fulfill all your needs. For you to see any results, the programmer who wrote the application you're using had to use the Voice Modem Extensions for Windows 95. The application needs to know how to use the capabilities that Windows 95 provides. Most of the answering-machine-type applications on the market right now still rely on those proprietary setups that I mentioned previously.

Voice modems use special command strings to activate their voice capabilities, just like any other service that they offer. If you've ever used a program like Procomm Plus or WinCIM, you're familiar with the Hayes command strings used to set up your modem. For example, `ATA` answers the phone and `ATH` hangs up the phone. There are other command strings to test the modem and even a few to ask it questions. Even though Hayes originated these command strings, they're now managed by groups such as ANSI (American National Standards Institute), TIA (Telecommunications Industry Association), and EIA (Electronics Industry Association). When the time came to implement voice capabilities into voice modems, there weren't any `AT` command strings for vendors to use, so they made up their own. Obviously this muddies the picture greatly because Windows can't depend on using a standard command string to work with a voice modem. There's a new standard now for voice modems: ANSI/TIA/EIA standard IS-101 (Facsimile Digital Interfaces—Voice Control Interim Standard for Asynchronous DCE). This standard defines a set of `AT+V` commands that modems should use to enable and use voice capabilities. When buying a new voice modem, make absolutely certain that it adheres to this standard, if you want to use it successfully with Windows.

So how does Windows get sounds recorded as messages out to the caller? Take a look at Figure 20.12. It shows a block diagram of the new connections that Unimodem V creates to connect various Windows 95 subsystems together so that you can use your voice modem in a variety of ways.

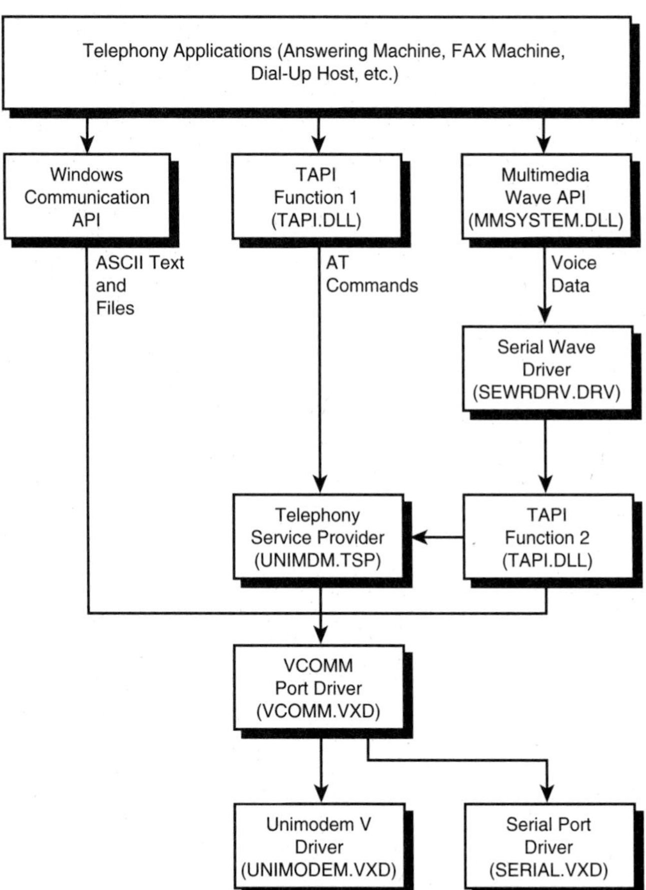

Figure 20.12.
Unimodem V creates new connections between various Windows 95 subsystems.

The following list provides an overview of the various Unimodem V subsystems:

- **Windows Communication API:** You're not likely to see a 16-bit application use the voice modem capabilities that Windows 95 provides—and as far as I can tell, Microsoft doesn't even make a provision for it. The Windows Communication API works the same here as it did in the earlier section "An Overview of the Communications Architecture."
- **Telephony API:** As with the Windows communications API, this part of the communications picture operates much as it did before. We do use it in a different way. Notice that the figure shows two different functions for TAPI now. We disguise the voice data so that

TAPI will work with it using the Serial Wave Driver. Even though there aren't any new TAPI files, we double the amount of work that it can do. (This particular feat is a real credit to the new modular approach that Microsoft has taken in designing Windows.)

- **Multimedia Wave API:** If you're wondering what this is doing here, you're not alone. It doesn't take long to figure out, though, that Windows has to have some way of converting the voice you hear on the phone into data that it can understand (and vice versa). Because we already have this capability built into Windows though the multimedia API, why not use it? As a result, the data you record by using a microphone or hear through a speaker goes through the multimedia API even when the source is a telephone call.
- **Serial Wave Driver:** This part of the picture can get a little confusing, so we'll talk about the simple version. If you've got a standard modem that adheres to all the standards, you'll use a serial wave driver that supports the International Multimedia Association (IMA) adaptive delta pulse code modulation (ADPCM) standard. All these fancy words mean is that the serial wave driver converts the digitized voice that it receives from the modem into something that the multimedia system can understand, and vice versa. This module uses a helper .DLL named VMODCTL.DLL to ease communications with the TSP. Some modems rely on a nonstandard hardware audio port to transmit digitized voice over the telephone. In this case, Microsoft adds another helper module named WRAP.DRV to coordinate voice and data transfers.
- **Telephony Service Provider (TSP):** This is the driver that takes care of things such as dialing the phone. It also issues all of the `AT+V` commands required to communicate with your modem. For example, there's one `AT+V` command to set the modem in voice mode and another to tell it to transfer data. (This module also supports some modems that use the `AT#V` command syntax, but you'll want to check the list I provided previously to make sure that your modem is supported.)
- **VCOMM Port Driver:** You'll find that this module is unchanged from the one discussed earlier, in the section "An Overview of the Communications Architecture."
- **Unimodem V Driver:** I discussed the overall purpose of this module previously—that hasn't changed one bit. The difference is that the Unimodem V Driver now has the capacity to use the specific voice commands supported by your modem.
- **Serial Port Driver:** As with many other modules, this one hasn't changed from the earlier section "An Overview of the Communications Architecture."

Remember that we've just looked at an overview of the new additions to the communications subsystem. There's a lot more going on than I've talked about, but this overview gives you enough information to better understand how Windows 95 works.

Using Microsoft Exchange

Microsoft Exchange is central command as far as communications go. You can perform almost any kind of communication that Windows 95 will support, just by opening Microsoft Exchange. As time goes on you'll see that, like Explorer, Microsoft Exchange pops up in the strangest places. Even if you think that each communications module under Windows 95 is a separate entity, it isn't. They all rely on Exchange for a user interface. The details differ from service to service, but the part that the user sees remains fairly constant.

Note: OSR2 users will notice a new name for Microsoft Exchange—it's Windows Messaging. Essentially, Microsoft Exchange and Windows Messaging are the same product. There are a few very minor differences, covered in this section. One of the differences that I'd like to cover now is performance related. Microsoft has made Windows Messaging faster than its predecessor. For example, there's a very noticeable difference in the rate at which the attachments are delivered. Fortunately, you can download this updated version of Microsoft Exchange from `http://www.microsoft.com/windows/software/updates.htm`.

Before we begin looking at specific communications services provided by Windows 95, I want to take you on a quick tour of Microsoft Exchange. I'm not talking about working through the intricacies of every service that it provides; I cover that in the individual service descriptions that follow. What I'll cover now is the generic core that you should know about. Once you get this part of the interface down, the little differences between components will seem a lot less intimidating.

Understanding the User Interface

The following discussion assumes that you have Microsoft Exchange installed. Later, we'll look at how you can install individual components. You'll use Microsoft Exchange to perform that work. What you want to do now is look at the user interface itself.

Figure 20.13 shows a typical Microsoft Exchange display. Of course, your display will probably vary from this one a bit, but you get the idea. The main thing to remember is that your interface will vary a little because of the settings you choose and the options you install.

Microsoft Exchange always defaults to your Inbox as the first location it shows. After it opens the Inbox, it updates any e-mail messages you have on the network (assuming that you're attached). You'll need to go online to update your other messages, but they all appear in this single Inbox (unless you change the settings that we'll discuss later).

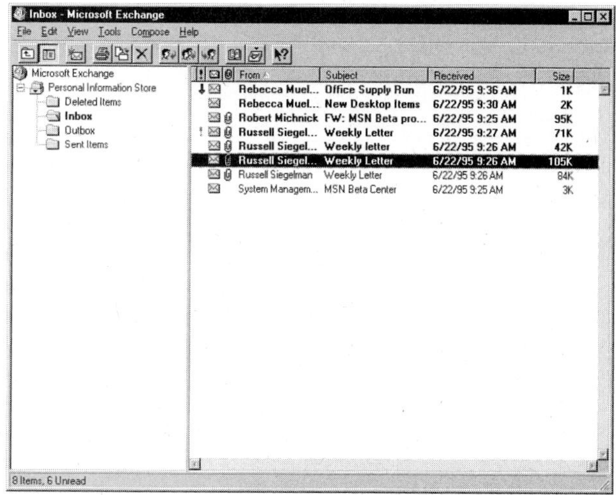

Figure 20.13.
The Inbox folder not only provides access to your messages, but helps you to organize them in a variety of ways.

Let's quickly look at how Microsoft Exchange presents your Inbox messages. This is the default setup of columns; I'll tell you how to change this setup later. We'll start at the very first column of the message header and work our way across. The first column can contain nothing, a red exclamation point (!) or a blue down arrow. Medium-priority messages receive no symbol. A red exclamation mark tells you that this message is high-priority, and a blue down arrow says that the message is low-priority. The second column tells you what type of item is stored there. In most cases it will be a message, as shown by the envelope symbol. The little paper clip symbol in the third column tells you that a message has attachments. You can either attach files outright or add OLE objects to your messages. I was surprised to find that you can add objects in such a way that they'll actually start an online session. You can also create an object that will access a file on the network. In the fourth column you'll find the name of the person who sent the message or item. The fifth column contains the message's subject line. The sixth column tells you when the message was received. Finally, the seventh column tells you how big the file is.

Tip: It almost always pays to change this default setup. Exchange provides a wealth of column headings that old versions of Microsoft Mail didn't. You'll at least want to see what's available and consider how you can use it to optimize your setup.

Sorting the messages in any given folder is easy. You'll notice that the column headings are actually buttons. Clicking a column heading sorts by that column. You can change the sort order by clicking a second time. Exchange displays an arrow in the heading that the messages are sorted by (if there's room in the heading). It uses an up arrow for ascending order and a down arrow for descending order. If you prefer a dialog box interface for changing the sort order, you can always use the View | Sort command to display the dialog box shown in Figure 20.14. It offers the same column selections that you see on the display. All you need to do is select one from the list box, click the order in which you want to sort, and click OK to complete the action.

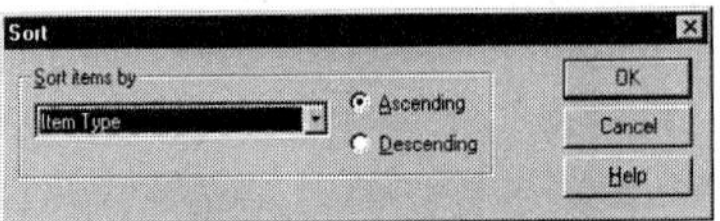

Figure 20.14.
The Sort dialog box allows you to select a sort order, but clicking the column headings is a lot faster.

Notice the use of bold text on the display. Whenever you see either a folder or a message name in bold, it means that you haven't read that message or completely viewed the contents of the folder. I find that this is the fastest way to see new messages on my system. Of course, this is a little less valuable when you use the default folder setup, but it can be quite valuable as you expand your system. Along with this use of bold text are two Edit menu options. You can mark a message as read or unread by using the two options on this menu.

Tip: It's important to use all the Exchange features to your benefit. For example, some people might view the Edit | Read and Edit | Unread commands as superfluous, but they're really quite useful. I don't often mark a message as read, but I do mark messages as unread from time to time. This is handy for times when you read a message, realize you don't have time to take care of it now, and mark it as unread so that you'll remember to look at it again later.

Looking at the default display, you can see a relationship between Exchange and Explorer. Certainly the hierarchy of folders is the same, and the messages equate to files in your post office. There are other similarities as well. For example, you can add folders to the default hierarchy to better organize your messages. I find that moving messages around into various project areas is a great way to make Exchange a lot easier to use. Use the File | New Folder command to display the dialog box shown in Figure 20.15. All you need to do is type in a name and click OK to complete the process. Moving messages from place to place is also as easy as using Explorer. Each entry has a context menu containing Exchange-specific functions that work the same as the Explorer equivalent. The bottom line is that if you know how to use Explorer, learning Exchange shouldn't be very difficult.

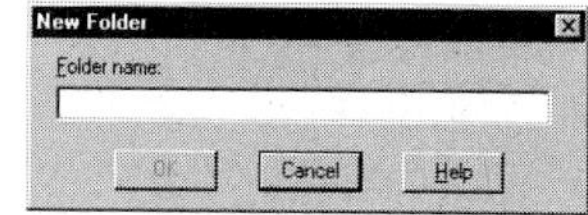

Figure 20.15.
Adding folders to the default Exchange hierarchy will let you organize your messages more easily.

Note: Exchange will let you remove folders you create by using the Delete command or by pressing the Delete key, just like Explorer. However, it stops short of allowing you to delete the default folders in the hierarchy. These folders have to remain in place to support the mail structure.

You might notice that the Recycle Bin doesn't change if you delete a message. That's because Exchange provides its own delete area in the Deleted Items folder. If you delete a message from any area of Exchange, it ends up in this folder. If you delete a message in the Deleted Items folder, you'll remove it from the system permanently. I usually disable this option to keep myself from removing old messages that I'll need later. You can't place Exchange messages in the Recycle Bin. We'll see later that you can make the process of removing old messages a little more automatic by changing the Exchange options.

Exchange also provides a fairly complete toolbar right under the menu bar. You'll notice some standard buttons here, but most of them are unique to Exchange. Chapter 2 discusses all these buttons, so I won't go through them again.

Using the Address Book

Microsoft Exchange provides an address book that helps you maintain a list of the people you normally contact. Before you send a message to anyone, it's usually a good idea to add his or her name to the address book, even if you intend to use the address only once. The reason is simple. I've often been in a situation where I think that I'll use an address only once, but then I have to look all over the place for it later when I need to send a second message.

Figure 20.16 shows the initial Address Book dialog box. Exchange defaults to using the Microsoft Mail Postoffice Address Book, but you can reset this default to any address book you like. It also adds all the names of people on your local network or workgroup, allowing you to send messages immediately without a lot of typing. The display normally provides the person's name as a minimum. Any other information it provides is format-specific (I cover that in detail later).

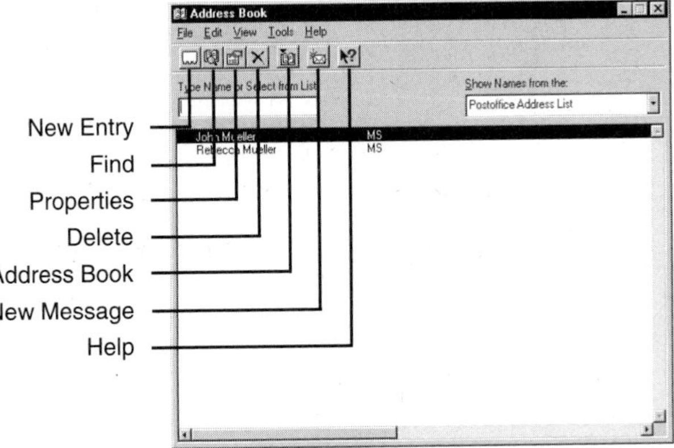

Figure 20.16.
The initial Address Book dialog box shows the addresses that you select as a default.

The toolbar below the menu bar provides access to the majority of the address book functions. In fact, I don't think I've ever had to use the menu itself. The following list provides an overview of each toolbar button:

- **New Entry:** This allows you to add new names to the address book.
- **Find:** You can use this button to filter the names displayed in the dialog box. It actually creates a new address book called Search Results.
- **Properties:** Use this to change the properties of the address book. You right-click a specific name to change its properties. The Postoffice Address Book doesn't provide any overall properties for you to change, so Exchange displays an error message if you select the Properties button in this case.

Note: As of this writing, the function of the Properties button tends to change with the address book you're using. In some cases it works, but in others it doesn't. In some cases it changes the properties of the address book itself, and in others it brings up the Properties dialog box for the individual entry. The definition provided here is consistent with the current Microsoft documentation.

- **Delete:** This button allows you to remove an entry from the address book. Unfortunately, there's no recovery area in case you accidentally erase a name that you needed.
- **Add to Personal Address Book:** Use this button to add a name from a public or other address book to your personal address book. Exchange always creates a personal address book for you. Of course, that doesn't restrict you from creating other personal address books, but this button works only with the default personal address book set up by Exchange.

- **New Message:** You can click one or more names in your address book and then click this button to send a message to the people you selected. The Message Creation dialog box automatically displays the selected list of names when you open it.
- **Help:** As with every Windows application, you can request help by using a variety of methods. Clicking this button displays the Help cursor. Point to whatever you need help with and click. Windows provides context-sensitive help that will aid you in using the Address Book dialog box.

Adding a New Address

Adding a new address is fairly easy. The only challenge is figuring out exactly what you need to provide. Each of the MAPI clients that Exchange supports uses a different address format because their methods of sending messages are different. However, aside from a few vagaries in the way that an address is stored for a specific type of MAPI client, there are a lot of similarities. The first step in adding a new address book entry is deciding what type of address it is (see Figure 20.17). Once you decide what type of address to add and where to add it, click OK to view the format-specific address page. Let's take a look at one or two specialty pages in the Address Book dialog box. Then I'll describe the pages that are common to all formats.

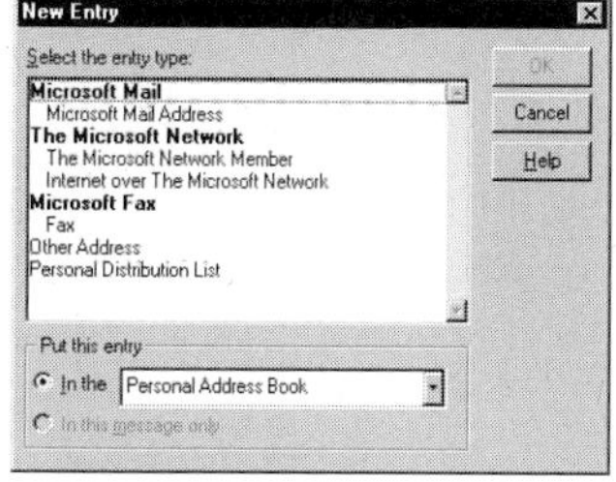

Figure 20.17.
You need to decide what kind of address to add before you can add it.

Figure 20.18 shows a new address book entry for Microsoft Mail. You'll need to use this page to add new entries only for users who are part of other workgroups. All the local workgroup names are entered automatically. This page has four blanks. Each one provides part of the routing information needed to send your message to its destination. The first field, Alias, is the person's login name. This might or might not be his full name. It could be a nickname or a shortened version of his full name if more than one person on the network has the same name. Type whatever name he uses to log into the network. The Mailbox field contains the person's nickname—the name that the Post Office Administrator used when entering his name in the post office. This field usually contains the same information as the Alias field. The Postoffice field contains the name of the post office. This might or might not be the name of the machine that actually contains the post office. Finally, the Network field contains the name of the network, workgroup, domain, or other identifying information. It's the name that you see at the root of a network entry in Network Neighborhood.

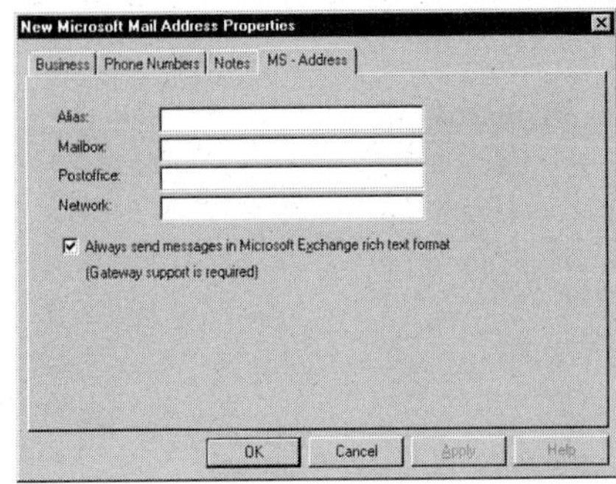

Figure 20.18.
A Microsoft Mail address entry requires just a few simple pieces of information about the network routing needed to reach a recipient.

A new fax address book entry probably contains less information than you would expect. Figure 20.19 shows an example of this entry. Notice that you need to supply only a name and some telephone information. The telephone number includes a country code, area code, and the telephone number itself. Be sure to define all three or you may end up calling someone you don't know. Fortunately, Microsoft Exchange provides default entries for the country code and area code. Note the Mailbox field. It's not a functional routing entry, but it could help the person at the other end direct the fax to the correct person. You can also choose to dial the area code, even if it's the same as yours, by checking the only check box on the page.

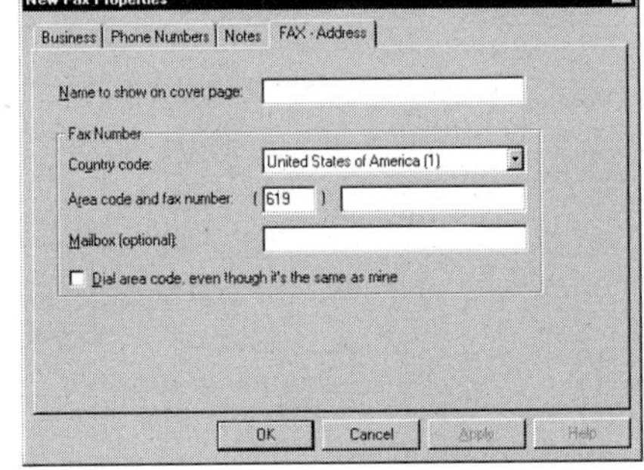

Figure 20.19.
A fax address entry requires the person's name and a telephone number.

Figure 20.20 shows a new Microsoft Network address entry. This is typical of most online service entries. It consists of a member name and an online identification number.

Figure 20.21 shows the last type of new address entry we'll cover. A new Internet entry contains three fields. The first contains the person's e-mail address. This is the same address that he would normally use if he were on that service. The second field contains the domain name. This might require a little explanation. It would be easy to think of the Internet as an entity. It really isn't. The Internet is composed of literally thousands of smaller networks, each providing common access. When you see an Internet address, it usually looks similar to this one: `71570.641@compuserve.com`. The "at" symbol (@) separates the e-mail address from the domain name. In this particular case, you would send a message to someone on CompuServe. If you wanted to send a message to America Online, you would use `aol.com` as the domain name. Every server has a unique domain name that allows it to receive messages. The third field contains the person's name.

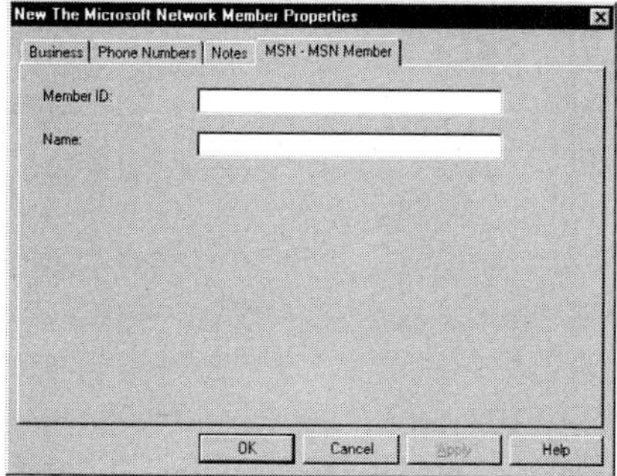

Figure 20.20.
The Microsoft Network address entry is the easiest to fill out so far. All you need is a name and identification number.

Note: CompuServe addresses require a period instead of a comma when accessed from the Internet. For example, if you have an address of 12345,678 on CompuServe, your Internet address would be 12345.678@compuserve.com. The change of a comma to a period is important.

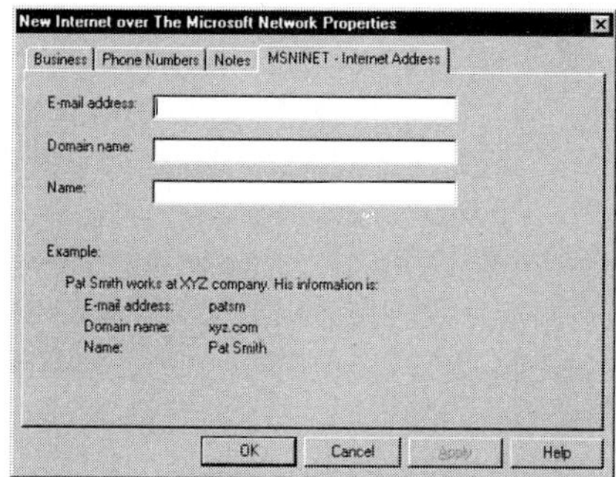

Figure 20.21.
A new Internet address page might look a bit strange at first.

Now that we've seen all the format-specific pages, let's look at the common pages that the address book provides. Figure 20.22 shows the Business page. It allows you to record all the specifics that you're likely to need for contacting that person. All of the fields are self-explanatory; you'll find them in any contact manager. One of the nice features of this particular page is the Phone Number field. You can select the location that you want from the list box and then enter a number. I'll describe all the locations in the next paragraph, but it's nice to know that you can record more than one. Another nice feature is the ability to dial that phone number right from this page, using the Phone Dialer utility discussed in Chapter 19.

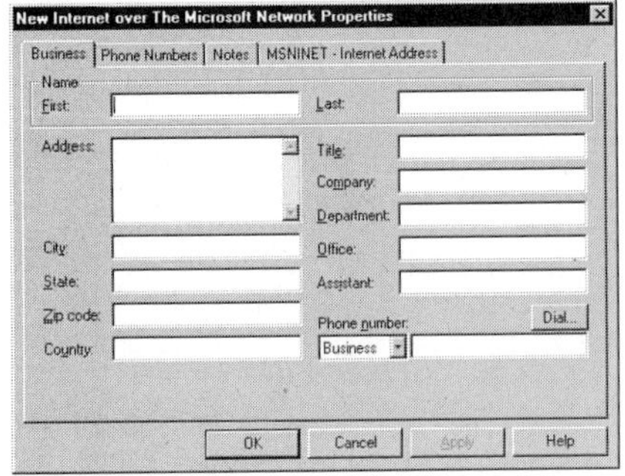

Figure 20.22.
The Business page provides a fast way of recording all the pertinent contact information you need in order to reach someone.

The Phone Numbers page shown in Figure 20.23 provides a quick list of all the phone numbers that you can use to contact the person. I felt that adding the assistant's phone number was an especially nice touch. Unfortunately, you can't record any more than the eight phone numbers shown here. In most cases this is enough, unless the person that you're trying to contact travels a lot or normally works in more than one location.

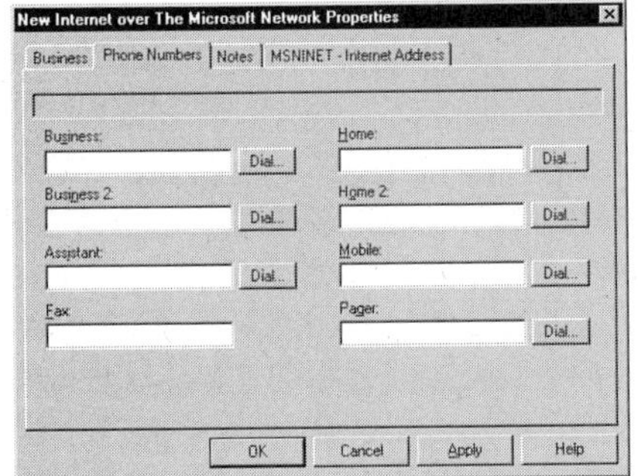

Figure 20.23.
The Phone Numbers page allows you to enter up to eight contact numbers for each person in your address book.

The final page, Notes, is a big notepad. You can enter previous contact information or any other free-form information here. I often use it to track the last date that I contacted someone and a brief note on what we talked about. This note-taker won't replace a contact manager, though. If you spend most of your time on the phone, and keeping track of all those contacts is important, I recommend a full-fledged contact manager in place of this solution. The notepad provided with the address book is more for the occasional user than anything else. However, you could store a customer ID or another number here to make it easier to find this person's record in your contact manager.

Note: Some services may include an additional page. For example, Figure 20.23 shows an additional page for the Internet service. You can be certain that this page will become prominent as third-party developers add their own MAPI drivers. Make sure that you follow the vendor-supplied instructions when filling out the contents of this page.

Finding Names in Your Address Book

Finding names in your address book is very easy. All you need to do is click the Find button on the toolbar to display the dialog box shown in Figure 20.24. Fill in the name or even part of the name. Clicking OK displays the list of names in a new address book called Search Results. You can switch between this address book and your original one by using the list box below the toolbar.

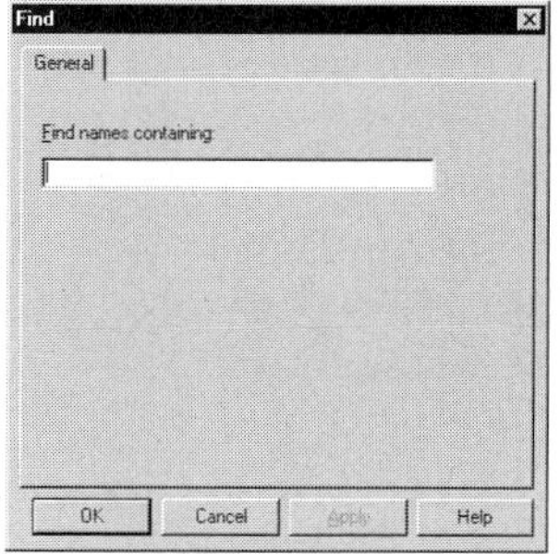

Figure 20.24.
You can use Find to whittle down a large address book into one containing just the names you need.

Changing the Address Book Properties

You can make a few configuration changes to each address book on your system except the Public Postoffice Address Book. You access the Personal Address Book Properties dialog box shown in Figure 20.25 by clicking the Properties button on the toolbar.

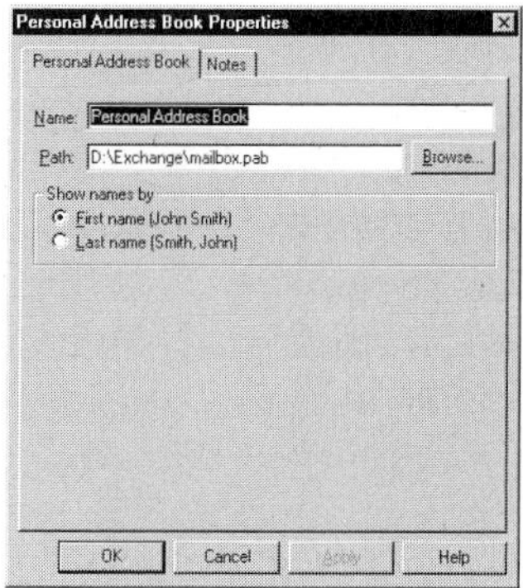

Figure 20.25.
The Personal Address Book Properties dialog box allows you to change the way that your address book works.

The first page contains three fields. The Name field allows you to change the name of the address book. In most cases you'll want to retain the name of the default personal address book that Exchange sets up for you, so that you can add names to it automatically. The second field contains the location of the actual address book file on disk. This, too, normally stays the same, unless you move the address book to a new location. The group of radio buttons changes the way that the address book lists names. I find this feature quite handy when I'm looking for a specific name. Changing the order makes it easier to find an entry for someone when I forget his last name.

Tip: You can create new address books with specific names by using the Find button. Use the Properties dialog box to change the name of that address book to something else so that Windows won't overwrite it the next time you need to create a special address book.

The Notes page of this dialog box contains a miniature notebook. You can use it to track the address book and anything you do with it. It might come in handy for writing a reminder of why you started this particular address book.

Adding and Configuring Address Books

One address book feature isn't covered by the toolbar. The Tools | Options command brings up the dialog box shown in Figure 20.26. This dialog box actually performs two different functions. The first is to configure Exchange to use your address books. The second is to create new address books as you need them.

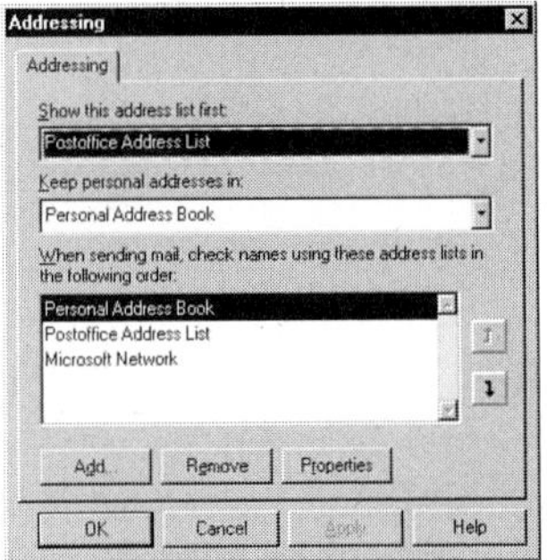

Figure 20.26.
Use this dialog box to configure Exchange to use your address books and to create new ones.

Let's examine the first purpose. The Show This Address List First field determines which address book Exchange shows first whenever you create a new message. If most of your messages go to the company e-mail, using the default setting of Postoffice Address List makes sense. However, if you're like me, you send messages to a variety of places, including the company e-mail. In this case, you might want to select your personal address list as the first location instead. The second field contains the name of your personal address list. Unless you want to personalize this setting for some reason, you'll want to keep the default setting. Exchange automatically creates this address list for you, so there's no real reason to change it later.

The second purpose for the dialog box is to add new address lists to your address book. The list box always shows a complete list of the current address lists that you have, except for any recent searches. You can add a new address list by clicking the Add button. Simply follow the prompts to create the new address list. In most cases, you'll find that the default address books provide more than sufficient flexibility.

Finding Specific Messages

Ever find yourself buried in a mound of messages with no real way to organize them and even less opportunity to quickly find the one you need? Exchange provides a handy search dialog box that looks similar to Explorer's Find dialog box (see Figure 20.27). This dialog box contains quite a few mail-specific features. Of course, it won't help you find any files on your drive.

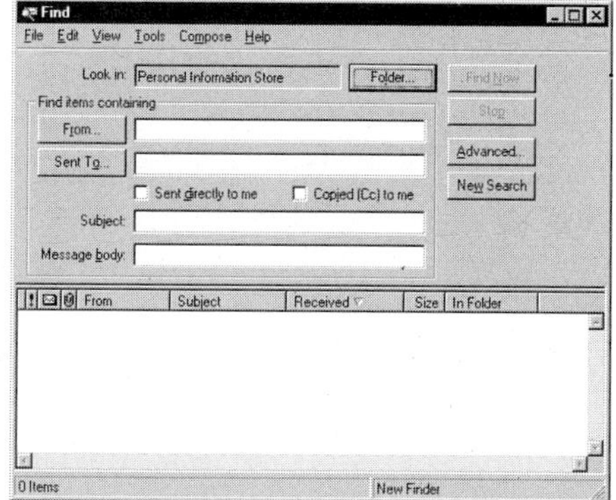

Figure 20.27.
The Find dialog box in Exchange looks similar to the one in Explorer, with some important exceptions.

Most of the fields in this dialog box are pretty self-explanatory, but using some of them might not be. For example, if you want to search through all your mail, you select the Personal Information Store folder. You can't search from the Exchange level. Of course, you can always go lower than this top level by looking through the folder hierarchy.

The Sent Directly to Me and the Copied (Cc) to Me check boxes aren't mutually exclusive. However, if you select the first one, you won't be able to ask for a specific person in the Sent To field, even though Exchange doesn't blank it out. You can combine the Copied (Cc) to Me check box and a specific Sent To name, though.

Using the various fields in tandem is the key to finding precisely the message you want. The Advanced button shows you some additional criteria that you can use to search for messages. It uses the dialog box shown in Figure 20.28 to allow you to perform a more stringent search.

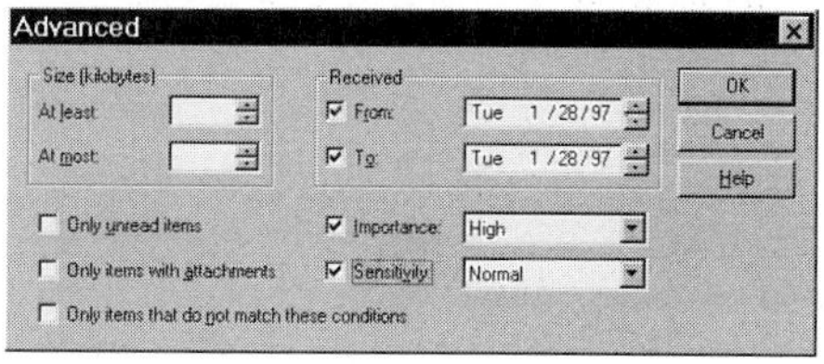

Figure 20.28.
You can perform a very detailed search of the message base by using the criteria in the Advanced dialog box.

Some of these options have interesting uses. For example, when it comes time to make room on the server containing the post office, you can get rid of the bigger messages by using the Size group. I use this option from time to time just to see how many large files I've accumulated. You'd be surprised how fast they can build up.

Getting back from vacation usually means that you have a lot more work to do than time to get it done. I start by categorizing the various things I need to do by placing them in separate folders. Then I use a high-priority search to find the items I need to get done right away.

You can also use the entries in this dialog box to search for messages you haven't read yet or messages received during a certain time span. The time span feature is nice when you know you received a message during a specific time period, but you can't remember much else about it. Any attempt to look through the entire message base will likely prove frustrating.

After you select all the search criteria, clicking the Find Now button displays a list of matching messages in the list box at the bottom of the Find dialog box. This list responds to all the usual actions, such as right-clicking and double-clicking. You can also delete messages in this list and respond to them in the normal way. The one item in this dialog box that surprised me a bit was the ability to create new messages. It certainly makes life a lot easier when you remember to write an important message in the middle of or as a result of looking for something else.

Working with the Exchange Services

Windows 95 comes with a limited number of MAPI servers. (Chapter 14 covers MAPI; a MAPI server simply provides access to a particular online service.) Each server uses Exchange as a front end. In other words, once you learn how to use Exchange, you pretty much know how to use all the generic pieces of each MAPI server as well. The big difference between servers and the interface that you get is the medium in which they operate. The medium determines some of the differences that you see in how the various MAPI servers operate.

Exchange might come with some or all of the servers added. The default servers are pretty much self-installing. But it's quite likely that you'll need to add new MAPI servers as third-party products arrive on the scene. For example, you might choose to use a MAPI server to access your local BBS instead of buying a full-fledged communications program. Not only would you ease the learning curve that such a product requires, but the software vendor will be able to provide similar functionality in a much smaller package.

Use the Tools | Services command to display the dialing Services dialog box, shown in Figure 20.29. The top of the dialog box contains a list of the current servers you have installed. In most cases, you won't need to install the Windows 95 servers individually unless Microsoft comes out with an update or the original server gets contaminated in some way. The five buttons below this list describe various actions that you can perform when adding, removing, or modifying a MAPI server.

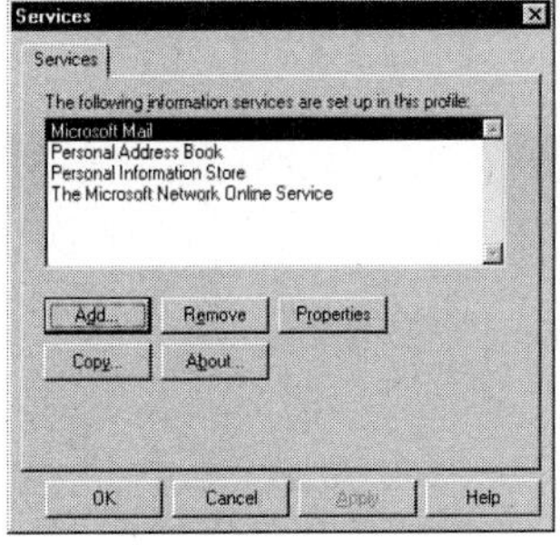

Figure 20.29.
The Services dialog box is where you manage the MAPI servers attached to your machine.

Adding a New Service

Adding a new Service to Exchange is very easy. All you need to do is click the Add button in the Services dialog box. Exchange displays a list of default services available for Windows 95, as shown in Figure 20.30. However, you can add third-party MAPI services by clicking the Have Disk button.

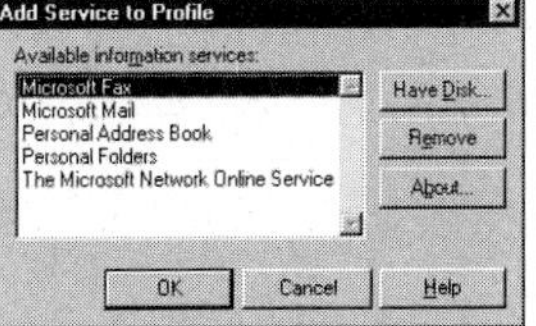

Figure 20.30.
The Add Service to Profile dialog box allows you to add new MAPI servers to Exchange with little effort.

Tip: More vendors are providing MAPI servers that you can use with Microsoft Exchange (Windows Messaging, for OSR2 users) every day. In some cases, that support isn't immediately evident, or you don't need to install the support as a separate item. For example, when you install Netscape Navigator, you have the option of using the mail reader that comes with the product, or using Microsoft Exchange. If you choose Microsoft Exchange, the Navigator install program automatically adds the appropriate MAPI client for you. Make sure that you fully understand how MAPI support gets added before you install a product; some vendors may use techniques other than the ones mentioned in this book for supporting MAPI. (Removing MAPI support almost always involves highlighting one of the services shown in the Services dialog box and clicking the Remove button.)

Normally the procedure would involve selecting the service you want to install and clicking OK. That's what you should do to install the service. However, I found an interesting piece of information in this dialog box. Clicking the About button displays a dialog box similar to the one shown in Figure 20.31. Notice that it lists all the files required to make this service operate. You can use this dialog box later if you need to know the names of the files to remove from your hard drive when a service is no longer needed. This dialog box also provides helpful diagnostic information if you have problems later. For example, you could use it to determine the size of the various files, the version number of each component, and who to call for help with a particular service.

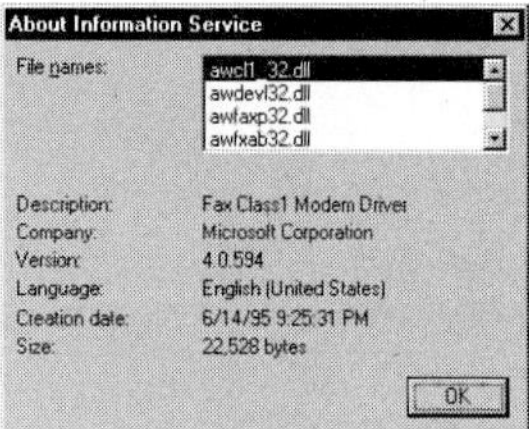

Figure 20.31.
The About Information Service dialog box tells you a lot more than the usual About dialog box.

After Exchange completes the installation of a new service, it usually asks whether you want to configure it. This usually involves providing routing information or perhaps some specifics about the equipment you plan to use. You don't necessarily have to configure the service right away if you don't have the required information. Clicking the Properties button later will allow you to configure the service to meet your needs. However, if the service requires some type of routing or equipment-specific information, you'll need to perform the configuration before you can use the service.

Customizing Exchange

Exchange provides a great deal of flexibility in the way that you access information. You've already seen much of that flexibility in this chapter. As third-party vendors create more MAPI servers, you'll only see that flexibility increase. However, the flexibility of Exchange goes beyond that. You can also configure just about every aspect of the interface itself. The Tools | Options command displays an Options dialog box like the one shown in Figure 20.32. This dialog box allows you to change the way that Exchange interacts with you.

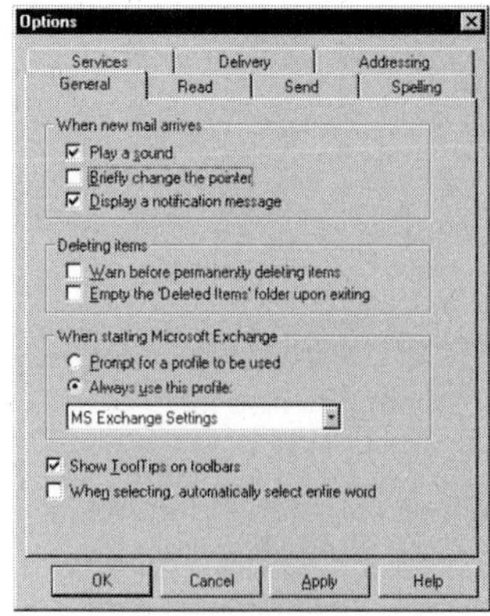

Figure 20.32.
The Options dialog box allows you to change the way Exchange interacts with the user.

The General page contains four main sections. The first tells Exchange how to notify you about new mail—if you do, in fact, want to be notified. The check boxes in this group are fairly easy to figure out. You can have Exchange play a sound, change the mouse pointer, or display a message to notify you of new mail. Of course, you can select combinations of all three if you like. The second section tells Exchange what to do with deleted items. The first selection tells Exchange to warn you before it permanently deletes anything, just in case you really want to keep something. By checking the second selection, you can automatically remove any deleted messages from the hard drive when you exit Exchange. The first setting in the third section allows you to choose the profile (list of services) that you'll use each time you start Exchange. You can keep more than one profile if needed, but I usually find that centralized control of my messages is far more valuable than the flexibility of using additional profiles. The default setting is to use the standard Microsoft Exchange Settings profile.

The final two check boxes on this page are miscellaneous settings. The first setting affects ToolTips. Those are the little dialog boxes that appear under each control if you rest your mouse cursor there long enough. They provide a quick description of that control's purpose. The second setting affects how the editor works. Checking this box means that Exchange selects an entire word at a time, instead of single characters. It comes in handy for block deletes, but I personally find that the editor works better without this option turned on.

The Read page, shown in Figure 20.33, contains two main sections. The first tells Exchange how to move the cursor after you read and either move or delete a message. The default setting moves the cursor to the next item in the list. This is very convenient when your message base is sorted by date because you waste a lot less time positioning the cursor this way. Of course, you might organize your list in reverse order to see the older messages first. In this case, the second setting would work better. Whichever way you organize your messages, selecting the right radio button can add a measure of convenience to the process of selecting and then reading your messages.

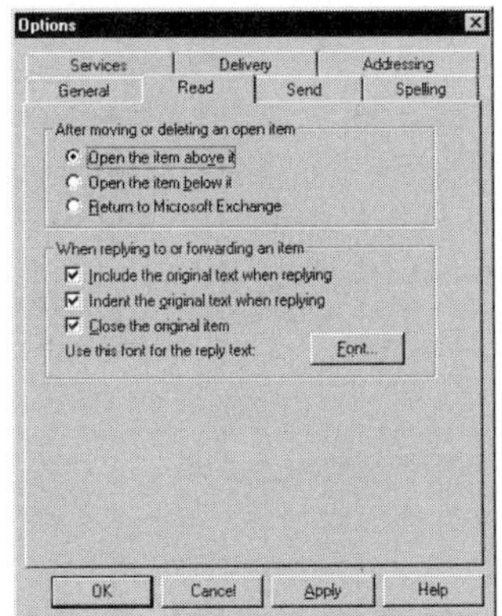

Figure 20.33.
Use the Read page of the Options dialog box to change the way that Exchange reacts when you read messages.

The second section of this page allows you to change the tasks that Exchange automatically performs when you answer a message. The first option allows you to include the original message in your response. The second option indents the original text to make it clearer that you're including the original text. If you use the first option, always include the second for the sake of clarity. The third option closes the original item after you respond to it. This allows you to move to the next message without wasting time. Finally, the Font button displays a list of fonts and font sizes in a dialog box. You should normally select a typeface and font size that will help the other person see your response clearly, but keep the font small enough to avoid unnecessary wrapping, which is annoying to read.

Peter's Principle: Quoting: A Waste of Money or a Friendly Gesture?

Exchange offers you the chance to include the text of the original message when you make a reply. This process is called *quoting* when you use it with an online service such as CompuServe. Other services might use different names, but the effect is the same. When you include part of the original message in your response, you're quoting the other person.

This particular policy generates a lot of controversy in some online services. Some people think quoting is a waste of time because the other person should know what you're talking about. Time spells money on some online services because they charge you for every minute that you spend actively using it. To the people who oppose this practice, downloading quoted material means wasting money. Other people—those who spend a lot of time online—really like this practice because it allows them to keep individual conversations separate. They believe that the small amount of additional text is the cost of maintaining a clear dialog box.

You can compromise to keep both parties happy. Simply enclose the significant part of the original text in angle brackets, like this: <<Some part of an original message.>> Be sure to place the quoted text on a separate line so that it's clear when you're quoting the other person. I usually use this measure if I'm not sure whether the other party likes quoting or not. My responses usually include quoted questions or perhaps a comment that caught my attention. I never include more than absolutely necessary to get my point across or to clarify my response.

What about your company e-mail? Quoting is always a good idea when you're carrying on a lot of conversations with one person. I find that it helps me to remember the exact nature of a particular discussion as I go from topic to topic. Whether or not you use quoting when you access an online service is a matter of personal preference. Using it with the people you work with is a matter of necessity.

The Send page shown in Figure 20.34 contains settings that change the way you send messages to other people. This dialog box has five main areas. The first setting allows you to change the font that you use to create messages. Clicking this button displays a list of typefaces available on your machine. Always select a typeface and font size that will allow the other person to read your message with a minimum of squinting. The second item allows you to determine whether the other party received and/or read your message. I almost never use the receipt feature unless I've been having communication problems. It tends to make the other person think that you don't trust him. The Set Sensitivity list box tells the other person how much secrecy to attach to your message. I usually include a lot more than just a sensitivity setting, though, if the information is very important or if it's critical that the other person guard the contents of the message. The next setting allows you to adjust the standard importance associated with a particular message. Unless you're the president of the company, you'll probably want to keep it at the Normal setting. Fortunately, you can easily adjust this setting on an individual basis when needed. I will tell you how later in this chapter. The final setting on this page places a copy of your message in the Sent Items folder. I always use this feature because people (or the mail system) often lose the messages I send. Most people have this problem. Keeping a copy of the message where you can grab it quickly changes a major headache into a minor nuisance.

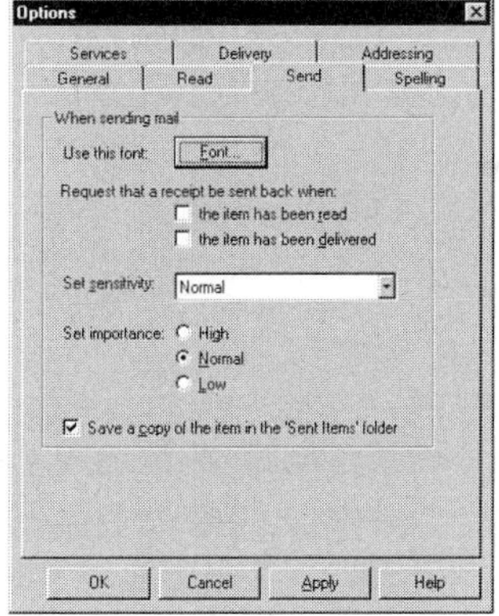

Figure 20.34.
The Send page of the Options dialog box allows you to change the way that Exchange sends messages you create.

The Spelling page shown in Figure 20.35 can save you more than time. It can save you the embarrassment of making a major spelling error on a message that you planned to use to impress someone. I often wonder what the other person was thinking when he wrote a message, because of the number of spelling errors. In fact, such a problem is almost inexcusable today because just about every product that works with Windows also includes a spelling checker of some type. Of course, a spelling checker can't catch some types of errors such as homonyms (to-too-two). They also won't catch grammar errors unless they're designed to do so, and then you can only count on them doing a very marginal job. If a message is so important that you can't afford any errors, get a second set of human eyes to look at it for you.

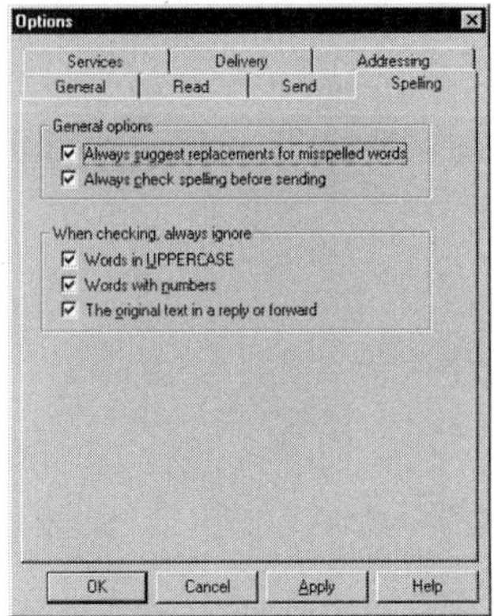

Figure 20.35.
The Spelling page determines when and how the spelling checker will keep your messages free of spelling errors.

Previous sections looked at the Addressing and Services pages. The Addressing page is where you add new address lists and define the default address list to use when creating a message. The Services page allows you to add new services to Exchange.

The Delivery page appears in Figure 20.36. The first two fields allow you to define a primary and secondary mail-delivery location. All you need to do is select the desired location from the list box. The third list box defines which address lists Exchange will use to process recipient addresses. You can change the order by highlighting the desired entry and using the arrows to move it up or down the list.

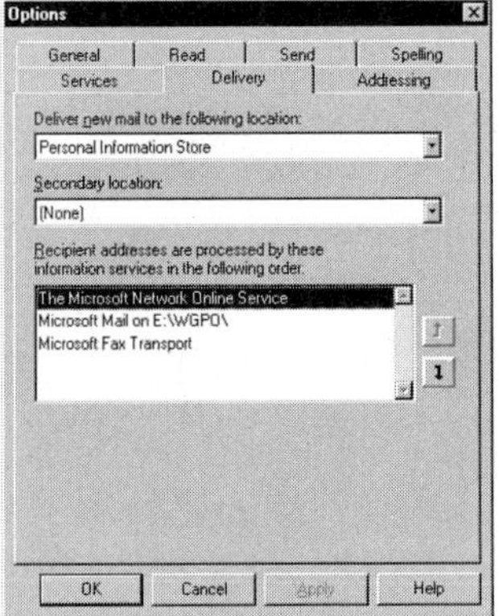

Figure 20.36.
The Delivery page allows you to define the delivery location for your mail.

Customizing the Toolbar

I like the way the Exchange toolbar is arranged. It seems to contain everything I need without getting cluttered with things I don't normally use. However, you might need to use different Exchange features to get your work done. That's one reason I was so happy to see the customization feature.

Use the Tools | Customize Toolbar command to display the dialog box shown in Figure 20.37. This is where you customize the toolbar. There are two lists. The one on the left includes all the commands and other features that you can include on the toolbar. The list on the right contains all the commands and other features that are on the toolbar right now. To add a new feature to the toolbar, simply highlight the position on the right list where you want it to appear and then highlight the item on the left list that you want to add. Click the Add button to add the new item. Likewise, if you want to remove an item from the toolbar, simply highlight it and click Remove.

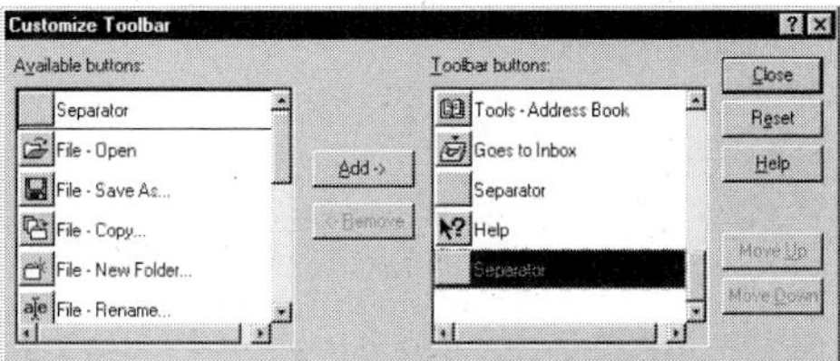

Figure 20.37.
Customizing the toolbar is as easy as a few clicks in this dialog box.

You can also move things around on the toolbar. Simply select the item you want to move and click the Move Up or Move Down button to make the change. If you decide that all the changes you made were in error, clicking the Reset button returns them to their previous state. Finally, click the Close button to make your changes permanent.

Customizing the Column Headings

Exchange even allows you to modify the amount and type of data it displays. You can easily change the column widths by moving the mouse cursor between two columns, waiting for the pointer to change to a line with two arrows (one pointing each direction), and dragging the column line wherever you want it. Once you get past column widths, though, you need to use the View | Column command to modify other column features. Figure 20.38 shows what this dialog box looks like.

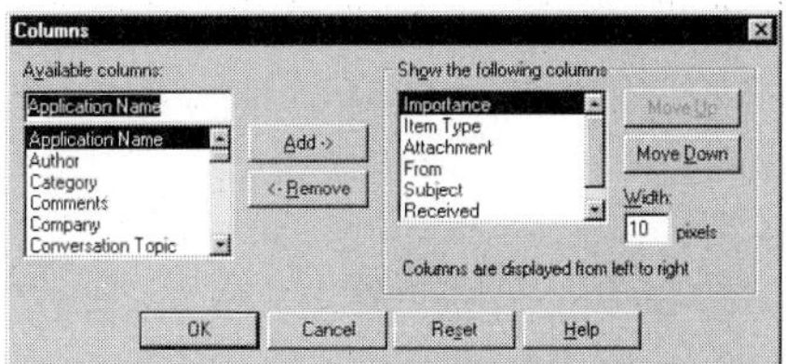

Figure 20.38.
There's no reason to keep data around that you don't need. Get rid of it by using the Columns dialog box.

There's no reason to keep specific columns around when you no longer need them. Likewise, you might find that Exchange provides some type of information you would really like to see. I usually err in favor of too much data if I have the screen real estate to support additional columns. It's better to have too much data than to miss something important because you don't have enough.

This dialog box works much like the Customize Toolbar dialog box discussed in the preceding section. To add a column to the display, simply select where you want it to appear in the right list, highlight the data you want in the left list, and click Add. Removing unneeded data is just as easy. In the right column, highlight the entry you want to get rid of, and click Remove.

If you find that you've added or removed too many columns, click Reset to restore things to their unedited state. Moving columns around is easy, too. Just select the desired column in the right list and use the Move Up and Move Down buttons to change its position.

This dialog box has one additional field. The Width field allows you to set the size of the columns in pixels. Personally, I find this a little counterintuitive. I prefer to use the mouse to change the column size, using the technique I described at the beginning of this section.

Understanding the Online Services

Now that you have a better understanding of Microsoft Exchange, it's time to look at some of the things that you can do with it. Exchange comes with three different MAPI servers: Mail, Fax, and Microsoft Network. Each of these servers uses Exchange as its front end to varying degrees.

Tip: The original version of Microsoft Exchange came with four MAPI servers, but Microsoft dropped the CompuServe service at the very end of the test cycle. There are rumors that CompuServe will pick up support for this particular server sometime in the near future. You'll probably want to keep your eyes peeled for it if Exchange is your medium of choice for online communications.

The following sections explore the MAPI servers that come with Windows 95. These servers can interact with each other through Exchange. All the messages you receive appear in one place, regardless of which server you used to retrieve them. In fact, from a user perspective, you might even be tempted to think that you're using a single product for all your communications needs. Of course, it's just the level of front-end integration that makes it appear that way.

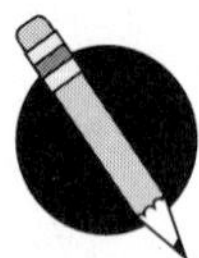

Note: Microsoft Plus!, the add-on product for Windows 95, includes additional MAPI servers. One of the servers provides complete access to the Internet. If Internet access is important to you, you might want to see what Microsoft Plus! has to offer. You can get an overview of what Microsoft Plus! provides by looking at Chapter 28.

Microsoft Mail

Microsoft Mail is the easiest of the MAPI servers to describe. We've already looked at all the interface elements in this chapter. The only thing you'll notice as far as Mail is concerned is that any changes to your local post office automatically appear in your setup as well. I find that Mail is probably the most integrated of all the MAPI servers.

Sending a Mail message is very easy. All you have to do is click the New Message icon on the Exchange toolbar to display the dialog box shown in Figure 20.39. Your dialog box might not have all the fields that mine does. I selected all the options in the View menu so that I could show you what they look like. As with every new Windows application, this one has a toolbar that provides access to just about every feature that Mail supports.

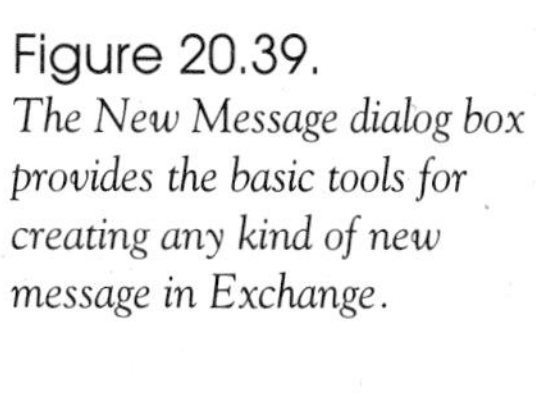

Figure 20.39.
The New Message dialog box provides the basic tools for creating any kind of new message in Exchange.

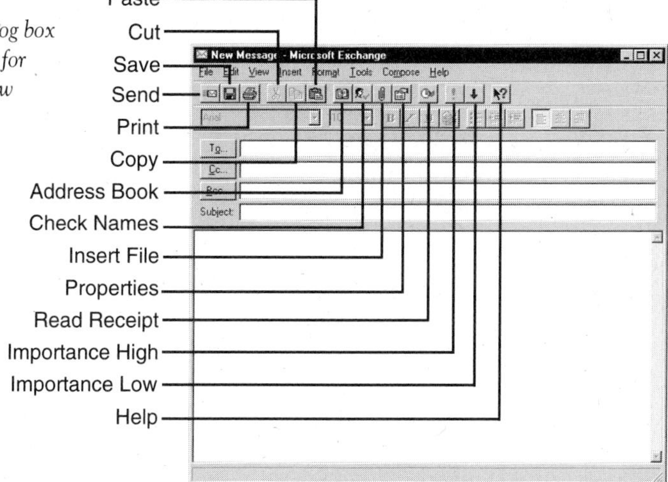

The following list provides an overview of what the features can do for you:

- **Send:** As soon as you get everything filled out in your message, click this button to send your message to the recipient.
- **Save:** Exchange allows you to save a copy of the message in an external file. You use this button to display the Save dialog box. You can use the File | Save As command to save this message under a different filename.
- **Print:** Clicking this button prints the current message, using the default print setup.
- **Cut:** This button removes the selected data and places it on the Clipboard.
- **Copy:** Use this button to copy the selected data to the Clipboard.
- **Paste:** This button places the data from the Clipboard at the selected position.

- **Address Book:** Use this command to open the address book and find any addressees for your message. You can perform the same thing by clicking any of the buttons next to the address fields on the message itself.
- **Check Names:** As soon as you come up with a list of people to whom you want to send a message, you can click this button to make sure that they're all correct. If Exchange finds that a name doesn't appear in one of your address lists, it displays a dialog box asking whether you want to add the name to an address list or correct it. Exchange usually supplies a list of substitutes for you. Of course, the size of this list depends on how many names in your address book are close matches to the one incorrect entry.
- **Insert File:** You can send someone a file as a message attachment by using this button. It displays a dialog box that allows you to browse your local and network hard drives. Any inserted files appear as icons within the message. Exchange doesn't actually place a copy of the file in the message; it uses an OLE link instead. You can link or embed objects in a message using the other techniques discussed in Chapter 12 as well.
- **Properties:** The Properties dialog box tells you the basics about a message. It also allows you to select the sensitivity and importance levels. Three check boxes allow you to select receipt types and whether Exchange saves a copy of the message in the Sent Items folder.
- **Read Receipt:** Clicking this button automatically requests a read receipt for this message. You'll get an acknowledgment from Exchange as soon as the recipient opens the message for reading.
- **Importance High/Importance Low:** You can select either of these buttons to send a message with other than a normal importance level. Exchange displays high-importance messages with a red exclamation point and low-importance messages with a blue down arrow.
- **Help:** Use this button to receive context-sensitive help about any items you don't understand.

In addition to all these toolbar options, there are other configuration options on the menu. All the configuration options you saw in the Exchange section also appear here. For example, you can configure the New Message dialog box toolbar to meet your needs. The service configuration option appears here as well.

Below the toolbar is a formatting toolbar. It includes everything that you might expect. You can select a typeface, font size, boldfacing, italics, underline, and font color. The toolbar allows you to format the paragraph by adding bullets and indentation. You can also specify the paragraph alignment: at right, center, or left.

Microsoft Fax

Microsoft Fax operates in essentially the same way as Microsoft Mail. You even use the same type of message editing box. However, the initial screens are somewhat different, so I'll cover them here.

You create a new fax by using the Compose | New Fax command in Exchange. Figure 20.40 shows the initial Fax Wizard dialog box. The first thing you need to do to create a new fax is to describe your location. Chapter 19 visited this issue (and we even looked at it again in this chapter), so I won't go though the details again.

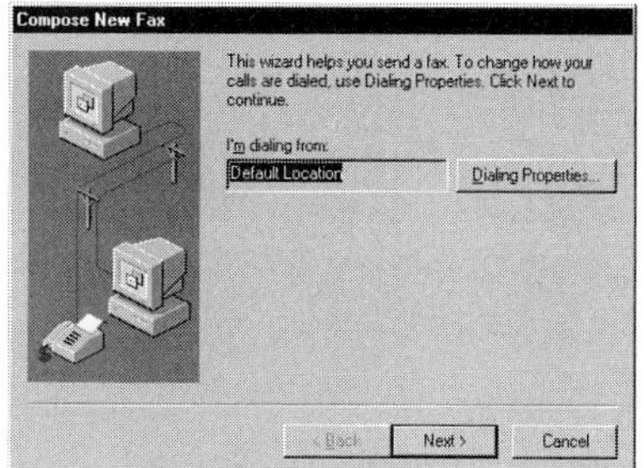

Figure 20.40.
Use the Compose New Fax dialog box to format the address portion of any fax you want to send.

After you describe your location, click Next to proceed to the next step of creating a fax. You'll see the dialog box shown in Figure 20.41. This is where you tell the Fax Wizard where you want the message sent. You can use the Address Book button to display any of your address lists and select a recipient from them. I use this method because it ensures that the address is correct and saves me time typing the required information. Notice the Add to List button. Clicking it adds the current name and telephone number to the Recipient List field. Use this option when you want to send the same fax to more than one person.

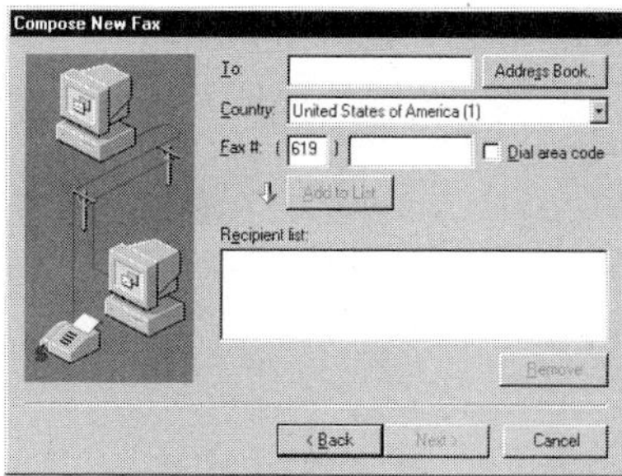

Figure 20.41.
You create a recipient list by using this dialog box.

Click Next when you complete this information to display the dialog box shown in Figure 20.42. It allows you to select a cover page. It also contains an Options button that displays a configuration dialog box. Optional items include the message format and when you want to send the fax.

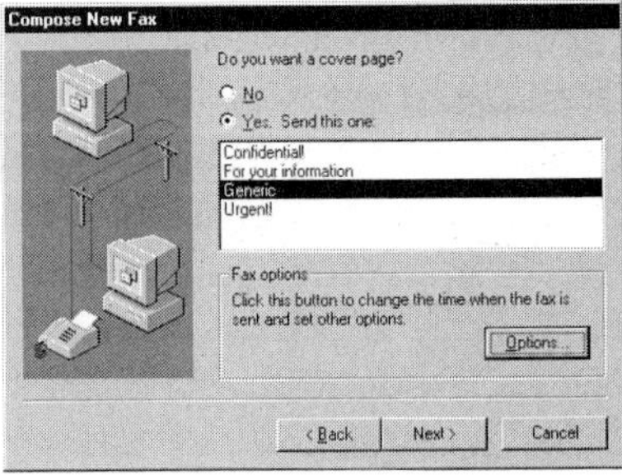

Figure 20.42.
Use this dialog box to set some of the optional features for your fax.

Click Next one more time to display the dialog box shown in Figure 20.43. This is where you'll define the subject and message content of this fax. It doesn't look very much like the Exchange format, but the finished fax will include all the same elements. In fact, if you had selected the Create New Fax option from the Create New Message dialog box, this display would look exactly like its Exchange counterpart. The Start Note on Cover Page check box allows you to place the beginning of your note on the cover page. If the entire note fits there, you'll save paper for the recipient because you only need to send a single page. Removing the check from this check box always sends the note on a separate page.

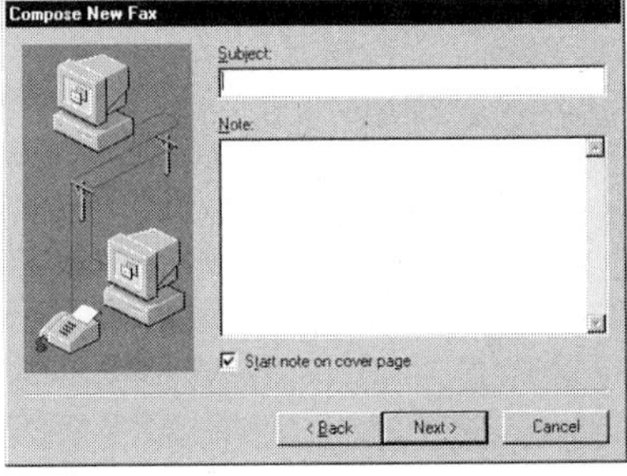

Figure 20.43.
This dialog box allows you to add a subject line and message to your fax.

Click Next to reach the next dialog box, shown in Figure 20.44. This dialog box allows you to attach a file to your fax. Of course, it won't appear as an OLE object this time. The attached file will be sent to the recipient as a file or an attached set of pages. The list box contains a list of files that you want to send. Clicking the Add File button displays a browse dialog box that you can use to select another file. Highlighting an entry in the list box and clicking Remove will remove that file from the list.

The next time you click Next, you'll see a dialog box saying that your fax is ready to send. All you need to do now is click Finish to send it. If everything goes well, you should either see a new entry in the Outgoing Faxes dialog box or hear the fax/modem as it whisks your message off to the recipient.

Figure 20.44.
Use this dialog box to attach files to your fax.

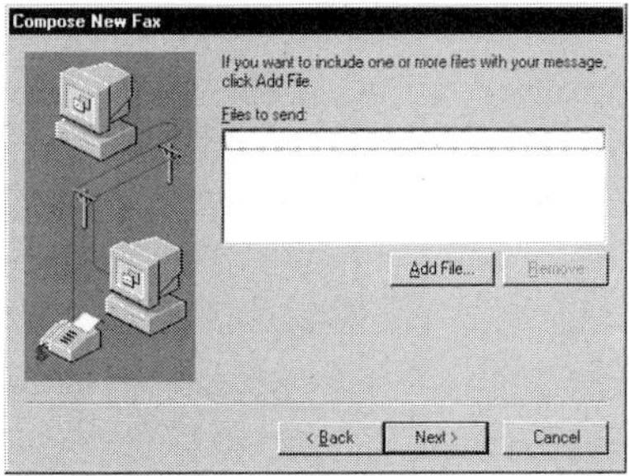

Note: One of the advantages of using Microsoft Fax instead of a standard fax machine is that you can send a fax late at night when the telephone rates are low. Unlike a standard fax machine, there are no pages to jam or other mechanical problems to overcome. Of course, problems at the other end can still prevent the recipient from actually receiving your fax.

Microsoft Network

The Microsoft Network (MSN) is Microsoft's attempt at creating an online service similar to CompuServe or America Online. It has actually turned out to be more than just another online service, though, as Microsoft has added features. The newest feature is an Internet front end. If you looked at MSN when it first came out, but then rejected it as too much of the same thing, you may want to take another look now.

Note: At the time of this writing, Microsoft was working on a newer Internet front end for MSN. OSR2 users will have a new version of MSN 1.3 on their machines that makes use of this new front end for sign-up purposes. Once you've signed up, everything else in this section should look the same. Existing Windows 95 users can use the Internet front end by going to this URL: `http://signup.msn.com/signup/signup.hts?`. Be sure to visit `http://www.msn.com/default.asp` as well to learn about future updates to MSN.

You can access MSN in a variety of ways. If you're currently using Exchange, use the Tools | Remote Mail option to display the dialog box shown in Figure 20.45. This is where all your MSN-specific messages are stored after you connect to the network. Notice that the indicator in the lower-right corner shows when you're connected or disconnected.

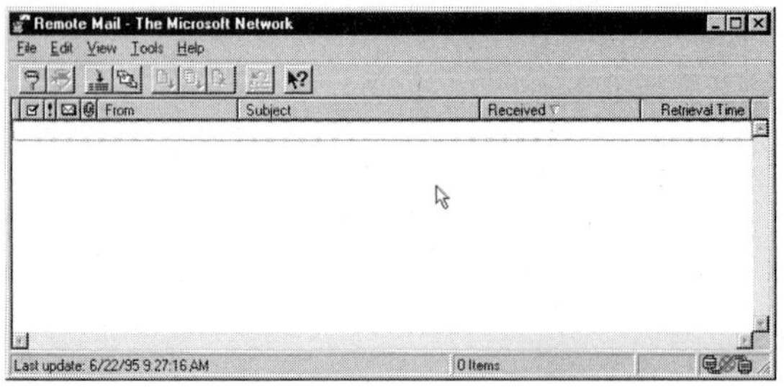

Figure 20.45.
The Remote Mail dialog box is where MSN stores any messages that you receive on the network.

Clicking the Connect button on the toolbar displays the dialog box shown in Figure 20.46. Notice that this dialog box contains three fields. The first field contains your name. The second contains the password for your MSN account. The check box tells Exchange to remember your MSN password between sessions. Notice the Settings button. Clicking it brings up a centralized dialog box with buttons for changing your modem and dialing properties. You've already seen both of the dialog boxes that clicking these buttons will bring up, so I won't describe them again. The only other setting that this dialog box changes is your access number—a single setting that allows you to access the Microsoft Network. You change this setting by selecting the city with an access number nearest your own.

Figure 20.46.
The MSN Sign In dialog box is where you enter your name and password prior to going online.

Note: Exchange remembers your MSN password between sessions only if you have some other form of Windows 95-specific password protection for your machine. If you use Windows 95 without enabling passwords, you'll have to enter your MSN password each time you use it. The reason for this safeguard is simple: It protects your account from misuse by other people.

After you enter your name and password and change any required settings, click Connect to proceed. You'll hear your modem attempt to access MSN. The dialog box also displays messages during this process in case your modem speaker is turned off.

This method of access doesn't show the full MSN display that we'll see in a few moments. All it does is allow you to access your e-mail. When you do finally make a connection, Exchange displays the Remote Mail dialog box again. Use the Update Headers button to collect all your message headers (this doesn't actually retrieve the messages). You'll use three buttons on the toolbar to mark the various message headers as you read them. The first retrieves the message and erases it online. The second retrieves a copy of the message but leaves the original in your online e-mail box. The third deletes the message without reading it. After you decide the fate of all your message headers, use the Transfer Mail button to retrieve any messages that you decide to keep. This will download them from MSN and place them in your Inbox.

Getting e-mail isn't the only reason to use MSN. Now that we've looked at the speedy way to get your mail, let's look at what you can do to browse through the features that MSN offers. You should see an MSN icon on your desktop. Double-clicking it displays the same Sign In dialog box that we saw before. However, instead of simply getting logged on and seeing the Remote Mail dialog box, you'll see a different display this time. Figure 20.47 gives you an idea of what you might see.

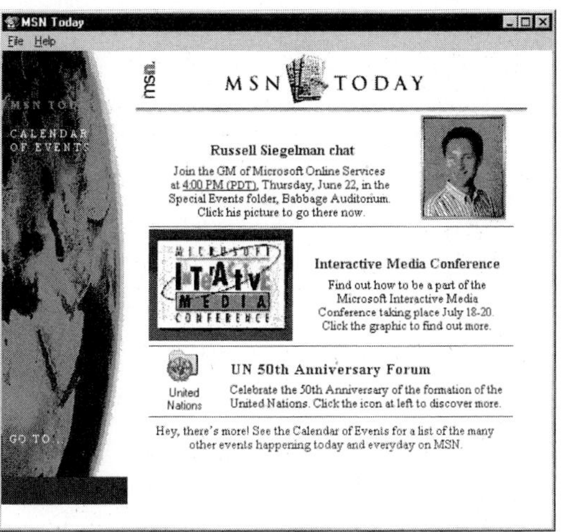

Figure 20.47.
The first thing you'll normally see when you sign in to MSN is MSN Today.

This is a brief description of the various events taking place on MSN today. You'll also get a quick summary of important news events and other information of this sort. When you get done looking at this page, you can use the MSN icon in the control area of the Taskbar to get back to MSN Central, shown in Figure 20.48. This is the starting point for all your adventures on MSN. From here you can check your e-mail, get some assistance with using MSN, or check out the categories of other places that you can visit on MSN. Notice the Favorite Places option. You can store the locations of places you visit frequently, so that you can find them quickly.

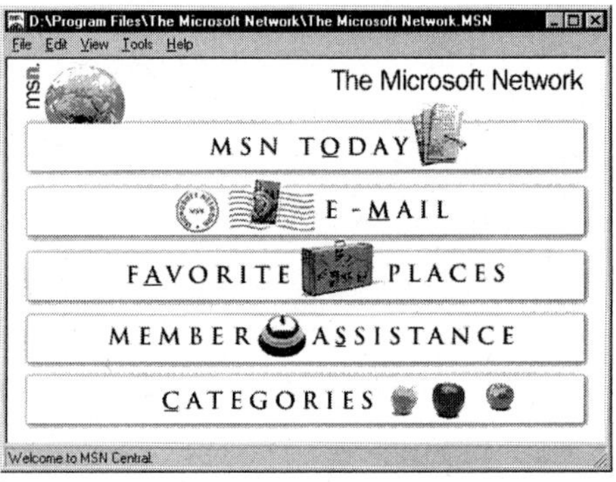

Figure 20.48.
MSN Central is the starting point for any online time on MSN.

Categories is where all the action is on MSN, so let's take a look there. Figure 20.49 shows an example of what you might see. However, Microsoft is constantly changing the features that MSN offers, so this view will change often. What's the first thing you noticed about this display? It should look just like an Explorer single-pane view with a little window dressing because that's exactly what it is. You'll navigate MSN by using an Explorer-type interface. Of course, this means that it's easy to use, but it also means that you'll spend some time boring down through the various folders to find what you want. That's why setting up some Favorite Places is so important.

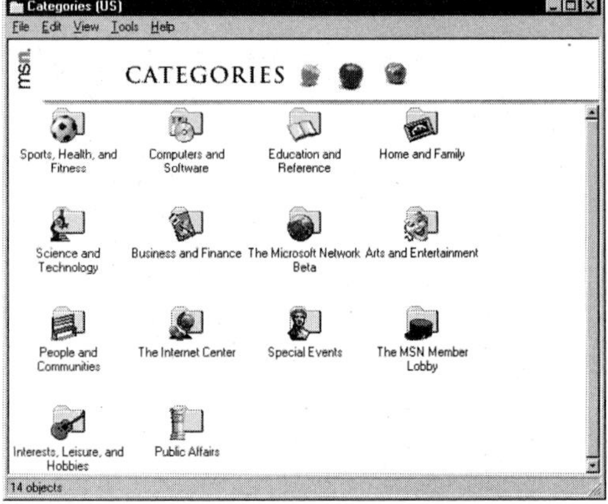

Figure 20.49.
It's no surprise that MSN uses a single-pane Explorer view to help you get around.

Tip: If you were a bit shocked to see the extensive change in MSN organization that Microsoft made recently, don't worry. You can still get the classic MSN look if you really want to, and this includes the classic category folder list. Simply open the MSN Classic Categories folder shown in Figure 20.38, and you'll see all the categories you know and love. Unfortunately, you'll have to set up this particular folder in your Favorite Places list to get there without having to go through the new Categories folder first. Hopefully, Microsoft will eventually add some kind of online configuration setting so that you get to choose one arrangement or the other.

I don't want to spoil all the fun of exploring MSN, but let's look at one of the categories you probably will want to see immediately. Suppose that you wanted to check the Internet listings for a new job. Double-clicking The Internet Center, then The Most Popular Newsgroups, then `misc.jobs.offered` would take you to a place where you could learn about new job possibilities. Figure 20.50 shows how the messages appear in a typical MSN forum. I've pulled down the folder list box here to show you that you can move through MSN by using the same techniques that you use with Explorer.

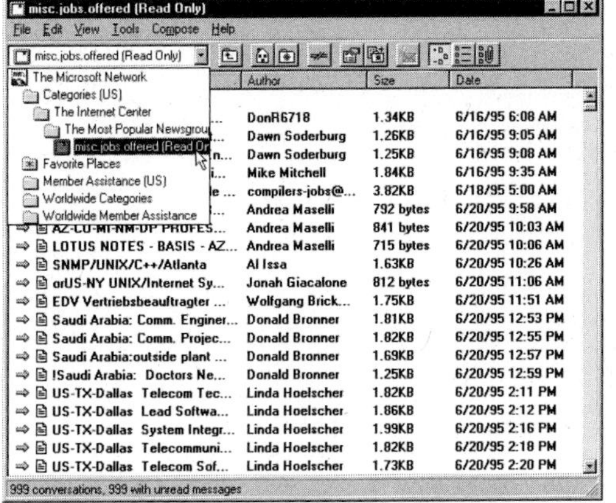

Figure 20.50.
A typical MSN forum contains a list of messages available for reading.

Warning: It's sad that the browser wars will affect your use of MSN for the time being. After several frustrating hours, I found that the only way to access many of the Internet links (such as Star Trek Continuum) provided by MSN is by using Internet Explorer. Any attempt to use Netscape Navigator (or any other browser, for that matter) results in an error message within the browser window. Hopefully, Microsoft will make MSN more open in the future so that people can use the browser that they want to use, rather than being forced to use Internet Explorer as their exclusive option. On the other hand, there are quite a few Internet sites that you can visit from MSN by using Netscape Navigator—the support just isn't 100 percent.

You can use the File | Add to Favorite Places command to add this location to Favorite Places. That way, the next time you wanted to view the listing of available jobs, it would be easy to get to this particular forum. Instead of "drilling down" through all those folders, you would gain direct access.

As with every other aspect of Exchange, you can retrieve messages from MSN and place them in your Inbox. Once you respond to them offline, you can upload the responses to the forum. Everything for MSN works the same as any other Exchange MAPI server.

Now that we have the basics of using MSN out of the way, let's talk about a few things that you'll need to really use this product. The following list tells you about the language of using an online product like MSN:

- **Forum:** This is a gathering place for people of like interests. One person leaves a message and someone else responds to it. You can look at the message header to determine what a particular discussion is about. In essence, you can think of a forum as a room in a house where people of like interests get together to talk. Finding the right forum can provide you with a wealth of information that you might not find elsewhere. It can also help you solve problems related to your software, your machine, or even your business.
- **Message:** A single note on a particular subject is a message. You use messages in e-mail and other places already, so the concept of a message shouldn't be new to you.
- **Thread:** A group of connected messages on the same topic. As each person responds to a message, he makes the list of messages about a given topic longer. You can read an entire list of messages (a thread) to discover the conversation that took place on a specific topic. The fact that the messages are written rather than spoken is an advantage, because you can read the messages when it's convenient. Threads are also a key way to store information for future use. Many people archive message threads about specific topics because that information can't be found easily anywhere else.

I don't want to make this a book about using online services; there are plenty of those on the market already. I suggest that you buy one or two of them to build your knowledge of online services. It's important to learn the rules of the road when it comes to reacting to other people's messages. You'll also need to learn rules of etiquette for forums. I've presented some of these ideas already. For example, many people frown on the practice of quoting on a forum.

Body language is a missing element of any online conversation. You can't really tell someone that a comment is tongue-in-cheek using a wry smile, because he won't see it. To help avoid conflict whenever possible, people have come up with something called an emoticon (pronounced *ee-MOTE-ick-on*). It's a little text icon that tells the other person what you mean by a certain comment. Just look sideways to see a facial expression in most cases, and a text version of a picture in others. Table 20.1 lists common emoticons that you can use to dress up any written communication. In fact, you could even use them on your company e-mail.

Table 20.1. A list of standard emoticons.

Emoticon	*Description*
`:-)`	A happy face
`:->`	An alternative happy face
`:-D`	Said with a smile
`:<)`	Humor for those with hairy lips
`:<)=`	Humor for those with beards too
`B-)`	Smiling and wearing glasses or sunglasses (or a message from Batman)
`8-)`	Smiling and wearing glasses or sunglasses; also used to denote a wide-eyed look
`:-1` or `:-,`	A smirk
`'-)`	A wink
`:-(`	Unhappy
`:-c` or `(:-(`	Very unhappy
`:/)`	Not funny: The receiver of a message sends this emoticon to show that a particular comment wasn't received as the sender intended.
`(:-&`	Angry
`:-) )-:`	Theatrical comments: Use this for comments that are either theatrical in nature or used for emphasis.
`;-)`	Sardonic incredulity
`(@ @)`	You're kidding!
`:-"`	Pursed lips
`:-C`	Incredulous (jaw dropped)
`:-<`	Forlorn
`:-B`	Drooling (or overbite)
`:-¦`	Disgusted
`:-V`	Shouting
`:-o` or `:-0`	More versions of shouting
`:-w`	Speaking with a forked tongue: You're lying to the other person in a whimsical sort of way. In other words, you're making a point sarcastically.
`:-W`	Shouting with a forked tongue
`:-r`	Bleahhh! (tongue sticking out)
`<:-0`	Eek! You can use this for a number of purposes. You can even use it to tell the network administrator that your equipment is down, and you can't do anything without it.

continues

Table 20.1. continued

Emoticon	*Description*
:-*	Oops! (covering mouth with hand)
:-T	Keeping a straight face (tight-lipped): Use this emoticon when you mean something in a serious way that the receiver could interpret as a humorous comment.
:-#	Censored: You'd love to use a little profanity but resisted the urge.
:-x	Kiss, kiss
:-?	Licking your lips
:~i	Smoking
:~j	Smoking and smiling
:/i	No smoking
:-) :-) :-)	A guffaw
:-J	A tongue-in-cheek comment
:*)	Clowning around
:-8	Talking out of both sides of your mouth
<:-)	For dumb questions: Everyone knows that the only dumb question is the one you failed to ask before trashing the network. However, some people might feel that they have a dumb question they want someone to answer.
00	Headlights on: Use this emoticon to show someone that you want him to pay special attention to a comment.
:-o or #:-o	"Oh, noooooo!" (à la Mr. Bill)
¦-(	A late-night message
(:-$	Ill
#:-)	Matted hair
:^)	A big nose
:-{#}	Braces
(:^(	A broken nose
:-(=)	Big teeth
&:-)	Curly hair
@:-)	Wavy hair
?-(	A black eye
%-)	Broken glasses
:	A fuzzy person

Emoticon	*Description*
`*:**`	A fuzzy person with a fuzzy mustache
`(:<)`	A blabbermouth
`+<:-¦`	A monk or nun
`(:-¦K-`	A formal message
`¦¦*(`	A handshake is offered
`¦¦*)`	A handshake is accepted
`<:>==`	A turkey
`@>—>——`	A rose
`(-_-)`	A secret smile
`<{:-)}`	A message in a bottle
`<:-)<<¦`	A message from a spaceship
`(:-...`	A heartbreaking message
`(:>-<`	A message from a thief: Hands up!
`...—...`	SOS
`:-I`	It's something, but I don't know what...: You can't figure out what the other person is trying to say or reference.
`@%&$%&`	Profanity

Hopefully you'll come to enjoy using online services as much as I have. MSN is just starting out, but you can use other online services as well. CompuServe seems to be one of the favorite places for business people to congregate, although there are forums to attract just about anyone's attention. America Online is extremely popular as well. Of course, the trick to selecting any online service is to find the one that meets your needs. Obviously, no one can determine that but you.

On Your Own

Set up Microsoft Exchange to handle your faxing, online communications, and mail needs. See whether you can tell any difference between the messages you receive from the three sources. In most cases, you won't unless the sender provides some kind of clue.

Check your SYSTEM folder to see whether you can identify the various pieces of the communications subsystem. This chapter provides you with a list of the major files and many hints on how you can find the other special files that pertain to your system.

Determine whether you or your company can use a voice modem to make using the computer easier and more efficient. Be sure to check out the various criteria covered in this chapter—especially adherence to standards. You'll also want to download the Unimodem V update for your computer if you're not using the OSR2 version of Windows 95.

I provided you with a list of standard emoticons in this chapter. One of the fun elements of online computing is coming up with your own set of special emoticons (of course, this means that you have to explain them to everyone). Try creating a few emoticons of your own. For example, one person recently created an emoticon that resembles Bill the Cat.

21

Getting Online

In the minds of some people, the Internet has become the singles bar of the 90s—a place to meet new people and exchange ideas. The media has certainly done nothing to discourage this idea; if anything, they encourage the idea by publishing the names of Internet sites helter-skelter. Just look at your television set. During one evening, a friend and I saw that no less than 80 percent of the new television shows include an Internet address as part of their programming. A few shows even depend on the Internet as a primary source of entertainment information. Of course, television isn't the only entertainment industry making use of the Internet. Many games and other products now include Internet capabilities of one sort or another as standard fare. Suffice it to say that entertainment's certainly one way to view the Internet, but not the only one by a long shot.

An equally interesting idea is that the Internet is some kind of a remote communications magic carpet. The trade press has recently filled its pages with the term *intranet*—a viable term when used in the right way. The problem is that if you read any three people's opinions on what this term means, you'll come away with three different definitions. The true meaning behind intranet is something different from what most people expect. I normally reserve this term for an extended form of wide area network (WAN), a business tool that allows employees to share information even when they're on the road.

Consider all the other uses for the Internet. One magazine that I looked at recently suggested that artists use the Internet in place of a gallery to show previews of their art for sale. I've also seen some articles that talk about how the fashion industry uses the Internet to tell people about new trends. Obviously, there are more mundane uses as well. You'll find a number of newsgroups on the Internet and more than a few people use it for research purposes, for example. In fact, the Internet started as a means for government and educational organizations to exchange information.

The Internet certainly fulfills some of these ideas. You can use it as an extremely valuable research tool. Exchanging ideas with other people has always been a part of the Internet. The idea that you can create a Web site for your employees at remote sites is also a possibility. However, none of these uses for the Internet really tells you what it's all about and how you can use it to your best advantage. That's what this chapter is all about. I'm going to spend some time telling you about the foundations of the Internet and the tools that you can use to explore it.

What you should come away with is a new appreciation for what the Internet is really all about. I think you'll find that it's a lot more than what you've been told. Surfing the Net should be an experience that helps you meet specific goals and broadens your horizons. The problem is, with such a large number of items on the menu, you could easily get lost.

A Little History

Some people are laboring under the misconception that the Internet is a relatively new technology. Actually, it's older than the technology in your PC. The first rumblings of the Internet started in the 1960s when computer scientists saw the need to connect their computers to exchange information. They weren't the only ones to see a need, though. The U.S. government saw that allowing researchers to communicate through a computer network would also advance the projects they were working on. The Department of Defense (DoD) was the first group on the bandwagon, with an Internet predecessor known as ARPANET (U.S. Advanced Research Projects Agency Network). Finally, educators saw a need to exchange information as well. Not only would a nationwide computer network help them keep up-to-date with current technology, but it would add another educational opportunity for students as well. What came of all this discussion was something known as NSFNET (National Science Foundation Network).

I'm getting a little ahead of myself, though. Let's take a look at some of the decisions behind these networks. Remember that at this time there wasn't anything like a local area network (LAN) around to look to for ideas, and WANs weren't even a glimmer in someone's eye yet. People were used to connecting dumb terminals to mainframes within a specific location; the idea of outside communication wasn't very common at all. For the most part, mainframes didn't even speak the same language—connecting one network to another was physically impossible in all but a few cases. The combination of proprietary mainframe architectures and lack of connections must have seemed like nearly impossible hurdles to overcome.

So, given the environment in the 1960s, how do you create a nationwide (and soon an international) network? Well, the first thing you've got to do is figure out a way to get all those computers talking to each other. That's where TCP/IP (transmission control protocol/Internet protocol) comes into play. TCP/IP is still the common language of the Internet today. TCP/IP allows computers to talk with one another even if their architectures are totally different. The TCP portion of the protocol tells the computers how to talk to each other, while the IP portion could be compared to an envelope used to transfer messages from one computer to the other. Two computers would establish communication and then exchange data. The only requirement for the data itself was that it appear in an IP envelope. If you think about it in the form of an envelope, the idea of the IP protocol is a lot easier to understand.

After computers had a common communications method, it was possible to start allowing users access to data. The mainframe interfaces of the time were less than user friendly, however. To give users something they could interact with, the developers of ARPANET starting putting together some of the services we take for granted today. The very first Internet services included FTP (file transfer protocol), e-mail (electronic mail), and remote login (Telnet). These services worked together to provide a front end—a user interface. Even though these utilities are still around today, you'll find that they've changed a great deal from the time when they were created. Suffice it to say that today's interface is both friendlier and easier to use.

Now that we have a common language and a method for accessing the data that a server contains, you might think that we have everything needed to create the Internet. A wide area network such as the Internet can't function without one additional feature. You need a method for adding and removing computers from the network in a way that doesn't disrupt communications. That was one of the main goals of the U.S. Advanced Research Projects Agency. They combined TCP/IP, the user interface, and the modularity to allow computers to connect and disconnect from the network with ease into something called ARPANET. That was the first name for the Internet as we know it today.

ARPANET wasn't an immediate success. As with any government project, by the time ARPANET was ready to go, there were already a lot of proprietary connections in place. What we had was a mishmash of disjointed connections that worked, but not very well. ARPANET did provide a central server for all these computers as they added TCP/IP to their list of connection types, however. Remember, too, that there were few reasons for anyone to get too excited about ARPANET, because access was still limited to defense contractors and associated research facilities. ARPANET still managed to grow mainly because these defense-oriented agencies needed to share information.

By the early 1980s, ARPANET became something less of a large single network. It closely resembled what we now call a backbone. A backbone on a network is the connection between major network sites—it's like the relationship between a freeway and city streets. Now you had a lot of local area networks (the city streets) connected to one major network (the freeway). Something else happened during this time as well. The last of the computer systems on the network converted to full TCP/IP support in 1983. When this last piece of the puzzle dropped into place, the Internet was born. You now had a lot of computer networks connected to a single backbone called ARPANET—essentially the same thing we're using today.

Okay, so now I've covered the basic single-network history of the physical Internet, but that still doesn't give you access to it or explain why there are so many networks in existence today. Something else had to happen before the average person would gain access to the government's networked computer system. One of those events was the emergence of supercomputing centers in the mid 1980s. The National Science Foundation (NSF) established these centers around the country at larger universities. There were only five centers in the beginning, because supercomputers are extremely expensive to build. The fact that this kind of computing power wasn't available to most people at the time meant that everyone wanted to use them. The NSF needed some way to connect universities and other educational centers without supercomputers to these centers. Just think about it for a second and you'll figure out that ARPANET provided a nearly perfect solution.

Unfortunately, connecting everyone directly to ARPANET didn't work out very well. The problem for the NSF was that ARPANET suffered from staffing problems and the usual amount of bureaucracy. The DoD didn't want just anyone connecting to their secure network. On the other hand, the ARPANET concept provided one of the few ways of connecting computers without too many problems. In the end, the NSF funded a backbone network called NSFNET to connect these supercomputer centers. Eventually, NSFNET and ARPANET were connected, even though they were managed separately (starting one of the basic principles of the Internet today—multi-network support).

By the late 1980s, the Internet (as it was now officially called) had grown too large for the NSF to administer. One of the problems was that the Internet provided an easy way for people to exchange ideas. The fact that everyone was using the Internet for things other than supercomputer center traffic didn't help matters much. To keep things under control, the NSF awarded a contract to a private company called Merit Inc. It was Merit's responsibility to manage and upgrade the Internet so that everyone could continue to exchange ideas and still use the supercomputing centers. Merit is actually a consortium of educational organizations in Michigan. They worked with MCI and IBM to complete the upgrade.

One of the big differences between NSFNET and ARPANET is that the NSF actually promoted the idea of spreading Internet access around (because the other network was defense-specific, access was understandably limited to folks who needed it). A university or other educational facility could gain access to the Internet only with a plan to spread that access around to staff and students. A few years after most universities got access to the Internet, there were already plans underway to connect primary and secondary schools. In addition, people who graduated from colleges and universities that were connected to the Internet told their employers about what kind of data was available. Now those companies wanted access as well.

All these requests for access prompted another contract award by the NSF in April of 1993. That's when a consortium of companies formed something called InterNIC (Internet Network Information Center), which was assigned to manage the daily running of the Internet. If you want to build a server and add it to the Internet, for example, then you have to contact InterNIC to get an IP address and register a domain name—so why is this management needed? Think about it this way: The IP address is equivalent to your mailing address. If your mailing address wasn't unique, the postal service would have a difficult time delivering your mail. The domain name has to be unique as well. A domain name is the first step in finding a particular resource on the Internet by using a browser (more on this topic later).

In the early 1990s, Merit proposed that the Internet be made public so that everyone could participate. At first, the NSF was reluctant to make something designed for educational use available to the public; however, after a lot of conversation, Merit and NSF reached an agreement. A commercial concern could access the network if it agreed to pay network usage fees. These fees would provide funds for NSF-sponsored projects and the upkeep of the network itself. That's how you get access. Your Internet service provider pays fees to access the network and you pay the service provider for your share of that access.

By now, you know that the Internet has also grown much larger than ARPANET or NSFNET. Such a large network needs management. Here's where two other groups come into play. The Internet Architecture Board (IAB) is the head honcho of network management. They're the ones who approve new network standards and protocols. Essentially, the IAB is a consortium of all the service providers on the Internet. The IAB includes several committees. The most important committee, from a user perspective, is the Internet Engineering Task Force (IETF). It's composed of scientists and engineers who design new Internet technology. I describe this group in more detail later in this chapter.

Protocols and URLS

I've already pursued the question of what the Internet is all about from a historical point of view. However, history gives you only a part of the picture—it tells you why some things are the way they are today. It's time to look at the Internet today—what you can expect to see when you log on. There isn't any way that I can cover in two chapters all the specifics that some authors take an entire book to cover. What is covered is specific to what you, as the user, need to know.

I'll begin with a discussion of one very important Internet topic—uniform resource locators (URLs). You can't get anywhere on the Internet without knowing something of this topic, yet very few texts really tell you much about them. I'm going to give you an overview of URLs from the layman's point of view—how they're put together and what you need to know to use them.

Another important topic is protocols. If you read through the history section of this chapter, you'll see that the Internet was founded on several protocols such as TCP/IP and FTP—one is used for communications purposes, and the other is used for the purpose of exchanging information. Today's computing is more complex, and the protocols you'll use have to provide more flexibility to keep up.

Note: From this point on in the chapter, I'm going to use Pacific Bell as my Internet service provider. If you've decided to use another service provider, your screens and addresses will probably differ from mine. The principles I'm trying to get across are the same, though, so don't worry about the differences too much. I'll also use Internet Explorer 3.01 as my browser for this chapter, though you'll see other browsers such as Netscape Navigator in other Internet-related chapters such as Chapter 22. There are a lot of other browsers on the market. I'm not saying that Internet Explorer 3.01 and Netscape Navigator 3.0 are better or worse than the others, but these are the two most popular browsers at the time of this writing.

Understanding Uniform Resource Locators (URLs)

The URL is the basis for movement on the Internet, so it's important to understand how it works. Let's begin by looking at the Microsoft home page address—that's where you'll check in before exploring the rest of the Internet:

```
http://www.microsoft.com/
```

At first, you might think that it's all gibberish, but there are some very definite standards for putting these site locations together.

Actually, this is a typical URL that identifies a particular server and clues you in about its capabilities. Let's begin with the `http://` portion of the URL. This tells you what kind of data exchange protocol you'll be using to access the server. In this case, you'll use hypertext transfer protocol. I describe the two major data transfer protocols (HTTP and FTP) in the next section. There are other data transfer protocols as well, such as Gopher and Archie, but I'll leave them for you to explore at your leisure. Knowing the data transfer protocol tells you a lot about what to expect from the server. An FTP site, for example, isn't going to provide much in the way of user-friendly graphics.

The next section contains the domain name system (DNS) address for the site you want to visit—in this case, `www.microsoft.com/`. There are three sections to every DNS address. (Some DNS addresses have a fourth section that contains the computer name, but you won't see this very often.) The first section of the DNS address tells you about the service (or, as some books call it, the subdomain). We're going to visit the World Wide Web (WWW) in this case. WWW sites almost always provide some type of graphical presentation. Nothing states you have to use WWW; for example, you can visit a site called `http://home.microsoft.com/` that takes you to the home page for Internet Explorer. Most sites use WWW as a convention because everyone expects to find their Web site on the World Wide Web.

The second section of the DNS address contains the domain name itself. In this case, it's `microsoft` for Microsoft. If you wanted to visit the Microsoft Network, you'd use MSN as a domain name. You'll find that most domain names are either full names or acronyms for the organization—some of which can be quite convoluted. The Internet site must register the domain name with InterNIC. The domain name is the unique identifier you use in place of an IP address. Imagine having to try to remember 32-bit numbers for each site you want to visit instead of a convenient name.

The third section of the DNS address is the domain identifier. Table 21.1 shows the basis for this part of the DNS address. InterNIC simply picks the one that fits the organization best. Note that this table won't contain every identifier that you'll ever see, but it does contain the more common identifiers.

Table 21.1. Common Internet domain identifiers.

Identifier	*Description*
`.com`	Any kind of commercial company such as Microsoft or CompuServe. Most online service Internet access providers have a `.com` domain identifier.
`.edu`	Nonprofit educational institutions use this domain identifier. (There is some discussion as to whether the school really does have to be nonprofit, but in most cases you'll find that they are.)
`.gov`	All government agencies use this domain identifier. If you see it, you know that you're dealing with someone from the United States government.

continues

Table 21.1. continued

Identifier	*Description*
`.mil`	The United States military uses this special domain identifier that keeps it separate from the rest of the government.
`.net`	Normally, this domain identifier is reserved for Internet access providers. The exception to the rule occurs if the access provider is a commercial concern. In that case, it normally uses the `.com` domain identifier. (As with every rule, you may find some crossover with this identifier between access providers and commercial concerns. For example, a telephone company may have a .net identifier even though it's a commercial concern, because its main focus is providing Internet access.)
`.org`	Some sites fall outside these other designations, and therefore use the `.org` domain identifier.

That's all there is to a basic URL. Some URLs are a lot longer than the one that I showed, however. What does the rest of the information mean? Let's look at another example. In this case, we'll look at a page for the National Science Teachers Association (NSTA):

```
http://www.gsh.org/NSTA_SSandC/nses_home.htm
```

Part of this address should already be familiar, so I won't cover it again. Let's start looking at the section after the domain name.

In this case, we're looking at an organization that has rented space on someone else's server. The NSTA SSC (Scope, Sequence, and Coordination Project)—`/NSTA_SSandC`—actually exists within a subdirectory on the `gsh` server. Think of those forward slashes in the same way you would subdirectories in a DOS path and you'll be miles ahead.

In this case, we're in a particular area of the NSTA SSC site—the `/nses_home` page that contains National Science Education Standards information. Notice the .HTM extension here. Some browsers extend this to .HTML, but Internet Explorer 2.0 and 3.x don't. HTML stands for hypertext markup language. I describe it more in the next section. For right now, all you need to know is that when you see this extension, you're looking at a page that has been formatted graphically by your browser.

There's one other form of the URL that I want to talk about, and it concerns e-mail addresses. Understanding how these addresses work is really easy if you understand a basic URL. You'll normally see something like this: `JMueller@pacbell.net`. The first part of the address is the person you want to contact—in this case, `JMueller`. The `@` (at) sign separates the receiver's name from the DNS address of the server used to hold the message. I've already covered how to decipher the DNS address, so I won't cover that again here.

A Quick View of Protocols

The basis for conversation on the Internet is the protocol. Just as the name implies, a protocol is a formal set of rules. Protocols define the way that we conduct business as humans. You can break them down in a number of ways, both formal and informal. A formal rule might be one that says that you must be in the office by a certain time to begin work. An informal rule could be as simple as not making disparaging remarks about someone's new haircut or clothes.

Computers also need rules. You'll never run into some of them, because they affect really esoteric things such as the distance between nodes on a network. Others, such as those used for Internet communication, might become very important to you. There are literally thousands of rules that affect Internet communications in one way or another, but I want to concentrate on some of the protocols that you'll see as a user. Table 21.2 shows some of the newer (and older) protocols that you'll run into while you're surfing the Net.

Table 21.2. Common Internet protocols.

Acronym	*Full Name*	*Description*
CGI	common gateway interface	This is a special method for accessing an application from a Web page. When a vendor asks you to enter information on a form, for example, you're using CGI. The most common use for CGI is database applications. This is the only Web-server-to-background-application standard currently supported by the IETF (I'll talk about them in a bit). Two other proposed methods are ISAPI and NSAPI.
CORBA	common object request broker architecture	You won't see this technology today (although it may be available by the time you read this). It may appear in a Java application that you see tomorrow, however. The purpose of this protocol is to describe data and application code in a way that a variety of computer types can use. It will eventually allow you to go to a Web page and download a mini-application (applet) as part of that page. This is the Object Management Group's (OMG) alternative to Microsoft's ActiveX. CORBA was originally designed by IBM for inclusion with OS/2, but other companies such as Sun Microsystems now support this standard as well. You can see a beta version of CORBA at `http://splash.javasoft.com/pages/intro.html`.

continues

Table 21.2. continued

Acronym	*Full Name*	*Description*
DCOM	distributed component object model	You may be more familiar with this term as ActiveX (they aren't precisely the same thing, but that doesn't matter much for this discussion). It's Microsoft's latest experiment in distributed mini-applications (applets). You'll be able to use OLE over the Internet in a new way. The applets provide all the features covered in Chapter 12. The big difference is that you'll be able to use these features over the Internet. ActiveX applications require Explorer 3.0; you can download a copy of Explorer 3.0 at `http://www.microsoft.com/ie/appdev/controls/default.htm`. The same site allows you to see some ActiveX controls in action.
FTP	file transfer protocol	I've already talked about this particular protocol to a certain extent. It represents one of the earliest forms of communication that the Internet recognized. There aren't any graphics to speak of at an FTP site—just files to download. This is the only file download protocol currently supported by the IETF. The limitations of this particular protocol have prompted other standards such as CORBA and DCOM.
HTTP	hypertext transfer protocol	Whenever you go to a Web site that begins with `http:`, you're using this protocol. It's the technology that enables you to download an HTML (hypertext markup language) document—the kind that includes fancy graphics and buttons. Essentially, HTTP allows you to download an HTML script—a document containing commands rather than actual graphics. Your browser reads these script commands and displays buttons, text, graphics, or other objects accordingly. That's why the capabilities of your browser are so important (and also the reason why you'll need a new browser if you want to use any of the new protocols I've mentioned in this table). However, some vendors are already complaining that the IETF standard versions of both HTTP and HTML are old and less than optimal for tomorrow's needs. That's why there's such a proliferation of other protocol standards and associated HTML script commands on the Internet today; people are looking for better ways of making information accessible.

Acronym	*Full Name*	*Description*
INFS	Internet network file system	Think of this protocol as you would the file system on your own computer. Whether you use NTFS, HPFS, or VFAT, they all represent a way to organize the information on your drive and provide fast access to it. This file system does essentially the same thing for Internet files. However, it has to have a connection to the data. That's done with TCP/IP—the networking standard I talk about elsewhere in this chapter.
ISAPI	Internet Server Application Programming Interface	This is another Microsoft protocol. I've talked about other types of application programming interfaces elsewhere. ISAPI does the same thing for an Internet server—it allows you to access the features that the server has to offer. In this case, a programmer would use ISAPI to allow you to access a host application through an Internet server. You'll probably see ISAPI restricted to database and e-mail applications at first, but I already see other application types on the horizon. You might see it used as part of a turn-based game or even an online word processor, for example.
NSAPI	Netscape Application Programming Interface	Not to be outdone by Microsoft (see ISAPI), Netscape came up with its own API for connecting Web servers to background applications. As with ISAPI, NSAPI enables you to write a data entry or other application for the Internet by using advanced HTML scripting commands, and allows it to interact with applications on your network. As with Microsoft's offering, the major application that I see for this API right now is some type of data entry or e-mail system.
ODSI	Open Directory Services Interface	The Microsoft Network (MSN) provides a somewhat better interface to the Internet than most of the other online services I've tried. At least it's faster than most and ODSI is part of the reason. It provides a common naming convention API that will eventually enable you to treat an Internet Web site like any other folder in Explorer.

I really haven't begun to scratch the surface of all the things you'll see out there on the Internet. It's probably better to look at Table 21.2 as a sampling of some of the more interesting technologies that you'll use. The problem with all this new technologies is that they aren't standardized. As I mentioned before, the Internet has its own standards committee called the Internet Engineering Task Force (IETF), responsible for providing a standard set of HTML script commands. The problem with all these new protocols is that they introduce new scripting commands that could cause problems in the future. How can a browser handle a propriety script command? In most cases, it will ignore it, but you can't be sure. Even if the browser does ignore the foreign command, you'll be stuck without access to some of the features on a given Web page. There are other problems with the current trend. What if a vendor simply modifies an existing script command? A browser won't know to ignore it in this case, and you could end up with a frozen machine as a result. I think you can start to see my point about the need for standards.

The problem is more severe than you might think. There are new Internet technologies cropping up that don't have any old standards to follow. Just about every vendor out there has its own form of Virtual Reality Modeling Language (VRML), for example. Without a standard way to access this feature, you might find support for your browser to be spotty at best.

It's frustrating to think about the way protocols will affect your ability to surf the Net in the future. However, I think that the problem is going to be short-term. I'm often reminded of the problems with graphic adapters when IBM decided to introduce the 8514 adapter instead of upgrading VGA. Sure, we'll probably go through several years of trying to figure out which standards are best, but in the long run some technologies will win out and we'll eventually end up with a standard. The trick for right now is to figure out which technologies are going to gain market share and stick with them.

Finding What You're Looking For

If you do a lot of research on the Internet, like I do, you'll realize the benefit of finding what you need quickly. Internet Explorer provides you with some really handy tools in this regard. Let's look at the most basic tool first. Just click the Search the Internet speed button, and you'll see a display similar to the one shown in Figure 21.1. The precise view you get will depend on whether you use MSN as your ISP. This figure shows the site you'll reach if you don't use MSN. Netscape Navigator also provides a search feature using the Net Search button—the Web page it uses appears in Figure 21.2. Although the Netscape site provides fewer search engines, the ones shown are the ones you'll use most often.

The search pages for both browsers work about the same way. You can choose one of the preconfigured links such as ZDNet Shareware Search (shown in Figure 21.1), or you can choose to find a site by using a keyword search. (The Netscape site also provides preconfigured links, although they don't appear in Figure 21.2.) These entries provide hyperlinks to other locations on the Internet. You'll find that a lot of Web pages work this way, but this is the first time we're looking at such an obvious example.

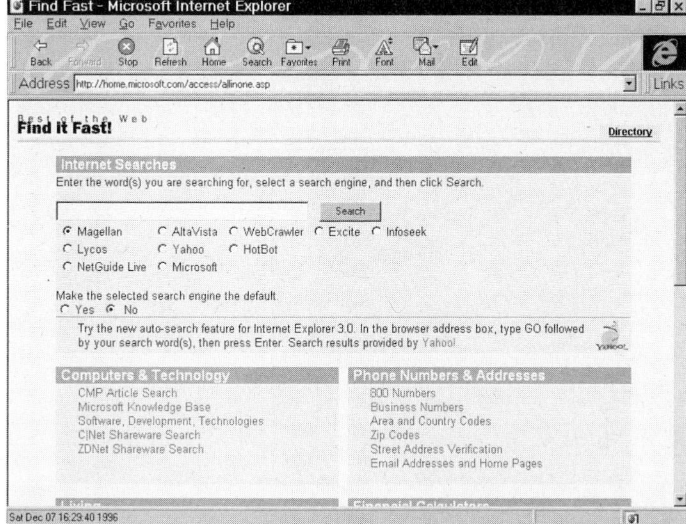

Figure 21.1.
Internet Explorer provides access to ten search sites on the Internet.

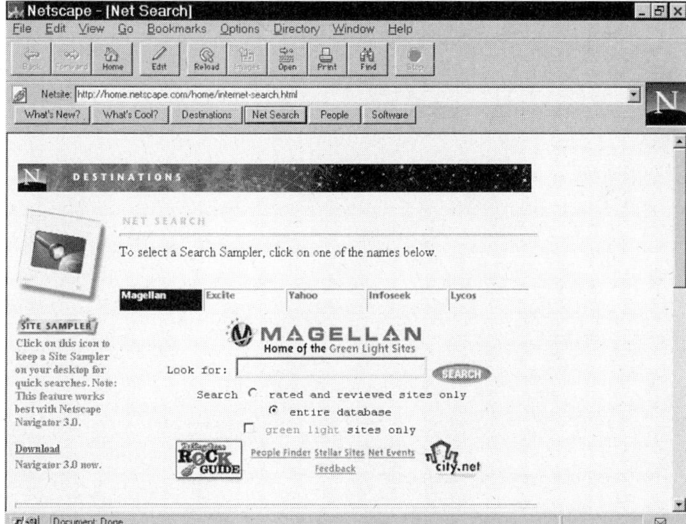

Figure 21.2.
Netscape Navigator also provides access to search sites on the Internet at the click of a button.

Let's talk about keyword searches for a second. All you need to do to perform a keyword search is to enter one or more keywords into the blank, select a search engine, and then click the Search button. Internet Explorer or Navigator then takes you to the appropriate search Web site and starts the search for you.

Tip: There are probably more Internet sites to visit than you can imagine when it comes to finding great additions to the Windows 95 environment. One of these sites is the NONAGS MAIN PAGE at `http://users.southeast.net/~itsvicki/nonags/main.html`. This site specializes in shareware utility-type programs for the most part, although you'll also find a variety of other offerings. As the home page title states, none of the software nags you to make a purchase. One of the more interesting aspects of this site is that you can find most of the software in both 16-bit (Windows 3.x) and 32-bit (Windows 95) versions. If you want a broader range of Windows 95-specific software to choose from, take a look at Windows95.com - Windows World on the Internet (`http://www.windows95.com/`). This site contains tutors on a variety of topics, an Internet hypertext glossary, an Internet TCP/IP connectivity guide, and even a full listing of Windows 95-specific hardware drivers.

Let's try a search. Select Lycos as your search engine, type **`ActiveX`** in the blank, and then click Search (this works with either browser). Depending on the security level you've selected, you may see a security dialog box before either browser does anything. (Both Microsoft's Internet Explorer and Netscape's Navigator provide security features. Use the View | Options command, and then select the Security page of the Options dialog to change your security level with Internet Explorer. Use the Options | Security Preferences command with Navigator to do the same thing.) Click Yes to clear it. You'll end up on a Web page like the one shown in Figure 21.3. There are a few things you should notice about this page. The first feature is that you can refine your search. Maybe a single keyword really didn't refine the search enough and you need to find something more specific. I haven't found a single search Web page that doesn't provide this capability in some form. In fact, many of them provide very detailed search mechanisms.

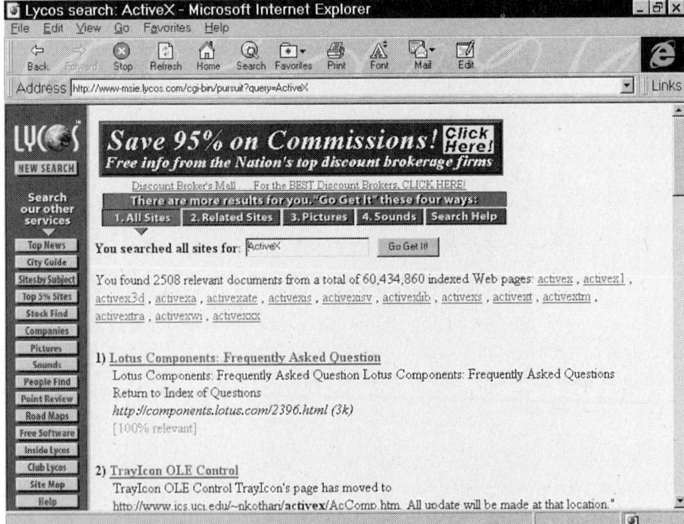

Figure 21.3.
A search Web page such as Lycos allows you to find specific information on the Internet.

There's something else you should notice. Each of the result entries (also called a hit) contains a confidence level. This tells you how confident the search engine is about the results it found. Normally, the search engine uses a variety of criteria to determine this number—such as the number of times the keyword appears in an article or other source of information. Obviously, a Boolean search starts to make a confidence calculation more difficult. (A Boolean search uses terms such as `"and"` and `"or"` to allow you to look for phrases in a specific way. If you say `"help and context"` the search engine looks for articles containing both the words *help* and *context*. On the other hand, if you told the search engine to look for `"help or context"` either word would satisfy the search criteria.) The method of determining a confidence factor is one of the things that determines which search engines you use. I use a variety of them for different purposes (more on that in a bit).

Web search pages normally don't list every site that the search engine finds. Notice that Lycos lists only 10 of them. (Other services allow you to change the number of entries listed as part of the search criteria). You have to click the Next Documents button to see the next group of 10 on the list. The confidence level assigned to the various hits usually determines which sites are listed first. Notice that Lycos defaults to listing the sites it finds by confidence level. This makes sense because you want to find the best sites first. If you want an alphabetical listing, click the Sort by Site button. Some search engines provide other sorting criteria. The Deja News site, for example, allows you to sort by author as well. I'll talk about that in a bit.

You might think that one search engine would be enough to fulfill your needs, but that simply isn't true. The problem with trying to come up with a "best fit" answer for any of these search engines is that they work differently. A search engine that works fine for my needs may not work at all for you. I thought it important, therefore, to provide a list of some of the more common search engines and a quick overview of how they work. I'd encourage you to try them all to see what works best for you and in what situations. The following list talks about the search engines I use; fortunately, most of them are accessed through the Search the Internet button in Internet Explorer or Navigator. I've provided URLs for those that you may have to access directly. To access the search engine page, click the Open button on the toolbar and enter the URL shown. (Once you find a search engine you like, you may want to add it to your Favorites or Bookmark list so that you can find it more easily the next time.)

- **Alta Vista (`http://www.altavista.digital.com/`):** One of the benefits of using this search engine is a lack of information overload. It returns only the amount of information you want about each hit. The service tends to focus on Web pages containing articles, meaning that you'll get some pretty narrow hits when using it. Alta Vista uses excerpts from the articles or other sources of information that it accesses. This service uses a somewhat esoteric Boolean search engine, making it difficult to narrow your search criteria with any level of ease.
- **Deja News (`http://www.dejanews.com/`):** I've used this particular search engine when I needed to find a lot of information fast. You'll notice a Power Search button on the page when you arrive. Power search may be something of an understatement; you'll literally

have to test it to see all that you can do. This is also one of the easier sites to use, despite its flexibility. It uses a lot of graphics, including radio buttons and other familiar controls. The only problem with this particular engine is that you may find yourself doing a search more than once to get everything it provides. There are so many search options that you'll find yourself thinking of new ways to search for a particularly tough-to-find bit of information. You can get two levels of detail—neither of which tells you much. All you can count on getting for each hit is an article title. This service doesn't provide either excerpts or summaries, but it does provide a very broad base of information, meaning that you'll find just about anything you search for; you'll just spend some time weeding out the entries that really don't fit.

- **Excite:** This service tends to focus on Web sites rather than pages on a particular site. In other words, you get to a general area of interest, and then Excite leaves it to you to find the specific information you're looking for. I find that this is an advantage when I'm not really sure about the specifics of a search. A wide view, in this case, helps me see everything that's available and then make some refinements. Excite also provides a summary of what you'll find at a particular site. It tends to concentrate on discussion groups and vendor-specific information.
- **Infoseek:** The strength of this particular service is that it provides just the facts. It uses excerpts from the articles or other sources of information from which it draws excerpts. The hits are a lot narrower than some search engines provide, because Infoseek concentrates on Web pages rather than sites. The only problem with this particular service is that your ability to narrow the search criteria is severely limited.
- **Lycos:** Of all of the search engines I've used, Lycos tends to provide the most diverse information. It catalogs both Web sites and pages but concentrates on pages whenever possible. Lycos provides a combination of summaries and excerpts to describe the content of a particular hit. The ability to narrow your search is superior to most of the search engines available right now. One of the downsides to using this particular search engine is that there's almost too much detail. You'll quickly find yourself searching false leads and ending up with totally unusable information, if you aren't sure what you're looking for.
- **Magellan:** You'll tend to find esoteric sources of information with this search engine. It doesn't appear to provide a very broad base of information, but it usually provides interesting facts about what you're searching for. Magellan concentrates on Web sites rather than pages, so the view you get is rather broad. You'll also find that it provides few methods for narrowing the search criteria. This search engine relies on summaries rather than extracts to convey the content of a particular hit. One of the more interesting features is the method used to rate a particular site; clicking a Review button gives you a full-page summary of how the information relates to similar information on other sites.
- **Open Text** (`http://search.opentext.com/`)**:** *Extremely comprehensive* and *flexible* are the best words to describe this particular search engine. I find that this is one of the easier sites

to use, and it provides a moderately broad base of information from which to choose. This particular search engine relies on extremely short excerpts, in most cases. It concentrates on Web pages rather than sites, meaning that you'll get a fairly narrow result.

- **Yahoo!:** This particular search engine provides the best organization of all those listed. It categorizes every hit in a variety of ways, making your chances of finding information contained in the search engine very high. However, this service doesn't provide the broad range of information that you'll find with other search engines. It also relies on very short summaries to tell you the content of a particular hit. In most cases, I rely on Yahoo! as a first-look type of search engine—something that gives me the broad perspective of a single keyword.
- **Web Crawler** (`http://www.webcrawler.com/`)**:** You'll find that this search engine requires a bit more work to use than most, because it doesn't provide much in the way of excerpts or summaries. On the other hand, it provides a full Boolean search engine and an extremely broad base of information. The only search engine that provides a broader base in this list is Lycos.

Using the Online Services Folder

The OSR2 version of Windows 95 comes with a new feature, the Online Services folder. You'll find access to a variety of online service providers by using this package. The two that you are most likely to know are America Online and CompuServe. Both of these companies provide services in addition to the Internet. (Appendix A takes a partial look at CompuServe.) You'll also find a sign-up kit for AT&T WorldNet. This is an Internet-only provider. Be sure to look in Appendix B for additional ideas on how to get your own ISP (Internet service provider).

Also included in the Online Services folder is a subscription to CompuServe WOW!. Unfortunately, the folder icon will probably last longer than the service, because CompuServe planned to end it in January 1997. In other words, disregard this icon if you see it in the Online Services folder.

Working with Internet Explorer

Now that we have some of the basics out of the way, let's take a look at what you need to do to get going on the Internet. Microsoft makes the task very easy if you go the route that they've set up for you. That includes using Internet Explorer as a browser and MSN as an Internet service provider. You could easily substitute your own choice for Internet service provider (I'll be using Pacific Bell) or use a different browser (Netscape Navigator appears in several chapters of this book, including Chapter 22). The next five sections cover installation and basic usage for Internet Explorer 3.01 and its companion programs Internet Mail and Internet News. (Internet Explorer 2.0 doesn't include either the mail or news programs.)

Note: The Service Pack 1 version of Windows 95 shipped with Internet Explorer version 2.0. This version of Internet Explorer also shipped with the Windows 95 Plus! pack discussed in Chapter 28. You can download an update of Internet Explorer from `http://www.microsoft.com/ie/`. The OSR2 version of Windows 95 comes with Internet Explorer 3.0 as part of the package. Even though I cover Internet Explorer 3.0 in the following paragraphs, most of the same principles apply to Internet Explorer 2.0.

Installation

Windows 95 doesn't automatically install the Internet Explorer software for you unless you select that option as part of a custom installation. However, installation couldn't be easier because Windows 95 does most of it for you. Be sure to install MSN first (or whatever other service provider you intend to use), and then install Internet Explorer using the following procedure:

1. Double-click the Add/Remove Programs applet in Control Panel. You'll see an Add/Remove Programs Properties dialog box similar to the one shown in Figure 21.4 (your list of programs will probably differ from mine). This is where you'll start most of your program installations—Internet Explorer is no different. We're going to add it using the standard application method on the Install/Uninstall page, however, rather than using the Windows Setup page.

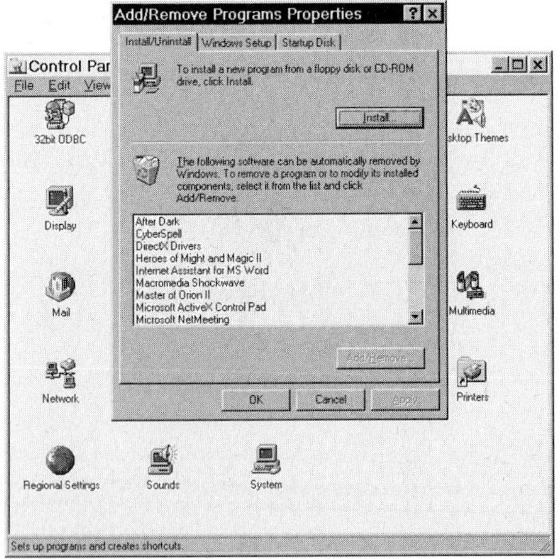

Figure 21.4.
The Add/Remove Programs Properties dialog box is the starting place for most program installations under Windows 95.

2. Click the Install button. You'll see a dialog box telling you to insert the installation floppy or CD. Insert your Windows 95 (OSR2 version) CD or Service Pack 1 CD into the appropriate drive if you want to install from there. You can ignore this step if you've downloaded the latest version of Internet Explorer and plan to install from a directory on your hard disk.
3. Click Next. Windows 95 displays a Run Installation Program dialog box and searches the various drives. It will eventually tell you that it found an installation program (in most cases, the Setup program on the Windows 95 CD). This isn't the one you're looking for. What you want to find is the Internet folder on the Windows 95 CD or the directory where you stored the latest version of Internet Explorer. (You won't have an Internet folder on the original version of the Windows 95 CD or the Plus! pack CD, but this folder does appear starting with Service Pack 1.)
4. Click the Browse button. Use the Browse dialog box (it looks and acts like a standard Open dialog box) to find the Internet folder or the directory containing the version of Internet Explorer you downloaded from the Internet. In most cases, you'll find an MSIE20.EXE, MSIE30.EXE, or MSIE301.EXE file. The 3.01 version of Internet Explorer appears in the MSIE301.EXE file. You'll find the older 2.0 version in the MSIE20.EXE file.

Note: The 2.0 version of Internet Explorer uses an installation procedure slightly different from the one shown in this section.

5. Click the Open button in the Browse dialog box to return to the Run Installation Program dialog box.
6. Click Finish to start running the Internet Explorer installation program. Windows 95 copies the files to your disk and then displays the Internet Explorer License Agreement dialog box shown in Figure 21.5. Read through the text in this dialog box before proceeding. It tells you how Internet Explorer is licensed for use on your machine.

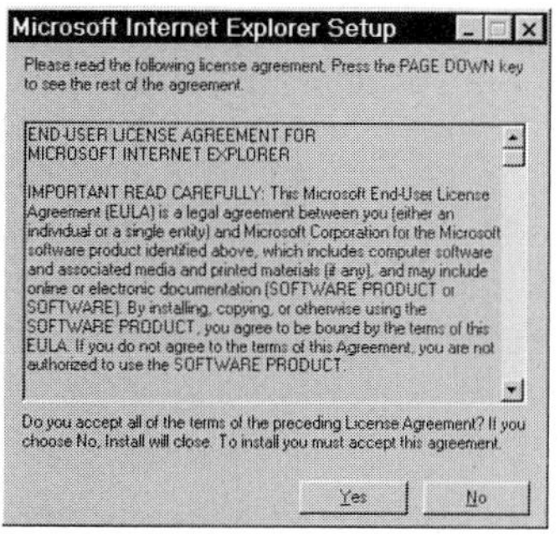

Figure 21.5.
The Internet Explorer License Agreement is where you agree to Microsoft's terms for using the product.

7. Click Yes. Windows 95 copies some additional files to your hard drive and then displays the dialog box shown in Figure 21.6. If you click Yes, Windows 95 allows you to decide which optional components to install. Otherwise, it makes the installation decisions for you. If you click No, you'll see the Internet Explorer Installation dialog box shown in Figure 21.8. (Skip to step 10 if you click No.)

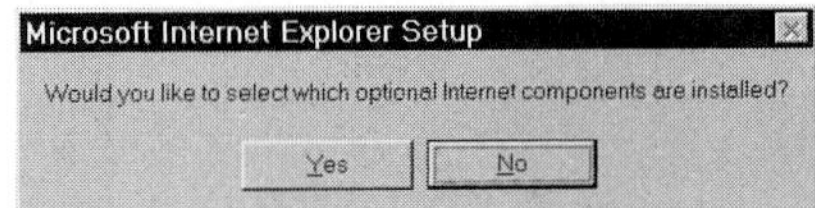

Figure 21.6.
This dialog box allows you to decide whether to customize your Internet Explorer setup.

8. Click Yes. You'll see an Optional Components dialog box like the one shown in Figure 21.7. This particular dialog box shows the options available for the 3.01 version of Internet Explorer. Your dialog box may vary from the one shown here. There are five options shown. I discuss the first three—Internet Mail, Internet News, and NetMeeting—later in this chapter. The ActiveMovie option is discussed in the "ActiveMovie Control" section of Chapter 2. We'll use the HTML Layout Control as part of our ActiveX discussion in Chapter 22.

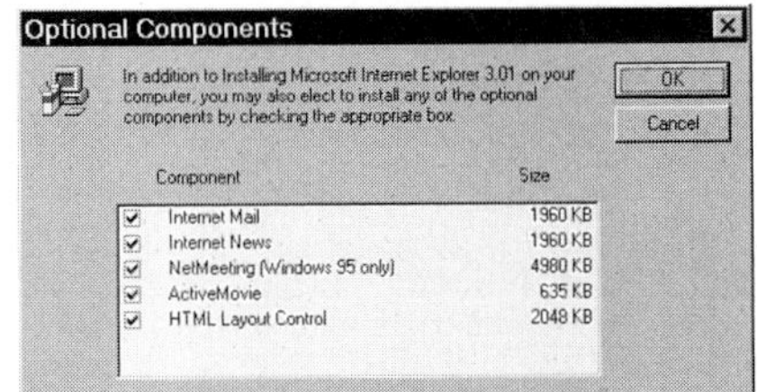

Figure 21.7.
The Optional Components dialog box allows you to choose which Internet Explorer features to install.

9. Select the components you want to install and then click OK. You'll see the Internet Explorer Installation dialog box shown in Figure 21.8.

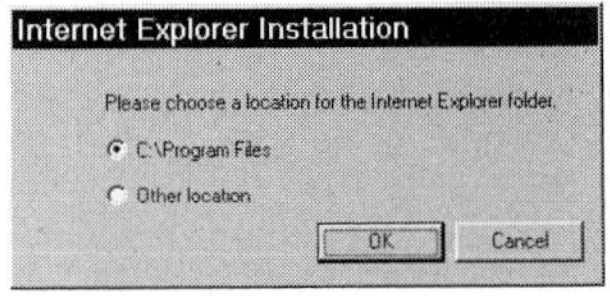

Figure 21.8.
Use this dialog box to determine whether you want to use the default or a special location for your Internet Explorer installation.

10. Select either the default or a special location for your Internet Explorer installation. If you choose the Other Location option, Setup displays a dialog box for you to choose the installation directory. Click OK after choosing an installation directory. You'll see Windows 95 copy more files from the installation CD to your drive. Windows then displays a completion message and asks you to reboot your machine.

11. Click Yes to reboot your machine after making sure that all your other applications are closed. Windows 95 restarts your machine after it performs some additional setup during the boot process. At this point, you should see a new icon on your desktop: The Internet. If not, shut down and reboot your machine. (Whether you have to reboot seems to depend on which network options you've installed. For example, Internet Explorer requires TCP/IP support.)

Setting Up Internet Explorer

Once you get Internet Explorer installed, you'll want to set it up for use. There are two routes to go here, but they're both essentially the same. What you need to do now is specify some type of Internet Service Provider (ISP). Microsoft provides full support for MSN as part of the Windows 95 package. An update to this support is available at `http://signup.msn.com/signup/signup.hts?`. You could also choose to use any other Internet service provider at this point; the only requirement is that you have the proper support installed for contacting them. See Appendix B for more details about ISPs. I used PBI (Pacific Bell Internet) in this case, because of its low cost and high level of support.

Tip: The first time you run Internet Explorer, you'll use the Internet Setup Wizard to install support for it. You can always rerun this program by using the Internet Setup Wizard option in your Internet Tools folder. This folder normally appears in the Accessories folder in the Start menu. Always run the wizard whenever you change Internet service providers or make some other major change to your Internet Explorer setup.

Note: This procedure uses Internet Explorer 3.01. However, if you're using Internet Explorer 2.0, you can follow the manual procedure starting in step 8. There are some slight variations between the 3.01 and the 2.0 versions of the manual procedure, but they're close. The big difference is that Microsoft no longer forces you to use MSN as an ISP.

1. Double-click the Internet Explorer icon on the desktop if this is the first time you're running it. Otherwise, select the Internet Connection Wizard option from the Internet Tools folder (see Figure 21.9).
2. Click Next. Figure 21.10 shows the first Setup Options dialog box. You'll need to decide how you want to connect to the Internet. As you can see, there are three ways to do so. The Automatic option lets Internet Explorer do everything for you, from selecting a modem to configuring your Internet settings. This option is probably the least time-consuming, but could produce unpredictable results if you're not using MSN as an ISP.

(Fortunately, Microsoft has fixed this problem with the latest release of Internet Explorer.) The Manual option works best if you use a LAN connection rather than a local modem to make the connection. The third option, Current, is the one that most people will use. It allows you to use a Dial-Up Networking connection that you've already configured. This particular option works best because you can set everything up with your ISP in advance.

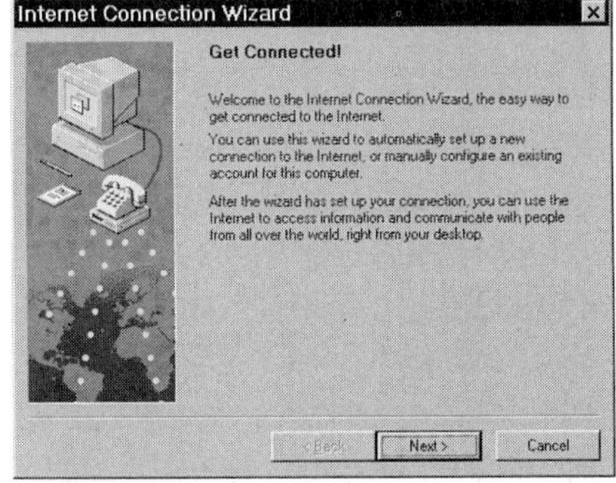

Figure 21.9.
The Internet Connection Wizard allows you to configure Internet Explorer for use.

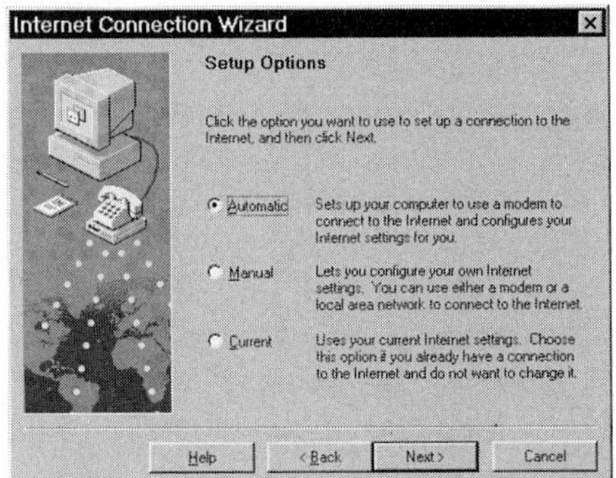

Figure 21.10.
The first Setup Options dialog box allows you to choose the method of creating an Internet connection.

3. Click Automatic, Manual, or Current. If you selected Automatic, proceed with step 4. If you selected Manual, proceed with step 8. If you selected Manual, you're all done creating a connection. The next thing you'll see is the standard Connect To dialog box.
4. Make sure the Automatic option is selected and then Click Next. You'll see a Begin Automatic Setup dialog box like the one shown in Figure 21.11.
5. Click Next. You'll see a dialog box similar to the one shown in Figure 21.12. The Internet Connection Wizard asks you for location information that it will use to download a list of ISPs in your area. This list is by no means comprehensive—you may not find an ISP that precisely suits your needs.

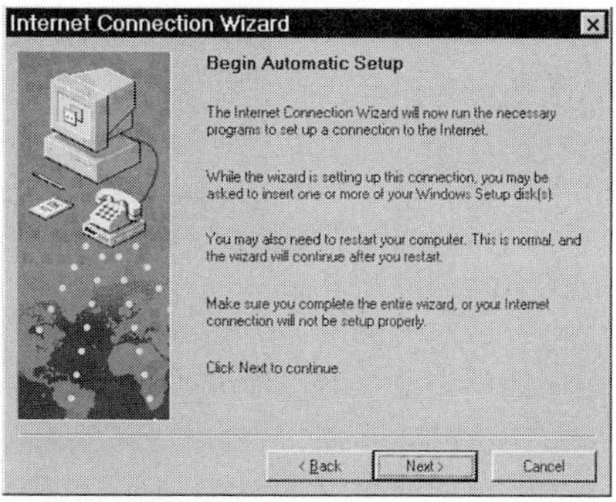

Figure 21.11.
The Begin Automatic Setup dialog box tells you that you're using the Automatic setup instead of the other two options.

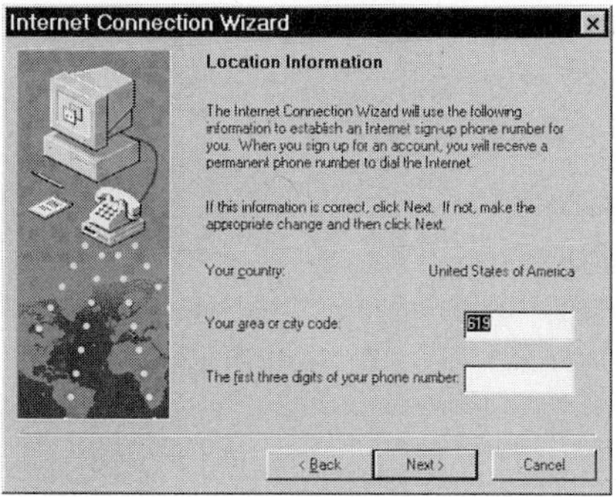

Figure 21.12.
The Location Information dialog box asks for the information needed to get a list of ISPs in your area.

6. Enter your area code in the first field and the first three digits of your telephone number in the second field. Click Next. At this point, the Internet Connection Wizard displays a Connecting dialog box, dials an 800 number, and downloads a list of ISPs in your area. When it finishes, you'll see a dialog box containing a list of ISPs in your area, similar to the one shown in Figure 21.13. All you need to do to sign up for an ISP is select the one you want, by clicking in the Sign Me Up column. Notice that you can get additional information about the ISP before you sign up, by clicking in the More Information column.
7. At this point, you'll need to follow the instructions for the ISP that you selected. Once you complete the sign-up process, the Internet Connection Wizard disconnects from the 800 number. You'll see a Connect To dialog box next. Simply type your user name for the ISP, along with a password, click the Connect button, and you'll be on your way to your first Internet session.
8. If you're reading this step, you must have selected the Manual option in step 3. Click Next at the initial dialog box shown in Figure 21.10 and you'll see a dialog box like the one shown in Figure 21.14. If you see this dialog box, you know that you've selected the manual connection method.

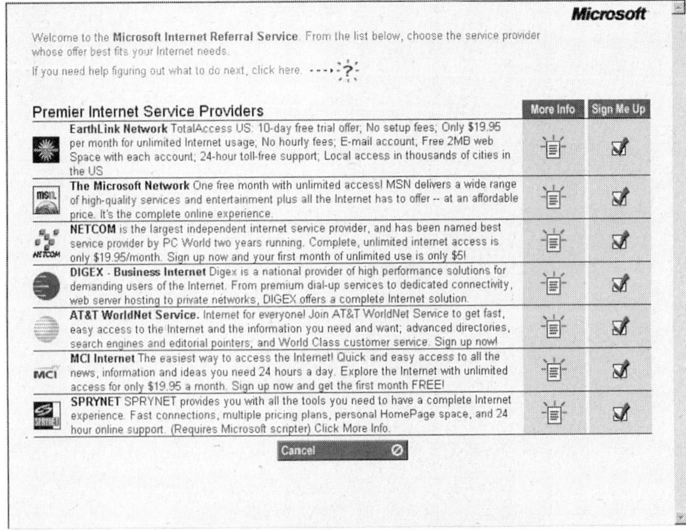

Figure 21.13.
The Microsoft Internet Referral Service can provide a list of ISPs, in case you don't already have one.

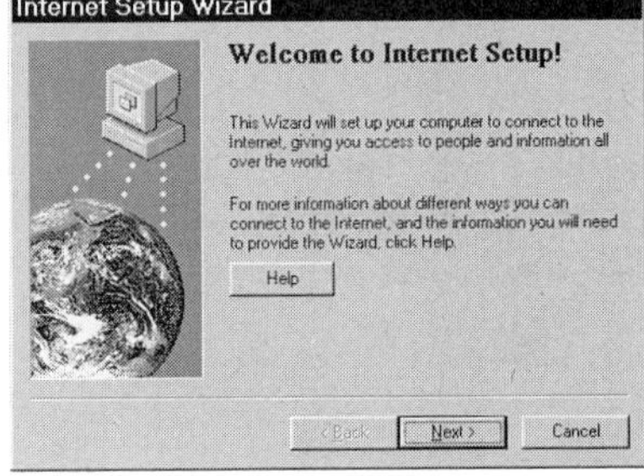

Figure 21.14.
This dialog box shows that you've opted to configure your Internet connection manually.

9. Click Next. Your first decision is how you want to connect your machine to the Internet (see Figure 21.15). There are two choices: locally, using the telephone lines, or remotely, through a network. I selected the Connect Using My Phone Line option in this case because I wanted to use a local connection.

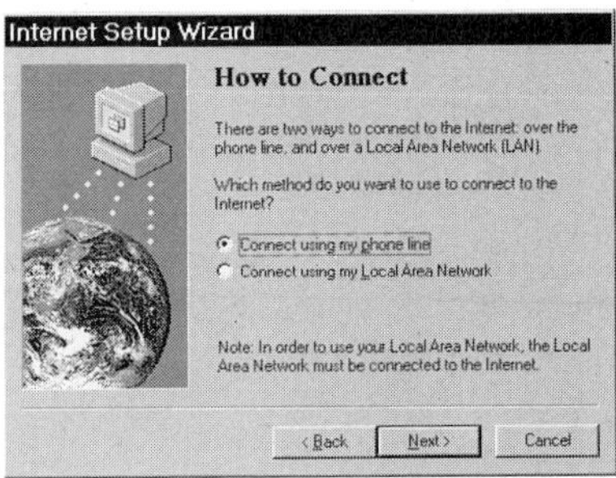

Figure 21.15.
Your first decision in setting up Internet Explorer is how to make the connection.

10. Click Next and you'll see a dialog box like the one shown in Figure 21.16. You'll need to decide whether you want to use Windows Messaging for your Internet messages. The advantage is that you'll need only one application to handle all your messaging needs. There are two disadvantages. Internet Mail provides an optimized interface that you won't get with Windows Messaging (the "Using Internet Mail" section of this chapter describes this). In addition, you'll need to spend more time managing your messages, because a lot more messages will go to one place.

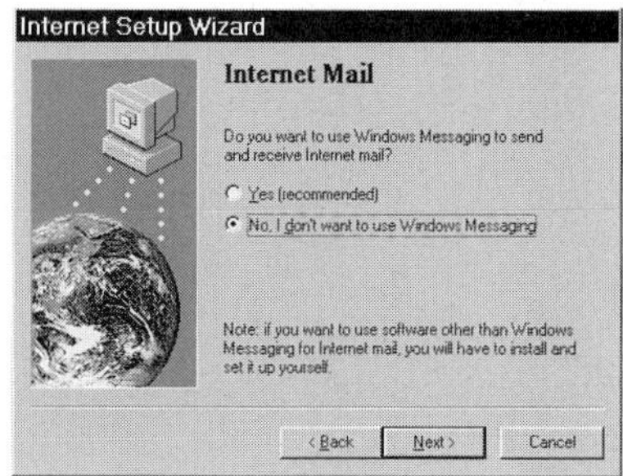

Figure 21.16.
The Internet Mail dialog box lets you choose between Internet Mail and Windows Messaging as your Internet mail handler.

11. Click Next. Now you need to decide on a service provider, as shown in Figure 21.17. Previous versions of Internet Explorer gave MSN a prominent position in this dialog box. This version has a simple drop-down list box where you choose the ISP you want to use. You should have a Dial-Up Networking connection configured before you reach this point in the configuration procedure. As an alternative, you can simply type the name of the ISP you want to use and the Internet Setup Wizard will help you create it.

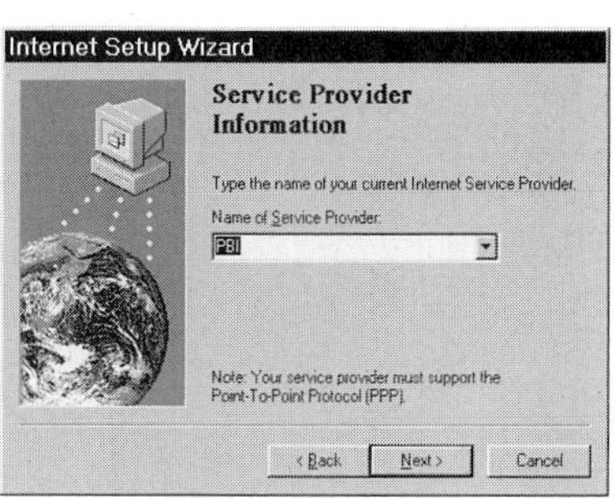

Figure 21.17.
If you want to use a local connection, you have to decide on an Internet service provider, using this dialog box.

Looking Ahead: Appendix B looks at several Internet service provider options. You can scan through these choices if you decide not to use MSN. I've also included some helpful hints on choosing an Internet provider, including some tradeoffs you'll make by going certain routes.

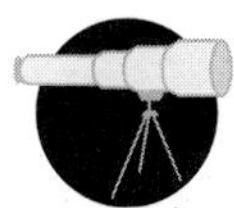

12. Click Next and you'll see the Phone Number dialog box shown in Figure 21.18. This is where you'll verify the calling information for your ISP. Unfortunately, there isn't any way to look up the information as you did when using the Automatic option—you must know the number in advance. Pay special attention to the Bring Up Terminal Windows After Dialing check box. I find that checking this box is handy for troubleshooting a connection that isn't working correctly. In some cases, the ISP provides an error message that Internet Explorer won't normally show. I usually check this box when I create the initial connection. Once I verify that the connection works, I uncheck it to keep my screen from getting cluttered.

Figure 21.18.
The Phone Number dialog box allows you to either verify or enter the access number for your ISP.

13. Enter the appropriate phone information. Click Next. You'll see the User Name and Password dialog box shown in Figure 21.19. The user name in this case is the one that you use for your Internet mailbox, not the one you use for logging into Windows. You'll also need to supply the password required to log into your account on the Internet.

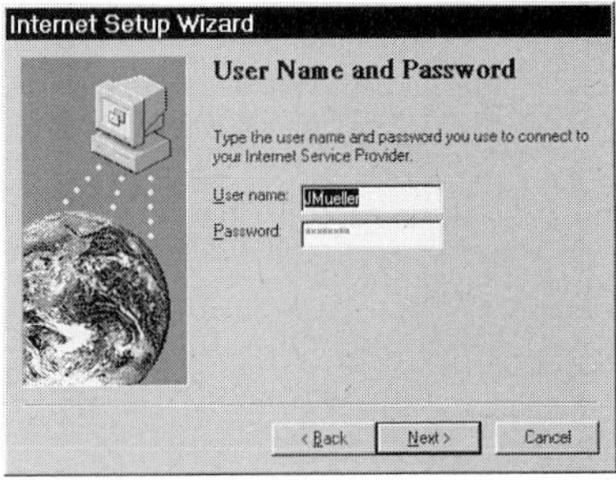

Figure 21.19.
Remember that the user name in this case is your Internet user name, not the one for Windows.

14. Click Next. You'll see an IP Address dialog box like the one shown in Figure 21.20. There are two different setups available; the one you use is determined by your ISP. Normally an ISP assigns you an IP address every time you log in from a cache of IP addresses on the Web server. However, some ISPs assign users a permanent number, and you can enter that number here. Check with the ISP first to determine which setting to use.

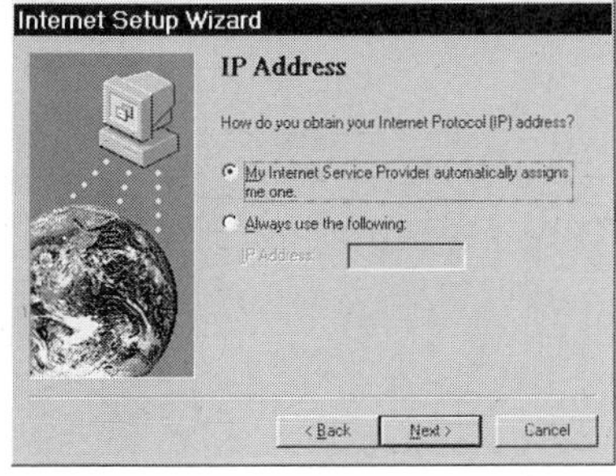

Figure 21.20.
Get your IP address from the ISP before you create a connection.

15. Select one of the two IP Address options. If necessary, enter the permanent IP address that the ISP assigned you. Click Next and you'll see a DNS Server Address dialog box like the one shown in Figure 21.21. This is one of the more interesting dialog boxes provided by the Internet Setup Wizard. Some ISPs provide a DNS Server Address; some don't. The Internet Setup Wizard always assumes that you need one, so you'll see a warning message if you don't provide this information. Simply bypass the warning message, and the Internet Setup Wizard allows you to proceed without any further questions. As with all IP addresses, your DNS server address consists of four sets of numbers from 0 to 255. You enter them like this: **`200-100-100-1`**.

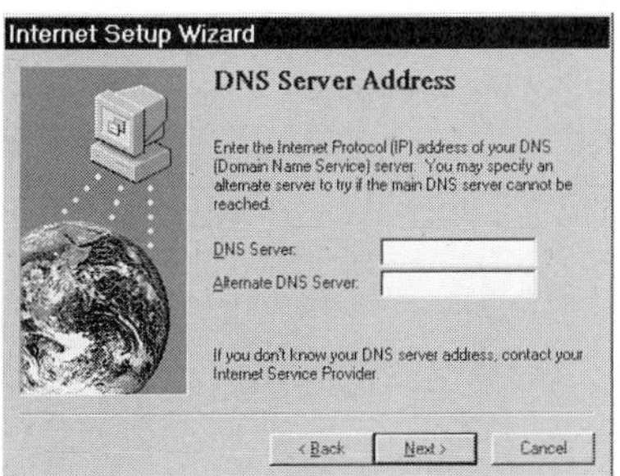

Figure 21.21.
In some cases, you won't need to enter any information here, even though the Internet Setup Wizard insists that you do.

16. You're done! At this point you'll see a Complete Configuration dialog box. Click Finish to close it. Unlike the other two setup options, you'll actually have to open Internet Explorer manually to check out the connection at this point. I'd suggest that you do so. Remember that you can always open the Dial-Up Networking connection in the Dial-Up Networking folder and change any settings without going through the Internet Setup Wizard a second time.

This procedure covered all three basic methods for gaining access to the Internet from Internet Explorer. I think that the Automatic option is the easiest method if you just want to look at what's available before you make any permanent decisions. Obviously, the LAN method that I didn't select in step 9 is for those folks who need to access the Internet from a server. Step 11 also shows that you could access the Internet using a third-party service provider. If you decide to go either route, you'll need to get some additional information from the service provider, such as your IP address.

Getting on the Internet

By this point, you're probably wondering what else you'll have to do to get online. Actually, the setup and configuration are all done. All you need to do now is double-click the Internet icon on your desktop. You'll see a Connect To dialog box like the one shown in Figure 21.22. The "Using Dial-Up Networking" section of Chapter 19 talks about this dialog box. Enter your name and password (if necessary) and click Connect to get started.

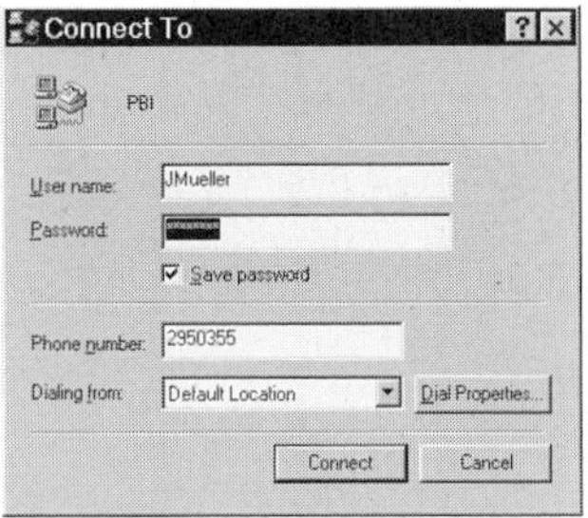

Figure 21.22.
You always need to connect to the Internet before you can surf it.

At this point, a number of things could happen, depending on how you created your Internet connection (you can also change the configuration of Internet Explorer to get a variety of results). In most cases, you'll start at the Welcome to Microsoft Internet Explorer Web page shown in Figure 21.23.

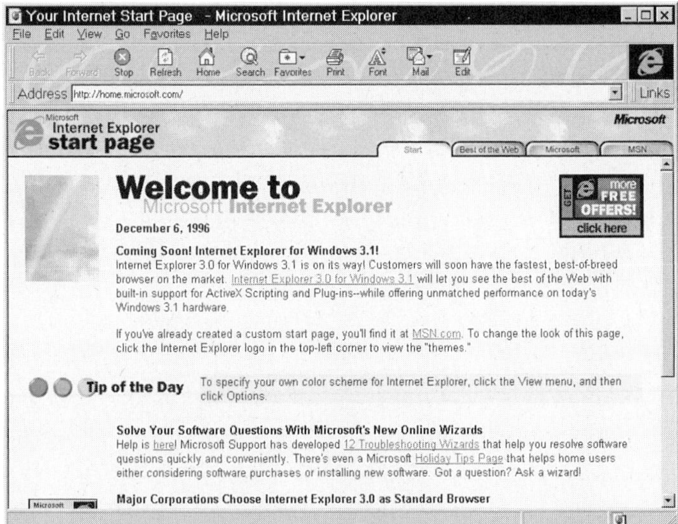

Figure 21.23.
You'll normally start your Internet session at the Internet Explorer home page.

Now that you're online, take a look at some of your controls in more detail. Everything you need is on the toolbar. I don't think I've ever used the menu system in Internet Explorer except to see what it contained. (There's always an exception to the rule. In this case, it's the Favorites menu that I describe in the next section.) The following list gives you a quick overview of the various controls on the menu. I cover some of them in detail as the chapter progresses:

- **Back/Forward:** These two buttons come in handy when you want to move quickly between several areas that you've already visited. I use the Back button most often to move from the current page back to the top level of an Internet site.
- **Stop:** Some Internet sites seem to provide more than the usual number of graphics. You could sit there waiting for them to all download, but I usually click this button instead. It tells the browser to stop downloading the graphics images on the page. The disadvantage is that you won't see all the neat graphics and buttons that the Web page designer placed on the page. The advantage is that you can get back to work faster.
- **Refresh:** Explorer, like most browsers, uses a cache to store images. Sometimes the Internet page changes without your knowledge, because your browser is looking at the cached page instead of the live page on the Internet. Use this button to update the current page contents. (This button also comes in really handy if part of the page got garbled during transmission and the browser didn't catch the error.)
- **Home:** Some browsers use the term *start page* for the place where you always start surfing the Internet—Internet Explorer uses the term *home page*. In my case, this is the Welcome to Microsoft Internet Explorer page shown in Figure 21.23. I prefer the term *home page* because it's a little more picturesque, and it's the term most people use to reference this part of the Internet. Clicking this button always takes you to your home page. (You can change your home page by using the View | Options command, and then selecting the Navigation page of the Options dialog box. Just type a new address in the Address field—you can even use a Web page on your local hard drive.)
- **Search:** I covered this button (and other search-related procedures) in the earlier section "Finding What You're Looking For." The short version is that this button opens an Internet page that you can use to search for things. Normally, you'll use some form of keyword search to accomplish the task.
- **Favorites:** Internet Explorer allows you to maintain a list of favorite places. For example, you might want to maintain a list of favorite Internet research sites or create a listing of sites related to a current project. This button displays a menu with a list of your favorite places. Using folders, you can also organize your favorite places into a hierarchy of submenus similar to the ones on the Start menu. There are also Add To Favorites and Organize Favorites options on the menu associated with this button. Use the Add To Favorites option to add an Internet site to your list of favorite places. Make sure that you're actually at the page you want to add, though, because Internet Explorer uses the URL of

the current site for the favorite place entry. The Organize Favorites option displays a dialog box that you can use to move your favorite places around and create folders (submenus) in which to store them.

Tip: You can save your favorite Web pages on disk for future reference, using the File | Save As command. The default save area is the desktop, making it easy for you to just double-click a favorite Web page the next time you need to access it. Clicking one of the hypertext links opens a connection. I use this feature to store the top-level page of places I visit on a regular basis, making it easier for me to find what I want in a pinch. If you don't want to clutter your desktop with a lot of Internet site locations, stick them in a folder on your desktop. You'll still be able to find them quickly by opening the folder when needed.

- **Print:** Use this option to send the current page content to the printer.
- **Font:** Generally, you'll find that Internet sites use an easy-to-read font. However, at times, you may need to see a little more or a little less of the text on a page. Use this button to change the font size. Each click cycles you through a set range of font sizes, starting at the smallest size and moving toward the largest.
- **Mail:** Clicking this button displays a menu containing four options: Read Mail, New Message, Send a Link, and Read News. The Read Mail option displays the Internet Mail program or Windows Messaging (depending on which you chose for your mail reader). Internet Explorer requests any new mail from your ISPs mail server and displays it in the window. The New Message option brings up a new message dialog box using the capabilities of either Internet Mail or Windows Messaging. The "Using Microsoft Exchange" section of Chapter 20 looks at Windows Messaging. I'll cover the messaging capabilities of Internet Mail further in the "Using Internet Mail" section of this chapter. The Send a Link option works much like creating a new message. However, in this case you send someone a link to your current Internet site in addition to the message. This allows you to have a discussion with someone else concerning the particulars of an Internet site. Finally, the Read News option brings up the Internet News program discussed in the "Using Internet News" section of this chapter.
- **Edit:** Clicking this button imports the current Web page into an editor. Internet Explorer automatically selects your favorite editor if you've got one of the Internet Assistants installed. (Chapter 22 discusses Internet Assistant for Microsoft Word—Office 97 includes Internet Assistants as a built-in feature.) Even if no application is set aside for editing Web pages, Internet Assistant looks for an appropriate editor, such as Notepad or WordPad.

Now that you've had an overview of the Internet Explorer connection features, let's take a more detailed view of specific features. The following sections give you a little more information about what I consider to be the essentials.

Using Internet Mail

Internet Mail is a special reader for your Internet mail. It's designed to work much like Windows Messaging, but provides a level of optimization for the Internet environment. For example, you can choose both plain text and HTML-based messages. Some of the file encoding options are a bit easier to understand as well. For example, you can set a specific MIME type or use UUENCODE to send binary messages.

Tip: If you're a road warrior, you know one of the problems with using any mail reader when you have two machines. Unless you take special precautions, you'll never have a complete copy of all your mail in one place; part of the mail appears on your laptop and the other part on your desktop machine. There are a couple of ways to handle this problem. The first way is also the easiest method. It allows you to read your messages on the road and respond to them, but keeps a copy of the messages on the server so that you can download them to your desktop machine. Simply use the Mail | Options command on your laptop setup to display the Options dialog box. Select the Server page and click the Advanced Settings button. Check the Leave a Copy of Messages on Server option. Of course, the only problem with this solution is that you still won't see a copy of your responses on the desktop machine (unless you CC: yourself in the message) and your laptop won't contain a complete copy of all your messages. The second method is a little more complicated and isn't automatic, but it has the advantage of allowing you to maintain a copy of all your messages and responses on both machines. Find the folder with your name in the Program Files\Internet Mail and News folder. The folder with your name should contain a Mail folder. In this folder you'll find a group of .IDX and .MDX files containing your mail messages. Copy these message files to the same location on your laptop when going on the road or to your desktop when arriving home.

Configuring Internet Mail for Use

The first time you start this program, you'll see an Internet Mail Configuration dialog box like the one shown in Figure 21.24. The procedure that follows takes you through this configuration process.

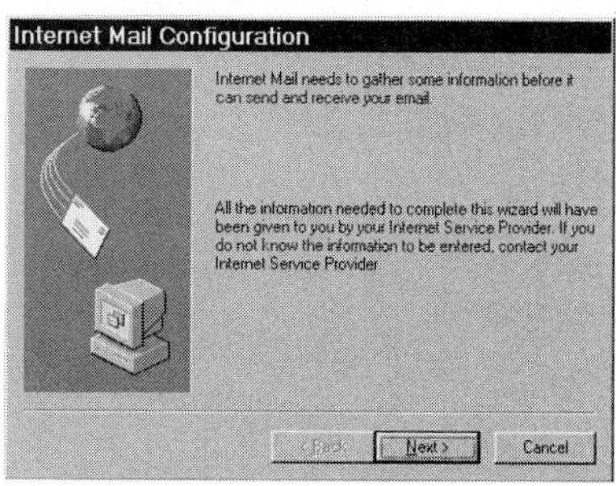

Figure 21.24.
The first step in using Internet Mail is to configure it.

1. Click Next. You'll see a dialog box like the one shown in Figure 21.25. This is where you tell Internet Mail how to access your mail on the ISP's mail server. The first field contains your name as you'd like it to appear at the top of your mail messages. Internet Mail usually suggests the name you used when you installed Windows 95. The second field begins with your Internet user name unless your ISP tells you otherwise. Next you add an `@` (at) sign. The second field ends with the name of your ISP's home page without the subdomain information (always make sure you check with your ISP regarding the contents of this field, if you have any questions). For example, if your ISP's home page is `home.msn.com` and your user name is Joe, you'd type **`Joe@msn.com`** in the second field. The second field is your Internet e-mail address.

Figure 21.25.
The first step in configuring Internet Mail is to tell it where to look.

2. Click Next and you'll see the dialog box shown in Figure 21.26. Now you've got to supply the name of the outgoing SMTP and incoming POP3 server that you'll use for your Internet mail. If this sounds as clear as mud, you're not alone. Let's make this simple. Unless your ISP tells you differently, you normally enter your ISP's mail server address as the incoming and outgoing mail server address. Using the previous example, you'd enter **`msn.com`** in the first field. Likewise, you'd enter **`msn.com`** in the second field.

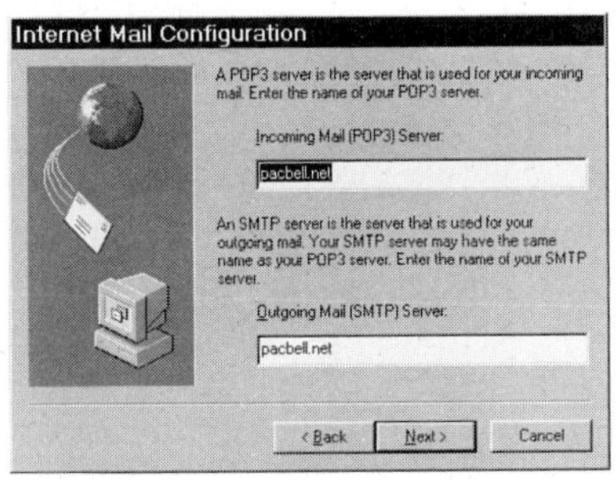

Figure 21.26.
This dialog box looks difficult, but it's simply a matter of knowing your e-mail address.

3. Click Next. The dialog box shown in Figure 21.27 asks for your e-mail account and password. Just enter your user name as the account name.

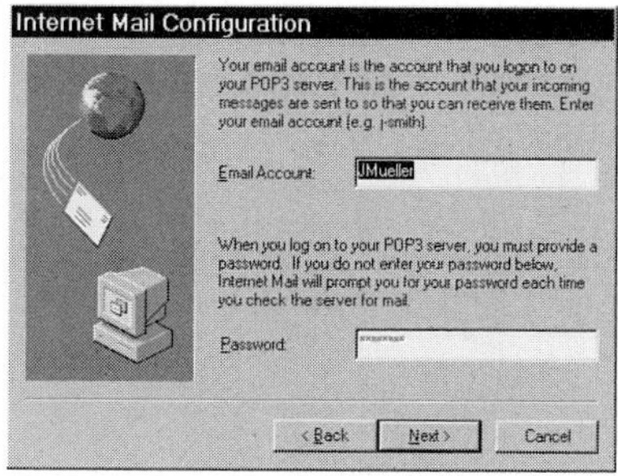

Figure 21.27.
Now you need to provide your e-mail account name and password.

4. Once you fill in your account name and password, click Next. You'll see the dialog box shown in Figure 21.28. As you can see, there are three different ways to connect to your mail server. Because you most likely want to create a dial-up connect, we'll pursue that route.

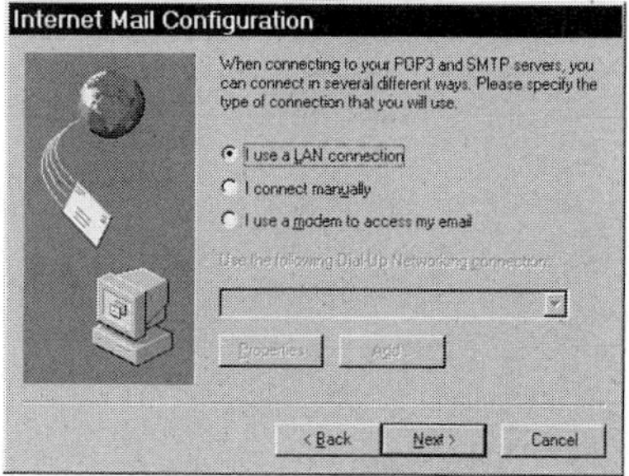

Figure 21.28.
Internet Mail provides three ways to connect to your mail server.

5. Select one of the three options (I chose Modem). If you select the third option, Modem, you'll also need to select a Dial-Up Networking connection. This is the same connection that you used when setting up Internet Explorer.
6. Click Next. At this point you'll see a completion message. You're ready to use Internet Mail.
7. Click Finish to complete the configuration process.

Figure 21.29 shows what Internet Mail looks like once you get it completely configured. Microsoft always places a welcome message in your inbox. You'll find a lot of valuable information in this message, so hold on to it while you learn how to use Internet Mail.

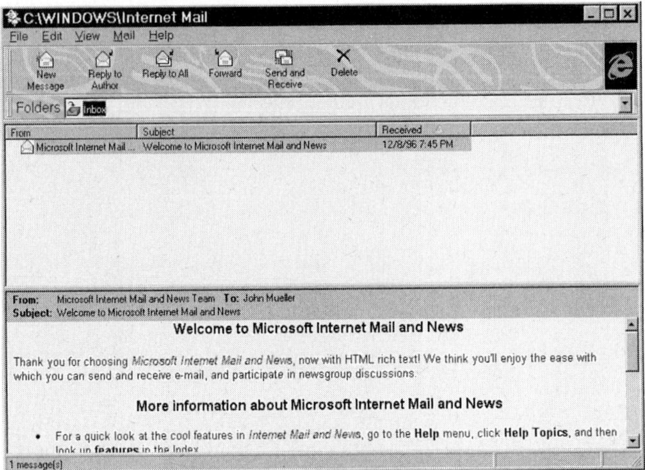

Figure 21.29.
Internet Mail provides many of the same features as Windows Messaging, but with a simpler interface.

Basic Internet Mail Usage

Let's begin looking at how Internet Mail works. In Figure 21.29, notice the six buttons in the toolbar. The following list describes the purpose of each button:

- **New Message:** Allows you to create a new message. As with Windows Messaging, you can include files with your message. You can also set priorities. In fact, the message editor works much like the one found in Windows Messaging.
- **Reply to Author:** Allows you to respond to an incoming e-mail message. This particular option sends the response only to the message author—not to anyone else who may have been on the message as a recipient. The author is the one that appears in the From section of the message. If multiple e-mail addresses are listed in the From section of the message, your response will be sent to all those recipients.
- **Reply to All:** Sends a response to everyone who received a copy of the original message, along with the message author.
- **Forward:** Sends a copy of the current message to someone else. What you'll see is a standard e-mail message dialog box with the forwarded message at the bottom. You can add your own message to the beginning of the forwarded message. This option also allows you to provide a CC: list.
- **Send and Receive:** This is the option you use to send any messages in your outbox folder. You'll also use it to receive any new messages from your ISP's mail server. Any new messages appear in your inbox folder. (See the next section for a discussion of folders.)
- **Delete:** Places the selected messages into the Deleted Items folder. If you're in the Deleted Items folder, this option permanently removes them from Internet Mail. This two-phase message-removal system should help reduce the number of messages you delete by accident, but it's also a little more work.

Working with Folders

It's time to talk about folders—one of the items you'll use to organize your mail. Internet Mail comes with the four basic folders shown in Figure 21.30. The purpose of each folder should be pretty self-explanatory. The Inbox receives all your new mail, the Outbox holds messages you want to send to someone else. The Sent Items folder holds a copy of the e-mail you send to other people so that you can refer to them later. The Deleted Items folder holds any messages that you deleted from other folders. Deleting a message in the Deleted Items folder removes it for good. Internet Mail always selects the Inbox when you open it so that you can see your current message list.

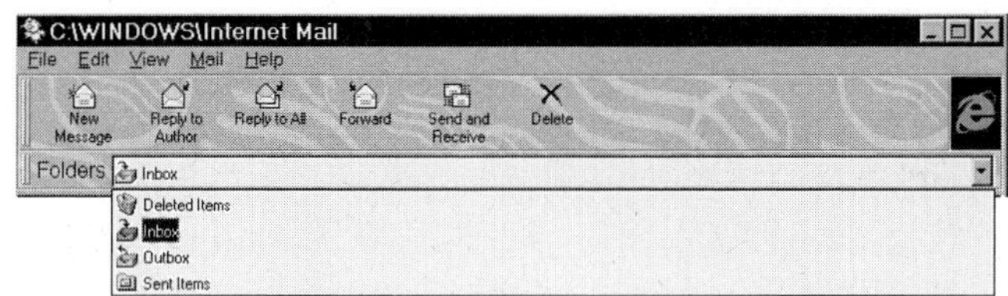

Figure 21.30. *You get four basic folders with Internet Mail, but you can add more.*

There are three folder-related commands on the File | Folder menu. The first allows you to create new folders. The second allows you to delete folders that you no longer need. Internet Mail won't allow you to delete the four default folders. Finally, there's a Compress option. Internet Mail doesn't actually recover the space used by old messages until you compress the associated folder. You can choose to compress all the folders or just one that's wasting a lot of space.

I usually organize my messages by project. Each project gets its own folder. This makes cleaning up easy when I complete a project—I just delete the associated folder. Let's look at the process for creating a new folder. Use the File | Folder | Create command to display the Create New Folder dialog box shown in Figure 21.31. Type the name of the new folder and click OK to create it. You'll see a new folder in the drop-down list box (refer to Figure 21.30).

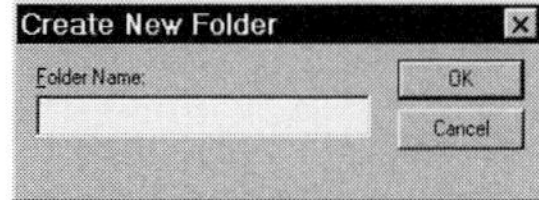

Figure 21.31. *Creating a new folder is easy using the Create New Folder dialog box.*

Tip: You can use project- or topic-related mailboxes to your advantage by creating a separate folder each time you need to separate a group of temporary messages. Internet Mail maintains two files for each folder that you create in the Internet Explorer\Internet Mail and News\<*user name*>\Mail folder on your hard drive. One has an .MBX extension and contains the messages. The other has an .IDX extension and contains index information for the folder. You can simply move these two folder files to a disk or other form of archive device when you complete a project. If you need to look at the project messages later, place a copy of the folder files into your Internet Mail folder. The mail utility for Netscape Navigator shares this particular Internet Mail feature. You'll find the Navigator files in the Netscape\Navigator\Mail folder.

By now you should be asking how to get your messages from the Inbox folder to a specialty folder. There are two ways you can do it. The manual method is to use the Mail | Copy To or Mail | Move To commands. Selecting either of these menu options displays a list of the folders on your machine like the one displayed in Figure 21.32. The big difference between the Move To and Copy To options is that the Copy To command leaves the selected message in the current folder as well as copying it to the new folder. Notice that Figure 21.32 includes a specialty folder named George's Project.

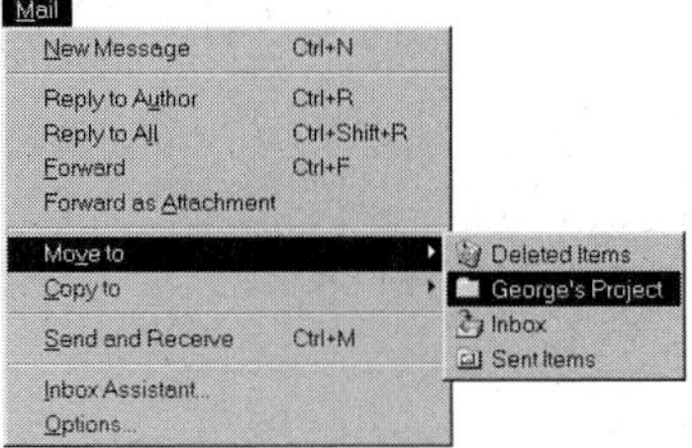

Figure 21.32.
You copy or move messages by using options on the Mail menu.

There's also an automatic method for moving messages around. Just use the Mail | Inbox Assistant command to display the Inbox Assistant dialog box shown in Figure 21.33. The Inbox Assistant uses rules to determine how to arrange your folders. Whenever you get a message in your Inbox folder from the ISP's mail server, Inbox Assistant looks through its list of rules to see whether the message meets certain criteria. As you can see, I've already defined a couple of rules in the dialog box shown in Figure 21.33 for George's Project.

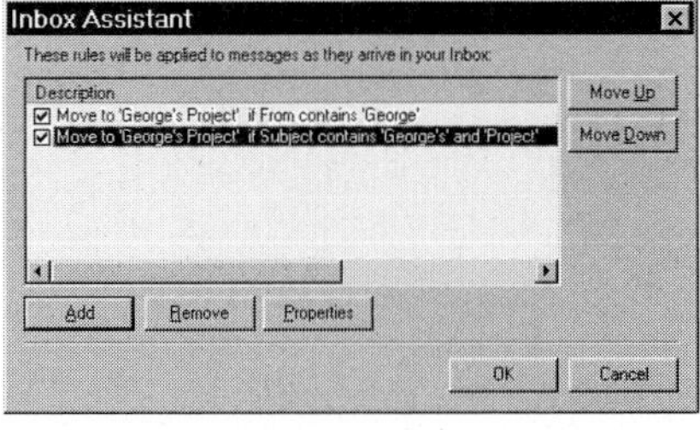

Figure 21.33.
The Inbox Assistant provides an automated method for moving messages to the right folder.

It pays to arrange the message rules in their order of importance, because Inbox Assistant takes some time to look at each rule and you want to reduce the amount of time you wait for it to get its work done. If a new rule that you've just added is more important than the others in the list, highlight it and use the Move Up button in the Inbox Assistant dialog box (refer to Figure 21.33) to move it. Likewise, if a rule becomes less important, highlight it, and move it by using the Move Down button.

Notice that there are three buttons along the bottom of the Inbox Assistant dialog box. The Add button displays a Properties dialog box like the one shown in Figure 21.34. Use the Remove button to remove a rule you no longer need. The Properties button allows you to edit an existing rule. Defining a new rule is very easy. All you need to do is tell Inbox Assistant what to look for in the message header. For example, you might want to send all messages from George to the George's Project folder. Right after you define what to look for, go to the Move To field and select one of the folders listed there. Click OK, and you'll see the new rule added to the Inbox Assistant dialog box.

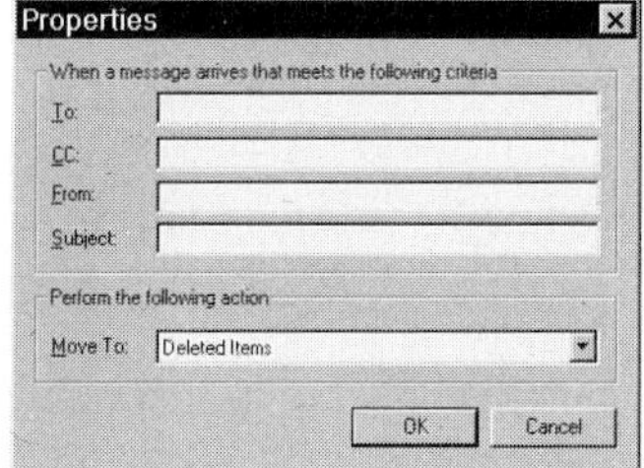

Figure 21.34.
Creating or editing a message rule is easy using the Properties dialog box.

There's one more matter to cover. What happens if you want to keep a rule, but you don't need it right this second? Notice that there's a check box next to each rule listed in the Inbox Assistant dialog box shown in Figure 21.33. If a rule is checked, Inbox Assistant uses it; otherwise, the rule is ignored. You can simply uncheck any rules that you don't need to use for the current session.

Sending a Message

Once you have Internet Mail installed and configured for use, you'll want to use it to send some messages. All you need to do is click the New Message button on the toolbar that I described earlier and you'll see a New Message dialog box like the one shown in Figure 21.35.

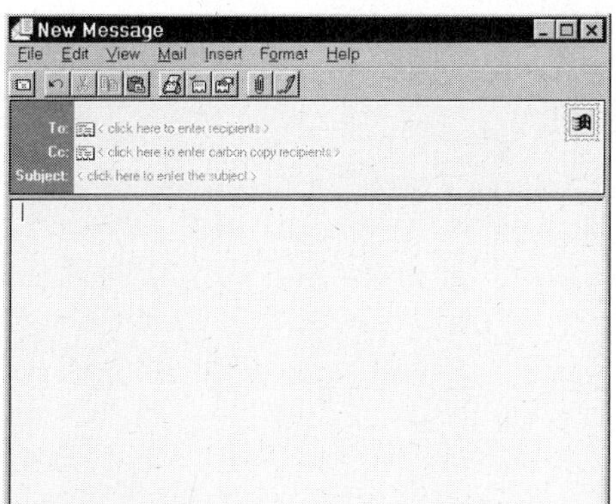

Figure 21.35.
The New Message dialog box allows you to create messages for the Internet.

Let's look at the buttons along the toolbar first, because they provide the features you'll use most often. The following list tells you about each button:

- **Send:** Sends the message you've just created. You must define a recipient in the To field before sending a message. In addition, Internet Mail checks the Subject field to make sure it's not blank. You can bypass this requirement by clicking Yes when Internet Mail asks you whether you want to send the message without a subject. Obviously, you'll want to make sure that the message contains some kind of information, although Internet Mail certainly doesn't check for any.
- **Undo:** Internet Mail provides one level of undo. Essentially, this means that you can undo your last action, but not much more. A second click of this button redoes your last action.
- **Cut/Copy/Paste:** These three buttons work much like they would with any Windows application. You can cut or copy information to the Clipboard. You can also paste information from the Clipboard into your message.
- **Address Book:** Internet Mail maintains a mailing list separately from the one maintained by Windows Messaging. Clicking this button displays the Internet Mail-specific address book. The later section "Managing Your Address Book" looks at managing an address book.
- **Check Names:** This is one of the nicer features offered by Internet Mail. Say you don't want to try and remember a lot of esoteric e-mail addresses when writing a message. All you need to do is type the person's name and then click the Check Names button. You'll see a dialog box like the one shown in Figure 21.36, which lists the names Internet Mail found in your address book that match the one you typed. Highlight the recipient you want to use, click OK, and Internet Mail adds the full form to your message heading. If Internet Mail doesn't find the name in the To field, it gives you the option of adding the name to your address book.

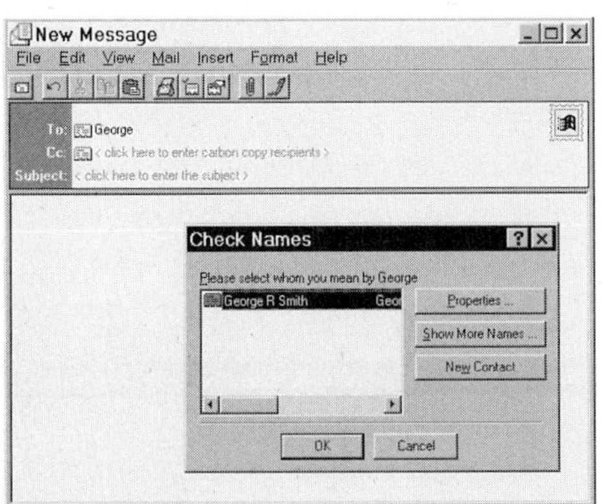

Figure 21.36.
The Check Names feature allows you to use real names instead of e-mail addresses in the To field of your message.

- **Pick Recipients:** Clicking this button displays a Select Recipients dialog box like the one shown in Figure 21.37. All you need to do is highlight one or more of the names and click the To-> or CC-> button as appropriate. Clicking OK places the names you selected in the appropriate fields of the message and closes the dialog box.

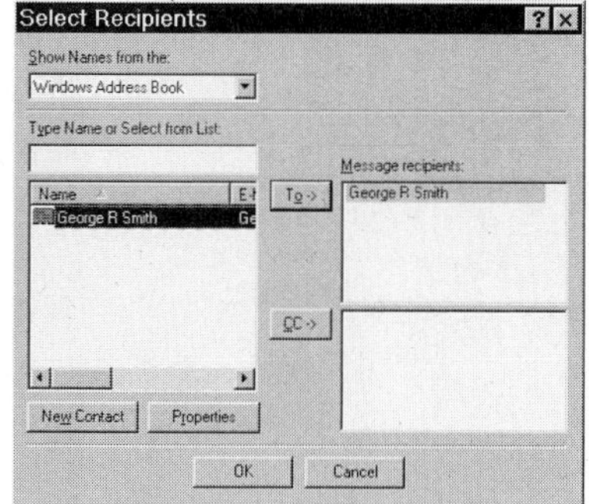

Figure 21.37.
The Select Recipients dialog box allows you to choose one or more people to receive your message.

- **Insert File:** Use this button to insert a file into your message. Internet Mail opens a standard File Open dialog box that you can use to select the file.
- **Insert Signature:** You can use this button only after you define a signature by using the Mail | Options command within the main Internet Mail dialog box. (For some reason, there's no Options option within the Mail menu in the New Message dialog box.) You'll find the signature options on the Signature page of the Options dialog box.

Once you've added a name or two to your recipient list, you need to type a subject for it. The first thing you'll notice is that the title for the New Message dialog box changes to match the message subject. You can also define the priority level for your message, although not all browsers and mail readers support this feature. Just click the stamp in the upper-right corner of the message area, and you'll see a menu like the one shown in Figure 21.38. There are three priority levels to choose from, with Normal Priority being the default. After you add some content to your message, click the Send button to send it. You'll see a Send Mail dialog box telling you that your message was added to your Outbox folder. It will be sent automatically the next time you click the Send and Receive button in the main Internet Mail window.

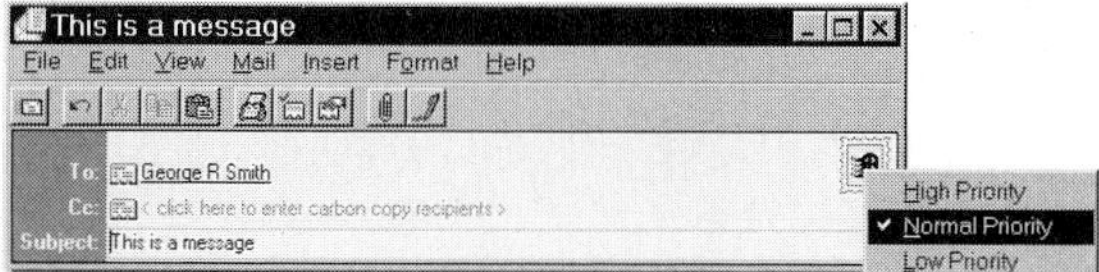

Figure 21.38.
Internet Mail allows you to define a priority level for the messages you send.

Managing Your Address Book

There are several ways to gain access to your address book, but the two most common methods are to use the File | Address Book command from within the main Internet Mail window, or click the Address Book button in the New Message dialog box. You'll use the Address Book dialog box to maintain your address book as shown in Figure 21.39.

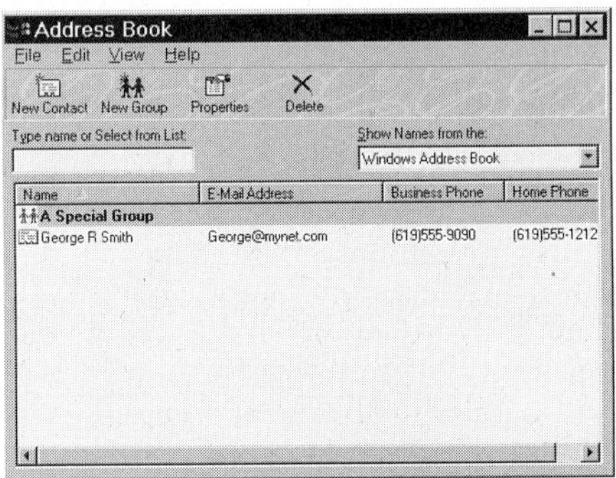

Figure 21.39.
The Address Book helps you maintain a list of contacts on the Internet.

As you can see from the figure, there are two kinds of e-mail address entries that you can create in the Address Book dialog box. The first is a single entry, like the George entry shown in the figure. Notice that this entry type uses a Rolodex page as an icon. The second is a group, which uses two people as an icon. Groups contain one or more of the single contacts that you create.

Creating a single contact is easy. All you need to do is click the New Contact button on the toolbar. You'll see a contact Properties dialog box like the one shown in Figure 21.40. (I've already filled this one out for explanation purposes—George isn't a real person.) There are four pages in this dialog box. The first page, Personal, contains all the personal contact information for the new entry, such as name and e-mail address. You can even add one or more e-mail addresses to the list. Notice that one e-mail address is designated as the default that you want to use. This is the address that Internet Mail uses, unless you specify an alternative address. You can specify a new default e-mail address by highlighting it and clicking the Set Default button. Adding a new e-mail address is easy. Just type it into the E-Mail Addresses field and click Add. Likewise, you can get rid of old e-mail addresses by highlighting the one you want to remove and clicking the Remove button. If you need to change an existing entry, highlight the e-mail address and click Properties.

The Home page contains all the personal information for your contact. It appears in Figure 21.41. Notice that it contains three personal contact numbers: home phone, home fax, and cellular. You can also enter the URL for a personal Web page. Notice the little world icon button next to the Personal Web Page field. Clicking this button opens your favorite browser, and then takes you to that person's personal Web page.

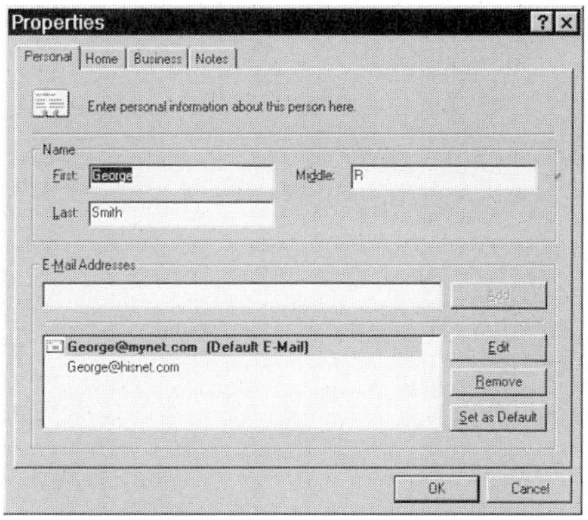

Figure 21.40.
The contact Properties dialog box allows you to add entries to your address book.

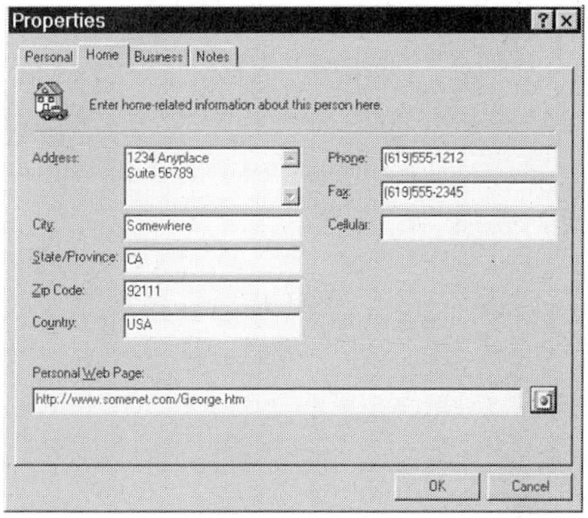

Figure 21.41.
The Home page of the contact Properties dialog box allows you to add a personal Web page URL for the contact.

The Business page looks a lot like the Home page. It contains three entries for business phone numbers, including office phone, office fax, and pager. You'll also find a Business Web Page field on this page that works just like the Personal Web Page field on the Home page. Clicking the World icon button on this page takes you to the client's business Web page.

Notes, the final page in the contact Properties dialog box, contains just that—notes about your contact. This page doesn't contain much more than a single notepad field, so I won't show it here. Suffice it to say that there aren't any fancy gadgets for maintaining contact information by date. You'll probably want to reserve this page for long-lasting notes and use a contact manager to keep track of current business information.

Let's get back to the main Address Book window. You can edit a group or single contact by highlighting the desired entry and clicking the Properties button in the toolbar. Getting rid of an unneeded entry is just as easy. Simply highlight the entries you no longer need and click the Delete button.

So how do you create a group? Click the Group button and you'll see a group Properties dialog box like the one shown in Figure 21.42. As you can see, I've already added one member to this group—our sample contact, George. The entries for a group include a group name, a list of members, and some notes. When you send an e-mail message to a group, every member gets a copy.

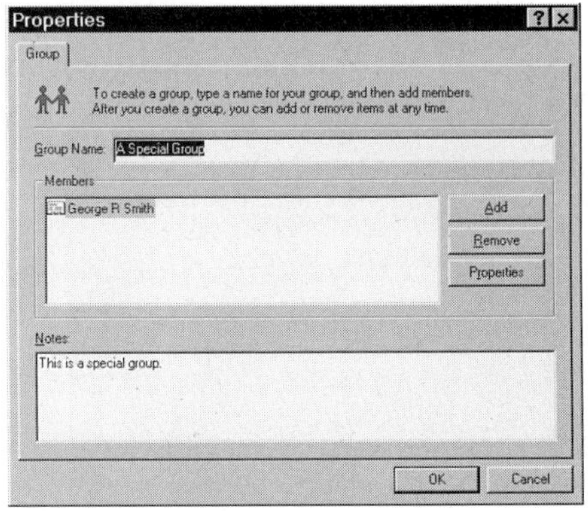

Figure 21.42.
The group Properties dialog box allows you to create a group, which allows you to send one message to multiple recipients.

There are three buttons along the side of this dialog box. If you want to remove a member entry, simply highlight the member name and click Remove. Highlighting a member name and clicking Properties displays a dialog box similar to the one shown in Figure 21.40 for that member. Finally, the Add button displays a dialog box like the one shown in Figure 21.43. Just select the contact or group that you want to add to your member list and then click the Add button. Click OK and you'll return to the group Properties dialog box. Notice that you can also add or edit entries from within this dialog box.

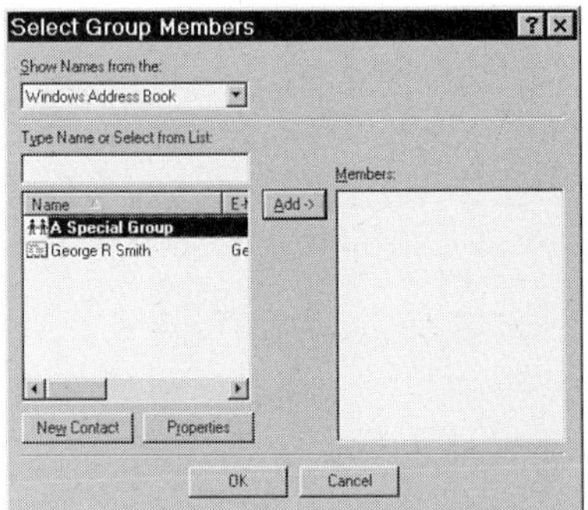

Figure 21.43.
The Select Group Members dialog box allows you to add members to a group entry in the address book.

Using Internet News

Internet News, like Internet Mail, is a separate application designed for use with Internet Explorer. Unlike Internet Mail, there isn't any replacement program for Internet News (unless you use a third-party news reader of some sort). The basic reason for using Internet News is to read the messages in a newsgroup and respond to them.

Tip: There are many sources of additional information on using Internet Mail and News. One of my favorites is the IMN User Tips site at `http://home.sprynet.com/sprynet/edm/`. You should also check out the two Internet Explorer-specific newsgroups: `microsoft.public.internetexplorer.beta.win95` and `microsoft.public.internetexplorer.win95`. (Notice that these groups are specifically designed to answer questions for Windows 95 users; there are other newsgroups for other versions of Internet Explorer.)

A newsgroup is a public forum for discussing issues or asking questions about a specific topic. One person begins the whole process by making a comment or asking a question. He or she uploads this information as a message. After you read the message, you can reply to it. A third person may see what you've written and respond to your message. Well, you get the idea. A series of messages forms what's known as a message thread. By reading the messages in a message thread in order, you can see a conversation.

Configuring Internet News for Use

The first thing you'll need to do when you start Internet News is configure it for use. The following procedure shows how to accomplish this task by using the Internet News Configuration Wizard. Figure 21.44 shows the initial dialog box that you'll see as soon as you start Internet News the first time.

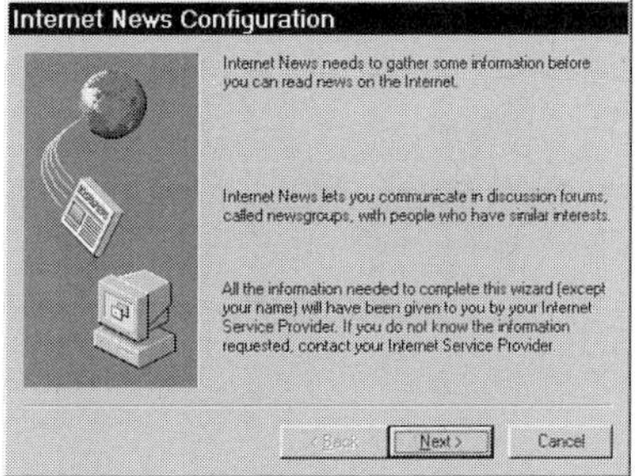

Figure 21.44.
You'll see the Internet News Configuration Wizard the first time you start Internet News.

1. Click Next and then supply your name and e-mail address. As previously mentioned, message threads depend on responses to existing messages. Providing an e-mail address enables someone to respond to your message. It also allows the Webmaster (the person who maintains the newsgroup site) to forward messages you haven't read. Figure 21.45 shows what this dialog box looks like.

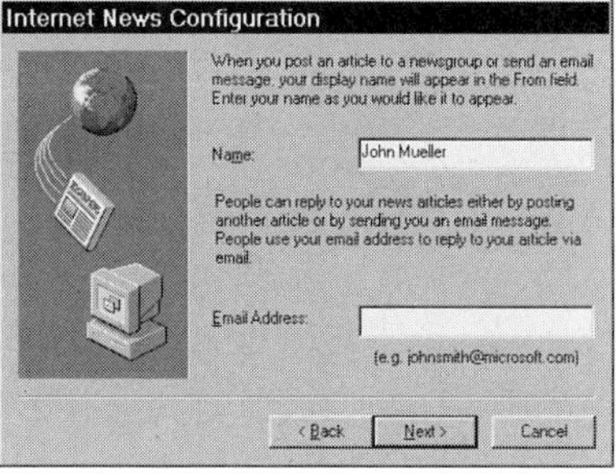

Figure 21.45.
You'll need to provide a name and e-mail address as part of the Internet News configuration process.

Note: Some people use false or modified addresses for newsgroups. (The most common method of modification is to add an asterisk in front of your e-mail address.) This tends to discourage some Internet users from sending junk mail to your e-mail address. The only problem is that it also prevents other people from responding to your message privately by using e-mail. It also prevents the Webmaster from forwarding unread messages to your mailbox. The bottom line is that you have to decide whether it's more of a hindrance to receive junk mail or not to get e-mail responses to your questions. In most cases, I think you'll find that using your correct e-mail address is worth the effort.

2. Enter your name and e-mail address and then click Next. You'll see a dialog box similar to the one shown in Figure 21.46. The one required piece of information here is your news server address. In most cases, your ISP provides you with an address. Many news servers use a simple modification of their home page address. For example, if your home page Web site is `http://home.mysite.com`, you'll probably find that your news address is `news.mysite.com`. This doesn't always work, but at least you can try it if the ISP didn't supply an address and isn't available to ask. Some news servers also require that you log in each time you use their service. The Logon Settings group allows you to enter a user name and password for the news server.

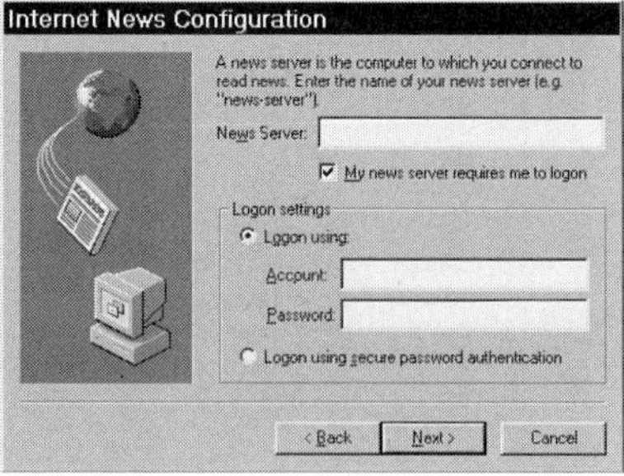

Figure 21.46.
This dialog box requires a News Server address as a minimum.

3. Type a news server address. Check the My News Server Requires Me to Logon check box and add user name and password, if required.
4. Click Next. You'll see a dialog box like the one shown in Figure 21.47. There are three connection options for Internet News. You can use a LAN connection, manually connect each time you want to read news, or use a modem connection. Because you probably will use a modem to connect to the Internet, I cover that option here.

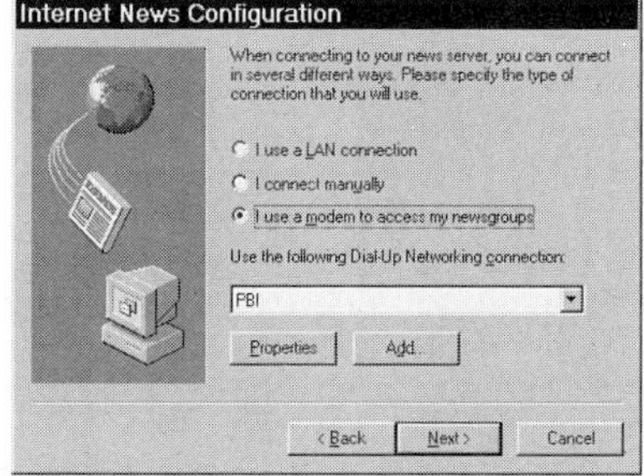

Figure 21.47.
Determining a connection method is the next step in the configuration process.

5. Select a connection method (and a Dial-Up Networking connection if you selected the modem option), and then click Next. You'll see an Internet News Configuration completion message.
6. Click Finish to complete the configuration process. At this point, you'll see a Connect To dialog box.
7. Click Connect. You'll see Internet News log on, and then see it download a list of newsgroups using a dialog box like the one shown in Figure 21.48. This process may take quite a while, so be patient.

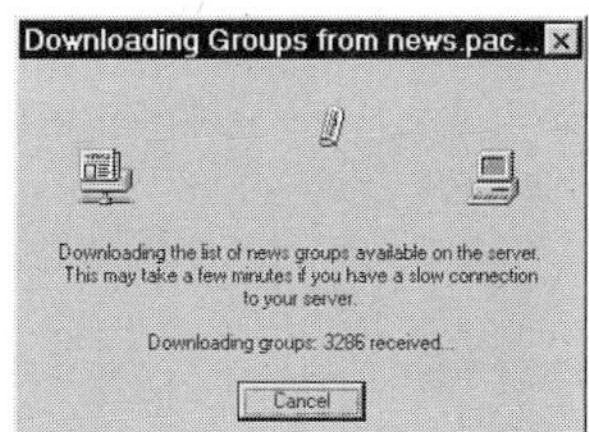

Figure 21.48.
After you configure your Internet News connection, it downloads a list of news-groups that you might want to join.

8. Wait until Internet News completes the download process. Once it does, you'll see a list of newsgroups like the one shown in Figure 21.49. Be sure to check out the next section, which tells you how to select and view newsgroups.

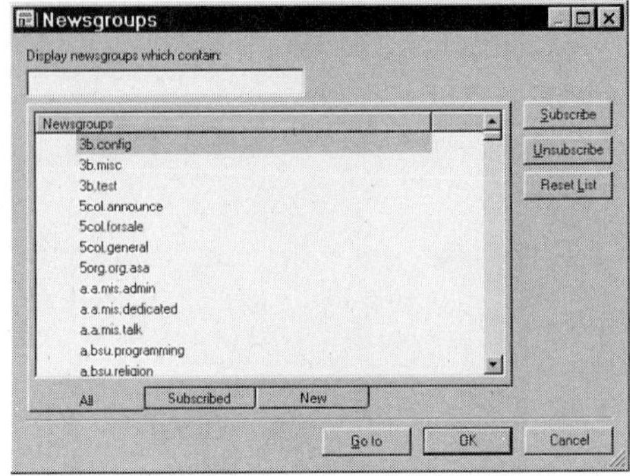

Figure 21.49.
The final phase of the Internet News configuration process is to select the newsgroups that you want to join.

Adding Newsgroups to Internet News

There are a couple of ways you can reach this section. You could have just completed the Internet News configuration process, which means that you have a Newsgroups dialog box like the one shown earlier (refer to Figure 21.49). Another way to get there is to use the News | Newsgroups command to display the Newsgroups dialog box. As your needs change, you'll use this dialog box to change the newsgroups you frequent.

The All page of the Newsgroups dialog box shown in Figure 21.49 displays all the newsgroups that you can join. If you're a bit worried about finding a specific newsgroup in the thousands that Internet Mail downloaded, don't worry. There are a few strategies you can use to quickly find what you need. It shouldn't be too surprising to find the Microsoft-specific newsgroups in a section starting with `microsoft`. In many cases, all you need is a vendor name or perhaps a good idea of what you're looking for. However, trying to find some newsgroups can be quite a trick. For example, what would happen if you wanted to find a special newsgroup for strategy game players? You could use the Display Newsgroups Which Contain field to narrow the choices. Figure 21.50 shows how I used this dialog box to find a few strategy game newsgroup choices. Notice that I didn't use complete words—phrases work best here, because not everyone will use the exact word you had in mind.

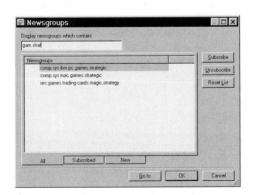

Figure 21.50.
Finding a newsgroup doesn't have to be hard, but it does take practice.

Once you find a newsgroup that you think sounds interesting, you can use the Subscribe button to subscribe to it. As soon as you do, you'll see a little newspaper icon appear next to the entry. If you later decide that you don't need this newsgroup, highlight it again and click the Unsubscribe button. Clicking the Reset List button downloads a new list of newsgroups from the ISP's news server.

You don't have to subscribe to a newsgroup without looking at it first. Just highlight something that looks interesting and then click the Go To button. Internet News displays the requested newsgroup in the browser (described in the next section).

Let's talk about the two additional pages listed in the Newsgroup dialog box. The second page, Subscribed, looks just like the page shown earlier in Figure 21.49. The only difference is that it shows only the newsgroups to which you've subscribed. This allows you to find a newsgroup quickly, in case you don't want to subscribe to it any longer. The New page of the Newsgroup dialog box allows you to find new newsgroups quickly. Obviously, it's a really handy feature—just imagine trying to dig through the thousands of newsgroups available to find the new newsgroup that you need.

Basic Internet News Usage

By the time you reach this section of the chapter, you should have Internet News configured and have a few newsgroups selected. The main Internet News window looks like the one shown in Figure 21.51. Notice that I've already downloaded the headings from one of the newsgroups.

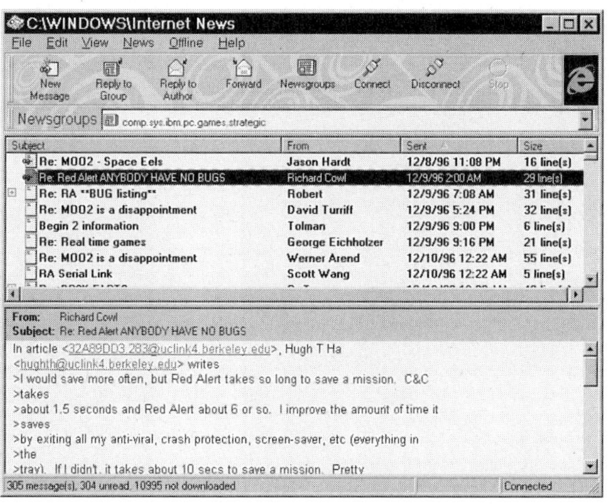

Figure 21.51.
The main Internet News window allows you to determine the current newsgroup and see the headings for messages that the newsgroup contains.

There are three sections to every Internet News window. The first is the Newsgroup drop-down list box, which tells you the current newsgroup name. The second contains a list of headings for the newsgroup. This is a list of the message subjects you'll find in the newsgroup. If you've already read a message, you'll see a thumbtack through it, like the `Re: M002 - Space Eels` topic shown in Figure 21.51. The third section contains the currently highlighted message. You'll see the message subject and its author at the top of this area. The message text follows.

Like most Windows applications, this one includes a toolbar. The following list tells you what the various toolbar buttons can do for you. I think you'll find that you'll have just about everything you need for daily message traffic:

- **New Message:** This button allows you to upload a new message to the newsgroup. It's almost like writing a message to someone by using Internet Mail, but in this case you're addressing the message to a group of people in a public forum. The next section talks more about this topic.
- **Reply to Group:** Use this option to send a reply for the current message to the entire group. In other words, you'll make a public response to a message that someone else left. You can use this option to ask for clarification of the previous sender's message, ask a similar question of your own, provide an answer to the initial message, or simply make a pertinent comment about the subject under discussion.
- **Reply to Author:** There are times when a public response to a question isn't ideal. For example, the author may specifically ask you to reply using e-mail, because he doesn't visit the newsgroup very often. You may also want to use this option when providing personal information, answering a personal question, or providing information that the rest of the group really isn't interested in hearing. I find that this particular method of responding is a two-edged sword. On the one hand, you may spare someone embarrassment; on the other hand, you remove the rest of the group from the loop. Not only does this prevent other people from providing additional information, but it's counter to the very concept of using a newsgroup in the first place.
- **Forward:** Occasionally you may want to make a colleague aware of some information you've found in a newsgroup that he or she doesn't read. This option allows you to do just that. You can forward a message containing the message from the newsgroup.
- **Newsgroups:** This button displays the Newsgroup dialog box that I described in the preceding section.
- **Connect/Disconnect:** I'm not sure why Microsoft included two separate buttons, but there's one for connecting and another for disconnecting from the news server. Clicking the Connect button again after you've already connected to the Internet doesn't do much. Likewise, you can disconnect only once.
- **Stop:** This button serves the same purpose as it does within Internet Explorer. It allows you to stop downloading a message or message headings from the news server.

There's one additional piece of information you need to know. If you'll look at the status line in Figure 21.51, you'll notice that only 305 of the message headers were downloaded. To download the next 300 messages, use the News | Get Next 300 Headers command.

Using Internet News to Write a Message

Getting a message uploaded to the Internet is much like writing a message for your mailbox. There are some differences, of course. For one thing, you're addressing a public forum. You don't need to specify a recipient for your message, because the entire group will look at it. I find it interesting that some people act as though they're addressing a specific person in a newsgroup, when in reality they can't. Always keep the idea of public versus private communication in mind when working in a newsgroup.

Let's take a look at a basic newsgroup message. Click the New Message or Reply to Group button on the Internet News toolbar and you'll see a dialog box similar to the one shown in Figure 21.52.

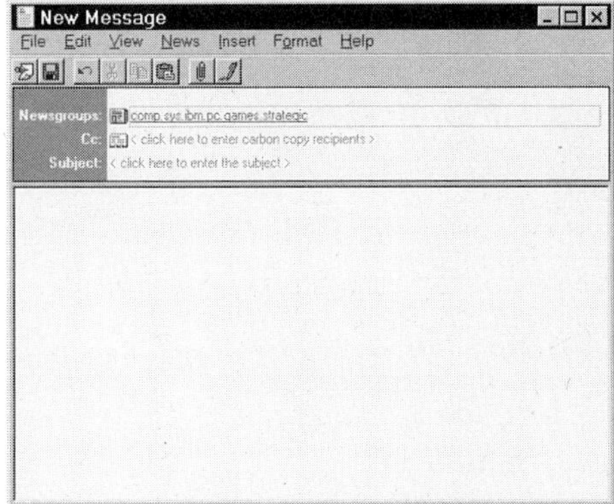

Figure 21.52.
You'll use the same dialog box for creating new messages or responding to existing ones.

The following list describes the functions of the various toolbar buttons:

- **Post Message:** Use this option to post your message onto the news server. You probably won't see the message appear right away. Some Webmasters monitor the messages they allow to appear on the newsgroup. However, even if the news server posts messages without any form of monitoring (as in most newsgroups), it still takes time for your message to arrive at the news server.
- **Save This Message:** Use this option to save the current message to a message file. Internet Mail allows you to use either a news (NWS) or e-mail (EML) file format.
- **Undo:** Internet News provides one level of undo. Essentially, this means that you can undo your last action, but not much more. A second click of this button redoes your last action.
- **Cut/Copy/Paste:** These three buttons work much as they would with any Windows application. You can cut or copy information to the Clipboard and paste information from the Clipboard into your message.
- **Insert File:** Use this button to insert a file into your message. Internet News opens a standard File Open dialog box that you use to select the file.

- **Insert Signature:** You can use this button only after you define a signature by using the News | Options command within the main Internet News dialog box. (For some reason, there's no Options option within the News menu in the New Message dialog box.) You'll find the signature options on the Signature page of the Options dialog box.

There are a few special features in your New Message dialog box. Click the newspaper icon next to the Newsgroups field and you'll see a dialog box like the one shown in Figure 21.53. This dialog box allows you to send your message to more than one newsgroup. I find it especially convenient when writing a new message that could be answered by people on several newsgroups. Notice that this dialog box defaults to showing only the newsgroups to which you've subscribed. Click the newspaper at the bottom left of the dialog box and you'll see all the available newsgroups. Using the dialog box is fairly straightforward. Just highlight a newsgroup in the left list and click Add to add a newsgroup. You can remove a newsgroup by clicking a newsgroup in the right list and clicking the Remove button.

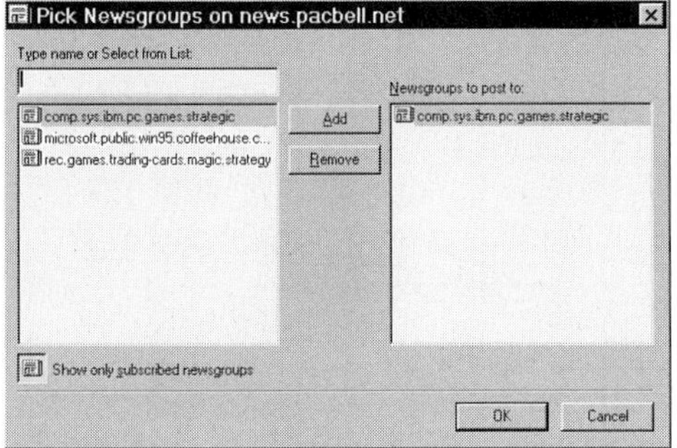

Figure 21.53.
Click the newspaper icon and you'll see a Pick Newsgroups dialog box.

Another dialog box like the one shown in Figure 21.54 appears when you click the index card next to the CC field of the New Message dialog box. You can use this dialog box to select people who will receive a copy of the message through e-mail. All you need to do is highlight a user or group name, and then click the Reply To or CC button. The earlier section "Using Internet Mail" describes the features of this dialog box, so I won't describe them again here.

Note: One thing you'll want to avoid on the Internet is sending messages to a lot of people you met in a newsgroup because you think that they might be interested in some new product, or even a particular Web site. This practice is called spamming, and most people react negatively to it. If you want to advertise a product, do so with extreme caution; you may want to simply post a single message on the newsgroup after you receive the Webmaster's permission to do so. Likewise, new or improved Web site announcements should appear as a single message on sites where you have the Webmaster's permission to post.

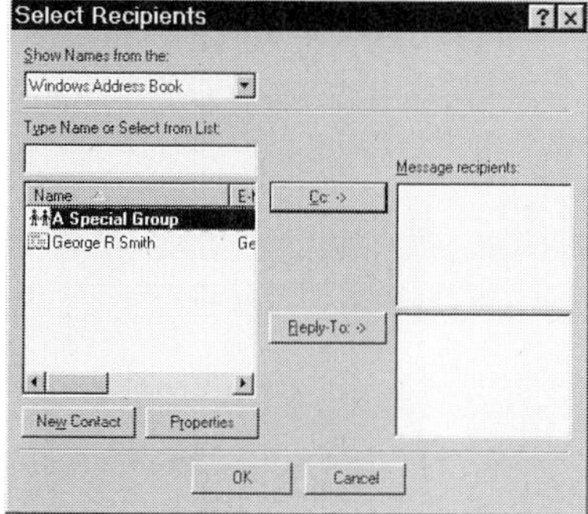

Figure 21.54.
In addition to sending a message to the newsgroup, you can send it to one or more people by using e-mail.

Working with Microsoft NetMeeting

Online conferencing is becoming more than just a convenience. Many companies are looking to this solution to reduce business travel costs. This section looks at the Microsoft solution to this problem—NetMeeting.

Tip: There isn't any need to limit the use of NetMeeting to the Internet. You can also use it to hold meetings over an intranet in a company setting. No longer will people feel left out as they strain to see what's going on from the last row of the meeting room. You can also use NetMeeting for training purposes. A company training specialist could hold company-wide training where anyone could join in. This would be a lot better than limiting the number of trainees by the size of a meeting room. Another use of NetMeeting is as a device for brainstorming sessions. Rather than wait until you can get everyone together for a formal meeting, you could discuss an idea with a few colleagues while the idea is fresh in your mind. In essence, you can use NetMeeting anywhere that you can use a standard meeting room. The only difference is that it's more convenient for everyone concerned.

Like most software in this category, NetMeeting is still more fluff than substance. You'll find that some meetings still require personal, face-to-face contact. Yet I find that NetMeeting is an outstanding tool in some situations. For example, if you have a meeting where everyone will need to provide some form of input, NetMeeting may actually be a better solution than a face-to-face meeting. Consider the possibilities for a moment. No one will feel inhibited because of the public nature of the meeting, and you'll find that people participate better when they can actually see what's going on. Whether or not online-meeting software will serve your company's needs is not the issue here. You'll need to decide that issue for yourself. What we'll look at are some basic usage techniques that you can use to reduce the NetMeeting learning curve.

Setting Up NetMeeting

The first time you use NetMeeting, you need to provide some information. This information is sent to other users when you join a meeting in progress. It also lets other users know what part of the country you're in, and so on. Figure 21.55 shows the initial screen. The following procedure takes you through the process of setting NetMeeting up for the first time.

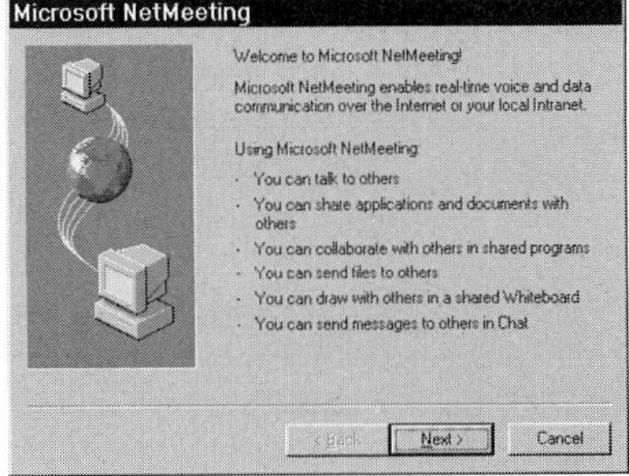

Figure 21.55.
NetMeeting automatically starts the configuration process the first time you start it.

1. Click Next to go to the next page. You'll see a dialog box like the one shown in Figure 21.56. This is where you supply the information needed to converse with other people. As a minimum, you'll have to provide your first name, last name, and e-mail address. I'd suggest filling out all the entries so you don't have to do it during long-distance meetings in the future.

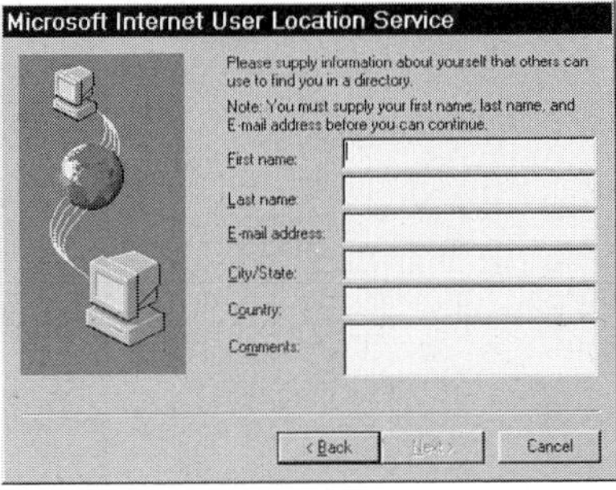

Figure 21.56.
You need to supply some personal information before you can converse with other people.

Tip: You could use the Comments field of this dialog box for a variety of purposes. Two of the more important items that you could include would be your position within the company and the department you work for. Coming up with a standard approach to using this field company-wide makes it even more useful.

2. Click Next. You'll see a dialog box like the one shown in Figure 21.57. This is where you decide whether you want to be part of a user location service. If you're only using

NetMeeting as part of a company approach to networking, it may not be important to join a user location service (ULS). On the other hand, if you're using NetMeeting as a company approach to meeting with individuals from a variety of places (including other companies), it makes sense to use this service. Microsoft is the only ULS provider, as of this writing.

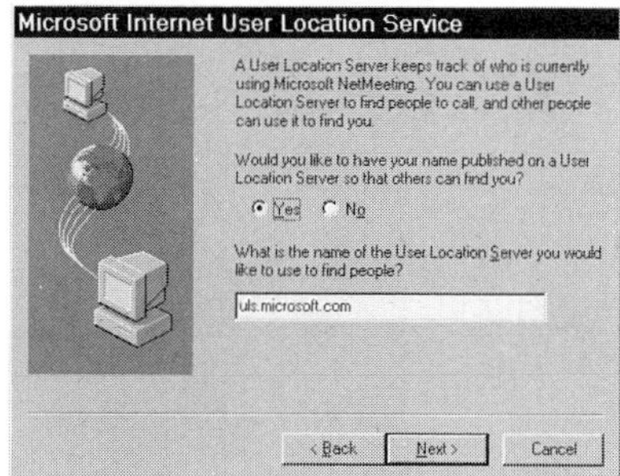

Figure 21.57.
A ULS can help you find other NetMeeting users.

3. Select Yes and then click Next if you want to use the ULS service. Otherwise, select No and click Next. At this point you'll see the first page of the Audio Tuning Wizard, as shown in Figure 21.58. This wizard helps you to adjust the audio qualities of your machine so that you get the best response possible when using the Chat feature of NetMeeting.

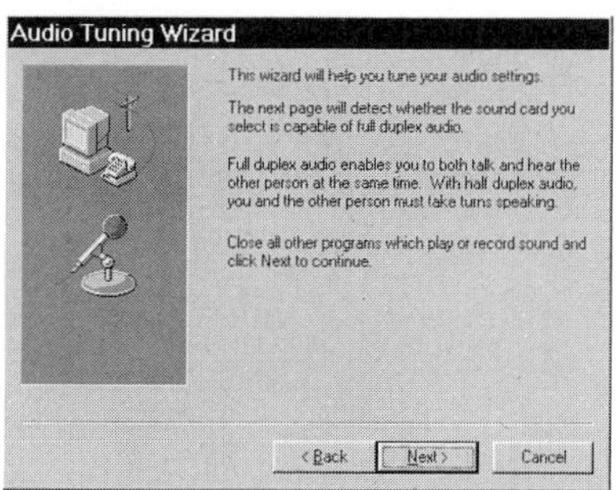

Figure 21.58.
Getting the right audio setup for your machine is the job of the Audio Tuning Wizard.

Tip: This would be a good time to check the status of your audio drivers. Some vendors, such as Creative Labs, didn't have duplex audio capabilities built into their drivers at the time OSR2 was released. This means that you'll experience problems using the NetMeeting Chat capability with some sound boards, such as the Sound Blaster. Fortunately, you can download updated drivers for most sound boards from the vendor. For example, Creative Labs makes its drivers available at `http://www.creativelabs.com/`.

4. Click Next. You'll see a dialog box like the one shown in Figure 21.59. This is where you select the audio driver that NetMeeting will use. Make sure that you select an updated driver, if you installed one.

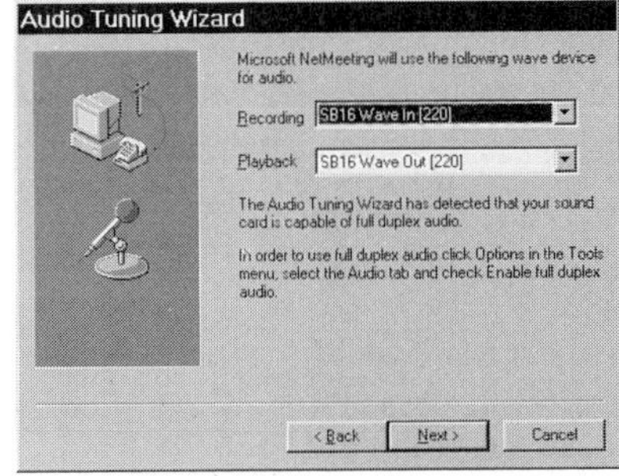

Figure 21.59.
It's important to select the correct audio drive, so that you can hear the other people in the meeting clearly.

5. Click Next. Figure 21.60 shows the dialog box you'll use to select modem speed. The speed of your modem affects the amount of data it can transfer. Even though audio compression algorithms have improved, the speed of your modem still affects the quality of the sound that you hear. (It also affects the quality of the sound you send to the other party and the speed of the connection as a whole.) As you can see, the lowest speed modem you can use with NetMeeting is 14.4 Kbps.

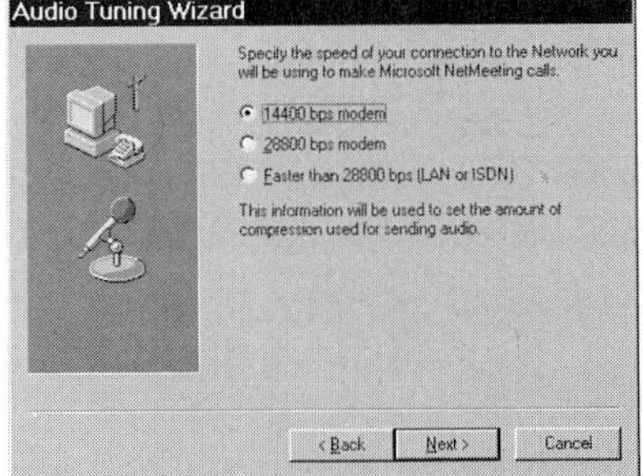

Figure 21.60.
Modem speed defines the quality of the voice connection you'll get.

6. Click Next. You'll see a dialog box like the one shown in Figure 21.61. NetMeeting automatically sets the volume level of your setup so that you can talk with other people without drowning them out (or seeming to whisper).

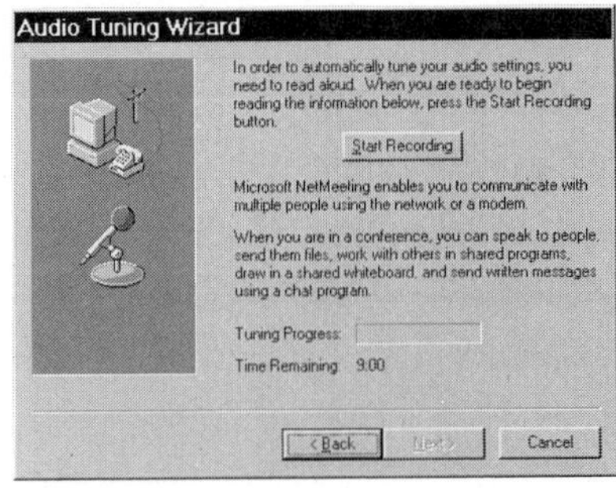

Figure 21.61.
Because NetMeeting provides a chat feature, you need to tune it to your voice qualities.

7. Make sure that you have a microphone attached to the microphone input of your sound board. Click the Start Recording button so that NetMeeting can get a sample of your speaking voice and set the volume properly. Keep speaking until the Audio Tuning Wizard tells you to stop (you'll see an indicator move as NetMeeting gathers the sound sample). If you haven't recorded any sound, the Audio Tuning Wizard displays an error message. Otherwise, the counter counts down to 0.
8. Click Next after you finish recording a sound sample. (If you see an error message, fix any problems and try to record the voice sample again.) You should see the successful completion message shown in Figure 21.62.

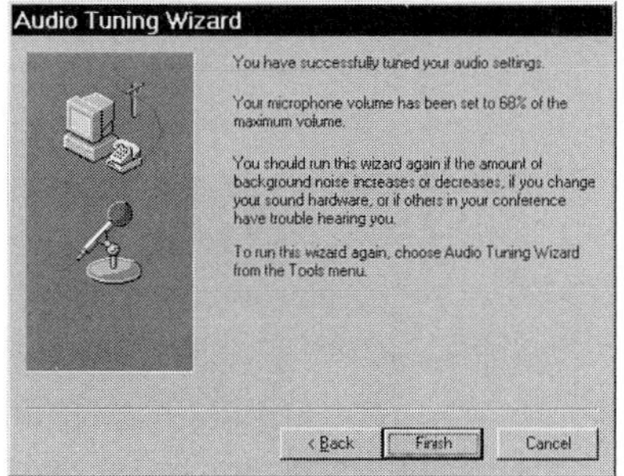

Figure 21.62.
This success message tells you that you've got the optimal audio configuration for your machine.

9. Click Finish to complete the audio tuning process. At this point, you'll see a standard Connect To dialog box. Connect to your ISP. The setup program takes care of a few additional setup requirements and then displays the main NetMeeting dialog box shown in Figure 21.63.

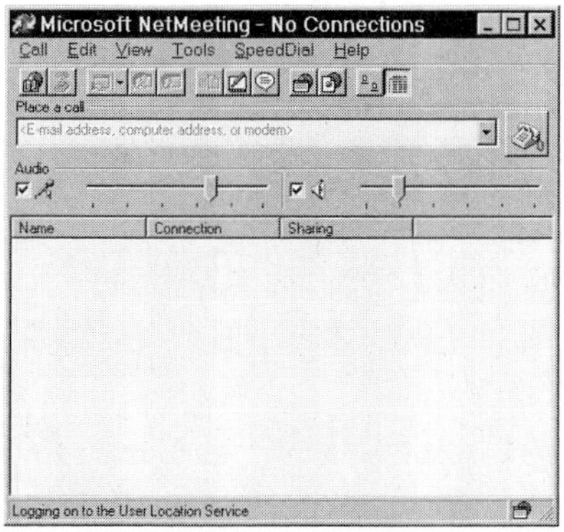

Figure 21.63.
There are a few additional configuration requirements before you have a complete NetMeeting setup.

Using NetMeeting with the Company Intranet

I don't see the Internet as the first place where you'll use NetMeeting. The speed at which we communicate right now is just a little too slow to get the high-quality connection that people expect. (At least a few people will occasionally use NetMeeting on the Internet.) The first place I expect to see this tool used is on an intranet or LAN. It doesn't actually matter where you use NetMeeting, though; the usage details are the same.

Let's begin by creating a simple conversation. Several people in the same company need to discuss a project, but there aren't any meeting rooms available at the moment. Each person has his or her copy of NetMeeting running, so calling someone over the company LAN isn't a problem. All you need to do is enter the name of the machine you want to call, and then click the Call button (telephone icon). When you receive a call, you'll see a dialog box like the one shown in Figure 21.64.

Figure 21.64.
Receiving or making a call is the first step in establishing contact with another person.

At this point, you decide whether to accept the call. If you accept the call, the NetMeeting display shows who is involved in the meeting, as shown in Figure 21.65. The initial connection is audio, as shown in the figure. What happens when someone talks? You'll see some sound waves coming out of the speaker. (Look at the speaker in the figure and you'll see some sound waves coming out.)

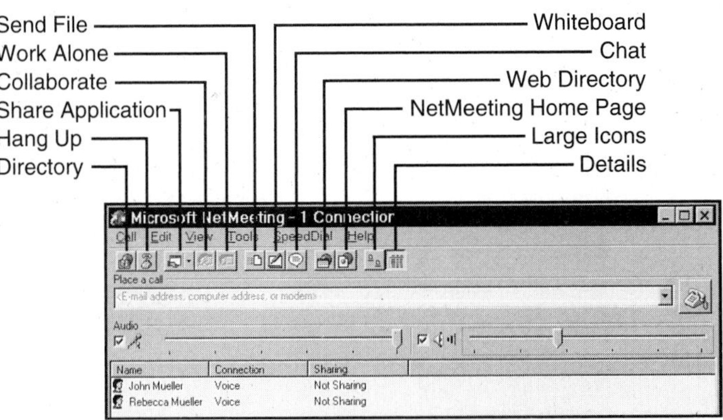

Figure 21.65.
The initial connection you get is audio.

Obviously, unless you just happen to be a gadget nut, seeing sound waves coming out of a speaker isn't all that exciting. You'll definitely get better sound quality from a telephone connection. That's where some of the other features of NetMeeting come into play. Before we go much further, though, let me introduce you to the buttons on the toolbar.

- **Directory:** During the setup process, you had the option of publishing your name on a ULS server. Clicking this button takes you to the ULS server that you chose during the setup process and provides a list of people who have registered there. If you see someone you want to call, just highlight his or her name on the list and click the Call button.
- **Hang Up:** Use this option to stop your participation in the current meeting.
- **Share Application:** I'll show you how this feature works later. Essentially, it allows two people to work together with an application. This doesn't necessarily mean that both people actually get to use the application. I really like this feature because a company training expert can show how to perform a task, and then ask a trainee to demonstrate the technique. Because everyone has his or her own machine, each person gets a maximum participation benefit.
- **Collaborate:** This button works with the Share Application option. It allows two people to work together on a project. Both parties have total control over the application.
- **Work Alone:** Like Collaborate, this button works with the Share Application feature. However, in this case, only the person who ran the application in the first place actually gets to use it.
- **Send File:** Use this button to send a file to someone else. Clicking Send File opens a standard File Open dialog box. Select the file you want to send, and then click OK. Everyone in the meeting sees a dialog box like the one shown in Figure 21.66 and can choose to accept or reject the file. Once the file is completely sent, you see a completion dialog box.

Figure 21.66.
You'll see a dialog box like this one if someone sends a file by using NetMeeting.

- **Whiteboard:** Every meeting needs some place for people to draw out their ideas. That's what the Whiteboard is for. Clicking this button displays a whiteboard similar to the one shown in Figure 21.67. Notice that you get a full set of drawing tools, including the normal circle and square drawing tools. Just so you don't get this confused with a regular drawing program, it also includes things such as a highlighter. One of the features I really like is the remote pointer. It looks like a great big pointing hand. You can use it to point at things on the Whiteboard in a way that everyone can see.

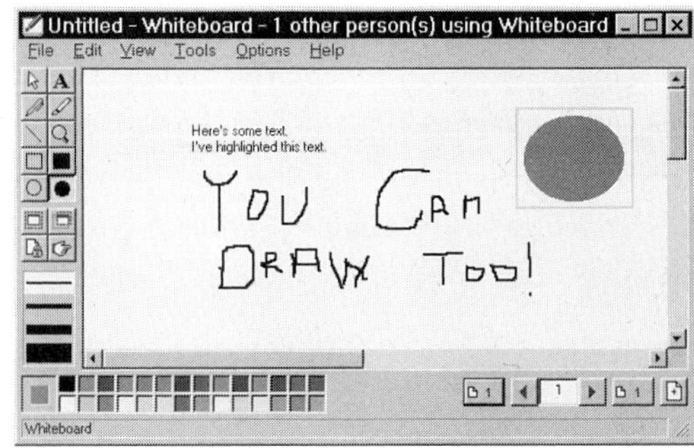

Figure 21.67.
The Whiteboard is one of the handier tools included with NetMeeting.

- **Chat:** Sometimes you can't hold a decent voice conversation, transfer files, use the Whiteboard, and share an application all at the same time. Even a LAN doesn't provide this kind of bandwidth. The alternative is to cut out one or more activities. That's where the Chat button comes into play. It opens a Chat dialog box like the one shown in Figure 21.68, which you can use to type text to other people. Sure, it's not as handy as talking, but it does work in a pinch.

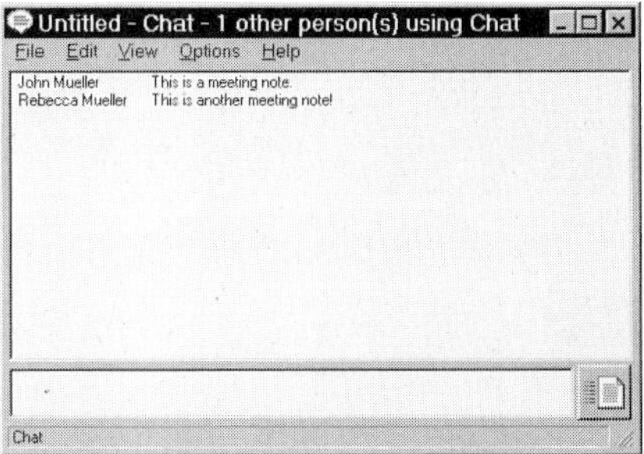

Figure 21.68.
The Chat dialog box allows you to type conversations to each other.

Tip: One way the Chat feature works better than voice communication is when creating minutes for a meeting. If you use the Chat feature, the meeting notes are already typed. I can guarantee that they'll be more accurate and in-depth than meeting notes that rely only on voice communication.

- **Web Directory:** Clicking this button takes you to another form of user directory. Instead of a dialog-box type of selection list, you get a Web page with links. I've found that this particular presentation provides more information about the individual, because it contains a larger comment section. You can also use this list to find people who have the same version of NetMeeting that you do. (Using the same version ensures that you'll have the same program features.)

- **NetMeeting Home Page:** This is one place you should visit. It takes you to the NetMeeting home page, which contains information about the current version. The current home page setup appears in Figure 21.69. I was surprised to see a list of third-party products and also a link for the developer's kit.

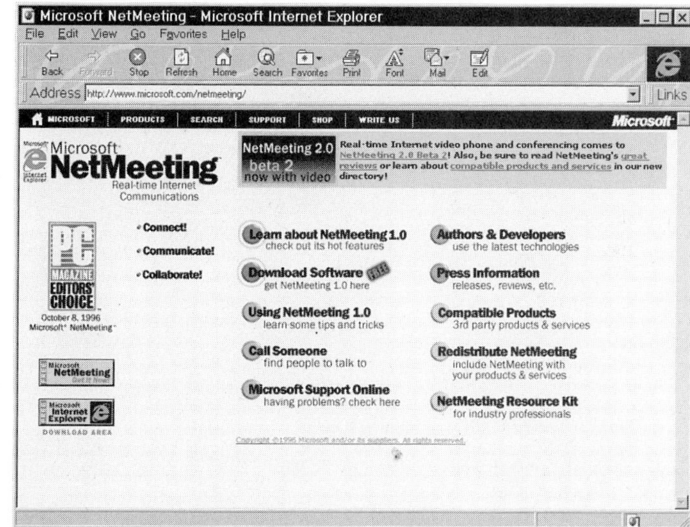

Figure 21.69.
The NetMeeting home page is one place you need to visit to keep up-to-date on the current product.

- **Large Icons/Details:** As in Explorer, you can choose to view the icons for people participating in a meeting using several icon sizes. The default view is Details, which tells you the current status of each connection. It's the view that I prefer, because the connection information is vital when you're using NetMeeting over the Internet. Figure 21.70 shows the Large Icons view.

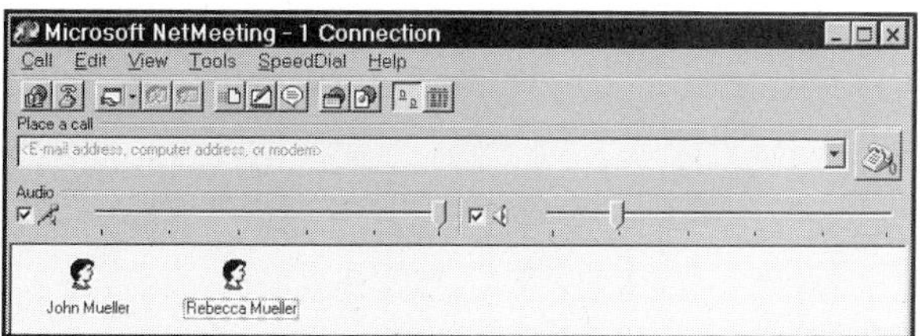

Figure 21.70.
The Large Icons view comes in handy for getting a simple overview of who is participating in a meeting, but it doesn't provide enough details.

Let's take a look now at sharing an application. I see this as one of the more important uses for the current version of NetMeeting, because there are so many ways you can use this feature.

How do you share an application? Begin by opening the application. You may also want to open any files that you intend to use, because the application could get a bit sluggish once you establish the NetMeeting setup. After the application is open, click the Share Application button in NetMeeting.

Select one of the running applications from the list that NetMeeting presents. You'll see a dialog box like the one shown in Figure 21.71. Click OK to establish a connection.

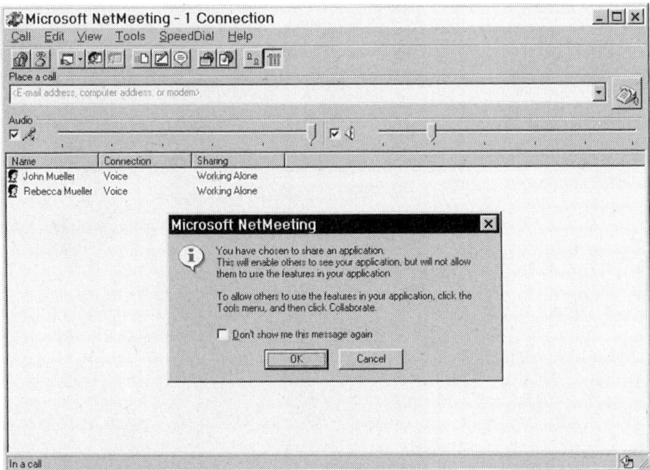

Figure 21.71.
NetMeeting usually displays the starting conditions for sharing an application, unless you tell it not to.

At this point, you're sharing the application with someone else in the work-alone mode. The way you can tell this from your machine is to look at the NetMeeting Sharing column (refer to Figure 21.71). The other party is able to tell by a message that NetMeeting displays when he or she places the cursor over the application title. Figure 21.72 shows what you'll receive. Notice also that this figure shows that the application has the initiating user's name at the top. This way, you can tell who "owns" the application.

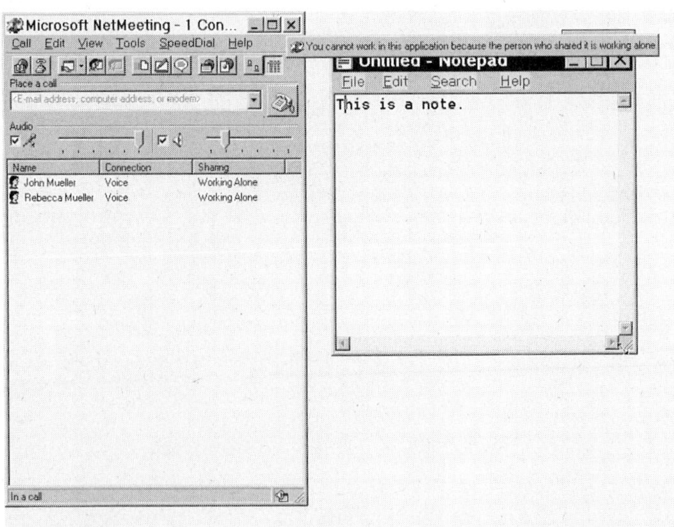

Figure 21.72.
NetMeeting tells you when you can't actually manipulate the application. It also tells who owns it.

Click the NetMeeting Collaborate button, and everyone involved in the meeting can now change the contents of the application. (They also need to click their Collaborate buttons.) By monitoring the NetMeeting window, you can always tell who is collaborating, who owns the target application, and who is working alone. Figure 21.73 shows what the NetMeeting window looks like when one person has control over an application and another is collaborating. Only one person can take control of the application at any given time. Everyone else has a pointer to click to take control. The pointer also contains the initials of the person who has control, so that you don't have to monitor the NetMeeting window.

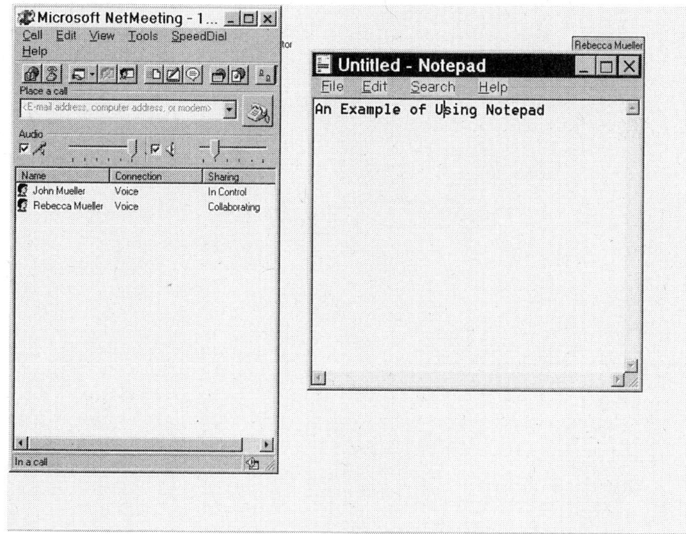

Figure 21.73.
NetMeeting allows several people to share an application and collaborate on the contents of a file, but only one person has control.

As you can see from the preceding paragraphs, NetMeeting is a powerful tool that allows companies spread over a large area to communicate as they never have before. It also helps small companies with a representative who needs constant updates on the road. Finally, a lot of people are using NetMeeting for non-business purposes. They just want to meet another individual on the Internet in a more personal way than e-mail allows. Whatever your use of NetMeeting, you can be sure that this is only the tip of the iceberg—online communications using multiple media are still in their infancy.

Understanding Browser Compatibility Problems

The browser wars certainly haven't done much for compatibility between the products offered by various vendors. For example, it doesn't take too much time to figure out that Netscape Navigator doesn't support ActiveX controls. You have to download a plug-in to do the job. (Most people add

ActiveX support to Navigator by using NCompass ScriptActive—you can download it at `http://www.ncompasslabs.com/showcase.htm`.) It may be an acceptable way to handle the situation from Netscape's viewpoint, but using a special plug-in for ActiveX doesn't do much for the user. Unfortunately, the NCompass plug-in uses an `<EMBED>` tag in place of the `<OBJECT>` tag used by Internet Explorer. This means that you can visit a site that's designed for ActiveX and still not be able to use it, even though you have the NCompass plug-in installed. There are rumors that Netscape plans to change this situation in the near future, so you may not have to live with plug-in support for ActiveX controls for the rest of your life.

There are quite a few scripting differences between the two browsers as well—some of which I cover in Chapter 22, when talking about the techniques for creating your own Web page. Just to give you an idea of how significant this problem is, though, consider the very basis for the Web pages you look at—HTML tags. Both Internet Explorer and Navigator support tags that are outside the mainstream specification for HTML. For example, Navigator implements plug-in support by using an `<EMBED>` tag that Internet Explorer doesn't recognize. On the other hand, Internet Explorer supports specialty tags such as the background sound (`<BGSOUND>`) tag that Navigator ignores. A site that wants to provide sound support for both Navigator and Internet Explorer has to include both an `<EMBED>` and a `<BGSOUND>` tag. Suffice it to say that testing every Web page using both browsers, and then figuring out why one won't work with it, is a major expenditure of time for Webmasters (the people who maintain Web sites).

Do the problems end there? No, that's really only the beginning. Take the very basic elements of a scripting language such as JavaScript as an example. The "Simple Scripting with JavaScript" section of Chapter 22 shows that the Netscape version of this scripting language is far more strict than the Microsoft version. According to Microsoft, Netscape released the specification for the language too late for Microsoft to incorporate it into Internet Explorer, so Microsoft came up with their own version. Again, it's the Webmaster—and, ultimately, the user—who loses in this conflict.

Given the politically charged environment of software development, you can almost understand some of the differences in implementation between browsers. Differences in product strategy have helped or hindered software developers from day one. For example, I use Word for Windows as a word processor because it supports writer-friendly tools, such as a great outliner. In days past, administrative assistants chose WordPerfect as their word processor of choice because it provided tools that met their needs. Lately, though, you'll find that there are even small differences in the way that various browser implementations from the same vendor work. For example, Microsoft recently released a VRML (virtual reality modeling language) tool for Internet Explorer. This product works fine with the English version of Internet Explorer, but users of some foreign-language versions of the product have experienced difficulty in getting it to do anything. I view this most recent level of browser incompatibility as almost inexcusable, because the Internet is an international environment. (Don't get the idea that Netscape Navigator is perfect in this regard—it has problems between various language versions as well.)

Incompatibility can also take other forms. Not everyone accesses the Internet using a PC. There are Macintoshes and Amigas out there, too. (Although the Amiga crowd seems to be thinning out somewhat, there isn't any reason to doubt that they're there.) Also consider the number of UNIX implementations. After all, UNIX was the very basis of the Internet until just recently. So why should you care whether someone with a Macintosh can access a Web site? The very nature of the Internet supposes that everyone can use the information that a Web site provides—not just a fortunate few. While it may not be possible (or even reasonable) to expect complete access to every site by every individual, it's important to make the effort. Unfortunately, browser incompatibilities make this nearly impossible.

Some Webmasters have started to handle the situation by adding alternate text to their sites. For example, if your browser doesn't support graphics for whatever reason, you might see some text that says that you'd be seeing a picture of a house if your browser could display it. This is a reasonable attempt to make the site more accessible to everyone, but let's face it: Seeing some text that tells you about the house isn't the same as seeing it.

Another form of browser-incompatibility repair by Webmasters is the use of "best when viewed by" icons. This little icon tells the person visiting a site that the site works best with a certain browser. It's frustrating to try to view a site designed for Internet Explorer when you have Netscape Navigator (or vice versa), but at least knowing that there isn't a problem with your software is a bit of a comfort.

Unfortunately, some Webmasters have started to abuse the intent behind the "best when viewed by" icon. For example, many of the Web sites I visit with ActiveX controls refuse to add the `<EMBED>` tag needed by the NCompass plug-in for Navigator. The result is that even though I have the plug-in installed, I still can't see the Web site as intended by the author. Considering the fact that NCompass does provide some of the tools required for the use of both the `<OBJECT>` and `<EMBED>` tags, it's hard to understand why a Webmaster would limit accessibility to the site to one browser (other than politically-charged reasons, of course). Suffice it to say that such sites are casualties of the browser wars—self-inflicted injuries in a war that makes little sense.

By now, you're wondering what all this has to do with you as a user. It means that you're going to be limited by browser incompatibilities of all kinds until browser vendors start to adhere to standards. You may need to keep two or more browsers installed on your machine if you spend a lot of time on the Internet (I certainly do). There are times when I need the information that a site provides; if that means using a different browser, that's the price I pay for the information. There's no magic bullet that will transform a single browser machine into something that can access every site on the Internet—at least, not as of this writing.

Will this multiple-browser situation last forever? I don't think so. Right now the Internet is in a state of growth. The various standards bodies are working to create new standards that address the needs for content people have expressed. Eventually there will be a standard for VRML. You'll eventually see a standard for ActiveX (provided that Microsoft keeps its promise and releases ActiveX to a standards body). Netscape is planning to loosen its hold on JavaScript as well. If it does so before too many versions are released on the market, we'll probably end up with a standardized scripting language. Unfortunately, all of this standardization takes time.

What do I suggest for a Windows 95 user? If you spend a lot of research time on the Internet, consider installing both Internet Explorer and Navigator on your machine. It sounds ridiculous—and it is—but that's the best solution available today. If you just can't live with two browsers on one machine, see which browser works most often for you. Simply list the sites you visit that are unusable with one or the other browser. Use the list to determine which browser to keep. Don't just base your decision on the number of sites you can't visit, but on the quality of each site in the list. If you're depending on the information provided by a particular site and it doesn't completely support one of the browsers in your list, then you'll just have to eliminate that browser.

On Your Own

Install Internet Explorer, using the instructions in this chapter. Try going online and looking around. The MSN home page is usually a good place to start, but don't limit your choices.

Try out another browser, such as the one provided for CompuServe. How does it differ from Internet Explorer? What about other browsers you may have used?

Try dismantling some of the URLs stored in your browser. What do these URLs tell you about the site that you've accessed? Spend some time on the Internet looking for various URL types.

Build a list of favorite Web sites. Don't forget to include Internet search sites such as Lycos.

Spend some time learning about the various institutions that manage the Internet. You can visit the InterNIC site at `FTP://ftp.internic.net` or `HTTP://www.internic.net`, for example. Appendix B also includes some of the other important sites. Just browse through the list in the "Public Service Access" and "Other Types of Service Providers" sections.

Try out the various Web search engines, using the same keyword, to see how they differ. What kind of results did you get? Use various keywords to see how each of these search engines helps you in a particular area of research. Try refining the search to find very specific information. How does each of the search engines work when it comes to refining the results you get from a single keyword?

Install several browsers on your machine to see how they work on various Internet sites. At a minimum, try both Netscape Navigator and Internet Explorer. You can download a free trial copy of Netscape Navigator at `http://www.netscape.com/`. Likewise, you can get a copy of Internet Explorer at `http://www.microsoft.com/ie/`. Be sure to try out some of the add-ons for both products, such as the sound-enhancing Real Audio Player (`http://www.realaudio.com/`). (If you install a sound related plug-in, be prepared for a few shocks. Some Web sites will try to blast you out of your seat with high-volume sound effects. Needless to say, such sound effects at midnight aren't much of a treat to you, or to anyone sleeping in your vicinity.) While Navigator does make heavier use of plug-ins than Internet Explorer does, both products benefit from third-party add-ons.

Download a copy of NetMeeting from the Internet at `http://www.microsoft.com/ie/download/ieadd.htm`. Install it at several workstations on a LAN or on a single workstation that has an Internet connection. Once NetMeeting is installed, try establishing contact with one or more people so that you can see how the product works. You'll find that a LAN connection works surprisingly well, but that the Internet connection is marginal at best, in most cases. Be sure to try out the various features such as the Whiteboard and Chat.

22

Creating Your Own Web Page

The previous chapter looked at the Internet from a surfing point of view. I answered the question of how to get the most information with the least amount of effort. We also looked at some interesting sites to see what they have to offer. You'd be wrong to think that the Internet ends there. The Internet isn't simply about grabbing information; it's also about exchanging information and presenting your own point of view about issues that affect you the most.

The Web pages we visited in the previous chapter didn't just spring up like mushrooms in the night. Someone had to put them together. In addition, not every Web site we looked at was commercial in nature; a good many Web sites have nothing to do with business, or even something of a scientific nature. A lot of Web sites talk about everyday events and interests. For example, I occasionally visit a Web site for cat owners and another for one of my favorite television shows—*Babylon 5*. Obviously there are a lot of commercial Web sites, such as CD Now, the music store that we visited elsewhere in the course of this book, but stores are still in the minority when compared to other kinds of Web sites.

Lest you think that you need to have something really interesting to say, consider the "silent" Web site used by professionals. There are more than a few authors who maintain their own Web pages, and I can guarantee that they don't pay anything in the form of money. Most authors who have a Web site simply want to learn who their readers are and exchange information with them. The same holds true for other kinds of professionals. Very seldom do you see them hawking their wares on an Internet site; the main purpose behind their Web pages is information exchange of some type. (Some computer authors also use their Web sites to make available special add-ons to their books, so you'll want to keep your eyes peeled for this kind of opportunity.)

Suffice it to say that creating a Web page doesn't have to involve a commercial enterprise; you may simply want to talk with someone about a topic of special interest to you. That's what this chapter is all about. We look at why you should even bother to put a Web site together, and then at the requirements for doing so.

Tip: Building a Web page isn't the same thing as building an Internet site or even an intranet site. Some Internet service providers (ISPs) allow you to upload your own Web page to their server. The only requirement in this case is that you maintain the content of your Web site. The ISP takes care of the server and everything else needed to create the actual Internet site. Obviously, there are some limitations when you take this route, and you may have to pay for the privilege of displaying your own Web site; but most non-commercial users find the costs low and the constraints minimal.

The bulk of this chapter looks at HTML, but I cover other technologies as well. HTML forms the basis of most Web pages, so it's important that you really understand this technology before you move on to more advanced topics. I also cover things such as cascading style sheets and ActiveX, but only at an overview level. Finally, I show you a little bit of scripting, using the two most popular languages, JavaScript and VBScript. Again, we'll only take an overview of how these scripting languages work—you'll probably want to experiment a lot before you go to other sources for additional information.

Why Bother?

Most people are fairly excited at the thought of creating their own Web site, until reality sets in. Maintaining a Web site is a lot of work and the benefits (at least at the outset) are of dubious value, at best. In addition to the work, some Web sites are so poorly thought out that other people won't even visit them. The typical response at this point is "Why bother?" Some people never begin their own Web site because they feel that anything they create is going to be a waste of time. If you're approaching your Web site with this kind of attitude, I have to admit that there isn't any reason for you to go forward.

Creating a good Web site is as easy as thinking about it first. Ask yourself what you want to get out of the Web site that you design and what you're willing to do to get it. If you don't have a good idea of what you want to achieve with a Web site, you'd better start gathering some ideas. It's pretty obvious to the veteran surfer when a site was just put together without too much forethought. If you can't come up with your own ideas, talk to other people with Web surfing experience. Better yet, visit other Web sites that appear to contain elements that you want to include with your site. Seeing what other people do can help you to figure out relatively quickly what you want to include.

There's another good reason to visit Web sites: You can quickly learn what works and what doesn't. If you find that you get annoyed waiting for a Web page to download, other people probably do as well. How does the Web page look from an aesthetic point of view? Is it inviting—do you want to come back? How hard is the Web site to look at—does it include glaring color combinations? Is the text easy to read? Asking yourself these questions as you visit other Web sites is about the best way to figure out what you want on your own. In fact, you may create the three folders of URLs (links) shown in the following list to hold your Web site ideas:

- **Content:** There are other people with interests similar to yours. Finding Web sites that offer the kind of content that you want to offer helps you learn how to present the information in the best way possible. You'll also want to see what's already been done, so that your Web site becomes a unique place to visit rather than a rehash of what everyone else has done.
- **Gimmicks:** I maintain a folder of Web sites that show how to do interesting things such as using animation or sound. These sites may not even interest me from a content point of view. There's one site that simply demonstrates various features of ActiveX and doesn't contain much in the way of content at all. Another site in my collection shows various kinds of animated GIFs.

- **Usability:** A site with great content and eye-dazzling gimmicks won't do much for you if it takes an hour to download. If someone has trouble getting from point A to point B of your Web site, you can be sure that he won't come back. Consistency is another problem that people face when working with Web sites. In one place you have to click a Submit button to get data; in another, you select a link. If a site looks confusing, you can be sure that some people won't be able to use it. Where am I going with all this? Make yourself a rogues gallery of sites that you find either very usable or so unusable that they aren't worth the time.

Tip: Remember that you can't assume anything about the computer that visits your site. Just because a gimmick or method of formatting content looks great on your machine doesn't mean that it will look great on a Macintosh. Some people get around this issue partially by saying something like, "This page looks best when viewed with Internet Explorer." A simple statement of the requirements for viewing a Web site may not win you any friends, but it reduces the number of hostile comments you'll get from people who can't use your site for whatever reason.

The bottom line is that you need to figure out what you want to do before you try to figure out whether a site is worth the effort. Most people take the time to set up and manage an Internet site because they expect to get something out of it. Whether that gain is in the form of new friends, contacts for a venture, information, or even monetary in nature is of little consequence. All that matters is that you see the value behind the site you set up and convey that value to people who visit it.

The Twelve Steps to Basic HTML

Every Web page you'll ever see uses some form of HTML (hypertext markup language) to display information. HTML is a combination of a formatting language with some built-in macro capability of sorts. A lot of vendors are working to expand the language to do more than it does now. For example, several companies are working on ways to create cascading style sheets (CSS)—a method for displaying information consistently and with a lot less effort on the part of the Webmaster. The later section "Using Cascading Style Sheets (CSS)" discusses this technology.

It's time to learn about the first tool that you'll use to fill out those folders I mentioned in the preceding section. Whenever I see an interesting idea, I use a special feature, built into most browsers, to view that page in its native form. If you're using Internet Explorer, you'll use the View | Source command to display the HTML used to create a page. On the other hand, if you're using Netscape Navigator, you'll use either the View | Document Source or View | Frame Source command. The later section "Advanced HTML Tags That Really Count" talks about frames. For now, all you need to know is that they subdivide the page you see into smaller, more manageable pieces. Figure 22.1

shows a typical Document Source dialog box for Netscape Navigator. Figure 22.2 shows the same thing for Internet Explorer.

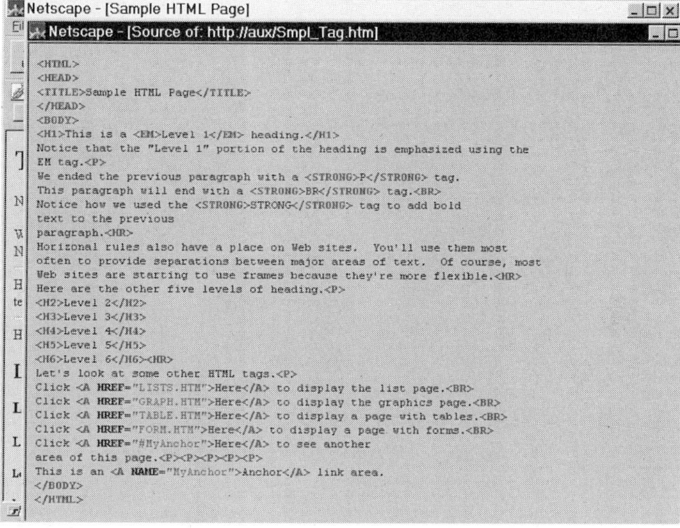

Figure 22.1.
Netscape Navigator provides a non-editable display with keywords highlighted.

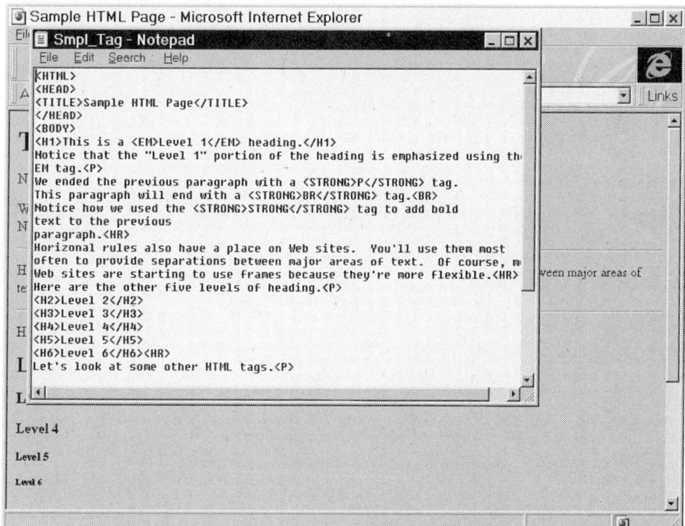

Figure 22.2.
Internet Explorer uses Notepad to display the HTML source, which makes it easier to save the source.

For the most part, both displays do the same thing—they allow you to view the source for a particular site. I like the fact that Netscape Navigator uses a special editor that highlights all the keywords in the source (at least, the ones that it recognizes as keywords). This makes it faster to figure out what's going on at a particular site and could save you time in learning new techniques. You'll also notice other forms of highlighting on this page. For example, links are highlighted, while some special link-related keywords appear in bold type. The negative side of using Navigator is that you can't save the page while viewing it in the source window—you have to use the File | Save As command instead. Sure, it's a small extra step, but an extra step that could confuse some users.

Internet Explorer takes a different approach. You see the source in a standard Notepad window. This means that you can save the source to a local hard drive without too much effort. It also means that you can change the code to meet your needs without using a separate text editor. The lack of highlighted keywords and other features provided by Navigator shouldn't be underestimated, though. If you're not used to looking for keywords, you could miss some special technique lurking within the source of an especially interesting Web site.

Let's take a closer look at the figures. You'll find some common elements in both figures, but the Navigator display in Figure 22.1 is the better of the two to look at because it highlights the keywords. An HTML page uses what's known as a tag. Essentially, a tag tells the browser that it needs to do something. For example, if the browser sees a `<P>` tag, it knows to create a paragraph. Notice that the tag begins and ends with angle brackets (`<>`). Every tag that you'll ever create uses the same delimiters—anything enclosed within angle brackets is a tag of some sort, no matter how long the tag is.

The most basic HTML document will likely contain 12 different kinds of tags. Some of these tags are mandatory; others are used only to provide specific types of functionality. In this section, we look at the tags in their simplest form—you can add modifiers to most tags to affect the way they work. For example, you could add a font specification or tell the tag to center any text it contains on the page. Table 22.1 provides a quick overview of the 12 basic tags that we look at in this section.

You should notice something about the tags in Table 22.1. Many tags come in pairs. For example, `<EM>` is the beginning of an emphasized section of text and `</EM>` marks the end. Whenever you see a tag pair, the end of the section that it marks uses the slash (`/`) symbol as part of the tag.

Table 22.1. Common HTML tags.

Tag	*Use*	*Description*
`<HTML>` and `</HTML>`	Mandatory	Every HTML document begins with `<HTML>` and ends with `</HTML>`. This is how the browser knows where to start and stop reading.
`<HEAD>` and `</HEAD>`	Normally used	When you look at any HTML document, you see a heading and a body. The heading normally identifies the Web site and defines the page setup.
`<BODY>` and `</BODY>`	Normally used	You place the main section of the content of your Web page within these two tags. The body normally contains the information that the user visited your site to find.

Tag	*Use*	*Description*
`<H*number*>` and `</H*number*>`	Optional	Books and other forms of text normally divide the information they contain into sections by using headings. This tag allows you to add headings to your Web site.
`<P>`	Optional	HTML always assumes that all the text you type, whether it appears on the same line or not, is part of the same paragraph. You use this tag to add a carriage return and two line feeds to mark the end of a paragraph.
` `	Optional	There are times when you'll want to go to the left margin without adding a blank line to the page. That's what this tag is for. It adds a carriage return with a single line feed.
`<HR>`	Optional	The horizontal rule tag places a line across the page. It also adds white space between paragraphs.
`<A HREF>` and `</A>`	Optional	Hyperlinks to other documents are the most common components of a Web page.
`<A NAME>` and `</A>`	Optional	Anchors allow you to move from one point on the page to another. The hyperlink to access this tag looks like this: `<A HREF="*current document#anchor name*">`.
`<EM>` and `</EM>`	Optional	Different browsers react differently to the emphasis tag. However, the majority simply display text in italic type.
`<STRONG>` and `</STRONG>`	Optional	As with the emphasis tag, it's up to the browser to determine how it will react to the `<STRONG>` tag. Most browsers display text in bold type when they see this tag.
`<PRE>` and `</PRE>`	Optional	There are times when you don't want a browser to reformat your text. The preformatted tag tells the browser to leave the text formatting alone.

Now that you have the basic idea of what these tags are about, let's look at a few of them in detail. The following sections talk about some of the tags that you'll use on a more-or-less consistent basis and that require more than a modicum of work to use in most cases. Don't worry if you can't quite grasp everything during this discussion; we'll look at actual usage details as we create simple HTML documents throughout the chapter. Seeing how the tags work will help you to understand how they interact with the browser.

An Initial Step

Table 22.1 tells you about the tags you use to create even simple HTML pages, but it doesn't tell you how to use them. Let's begin with the simplest HTML page that you can construct. The following code is how we'll create a blank HTML page:

```
<HTML>
<HEAD>
</HEAD>
<BODY>
</BODY>
</HTML>
```

Notice that it includes only six tags. You must have these six tags present in every Web page you create. If you don't have them, the browser won't be able to read your page at all. This particular set of tags merely displays a blank page within your browser; it doesn't contain any user-readable information.

Figuring out what the tags do is fairly simple. The `<HTML>` tag tells the browser that everything between this tag and the `</HTML>` tag is displayed within the browser window. Theoretically, the browser will ignore anything before the `<HTML>` tag and after the `</HTML>` tag. I say "theoretically" because not all browsers follow the rules when reading a Web page. If in doubt, always test your page by using several different browsers. Always test your page with Navigator and Internet Explorer, at minimum.

Immediately after the `<HTML>` tag is a `<HEAD>` tag. This is the beginning of the area where you normally place information that the user won't see as document text. It's also the area that I use for storing scripts or other non-display tags. For example, you'll run into a `<META>` tag on more than a few sites. This is an advanced tag that we won't discuss in this chapter, because it's for advanced users who want to create specialized command sequences. In most cases, you'll find that scripts are a lot easier to use; that's why I cover them instead.

The heading ends with the `</HEAD>` tag. You must use tag pairs carefully or you'll get unexpected results (nothing disastrous, but a visitor to your site will find it totally unusable). In this case, you have to explicitly tell the browser that you're ending the heading section and moving on to the body of the page.

Anything you want the user to see within the browser window appears after the `<BODY>` tag. This includes any freeform text, graphics, and gimmicks such as sound bytes. You don't always have to use a `<BODY>` tag. The later section "Advanced HTML Tags That Really Count" shows an example that uses frames instead of a `<BODY>` tag. Even though you can replace the `<BODY>` tag with something else, you'll normally need some place to put the information that you want to present to the user.

Creating Your First Useful Page

Okay, now that you know what you need to create a Web page, let's use some of the other tags shown in Table 22.1 to create something more useful.

Plain text is the first thing that most people think about adding to a Web site. There are a few rules here that may seem counterintuitive at first, but most people don't have any problem adapting to them. The first is that text is continuous. In other words, it doesn't matter whether you press Enter at the end of a line. The browser you use will always see the text as continuous. So, the question is how you create the end of a line. There are two tags for doing this. The first is the `<BR>` tag, which you use at the end of a line. The second is the `<P>` tag, which you use at the end of a paragraph. Let's take a look at these two tags in action. I'll use the following code to produce the display shown in Figure 22.3. (Notice the `<TITLE>` tag that I've added. It's used to display something in the title bar, as shown in the figure.)

```
<HTML>
<HEAD>
<TITLE>Creating Your First Useful Page</TITLE>
</HEAD>
<BODY>
This is some text and it won't end because I've pressed a
carriage return,<BR>
but it does start a new line because of the BR tag.<P>
This is a new paragraph.
</BODY>
</HTML>
```

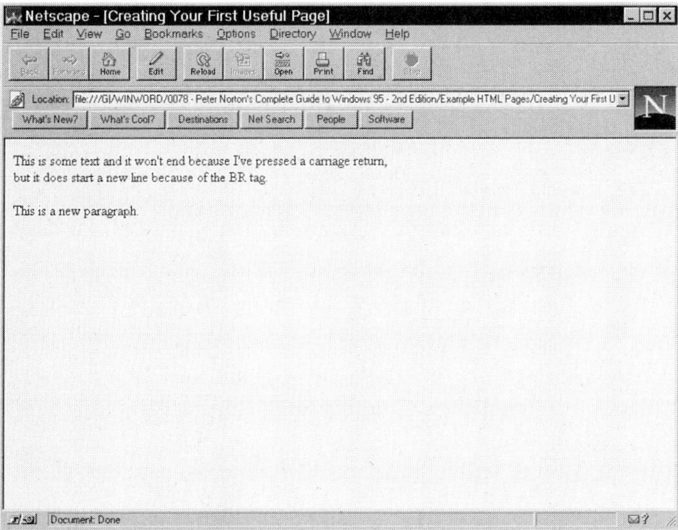

Figure 22.3.
Learning how to work with text is the first step in building a Web page.

Headings are the first thing that most people want to know about, once they learn basic text skills. There are six different sizes of headings recognized by most browsers. Using them is simple. All you need to do is add a `<Hnumber>` and `</Hnumber>` tag pair to your Web page. Here's how you would add the six headings to our previous code. Figure 22.4 shows what they look like when displayed. Notice that I've added a comment to the code in this case. The exclamation point (`<!>`) tag is recognized as a comment by most browsers. We'll see how this particular tag comes into play for a variety of purposes in the scripting and ActiveX sections of the chapter.

```
<!-Let's add some headings to the page.->
<H1>This is heading level 1.</H1>
<H2>This is heading level 2.</H2>
<H3>This is heading level 3.</H3>
<H4>This is heading level 4.</H4>
<H5>This is heading level 5.</H5>
<H6>This is heading level 6.</H6>
```

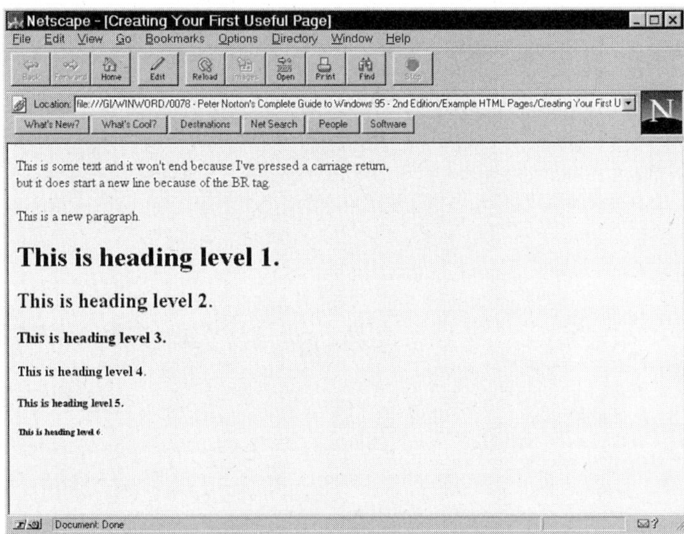

Figure 22.4.
Headings allow you to separate major areas of text, just like they do in a book.

Note: There isn't any real way to guarantee that a browser will use a specific typeface or style when displaying a heading. For that matter, there isn't even any guarantee that you'll get six levels of heading support. About the only thing you can guarantee when using a heading is that you should see some form of emphasis that tells the user that this bit of text is different from everything else.

In addition to headings, you can also emphasize your text by using a variety of tags. The three most common tags are <EM> (emphasis), <STRONG>, and <PRE> (preformatted). Let's take a look at all three of these tags in action. I added the following code to the page we've been looking at throughout this section. Figure 22.5 shows the results.

```
<!-Here are some ways to emphasize your text.->
This text is <EM>emphasized</EM>.<BR>
This text is <STRONG>strong</STRONG>.<BR>
This text is both <STRONG><EM>strong and emphasized</EM></STRONG>.
<PRE>
This text is
preformatted.
</PRE>
```

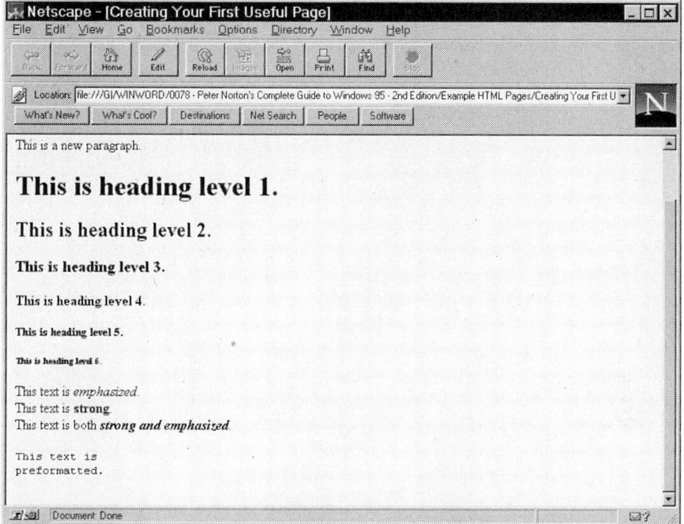

Figure 22.5.
You'll want to use text-formatting tags with care, because they may appear different under every browser that you test.

Note: There are a variety of basic formatting tags that you can use; I'm simply presenting the most common tags in this chapter. In addition to the tags I discuss here, some browsers recognize the <B> (bold), <S> (strikethrough), <I> (italics), <U> (underline), <SUB> (subscript), and <SUP> (superscript) tags. You need to use these variants with caution, though, if compatibility with all browsers is a major concern. Avoid using the underline (<U>) tag in most cases, because people could confuse the underlined text with a link to another Web page.

Besides the text formatting tags, you should notice something else about the sample code. I had to use a <BR> tag at the end of every sentence except the one right before the <PRE> tag. The <PRE> tag always signals the beginning of a new paragraph. There are other HTML tags like this one, so always double-check your page for extra spaces when learning how to use a new tag. (I cover several other tags that start a new paragraph within this chapter, but I don't cover them all.)

Basic Formatting Tags for Everyone

Once you get past basic headings and text formatting, you'll find the need to do other things. For example, bulleted lists are one item that just about everyone uses. How many technical books have you seen that don't include any form of bulleted lists or procedures? Putting complex ideas into easily grasped pieces is one of the most basic tasks that any writer can perform. Lists—short bits of text that enumerate ideas—are the answer in most cases. Considering the size limits of most Web pages, lists become even more important. HTML supports three different kinds of lists, as shown in Table 22.2.

Table 22.2. Tags used for lists.

Tag	*Description*
<UL> and </UL>, plus <LI>	The unordered list uses bullets. You start it with the <UL> tag and end it with the </UL> tag. Items within the list use the <LI> tag.
<OL> and </OL>, plus <LI>	Procedures and other numbered forms of text are considered ordered lists. This list format depends on the <OL> and </OL> tags. As with unordered lists, each item begins with the <LI> tag.
<DL> and </DL>, plus <DT> and <DD>	Sometimes you need a small, table-like list to display a short phrase (even a single word) and then its meaning. Glossary lists fulfill that purpose very well. This particular list uses two kinds of item entries surrounded by a <DL> and </DL> tag pair. The term that you want to define is preceded by a <DT> tag. The definition gets a <DD>tag.

Even though there are only three list types, you can still get a variety of effects by nesting them. For example, you could place an ordered list within an unordered list to create a fairly complex display. You'll see an example of how to do this later in this section, when I discuss the sample page code.

Of the three list types, the glossary list type is the most flexible in some ways. The use of two list element types can provide a little more in the way of aesthetics when you try to display text. The big difference between the <DT> (term) and <DD> (definition) tags is that one of them is indented. You can use this feature to create special effects not related to the display of glossary-type entries. As with some of the other special text tags discussed in this chapter, list tags (<LI>, <DT>, and <DD>) automatically insert a <BR> tag for you at the end of the line. Using a <BR> tag advances the text to the next line but keeps the list together.

It's time to take a look at some examples of list coding. The following code shows the three list types by themselves, and then one complex example. Figure 22.6 shows the results you'll see when viewing the page.

```
<HTML>
<HEAD>
<TITLE>Basic Formatting Tags for Everyone</TITLE>
</HEAD>
<BODY>

<!-Begin with an unordered list.->
<H3>This is a Bulleted List</H3>
<UL>
    <LI>Notice that every line with an LI tag has a bullet in front of it.
    <LI>However, you can split <BR>
           a line in two if so desired.
</UL>

<!-This is an ordered list.->
<H3>This is an Ordered List</H3>
<OL>
    <LI>Ordered lists are normally used for procedures.
    <LI>But you can use them any time that numbers are needed.
</OL>

<!-Create a glossary list.->
<H3>This is a Glossary</H3>
<DL>
    <DT>Glossary Lists
    <DD>You can use these lists as a form of mini-table.
</DL>

<!-Build a complex list.->
<H3>This is a Combination of Ordered and Unordered Lists</H3>
<UL>
    <LI>You could have a bullet.
    <OL>
        <LI>With a numbered list of features below it.
        <LI>Or even a procedure.
    </OL>
</UL>
</BODY>
</HTML>
```

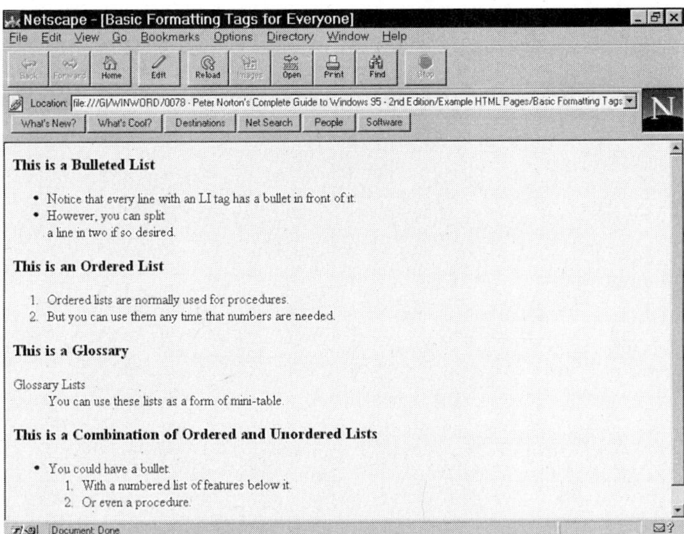

Figure 22.6.
Lists are one of the handier elements of a Web page.

Lists are nice, but they won't fulfill every text-formatting need that you'll have. Tabular data is part of just about any kind of business display. Spreadsheets are just one example of the accountant's ledger sheet brought to life in the computer. It makes sense, then, that you can create tables on an HTML page. However, you need an entire set of tags to make tables work, as shown in Table 22.3.

Tip: The `<TABLE>` tag includes a special `BORDER` attribute that allows you to enclose the table within lines. The default border size is a width of 1, but you can usually set this value to any width between 1 and 6, depending on the browser.

Table 22.3. Table-formatting tags.

Tag	*Description*
`<TABLE>` and `</TABLE>`	This set of tags defines the beginning and end of the table as a whole.
`<TD>` and `</TD>`	Every data element (column) is enclosed within this tag pair.
`<TH>` and `</TH>`	With this pair of tags, you create headings for each table row or column.
`<TR>` and `</TR>`	Each row is defined with these tags. Normal procedure is to define rows and then columns.
`<CAPTION>` and `</CAPTION>`	These tags define the table's title.

Let's take a look at some sample code for creating one of the more common types of table. I'm going to mix in a few new tags here to show you how you can start using tags together to create special effects. It's important to realize that none of the tags I've shown you so far stands alone. Almost all of them are designed to work together. That's why it's so important to visit other Web sites. Visiting Web sites with unique displays can help you to learn valuable techniques for formatting the information you have to present. (Just about every browser on the market allows you to view the source code for a site, because you have to download the source code to view it.) Figure 22.7 shows the results of this example when viewed in a browser.

Tip: You can center the text in a table by using the `<CENTER>` and `</CENTER>` tag pair, as shown in the code for this example. This tag pair works with any text that you may want to place within a document. It also works with graphics.

```
<HTML>
<HEAD>
<TITLE>Basic Formatting Tags for Everyone</TITLE>
</HEAD>
<BODY>

<!-Let's center everything on the page.>
<CENTER>

<!-Create a page header->
<H2>A Basic Table</H2>

<!-Let's create a basic table->
<TABLE BORDER=2>
    <CAPTION>Table Example.1. Here's the Table Caption</CAPTION>
    <TR>
        <TH></TH>
        <TH>Column 1</TH>
        <TH>Column 2</TH>
        <TH>Column 3</TH>
    </TR>
    <TR>
        <TH>Row 1</TH>
        <TD>Some simple text.</TD>
        <TD><CENTER>Centered Text</CENTER></TD>
        <TD>Some more simple text.</TD>
    </TR>
    <TR>
        <TH>Row 2</TH>
        <TD>Another row of text.</TD>
        <TD>You aren't limited to text; you can use <EM>graphics</EM> as well.</TD>
        <TD>Tables can use <STRONG>any visible element</STRONG> you want.</TD>
</TABLE>

<!-Stop centering the table.->
</CENTER>

</BODY>
</HTML>
```

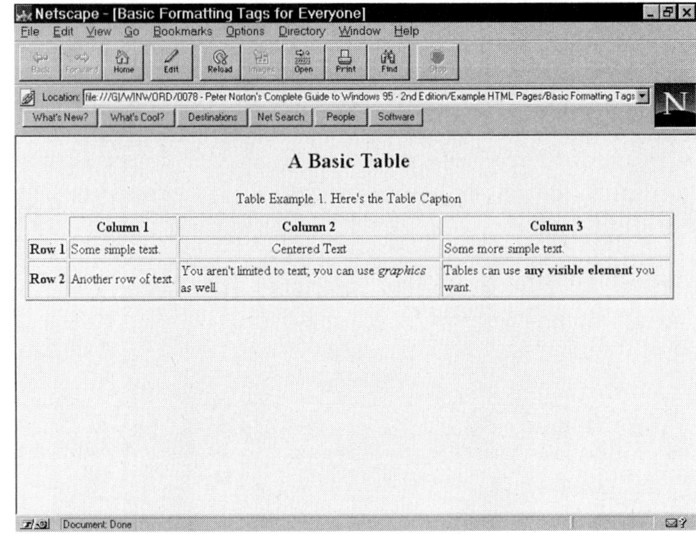

Figure 22.7.
Tables can be used for a variety of purposes; they're one of the more flexible Web page construction elements.

For the most part, this is just a simple table. I've used the various table tags such as `<CAPTION>` and `<TH>` to create the headings needed to identify table parts. However, you'll notice that there's a `BORDER` attribute for the `<TABLE>` tag. The `BORDER` attribute is used with a variety of tags—not just this one. An attribute changes the behavior of the tag in some way. In this case, we're changing the size of the lines between various table elements. I used the `<CENTER>` tag to center the text in the second column of the first row. Notice that I've also used the `<STRONG>` and `<EM>` tags to modify text in the second row of the table. As I mentioned previously, it's not always the number of tags you know how to use, but how you use them.

Making Your Page Work

To this point, we've simply looked at getting some text on the page, but anyone who spends time on the Internet knows that presenting information is only part of the process. Links and anchors provide the special feeling of visiting a Web site. (I mentioned links and anchors in Table 22.1 as part of the basic tag set that you'll see on every site.) Every time you visit a Web site and see some text underlines, you're probably looking at a link. A link connects your current location with some other location. In fact, two common forms of links are used on most Web pages. One creates a link to another page (an URL in Internet terminology), and it's the one that you'll see most often. The other type creates a link to another section of the current page or a specific area of another page. You'll use it to find an anchor (which we'll look at in a few seconds). Here's an example of the two common types of links. Notice that they both use the `HREF` keyword along with the `<A>` tag:

```
This is a <A HREF="http://www.mysite.com">Document</A> link.

This is an <A HREF="http://www.mysite.com#MyAnchor">Anchor</A> link.
```

In both cases, the text that appears between the <A> and </A> tags is the part of the sentence that appears underlined on the Web site. You should always place some text here or else your link will appear invisible to the user. Notice that the links look exactly alike except for one difference—the anchor link uses a number (#) sign to separate the URL from the anchor name. In this case, we've used MyAnchor as the anchor name. The second link would look for the URL first, then for a specific anchor location on that page, before displaying any content to the user.

> **Tip:** If you want to create an anchor link to an anchor on the current page, you don't need to provide the URL part of the <A> tag. You can abbreviate it as `<A HREF="#anchor name">`.

An anchor link also requires you to create an anchor somewhere on the page that you specify as part of the <A> tag. For example, we just looked at a link to MyAnchor on `http:www.mysite.com`. Here's how an anchor for this location would look:

```
This is the <A NAME="MyAnchor">Anchor</A> for this page.
```

As you can see, the big difference between an anchor and a link is the `NAME` keyword. An anchor always uses `NAME` in place of `HREF`. In addition, most browsers won't highlight or underline the text between the <A> and </A> tags, because you really can't use them for anything.

> **Note:** A specialized form of the <A> tag that I don't cover in this book is designed specifically for use with frames. It's the `<A target>` tag. You use it to load a Web page into a specific area of the browser window. This is a very advanced technique that you'll probably want to use after you've gained a little experience in creating Web pages.

There are a lot of specialized ways to use the <A> tag. For example, have you ever noticed the little message about sending e-mail to someone at the bottom of a Web page? That's actually a specialized form of the <A> tag. It uses the keyword `"mailto:"` as part of the `HREF`.

Let's take a look now at some links and anchors. The source code for this example appears as follows. Figure 22.8 shows what the example looks like when displayed in a browser.

```
<HTML>
<HEAD>
<TITLE>Making Your Page Work</TITLE>
</HEAD>
<BODY>

<!-Display a heading.->
<CENTER><H1>An Example of Links and Anchors</H1></CENTER>
<CENTER><STRONG><PRE>
There are a variety of ways to use links and anchors on a Web page,
but you'll find that some techniques are used more often than others.
</PRE></STRONG></CENTER>
```

```
<!-A link to another page.->
<CENTER><H3>Links Can Go to Another Web Site</H3></CENTER>
Here's a link to <A HREF="http://aux/default.htm">another page</A> on a test web site.

<!-A link to another page in the same directory.->
<CENTER><H3>You Can Make Links to Pages in the Same Directory</H3></CENTER>
The <A HREF="Basic Formatting Tags for Everyone.htm">Basic Formatting Tags
for Everyone</A> page is in the same directory as this page.

<!-This is a link to an anchor on this page.->
<CENTER><H3>Anchors Help You Move From One Area of a Page to Another</H3></CENTER>
You can also create links to <A HREF="#ShowAnchor">anchors</A> on the same page.

<!-Create a mailto address>
<CENTER><H3>Mail To Links are Really Handy</H3></CENTER>
<ADDRESS>
Send me some <A HREF="mailto: administrator@aux">email</A> if you like the site.
</ADDRESS>

<!-Here's the anchor for the on-page link.->
<CENTER><H3>Here's an Anchor</H3></CENTER>
Here's what an <A NAME="ShowAnchor">Anchor</A> looks like.
</BODY>
</HTML>
```

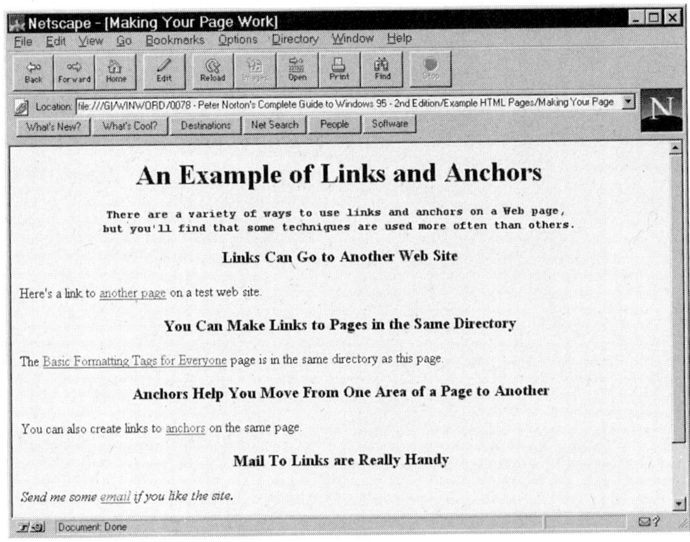

Figure 22.8.
There are a lot of ways to use links; this sample page shows just a few.

Notice that I've added a few additional techniques to this page. For example, I've combined `<CENTER>`, `<STRONG>`, and `<PRE>` to create a subtitle for the page. Notice how I've used the `<ADDRESS>` tag to display an address that people can send e-mail to. In most cases, the text appears as it does in Figure 22.8. Some browsers treat address text in other ways, but for the most part, you can count on the text looking a lot different from the other text on the page.

Automated Methods for Creating Pages

This section looks at a couple of ways that you can automate the process of creating Web pages. These methods don't represent everything on the market, by a long shot, but they do represent the techniques that I used for creating the HTML code in this book. In addition, you can download either of these products from the Internet—a real plus if you simply want to take a look at building a Web site without incurring all the cost at the outset. If you decide to build a permanent Web site, you'll want to shop around for a product that meets your needs completely (if these don't).

The first product we'll look at is ActiveX Control Pad. As the name implies, it excels at helping you to use ActiveX Controls on your Web site, although I find it a good tool for scripting as well. This product is best suited to people who have at least a modicum of programming experience, so you may want to take a look at the Internet Assistant for Microsoft Word instead, if your experience is limited. You can download ActiveX Control Pad at `http://www.microsoft.com/workshop/author/cpad/`.

The second product is the Internet Assistant for Microsoft Word (there are similar versions of this product for all the Microsoft Office suite applications, such as Excel). The advantage to using this product is that many of the formatting steps are completed for you. All you need to do is format your document by using the standard Word feature set. You may also choose to retain your page in .DOC format when using this solution, but that limits your audience to Internet Explorer users who have a Word viewer of some kind installed on their machines. This solution is also a little less flexible in some ways than using ActiveX Control Pad. You don't have the low level of control over the HTML that gets generated (although you can certainly edit the code later if you want). You can download the Internet Assistant at `http://www.microsoft.com/word/Internet/ia/default.htm`.

Using ActiveX Control Pad

ActiveX is a new technology that Microsoft hopes will take the Internet by storm. The short definition of ActiveX is that it's the updated version of OLE. There's more to it than that, but you can read all about ActiveX in the "ActiveX—An Internet Strategy" section of Chapter 12. Make sure that you understand ActiveX from a user perspective before you attempt to use it on your Web site.

Let's discuss ActiveX for just a moment before I show you how to use it within the confines of ActiveX Control Pad. You can do anything with an ActiveX control on a Web page that you can do with the same control on a desktop machine—within limits. For example, unlike the scripting languages I show you later, you can use ActiveX controls to access the hard disk or to retrieve information about the users of your site. Herein lies the danger that most people are worried about when using ActiveX controls. Unless an ActiveX control is monitored by someone, it could do grave damage to your machine. Microsoft and other companies are working on ways such as certificates and browser monitoring to help a user feel comfortable using ActiveX controls. I discuss this security aspect of ActiveX controls in more detail in the "Sandbox Approach Versus Open Access" section of Chapter 24. Suffice it to say right now that some users may actually avoid your site because of the added capability provided by ActiveX.

Another problem with ActiveX controls is that they're a Windows-specific technology. As I write this, Microsoft is busy trying to gain support for ActiveX on a variety of platforms, but that doesn't help you today. As things stand, you're going to lock some people out of your site if you use ActiveX controls.

The browser wars will approach your doorstep if you don't provide at least Netscape Navigator and Microsoft Internet Explorer support when using ActiveX controls. Fortunately, there's a way around this problem that I tell you about in the "Using NCompass ScriptActive" section of this chapter. Suffice it to say that the HTML pages you create using ActiveX Control Pad won't work with Navigator. You have to take some extra steps to make sure that ActiveX-enabled pages work with both browsers.

Now that I've filled you with doom and gloom, let's look at this technology and what it can do for you. Remember that I'm only showing you an overview of the controls that come with ActiveX Control Pad. A lot more controls are available from a variety of vendors. In fact, you can view the ActiveX Component Gallery at `http://www.microsoft.com/activex/gallery/default.htm`. This site can lead you to others that demonstrate various types of ActiveX controls. In most cases, you can also download a sample version of the control and any server software required to work with it. The important thing to remember is that, as with any technology, you need to weigh the benefits that ActiveX can provide versus the negative aspects. The following list is just the tip of the iceberg when it comes to benefits.

Tip: Microsoft provides an ActiveX Directory Search page that helps you find controls you need. Just go to `http://www.microsoft.com/activex/` to find more information.

- **Reduced development time:** ActiveX will do for the Internet what OCXs (OLE Control eXtensions) have done for the desktop. (An .OCX is the special form of control used by products such as Visual Basic to reduce the amount of work that a programmer has to do. For example, a single .OCX might reduce to a few lines of code the effort required to access a database.) However, you'll find ActiveX controls in places that you hadn't really thought about in the past. For example, NetManage, Inc. plans to create a new e-mail client called Z-Mail Pro. This package supports ActiveX technology in a way that allows users to exchange, create, and view HTML documents directly in the message viewing window. What this means to users is that they now have the ability to create dynamic Web pages, something that you really have to work at today.

- **Improved accessibility of remote data:** Remote connections will also benefit from the use of ActiveX. For example, Proginet Corporation is currently working on ActiveX technology that will bring mainframe data to the desktop. Their Fusion FTMS (File Transfer Management System) will work with any development language that supports OLE containers, such as Delphi, Visual C++, and PowerBuilder. Essentially, you'll place an ActiveX control on a form, define where to find the data, and then rely on the control to make the connection. No longer will remote access over the Internet require the user to jump through hoops. A special transfer server on the mainframe will complete the package by automating all transfer requests. No longer will an operator have to manually download a needed file to the company's Web site before a client can access it.
- **Enhanced mail service capabilities:** Even Microsoft Exchange will benefit from ActiveX. Wang Laboratories, Inc. and other companies are creating new add-ons that mix Exchange and ActiveX together. Wang's product is a client/server imaging add-on. It will allow users to scan, view, annotate, manipulate, or print graphic images, no matter where they're located. This same product will include a hierarchical storage-management ActiveX control. The two technologies will work together to make graphics easier to access and use in a large company. They'll also make it easier to find a needed graphic—which should ultimately result in storage savings to the company.
- **A head start for programmers:** Microsoft itself has issued a whole slew of ActiveX controls. You can download some of these controls from the Microsoft section of their Web site at `http://www.microsoft.com/activex/gallery/`. Examples of these new controls include Animation Player for PowerPoint and Internet Assistant for both Access and Schedule+. The Internet Assistant for Access creates a snapshot of a database table that's uploaded as a static image. The snapshot automatically updates every time the user accesses the page. The Internet Assistant for Schedule+ allows you to upload scheduling information to a Web page. Because the data gets updated every time a user accesses the site, you no longer have to worry about compute-at-home employees missing meetings. Finally, the PowerPoint Animation Player allows you to play a PowerPoint presentation from within any ActiveX-compliant browser.
- **Enhanced network security:** If you think ActiveX won't help with network security, think again. A lot of new firewall and certificate strategies are making the rounds these days. One of those new strategies is Net2000. It's a set of APIs that allow developers to tie NetWare core services (including directory, security, and licensing) into their applications. You'll be able to tap this API set through ActiveX controls over an intranet. How will this help users and developers alike? With the proper programming constructs, a network administrator will be able to track license usage throughout the entire network—even across Internet connections. This is going to become a much bigger issue as more people compute from home rather than the office.

- **Increased Web page capabilities:** Users will find that they have more features to choose from on a typical Web page implementing ActiveX. That's because a lot of the programming constraints that you used to have with standard HTML are gone. Just about anything you can do with an .OCX, you can do with an ActiveX control. This means that you can add specialized forms features such as a spelling checker, graphics, or even live data to your repertoire.
- **Decreased response time:** Right now users must rely on CGI scripts to get any kind of interactive feedback from a Web server. Every request is handled separately. Adding a new piece of information to a field requires another call to the server. Using ActiveX allows programmers to maintain a live data connection that requires a minimum of network traffic and therefore increases perceived performance.
- **Application integration:** A lot of vendors are coming out with ActiveX-type controls that you can include with local applications, just as you can include an .OCX. For example, you could include an ActiveX control that automatically creates a connection to a Web site as needed to get remote information. As far as the user is concerned, that data might be coming from a local hard drive or the LAN; only the programmer knows that it's really coming from the Internet somewhere. The bottom line is that an application such as a word processor or database manager could become a browser as well—it's simply a matter of including the right ActiveX controls with your application.
- **Enhanced application and browser security:** Right now there are a lot of problems with maintaining security on the Internet. A good portion of that problem is due to the way in which the Internet currently implements IP (Internet protocol). There are a ton of very "messy" solutions to fix the problem, but most of them are going to require a lot of work on the part of the user. Consider something as simple as certificates, which require users to perform a lot of additional setup on their machines. An ActiveX control may not provide the ultimate in security, but there are ways of writing these controls so that they provide a modicum of security in a totally seamless manner.
- **Reduced waiting for application updates:** Using ActiveX to provide canned modules for common application pieces will reduce the workload on you as a programmer. Think about it this way: You'll let someone else write and debug pieces of your application for you. The only thing you really need to worry about is putting the modules together and adding any custom code. What users will see is faster updates—something everyone wants and needs in today's competitive environment.

ActiveX Control Pad is little more than a specialized editor in some ways. Figure 22.9 shows what you'll see when you open this utility program for the first time. Notice that ActiveX Control Pad automatically starts an HTML page for you.

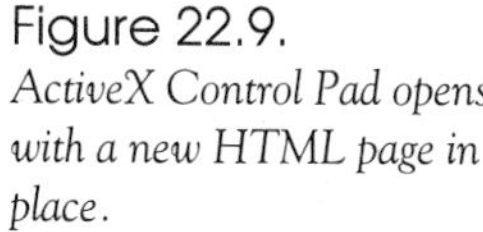

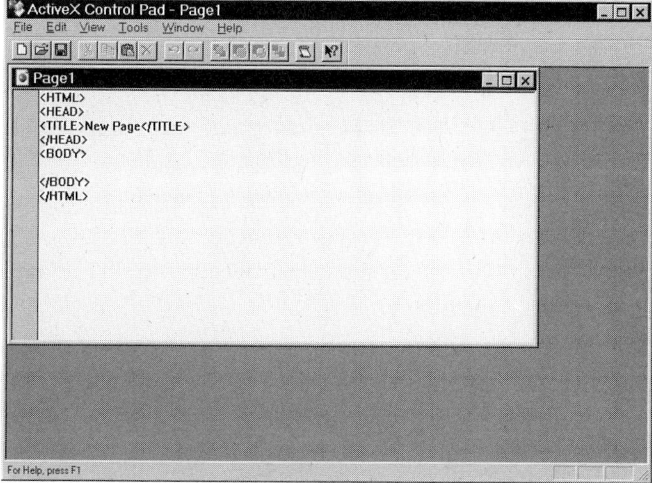

Figure 22.9.
ActiveX Control Pad opens with a new HTML page in place.

Take a look at the toolbar across the top of the dialog box. The following list tells you about each button, starting from the left:

- **New:** Creates one of two new document types. The first is an HTML document like the one shown in Figure 22.9. The second is an HTML Layout (discussed in the later section "Creating an HTML Layout for Microsoft ActiveX Controls").
- **Open:** Opens an existing HTML document (with an .HTM or .HTML extension) or HTML Layout (with an .ALX extension). Because this is a text editor, you can also use it to open standard ASCII files, although Notepad is probably a better option because it takes less memory.
- **Save:** Saves an existing HTML or HTML Layout document. ActiveX Control Pad chooses a default extension for you, based on the kind of document you're editing. As with all other Windows applications, this one displays a Save As dialog box if you haven't saved the document in the past.
- **Cut:** Removes selected text or ActiveX controls from their current location and places them on the Clipboard.
- **Copy:** Places a copy of any highlighted text or ActiveX controls on the Clipboard.
- **Paste:** Copies any text or controls from the Clipboard into the current document. Needless to say, you can't copy an ActiveX control from an HTML Layout and paste it to an HTML document.
- **Delete:** Permanently removes the highlighted text or ActiveX controls without placing them on the Clipboard.
- **Undo:** ActiveX Control Pad provides a single level of undo. In other words, you can undo only a single action. Unfortunately, some activities such as highlighting text count as an action. This places a fairly grave limitation on your ability to undo some kinds of tasks.

- **Redo:** Allows you to redo the previous action. Like the Undo button, there's only one level of redo. In other words, you can't use this button to perform a repetitive task, as you could in some applications.
- **Bring to Front:** You can use this button (and the following three buttons) only when working with an HTML Layout. It allows you to move the selected element from any position to the front position in a stack of elements. Stacking elements allows you to build a complex page by using many simple elements.
- **Move Forward:** Moves the selected element one position forward (toward the front) in the stack.
- **Move Backward:** Moves the selected element one position back (toward the back) in the stack.
- **Send to Back:** Moves the selected element all the way to the bottom of the stack.
- **Script Wizard:** Use this option to display the Script Wizard. The "Creating Simple Scripts" section of this chapter covers this feature.
- **Help:** Displays online help.

At this point, you could use ActiveX Control Pad as you would any editor to type HTML code. However, that would be a real waste of the capabilities that this product provides. Let's review some of the features that you'll use just about every time you open up this utility.

Note: The remainder of this section assumes that you've obtained a copy of ActiveX Control Pad and installed it on your machine. You should be able to follow along with the procedures even if you don't have the product installed, but you won't be able to get any hands-on experience.

Inserting ActiveX Controls

I've already covered a wealth of HTML tags, so I don't cover too many new ones in this section. You can do quite a bit using the tags I've shown you already, but even the most experienced Webmaster will tell you that standard HTML tags are limited at best. That's why technologies such as ActiveX are becoming so popular. They allow you to extend a Web site without a lot of extra work. That's why ActiveX Control Pad is such an important product. It allows you to add ActiveX controls to your Web page with only a modicum of additional work.

Let's take a look at the technique you use to add an ActiveX control to a standard HTML page. You can use the same procedure no matter which control you want to install, but I'll use a standard button for the purposes of this example:

1. Open ActiveX Control Pad. Use the File | New command to create a new HTML document or the File | Open command to open an existing document.
2. Position the cursor where you want the control to appear in the document. As with every other kind of HTML tag, the `<OBJECT>` tag used by ActiveX is position-dependent.
3. Use the Edit | Insert ActiveX Control command to display the dialog box shown in Figure 22.10. This is where you select the control that you want to use. If you don't see the control, make sure that it's installed properly and that you registered it. You can register a control by hand by typing **`RegSvr32 <OCX name>`** in the SYSTEM folder at the DOS command prompt. (Unregistering a control before you erase it is just as easy—simply type **`RegSvr32 -U <OCX name>`** at the DOS command prompt.) RegSvr32 always displays a success message when it registers a control for you.

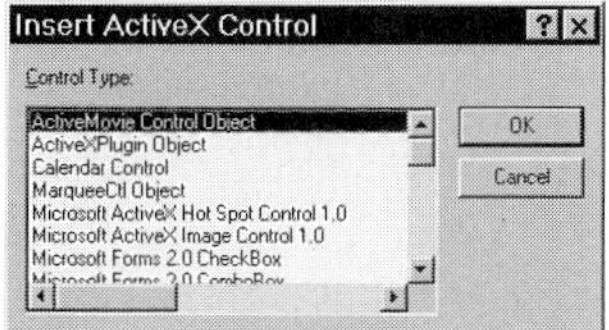

Figure 22.10.
The Insert ActiveX Control dialog box allows you to select from one of the ActiveX controls registered on your machine.

4. Highlight the control you want to use, and then click OK. You'll see the control in the Edit ActiveX Control dialog box, along with a Properties dialog box, as shown in Figure 22.11. Because I chose a command button, that's what you see in the figure.

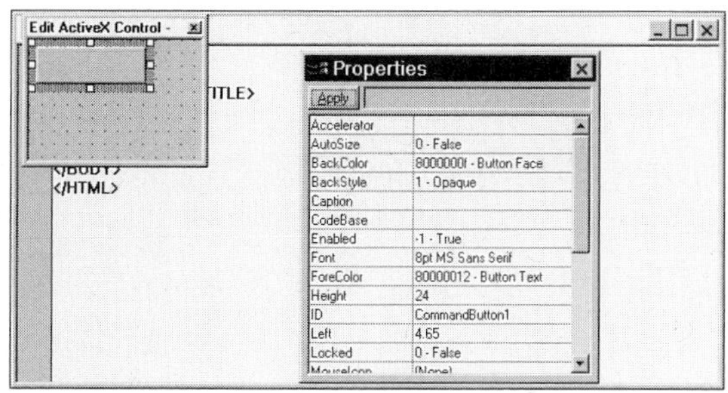

Figure 22.11.
ActiveX Control Pad displays a copy of the ActiveX control and its Properties dialog box.

5. Set any properties needed to make the control work. For example, I added a caption to my command button. Every ActiveX control you use will also have a `CodeBase` property, which is the directory where you store the control on the Web server. You must set this property or the user won't be able to download the control from your Web site. I always store my controls in a special directory on the server. The controls you get with ActiveX Control Pad appear in the ISCTRLS.OCX file. You must specify the name of the .OCX as well as the location on your Web site. For example, my local experimental Web site uses a `CodeBase` property of `http://aux/controls/ISCTRLS.OCX` for the controls that come with the ActiveX Control Pad.

6. Click the Close button in the Edit ActiveX Control dialog box. The dialog box displaying the ActiveX Control and its associated Properties dialog box should close. What you'll see is a new `<OBJECT>` tag in the HTML document, like the one shown in Figure 22.12. Notice the special button next to the `<OBJECT>` tag. Clicking this button reopens the Edit ActiveX Control dialog box so that you can modify the control properties.

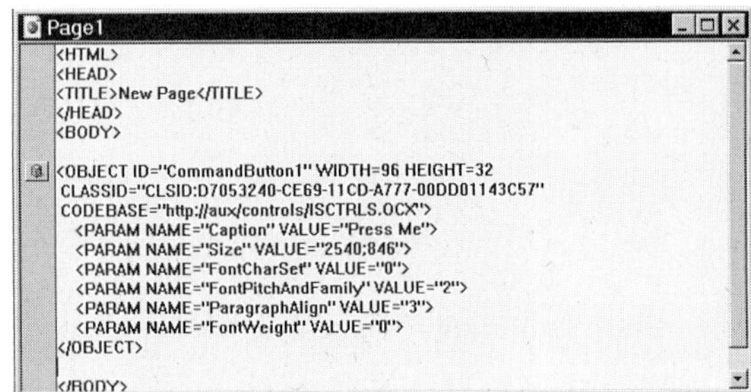

Figure 22.12.
The final result of adding an ActiveX control to your HTML document is an `<OBJECT>` *tag.*

That's all there is to it! Using ActiveX Control Pad makes the job of adding ActiveX controls to your Web page easier. This control still won't do anything, but we can at least display it. Open the sample page, using Internet Explorer. We haven't yet converted this page for use with the NCompass ScriptActive plug-in, so it won't work with Netscape Navigator. Figure 22.13 shows the results of adding a command button to a page.

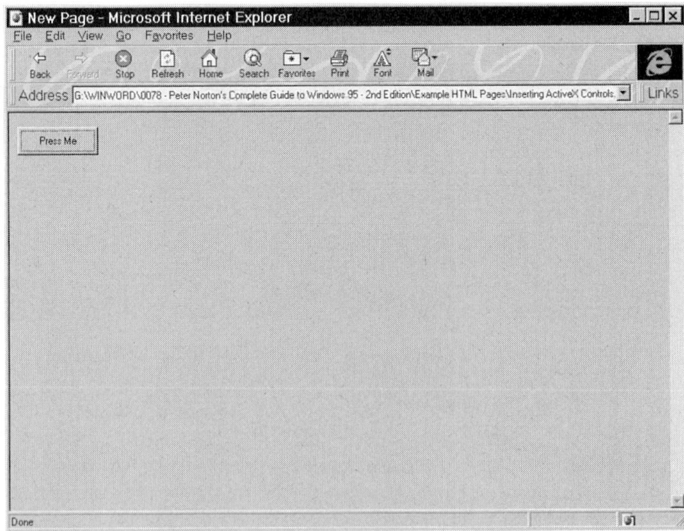

Figure 22.13.
Our sample ActiveX control displays just fine, but it won't do anything just yet.

Creating an HTML Layout for Microsoft ActiveX Controls

One of the problems with using straight HTML for your Web pages is that you can't control the location of the various display elements very easily. Fortunately, you can use an HTML Layout to get around this problem if you're willing to devote the site to ActiveX. The advantage to using this particular technique is that you can create and display Web pages in much the same way that programmers have displayed forms within products such as Delphi and Visual Basic for quite some time now. The disadvantage is that, on top of all the constraints for ActiveX, you now have the added constraint of the user's machine. Using an HTML Layout means that the user's machine must now display the page as you've laid it out. If you don't plan ahead, you could have the user scrolling back and forth across the page in an effort to see it.

Despite the problems that HTML Layouts could cause on a Web site, creating one is just too fast and easy to ignore. Add to that the flexibility and other features of ActiveX and you have a winning combination. My personal take on all this is that HTML Layouts are best used on company intranets where you have complete control over the type of machine and browser used to access the Web site. There are just too many variables to consider outside of the intranet environment to make this a practical solution—at least for the time being.

Let's take a look at what you'd need to do to create an HTML Layout using ActiveX Control Pad. Obviously you'll need to open ActiveX Control Pad to get started.

1. Use the File | New HTML Layout command to create a new HTML Layout like the one shown in Figure 22.14. Notice that this layout looks much like the forms used by products such as Delphi and Visual Basic. You'll also want to take a look at the toolbox at the right side of the figure. It contains all the standard tools provided with ActiveX Control Pad: Label, TextBox, ComboBox, ListBox, CheckBox, OptionButton, ToggleButton, CommandButton, TabStrip, ScrollBar, SpinButton, HotSpot, and Image. The Additional page of the toolbox contains two controls: ActiveMovie and WebBrowser. I'll show you how to add additional controls in just a bit.
2. Click a control in the toolbox. For purposes of this example, I chose a command button. You can choose any of the controls shown in the toolbox. Your mouse cursor will change to a plus (+) sign and you'll also see next to the cursor a small version of whatever control you've chosen. The plus sign shows where the upper-left corner of the component will appear when you click the layout.
3. Select a position on the layout and click. The control appears as shown in Figure 22.15. Notice that you don't see a Properties dialog box.

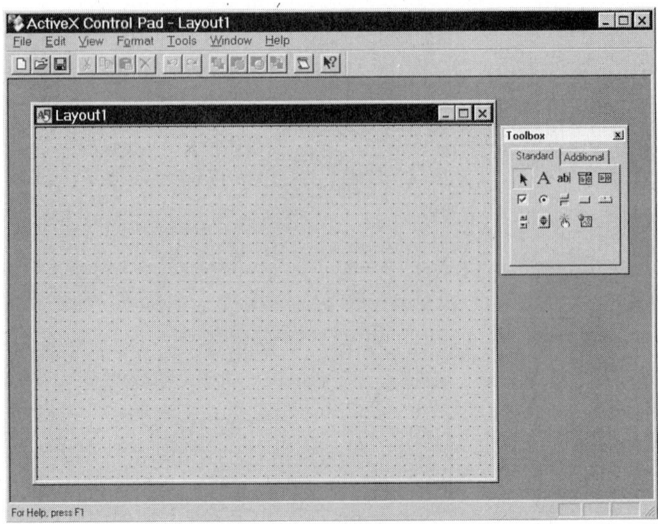

Figure 22.14.
The initial screen for an HTML Layout looks much like the forms used by RAD programming languages such as Delphi and Visual Basic.

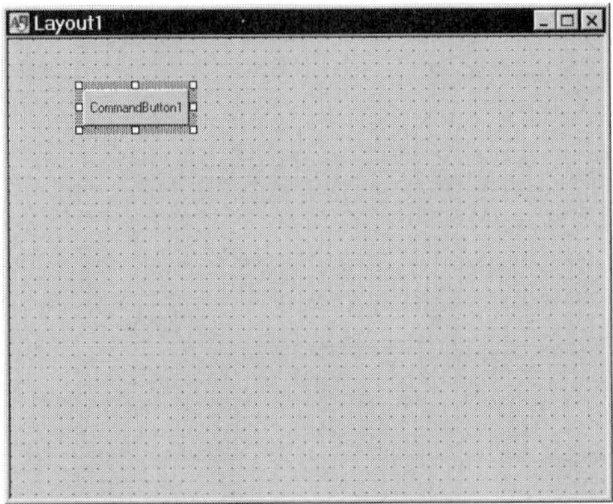

Figure 22.15.
Positioning a control on an HTML layout is as easy as pointing to where you want to place it.

4. Display the Properties dialog box shown in Figure 22.16 by double-clicking the control. You could also right-click the control to display the context menu shown in Figure 22.16, and select Properties. Notice that the context menu also contains options for cutting, copying, and pasting the control. You can also display the source code required to create the control—an HTML Layout still relies on `<OBJECT>` tags (as you'll see by the end of this procedure). The Script Wizard option helps you create scripts for this control (see the later section "Creating Simple Scripts").

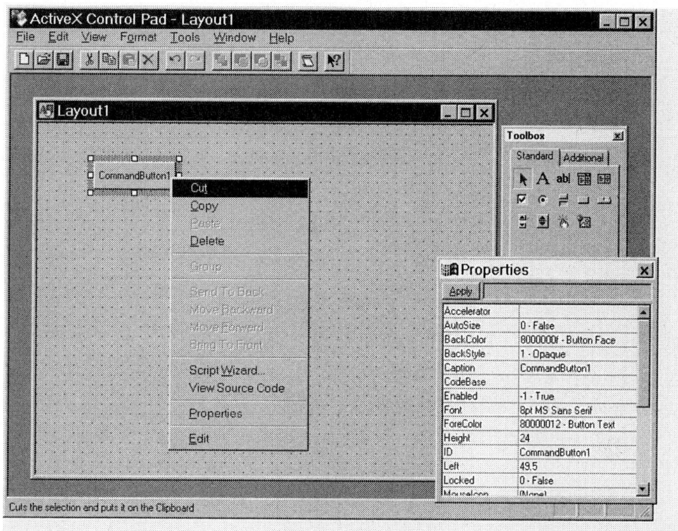

Figure 22.16.
Double-clicking the control displays the Properties dialog box—you can also use the Properties entry on the context menu.

5. Define any properties needed to use this control. Every control you use will also have a `CodeBase` property. You must set this property or the user won't be able to download the control from your Web site. I always store my controls in a special directory on the server. The controls you get with ActiveX Control Pad appear in the ISCTRLS.OCX file. You must specify the name of the .OCX as well as the location on your Web site. For example, my local experimental Web site uses a `CodeBase` property of `http://aux/controls/ISCTRLS.OCX` for the controls that come with ActiveX Control Pad.
6. Add controls as needed to complete the layout. Figure 22.17 shows the layout that I created for this example. Notice that I simply added a text box control. I centered the text within the control by selecting a value of `Center` for the `TextAlign` property. Centering the text within a control or a layout doesn't guarantee that it will appear centered within the browser, however.

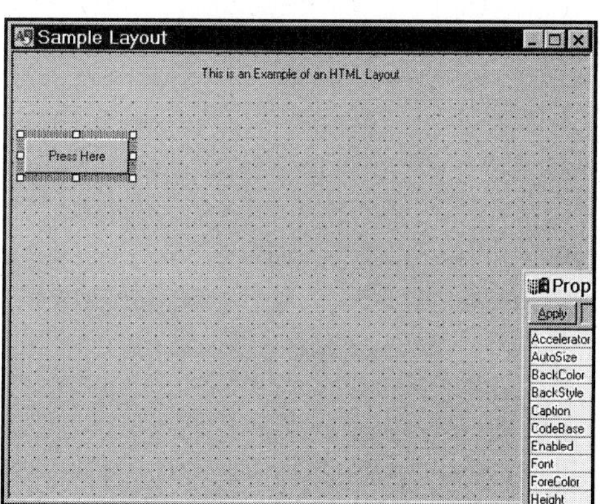

Figure 22.17.
Our sample layout isn't very complex, but it gives you an indication of what you can do with HTML Layouts.

7. At this point, you can add scripts by hand or use the Script Wizard to add them. (The later section "Creating Simple Scripts" looks at the Script Wizard.) However, even with the Script Wizard, there are times when you'll need to add code by hand. Right-click the layout and select View Source Code from the context menu. You'll see a dialog box telling you that you have to save the layout before looking at the source. If you see this dialog box, click Yes to display a standard Save As dialog box. Save the layout and you'll see the source code for your layout displayed in Notepad. Figure 22.18 shows the source code for this example. Notice that we're still using `<OBJECT>` tags. You should also notice the `<DIV>` and `</DIV>` tag pair. The `<DIV>` tag is what differentiates an HTML Layout from a standard HTML page. (The layout also uses an .ALX extension.)

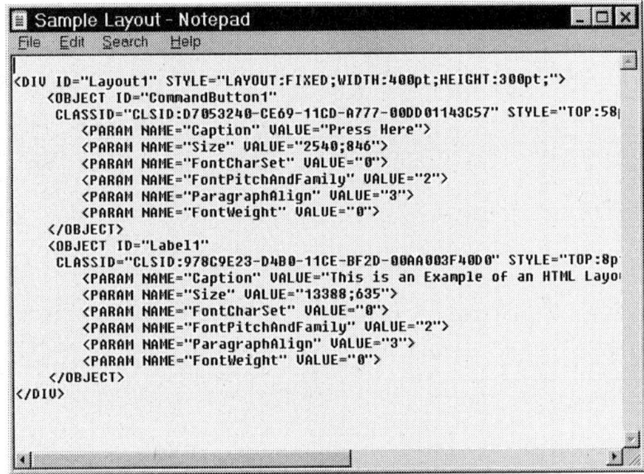
Sample Layout - Notepad
File Edit Search Help
<DIV ID="Layout1" STYLE="LAYOUT:FIXED;WIDTH:400pt;HEIGHT:300pt;">
<OBJECT ID="CommandButton1"
CLASSID="CLSID:D7053240-CE69-11CD-A777-00DD01143C57" STYLE="TOP:58
<PARAM NAME="Caption" VALUE="Press Here">
<PARAM NAME="Size" VALUE="2540;846">
<PARAM NAME="FontCharSet" VALUE="0">
<PARAM NAME="FontPitchAndFamily" VALUE="2">
<PARAM NAME="ParagraphAlign" VALUE="3">
<PARAM NAME="FontWeight" VALUE="0">
</OBJECT>
<OBJECT ID="Label1"
CLASSID="CLSID:978C9E23-D4B0-11CE-BF2D-00AA003F40D0" STYLE="TOP:8p
<PARAM NAME="Caption" VALUE="This is an Example of an HTML Layo
<PARAM NAME="Size" VALUE="13388;635">
<PARAM NAME="FontCharSet" VALUE="0">
<PARAM NAME="FontPitchAndFamily" VALUE="2">
<PARAM NAME="ParagraphAlign" VALUE="3">
<PARAM NAME="FontWeight" VALUE="0">
</OBJECT>
</DIV>

Figure 22.18.
HTML Layouts still rely on `<OBJECT>` tags to display ActiveX controls.

8. Before you can use an HTML Layout, you must insert it into a standard HTML page. Begin by using the File | New HTML command to create a new HTML page.
9. Use the Edit | Insert HTML Layout command to display a standard File Open dialog box. (The dialog box title won't match, but the functionality is the same.) Double-click the HTML Layout file that you just created. ActiveX Control Pad inserts the layout by using an `<OBJECT>` tag, as shown in Figure 22.19. The first thing that you should notice about this `<OBJECT>` tag is that the button on the left side of the edit window is different. Clicking this button opens the HTML Layout window shown earlier in Figure 22.17.
10. Save the HTML file by using the File | Save As command. Figure 22.20 shows what this HTML Layout looks like when viewed within Internet Explorer. You should notice two things about this display. First, the relationships between the controls in the layout are exactly the same as when we designed the HTML Layout. Second, the heading at the top of the layout isn't centered within the browser, although it's still centered within the layout. (Internet Explorer makes layout incorporation completely seamless.)

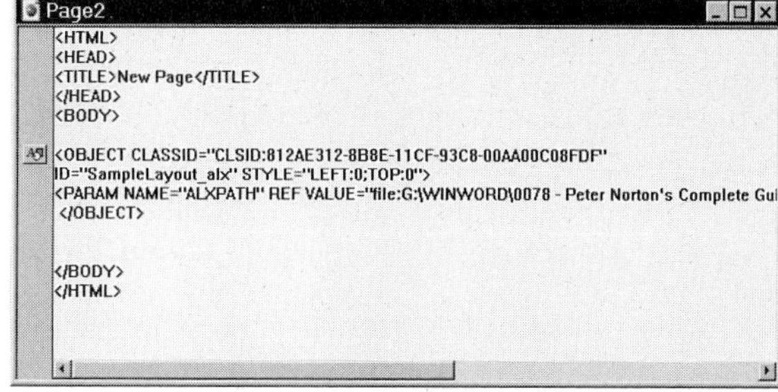

Figure 22.19.
An HTML Layout uses a special form of `<OBJECT>` *tag.*

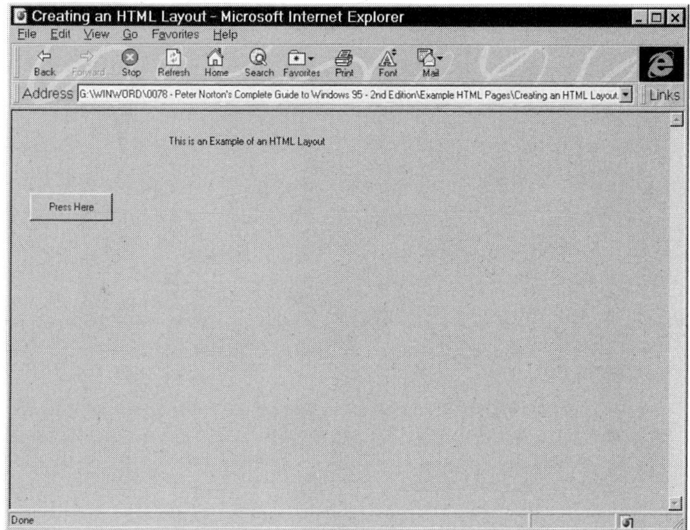

Figure 22.20.
The final result of creating an HTML Layout is a display like this one.

Tip: You can use the `<CENTER>` tag to center an HTML Layout within the browser window.

Now that you've got a good idea of how to create your own HTML Layouts, let's look at what you need to do to add a control to the toolbox. Select the page of the toolbox where you want to add a control. Right-click the toolbox and select Additional Controls from the context menu. You'll see a dialog box like the one shown in Figure 22.21.

This dialog box displays a list of the controls and insertable objects registered on your machine. (You can uncheck either of the two top check boxes to limit the number of items displayed. The third checkbox in the dialog box displays only the selected items—those currently shown in the toolbox.) You can't use every control or insertable object within an HTML Layout or as an ActiveX control, so it's better to know ahead of time which control you want to add. Check a control to add it to the toolbox. Likewise, unchecking the control removes it from the toolbox. Click OK in the Additional Controls dialog box to complete the action.

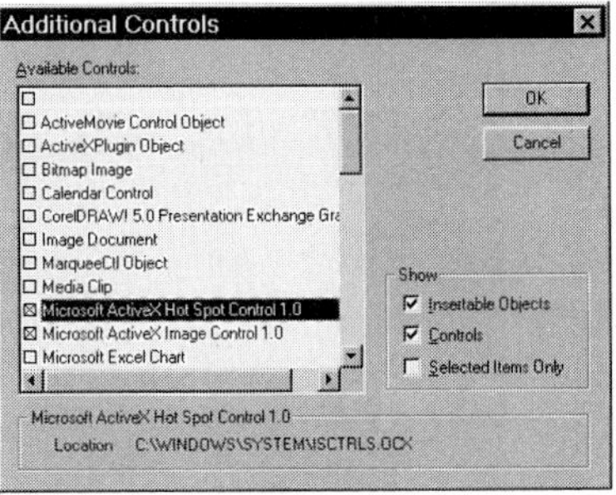

Figure 22.21.
The Additional Controls dialog box allows you to add or remove controls in the toolbox.

Tip: Highlighting a control displays the location of the file you need to use to implement it. For example, if you select the Microsoft ActiveX Hotspot Control 1.0 entry shown in Figure 22.21, you'll notice at the bottom of the Additional Controls dialog box that the control appears within the ISCTRLS.OCX file in the SYSTEM folder.

Creating Simple Scripts

ActiveX Control Pad can help you create simple scripts by using Script Wizard. It does a great job if all you want to do is change the color of the background or change a control property. Script Wizard doesn't work very well if you need to perform complex tasks such as sending data to your Web server. In fact, about the only thing you can count on it to do is to make static changes to the elements of the Web page itself. Anything else is really outside the range of things that you can do with Script Wizard. We're going to look at simple scripts in this section. Take a look at the later sections "Simple Scripting with VBScript" and "Simple Scripting with JavaScript" for more complex scripting needs.

I created a simple HTML page with a single command button on it in the "Inserting ActiveX Controls" section of this chapter. Let's take another look at that example. What I'd like to do is tell the command button control to change the display color when a user clicks it. As any Webmaster will tell you, it's impossible to change the background color of a Web page once it's displayed. This script allows us to get around that limitation. Before we do that, however, I'd like to show you how to set up the Script Wizard. Use the Tools | Options | Script command to display the Script Options dialog box shown in Figure 22.22.

Figure 22.22.
Always check your Script Wizard options before starting a script.

The first set of option buttons controls the Script Pane view. In List view, it shows you a list of scripts associated with each object. In Code view, it displays the actual code associated with an object. You'll want to keep it in List view until you actually create some scripts to look at. Fortunately, you can change this setting within the Script Wizard dialog box. The Script Pane Font button in this area displays a standard Font dialog box that you can use to change the font used to display objects and associated code.

The second set of option buttons controls the language produced by the Script Wizard. It defaults to producing VBScript, a true subset of Visual Basic for Applications. You can also choose to produce JavaScript.

When you're ready to create a script, use the Tools | Script Wizard command to display the Script Wizard dialog box shown in Figure 22.23. On the left side of the display is a list of objects that respond to events. If you click the plus (+) sign next to an object, you see a list of events that it supports. For example, Figure 22.23 shows that `CommandButton1` responds to a `Click` event. On the right side of the dialog box is a list of objects with properties. Clicking + here displays a list of properties, methods, and other objects controlled by that object. For example, the Window object supports an `alert` method, a `defaultStatus` property, and contains a `document` object.

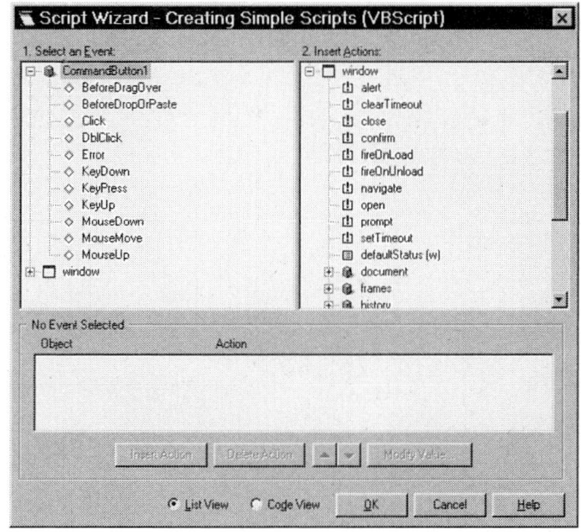

Figure 22.23.
The Script Wizard window displays all the objects you can access from the current HTML document.

Let's create the simple script that I mentioned previously:

1. Click the `Click` event for `CommandButton1` in the Select an Event section of the dialog box. Next, click + next to `CommandButton1` in the Insert Actions section. You should see a `Caption` property.
2. Click the `Caption` property to select it. Now that we've selected an event and a property, we have to tell Script Wizard what to do.

3. Click the Insert Action button. You should see a dialog box similar to the one shown in Figure 22.24. This dialog box allows you to do one of three things. You can assign a color to `Caption`. Normally, you'd use this to change the document background or something of a similar nature. The Script Wizard always allows you to perform a custom action as well, but this can get tricky. You'll often find that writing a custom script at this point is easier than trying to use Script Wizard. Finally, you can do what we need to do—assign a string to the `Caption` property.

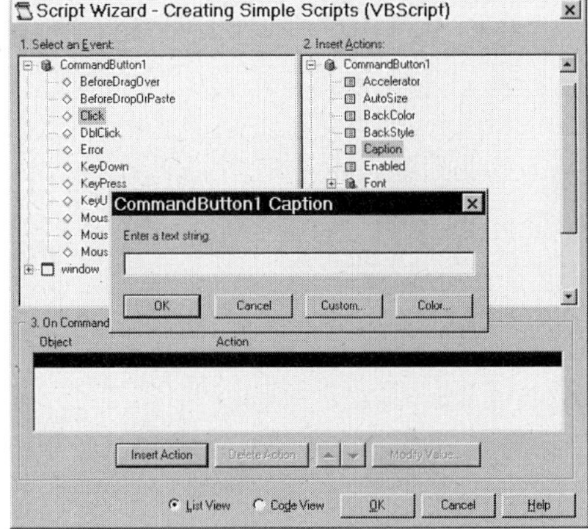

Figure 22.24.
You'll see a dialog box like this one whenever you want to assign an action to a particular event.

4. Type **`"I've Been Pressed"`** in the Enter a Text String field, and then click OK. You'll see a new action associated with the `CommandButton1 Click` event, as shown in Figure 22.25. Notice that the little diamond next to the entry is black now. Whenever you see a black diamond next to an event, you know that it has an action associated with it.

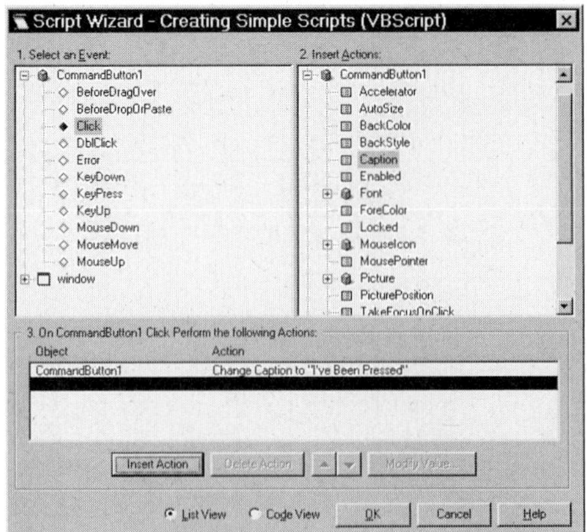

Figure 22.25.
The Script Wizard shows you which events have actions associated with them by making the diamond next to the event black.

5. Click OK to complete the action. You should see a VBScript entry in the HTML document like the one shown in Figure 22.26. (The later section "Simple Scripting with VBScript" talks about the inner workings of VBScript.)

Figure 22.26.
The Script Wizard creates a VBScript to match the actions you specified.

Creating Simple Scripts

```
<HTML>
<HEAD>
<TITLE>Creating Simple Scripts</TITLE>
</HEAD>
<BODY>
   <SCRIPT LANGUAGE="VBScript">
<!-
Sub CommandButton1_Click()
CommandButton1.Caption = "I've Been Pressed"
end sub
->
   </SCRIPT>
   <OBJECT ID="CommandButton1" WIDTH=96 HEIGHT=32
    CLASSID="CLSID:D7053240-CE69-11CD-A777-00DD01143C57"
    CODEBASE="http://aux/controls/ISCTRLS.OCX">
      <PARAM NAME="Caption" VALUE="Press Me">
      <PARAM NAME="Size" VALUE="2540;846">
      <PARAM NAME="FontCharSet" VALUE="0">
      <PARAM NAME="FontPitchAndFamily" VALUE="2">
      <PARAM NAME="ParagraphAlign" VALUE="3">
      <PARAM NAME="FontWeight" VALUE="0">
   </OBJECT>
</BODY>
</HTML>
```

6. Save the modified version of our simple HTML page with an ActiveX control. Open the page in Internet Explorer and you'll see the same display you saw in Figure 22.13. However, when you click the Press Me button now, you should see a change in the Press Me button caption.

As you can see, creating a simple script using Script Wizard doesn't require much more skill than the ability to choose items from a list. A script can quickly get more complicated, though, and I cover some of those situations later in the chapter. The bottom line is that even if you can't use Script Wizard to complete a script, you might want to consider using it as a starting point. At least you'll save yourself the time of creating a script shell.

Using NCompass ScriptActive

So far, none of the ActiveX coding we've done will work with browsers other than Internet Explorer. Before you can use a page containing ActiveX controls with Netscape Navigator, you have to perform two steps. The first is to use a special utility on the HTML page itself. The second is to install a plug-in for your browser. The most common solution you'll find right now for performing both steps is the ScriptActive plug-in from NCompass Labs. You can download an evaluation copy of this plug-in (and associated HTML conversion utility) from `http://www.ncompasslabs.com/showcase.htm`.

How does ScriptActive work? It relies on an `<EMBED>` tag to replace the `<OBJECT>` tag that Navigator doesn't understand. The `<EMBED>` tag is used by browsers to start a helper application such as the multimedia player. In this case, it starts ScriptActive, which interprets the contents of the `<EMBED>` tag much as Internet Explorer would do natively.

Tip: There are many different ways to use helper applications within browsers such as Netscape Navigator and Internet Explorer. You may find that a colleague doesn't have one of the Microsoft applications you used to create a document. Don't bother to convert the document. Simply have the colleague download an appropriate viewer. (You could also add the URL for the viewer to your Web page.) You'll find the viewers for Excel, PowerPoint, and Word at these sites, respectively:

```
http://www.microsoft.com/excel/internet/viewer/

http://www.microsoft.com/powerpoint/internet/viewer/

http://www.microsoft.com/word/internet/viewer/
```

Let's look at an example of this plug-in in action. You'll need to download and install the plug-in, using vendor instructions. In most cases, this means downloading the file, double-clicking it, and then following the prompts. Once you have ScriptActive installed, you need to restart Windows. When you return, you should have a new context-menu entry called NConvert, as shown in Figure 22.27. All you need to do to add `<EMBED>` tags to an existing HTML document is to right-click it and then select the NConvert | Convert command from the context menu.

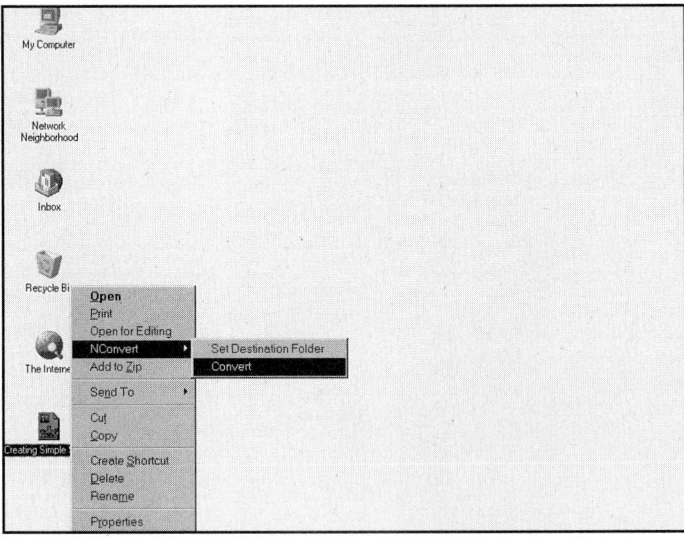

Figure 22.27.
The NCompass NConvert utility helps you to create ActiveX-enabled documents that both Internet Explorer and Navigator can use.

I tried this with the example in the previous section. Because that example also included a VBScript file, NConvert also created a separate .AXS file for it. The .AXS file contains any scripts associated with embedded ActiveX controls, so you need to copy it to the same directory as the HTML document on your Web server. Figure 22.28 shows the resulting source code.

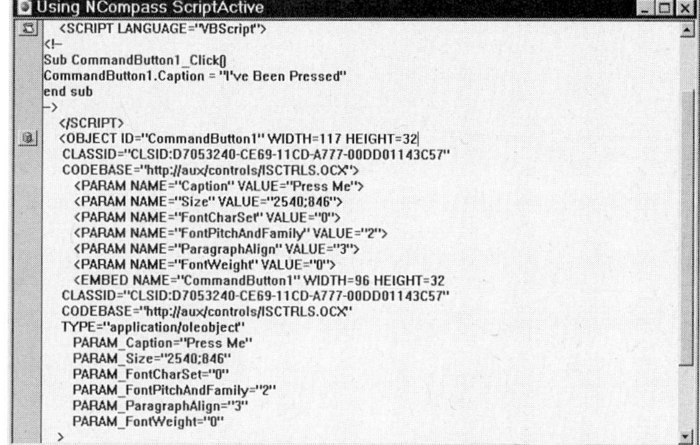

Using NCompass ScriptActive
<SCRIPT LANGUAGE="VBScript">
<!--
Sub CommandButton1_Click()
CommandButton1.Caption = "I've Been Pressed"
end sub
-->
</SCRIPT>
<OBJECT ID="CommandButton1" WIDTH=117 HEIGHT=32
CLASSID="CLSID:D7053240-CE69-11CD-A777-00DD01143C57"
CODEBASE="http://aux/controls/ISCTRLS.OCX">
<PARAM NAME="Caption" VALUE="Press Me">
<PARAM NAME="Size" VALUE="2540;846">
<PARAM NAME="FontCharSet" VALUE="0">
<PARAM NAME="FontPitchAndFamily" VALUE="2">
<PARAM NAME="ParagraphAlign" VALUE="3">
<PARAM NAME="FontWeight" VALUE="0">
<EMBED NAME="CommandButton1" WIDTH=96 HEIGHT=32
CLASSID="CLSID:D7053240-CE69-11CD-A777-00DD01143C57"
CODEBASE="http://aux/controls/ISCTRLS.OCX"
TYPE="application/oleobject"
PARAM_Caption="Press Me"
PARAM_Size="2540;846"
PARAM_FontCharSet="0"
PARAM_FontPitchAndFamily="2"
PARAM_ParagraphAlign="3"
PARAM_FontWeight="0"
>

Figure 22.28.
Prepare for a lot of additional source code—the `<EMBED>` *tag is just as large as the* `<OBJECT>` *tag.*

How does this utility work? Figure 22.29 shows the same page we saw earlier in Figure 22.13. This time, it's displayed in Netscape Navigator instead of Internet Explorer. All the simple scripts I tried appeared to work fine—although I did seem to run into problem areas when the scripts became too complex. Part of the problem is that ScriptActive doesn't appear to support all the VBScript statements in precisely the same way as Internet Explorer. You'll also find that ScriptActive doesn't support all the properties that Internet Explorer does. For example, try to use the `window.document.bgColor` property and you'll find that it isn't supported. I also ran into a few minor problems with custom-built ActiveX controls. In most cases, this appears to be a problem with the way in which the control interfaces were implemented, rather than ScriptActive itself. The worst culprits are older controls that don't fully adhere to the ActiveX standard.

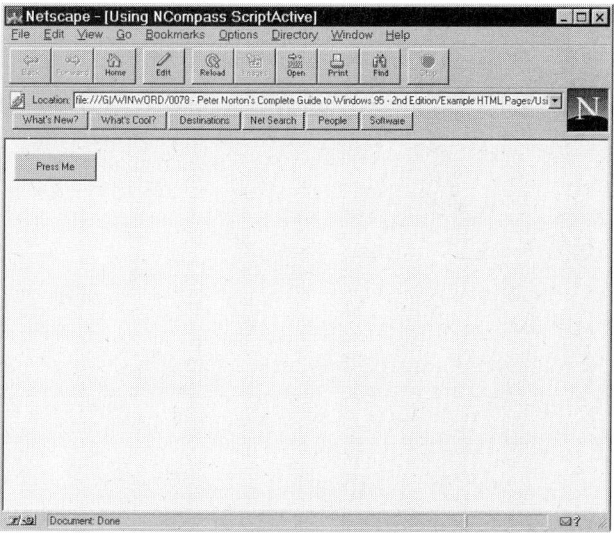

Figure 22.29.
The Internet Explorer-specific version of the test HTML document now works with Netscape Navigator as well.

Using Internet Assistant for Microsoft Word

Programming by hand isn't the only way to create HTML documents. There are a number of products on the market that allow you to create HTML, using tools you might find more familiar. One of those tools is designed to work with the Microsoft Office suite of products—Internet Assistant. You'd need a different version of the program for each Office product, but they all do one thing—reduce the complexity of creating Web pages.

Unlike ActiveX Control Pad, Internet Assistant is end-user-oriented. It provides a lot more in the way of hand-holding for the first-time developer. You'll also find that Internet Assistant isn't nearly as flexible as ActiveX Control Pad—it controls the appearance of your final Web pages in a number of ways. Internet Assistant is also somewhat limited. For example, it doesn't support incorporation of objects and you can't use it to create ActiveX control-enabled pages. In essence, Internet Assistant is a great tool for creating content pages, but not such a good tool for creating things such as forms.

We can't look at every nuance of Internet Assistant, but I'd at least like to give you an overview of how it works. This section covers the Microsoft Word version of Internet Assistant. You can download it at `http://www.microsoft.com/word/internet/ia/`.

Tip: You can find Internet Assistant for Access at `http://www.microsoft.com/access/internet/ia/`. The Excel version of Internet Assistant is at `http://www.microsoft.com/excel/internet/ia/`. There are versions of Internet Assistant for PowerPoint and Schedule+ as well. You'll find the PowerPoint version at `http://www.microsoft.com/powerpoint/internet/ia/` and the Schedule+ version at `http://www.microsoft.com/scheduleplus/internet/ia/`. Any of these versions allows you to convert standard documents to HTML pages.

Some Usage Details

Once you install Internet Assistant for Word, you'll find a couple of new features in the word processor. The first feature appears on the File menu. There are two new menu entries. The first entry is Open URL. Selecting this entry displays a dialog box similar to the one shown in Figure 22.30. If you enter an URL in this dialog box, Word literally takes you to the Internet site you've requested. (Obviously, Internet access must be set up on your machine before you can use this feature.) The first thing you see is the standard connection dialog box that you're accustomed to seeing when using your browser. After Word makes a connection, it downloads the Web page you've requested and converts it into something that Word can use for display purposes.

Figure 22.30.
The Open URL dialog box takes you to your favorite Internet site without opening your browser first.

Being able to surf the Web without leaving your word processor probably sounds perfect. Lest you think that you can replace your browser with Microsoft Word, however, let's take a look at an actual Web site. Microsoft's Word home page seems appropriate for this section. Figure 22.31 shows how this site looks when viewed from within Microsoft Word. All the links work, but, as you'll notice, not everything converted. (As an example of the conversion problem, notice the `Display Text cannot span more than one line` error messages displayed in the figure.) Figure 22.32 shows how this same site looks when viewed from Internet Explorer. This is more of what you'd expect to see. It's a good idea to think of Internet Assistant as a work in progress—a tool that you can use, albeit an imperfect one.

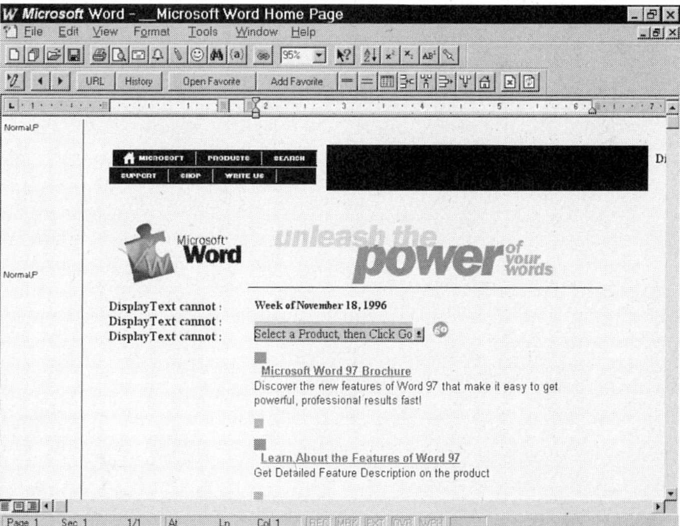

Figure 22.31.
Word can't convert some of the elements on this Web site.

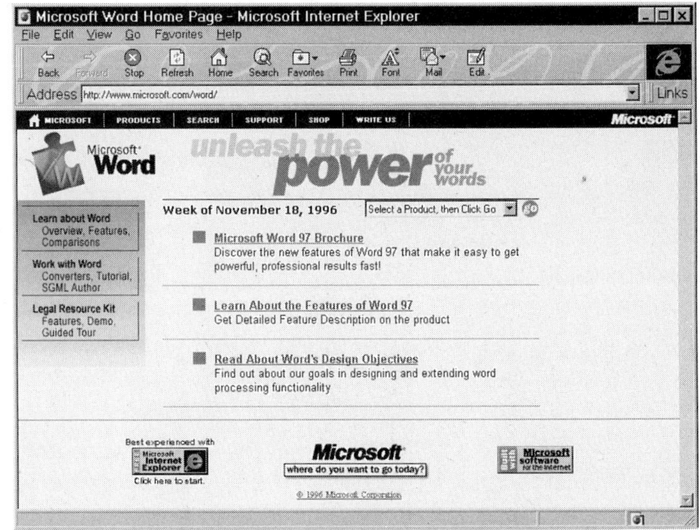

Figure 22.32.
This is how the same site looks when viewed from Internet Explorer.

The second new menu item that Internet Assistant places on the File menu is a bit more complicated. It's the Browse Web entry that allows you to move from your company network to an intranet, or even to the Internet, without really thinking about it. The secret is hyperlinks—the link and anchor tags that I talked about previously. You can create a link to anything, just about anywhere. Selecting the Browse Web entry of the File menu automatically displays the DEFAULT.DOC file in your Internet Assistant folder (normally located within the Program Files folder). Figure 22.33 shows the first version of DEFAULT.DOC that you'll see. (You can also modify this page to take you anywhere you need to go.) Remember, though, that the display you'll see of some Web sites will be less than perfect. Because the process for modifying this default Web link page is the same as working with any other document you want to create, I'll cover it in the "Starting a Document" section of this chapter.

Let's look at the third new element that Internet Assistant adds to the standard Word interface. It's a button on the left side of the Style list box. The button allows you to move from Web Browser view to Edit view. You can see a Switch to Edit View version of this button in Figure 22.31. The Switch to Web Browser View version appears in Figure 22.33. You should see something else when comparing these two figures—the toolbar changes. When you go to Web Browser view, the toolbar contains the tools that you need to create a Web page. Moving back to Edit view allows you to modify the content of the page by using standard editing tools.

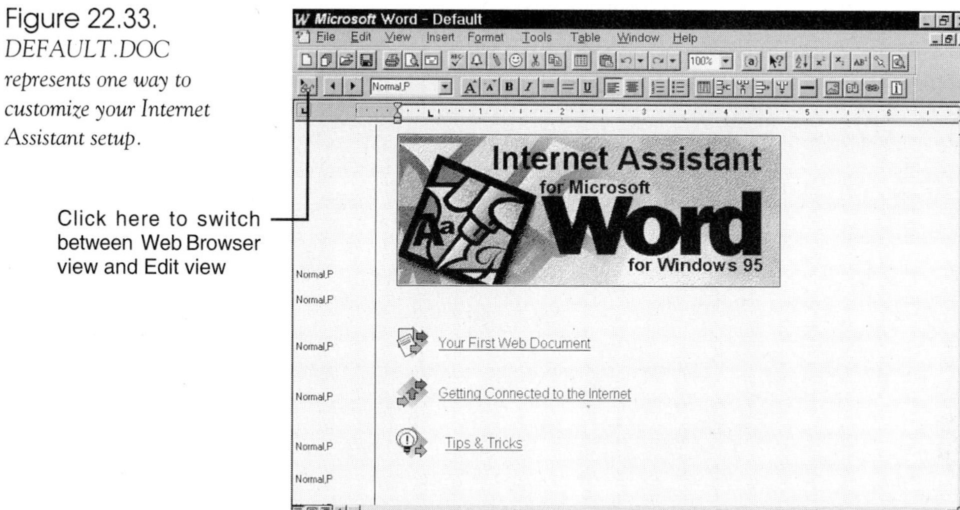

Figure 22.33. *DEFAULT.DOC represents one way to customize your Internet Assistant setup.*

Tip: You can use the View | Web Browse command to move to the Web Browse view. The View | HTML Edit command takes you to the Edit view. While using the button on the toolbar is easier, the menu option comes in handy for creating macros.

There are four buttons on the Web Browse version of the toolbar that I'd like to talk about. You can see them in Figure 22.31. The URL button displays the same Open URL dialog box as in Figure 22.30. Clicking the History button displays a dialog box similar to the one shown in Figure 22.34. The History List serves three purposes. First, you can use it as a means of identifying places you visit quite a bit. Every time you visit a site, it's recorded in the list—until you erase the history. You can also use this dialog box to visit a site by double-clicking the site name or highlighting and clicking the Go To button at the bottom of the dialog box. Finally, you can copy the URL for a site to the Clipboard. We'll see several ways in which you can use this copy in the "Starting a Document" section. You can also use it with the Favorites dialog box that I discuss next.

There are two "favorite places"-related buttons on the Web Browser version of the toolbar. The Open Favorite button displays the document shown in Figure 22.35. You'll also find this document in your Internet Assistant folder as FAVORITE.DOC. Adding new URLs to this document is easy. All you need to do is click the Add Favorite button. (You can also copy an URL to the Clipboard, and then paste it into the document.) Be sure to save the FAVORITE.DOC file while in Edit view, or your changes will be saved as an HTML page.

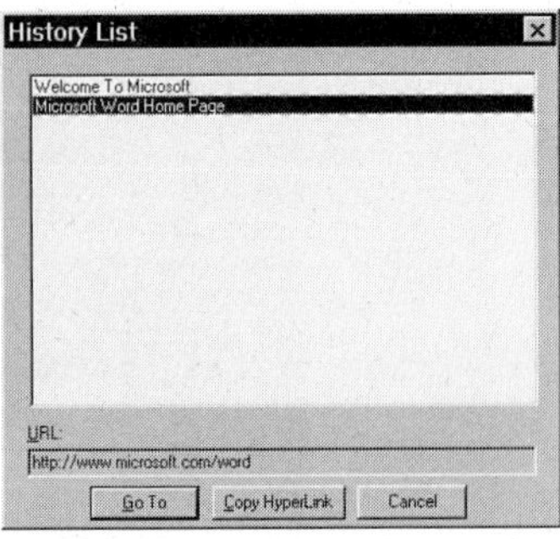

Figure 22.34.
The History List dialog box allows you to get back to a site you've already visited.

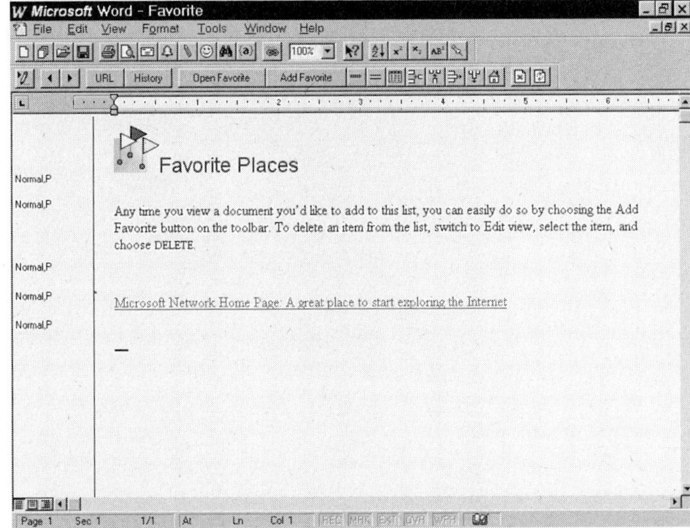

Figure 22.35.
The FAVORITE.DOC file contains a list of the places you like to visit often.

The Web Browser version of the toolbar also contains several Internet-specific buttons. There is a group of three buttons located on the right side in the second row in Figure 22.31. The Home button has a house icon. It always takes you back to DEFAULT.DOC. The Stop button looks like a document with a red X through it. This button stops loading the URL you've selected. Press it if the Web page seems to be taking an extraordinary amount of time to load. Finally, the Reload Document button, which shows a document with two green arrows, reloads the current document, whether it's an URL or a document located on a local server. (The only time you need this is if you're on the Internet and want to make sure that Word downloads the page from the Internet instead of displaying the page stored in the local cache.)

The final two buttons are located in the top row of buttons in Figure 22.31. Word normally hides all the HTML details of a page from you. That way, you don't have to wade through a lot of additional text to find what you need. In some cases it's actually better to see the HTML. Clicking the HTML Hidden button (an "a" between braces, like this: {a}) displays the hidden HTML code for you. The next button to the right is the Copy Hyper Link button, which looks like a pair of anchor chains. You can click this button when visiting a Web site, to place its URL on the Clipboard. We'll see later that you can paste an URL into the FAVORITE.DOC file or use it as part of a new Web page.

Creating an HTML Document with Internet Assistant

Like everything else in Word, creating an HTML document with Internet Assistant starts when you create a Word document. You'll find that there's a new HTML-specific template available in your Template folder named HTML. Use this template to create your page—it contains special styles designed to make converting your .DOC file into an HTML document as easy as possible.

The first thing you'll want to do is give your document a title. That's the same as the `<TITLE>` tag that we talked about earlier. The easy way to do this is to display the HTML Document Head Information dialog box shown in Figure 22.36, by using the File | HTML Document Info command. (This command shows up only if you use the HTML template; you can achieve the same effect by defining a value for the `Title` field in the document Properties dialog box. Display this dialog box by using the File | Properties command and select the Summary page.) You won't see this title in the browser window, just as you don't when you use the `<TITLE>` tag. The title affects the browser's title bar.

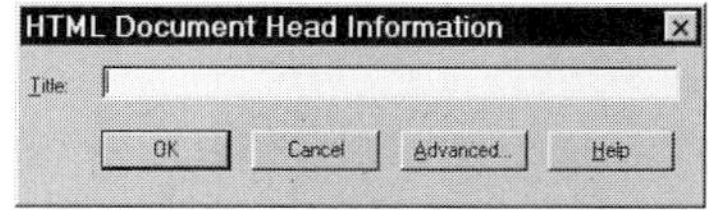

Figure 22.36.
One of the first steps in creating an HTML page using Internet Assistant is defining a title.

Once you have a title in place, you'll probably want to define the overall content of the page by using headings. Make sure that you're in Edit view so that you have access to the Style drop-down list box. Remember that most browsers recognize six different heading levels using the `<H`*`number`*`>` tag. The HTML template provides six heading levels as well. You can even use Word's Outline view to organize your page by clicking the Outline View button in the lower-left corner of the screen. You'll also notice that only the Align Left and Center buttons are available on the toolbar. That's because you can't justify or right-align text on the Internet. Figure 22.37 shows the general outline I created for this example.

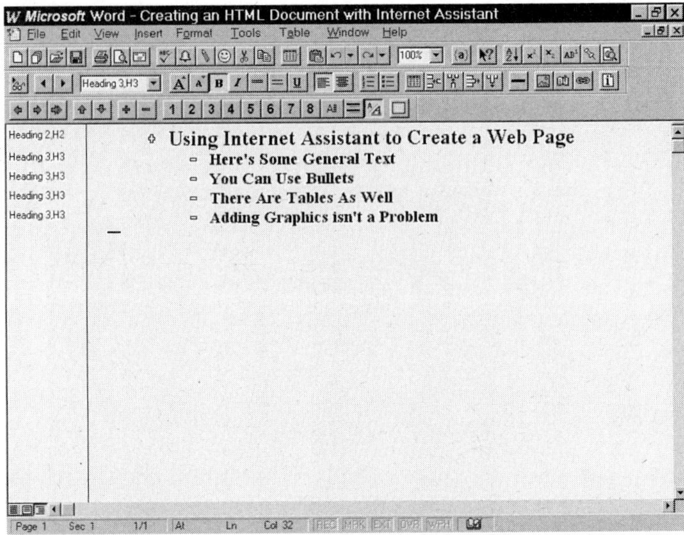

Figure 22.37.
A good way to start designing your Web page is to create an outline.

With the headings in place, you can start filling in the document by using various styles provided by the template. General text uses the Normal,P style. Let's talk about the styles for a second. Normal is the type of paragraph and P stands for the HTML tag associated with the style. In this case, the template is telling you that every paragraph will end with a `<P>` tag.

The earlier section "Creating Your First Useful Page" covered character-formatting tags such as `<EM>` and `<STRONG>`. You can use these same styles when using the HTML template. Simply highlight the text you want to format, and then select the appropriate character-formatting style from the Style list box. For example, if you want to use the `<EM>` tag, you select the Emphasis style.

Tip: You can use the Bold (labeled **B**) and Italic (labeled *I*) buttons on the toolbar to add the `<STRONG>` and `<EM>` tags to highlighted text. The styles listed in the Style list box don't include combinations of tags—only one tag is used at a time. You may want to add new styles that allow you to add multiple tags to specific areas of text.

Earlier, I covered the various kinds of bullet lists that you can create for HTML pages: unordered list, ordered list, and glossary. There are styles for each kind of list in the HTML template. For example, the unordered list uses the List Bullet,UL style. Notice that we didn't have to define the `<LI>` tag for an unordered list—that's because Internet Assistant adds it for you automatically. Whatever you see on the page is what you'll see in the browser. In essence, this means that you don't need to add any additional tags if the output looks correct—it's safe to assume that Internet Assistant adds them for you automatically in most cases.

The only type of list that may be a bit difficult to figure out at first is the glossary list. The HTML template provides four styles here: Definition Compact,DL COMPACT; Definition List,DL; Definition Term,DT; and Definition,DFN. If you're a bit confused about the lack of a `<DD>` tag, don't be. For whatever reason, it's not included as part of the template, so you have to define it (especially if you plan to use your site with Netscape Navigator, which doesn't appear to support the `<DFN>` tag). Defining a new tag style is relatively easy in this case. Just use the Format | Style command to display the Style dialog box. Highlight the Definition Term,DT entry in the Styles list and then click New. You'll see a New Style dialog box. At this point, select Character in the Style Type field. Type **`Definition Data,DD`** in the Name field. If you want, you can choose a different character format (I chose italic) by using the Format | Font command. Click OK in the New Style dialog box to add the style, and then Cancel to close the Style dialog box. The process for creating a glossary list is also a little different. Start by selecting either the Definition Compact,DL COMPACT or the Definition List,DL paragraph style. You type both the term and the definition on one line. Highlight the term and then select the Definition Term,DT character style. Do the same for the definition, but use the Definition,DFN or Definition Data,DD style.

Tables are a real cinch when using Internet Assistant. Remember the really long set of tags we had to write by hand in the "Basic Formatting Tags for Everyone" section of the chapter? All you need to do in Word is create a table the same way you always have. You have total control over the width of each column, the kind of text, and the width of the border elements. The only limitations that you'll suffer are the ones placed on you by HTML. There are a few things that you'll want to remember. Tables are a bit hard to read in a browser if you don't use a border. Unfortunately, that's the default setting for Internet Assistant, so be sure to set up the border before saving your document. There isn't any way to define the space between columns, either. This means that you'll want to define the table in such a way that the text is still easy to read without this adjustment. If nothing else, widen the border that you use, to make the text easier to read.

Now we come to a special part of the page composition process. Adding graphics, links, horizontal rules, and other special page features is easy. All you need to do is look on the Insert menu to see the entries required to get the job done. We'll look at two of the more common tasks: adding hyperlinks and adding graphics. First, let's look at the task you'll always have to do on a Web site—adding hyperlinks. You'll see a Hyperlink dialog box like the one shown in Figure 22.38.

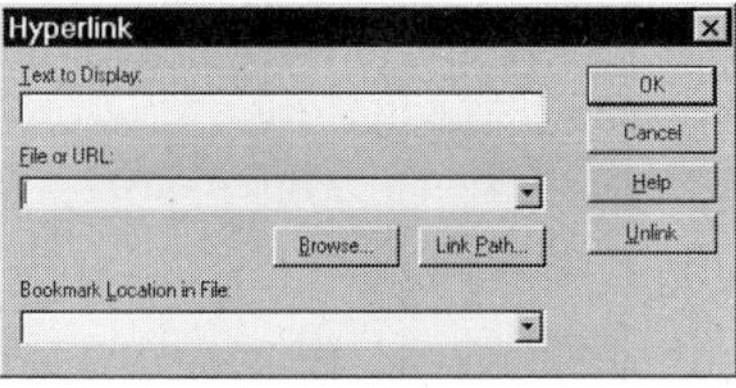

Figure 22.38.
The Hyperlink dialog box allows you to add links and anchors to your Web page.

There are three different kinds of basic links you can create using this dialog box. In the first case, you type the URL of a Web site in the File or URL field. In the second case, you type the name of a file in the same field. Notice the Browse button right under the File or URL field. This allows you to find a file on your local drive or network instead of typing it in by hand. (Theoretically, you can use this to find URLs as well, but this feature probably won't work right until Microsoft releases Internet Explorer 4.0.) The third type of link takes you to an anchor on the same page. However, instead of actually defining an anchor, you define a bookmark instead. Just select one of the bookmarks in the Bookmark Location in File field. Don't type anything in the File or URL field unless the bookmark is located in a different document. All three link types require you to type something in the Text to Display field. This is the text that appears underlined on the Web page.

Inserting graphics isn't very difficult, either. All you need to do is use the Insert | Picture command to display the Picture dialog box shown in Figure 22.39. Adding a picture consists of typing the location and graphic name into the Image Source field. You'll also want to supply some text in the Alternative Text field. This text is displayed if the user's browser doesn't support graphic images. Make this text as descriptive as possible, because you can never be sure when someone will at least want to get a mind's-eye view of the picture you supplied.

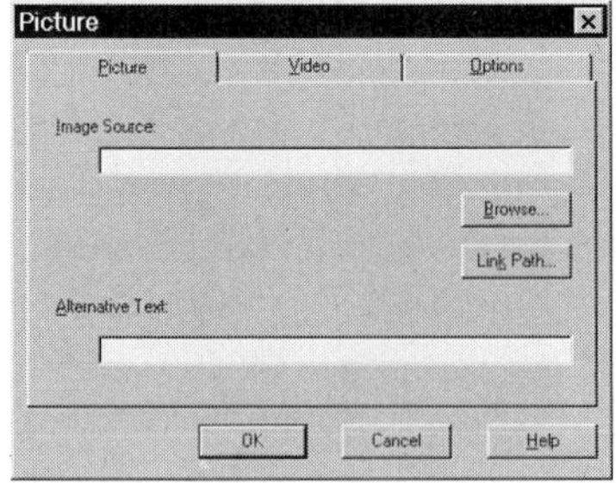

Figure 22.39.
Adding pictures is a two-step process.

Tip: You may be used to using .BMP or .PCX pictures for everything under Windows, but the Internet doesn't use those formats. The standard Internet formats for graphics are .JPG and .GIF. Of the two, .GIF is probably the most-used graphic type for small images. The "Creating Animated .GIFs" section of this chapter discusses a special animated form of this graphic. .JPG (JPEG) is designed for photographic-quality images.

If you want your pictures to be a certain size or shape, you need to select the Options page of the Picture dialog box shown in Figure 22.40. This page allows you to change things such as the picture size. It also allows you to define a frame. I find this particular feature extremely handy, because it gives the person visiting your site some idea of what size picture to expect.

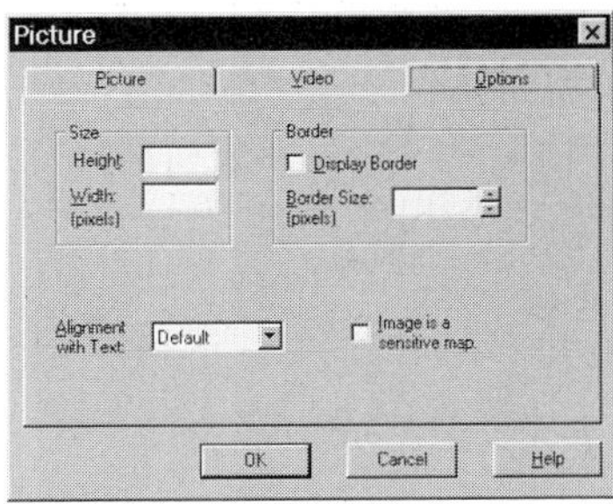

Figure 22.40.
The Options page of the Picture dialog box allows you to refine the image presentation.

Once your page is put together, it's time to save it. Make sure that you're in Edit view (the one where the glasses show in the Switch to Web Browser View button on the toolbar). Using this mode saves your document as a .DOC file. Now click the Switch to Web Browser View button and save the document again. This time, you'll end up with an .HTM extension document that you can view within a browser. At this point, you'll want to test your Web page to make sure that it looks as anticipated. Figure 22.41 shows the sample page I created using Internet Assistant while writing this section of the chapter.

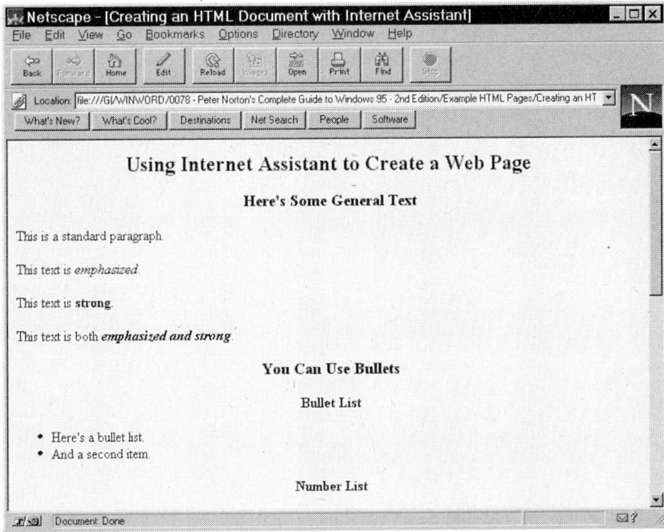

Figure 22.41.
Internet Assistant makes it possible to put Web pages together without worrying about a single tag.

Advanced HTML Tags that Really Count

There are more HTML tags out there than we can ever attempt to cover in one chapter of a book. What we've looked at so far are the tags that you'd have to know to do just about anything on the Internet. What about those tags that are nice to have, but not absolutely essential? That's what we talk about in this section of the chapter. We look at some tags that add pizzazz to your Web site.

Tip: The average user visiting your Web site probably has a 14.4 Kbps modem, which can download information from the Internet at 1 Kbps on a good day. That means that if you have a 10KB .GIF on your site, it will take ten seconds for the user to download. It doesn't take too many of these small files to convince the user to click the Stop button and go to the next site. A good rule of thumb to follow is that a user will wait no longer than 60 seconds to download a Web page.

Let's begin with a very simple tag. If you've visited Web sites very much, you've noticed that a lot of them use horizontal rules to separate sections or provide a visual pause in the display. The `<HR>` tag is responsible for the rules you see. There are several ways to enhance this particular tag, but the two most common methods are the `WIDTH` and `SIZE` attributes. Unfortunately, using these attributes is a bit counterintuitive, so I set up a Web page of horizontal rules to show you the effects you can achieve. Figure 22.42 shows the result. As you can see, increasing the value of the `SIZE` attribute changes what many people would associate with the width of the line. The `WIDTH` attribute changes are normally associated with length. One of the rules of thumb you should remember is that when designing Internet pages, the `WIDTH` attribute normally refers to the x axis. Look at the last horizontal rule. Instead of a measurement in pixels, I used a percentage. This line resizes itself as the user resizes the browser window. You can usually use a percentage in place of a specific pixel or character measurement whenever the `WIDTH` attribute is used. Notice that I've used the `<CENTER>` tag to center the rules on the page—a combination that you'll normally see.

Tip: Internet Explorer allows you to use two other attributes with the `<HR>` tag that Netscape Navigator doesn't appear to support. The first is `COLOR`. You can use this attribute to make the horizontal rule something other than the default colors. The second is `ALIGN`. You can use this attribute to align the horizontal rule at right, left, or center.

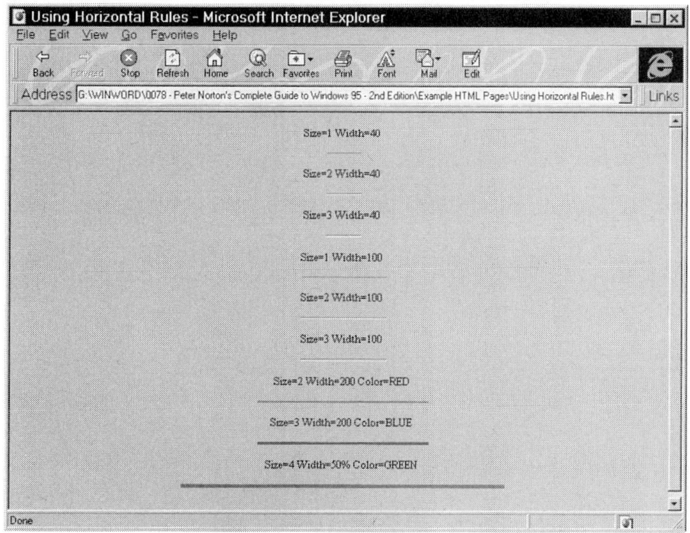

Figure 22.42.
Horizontal rules are an extremely efficient way to add a little pizzazz to your Web page.

Sound is another feature that people really like to add to their Web sites. Unfortunately, this is yet another area where the browser wars force you to do more work than needed. The following code shows what I'm talking about:

```
<HTML>
<HEAD>
<TITLE>Using Sound</TITLE>
</HEAD>
<BODY>

<!-Play a sound sample.->
<CENTER><H2>Playing the Twilight Zone Theme</H2></CENTER>

<!-Internet Explorer specific->
<BGSOUND SRC="TwilZone.WAV" LOOP=1>

<!-Netscape Navigator specific->
<EMBED SRC="TwilZone.WAV" LOOP=1 HIDDEN=TRUE>

</BODY>
</HTML>
```

Playing the sound isn't difficult, but getting it to play in different browsers is another story. I had to use an `<EMBED>` tag to get the sound to play in Navigator. On the other hand, Internet Explorer ignores the `<EMBED>` tag and uses the `<BGSOUND>` tag instead. You don't get precisely the same results when using these two tags, either. Navigator downloads the entire sound byte before playing it. Because it relies on a helper application, you can't interrupt the sound once it begins to play. Internet Explorer appears to start playing the sound as it downloads. In addition, because the `<BGSOUND>` tag is handled locally, you can interrupt the sound—a convenience factor for people working in an office environment. Notice that I've also introduced a new attribute in this example. The LOOP attribute tells a tag how long to play. In this case, I played the sound file once, and then stopped. The HIDDEN attribute tells the browser that you don't want to display an icon for this file—it's a hidden element on the page.

Graphics are another big source of pizzazz for Internet sites. The downside to using graphics is that they tend to consume a lot of space and can greatly increase the download time for a page. The idea of getting great-looking graphics to your screen fast has spurred more than a few conversations. A whole range of vendors has worked on solutions from graphics compression to an assortment of display techniques. Suffice it to say that using graphics on a Web page is one of those items that you'll have to consider carefully. A well-designed graphic can take an otherwise drab Web site and spark it up.

We're not going to look at even a small percentage of the graphics solutions in this chapter. The two kinds of graphics that most people use are .JPG and .GIF. As previously mentioned, .JPG graphics are normally reserved for photographic-quality images. Most people use .GIF files for things such as clip art, because they consume less space. Using either kind of graphic requires the same technique: You add an <IMG> tag to your code to display the image. There are a whole range of attributes associated with the <IMG> tag as well. The most important (and only required) attribute is SRC. You must specify a source for the image. Other attributes include WIDTH, HEIGHT, ALIGN, ALT, BORDER, and LOOP. The WIDTH and HEIGHT attributes determine how big the image is drawn. The ALIGN attribute specifies how the graphic will be aligned with respect to text and other graphics. The three common alignment values are top, middle, and bottom. I consider the ALT attribute very important even though it's not required. This attribute provides a text description of the graphic in case the browser doesn't support graphics. The reason that this particular attribute is so important is that blind users can at least get a mental picture of what you're talking about on the Web site. A lot of users are also turning off graphics as Web sites become more complicated and therefore more time-consuming to download. The BORDER attribute is also more than a simple convenience item. It draws a border around the graphic. Because this border is displayed before the graphic, a user can determine how big the graphic will be and whether he wants to wait for it to download. The LOOP attribute isn't used with static images; I discuss it in the "Creating Animated .GIFs" section of the chapter.

I previously mentioned that graphic download size could become a problem when someone visits your Web site. (Sound files present similar problems, though not to such a degree, because you'll have one or perhaps two sounds on your site, at most.) There are things that you can do to make your site attractive and still reduce the time needed to download the page:

- **Reduce image size:** A number of products on the market help you shrink the size of an image. In many cases, you can shrink the image by half in each direction without making it hard to see or too grainy. A reduction of that amount reduces the size of an image by a factor of 4. A 100KB image will take only 25KB when you finish shrinking it.

- **Reduce the number of colors:** Some people think that every image has to use 24-bit color, but how many computers can actually display that many? A good rule of thumb is to use 256 colors for art and 16 colors for icons. Pictures—actual images that are captured with a camera—probably need more colors, depending on the quality of the image you want to present. A color reduction usually reduces your image size by a factor of 2.
- **Avoid realistic art:** You may want to see that picture of your best friend displayed on your Web site, but it's pretty safe to say that no one else will be too thrilled about it. Unless you absolutely must have a pictorial image of some idea or concept, use art instead. Try to present your ideas in the simplest ways possible. Using realistic art almost always increases image size by a factor of 10.
- **Use compression if possible:** This may seem a bit weird when you first think about it, but what stops you from downloading compressed graphics to a user's machine and then blowing them back up by using an ActiveX control? Compression can reduce an image by a factor of 5 or more. Even if you don't want to go this route, some Netscape plug-ins will help you accomplish the same thing. But you will have to give up something to get the incredible space savings that compression can provide—compatibility.
- **Use animation sparingly:** Animated .GIFs are actually created using a series of images. Even if you use the image-cropping techniques, you'll find that an animated .GIF can quickly become more bother than it's worth. Make sure that you keep animated images small and pertinent.
- **Give users a method of escape:** There are many ways to do this, but most Web sites simply provide a link that turns off the graphics display. Users still get the use of the site, but they see text instead of graphics. You could even provide an intermediate level of user interface by including a tag that allows users to turn off animation without affecting the rest of the graphics they see.

Internet Explorer users have another trick up their sleeves when it comes to adding pizzazz to a Web page. The `<MARQUEE>` tag displays scrolling text. You can scroll the text horizontally or vertically. In addition, there are attributes to control the rate and direction of scroll. This tag is an extremely easy method for adding animated text to your Web page. Unfortunately, Navigator doesn't support this tag, so I usually refrain from using it. (I haven't even seen this tag used on Microsoft sites.)

Creating Animated .GIFs

Even if the previous section didn't show you enough techniques to make your Web site sparkle, there are other ideas that you can use. A favorite idea of Webmasters the world over is the use of animated .GIFs. An animated .GIF packs several pictures into one file. The browser plays these pictures back, one at a time—allowing you to create the illusion of continuous animation. You can also use special effects to create a slide show using a .GIF. The only problem with this approach is the download time—a slide show tends to put quite a strain on the user's download capability.

Note: This section shows you how to create a .GIF by using GIF Construction Set from Alchemy Mind Works. You can download it from several places. The best place is straight from the vendor at `http://www.mindworkshop.com/alchemy/gifcon.html`.

We'll use GIF Construction Set for this section for two reasons. First, because it's shareware, you can download it from the Internet and follow along with the examples. Second, it's a really great program, and most people find that it works just fine for creating animated .GIFs. At most, you'll notice the lack of an actual drawing program with this program, but Windows already supplies that in the form of Paintbrush or MS Paint. You also need a graphics conversion utility if your drawing program doesn't support the .GIF file format directly (neither Paintbrush nor MS Paint does). Both Graphics Workshop from Alchemy Mind Works and Paint Shop Pro by JASC, Inc. are excellent graphics-conversion programs. Both vendors provide shareware versions of their product. You can find Alchemy Mind Works at the Internet site provided in the previous note. The JASC product appears on various BBS and CompuServe forums (GO JASC). You can reach them on the Internet at `http://www.jasc.com/`. Figure 22.43 shows the initial screen that you'll see when you open GIF Construction Set. This is the display that you'll normally use for opening files.

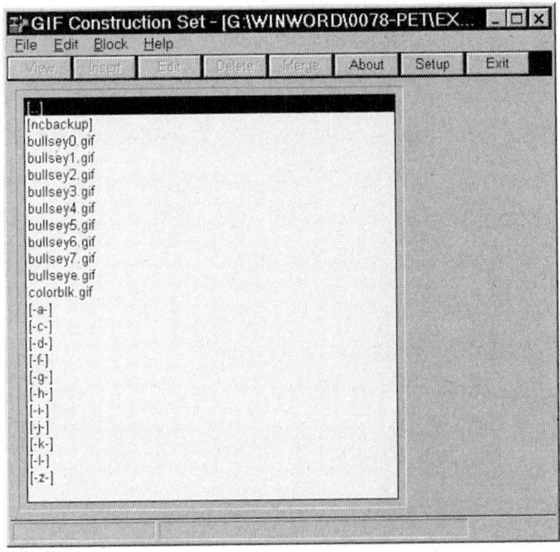

Figure 22.43.
GIF Construction Set displays this dialog box whenever you need to look for files.

Notice that the directory shown has several .GIF files in it already. For this example, I show you how to create a short animation that draws a bullseye on the screen and then displays the word **BULLSEYE** in capital letters. BULLSEYE.GIF is a base file—a blank used to create the animation effect. You can save a substantial amount of time by creating such a blank whenever you create an animation. In fact, cartoonists use this very technique. They draw the common elements of an animation once on separate sheets, and then combine them to create the animation. Only unique items are drawn one at a time. BULLSEY0.GIF through BULLSEY7.GIF are the actual animation files—think of each one as an animation cel. (A cel is one picture in the animated series.)

Tip: You can see animated .GIFs in action on many Internet sites. One of the more interesting places to look is `http://www.wanderers.com/rose/animate.html`. This site offers an index of sites that you can visit to see various kinds of animated .GIFs. Looking at a variety of sites helps you understand what works and what doesn't. You can also download an animated .GIF wizard, make your own animated .GIF online, and learn all about how to make animated .GIFs.

Let's create an animated .GIF using these "cel" files. The following procedure isn't meant to lock you into a particular regimen, but it does show one way to use GIF Construction Set to create an animated .GIF:

1. Use the File | New command to create a new .GIF. You'll see a blank dialog box like the one shown in Figure 22.44. A .GIF always contains a header, which tells an application what kind of compression technique the .GIF uses and other factors such as the size of each cel in the file. The GIF Construction Set always assumes a standard display size of 640 × 480 pixels. You need to change that value.

Figure 22.44.
A new .GIF file is blank except for the header entry.

2. Double-click the HEADER entry. You'll see the Edit Header dialog box shown in Figure 22.45, which allows you to change characteristics associated with the .GIF—for example, its size.

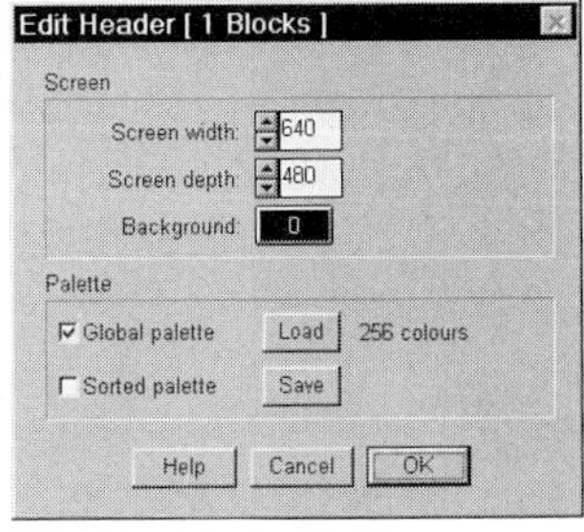

Figure 22.45.
The Edit Header dialog box allows you to change the .GIF characteristics.

3. Type a new size in both the Screen Width and Screen Depth fields to match the size of your image. (Your paint program should supply this value—make sure that all the cels that you plan to use in the .GIF are precisely the same size.) For this example, use a value of 150 for both fields. Let's take a quick look at the other fields. The Background field allows you to change the background color used when you can see through various areas of the cels you've provided (for example, the transparent color used in drawing icons). The Global Palette check box tells other applications that you're using a global palette. If all the cels use the same color settings, checking this box reduces the size of the overall .GIF, because you won't have to store a palette with each image. The Load and Save buttons allow you to load and save previously stored palettes. The final check box, Sorted Palette, indicates that the global palette is sorted. This particular check box won't help much when creating animated .GIFs for the Internet—don't set it.
4. Click OK to make the change permanent. The dimensions shown in the .GIF header should change to the new settings. For the purposes of this example, they've changed to 150 × 150. Now it's time to start adding images.
5. Click the Merge button. This allows you to add an image to the .GIF. You'll see a standard File | Open dialog box.
6. Double-click the first file you want to use in the animation. In this case, double-click BULLSEYE.GIF to set up the standard background. In most cases, the palette for any graphics you draw won't match the standard palette used by GIF Construction Set, so you'll see the Palette dialog box shown in Figure 22.46.

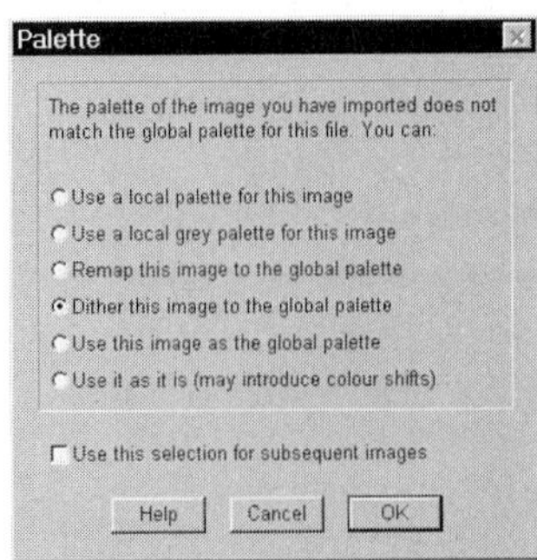

Figure 22.46.
The Palette dialog box is displayed if the palette of your drawings doesn't match the palette used by GIF Construction Set.

7. Because all the images in this animation use the same palette, you'll want to select the setting Use This Image as the Global Palette. If you want to use a different palette for each image (or a special palette for some images), select Use a Local Palette for This Image. Likewise, if the palette of this image is supposed to match the palette used by the other images, select Remap This Image to the Global Palette.
8. Click OK to complete the process. GIF Construction Set inserts a new graphic into the .GIF, as shown in Figure 22.47. Notice that you can see a preview of the image to the right of the entry. You can use this feature to make sure that you're loading the images in order. Numbering the images (as I've done in the example) helps as well. Notice that the image entry also tells you the size of the image and the number of colors it uses.

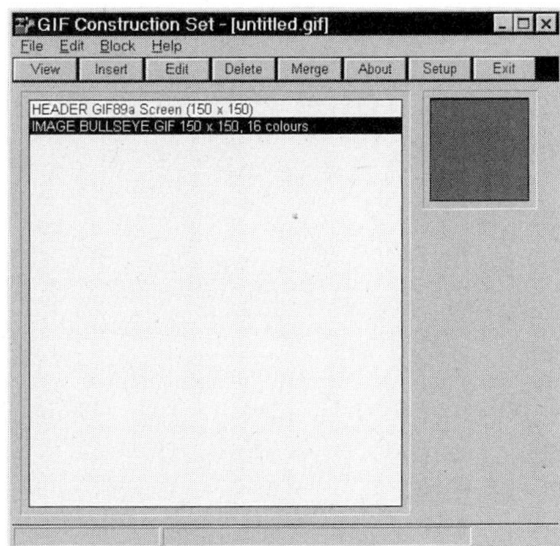

Figure 22.47.
Every image entry in an animated .GIF tells you about itself.

9. Click the Merge button. You'll see the same File | Open dialog box as before.
10. Select the next image in the series and click OK. Click OK again if GIF Construction Set asks you about the palette setting. GIF Construction Set automatically inserts the image in the next position of the animation sequence.
11. Repeat steps 9 and 10 for the remaining .GIFs in the animation. Once you complete this step, your dialog box should contain a list of cels (drawings). Figure 22.48 shows the list of drawings for my example .GIF. Notice that all nine images are in order. Now we have to insert some controls to make this image work properly.

Figure 22.48.
Adding all the drawings required to create the animated .GIF is only the first step.

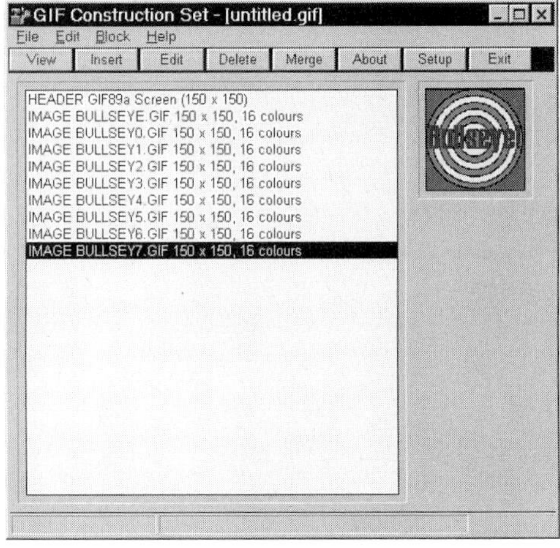

12. Click the Insert button and you'll see the menu shown in Figure 22.49. This menu contains every kind of object you can insert into an animated .GIF. The two you'll use most often are Loop and Control. A loop allows you to define how long the animation continues to go through a sequence of pictures. Wise use of `Loop` objects can create some pretty interesting effects. Unfortunately, many browsers ignore this particular entry, so you may want to use it sparingly. (If a browser ignores the `Loop` object, it simply keeps the animated .GIF looping forever.) Controls allow you to modify the behavior of the animated .GIF. For example, you can use a control to set the time between pictures. The Image entry is pretty obvious; every picture you want to add to the animated .GIF is an image. You'll use comments to document the behavior of your animated GIF, which is especially important if you plan to allow other people to use it. Plain text is simply that—text that's displayed as part of the animation.

Figure 22.49.
The Insert Object menu shows the kinds of objects that you can insert into the animated .GIF file.

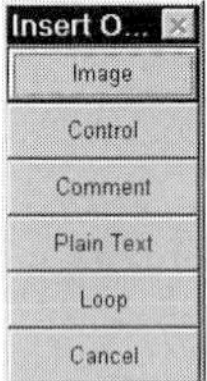

13. Select the Loop entry in the menu. GIF Construction Set automatically places it under the Header entry. Now we need to place `Control` objects between each picture to time the animation sequence. The rule of thumb here is that the `Control` object immediately preceding an image controls how that image appears.
14. Click the Loop entry. GIF Construction Set normally places the next entry right below the one you click.

15. Click the Insert button and select Control from the menu. You'll see a `Control` entry added to the list, as shown in Figure 22.50.

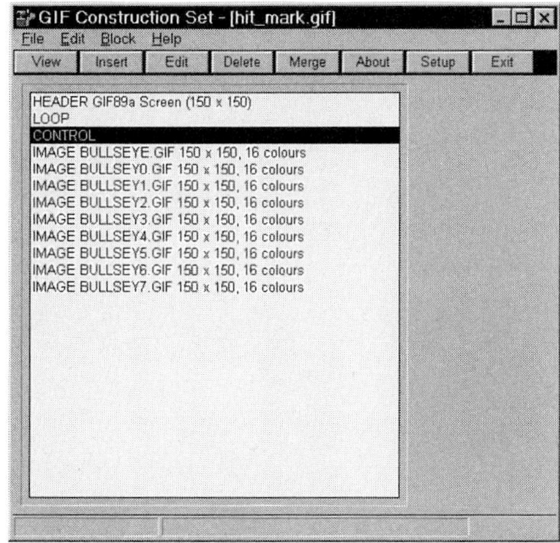

Figure 22.50.
Make sure that you get the `Control` *entries before each image.*

16. Click the next image entry.
17. Repeat steps 15 and 16 for each of the images. You'll end up with a series of `Image` and `Control` objects, as shown in Figure 22.51. (Be sure to add a `Control` object after the last image, because the animated .GIF automatically loops back to the first image.) Now we need to set up the `Control` objects so that our animated .GIF "plays" the way we want it to.

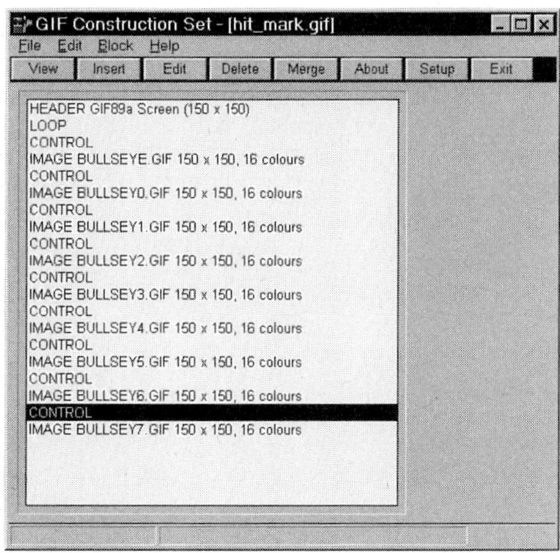

Figure 22.51.
The animated .GIF now contains all the drawings and `Control` *objects needed to make it run properly.*

18. Normally you'll find that the default time period between pictures works pretty well. However, let's take a look at what you'd need to do to change the setting. Double-click the last `Control` object entry. You'll see the dialog box shown in Figure 22.52. The most commonly used entry is the `Delay` field. You can use it to control the speed of the animation. The Transparent Color check box allows whatever appears below the .GIF to show through in the areas that are displayed with a certain color. Clicking the button allows you to select the transparent color. The Wait for User Input check box tells the animation to pause at this point in the animation and wait for the user to provide some kind of input. Normally, the user will press a key. Finally, the Remove By field allows you to determine what to do with this animation cel once the browser displays it. Make sure that you leave this entry alone; otherwise, you'll get unpredictable results from some browsers.

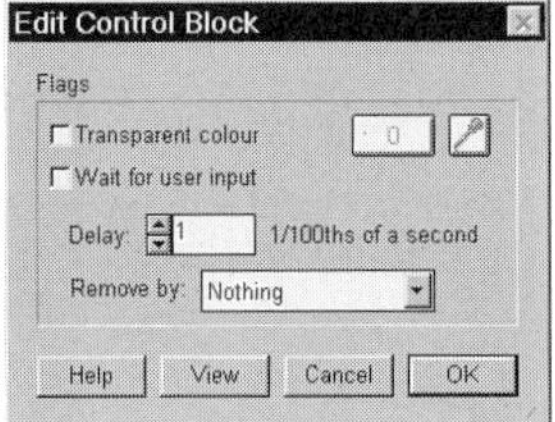

Figure 22.52.
The Edit Control Block dialog box allows you to change animated .GIF features such as the delay between drawings.

19. In this case, I want the animated .GIF to pause after it displays the word BULLSEYE, so I changed the Delay field setting to 50. Remember that a user needs time to read text, so you should add an extra delay for any text screens.
20. I also wanted a slight pause before BULLSEYE is displayed, so I double-clicked the `Control` entry right before the BULLSEY6.GIF image entry. In this case, I changed the Delay field to 100. This is just enough time to add that bit of "suspense" that people associate with some of the better animations. The bottom line is that the `Control` entry settings you choose between the images in an animation depend a great deal on the effect you want to achieve.
21. Let's view the completed animation. Click the View button, and you'll see a screen similar to the one shown in Figure 22.53.

Note: Some animated .GIF features may not work the same when viewing them within GIF Construction Set as they do in a browser. This is especially true of time delays set by `Control` objects, which are greatly exaggerated in GIF Construction Set. The best idea is to check the animated .GIF within GIF Construction Set for general features, and then use a browser for final testing.

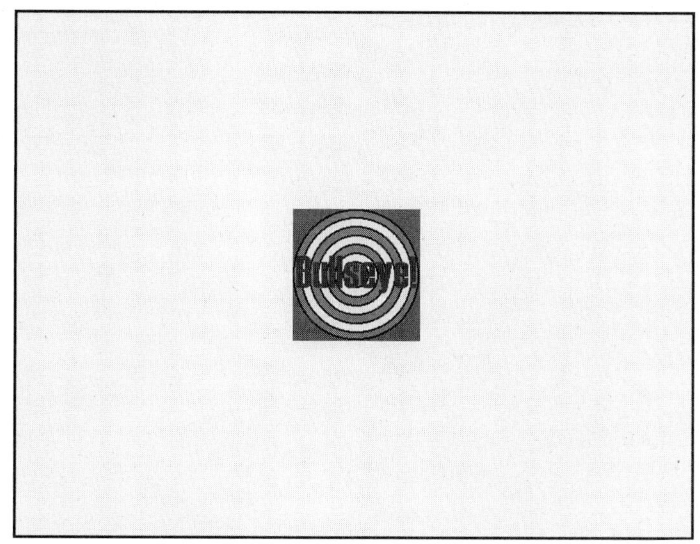

Figure 22.53.
Once you complete your animation, use the View button to see how it acts. You may want to make some changes.

22. Press Escape to exit the viewing area.
23. The only thing left to do is save your animated .GIF file. Use the File | Save As command to do that. You could use any filename, but for the purposes of this example, save the file as Hit_Mark.GIF.

If you look at the size of even the modest animation created for this example, you'll find that it consumes about 13.3KB of disk space. That's almost one third of your budget for a typical Web page (if you want the user to download it in a reasonable amount of time). What you've got to consider at this point is whether the animation is worth the added memory burden. Fortunately, there's another way to deal with the problem. Double-click any of the `Image` objects and you'll see an Edit Image dialog box like the one shown in Figure 22.54.

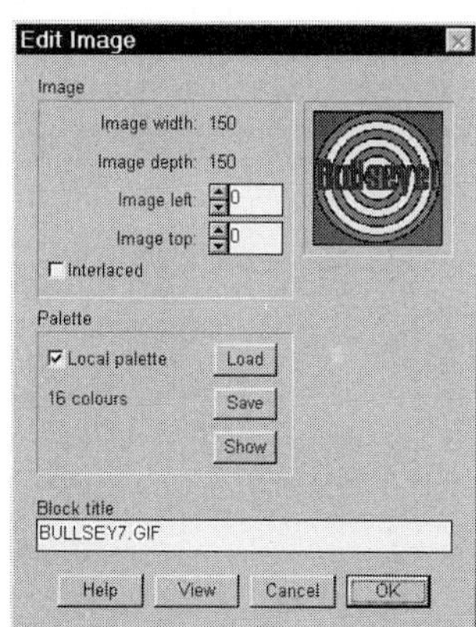

Figure 22.54.
The Edit Image dialog box allows you to change the way an animation is drawn.

Notice the Image Left and Image Top fields. These fields allow you to choose a starting point for each image in the animation. You really don't need to redisplay the entire bullseye every time the animation cel changes. You only need to overwrite the previous circle within the center of the bullseye and replace it with the next one in the series. Cropping each image so that the previous circle is covered and the new one displayed could reduce the size of your animated .GIF by 75 percent. In other words, that 13.3KB file would be reduced to about 3.3KB. The only thing you need to do is crop the image with your paint program, reinsert it into the animated .GIF file using the procedure just covered, and then use the Image Top and Image Left fields to place the cropped image correctly on the display. This dialog box also allows you to choose a new palette for the picture and assign it a different name.

Tip: Unless your animated .GIF is very large or your download budget very small, you won't want to take the time to crop every image individually. For example, our sample .GIF would probably work fine if it were the only image on the page.

The Interlaced check box is pretty interesting, too. If this .GIF were designed as a static image, you'd want to check this box. Interlaced images are displayed one line at a time. It's the effect you see on most Web sites when downloading a large graphic. Using an interlaced graphic gives users some visual feedback during the download process, letting them know that the machine hasn't frozen. You'll want to leave this box unchecked for animated .GIFs, though, because displaying an interlaced image takes more time. Checking the Interlaced check box could actually make the animation look pretty jumpy in this case.

Okay, so you don't want to check the Interlaced check box, because it makes your animated .GIF look jumpy and the idea of hand-editing each picture doesn't really appeal to you. There's one additional way to reduce the size of your image, and it's very easy. Notice that the Local Palette check box is checked in this example, yet we planned on using a global palette. A lot of the tools that you use to create animated .GIFs have this problem. As you import images, the first one uses the global palette and the rest use a local palette. Those local palettes consume disk space. Uncheck the Local Palette check box for each of the images. In this case, I managed to reap a .4KB savings—making the size of the file 12.9KB. The savings will be a lot larger if you use a 256-color palette instead of the 16-color palette that I used here. In fact, you can calculate the approximate savings as follows: 3 × number of colors × number of pictures. So, if you had a 256-color palette and 8 pictures, you could save up to 6KB by using a global instead of a local palette for all the images. To give you a better idea of what this 6KB means, it's equivalent to 6 seconds of download time if the user has a 14.4 modem and an average connection.

Simple Scripting with VBScript

Visual Basic Scripting Edition (VBScript) is a full-fledged subset of Visual Basic for Applications (VBA). If you already know how to use either Visual Basic or VBA, you know how to use VBScript. It's that simple.

One of the more interesting uses that Microsoft sees in VBScript's future is using it as a hardware-independent batch-processing language. A hardware vendor could potentially use it as part of an installation program. This may work out eventually, but so far no hardware vendors are using VBScript in place of more standard languages. Likewise, I haven't seen too many software developers using VBScript for anything other than Web site development. One place where VBScript could work out is with Windows CE, the new hand-held PC (HPC) operating system recently introduced by Microsoft. The small, fast-form factor would really help on such a small machine. Of course, Microsoft is quick to point out to everyone that VBScript is free—certainly a plus if you need a small programming language to write an installation routine.

Tip: Internet Explorer supports VBScript right out of the box. You can get Netscape Navigator to use VBScript in some instances if you use a plug-in such as the NCompass ScriptActive product discussed in the earlier section "Using NCompass ScriptActive." You can download a copy of the VBScript documentation from `http://www.microsoft.com/vbscript/`. Microsoft also sponsors a VBScript-specific newsgroup.

Unfortunately, the fact that VBScript is only a subset of VBA means that there are some restrictions on what you can do. Table 22.4 shows how VBScript differs from VBA. As you can see, some of the restrictions are pretty severe, but they're in line with the goal for VBScript—to create a small, fast version of Visual Basic for use with browsers. Microsoft recommends that you use the more capable VBA or Visual Basic if you want to write applications. VBScript is better used as a form of advanced macro language. Fortunately, you can overcome many VBScript limitations through wise use of ActiveX controls. For example, an ActiveX control can help you get around all the file limitations listed in the table.

Note: This table lists both programming and runtime features provided in VBA that don't appear in VBScript.

Table 22.4. VBA features not found in VBScript.

Feature Category	*Missing Features*
Arrays	`Option Base`, declaring arrays with a starting point other than 0
Calling .DLLs	`Declare`
Classes	`TypeName`, `With...End With`
Clipboard	Clipboard object
Collection	`Add`, `Count`, `Item`, `Remove`
Collection access using `!`	`MyCollection!Foo`
Conditional compilation	`#Const`, `#If...#Then...#Else...#End If`
Constants (data types)	`Currency` type, `CCur`
Constants (module level)	`Const`, `Private`, `Dim`, `Public`, `Global`
Constants (procedure level)	`Const`
Constants (runtime)	For the most part, you can't use the full capabilities of constants in the runtime environment. As of this writing, Microsoft hasn't listed all the shortcomings of VBScript in this regard.
Control flow	`DoEvents`, `GoSub...Return`, `GoTo`, line numbers and labels, `OnError...GoTo`, `Select Case`
Conversion	`Chr$`, `Hex$`, `Oct$`, `CVar`, `CVDate`, `CCur`, `Format`, `Format$`, `Str$`, `Str`, `Val`
Data types	`Boolean`, `Byte`, `Currency`, `Date`, `Double`, `Integer`, `Long`, `Object`, `Single`, `String`, type suffixes (`%`, `$`, `!`, etc.), user-defined classes (no `Me`)
Date	`Date` statement, `Date$`, `Timer`
DDE	`LinkExecute`, `LinkPoke`, `LinkRequest`, `LinkSend`
Debugging	`Debug`, `Print`, `End`, `Stop` (essentially no debugging)
Error trapping	`Erl`, `Error`, `Error$`, `On Error...Resume`, `Resume`, `Resume Next`
File I/O	There are too many missing features to mention here. Suffice it to say that if you want to perform file I/O outside of using the cookie, you'll need to include an ActiveX control in your Web page. The cookie is a special file that contains Web site-specific information.
Financial	Most of the financial functions don't work at all or provide very limited functionality. As of this writing, Microsoft hasn't listed all the shortcomings of VBScript in this regard.

Feature Category	*Missing Features*
Graphics (programming)	`Cls`, `Circle`, `Line`, `Point`, `PSet`, `Scale`, `Print`, `Spc`, `Tab`
Graphics (runtime)	`TextHeight`, `TextWidth`, `LoadPicture`, `SavePicture`, `QBColor`, `RGB`
Literals	Based real numbers such as `1.2345E+100`, dates such as `#4/7/96#`, trailing type characters such as the highlighted ampersand (`&hFF&`)
Miscellaneous	`Environ`, `Environ$`, `SendKeys`, `Command`, `Command$`, `DoEvents`, `AppActivate`, `Shell`, `Beep`
Named arguments	Named arguments in calling members. For example, you can't use the call `MyFunction(Variable1:=4)`
Objects (general)	`GetObject`
Objects (manipulation)	`Arrange`, `ZOrder`, `SetFocus`, `InputBox$`, `Drag`, `Hide`, `Show`, `Load`, `Unload`, `Move`, `PrintForm`, `Refresh`, `AddItem`, `RemoveItem`
Operators	`Like`
Options	`Def <type>`, `Option Base`, `Option Compare`, `Option Private Module`
Printing	`TextHeight`, `TextWidth`, `EndDoc`, `NewPage`, `PrintForm`
Procedures (declaring)	`Property Get/Let/Set`, Specifying `public/private`
Procedures (exiting)	`Exit` property
Procedures (parameters)	`ParamArray`, `Option`
Strings	Fixed-length strings, `Mid`, `LSet`, `Rset`, `Lcase$`, `UCase$`, `Space$`, `String$`, `Format`, `Format$`, `Left$`, `Mid$`, `Right$`, `Trim$`, `LTrim$`, `RTrim$`, `StrConv`
Structs	`Type...End Type`, `LSet`, `RSet`
Time	`Time` statement, `Time$`, `Timer`
Types	`TypeOf`
Variables (data types)	`Currency` type, `CCur`
Variables (module level)	`Const`, `Private`, `Dim`, `Public`, `Global`
Variables (procedure level)	`Const`
Variant support	`IsMissing`

Even despite the limitations listed in Table 22.4, there are a lot of things that you can do with VBScript to enhance your Web site. We won't visit every possibility for using VBScript in this chapter, but we can certainly take a look at a simple script.

One of the major failings of HTML is that you can't change it dynamically. What this means is that once a page is displayed, you're basically stuck with it. Wouldn't it be nice if you could change things as needed to fit a particular situation? For example, what if you had a form and you wanted to add additional blanks if a user answered one way or remove them for other answers? The following code shows how you could handle an example like this. (I use ActiveX Control Pad in this example. You don't absolutely have to have it to write HTML code or even VBScript, but you should have a productivity tool of some kind to make scripting easier.)

```
<HTML>
<HEAD>

<SCRIPT LANGUAGE="VBScript">
<!--
Sub CheckBox1_Click()
    if CheckBox1.Value = True then
        CommandButton1.Enabled = True
    else
        CommandButton1.Enabled = False
    end if
end sub

Sub CommandButton1_Click()
    if CommandButton1.Caption = "Press Me" then
        CommandButton1.Caption = "Pressed"
        Window.Document.bgColor = "#FFFFFF"
    else
        CommandButton1.Caption = "Press Me"
        Window.Document.bgColor = "#C0C0C0"
    end if
end sub
-->
</SCRIPT>

<TITLE>Simple Scripting with VBScript</TITLE>
</HEAD>
<BODY>

<!-Display a heading.->
<CENTER><H2>VBScript Programming Example</H2></CENTER>

<!-Display a check box.->
<OBJECT ID="CheckBox1" WIDTH=144 HEIGHT=24
    CLASSID="CLSID:8BD21D40-EC42-11CE-9E0D-00AA006002F3"
    CODEBASE="http://aux/controls/isctrls.ocx">
    <PARAM NAME="BackColor" VALUE="2147483663">
    <PARAM NAME="ForeColor" VALUE="2147483666">
    <PARAM NAME="DisplayStyle" VALUE="4">
    <PARAM NAME="Size" VALUE="3810;635">
    <PARAM NAME="Value" VALUE="False">
    <PARAM NAME="Caption" VALUE="Enable Pushbutton">
    <PARAM NAME="FontCharSet" VALUE="0">
    <PARAM NAME="FontPitchAndFamily" VALUE="2">
    <PARAM NAME="FontWeight" VALUE="0">
</OBJECT>
<P>
```

```
<!-Display a pushbutton.->
<OBJECT ID="CommandButton1" WIDTH=96 HEIGHT=32
    CLASSID="CLSID:D7053240-CE69-11CD-A777-00DD01143C57"
    CODEBASE="http://aux/controls/isctrls.ocx">
    <PARAM NAME="VariousPropertyBits" VALUE="25">
    <PARAM NAME="Caption" VALUE="Press Me">
    <PARAM NAME="Size" VALUE="2540;847">
    <PARAM NAME="FontEffects" VALUE="1073750016">
    <PARAM NAME="FontCharSet" VALUE="0">
    <PARAM NAME="FontPitchAndFamily" VALUE="2">
    <PARAM NAME="ParagraphAlign" VALUE="3">
    <PARAM NAME="FontWeight" VALUE="0">
</OBJECT>

</BODY>
</HTML>
```

Let's take this example apart. What the user will see is a check box and a button. The button is disabled when you first display the Web page. However, as soon as the user checks the check box, the button is enabled. That's what the `CheckBox1_Click()` procedure is all about. Once the button is enabled, the user can click it. Clicking the button changes the button's caption. It also changes the background color for the window. That's the whole purpose behind the `CommandButton1_Click()` procedure.

Now let's talk about a few nuances of programming with VBScript. I used very specific procedure names in this example. The reason is simple: Internet Explorer recognizes certain kinds of procedure names as being event-specific. If you look at the code in the body of the Web page, you'll notice that I haven't done anything to associate the VBScript procedures with the controls. When you want to associate an event with a particular control, you type the control name, followed by an underscore, and ending with the event name. In this example, I associated the `Click` event for `CommandButton1` with the `CommandButton1_Click()` procedure. Likewise, the `Click` event for `CheckBox1` is automatically associated with the `CheckBox1_Click()` procedure. Figure 22.22 in the earlier section "Using ActiveX Control Pad" shows how you can determine which events are supported by each control on your Web page. This includes both ActiveX controls and those that you create using the HTML `<INPUT>` tag.

You should notice something else about the code in this example. To access a particular control value or method, you have to use a dot-naming sequence. What does this mean? Look at the `CheckBox1_Click()` procedure. To change the `Enabled` property for `CommandButton1`, I access that property like this: `CommandButton1.Enabled`. You can also access HTML page-specific properties this way. For example, look in the `CommandButton1_Click()` procedure. I change the background color of the document by using this syntax: `Window.Document.bgColor`. Be sure to spend some time in Script Wizard (if you're using ActiveX Control Pad) discovering the properties that you can access on a Web page. That's the secret to using VBScript efficiently.

Simple Scripting with JavaScript

JavaScript is another scripting language that you can use to enhance your Web pages. Like VBScript, you'll find that it's severely limited in the way that you can interact with the host machine's hardware. If anything, JavaScript is even more limited than VBScript. However, JavaScript has one important advantage over VBScript—both Netscape Navigator and Internet Explorer support this language natively. I view this as a very important consideration if maximum compatibility is your main objective. Suffice it to say that I've seen more JavaScript sites on the Internet for this very simple reason.

Some people think that JavaScript is just another form of C. It's not really like C at all—although it does contain C-like elements that make it easier for C programmers to learn. JavaScript has also been compared to Java. Again, there isn't any real comparison—the name similarity is the result of a marketing decision on Netscape's part. JavaScript's original name was LiveScript. (Java was originally developed by Sun.) Java programmers won't have much more of an advantage than C programmers do when it comes to learning JavaScript. The important thing to remember during this discussion is that JavaScript is just that—a scripting language, originally developed by Netscape, that you can use to enhance your Web pages. You'll find that it has many of the same advantages and disadvantages as VBScript when it comes to the mechanics of creating a Web site. In fact, you'll even find some similarities in the way that you'd use the two languages, although a direct comparison really isn't possible (or even reasonable).

Tip: There are many places to learn about JavaScript. The best place to view the language guide is `http://home.netscape.com/eng/mozilla/gold/handbook/javascript/index.html`. You'll find not only a language guide there, but good discussions on various language elements. (Netscape used to provide a ZIPped copy of their documentation, but the site isn't active anymore.) Fortunately, you can get a tutorial-sized version of the JavaScript documentation in Windows Help format from `http://www.jchelp.com/javahelp/javahelp.htm` or an Adobe Acrobat version from `http://www.ipst.com/docs.htm`. (You can also get a free Acrobat reader or plug-in from `ftp://ftp.adobe.com/pub/adobe/applications/acrobat`.) Another good resource page is `http://www.c2.org/~andreww/javascript`. This site contains source listings and a wealth of other information. It's also important to find a place where you can share information about JavaScript with other people. You'll find a great newsgroup at `Comp.Lang.JavaScript`.

JavaScript takes an object-map approach to working with HTML documents. It builds a hierarchy of objects starting with the window, the documents within the window, forms within the document, and finally any objects within the form. Using JavaScript allows you to communicate with each object by defining a path to it. For example, if you wanted to do something with a form, you'd separate the name from the window name like this: `Window1.Document1.Form1`. Notice that everything starts at the window level and that there's a very distinct hierarchy to work with. As with VBScript, this kind of notation is called *dot syntax reference*. However, don't confuse VBScript's way of doing things with the way that JavaScript handles the same task.

I previously mentioned that JavaScript and C are two very different languages. Let's look at some of those differences. JavaScript is a loosely-typed language. This means that you don't have to declare your variables before you use them. JavaScript creates a variable of the right type for you as you use it. However, it's still a good idea to declare your variables before you use them—if for no other reason than to document their purpose.

JavaScript does support objects; however, you can't create new object types in JavaScript, because there aren't any classes or inheritance provided. You're stuck with whatever objects the browser chooses to support. (Thankfully, these objects are fairly standardized, and you'll find that they'll meet all your needs, in most cases.) JavaScript allows you to add classes to those that the browser supports. One way to do this is by adding ActiveX controls or Java applets to your Web page. If you find that you can't get a particular task done with JavaScript by itself, you'll want to develop (or purchase) an ActiveX control or Java applet to get the job done.

A final difference between JavaScript and C is in the way that the two languages handle objects. The reason that you can add functionality to JavaScript by adding ActiveX controls to a Web page is that it's dynamically bound. That means that JavaScript doesn't look for any of its objects until runtime—it assumes that you know what you're talking about until it actually needs a resource. C, on the other hand, is statically bound. If you want to work with an object, it had better be available while you're writing and compiling your code.

There are four different kinds of variables supported by JavaScript: numbers, strings, Boolean, and a special `null` value. You can use function calls to convert one variable type to another. However, you can just as easily mix and match the variables in most cases—JavaScript automatically performs any required conversions if it can figure out what you want to do. For example, you can write a line of code in JavaScript that looks like this: `MyValue := "My Value is: " + 100`. JavaScript will automatically convert the number `100` to a string for you.

Now that you've got at least some idea of what JavaScript is like, let's take a look at some code. This is a very simple example of what you can do with JavaScript. I'm using all HTML code in this example, but you could just as easily use ActiveX controls as we did with the VBScript example in the previous section.

```
<HTML>
<HEAD>
<SCRIPT LANGUAGE="JavaScript">
<!--
function ChangeColor(sColor)
{
    document.MyForm.TextInput.value = 'The background is ' + sColor + '.'
    document.bgColor = sColor
}
// -->
```

```
</SCRIPT>
<TITLE>Simple Scripting with JavaScript</TITLE>
</HEAD>
<BODY>

<!-Display a heading.->
<CENTER><H2>A Simple JavaScript Example</H2></CENTER>

<!-Netscape requires all INPUT tags be within a form.->
<FORM NAME="MyForm">

<!-Display a simple textbox.->
This textbox will change as you click the radio buttons.<BR>
<INPUT TYPE="text" NAME="TextInput" VALUE="Click a radio button" SIZE=40><P>

<!-Display some radio buttons for changing the textbox.->
Click a radio button:<BR>
<INPUT TYPE="radio" NAME="Radio1" VALUE="Aqua"
    ONCLICK=ChangeColor("Aqua") CHECKED>Aqua<BR>
<INPUT TYPE="radio" NAME="Radio1" VALUE="Blue"
    ONCLICK=ChangeColor("Blue")>Blue<BR>
<INPUT TYPE="radio" NAME="Radio1" VALUE="Gray"
    ONCLICK=ChangeColor("Gray")>Gray<BR>
<INPUT TYPE="radio" NAME="Radio1" VALUE="Lime"
    ONCLICK=ChangeColor("Lime")>Lime<BR>
<INPUT TYPE="radio" NAME="Radio1" VALUE="Navy"
    ONCLICK=ChangeColor("Navy")>Navy<BR>
<INPUT TYPE="radio" NAME="Radio1" VALUE="Purple"
    ONCLICK=ChangeColor("Purple")>Purple<BR>
<INPUT TYPE="radio" NAME="Radio1" VALUE="Silver"
    ONCLICK=ChangeColor("Silver")>Silver<BR>
<INPUT TYPE="radio" NAME="Radio1" VALUE="White"
    ONCLICK=ChangeColor("White")>White<BR>

</FORM>
</BODY>
</HTML>
```

There are quite a few fine points of working with JavaScript and HTML shown here. First, look at the `<INPUT>` tags. This is the first time I've introduced them. If you don't use ActiveX controls on your Web site, you'll likely use the `<INPUT>` tag to create various kinds of controls. I show you how to create two here: radio buttons and text boxes. You can also create buttons and check boxes. When creating radio buttons, it's important to give the same name to all the radio buttons in the same group. Otherwise, when the user clicks on a new radio button, the first radio button remains selected. Notice how I've used the `ONCLICK` attribute along with a call to the JavaScript function `ChangeColor()`. Unlike ActiveX controls, HTML controls need a direct link to the function that you want to use with them. I've also selected one of the radio buttons to be checked by default, using the `CHECKED` attribute. Normally you'll want to do this for the sake of appearances.

Notice that I had to place all the `<INPUT>` tags within a form. This is a Netscape requirement. You can use `<INPUT>` tags with Internet Explorer without placing them in a form. You create a form by using the `<FORM>` and `</FORM>` tag pair.

It's time to look at the `ChangeColor()` function. Unlike the VBScript example I showed previously, this function requires that a value be passed to it. The reason is simple: Trying to determine which button is pressed takes a lot more code than simply passing a value. Notice that I've placed the function code within braces. JavaScript, like C, uses braces to mark off various program areas. If you know C, then you'll know where to use these braces within JavaScript.

Remember the strict hierarchy that I talked about at the beginning of this section? Notice how I've had to format the dot reference syntax for the two statements in our function. Netscape is a little more particular than Internet Explorer about how you do this. One interesting difference between the two browsers is that Netscape is case-sensitive—Internet Explorer isn't, for the most part.

The code itself is fairly easy to understand. All I do is take the value passed to the function and use it to change two items. The first is the string that you see in `TextInput`. The second is the background color of the document. The beauty of this example is that it works equally well in Navigator and Internet Explorer without a single add-in.

On Your Own

Visit a variety of Web sites. Use the three kinds of folders—Content, Gimmicks, and Usability—that I talked about in the "Why Bother?" section of the chapter to store comments about each site. Now try to determine which site most closely matches the kind of site you'd like to build. You might want to classify sites in other ways as well. For example, which site displays the best use of animated .GIFs? Is there a site in your list that shows how to use sound especially well? What about an ActiveX site or two?

Now might be the time to learn a few Web page creation techniques. Use the material in the section "The Twelve Steps to Basic HTML" to create your own Web page. Use a basic editor such as Notepad, or something a little more suited to creating Web pages, such as Internet Assistant or ActiveX Control Pad.

Download a copy of GIF Construction Set from the Internet site listed earlier in the chapter. Try creating your own animated .GIFs for use on a Web page. Make sure that you test the resulting file by using a browser. (The tag for displaying an animated .GIF is `<IMG SRC="filename">`, where *`filename`* is the name of the file you created.

Try adding some functionality to the Web page you're creating by using either VBScript or JavaScript. Be sure to download any required documentation before you begin the project. Join a newsgroup as well so that you can get help from other programmers. You may even want to try both languages to see which one you like best.

VI Networking with Windows 95

23 Networks

Just about every business, large or small, has a network these days. The benefits of linking a group of computers to share peripherals and some data are just too great to ignore. Even two- and three-person shops commonly have a network installed—if for no other reason than to share a laser printer and a few documents. I'm often surprised at the number of home networks that I see as well. It doesn't come as too much of a shock, though. Just think about the benefits to mom and dad of having a modern home workstation with a large hard drive, fast processor, and other new-machine features. Using a peer-to-peer network allows the parents to give that old machine to the kids. Even if the kids' workstation has a hard drive large enough for only the Windows system files, their application files can reside on the larger hard drive of the machine used by their parents. Keeping the parents' machine separate from the kids' machine is a good way to keep your work separate from their play.

No matter the size of your network, there's bound to be some native support for it in Windows 95. You can even install limited support for some of those older real-mode peer-to-peer networks on the market. A few of these older networks don't provide the same level of features that they did under Windows 3.x, but at least they work well enough to get the job done.

This chapter talks about the networking capabilities that Windows 95 provides. For the most part, I purposely avoid talking about networks in general or even comparing the various options you have. The reason is simple: A single chapter can't possibly contain everything you'll ever need to know about networking. There are literally volumes of information about this topic—and some people think that these are just barely adequate.

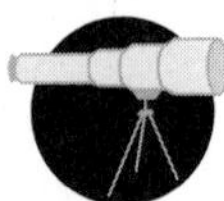

Looking Ahead: Chapter 27 covers network troubleshooting aids and techniques—especially those that work with Novell NetWare, Windows NT, and Windows 95 peer-to-peer networks. We also look at some networking issues such as differences between Novell's Client 32 and Microsoft's NDS client for Windows 95. If you still have trouble finding what you need, you may want to look at the `microsoft.public.win95.networking` newsgroup.

In this chapter, I provide you with some insights into the way that Windows 95 provides network services—and that's something that you'd be hard-pressed to find in one of those networking tomes. That's the whole reason for this chapter—to give you the Windows 95 view of networking. I strongly suggest that you also spend some time learning about networks in general before you install one.

The discussion in this chapter also assumes a certain level of knowledge on your part. I assume that you've already spent some time on a network and know some of the basics. You don't need to be a networking guru to understand this chapter, but you need to know what logging in is all about and some of the easier terms such as *network interface card* (NIC).

The Client Module

This section of the chapter looks at the "how" of network support under Windows 95. What can you expect, and why do things work the way they do? These are just some of the questions I answer here. Before we become too embroiled in some of the details of using the Windows 95 network capabilities, though, I'd like to spend a little time looking at its architecture. Figure 23.1 shows the Windows 95 network architecture. Notice that a request can follow two discrete paths. Windows 95 provides a 32-bit protected-mode path for any networks that it supports directly and uses a real-mode path for drivers that it doesn't support. Both paths end up at the NIC driver.

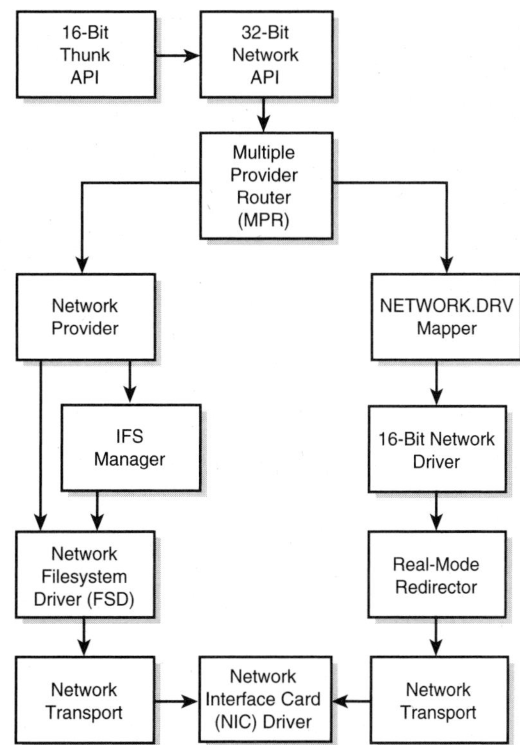

Figure 23.1.
An overview of the Windows 95 network architecture.

The following list describes the individual components:

- **16-Bit Thunk API:** Windows 95 provides full network support using 32-bit code. However, there are a lot of 16-bit applications out there to support as well. This module replaces the standard 16-bit API with calls to the 32-bit API. It has to provide thunk support in order to do this. Chapter 6 looks at the thunk process, so I won't go into it again here.

- **32-Bit Network API:** All application requests start at this module. I won't go into details about the API, but Microsoft has gone to great lengths to reorganize and simplify it. A user won't notice these details—except in the way that they affect network performance—but they make a definite impact on the effort required to program. The API translates one application request into one or more standardized network requests. Quite a few files are involved in creating the network API under Windows 95. The two most prominent are NETAPI.DLL and NETAPI32.DLL. Loading NETAPI32.DLL also loads NETBIOS.DLL, which provides most of the low-level functionality that the API requires.
- **Multiple Provider Router (MPR):** You can use more than one protocol with Windows 95. In fact—theoretically, at least—you should be able to mix and match protected-mode and real-mode drivers on the same network. The current Windows 95 implementation always allows you to perform the first function. For example, you can mix NetBEUI and IPX/SPX on the same network. However, it usually won't allow you to do the second without some restrictions. For example, you can't mix LANtastic with a Microsoft network, but you can mix it with other systems in some cases. (Some people have successfully mixed the Windows 95 version of LANtastic with a Microsoft network, but this compatibility is by no means guaranteed, and you probably shouldn't count on it.) All network protocols require a network provider. The whole function of the MPR is to accept network requests from the API and send them to the appropriate network provider (NP). Part of each request states which NP to use. This is how the MPR knows which one it should send the request to. However, some requests are generic. For example, a request for the status of the entire network falls into this category. In that case, the MPR calls each NP in turn to fulfill the application request. In still other cases, a request might not include enough information for the MPR to know which NP to use to fulfill the application requirement. In this case, the MPR will "poll" the NPs to see whether one of them can fulfill the request. If none of the installed NPs can do so, the MPR returns an error message. You'll find that the MPR functions appear in the SYSTEM folder in MPR.DLL. This .DLL is loaded when Windows 95 executes MPREXE.EXE during startup. An intermediate file, MPRSERV.DLL, performs the loading process. Interestingly, loading this set of .DLLs also loads ADVAPI32.DLL. The MPR uses the functions in this .DLL to view the contents of the Registry to determine which NPs and other network resources are available. The MPR also loads MSPWL.DLL. This module checks for your password and performs other security-related activities. There's also a path from the MPR to NETWORK.DRV. This path becomes active when you use a real-mode driver in place of a Windows 95-specific NP. The MPR can't poll the real-mode driver or perform any of the other NP-specific tasks that I described earlier. NETWORK.DRV provides the NP services that Windows 95 requires. I describe this particular part of the network a little later in this chapter.

- **Network Provider (NP):** The Network Provider performs all the protocol-specific functions that an application requires. It makes or breaks connections, returns network status information, and provides a consistent interface for the MPR to use. An application never calls the NP; only the MPR performs this function. Even though the internal structures of NPs vary, the interface that they provide doesn't vary. This mechanism allows Windows 95 to provide support for more than a single protocol. The code used by the MPR can remain small and fast because none of the NPs require special calls. If an NP can't fulfill a request because of a limitation in the network protocol, it simply tells the MPR that the required service is unavailable. The NP also keeps the IFS Manager up-to-date on the current connection status. This is how Explorer knows when you've made a new drive connection.
- **IFS Manager:** When the IFS Manager obtains new status information from the NP, it calls the Network Filesystem Driver (FSD) to update file and other resource information. For example, when the NP tells the IFS Manager that it has made a new drive connection, the IFS Manager calls on the Network FSD to provide a directory listing. The same holds true for other resource types such as printers. In addition to this function, the IFS Manager performs its normal duties of opening files and making other file system requests. The MPR doesn't know what to do with a pathname, so it passes such requests through the NP to the IFS Manager to fulfill. Of course, applications also access the IFS Manager in other ways. The only time that the MPR becomes involved is when a network-specific request also requires its intervention.
- **Network Filesystem Driver (FSD):** Each server on the network could use a unique file system. For example, if you make a connection to an OS/2 server, you could require access to an HPFS drive. NetWare and other client/server networks all use special file systems that the vendor feels will enhance performance, security, reliability, and storage capacity. Because Windows 95 understands nothing about HPFS or any other special storage system, it needs a translator. The Network FSD performs this task. It translates the intricacies of a foreign file system into something that Windows 95 can understand. A Network FSD is usually composed of a file-system-specific driver and VREDIR.VXD. The second file provides the Windows 95 interpretation of the file-system specifics. Normally there's only one Network FSD for each NP. However, there's nothing to enforce this limit. An NP might require access to both a FAT and an NTFS Network FSD for a Windows NT Server. If so, both drivers will be installed when you install network support. The IFS Manager will also call on the Network FSD for support. While the NP usually makes requests for network status or connection information, the IFS Manager takes care of application needs such as opening files and reading their contents. These two modules—NP and IFS Manager—work in tandem, each fulfilling completely different roles.

Note: You might wonder why Microsoft didn't combine the NP and the IFS Manager into one module. After all, from this discussion it appears that the IFS Manager is simply part of an access strategy for network drives. Remember to take the whole picture into account. The IFS Manager also works with local drives. In addition, combining the modules would have produced a lot of replicated code. In essence, using two separate modules to access the drive status information and contents is the only way to get the level of flexibility that network requests require, with the minimum amount of code.

- **Network Transport (NT):** I placed a single module called Network Transport (NT) in Figure 23.1. Actually, this module is made up of many smaller modules and drivers. The number of pieces in an NT is determined by the complexity of your setup and the requirements of the protocol. The smallest NT could consist of a mere four drivers. For example, you could create an NT for the NetBEUI protocol by using the following files: VNETBIOS.VXD, NETBEUI.VXD, NDIS.VXD, and NE2000.SYS. These are just the drivers, but let's take a quick look at them.

  VNETBIOS.VXD virtualizes access to the protocol. This is the reason that more than one virtual machine running on your system can access the network drives at the same time. NETBEUI.VXD performs the task of talking with the NDIS (network driver interface specification) module. It takes protocol-specific requests and translates them into smaller, standardized network requests. NDIS.VXD translates each Windows 95-specific request into a call that the NIC driver can understand. Finally, the NIC driver talks to the NIC itself. The driver can take things such as port addresses and interrupts into account—everything needed to talk to the NIC. Of course, the NIC converts your request into an electrical signal that appears on the network.

  NT requires other files as well. For example, NDIS30.DLL provides the API support for NDIS.VXD and NETBIOS.DLL performs the same function for VNETBIOS.VXD. In essence, it takes a lot of different modules to create one transport. The reason for all these files is fairly easy to understand. For example, what if you want to use a different NIC? All you need to do is change the NIC driver—not any of the protocol-specific files. What if you wanted to use two different levels of NDIS support (Windows 95 supports two)? You would add an additional driver and its support files to the equation. Rather than going into too much additional detail, let's close the book on the NT for now. All you need to know is that the NT takes care of the "transportation" details for your network installation.

Tip: The OSR2 version of Windows 95 provides support for the NDIS 4.0 NIC drivers. Unfortunately, you can't download this support as a separate package. You'll also find support for the 32-bit DLC (data link control) protocol for SNA (simple network architecture) host connectivity (mainly IBM) in OSR2. Users of older Windows 95 versions can download this support from `http://www.microsoft.com/windows/software/dlc.htm`. They can also obtain the updated ISDN (Integrated Services Digital Network) support found in OSR2 from `http://www.microsoft.com/windows/software/isdn.htm`. Finally, you can download the NDS (NetWare Directory Services) support that I mentioned earlier at `http://www.microsoft.com/windows/software/msnds.htm`. Be sure to read any update instructions before you attempt to install this new support. You'll also need to make certain that your hardware and drivers are capable of supporting the features provided by these updates.

- **Network Interface Card (NIC) Driver:** I make special mention of this part of the NT here for a reason. This particular driver is hardware-specific. It has to communicate with the NIC on a level that the NIC can understand. That's the first problem—trying to find a driver that provides a standard Windows 95 interface, yet talks with the NIC installed in your machine. The second problem is that there can be only one driver. I mentioned earlier that there was a chance that a real-mode and a protected-mode network could coexist, but that it wouldn't happen in a lot of cases. Here's the reason why. If you can't load a Windows 95-specific NIC driver because it interferes with a driver that the real-mode product requires, you're faced with a decision as to which network to use.

Tip: Even if you've invested in a real-mode networking product such as LANtastic, the performance and reliability increase that you'll get from a Microsoft network running under Windows 95 might make it worth the effort to switch. Of course, you have to consider the tradeoffs of making that decision versus the loss of features. Windows 95 doesn't provide many of the features that people switched to other networks to get. For example, Artisoft provides a DDE Link Book that helps you make OLE links to other machines. You'll also find that the Windows 95 mail and scheduling features are inadequate when compared to products such as Artisoft Exchange. In addition, there's a very good chance that vendors such as Artisoft will eventually provide Windows 95-specific solutions to replace their current product. (As of this writing, there's a new version of LANtastic available for Windows 95 users.) Even if you decide not to switch, it might be beneficial to see whether the real-mode network vendor can provide the required Windows 95 NIC driver to allow you to use multiple networks.

- **NETWORK.DRV:** The reason for this file is simple. You need to have an NP to gain access to a network under Windows 95. When you install the real-mode LANtastic client in the Network applet, this is one of the files that gets installed. (The Windows 95 version of LANtastic uses the same protected-mode elements as its Microsoft network counterpart.) NETWORK.DRV provides the interface to your real-mode network that Windows 95 requires in order to use the network. In this case, the NP also acts as a mapper—a module that maps the Windows 95-specific calls to something that the 16-bit driver will understand. It also provides a thunk layer to translate the 32-bit requests into their 16-bit equivalents. Remember that you still need to install the old 16-bit Windows version of the network drivers. In the case of LANtastic, you need the LANTASTI.386 and LANTNET.DRV files from your distribution disks.
- **16-Bit Network Driver:** As I mentioned in the preceding paragraph, you'll still need a Windows driver for your real-mode network. Otherwise, there's no magical way that Windows 95 will be able to talk to it. There has to be a framework for discussion before a discussion can take place. The 16-bit network drivers typically translate any requests into something that the real-mode redirector can understand. Then they ask Windows 95 to make the transition to real mode so that the redirector can do its job.

Tip: In some cases, it's nearly impossible to get a good real-mode network installation under Windows 95. Some of the problems include the real-mode network setup program overwriting Windows 95-specific files, and the use of undocumented Windows 3.x features. A few setup programs also require Program Manager to complete their installation, so you might want to start a copy of Program Manager before you begin. I've found that the best way to get a good real-mode network installation under Windows 95 is to install a copy of Windows 3.x first, install the real-mode network there, and then install the copy of Windows 95 over the Windows 3.x installation. It seems like a roundabout way of doing things, but it will ensure that you'll have a minimum of problems.

- **Real-Mode Redirector:** This network component translates your requests into network calls. It works with the real-mode network transport to create an interface with the NIC. Essentially, it performs about the same function in real mode that the IFS Manager and Network FSD do in protected mode.

This might seem like a lot of work just to create a workstation, but that's only half the picture on many peer-to-peer installations. Once you get past being a workstation, you have to take care of network requests as well. The next section shows you how Windows 95 provides peer-to-peer network services. We look at Windows 95's peer-to-peer support from a server level. We also look at a lot of the implementation details. For example, how do you share your printer or local hard drive with someone?

Peer-to-Peer Support

Peer-to-peer networks represent the easiest and least-expensive way to get started in networking. Everyone starts with a workstation, just like you would normally need in any business environment. However, you can't share resources on stand-alone workstations; you need to connect them in order to do that. In the past, the standard method for sharing resources was to buy additional machines (called *servers*) and place the common components there. The investment in hardware and software for a full-fledged network can run into tens of thousands of dollars—prohibitively expensive for many companies and out of reach for others. Peer-to-peer networks take a different route. One or more workstations also act as servers. In fact, if you work things right and the network is small enough, everyone will probably have access to everyone else's machine in some form. This means that, except for the NICs and cabling you'll need, a peer-to-peer solution under Windows 95 is free for the asking.

Windows 95 provides peer-to-peer networking capabilities right out of the package. All you need to do is install a NIC in each machine, run some cable, and add a few drivers to your setup. Of course, once you get everyone set up, you'll want to install a few extra utilities, such as a centralized calendar and e-mail.

I was actually a little disappointed with the network utility feature set that Microsoft decided to provide for Windows 95. Exchange is a wonderful e-mail system. However, past versions of WfW (Windows for Workgroups) came with Schedule+. Windows 95 doesn't provide this feature, and almost everyone will notice. Microsoft has introduced a Windows 95-specific version of Schedule+ as part of Office 95. Of course, this brings up another problem—that of incompatibility between the old and the new version of Schedule+. No matter which way you look at it, Schedule+ will become a thing of the past unless you're willing to perform a major upgrade of all your PCs at the same time—something I doubt that most businesses could do even if they wanted to and had the required resources. I see a definite third-party opportunity here. People will still need a centralized calendar for planning meetings, and with Schedule+ gone, some third-party vendor will fill the gap.

Peter's Principle: Grabbing a Piece of the Past

You don't have to do without Schedule+ in your new Windows 95 installation if you still have the files from your old version of WfW lying around. Even though that version of Schedule+ won't work with Exchange, you can still share information with other people on the network by copying the required files to your drive. Here are the files you should copy to your \WIN95 folder (more on the next page):

*.CAL
DEMILAYR.DLL
MSCHED.DLL
MSMAIL.INI

MSREMIND.EXE
SCHDPLUS.EXE
SCHDPLUS.HLP
SCHDPLUS.INI
TRNSCHED.DLL

You'll also need to copy the following files to your SYSTEM folder:

AB.DLL
FRAMEWRK.DLL
MAILMGR.DLL
MAILSPL.EXE
MSSFS.DLL
STORE.DLL

If the new version of Microsoft Mail doesn't exactly meet your specifications, you can still use the old version under Windows 95. Simply copy these files to your \WIN95 folder:

MSMAIL.EXE
MSMAIL.HLP
MSMAIL.PRG

You'll also need to copy VFORMS.DLL to your SYSTEM folder.

Once you copy all these files, make any required changes to the .INI files. For example, you'll want to change the directory names so that they match the new location. The only problem I've detected with this arrangement so far is that Schedule+ won't remember your password. This is a small price to pay for using an old and familiar utility program.

Another way around the problem of using the old Schedule+ files is to use Microsoft Outlook, included with Microsoft Office 97. This product can import Schedule+, Lotus Organizer, Act, and other files.

A Little History

Before we delve into all the details of how Windows 95 supports peer-to-peer networking, let's take a brief look at the history of this networking system. Apple actually introduced peer-to-peer networking in a covert manner in 1985. They included AppleTalk in every Macintosh sold. Most people didn't realize that they were actually using a network when they printed a document using the LaserWriter.

Peer-to-peer networking continued to be a cult classic in the years that followed. Many companies wouldn't recognize peer-to-peer networking as much more than a kludge or a poor man's network. Novell NetWare used a client/server model that mimicked the big iron that corporations were used to using. It was comfortable using a network operating system that provided the look and feel of something substantial. In the PC world, many people thought that it was client/server or nothing at all.

Note: Don't get me wrong. I'm not saying that peer-to-peer networking is the end-all solution for everyone. However, it's a very good solution for those on a limited networking budget who need to connect anywhere from 2 to 10 workstations. You might even want to look at it for workgroup connections (the very reason that Microsoft came out with Windows for Workgroups). You can combine the benefits of a client/server network with those of a peer-to-peer network under Windows 95. Although I would probably set an upper limit of 10 workstations for an 80486-based peer-to-peer network, it might also work for larger numbers of workstations if the network load is very light. (Many Pentium-based peer-to-peer networks now support up to 20 workstations without any problems.)

A group of companies began distributing peer-to-peer networking solutions for the PC. One of the bigger contributors to this ground swell of alternative networking technology was Artisoft, which still sells LANtastic today. Other vendors contributed products such as 10Net and TOPS. The Software Link even marketed a processor-sharing operating system for the 80386 called PC-MOS/386. This solution and others allowed people to share system resources without having to purchase a file server to do so. In addition, the cost of a peer-to-peer network operating system was a lot lower because these vendors faced stiff competition from Novell.

I'm not sure whether Novell helped or hindered the expansion of peer-to-peer networking with its introduction of NetWare Lite in 1991. This product was designed not to interfere with Novell's client/server product. As a result, NetWare Lite wasn't well-designed or well-implemented. It couldn't even compete with other peer-to-peer products such as LANtastic. However, the introduction of a peer-to-peer networking product by a major vendor such as Novell at least put this type of networking on some people's agenda for the first time.

Things started to change for the better in the peer-to-peer market when Microsoft introduced Windows for Workgroups at the 1992 fall COMDEX trade show. This show of support by Microsoft legitimized the use of peer-to-peer networking for some corporate applications. Of course, Microsoft didn't go so far as to say that you could use it for more than a few people. Still, it was a step in the right direction.

So has everyone bought into the peer-to-peer networking technology? Not by a long shot, and I doubt that peer-to-peer networking will ever take over the market. However, using a solution such as Windows for Workgroups or Windows 95 in the right place could make a big difference at a very small cost. Windows 95 goes a long way toward making dual solutions—a combination of client/server and peer-to-peer networking—a viable solution.

A Look at the Architecture

We've already taken a detailed look at what it takes to provide workstation support under Windows 95. However, what happens if you also want the workstation to act as a server? Providing server support means that your machine must accept requests from other workstations, process those requests, and return the requested information. Figure 23.2 shows the Windows 95 peer-to-peer network server support.

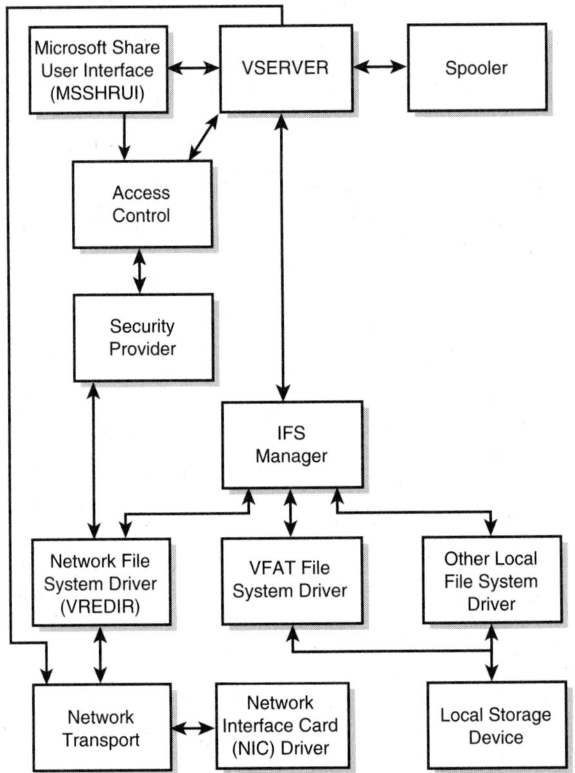

Figure 23.2.
An overview of the Windows 95 server architecture.

The following list describes each component in detail:

- **Microsoft Share User Interface (MSSHRUI):** This module responds to external requests from the user for network resource configuration. Every time you right-click a resource and tell Windows 95 that you want to share the resource, this module fields that request. It works with the access control module to set password protection. An interface to the MPR and ADVAPI32.DLL allows the MSSHRUI to set the proper entries in the Registry. You'll find it in the MSSHRUI.DLL file in your SYSTEM folder.
- **VSERVER:** The central point of all activity for the server is the virtual server driver, VSERVER.VXD. As with all the other drivers in this chapter, you'll find it in your SYSTEM folder. This component provides network requesters direct access to all local resources through the Network Transport. It works with the IFS Manager and access control modules to limit access to shared resources and to ensure that any access is

performed properly. Each access to shared system resources is maintained in a separate thread. This means that access by one requester need not interfere with any other request. In addition, a single requester can make multiple requests. Of course, the number of actual requests is usually limited by the protocol settings you provide.

- **Spooler:** If you grant someone access to your printer, VSERVER will send any requests for print services to the spooler module. This module works just as it would for a local print request. As far as the spooler module is concerned, the request originated locally. There are three spooler-specific files in your SYSTEM folder: SPOOLSS.DLL, SPOOL32.EXE, and WINSPOOL.DRV.
- **Access Control:** Windows 95 uses this module for a variety of purposes, not just network access control. For example, Windows calls on this module to verify your initial logon password, even if you don't request access to a network afterward. Unlike the other modules discussed so far, the access control module makes use of .PWL files on your drive as well as Registry entries to verify and set security. You'll find access control in the SVRAPI.DLL file in the SYSTEM folder.

Tip: You can get around a potential security problem by removing user access to all the .PWL files on your drive. If a user erases one of these files, it becomes a lot easier for him to override any security you provided. In addition, you can erase a user's .PWL file to give him access to Windows 95 if he forgets his password. Unfortunately, this means that you'll also have to perform the setup required to re-create that .PWL file. If security is a major concern, be sure to install Service Pack 1 as well. It contains several fixes to the Windows 95 password system. One of the most dangerous problems that this patch addresses is the ability of other people to decrypt your encrypted .PWL files (especially since the algorithm for doing so was posted on the Internet). The new algorithm used by the patch is 96^2 times more difficult to decrypt. (The OSR2 version of Windows 95 includes these fixes as a default.)

- **Security Provider:** There are a number of sources for this module. In fact, even if you install a Microsoft network, you can still choose between the Microsoft network client and the Windows 95 Login module as a security provider. The Microsoft network client is a network-specific security provider that might include features that the Windows 95 Login module (a generic dialog box) might not provide. You can always access the Windows 95 Login module, even if the network isn't running. The advantage of using it is that the Login module will always be available, even if you change the network setup or remove it altogether. The security provider performs two tasks. First, this is the module that asks you for a password. Second, it combines the user's login name and the password she provides to verify any network requests.

- **VFAT File System Driver (FSD) and Other Local File System Driver:** Chapter 9 covers both of these modules in detail.
- **IFS Manager, Network FSD, Network Transport, and NIC driver:** I talked about these modules at the beginning of this chapter.

Understanding the server capabilities that Windows 95 provides is pretty straightforward from a conceptual point of view. However, once you get past theory, implementation becomes another story altogether. The problem isn't due to a poor plan, but due to all the compatibility issues that come into play. Fortunately for the user, the design of the server capabilities makes all these details fairly seamless.

Sharing Files and Printers

Sharing is the main reason to install a network. The very concept of networks came from the need to share expensive peripheral devices and files. Windows 95 provides an easy-to-use interface that allows you to share just about everything on your network with a few clicks of the mouse. Let's take a look at what you'll need to do to share files and other resources located on your machine.

The first thing you'll need to do is install support for file and printer sharing. Right-click the Network Neighborhood icon and select Properties. If you have a peer-to-peer network installed, the File and Print Sharing button will be enabled. Click it to display the dialog box shown in Figure 23.3. Notice that you can select file and printer sharing individually. Of course, installing support doesn't give everyone access to your system. You still have to select the specific items that you plan to share.

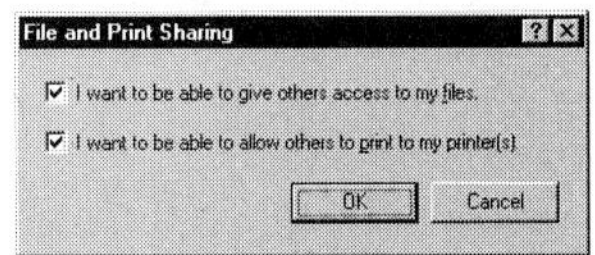

Figure 23.3.
The File and Print Sharing dialog box allows you to determine what level of sharing support Windows 95 will install.

Tip: The NETCPL.CPL file in your SYSTEM folder provides the interface that you use to configure the network. Some real-mode or older 16-bit Windows network installation programs insist on changing this file. If you ever lose your Network icon (as I once did), check to make sure that this file didn't get overwritten or otherwise corrupted. In fact, you might want to make a copy of this file before you install any real-mode network on your machine.

After Windows 95 enables file and printer sharing, you need to select the items to share. Right-clicking any of your drive or printer icons and clicking Properties (depending on what support you installed) displays an additional Sharing page like the one shown in Figure 23.4. (The context menu also includes a Sharing option that takes you directly to this page.)

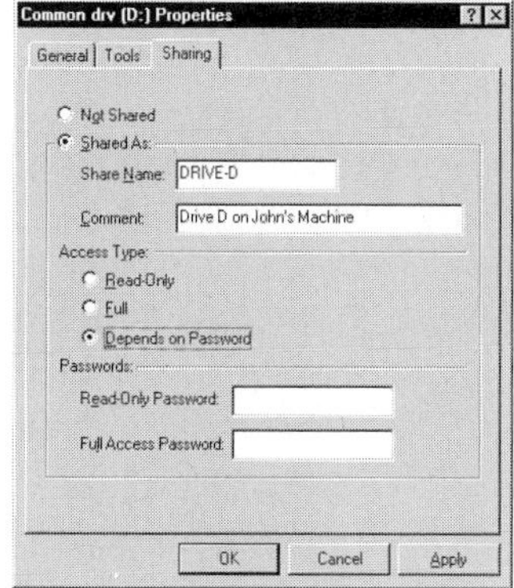

Figure 23.4.
The Sharing page of the printer or drive Properties dialog box lets you define the level and type of sharing for that device.

The first two radio buttons on this page allow you to determine whether the resource is shared. Selecting Not Shared means that no one can see the resource, even if they have other access to your machine. If you select shared access, some additional blanks become available.

You need to provide a resource name in the Share Name field. This is how Windows 95 presents the resource in dialog boxes, such as with the Drives field of the File Open dialog box. The optional Comment field allows you to provide a little more information to someone who wants to share the resource. I normally include the precise resource name, my name, and a telephone number where I can be reached as part of the comment. This reduces the chance that someone will accidentally try to use a resource on my system. You may want to include a location, especially for printers, because someone could potentially select a printer that isn't even in the same building.

Use the Access Type group to define the level of access to a particular resource. You can provide two levels of access: read-only and full. The third option allows you to assign two different access passwords. This would allow one person full access, while another could read only the contents of the drive or other resource. The two password fields allow you to define the password required to access that resource.

Windows 95 doesn't limit you to providing access to an entire drive or printer. You can define access to an individual directory as well. I find it very convenient to set aside a temporary directory on my machine for file sharing. People can upload their files to a specific directory and avoid changing the contents of the rest of my drive. You can use the same principle for other resources. The key is to maintain control of your system.

Peter's Principle: Maintaining Control of Your System

Sharing doesn't always mean that you allow everyone to access every resource on your machine. It's easier to simply provide access to an entire drive than it is to set the required level of security folder by folder, but the drive strategy might not be the best way to go when it comes to your company's health.

Many of us work with confidential information that we must keep safe, but we also work with other people who need to see some of the things that we work with. For example, someone working in the Accounting department might need to share analysis files with a workgroup. However, can you imagine what would happen if she also shared access to the payroll files? What about the new plans that your company might be working on? Even though you need to share access to the current project, you'll want to keep that new project a secret. A little bit of discretion can save you a lot of headaches later.

It's important that you provide the right level of access to everyone in your workgroup. I won't cover every bit of security in this chapter (I look at this in detail in the next chapter), but you might want to put on your thinking cap now. Where are the potential security leaks in your company? It's a well-known fact that people complain when they don't have enough access to the network. Have you ever heard anyone complain about having too much access?

Finding the areas where people have too much access will give you the most trouble. Audits and other forms of security-checking are just as important as the sharing itself on your network. Performing an audit takes time and resources that might be very difficult to defend when management asks for an accounting. Of course, having a security breach is even more difficult to defend. Allow others to use the resources that you have available, but don't allow misuse of those resources. It's up to you to do your part in maintaining the proper level of security on your network.

Login Scripts

Windows 95 provides several support mechanisms for login scripts. The best support is for most versions of Novell NetWare, but the same principles hold true (for the most part) with any other network operating system (NOS) that Windows 95 supports. This support doesn't extend to real-mode networks such as the older version of LANtastic. You need to perform any login script requirements as a call from AUTOEXEC.BAT before you enter Windows 95. In most cases, this means running STARTNET.BAT for LANtastic. Check the vendor documentation for any requirements for using a login script with your real-mode network. You follow the same procedure that you did prior to installing Windows 95.

Now that we have the real-mode networks out of the way, let's look at the kind of support that you can expect for supported networks such as NetWare. The first thing you need to do is disable any AUTOEXEC.BAT or other batch files that you used under Windows 3.x. You don't need to log into the network before entering Windows 95. Any workstations that use NetWare must have an account on the server before you try to install Client for NetWare.

Note: I was surprised to find that the protected-mode Client for NetWare Networks isn't under the Novell entry of the clients listing. You'll find it in the Microsoft list of clients. Novell didn't supply the protected-mode client for NetWare that comes with Windows 95—Microsoft did. If you install either of the entries from the Novell listing, you'll be using real-mode drivers. Not only will this reduce performance and cause some level of system instability, but it also will remove many of the positive benefits of using an integrated approach to networking. For example, you won't be able to use a single login screen for both NetWare and Microsoft; you'll have to enter them separately. Always try the protected-mode drivers first, just to see whether they'll work with your system setup. Fortunately, you can download the Novell version of the NetWare client at `http://support.novell.com/Ftp/Updates/nwos/nc32w952/Date0.html`. This site includes other Novell-supplied Windows 95 fixes and patches as well. Make absolutely certain that you read any update files associated with the drivers before you install them. Chapter 27 discusses the Novell 32-bit client for Windows 95 in more detail.

Once you get Client for NetWare installed, select it in the Primary Network Logon field of the Network Properties dialog box. You access this dialog box by right-clicking the Network Neighborhood icon and selecting the Properties option. The first time you run Client for NetWare, you see two login dialog boxes. The first dialog box logs you into a preferred server. The second login dialog box takes care of the Windows 95 security requirement. As long as the user name and password for NetWare and Windows 95 are the same, you see this dual-login dialog box only once. The next time you log in, you see only one dialog box that takes care of both login needs.

To enable login script processing on the NetWare server, you need to use the Client for NetWare Networks Properties dialog box shown in Figure 23.5. This dialog box has three fields. The one that you're interested in is a check box that enables login script processing. You also see fields for the preferred server and the first network drive.

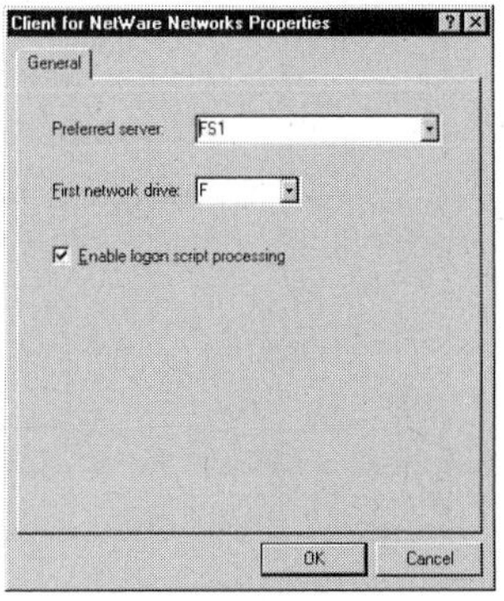

Figure 23.5.
The Client for NetWare Networks Properties dialog box allows you to enable login script processing.

Tip: You can reduce your need to use the MAP command (or anything similar) by using the persistent mapping capability available by using Explorer or the context menu of Network Neighborhood. Chapter 2 covers the Explorer part of the equation. You'll find Network Neighborhood described in this chapter. Using the native Windows 95 capability means less chance of error if an individual workstation's configuration changes.

Enabling login script processing allows an administrator to maintain the pre-Windows 95 security policy on the server. It also provides a means for creating automatic drive mapping and other NOS-specific features. Check the documentation that came with your network to see exactly what types of script file processing you can perform.

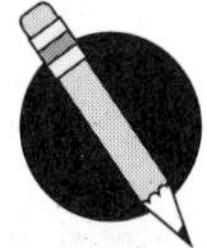

Note: Windows 95 doesn't currently support the NetWare 4.x NDS style of login-script processing. You must use the bindery-style login scripts provided by NetWare 3.x and below. This means placing your NetWare 4.x server in bindery emulation mode. The system login script for a NetWare server is stored in NET$LOG.DAT. You'll find it in the \PUBLIC directory. The individual user scripts appear in the \MAIL directory. Keep in mind that NetWare 4.x utilities run only under true NDS.

Warning: The Windows 95 protected-mode script processor can't run TSRs. The TSR starts in a separate virtual machine, which terminates with an error when the script-file processing completes. This lack of TSR processing in your script files means that you have to come up with a different way to install backup agents and other files that you normally install by using the login script. In most cases, you need to install such files as part of the AUTOEXEC.BAT or within a DOS session after you start Windows 95.

TCP/IP and PPP—It's in There!

Windows 95 provides a fairly complex and complete set of features related to Transmission Control Protocol/Internet Protocol (TCP/IP). Think of a protocol as a set of rules for a game. The rules tell you how to play the game and give you a basis for playing it with someone else. A protocol performs the same task on a network. It establishes rules that allow two nodes—workstations, mainframes, minicomputers, or other network elements such as printers—to talk to each other. TCP/IP is one of the more popular sets of network communication rules. Windows 95 also provides support for Point-to-Point Protocol (PPP). Just like TCP/IP, PPP is a set of communication rules. However, in this case the rules provide a method of conducting online (from one point to another) communications. Both of these features allow you to connect to a UNIX host or the Internet or enhance your dial-up networking capability. In almost all cases, the support that Windows 95 provides deals with remote communications, but there are exceptions. For example, the monitoring capability provided by SNMP could work in a local server setup.

There are two reasons that it's important to include this support as part of the operating system. First, adding TCP/IP and PPP to the operating system makes it easier for software developers to write agents (special drivers or applications that use the rules that these protocols establish to perform useful work). If you added either protocol as a third-party product, there wouldn't be any standardization, making it nearly impossible for other third-party vendors to write standard agents. Second, adding this level of protocol support to the operating system means that Microsoft can incorporate an additional level of support as part of its utility program offerings. For example, you'll find that both protocols are important when communicating with the Internet through Microsoft Network (MSN). Before you can use TCP/IP, you have to install it. Let's quickly go through a few of the things you need to do to install TCP/IP support.

Tip: Installing TCP/IP support before you install Dial-Up Networking saves some extra steps later. The Dial-Up Networking installation routine automatically installs the required protocols for you if you install TCP/IP support first.

1. Right-click the Network Neighborhood icon and select Properties.
2. On the Configuration page, click the Add button. You'll see the dialog box shown in Figure 23.6.

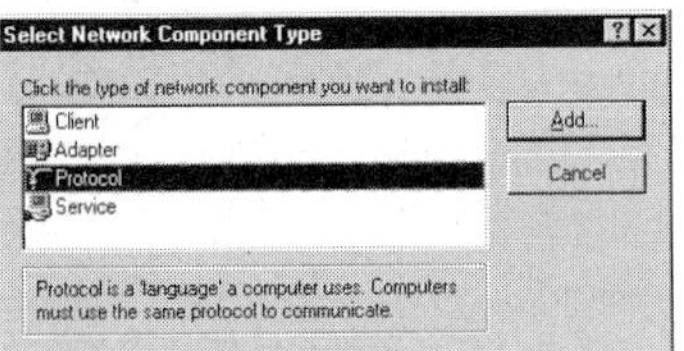

Figure 23.6.
The Select Network Component Type dialog box allows you to choose the type of network component to install.

3. Select Protocol and click Add. Scroll through the list of vendors and select Microsoft. Then select TCP/IP in the listing on the right side. You'll see the dialog box shown in Figure 23.7.

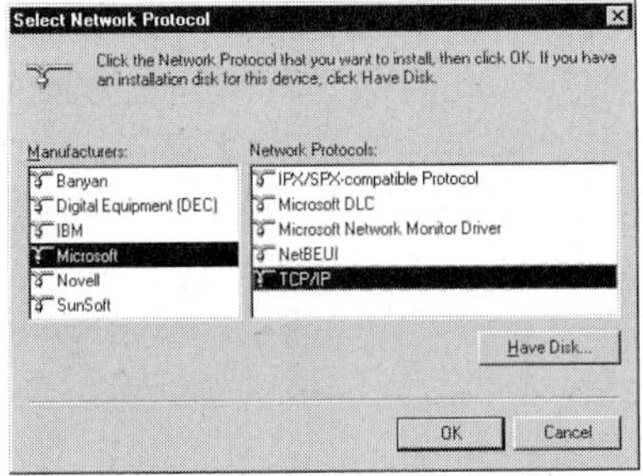

Figure 23.7.
Use the Select Network Protocol dialog box to select TCP/IP as the protocol you want to install.

4. Click OK to complete the selection. Click OK again to close the Network Properties dialog box. Windows 95 prompts you for installation floppies or the CD-ROM as needed. After it installs the required files, Windows asks whether you want to restart the system. Click OK to complete the installation process.

Once you get it installed, configuring the TCP/IP support is easy. All you need to do is select the TCP/IP entry in the Network Properties dialog box and click the Properties button. You'll see a dialog box similar to the one shown in Figure 23.8. (Table 4.1 in Chapter 4 discusses the various TCP/IP setup options.) Essentially, all the pages in this dialog box allow you to set the addresses and other TCP/IP properties for your machine. All the setup options available for automatic setup are present when you use this manual technique.

Once you complete this initial installation process, you need to perform other installations to provide specific levels of support. For example, you need to install Dial-Up Networking and then the TCP/IP support that Windows provides before you can access that support for a remote connection. The following sections show you how to configure Windows 95 to use both TCP/IP and PPP. I also cover a few of the usage issues that you need to know about.

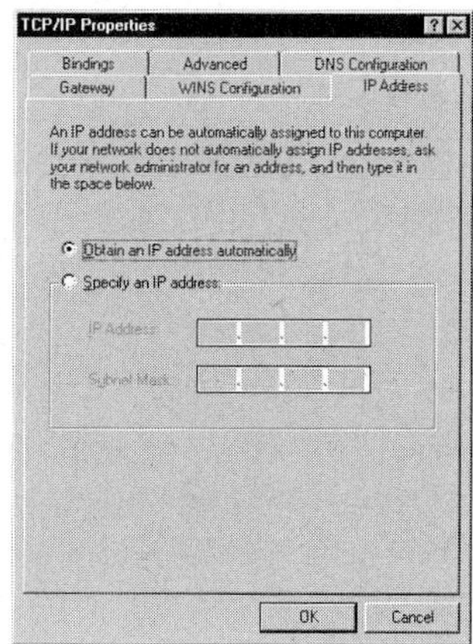

Figure 23.8.
The TCP/IP Properties dialog box allows you to configure TCP/IP support under Windows 95.

SNMP Support

Windows 95 provides remote monitoring agent support for agents that use the Simple Network Management Protocol (SNMP). SNMP was originally designed for the Internet. It allows an application to remotely manage devices from a variety of vendors, even if those devices don't normally work with the managing device. For example, a mainframe could use SNMP to send updated sales statistics to a group of satellite offices in a large company. You can use an SNMP console to monitor a Windows 95 workstation once this support is installed. SNMP support under Windows 95 conforms to the version 1 specification. Microsoft implements SNMP support for both TCP/IP and IPX/SPX by using WinSock (which I describe later). The following procedure allows you to install SNMP support under Windows 95:

1. Right-click the Network Neighborhood icon and select the Properties option.
2. From within the Network Properties dialog box, click Add and then double-click Services. You should see the dialog box shown in Figure 23.9.

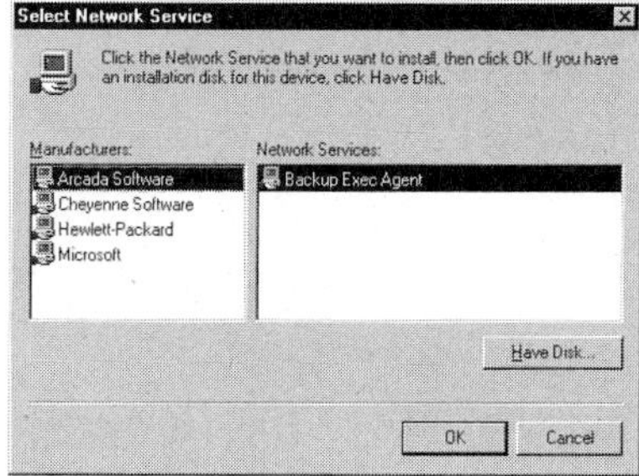

Figure 23.9.
You'll find a list of the common network services in the Select Network Service dialog box.

3. Click Have Disk and then click Browse. Search for the \ADMIN\NETTOOLS\SNMP folder, as shown in Figure 23.10. Notice that the dialog box automatically finds the .INF file required to install this service.

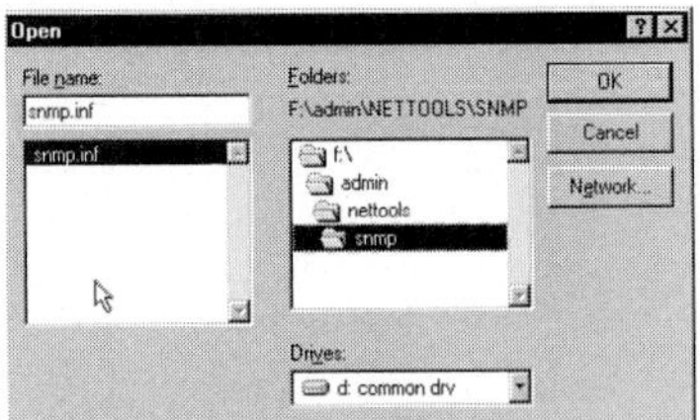

Figure 23.10.
Browsing is the easy way to find the network component you need to install.

4. Click OK twice. You should see the dialog box shown in Figure 23.11. It allows you to select from the list of network components that the .INF file will install. In this case, there's only one on the list—SNMP support.

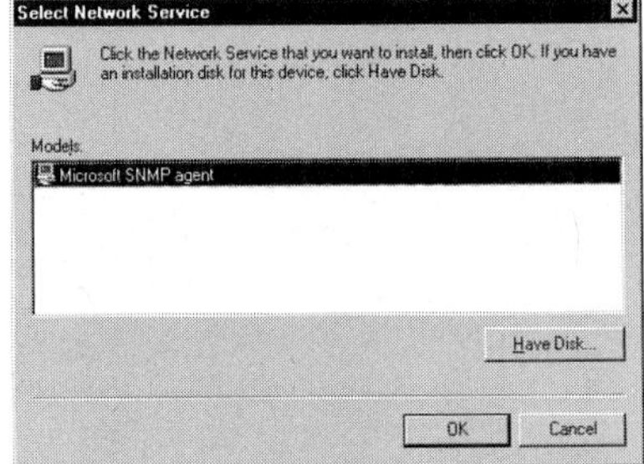

Figure 23.11.
This second Select Network Service dialog box presents a list of services supported by the .INF file that you selected.

5. Select the new service and click OK. You'll see that SNMP support is part of the installed component list of the Network Properties dialog box.
6. Click OK to close the dialog box. Windows 95 installs the required files from the CD. When it completes this task, Windows 95 asks whether you want to shut down and restart the operating system. You need to do this before SNMP support will take effect.

Unlike just about every other feature in Windows 95, there's no Properties dialog box for SNMP support. You need to edit the various properties by using the System Policy Editor. Simply open the System Policy Editor and use the File | Registry command to open the Registry. You can install the System Policy Editor by using the procedure in the section "Special Utility Installation" in Chapter 11. The System Policy Editor appears in the \ADMIN\APPTOOLS\POLEDIT folder on the CD-ROM. Double-click the Local Computer icon and select the SNMP option of the Network policy, as shown in Figure 23.12. There you can change all the SNMP policies for your machine. Notice that there are two change areas. The first is where you check the property that you want to enable. If this property has other settings, they appear in the box at the bottom of the dialog box. All you need to do is click the button you find there to display a dialog box containing any options for that property.

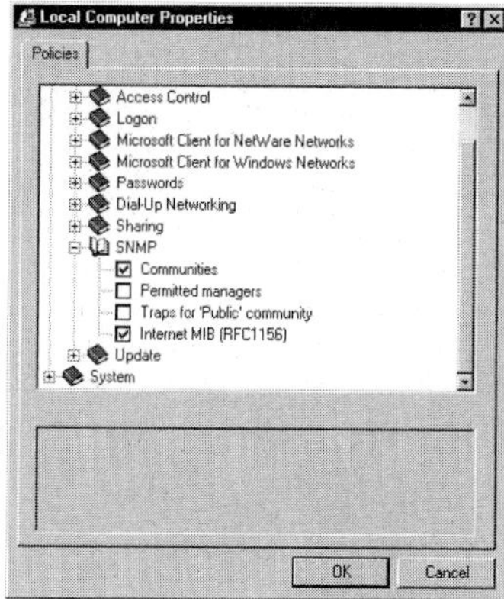

Figure 23.12.
The System Policy Editor provides the only method for changing your SNMP configuration.

As you can see from the figure, you can change four different settings. The following list tells you which setting each item affects:

- **Communities:** Defines the hosts that your computer can connect to for administration purposes. You must belong to a community before you can use SNMP services on it. Even though they aren't exactly the same, you could look at a community as a NetWare group or a Windows NT domain.
- **Permitted Managers:** This setting defines a list of IP or IPX addresses that can query the SNMP agent installed on your machine. If you don't provide a value here, any IP or IPX address can query the agent.
- **Traps for 'Public' Community:** Use this setting to define a list of host IP or IPX addresses to which you want to send SNMP traps. In essence, a trap is an automatic monitoring method. It automatically updates the host when specific events occur on your machine.
- **Internet MIB (RFC1156):** Determines a point of contact and location if you're using the Internet MIB.

The System Policy Editor configuration procedure comes in handy for more than just SNMP installation and configuration. I refer to it several times in this chapter. You can also use the System Policy Editor to affect the condition of other network settings. However, I usually find that the Properties dialog box that comes with this feature provides an easier-to-use interface.

Using the FTP Utility

Using the Internet requires some form of browser support if you want to download files or upload messages. FTP is actually a utility program that Windows 95 installs for you along with TCP/IP support. It's a DOS application that uses a standard character-mode interface. The syntax for FTP is as follows: `FTP [-V] [-N] [-I] [-D] [-G] [<host>] [-S:<filename>]`.

Tip: Once you get more familiar with the Internet, you'll find that the FTP and Telnet utilities provided with Windows 95 are pretty limited as far as browsers go. For example, some of the page links didn't work properly, and I didn't see the same level of graphics that Mosaic provides. A lot of other browsers, such as Mosaic, Gopher, Archie, and WAIS, can make your life a lot easier. You can get any of them commercially or as shareware from Internet servers. You can also get the WWW (World Wide Web) Browser from a variety of sources. The Microsoft Plus! pack also provides an enhanced browser from Spyglass that's specially designed for the Windows 95 interface. The bottom line is that you need an easy-to-use browser that meets your particular needs in order to make the best use of the resources that the Internet makes available.

The following list defines each option:

- `-V`: This switch disables the display of remote server responses. It comes in handy if you want the download to progress in the background without disturbing your foreground task.
- `-N`: Use this switch to disable autologon upon initial connection.
- `-I`: You can use this switch to remove interactive prompting during multiple file transfers. This allows you to automate the file transfer process.
- `-D`: Use this switch to display all FTP commands passed between the client and server. This allows you to debug script files.
- `-G`: This switch disables filename globbing, which permits the use of wildcard characters in local filenames and pathnames.
- `<host>`: Replace this parameter with the name or address of the host with which you want to connect for a file download.
- `-S:<filename>`: Replace `<filename>` with the name of a text file containing FTP commands. In essence, this switch allows you to create a script for your FTP download. Use this switch instead of redirection (`>`).

The FTP utility provides a surprising array of commands that you can use once you run it. There really are too many to list here, but you can get a list easily enough. All you need to remember is one command, the question mark (`?`). If you type a question mark, you'll see a list of all the things that you can do with FTP.

SLIP Support

Windows 95 provides support for both SLIP (Serial Line Internet Protocol) and CSLIP (Compressed Serial Line Internet Protocol) for remote network connections. This is the type of connection supported by older UNIX remote servers. The operator of the host machine will let you know if you require this level of support, so don't install it unless you need to do so. You access both types of connections by using the Dial-Up Networking utility described in Chapter 19. Before you can use either level of support, you have to install it. Unfortunately, like most of the features in this chapter, it's not one of the things on the standard Windows installation menu. You have to use the following procedure to install SLIP and CSLIP support (they both get installed at the same time).

Note: Be sure to install the Dial-Up Networking utility before you install SLIP support. Otherwise, the SLIP and CSLIP options won't appear in the Connection Properties dialog box when you need to configure the connection. You also need to reinstall SLIP support if you update or otherwise change the Dial-Up Networking utility.

1. Open the Control Panel and double-click the Add/Remove Programs applet.
2. Select the Windows Setup page and click the Have Disk button.
3. Use the Browse button to display an Open dialog box like the one shown in Figure 23.13. Find the \ADMIN\APPTOOLS\SLIP folder and select the RNAPLUS.INF file. Notice that it's the only file shown in this dialog box.

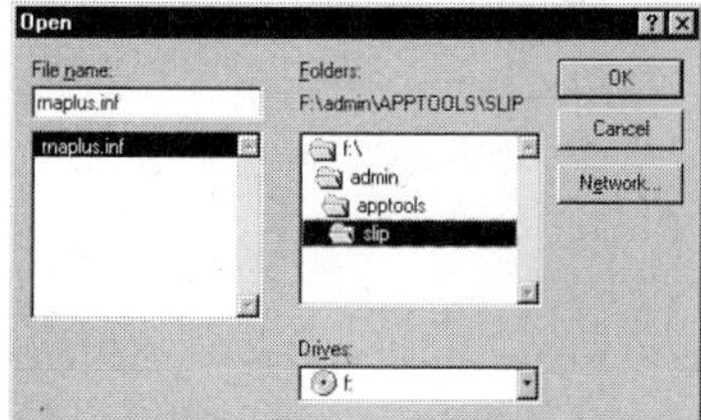

Figure 23.13.
Use the Open dialog box to find the .INF file needed to install SLIP support.

4. Click OK twice to select the .INF file. You'll see the Have Disk dialog box shown in Figure 23.14. Notice that it contains only one entry. There would normally be one entry for each installation option that the .INF file supports.

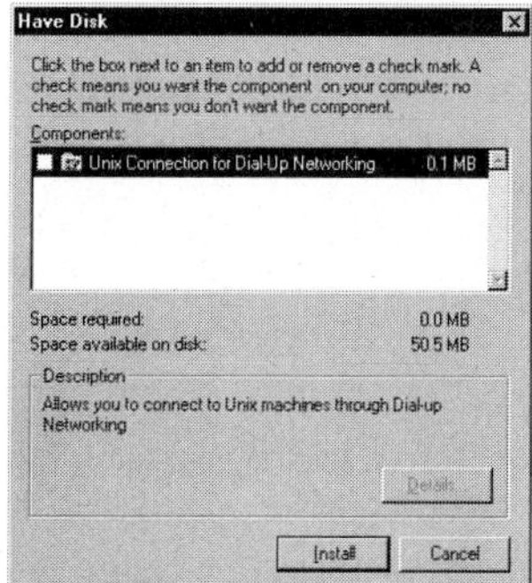

Figure 23.14.
The Have Disk dialog box shows you which installation options the .INF file provides.

5. Click the option you want to install, and then click the Install button. Windows 95 copies the required files from the CD and lists the new option on the Windows Setup page of the Add/Remove Programs Properties dialog box.
6. Click OK to exit the dialog box. You'll probably want to shut Windows down and reboot the machine so that any Registry changes take effect.

You don't configure SLIP support like most of the Windows 95 features, either. The first thing you'll need to do is open Dial-Up Networking and create a new connection. Chapter 19 covers this procedure, so I won't go over it again here. Once you get this done, right-click the new connection and select the Properties option. Click the Server Types button. You'll see the dialog box shown in Figure 23.15. Notice that the list of available server types includes both SLIP and CSLIP support.

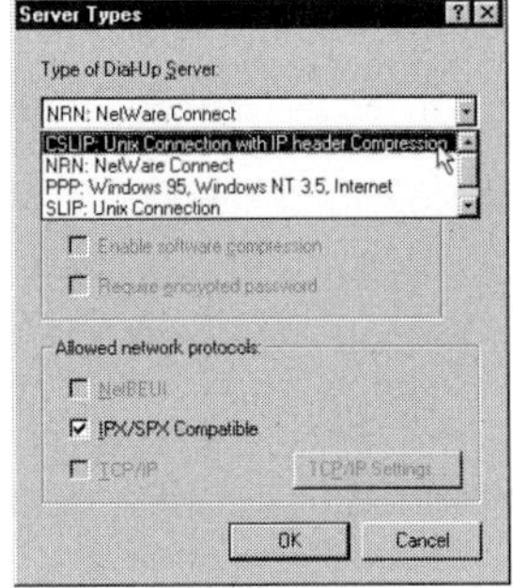

Figure 23.15.
You add SLIP and CSLIP support to a connection through the Server Types dialog box.

After you select a SLIP or CSLIP server, it's time to configure it by clicking the TCP/IP Settings button. You should see the dialog box shown in Figure 23.16. Notice that it contains all the familiar TCP/IP address information required by the host computer. Chapter 4 covers all the options listed here.

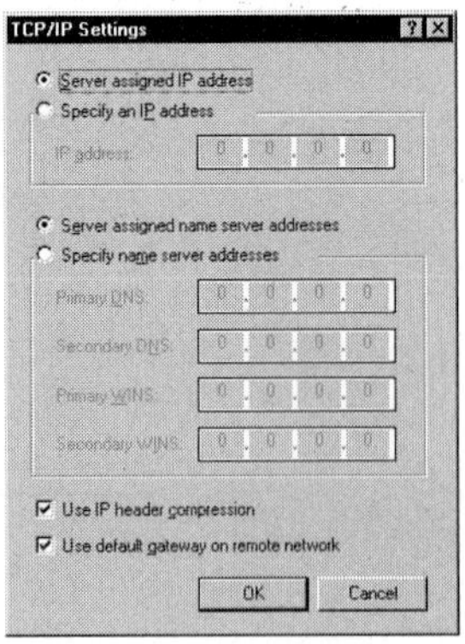

Figure 23.16.
After adding a SLIP or CSLIP server to your connection, you need to configure it by using the TCP/IP Settings dialog box.

Using the Telnet Utility

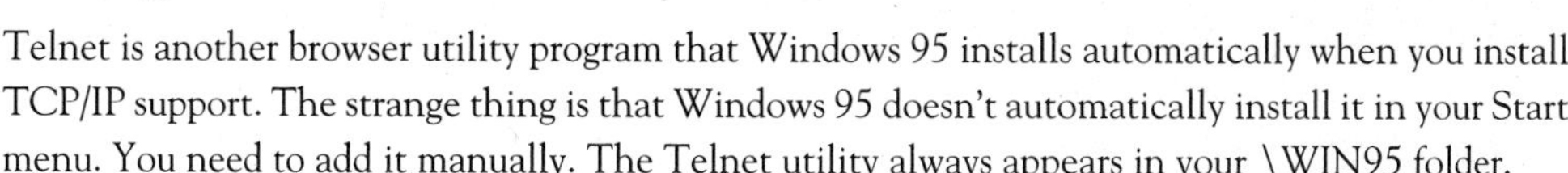

Telnet is another browser utility program that Windows 95 installs automatically when you install TCP/IP support. The strange thing is that Windows 95 doesn't automatically install it in your Start menu. You need to add it manually. The Telnet utility always appears in your \WIN95 folder.

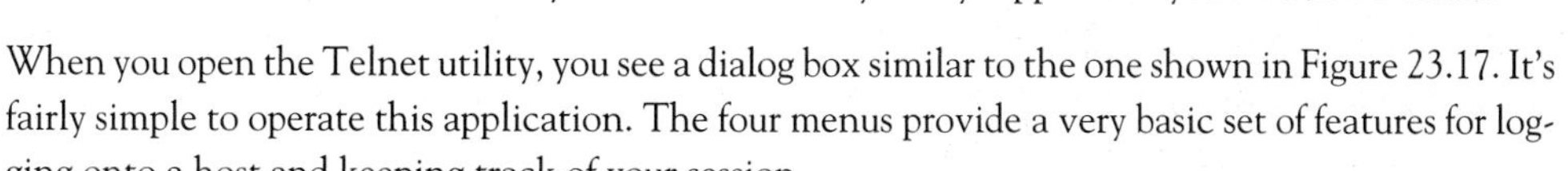

When you open the Telnet utility, you see a dialog box similar to the one shown in Figure 23.17. It's fairly simple to operate this application. The four menus provide a very basic set of features for logging onto a host and keeping track of your session.

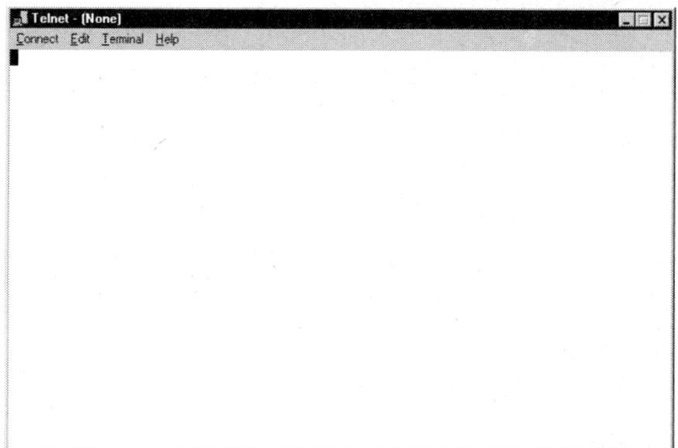

Figure 23.17.
Telnet provides a very basic terminal-like front end for a host connection.

The Connect | Remote System command displays the Connect dialog box shown in Figure 23.18. This dialog box has three fields. The first contains the name or address of the host you want to connect to. The second field contains the host type. The third field specifies a terminal type. In most cases you won't have much of a choice about terminal types, but I find that the ANSI terminal is usually a bit easier to use if you can gain access to a host that supports it. Disconnecting from the host is very easy. Just use the Connect | Disconnect command.

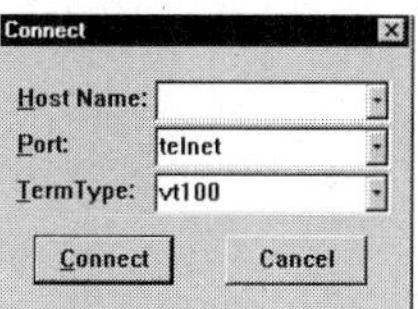

Figure 23.18.
The Connect dialog box is where you tell Telnet how and where to make a connection.

The Edit menu contains the normal Copy and Paste commands, so I won't spend any time discussing it here. The Terminal menu provides a few options that you should know about. For example, you can use the Start Logging and Stop Logging options to keep track of your session. The Start Logging option displays a File Open dialog box that you can use to find or create a log file.

Figure 23.19 shows the dialog box that appears when you select the Terminal | Preferences command. The Terminal Options and Emulation groups are pretty self-explanatory. They configure the way that the host machine interacts with the terminal emulation program. The Fonts button allows you to select a different font than the default Fixedsys. You can also add a little color to the display by clicking the Background Color button. I normally keep it set as is because you can't change the foreground color. The Buffer Size field allows you to change the number of lines of text that you see in the terminal window. Telnet uses a default setting of 25, which seems to work well with most hosts.

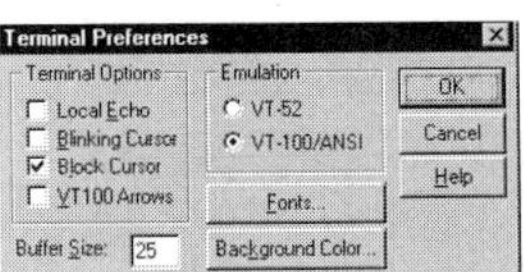

Figure 23.19.
Use the Terminal Preferences dialog box to configure Telnet for the host that you plan to connect with.

Desktop Management Interface (DMI) Support

Have you ever wondered how you were going to figure out which computers on the network required new hardware before you could make an upgrade? For example, will your current hardware run Windows 95? You might ask just that question in the next few months, after you've had time to evaluate Windows 95. Desktop Management Interface (DMI) is part of Systems Management Server. It's the hardware auditing component of this utility and follows the standards set by the Desktop Management Task Force (DMTF).

Note: The OSR2 version of Windows 95 provides support for the 1.1 version of DMI. This new version of DMI gives network administrators a better look into the hardware by examining dependencies. For example, a fan failure might cause a hard drive to fail. It's also designed to work with servers, even if they aren't running Windows 95. (Of course, the server hardware has to be DMI-compliant.) Even though a download site wasn't available at the time of this writing, Microsoft does plan to make the update available to users of older versions of Windows 95. You can contact the Desktop Management Task Force (DMTF) Web site at `http://www.dmtf.org/` for further details on this update.

A vendor writes a Management Information File (MIF) that contains all the particulars about a piece of equipment. When the System Management Server looks at a workstation and finds this file, it adds the file contents to a SQL database that you can open with any number of products. In addition to the hardware information, System Management Server adds the software auditing information that it finds to the database. The combined software and hardware information gives you the data required to know whether a particular workstation can run a piece of software without an upgrade.

Unfortunate as it might seem, none of this is fully implemented in Windows 95 as of this writing. DMI client support is present, but you won't find System Management Server anywhere on your Windows 95 CD. (The client support level for the original and Service Pack 1 versions of Windows 95 is 1.0; OSR2 provides version 1.1 support.) Adding server support is a future upgrade that Microsoft might make to Windows 95. Although it might not help you much right this second, it's good to know that help is on the way. However, if you have all of the following equipment, you can implement System Management Server today:

- Windows NT Server version 3.5 or later
- Microsoft SQL Server version 4.21 or later
- A 486/66 or better processor
- 32MB of memory (recommended)
- A hard disk with at least 100MB disk space available
- A network-accessible CD-ROM drive
- A network adapter
- A Microsoft mouse or compatible pointing device (a mouse is recommended, but optional)

Remote Procedure Calls (RPC) Support

Remember near the beginning of this chapter when I talked about network transports and the way that Microsoft implements them? I mentioned then just how complex a network transport could get if you added a few features. Remote procedure calls (RPCs) are a somewhat new concept for Windows 95. They're implemented as a network transport mechanism using named pipes, NetBIOS, or WinSock to create a connection between a client and a server. RPC is compatible with the Open Software Foundation (OSF) Data Communication Exchange (DCE) specification.

So what does RPC do for you? OLE uses it, for one. Actually, OLE uses a subset of RPC called light RPC (LRPC) to allow you to make connections that you couldn't normally make. The "Differences Between OLE 1 and OLE 2" section of Chapter 12 discusses the whole OLE 2 connection issue in detail, so I won't talk about it again here. (You'll also find some information about the appearance of LRPC in the Registry in the "`HKEY_LOCAL_MACHINE`" section of Chapter 7.) However, OLE is only the tip of the iceberg. There are other ways in which RPC can help you as a user.

Think about it this way. You're using an application that requires any number of resources in the form of .DLLs, VxDs, and other forms of executable code. Right now, all that code has to appear on your machine or in a place where Windows will be certain to find it. What this means is that every time a network administrator wants to update software, he has to search every machine on the network to make sure that the job gets done completely. What if you could "borrow" the .DLL from someone else's machine? That's what RPCs are all about. An RPC lets your application grab what it needs in the form of executable code from wherever it happens to be.

You won't find a lot of RPC support in Windows 95 right now, but there's one way to see how it works. If you're running a Windows NT network, Microsoft provides a remote print provider utility in the \ADMIN\APPTOOLS\RPCPP folder. Installing this utility allows a Windows 95 client to administer printer queues on Windows NT servers. Using this print provider, a Windows 95 client can obtain complete accounting and job status information from the Windows NT server.

Windows Sockets (WinSock) Support

Windows sockets (WinSock) started out as an effort by a group of vendors to make sense out of the conglomeration of TCP/IP protocol-based socket interfaces. Various vendors had originally ported their implementation of this protocol to Windows. The result was that nothing worked with anything else. The socket interface was originally implemented as a networked interprocess communications mechanism for version 4.2 of the Berkeley UNIX system. Windows 95 requires all non-NetBIOS applications to use WinSock if they need to access any TCP/IP services. Vendors may optionally write IPX/SPX applications to this standard as well. Microsoft includes two WinSock applications with Windows 95: SNMP and FTP.

Before I go much further, let me quickly define a couple of terms used in the preceding paragraph. Earlier, we looked at what a protocol is: It's a set of rules. TCP/IP is one common implementation of a set of rules. Think of a socket as one of the tube holders found in old televisions and radios. An application can plug a request (a tube) for some type of service into a socket and send it to a host of some kind. That host could be a file server, a minicomputer, a mainframe, or even another PC. An application can also use a socket to make a query of a database server. For example, it could ask for last year's sales statistics. If every host uses a different size of socket, every application will require a different set of tubes to fit those sockets. WinSock gets rid of this problem by standardizing the socket used to request services and make queries.

Besides making the interface easier to use, WinSock provides another advantage. Normally, an application has to add a NetBIOS header to every packet that leaves the workstation. The workstation at the other end doesn't really need the header, but it's there anyway. This additional processing overhead reduces network efficiency. Using WinSock eliminates the need for the header, and the user sees better performance as a result.

Sockets are an age-old principle (at least in the computer world), but they're far from out-of-date. The WinSock project proved so successful that Microsoft began to move it to other transports. For example, Windows 95 includes a WinSock module for both the IPX/SPX and NetBEUI transports.

Of course, WinSock is really a stopgap measure for today. In the long term, companies will want to move from the client/server model for some applications and use a distributed approach. This will require the use of a remote procedure call (RPC) interface instead of WinSock. We've already looked at the implications of RPC in this chapter.

So what does it take to implement WinSock on your system? A group of five files in your SYSTEM folder are used to implement WinSock. The following list tells you what they are and what tasks they perform:

- WINSOCK.DLL: This 16-bit application provides backward compatibility for older applications that need it. For example, an application such as PING would use this .DLL.
- WSOCK32.DLL: 32-bit applications use this .DLL to access the WinSock API. It provides support for newer socket applications such as Telnet.
- VSOCK.VXD: Windows uses this driver to provide both 16-bit and 32-bit TCP/IP and IPX/SPX WinSock support. It provides virtualized support for each virtual machine, enabling Windows to perform more than one WinSock operation at a time. This is the general driver used for both protocols. If Microsoft added more WinSock interfaces later, they would all require this file for interface purposes.
- WSTCP.VXD: TCP/IP requires a protocol-specific driver. This file provides that support.
- WSIPX.VXD: IPX/SPX requires a protocol-specific driver. This file provides that support.

Configuring TCP/IP— The Short Form

Windows 95 provides a lot of capabilities as far as TCP/IP goes, and it's really not possible to cover them all in one short section of a chapter. The same flexibility that makes Windows 95 so easy to use with TCP/IP, however, makes it nearly impossible for an inexperienced user to configure it. With this in mind, I decided to provide a very fast and easy method for you to configure TCP/IP for a local intranet. I assume that you're going to use Personal Web Server on a LAN in this section, but the principles apply equally well to other kinds of setups.

The first thing you have to do is install TCP/IP, as shown in the earlier section "TCP/IP and PPP—It's in There!" You'll also find some subsections there that tell you about some of the utilities provided with TCP/IP. You don't have to understand all of that additional information to use this section—your only concern is installing the required TCP/IP support.

After you have TCP/IP installed, you'll want to modify its properties so that other computers can see yours. Just right-click the Network Neighborhood icon, choose Properties from the context menu, and then select the TCP/IP protocol on the Configuration page of the Network Properties dialog box. (You may have more than one entry here—select the TCP/IP entry for your NIC and ignore any dial-up connections that you may see.) Click the Properties button and you'll see the TCP/IP Properties dialog box. Select the IP Address page and you'll see a dialog box like the one shown in Figure 23.20.

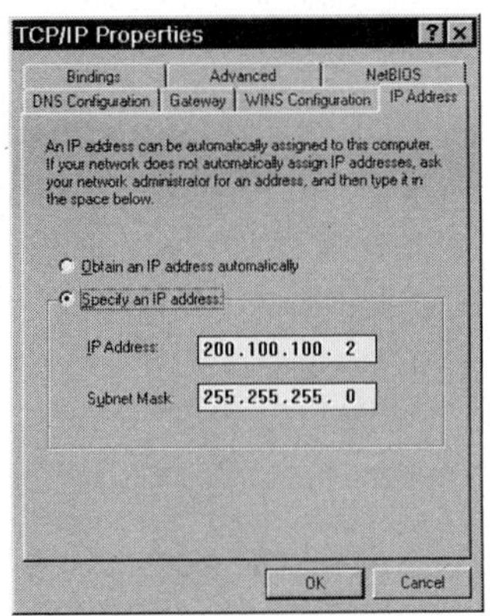

Figure 23.20.
You use the TCP/IP Properties dialog box to set up TCP/IP on your machine for local intranet use.

Look at how I've configured the IP Address page in my dialog box. There are only two fields you need to worry about: The first is the IP Address field; the second is the Subnet Mask field. These two fields work together. An IP address is really composed of two parts. The first part defines your organization and the second part defines your individual computer.

Notice that the IP address is actually composed of four numbers separated by periods. You can choose up to three of those numbers to represent your organization. The remaining numbers represent your computer. A single entry can contain any value from 0 to 255. All four entries combined make up the IP address. If you were on the Internet, you'd have to apply to InterNIC to get an IP address. On a local intranet, however, you're not really talking to anyone but your own organization. You can use any set of four numbers that you want.

I normally select three easy-to-remember numbers for my organization and then use the remaining IP address entry to number the computers on my network sequentially. In this case, I've chosen 200.100.100 to represent my organization and 2 to represent the workstation.

Now comes the question of how the computer knows how to read this address. That's where the subnet mask shown in Figure 23.20 comes in. Like the IP address, it contains four numbers separated by periods. Unlike the IP address, however, you can only choose 0 or 255 for each number. A value of 255 represents an organization entry in the IP address, while a value of 0 represents a node (workstation) in the IP address. As you can see from the figure, I've placed a value of 255 for the first three numbers because I've used those numbers to represent my organization. I placed a 0 in the last position because it represents my workstation.

The final step is getting one computer to talk to another. Every computer on your network must use the same organization number or it won't be able to hear the other computers. In addition, every computer must have a unique node number. Because 1 is already in use by another machine that I've set up, I'll use 2 for the next node. You must configure all the computers on your network before they can talk to the Internet server on your workstation.

Checking these connections is relatively easy as well. Windows 95 provides a DOS utility called PING (Packet Internet Groper) to check your capability to communicate with other TCP/IP workstations. All you need to do is type **PING *<workstation IP address>***. If you want to check the first workstation in the network, for example, you'd type **PING 200.100.100.1**. PING transmits three packets and listens for a response. If you see three responses from a particular workstation, you'll know that you've configured it properly.

Personal Web Server

Personal Web Server is the smallest and newest version of Internet Information Server (IIS) provided by Microsoft. It's not designed for running an Internet site—you'd use it for testing purposes or perhaps a small in-house intranet Web site. I use it to test my Web pages before uploading them to a live site. This is a new feature for the OSR2 version of Windows 95, but you can use it with older versions as well. All you need to do is download the Personal Web Server files from `http://www.microsoft.com/ie/download/ieadd.htm`.

Note: What Is an Intranet?

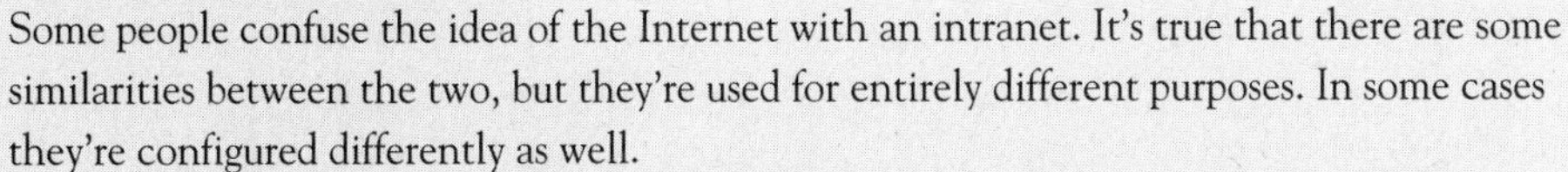

Some people confuse the idea of the Internet with an intranet. It's true that there are some similarities between the two, but they're used for entirely different purposes. In some cases they're configured differently as well.

First let me clear up the major difference between the two. An intranet is normally private—I don't think I've ever seen a public one. The Internet, on the other hand, is always public. Private versus public access makes a great deal of difference in the way that you configure the two setups.

Another difference is size. The Internet invites literally thousands of people to view your site. The private nature of an intranet precludes inviting thousands of people—you may be inviting hundreds instead. This consideration affects the amount and type of equipment you buy. You'll find yourself spending more on security and less on hardware when setting up an intranet.

Compatibility considerations are another area where the Internet is different from an intranet. If you set up an Internet site, you'll want to make it as compatible as possible with a broad range of browsers. Intranet sites concentrate on flexibility and power. Because you control the browser used for the site, you also get to use all of the capabilities and features that it provides.

Finally, the Internet is always available through a worldwide connection. You can keep an intranet company-based and not make it available to anyone but the few people in one location. For that matter, an intranet can simply become an extension of your LAN and nothing more.

This section of the chapter looks at what you need to do to install Personal Web Server. We also look at some configuration and testing issues. The one thing we don't look at is designing Web pages; see Chapter 22 for that information. I also won't spend any time on Internet server-specific issues because Personal Web Server isn't designed for that purpose (you'll be very disappointed by the results if you even attempt to use it in that way).

Installation

Installation of this product couldn't be easier. There are two techniques that you can use. The first is for OSR2 users. All you need to do is right-click the Network Neighborhood icon and select Properties from the context menu. When you see the Network Properties dialog box, click the Add button. Select Service in the Select Network Component Type dialog box, and then click Add. You'll see a Select Network Service dialog box. Highlight the Personal Web Server entry in the Microsoft section as shown in Figure 23.21. Click OK. Windows 95 will ask you to restart the machine.

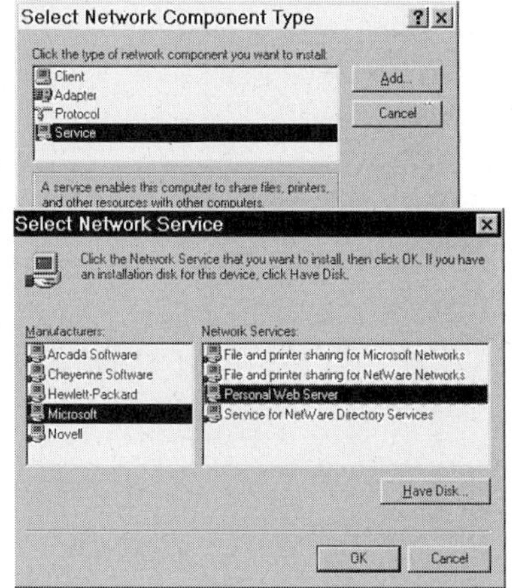

Figure 23.21.
Personal Web Server installs much like any other service under the OSR2 version of Windows 95.

The second method for installing Personal Web Server is even more automatic. Download the PWS10A.EXE file from the Internet site I mentioned earlier in this section. Double-click the icon. You'll see the program copy some files. Once it completes this task, it asks you to restart your machine.

Immediately after you restart your machine, you'll notice a new Personal Web Server icon on the Taskbar. Right-clicking this icon displays a context menu with three entries, as shown in Figure 23.22. The later "Configuration" section shows how to use these options.

Figure 23.22.
The Personal Web Server icon appears on the Taskbar once you successfully install it.

Testing Your Setup

Personal Web Server normally runs right out of the box. You don't have to do anything more at this point if you don't want to. People will be able to display any Web pages that you create. Every link will work as expected. In short, Personal Web Server's default configuration is more than enough to set up a help desk or perform other tasks that you can perform by using HTML pages. I find it helpful to test my setup right after installation to see if it works at all. Regular testing after that point ensures that I get the results I'd hoped for.

You need a browser to test your setup. The first thing you need to know is how to access the Web site. It's easy; just type **`HTTP://`*`<name of machine>`*** when asked for an URL. For example, I have two machines on a test network named MAIN and AUX. Personal Web Server is installed on MAIN, so I'd use **`HTTP://MAIN/`** as an URL. Make sure that you perform this initial test from every computer that needs to access the Web site. That way, you can fix any communications problems before you perform a lot of setup. Figure 23.23 shows the initial screen for the default Web page that Microsoft provides.

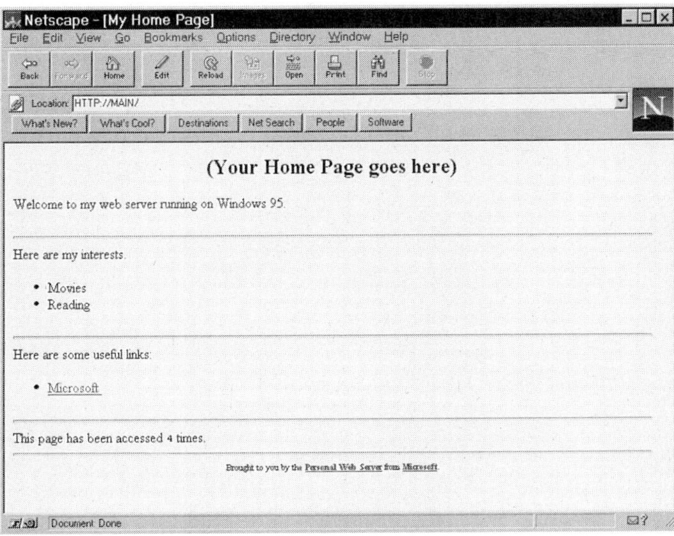

Figure 23.23.
Always test your Personal Web Server setup before you invest a lot of time in configuring it.

At this point, you'll want to turn on your FTP server if you intend to use it (Microsoft installs Personal Web Server with the FTP server shut off). Double-click the Personal Web Server icon on the Taskbar and you'll see a Personal Web Server Properties dialog box. Select the Services page, as shown in Figure 23.24. This is where you decide which services are on or off. For example, you may simply want to provide a central download point for everyone in the company. In that case, you can turn off the HTTP service. All you need to do to start the FTP service is highlight the FTP entry in the Services list box, and then click the Start button. The Status column entry changes from Stopped to Running.

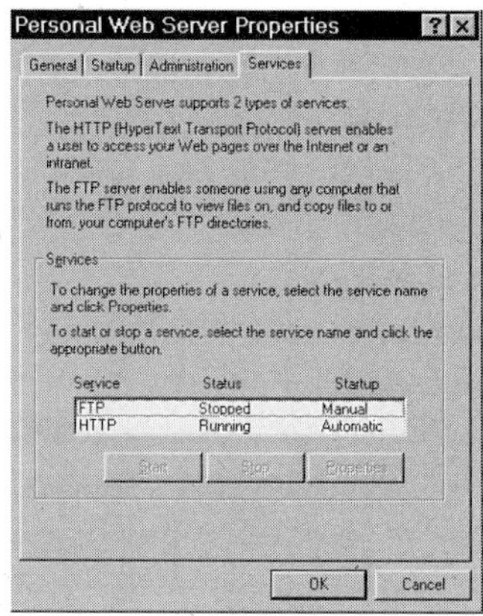

Figure 23.24.
Starting a service is relatively easy—simply select the service you want and click Start.

Notice that this dialog box shows that the FTP service is set up to start manually (look in the Status column). If you want to use the FTP service every time you start Personal Web Server, highlight the FTP entry and click the Properties button. You'll see an FTP Properties dialog box like the one shown in Figure 23.25. Change the Startup Options setting from Manual to Automatic. Notice that you can also use this dialog box to change the home directory for the FTP server. I talk about this setting in the later "Configuration" section of the chapter. Once you make any needed changes on this page, click OK to make the change(s) permanent. You'll want to verify that Personal Web Server accepted the change, by looking at the Startup column in the Services list box. The FTP entry should now say Automatic instead of Manual. Click OK to close the Personal Web Server Properties dialog box. (You don't have to restart Windows 95 for the changes to take place—in fact, you won't want to if you didn't set the FTP server to start automatically.)

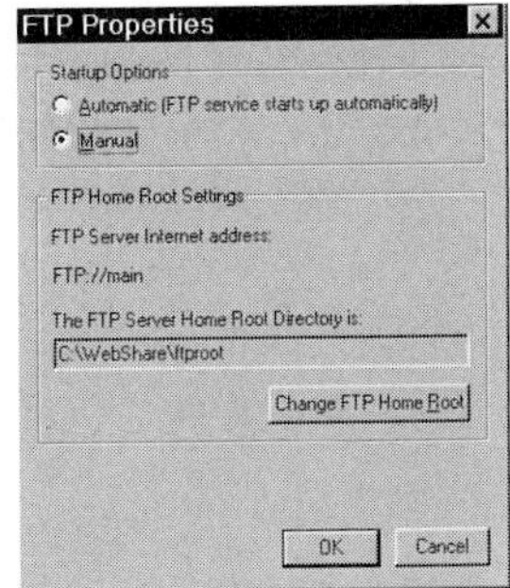

Figure 23.25.
If you plan to use the FTP server every time you start Personal Web Server, be sure to change the Startup Options entry in the FTP Properties dialog box.

Even though there aren't any files in our FTP directory, we can still see whether the site works. In this case type **FTP://*<name of machine>*** when entering the URL. Figure 23.26 shows what the FTP site on my test machine looks like. Notice that the directory contains a single file placed there during installation. It contains the single statement `"Microsoft Personal Web Server FTP Service"`. (You'll see this string in the browser if you click the entry.)

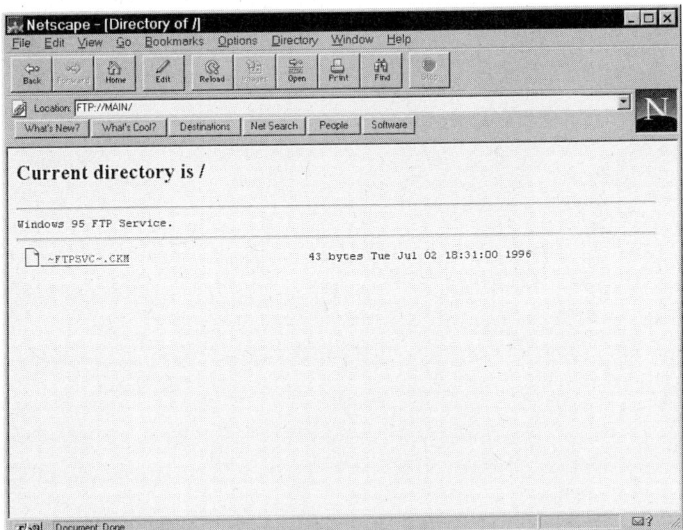

Figure 23.26.
Your FTP directory contains a single default file.

Remember that this initial test isn't the end of the process. You'll want to continue testing your Web site as you develop it. Make sure that you maintain private areas for testing new pages if you plan to actually use this as a small intranet for your office. Otherwise, you can treat the site as you would your production site. You'll be able to test new pages by using the same links that a visitor to your site would use.

Configuration

There are a lot of configuration options in Personal Web Server, though not nearly as many as you'd find with other versions of Internet Information Server (IIS), such as the one that comes with Windows NT Workstation. In fact, I was able to run Personal Web Server using HTTP without changing any configuration items at all. As soon as you want to do anything other than display HTML pages, though, you need to change the default configuration. You'll likely want to at least tune your setup once you get it going—even if your only goal is displaying HTML pages.

The following sections look at how you'd perform the three most common tasks using Personal Web Server. Make certain that you have Personal Web Server installed and working before you attempt to display any of the pages shown. You need to start the FTP server using the procedure in the earlier "Testing Your Setup" section if you want to view the FTP-specific configuration page. If you want to maintain local security over the Web site, you need to disable file and print sharing—this is one of the reasons I previously mentioned that you would want to keep your intranet site on a different workstation than the directories you normally use to share information. (To disable file and print sharing, right-click Network Neighborhood, select Properties from the context menu, click the File and Print sharing button in the Network Properties dialog box, and uncheck all of the boxes. Click OK twice to close the two dialog boxes, and then restart your machine.)

All the Personal Web Server configuration features are viewed from the Internet Services Administrator Web page installed as part of the initial setup. To view this administration page, right-click the Personal Web Server icon on the Taskbar, and select Administer from the context menu. Figure 23.27 shows the initial Web page that you'll see. Note that using a Web page to administer your site allows you to make changes from any workstation on the network that has access to the Personal Web Server site.

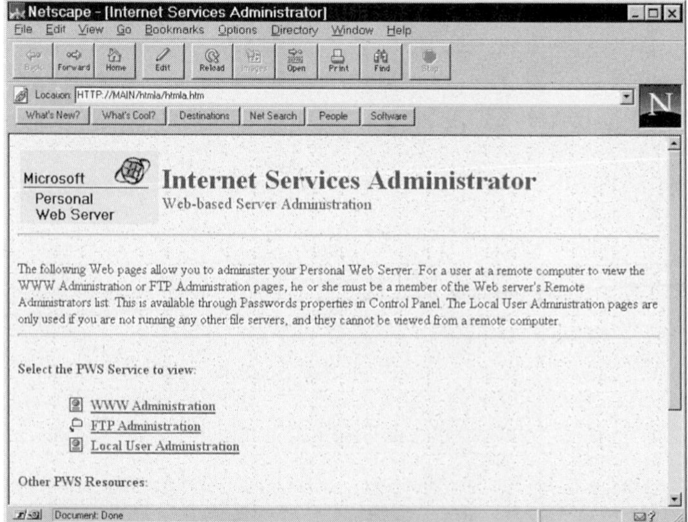

Figure 23.27.
The main administration Web page allows you to configure your Personal Web Server setup.

Note: Even though there's an applet in the Control Panel for Personal Web Server and a Properties page accessible from the Taskbar icon, all the configuration options are on the Internet Service Administrator Web page. Any time you access a configuration item from the Personal Web Server Properties page, you'll start a copy of your default browser. Therefore, you must have a browser installed on the Web server if you intend to maintain the site from that location. The earlier section "Testing Your Setup" covered all the unique Personal Web Server Properties dialog box settings.

HTTP (WWW) Administration

Even though Personal Web Server works right out of the box, you need to spend a little time optimizing your HTTP site before it's ready to use in a production environment. You access the configuration for this part of Personal Web Server by clicking the WWW Administration link shown in Figure 23.27. Figure 23.28 shows the Web page you use to perform the configuration. I scrolled the image so that you could see all of the controls—the page normally contains a header. Notice that this Web page contains several tabs; each tab relates to a different part of the configuration process.

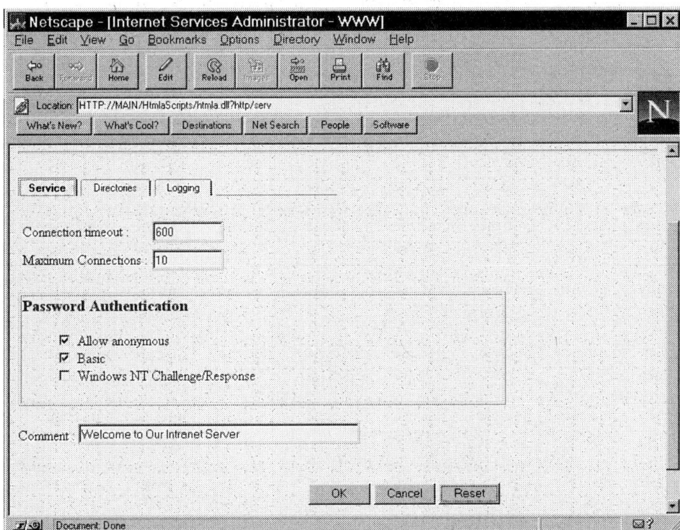

Figure 23.28.
The Internet Services Administrator - WWW page allows you to configure the HTTP settings.

Tip: Notice that we're actually accessing a .DLL to display the Internet Services Administrator - WWW page. You'll also figure out that this page doesn't appear in your WEBSHARE folder. It appears in the \Program Files\WEBSVR\HTMLASCR folder. In addition to the .DLL, you'll find a wealth of .HTR files in this folder. These files use standard HTML code that you could potentially modify if needed. For example, you may want to add a quick link between the HTTP configuration page and the FTP configuration page. Be sure to take the time to make a copy of the .HTR files before you modify them.

The Connection Timeout field defines how long Personal Web Server will wait before terminating a connection that hasn't had any activity on it. Here's one of the problems that you need to consider. If you set this value too high, one user could end up with multiple connections to your server. On the other hand, if you set it too low, people will have connections terminated as they use the Web site as an information resource. I find that the default value of 600 seconds (10 minutes) works fine in most cases.

You use the Maximum Connections field to limit the number of people using the Web server. The astronomical value of 300 that Microsoft uses as the default value probably won't work very well because the server will bog down. I've set a limit of 10 in the figure, which is probably a little low. You'll need to experiment with this setting to see how many users you can add without bogging down the server. (The server may require a few extra connections to allow people to use multiple sessions.)

The next section relates to security. Even though the figure shows that you can use anonymous connections, I usually disable this feature on the small networks that use Personal Web Server. Maintain strict control over access by forcing everyone to use his or her name. This will prevent more problems than it causes. For one thing, you'll get better log files, because they'll contain actual names instead of anonymous entries. Checking the Basic option in this group tells Personal Web Server that you want to use passwords using standard base 64 encoding. This isn't very secure because someone can easily break into your system by decrypting passing messages and using stolen passwords. Using the Windows NT Challenge/Response option enhances security through the use of fully encrypted passwords. You can also choose both options, although this doesn't provide much added security.

You'll also find a Comment field on this page. You can use this for just about anything that you want other administrators to see—no one else will see it. I usually put a last-modified date here, but you could simply type in a friendly message as shown in the figure.

Once you've configured this page you need to send the information to Personal Web Server. To send the information on this page, click OK. Otherwise, click Reset. This returns any values to their original settings. Click Cancel to leave the Web page without making any changes.

Personal Web Server also requires you to set aside a number of directories to store content and specialty pages such as the administration pages we're looking at right now. Figure 23.29 shows the

Directories tag and the default entries for it. You must maintain these directories or some of the links for Personal Web Server itself will be broken. However, you can add to or edit the links shown here as changes in your setup occur.

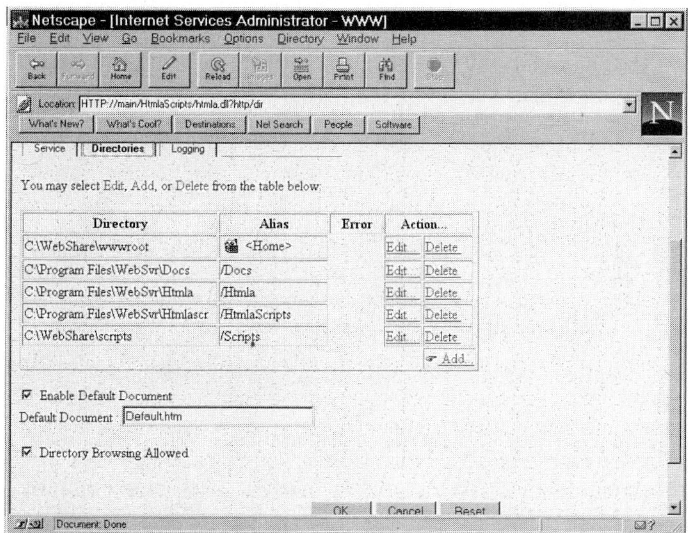

Figure 23.29.
The default directory setup used by Personal Web Server should meet all your needs.

Normally you'll find that these directories work just fine. However, what happens if you move a directory to another drive? Click the Edit entry next to the affected directory and you'll see a dialog box like the one shown in Figure 23.30. At the very top of this page is the Directory field. It contains the directory location on your hard drive. The Home Directory option allows you to choose which directory a visitor to your site will see first. Below it you'll see the Virtual Directory section. This is how someone would refer to the directory if he or she accessed the Web site. The Virtual Directory setting doesn't necessarily have anything to do with the actual directory location—it's a way to refer to the directory in reference to the root Web page. For example, I may have a \Stuff\Good folder on my machine that has a virtual setting of \GoodStuf. You'd access this directory as `http://main/GoodStuf/` if you were using a browser on my test Web site. (My Web site is `http://main/` in this case.) Finally, you'll see an Access section. This defines what kinds of things someone can do in the directory. You'll notice that this directory is marked as Read. If you place applications in the directory, you'll also want to mark the Execute option.

Adding a new directory to the mix follows essentially the same course as editing. However, you'd click the Add link instead of an Edit link in this case. You'd see the same form shown in Figure 23.30. You can click the Browse button if you want to select an existing site on the hard drive without typing it in. The Select Directory page also contains an option for creating a new directory. Interestingly, you can select a location on any hard drive that the Personal Web Server workstation can access.

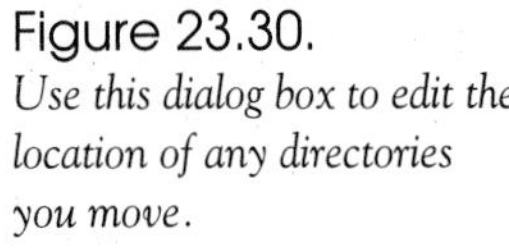

Figure 23.30.
Use this dialog box to edit the location of any directories you move.

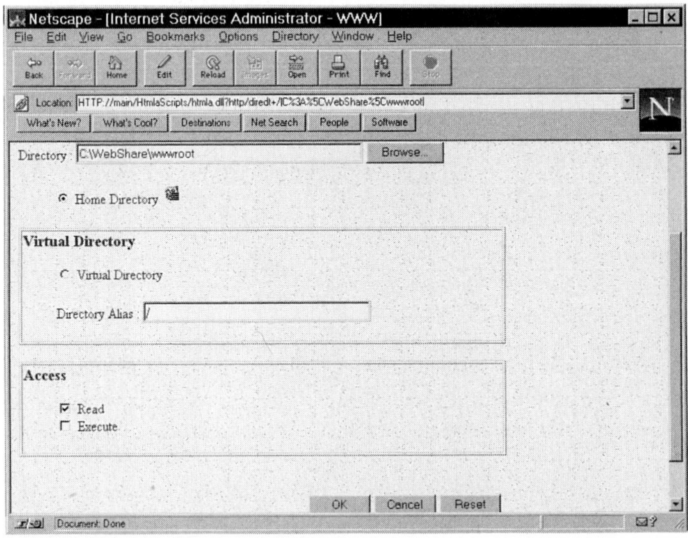

Deleting a directory is almost too simple. All you need to do is click the Delete link next to the directory you want to get rid of. Use this feature with extreme caution, though, because you don't get any kind of warning about deleting essential directory entries. In other words, you could delete your link to the administration directory and find it difficult to regain access later.

There are two more entries on the Directories tab shown in Figure 23.29. The first is the Enable Default Document option and associated Default Document text box. You use this entry to set a default document. In most cases, the default setting works just fine. All you need to do is edit the existing document to meet your needs. The final option, Directory Browsing Allowed, allows the visitor to move from one directory to another. This is a fairly dangerous option to enable on a Windows 95 machine, because your ability to truly control access is somewhat limited. A better choice is to offer more virtual locations for the visitor to look at.

The final tab on the Internet Services Administrator - WWW page is Logging. Figure 23.31 shows what it looks like. The first option, Enable Logging, tells Personal Web Server to maintain a record of special events such as someone logging in. Once you enable logging, you need to determine how often Personal Web Server creates a new log. The default setting is once a month. Finally, you need to select a location for the log. Personal Web Server defaults to using your Windows directory, but you can choose any other option you like. (I usually change this setting to a special log directory to keep my Windows directory from getting any more crammed than it already is.)

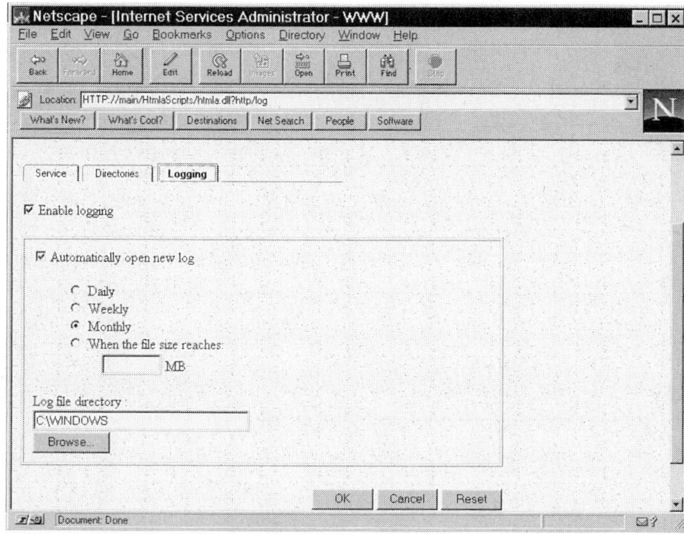

Figure 23.31.
You'll find that maintaining a log of special events can help you locate problem areas such as security breaches.

FTP Administration

Once you work with the HTTP (WWW) administration for a while, the FTP administration should come fairly easily. Figure 23.32 shows the initial page that you'll see. As with the Internet Services Administrator - WWW page, this one uses tabs. You'll find that the Directories and Logging tabs work just like the ones discussed in the preceding section, so I won't discuss them again here.

Figure 23.32.
The Internet Services Administrator - FTP page works much like its WWW counterpart.

The Connection Timeout and Maximum Connections fields work just like they do on the Internet Services Administrator - WWW page. However, you have to tune these pages differently. Notice that I'm using the default value here. You don't want people to try multiple downloads from your FTP server, so watch the number of connections closely. You'll also find that you need a longer timeout value, because a download could get delayed. (Just watch how hostile users get if you don't set this value for a long enough interval.) Unlike the HTTP connections, it's less likely that someone will leave a lot of connections open when using the FTP portion of your intranet site.

It's not uncommon for people to log in using an anonymous connection to an FTP site. However, as before, you'll probably want to disable this option on your intranet to improve security. Notice that this page also contains an Allow Only Anonymous Connections option. This feature is more designed for Internet pages. If you allow only anonymous connections, it's a lot harder for hackers to get in by using the supervisor account.

The last entry on this first page is Show Current Sessions. Clicking this link displays a page like the one shown in Figure 23.33. The center portion of this page is taken up with a table containing a user name, IP address, and the time he or she logged on to the FTP site. You'll also see a Disconnect link next to each entry in the last column of the table. Clicking this link terminates that user's connection. You can also choose to disconnect everyone by using the Disconnect All link near the bottom of the page. The Close link closes the page without making any changes.

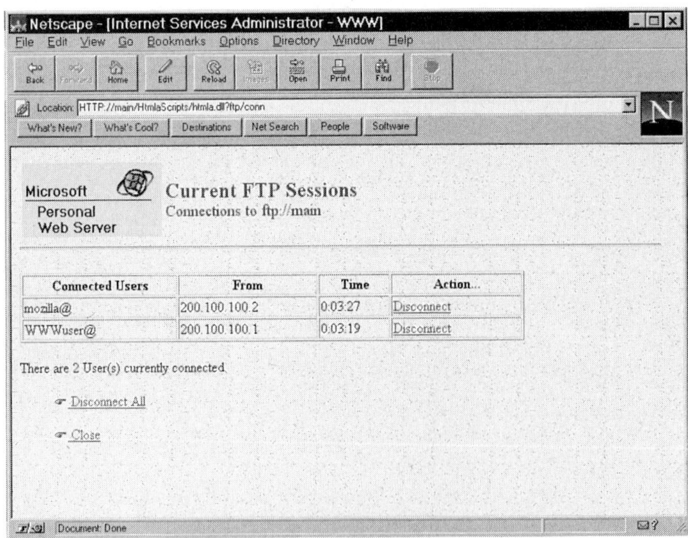

Figure 23.33.
You can use this page to monitor FTP site status or to disconnect an errant connection.

The next tag we'll look at is Messages. Figure 23.34 shows this page. There are only three messages you need to worry about when using an FTP site. The first welcomes the user to your site. The second tells him goodbye when he completes his file download. The final message tells him that the number of connections has been exceeded and he'll need to try again later.

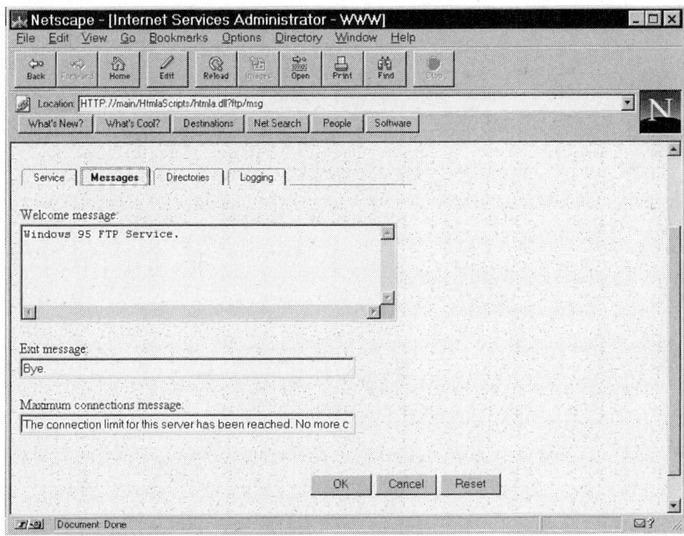

Figure 23.34.
The FTP Administrator - Messages page contains the three messages you'll need to send to visitors at your site.

Working with User Accounts

Maintaining security is a major concern on the Internet and an even bigger concern on local intranets. Personal Web Server provides a very simple security mechanism modeled after the one you already use under Windows 95. Figure 23.35 shows the main page for this feature. Notice that we have three tabs to look at in this case.

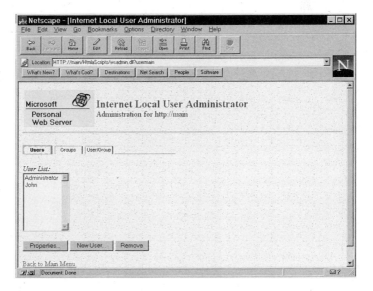

Figure 23.35.
You can work with both users and groups when using Personal Web Server.

Notice that Figure 23.35 shows two users in the User List field. Let's add another user to the list. Click the New User button and you'll see the options shown in Figure 23.36. All you need to do is type a user name in the User Name field, and then type the password for that user twice (once in the User Password field and again in the Confirm Password field). Click Add to complete the process. You'll return to the Internet Local User Administrator page and see the new user added to the User List field.

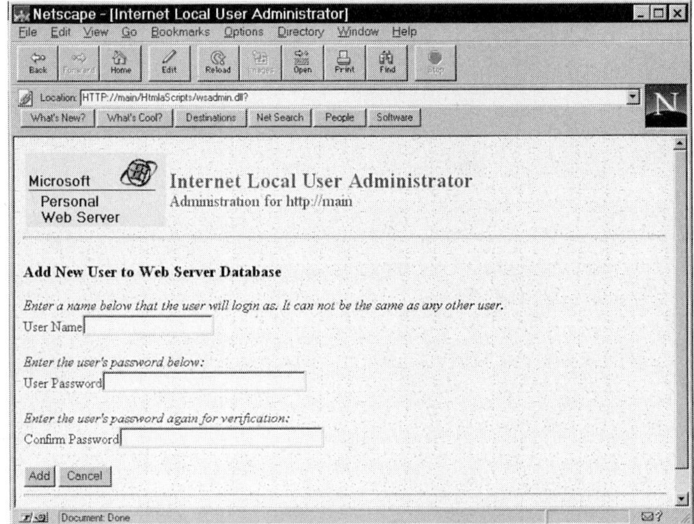

Figure 23.36.
Adding a new user is a four-step process.

Warning: The current version of Personal Web Server doesn't support null passwords. You must assign a password to every user.

The Properties button displays a page similar to the one shown in Figure 23.36 for the user you select. There's only one major difference: At the bottom of the page, you may also see a list of groups that the user belongs to. You can use the Properties button to change the user's name or password as needed. Removing a user is fairly simple; just highlight the user you want to remove, and then click the Remove button. There aren't any safety messages, so make sure that you really want to remove a user before doing so.

Let's look at the Groups tab in Figure 23.37. I've already entered a group into this page as well. As before, there are three buttons: one that allows you to add new groups, another for viewing the properties of existing groups, and a third for removing groups that you no longer need.

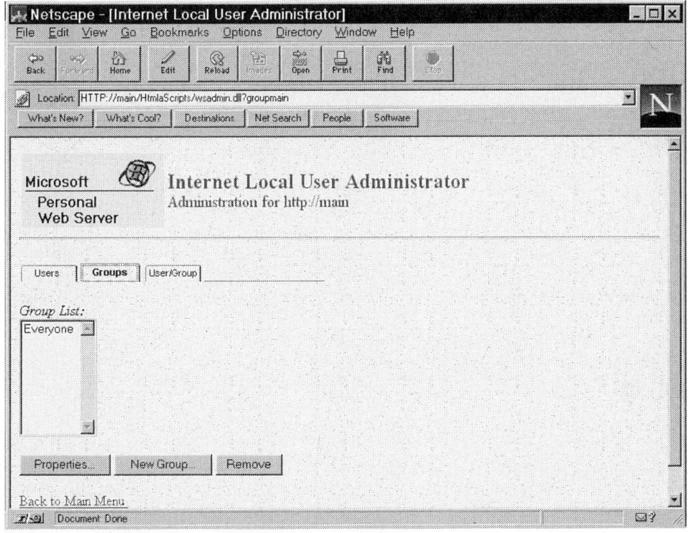

Figure 23.37.
The Groups tab allows you to add new groups to your setup.

Figure 23.38 shows the view that you'll see when adding or modifying groups. As you can see, it consists of a single field for adding the group name.

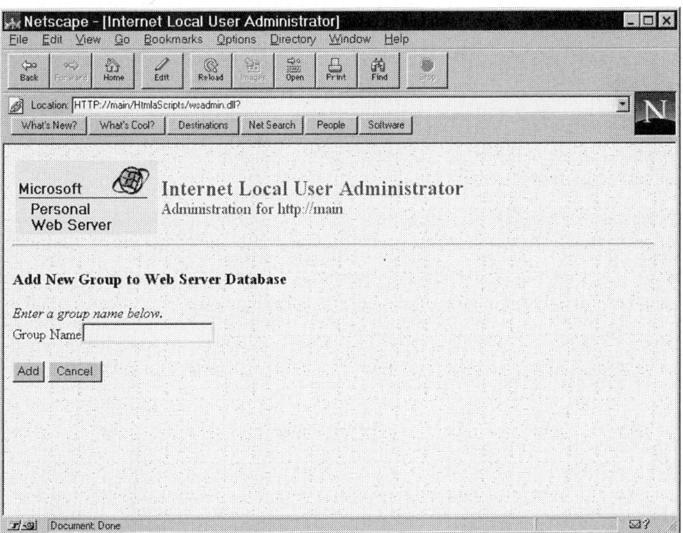

Figure 23.38.
Adding a new group is as simple as typing a name.

The last security-related task that you'll perform using the Internet Local User Administrator appears on the User/Group page shown in Figure 23.39. To assign a user to a group, select a user from the User List field and a group from the Group List field. Click the Add User to Group button to complete the process. Likewise, to remove a user from a group, click the Remove User from Group button.

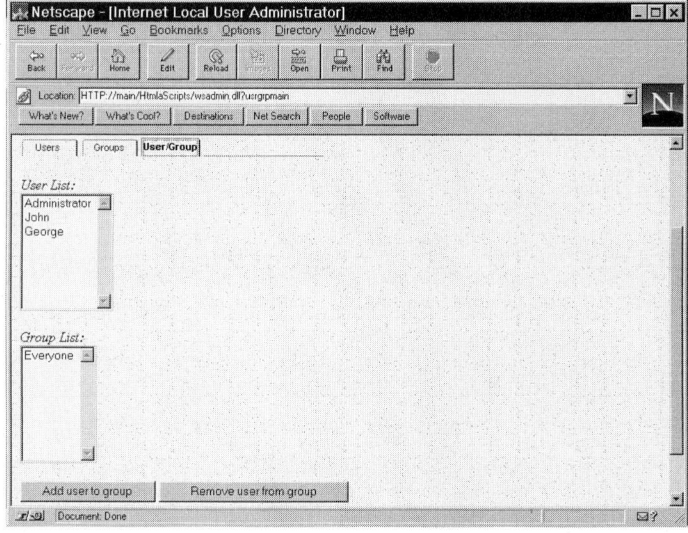

Figure 23.39.
Assigning a user to a group consists of selecting one of each and clicking the appropriate button.

There's one last task you need to perform to make security work. You need to give these users and groups access to specific areas of your Web site. Let's say that you want to share the WWWROOT folder so that people can access the content of your Web site. Open the appropriate folder in My Computer. Right-click the folder you want to share and select Sharing from the context menu. You'll see a dialog box like the one shown in Figure 23.40.

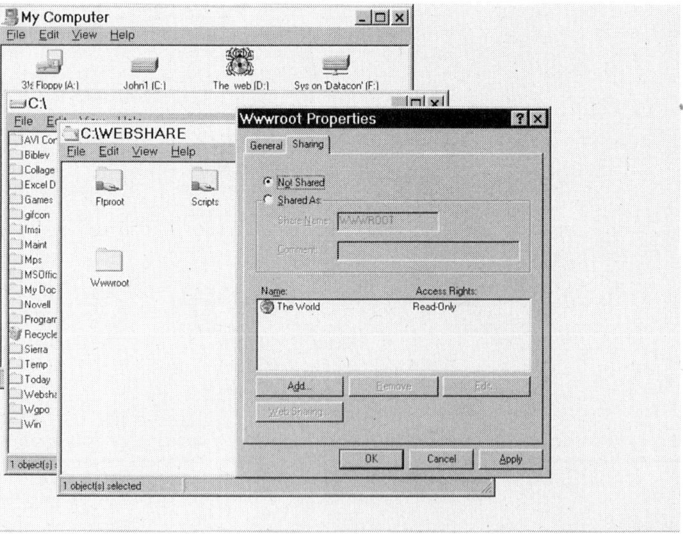

Figure 23.40.
You have to share a folder before it's accessible from your Web site.

Click the Shared As radio button and the Web Sharing button at the bottom of the page becomes active. Click this button and you'll see a dialog box like the one shown in Figure 23.41. This is where you decide on what level of intranet sharing you'll provide. As you can see, there are several levels for both HTTP and FTP access. The "Internet Security" section of Chapter 24 covers the advantages and disadvantages of specific levels of access. Once you've made a decision as to the level of Web access, click OK.

Figure 23.41.
Deciding on what level of intranet access to provide is an important security issue.

Now you need to decide who should have access to your directory. Click the Add button in the folder's Properties dialog box. You'll see a dialog box like the one shown in Figure 23.42. This is where you add users or groups to the access list. All you need to do is highlight a user or group name, and then click the level of access you want to grant. Read-only access means that the user can read the directory and scan its contents, but nothing else. Full access means that they can do everything. The meaning of the Custom button differs by drive type, but you'd normally use it for a special level of directory access. For example, you could use it to grant someone write access and not read access for surveys. That way, they could submit a survey, but not change their responses later. Notice that all the users we created in the Internet Local User Administrator appear in this dialog box. Once you select a group of users, click OK twice and you're done.

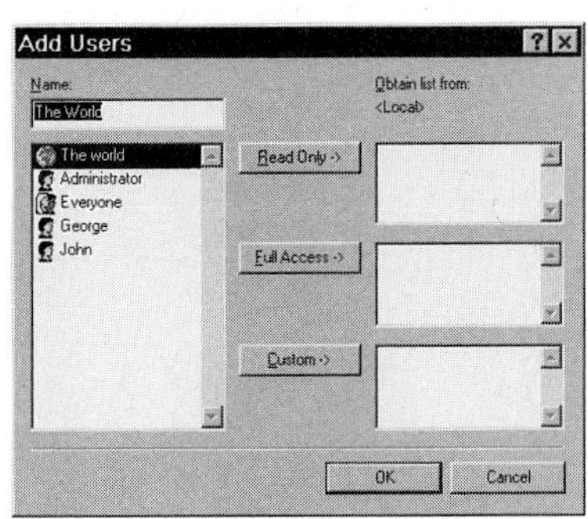

Figure 23.42.
This dialog box allows you to decide who gets access to your Web site.

Limitations

Personal Web Server doesn't include many of the supplementary features that you'll find in other versions of IIS. For example, it doesn't include some of the less-used protocols such as Gopher. However, I consider this particular lack of minimal importance for Personal Web Server's intended purpose.

One of the more important differences between Personal Web Server and a full-fledged setup is that you can't manage several Web servers from one site by using Personal Web Server. In addition, this server won't appear in the Microsoft Internet Service Manager utility provided for Windows NT. As I mentioned earlier, this product is designed for very small intranets. You wouldn't want to use it in places where you need several Web servers.

You'll also want to limit the number of users attached to Personal Web Server. Setting up a Personal Web Server generates more traffic on the network and results in more work for the host. A machine that could normally support 20 network connections will probably support 10 to 15 Personal Web Server connections. In other words, use this option with care. Installing your local intranet on a machine other than the one you use for file and print sharing is always a good idea.

On Your Own

Use the information in this chapter to determine which of your system resources are shared and which aren't. You might want to create a written list of who has access (and where) for future reference. This allows you to plug any security leaks whenever someone leaves the company.

Once you determine who has access to your machine, look for any security leaks. Be sure to change passwords on a regular basis, especially after someone leaves the company. Check to see how the use of your system resources by others affects system performance and overall usability.

We discussed the network subsystem architecture in this chapter. Go through your SYSTEM folder and see whether you can identify the components that comprise it. See if your network needs any specialty components because it uses a different protocol than normal. You might also want to take this opportunity to look for any real-mode drivers that are still lurking around your hard drive.

Download and install Personal Web Server so that you can learn some of the ins and outs of managing your own Web site. It's very helpful when the time comes to work on a Web site within your company. You'll also find that Personal Web Server comes in handy when it's time to design your own Web pages and test them out.

24 Setting Up Security

Network security is a major thorn in most network administrators' sides. Even a small network requires some level of planning, and many managers fail to see the value of implementing the type of security they really need. Of course, I've seen the opposite side of the coin as well. Some administrators wrap the people who use the network in a tight cocoon of regulations and passwords. The choke hold that these people create inhibits any kind of creative resource management and often impedes work as well.

It's difficult to create a bulletproof network setup that offers the level of flexibility that most users require. Adding a bit of flexibility normally means that you also open a security hole. I find that a network administrator must reach an important balance. The first thing you need to realize is that there's no such thing as a bulletproof security system. Any security system that you design can be breached by someone else.

So what do you do—just leave the network open to whoever might want to access it? That's not the way to go, either. The real goal is to put reasonable security restraints in place. You need to assess your security risks and do whatever it takes to reduce your risk to an acceptable level.

More important than physical security and password protection is the cooperation of those around you. I recently went into a client's office to check on his network setup. He let me use one of his employee's desks to get the work done. Right in front of me was one of those yellow reminder pads. It contained not only the employee's password, but the superior's password as well. Names were all over the desk. Anyone could have simply walked into the office and gained access to the network because of this security breach.

This incident reminded me of the importance of the "human" factor in any security plan. To implement a good security system, you need to consider the following elements:

- **Physical security:** Place your file server in a locked room. I can easily break the security for a NetWare setup (or most other networks, for that matter) if I have access to a running file server. If you lock up the file server, I can't access it unless I have a key.
- **Software protection:** Using passwords and other forms of software protection is your next line of defense. Make sure that all the right kinds of security measures are in place. I cover this particular topic in greater detail later, but this is one area where Windows 95 can really help. It contains all the right features; all you need to do is implement them.
- **Cooperative security:** You can't secure the network by yourself. The larger your network, the more you need every user's cooperation. If you expect the user to cooperate with you, you need to actually talk to him and find out what's reasonable. No one will use an unreasonable security plan. This cooperative strategy also extends to management. If you don't talk to management and tell them what your security problems are, they won't be able to help. You also need to make sure that management knows what kinds of security risks are present in the current setup. This reduces the chance of someone being surprised later.

- **Training:** It's never a good idea to assume that users know how to use the security features that Windows 95 provides. You can implement a lot of the physical security, but it's the user who will use the software part of the equation. An untrained user might not use a particular security feature correctly or might not even know that it exists. In addition, untrained users often resist using security features because they don't understand their purpose.
- **A written security plan:** I don't find this particular step necessary on small networks. However, as your network becomes larger, it becomes vitally important to get the rules put down in writing. Otherwise, how will a user know what's expected or how to react in a crisis? Writing everything down also makes management aware of the security that you have put in place.

This might seem like a lot of work to implement security, but it isn't when you consider the loss that a single security breach can cause. A pirate isn't going to steal last week's letter to the general public; he's going to steal something valuable. The more secret something is, the better the pirate likes it. Just think about what a competitor could do with your new marketing plan or the design for that new widget you plan to produce. Even if a pirate doesn't take anything, he could leave something behind. What would a virus do to your network? It doesn't take too much thought to imagine your entire setup crumbling as a virus infects it.

The next section of this chapter addresses network security in the broad scheme of things. In other words, it actually goes a little beyond what you would need to implement in Windows 95 itself. The reason I'm including it is that security needs to be cohesive. You can't create little security groups in a network. The entire network must use a consolidated plan to ensure that your security net is consistent and has no holes. Anything less is an open invitation to whoever would like to circumvent your security to gain access to sensitive information.

Once we get past these general guidelines, I show you the features that Windows 95 provides to help you implement a company-wide plan. I've looked at many of these features elsewhere in the book, so I don't go into a lot of detail in some areas. (I tell you where the detailed information does appear in this book, though.) Even if you're running a small network, you'll want to read both sections. The first section tells you what to implement, and the second tells you how to do it.

Creating a Security Plan

To run a network efficiently, you need to have a plan. Ad hoc solutions to any problem are simply that—ad hoc. They won't go very far in helping you to plug a security leak or tell someone why he needs to observe a particular rule. Without a plan, you won't know what your security goals are or what steps you need to take to meet them. The problem that most administrators face is that they really aren't sure what goals a security plan helps them achieve. Figuring out what a security plan does for you is almost as important as creating it. A security plan will help you achieve at least the following five goals (in order of importance):

1. A security plan helps you define and organize your security system into manageable pieces. "Divide and conquer" is the technique used by many generals to win wars. Instead of trying to fight an entire army of problems by working on them all at the same time, take them on one at a time. You can win the war against security leaks by using this tried-and-true strategy. A network security plan is the map you need to see where to break the problem into smaller pieces.
2. Most networks have security problems from time to time. An old employee leaves and a new one takes her place, creating a potential gap in your security net. Someone gets promoted and you need to extend his rights on the network. Will he know how to handle these new responsibilities if you don't train him? What if someone gets transferred from one department to another? Do you really want him to have access to both departments' data? The network administrator might not even know that these problems exist. What if a manager inadvertently gives someone rights to a sensitive directory? One way to find problem areas quickly is to compare the current network state with a baseline condition. A network security plan can provide that baseline. It captures the network's ideal state rather than its current state.
3. If you're like most administrators, users constantly ask why you implement one procedure over another. They might want to legitimately ferret out ways to increase their freedom on the network. (Some users equate increased freedom with increased productivity—an inaccurate assumption on a properly designed network.) So how do you answer these questions? A network security plan can provide a historical context that tells why you implemented a specific procedure or network rule. Recording a rule and why you implemented it often helps you keep the network security plan up-to-date. Keeping old rules without apparent reason is counterproductive. On the other hand, too much freedom is an invitation to security problems.
4. You might find that the goals of management and the network's users don't reflect the goals of the network administrator. A network security plan provides an opportunity for you to express these differences. It also provides the means to discuss reasonable alternatives and compromises. Arguing a particular course of action once you study the ramifications of that action is the only way to create a network that everyone will enjoy using. Rules based on knowledge rather than personal feelings is the best way to later ensure that you know why the rule is in place.
5. Evenhanded administration of the network means that you enforce the network rules in the same way each time someone breaks them. (Some network operating systems even provide you with the tools required to detect security breaches in your system. For example, NetWare provides the SECURITY utility for this purpose.) It also means that you explain the rules in the same way to everyone who uses the network. Unless you write down the rules, someone could legitimately say that you show a bias toward certain network users or that you make arbitrary decisions regarding some infractions. Clearly-written rules alleviate this problem by making the rule, the implementation, any penalties, and the historical context clear to everyone.

Tip: A small company doesn't necessarily need a written security plan. However, you should at least think through these issues before you start setting up Windows 95. A peer-to-peer network needs some type of security plan, too. Trying to implement a security plan after installation is fine, but it will probably cost you extra time to do things this way. Just as you plan your installation in advance, take the time to consider the security needs of your network, too.

As you can see, a properly designed and implemented security plan can change the way that everyone views the network. There's always a group of people who fail to understand that a security problem on the network costs everyone money. A security plan can handle this situation as well. Even if a user doesn't agree with the implementation of a security feature, he won't want to face any penalties that management assigns for failure to follow the rules. Of course, this is the last course of action you want to take. Assigning a penalty might show that a user failed to follow the rules, but it also shows that your plan failed to work in this instance. It's unlikely that you'll ever create a plan that everyone agrees with and no one disobeys, but getting as close as possible to this ideal is the goal that you should seek to attain. The following paragraphs provide you with more details about designing and implementing a security plan for your company.

Breaking the Company into Groups

Many companies use a combination of workgroups and a client/server architecture. The workgroup might use Windows 95 to implement a small peer-to-peer network just for the people in that section. The client/server network might use NetWare or some other network operating system (NOS). It allows the company to communicate as a whole.

Tip: It's easy to get confused about the ways in which you need to split your company's various security needs into manageable pieces. Think of workgroups in terms of a group of people working together on a single project. This is a key concept, because they don't necessarily have to come from the same department to be in the same workgroup. Think of security groups as people with similar security needs. You can assign a person to more than one group. For example, he or she could be part of the engineering workgroup but also be part of the managerial security group. These ideas are separate, and you need to consider them separately.

Whether your company uses several small networks or simply has everyone log into one file server, you need to break a large network into smaller pieces before you create a security plan. This helps you organize your company into functional security areas. By breaking the security task into smaller pieces, you can reduce the overall complexity of making your system secure. There are many ways to break the problem into smaller pieces, and you'll probably need to employ more than one of them. The following paragraphs provide some ideas on how to accomplish this task:

- **Department/workgroup:** Because users who work together are apt to require similar access to the network, you can easily break the company into groups along this natural line. For example, people working in Personnel are unlikely to require access to financial records. Likewise, the company's accountants won't require access to the personnel records. This is the best way to go if your company already uses peer-to-peer networks to connect small workgroups.

Tip: Always assign someone to manage every workgroup on the network (if you have more than one). Let this person take care of some security details by allowing him or her to assign access for the local workgroup resources. It might also be a good idea to assign someone from the group to manage the print server, if the group has one with more than one printer attached. You can't take the time to see to every networking detail, especially when a network starts to grow beyond 100 or so workstations. It takes a lot of time just to keep the network applications current, keep the workstations up and running, and attend to the myriad of other details that a network administrator needs to worry about. Making someone in the local workgroup responsible not only reduces your workload, but also helps keep any security measures in place.

- **Seniority/longevity:** Some companies assign tasks based on a person's seniority. For example, when a manager leaves town for a few days to attend a convention, he might assign the senior employee in that section to act in his stead. You might need to give that employee access to certain managerial areas of the network to allow him to perform these duties. Even though the person doesn't need to have access to these areas as a result of department or workgroup affiliation, he needs to have them as a substitute manager. As with many security considerations, this scenario is definitely an exception to the rule.
- **Job function:** Another natural way to break the company into groups is by job function. For example, management might have one area set aside on the network for managers. Another area might contain information of vital importance to people who maintain print servers on the network. A foreman might require access to an area set aside for all the foremen in the company. As you can see, some of these job function areas cross department and workgroup lines.
- **Special designation:** Some companies give individuals special designations. For example, you might have a person on staff who wears more than one hat. She might require access to records from more than one department. You might need to accommodate the needs of a consultant from time to time as well. All these people fall outside the normal security boundaries. You need to list these special considerations.

Security Plan Considerations

Once you break a company into functional groups, it's a good idea to figure out the security needs of each group. Accounting will need much more stringent security than someone who takes care of the company's correspondence. Sometimes you might be able to get by with read-only access for this group. For example, no one would need to edit last year's accounting records, but they might need to refer to them. You might need extra flexibility in an engineering section to promote the flow of ideas from one person to another without giving away new ideas to a competitor. One engineer might have one piece of the puzzle, and that piece could trigger someone else's creative abilities to come up with yet another piece. Inhibiting an engineer with a straitjacket of rules is never a good idea. A management group needs very tight security but also needs the maximum level of access within the group. You can provide management with a straitjacket and actually expect that they'll use it. Hopefully, a manager will understand the need for tight security when discussing the company's future plans.

In addition to these considerations, you need to think about special security items within your company. You'll also want to start implementing your security plan. The following steps help you with both processes. They help you complete a security plan and present some additional ideas that you should consider as you implement it.

1. **Assessing company tasks:** Even if you do a perfect job of identifying all the groups in your company, you might find that there are still a few tasks that the company must perform that fall outside the purview of a group. In many cases, more than one group performs these tasks. For example, creating the end-of-year report might require the efforts of several departments in the company. Because this isn't a task that the company performs every day, there's no need to create a special group to do it. However, you need to consider this type of task when you create your security plan. Other examples of task-related groups include special committees and research groups. In this case, several specialists get together to work on a specific problem or idea.
2. **Appointing each person to one or more groups:** Once you break the company into groups and decide what major additional tasks the company needs to perform, it's time to assign people to them. For example, the Financial group maintains accounting records, and the Personnel group maintains employee records. In many cases, the assignments you need to make are very straightforward. It's easy to see that everyone in the Accounting department will easily fit within the Financial group. However, there are some assignments that you might not think about at first. For example, you might have someone in Personnel who needs assignment to both the Financial and the Personnel groups. She might need to make entries into the financial program regarding employee raises or terminations.
3. **Brainstorming special user needs:** There are other ways to look at your company's security needs, not just from an organizational point of view. Breaking the company into physical and logical units is fine for most security needs. Doing so allows the network administrator

to work with both management and network users to make reasonable security assignments based on fact. In some situations, however, a lack of information prevents you from making reasonable assignments. For example, what if a user is just starting a new project? He certainly won't know what types of access he'll require on the network, because he's never tried to perform that task before. The manager might have a reasonable idea of what type of access the user requires, but this is mere conjecture. Without more information, you'll find yourself at a loss to make a reasonable assignment. Unless you want to spend a lot of time retuning your network to compensate for these situations, you might want to take the time to brainstorm the user's needs.

I'd like to look at that third step in more detail. It's the last one you need to complete your security plan. Once you figure out special user needs, you have all the information required to make the plan work. Brainstorming is a think-tank approach to network management. It's a tried-and-true method used in many other ventures. Essentially, you define a task based on past knowledge of similar tasks and on future goals. You answer questions such as "What do we plan to achieve?" and "How do we plan to achieve these goals?" You must consider what tools you have available on your network to get the job done. This includes both hardware and software resources. You also throw out ideas for consideration. Someone might need to play the part of devil's advocate to make sure that you consider both the positive and negative aspects of a particular decision. Of course, you want to use this approach only if there's insufficient information on which to base a decision by using standard techniques. You can take a number of steps to make this process work properly:

1. Break the user's task into logical elements. For example, what types of applications does the user need to use? Each application involves a different set of security rights. Perhaps one or more groups already provide these rights on the network. (Whenever possible, try to avoid making non-group assignments. Using non-group assignments increases the amount of work you need to do to maintain the network and could cause potential security gaps as an employee changes jobs in the company.)
2. Create a list of equipment that the user needs to access. For example, does the user need to use a fax or a special printer? If the security system on the network limits access to these items, you might need to provide the user with the special access required to use them.
3. Write down a list of tasks that the user needs to perform. Sometimes you'll see a special application or a piece of equipment that the user will need to use to accomplish a task. Don't just list these tasks; describe the tasks so that everyone is talking about the same task.
4. Look for areas where the user might have too much access. Once you figure out where the user might need access, trim your list to areas where the user must have access to get the job done. There's no reason to give someone too much network access simply because he's starting a new project.

As you can see, brainstorming a task can really help in a situation where you lack the information needed to make a good decision by using just the available facts. What you need to realize is that your group bases such decisions on conjecture and derived information. Keep in touch with the user as he gets further into his project. You might find that you can reduce his access in some areas and that he requires additional access in other areas. (The user normally will tell you when he doesn't have enough access, but seldom will he tell you if he has too much access.) Remember that it's your responsibility to make sure that the user has enough access but not too much. Some users will try to convince you that they need additional rights to certain areas when they really don't.

Peter's Principle: Delegating Network Administration Tasks

You have your network installed, and all the Windows 95 workgroups are in place. So why are you still running around like the proverbial headless chicken? Windows 95 provides a lot of tools to help the administrator manage a network. Chapter 23 explains that these tools pertain not only to Windows 95 peer-to-peer installations, but to other types of networks as well. You can install agents to monitor the status of a workstation remotely or through a local host. You can use all kinds of connections to get a bird's-eye view of your network. Yet even with all these aids, you feel out-of-touch and barely able to maintain the system.

Some network administrators are under the impression that they can maintain the entire network themselves, given enough time and tools to do the job. The truth of the matter is that only Superman could fulfill all the needs of some networks. This includes the area of network security. Although you don't want to give anyone rights that he doesn't need, you might find that you need someone to help you maintain a large network—and you'll have to decide what kind of rights to give that person. How much help you need and what size of network can be defined as "large" is primarily a matter of network complexity and whether you're a full-time network administrator. If management gives you a few hours each day to perform network duties and you wear another hat for the rest of the day, a large network could be as few as 20 users. Even a full-time administrator will begin to feel the pinch at around 100 users, especially if your company performs a wide variety of tasks with a conglomeration of equipment.

There are a few problems in allowing other people to help you maintain network security. Centralized control of the network for security purposes is a real advantage. If one person is responsible to management for ensuring that network security remains high, there's little possibility that he'll do a halfhearted job. In addition, centralized control means that fewer problems will slip through the cracks. Users will never wonder whom to ask for more rights on the network. They'll always know the one person who can help them out.

I always follow a simple principle when it comes to network security: Always maintain control. When you can't maintain control, find out why. You might find that it's a problem with a network administrator who's overwhelmed with requests for service and little time to really take care of the network. Don't kill the security plan that you worked so hard to create. Give the network administrator sufficient help to get the job done.

Local Security

Now that we've had a bird's-eye view of security, let's look at what Windows 95 can do to help. I was pleasantly surprised by some features, but a bit dismayed by others. For example, the ability to assign two levels of password protection to every resource is nice and will probably work fine for a peer-to-peer network. The inability to assign a password to a specific file didn't sit well with me. Sometimes you need to protect one file in a directory but not another. Some older applications really need to have their configuration files in the same directory as the rest of the executables. I usually like to make my executable files read-only so that the user doesn't erase them.

However, putting these inconveniences aside, you can still implement a significant security strategy by using Windows 95's built-in capabilities. The following sections describe these features. In most cases, I've described how to use and implement these features in other chapters, so I won't cover that aspect again here. I'll show you how to use the features that Windows 95 provides to implement the security plan that I talked about in the preceding section.

Logon

The best way to prevent a security breach is to keep someone from getting onto the network in the first place. The dialog box that you see when you start Windows 95 is your first line of defense against someone who would try to break into your system. I've talked about the logon feature of Windows 95 in several places. We look at it as part of the Control Panel applets in Chapter 11 and again in Chapter 23. We also look at how you can change the source of the network logon by using the Network Properties dialog box (also in Chapter 23). Let's take a look at how you can use the Logon dialog box to help implement a security strategy.

Stand-Alone Security

It always amazes me when someone asks why it's important to take the time to protect a stand-alone workstation. Does the fact that a workstation doesn't connect to the network reduce the quality of the data it contains? The only part of the security picture that has changed is that a stand-alone workstation will at least keep someone from accessing your data on the network. The fact that many stand-alone workstations contain valuable data is still very important. In fact, I think you'll find that most stand-alone machines at your company are either relics that no one wants to use or engineering workstations that no one wants to expose to the security risks of network use. Either way, if your stand-alone machine has Windows 95 on it, it's pretty certain that the data it contains is valuable. The initial strategy to follow for a stand-alone workstation is to enable password protection by using the Passwords Properties dialog box, shown in Figure 24.1. Simply open the Control Panel and double-click the Passwords applet.

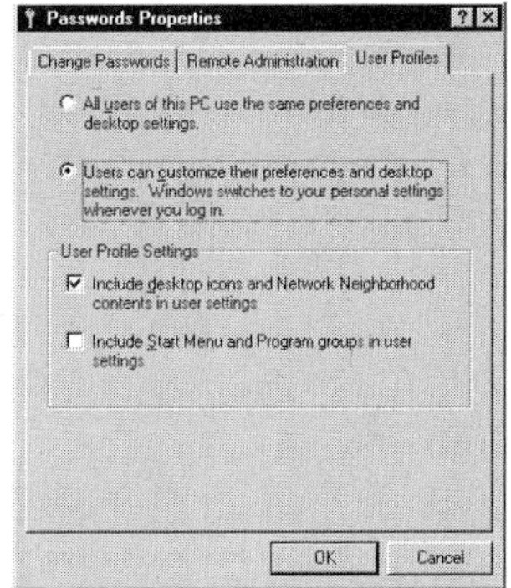

Figure 24.1.
Protecting a stand-alone machine might require you to enable the multiple-desktops feature, which requires each user to log in.

Tip: If security for a specific workstation is so important that software alone won't take care of the problem, consider one of several alternative solutions. For example, you could add a locking bolt to the back of the machine to prevent people from opening it up, and use the BIOS-password feature to prevent access by any means until the user provides the correct password. Physical locking mechanisms are also available. One of them goes over the floppy disk drive to prevent the user from accessing it. You can also add a lock to a standard PC's On switch. Unfortunately, most of these solutions are either expensive or inconvenient or both. It's almost always worth your while to seek other solutions to the problem.

Note: You'll need to install the System Policy Editor by using the Special Utility Installation procedure described in Chapter 11. The required .INF file appears in the \ADMIN\APPTOOLS\POLEDIT folder. Once you get the System Policy Editor installed, you can access it from by choosing Start | Programs | Accessories | System Tools.

Of course, just enabling passwords doesn't help you very much. What would prevent someone from coming along and turning off the settings? I always back up my configuration changes with a policy change. The policy change reinforces the password setting. This means opening the System Policy Editor and turning off various types of access. For example, you can turn off the Control Panel settings by using the options shown in Figure 24.2. Notice that one of the settings in this list is the Passwords applet. Use the File | Registry command to load the current settings from the Registry. The File | Save command will save any changes that you make in the Registry before you exit the System Policy Editor. You'll see two icons after loading the Registry—one for the user and one for the machine. It's the user settings that you'll want to modify. You'll need an administrator account to use the System Policy Editor in this way.

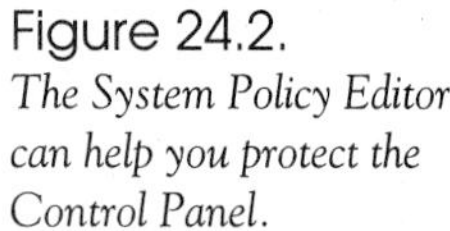

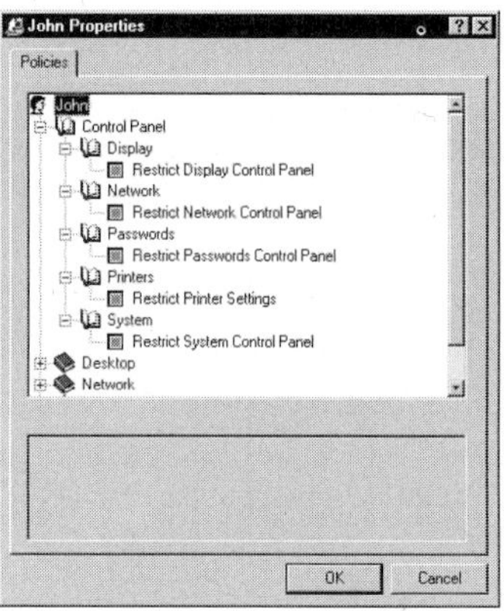

Figure 24.2.
The System Policy Editor can help you protect the Control Panel.

The following paragraphs explain each Control Panel restriction in detail:

- **Restrict Display Control Panel:** You can choose to disable the entire Display applet, or you can select which pages in the Display Properties dialog box are disabled. The first option in the list disables the entire applet. Every other option disables a single page at a time. This particular setting comes in handy for setting a screen saver password and then shutting off the page so that the user can't disable it.
- **Restrict Network Control Panel:** As with the Display applet, you can choose to disable the entire applet or individual pages. The Access Control page is the one to check here, but it really applies only when you have a network setup on the machine.
- **Restrict Passwords Control Panel:** This is one of the few applets that I would consider disabling completely. Every page on this one could produce potentially harmful effects for your setup. Of course, the big ones in a stand-alone setting are the User Profiles and Password pages.
- **Restrict Printer Settings:** The only good reason to implement this policy is if you're afraid that the user will add a nonexistent printer or delete one installed on the machine. This particular policy affects only the General and Details pages.
- **Restrict System Control Panel:** This policy affects the Device Manager and Hardware Profiles pages. It also removes the Virtual Memory and File System buttons. Whether you disable these settings depends largely on the user's expertise. In most cases, you probably gain more than you lose by leaving these settings alone, because the user will be able to help you troubleshoot many system problems if he can access the information that these pages provide.

I mention in Chapter 23 that a user could circumvent the password by erasing the .PWL file. You can keep this from happening by taking another preventive measure. Figure 24.3 shows the System Restrictions policy. Checking all four of these items prevents the user from accessing the hard drive in any manner other than the one you allow. You could restrict access to applications to only those required to complete the user's work. Disabling the DOS prompt will also prevent the user from erasing the .PWL files that way. Of course, the user who has to live with these restrictions might see them as very constricting. Even though this strategy gives the network administrator the tools needed to prevent user meddling, it could backfire somewhere along the way.

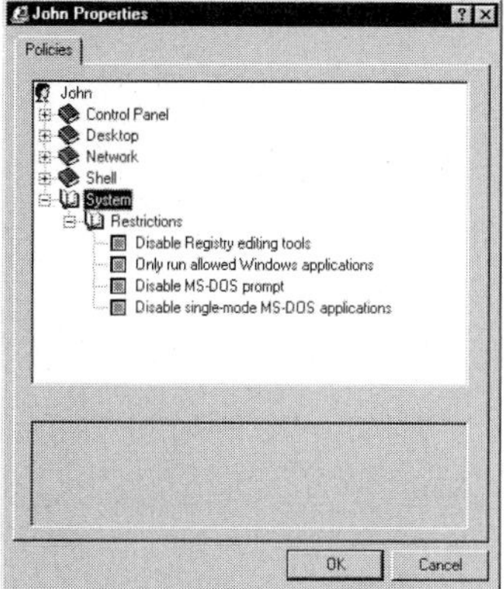

Figure 24.3.
The System Restrictions policy allows you to control user access to potentially harmful applications.

Tip: Disabling the user's access to the hard drive after he starts Windows 95 won't prevent other forms of access. For example, a user could boot his system using a floppy and remove both the .PWL and .POL files. (The System Policy Editor stores its data in the .POL file, and the system passwords appear in the .PWL file.) This would effectively disable any restrictions that you placed on the user. Removing the floppy drive would disable this form of access but would make it very difficult to troubleshoot the machine or add new applications. You also need to set specific MSDOS.SYS settings to prevent the user from exiting the boot sequence. Refer to Table 6.1 for a complete list of MSDOS.SYS switches.

Using a combination of these settings will allow you to restrict user access to most of the "harmful" features that Windows 95 provides. It would be a lot better, though, if you could participate in a cooperative form of security rather than resorting to these very harsh measures that will likely cause a lot of user unhappiness.

You can impose a final level of restrictions on the user of a stand-alone machine. Figure 24.4 shows the Shell Restrictions policy options. As you can see, most of these options will effectively prevent a user from exercising any form of control over the shell itself. Notice that these policies also provide some network settings. I'll refer to them again in the next section.

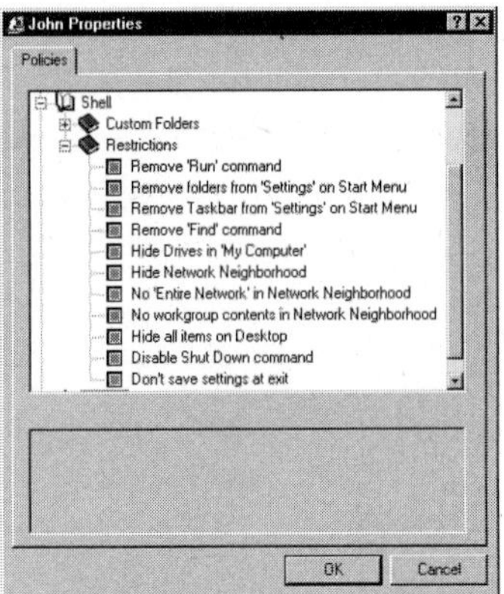

Figure 24.4.
The Shell Restrictions policy allows you to control user access to the shell itself.

Of all the policies presented here, disabling the Run command is probably the most reasonable. It allows you to restrict the user from starting applications on the hard drive. This is especially important if you maintain a set of diagnostic tools locally. For example, it's fairly likely that you wouldn't want the user to access the Registry Editor or the System Policy Editor. Most of these settings are pretty self-explanatory. The one that really caught my attention, though, was the Hide All Items on Desktop policy. About the only use I can think of for this setting is when you create the general system policy. You could disable access to everything, including the desktop. That way, if someone did manage to bypass the Logon dialog box, he wouldn't see much of value when Windows 95 did start.

Peer-to-Peer Security

All the policies I covered in the preceding section apply here as well, but there are several important differences. First, you'll probably load the system policies from a .POL file instead of directly from the Registry. Second, you'll probably see more than just one user; this dialog box will include groups as well.

Whether you set policies by groups or by the individual (or even a combination of both), the settings covered in the preceding section are the same. You can restrict the user from doing just about anything by implementing the right set of policies. The problem is that the more you restrict the user, the harder it is for him to get anything done. As I mentioned at the beginning of this chapter, creating a security plan is often more a matter of considering an acceptable risk than trying to seal all the holes.

I'd like to again direct your attention to the Shell Restrictions policy shown earlier in Figure 24.4. I wanted to talk about quite a few network restrictions in this section because they don't really apply to stand-alone machines. There are three Network Neighborhood-specific settings here. The problem with implementing these policies is that they restrict the user from exploring the network. This could be a good policy if you're working with a computer novice who has managed to damage network files "by accident" in the past. However, restricting a user from exploring his computer only removes any reason for him to really learn about it. Training a user is almost always a matter of sparking his interest in what the computer can do. Inhibiting that interest is about the most counterproductive thing that you can do. That said, you'll probably want to think twice about implementing these policies for most users.

There's one set of policies that you should probably consider implementing on a structured network, especially if you manage a lot of machines. Figure 24.5 shows the Network Sharing policies. There are two of them—one for printers and one for drives. Disabling the user's ability to share (or not share) resources on his machine could save you a lot of trouble in the long run. A user might not always understand why you granted someone else access to his hard drive. Unless you want to explain each and every setting on every machine on the network to every user, you'll probably want to disable these settings.

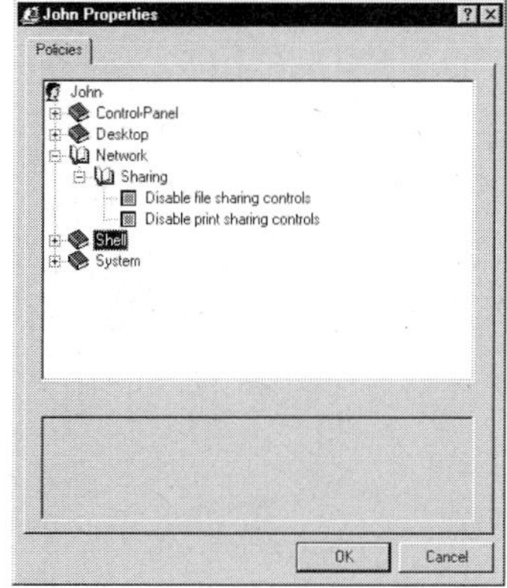

Figure 24.5.
The network administrator, not the user, should set the policy regarding drive and printer sharing.

Peer-to-peer networks also need to consider the machine settings. For example, how do you want the various machines to talk to each other, and which protocols will they use? Chapter 23 covers many of these issues. Other settings are discussed in the following sections. The important thing to see right now is the overall picture. Figure 24.6 shows the overall settings picture for the machine network settings.

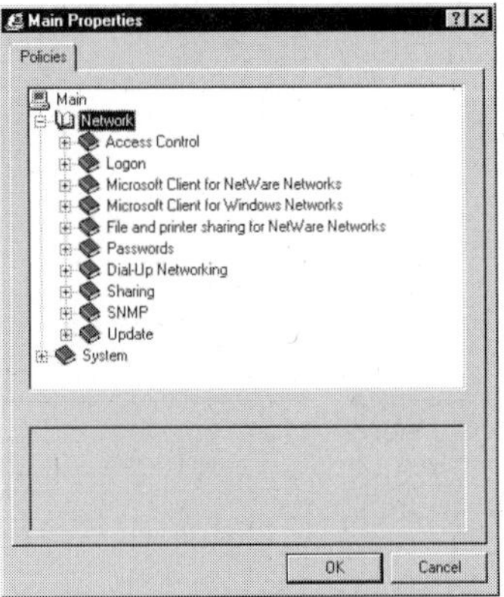

Figure 24.6.
Machine-specific settings become important in a peer-to-peer networking environment.

The Access Control setting performs the same function as that page in the Network Properties dialog box. It's included here so that you can set that policy by using a remote terminal. (In fact, every important setting that you can change with a Properties dialog box also appears somewhere in the System Policy Editor so that you can change it remotely.)

The System policies for a machine can provide some additional security as well. Figure 24.7 shows the various settings that you can change. One of the settings I use quite a bit is Network Path for Windows Setup. This particular policy allows you to place a copy of Windows 95 on a file server and then prevent the user from accessing it. The network administrator can update a system with ease, but the user is restricted from adding new Windows 95 features.

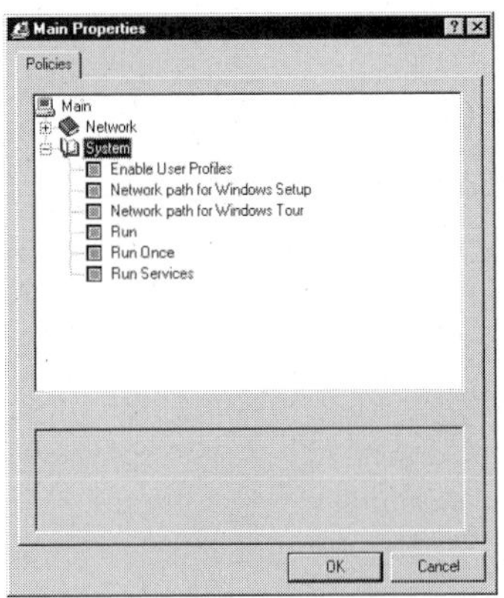

Figure 24.7.
Although it's not immediately apparent, the System policy can help you implement a security strategy.

The three Run policies provide an opportunity to load network monitors and other applications. A monitor can help you keep track of both how the user interacts with the network and the current status of the workstation itself. Of course, you can also use this policy to add default applications to the user's setup. For example, company policy might dictate that everyone use a specific contact manager or e-mail program. You could add either one to the Run policy in order to load them automatically for the user.

Client/Server Security

As mentioned earlier, you can use the settings described in the "Stand-Alone Security" section with a client/server security setup for a network operating system such as NetWare or Windows NT. You can also add the peer-to-peer networking security described in the preceding section. Windows 95 provides some additional capabilities for client/server setups that I didn't describe earlier. Some of these settings appear in Chapter 23. For example, you can implement a remote monitor by using SNMP.

The major addition to security that Windows 95 provides for client/server networks is the ability to download system policies from the file server. You must install the Group Policy features by using the procedure provided in the "Special Utility Installation" section of Chapter 11. Placing the GROUPPOL.DLL file in your SYSTEM folder enables Windows 95 to download group policies included in your .POL file to the local workstation.

You need to know some things about group policies. First, Windows 95 won't override an individual user policy with a group policy. If you want to use groups, don't define any individual policies for that particular user.

Second, Windows 95 processes the groups in the order of precedence that you set using the Options | Group Priority command. The Group Priority dialog box, shown in Figure 24.8, allows you to change the way in which Windows 95 views each group policy. A policy in a high-priority group always overrides a policy in a low-priority group. This means that you'll have to set the priorities to reflect the security requirements of the network. Otherwise, you could accidentally give a user access to something that he wouldn't normally need to access.

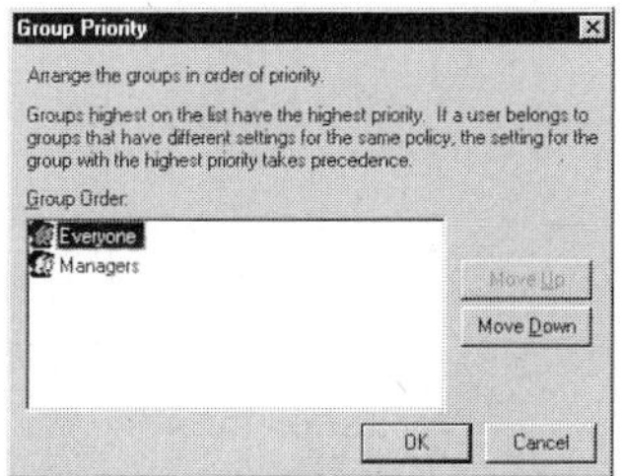

Figure 24.8.
Use the Group Priority dialog box to change the order in which Windows 95 interprets each group policy.

The Password Cache

Windows 95 implements something called a password cache. The .PWL or password list file in either the main Windows 95 or your individual profile folder contains more than just the password for your system. This file also remembers the password for Microsoft Network (MSN) or any of the resources that you need to access. Your password unlocks this file, which in turn contains the passwords that unlock all the other resources you can access.

Setup normally provides password caching as a default. (This means that Windows 95 remembers your password when you use programs such as Microsoft Network.) In fact, there isn't any place to turn it off in a Properties dialog box. However, if you open the Network Passwords property of the Local Computer Properties dialog box by using the System Policy Editor, you'll see an option for disabling password caching (see Figure 24.9).

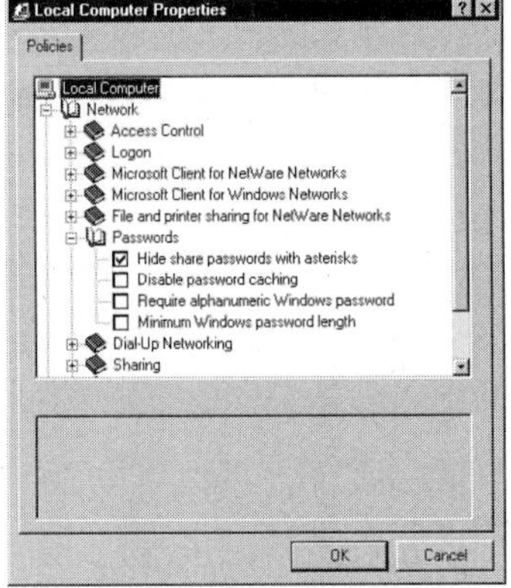

Figure 24.9.
Normally you'll want to keep password caching turned on to make life a little easier for the user.

The other three policies here are pretty self-explanatory. Notice the Minimum Windows Password Length policy. It can help you make it more difficult for a hacker to break into the network. It's a proven fact that some people use a single-character password—or none at all. This isn't just under Windows 95; it's everywhere. Setting a minimum password length of five characters greatly reduces the chance that a hacker will guess a user's password and break into the system. In fact, the longer the password, the harder it is to break in. Of course, there's a point at which you'll spend a lot of time bailing out the user because he forgot his password. Setting a reasonable length—between 5 and 10 characters—is usually sufficient. (In fact, passwords over 10 characters in length usually encourage the user to write down his or her password. Passwords stolen from desktops is one cause of network break-ins.) You should also set a policy of using a combination of letters and numbers that don't form birth dates or other combinations that a hacker who knows the user could easily guess.

What happens, though, if the .PWL file becomes corrupted? Windows 95 also provides a Password List Editor, shown in Figure 24.10, to remove corrupted passwords from the file. As you can see, there's no way for the administrator to know the user's password, but he can remove a specific password from the list. In this case, the .PWL file contains two Microsoft Mail passwords and one for MSN. You'll find the Password List Editor in the \ADMIN\APPTOOLS\PWLEDIT folder.

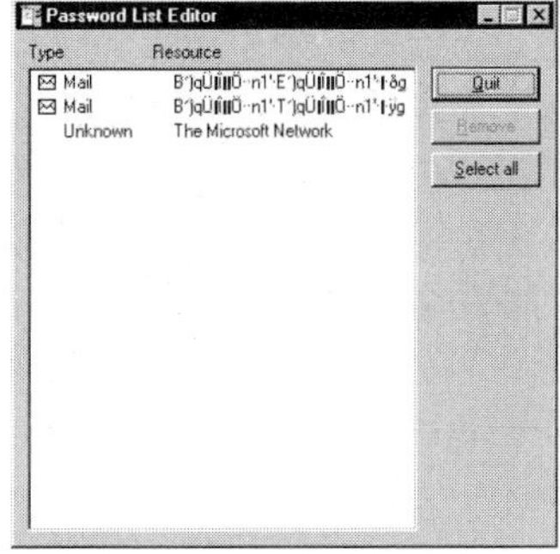

Figure 24.10.
The Password List Editor is a simple utility for removing old or corrupted passwords from the user's .PWL file.

Warning: There are a few caveats about using the .PWL editor. First, the user needs to log in to "unlock" the file. This means that you can't edit a .PWL file remotely. You must do it at the user's machine. Second, the Password List Editor might corrupt a .PWL file if an application adds a password in an unknown format. Be sure to create a backup of the .PWL file before you edit it.

Network Security

Let's get back to peer-to-peer networking for a while. Windows 95 provides several levels of security that fit different kinds of networking needs. You can select only one level at a time, so it's important to select the correct one. Changing your policy later will prove time-consuming, at the least.

The following sections provide the details of Windows 95 security. This information is very peer-to-peer-network-oriented, but I do throw in a few bits of information that you can use with client/server networks as well.

Tip: Under DOS, you could use the hidden and read-only file attributes to marginally hide files and directories from a user. Windows 95 exposes these files through Explorer, making it easier for a novice to delete much-needed files without much thought. Win-Secure-It is a new product that helps you get past this new set of problems. It allows you to hide and optionally protect files as needed. You can get all the details and download a shareware version of this product from Shetef Solutions at `http://www.shetef.com/`. This same vendor makes a variety of other useful Windows 95 utility programs, including products like THE Security Programmable Interface for Windows 95, which is a special set of libraries for programmers who want full control over file security on Windows 95 machines.

Share-Level Versus User-Level Security

The first level of security that Windows 95 provides is share-level access control. You get to this setting by using the Access Control page of the Network dialog box, shown in Figure 24.11. The other security level is user-level access control. Each of these security levels provides a different set of features, and each has different qualities that make it useful in a given situation.

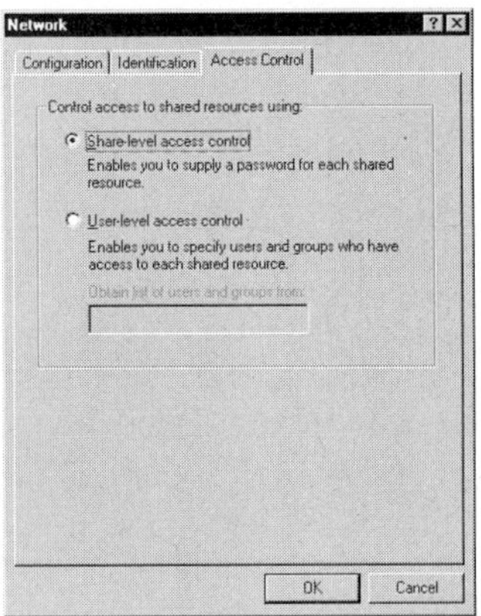

Figure 24.11.
Windows 95 provides two levels of security: share and user.

Share-level access control allows you to assign a password to each resource on the network. You can use the same password for each resource, or a variety of passwords. Share-level access control also allows you to determine whether a user gets read-only or full access based on a password. This is my favorite form of access on a small network. I normally use three different levels of security:

- **No password:** Since the user has to log into the network in the first place, you can assume that she already has a certain level of security. I don't assign an additional password to low-priority resources. The user has already proven that she's supposed to be on the network, so why ask her to prove it again?
- **Read-only:** When I do assign a password to a resource, I give it both a read-only and a full-access password. The read-only password allows me to give people quick access to documents that they can either copy to their hard drive or simply read online. This works well with applications that don't provide a revision-marks feature, because I can see who made what comments. Of course, I still have to go to the trouble of consolidating the comments later.
- **Full:** Anyone who is working on a sensitive project with me usually gets full access to the resource. This allows us to work together on a single document. I normally use Word for Windows for group projects. (Of course, if you're working on a financial projection, you'll probably use something like Lotus 1-2-3 instead.) Turning on the revision-marks feature allows me to see who made what changes. It also allows all of us to interact without actually setting up a meeting.

User-level access control allows you to set resource access by user name or group. This is the same type of access that client/server products such as NetWare use. I use this form of access control when the user will also interact with a larger network. The advantage is obvious. I don't have to spend a lot of time retraining the user to use the peer-to-peer setup. He already knows how to use it based on his previous experience with NetWare.

There's a more important reason to use user-level access control. This is the method that allows you to use a policy file created using the System Policy Editor.

Master Key

What do I mean by a master key? This is a policy more than a feature. Suppose that your company uses a combination of client/server and peer-to-peer networks. It's important to keep things as simple as possible for the user, yet make maximum use of company resources and still provide the needed level of flexibility.

Trying to get any user to remember more than one login password is difficult. It also wastes time in some respects because the user will spend a lot of time logging in to the various networks he needs to access. Also, there's a frustration factor to consider as the user goes from login screen to login screen. Do you really want to frustrate a user who is trying to help you implement a security strategy?

Windows 95 provides the capability to use one "master key" to get to all the networks that a user can access. A master key allows users to enter one password to access all the resources they need. The old system was to use a different password for each resource. If you needed to log into the workgroup network, you needed one password. Another password would give you access to the company network. You needed another password for your mail program and yet another for your communications program. Even if you used the same password for every access, it was inconvenient to say the least to enter a password every time you required access to something. Windows 95 remembers all the user's passwords and enters them automatically as needed. All the user needs to do is enter the initial password when starting Windows 95. Implementing a master key strategy is simple. All you need to do is have the user provide precisely the same password to every login screen the first time she goes through them. I stress the word "precisely" here because capitalization makes a difference on some networks.

After you do this the first time, Windows 95 will remember the master key and use it to log the user into every network that she has access to. Instead of going through a long, frustrating procedure, the user will see one consolidated Logon dialog box at the beginning of her Windows 95 session. This one password is all she'll need to use the full flexibility of the network.

Internet Security

The question of Internet security has generated a lot of press lately and I imagine it will get a lot more before anything is resolved. In a lot of respects, it's not even a matter of security we're talking about here—it's a matter of access. Security implies that you're locking something up, and that's clearly in opposition to how people actually use the Internet. Shared information—but shared with only the people you *want* to share with—is what Internet security is really about. In sum, it comes down to a matter of access.

What kinds of access are we talking about? There are a number of ways to look at information exchange. You can either exchange information willingly, or someone can try to steal it from you. Just consider one form of information exchange that people considered stealing. You register your software electronically instead of using the mail-in card as usual. Getting online is easy, but it seems to take a long time. Only after you actually look at what was transferred do you begin to realize that the vendor not only received the information you provided (such as your name and address), but conducted a complete survey of the contents of your machine as well. The mail-in card didn't request any of this information and the vendor didn't bother to tell the user that she would have to supply this information when registering online. That's one form of stealing that's somewhat widespread. Knowing exactly what kind of hardware you use and the type of software on your machine is a big advantage to the vendor that gets the information.

There are other forms of unintentional access as well. For example, a user may decide to visit an Internet site. During the process of downloading the Web page, he also downloads a destructive ActiveX control that wipes out his hard drive. An investigation by authorities shows that there wasn't any malicious intent on the part of the control's author—the control simply conflicted with a disk utility running in the background. Who's to blame? What could you have done to prevent the unauthorized access of your hard drive by a foreign ActiveX control? Damage to both hardware and software becomes a very real issue when you start running those cute-looking controls springing up on Web pages all over the world.

The effect of unrestricted access on your machine's hardware and software isn't the only consideration. Many people are beginning to shop online—I'm one of them. How do you know that the vendor is using your credit card information correctly? For that matter, how do you know that someone isn't monitoring your "conversation" with the vendor and copying down that number? You could end up paying for someone's new car or clothing with your credit card. The most insidious part of this whole plot is that your credit card is still in your pocket. At least if someone had stolen it outright, you'd have a chance of canceling it before he used it. If someone stole your credit card number through an insecure Internet connection, the first sign of trouble would be the end-of-the-month statement or your inability to use the card at a store.

The need to restrict access doesn't affect just the user. What happens to companies that lose their competitive edge when someone snoops through their supposedly secret files? It happens. Just look at all of the news in the trade presses regarding updated firewalls and other security items. A lot of the security software that people depended on the most ended up having some flaw that rendered the security features useless. (Fortunately, firewall and other security software are becoming a lot more secure due to the hard work of both vendors and users.)

It doesn't take too long to realize that creating a secure environment on the Internet may be more difficult than you first thought. I'm not going to spend a lot of time telling you horror stories of companies that lost millions of dollars due to the seemingly petty crimes committed by hackers. Nor will we explore the test cases of home users who let their guard down for a few moments only to discover that those were the most important few moments of their computer's history. You can find stories like that in any number of books on the market, not to mention the ones that will appear in the trade presses you read on a weekly basis. What we'll concentrate on instead are the security measures that you can take to protect yourself when using a standard browser under Windows 95. After all, preventing a break-in is at least as important as recovering once one occurs.

Peter's Principle: When Will a Hacker Break Into Your Machine?

The first sign of trouble, at least for me, when I visit a site to offer advice on security, is the level of confidence that I find. If someone is confident that a hacker can't break into her system, I'm almost positive that the hacker will find a way to do so. The only sure thing about security software of any kind is that it will keep an honest person from going down the wrong road. If someone really wants to find a way to break into your system, he'll find a way to do it.

Think about the very concept of security software for a second. That software you're using is designed by a programmer who wants to provide you with the best protection he can think of. Any software designed by a programmer can be overcome by an equally competent hacker thinking along the same lines. All that the hacker really needs to do is figure out what line of reasoning the programmer followed when creating the security software, and then think of a way around it. The idea that anyone can overcome your security precaution is an important concept to remember. In other words, the very idea of a secure system is an illusion and a very dangerous one at that.

So, if you can't count on your security software to prevent a break-in, what good is it? There are three ways that security software can help. First, it does act as a direct deterrent to people who are basically honest and really don't want to cause problems. Second, it can slow down even a good hacker, which gives you time to react and prevent any major problems. Finally, good security software admits that it didn't stop the hacker, alerting you to the problem at hand. The one way in which security software won't help is to deter a hacker from breaking in at all. The better your security, the more a hacker will want to break it. In most cases, the hacker is after the thrill of killing your security; he doesn't even know what he'll find on your system.

The number one way to stop a hacker in his tracks is to start out by thinking that he's going to get past your security software. Once you get that idea in mind, you can start looking for breaches in your security. A good piece of security software will work with you to help you locate holes or unauthorized entry (which could be as simple as a break in someone's normal pattern of system access or an unusual number of password retries). Looking for holes is unfortunately the only way that you'll keep someone from damaging your system.

Understanding Certificates and Digital Signatures

The beginning of this section noted some very distinct problems with the current Internet setup when it comes to secure downloads. How do you know that an ActiveX control won't destroy your hard drive while you're using it? There are efforts underway right now to make downloading ActiveX controls, Java applets, or anything else from the Internet just a little safer. Some of the trade press calls this new technology a *certificate*, while other people use the term *digital signature*. I view *certificate* as a friendly but imprecise term, so I'll use digital signature throughout this section. So what exactly is a certificate or digital signature all about?

Right now, figuring out the precise technology behind digital signatures is a little like nailing Jell-O to the wall—you might be able to do it, but who would want to try? Suffice it to say that the precise details are changing on an almost daily basis. However, there's a simple way to look at a digital signature from a user perspective. Think of it as you would a driver's license or an identification card, because it has the same function. A digital signature identifies some Internet object such as a Java applet or an ActiveX control, who created it and when, and potentially a wealth of other information. For example, if the object happens to be a client or server, a digital signature shows the current owner. In other words, you'd know the true identity of the person or company that you're dealing with.

Giving someone a digital certificate for the life of an object leaves a few things in doubt. For example, what if a company sold the rights to an ActiveX control to another company? To alleviate this problem, the digital signature, like a driver's license, also expires—forcing vendors to keep proving that they are who they say they are. The expiration date also gives hackers a lot less time to figure out how to steal the certificate. (Because each certificate is a separate item, learning how to steal one won't necessarily buy the hacker anything.) Using a digital signature helps to keep everyone honest, because it forces everyone to go through a central verification point. A digital signature avoids the one big problem with the honor system used by the Internet to date—it doesn't rely on one person to maintain the security of your machine. Now you have direct input into who gets access and when. (This implies some level of user training to ensure that people actually know how to use this feature.)

Looking for Digital Signatures

How do you identify someone who has a digital signature versus someone who doesn't? You'll always see some kind of warning dialog box when accessing an insecure site. Figure 24.12 shows one of the warnings that you'll get. In this case, the site doesn't have a digital signature for the ActiveX control on its page. Likewise, accessing a site with a digital certificate always looks the same. You'll see a digital certificate dialog box like the one shown in Figure 24.13. Make absolutely certain that the date is current and that the digital signature belongs to the person or company that you thought it belonged to.

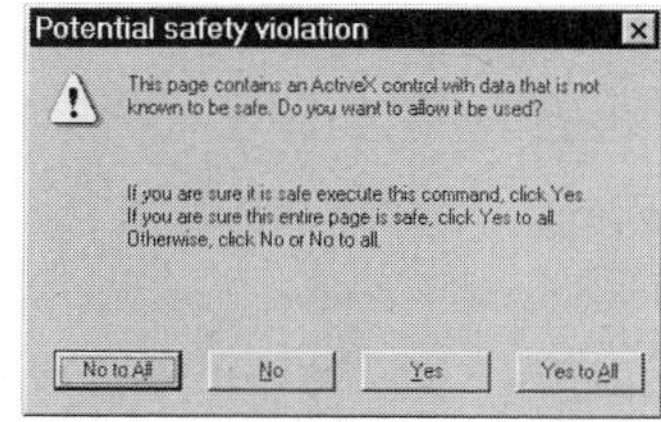

Figure 24.12.
You'll get a warning message if you try to download an ActiveX control or other object that doesn't have a digital signature.

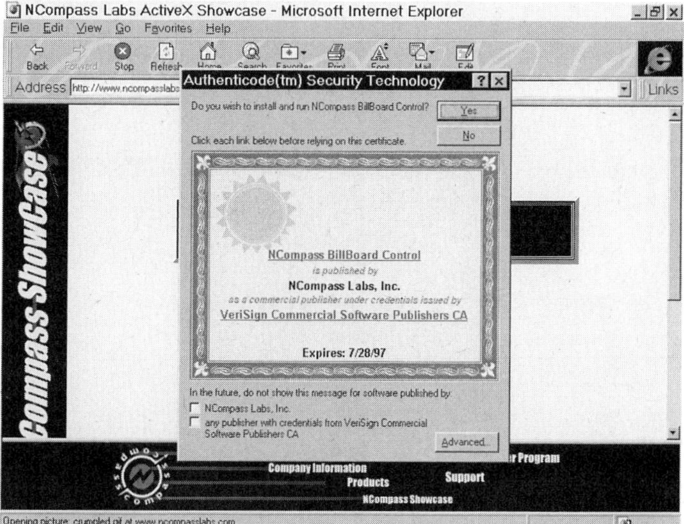

Figure 24.13.
The first time you visit a site that has a digital signature, your browser should display a dialog box showing it to you.

Warning: If the digital signature you see doesn't look like the one shown in Figure 24.13, it isn't a real digital signature. The capability to display these certificates isn't part of the browser itself—it's part of a lower-level Windows API. The browser calls this API to test the certificate and see whether it's real. As a result, you'll get the same certificate dialog box no matter which browser you use.

Notice that the Authenticode™ Security Technology dialog box gives you a few options for optimizing your system. First, you'll want to check the certificate to make sure that it's valid. For example, check to see that the vendor listed is the one that you expected. Also check the date to make sure that the certificate hasn't expired. Second, you'll have the ability to bypass the verification stage for this vendor if you want to. The first check box below the certificate always allows you to add a particular company to the list checked by WinVerifyTrust—this is a special API function designed to check the security of the certificate. If you check this box, you won't be asked each time you request a download from that particular vendor. This is a good risk with some vendors, but may not be such a smart thing to do with others. What you have to determine is how far you trust the vendor. The second check box always allows you to accept all access from any vendor certified by a specific certificate authority, such as VeriSign (the vendor shown in this case). Unless you're very comfortable with the certification process, you'll probably want to leave this box unchecked.

The Authenticode™ Security Technology dialog box also has an Advanced button. Figure 24.14 shows what you'll see when you click it. This is a list of the trusted companies in your Registry. Every time you check one of the two options in the first dialog box, you'll get another entry in this one. Notice that I don't have any entries here. I prefer to take the extra time to view each certificate. You may not feel the need to take this extra precaution, but it never hurts to do so. The dialog box shown in Figure 24.14 also contains a Remove button. You should remove any vendors that you don't trust or whose certificates you haven't used in a while. Never take chances when it comes to security on the Internet.

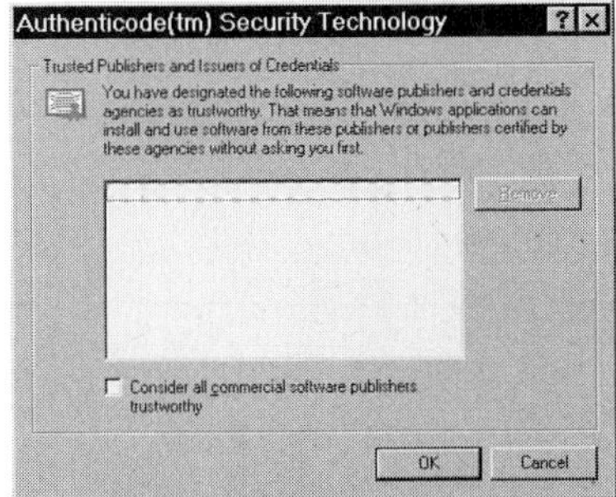

Figure 24.14.
The Advanced button shows a list of vendors that you trust.

Obtaining a Digital Signature

Just as you want to know who you're dealing with, people are going to want to know who *you* are. For that reason, VeriSign (and any other digital signature providers that may be around when you read this) provide a way for you to get a digital signature as well. All you need to do is visit their Web site at `https://digitalid.verisign.com/`. Figure 24.15 shows what the Web page looks like.

(You'll see a Security Information dialog box saying that you're about to request a secure document when you visit the site—don't worry about clicking Yes. The secure document helps to ensure that the information you send to VeriSign remains secret.)

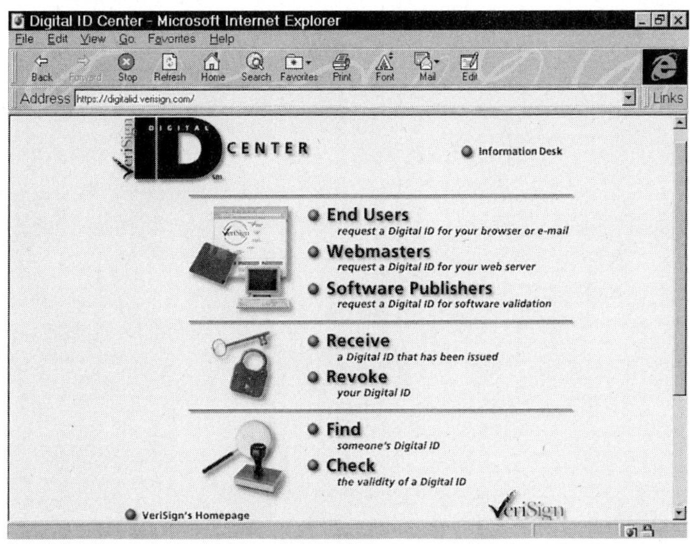

Figure 24.15.
The VeriSign Digital ID Center gives many different kinds of people digital signatures for a variety of purposes.

Tip: You can always tell when you're making a secure transmission by looking for special icons provided by your browser. Internet Explorer shows a lock on the right side of the status bar. Navigator shows a key on the left side of the status bar. The more teeth in the key, the higher the security level (one and two teeth are all you'll see). A missing lock or broken key usually signifies an insecure connection—you'll want to exercise extra caution when transmitting data if you see a missing lock or broken key.

Unless you're a Webmaster, you'll want to select the first option in the list—End Users. Figure 24.16 shows the application selection page that you'll see next.

Choose one of the three application types. The two browser application paths follow the same route. (I don't cover the procedure for the S/MIME-enabled applications in this chapter.) You'll see the selection dialog box shown in Figure 24.17. This is where you select the class of digital signature that you want. There are two classes of digital signatures you can choose from.

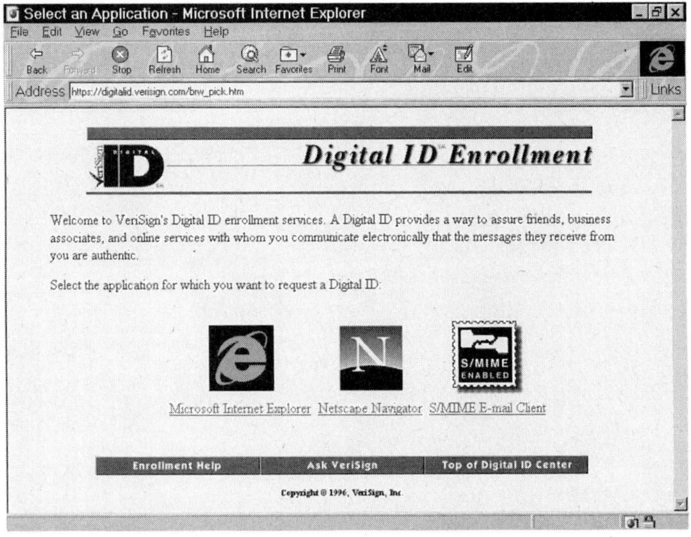

Figure 24.16.
You'll need to tell VeriSign which browser you plan to use the digital certificate with.

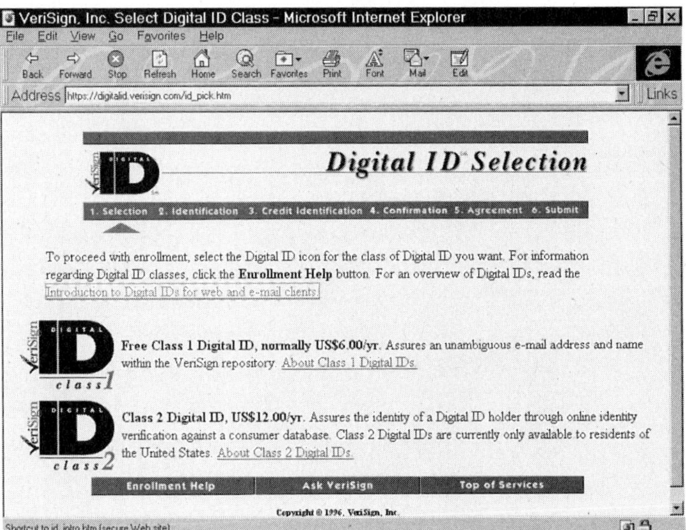

Figure 24.17.
The class of digital signature you choose determines the level of security it provides.

The following list explains what each type provides in the way of security:

- **Class 1:** Provides the user with a unique name and address within a repository. VeriSign (or whatever certificate vendor you choose) will be able to verify that the person and the address go together. The mail-back process is the only verification that VeriSign uses in this case. You have to own an e-mail address to receive the certificate, making it hard for a hacker to obtain a fake certificate. This class of certificate normally costs $6 per year to maintain.

- **Class 2:** To obtain a Class 2 certificate, you must provide third-party evidence of your identity. (At the moment, this limits access to a Class 2 certificate to people in the United States.) The big difference between a Class 2 certificate and a Class 1 certificate is that VeriSign actually checks information you provide against a consumer database maintained by EquiFax. You'll also go through a hardware-signing process, which requires multiple keys instead of one. This class of certificate costs $12 per year to maintain.

Notice that the Class 1 digital signature is free at the moment, to promote the use of digital signatures. That's going to change in the future, but VeriSign hasn't told anyone when. However, you can't really argue with a free digital signature and the security it can provide.

At this point you select one of the two classes of digital signature (certificate). I'm going to follow the Class 1 route because that's what you'll probably use the first time. Click the Class 1 icon on the left side of the window. The next thing you see is an identification page similar to the one shown in Figure 24.18. (I've scrolled the page down in this case so that you can see all the blanks.)

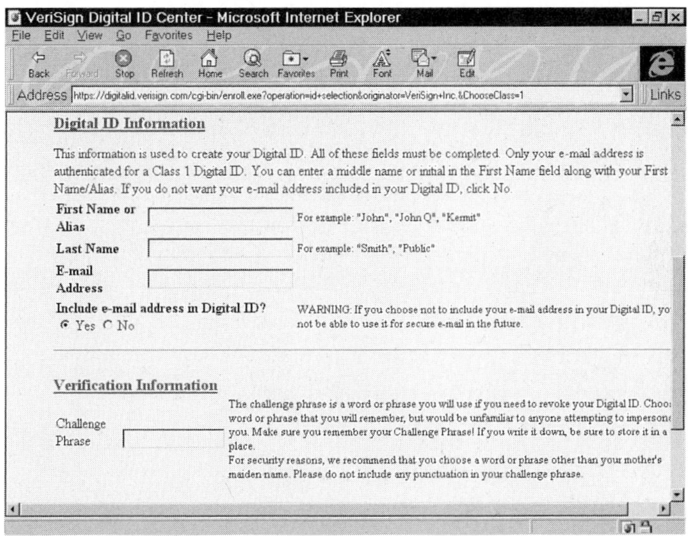

Figure 24.18.
Part of the process of obtaining a digital signature is to tell VeriSign who you are.

The form isn't all that difficult to figure out. All you need to do is type in a first and last name. You must supply an e-mail address—that's how your certificate is issued. After you fill in this minimal information, you need to decide whether to include your e-mail address as part of the certificate. For the most part you don't have a choice. In many cases people simply won't accept your certificate if it doesn't include the e-mail address as part of the package. Because a Class 1 digital signature counts on e-mail address verification, it's not too difficult to figure out why this is such a big issue. The final blank is a challenge phrase. I prefer to look at this as a password. You'll definitely want to choose something out of the ordinary, because VeriSign will use the challenge phrase when you need assistance with your certificate.

Even though Figure 24.18 doesn't show it, there's a Continue button at the bottom of the page. Click it and you see a verification page that contains all the information for your certificate. Verify that everything is correct, and then click Continue again. At this point you see an agreement page like the one shown in Figure 24.19.

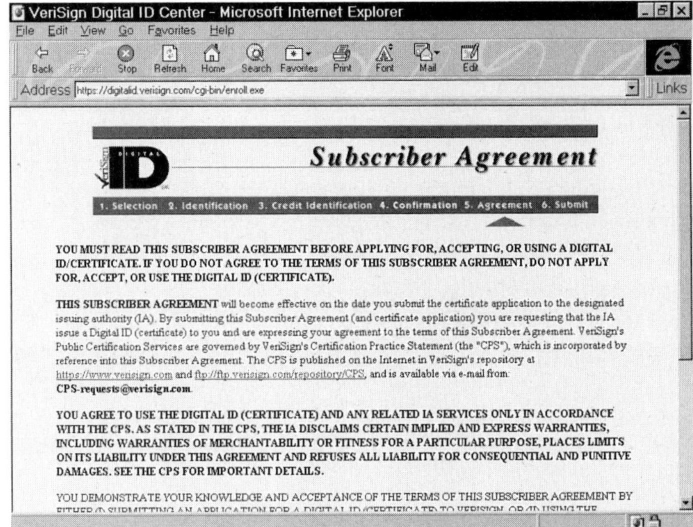

Figure 24.19.
The agreement page tells you about the requirements for using your digital signature.

If you agree with the terms of the license, click Accept at the bottom of the page. The next page you see will tell you that you've completed the enrollment process and that it's time to send your information to VeriSign. At this point you need to start the process of creating a private key, the one on your hard drive that's used for encryption purposes. Simply click the Submit button to see the Credentials Enrollment Wizard dialog box shown in Figure 24.20.

Click Next to get past the first page of the Credentials Enrollment Wizard. You need to provide the name of your private key. The Credentials Enrollment Wizard defaults to MyPrivateKey, but you can use anything you'd like.

Click Finish once you've entered a private key name. That's it! At some time in the near future, you'll receive a confirmation e-mail from VeriSign. This e-mail contains a link to a Web site where you can download your digital signature. It also contains a special PIN (personal identification number) that you have to use at the download site.

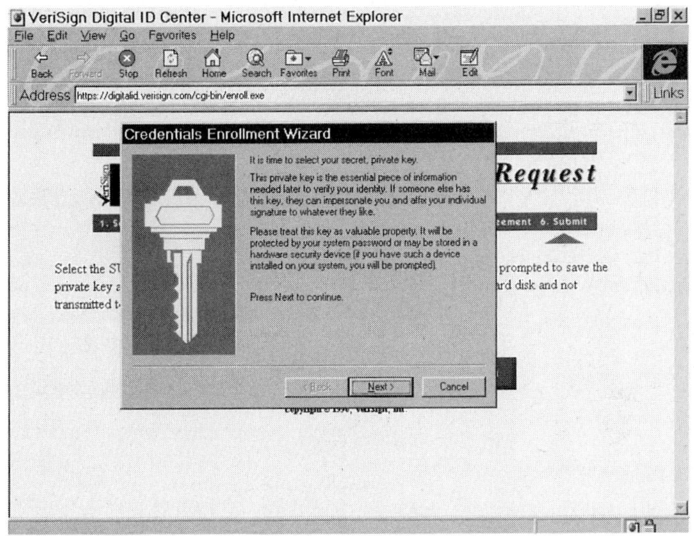

Figure 24.20.
The Credentials Enrollment Wizard helps you to create a private key.

Once you've got your PIN, go ahead and follow the link to the Web page shown in Figure 24.21. Simply copy the PIN number you got in your e-mail, and then paste it into the blank provided.

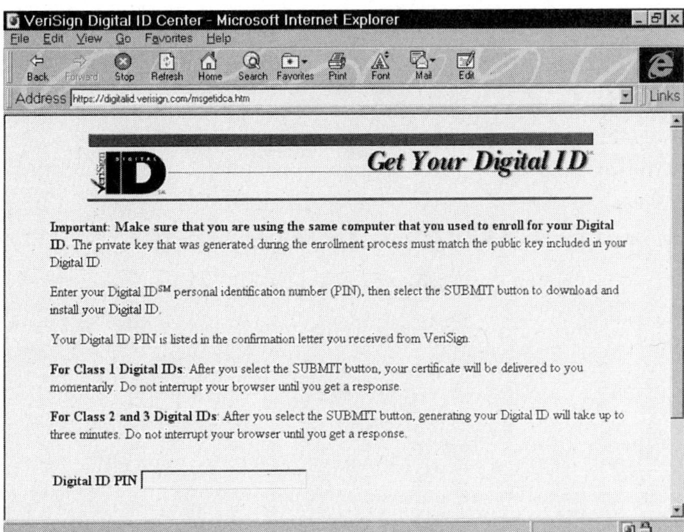

Figure 24.21.
Getting your digital signature is as easy as entering the PIN you get in your e-mail.

Click Submit. After a few minutes you'll get a success page like the one shown in Figure 24.22. Make absolutely certain that you don't disturb the browser during this period of time. Simply wait for the transaction to complete. Click the Install button at the bottom of the page to complete the process. You see a simple message stating that your digital signature has been installed.

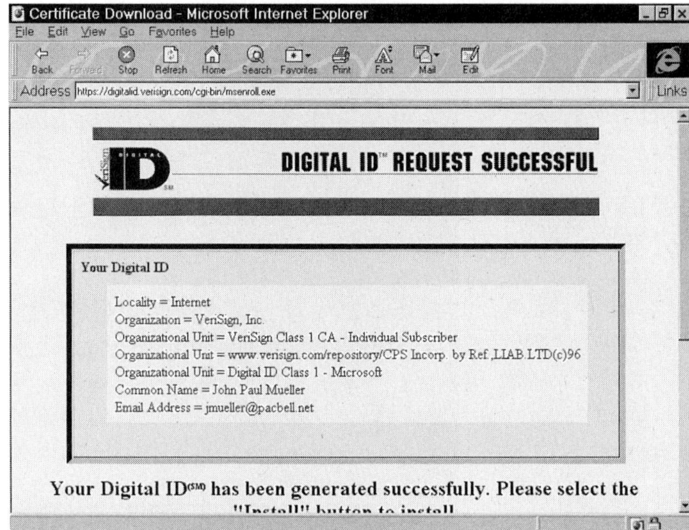

Figure 24.22.
The process is complete when you retrieve your digital signature from the VeriSign (or other certificate provider) site.

The Cookie Monster

If you spend very much time in some of the browser-oriented newsgroups on the Internet, you'll find some amount of talk about cookies. What precisely is a cookie? It's a small file with configuration information that a Web site can write to.

Normally you'll find this file in a special directory that you can monitor, and the Web site will use it for things such as your name and site preferences. However, there aren't any real limitations on what kind of information a Web site can write to the cookie, and that can create problems. For example, what would prevent a Web site from writing executable code to the cookie and then fooling the operating system into executing it? This particular problem actually occurred, but fortunately the results were more along the lines of a bad joke than actual damage to the system. It could have been different, though, and that's why people are concerned about cookies.

There are two approaches to the storage of cookies. The Netscape Navigator approach is to place all the cookies in one file named COOKIES.TXT in the Navigator folder. You can examine this file if you'd like, but make sure that you don't change anything it contains. The disadvantage of the Navigator approach to cookies is that you have to erase the entire file to get rid of an offending site. On the other hand, this approach is very space-efficient and it's easy to locate the file you want.

Internet Explorer stores the cookies in separate files in the Cookies or Temporary Internet Files folder within your main Windows folder. Each cookie is represented by a user name followed by an at sign (`@`), followed by the site name. For example, if a person named Ted visited the `http://www.msn.com` site, MSN would download a cookie to his machine, and then he'd have a cookie file named Ted@MSN in his Cookies folder. The main advantage of this approach is that each user can have his own configuration settings for the same site, even if they all use the same machine to visit it. In addition, getting rid of the settings for a site you no longer use is as easy as erasing a single cookie file. The disadvantages include inefficient disk use and the fact that some users find it difficult to figure out which cookies to get rid of (if they even know that the Cookies folder exists). Obviously, neither the Internet Explorer nor the Navigator approach is perfect.

The point is that you know where the cookies are stored and how to reject them if desired. Both Internet Explorer and Navigator provide the means to reject cookies you don't want. In Internet Explorer you use the View | Options command to display the Options dialog box. Select the Advanced page. On that page you'll find a Warn Before Accepting Cookies check box. Normally this check box isn't checked because cookies are a normal part of life on the Internet. Getting to the appropriate option when using Navigator is just as easy. Simply use the Options | Network Preferences command to display the Preferences dialog box. Select the Protocols page. You'll find an Accepting a Cookie check box here that tells Navigator to display a message before accepting a cookie. As in Internet Explorer, this box normally isn't checked.

So, if accepting cookies is a normal part of surfing the Internet—yet accepting them could be dangerous—how do you work with cookies on a daily basis? I normally keep cookies enabled because I'm visiting sites that are business-oriented. I disable cookies when I visit a small site that I'm not sure of or perhaps a non-business site that I haven't looked at before. Normally cookies are pretty safe, though, so you'll probably want to give them a wide latitude with regard to security. Because this is the only file that a standard Web page can write to, you'll find that most cookies do just what they're supposed to do—store configuration settings. Because the advent of ActiveX controls and Java applets gives more power to hackers who really want to harm your system, I'd spend more time worrying about these potential breaches in your security.

Sandbox Approach Versus Open Access

Security is more complex than it really needs to be right now because the Internet is going through a lot of changes with regard to capability and flexibility. The two main players in all this are ActiveX controls and Java applets. (Scripting languages also play a role, but they normally interact with ActiveX controls or Java applets.)

Java applets take what's known as the sandbox approach to security—they don't do anything outside the purview of the applet. For example, accessing the hard drive isn't allowed because the applet would have to use the operating system to do so. Some developers complain that the sandbox approach hinders them from writing fully-functional applications, and to a certain point they're right.

If an applet can't access system resources, it can't really do much more for you from a system level than standard HTML can. On the other hand, many users feel safer knowing that the Java applet they just downloaded won't erase the contents of their hard drive or something else equally devious.

There's another good reason to use the sandbox approach. It allows a developer to write a single applet that works on a lot of platforms. Because the applet doesn't rely on system services, everything it needs is provided by the Java engine. In other words, a Java applet is self-contained and doesn't rely on anyone else. (The Java engine is obviously platform-specific.)

Microsoft has taken a different approach with ActiveX. It's actually an extension of OLE technology. Unlike a Java applet, ActiveX controls can interact with applications on your machine, access the hard drive, and look into the Registry. This makes ActiveX controls a lot more flexible from the developer perspective. It makes them more useful from the user perspective as well. The problem lies in the level of access that they obtain. An ActiveX control has the same level of access as any other application on your machine. This means that an ill-behaved control could cause more than a little damage. In addition, it means that the user can't simply download a control without thinking about its origins first.

At first glance, it would seem that the distinction between ActiveX controls and Java applets is pretty clear. You'd accept Java applets if security was foremost on your mind. ActiveX controls would provide added capability, but only if you were willing to accept the consequences of a reduced security net. Let's look at that dividing line, though; it's not as clear as you might think. People have had Java applets use back doors to access the system. There have been a few documented cases where they've actually caused damage. Supporters of Java have stated that these security holes are all sealed up, but how can you be certain?

ActiveX supporters further muddy the waters by stating that an ActiveX control falls under the same guidelines as any OLE control. In addition, the author has to sign the control—showing the user downloading it who created the control. (You can still download the control if the author doesn't sign it, but both Internet Explorer and Navigator display warnings against this practice.) The use of digital signatures means that you'll always know who created an ActiveX control and can make a reasonable decision about downloading and using it. (Java controls are downloaded automatically—you don't get a chance to review a digital signature for them in advance and very often don't even know who created them.)

The only thing that you can say about the sandbox versus the open approach right now is that neither one is clear-cut. About the only thing you can do is watch where you download controls from. If you're uncertain about a site, then don't take the risk of using it. Security is a user matter right now. Look before you leap. Make sure that you know who created that Java applet or ActiveX control before letting it run on your machine.

Tip: You can avoid the whole question of downloading Java applets you don't want—by disabling them. Navigator provides this capability on the Languages page of the Preferences dialog box. You access it by using the Options | Network Preferences command. (If you don't want to use ActiveX controls, don't install a plug-in like NCompass's ScriptActive.) Likewise, you can disable both ActiveX and Java on the Security page of the Options dialog box for Internet Explorer. You access this dialog box by using the View | Options command.

On Your Own

Take this opportunity to design your own security plan. Work with network users and management to come up with a plan that's both fair and reasonably secure.

Analyze the plan that you created for leaks and potential security risks. Make sure that you tell management about these risks and their effect on the network. Also come up with contingency plans to plug the leaks if management decides the risk is too great.

Spend some time training the users on your network about security. It's very important that you also take the time to explain what types of passwords are acceptable. Spend a little time with each user who has problems understanding the security plan.

If you're a home user, try setting up a variety of security options on your machine. For example, you might want to create a security profile for young users that gives them access to programs that they can use but removes access to programs that could damage your machine. Try using the System Policy Editor and the other tools described in this chapter to make the process of creating a home security plan easy.

Anyone who uses the Internet for more than just casual browsing should have his or her own digital signature. Use the procedure in the "Obtaining a Digital Signature" section of this chapter to get your own digital signature. Be sure to reread the rest of the section as well. It's always good to know when you can trust the party at the other end of the connection.

VII Troubleshooting Windows 95

25

Software Problems

It would be nice to say that Windows 95 takes care of every problem and that you'll never again experience any kind of software error, but that wouldn't be reality. Windows 95 does provide a level of safety you've probably never seen before. It certainly isn't as safe as Windows NT, but it's a lot better than Windows 3.x.

When you look at Windows 95, you're seeing a middle ground of reliability, not the best there is. Microsoft had to make some concessions to allow all the products you used under Windows 3.x to run under Windows 95 as well. In addition, there was a problem with getting enough security in a package that also runs under 4MB of RAM. (Of course, even though Windows 95 will probably start with 4MB, we've already discussed the practical recommendations for RAM.)

So how do these limitations affect you? First, you'll still have problems with GPFs. Windows NT provides a very strict environment for sensing programs that make illegal calls and recovers from them by terminating the offending application. This won't quite work with some applications that depend on those illegal calls to run. The result is that you'll experience some GPFs because Windows 95 relaxes the rules to allow more applications to run—even those that aren't necessarily good citizens.

Another problem occurs with DOS support. As in any Windows environment, when your application switches to real mode to run, the operating system is vulnerable to attack. Windows NT handles this problem for the most part by implementing a strict set of rules. As with the Windows applications, Windows 95 relaxes these rules so that more applications can run. The result is that an errant application can crash the system.

Fortunately, you'll still notice a superior level of support from Windows 95. It recovers from a great many more problems than Windows 3.x. In addition, the more 32-bit applications you use, the less your chance of having the system crash.

I've been testing the latest release of Windows 95 pretty thoroughly over the course of writing this book and compared it to the previous releases. I've changed the Registry and tested what will and won't work. Setup has also gotten a good workout as I've added and removed applications. I even changed the network setup quite a few times to test different configurations. If Windows 95 ever had a good reason to crash, it was while I kept changing its configuration. During this time, I've experienced less than one system crash per day. That's pretty good, considering what I put Windows 95 through. Of course, it would have been better if the record were perfect, but you'd need something a little more robust in the protection area, such as Windows NT, to accomplish that.

The bottom line? You don't get anything for free. That applies to operating systems as well. People don't want an operating system that places their applications in a straitjacket and forces them to buy new ones. They want something that will run their old stuff well and their new stuff even better. That's what Windows 95 provides, but it comes at the cost of system stability.

This chapter covers from a software perspective some of the problems you'll experience. I also tell you about some of the fixes that Microsoft provides to alleviate those problems. Will these fixes always work? Probably not. During one incident, I actually had to reinstall Windows 95 and all the applications I use, because the Registry got trashed beyond recognition. An application decided to overwrite some files that would have been fine under Windows 3.x, but not under Windows 95. Suffice it to say that you'll experience fewer problems under Windows 95 and that the cures Microsoft provides work most of the time, but thinking that they'll cure every problem just isn't realistic.

Startup and Configuration Errors

Configuration problems normally manifest themselves in several ways. The most devastating is during system startup. Have you ever seen the infamous blue screen? If you reconfigure your machine as often as I do, you're definitely going to see it.

The other types of configuration problems are a lot more devious. They usually rob your system of its flexibility or make some of its components unusable. You might find yourself running in circles trying to identify the culprit, only to find that it wasn't any of the things you suspected at all. One of the problems I found in this category was my sound board. I couldn't figure out what was wrong. The Midi Balance setting kept getting out of whack. I looked at the driver—no luck. The same held true with the hardware itself. I thought there might be a problem in the way that the CD software was working, so I disabled it. No luck there either. After several days of searching, I found that the problem occurred only when I ran a specific version of After Dark. Problems such as these can really make you want to pull your hair out.

Don't get the idea that configuration problems are always obvious. It was pretty easy to figure out when my sound board wasn't working correctly—especially with my previous problems. Even my neighbors knew I had a problem with my sound board. But what about the problem I was having with another application? It would work just fine—at least just fine on most days. What would happen on the other days is almost indescribable. My machine would make a strange noise, the screen would look funny, and then the system would reboot. I couldn't figure out what was going on. The solution to this problem turned out to be a Control Panel setup problem. One of my applications had overwritten the standard ODBC files. The new files were incompatible with this application in certain low-memory situations. I discovered that the problem always occurred when I had my word processor or any other large application open.

Tip: I could've had a lot less grief fixing the ODBC file problem if I'd recorded the time stamp for the files in that section or at least made note of the time stamp for my Windows 95 files. You can do the same thing. Throughout this book I've made every effort to tell you which files affect what functions. You can use this information when you're troubleshooting. It also comes in handy when you're recording information for a setup that works. When you get into a situation where the setup no longer works properly, one of the things you can do is go back to your notes to find a potential source of trouble.

If you have plenty of disk space, you can give yourself a measure of security against this sort of problem. Just before you install a new program or a piece of hardware, make a .ZIP file (a compressed archive) of all the files in your Windows and Windows\SYSTEM directories. If anything goes wrong, you can compare the files in those directories with what they used to be back when your system was working okay. If you can't afford to use that much disk space, zip up just your .INI files (and also your CONFIG.SYS and AUTOEXEC.BAT files) and then use the `DIR` command redirected to a file (`DIR > filename`) to save at least that much information about how things were. This won't prevent the problems or even give you copies of the files as they used to be, but at least you'll know which ones were changed. Sometimes that helps point you toward the proper steps to recover from a problem.

As you can tell, I've had lots of fun digging up these real-life problems for you to learn about. The next few sections describe some of the types of problems that you'll run into when your machine's configuration gets out of whack. I'll also provide you with some ideas on how to fix these problems.

Startup Problems

Startup problems are the very worst kind of configuration problem to fix because you can't very easily use the tools that Windows 95 provides to find the problem. What usually happens is that the settings for one or more devices conflict, get lost, or are somehow incompatible with the device you're using. When a device conflict affects the display adapter or your hard drive, you see a blue screen. This blue screen means that Windows 95 can't recover from this sort of problem.

So how do you get around this? The best way is to start the machine in fail-safe mode. This mode starts your machine with the bare minimum of devices installed. That should get rid of the majority of your problems. The only two devices that you really *must* have to start Windows 95 are the display adapter and the hard drive. It's extremely unlikely that these two devices will have any conflicts. Windows also uses a generic VGA display driver. This will get rid of the rest of your problems. Even if your display driver is somehow corrupted or you've used the wrong settings, the generic VGA display driver will work. Figure 25.1 shows a machine in fail-safe mode. Notice that you'll always know when you're in this mode because `Safe mode` appears in all four corners of the screen.

There are two ways to get into this mode. The first is automatic. When Windows 95 detects a problem in booting, it automatically sets the machine up to reboot in fail-safe mode. Of course, that depends on Windows 95 actually detecting the problem. Sometimes it doesn't. For example, if you make it most of the way through the boot process, Windows 95 might not detect a startup problem. The most difficult situation to detect is a sound board problem. The system is most or all of the way through the boot sequence before a sound board problem occurs. If Windows fails to detect the startup problem, use the manual startup method. You can force a manual fail-safe boot by pressing the F8 key when you boot your machine. Normally, pressing F8 displays a menu. This menu will have one or more entries for fail-safe mode.

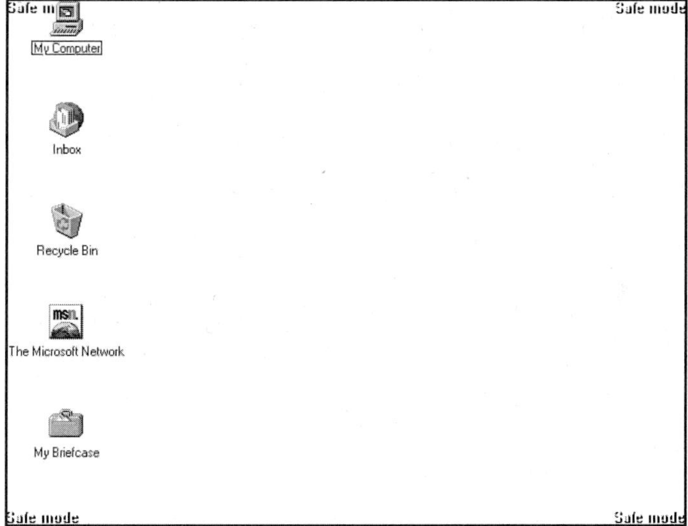

Figure 25.1.
It's easy to see when you're in fail-safe mode.

The following is a complete list of the items you can expect to find on the boot menu:

- **Normal:** Allows you to boot the machine normally. The only reason you would need this entry is if you pressed F8 by accident during the boot process.
- **Logged (\BOOTLOG.TXT):** I've discussed this particular feature in earlier chapters. You can use the contents of BOOTLOG.TXT to determine precisely where the boot sequence is failing. Of course, it takes a little time to analyze the contents of the files, so you should rely on this as one of the later troubleshooting methods. The advantage of this method is that it gives you the best picture of exactly what's going on during the boot process.
- **Safe mode:** This is the entry you would normally select to find boot problems. It starts your machine with the minimum number of devices enabled. Windows 95 doesn't process the contents of CONFIG.SYS or AUTOEXEC.BAT. None of your Startup folder entries will be processed, either.
- **Safe mode with network support:** Use this entry if safe-mode startup doesn't really tell you where the problem is and you suspect your network card. Always use this startup after you try safe mode; otherwise, you can't be certain that the failure isn't being hidden by something else. For example, I had a conflict with my COM port. The fault showed up as a mouse not responding. The COM port didn't show any errors at all. If I hadn't taken the time to really look at what was going on, I could have missed the conflict and replaced my mouse, thinking that it had finally bit the dust.

- **Step-by-step confirmation:** If you must use real-mode drivers, this option allows you to find a real-mode driver conflict. You can restart your machine several times, excluding a different driver each time, until you find the one that's causing problems with your Windows setup. Of course, the best way to get rid of these types of conflicts is to get rid of the real-mode drivers so that Windows can help configure your machine.
- **Command prompt only:** Use this option if you need to get to the command prompt to check something out. It does process your CONFIG.SYS and AUTOEXEC.BAT entries, so any real-mode drivers you need will be loaded. This is a great setting to use if you need to install an older DOS application that insists on not having anything else loaded. I also found it handy when installing the NetWare client software.
- **Safe mode command prompt only:** I find this setting handy if I need to get to the DOS 7.0 prompt for some reason. For example, if a CONFIG.SYS or AUTOEXEC.BAT entry is causing problems, I can get to the DOS prompt, make any required modifications, and reboot the machine. Windows 95 boots to a DOS prompt without processing either CONFIG.SYS or AUTOEXEC.BAT when you select this option.
- **Previous version of MS-DOS:** You'll see this option only if you include the `BootMulti=1` setting in MSDOS.SYS. It allows you to boot the previous version of DOS. Of course, this assumes that your previous version of DOS is still available. Removing the previous version should disable this feature. Also remember that some types of installations will remove your ability to boot your old version of DOS.

Note: Some MSDOS.SYS settings disable the user's ability to use the F8 key. A network administrator could use this setting to prevent users from circumventing network security. If this happens, you'll need to use your startup disk to start the machine from a floppy. Go to the hard drive and edit the MSDOS.SYS file, using the settings described in Table 6.1.

Tip: Several other boot modes are available on the F8 boot menu. One of them allows you to boot into MS-DOS mode. This is handy if you need to access a diagnostic program to locate a problem. You can also select which CONFIG.SYS and AUTOEXEC.BAT entries are executed (this works the same as the F8 feature under DOS). You can use this feature to find a real-mode driver or a TSR that might be preventing your system from booting.

Once you get your machine booted in fail-safe mode, start looking for hardware or software conflicts. You might want to begin by removing all the applications and data files from your Startup folder. Also check WIN.INI to make sure that there are no `LOAD=` or `RUN=` lines in it. Go ahead and `REM` out any lines you do find so that the application won't run the next time you start Windows. After you make sure that all the conflicts are resolved, start your machine again.

Hardware Configuration Problems

Hardware-specific configuration problems are fairly easy to find because Windows makes most of them pretty obvious. All you need to do is right-click the My Computer icon. Look at the Device Manager page of the System Properties dialog box to see whether there are any conflicts. (Chapter 14 covers the ways of using this dialog box.) Look for conflicting devices and change their settings as required. Windows 95 displays the conflicting device as shown in Figure 25.2.

In most cases you can figure out the cause of the conflict by looking at the Resources page shown in Figure 25.3. Notice that this particular page lists two conflicts, but there could just as easily be three or even four conflicting devices. You need to clear the ones that Windows 95 detected the first time around to see whether there are others.

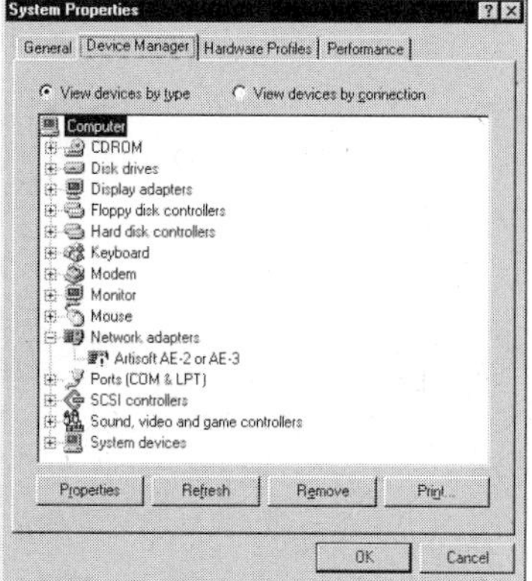

Figure 25.2.
Hardware conflicts that Windows 95 can detect are pretty easy to find.

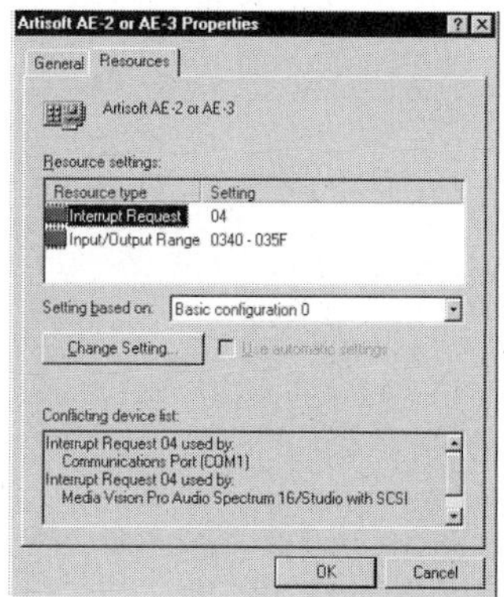

Figure 25.3.
IRQ conflicts are the most common hardware configuration problem.

The problem with some hardware conflicts is that you might not see them immediately. For example, if Windows 95 doesn't manage a particular device, it might not know that a conflict exists. Any device that requires a real-mode device driver to operate generally falls into this category. What this means is that you'll need to find the configuration problem by scanning through the documentation that came with all the pieces of hardware in your system, looking for which DMA channels, IRQ lines, and port addresses they use. Then you'll have to manually set them to non-conflicting values.

Another problem could occur if Windows 95 provides a generic driver for a specific device, and the vendor introduces a version of that device that conflicts with the driver. For example, there's only one driver for the Pro Audio Spectrum 16 Plus sound card, but there are four revisions of that board and even more of that driver. The revision that you use could make a difference in how compatible the device driver and board really are.

Even more problematic is if you think you disabled a device feature, but really didn't. Take another look at that Pro Audio Spectrum sound board. It includes a game port that really doesn't work all that well on high-speed machines. You might disable the game port and use those same settings for an adjustable game port. What happens, though, if the driver fails to do its job properly? I actually ran into this problem. The only solution was to reinstall the driver, but I was probably lucky in this case. Even if Windows thinks it has disabled a specific feature, you might want to view it as a potential area of conflict.

Windows Software Configuration Problems

There are many ways in which a Windows application configuration can go wrong. For example, I recently installed an older 16-bit application that required Program Manager in order to install properly. For whatever reason, the Setup application didn't signal its need for Program Manager, and I thought the installation was a success.

Quite the contrary. The setup program had actually quit before it completed the installation, so I was missing an important .INI file. The result was a piece of software that kept freezing my machine. I fixed the problem by reinstalling the software with Program Manager running. The moral of the story is to always install 16-bit Windows applications with Program Manager running. That way, you'll avoid any problems. Even if the application doesn't actually need Program Manager, you won't lose anything by running it.

There are other Windows application problems as well. For example, have you ever noticed that many applications want to modify your PATH statement in AUTOEXEC.BAT? If you let every application have its way, you'd probably have a mile-long path. Unfortunately, there's a definite limit to how long the path can be and still work. Many applications run just fine without a PATH statement. However, there are two ways in which an application can fail.

I ran across the first problem area by accident. I added the file association required for a new application I installed. Whenever I double-clicked a data file, though, I got a message that the application couldn't find the data file. The application started just fine, but it wouldn't load the data file. After a few hours of troubleshooting, I found that I could get rid of the problem by adding the application's location to my path.

Some applications fail in a big way if you don't add them to the PATH statement. CA-Visual Objects and some other large applications fall into this category. They usually provide some nebulous error message and quit before you can get them going. Or the application will load and then refuse to load any add-ons because it can't find them. You might see symptoms of this problem when an application refuses to maintain the settings you save from session to session. Whenever you're in doubt, try adding the application to your PATH statement to see whether the problem goes away.

Corruption of .DLL or other shared files is another problem area. The .DLL might not actually contain any bad data. It might work just fine with several other applications. However, one application might require an older version of the .DLL, because it uses an undocumented feature of that .DLL or makes use of some bug to its advantage. Sometimes you'll need to keep the old version of a .DLL on disk to satisfy the needs of a particular application.

What happens if one application needs the new version of the .DLL and another application requires the old version? Unless one or both applications keep their own version of the shared .DLL in their own separate directory (which is a regrettably uncommon practice), you must make a decision about which application to keep. In most cases, I use this situation as an excuse to upgrade my software. There usually isn't any reason to keep an old application around if it refuses to work with all your newer applications. In fact, an incompatibility of this type usually means that it's really time to retire that old application and get the newer version.

I ran into a really strange problem with one application on my machine. It was a communications program, but I imagine the same thing could happen with any application. Every time I tried to open this application, it would fill the screen—and then some. I had recently lowered my screen resolution to capture some screen shots, but I needed to run this application quickly to download a needed file from CompuServe. No matter what I did, as soon as the main application window appeared, the machine would freeze and I'd have to reboot. This was yet another example of an application that failed because its environment wasn't set up correctly. The point I'm trying to make is that the cause of failure isn't always obvious. You usually need to spend some time looking for the potential cause of a problem. Some of these causes can lead you down blind alleys into places you thought would never fail.

If you thought Windows software had a lot of failure points, you haven't worked with enough DOS software recently. There are some applications that you'll never get to run under any version of Windows. Most of these applications fall into the games category, but I've seen others in this situation as well.

An application that assumes that it has the machine to itself, combined with users who keep asking for better performance, equals a situation in which the programmer is going to access the hardware directly in ways that the programming community as a whole would never recommend. This is precisely the situation that some game and utility program vendors get into. Users demand faster games with better graphics and sound, yet they want to run these programs on very outdated hardware. The game programmers usually have to resort to register-level programming to get the speed that the user wants. Of course, this usually means that any mistake in programming, even a small one, will result in a frozen machine—or worse.

Applications that fall into this category can be fixed in only one way: You have to run them in MS-DOS mode. I covered MS-DOS mode earlier, so I won't cover it again here. The thing to remember is that running an application in MS-DOS mode means that you can't allow it to interact with any of your other applications. Using MS-DOS mode is the very last alternative you should try.

If MS-DOS mode is the last resort, what should you try first? I usually look at the application settings to see whether I can find and fix any potential problems. Here's one scenario. You have a game program that always freezes when you run it in Windows, but it works fine from the DOS prompt. What's the problem? I found several settings-related problems that can wreak havoc with a game. One of them is that you can't assume that the sound board settings that you use in DOS are the same ones that Windows will use. Checking all your settings is an important part of getting a DOS application to run.

There are other settings-related problems as well. For example, many of my games require that I add a Sound Blaster setting to my AUTOEXEC.BAT. They read this setting and configure themselves appropriately. If you don't include the `SET` statement, the game freezes because it doesn't know what settings to use.

Speaking of settings, most DOS applications are very sensitive to the environment settings. I find that compilers are the worst culprits in this area, but other applications can be quite challenging as well. It's usually a good idea to run every application that requires a complex environment setup from a batch file. Add all the required environment settings to the beginning of the batch file and make running the application the last step. You might have to change the program's environment size setting to make this work. See Chapter 13 for more details on the DOS application memory settings.

Once you get past settings and strange hardware-access problems, you might face a few other problems. One of the big problems, especially when talking about games, is a lack of conventional memory. Chapter 13 covers this issue fairly well, but it pays to mention it again. Using a memory manager probably isn't the solution—get rid of unneeded TSRs and device drivers instead. You can save a lot of memory by getting rid of TSRs such as DOSKey. Installing it as part of a batch file from any DOS sessions you start makes more sense. It also makes sense to get rid of ANSI.SYS, because you no longer need it. Windows 95 provides this functionality for you automatically, so loading an additional device driver doesn't make sense.

Memory-Related Problems

You could have quite a few memory-related problems under Windows 95. They fall into several categories. It's important to know which one you're dealing with before you attempt to fix it. The following list categorizes the various memory-related problems you could have when using Windows 95. Go through the list to see whether you can find the symptoms that match your particular problem.

- **Real-mode memory manager conflict:** Some memory managers, such as 386MAX and QEMM, could cause problems when you're using Windows 95. The benefit of using them is a few additional kilobytes of conventional memory. Admittedly, they do a better job in this area than Windows 95 does. The problem is that you now have two very different memory managers fighting for control of the machine. The loser is always the user. Some of the symptoms of this type of problem are a failure of Windows 95 to boot, a sudden freeze-up of the machine, or abnormal device problems such as errors in displaying data. If you experience this problem and your application really needs the additional conventional memory, consider creating an MS-DOS mode setup for using the memory manager with that particular application.
- **Memory leaks:** A few Windows applications don't manage memory properly. They grab a lot of memory from Windows, and then don't release all of it when they terminate. The result is a gradual loss of memory capacity that you can actually track by using the memory field of the application's Help About dialog box. You'll also notice that your other applications start to slow down after a while, as the system starts using a larger swap file to make up for the memory loss. If you have an application that shows a gradual loss of memory, the best way to use it is to start it once and leave it open the entire time you need to use it. Such an application will still gradually bleed memory from the system, but the loss is more gradual if you don't open and close it very much. Eventually you'll need to reboot the system.

Note: Selecting the Reboot the Computer option isn't sufficient. You need to restart the system from scratch, either by using the reset button or by powering the system down and then back up again.

- **Too many frills:** Some types of memory problems are created when you have too many frills on your machine. For example, you might find that Access or another large application is running very slowly or could even GPF a lot after you add a screen saver or another frill to the system. Most people associate utilities with small memory requirements, but this isn't necessarily true. You'll find that many DOS applications had to stay small to keep their conventional memory requirements to a minimum. Windows utilities have no such limitation. Their designers have fewer reasons to keep their applications small, because Windows is designed to allow for better memory management. As a result, I have one screen saver that actually grabs an entire megabyte on my system and more than a few percentage points of system resources as well.

- **Windows system space corruption:** I find it incredible that some vendors put so little effort into testing their products that this type of problem could actually go unnoticed. What usually happens is that an errant pointer in the application starts overwriting the Windows system area. Most of the time, Windows 95 detects this problem and displays an appropriate message. It recovers by terminating the application. On a few occasions, Windows 95 won't detect the problem and will simply freeze. In most cases, you'll want to contact the vendor about this kind of problem and see if a workaround or fix is available.
- **Disk thrashing:** If you try to use an application that your system can't really support, you might experience something called *disk thrashing*. This happens more under Windows 95 than it did under Windows 3.x. You'll know your system is thrashing if the hard disk light stays on for abnormally long periods of time and the application runs really slowly. The only way to fix this problem is to add more memory. Of course, you could also look at some of the memory-saving techniques discussed in Chapter 3.
- **Display memory corruption:** Some older Windows applications might experience problems when writing to the display. Even though they use a different method than DOS, there are situations in which a Windows application can cause problems with the entire display. One of these situations is when it changes the palette (the display colors) without regard for any other applications running on the system. You can't do much about this problem. What you'll see is that the application window will probably look fine, but everything else around it will use really strange color combinations that might produce unreadable text. The big problem occurs when an application leaves the display in this state, even after it exits. You might see other forms of display corruption as well. For example, it's possible for an application to corrupt the icon cache. Icons no longer match the associated functions, or might disappear altogether. The fix is to exit the application and reboot the system. Sometimes that doesn't work. If you find that the problem persists, you might have to erase the ShellIconCache file in your main Windows 95 folder and reboot the machine again. The ShellIconCache file contains an archive of the most-recently-used icons. Windows 95 loads this file when it starts in order to reduce the time it spends reading the icons from disk. Some types of corruption become embedded in this file when Windows exits with a corrupted icon cache in memory.

There are probably other ways to corrupt memory. For example, Windows 95 uses other cache files. Any of these caches could become corrupted and cause problems for your system. You'll need to spend some time looking for the particular cache files on your system. In addition to the ShellIconCache, I also had a ttfCache and a frmCache.dat file on my system. ttfCache affects the fonts listed in the Fonts folder. You might find that the fonts listed no longer match the fonts actually in the directory, if certain types of memory corruption occur. The same holds true for the frmCache.dat file. Any type of cache corruption is easily cured by erasing the corrupted file and allowing Windows 95 to rebuild it during the next boot cycle.

Once you identify and clean up a memory corruption problem, it's usually a good idea to find the responsible application. Most memory corruption problems won't simply go away. You'll find that the corruption occurs over and over again—at the very worst possible moment. After you identify the culprit, you usually have to contact the vendor to find out whether a fix is available. If none is available, you need to decide whether to live with the corruption problem or just get a new application—one that hopefully doesn't exhibit the same memory corruption problem.

So how do you find the culprit? You can't simply assume that the culprit is the foreground application; it could be a background application. For that matter, it doesn't have to be an application at all. A device driver could be causing the memory corruption as you use a specific device. A third class of problem is some type of interaction between two applications or an application and a device driver. However, you have to start somewhere, and looking at the applications you have running is a good place to start. You can follow this simple procedure to find many—but not all—of the memory corruption problems on your system:

1. Start a list of potential problem applications. I usually make note of all the applications I had running when a memory corruption problem occurred. It's also important to make notes on any devices you had running. Of course, some devices are always running. It doesn't pay to list those.
2. Run the suspect applications one at a time to see whether you can get the problem to repeat. Be sure to start Windows with a clean Startup folder and no applications loaded using WIN.INI. It's also important to reboot after each test to make sure that you're starting with a clean memory environment.
3. If you still don't find the culprit, go back to your normal setup and try various combinations of applications. You could be seeing some type of interaction problem.
4. Test the various devices on your machine one at a time to eliminate any device drivers.
5. Keep a running list of active applications each time the memory problem appears. Eventually, you'll see a pattern of one or more applications that are always present when the problem occurs. Try loading just this group of applications and see whether you can get the problem to happen again. Keep whittling the list until you end up with one or two applications that won't work together. The solution is to avoid running them at the same time.
6. If you don't see an application pattern emerge, the problem is definitely device-driver-related. Try disabling one peripheral device at a time to see whether you can find the problem. Don't discount the effects of real-mode drivers on Windows; be sure to check those first.

This kind of testing is time-consuming, but if you do it right you can usually track down a stubborn problem in a matter of days. Unfortunately, memory problems are incredibly difficult to locate in an environment like Windows 95, because so many different things are happening at once. Each application and device driver interact. You'll find that the hardest problems to find are those that result from three or four applications or device drivers working against each other. It always pays to take your time and do a thorough job of testing each potential problem area.

Of course, once you come to a conclusion, finding a permanent fix could prove to be the most difficult part of the journey. You've probably gone through this before—waiting on the phone as each vendor points the finger at someone else. The reality of the situation is that there might not be an easy fix for some types of memory problems. You might just have to avoid the situations that cause them in the first place, get a newer version of the same application, or even go so far as to update your hardware.

On Your Own

Reboot your machine and press F8. See which menu settings discussed in this chapter are present. If you don't see all eight options, find out why. Check your MSDOS.SYS file to make sure that you can access this important feature when needed, if the F8 key doesn't work. You might want to check with your network administrator regarding company policy for this particular setting.

Look at the Device Manager page of the System Properties dialog box to familiarize yourself with its contents. Chapter 14 discusses this feature, but it's a good idea to know what this particular dialog box can do for you. It's one of the major troubleshooting aids that Windows 95 provides.

If you have an application that you currently run in MS-DOS mode, try to find out whether you can make it run under Windows. You might find that the sound board or other device settings that you're using don't match those used by Windows. If there's a conflict, try changing the DOS application settings to those used by Windows to see whether that will allow you to run the application normally. Also check for environment settings that could affect your ability to use the application from within Windows.

26 Hardware Problems

Hardware problems usually are less of an issue under Windows 95 (or any operating system, for that matter) than software problems. The reason is fairly easy to understand. Hardware problems usually fall into two easily recognized groups: compatibility and catastrophic.

Catastrophic errors can include subtle problems such as loss of functionality. By and large, though, you can quickly determine that a catastrophic failure has occurred because the device no longer works. You try to access a hard or floppy drive and nothing happens. Trying to use a faulty modem might mean that it picks up the phone line but refuses to dial. Figuring out the sources of these kinds of problems is easy; fixing them is even easier (albeit expensive, for the most part).

Even compatibility problems are fairly easy to fix under Windows 95. You'll probably get a symptom in which a device looks as if it failed, but later testing shows that it hasn't. We've already looked at some of the fixes for this type of problem. For the most part, you'll find that they're easy to trace and fix.

A Quick Look at Catastrophic Failures

Figuring out a catastrophic error usually takes a little time and a few hardware and software tools. You also need the knowledge required to use these tools. Here's a typical scenario. You start your machine in the morning and Windows 95 comes up fine, but you can't use the mouse. After a little looking around, you find that there aren't any conflicts and you haven't installed anything new recently. The most probable cause of your problem is some type of hardware failure. At least, that's a good place to start searching for a problem that doesn't appear on the Device Manager page of the System Properties dialog box as some type of conflict or other problem.

All kinds of problems fall into the catastrophic category. For example, severely crimping a cable (putting an obvious dent in it) will normally cause some type of hardware failure. It might be as simple as a device that won't respond or a network connection that seems to work intermittently. Port failures don't happen often, but they do happen. You'll also find that NICs fail from time to time. Everyone knows that hard drives fail.

Part of the problem for a network administrator or a home user is figuring out how to find the problem for certain. "Easter-egging" is the solution that some people use. They just try replacing one component at a time until they locate the problem. Unfortunately, that's really not the best way to do things. Using diagnostic aids and other troubleshooting tools will save you a lot more time than they cost. It's also a lot less expensive to find the right component the first time and replace it.

Tip: Never discount the usefulness of hardware-specific diagnostic aids. Most sound board and display adapter vendors include a complete diagnostic for their product as part of the package. Some hardware vendors are starting to include this feature as well. I even found one motherboard vendor—Hauppauge—that provides a diagnostic disk with its products. The diagnostic tests basic motherboard functionality and any installed memory.

Let's look at some of the diagnostic aids I've found helpful in the past. The following sections aren't designed to be an inclusive list of every tool that you'll ever need, but you might find that they provide just enough help so that you can get through a repair with a minimum of effort.

Peter's Principle: Using a DOS-Based Versus a Windows-Based Diagnostic Program

Windows applications provide an ease of use that makes most DOS applications look totally unusable. That's the point in their favor. You can rely on most Windows diagnostics to provide very useful and easy-to-read information. They also find a great majority of the hardware problems you could experience. Early entries in this field were unsuited to this task, but I could probably feel comfortable using a Windows diagnostic aid for many types of troubleshooting today.

However, there isn't any reliable way to completely test your hardware from within Windows. The multitasking nature of the operating system makes this impossible. Some diagnostic programs need total access to the hardware as well, and Windows won't allow this kind of access. In fact, getting rid of the operating system altogether is probably the best way to go. Some software tools out there do just that. Others run from the DOS prompt, where they have better control over the hardware.

There's another problem with Windows diagnostic programs—something that won't occur to most people until it's too late. What happens if you can get DOS up and running, but a hardware conflict or failure prevents Windows from starting? I've had this particular problem more than a few times. Using a DOS diagnostic means that if the system will boot at all, you can at least figure out what's going on.

Here's the bottom line: If you're going to rely on only one diagnostic program, choose a DOS-based one rather than a Windows-based one. Use the latter only if it's a supplement to the DOS-based one.

Note: Although you could probably run at least the DOS diagnostic products from within Windows, the results you'll get will be inaccurate, at best. Always run your diagnostic programs in MS-DOS mode, preferably from the DOS prompt before Windows 95 starts. You can access the Windows 95 DOS prompt by pressing the F8 key and selecting the Safe Mode Command Prompt Only option. Chapter 25 covers this topic in greater detail.

Microsoft Diagnostic (MSD)

Microsoft Diagnostic (MSD) has been around for a long time. Microsoft includes it with both DOS and Windows, but doesn't install it to your hard drive with Windows 95. The current product version shipping with Windows 95 is 2.13. That's the same version that's been around for quite some time now. (Users of the OSR2 version may not get a copy of MSD as part of the operating system package. You'll want to get one of the other diagnostic programs covered in this chapter if you don't have MSD on your machine.)

Tip: Windows NT includes a Windows version of MSD called WinMSD that appears to work just fine with Windows 95. You might want to consider using this product instead of MSD if your system is running a Windows NT file server. This version of MSD won't work with your Windows 3.x workstations, because it uses the Win32 interface.

The original purpose of creating MSD was to provide Microsoft technicians and beta support staff with a full accounting of the capabilities that your machine provides. Figure 26.1 shows that this is still the main purpose of this program. It helps detect any hardware you have installed on your machine. It also has command-line parameters for compiling this information into a file that you can use for future reference, as shown in Table 26.1.

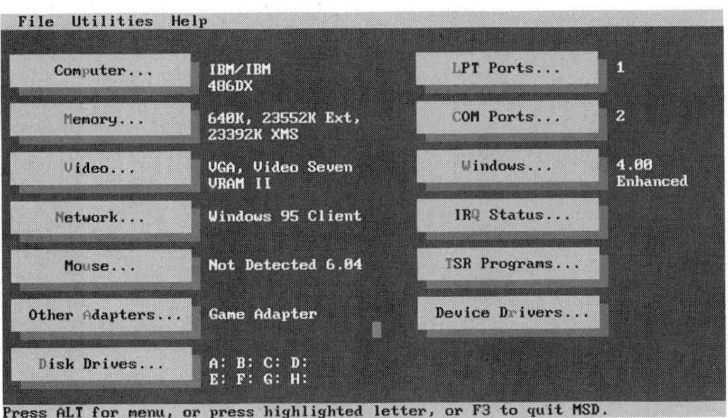

Figure 26.1.
The opening MSD display shows the types of hardware it will detect for you.

Table 26.1. MSD command-line switches.

Switch	*Description*
/B	Switches MSD to a white-on-black display mode. This comes in handy for running MSD on LCD displays.

Switch	*Description*
`/I`	Tells MSD to bypass initial hardware detection. Use this setting if your hardware seems to freeze every time you enter MSD. Some detection phases interfere with normal hardware operations on some machines.
`/F` *<drive>*:*<path><filename>*	This is one of the automated report settings. It asks the user to provide a name, address, and telephone number before it produces the report. MSD inserts these items into the report. I find it handy to use this feature to insert a machine name and location instead of the intended information. You also need to supply the drive letter, path, and filename. Notice the space between the `/F` and the drive letter. MSD won't recognize the switch if you don't include the space.
`/P` *<drive>*:*<path><filename>*	The `/P` switch does the same thing as the `/F` switch, except it doesn't ask for the user's name and address first.
`/S` *<drive>*:*<path><filename>*	Use this switch to produce a summary instead of a full-length report. The summary report contains only the basics about your computer: processor type, memory types and sizes, video type, network type and vendor name, operating system version numbers, mouse type and vendor, other adapter type, drive listing, and port listing. Omitting the filename sends this report to the screen.

The main reason for using MSD is that it will detect all your functional hardware. The key word, of course, is *functional.* If you run MSD and find that it doesn't detect something, there's a pretty good chance that one of two things occurred: Either the driver required to turn on the device isn't present, or the device has failed. If you can eliminate the first cause, you'll have found the cause of a hardware failure.

MSD is pretty limited as far as diagnostic aids go, but you can use it in a pinch. I'd recommend that you use MSD for its intended purpose—hardware inventory—and go with a diagnostic aid that provides just a little more input.

TouchStone CheckIt

Finding an inexpensive troubleshooting aid can be quite difficult. At about $45 for the DOS or Windows version, CheckIt is quite a deal for someone who needs to find simple workstation problems quickly. It's much more than a hardware inventory program. It also includes a variety of diagnostics, a virus scanner, a hard disk formatter, and a floppy disk alignment checker. (The latest version includes even more.) CheckIt is essentially a total workstation diagnostic on a disk. In fact, you can place both of the DOS version CheckIt Pro 3.x 360KB floppies on one 1.2MB or 1.44MB disk and have plenty of room left over for the DOS boot file and your network drivers. The latest version, CheckIt 4, requires a bit more space, but you can still run it from a set of 1.44MB floppies (one boot, one for CheckIt, and a third for SysTest).

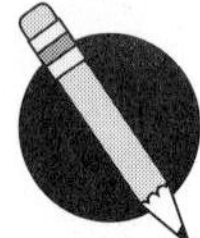

Note: TouchStone has recently released the new version of CheckIt. This version offers expanded test features that the original product doesn't include. For example, you can use it to test your CD-ROM drive. The amount of memory you can test has also increased, along with the capabilities of just about every other test. I plan to concentrate on the new version of the product in this section. Be sure to contact TouchStone for the updated version at `http://www.checkit.com`. You can also call (714) 374-2801.

CheckIt Pro is the venerable version that most people will recognize—it has been around for a very long time. The latest version of the product includes a much-enhanced version of CheckIt Pro and WINCheckIt in one package. However, even the original CheckIt (version 3.0) is still good enough for most purposes. We'll look first at the older version of CheckIt Pro in the next section, and then see in the sections that follow what the latest version has to offer.

A Quick Look at CheckIt Pro 3.x

CheckIt provides three important pieces of machine configuration information. All three of them appear on the SysInfo (system configuration) menu. First, the configuration display shown in Figure 26.2 helps you see exactly how much memory the workstation has installed, and gives you an overview of how the memory is used. This same display provides basic workstation configuration information. For example, it tells you whether the workstation has a mouse installed.

```
CheckIt 3.0
  SysInfo     Tests     Benchmarks     Tools     Setup     Exit
Configuration Information
       DOS Version: 7.00
          ROM BIOS: (Standard)                    BIOS Date: 11/30/87

    Processor Type: 80486 AT Machine
  Math Coprocessor: 80486 FPU
       Base Memory: 640K                          Available: 422K
   Extended Memory: 23552K                        Available: 23552K
   EXPANDed Memory: No EMS driver installed
     Video Adapter: VGA                        EGA Switches: 0110
     Video Address: A000h                    Video RAM Size: 256/512K
     Hard Drive(s): Drive 0 (C:) = 539M, Drive 1 (D:) = 345M
   Floppy Drive(s): A:1.44M(3½"), B:1.2M(5¼")
    Clock/Calendar: CMOS Clock
  Parallel Port(s): LPT1=378h
    Serial Port(s): COM1=3F8h, COM2=2F8h
             Mouse: None                        Joystick(s): 1

              F2 - Copy to Activity Log ■ ESC - Cancel
```

Figure 26.2.
CheckIt version 3.0 provides a variety of information about the devices installed on your machine.

The memory display shown in Figure 26.3 gives you a detailed look at how the workstation uses the memory it has installed. You can use this display to find the location of ROM chips in the CPU's memory address space and to help you optimize the workstation's environment. More importantly, it might alert you to special hardware needs that you should consider when configuring Windows 95. For example, are there any hidden BIOS areas that you'll need to worry about if you decide to use a third-party memory manager?

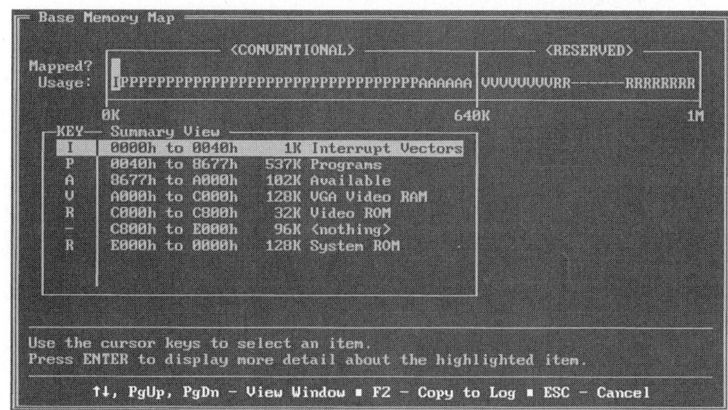

Figure 26.3.
You can use CheckIt to determine your current memory settings, but this display is a little out-of-date.

The final display, shown in Figure 26.4, depicts interrupt usage. This is another factor that you should take into consideration when you need to make an update to the system. You need to know whether the machine has a free interrupt to use as required by the new hardware. Notice that this display also includes DMA channel usage. Few products provide this information, but it's essential to the PC user of today. For example, many multimedia cards rely on one or more IRQ lines and one or more DMA channels to perform their work. Fortunately, Windows 95 provides a detailed listing of port addresses, interrupts, and DMA addresses. However, this display could help you find out about devices that still use real-mode drivers—an important consideration when you're experiencing some type of hardware conflict.

```
CheckIt 3.0
  SysInfo    Tests    Benchmarks    Tools    Setup    Exit
Interrupt Usage
INTERRUPT ASSIGNMENTS:                    DEVICES WITH NO IRQ
IRQ 0   System Timer,SNAP                 None
IRQ 1   Keyboard
IRQ 2   [Cascade]
IRQ 3   COM2
IRQ 4   COM1
IRQ 5   Available
IRQ 6   Floppy Disk
IRQ 7   LPT1                              STANDARD DMA ASSIGNMENTS:
IRQ 8   Clock/Calendar                    DMA 0
IRQ 9   VGA, (Active)                     DMA 1
IRQ 10  Available                         DMA 2  Floppy Disk
IRQ 11  Available                         DMA 3
IRQ 12  Available                         DMA 4  [Cascade]
IRQ 13  80486 FPU                         DMA 5
IRQ 14  Hard Disk                         DMA 6
IRQ 15  Available                         DMA 7
          F2 - Copy to Activity Log ■ ESC - Cancel
```

Figure 26.4.
Windows 95 provides a complete picture of your system, but this CheckIt display could help with devices that use real-mode drivers.

The System Configuration menu has two other items of interest. The most important one allows you to see the current CMOS setup. A less useful item is the device driver listing. Keeping a record of the settings in your CMOS will make it much easier to recover when the battery that maintains that information dies, or if your PC loses the information in some other way (this happens from time to time). The device driver list, on the other hand, provides additional information, but none that's essential to completing the inventory.

The Tests menu includes the ability to run tests alone or as part of a batch process. Figure 26.5 shows the batch test display. As you can see, it includes all the tests that CheckIt will run. The memory test provided with this particular product is exceptional. The only test I've found that's more complete is the one included with the KickStart2 card, which I discuss later.

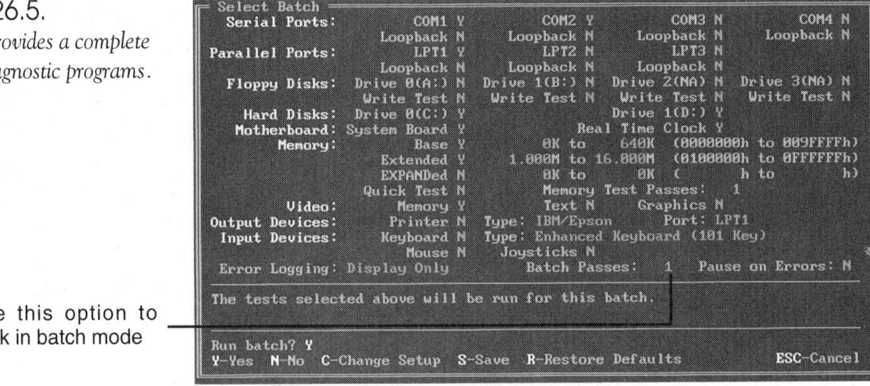

Figure 26.5.
CheckIt provides a complete suite of diagnostic programs.

One other feature that you'll see on this test screen is the batch mode capability. You can run a set of tests over and over until you find a particular error. Some types of hardware faults are intermittent in nature or occur only after the machine has been running for a while. CheckIt helps you find both types of errors.

I was also impressed by some of the other features under the Tools menu, shown in Figure 26.6. The Locate RAM Chips option helps you find a bad set of RAM chips on the motherboard. All you need to do is enter the motherboard chip configuration; the locater takes care of the rest. The virus checker and other options are nice touches as well. (Just don't forget to get updated virus signature files frequently.)

Using Checkit 4

The latest version of CheckIt has a different look from its predecessor, as shown in Figure 26.7. Notice that there are four basic tasks that you can perform: Collect data about your machine, Load an existing configuration file, Skip the data collection process, or Exit the diagnostic program. In most cases you'll want to select either the Collect or Load option, because there isn't a lot you can do without knowing the configuration of the machine. (The Collect, Load, and Skip options all end up at the testing screen.)

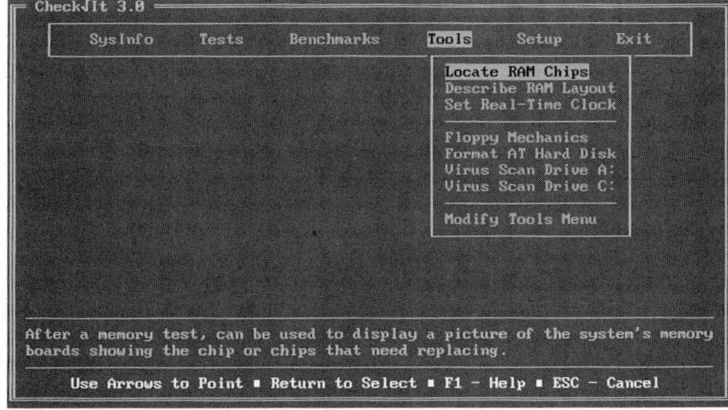

Figure 26.6.
The Locate RAM Chips feature helps you find a bad RAM chip fast.

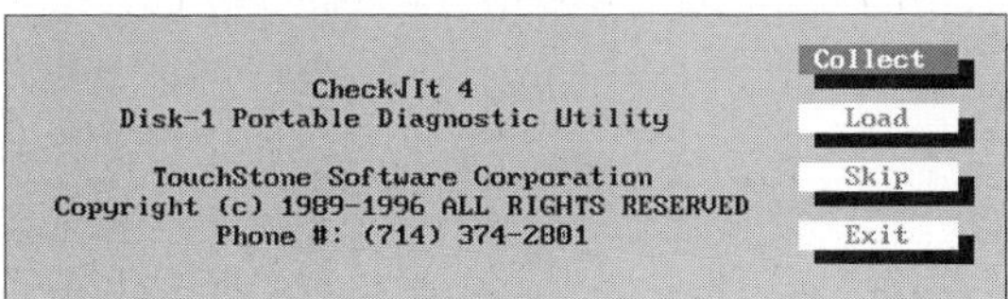

Figure 26.7.
The latest version of CheckIt uses a straightforward front end that makes it easy to figure out what you want to do.

Tip: Unlike its predecessor, CheckIt 4 includes a separate burn-in and batch testing utility named SysTest. It provides a lot more flexibility than the old combined version of CheckIt. The next section looks at this program.

If you do choose to use the Skip option, you go immediately to the testing screen. Fortunately, you can use the options on the File menu to either load or collect data later. Selecting the Load option displays a standard File Open-type dialog box that you can use to choose an existing configuration file. You have to collect data and save it to disk before this option will work.

The Collect option displays a dialog box like the one shown in Figure 26.8. This is where you choose what to collect and how in-depth to look. There are two or three columns of options for each device on your machine. The Exclude column tells CheckIt not to look at the selected hardware feature. A Standard look provides an overview of hardware statistics such as hard drive settings—CheckIt looks exclusively in the system CMOS for this information. This is the option to use if you have problems when CheckIt takes a look at a specific piece of hardware. You can also use it when an in-depth look at the hardware isn't required. (For example, you might need to know only the basic settings for the hard drive.) Selecting the Advanced option (for devices that provide this option, such as the COM ports) gives you in-depth information about a particular piece of hardware. CheckIt actually tests the hardware to see what it can do. You'll get information such as the IRQ that the hardware actually uses (rather than the setting that Windows may think it uses). Getting this information can take quite a bit of time, though, so you'll want to use the Advanced setting with care. In addition, because the Advanced option actually tests the hardware, you may find that there are conflicts with any software you have loaded.

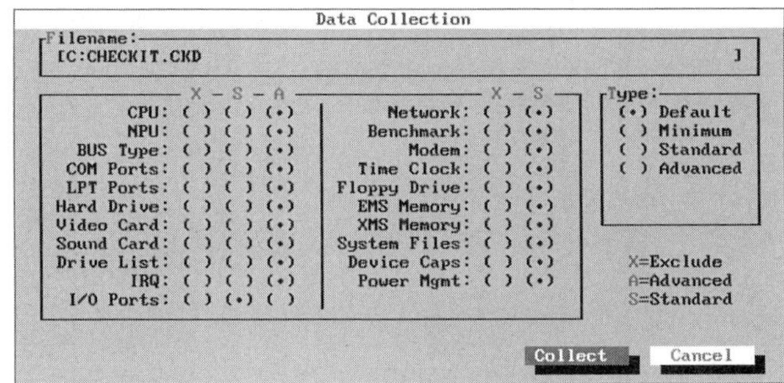

Figure 26.8. *CheckIt allows you to determine how much time you want it to spend collecting data.*

You'll also notice some preset defaults in the Type group. I find that the Standard option provides me with just about everything I need to know on a regular basis, without spending a lot of time to get it. I use the Advanced option if I need to troubleshoot a specific hardware-related problem. In this case, getting all the information you can is a good idea if you don't want to overlook the obvious. The Default setting in the Type group selects a combination of Standard and Advanced options that TouchStone feels that most people will need. The Minimum setting obtains the level of information that you absolutely must have to use CheckIt to its fullest potential.

Once you choose the level of hardware information you need, click the Collect button. CheckIt displays a series of screens as it checks your hardware. What you'll see next is the testing screen mentioned earlier. Figure 26.9 shows a typical example, although your screen will contain different information than mine. At this point you're ready to use CheckIt for a variety of purposes, such as single-component testing or verifying your hardware settings.

```
File    SysInfo    Tests    About

              System Summary  (C:\MAINT\CHECKIT.CKD)
                   Collected  12-05-1996  14:14
                     Default Check of System

   OS Version : DOS Version 7.10
     Main CPU : Intel Pentium 166.0MHz
          NPU : Integrated NPU 166.0MHz
   Active Bus : ISA, PCI
 Total Memory : 32MB
Video Adapter : VESA 1024K VGA Color, Secondary : None

 Floppy Drive : 1.44M(3 1/2")
   Hard Drive : 0: 1622M
    I/O Ports : 3  Serial  1  Parallel
     Keyboard : 101-key Enhanced
        Mouse : No Active Mouse Device Found.
        Sound : Sound Blaster Adlib
       CD-ROM : No Active CD-ROM Device Found.
        Modem : Port Used: COM2 (2F8h)
     FAX Type : CLASS 1
 Network Type : No Network Driver Loaded

      Use Alt+Letter for menu option, Arrow keys, ESC to exit
```

Figure 26.9. *CheckIt provides an overview of the information it collected in the initial testing screen.*

The two menus that we're most interested in are SysInfo and Tests. The SysInfo menu appears in Figure 26.10. It allows you to obtain concise details about the various facts that CheckIt collected about your machine. Figure 26.11 shows an example of what you might see for the modem. Notice that the check not only determines the address of the modem port, it also tells you whether buffers are available (an important consideration in a multitasking environment such as Windows 95). This screen also shows the results of various AT information commands.

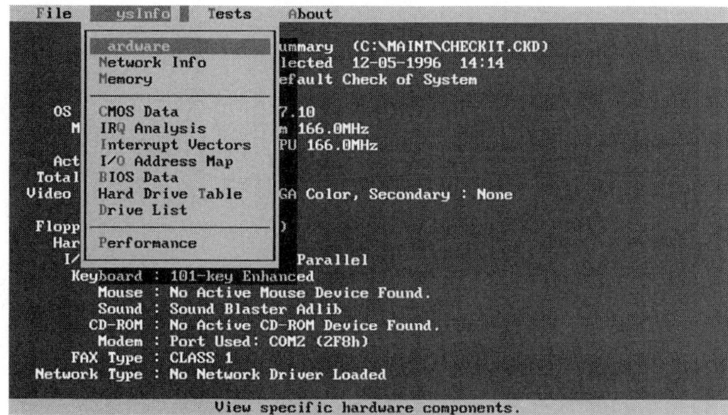

Figure 26.10.
You can get information about any part of your system by using the SysInfo menu options.

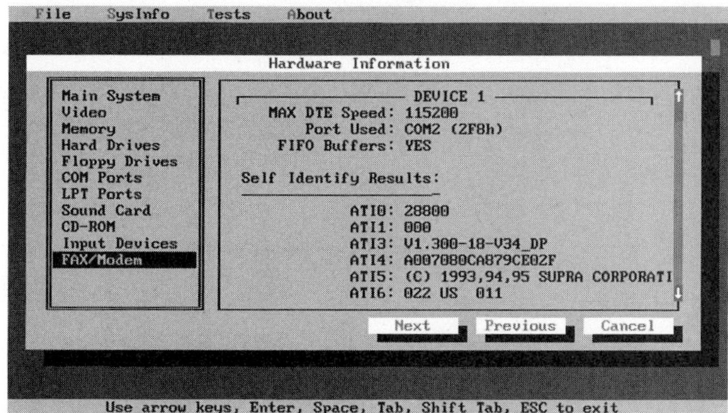

Figure 26.11.
A typical information display provides every piece of information you need to know about the device in question.

The Tests menu acts much as its name implies. It provides a list of tests that you can run by using CheckIt. Figure 26.12 shows a list of the tests that CheckIt currently supports. Notice that along with standard tests such as those you'd run on the system board or ports, you can test your CD-ROM drive or modem.

Every test on this list is fully configurable. Figure 26.13 shows a typical example. In this case, we're looking at the Memory Test configuration dialog box. Notice that you get to choose the area of memory to test, along with the level of test you want to perform. Unlike the previous version of

CheckIt, you can't choose a precise memory range to test. This is one of the few areas where the new version of CheckIt doesn't quite perform as well as its older sibling, but the loss in functionality is minimal.

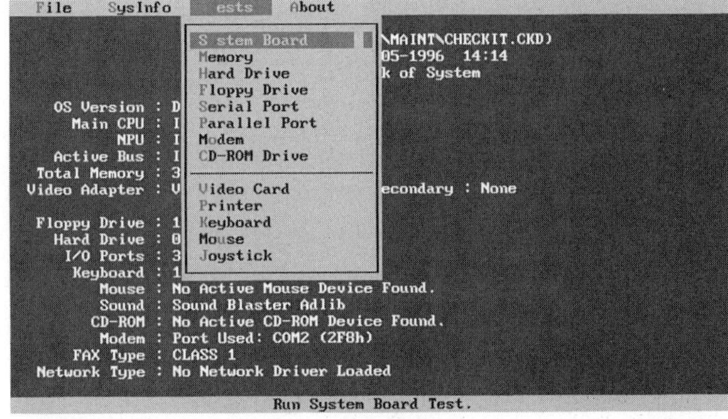

Figure 26.12.
The Tests menu provides a complete list of the kinds of tests that you can run with CheckIt.

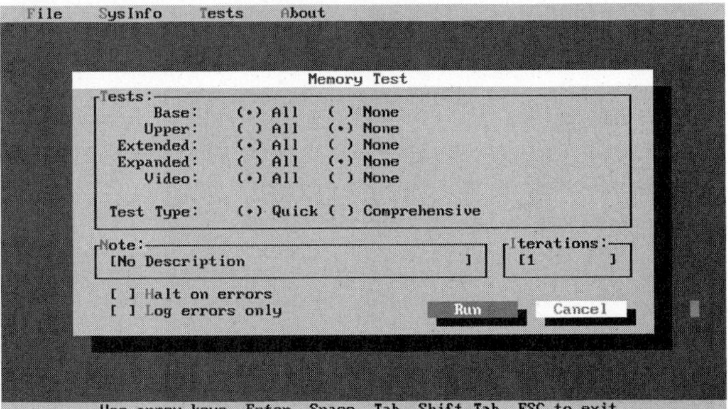

Figure 26.13.
You need to decide how to run the various diagnostic tests.

Burn-In and Batch Testing Using SysTest

The CheckIt 4 disks include a separate batch-testing program named SysTest. Figure 26.14 shows the initial display for this program. The main reason for using this program in place of CheckIt is for burn-in or certification testing. You can also use it to find intermittent problems with hardware. For example, you may have a memory problem that shows up only in certain conditions, or a partially failed part may give you problems. Batch testing can help find it. You may even want to use batch testing to verify that you've completely fixed a problem. There have been a few cases where two bad components caused a system failure and finding the second component proved problematic after fixing the first one.

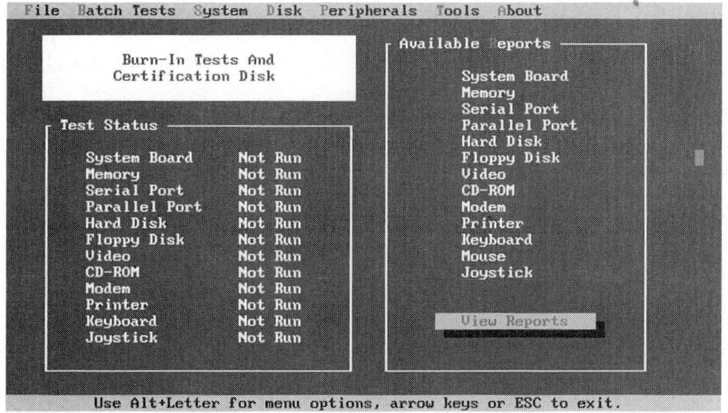

Figure 26.14.
SysTest allows you to perform burn-in, certification, and other forms of batch testing.

The menu system for this utility looks a bit more complicated than the one used for CheckIt, but you can break it down into four areas. The File menu allows you to look at reports. It's also where you select a custom batch file that you want to run, or change the location of program output. (You may want to use a printer rather than the screen for batch testing, because the printer can provide a history of each test.)

The next menu entry, Batch Tests, allows you to run and create various kinds of batch and burn-in tests. We'll look at this menu in a few minutes. Suffice it to say that this is the heart of the SysTest utility.

The next set of menu entries includes System, Disk, and Peripherals. These options work much like the Tests menu did for CheckIt. In fact, you'll find that SysTest uses the same configuration menus for the various tests. The only difference is how the tests are arranged on the menu. You use these menu selections if you want to test one hardware item multiple times.

Finally, there's a Tools menu. It allows you to save the contents of your CMOS to disk—a handy feature if you think you might run out of battery backup power sometime in the future (and who won't?). You can use this same tool to restore a CMOS configuration file that you've saved to disk. Figure 26.15 shows the Save/Restore CMOS dialog box that you see when using the Tools | Save CMOS command. The Tools menu also contains entries for the RAM Exam utility (an advanced memory-testing program) and Rescue Disk (a program that creates a boot disk that you can use in case of emergency).

Now it's time to look at the meat-and-potatoes of this utility—the batch-creation utility. You use the Batch Tests | Custom command to display the dialog box shown in Figure 26.16. This is where you decide which tests to run and how. As you can see, there are two option groups. The first group, Select Test, selects a basic test such as the System Board Test. Once you select a test, you can choose it in the Configure Test option group. Normally you'll get a dialog box just like the one shown earlier in Figure 26.13 for the memory test. Notice the FileName field in Figure 26.16. The output of this custom batch-testing process is a .BAT. Once you create it, you don't even have to enter SysTest or CheckIt to perform a standard test of your system. Simply type the batch file name at the DOS prompt, and you're ready to go. You lose the capacity to view reports within the CheckIt environment, but you can still use a standard text editor to view the test results file.

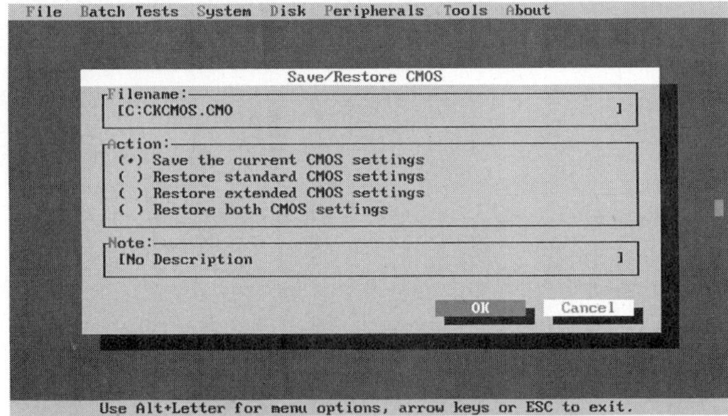

Figure 26.15.
The Save/Restore CMOS dialog box allows you to save or restore your hardware configuration settings.

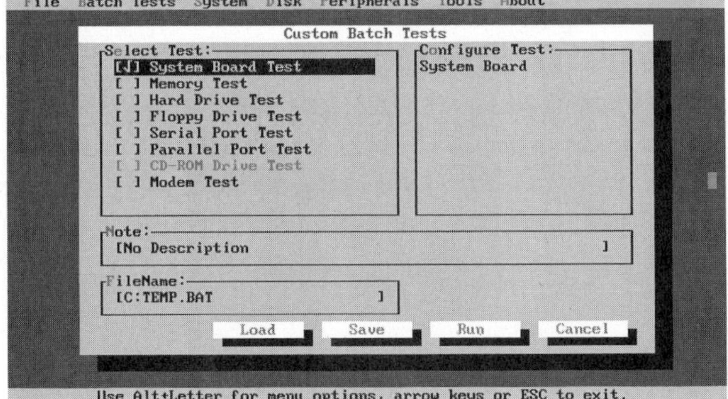

Figure 26.16.
Creating a custom batch testing job results in a .BAT file that you can run from the DOS prompt.

TouchStone WINCheckIt

Nothing beats a Windows diagnostic program for ease of use. At $50, WINCheckIt is only slightly more expensive than its DOS counterpart, and you gain the benefit of the Windows interface. In addition, the 4.x version of WINCheckIt provides full 32-bit support and some special Windows 95 features. What you lose in exchange are some of the detailed diagnostics that the DOS version of the product provides, but I'll get into that in a few moments.

When you start WINCheckIt for the first time, it does an inventory of your machine. I found that the inventory was fairly complete, but it missed some of my hardware the first time around (a second run of the check found the missing hardware). The program also misinterpreted my network, informing me that I had NetWare installed when I was using a Microsoft Network for the purposes of this test. WINCheckIt did figure out what kind of serial ports I had and properly noted that I had one bidirectional parallel port. (You can rerun the inventory any time by clicking the Collect button.)

After WINCheckIt collects all this information, you see a main screen like the one shown in Figure 26.17. Notice the four dial indicators. They tell you about your current resource status, including the largest available block of system memory, system resource status, free memory below 1MB, and disk space used. A DOS program wouldn't provide this type of information. Then again, you can easily obtain this kind of information from other sources, although in a less user-friendly format. The System Summary information is on a par with the DOS version of CheckIt Pro (WINCheckIt doesn't even begin to touch the thoroughness of the CheckIt 4.0 version). Essentially, it tells you what you have installed on your machine in the barest possible terms. I find that this display comes in handy for a quick check of the system. I've been able to fool WINCheckIt in several ways in the past, however. Using some types of communications programs before I run the collection utility, for example, causes WINCheckIt to tell me that I don't have a modem installed. As previously mentioned, it never did figure out what kind of network I had installed.

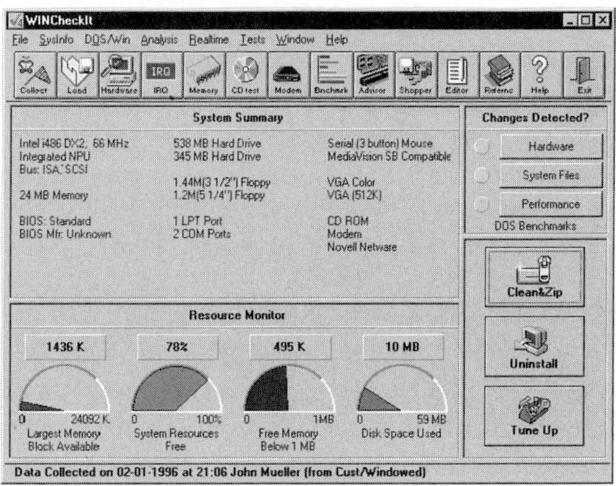

Figure 26.17.
WINCheckIt provides quick access to its features and gives you a summary of your system's resources.

Across the top of the display you'll find some very handy buttons. I'm not going to show you every one of them, but a few deserve special mention. Clicking the CD Test button displays the dialog box shown in Figure 26.18. Notice that this isn't just a CD-ROM drive test; it's an actual check of your machine's capability to run multimedia programs. There are three levels of compliance that you can check, as shown in the figure. My test machine failed the second two Multimedia PC Marketing Council (MPC) compliance tests because of the way that WINCheckIt performed the check. It looked only at my first hard drive partition. Even though the test machine had more than 850MB of drive space available, WINCheckIt reported a mere 60MB—the amount on the first drive partition.

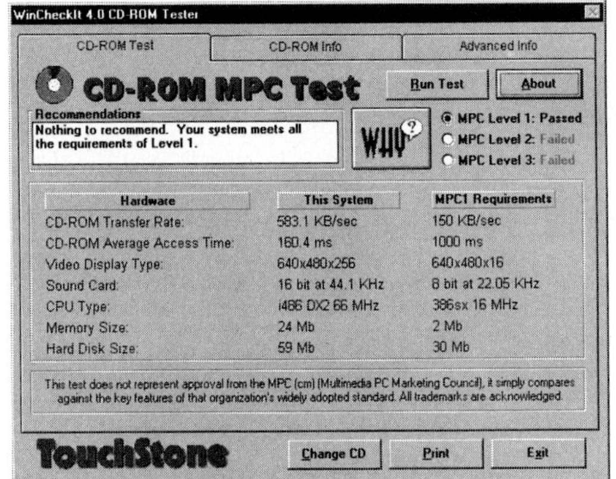

Figure 26.18.
You can use WINCheckIt to determine the multimedia status of a workstation.

I found that the modem tester provided in this utility far exceeded anything I could find in a DOS utility, except in CheckIt 4.0. Not only does it test local modems, but it can test a remote connection as well. To access this test, click the Modem button. WINCheckIt displays a dialog box that asks whether you want to run a local or a remote test. If you select a remote test, you need to provide a telephone number to access the remote modem. When WINCheckIt completes the test, you see a dialog box like the one in Figure 26.19. I found that the report provided by WINCheckIt is superior to the one you can get from Windows 95; the tests are also a little more thorough. (Obviously, Windows 3.x doesn't even provide modem diagnostics.)

Now let's get down to the feature that you really wanted to hear about: The capability to test your hardware. Unlike most of the other features, you'll actually have to use the Tests menu to check a piece of hardware. This menu has a Test Everything option, along with the capability to test separate subsystems. WINCheckIt examines everything you ask it to and then displays the test results window shown in Figure 26.20. You can scroll through the entire report or simply select specific subsystems by using the drop-down menu.

In addition to the things I've already shown you, WINCheckIt provides a wealth of user-related features that don't have a lot to do with diagnosing hardware problems. The Software Shopper utility is a database of more than 2,000 products. You can use WINCheckIt to compare the capabilities of your system with the needs of the product. WINCheckIt provides a list of any upgrades that you need to make to your system before you can use the software product. Clicking the Benchmark button takes you to a display that allows you to test your system extensively. It also includes the capacity to compare your system to a variety of test systems. This is nice to have, but it's not really essential.

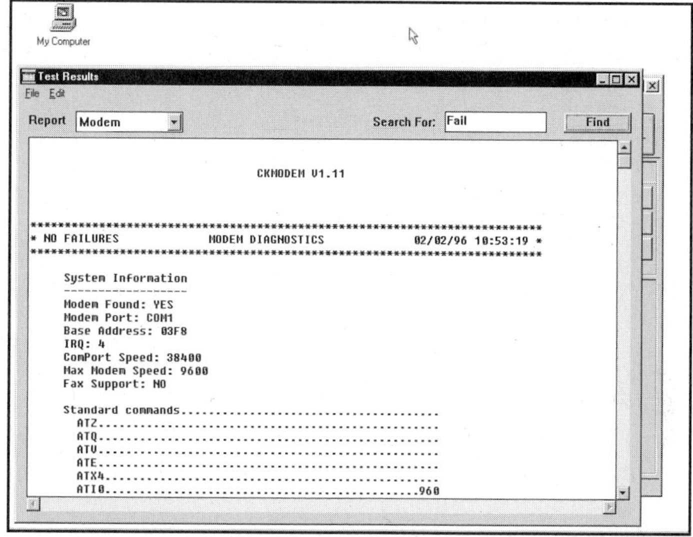

Figure 26.19.
Checking the status of your modem is one of the better features of WINCheckIt.

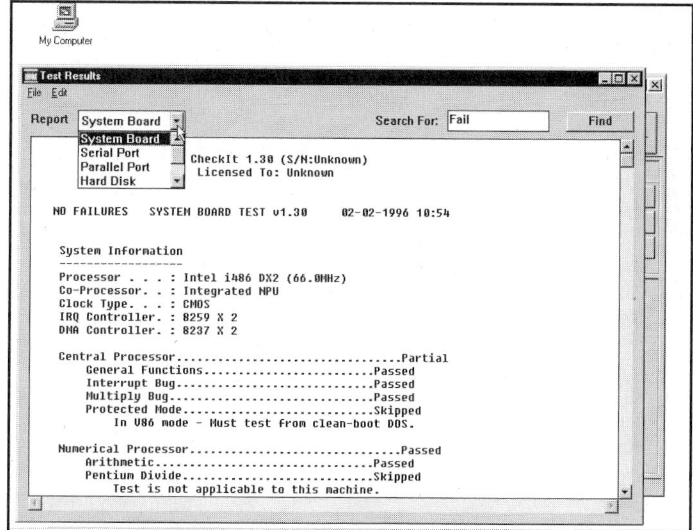

Figure 26.20.
WINCheckIt provides a detailed list of the tests it performed, along with the test results.

Of all the features that WINCheckIt provides, the Tune-Up button seems the least useful. It's supposed to defragment system memory and enhance performance. The monitor did display a slight improvement on my test systems, but I couldn't see it in any concrete way. Your results might vary from the ones I received, but this particular feature of other programs has certainly received a lot of bad press lately.

What's missing from this program? If you haven't noticed already, I haven't said a word about burn-in tests or any of the other things you'd normally associate with a heavy-duty diagnostic program. You won't find these features in WINCheckIt. Overall, it's a lightweight diagnostic aid at best. You'd probably be better off looking at TouchStone's DOS product if you need something substantial.

Windsor Technologies, Inc. PC-Technician

Running a diagnostic using any operating system is risky business. The problem is that the operating system can actually interfere with your ability to find a problem. This is less of a problem under DOS than Windows, because the diagnostic can simply bypass the operating system, but the problem is still there.

PC-Technician seemed a little expensive when I first looked at it. Expect to pay at least $200 for this comprehensive diagnostic. The thing that sets it apart from CheckIt and WINCheckIt isn't the tests that it runs, but the fact that it runs them without an operating system such as DOS. All you do is place the floppy in a drive and boot the machine. The next thing you'll see is the PC-Technician display.

The fact that PC-Technician doesn't need an operating system is a big advantage in several ways. First, you can use PC-Technician on any machine, even if your company uses several different operating systems. Second, using this product means that you don't need to have a functional hard drive to test the machine. Of course, CheckIt can say the same thing if you use the DOS version of the product. Third, you don't need to worry as much about viruses affecting the results of your tests. The non-DOS format of the PC-Technician disk makes it more difficult for a virus to infect it. Still, Windsor Technologies does provide some information on virus prevention that you should follow.

Landmark Research International KickStart1

What do you do when your machine won't boot at all? You can't use a diagnostic aid such as PC-Technician because to do its work it needs a functional floppy drive system and a machine that will boot at least marginally. Easter-egging the problem might seem like the only way to go in this situation. After all, only a few things can keep a PC from booting at all, and it wouldn't take very long to replace them. However, there's a better way.

There are many ways to monitor a PC. One of them is to check the POST (power-on self test) results by intercepting the contents of port 80h. Using this port is a well-documented method of monitoring the progress of your system startup tests. As your system tests itself, it sends the number of each test to an output port, usually port 80h. All you need to do to find a particular system fault is see which test number the machine stops at. You'll also need a listing of the test numbers from the vendor or the test card manufacturer. Fortunately, Landmark provides a book that contains the POST codes for most of the common BIOS chips. You can refer to this book whenever you need to test a machine that won't boot.

The KickStart1 card is an unimposing diagnostic aid. It contains only 12 LEDs and three chips. The first four LEDs monitor the power supply to within 10 percent of its specified rating. If one of the lights is out, it's time to replace the power supply.

The other eight LEDs provide output from port 80h. They read as a binary counter. The first four LEDs form the first number, and the second set of four LEDs forms the second number. For example, if lights 1, 2, and 4 are lit, the first number is Bh. This decoding process is somewhat error-prone, however. You could easily see the POST code as 1Ah when in fact it's 1Bh. This difference of 1 can make all the difference in the world in finding the problem.

Some BIOS chips don't provide a port 80h output. In that case, you need a special test BIOS that Landmark sells to go with its KickStart cards. The advantage of using this special BIOS is that it's fully documented—better documented, in fact, than just about any other vendor's BIOS that you'll find. It's unfortunate that you have to buy it as a separate item. Landmark currently sells one test BIOS for each major type of PC. Just plug in the appropriate test BIOS ROM chip in place of the regular BIOS chip on an ailing motherboard, and it will subject all the hardware to a much more thorough power-on self test. (Another option for PCs that report their POST codes to a different port than 80h is to use a card such as the PocketPost card, which includes jumpers to select the correct port for almost any brand or model of PC.)

The advantage of this model of KickStart card is price. You can get a KickStart1 card for less than $100. The disadvantage is that it provides only the bare bones of diagnostic aid. It won't help you find anything beyond power supply failures and clues that the POST codes can supply.

Landmark Research International KickStart2

The KickStart2 card is the younger brother of the KickStart1 card. This diagnostic aid also monitors port 80h and provides you with four LEDs for monitoring the power supply. However, instead of using LEDs for the port 80h output, this card outputs the actual numbers, making it less likely that you'll misinterpret the POST results. (Two alphanumeric LEDs are mounted on the board.) The power supply LEDs also provide a little more flexibility. A switch allows you to choose between monitoring power of 2.5 percent or 5 percent of the rated voltage. This means that you can monitor a power supply to a closer tolerance than you could with the KickStart1 board.

In addition to these enhanced features, the KickStart2 board provides an assortment of additional features. For example, the diagnostic aid doesn't end with monitoring port 80h and checking the power supply levels. This card also provides a set of intense diagnostics in ROM. One of the reasons to use a ROM-based diagnostic is that these diagnostics are unaffected by the operating system or other software problems. The ROM-based diagnostics on the KickStart2 card initialize before the system loads the operating system—a handy feature for times when you need to decide whether the hardware or software is the source of the problem with the workstation.

The diagnostics on the KickStart2 board do a lot more and less than standard software diagnostics. The memory tests are much more intense. For example, you can find a problem in the memory support chips—a problem that most software solutions can't locate. Some of the video and input device tests are less powerful than those provided by software aids, but this is a minor problem considering the purpose of buying such a card.

If you want to communicate with the outside world, the KickStart2 card provides the means. It comes equipped with both a parallel and a serial port. The parallel port allows you to troubleshoot a motherboard even if no other peripheral cards are attached. By default, the KickStart2 card sends the results of every test it runs to both the display and the seven-segment LEDs on the card. This provides you with two ways of viewing test results. Unfortunately, you can't obtain detailed test results by viewing the LEDs. However, you can choose to send the test results to the printer. Even though this might waste a little paper, it allows you to see what's happening with the faulty workstation. You can use the serial port to connect the test machine to another machine. This allows you to use the other machine's display and input devices to troubleshoot a nonfunctional workstation. In fact, you could even use this technique to have your PC call a PC that has an intermittent problem, via modem. To catch such an error, simply tell the remote user to let you know when the problem appears, and then place the call. Rebooting the failed machine takes you directly to the KickStart diagnostic program.

As you can see, the KickStart2 board is a formidable aid in diagnosing difficult workstation failures. It can save you a lot of time and effort in finding problems that software solutions can't handle. In addition, it might provide one of the best ways to separate the hardware from the software so that you can see which component is causing your problem.

Serial and Parallel Port Loopback Plugs

You can't fully test the serial and parallel ports in a workstation without loopback plugs. These plugs pass the signal from the port's output back to its input. To create a loopback plug, use a blank connector without wires and then connect wires between specific pins. Most of the high-end diagnostic programs you buy (such as PC-Technician, AMI Diags, or the Norton Utilities) provide these plugs. Others, such as CheckIt, don't provide them. However, TouchStone tells you how to build them, and will sell them to you as a separate product.

Tip: The list of modems supported by Windows 95 grows with every release. However, you won't find a NULL modem driver for Windows 95 in the standard list of hardware options. This makes it impossible to create a Dial-Up Networking connection that requires a NULL modem setup. Don't worry, though—you can download a NULL modem driver from `http://www.vt.edu:10021/K/kewells/net/index.html` that works up to 115 Kbps.

Table 26.2 provides the pin connections for a parallel port. Every parallel port uses a 25-pin male connector. Another designation for this type of connector is DB25P. You need to create two connectors to test serial ports. There are 9-pin and 25-pin serial ports. Every serial port uses a female connector. The designation for a 9-pin serial port is DB9S. Table 26.3 lists the pin connections for a 9-pin serial port. The designation for a 25-pin serial port is DB25S. Table 26.4 gives the pin connections for a 25-pin serial port. You can find the blank connectors and wire you need at most electronics stores.

Table 26.2. Parallel port (DB25P) loopback plug connections.

First Pin	*Connected to Second Pin*
11 (Busy +)	17 (Select Input –)
10 (Acknowledge –)	16 (Initialize Printer –)
12 (Paper Out +)	14 (Autofeed –)
13 (Select +)	01 (Strobe –)
02 (Data 0 +)	15 (Error –)

Table 26.3. 9-pin serial port (DB9S) loopback plug connections.

First Pin	*Connected to Second Pin*
02 (RD: Received Data)	03 (TD: Transmitted Data)
07 (RTS: Request to Send)	08 (CTS: Clear to Send)
06 (DSR: Data Set Ready)	01 (CD: Carrier Direct)
01 (CD: Carrier Detect)	04 (DTR: Data Terminal Ready)
04 (DTR: Data Terminal Ready)	09 (RI: Ring Indicator)

Table 26.4. 25-pin serial port (DB25S) loopback plug connections.

First Pin	*Connected to Second Pin*
03 (RD: Received Data)	02 (TD: Transmitted Data)
04 (RTS: Request to Send)	05 (CTS: Clear to Send)
06 (DSR: Data Set Ready)	08 (CD: Carrier Direct)
08 (CD: Carrier Detect)	20 (DTR: Data Terminal Ready)
20 (DTR: Data Terminal Ready)	22 (RI: Ring Indicator)

As you can see, the pin connections are relatively easy to make. Whether you buy prefab loopback plugs or make your own, this is an essential tool for your toolkit. Without loopback plugs, you'll never know whether the serial or parallel port you tested really works.

Cable Scanner

Network administrators, especially those managing large networks, can spend a lot of time tracing cables. People are forever abusing cables in ways that would seem impossible unless you actually looked at the damage. If you're in this position, a cable scanner is the most important tool you can get for your toolkit. An average cable scanner costs about $1,000, although you can usually find one a little cheaper. Alternatively, you could build your own cable scanner for about $200, using plans in some electronics magazines. For example, *Circuit Cellar INK*'s October/November 1992 issue contains a set of plans on page 22.

One of the better cable scanners on the market is the Cable Scanner from Microtest. (Microtest provides many other cable scanners with more features, but the Cable Scanner model provides the minimum feature set you need to maintain a network.) This product tests for opens, shorts, and improper terminations. It tells you the distance from your current location to the cable fault. In most cases, all you need to do is track the cable for the required distance and you'll find the problem. To help you trace the signal, the main unit outputs a signal that you can pick up on a remote unit. Instead of taking down every ceiling tile in your office, you simply use the remote unit to trace the cable.

You can send the data collected by the Cable Scanner to a serial printer. The unit collects the data, stores it, and allows you to output it later. The Cable Scanner provides both text and graphic output. This is a handy feature for maintaining records on your system. All you need to do is print the results of the cable check and add the printout to the network documentation.

The Cable Scanner provides a few other unique functions that you might not use very often. For example, it can detect the noise level of the cable on your system. This means that you can reduce the number of packet errors by simply reducing the noise that the packet signal must overcome. You can also interface the Cable Scanner with an oscilloscope. This allows you to actually monitor the signal that flows across the network. An experienced network administrator could use this information to troubleshoot problem installations.

Incompatible Hardware

For the most part, any hardware that runs under the DOS and Windows 3.x environment will also run under Windows 95. Even if you have to use a real-mode driver (which I talk about in the next section), you should be able to use that old device if you really want to. The problems start when you mix that old hardware with new hardware or when the old device uses some of the undocumented features provided by previous versions of DOS.

Windows 95 really does try its best to figure out which interrupts and port addresses are in use, but it doesn't always succeed if you have an eclectic mix of old and new. Older devices often require real-mode device drivers to work at all; that's not a problem. Unfortunately, some of these devices don't register themselves properly. A device driver is supposed to register itself in a device chain and provide certain types of information as part of that registration process. If the device doesn't provide the right level of information, Windows 95 can't detect it. What happens next is inevitable, given such circumstances. If Windows 95 doesn't see the device driver, it might assume that the interrupts and port addresses it uses are free. The result is that you might find two devices trying to share the same interrupt or port address.

Of course, one of the best ways to eliminate some of the problems is to make a checklist of all your hardware and the settings that each device uses. You need to include port addresses, interrupts, and DMA addresses. Physically check the settings on cards that use jumpers. You might want to take this opportunity to physically check your card's BIOS revision. An undocumented update could make a big difference in the settings you need to use with Windows 95. Make sure that you double-check any settings included in CONFIG.SYS or AUTOEXEC.BAT. A software-configurable device always includes the current settings as part of the command line. All you really need to do is get out the vendor manual and determine what the settings mean. Because some device drivers provide a default setting, you need to check for the default if the entry in CONFIG.SYS or AUTOEXEC.BAT doesn't contain a complete list of settings.

Once you get all the settings written down, check your list for potential conflicts. Windows 95 might tell you that there aren't any, but it's possible that you'll find some anyway. For example, someone I know recently tried to install Windows 95 but found that he couldn't. The machine he was using included two SCSI adapters. Windows 95 recognized one adapter, but not the other. As a result, Windows 95 didn't recognize the CD-ROM drive attached to the second adapter and therefore couldn't install itself properly. Removing the second SCSI adapter and connecting the CD-ROM drive to the first one cleared up part of the problem. At least Windows 95 would install. However, performance on the network was very slow, and the user still experienced some problems. A check of Windows didn't show any device conflicts. However, a physical check of the remaining SCSI adapter showed that it was using the same interrupt as the NIC. (Windows 95 had claimed that the NIC was using interrupt 5 and that the SCSI adapter was using interrupt 3.) Physically changing the SCSI adapter's interrupt setting cleared up the remaining problem.

Sometimes you might not be sure that you got all the settings right during the first check. You can determine the equipment settings by viewing the port and interrupt addresses that a device uses, with MSD or a diagnostic program such as CheckIt. In fact, using this technique coupled with physical inspection of your CONFIG.SYS and AUTOEXEC.BAT will ensure that you have all the settings for each device. Even if there aren't any conflicts, you'll still want to maintain a complete record of your hardware and any real-mode drivers you need to use. Avoiding problems with real-mode drivers starts with the detective work you perform during this phase of the installation. Record real-mode driver settings and then avoid using the address and interrupt, even though Windows 95 says it's free. This also means that you'll have to configure your setup manually, rather than relying on the Windows 95 automatic configuration features.

Tip: Watch out for older plug-in cards and some of the cheaper "no-name" ones. In the early days of PCs, no one used any port addresses above 3FFh, and most cards decoded only the low-order 10 bits of a port address to find out whether a command was intended for that card. Now many cards use higher addresses (all the way up to FFFFh). If you have one of these newer cards and an older one in the same PC, you could run into a very subtle sort of problem. If the addresses used by the newer card are the same in the low-order 10 bits as those used by the older card, each card will think that commands meant for the newer card were meant for it. There's no telling what will happen in this case, but it might not be pretty!

Some devices simply won't work with Windows 95. Unlike your old DOS setup, Windows 95 is a lot less forgiving about adapters that try to share the same address or interrupt. You simply can't do this under Windows 95 and expect the device to work. If that device happens to be a hard disk drive controller, you might find it impossible to boot all the way into Windows 95.

Some of those real-mode device drivers will cause problems, too. A well-behaved device driver makes direct access only to the hardware it controls. It calls on the ROM BIOS routines for other types of service. An older device might use direct hardware access to other devices as well as the device it controls in order to make the driver faster. Windows 95 normally ignores the device if you try to use a device driver of this type. Sometimes a device driver of this type can actually cause the system to freeze when Windows switches to running a real-mode interrupt service routine. Previous chapters covered many of the architectural aspects of this problem.

Unfortunate as it might seem, an ill-behaved device driver normally looks like a malfunctioning device rather than a piece of software that Windows 95 won't work with. I was surprised when I found myself in this position with an old CD-ROM drive. Fortunately, I was able to get a newer driver that did work from the vendor. This is the solution you should try as well. Many vendors will even allow you to download the upgrade directly from their own BBS for the price of a phone call. They also might make the upgrade available through a commercial information service such as CompuServe or America Online. Some even make it available on an Internet FTP site.

Some older devices include their own BIOS. Sometimes the BIOS routines conflict with Windows 95 and cause various types of system failures. Most vendors upgrade their BIOSes as time goes on. They fix bugs and perform some types of optimizations. I've never been able to understand why, but hardware vendors are notoriously reluctant to tell anyone about these fixes. If you have an older piece of hardware with a BIOS that's causing problems with Windows 95, see whether the vendor has some type of BIOS upgrade that might fix the problem. Installing a new chip is usually cheaper than buying a new peripheral.

By now it should be apparent that hardware incompatibility can cover a lot of ground. Everything from misinterpreted settings to a poorly designed device driver can make it appear that your hardware is incompatible with Windows 95. Let's take a look at the hardware compatibility problem from a procedural point of view:

1. Get into MS-DOS mode and test the hardware to ensure that there's no problem with the device itself. It's important to test the hardware with the same device driver that you plan to use with Windows 95, if you intend to use a real-mode driver for it under Windows 95.
2. Check the device settings to see whether there's a conflict with any of the devices that Windows supports directly. This is especially important when you try to mix older hardware with new plug and play-compatible hardware. If Windows insists on using a specific setting for a plug and play-compatible board, see whether your old board can use a different set of unused settings.
3. Once you determine that the hardware is working and that it doesn't conflict with anything, see whether the vendor documentation provides any insights as to the requirements for using the device driver. For example, you'll probably find that device drivers written to work with versions of DOS prior to 3.3 will have some level of problem with Windows 95. These older device drivers often wrote directly to the hardware and definitely didn't use all the features that newer versions of DOS provide to support device drivers. See whether the vendor can provide a new set of drivers.
4. Check your BIOS revision level. Many adapter cards that have a BIOS extension ROM on them display a version number on-screen during the boot process. With other pieces of add-in or connected hardware, you'll have to determine the revision level in some other way. Vendors provide a variety of ways to detect this information, so you'll have to check your documentation for details about your particular device. My modem uses a Hayes-compatible AT command to display the BIOS revision number. A display adapter that I own has an actual program that I run to display the BIOS and setup information. Check with the vendor to see whether a newer version of the BIOS is available. You might have to send the device to the vendor's repair facility to get the BIOS replaced. It depends on the vendor's policy concerning sending BIOS updates to customers.
5. If all else fails, see whether replacing the board with a similar board from another vendor helps. In this way, you might find that a software or other conflict is disguising itself as a hardware problem. For instance, my mouse example at the beginning of this chapter was an example of a problem with a serial port that disguised itself as a faulty mouse. You might find that other types of problems disguise themselves.

Tip: Actually, there's a very easy way to distinguish a serial mouse problem from a serial port problem. To do so, first run a diagnostic on the serial port with a loopback plug installed. If the port passes the test, then test the mouse. Incompatible hardware rarely is incompatible. There's usually some problem that you can define, given enough time and resources. The question that you have to ask yourself is whether that old hardware is really worth the effort. In my case, I replaced the hardware that was giving me problems, which probably saved me time and frustration. Some types of expensive hardware might be worth the effort involved in looking for the cause of incompatibility, but make sure that you'll get some type of payback.

Using Real-Mode Device Drivers

I never use real-mode device drivers under Windows 95 if I can help it. I've discussed this topic several times throughout this book. I've shown you that real-mode device drivers are less reliable and a lot slower than their 32-bit protected-mode counterparts.

Still, you really don't want to get rid of those drivers, and here's why. What happens if you experience some type of failure on your machine? Say that Windows 95 can't start because of a corrupted file. You could restore it using Backup, but Backup needs Windows 95 to run. So what do you do now?

Getting a new copy of the corrupted file from a floppy setup of Windows 95 wouldn't be too hard, but you're using the CD version and you need Windows 95 to gain access to that, too. Now you're really in trouble—or are you? You really need a boot disk that contains all the drivers needed to activate your hardware. Make sure that you include all the real-mode driver equivalents for your CD-ROM drive and sound board. In fact, you'll want to include on this disk everything needed to make your computer fully functional.

You'll also want to keep a copy of those real-mode drivers around if you test your system by using a DOS-based diagnostic program such as CheckIt. Of course, you can't use a memory manager to load the devices high. Memory managers and diagnostic programs usually don't get along very well. Just load the drivers in low memory to get your testing done. A diagnostic program is usually fairly easy on memory anyway, because the vendor wants it to run on the maximum number of machines possible.

Device Conflicts Under Plug and Play

As I mentioned earlier, Windows 95 does an outstanding job of managing a system if it can see all the devices. When nothing is hidden, Windows 95 will do the best job it can to find alternative settings for every device. It will provide a set of port addresses, DMA addresses, and interrupts that will meet the device's needs and yet avoid conflict with everything else on the system. Unfortunately, there are limits to what Windows 95 can do. That's where you come in.

What if you have one too many devices installed on your machine and there isn't a free interrupt for one of the devices? Windows 95 will try to come up with the best solution possible and then leave one device turned off because it can't find an interrupt to service it. There's one exception to this rule. Printers might not need an interrupt. In this case, Windows 95 will let that device operate without an interrupt, if none is available for its use. You have only 16 interrupts on your machine, and many of them are used before you install the first device.

That's where looking at the Device Manager page of the System Properties dialog box comes into play. You've seen this dialog box many times throughout this book, and you'll probably use it a lot when you're configuring your system for the first time. Windows 95 will display the device it chose to leave out of the computing picture, by using the same technique that it uses to display any conflict. You'll see the device name with either a yellow exclamation point or a red "not" sign through it.

It's quite likely that you'll want all the devices installed on your machine to work, but that might not be possible due to a shortage of interrupts. What you need to do is decide which device to get rid of, remove it, and reboot Windows 95. Check the Device Manager page again to make sure that Windows has reconfigured itself and that the remaining devices are functional.

There are alternatives to getting rid of an important device. For example, most sound cards come with a game port. If you don't use that game port, you might have an additional port address free that you really hadn't thought about. If you normally use a network printer instead of a local printer, you might consider disabling your printer port so that you can use its interrupt. The same holds true for any other unused port. Look for something you don't need before you remove something you do need.

Windows 95 provides a special device view for just this purpose. Figure 26.21 shows the interrupt version of this special view. (There are three other views as well.) To see it, highlight Computer on the Device Manager page of the System Properties dialog box and click Properties.

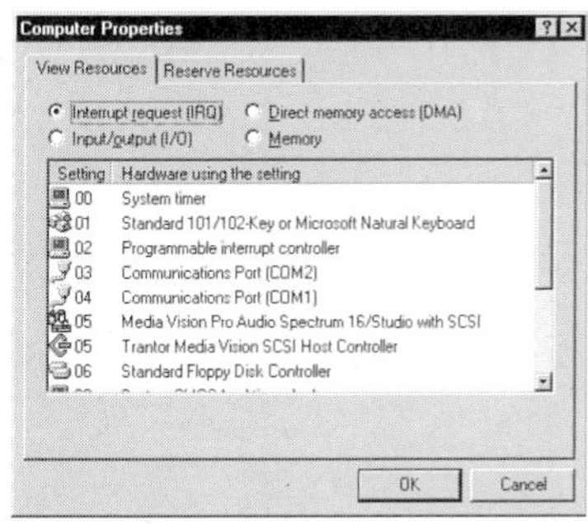

Figure 26.21.
Windows 95 gives you an easy way to find open interrupts, DMA addresses, and port addresses.

This dialog box has a second page. I strongly recommend that you not use it unless you absolutely have to do so, although it could help you to resolve some types of conflicts. Figure 26.22 shows the Reserve Resources page of the Computer Properties dialog box. This is where you can reserve various system resources. The problem with this solution is that it interferes with the normal arbitration process that Windows 95 uses and might make the situation even worse than before. I've tried this particular feature quite a few times and have found that it's in the "still needs work" category for most situations.

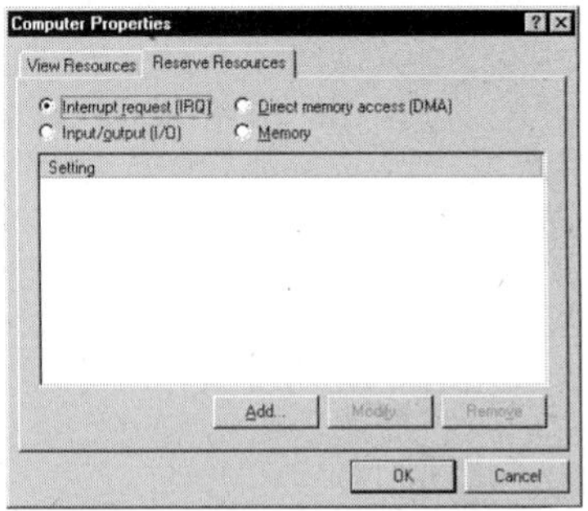

Figure 26.22.
You can use the Reserve Resources page of the Computer Properties dialog box to reserve interrupts, DMA addresses, or port addresses used by real-mode devices.

Warning: Never reserve a resource used by a system device. In general, this includes the real-time clock, system timer, system CMOS, keyboard, and programmable interrupt controller. Doing so will cause the machine to freeze, and at best you'll find it difficult to correct the problem. In some cases, you can fix the error by starting the machine in safe mode, but there's no guarantee that this will work. If the safe-mode method doesn't work, the only way to fix the problem is to install a new copy of Windows 95 over your current copy. Sometimes even that measure doesn't work, because the setting was saved in the Registry. When this happens, you have to start your Windows 95 installation from scratch.

To add a new reservation to the list, simply click the Add button. This displays a dialog box similar to the one shown in Figure 26.23. This is the interrupt-specific Edit Resource Setting dialog box, but the other ones look about the same. All you need to do is tell Windows 95 which resource you need to save and then click OK. You'll get an error message if the resource you want to save is already in use. Saving the setting anyway could stop your machine from running. The best course of action is to find out which device is using the resource, manually change it, reboot the machine, save the resource, put the device back into automatic, and reboot again. This whole procedure ensures that the arbitration process will continue to function smoothly.

Clicking the Modify button displays the same dialog box you got when you clicked the Add button. The only difference is that you'll modify the current setting rather than add a new one. If you decide later to remove a saved setting, all you need to do is highlight it and click the Remove button.

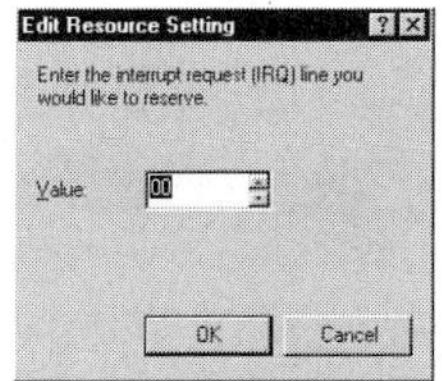

Figure 26.23.
Adding or modifying a saved resource is easy, using the Edit Resource Setting dialog box.

EISA Configuration Requirements

Under DOS, an EISA machine will run fine even if you don't run the EISA configuration utility. Running it could help you resolve some resource conflicts, but it isn't essential. You really should run it for Windows 95 to function properly. Part of the plug and play functionality of Windows 95 depends on being able to poll the EISA configuration to find out what kind of devices you have installed.

What does the EISA configuration utility do? It places information about each adapter in your machine in an area of CMOS. When you run the configuration utility, you see one blank for each slot that your EISA bus provides. The EISA configuration utility comes with a list of adapters that it supports. All you need to do is select a slot and then select a device from the list of available devices. This tells your motherboard the specifics of the adapter installed in that slot. The configuration utility automatically displays a device name in each slot that you define. After you tell the configuration utility the contents of each slot, you have to supply it with the interrupt, port address, DMA address, and any other configuration information for that device. Windows 95 uses this information to configure your machine, even if the real-mode device drivers or the adapter itself can't supply the required information. This information also helps Windows 95 to locate some types of problems. For example, if Windows 95 can't detect a device that the EISA bus says is present, it displays an error message telling you so, instead of simply ignoring the device. The configuration utility also allows you to enable or disable some types of motherboard features, such as installed ports. You need to consult the manual that came with your motherboard for full details on how to use the configuration utility.

Will anything terrible happen if you don't run the configuration utility? It won't be terrible, but it will hinder you from making full use of your machine. Without this information, Windows 95 won't be able to perform some types of optimizations that it would normally provide for your system, and it could end up running more slowly as a result.

The problem for most people is that their EISA configuration utilities are out-of-date, and some peripheral device vendors don't provide the files needed to configure the bus. For example, it's unlikely that you'll find a configuration file for your modem. To solve the first problem, you need to contact the vendor to get a new set of configuration files, and perhaps a new utility program as well. The second problem might prove a little more difficult. In some cases, your motherboard vendor will be able to help you with a generic file that will take care of the peripheral. In other cases, the vendor who designed the peripheral might have a configuration file that you can use; they just didn't include it with the device. In some situations, though, despite your best efforts, you won't be able to find a configuration file. The thing to do in these cases is to configure everything else and leave that particular spot blank. Windows 95 will still pick it up during its scan of the system.

PCMCIA Conflicts

The last kind of hardware I'll address in this chapter is the PCMCIA bus. There's been a problem with this bus since the day it came out. Some cards won't work with your bus. You might plug a card into the slot and it won't work at all. Of course, when you take it back to the place where you bought it, they'll show you that it does work. (This is one of the reasons that you should take your machine with you if at all possible when you suspect some type of compatibility problem.) Even worse, some cards will work with your bus, but only in a certain slot or only with certain other cards. You might find that a modem card works fine in the first slot but not in any of the others.

Most people have heard about the problems with getting PCMCIA cards to work properly. Finally there are some standards for making the cards compatible, but only the new cards adhere to these standards. Unfortunately, many cards have already gone out that won't work together, so you need to choose your cards with care. The best piece of advice I can offer is to buy new cards from a vendor who will actually allow you to test them with the other cards in your machine.

Make sure that you run a thorough test, using several combinations of cards to check the new one for compatibility problems. The test should include checking the card in different slots. I usually test the card under both DOS and Windows. You never know when you'll need to access that card outside of the normal Windows environment to take care of some kind of diagnostic.

On Your Own

Use MSD to find out about the components installed in your machine. The following procedure will guide you through the process:

1. Copy MSD from the \OTHER\MSD folder on your Windows 95 CD to the COMMAND folder within your main Windows 95 folder.
2. Shut down Windows and reboot your machine. Press F8 when you see the "Starting Windows 95" message.
3. Select Safe Mode Command Prompt Only from the boot menu.
4. Change directories to the \WIN95\COMMAND directory. Type **MSD** and press Enter.

5. Look through the various options that MSD provides. For example, what type of serial ports do you have? Do they use an 8250 UART or a 16550 UART? How many cylinders, heads, and sectors per track are listed for your hard drives? Check your system to see what features it provides.
6. Use the File | Exit command to exit MSD.
7. Reboot your machine into the standard Windows 95 setup.

Buy a diagnostic program and completely test your system, especially the hard drives. Be sure to get a diagnostic that's easy to use and that tests everything your machine has to offer. Use the loopback plugs provided with the diagnostic program to test your ports, or create your own loopback plugs by using the procedure in this chapter.

Check any real-mode device drivers installed on your system. Make sure that they're the most current drivers that the vendor has to offer. Do the same with any peripherals that provide their own BIOS. This includes both modems and display adapters. You'll also find a BIOS on most hard-disk controllers and many other devices installed on your machine. Using the most current BIOS not only ensures that you'll have the least number of bugs to contend with, it could also mean a slight speed boost because of optimizations that the vendor made to it.

Don't wait until you have a problem to make this detailed checklist of all the device drivers in your system. This can be much easier to do when your PC is working normally. Then, when it fails in some way, you'll already be a good ways down the path toward a solution to the problem.

27

Network Problems

There aren't many places where you'll find stand-alone computers anymore. Even home users are networking their computers, for a variety of reasons—games are one of the big ones. Parents also like to keep the kids out of their business machine by providing a networked PC specifically for the kids. Outside of the home, you'll find few businesses that lack a network anymore, because the advantages of having one are just too great to ignore. A lot of people are looking at networking as a necessity now, and it's not too much of a surprise that the number and variety of network problems are increasing as a result.

This chapter looks at several aspects of network troubleshooting and the problems you may encounter. We'll view four different network problem areas: hardware, Novell NetWare, Windows NT, and simple peer-to-peer using Windows 95 workstations. Don't think for a second, though, that one section is necessarily exclusive of the others. Hardware problems can certainly affect any network. You may also have a combination of networks such as a peer-to-peer and NetWare setup. Combination networks often have problems that appear to be more than the sum of their parts. Be sure to look at all the possibilities in this chapter before throwing in the towel and calling in a professional (although calling in a professional is certainly a step you should consider when a problem becomes too difficult for you to solve alone).

Tip: One of the places you should look for patches to solve network-related problems is `http://www.microsoft.com/windows/common/aa2719.htm`. This is the site where Microsoft adds any new Windows 95-specific patches. Those of you who are encountering memory leakage problems when using the network will especially want to download the kernel patch at this site (if you aren't using the OSR2 version of Windows 95 that includes this patch as part of the package).

What are you going to walk away with when you're done reading this chapter? I've based the contents on real problems that have happened on a variety of networks, not just one particular type. In most cases we'll look at common problems or those that you'll run into under special circumstances. The information you'll get here is real-world, but remember that you need to take the peculiarities of your own network into account. That's why I've isolated the problems into specific areas. You can view the problems and solutions that pertain to your network and use them to come up with a strategy tailored to your network setup.

I think it's equally important to understand what this chapter *won't* do for you. There isn't any way that I can help you to become a network professional in one chapter of a book. Some books on this subject are well over a thousand pages and cover a single network operating system (not the three I cover here). Networks can become very complex. The information you get here is going to help you find minor problems, but you still need to call in a professional for the really big problems. I also don't cover esoteric problems—those that happened to one person in a million. Be sure to spend some time reading through the Microsoft Knowledge Base for this kind of information (Appendix A tells you how to do this).

Peter's Principle: Starting Your Network on the Right Foot

If you think that setting up a network is the connecting of a few cables and the installation of some software, you're probably wrong. All networks rely on drivers of some sort to get the job done. Because those drivers have to be tailored to your specific network operating system (NOS), hardware, and cabling setup, it's not too surprising that vendors have to try a few times before getting them right.

One of the first things that Novell (or any other NOS vendor) will ask when you call in is whether you have the most current drivers installed on your machine and your file server. Don't be surprised that they ask. After all, an old driver gets replaced when the vendor introduces a new one with additional features and bug fixes. Trying to fix a network that doesn't use the most current drivers is a little like fixing an old rusty car. Some people actually manage to do it, but the most of us would rather trade in the old car for a new one. The time you'll waste getting that old driver to work could be used for something a little more productive—like getting your real work done.

The first thing you should always do before installing your network is to make sure that you have all the current drivers. Unfortunately, this isn't always as easy as it might seem. Take the NIC driver as an example. Very rarely will the driver that you get in the box be the most current driver available. Count on downloading a new driver from the vendor's Internet site or BBS. Sometimes the problem is compounded when one vendor has a different view of the world than another. You may find that your hardware vendor provides one version of the driver that works in one way and the NOS vendor provides an entirely different version that they claim works better. Which should you choose? The one that works. In many cases, you'll find that one of the two drivers works better, so it's a good idea to have both on hand.

Another situation you'll run into that affects how your network runs is the choice of client. This chapter covers the Novell version of the Windows 95 client. Is it better than its Microsoft-supplied counterpart? You may be surprised to find out that the Microsoft client isn't always the best choice. There are times where the extra features or reliability provided by the Novell client are exactly what you need to get your network running. In other cases, the extra memory required by this client could keep a much-needed application from working properly.

The bottom line is that you'll need not only the most current drivers and other software available for your network, but all of the varieties as well. Somewhere in all of the various combinations that you'll find is a network setup that will work perfectly for you. The problem is that many people don't take the time to find it.

A Look at the Hardware

Ask anyone who just spent an afternoon ensuring that his hardware is configured correctly and you'll find that it's probably the most frustrating experience he has ever had. Yet the level of frustration doesn't make sense to many people until they actually experience it in some way. After all, network hardware setup and configuration looks very simple. All you have in most cases is a network interface card (NIC), a length of cable, and some kind of an adapter. (Some networks require the use of hubs and others use terminators, but first let's look at the specifics of the hardware attached directly to your PC.) The fact is that hardware is more than just a simple set of connectors, a cable, and a card. There are configuration issues that affect the hardware in ways that you really can't understand until you've spent that afternoon reconfiguring your setup.

Take, for instance, the problem of assigning network addresses for cards that still require you to assign them manually. Keeping track of all those addresses can be a chore. However, it doesn't take long to figure out what happens when two workstations have the same address. The results are usually easy to track down, but it's still a problem that most administrators don't want to deal with. (Fortunately, most cards don't require any form of manual address configuration now, and even the configuration settings are all done through software.)

Some hardware problems are a little more difficult track down, yet they're fairly apparent once you find them. For example, a crimped cable is easy to detect if you look for it, but how many people would associate lost data packets with a cable? A simple check with an ohmmeter might show that the cable is good, but a connection isn't all you need. (Crimped cables are one of the more common problems that I've seen administrators fail to find.) There are simple troubleshooting guidelines that you can follow for all hardware in general. The following list shows you the things I look for most often, in addition to the hardware-specific tips in Chapter 26.

- **Hardware in a package isn't always good:** I actually run into this problem frequently. For example, consider a short length of coaxial cable required to connect two workstations in the same room. The old cable goes bad, so you go to the store and get a new one. After installing the new cable, nothing changes, so you start to think that the old cable wasn't bad after all. If you don't check the cable at this point you may be opening yourself up to many hours of needless troubleshooting. I've had more than a few cables show up bad right out of the package (and they always look good).
- **Few components really look bad when they are:** It used to be that you could look at a resistor or capacitor and pretty much know that it was bad. Even older chips tended to scorch themselves in the process of dying. Looking for a bad component is a waste of time today. In most cases, the old component looks just as good as the one that replaces it. In fact, if you see a component that looks bad, you'd better start looking for the ones that went with it.

- **Good connections are a must:** Coaxial cables are especially prone to this problem, but you'll find it with other kinds of cabling as well. When you connect a tee adapter to the end of a thin net Ethernet connection, be sure to give it a twist. If you don't, then there isn't any kind of mechanical connection between the tee and the adapter. The same holds true for cables. Make sure that you connect them firmly to the adapter. It may seem like this is a piece of worthless information, but I've actually found more loose connectors than I care to mention. Always check e your connections when you start to see a cable-related problem.
- **Keep the noise down:** There was one installation that I looked at where the network was constantly going down or acting erratic in some way. I found that the cause of the problem didn't have anything to do with the network hardware. The problem was a power panel and associated transformer on the other side of the wall. Only when we moved the PCs away from the wall did the network problems dissipate. However, you don't need to have a really strange setup to get noise problems. A simple problem such as passing a cable near the transformer for the light fixtures in your office can cause problems. Noise is one of your biggest enemies. It doesn't matter what kind of setup you have—enough noise can cause all kinds of strange problems.
- **Out with the old, in with the new:** You may think that the old 8-bit Ethernet card hanging around on your network will work just fine, but in some cases it won't. If you've got a lot of nice new 32-bit cards in the workstations on your network sending data to an 8-bit card in a print server, you're in for trouble. The old card will lose packets and give you all kinds of other grief. Even if it manages to keep up, the old card is costing you part of the performance you're supposed to get with the new cards. I usually install cards of the same type and from the same vendor (if possible) throughout the network. To do so will save you a lot more time and effort than it will cost you in new cards.

There are some other tools you can use to help yourself in the hardware area. For example, people who use twisted-pair cabling require a hub in most cases. Trying to figure out whether a hub or a NIC is bad might be a time-consuming task if you couldn't eliminate one of the two. There are some situations where the hub has gone bad in such a way that you'll spend days trying to figure things out. One of the techniques that I use to eliminate or confirm a bad NIC is to connect two PCs together by using a null hub cable. If the PCs can communicate without the hub in place, then the hub is bad, not the NIC. By the way, you can also use this handy cable to get by without using a hub at all, if you only need to connect two machines together for game play. The same cable works great if you want a high-speed connection between a stand-alone desktop machine and your laptop (you'll also need to provide NICs in both machines). Table 27.1 shows the connections to make for a null hub cable for twisted-pair 10Base-T Ethernet. It uses the color code specified by the EIA/TIA T568B standard. Remember that you'll need a length of 10Base-T cable and two RJ45 plugs.

Tip: If you perform a lot of network cabling, you may want to check out the data communications cabling FAQ sheets available at `http://www.cis.ohio-state.edu/hypertext/faq/usenet/LANs/cabling-faq/faq.html`. Another good place to visit is the `comp.dcom.cabling` newsgroup. Here you'll find a lot of helpful advice on how to get around cabling problems. If you want to find out more about standard commercial-grade 10Base-T cabling, look at the ANSI/EIA/TIA-568-1991 standard.

Table 27.1 Ethernet 10Base-T null hub cable.

Plug 1 Pin	*Wire Color*	*Plug 2 Pin*	*Wire Color*
1 (Tx+)	White/Orange	3 (Rx+)	White/Green
2 (Tx-)	Orange	6 (Rx-)	Green
3 (Rx+)	White/Green	1 (Tx+)	White/Orange
4 (R1)	Blue	4 (R1)	Blue
5 (T1)	White/Blue	5 (T1)	White/Blue
6 (Rx-)	Green	2 (Tx-)	Orange
7 (T4)	White/Brown	7 (T4)	White/Brown
8 (R4)	Brown	8 (R4)	Brown

Note: The NorTel Digital Patch Cable (DPC) colors are as follows: 1 yellow, 2 black, 3 blue, 4 red, 5 green, 6 orange, 7 brown, and 8 gray. These cables use stranded wire in place of the solid wire used by the EIA/TIA T568B standard.

One of your best tools for detecting cabling problems is a time-domain reflectometer (TDR). This is a special device used to check out network cabling. It can help you to detect crimped cables and all kinds of other problems on your network. Not only will it detect the crimp or other cabling problem, but a TDR can tell you the distance to the problem area. Knowing this information will save you hours of crawling through cable runs. In fact, the better TDRs can also tell you about noise problems and other cable-related network troubles.

NetWare Server Connections

Novell NetWare is one of the more common network operating systems in the corporate environment. In fact, you'll occasionally find it in a smaller company as well. The reason is simple: NetWare provides superior file and print-server capabilities. (Most network administrators give Windows NT the nod when it comes to application-server capabilities.) Few people would argue that if you plan to work with networks, you need to know how NetWare fits into the picture.

Tip: You can view a list of current NetWare (and other Novell product) patch files at `http://support.novell.com/search/patlst.htm`. Be sure to download and install all patches for your file server before you call Novell support. In many cases, a patch file will fix a problem you're having.

There are a few common problems that you'll find when using Windows 95 in a large computing environment, especially when it comes to a WAN environment. Obviously, NetWare users will also experience problems even in a smaller network; I'll cover some of those situations as well. The following list shows some of the more common problems I've seen:

- **Network Neighborhood doesn't show all servers:** If you're working with a very large network, you may not see every server on your network the first time you open Network Neighborhood. In fact, you may find out that there are some servers that won't show up for a day or two. The problem is one of information-gathering. If you're working in a WAN environment with servers spread over several sites, relying on Network Neighborhood to display the available servers probably isn't the best idea. You'll want some software such as Novell ManageWise or Intel LANDesk to get the job done. Even so, you'll probably need to wait a while for this specialty software to find all the servers on the network. If you happen to know the name of a server that you want to find, use the Find Computer option of the Network Neighborhood context menu to locate it.
- **Can't make an NDS connection:** You definitely can't use the Novell client that comes with the older version of Windows to create an NDS connection. Both Microsoft and Novell released 32-bit NDS clients after the original Windows 95 release date. (OSR2 users get a copy of the Microsoft 32-bit client as part of the package.) Be sure to download Service Pack 1 to update your NDS client before attempting to make a connection. Unfortunately, you may find that the Microsoft client still doesn't work. In that case, try the Novell 32-bit client. The later section "Using Novell Client 32" tells you all about this client.
- **Long filenames don't work:** NetWare doesn't support long filenames unless you do a little extra work. First, make sure that you have the most current OS2.NAM name-space file. Once you get the needed driver, you can get it installed. There are two console commands you need to use (at the server, not your workstation). First, you need to load name-space support for long filenames by typing **`LOAD OS2.NAM`** at the file server console. Once the name space is loaded, you need to tell NetWare to use it. You do this by using the **`ADD NAME SPACE OS2 TO`** ***`<volume name>`*** command. For example, if you want to add long filename support to volume SYS, you type **`ADD NAME SPACE OS2 TO SYS`**. Once you get

name-space support added to the volume, you need to down the server. Add the OS2.NAM file to the DOS directory containing the rest of your server software. Restart the server.

- **The connection type is always Bindery:** Obviously, you have to use NetWare 4.x with NDS installed before you'll get anything other than a bindery connection. You'll also need to use a 32-bit client. If you've set up your machine correctly and still can't get an NDS connection, you may want to check one other setting. Look at the NetWare client Properties dialog box (the exact name of this dialog box varies by the client you're using). Make sure that you don't have anything entered in the Preferred Server field, but that you entered a Preferred Tree and Name Context. These fields appear on the Client 32 page of the Novell client. The Preferred Server setting appears on the General page of the Microsoft client; you'll need to install the Service for NetWare Directory Services service to add a preferred tree and name context when using the Microsoft client.
- **Can't get NWAdmin utility to work:** Older versions of the Microsoft client didn't support this utility at all. The newer versions are supposed to support it, but many people have had trouble getting NWAdmin to work properly. Because you need this utility to administer a NetWare file server, it's usually better to use the Novell 32-bit client on the administrator's machine.
- **NPrinter utility doesn't work:** As of this writing, Novell has a beta version of a new NPrinter utility that's specifically designed for Windows 95 available for download at `http://support.novell.com/Ftp/Updates/nwos/nc32w952/Date0.html`. You must have all the Client 32 updates installed before this program will work. If you get a message stating that NPrinter can't find PRTWIN32.DLL, you're still missing the second update for Client 32.

Security-Related Network Concerns

Once you get past some of the standard problems, a few problems appear to plague administrators because they don't understand what's required. For example, NetWare provides an extensive array of security options. Administrators who feel very comfortable in a peer-to-peer setting may find the number of choices a bit daunting at first. The biggest problem that administrators suffer is giving the users on a network enough rights to do their work, but not enough to damage the file server. There's a simple way to check what rights a user has: by using the NWAdmin utility found in the PUBLIC folder of the file server. Let's take a quick look at what you need to do to verify a user's rights. (The later section "Using Explorer with Client 32" looks at a way that you can use Explorer to do this.)

1. Load NWAdmin. You'll see a complete listing of all the items you have rights to within your organization.
2. Open one of the Volume objects. Select the directory or file that you want to check. Right-click to see a context menu like the one shown in Figure 27.1.

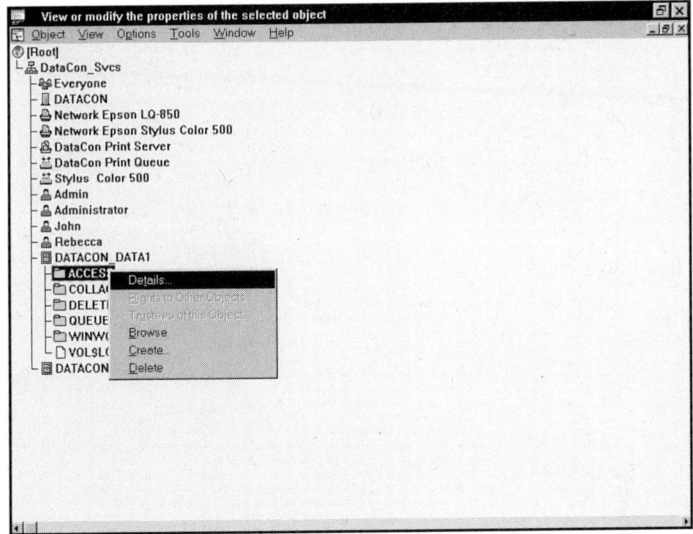

Figure 27.1.
Just about every object within NWAdmin has a context menu that contains the Details option.

3. Select Details. You'll see a details dialog box. In my case I chose a directory, but you could just as easily select another object.
4. Click the Trustees of this Directory or Trustees of this File button. You'll see a dialog box similar to the one shown in Figure 27.2. Notice that there's a list of trustees that are directly assigned to this directory. However, knowing the direct assignments is never enough. There are a lot of indirect assignments that you can assign in NetWare. For example, if you look at the figure you'll notice that user Rebecca doesn't appear in the list. Let's see what you need to do to find out what her rights are.

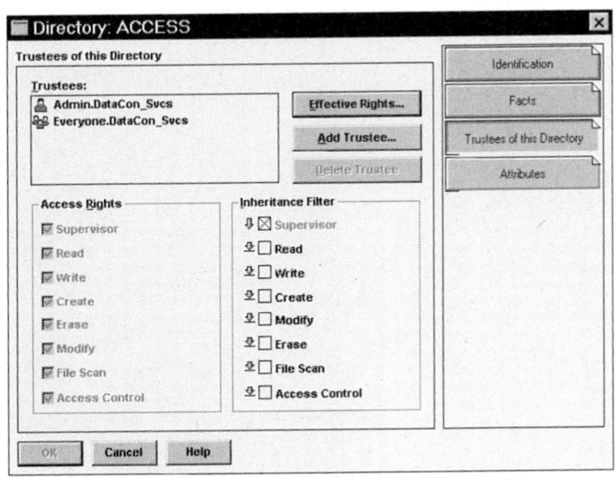

Figure 27.2.
The trustees listing doesn't always give you all the information you need; it's important to dig deep.

5. Click the Effective Rights button. You'll see an Effective Rights dialog box like the one shown in Figure 27.3.

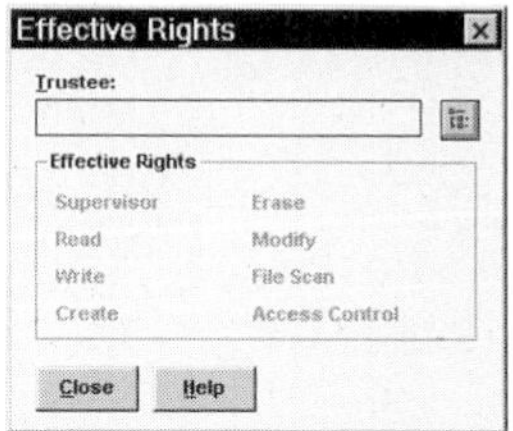

Figure 27.3.
The Effective Rights dialog box can tell you who has rights to the current object.

6. Click the Organizational Unit button (the one that appears right next to the Trustee field in Figure 27.3). You'll see a Select Object dialog box like the one shown in Figure 27.4.

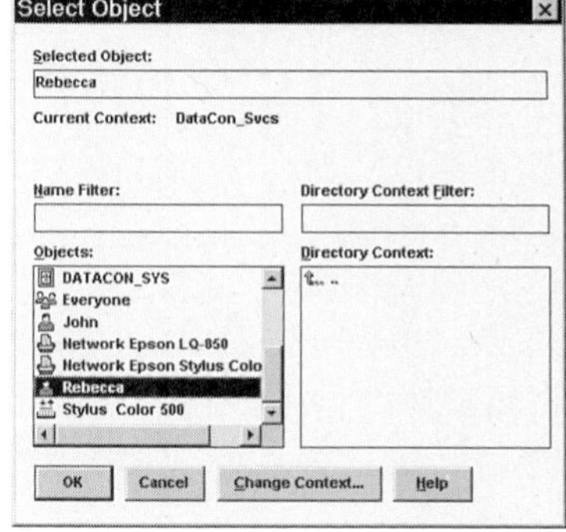

Figure 27.4.
The Select Object dialog box allows you to choose the user or other object that you want to check.

7. Highlight a user or other object that you want to view. In my case, I chose user Rebecca. However, you could just as easily select other objects to see what rights they have to the current directory.
8. Click OK to return to the Effective Rights dialog box. In this case, you'll see the rights that the selected object has to the current directory or file. The example in Figure 27.5 shows the rights that user Rebecca has to the Access directory, but this same technique works in all other cases as well.

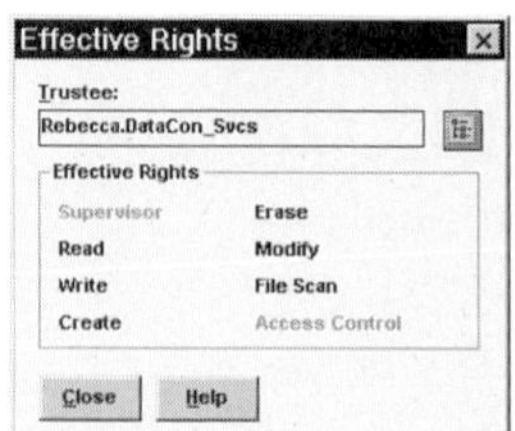

Figure 27.5.
Learning the effective rights that a person has to a directory or file is the first step in fixing access problems.

9. Close the Effective Rights dialog box. Click the Cancel button to close the details dialog box.

At this point, you need to figure out why user Rebecca (or any other user, for that matter) has rights to this directory. If you look carefully at Figure 27.2, you'll notice that the group Everyone has rights to the directory. If you looked at the members of this group, you'd see that user Rebecca is a member. She inherits her rights to the group through group membership.

You can always find out about a user who has too little access to a directory or file. However, finding out about situations where a person has too many rights will take a little detective work. What you've just seen is one way to do it. Obviously, this isn't the only tool at your disposal, but it does come as part of NetWare.

Hardware-Related Problems Such as Printers

Let's look at another potential problem scenario: You can't get your printer to work. The NWAdmin utility can help out in this case as well. Every printer setup for a NetWare network has three elements: a print server, the printer itself, and a print queue. You have to organize these three units to work together. The easiest way to make sure that you have everything right is to double-click the Print Server object in NWAdmin. You'll see a Print Server dialog box. If you click the Print Layout button, you'll see a dialog box like the one shown in Figure 27.6.

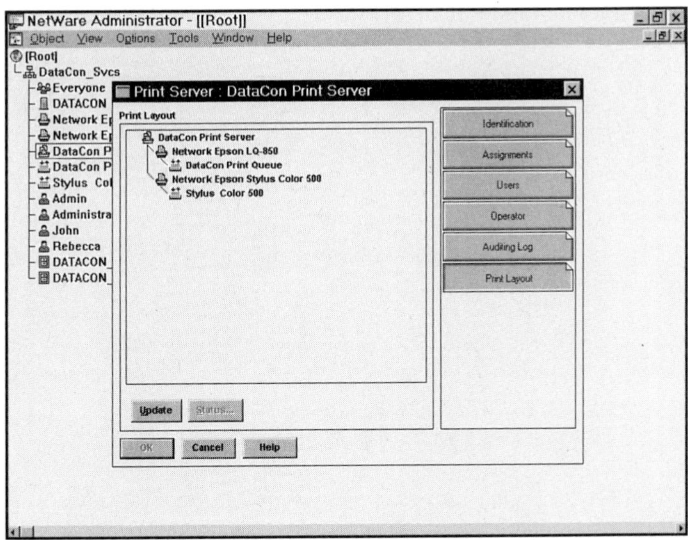

Figure 27.6.
The Print Layout page of the Print Server dialog box shows you all the details of your printer setup.

Notice how the various queues and printers are connected to the server in the figure. That's the kind of setup that you need to establish on your server as well. The way you do it is by assigning a queue to a printer, and then a printer to the server. Figure 27.7 shows the Assignments page of the Print Server dialog box. You'll find a similar page in the Printer dialog box.

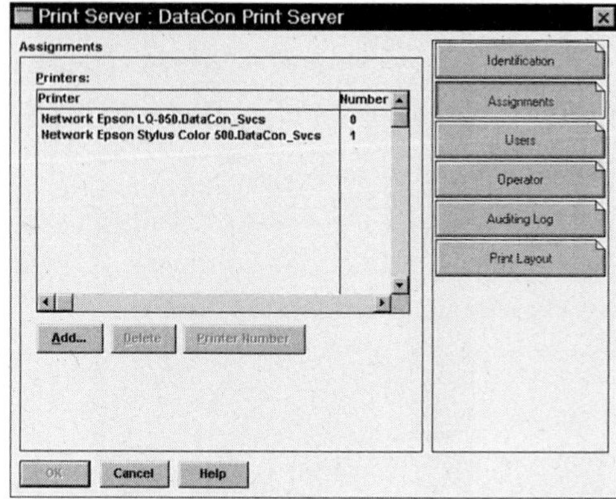

Figure 27.7.
Getting your printer setup going is a matter of making the right assignments.

Let's go back to Figure 27.6 for a moment. You can click any of the objects shown in the printer layout. As soon as you do so, the Status button is enabled. Clicking that button displays a dialog box like the one shown in Figure 27.8. This dialog box helps you to determine the current status of your queues, printers, and servers. In this case, the printer is working fine. However, the Status dialog box could just as easily report some type of problem with a particular object. Knowing which object is down is the first step in troubleshooting the problem.

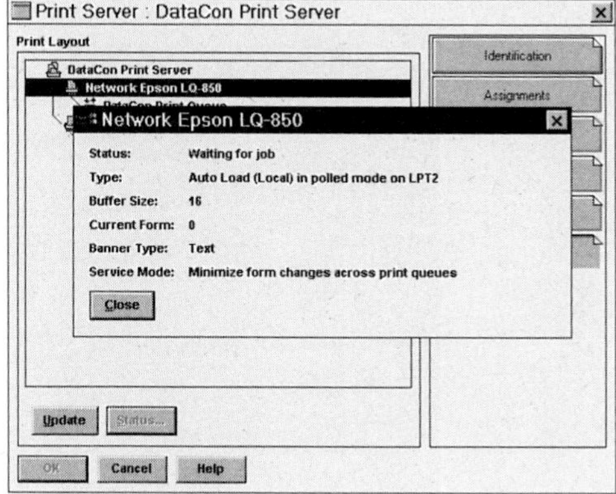

Figure 27.8.
When in doubt, check the status of the various print objects on your network.

Using Novell Client 32

When Microsoft first introduced Windows 95, there weren't any 32-bit NDS clients for Novell NetWare. It didn't take long for users to get irate over the situation. After all, one of the benefits of using NetWare 4.x was NDS—the idea that you could manage a large network from one location, using one utility.

Microsoft's client arrived on the scene a short time after Windows 95 appeared on the market. Unfortunately, the client was buggy and very limited from a capability perspective. The first version of the Microsoft client barely allowed you to log into an NDS-enabled NetWare server.

Sometime after the Microsoft client appeared on the market, the Novell version appeared. This client was just as buggy as the Microsoft offering, but at least it offered all the features that a user might need to manage her NetWare server.

As time has passed, both clients are getting better, although neither client is bug-free even to this day. Both Microsoft and Novell are working on patches that fix various problems that users have noted with the client software. Suffice it to say that you're going to need an update or two, no matter which client you select.

So, what precisely are the differences between the two NDS clients? I see the big difference as one of capability. Microsoft's client is very lean. It consumes very few system resources when compared to the Novell offering, but it doesn't offer many of the features you'll need, either. For example, the "Using Explorer with Client 32" section of this chapter explains that the Novell client modifies the way that Explorer works. It allows you to view and assign user rights to directories and files (provided that you have the proper rights). The Network Neighborhood display is much enhanced as well. We'll look at that in the "Differences in Network Neighborhood" section. You'll also see that the Novell offering provides a lot of configuration flexibility—something that you'll really need if you want to get the most out of your network. The added flexibility also comes in handy when you start experiencing compatibility or other network-related configuration problems. Finally, you absolutely have to have the Novell client if you want to use the NWAdmin utility. Microsoft's latest client is supposed to provide support for this essential utility program, but the level of support you get is minimal, at best.

Obviously, all these added features come with a price. While the Novell client helps you find things faster and provides a generally faster interface, you're going to pay a heavy penalty in memory usage. Don't even attempt to use this client with a minimal machine configuration. In fact, you'll want to make sure that every machine using the Novell client has at least 32MB of RAM installed. You'll also give up some hard disk space. The current version of the Novell client (including patches) consumes 3MB of hard disk space, not including all the files it places in your SYSTEM folder. Finally, even though I find that the Novell client is a little more reliable than the Microsoft offering once you get it set up, you'll find that all the features this client offers can get confusing. At a minimum, you'll find that users have more questions when it comes to Network Neighborhood, not less, once you get this client installed. Be prepared to spend a little more time holding the user's hand once you install the Novell client.

Tip: There isn't any rule that says that you have to use only one client on your network. In most cases, I use the Microsoft client on the vast majority of machines. It's small and easy to use, so users feel more comfortable with it. I install the Novell client if a machine has problems accessing the network or needs added flexibility. Every network administrator machine also gets the Novell client, as do manager machines where the manager needs to have some kind of access to NDS.

Installing the Client

Getting Client 32 installed on your machine is about as easy as software installation gets. You download the required software from `http://support.novell.com/Ftp/Updates/nwos/nc32w952/Date0.html` or from CompuServe. Once you download and unpack the software, double-click the Setup icon. You'll see a dialog box similar to the one shown in Figure 27.9.

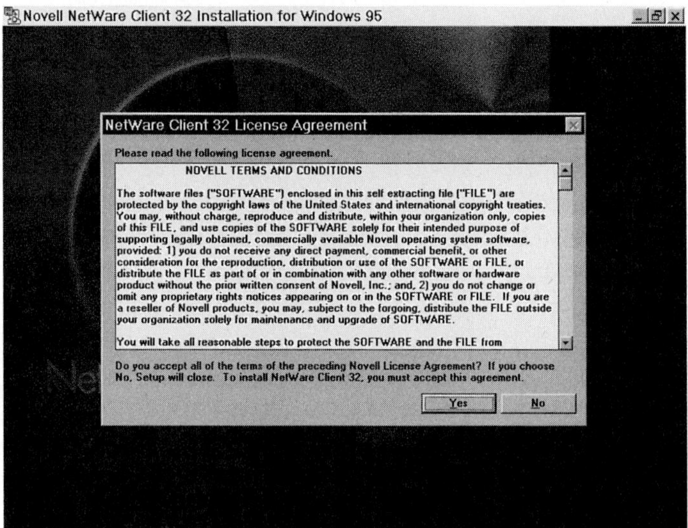

Figure 27.9.
The license agreement is the first thing you see when you start the Client 32 installation.

Click Yes if you agree to the license terms. You'll see a dialog box like the one in Figure 27.10. Just click Start and the Setup program takes care of all the details.

The first thing that Setup does is remove your old client. I mention this because you may want to run the installation from a local drive instead of the network. While Setup doesn't actually disconnect you from the server, at this point a failure that requires a reboot could leave you without any client at all (making the file server inaccessible).

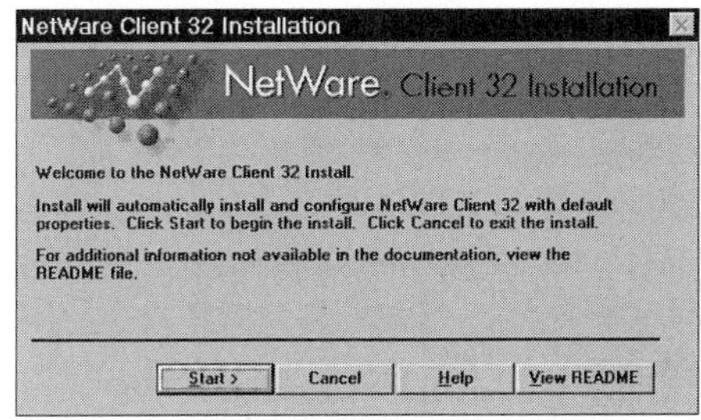

Figure 27.10.
Just click Start at this dialog box, and Setup takes care of the rest.

Once the old client is removed, Setup installs a few new files in the Windows INF folder. At this point, it forces Windows 95 to rebuild its drivers list, based on the contents of the new INF file. Setup automatically selects the new client for you and gets it installed. You'll see another rebuild of the driver list after the new client is installed.

After all the files are copied and Setup performs a basic setup, you'll be asked to reboot your machine. When you restart your machine, you'll be using the new client. Getting started couldn't be much easier than that.

Tip: Make sure that you know your current context and NDS tree. You'll need this information the first time you restart your machine with the Novell client installed. The preferred tree and context information is recorded so that you don't have to enter it again.

Configuration Options

Configuring Novell's Client 32 is much like configuring any other network-related driver. You begin by opening the Network Properties dialog box (right-click Network Neighborhood and select Properties from the context menu). Select the Novell NetWare Client 32 entry in the components list shown on the Configuration page, and then click the Properties button. You'll see a Novell NetWare Client 32 Properties dialog box similar to the one shown in Figure 27.11.

The Client 32 page of this dialog box contains four fields. Notice that I've left the Preferred Server field blank. You need to leave it blank unless you want a bindery connection in place of an NDS connection. The Preferred Tree field contains the name of the tree you want the client to search for your name. The Name Context text box normally contains the name of your organization and workgroup. (Figure 27.11 shows only the organization name.) Finally, you need to select the first network drive. Unlike the Microsoft client, you can actually select a drive below F if you want to. For example, you may have only a hard drive and CD-ROM installed on your machine. Selecting E as the first network connection saves one drive letter.

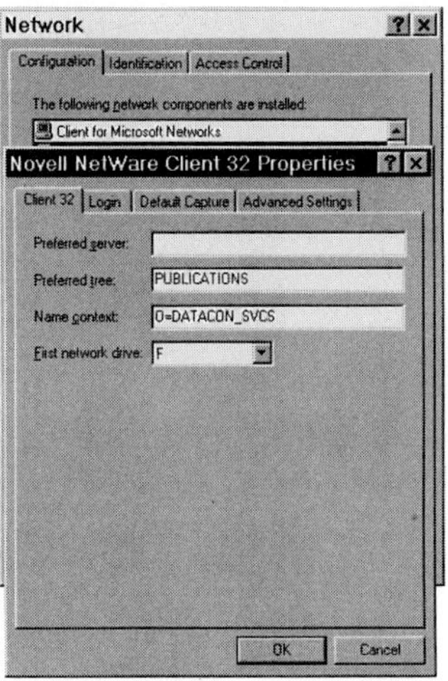

Figure 27.11.
The Novell NetWare Client 32 Properties dialog box allows you to configure the client.

The Login page appears in Figure 27.12. Normally, when you log into the network, you see a single page login similar to the one used by the Microsoft client. This page allows you to enter a user name and your password. It works fine if you have only one user working with a machine, who uses the same network configuration each day. However, if you have a user with special needs, you'll want to modify one or more of these settings.

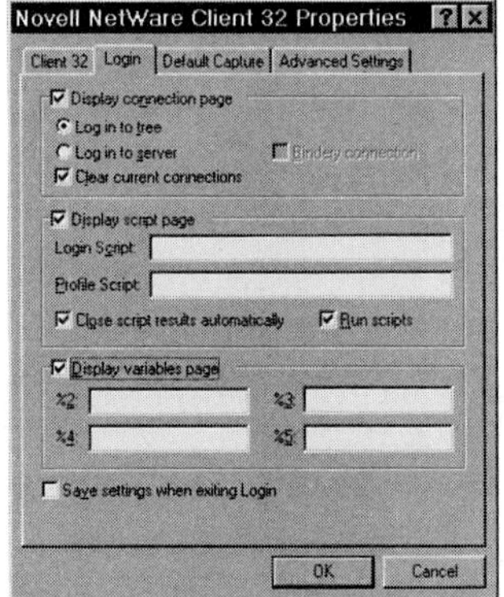

Figure 27.12.
The Login page allows you to modify the appearance of your login dialog box when Windows 95 first starts.

Let's look at the three additional page types. The Display Connection Page option tells Client 32 that you want to see the page for selecting a preferred server, tree, and context each time you log in. This allows you to change the default server you use each day and provides some added flexibility for those times when you have to log in as the network administrator versus a regular user. This group includes two additional options. The first clears all the connection information each time you log in. I normally uncheck this selection on my machine because I use the same server each day, unless I'm performing administrative duties. However, you'll probably want to keep it checked for security reasons if several users use the same machine. Using this feature would enable you to keep a hidden server hidden. The other check box isn't highlighted in this case. If you select the Log in to Server option, you'll enable the Bindery Connection check box. This check box forces a bindery versus an NDS connection to the server.

Normally, the administrator assigns a default set of scripts to each user on the network. These scripts set up any drive mappings or other essential network configurations. Client 32 allows you to select one of the NDS scripts by using a Script page during login. That's what the second section of the Login page is all about. Notice that there are two separate fields for script names—one for the login script and another for the profile script. You can choose NDS script objects or a simple batch file on your machine—Client 32 will work with either one. There are two check boxes that affect the way the scripts are run. The first automatically closes the script window when it's complete. In most cases you'll want to keep this checked. Unchecking the check box would allow you to observe results of a script during debugging. The second check box, Run Scripts, tells Client 32 to run the scripts you've selected. You can uncheck the box if you don't want to run any scripts during the login process.

The third section of the Login page relates to scripts as well. The Display Variables Page option displays a third additional page during the login process. You can use the fields on this page to pass variable information to your scripts. This is especially handy if you want to build one script file to serve a number of purposes.

Printing is another major problem in some situations. The Default Capture page of the Novell NetWare Client 32 Properties dialog box allows you to get around some of them. Figure 27.13 shows this page. If you've worked with printers before, you should recognize this page as a generic form of the one discussed in the "Installing a Printer" section of Chapter 15. Because the settings perform the same purpose, I won't discuss them here again. The thing to remember is that these settings affect the network printers as a whole. They won't affect the settings of printers you have already installed—Windows 95 overrides any settings you may make on this page.

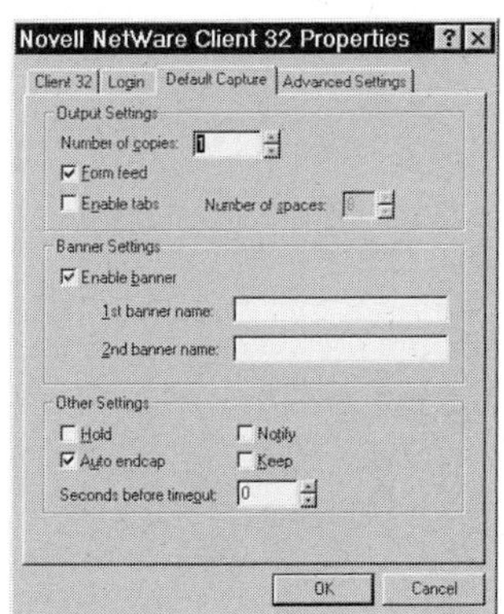

Figure 27.13.
The Default Capture page allows you to change the default settings for new network printers.

The final page in the Novell NetWare Client 32 Properties dialog box is the Advanced Settings page shown in Figure 27.14. In most cases you'll never have to adjust these settings. However, some of the settings can help you fine-tune the way Client 32 works. For example, the Delay Writes setting can help in situations where an application repeatedly opens and closes files on the server (such as overlays). The client will hold the file write for a given number of clock ticks to ensure that the application actually wants to write the information. In essence, this setting works as a disk cache. One of the handier troubleshooting aids is the Log File setting. You can tell Client 32 to generate a log of any errors it encounters. The Log File Size setting allows you to keep the file size under control.

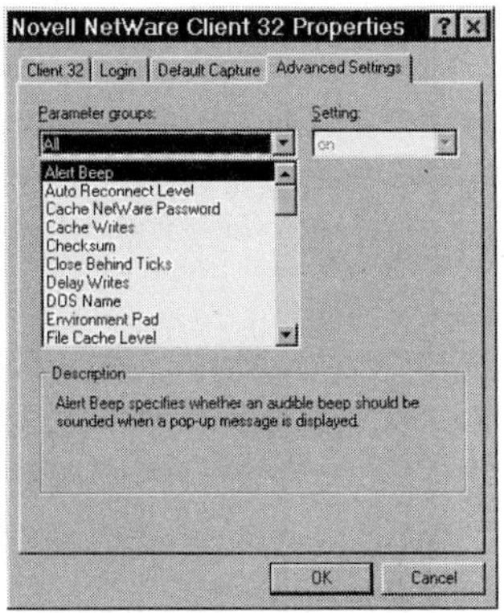

Figure 27.14.
The Advanced Settings page allows you to fine-tune your Client 32 settings.

Differences in Network Neighborhood

Novell's Client 32 does things a bit differently than Microsoft's client when it comes to Network Neighborhood. The first thing you'll want to look at is the NetWare Connections option on the Network Neighborhood context menu. Selecting this option displays a Current NetWare Resources dialog box like the one shown in Figure 27.15.

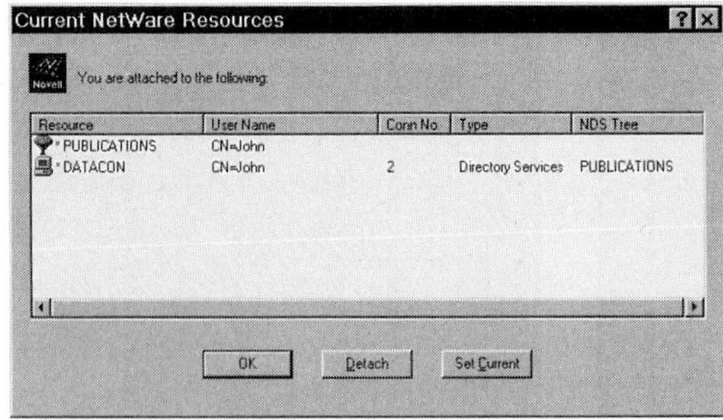

Figure 27.15.
The Current NetWare Resources dialog box provides more information than its Microsoft counterpart.

Notice that this dialog box tells you all about your connection. Not only does it tell you what server you're connected to and the type of connection, but it tells about your context, including the tree that you're logged into. This dialog box provides a lot more information than its Microsoft counterpart. The only problem is that a novice user will think that he's using two connections. Even though it may appear that you're using two connections, you're actually using one. Look at the Conn No. column of the dialog box. It contains the actual connection number that you're using.

Double-clicking Network Neighborhood presents a few surprises as well. Figure 27.16 shows a typical setup. Notice that there are three NetWare-specific entries here instead of the usual one. The first looks like a standard computer and shows the file server itself (DataCon). The second looks like a tree; it's the NDS tree that you're logged into (Publications). Finally, you'll see the default context that you're logged into (which looks like a white square in the figure). Each of these icons serves a different purpose, but the one you'll use most is the server icon.

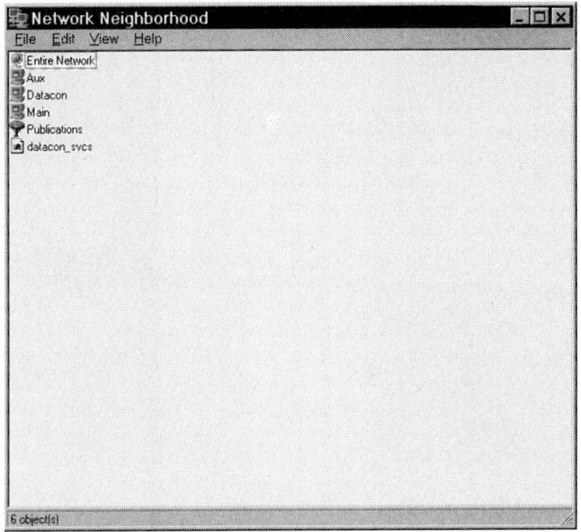

Figure 27.16.
Network Neighborhood takes on a slightly different appearance when you use Client 32.

If you double-click a server icon, you'll see something similar to the display shown in Figure 27.17. As you can see, this is a typical Explorer display like the ones we've looked at elsewhere. However, there's one word of advice here. Get all your drive mappings from this view of your server—don't use the resource view that you'll get by double-clicking the content icon. The reason is fairly simple: You'll get friendlier names in Explorer if you use this view. For example, if you map the SYS volume shown in Figure 27.17, the name you'll see in Explorer is \\DataCon\SYS. Try to map that same drive from the context view of the server resources and you'll get something like \\PUBLICATIONS\.DATACON_SYS.DATACON_SVCS. It's still readable, but less so than the standard UNC name you get in the server view.

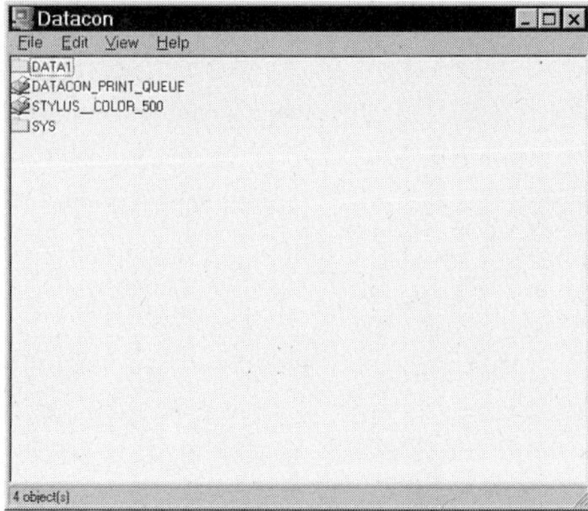

Figure 27.17.
Double-clicking the server icon displays a standard Explorer view of resources, like the one shown here.

The context view provides some information that you won't find by using the more standard server view. Figure 27.18 shows what you'll probably get if you double-click the context icon. There are two things that you should notice. First, this view of server resources uses long names. I find that it's more readable when I need to search for a system resource. In addition, notice that you get to see all the resources. The standard server view in Figure 27.17 shows just the print queues. The context view in Figure 27.18 shows both the print queues and the printers.

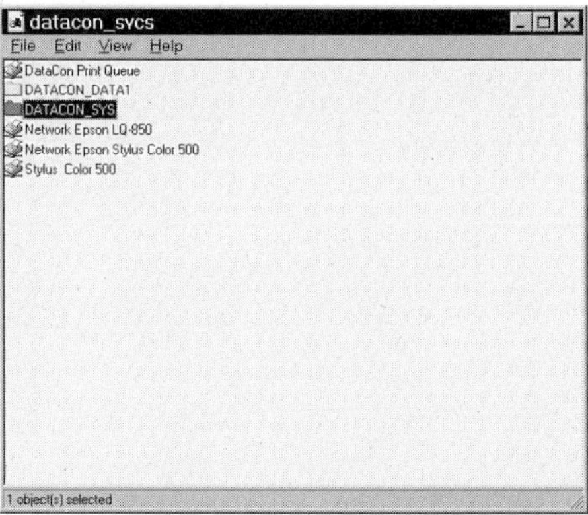

Figure 27.18.
The context view of your server resources provides more information than the server view.

Each of the three icons provides some different context menu entries as well. Figure 27.19 shows the context menu for the server icon. Notice that you can use this context menu to log in, log out, display a dialog box showing who you are on the network, and authenticate your server connection. (Authentication ensures that you're actually connected to the server that you think you're connected to, and in the proper context.)

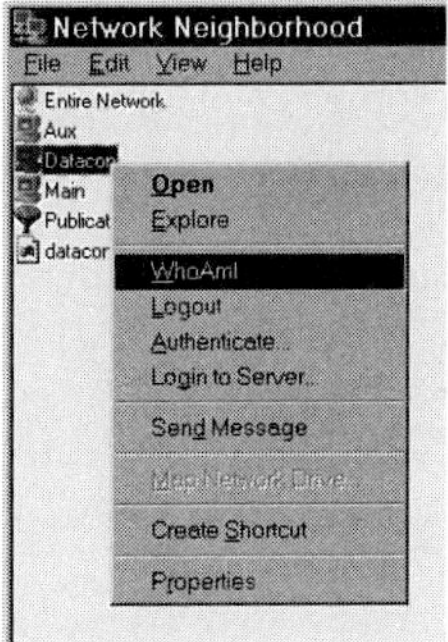

Figure 27.19.
The server icon context menu helps you maintain your server contact.

Let's look at the NDS Tree context menu next. Figure 27.20 shows what you'll see here. Notice that you can log in and log out as before, but this time it's to the tree rather than the server. You can also display a dialog box showing who you are, and authenticate your connection as before. There's another entry here, though, that allows you to change your context. Select it and you'll get a dialog box that asks you to change your context. You can type a number of entries here, but let's take [ROOT] as an example. Using this context takes us from the organizational level (my normal login level) to the root of the NDS tree.

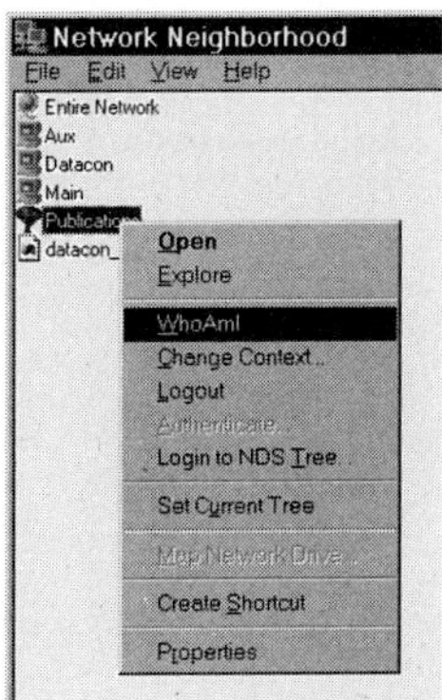

Figure 27.20.
The NDS tree context menu contains a special entry for changing your current NDS context.

The final context menu we'll look at belongs to the context icon. It appears in Figure 27.21. About the only thing that this context menu will do for you is set the context to the default that you provided in the Novell NetWare Client 32 Properties dialog box shown in Figure 27.11.

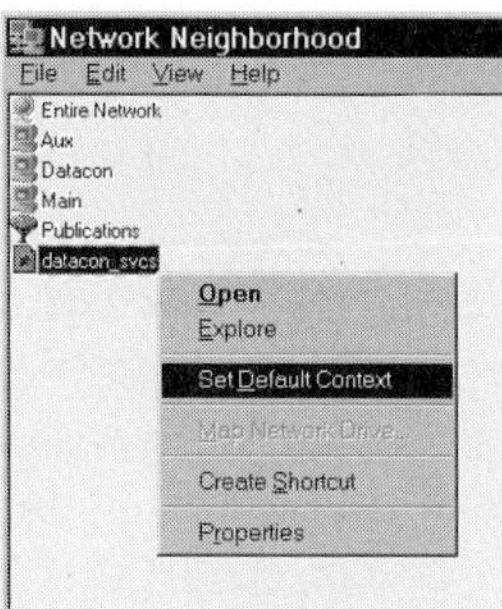

Figure 27.21.
The context icon context menu allows you to reset your NDS tree context to its default value.

Using Explorer with Client 32

Client 32 affects the way that Windows Explorer displays the Properties dialog box for a network drive. Figure 27.22 shows a typical example. Notice that you have several new pages to use, including the NetWare Volume Information page shown here. As you can see, this page provides statistics on current disk usage and amount of resources left.

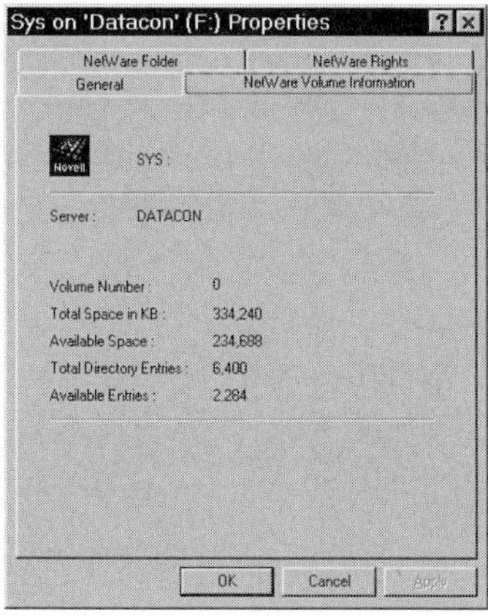

Figure 27.22.
Client 32 adds three new pages to the standard Explorer display.

The NetWare Folder page shown in Figure 27.23 gives you access to the volume attributes. (Files provide a similar page with file-specific rights such as Transactional, so I won't discuss it in this section.) Notice that you can change NetWare-specific attributes such as Don't Compress and Immediate Compression. Normally, you'd have to open the NWAdmin utility to change these settings. There are two other important pieces of information shown on this page. The first tells who owns the folder (or file). In this case it's Supervisor. Notice that the page also includes a Name Space field. You can use this information to determine which directories would be affected if you decided to remove the OS2 name-space support required for long filenames from a volume. Finally, you get to see the folder's creation date, last update, and the date it was last archived. Unfortunately, you have to perform your backups from the server to keep this information current.

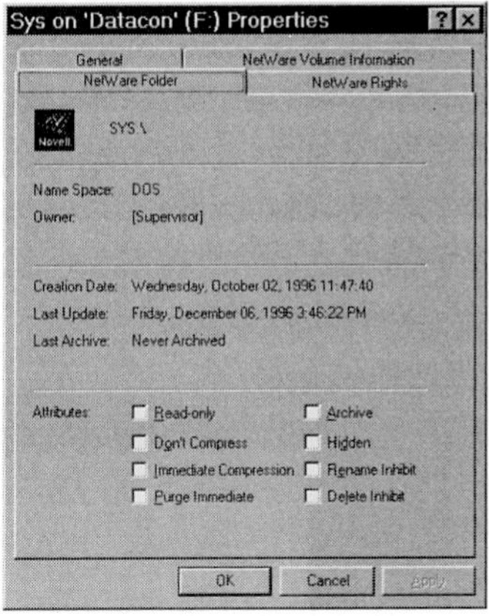

Figure 27.23.
The NetWare Folder page allows you to control the folder attributes and presents statistical information.

You'll really like the NetWare Rights page shown in Figure 27.24. It allows you to view and assign the trustee rights for users of a folder or file. Notice that this dialog box shows two trustees and the rights they have to the folder in the Trustees list. To change the rights for a particular individual or group, just check or uncheck one or more of the rights check boxes. Removing a trustee is equally easy. Just highlight the trustee you want to remove and click the Remove button.

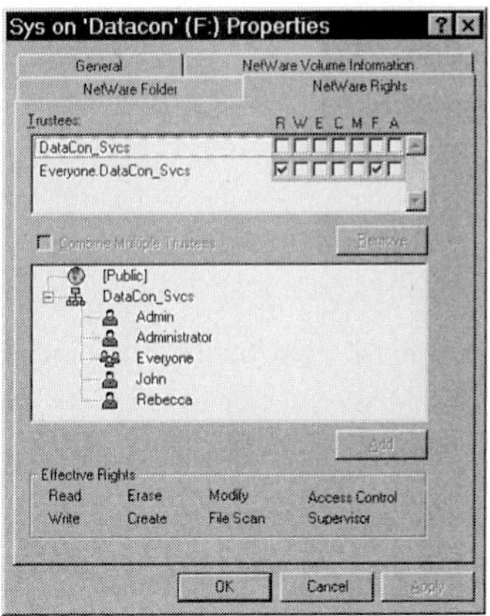

Figure 27.24.
The NetWare Rights page provides the most capability when it comes to administering a network.

The second section of the NetWare Rights page provides a list of groups and users in the current context. (You'll need to change your context if you want to see users and groups in other parts of the NDS tree.) To add a user to the Trustee list, just highlight his or her name and then click the Add button. He or she will automatically get a default set of rights assigned, but you can just as easily change those rights. You'll need to click Apply or OK to make the changes permanent.

The final section of the dialog box shows effective rights. At first it's easy to think that it shows the effective rights of the highlighted trustee. The fact is that it shows *your* effective rights to the folder or file. Even if a user can't change trustee rights, she can use this page of the dialog box to see what *her* rights are to the folder.

Peer-to-Peer Network Connections

Normally peer-to-peer network connections are extremely reliable and easy to configure. The low cost of these networks is another reason that they're so popular. However, there are things that can affect a peer-to-peer network that you may never see on a client/server network model such as NetWare.

Let's take a look at one of the more interesting examples. You set up a five-node peer-to-peer network, testing each node as you add it in. Everything works great. You get every workstation online and configured. As you add each workstation, you check to make sure that it can see all the other workstations and can access their shared resources using Network Neighborhood. Everything looks like it's going to work great. However, you get to that final test stage, testing every workstation one more time to make sure that the connections work, and find that the first workstation can no longer see any of the others. The same holds true of the second workstation. In fact, the only workstation that can see any of the others is number three.

By the way, this failure actually happened to someone who spent several hours looking for some common cause of failure for the other four workstations. The cabling, network cards, terminators, tees, and just about anything else that was common to all four workstations checked out fine. In this case workstation three was the culprit. At this point, you're probably asking yourself how it could be the culprit when it was the only one working. It seems that workstation three was configured for user-level security on the Access page of the Network Properties dialog box. The rest were configured for share-level access. In other words, you need to configure all the workstations to use the same level of access control, or they won't work together.

So, how could we have made this problem a little easier to troubleshoot? There are several ways in which peer-to-peer networks differ from the large setups that many of you may be used to working on. The following list gives you some idea of how to optimize your troubleshooting strategy for this environment:

- **Make things easy:** A peer-to-peer network is unlikely to affect a large number of users. Simply take everything offline and look for the simple one-to-one connection first. Turn off everything except machines one and two. Look for a connection from machine one (the first one on the network) to machine two. If that works, turn off machine one, turn on machine three, and then look for a connection from machine two to machine three. If you can get through the entire network this way, then it's unlikely that cabling or network cards are the problem.

- **Look for odd man out:** Unlike large networks, you'll find that peer-to-peer networks tend to fail in one area. In the example we just looked at, one workstation worked while the others didn't. It was the odd man out and turned out to be the cause of the problem, even though it appeared to work just fine.
- **Configuration is key:** Smaller networks are usually more open than large ones. Users normally have a greater range of freedom than they would on a large network setup, because there simply isn't as much to watch. Unfortunately, this open atmosphere can cause the most absurd problems you've ever seen. Someone will change a simple setting that doesn't appear to hurt his computer, but affects everyone else's. For example, a user of a small peer-to-peer network could decide to change the share name of a drive or folder (the change could even happen accidentally, in some cases). This would have the effect of making that drive or folder unavailable to anyone else, yet nothing would change on the machine where the problem occurred. Remember that small networks are usually reliable because they use proven technology and very few new pieces of hardware. If everything looks like it should work, then you're probably looking for a configuration problem.
- **Make changes only when needed:** The problem with many small networks isn't in the software, the hardware, or even in the configuration. It's a problem with the person assigned to maintain the network. There's a simple axiom that I've always followed—if it works, don't fix it. Peer-to-peer networks are very popular because of their simplicity. Yet, this simplicity leads to the tinkerer—the person who wants to make everything just a bit faster or better. Once you get your network running, leave it alone until it actually requires some kind of service. When you do make a change, record it in a log. That way, you can refer to the log when a problem occurs. Always ask yourself this question: What changed right before this problem started cropping up?
- **Run diagnostics on a regular schedule:** I use a product such as CheckIt on a weekly basis to ensure that each machine on the network is functioning properly. A single machine failure on a peer-to-peer network affects everyone. That's one of the problems with using this kind of network instead of a centralized file server. As a result, even a minor problem on a single machine can have a big effect. When the time comes to troubleshoot problems on your network, run the diagnostics again. You have to make sure that every machine is operating properly or there isn't any way to ensure the problem isn't hardware-related.
- **Don't overlook the obvious:** There are problems that will drive you absolutely crazy because they're obvious. Peer-to-peer networks seem to have more of this kind of problem than anything else. Consider for a second what would happen if a terminator went bad or a cable got squeezed. Both of these failures happen on a regular basis on peer-to-peer networks. The cable problem is especially bad because the cables usually aren't run through the walls. Someone steps on a cable in just the wrong way and the network stops running.

Windows NT Server Connections

You may think that Windows NT is going to be a completely different story from everything covered so far in this chapter, but that isn't true. You'll find that Windows NT Server shares many of the same characteristics of both the NetWare client/server architecture and Windows 95 peer-to-peer networks that I've talked about so far. In reality, while NetWare uses a true client/server architecture, Windows NT is peer-to-peer based. To say that Windows NT is at the same level of most peer-to-peer networks, though, would be to deny the power of this particular NOS. The real-world view is that Windows NT lies somewhere between the two extremes (if you want to take a simplistic approach to the problem).

So, what makes Windows NT special? I could probably tell you about all of the intricacies of that particular NOS, but that would take an entire book. Here's a summary of what I see as the main differences between NetWare and Windows NT. While NetWare provides very fast file and printer services, Windows NT is a much better application server. For example, if I were to set up a Web or database server, I'd choose Windows NT instead of NetWare.

Windows NT also boasts a better interface than NetWare, but that may be short-lived. Novell is constantly improving the NetWare interface and as of this writing there are rumors that NetWare may soon boast a GUI similar to the one used by Windows.

Finally, the thing that makes Windows NT so much better than Windows 95 as a server is the level of security it provides. You'd be hard-pressed to find a more secure NOS—even NetWare doesn't provide some of the security features that you'll find in Windows NT.

How does all this affect the kinds of problems you'll find when using Windows NT? The following list provides some of the special problem areas that I've noted when using Windows NT:

- **Can't see the Windows NT server:** Open the Client for Microsoft Networks Properties dialog box. (You can access this dialog box through the Network Properties dialog box—just right-click Network Neighborhood and select Properties from the context menu.) Make sure that you have Log On to Windows NT Domain checked and have the domain name entered in the Domain field.
- **No WINS browse capabilities for the Internet through Network Neighborhood:** Make sure that you have a WINS account established on the Windows NT Server. (You can experiment with the user end of the WINS configuration using a public-access Winserve account—see the tip that follows.) You'll want to enter the Windows NT domain name in the Domain field of the Client for Microsoft Networks Properties dialog box. Make sure that you have the Quick Logon option selected, especially if you don't have a permanent connection to the Internet. You also need to check the TCP/IP Properties dialog box. Check the one associated with the Dial-Up Adapter if you use Dial-Up Networking. Otherwise, check the one associated with your network card. Select the Obtain IP Address

Automatically option on the IP Address page. Look at the WINS Configuration page. You should have the Enable WINS Resolution option selected and an Internet address for both the Primary WINS Server and Secondary WINS Server fields. The Disable DNS option on the DNS Configuration page should be selected. You'll also want to look at the Bindings page and make sure that both the Client for Microsoft Networks and the File and Printer Sharing for Microsoft Networks bindings are checked.

Tip: If you or your company need Windows NT Internet services, check out the site at `http://www.winserve.com/`. They offer both public and commercial services such as disk space and post offices. You can also use this service to see how your workstation would look as part of a worldwide Internet-based workgroup. Setting up your machine as suggested will allow you to browse the Internet workgroup through Network Neighborhood.

- **Inaccessible Windows NT server:** Even if you can see the Windows NT server in Network Neighborhood, that doesn't mean that you can use it. Some people really don't think about the added level of security that Windows NT provides in comparison to Windows 95. You must have an account on the Windows NT server to use it at all. However, simply having an account isn't enough. You must also have access to the various resources on the Windows NT server. This means that your name has to appear on an access list or as part of a group that has access to the resources you need. In this respect a Windows NT server works much like a NetWare server.
- **Internet Explorer can't find the company intranet:** More and more, companies are using intranets today in place of more traditional forms of data-sharing. However, there are some problems that you may experience in getting your favorite browser to cooperate. Internet Explorer seems to have more problems in this regard than Netscape Navigator. In some situations, it will report that it can't find your Windows NT-based intranet server. There are two ways to fix this problem. The first is to open the Internet applet in the Control Panel. Select the Connection page and uncheck the Connect to the Internet as Needed check box. Second, you can try using the computer name or IP address of the Internet server in place of the DNS name that you'd normally use.
- **Windows NT Crashes after a workstation issues the `PING` command:** This is a well-known problem and Microsoft is working on a solution in the form of an updated PING.EXE file. In the meantime, ensure that you issue legal-sized ping packets. Using a ping packet that's too large will overload the file server or firmware. This problem isn't limited to Windows NT servers, either. Bay Networks Inc., Galacticomm Inc., Storage Technology Corp., and Linux are issuing patches for their software as well. You can find out more information about this problem at `http://www.sophist.demon.co.uk/ping/`.

- **Printers don't work after you install the software from a Windows NT server:** Make sure that you have the Windows 95 as well as the Windows NT drivers loaded on the server. In some cases, the server will send the Windows NT drivers if you don't have the Windows 95 equivalent loaded. This particular problem occurs only if you install the printer through Network Neighborhood instead of the Printers folder.

On Your Own

Any network administrator who manages more than 10 workstations should probably consider getting a TDR for his toolkit. You'll find that this useful instrument is worth its weight in gold when it comes to finding cabling problems. You can normally get a decent TDR such as the Fluke 620 LAN CableMeter for around $750.00, although the TDRs with advanced features can cost as much as $4,500.00. If a TDR is out of your budget, you may want to consider one of the cable testers, such as the Multi-Network Cable Tester (which costs around $125.00). The only problem with this solution is that you can't detect crimped cables and a variety of other problems such as noise. This simple tester checks only continuity, miswiring, and polarization of your network cables. In addition, the Multi-Network Cable Tester will require coordination between two testers, whereas a TDR allows one-person operation. Specialized Products Company sells a wide range of network test equipment, including these two cable troubleshooting aids. You can reach them at: (800) 866-5353.

If you have a NetWare file server on your network, spend some time learning how to use the diagnostic tools that it provides. For example, if you have a NetWare 4.x server, you'll want to spend some time working with the NWAdmin utility. Make sure that you know how to use these utility programs before you actually need them to troubleshoot a network problem.

Perform a security review of your file server. (It doesn't matter what kind of network you have in this case, although a review of share-level security on a Windows 95 workstation set up to meet the needs of a workgroup will certainly take a lot less time than performing a full audit of a Novell NetWare WAN.) Make sure that every user has the rights she needs to get her work done. At the same time, make sure that you plug any security breaches that may have occurred as you changed the system setup. Be sure to review any loss of rights with the user before you actually make the required changes.

If you own a peer-to-peer network that's experiencing even minor problems, try looking at the configuration for each machine on the network. Do they all use the same configuration? If not, is there a good reason why they don't (such as hardware)? Spend some time trying to figure out where the source of the problem is by using the troubleshooting guidelines discussed in the "Peer-to-Peer Network Connections" section of the chapter.

Check your Windows NT server to see whether you have all the right printer drivers available. Make sure that you have both Windows 95 and Windows NT versions available for download. You'll also want to download any updated drivers for your Internet server. Download the new PING.EXE utility as soon as Microsoft makes it available, if you use your Windows NT server as a company intranet.

VIII Microsoft Plus!

28

Microsoft Plus!

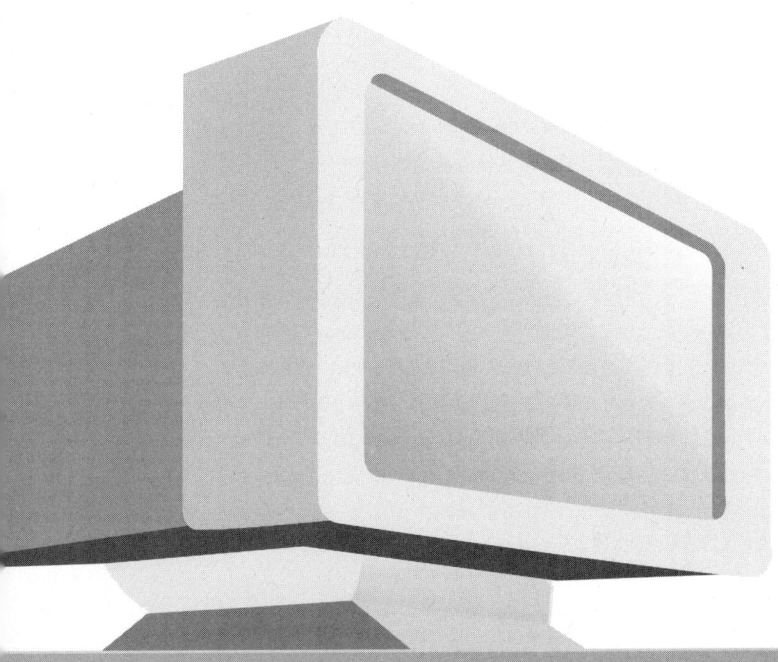

Microsoft calls its Plus! package a companion to Windows 95 for computers with 486 or Pentium processors. Plus! makes a good companion indeed. With Microsoft Plus! added to your machine, you can do the following:

- Keep your desktop lively and interesting through visual and other multimedia enhancements.
- Automatically perform system maintenance in the background while you work or even while you sleep.
- Add powerful enhancements to the standard disk compression facilities provided by Windows 95.
- Bring data and information from around the world to your desktop through its network and Internet features.
- Sit back and relax with a game of 3D Pinball.

This chapter discusses each of these features in detail.

Installing Microsoft Plus!

Installing Microsoft Plus! couldn't be easier, but you must have a computer with a 486 or Pentium processor. The features are simply too powerful to run on lesser machines. To take advantage of many of the features, your computer must have a graphics card that can support at least 256 colors.

Tip: The number of colors displayed by a graphics card usually depends on the display resolution it's set at. The resolution is the number of pixels, or the smallest unit of light, displayed across your monitor from left to right and from top to bottom. For instance, some cards can display only 16 colors at a resolution of 1024 × 756 pixels but can display 256 colors at a resolution of 640 × 480 pixels.

It's desirable to have a high-color graphics card so that you can have dazzling graphics on your desktop. You also deprive yourself if you don't have a sound card and speakers (which would result in pinball without a lot of noise).

Installing Microsoft Plus! from CD-ROM

To install Microsoft Plus!, put the CD in your CD-ROM drive. You'll hear a soothing jingle (if you have a sound card) as Microsoft Plus! for Windows 95 automatically launches. The window displays three buttons floating in clouds. Click on the Install Plus! button at the top right, as shown in Figure 28.1, and follow the instructions.

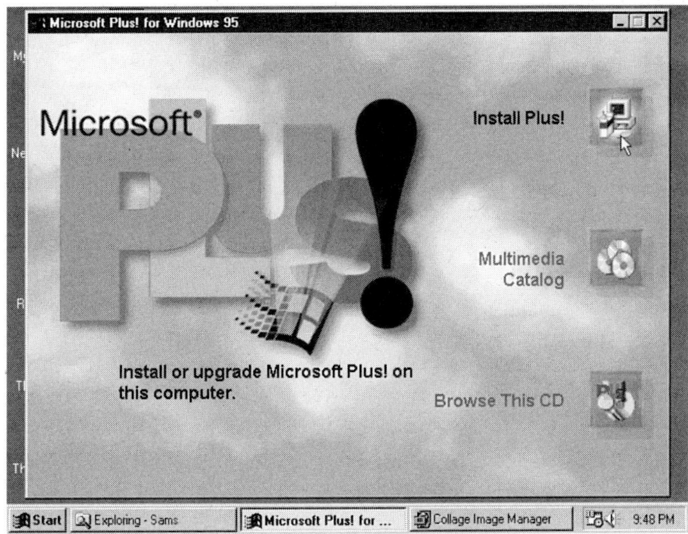

Figure 28.1.
From the Microsoft Plus! splash screen, you can click on a button to install Plus!, get information on other Microsoft products, or browse the Plus! CD.

CD auto-launch doesn't work on some computers. In this case, simply run SETUP.EXE from the Plus! CD. For instance, if your CD-ROM drive is drive D:, you would do the following:

1. Choose Start | Run.
2. Type `d:\setup` in the Open text box.
3. Click OK.

Alternatively, you can double-click the My Computer icon on your desktop and then double-click CD-ROM Drive, which should show up as a Plus! icon. Double-click the setup.exe icon to start the Plus! setup.

Installing Microsoft Plus! from Floppy Disks

To install Microsoft Plus! from floppy disks, insert disk 1, the setup disk, into a disk drive and run SETUP.EXE from that disk. For instance, if you inserted disk 1 into drive A:, you would then do the following:

1. Choose Start | Run.
2. Type `a:\setup` in the Open text box.
3. Click OK.

Alternatively, you can double-click the My Computer icon on your desktop and then double-click A: Drive, which should show up as a 3½-inch floppy icon. Double-click the setup.exe icon to start the Plus! setup.

Using the Typical or Custom Installation

The Microsoft Plus! for Windows 95 Setup will ask you to select the typical or custom installation. The typical installation, the choice for most people, simply installs all components. There are a few instances in which you might want to use the custom installation.

If there's a specific option you know you won't use and you don't want it to take up space on your desktop or disk drive, use the custom installation so that you can deselect that option. In the Microsoft Plus! for Windows 95 - Custom dialog box shown in Figure 28.2, click the check box to the left of each option in the Options list that you want to deselect. If you're running low on disk space, you might need to do this so that you can load only the features that you need the most.

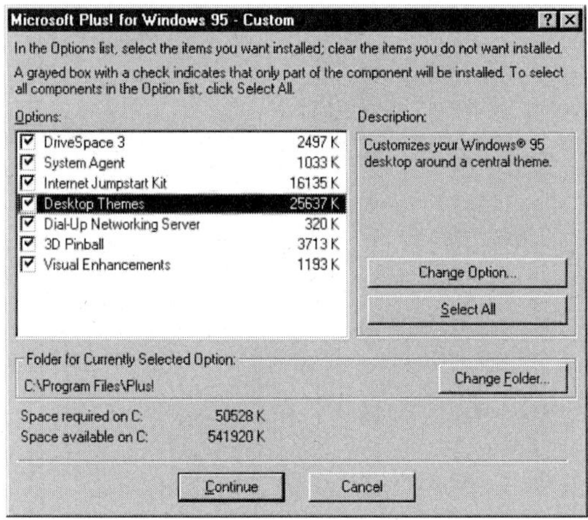

Figure 28.2.
All options in the Options list are selected by default. To deselect an option, click the check box to the left of the option.

Table 28.1 lists the Plus! options you can select or deselect during the Plus! custom installation.

Table 28.1. Microsoft Plus! options available during custom installation.

Option	*Disk Space Required*	*Description*
DriveSpace 3	2497KB	Provides enhanced disk compression, including Compression Agent, to create more hard disk space.
System Agent	1033KB	Runs system maintenance tasks and other programs at regularly scheduled times or when your system is idle.

Option	Disk Space Required	Description
Internet Jumpstart Kit	16135KB	Makes configuring access to the Microsoft Network, the Internet, and Internet Mail quick and easy.
Desktop Themes	25637KB	Customizes your Windows 95 desktop around a central theme.
Dial-Up Networking Server	320KB	Configures your computer server so that you can dial into it from another location.
3D Pinball	3713KB	The classic arcade game, including great graphics and sound.
Visual Enhancements	1193KB	Enhancements for high-end systems to maximize graphics capabilities.

When you select the Desktop Themes or the Visual Enhancements option, you're given the opportunity to see additional options by clicking the Change Option button. When you click the Change Option button while Desktop Themes is selected, the list of options shown in Figure 28.3 appears. Table 28.2 lists all the Desktop Themes options.

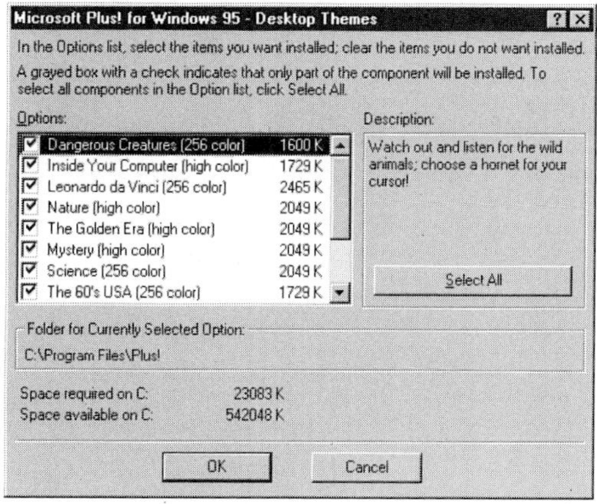

Figure 28.3.
You might want to deselect some of the Desktop Themes options if you have limited disk space or if your video driver can display only 256 colors.

Table 28.2. Microsoft Plus! Desktop Themes you can install during custom installation.

Desktop Theme	*Disk Space Required*	*Description*
Dangerous Creatures (256 color)	1600KB	This wild-animal motif focuses on mountain lions, poisonous frogs, hornets, and so on.
Inside Your Computer (high color)	1729KB	This theme revolves around motherboards, chips, and other computer guts.
Leonardo da Vinci (256 color)	2465KB	The Master's work becomes part of your desktop, animated cursors, and an animated screen saver.
Nature (high color)	2049KB	This theme includes docile animated caterpillars crawling around in leaves.
The Golden Era (high color)	2049KB	This theme is set in the 1940s industrial, art deco "Golden Age of Radio."
Mystery (high color)	2049KB	Microsoft writes "Col. Batwing did in your computer's haunted library with the knife!" What does it mean?
Science (256 color)	2049KB	This theme covers the physical sciences. You'll find atoms, stars, and beakers.
The 60's USA (256 color)	1729KB	This theme features tie-dyed wallpaper, love bugs, and revolving peace signs. What would the hippies think if they saw this?
Sports (256 color)	2602KB	Every time you click the mouse button, you return a serve. When your screen saver appears, football strategy is scrawled on the blackboard.
Travel (high color)	2272KB	Trains, planes, and cars move around to take you virtually anywhere.
Windows 95 (256 color)	2908KB	This theme is full of Windows 95 images.
More Windows (high color)	3018KB	The high-color Windows 95 desktop.

When you click the Change Option button while Visual Enhancement Options is selected, the list of options shown in Figure 28.4 appears.

Table 28.3 lists all the Visual Enhancement options. You'll probably pick-and-choose items in these lists if you need to conserve disk space or if you don't have video hardware that can handle high-color graphics.

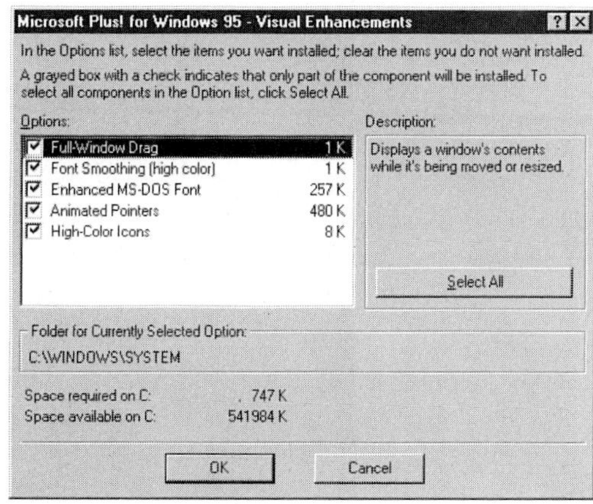

Figure 28.4.
Some Visual Enhancement objects require high-color capacity, but none use much disk space. Deselect an option if you can't use it.

Table 28.3. Microsoft Plus! visual enhancements you can install during custom installation.

Visual Enhancement	*Disk Space Required*	*Description*
Full Window Drag	1KB	Displays a window's contents while it's being moved or resized.
Font Smoothing (high color)	1KB	Smoothes jagged screen fonts to improve their appearance and legibility.
Enhanced MS-DOS Font	257KB	Uses the more-legible Lucida font for the MS-DOS Command Prompt window.
Animated Pointers	480KB	Additional animated mouse pointers.
High-Color Icons	8KB	Replaces the standard Windows 95 icons with high-color icons.

You might have hardware limitations that make some Plus! features irrelevant to your system. For instance, my laptop displays only 256 colors; therefore, it makes no sense to load the high-color Desktop Themes provided by Plus!. In this instance, I selected custom installation and deselected all high-color themes from setup, thus saving about 18MB in disk space.

Note: As this book was going to press, I received the following new, undocumented information directly from Microsoft about high-color themes. If your video handles only 256 colors, high-color images in high-color Desktop Themes are dithered down to 256 colors. When images are dithered, they are filled in with fewer colors by using the closest matching colors available. However, icons can't be dithered. So, under 256-color video, you'll get 16-color icons and 256-color dithered versions of the 16-bit (high-color) bitmaps.

Running System Maintenance Tasks at Night

The next thing Microsoft Plus! setup asks is whether you want to run system maintenance tasks at night (see Figure 28.5). Plus! comes with a tool, System Agent, that will run system maintenance tasks at preset times. If you usually leave your computer on overnight, you should answer Yes when setup asks if you want to run system maintenance tasks at night so that maintenance programs will be run while you're not using the computer. This avoids any computer slowdown during your workday. Otherwise, if you shut your computer down at night, answer No, and system maintenance will be scheduled during the day. Of course, you can specify your own times to run each system maintenance utility. See the section "System Agent."

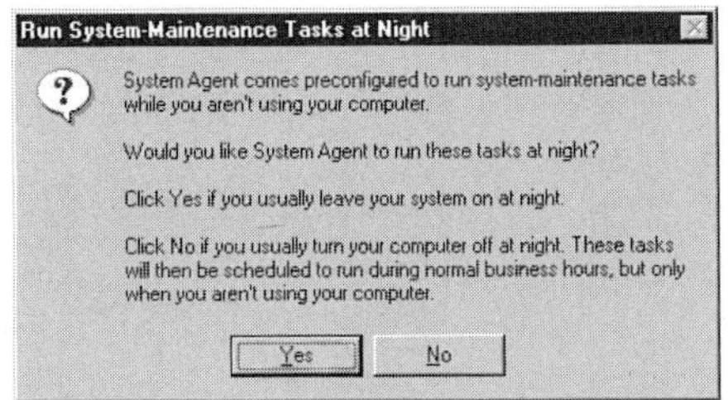

Figure 28.5.
If you leave your computer on all the time, you'll like the option of having Microsoft Plus! set up preset nighttime system maintenance for you.

If There's Not Enough Disk Space

Setup then checks for the necessary disk space. If there's not enough space, the Microsoft Plus! for Windows 95 dialog box shows you a list box of the options selected and lets you change them. The first options to consider deselecting are those that you know you'll never use. For instance, if you know you'll never use disk compression, deselect DriveSpace 3, and you'll save nearly 2.5MB of disk space. However, if you're tight on disk space, disk compression might be just the ticket. You might want to exit the Plus! setup and compress your drive (see the section "Disk Compression with DriveSpace 3"). Now, with all your new drive space, you can run the Plus! setup again without deselecting anything.

The Internet Setup Wizard

If you told Plus! setup to install Internet facilities, you'll be taken through the Internet Setup Wizard at this time during the initial installation process. The first page of the Internet Setup Wizard will appear, as shown in Figure 28.6. For details on using the Internet Setup Wizard, see the section "Internet Setup Wizard."

Figure 28.6.
The first page of the Internet Setup Wizard greets you after Microsoft Plus! setup copies most of the Plus! files to your disk.

Choosing a Desktop Theme

Your final task while installing Plus! is to choose a Desktop Theme. Use the Themes drop-down list in the upper-left corner of the Desktop Themes dialog box, shown in Figure 28.7, to select a theme. Be sure to select high-color themes only if you have your display set to 16-bit color (high color).

Figure 28.7.
The Desktop Themes dialog box.

When you select a theme, you'll see a preview of how your desktop will look in a large area under the Theme drop-down list. Figure 28.7 shows a preview of the 256-color theme The 60's USA. When you find a theme you like, click the OK button to complete the setup. Don't worry if you're not sure that the theme you chose is your favorite. It's easy to change themes later, or even create your own themes.

The Desktop Environment

The new desktop environment in Windows 95 is considerably improved, both functionally and aesthetically. Plus! adds many features that allow you to customize almost every aspect of your desktop environment to match your mood, your interests, and your artistic tastes.

Desktop Themes

Desktop Themes are complete, prepackaged desktop environments designed with a particular theme, or subject, in mind. Plus! gives you 12 Desktop Themes (listed in Table 28.2) plus a Windows default.

Naturally, you must have the right hardware on your computer to use a theme. If you have a graphics card capable of high color (16-bit color), you can use any of the 12 themes. Otherwise, you must have a card capable of 256 colors (8-bit color) to run the six 256-color themes and the Windows default.

Each theme is more than just a background image. If you've used previous versions of Windows, you're familiar with wallpaper. To spruce up the old Windows desktop, you would find a bitmap that you liked and add it to the desktop—the whole screen area behind all the windows. If you were especially determined to customize the look of your desktop environment, you might have added custom icons to certain programs. In Windows 95, virtually every aspect of your desktop environment can be modified, and each theme does just that.

A theme changes the entire look and sound of your desktop. (Yes, even sound, if you have a sound card.) Each theme has its own desktop wallpaper and icons, but it goes much further than that. Each theme also has a custom screen saver, sound events, mouse pointers, colors, font names and styles, and font and window sizes. Many of the pointers are animated, and all the screen savers have animation and sound.

If you feel that your creativity is stifled by prepackaged themes, never fear. You can customize every aspect of your desktop. Creating a desktop that's completely your own takes a bit of work, but once you've designed it, you can save it as your very own Desktop Theme.

Selecting a Theme

Plus! setup asks you to select a Desktop Theme. If you canceled theme selection during setup or if you want to change your Desktop Theme, you must open the Control Panel. Choose Start | Settings | Control Panel. Double-click the Desktop Themes icon in the Control Panel. The Desktop Themes dialog box shown in Figure 28.8 opens and shows what the current theme looks like.

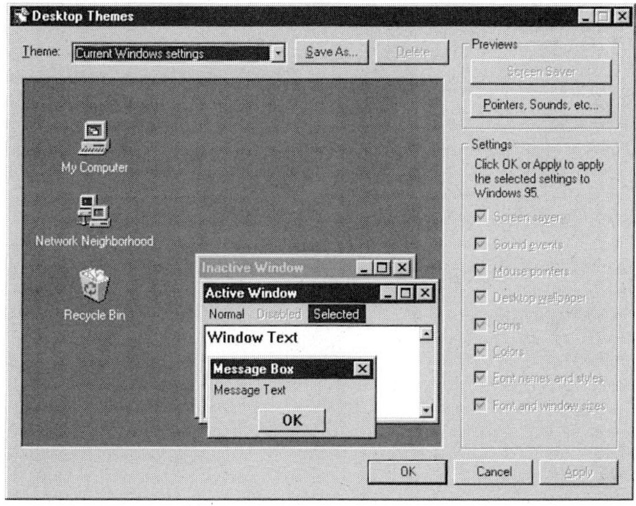

Figure 28.8.
Current Windows Settings is listed in the Theme drop-down list. Beneath this list is a window showing what the current theme looks like.

You can select from the themes listed in the Themes drop-down list at the upper-left corner of the Desktop Themes dialog box. When you select a new theme, it's loaded into the preview window, as shown in Figure 28.9. In this case, the Sports theme is selected.

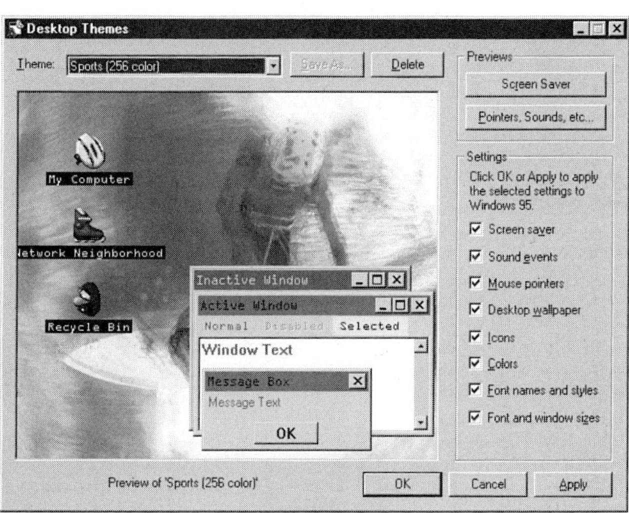

Figure 28.9.
Sports is selected in the Theme drop-down list. A preview of this theme is shown in the area below the Theme drop-down list.

If you like what you see in the preview, click OK to apply this theme to your desktop and to close the Desktop Themes dialog box. If you prefer to keep the Desktop Themes dialog box open after you apply the theme, click the Apply button. Otherwise, try another theme or, if you decide that you don't want to change your Desktop Theme, click the Cancel button.

Customizing Desktop Themes

There are two ways you can create your own customized desktop theme. Relatively minor adjustments to existing themes can be done inside the Desktop Themes dialog box. For more ambitious customization jobs, you'll want to work with most of the tabs in the Display Properties dialog box and perhaps use the Desktop Themes dialog box to give your new Desktop Theme a name. Using either method, you can customize virtually every aspect of your desktop environment.

Note: To open the Display Properties dialog box, right-click the Desktop icon and select Properties from the context menu.

Using the Desktop Themes Dialog Box

The desktop's current settings are always listed in the Desktop Themes dialog box as Current Windows Settings in the Theme drop-down list. After you select and apply a theme such as Dangerous Creatures to your desktop, all your settings will reflect those specified by the Dangerous Creatures theme and will be saved as the Current Windows Settings. You'll see in a moment why this is an important step.

Suppose that you like the Dangerous Creatures theme that you've applied to your desktop, but the colors are just too dark for your laptop computer (see Figure 28.10).

Figure 28.10.
The Dangerous Creatures Desktop Theme uses dark colors. (Of course, in this black-and-white book, the colors in these schemes are relatively indistinguishable. On-screen, you'll notice the difference.)

By contrast, the color scheme in the Leonardo da Vinci theme looks just right (see Figure 28.11).

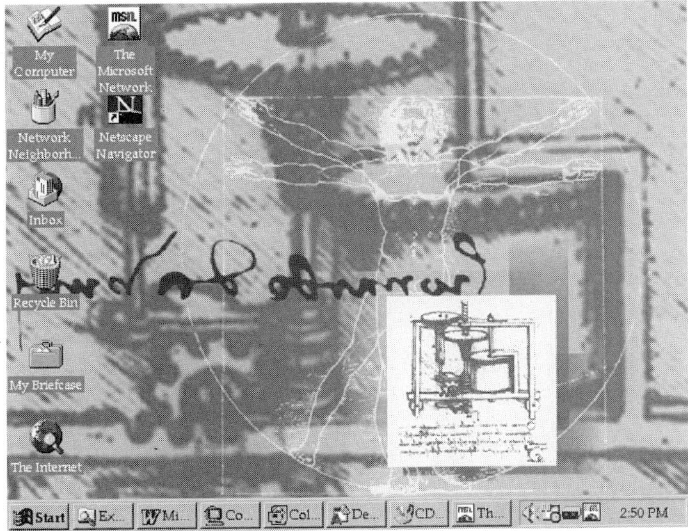

Figure 28.11.
The Leonardo da Vinci Desktop Theme uses relatively light colors.

You can remedy this problem easily. Open the Desktop Themes dialog box. Notice that the Theme drop-down list says Current Windows settings (see Figure 28.12). Notice also that the preview window shows the same desktop configuration as the Dangerous Creatures theme would if you had selected it.

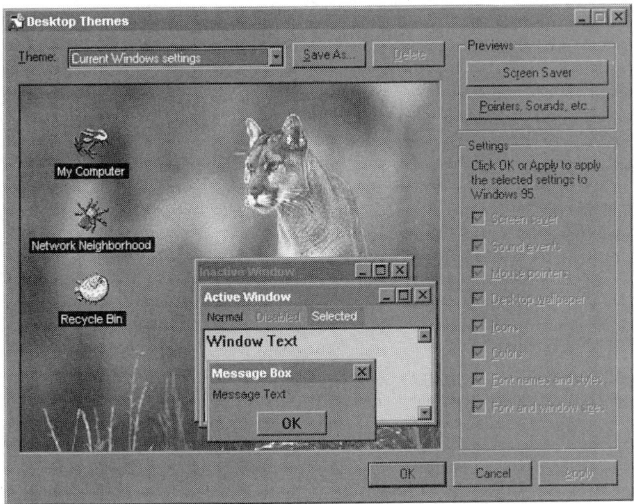

Figure 28.12.
The Current Windows Settings are now the same as if you had selected the Dangerous Creatures theme.

To change the color scheme in your Current Windows settings to the color scheme in the Leonardo da Vinci theme, select the Leonardo da Vinci theme in the list box, as shown in Figure 28.13.

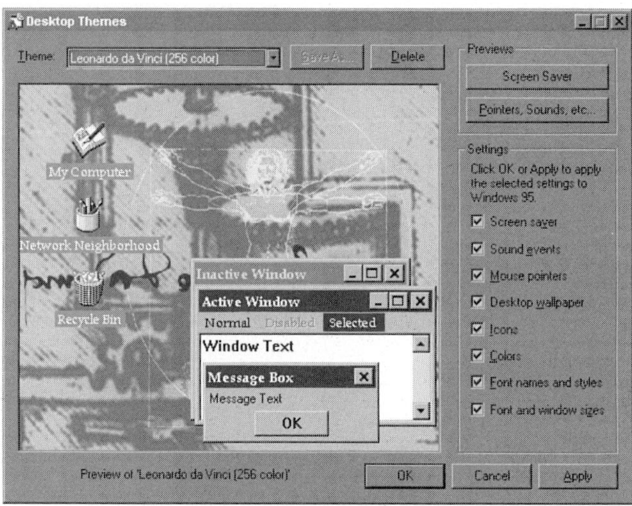

Figure 28.13.
The Leonardo da Vinci theme.

Notice that the preview window shows the full Leonardo da Vinci theme. Your Current Windows Settings would change to reflect all the settings in the Leonardo da Vinci theme if you were to click the Apply button or the OK button now. However, all you want to change in the Current Windows settings is the color scheme. Notice the Settings check boxes on the right side of the dialog box. All of them are checked. Click the check box to the left of Desktop Wallpaper. The Leonardo da Vinci wallpaper disappears, and the wallpaper specified in your Current Windows Settings, the picture of a mountain lion, appears (see Figure 28.14).

Figure 28.14.
The Leonardo da Vinci theme with wallpaper deselected.

Only the selected settings—the settings with check marks next to them—are applied to your Current Windows Settings. Since you want to change only the color scheme, remove the check marks next to all of the settings except Colors, as shown in Figure 28.15.

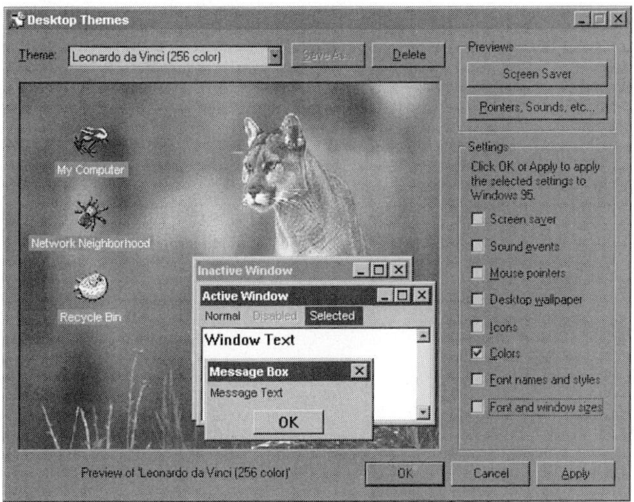

Figure 28.15.
The Leonardo da Vinci theme with every setting deselected except Colors.

The preview window should now look a lot like the Dangerous Creatures theme, except that the colors are from the Leonardo da Vinci theme. Click the Apply button, and your Current Windows Settings now include the new, lighter colors.

You might be very happy with your new creation, but you're also eager to try other combinations. If you simply apply new settings to your Current Windows Settings, you'll lose any particular combination that previously existed unless it's saved as a Desktop Theme. You can create a new theme from the Current Windows Settings at any time. Select Current Windows Settings in the Theme drop-down list. Notice that the Save As button to the right of the Theme drop-down list is now activated, as shown in Figure 28.16.

To save the Current Windows Settings as a Desktop Theme, click the Save As button. The Save Theme dialog box appears, as shown in Figure 28.17. Give the theme a name—Dangerous Creatures Light (256 color), for instance—and click the Save button.

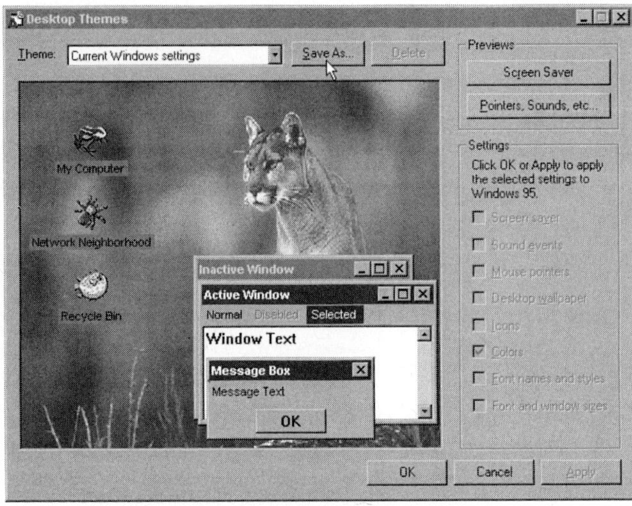

Figure 28.16.
Click the Save As button to save the Current Windows Settings.

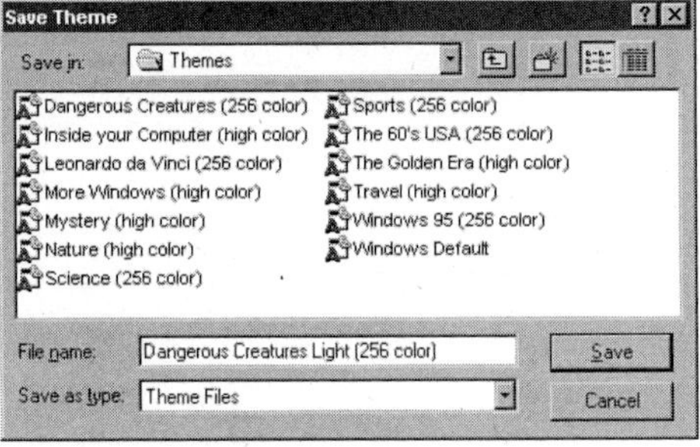

Figure 28.17.
The Save Theme dialog box.

Tip: It's a good idea to continue the naming conventions that Microsoft started and include the color requirements in parentheses after the theme's name.

When you save the new theme, it becomes the selected theme in the Theme drop-down list. Notice that the Save As button is now deactivated, but the Delete button is activated. If you don't like a theme, you can delete it by clicking the Delete button. You can save only the Current Windows Settings.

Using the Display Properties Dialog Box

You can completely customize your desktop environment by using the Desktop Themes dialog box. However, combining settings sprinkled across many or all of the existing themes can become clumsy. Also, maybe you'd like to use settings that aren't included in any existing theme. In either case, you'll want to change your Current Windows Settings by using the Display Properties dialog box.

Windows 95 allows nearly complete customization of its desktop environment without Plus!. However, there is no way to save multiple desktop environment configurations under the same user profile, and there is no way to customize the standard desktop icons without Plus!.

Note: You can create multiple desktop configurations without Microsoft Plus! by creating multiple user profiles. On a machine used by more than one person, each person can set up his desktop just the way he wants it. However, a single user must use only one desktop configuration or log on using different user IDs to save different desktop configurations. Using Microsoft Plus! allows a single user to save multiple desktop configurations under a single user profile.

Plus! adds a Plus! tab to the Display Properties dialog box, as shown in Figure 28.18. This tab lets you change the standard desktop icons to anything you like.

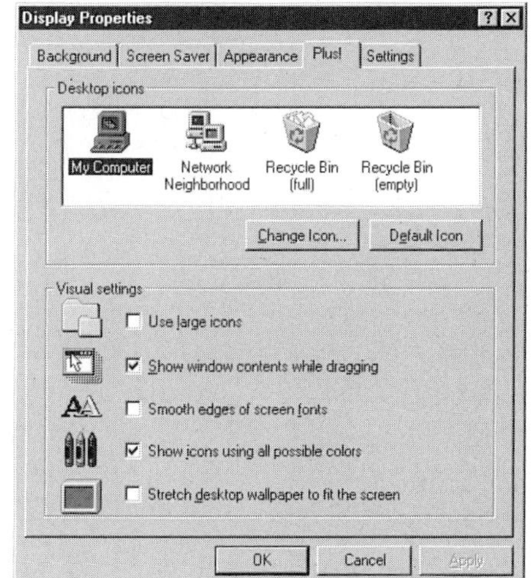

Figure 28.18.
The Display Properties dialog box lets you change the standard desktop icons and other visual enhancement options.

Note: There are other features on the Plus! tab of the Display Properties dialog box. These will be discussed later.

The four standard desktop icons are

My Computer
Network Neighborhood
Recycle Bin (full)
Recycle Bin (empty)

The Background, Screen Saver, and Appearance tab settings in the Display Properties dialog box are discussed earlier in this book. There's one major drawback to using the Background tab: You can't select from the different Plus! Desktop Theme wallpapers. You can select Plus! from the Background tab's Wallpaper list and use the wallpaper from the last Desktop Theme you selected, as shown in Figure 28.19.

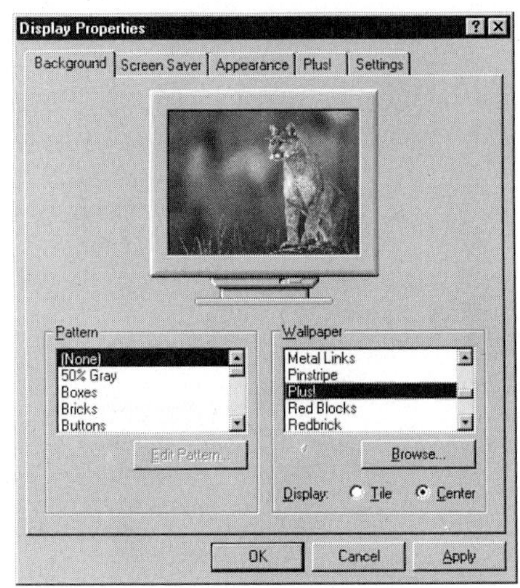

Figure 28.19.
Selecting Plus! from the Background tab's Wallpaper list selects wallpaper from the last Desktop Theme you used.

The reason for this is that Microsoft has set up the Plus! Desktop Themes in a way that saves disk space. Wallpaper for all of the themes is stored in the Program Files\Plus!\Themes folder as JPEG (.JPG) files. You'll find wallpaper listed as the theme name followed by the word "wallpaper." For instance, the Dangerous Creatures theme wallpaper is listed as "Dangerous Creatures wallpaper." When you select a Desktop Theme, the theme's JPEG wallpaper file is converted to a bitmap (.BMP) file in the Windows folder (see Figure 28.20). You can find a bitmap of the last Desktop Themes wallpaper you used as the Plus! bitmap (.BMP) file in your Windows folder.

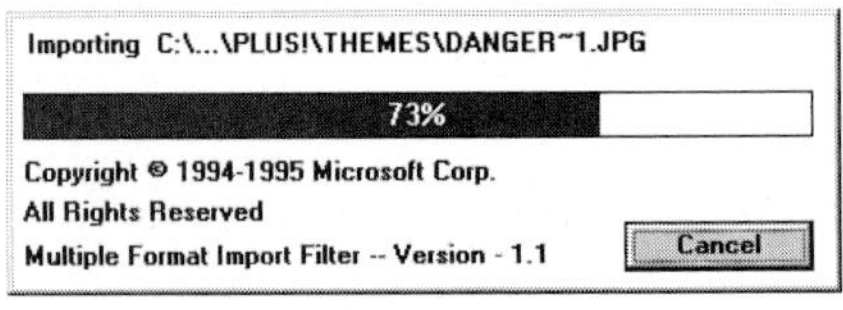

Figure 28.20.
When you switch to a new Desktop Theme in the Desktop Themes dialog box, the new wallpaper is converted from a JPEG file to a bitmap file.

Bitmap files are larger than JPEG files, but you can work with bitmap files only from the Background tab of the Display Properties dialog box. The Dangerous Creatures wallpaper JPEG file in the Program Files\Plus!\Themes folder is 97KB. The same wallpaper as the Plus! bitmap file in the Windows folder is 301KB. This saves disk space, but you'll either need to use the Desktop Themes dialog box to change between different Desktop Theme wallpapers or convert the Desktop Theme wallpaper JPEG files to bitmap files by using an image conversion program.

Create a new Desktop Theme when you've finished making your Current Windows Settings just the way you want them by using the Display Properties dialog box. Open the Desktop Themes dialog box and, with the Current Windows Settings selected in the Theme list, click the Save As button to save your new Desktop Theme.

Animated Mouse Pointers

Plus! gives you several animated mouse pointers with its Desktop Themes. Plus! also places several other animated pointers in the Windows\Cursors folder. You can access animated mouse pointers by doing the following. Open the Control Panel and double-click the Mouse applet to open the Mouse Properties dialog box. Select the Pointers tab, as shown in Figure 28.21. Select the type of mouse pointer you want to change. The Busy pointer is selected in Figure 28.21.

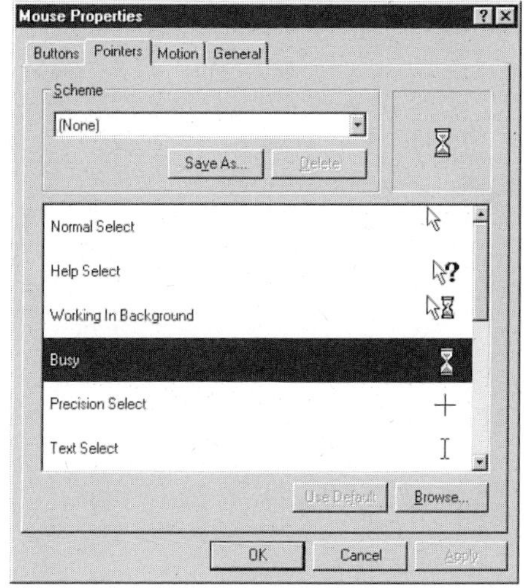

Figure 28.21.
Select the Pointers tab in the Mouse Properties dialog box to customize your mouse cursor.

Click the Browse button to open the Browse dialog box shown in Figure 28.22. The Browse dialog box opens to the Windows\Cursors folder by default. If you want to use the animated mouse cursors included in the Desktop Themes, go to the Program Files\Plus!\Themes folder in the Browse dialog box. Select a cursor. The Banana cursor is selected in Figure 28.22.

The Files of Type drop-down list says Cursors (*.ani, *.cur). You might recognize the .Cur type as the typical cursor type. The .Ani type is the animated cursor type. When you select a cursor, it is displayed in the Preview area at the lower-left corner of the Browse dialog box. If it's an animated cursor, it will be animated in the Preview area.

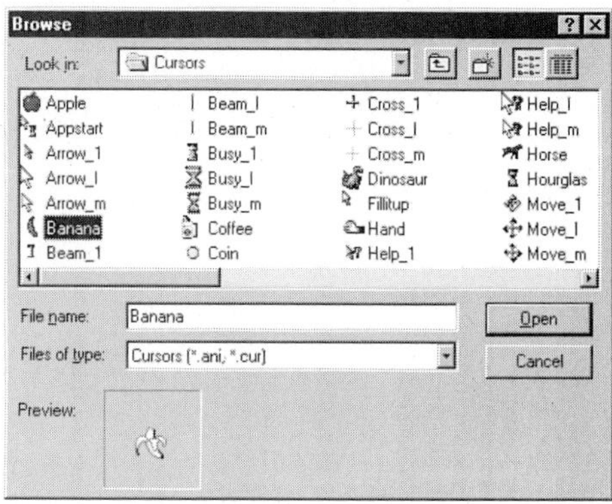

Figure 28.22.
The Browse dialog box opens to the Windows\Cursors folder. The animated Banana cursor is selected in this case.

Click the Open button. You should be back in the Mouse Properties dialog box with the new cursor added to the cursor type you selected earlier (see Figure 28.23).

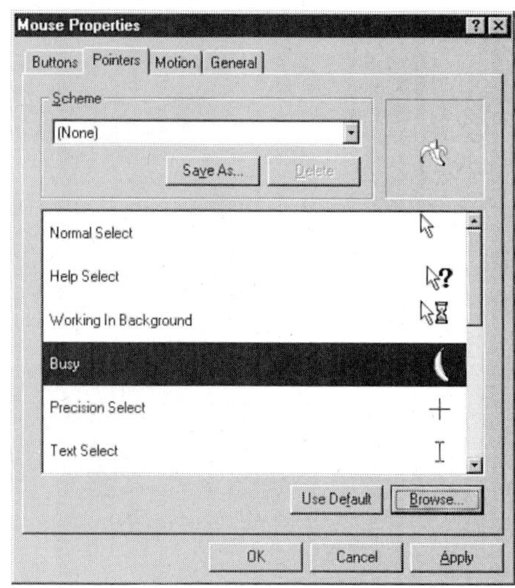

Figure 28.23.
The Busy cursor is now the animated Banana cursor.

Click the Apply button to add the cursor to your current list of cursors and to leave the dialog box open so that you can modify other cursor types. Otherwise, click OK to add the cursor to your list and exit the dialog box.

Full-Window Drag

With Plus! installed, you can set your desktop environment so that it shows a window's contents rather than just an outline when you drag or resize the window. You can find the Show Window Contents While Dragging option on the Plus! tab of the Display Properties dialog box, inside the Visual Setting frame.

Font-Smoothing

Font-smoothing gets rid of any jagged edges that large fonts sometimes display. You must be running your video at 16-bit color (high color) or better to take advantage of font-smoothing. You can find the Smooth Edges of Screen Fonts option on the Plus! tab of the Display Properties dialog box, inside the Visual Setting frame.

Stretching the Wallpaper

Have you ever found an ideal wallpaper image, only to discover that it's either too small or too large for your desktop? Plus! gives you the ability to stretch the image to fit your desktop. This setting also shrinks images to fit your desktop. You can find the Stretch Desktop Wallpaper to Fit the Screen option on the Plus! tab of the Display Properties dialog box, inside the Visual Setting frame.

Fun with 3D Pinball

I felt compelled to do extensive research on this Plus! feature, and I'm happy to report that 3D Pinball is fun. Start the program, select Options | Full Screen to hide all of that pesky work, and launch the ball using the spacebar (see Figure 28.24).

Figure 28.24.
3D Pinball in action. Just imagine all the bells, clangs, and flashing lights! You can start your copy by choosing Accessories | Games.

The left flipper is the Z key, and the right flipper is the slash (/) key. If someone tries to interrupt your game, ignore him. If he breaks your concentration, press the F3 key to pause the game and regroup, and then press F3 again to resume playing. If it's your boss, however, you can press the Esc key to quickly minimize and pause the game. Remember the work you hid beneath the game? It's prominently displayed until your boss disappears. Click the 3D Pinball button on the Taskbar, press F3, and resume playing.

What good is a game of pinball if you can't knock the machine around a bit to persuade the ball to go to the right location? The X key knocks the machine to the right, the period (.) key knocks it to the left, and the up arrow pushes it. Be careful, though! You can tilt the machine.

Program Scheduling and Monitoring Disks

If you're like me, you probably fire up a disk defragmenting program once a day and maybe test the disk for any errors while you're at it. These tasks typically take a long time to run and often make the computer unusable while they operate. Why not perform them automatically while you eat lunch or sleep? System Agent, a new program included in the Plus! package, does just that and more.

System Agent

System Agent is probably already installed and running on your machine if you've installed Plus! (unless you specifically deselected it during a custom installation). Plus! installation automatically installs System Agent preset to run the ScanDisk for Windows, Disk Defragmenter, and low-disk-space notification programs at times that are generally best for most people. During installation, you're asked if you'd like to run system maintenance tasks at night (refer to Figure 28.5). If you click Yes, ScanDisk for Windows and Disk Defragmenter will be set to run at night. Otherwise, they'll be set to run during the workday at times when you're least likely to be using the computer. Just to be sure that the system maintenance tasks don't interrupt anything, System Agent runs them only after the computer hasn't been used for a set amount of time. The low-disk-space notification program runs in the background once an hour to check on your disk space. You'll never notice that it's running unless it finds that your drive has less than the preset amount of space left on it. Then it will notify you of the space squeeze. Finally, if you compressed a drive to alleviate disk-space squeeze, Plus! will automatically schedule Compression Agent to run once a week. We'll look at each of these programs in detail later. First, let's see how System Agent does its job and how you can use it to schedule other software to run repetitive jobs.

Scheduling Backups Using System Agent

Backing up hundreds of megabytes of hard disks is something that no one enjoys doing even once, let alone on a regular schedule. How many times have you wished that you could back up everything the way you should? Do you? Of course not! This is a perfect task for the System Agent to perform.

Backing up files to floppy disks requires someone to remove filled disks and enter fresh, empty disks into the drive, so a mass storage device is the one special hardware requirement for automated backups. These include tapes and WORM drives. (A WORM drive writes once and reads many times from its storage medium.)

Using Backup is covered in detail in Chapter 9. You'll need to define backup sets and how often you want to run each backup set. You'll also need to set a time and day or days on which you want to run the backup. Simply build a backup set for each type of scheduled backup you want.

Scheduling a New Program in System Agent

After you've defined your backup sets, you can automate the backup process using System Agent. Open System Agent by double-clicking the System Agent icon on the right side of the Taskbar. Open the Program menu and click Schedule a New Program to open the dialog box shown in Figure 28.25.

Figure 28.25.
Add a program to System Agent by using the Schedule a New Program dialog box.

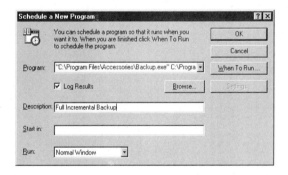

In the Program box, type

```
"C:\Program Files\Accessories\Backup.exe" C:\Program Files\Accessories\setname.set
```

where `setname.set` is the name you assigned to the backup set. Be sure to include the quotation marks.

Fill in the Description box with an easy-to-understand description of your backup set, as shown in Figure 28.25. Click the When To Run button on the right to schedule the backup. The Change Schedule dialog box shown in Figure 28.26 will appear.

Tip: Wait Until I Haven't Used My Computer for *x* Minutes is a handy feature supplied in the Change Schedule dialog box. Click the check box next to this feature and fill in the amount of time. System Agent will run the program at the scheduled time. However, if you're using the computer when the program was scheduled to run, System Agent waits until you stop using it for the amount of time you specify before it starts the scheduled program.

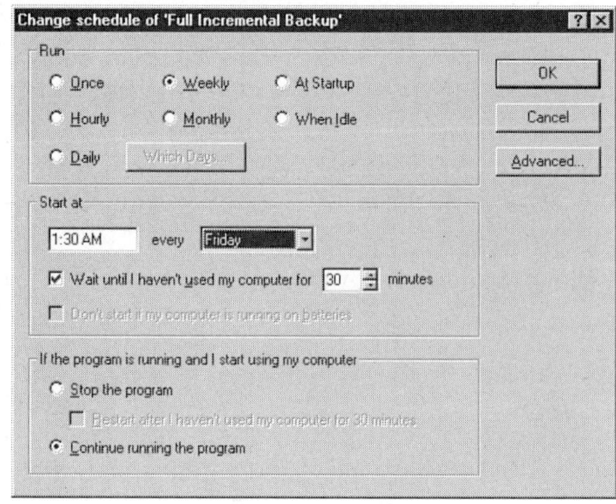

Figure 28.26.
Select the times and days that you want Backup to run a particular backup set in the Change Schedule dialog box.

Click OK. Repeat these steps for every backup set that you want to schedule.

Tip: Making sure that you have a complete backup of each drive is important. However, you probably won't want to back up every file repeatedly. I find that the best approach is to do a complete backup of a drive and then have System Agent periodically run an incremental backup of the entire drive. How often will depend on how quickly changes accumulate on your drives.

The Low-Disk-Space Notification Program

System Agent runs the low-disk-space notification program in the background while you work to alert you to any drive that might be getting full. Its default setting upon installation is to run once an hour.

Using Your Computer as a Dial-Up Server

Windows 95 wasn't built to be a powerful dedicated server. If that's what you want, you need Windows NT Server. Nevertheless, there might be times when you'd like to access data on your computer while in another town or country, especially if you're on the road with your laptop. Alternatively, you might want to give friends or colleagues access to certain files or directories on your machine. The Plus! pack provides a program that allows telephone access to your computer. Of course, you must have a modem.

Setting Up Dial-Up Server

You can find the Dial-Up Server settings by opening the Dial-Up Networking window. Double-click the My Computer desktop icon and then double-click the Dial-Up Networking folder (or choose Start | Programs | Accessories | Dial-Up Networking). In the Dial-Up Networking window, open the Connections menu and select Dial-Up Server to open the Dial-Up Server dialog box. To allow dial-up access, select the Allow Caller Access radio button. You must share any folders that you want to give dial-up access to (see Chapter 23), and don't forget to leave the computer on!

Disk Compression with DriveSpace 3

Unlike with some previous versions of Windows, disk compression in Windows 95 is very reliable and is an excellent option to use when you need more disk space—and who doesn't? I especially like to use disk compression on my laptop computer. My 0.5GB drive gives me nearly 1.5 gigabytes of space when I use the compression facilities that come with Windows 95 and the Plus! pack. Windows 95 comes with the disk compression program DriveSpace. Plus! upgrades the standard DriveSpace to DriveSpace 3. Additionally, it adds the compression utility Compression Agent, which is run by System Agent when you're not using your computer, to optimize disk space and performance.

There are several advantages to using DriveSpace 3 disk compression instead of the standard DriveSpace. Perhaps the most important advantage is that you can create compressed drives larger than 512MB. DriveSpace 3 supports compressed drives of up to two gigabytes. With the ever-growing size of programs, this is a welcome capability. DriveSpace 3 uses all the free space on your drive, even if it's fragmented. The standard DriveSpace can use only contiguous, unfragmented disk space to compress files. DriveSpace 3 allows you to achieve maximum compression, called *UltraPack compression*, on files you don't use often, further increasing storage efficiency. Finally, DriveSpace 3 is built to work with Compression Agent to maximize your storage efficiency and performance.

Compressing a Drive with DriveSpace 3

Compressing a drive with DriveSpace 3 is essentially the same as compressing it with the standard DriveSpace, except that you get the advantages of the extra features just discussed. If you want to create a compressed drive larger than 512MB, you must use DriveSpace 3. This substantial increase in capacity is welcome, but, sadly, there is still a limit—2GB. This means that you can compress up to between half a gigabyte and one gigabyte of uncompressed drive space. This number is sure to be closer to half a gigabyte since, in my experience, DriveSpace 3 really gives you about three times your original disk space.

Upgrading a Compressed Drive with DriveSpace 3

Like compressing an uncompressed drive with DriveSpace 3, upgrading a compressed drive using DriveSpace 3 is essentially the same as upgrading it with the standard DriveSpace. The exception is that you must also upgrade drives compressed with the standard DriveSpace to get the added features of DriveSpace 3.

Balancing Disk Space and Speed with DriveSpace 3

DriveSpace 3 allows you to fine-tune how your drive is compressed, giving you control over trade-offs between disk space and operation speed. Three compression types used by DriveSpace 3 form the basis of these adjustments: standard compression, HiPack compression, and no compression at all.

Standard Compression

With standard compression, DriveSpace 3 typically compresses files to just over half of their uncompressed size. A special Plus! feature of standard compression is that more of the disk drive is searched for repetitive data. This results in better compression ratios and relatively fast disk reads and writes.

HiPack Compression

With HiPack compression, files are typically compressed to just under half their uncompressed size. Reading data from HiPack compressed files is relatively fast. However, writing data to HiPack compressed files is relatively slow.

Tip: You get the highest compression ratios from UltraPack compression. Only Compression Agent can pack your files using UltraPack. See the later section "Compression Agent."

Balancing Optimization and Compression with DriveSpace 3

Nearly everyone will want to optimize his or her compressed drive for a balance between speed and drive space. Nevertheless, it's possible to fully optimize your compressed drive for either speed *or* space. We'll consider these extreme optimizations first, because they're easy to understand and they demonstrate the principles behind disk compression optimization well.

Compression Optimized for Speed

If you want your machine to run at the maximum speed possible, then you want your programs to load files from disk as rapidly as they can, and you want to optimize your compressed drive for speed. That's silly, you say—everyone wants that! Right you are. The "gotcha" is that, in this extreme example, you don't care at all about disk space. Presumably, you have plenty of it. To maximize speed, configure DriveSpace 3 to save files uncompressed. That's right—compress your drives with DriveSpace 3 set so that it doesn't compress your files! Naturally, this is the fastest compression option. It also seems a bit silly. However, we'll see later that there are times when this setting can be useful.

To compress a drive for maximum speed, open DriveSpace 3. Select Advanced | Settings to open the Disk Compression Settings dialog box shown in Figure 28.27. Select the No Compression (Fastest) radio button. Click OK and compress the drive in the usual way.

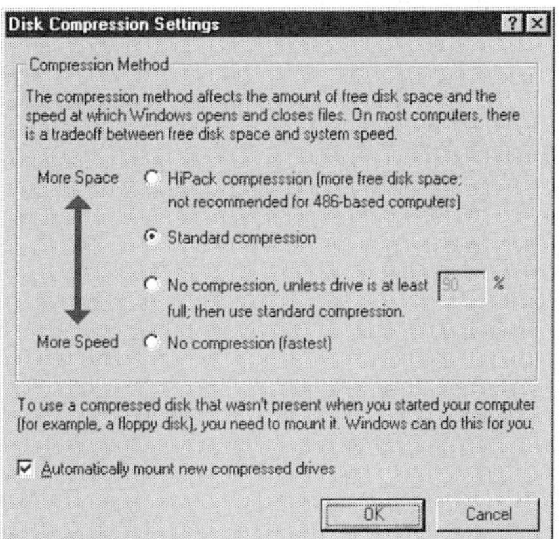

Figure 28.27.
Select DriveSpace 3 compression features in the Disk Compression Settings dialog box.

Compression Optimized for Drive Space

If you're trying to squeeze a lot of program and data bytes onto a small disk drive, you'll want to maximize your disk compression with drive space. You can set DriveSpace 3 to maximize drive space while, for the most part, ignoring performance considerations. Of course, you'll take a performance hit if you do this, but it might be worth it if you need the space. Actually, the default DriveSpace 3 compression method compresses every file. However, it compresses them using standard compression, which should show a small (if even noticeable) performance hit. You can squeeze even more space onto your drive if you select the HiPack compression method. You should compress your entire drive with HiPack compression only if you desperately need the space, because this setting causes a substantial slowdown in writing data to the drive. You might find HiPack tolerable if your machine has a Pentium or faster central processing unit.

To compress a drive for maximum space with very little degradation in performance, open DriveSpace 3. Select Advanced | Settings to open the Disk Compression Settings dialog box (refer to Figure 28.27). Select the Standard Compression radio button. Click OK and compress the drive in the usual way.

To compress a drive for maximum space while throwing performance concerns to the wind, select the HiPack Compression radio button instead.

Compression Optimized for a Balance Between Speed and Drive Space

I like this option. Balance always seems to be a good thing; extremes often get us into trouble. DriveSpace 3 lets you have a balance between speed and drive space that best suits you and your computer hardware. It works like this: You tell DriveSpace 3 to use the uncompressed method on files until a specified percentage of the drive, predefined by you, fills up. Then DriveSpace 3 begins compressing files, using standard compression. The default is set so that when 90 percent of the compressed drive is filled, DriveSpace 3 begins compressing files. However, you can fill in your own percentage. At the 90 percent setting, DriveSpace 3 is optimized to favor speed over space until it's absolutely necessary to have more room. In contrast, if you set it to 10 percent, you'd be optimizing DriveSpace 3 in favor of drive space over speed.

To compress a drive for a balance between space and performance, open DriveSpace 3. Select Advanced | Settings. In the Disk Compression Settings dialog box, select the No Compression, Unless Drive Is at Least 90% Full radio button. Modify the percentage if you wish. Click OK and compress the drive in the usual way.

Compression Agent

Using Compression Agent can significantly increase the storage efficiency and performance of your drive compressed by DriveSpace 3. As we've seen, DriveSpace 3 compresses uncompressed drives, upgrades drives previously compressed using DoubleSpace or DriveSpace, and sets the compression method of saving new files to disk, allowing you to specify some optimizations for drive space and performance. Compression Agent picks up where DriveSpace 3 leaves off and works with DriveSpace 3 to optimize drive space and performance better than DriveSpace 3 can on its own.

In particular, Compression Agent scans your compressed drive and looks at each file for the time it was last accessed and how it is compressed. If the file is seldom accessed, Compression Agent will compress it at the highest compression ratio—UltraPack compression. Only Compression Agent can compress files using UltraPack. If the file is used often but has been compressed, Compression Agent will probably uncompress it to increase system performance.

DriveSpace 3 sets the standard compression method, as discussed earlier. Compression Agent optimizes the compression method set through DriveSpace 3 by checking individual file usage against compression type.

The Compression Tab

Plus! adds a Compression tab to your disk drive's Properties dialog box. The Compression tab contains different information, depending on whether the drive is compressed or not. If your drive isn't compressed, the Compression tab shows you the amount of used and free space currently on your drive and how much you would have of each if you compressed the drive (see Figure 28.28).

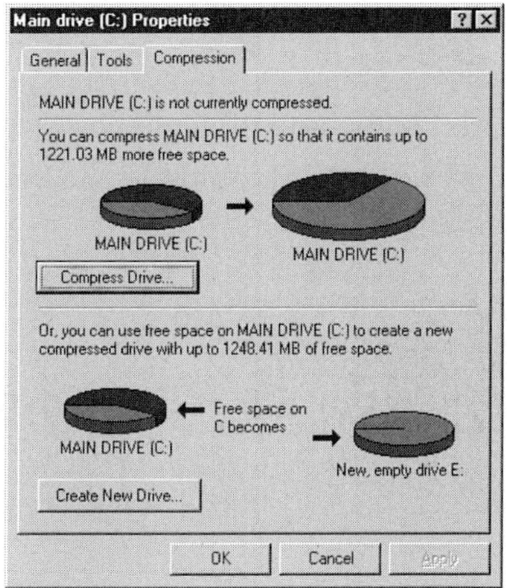

Figure 28.28.
The Compression tab in the Properties dialog box of an uncompressed drive.

It also tells you the approximate size of a new drive that could be built by compressing your drive's remaining free space. This is the perfect option if you want to compress files on your boot drive but don't want to risk having your whole boot drive compressed. Buttons on this tab allow you to compress the drive or make a new compressed drive. If your drive is compressed, the Compression tab is filled with statistics on the percentage of files compressed, with various compression types and the amount of disk space you've gained.

When you select the Compression tab from the Properties dialog box of a compressed disk drive, all sorts of drive statistics are calculated, as shown in Figure 28.29. Beware: This can take a while. You can cancel the operation if you want, however.

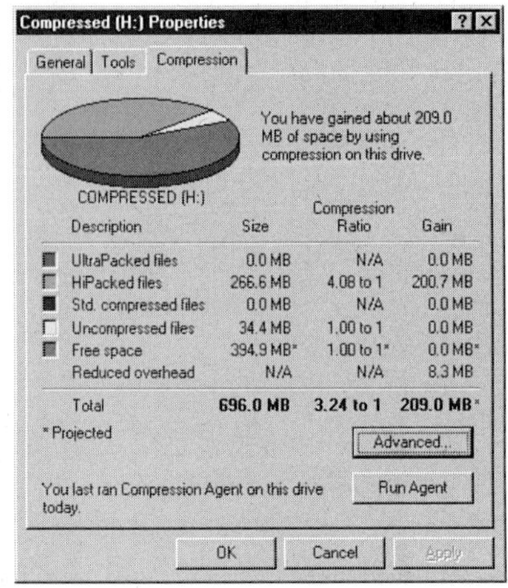

Figure 28.29.
You can obtain information about your compressed drive in the Compression tab of the Properties dialog box.

The Compression tab will tell you how many megabytes of files are taken up by each compression type on your drive. It will also tell you the compression ratio achieved for each compression type and the number of megabytes you've gained by compressing the files.

In the disk drive's Properties dialog box, you have the option of clicking the Run Agent button to run Compression Agent to optimize disk compression. You can also click the Advanced button to open the Advanced Properties dialog box shown in Figure 28.30, where you can elect to hide the host drive or click the Run DriveSpace button to reset various parameters inside DriveSpace 3.

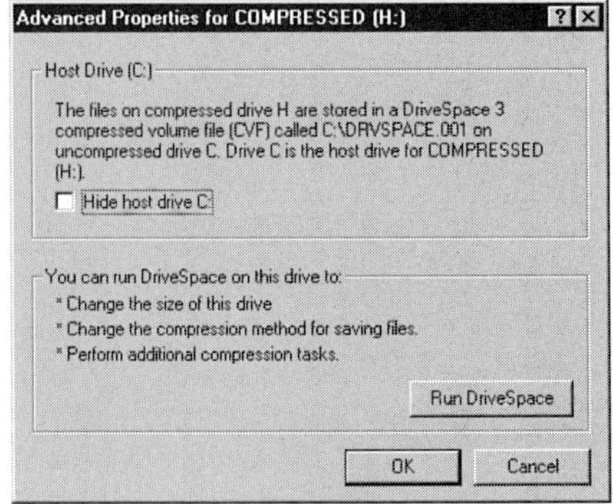

Figure 28.30.
You can hide the host drive by using the Advanced Properties dialog box.

The Internet

You've no doubt heard about the Internet—the Information Superhighway. Microsoft Plus! makes it easy for you to use the Internet. Microsoft built in everything you need to connect to the Internet, over a telephone or through a local area network (LAN), in Windows 95. However, knowing how to set up and use these resources can be difficult for most people. All it takes is one trip to the bookstore to see all the Internet titles to realize that this is true. Microsoft's Plus! package includes tools that make both setting up Internet access and using the Internet a breeze.

The Internet Setup Wizard is the principal tool that Plus! provides to take the pain out of setting up Internet access on your computer. Once you've run the Internet Setup Wizard, you can perform adjustments to your Internet connection settings using the Internet Control Panel applet provided by Plus!.

The Internet Setup Wizard

The Internet Setup Wizard is typically run during Microsoft Plus! setup. Using the Internet Setup Wizard can be anything from a no-brainer to a bit more involved, depending on the Internet service provider you decide on. An Internet service provider is a person, business, company, or even a university that provides you with Internet access, either through a LAN or through the telephone using PPP (Point-to-Point Protocol). The Internet Setup Wizard doesn't support the Serial Line Internet Protocol (SLIP). You can set up a SLIP connection using Windows 95, but you'll need to do that without the help of the Internet Setup Wizard.

Note: SLIP is a simple dial-up protocol that turns your telephone line into a serial connection to the Internet. With SLIP, you must have an IP address and DNS addresses before you can connect to the Internet. PPP is a newer dial-up protocol that builds in several advanced features that allow the automatic setting of your IP address and DNS addresses by your Internet access provider.

If you're running Microsoft Plus! setup and have selected the Internet Jumpstart Kit, you'll get to the first page of the Internet Setup Wizard after Setup copies most of the Plus! files to your hard disk (refer to Figure 28.6). Otherwise, you can start Internet Setup Wizard by choosing Start | Programs | Accessories | Internet Tools | Internet Setup Wizard. When Internet Setup Wizard starts, it opens to the same first page that it does during Microsoft Plus! setup (refer to Figure 28.6).

Click Next. If you have both a modem and a networking card installed on your computer, an Internet Setup Wizard page will appear, asking whether you want to connect by using your phone line or by using a direct networking connection. If you have only a modem installed on your machine, select Connect Using My Phone Line and go to the next section of this chapter, "Dial-Up Networking." If you have only a networking card installed on your machine, select Connect Using a LAN or CERN-Compliant Proxy Server and go to the section "Local Area Network Access."

Dial-Up Networking

If you have a modem installed but not a network card, the Internet Setup Wizard's second page will be the How to Connect page shown in Figure 28.31. If you choose to use a dial-up connection on the second page of the Internet Setup Wizard, this same page will be displayed even if you have both a modem and a network card installed. At this point, you need to make a decision about who you want to use as an Internet access provider. The next three sections cover your options.

Figure 28.31.
You can use either the Microsoft Network or another Internet access provider to connect with the Internet over the telephone.

Accessing the Microsoft Network and the Internet at the Same Time

The easiest way to set up access to the Internet is to use Microsoft Network's Internet access. Of course, Microsoft hopes you'll use this method. Microsoft Network offers excellent Internet connections through 28.8 Kbps modems. However, at the time of this writing, the number of cities with Internet access was limited.

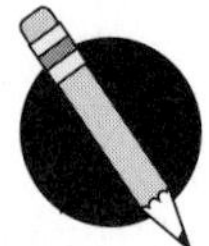

Note: Microsoft has promised to eventually offer 28.8 Kbps Internet access as a local call from anywhere in the continental U.S. But they're far from achieving this goal.

A unique feature of the Microsoft Network is that you can surf the Internet and the Microsoft Network at the same time. Suppose you hear about a particular page on the World Wide Web during a chat session on the Microsoft Network. While you continue chatting, you can fire up Microsoft's Internet Explorer and check out the Web page. Microsoft Network was the first online commercial network to allow simultaneous access to its online services and the Internet.

To set up an Internet account on the Microsoft Network, select the Use The Microsoft Network radio button on the How to Connect page of the Internet Setup Wizard (refer to Figure 28.31) and click the Next button. The rest is easy!

Dialing Up Other Internet Access Providers

The Internet Setup Wizard lets you set up dial-up Internet access with providers other than Microsoft. The only stipulation is that the provider must allow Point-to-Point Protocol (PPP) connections. Internet Setup Wizard doesn't support Serial Line Internet Protocol (SLIP). The procedure for setting up Internet access through providers other than Microsoft is a bit more involved, but not exceedingly so.

Note: Your Internet access provider will give you specific instructions on how to connect to their service. Be sure to follow your provider's instructions to the letter for a Windows 95 connection.

You'll need four pieces of information before running Internet Setup Wizard to set up dial-up PPP access to an Internet access provider other than Microsoft. First, you'll need the provider's name—CompuServe, for instance. Then you'll need the number of the provider's modem through which you'll access the Internet. You can get access numbers from your provider. Be sure to check the speed of the modem. Surfing the Internet gets unbearably slow at less than 14.4 Kbps; 28.8 Kbps is better. Third, you'll need your user name and password. Finally, you'll need the Internet Protocol (IP) address of the access provider's Domain Name Server (DNS). Again, your Internet access provider should give you this information.

Your Internet service provider might provide POP/SMTP mailboxes. You can use Microsoft Exchange for your Internet e-mail. If you do, you'll need your e-mail name and password and the address of your e-mail server.

To set up an Internet account using an Internet service provider other than Microsoft, select the I Already Have an Account with a Different Service Provider radio button on the How to Connect page of the Internet Setup Wizard (refer to Figure 28.31) and click Next.

On the Service Provider Information page, type the name of your service provider, as shown in Figure 28.32, and click Next.

Type the telephone number of the modem you'll be dialing on the Phone Number page, as shown in Figure 28.33.

Figure 28.32.
Type the name of your Internet access provider in the Name of Service Provider drop-down list box.

Figure 28.33.
Be sure to include the area code of the Internet access provider's modem.

Local Area Network Access to the Internet

If your computer is part of a LAN, and if it's already connected to the Internet, there's no need for you to connect to the Internet over the phone. In fact, direct connections are much faster and therefore more desirable than phone connections. Plus! also supports using a CERN-compliant proxy server to connect your LAN to the Internet.

Direct LAN-to-Internet Connection

To use the Internet Setup Wizard to make a direct LAN-to-Internet connection, you'll need at least two pieces of information. First, you'll need the Internet Protocol (IP) address of your Domain Name Server (DNS). You might have more than one DNS address. In that case, you can specify a main and an alternate server. Second, you'll need the IP address of the Internet gateway computer on network. If you have a POP/SMTP mailbox on your LAN, you can use Microsoft Exchange for Internet e-mail. You'll need your e-mail name and password and the address of your e-mail server. You might also need an IP address and subnet mask for your computer. Ask your network administrator if you need one or if your network supports automatically assigned IP addresses. Once you have this information, start the Internet Setup Wizard and click Next to go to the second page.

If you have only a networking card installed on your machine, select Connect Using a LAN or CERN-Compliant Proxy Server and go to the "Local Area Network Access" section. If you have both a modem and a network interface card installed on your machine, select the Connect Using My Local Area Network radio button on the How to Connect page. Click Next to open the IP Address page.

If your network supports automatically assigned IP addresses, leave the Use DHCP to Choose One Automatically (Recommended) radio button selected. Otherwise, select the Always Use the Following radio button and fill in your IP Address and subnet mask in the proper fields. Click Next to go to the DNS Server Address page.

Fill in the DNS Server field with the address of the DNS server given to you by your network administrator. If you have an address for a second DNS server, type it into the Alternate DNS Server field. This field is optional. Click Next to go to the Internet Gateway page.

Fill in the Gateway Address field on the Internet Gateway page with the gateway address given to you by your network administrator. Click Next to go to the Internet Mail page.

If you've been given an e-mail account on a machine with a POP server, click on the Use Internet Mail check box and enter your complete e-mail address in the Your Email Address field. Enter your server's address in the Internet Mail Server field. Click Next.

If you checked the Use Internet Mail check box, skip this paragraph. After filling in your e-mail address and your mail server's address and clicking Next, you should be at the Exchange Profile page. You can either use an existing profile or create a new Internet mail profile by clicking the New button. If you click the New button, the default Internet Mail Settings will be in the Profile Name field of the Profile Name dialog box. Click OK and then click Next on the Exchange Profile page.

You should be on the Finished Setup! page of the Internet Setup Wizard. Click the Finish button, and your direct Internet connection is ready.

LAN-to-Internet Connection Through a CERN-Compliant Proxy Server

Configure proxy support by opening the Internet Control Panel applet after running the Internet Setup Wizard, and choose the Advanced tab in the Internet Properties dialog box.

If you have a POP/SMTP mailbox on your LAN, you can use Microsoft Exchange for your Internet e-mail. You'll need your e-mail name and password and the address of your e-mail server.

Adjusting Connection Settings with the Internet Applet

Plus! installs the new Internet icon in the Control Panel. You'll use the Internet Control Panel applet if you want to change settings or add connections to other Internet providers after you've installed Plus! and used the Internet Setup Wizard.

Double-clicking the Internet icon in the Control Panel opens the Internet Properties dialog box. The tabs contained in this dialog box depend on the type or types of Internet connections you've specified.

The AutoDial Tab

If you're accessing the Internet over the phone, you'll see an AutoDial tab in your Internet Properties dialog box, as shown in Figure 28.34. When AutoDial is on, whenever you launch an application that tries to access the Internet, AutoDial is alerted and automatically launches Microsoft Network's Sign On dialog box or Connect To dialog box, depending on your Internet access provider. In the Settings section, select the provider that you want AutoDial to call. To dial your Internet provider's modem, you simply click the Connect button.

Note: Not all Internet applications are compatible with the AutoDial feature. As of this writing, the Microsoft Internet Explorer, Netscape 1.2, Windows 95 Telnet and FTP, and Microsoft Exchange definitely support it.

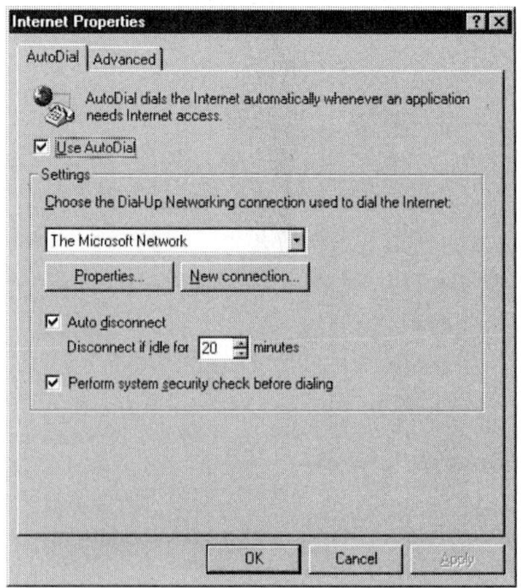

Figure 28.34.
The AutoDial tab in the Internet Properties dialog box.

The Advanced Tab

The Advanced tab shown in Figure 28.35 is used to set up a connection through a proxy server. You'll use this if you're connecting to the Internet from a LAN through a CERN-compliant proxy server.

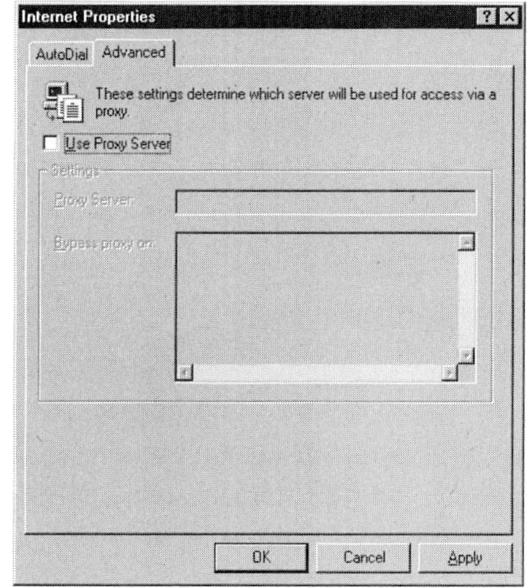

Figure 28.35.
The Advanced tab in the Internet Properties dialog box.

Surfing the Internet with the Internet Explorer

Now that your Internet access is set up, you can have fun. Microsoft has carried its concept of "information at your fingertips" to the Internet. The idea is that you focus on the information, not the gritty details of the technology used to retrieve it. For example, sometimes you arrive at a point where you need more information in order to continue. If you were writing a document on mountain gorillas, you would simply ask your computer how many mountain gorillas were left in the world. The data would show up in your document, and you would continue working, incorporating the data into your discussion. Unfortunately, technology isn't that far along. Nevertheless, Windows 95 goes a long way toward this goal, and the way Microsoft integrated its Internet tools—especially the Internet Explorer—with your desktop environment is no less innovative.

Introducing the World Wide Web

The World Wide Web (WWW for acronym lovers and the Web to the rest of us) is an interactive way to visually move through the huge virtual space of the Internet. The Web is visual because each piece is similar to a page in a glossy picture book, but it's much more than that. Each page almost always contains text and graphics, but often you can also play movies or listen to sound. The Web creates a multimedia environment that extends to your Windows 95 desktop environment and to your room through your monitor and speakers.

The Web is interactive. Each page usually has icons, graphics, and text that you can point to in order to get to other pages on the Web, see a picture, play a sound, or retrieve a file. When you click something and end up on another page, you're experiencing the fundamental interaction that the Web was named for. Whatever you click is linked to another page. If you visualize each page as a dot sitting somewhere in virtual space and a link as a string that connects one dot to another, you'll understand why it's called the World Wide Web. Literally millions of pages (or dots) are connected through an unimaginable number of links or strings that form a virtual web spanning the globe.

The Web is always changing. The *Wall Street Journal* has daily Money and Investing pages. There are many continuously updated weather pages. Most Web pages update or change their contents to remain interesting.

If my definition of the Web still doesn't seem that precise, perhaps it's because the World Wide Web can be precisely defined only by the protocols and other technical underpinnings that go into building each part of it, each page, and the interactions between its many millions of pages around the world. However, the sum of the Web is greater than its parts. You don't need to know a lot of technical jargon to use the Web effectively.

Web Browsers

Web browser is the nontechnical term applied to programs used primarily to browse pages on the Web. Browsing the Web is sort of like browsing through pages in a book or magazine. Microsoft Plus! includes a very good Web browser, aptly named the Internet Explorer, that provides all the features you need to explore the Internet thoroughly.

Addresses on the Web

Just as each house is associated with a unique address so that a mail carrier can deliver a letter there no matter where it's from, each Web page is associated with a unique address called its Universal Resource Locator, or URL. If you know a Web page's URL, you can find it. If you don't know any URLs or Web pages, you can still use the Web. You can usually find what you're looking for, but you'll be much more efficient and far more confident during your navigations if you understand something about URLs.

A good place to start learning about URLs is to look at one, and a good URL to start with is the address of Yahoo!. Yahoo! is a comprehensive compilation of Web sites around the world, grouped into hierarchical categories according to subject matter. You'll find Yahoo! at `http://www.yahoo.com/`. We'll talk more about Yahoo! later. First, let's take a closer look at this URL.

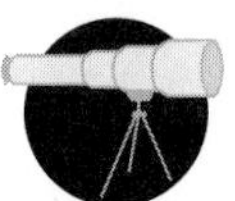

We'll look at Yahoo! using the Microsoft Internet Explorer. We'll also see how the Internet Explorer uses URLs. Flip forward a few pages for a second, to Figure 28.43, to see the Yahoo! home page. Notice Yahoo!'s URL listed just below the Internet Explorer's toolbar in the Address field.

At the highest level, an URL can be divided into two parts by a pair of slashes (//). Information to the left of the slashes identifies the protocol name (in this case, `HTTP`), and the information on the right is the address of the computer where the Web page that you want is stored.

First, let's find out what HTTP means and why the URL must identify a protocol. HTTP stands for Hypertext Transfer Protocol, the name given to the technical specifications behind the mechanisms that make the World Wide Web work. It's not important for you to know these specifications in order to use the Web. The only thing that's really important is that when you see `HTTP`, you know you're using the Web.

Since the first part of the URL specifies a protocol, maybe you've theorized that a Web browser can use more than one protocol—and you're right. Protocols define how computers talk to each other and the computer user. The Web protocol is a newcomer to the Internet community. When the Web started, popular protocols such as the e-mail protocol SMTP (Simple Mail Transfer Protocol) were already in use. If Web browsers (such as the Microsoft Internet Explorer) supported only the new Web protocol and ignored the others, they couldn't use much of the existing Internet. This would severely limit the usefulness of a Web browser. Luckily, the designers of Web browsers thought of this and included the ability to use many existing Internet facilities by defining protocols.

HTTP will probably be the most common protocol that you'll use, especially if you stick to looking at Web pages. However, you can use six other protocols (see Table 28.4). Of these, the most common are FTP and Gopher. We'll return to these, and others, later in this chapter.

Table 28.4. Protocols used by a Web browser.

Protocol	*Description*
`ftp://`	Takes you to a File Transfer Protocol site, a site set up so that you can transfer files back to your computer.
`gopher://`	Takes you to a Gopher menu system.
`http://`	Loads Web pages.
`mailto:`	Used to send e-mail.
`news:`	Used to read UseNet news groups.
`telnet://`	Starts a Telnet session, in which you can log onto another computer on the Internet.

Let's look again at that URL for Yahoo!, `http://www.yahoo.com/`. Again, the part of the URL to the right of the two slashes specifies the address of the computer where the Web page that you want is stored. The computer, usually called the *server*, is found on the Internet at `www.yahoo.com`. This address is actually a human-friendly form of what is technically an Internet Protocol (or IP) address that consists of a string of four numbers separated by periods. The IP address for `www.yahoo.com` is `205.217.231.67`. For our purposes, we never need to look at a string of numbers again. The human-readable address, like the string of numbers, is broken up by periods. Each part of the address specifies a computer's Internet site, starting with the most specific information on the left through the most general on the right. In general terms, the part of the address before the first period usually gives the name of a specific computer; the next one or two parts usually gives the name of a subnet or institution; and the final part of the name, the suffix, identifies the kind of institution that maintains the site. Common suffixes are listed in Table 28.5.

Table 28.5. Common Internet address suffixes.

Suffix	*Host*
`com`	A commercial site
`edu`	An educational site
`gov`	A government site
`mil`	A military site
`org`	An organization such as the United Nations

You might see other information in an URL. Most of this information will be to the right of the Internet address. For instance, as you move through Web pages at a particular Internet address, you'll see directory information appear in the URL. You're also likely to see a file listed on the far-right side of an URL after a list of directories. Often this will be an HTML file—a Hypertext Markup Language file. HTML is the language that Web pages are programmed in. It's not important for you to know HTML in order to use the Web, but if you see an URL ending with `.html` or `.htm`, you know it's an HTML file. You don't need to know every last thing about an URL to surf the Web effectively, so I'll point out some of these subtleties later when we surf.

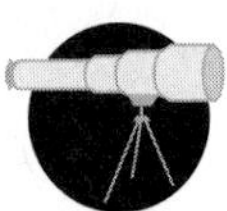

Looking Ahead: To see what an URL with a directory listed looks like, jump forward a few pages to take a look at the URL in the Address box in Figure 28.46. Here we're in the Science directory. Figure 28.48 shows an URL with the HTML file `alife.html` listed at the end of the directory `cb`. Notice also that this page is at a new address, `www.fusebox.com`.

Browsing the Web with the Microsoft Internet Explorer

Let's look at the premier Internet tool that's provided in Plus!—the Microsoft Internet Explorer. While we're at it, let's go surfing!

If you installed the Internet Jumpstart Kit during the Microsoft Plus! setup, you should see the icon "The Internet" on your desktop (see Figure 28.36).

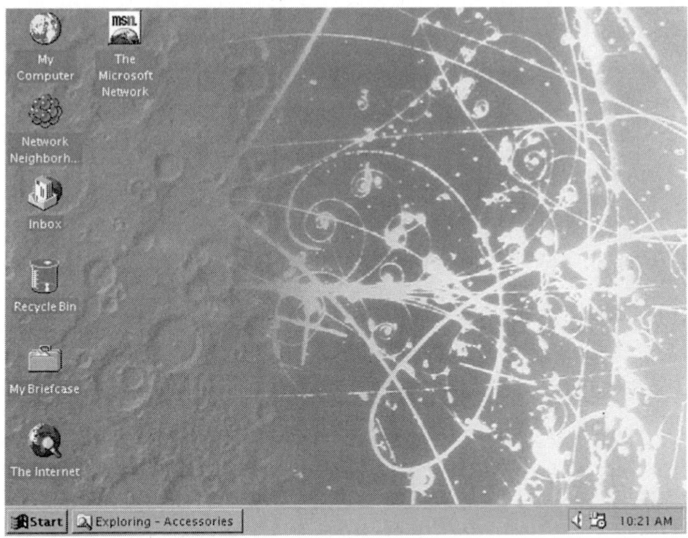

Figure 28.36.
You'll find a quick way onto the Internet by double-clicking the Internet icon on the left side of the screen. (This figure shows the Science Desktop Theme.)

Double-click the Internet icon to launch Microsoft Internet Explorer. If you're using a dial-up connection to the Internet but you're not connected when you launch Internet Explorer, a Sign In dialog box, shown in Figure 28.37, will appear.

Figure 28.37.
When the Microsoft Internet Explorer is launched from the Desktop, a Sign In dialog box appears. In this case, the dial-up Internet access provider is Microsoft Network.

Click the Connect button. Otherwise, if you're connecting directly to the Internet or through a LAN, you must already be communicating properly with the Internet before launching Internet Explorer. When Internet Explorer opens, it automatically loads the Microsoft Network's home page on the Internet, as shown in Figure 28.38.

Let's take a closer look at the Microsoft Network's home page. It shows several general features that are common or even ubiquitous on the Web, using different Web browsers and some features that are specific to Internet Explorer.

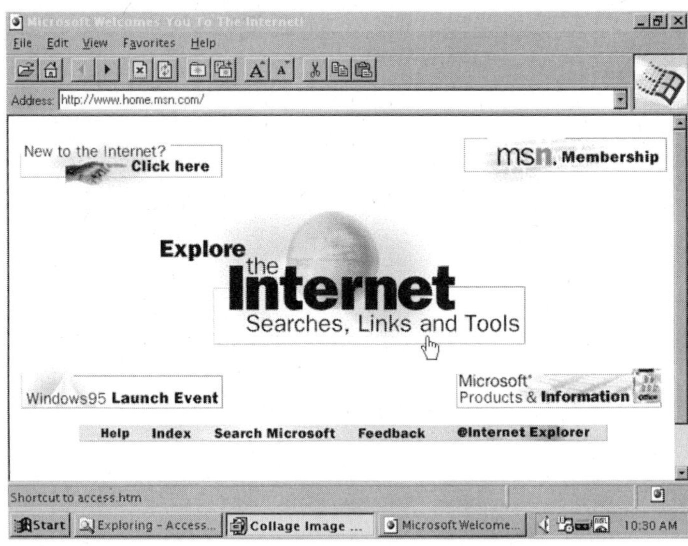

Figure 28.38.
The Microsoft Network's home page is loaded when you launch Internet Explorer. (Like most Web pages, this one is constently changing. Your version probably will look different, when you get to this page.)

A central feature of browsing the Web is something called the *link*. Text objects and graphic objects on a Web page can be linked to other Web pages or files in such a way that when you click the text object or graphic object, it either takes you to another Web page or loads the file on your computer.

The Microsoft Network's home page has several links. You can tell when something on a Web page is linked by passing the mouse pointer over it. If the pointer icon turns into a hand, the object is linked. You can see in Figure 28.38 that the Explore the Internet: Searches, Links and Tools graphic in the middle of the Microsoft Network home page is linked because the hand pointer is pointing to it. Notice also that the status bar at the bottom-left corner shows the message `Shortcut to access.htm`. When you point to a linked object, Internet Explorer's status bar tells you where the object is linked to—in this case, an HTML page named "access." Can you find the other links on this page?

Tip: If you don't see a status bar when you open Internet Explorer, select View | Status Bar. The status bar is displayed when there's a check mark next to this option on the View menu. Notice that Toolbar and Address Bar are also on the View menu. Each is displayed according to whether it's checked on the View menu.

A couple of other general features of the Web browser are worth mentioning. Notice that the title bar displays the name of the Web page you're viewing. You can see Microsoft Welcomes You To The Internet! displayed at the top left in the title bar in Figure 28.38. I'll point out items of interest in the menu bar and toolbar as we go along. Below the toolbar you should see the address bar, which displays the address or URL of the current page. You can also type in a page in the Address field. All of the typical text-editing features are available in the Address field. Just right-click inside the Address field to highlight the URL and display a shortcut menu that lists familiar editing commands. If you find a great new Web page that you must share with a friend, simply right-click in the Address field, select Copy (as shown in Figure 28.39), paste the address into an e-mail message, and send it off. Likewise, you can paste an URL you receive in e-mail by using the e-mail's Copy command, the same shortcut menu in Microsoft Exchange, and the Paste command in the address bar.

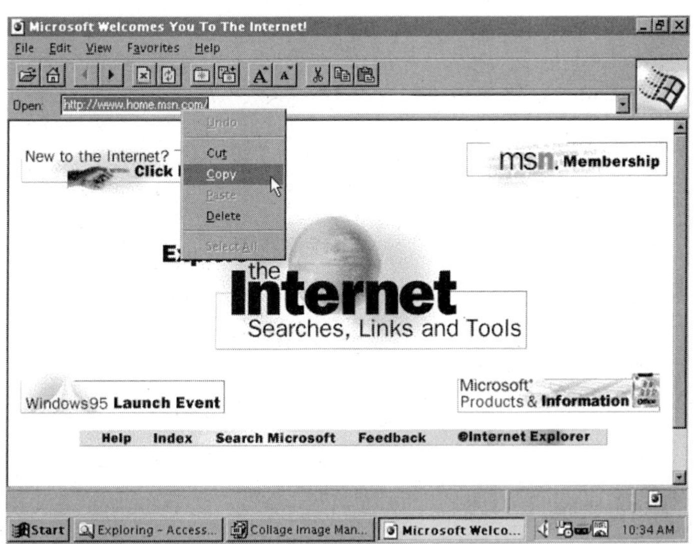

Figure 28.39.
You can use familiar editing commands with a click of the right mouse button in the address bar's Address field.

Tip: You can also use Internet Explorer's Edit menu while editing the address field.

Some features make Internet Explorer special. The most important of these is its OLE support. We'll look at all of the Internet Explorer's special features as we move through the Web. For now, let's take a break from surfing to look at what OLE support will do for you.

To see what OLE can do, make sure that the Internet Explorer window takes up only a portion of your desktop, and point to the Explore the Internet: Searches, Links and Tools link in the center of the Microsoft Network's home page (refer to Figure 28.38). Hold down the left mouse button while you move the mouse pointer anywhere over your desktop where no desktop icon is showing. Release the left mouse button. You should now have a .GIF image icon sitting on your desktop with the name "internet" under it, as shown in Figure 28.40.

You can do this with any graphic object on the Web page. Just don't release the left button before you get to the desktop, or you'll go to the place that the object is linked to.

Figure 28.40.
Dropping a graphic object from a Web page onto the upper-right corner of the Windows 95 Desktop results in a .GIF file named "internet" being placed on the desktop and shown as an icon.

You can also drag and drop text from a Web page. Open an OLE-enabled word processor, such as Microsoft Word version 6 or later, to test this. When you move the mouse pointer over text in a Web page while using Internet Explorer, the pointer changes into the bar cursor. Highlight the text you want to drag and drop, and then point the mouse cursor at the highlighted text. Hold the left mouse button down and drag the text to a page in your OLE-enabled word processor. Let go of the left mouse button. Now the text is included in your document. OLE lets you grab just about anything from a Web page and drop it into any OLE-enabled container. Just think how handy this will be when you need to grab the latest weather statistics from a Web page and add them to your report. Microsoft Exchange is also an OLE application.

Note: WordPad, the OLE-enabled word processor included with Windows 95, should be able to handle text dragged from Internet Explorer. However, I got a blank page when I tried this. On the other hand, dragging and dropping text from Internet Explorer worked perfectly when I dropped it into a Microsoft Word or a Microsoft Excel document. If you want to use WordPad, you can use the shortcut menu by pointing to the highlighted text in Internet Explorer, right-clicking, and selecting Copy. Now activate your WordPad document and select Paste from the Edit menu or WordPad's shortcut menu.

I was recently reading the online version of the *Wall Street Journal* when I saw a quote that I thought a friend would appreciate. I simply highlighted the quote on the Web page, dragged and dropped it into a note I was composing under Microsoft Exchange, and sent the message to her. OLE is a key feature in integrating the Internet with your desktop.

Tip: As an alternative, you could have selected File | Save to save the whole Web page on your PC as an HTML or a text file, and then dragged and dropped or cut and pasted your text later, offline.

Note: You can find the online version of the *Wall Street Journal* at `http://update.wuj.com`.

Okay, we've taken our first step into the Web and looked at some features of our Web browser. Now let's get into some serious surfing. Back on the Microsoft Network's home page, click Explore the Internet: Searches, Links and Tools at the center of the page to get started. This should take you to the Microsoft Network's Explore the Internet page, shown in Figure 28.41.

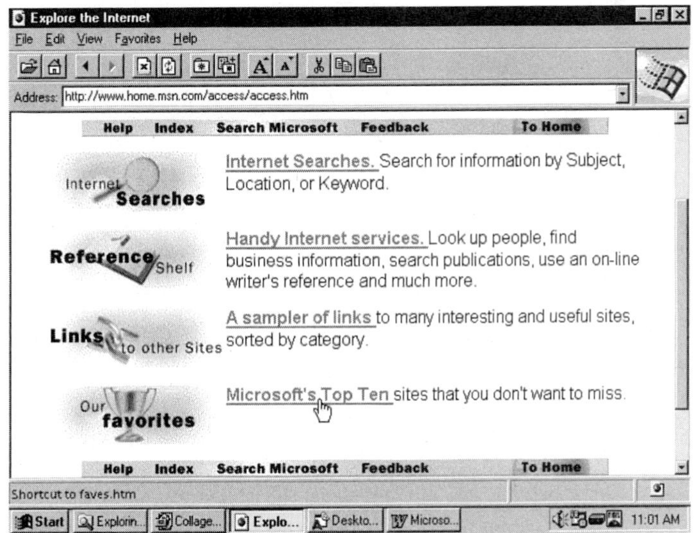

Figure 28.41.
The Microsoft Network's Explore the Internet page, scrolled down a bit to view Microsoft's Top Ten (favorite) sites.

Click the linked text that says Microsoft's Top Ten or click the linked Our Favorites graphic. You should now see the Microsoft Network's Our Favorite Websites page, shown in Figure 28.42. Right under the listing for ESPNET Sports Zone is our old friend Yahoo!, listed as the Yahoo! Search Server.

Click on Yahoo Search Server to load Yahoo!, as shown in Figure 28.43. Yahoo is a good place to start browsing the Web because from here you can find Web pages on nearly any subject. This is a good time to look at Internet Explorer's favorite places facilities.

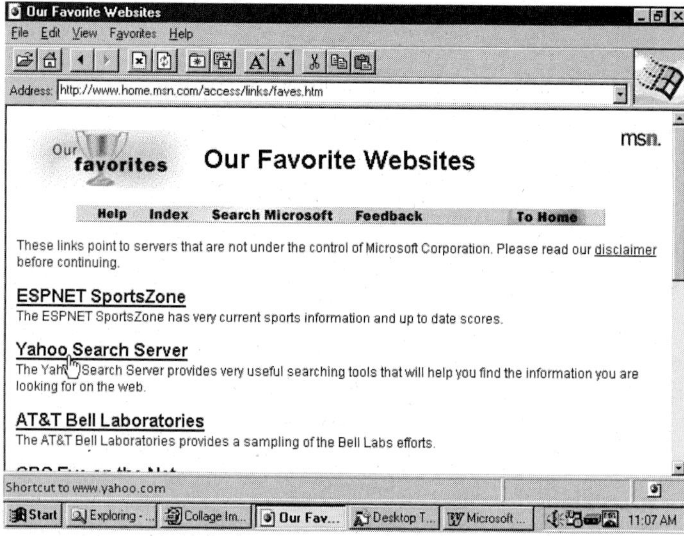

Figure 28.42.
Find out Microsoft's favorite Web sites from the Microsoft Network's Our Favorite Websites page.

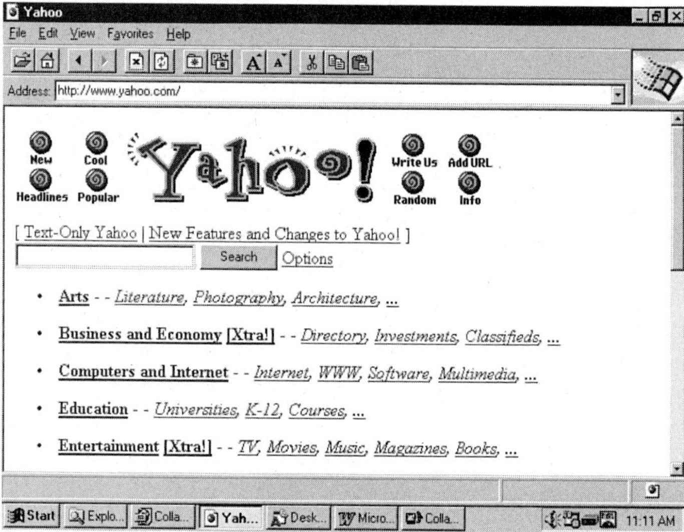

Figure 28.43.
From this Yahoo! Web page you can find Web pages on nearly any subject.

Wouldn't it be handy to be able to jump to the Yahoo! page wherever you were on the Web and whenever you needed to find a page by subject? You could do this by saving the Yahoo! page address or URL. Internet Explorer makes this easy with its favorite places facilities. While you're viewing Yahoo!, either click the Add To Favorites button on the toolbar or select Favorites | Add To Favorites. The Add To Favorites dialog box shown in Figure 28.44 will appear.

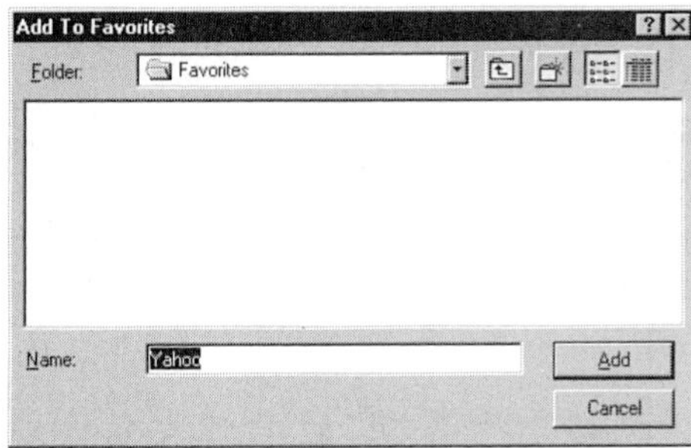

Figure 28.44.
Add to your list of favorite places using the Add To Favorites dialog box.

In the Name text box, accept the default name of the Web page or change it to something that makes sense to you, and then click the Add button. Now, when you open the Favorites menu, the favorite page you just added—in this case, Yahoo!—will be listed at the bottom, as shown in Figure 28.45. When you want to go to Yahoo!, simply open the Favorites menu and select Yahoo!.

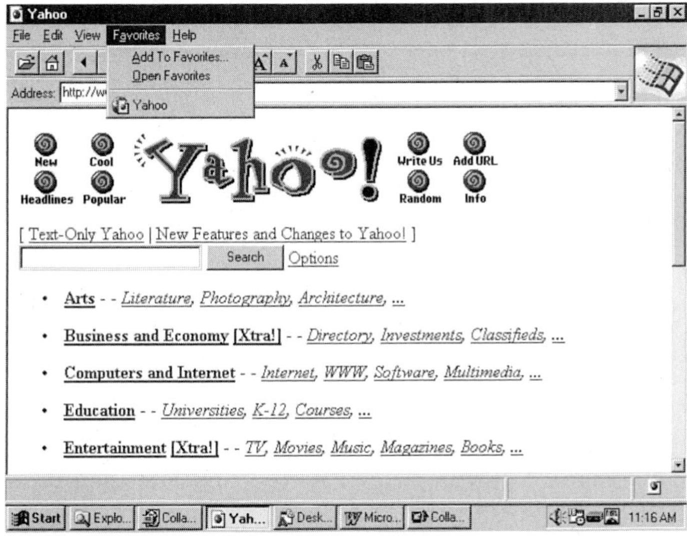

Figure 28.45.
All the pages you add as favorites will be listed at the bottom of the Favorites menu.

Tip: Your favorites are saved in the Windows\Favorites folder. Each time you save a favorite, a .URL file is created in the Favorites folder. You can open your Favorites folder from Internet Explorer either by clicking the Open Favorites button on the toolbar or by selecting Favorites | Open Favorites. Each .URL file is given the name of the Web page it's associated with. You can manipulate these files in the normal way. Right-click the file and select Properties from the context menu to see the URL. Drag and drop a .URL file to your desktop. Then, when you want to go directly to that page, double-click the .URL file.

You can also send a .URL file to friends so that they can drag and drop it into their Favorites folder. Finally, you can organize your favorite files by creating folders inside your Favorites folder and dropping .URL files into them. These folders will show up as submenus in your Favorites menu. Any .URL files that you drop inside a folder will be listed under the submenu named after that folder.

Now we'll continue browsing until we get to an interesting page. Suppose we want to find out what science resources are listed at Yahoo!. Scroll down the list on the Yahoo! Web page until you see Science, and then click the listing to go to the Yahoo! Science page shown in Figure 28.46.

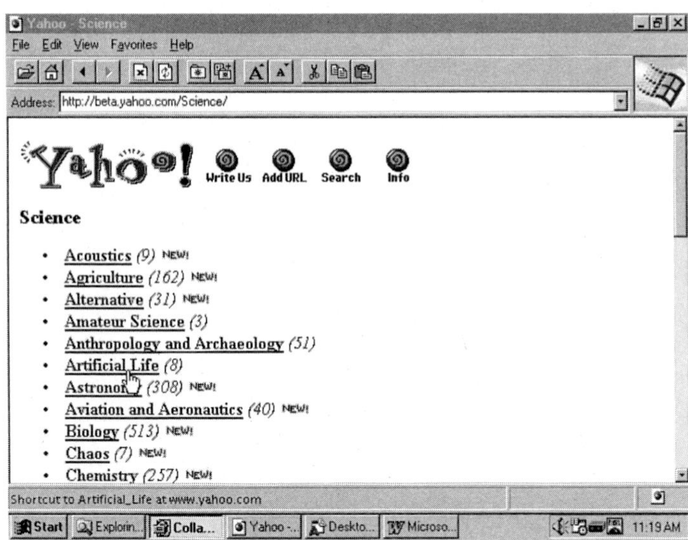

Figure 28.46.
The Yahoo! Science page.

Artificial Life looks interesting; let's click the Artificial Life link. Now you should see the Science:Artificial Life page shown in Figure 28.47.

The Live Alife page looks interesting. Click Live Alife.

Note: Alife is short for artificial life. Therefore, the page we're going to has live artificial life!?

You should now be in the Live Artificial Life Page shown in Figure 28.48.

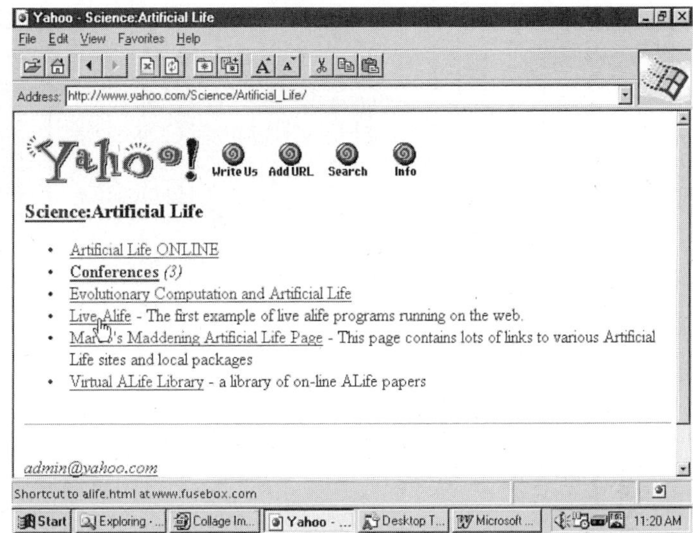

Figure 28.47.
The Yahoo! Science: Artificial Life page.

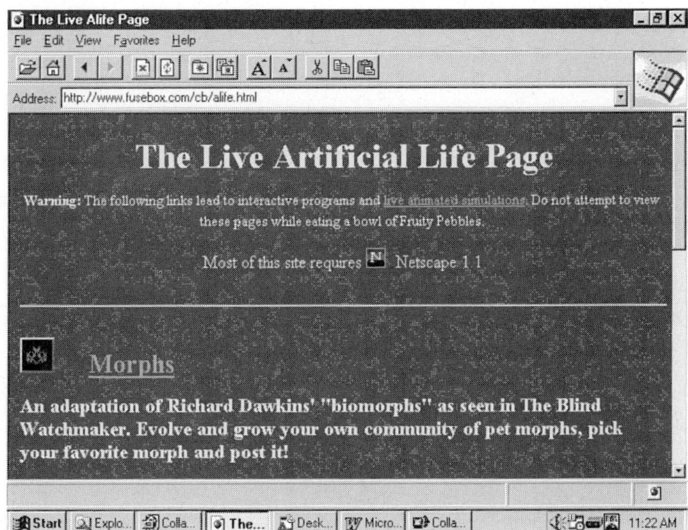

Figure 28.48.
The Live Artificial Life page.

You can learn a lot about artificial life here and, better yet, you can do real experiments in artificial life at this site. For instance, you can click Morphs and then click Morphs Lab to evolve your own Morphs. But wait! Why is there a red dot with an X in it on the Morphs Instructions page, shown in Figure 28.49?

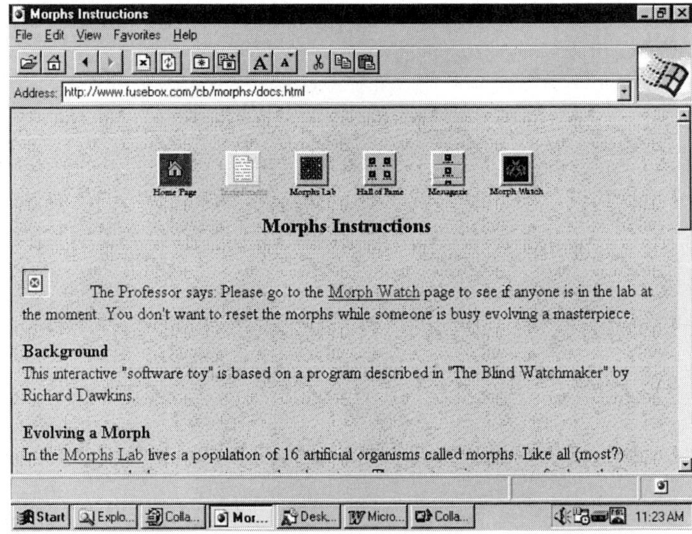

Figure 28.49.
The Morphs Instructions page demonstrates a limitation of Internet Explorer.

Perhaps you noticed a warning on the Live Artificial Life Page in Figure 28.48, which said "Most of this site requires Netscape 1.1." Every Web browser has common features, but, as we've already seen, each browser can have special features not found on other browsers. Internet Explorer is the only OLE browser that I know of to date. Netscape Navigatior has typically been an innovative leader. In my experience, Internet Explorer does almost everything that Netscape can do. However, one thing Internet Explorer can't deal with is a kind of real-time animation used at this Web site. Netscape also has security features that Internet Explorer doesn't.

If you're now set on seeing all the animated features at the Live Artificial Life Page site, don't despair. You can download the latest Netscape browser from the Internet and evaluate it at no charge. Netscape is shareware, so if you decide to keep it, be sure to register it and pay the shareware fees. Currently, several Windows 95 versions are available. Go to `http://home.netscape.com/` to find out more about it. Figure 28.50 shows the Morphs Instructions page using Netscape.

Tip: When possible, always use 32-bit applications under Windows 95. Netscape is available in both 16-bit and 32-bit formats. Either of them will run under Windows 95, but 16-bit applications actually cripple Windows 95. For instance, multitasking is far less efficient when you run a 16-bit program. The bottom line is that you'll get your best performance when using 32-bit programs under Windows 95.

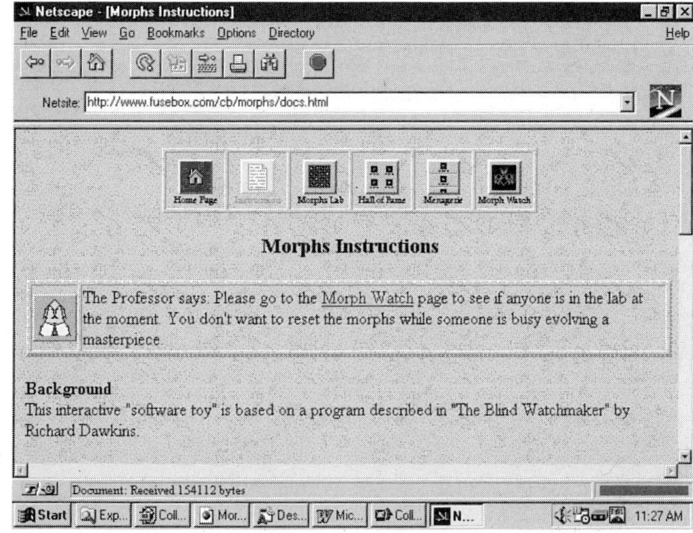

Figure 28.50.
The Morphs Instructions page using a 32-bit version of Netscape. Notice that the icon on the far left is different from the one in Figure 28.49.

Now that you've surfed through a small portion of the Internet, you can look at Internet Explorer's history feature. You should see the previous Web pages you've visited at the bottom of the File menu. Number 1 is the most recent. At the end of the list you'll see the menu selection More History. When you select it, the History folder opens. (Your History folder can be found under Program Files\Plus!\Microsoft Internet when you use Explorer.) Your History folder contains .URL files from the Web sites you've visited. You can drag and drop files from your History folder into your Favorites folder, your desktop, or anywhere else that's OLE-enabled.

In the Options dialog box, you can set the number of Web pages that are saved in your History folder. Choose View | Options to open the Options dialog box. Select the Advanced tab, shown in Figure 28.51. Within the History frame, the default setting of Remember the Last *x* Places Visited is 300. Reset this number to the number of sites you want remembered. You can also change the History folder from the default by using the Change button, and you can empty the History folder by clicking the Empty button.

You're now ready to step out into cyberspace on your own. If you're interested in artificial life, you can connect to other pages on the subject through links from the Live Artificial Life Page, or you can hunt for pages centered on your own favorite subject. Just select Favorites | Yahoo.

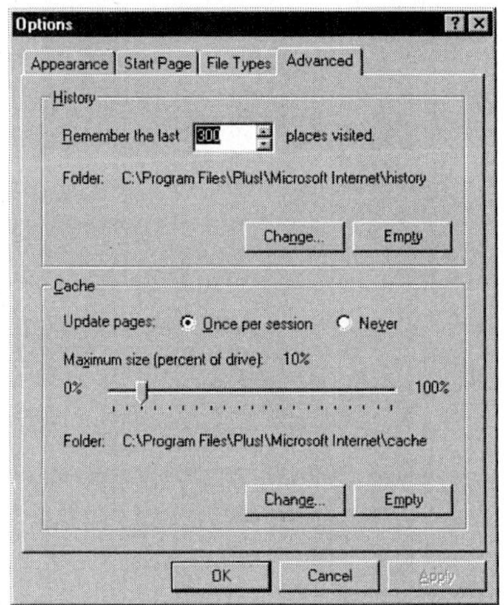

Figure 28.51.
You change history settings by using the Options dialog box in Internet Explorer.

Using FTP and Gopher

Web browsers were built to utilize not only the World Wide Web but also various Internet facilities that were already in place when the Web was first conceived.

Using FTP

FTP, or File Transfer Protocol, is a set of technical specifications that define a protocol that allows you to transfer files from one computer to another over the Internet. Luckily, you don't need to understand these specifications to use FTP. Internet Explorer makes it easy to gather files by using FTP.

To use FTP from Internet Explorer, you'll need to either click a link from a Web page to an FTP site or enter an URL into the address bar's Address field with the `FTP` protocol type (refer to Table 28.4) and the address of an FTP server.

Let's say you want to try out the Netscape browser to compare it with the Internet Explorer. Type

`ftp://ftp.netscape.com/pub`

into the Address field and press Enter.

Note: Netscape is a shareware program. This means that you can download the program and evaluate it for free, but if you decide to keep it, you must pay for it.

If the site isn't too busy, you should see a page with the words `pub Folder` in bold at the top left, as shown in Figure 28.52.

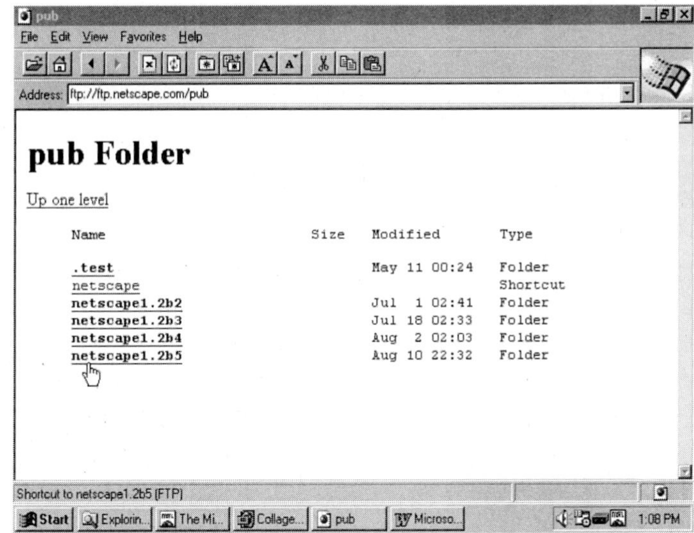

Figure 28.52.
The pub folder at one of Netscape's FTP sites.

As of this writing, the most recent release of Netscape is version 1.2b5 (1.2 beta 5). "Beta" means that this version of Netscape is still under development and that the program is bound to have some glitches. New betas are coming out fast and furious, so when you access this page, just look for the highest-numbered release. Click on `netscape1.2b5` (or the most recent release). You should see a page that looks like the one shown in Figure 28.53.

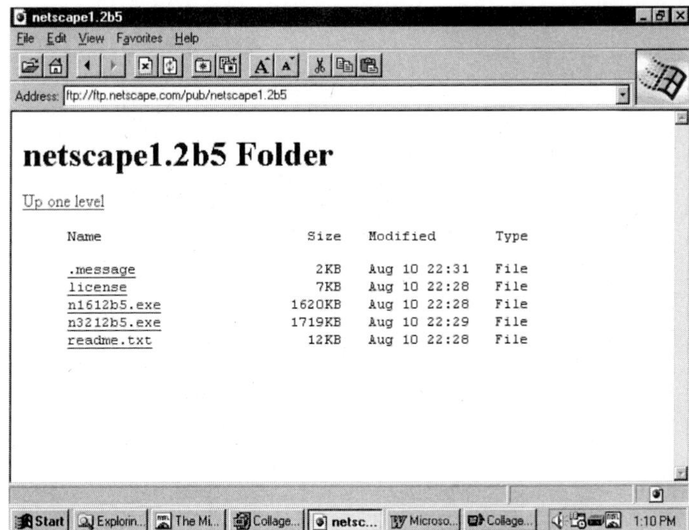

Figure 28.53.
This folder at Netscape's FTP site contains only 16-bit and 32-bit versions of Netscape 1.2b5.

You're now in a bottom folder at Netscape's FTP site that contains only files. Click `.message`, `license`, or `readme.txt` to read the contents of these files. Files that contain text are loaded directly into the browser. This can get annoying when you want to read a text file but you also want to stay in the same page. Internet Explorer solves this problem by letting you open as many windows as you want. For example, if you hold down the Shift key and click `readme.txt`, another Internet Explorer window will open with `readme.txt` loaded, as shown in Figure 28.54.

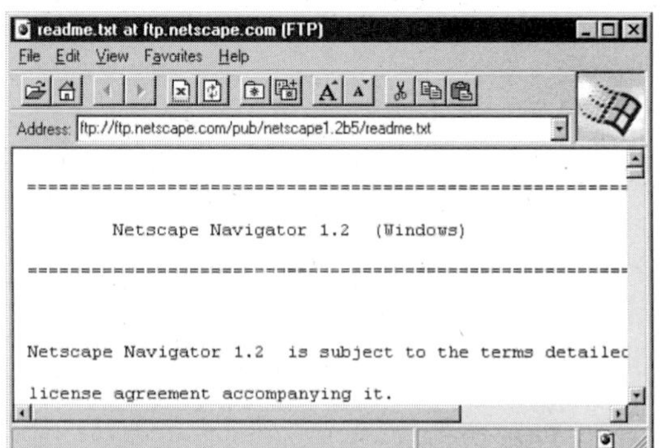

Figure 28.54.
You can open as many Internet Explorer windows as you want. You can do this anywhere on the Internet, not just at an FTP site.

You can do the same thing by right-clicking while pointing to `readme.txt` and selecting the Open In New Window command from the shortcut menu. This command is available for any link you find on the Internet. You can save the text loaded into an Internet Explorer window by selecting File | Save As.

The other two links in the netscape1.2b5 folder shown in Figure 28.53 are links to the executable files n1612b5.exe and n3212b5.exe. The `n` stands for Netscape, the `16` and `32` tell you the bits your operating system must be able to handle in order to use the program, and the `12b5` stands for version 1.2b5. Since you're running Windows 95, you definitely want the 32-bit version, so click `n3212b5.exe`. Internet Explorer doesn't load executable files. When you click a link to an executable file or other binary files that Internet Explorer doesn't open, a Confirm File Open dialog box appears, as shown in Figure 28.55.

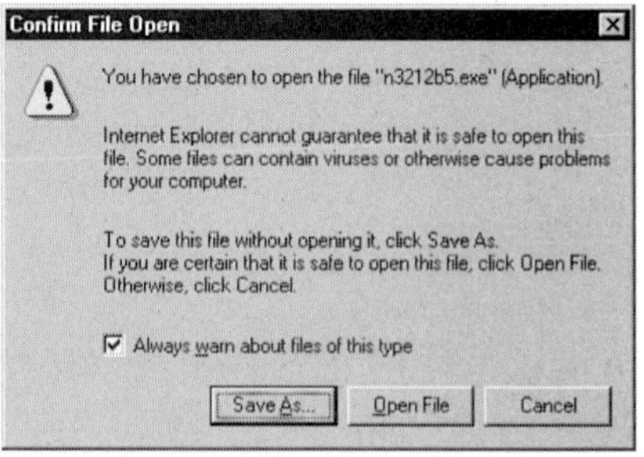

Figure 28.55.
The Confirm File Open dialog box opens for files that the Internet Explorer doesn't normally open.

Since you want to load this file to your local disk drive, click the Save As button. The Save As dialog box opens. Go through the usual procedures to save a file. When you click the OK button, Internet Explorer downloads the file to your computer. You should see a `Copying file` message in the status bar, telling you the filename and size of the file being transferred. Also, on the right side of the status bar, you should see a progress bar indicating the relative percentage of the file downloaded.

Tip: If you want to continue browsing the Web while downloading a file, try opening a new window by holding down the Shift key while clicking the link to the file you're going to download. A new Internet Explorer window opens, and the Confirm File Open dialog box appears. Go through the usual procedures and then, while the file downloads, continue browsing the Web in the other Internet Explorer window.

You have now used Internet Explorer's built-in FTP capabilities. If you want to try out the program you just downloaded, follow the installation instructions provided by Netscape in its readme.txt file.

Using Gopher

Gopherspace is something like the Web without the graphical interface. Gopher predated the World Wide Web and was built mainly for easy text-based Internet navigation, using links. Internet Explorer provides access to Gopherspace when you click a link to a Gopher server or if you enter an URL into the address bar's Address field using the Gopher protocol identifier `gopher` (refer to Table 28.4) and a Gopher server's address. One major advantage of using Gopher is its speed. Without the graphics overhead, you'll find moving around Gopherspace noticeably faster than on the Web.

Maybe after hearing so much about the United Nations in the news, you decide that you want to learn more about what they do in troubled areas around the world. Enter the URL `gopher://nywork1.undp.org/11/` into the Address field and press Enter. You should see the Gopher page shown in Figure 28.56.

The link `The United Nations, what it is and what it does` looks promising. When you click the link, the Gopher page shown in Figure 28.57 appears.

At the bottom of the list is a link to information about United Nations Peace-Keeping Operations. When you click it, the Gopher page shown in Figure 28.58 appears.

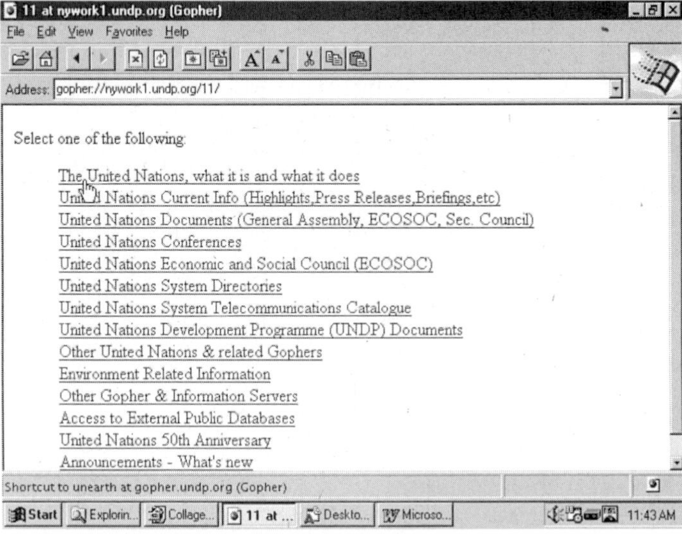

Figure 28.56.
The United Nations Gopher server.

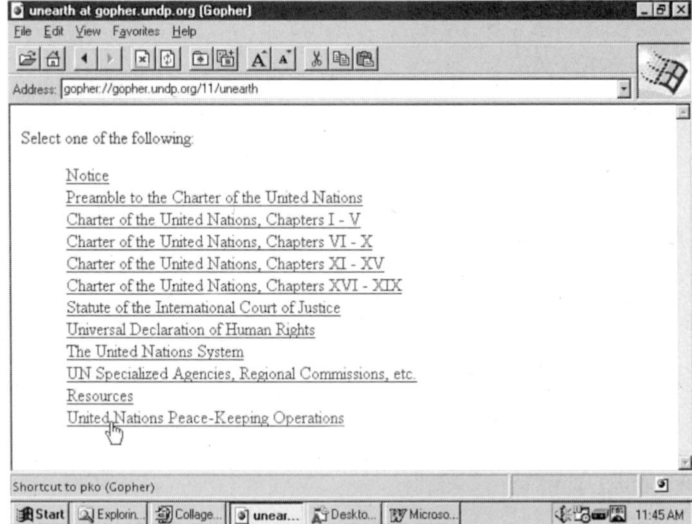

Figure 28.57.
This Gopher page contains links to information about what the United Nations is and what it does.

This page lists a collection of links to files describing UN peace-keeping missions around the world and files that describe current situations in various trouble spots. Click the link `Information notes on Yugoslavia (July 95)`, for instance, and you see the document shown in Figure 28.59.

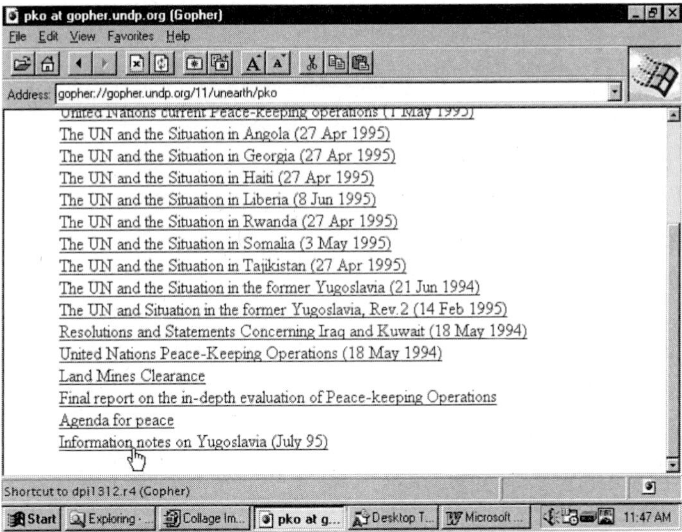

Figure 28.58.
This Gopher page lists a collection of links to files describing United Nations peace-keeping missions and situation reports from around the world.

Note: Due to the nature of the reports shown in Figure 28.58, you're likely to see a different screen. The world situation is constantly changing. This Gopher page reflects those changes through constant updates.

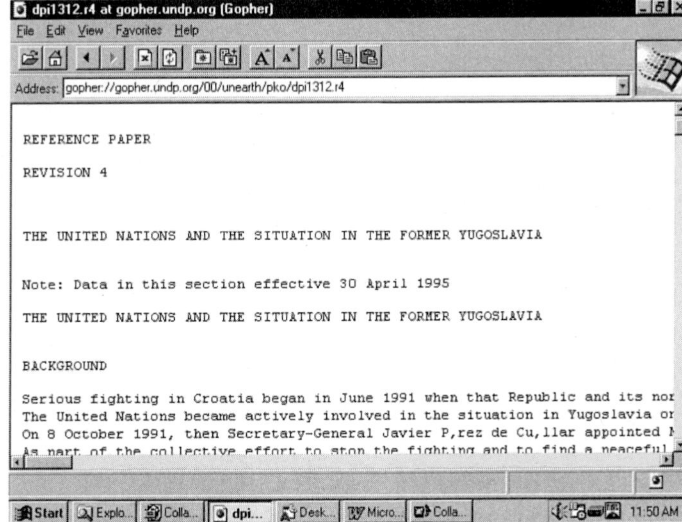

Figure 28.59.
Information on Yugoslavia from the United Nations Gopher server.

Using Helper Applications with Internet Explorer

Because the Internet's content is constantly changing, Web browsers need to be flexible in the way they handle files found on the Internet. For instance, initially the most common audio file on the Web had a low-fidelity 8-bit mono format and an .AU extension. This form of audio file has the advantage that the files remain relatively small, but has the disadvantage of poor sound quality.

Other formats began to proliferate for various reasons. When the Windows 3.x multimedia extensions were released, wave files began showing up on the Web. Wave files, with the .WAV extension, have the advantage of very good sound quality, but their disadvantage is that they can be very large. You can compare advantages and disadvantages among half a dozen formats.

Internet Explorer is configured at setup time to run most audio formats you'll encounter, including .AU, .AIFF, and .WAV. Additionally, it's preconfigured to run RealAudio files with the .RAM extension. All the other sound file formats mentioned force you to download the whole file before listening to it. A couple of minutes of sound can form a file of several megabytes. If you're using a dial-up network to connect to the Internet, it could take a huge amount of time to download. RealAudio feeds the sound file to your player through the Internet in real time, even over a 14.4 Kbps connection! Sites that use RealAudio are often radio-show-style talk shows that might last an hour or more.

The way that the Web browser built in flexibility to take advantage of the tremendous changes and growth in technology was to use what are often called *helper applications*. When you try to link to a file that Internet Explorer can't display or play directly, it looks at the Windows 95 file registration list to see whether another application can handle the file. If so, Internet Explorer launches that application and displays or plays the file with it. Otherwise, Internet Explorer displays the Unknown File Type dialog box. Usually, if you don't have a helper application that will play a file, you can find a helper application on the Internet that will play it.

To see the list of registered files from within Internet Explorer, select View | Options and then click the File Types tab in the Options dialog box, shown in Figure 28.60.

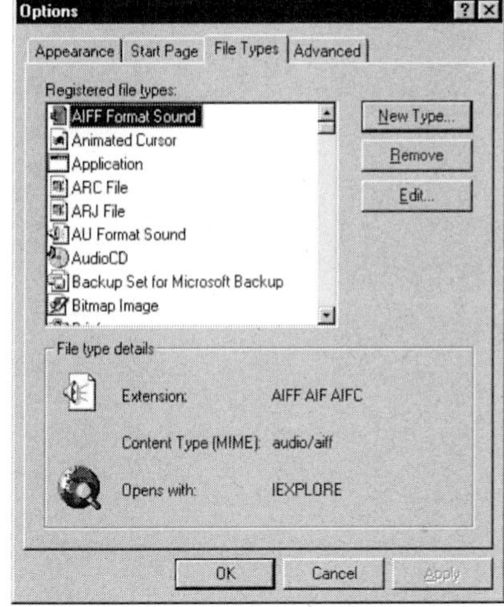

Figure 28.60.
The File Types tab in the Options dialog box lists registered file types from within Internet Explorer.

Reading Newsgroups with Internet Explorer

Perhaps you've heard of Internet newsgroups or UseNet. If you use the Internet Explorer with the Microsoft Network, you can access newsgroups through links in the Web. Internet Explorer has been integrated with the newsgroup services offered through MSN itself. When you click a link to a newsgroup—`bionet.neuroscience`, for instance—a window for the newsgroup pops up. It contains a list of all of the newsgroup's messages.

Note: Where did I come up with `bionet.neuroscience`? It's one of the newsgroups blocked by MSN until you give MSN a release for full newsgroup access. For more information, go to MSN's Internet forum.

Internet Mail and Microsoft Exchange

When you install the Internet Jumpstart Kit, the Internet mail service is added to Microsoft Exchange.When you want to send or receive Internet mail through a POP/SMTP server, open Microsoft Exchange. When the Choose Profile dialog box appears, select the Internet Mail Settings profile in the Profile Name list box.

Note: You don't need the Internet mail service to send or receive Internet mail through the Microsoft Network. It's provided for your SMTP (Simple Mail Transfer Protocol) accounts that you might have with other Internet access providers.

When you use the Microsoft Network, Microsoft Exchange is closely integrated with Internet Explorer. Remember the `mailto:` protocol in Table 28.4? When you click a link to an e-mail address on a Web page, Exchange's New Message window opens, and the To field is filled in with the e-mail address you clicked. After you fill in the Subject field, fill in the body of the message, and click Send, the addressee will receive your e-mail message.

Summary

The Microsoft Plus! package is greater than the sum of its parts. There are endless ways that you can use different features of Microsoft Plus! with standard Windows 95 features to enhance your productivity and pleasure. You'll be mining Microsoft Plus! for new ways to do things long after your introduction to this handy program.

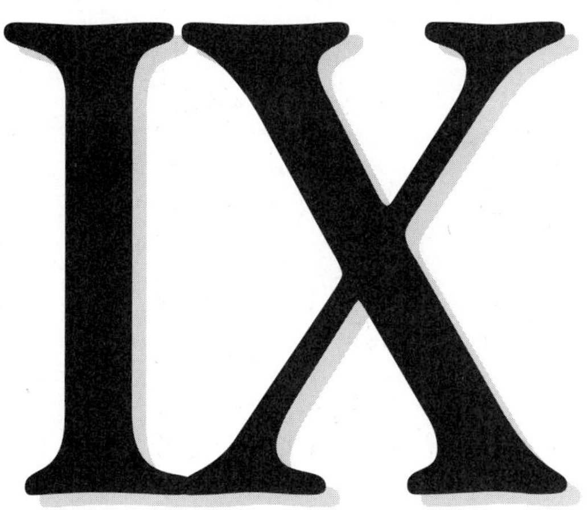

Appendixes

A

Online Resources

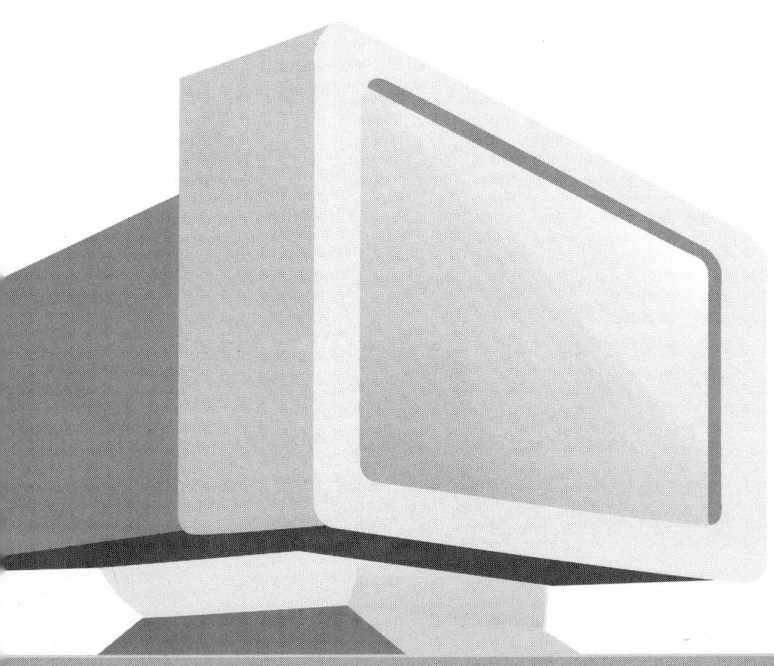

Local user groups provide a valuable source of information for the average user, but they can be a little limited. There's only so much information that you can expect to get from the members of your user group. Even if it's a larger group, you'll see a lot less than the literally thousands of people on the Internet who work specifically with Windows 95. CompuServe and other online services also provide a wealth of resources for the typical user. The types of information provided by online services vary, but in the long run you'll find that most of them provide a level of information superior to that found in a local user group. (The place where user groups still fill an important role is in the form of hands-on assistance. No matter how informed your online buddy is, he'll have a hard time actually showing you what to do on your machine.)

I won't say that every person you run into when using an online service will be an expert. Most of them are just average users like you. However, I've had the pleasure of running into some truly remarkable people from time to time while browsing through the messages. In fact, some people are constantly looking for ways to make Windows better in their spare time. You'll usually find them in a forum somewhere, just waiting to share this information with you.

Online services offer other things of value as well. For example, if you talk with your local user group, you're getting the local view of Windows 95. On the other hand, talking with someone on an online service, such as CompuServe or the Internet, might give you the English, Australian, or Japanese view of Windows 95. This international flavor will give you a better appreciation of features you might not have considered important. In addition, the cultural differences actually work together to help you see new ways of using features you might not have seen.

Aside from all the talking you'll do with other users, an online service also gives you access to vendor representatives. There have been times when I've started a conversation with three or even four people who work for the company whose product I'm using. You'll find that the expert knowledge that the vendor representative provides often gets mixed in with the real-world view of the other users. The result is that you actually get better information from the online service than you could have received from the vendor's technical support line.

Is this all there is? Not by a long shot. Online services provide many of the features you've come to expect from a vendor BBS. For example, you can go online to CompuServe, the Internet, or MSN (Microsoft Network) and download the latest patches for just about any Microsoft product. The same holds true for other vendors as well (though many of them provide only CompuServe or Internet access, so you'll have to check to make sure you'll find the vendor you need on the service to which you subscribe). I've often found a needed NetWare patch on the NetWire forum on CompuServe.

Tip: As of this writing, the best place to go for both patches and information is the Internet. CompuServe used to be the place to go to contact Microsoft, but they've moved from there to the Internet. Older application documentation still lists CompuServe as a source of information, and it is, but you won't get vendor-specific help there any longer.

WUGNET does maintain many of the forums that you used to find staffed by Microsoft employees on CompuServe, so the CompuServe GO word in your manual may still work. In addition, Microsoft does maintain certain features on CompuServe, such as the Microsoft Knowledge Base.

If you think CompuServe or any other online forum is all software, think again. Practical Peripherals, AST, Hewlett-Packard, IBM, and other hardware vendors provide valuable services there too. I think you'll find this hardware presence useful each time you need to download a new driver or ask a configuration question regarding Windows 95. You'll find the same level of expertise in those areas that you find in the software areas.

CompuServe and other online forums aren't all work. You'll also find several areas that deal specifically with the fun end of life. For example, some CompuServe forums deal with travel and hobbies. Some online services, such as the Sierra Network, specialize in games or other forms of entertainment. The list goes on and on. I dare say that if you get online, you'll never visit every forum there is—or even scratch the surface of the knowledge you could use. An online forum can provide a wealth of information and enhance the way you work. If you're really interested in all these other activities, I suggest that you get one of the many books on the market that deal specifically with online computing.

The Microsoft Network

Windows 95 comes with the capability to use Microsoft Network (MSN) as part of the installed features. Chapter 20 takes an initial look at what you can expect to find. Actually, that chapter covers more of the usage end of the product—how to get something done. Let's take a look at MSN from another perspective.

I don't want to tour every nook and cranny of MSN, but I'd like to give you an idea of what's available. The problem is that even the look I give you right now won't be quite complete. Microsoft is constantly changing MSN in an effort to make it easier to use. In addition, their marketing staff has changed direction several times since the inception of MSN, so this online service is very much a moving target at this point. With that in mind, let's take a look at what you'll find today. (At least you'll know what features are available right now.) It's important to remember that this appendix provides more of an overview of the features you'll find on MSN, rather than a precise description of content.

The top menu, Categories, is the place to begin with MSN. One of the things I've noticed recently is Microsoft's trend toward simplifying MSN. Readers of the first version of this book will notice that MSN has a much cleaner appearance now. There are fewer top-level icons, but they're better arranged now and offer quality features that make finding what you need faster and easier. MSN still doesn't offer even a modicum of what you'll find on some online services such as CompuServe and

America Online, but their services may actually be more in line with the direction that users are taking. A few minutes of using this service will show a lot of Internet connections. In other words, MSN provides a kind of organized gateway to the Internet, more than anything else. (Don't get me wrong. MSN isn't exclusively a front end for the Internet, but it does rely heavily on connections to the Internet.)

Like any online service, MSN uses a hierarchical format to allow you to "drill down" to the specific areas you want to find. Unlike many other services, though, using the hierarchical format is easy with MSN. In fact, you really can't get away from it because of the Explorer interface that MSN uses. Figure A.1 shows how this top-level folder grouping looks. The following sections tell you a little about each entry.

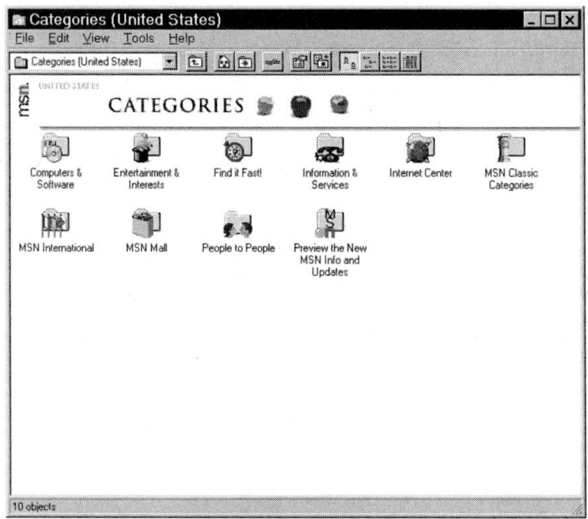

Figure A.1.
The top level of the MSN Explorer interface tells you about the major features you'll find here.

Note: This section of the appendix looks at the new MSN layout. I also describe how you can use the classic layout in place of this new one, if desired. Skip to the later section "MSN Classic Categories" for a quick look at the older layout method.

Computers & Software

This folder contains the kinds of entries that you'd expect: hardware, software, training, and access to more than a few magazine vendors, such as Pinnacle Publishing, Windows Source, Computer Gaming World, and *PC Magazine*. Figure A.2 shows an overview of the Computers & Software folder, but you'll want to explore all of the entries here to find everything that MSN has to offer. Some of the folders, such as Computer Forums, are simply packed with places to go to find user-provided information. Other forums offer a good source of vendor-specific information. Look under the Software folder and you'll find a broad range of topics—everything from desktop publishing to the latest game—the kinds of things you would expect to find. There are some very interesting offerings in the Software folder as well, such as the Safe Computing Forum and the Engineering Software folders.

Figure A.2.
The Computers & Software folder contains locations for just about everything you'd want to know about your machine.

Standard folders such as Software and Hardware might be the meat-and-potatoes of online computing, but most people want more. It's the other folders, such as On Computers w/Gina Smith, that you'll find interesting. One folder is devoted to multimedia and another to networking and telephony, for example. There's even a special folder named Preview the New MSN Info and Updates that allows you to take a peek at what Microsoft is doing. Some online services, such as CompuServe, keep this type of information completely hidden.

The Altair Pavilion is a good place to go if you have questions about your computer or the computer industry in general. It appears that they have an online chat section where you can ask questions during a live session, but it wasn't active when I checked. You'll see announcements in MSN Today regarding the various seminars and other services provided at the Altair Café. You can also look in the TODAY'S EVENTS in C&S section for information on what you can expect to find in Altair Café and other places on MSN.

Overall, you'll find everything a home user will need in the Computers & Software folder if all you're looking for is help from other users or a basic level of vendor support. On the other hand, if you need extensive help from a vendor, or your vendor isn't one of the lucky few that appear on MSN, you'll probably have to use an online service such as CompuServe—at least in the interim, until Microsoft garners the support it needs. There were only 2 hardware vendors and 16 software vendors as MSN neared its opening date of August 24, 1995. As of this writing, you'll find at least 46 software vendors and 14 hardware vendors at your disposal—a vast improvement over the past few months, but still far short of the offerings provided by other online services such as CompuServe.

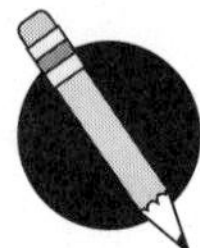

Note: Despite the very long way that Microsoft has gone in improving this particular folder, it's still far less complete than similar offerings on other online services. For example, you won't find anything from IBM here for hardware-related help. Similarly, Borland is missing for software-related help. Interestingly, Corel offers support on MSN, which only goes to show that you should check before you assume that some level of support is either supplied or missing. In addition, you'll want to verify whether that support is provided on MSN itself or is simply an Internet link. More than a few of the icons connect you to the Internet rather than to an MSN-specific forum.

Entertainment & Interests

You'll find much of what you'd expect here. Many of the folders are devoted to writers, musicians, artists, comedians, and a variety of other entertainment-related fields. Figure A.3 shows an overview of the Entertainment & Interests folder. You can also find out about television, radio, and the theater here. In fact, you'll find just about any artistic endeavor that also deals with entertainment. There's also a well-designed section devoted to movies. It includes not only a forum for aspiring movie makers, but a movie review BBS and other movie-related features. I was happy to see sections specifically devoted to kids, teens, and adults. Two special sections allow you to voice your opinion about movies in the theater or on video.

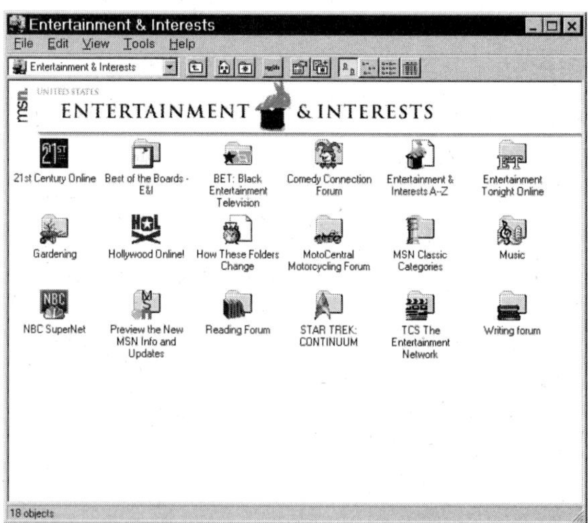

Figure A.3.
You'll find all of the non-computer recreation-related MSN offerings in the Entertainment & Interests folder.

Don't get the idea that you'll find only entertainment or artistic topics here. The Gardening folder provides a wealth of information in several areas. For example, one of the folders contains tips on starting seedlings indoors. There's even a special folder for kids in this section. Unlike some areas of

MSN, the Internet connections are clearly labeled. You get to decide whether to use MSN or another ISP for these offerings before you attempt to open them.

Science fiction fans will probably notice the STAR TREK: CONTINUUM folder almost immediately. Unfortunately, this particular folder links to the Internet, not to science fiction-specific sections on MSN. Another folder named 21st Century Online offers a tad more substance. At least you can converse with other people interested in science fiction. This folder contains an interesting picture gallery and a link to a chat section as well. There are also the requisite Internet links, which in this case are clearly marked.

Find It Fast

In line with Microsoft's new commitment to make finding information as fast as possible on MSN, you'll find that this new section contains a wealth of search aids. There are two basic ways of searching: Either you can look for information in a specific category, or you can search MSN as a whole. Figure A.4 shows an overview of Find It Fast.

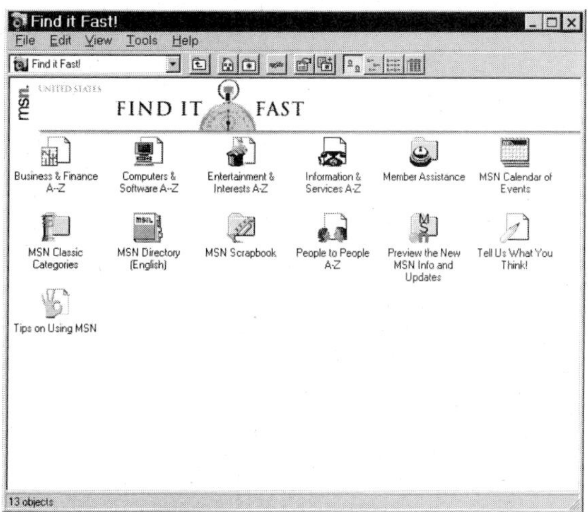

Figure A.4.
Trying to find something fast is pretty hard on any online service—the Find It Fast folder makes life a lot easier on MSN.

Let's talk about category-specific searches first. You'll notice that there are several folders that end in A–Z, such as the Computers & Software A–Z folder. Opening any of these folders presents a Help-like display of the various offerings in that particular category. All you need to do is click one of the underlined entries to go to that section of MSN. Figure A.5 shows what you'd see if you opened the Computers & Software A–Z folder. Notice that all the entries are in alphabetical order and include a short description. I like to view this format as the encyclopedic form of searching. It allows you to determine whether the entry is really the one you wanted in the first place, before you actually go there.

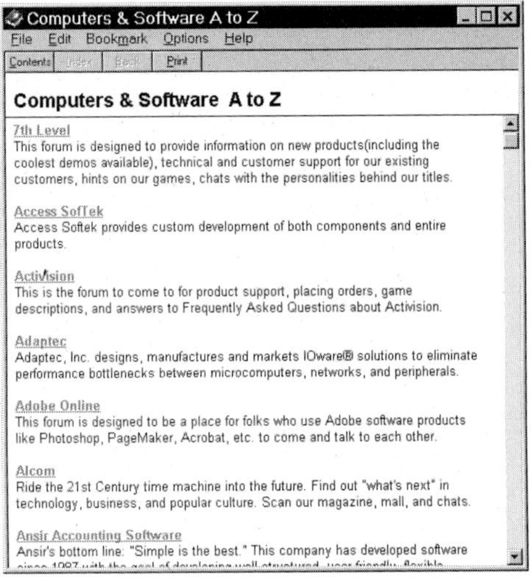

Figure A.5.
Use one of the A–Z folders to conduct an encyclopedic-type search for specific information.

Everyone knows how useful the telephone book is when it comes to finding a telephone number. The MSN Directory works much like a telephone book. Figure A.6 shows what it looks like when using the alphabetical order option. As with the telephone book, you have a couple of ways to search for information. Using the alphabetical option is much like using the white pages—if you know what you're looking for, this presentation is both fast and efficient to use. On the other hand, using the category option is much like using the yellow pages. MSN features are grouped together by type. This option comes in handy if you're pretty sure of what you're looking for, but aren't quite sure which MSN folder provides that kind of information. All you need to do is click the desired link, once you find it, and MSN displays it for you. This search method doesn't offer any kind of description for the various entries.

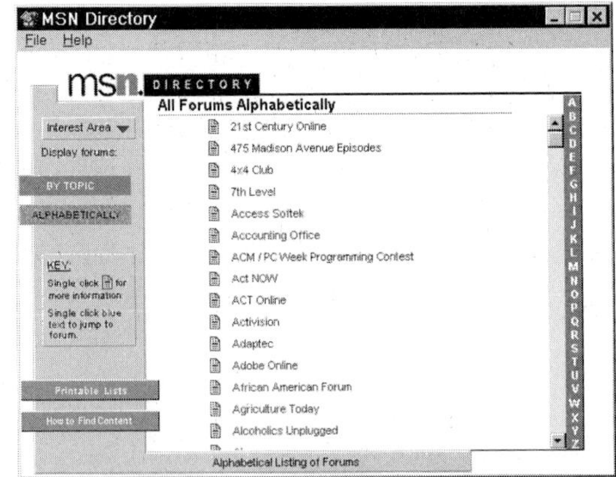

Figure A.6.
Think of MSN Directory as a telephone book—it allows you to find just the name of the feature you want to use.

Information & Services

This folder turned out to be a junk drawer of various MSN offerings that really didn't fit anywhere else. (Even if they did fit somewhere else, like Computers & Software, they also showed up here.) Figure A.7 shows an overview of this folder, but you won't really know too much about it until you take the time to explore. We'll take a quick trip now so that you at least have some idea of what to expect.

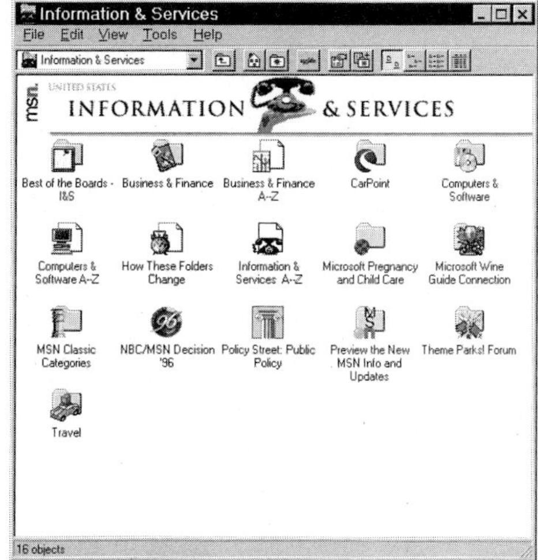

Figure A.7.
The Information & Services folder contains everything but the kitchen sink.

Let's talk about the Business & Finance folder first. My first thought about this area was that it would offer access to *The Wall Street Journal* and other sources of financial information. (Admittedly, there's a rather anemic section called Investing that doesn't really tell you much except the stock prices for the day and some business news.) Don't get me wrong—this section does contain a lot of interesting entries. If you run a small business out of your home, for example, you'll find a forum specially designed to meet that need. A folder in the MSN Small Office/Home Office (SOHO) area contains all kinds of business services. You'll find an Ask a Lawyer forum here, as well as access to TRW. I was also very pleased to see a both a Federal Express and a UPS forum. You can schedule packages for pickup or check on the status of a package while online. One of the more unusual offerings was access to the PhotoDisk service. Once I got out of the Small Office/Home Office folder, I found that the Business & Finance folder includes an area where professionals of various persuasions could meet to discuss their trade. It includes 15 professional category folders, such as real estate and accounting. Each category folder contains professions as diverse as airline pilots, doctors, and fashion designers. Overall, the Business & Finance folder seems tuned to the needs of a small business or a home user. This area needs a lot of work if you plan to find anything of a high-end or serious nature.

Another major area in this folder deals with travel. You can open the Travel folder if you need general travel information. For example, you'll find United Airlines here. There's also a folder called Time Sharing, which allows you to hook up with other people who want to go in on a time-share condo or house. Need to find out about the place you're going to? The On the Spot Travel Guides folder may contain exactly what you need. If you're going to Europe, you won't want to miss the Friends of Europe Forum folder. The Travel folder contains a Theme Parks folder. This same folder appears one level up in the Information & Services folder. As the name implies, you can find out about any theme park here before you actually travel to it. There are special folders here for the bigger theme parks like The Disney Parks and Six Flags. You can also check out the Theme Parks File Library folder if you want to see a picture of the theme park before you go there. One folder even contains short videos of the various theme parks in AVI format.

Some of the less impressive areas of the Information & Services folder include Microsoft Wine Guide Connection and Microsoft Pregnancy and Child Care. The Microsoft Wine Guide Connection folder gives you access to both present and past issues of an online magazine. There's also a connection to the Internet where you can find additional information. Likewise, the Microsoft Pregnancy and Child Care folder contains links to several chat sections, a BBS or two, and the Internet. Neither folder is very extensive—a real disappointment after seeing the much-improved areas that MSN provides.

Rounding out this folder are a couple of interesting entries. I've already discussed the Computers & Software folder in this appendix, so I won't discuss it here again. Notice that you can also access several of the A–Z folders that I described earlier, in the "Find It Fast" section. From time to time, you'll also find some floating folders. For example, because it was an election year as I wrote this, I found an NBC/MSN Decision '96 folder. Obviously this folder will be gone by the time you read this, but expect it to be replaced by other folders as world events take place.

The Internet Center

I'll take a complete look at this area in Appendix B, but let me give you a quick rundown. The Internet Center allows you to access the Internet. Figure A.8 provides an overview of what you can expect to find here, though the exact contents of this folder appear to change on a daily basis. It also provides quick access to many of the news services on the Internet. It's especially important to look at the Getting on the Internet folder, because it provides special news and information regarding any Internet. The document you download will also contain an icon that requests full access to any Internet resources that MSN provides, including adult material that you won't normally see. Not surprisingly, this was the most active area on MSN during my visits there.

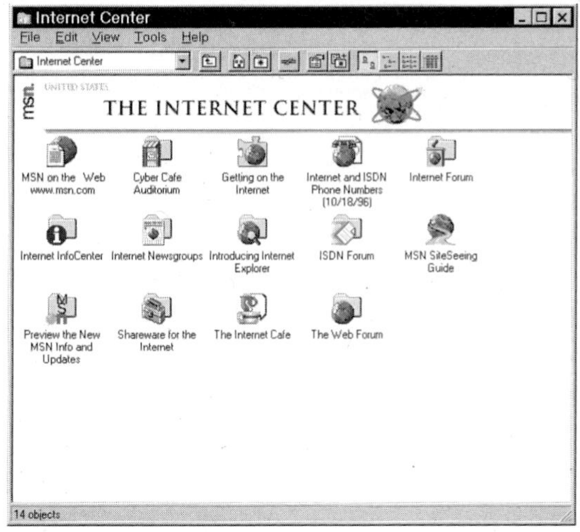

Figure A.8.
Like the Internet itself, the contents of the Internet Center folder change on an almost daily basis.

MSN Classic Categories

A lot of folks really hate change. When Microsoft dramatically changed the layout of MSN to the one described in this appendix, a lot of people didn't like it at all. If you can't find anything on MSN after the change, open the MSN Classic Categories folder shown in Figure A.9. This folder contains the old layout that you know and love. Be sure to add the location to your Favorite Places. That way, you won't have to go through the new layout to view the MSN Categories.

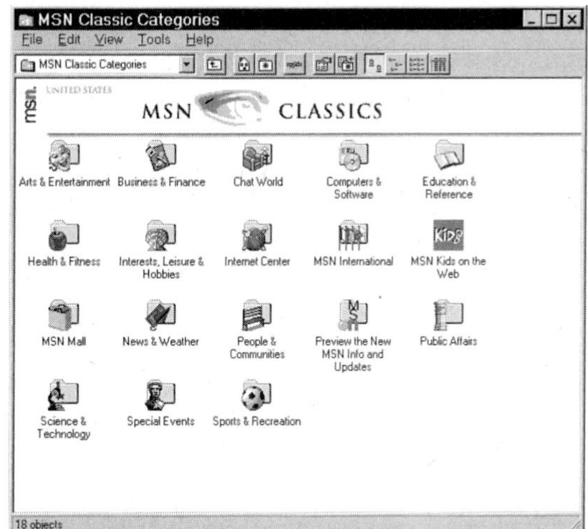

Figure A.9.
People who hate change will like the MSN Classic Categories folder.

MSN International

One of the things that's most attractive about online services is their international appeal. One of the ways that I feel MSN is ahead of the game is in this particular area. Unlike other online services, where you may be stuck trying to work in English even if you speak German, this section allows you to access sections in other languages. Instead of a Health and Fitness section, for example, the German Categories listing contains Gesundheit and Fitness. In other words, you get to use MSN in the language you know best. Figure A.10 shows an overview of the MSN International folder at the time of this writing. Fortunately, Microsoft seems determined to address the needs of every major language on the planet.

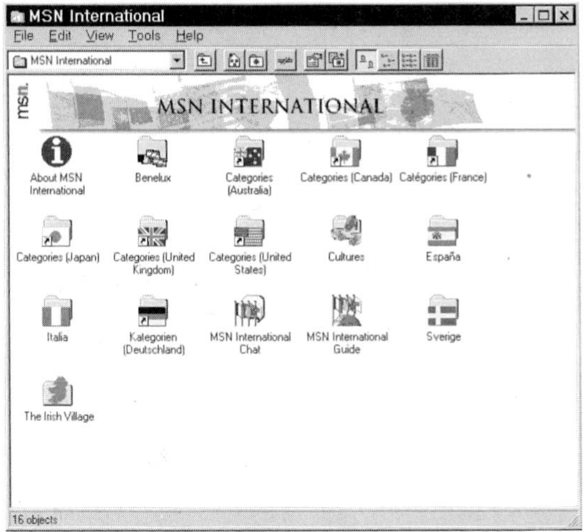

Figure A.10.
Don't worry about using MSN if you speak another language—MSN provides a set of categories in the language you need.

MSN Mall

Just like any other mall, you'll find a lot of stores here. Figure A.11 provides an overview of the MSN Mall folder. I found a few unexpected offerings, such as Gourmet Gift Net, with stores like Bella Java and Sweet Decadence. For the most part, though, you'll find the expected offerings, such as American Greetings and Columbia House. Of course, it wouldn't be much of a mall without an MSN Gift Shop; you can buy T-shirts and other MSN gifts here. The MSN Mall is a lot smaller than I anticipated. I'm attributing the size to the relative newness of the online service at the moment. Hopefully, Microsoft will entice other businesses to frequent the mall as well.

Figure A.11.
MSN Mall provides an online version of the real thing.

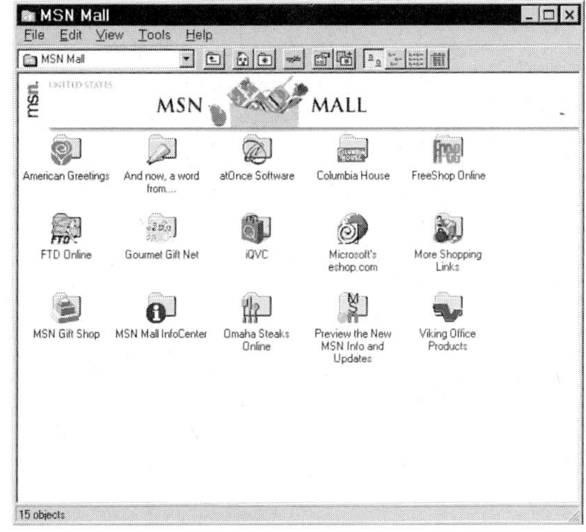

People to People

Interpersonal relations over an online service can be a fairly confusing, not to mention error-prone, kind of contact. Consider the lack of body language and other problems of trying to get your meaning across over a wire instead of face-to-face. That's why this particular folder is so important. It provides the tools you need to perform various kinds of online communication. Figure A.12 provides an overview of the People to People folder.

Figure A.12.
The People to People folder provides a variety of ways to talk with other people online.

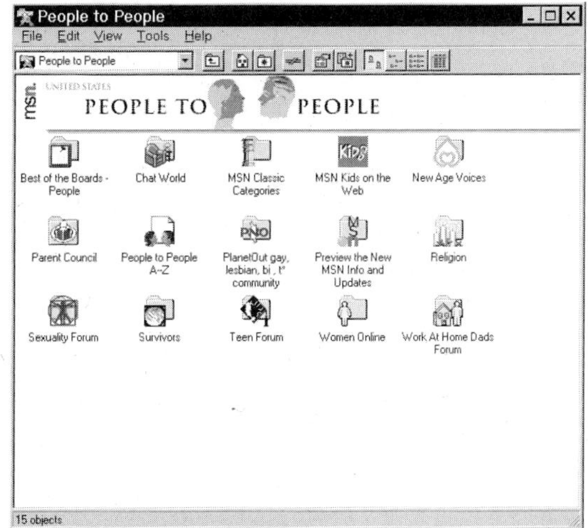

You'll want to come to Chat World area of MSN to talk with other people. I'm not talking heavy business discussions, but the kind of light conversation you might have with your next-door neighbor. In fact, there's even an Atrium Restaurant you can visit. There are seats here for two, five, or ten people, just so you can have an intimate discussion with someone without having the entire world barge in on your conversation. If you prefer a garden to a restaurant, Chat World has one of those, too. For a little more open discussion, you can go to places like the Games and Casino section. Section names such as CheyAnne Dance Hall and Karaoke Bar don't really say much about what's going on, but they do inspire the imagination.

In addition to the general-purpose Chat World folder, the People to People folder contains some special-purpose folders. Unfortunately, MSN currently supports only a few of the items you would see on other online services. There's a section for men who work at home, another for women, and one for discussing religion. You'll also find support groups here. For example, the Survivor folder helps those who have lived through some type of trauma in their lives. The Teen Forum can help teens talk out some of the issues they face. There also are forums for holidays and special occasions (where you can discuss the holidays or other events practiced by your culture or a culture in another country).

Preview the New MSN Info and Updates

I've always liked to get prepared for changes as they occur. That's one of the reasons I applaud Microsoft's efforts by providing this particular folder. It allows you to decide whether to wait until a change happens or to prepare for it now. Figure A.13 shows the kinds of folders that you'll find here as of this writing. (For obvious reasons, the contents of this folder are extremely volatile.)

Figure A.13.
Microsoft keeps you informed about future MSN updates through the Preview the New MSN Info and Updates folder.

You can more or less count on seeing at least two of these folders at all times. The Internet and ISDN Phone Numbers icon downloads updated access phone numbers to your computer. You can use this option if you want to keep MSN up-to-date without doing a lot of reading. The Update Your MSN Phonebook Now! icon displays some instructions for completing the update. It also displays a complete list of the current access numbers—just in case you need to find a new one in your area.

WUGNET (Windows Users Group Network)

Windows Users Group Network (WUGNET) isn't an online service, but it's an important group to get to know. They have a forum on CompuServe and many user groups throughout the United States. WUGNET also has its own newsletter, *Windows Journal*. They encourage people to contribute articles. If you're interested, contact Howard Sobel at 76702,1356 or at sobel@libertynet.org. Sobel is also your contact on CompuServe for many forum-related activities.

WUGNET was founded in 1988 as an independent organization devoted to providing technical resources for Windows users. Their main goal is to communicate trends and developments in Windows programming and usage to the user community on an international level. They also get involved in some standardization efforts, but their actual participation isn't as easy to see here as it is elsewhere.

What will working with WUGNET buy you? They provide presentations about Windows in general through CompuServe, conferences, trade shows, publications, trade books, and various membership interactions. You can access their forum using the command `GO WUGNET`. You'll also find that their members are very active on the WinNews forum. This is a special forum that Microsoft developed just for the Windows 95 beta prerelease program. Now that Windows 95 is a released product, WUGNET maintains the WinNews forum as a place to get the latest news on Windows 95 updates and support software.

Note: Joining WUGNET is easy. All you need to do is fill out a membership form that you can download from the CompuServe forum. They offer a range of membership levels, including both personal and corporate rates. WUGNET also provides a few points of contact outside of CompuServe. Here's the information for their main membership contact:

Jim Herndon
Windows Users Group Network
126 E. State St.
Media, PA 19063

E-mail: CompuServe 76702,1356
Internet e-mail: sobel@libertynet.org

Telephone: (215) 565-1861
Fax: (215) 565-7106

Direct membership enrollment: 800-WIN-USER (1-800-946-8737)

When you become a member of WUGNET, you'll receive a toolkit. It contains a variety of things, including online Windows Help versions of the Microsoft Windows 3.1 and Windows for Workgroups resource kits, WUGNET System Engineer, and a support-oriented CompuServe forum with a private library for members. System Engineer is the most interesting tool of the group. It allows you to decipher the myriad entries in the SYSTEM.INI and WIN.INI files on your machine. System Engineer also provides a variety of performance and resource-monitoring tools. Overall, you'll find this a helpful tool for any version of Windows, but it is admittedly Windows 3.x-specific for the moment. Hopefully, they'll come up with a version of this valuable tool for Windows 95. Of course, this toolkit also includes *Windows Journal,* which I mentioned earlier.

In addition to the direct benefits you get from being a WUGNET member, there are other bonuses. The one that most people will really appreciate is reduced prices for software and hardware from a variety of vendors. Some of these vendors include Lotus, Artisoft, Knowledge Garden, hDC, and Micrografx. This is just a short list, but it shows the wide variety of vendors who provide support for WUGNET.

There's also a CD offering for Windows 95 users. It contains a wealth of shareware and freeware utilities. These are demo versions of programs from people you don't know. In addition to the shareware and freeware, you'll find some fully-functional utilities from name-brand vendors. Some of the companies who provide software for this CD include Attachmate, American Megatrends, Inc. (AMI), Micrografx, and yours truly. Yes, that's right: You'll see a Personal Training Systems Product—*Peter Norton Presents Windows 95 Made Easy Tutorial*—as part of the WUGNET Windows 95 CD.

Microsoft Knowledge Base

Before I get into a full-fledged look at the Microsoft offerings on the Internet in detail, I'd like to look at one special Microsoft URL called the Microsoft Knowledge Base. (You can also access the Knowledge Base using CompuServe.) This isn't a standard Web site like the others you find on the Internet. Rather, it's a library of articles, white papers, and other sources of information that you need to use specific Microsoft products. We'll see later how this special forum fits into the overall scheme of things. Right now, I'd like to cover why it's important and how you use it.

I often look at the Microsoft Knowledge Base for information about the future direction of Microsoft products. For example, I was able to find a white paper dealing with Program Manager issues in Windows 95. You can also find out a lot about problems people are having—people just like you—and Microsoft's suggested solutions. One white paper told me about Windows 95 and After Dark 2.0 issues that I could expect. Finally, you can find out the technical details of a product. While browsing through the Knowledge Base, I found a white paper that provided an explanation of system resources in Windows 95. It's not too difficult to figure out that the Knowledge Base is more like a fax support line than anything else. However, the method you use to interact with it is a lot different.

The problem with using automated support in most cases is that unless you really know what you're looking for, it's not very likely that you'll find it. I've been through some fax support lines that are so unfriendly you won't get any information at all unless you know a specific article name or its number. Microsoft Knowledge Base is different. It provides a search engine that you can use to actually find the information you're looking for. So how do you use this nifty Microsoft offering? The first thing you need is an Internet (or CompuServe) account. Follow the specific guidelines from your software vendor for getting an account set up and your communications software installed. Many ISPs use Netscape Navigator or Microsoft Internet Explorer. CompuServe accounts normally come with CompuServe Information Manager, though many other programs are available for this online service.

Once you get completely set up, you need to get online. If you plan to access the Knowledge Base from within CompuServe, you'll need to use terminal mode. (Products such as CompuServe Information Manager use this mode as a default. Other products, such as TapCIS and OZWin, require you to enter a special command to get into terminal mode.) After you get online, Internet users go to `http://www.microsoft.com/kb/`. CompuServe users use whatever command your communication package provides to `GO MSKB`. When you get there, you see a menu with the following options:

Note: The menu options may vary, depending on how you access the Knowledge Base. These bullets provide the entries that you'll normally see online. CompuServe and the Internet use similar menus, but there are enough differences that they're noted here, along with the online service that supports them.

- **What's New in the Knowledge Base (CompuServe):** This option displays a help screen that tells you about the features provided by Microsoft Knowledge Base and any new articles you need to know about. It also keeps you up-to-date on future article additions. You can download this help screen by typing `DOWN` at the prompt.
- **Description of Database (CompuServe):** Use this option to display a general help screen telling you what kinds of information Microsoft Knowledge Base provides. As with the preceding selection, you can download it to your hard drive for future reference by typing `DOWN` at the prompt.

- **Online User's Guide (CompuServe):** You can use this option to get detailed information about the various search engine features and how to use them. It's a lot more detailed than the first menu option and goes through every menu entry that you'll see. Downloading this help screen also means typing `DOWN` at the prompt.
- **Find Out About Support (Internet):** This entry takes you to a page that describes the various support options that Microsoft provides. You can look at specific product support options. A menu along the side allows you to move between the Knowledge Base and other support options like Software Library.
- **Check Our Frequently Asked Questions (Internet):** Use this entry if you want to download a list of the questions asked most often by users (along with the answers you'll need). FAQ (Frequently Asked Question) sheets can save you a lot of search time, because it's likely that other users will have had the same problems you have. Obviously, this isn't going to work all the time, but it beats spending hours looking for just the piece of information you need using the Knowledge Base.
- **Search the Knowledge Base (Both):** This is the option that most people will use. It displays a menu-driven method of obtaining the name and number of various articles. You can choose to download the article immediately or save the number for future reference. A little later in this section, I discuss the search criteria that this option provides.
- **Search Using Expert Mode (CompuServe):** Some people hate menus. Once you gain a little experience with the Microsoft Knowledge Base, you can use the expert mode to search for articles without using the menu. I don't find this particular method any faster than using the menu-driven approach, but you can use it to automate your searches, using script files.
- **Quick Search by Document ID Number (Both):** Sometimes a support person on one of Microsoft's forums will tell you to download a specific Knowledge Base article for more information about a particular problem. Some questions are asked so often that it's easier to provide a complete answer in an article and allow the user to download it as needed. In addition, some problems are a little more complex than others. This method allows a support person to provide a complete answer even when the question is very complicated. A message on one of the forums just wouldn't provide the same level of information. CompuServe provides an option where you can enter the "Q" number of the document directly. The Internet requires URLs. Fortunately, there's an order to the URLs. For example, if you need to find the article that I mentioned earlier about Windows 95 and After Dark 2.0, the URL is `http://www.microsoft.com/kb/peropsys/win95/q116452.htm`. The beginning part of the URL takes you to the Knowledge Base, the next part (`peropsys`) takes you to the Personal Operating System section, the next part selects Windows 95, and finally you enter the "Q" number of the document. Yes, it's less convenient to use the Internet in this case than CompuServe, but it works.

- **Microsoft Software Library/Download Driver, Patch, or Sample File (Both):** Sometimes you need a new driver or patch to take care of a problem. The Knowledge Base articles you download might contain an "S" number. You can use this number to download the correct software. All you need to do is select this option and provide the number when asked.
- **Visit Our Newsgroups (Internet):** This option takes you to a page that helps you select the right newsgroup for your product. It sure beats searching for the newsgroup by hand. I also find it slightly easier than trying to find the right `GO` word on CompuServe.

The Search the Knowledge Base selection is probably the most likely choice unless someone from Microsoft directs you to a specific article or you use the search engine quite a bit. Once you choose this option, you see a menu of choices for limiting the number of articles that the Microsoft Knowledge Base displays. This menu allows you to choose the following criteria: product name, product version, publication date, operating environment, document type, document text, and title text. The last two options allow you to display all the articles that Microsoft Knowledge Base found and start a new search.

CompuServe Forums

CompuServe is absolutely huge. I don't think I've ever really seen everything it has to offer. There's something here for everyone, no matter what your occupation, hobbies, or interests. Seeing really is believing. In fact, it's so large that most people seem to stick to one or two areas because of the number of features that CompuServe has to offer. Besides news, weather, and the stock market, you can shop online and access other services such as Delphi. I even use CompuServe to access the Internet and look for reference materials in Books in Print.

One of the biggest areas that CompuServe offers is software. I've seen vendors here that you would never expect to see online. Just about every game and utility vendor that has any market share at all is here. Many shareware vendors are here as well. You'll also find big companies such as Borland, Computer Associates, and Lotus. Some companies have more than one forum to offer. For example, both Computer Associates and Novell occupy more than one forum area.

Suffice it to say that the rumor of CompuServe's immediate demise is greatly exaggerated. On the other hand, Microsoft has removed a great deal of its presence from CompuServe and either turned it over to WUGNET or moved it completely to the Internet. You're going to find that some of the `GO` words you used in the past won't work anymore. At least Microsoft left behind warning messages like this one to help you find what you need:

```
The area you are trying to access has been removed. Please type
GO MICROSOFT or GO WINSUPPORT to access Microsoft products. We
apologize for any inconvenience.
```

Even though a few vendors have moved to the Internet, CompuServe still represents a very viable place to get information. In fact, it would be difficult to describe in an appendix what some entire books have a problem describing. Some of these books are as large as or even larger than this one, and still can't provide a complete listing of all the features that CompuServe provides. With that in mind, I want to concentrate on one area. Since this book is about Windows 95, I'll tell you what kinds of services Microsoft and WUGNET have to offer. (If you want the exclusive Microsoft view, look at the later section "Microsoft's Presence on the Internet.")

This section covers Microsoft's CompuServe forums (or those managed now by WUGNET), a vast array of places you can use to get answers for every conceivable question. These forums also offer download services that provide free updates to Microsoft products. (Of course, you see this service only when the update is free of charge.) Figures A.14 through A.16 provide an overview of Microsoft's CompuServe forums.

As you can see from these figures, Microsoft's CompuServe offering is huge—and this doesn't even include all the beta forums that Microsoft supports. If you feel a little overwhelmed by the number of services that Microsoft offers, you're not alone. You could spend days just trying to find the right forum for your particular needs. For that matter, unless you use a product such as WinCIM (a Windows-based communication program specifically designed for use with CompuServe) to maneuver through the labyrinth of CompuServe menus, you might not even reach your destination. Using Figures A.14 through A.16 should make your job easier and allow you to use more cost-conscious tools such as TapCIS to find your way through CompuServe. Microsoft also offers some special forms of WinCIM that include all the required `GO` words as part of the Favorite Places listing. One of these appears on the Microsoft Developer Network (MSDN).

Figures A.14 through A.16 are arranged in a hierarchical format. This means that the upper-level menus appear first. The actual forums appear at the bottom of the hierarchical tree. Notice the `GO` words in parentheses beside each menu or forum name. A `GO` word provides a shortcut on CompuServe. If you know the `GO` word, you can go directly to the menu or forum that you want to see. Not every menu entry has a `GO` word, but enough are provided in Figures A.14 through A.16 to greatly decrease your search time. Every forum has a `GO` word, making it easy to get to any forum you want to visit. You type **`GO`** ***`<forum name>`*** to get to your destination. Some software programs such as WinCIM, OzWin, and TapCIS automate the `GO` part of the command for you, but you still need to provide the forum name. Most of the CompuServe-specific communications software allows you to add the forum name to a list so you don't have to remember it each time you want to access the forum.

Notice that the upper-level menu doesn't list product areas or forums. What this level provides is access to Microsoft forums in various languages. This allows you to communicate with Microsoft even if you don't understand English. Unfortunately, not every language provides all the services that the Microsoft US section does, so you might need to use this section in some cases.

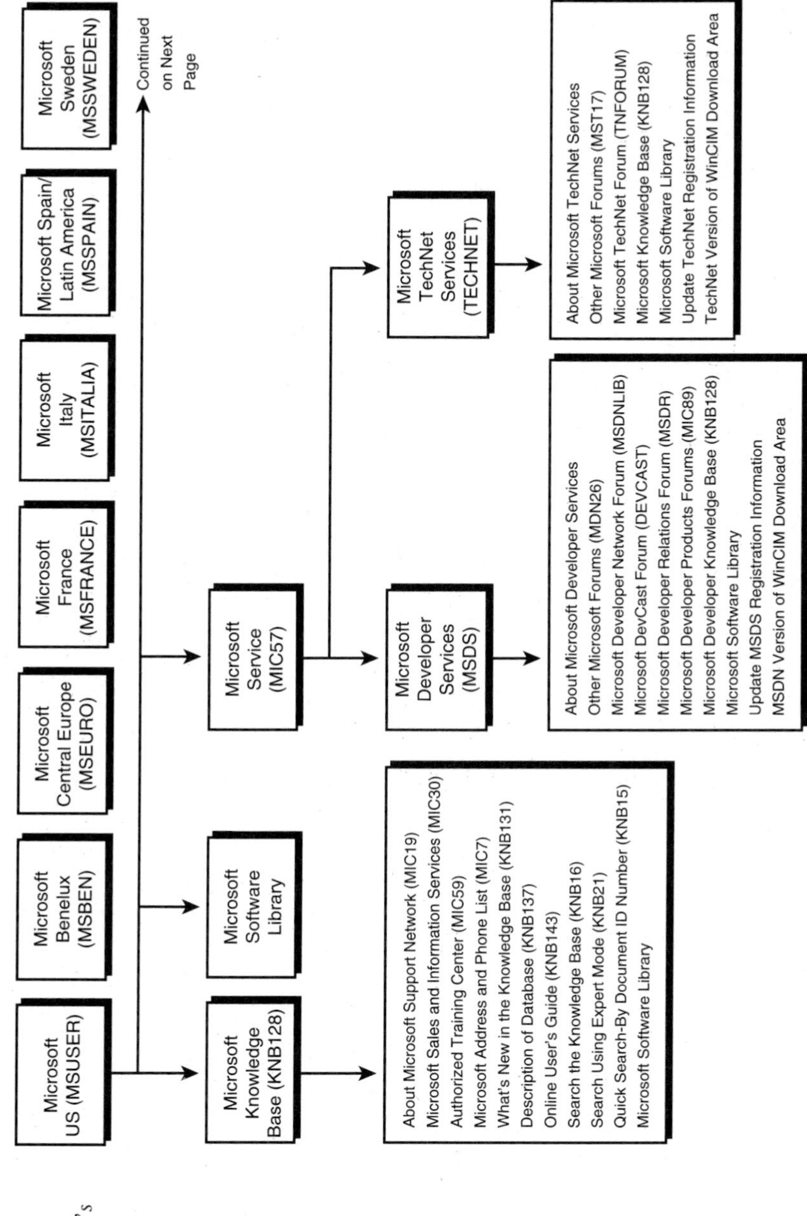

Figure A.14. *A hierarchical view of Microsoft's CompuServe offering.*

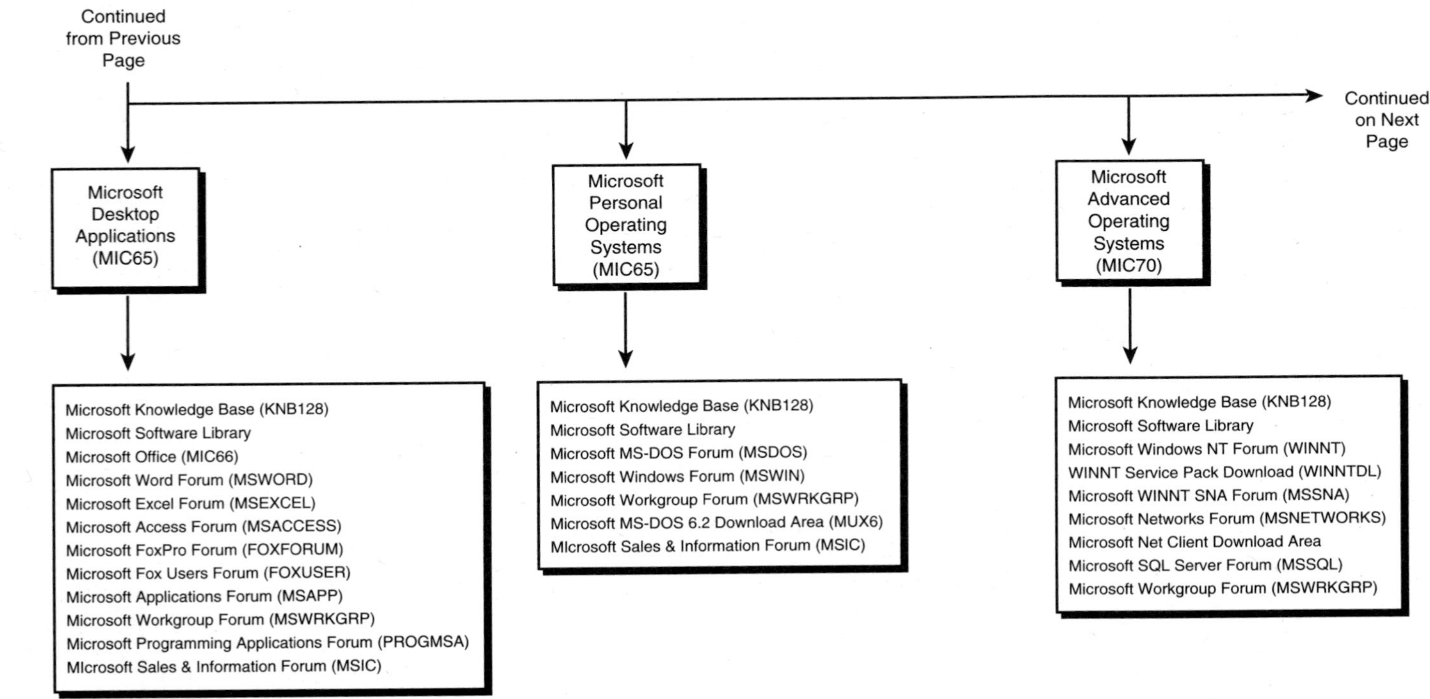
Continued from Previous Page
Continued on Next Page
Microsoft Desktop Applications (MIC65)
Microsoft Knowledge Base (KNB128)
Microsoft Software Library
Microsoft Office (MIC66)
Microsoft Word Forum (MSWORD)
Microsoft Excel Forum (MSEXCEL)
Microsoft Access Forum (MSACCESS)
Microsoft FoxPro Forum (FOXFORUM)
Microsoft Fox Users Forum (FOXUSER)
Microsoft Applications Forum (MSAPP)
Microsoft Workgroup Forum (MSWRKGRP)
Microsoft Programming Applications Forum (PROGMSA)
MIcrosoft Sales & Information Forum (MSIC)
Microsoft Personal Operating Systems (MIC65)
Microsoft Knowledge Base (KNB128)
Microsoft Software Library
Microsoft MS-DOS Forum (MSDOS)
Microsoft Windows Forum (MSWIN)
Microsoft Workgroup Forum (MSWRKGRP)
Microsoft MS-DOS 6.2 Download Area (MUX6)
MIcrosoft Sales & Information Forum (MSIC)
Microsoft Advanced Operating Systems (MIC70)
Microsoft Knowledge Base (KNB128)
Microsoft Software Library
Microsoft Windows NT Forum (WINNT)
WINNT Service Pack Download (WINNTDL)
Microsoft WINNT SNA Forum (MSSNA)
Microsoft Networks Forum (MSNETWORKS)
Microsoft Net Client Download Area
Microsoft SQL Server Forum (MSSQL)
Microsoft Workgroup Forum (MSWRKGRP)

Figure A.15.
Microsoft's CompuServe offering, continued.

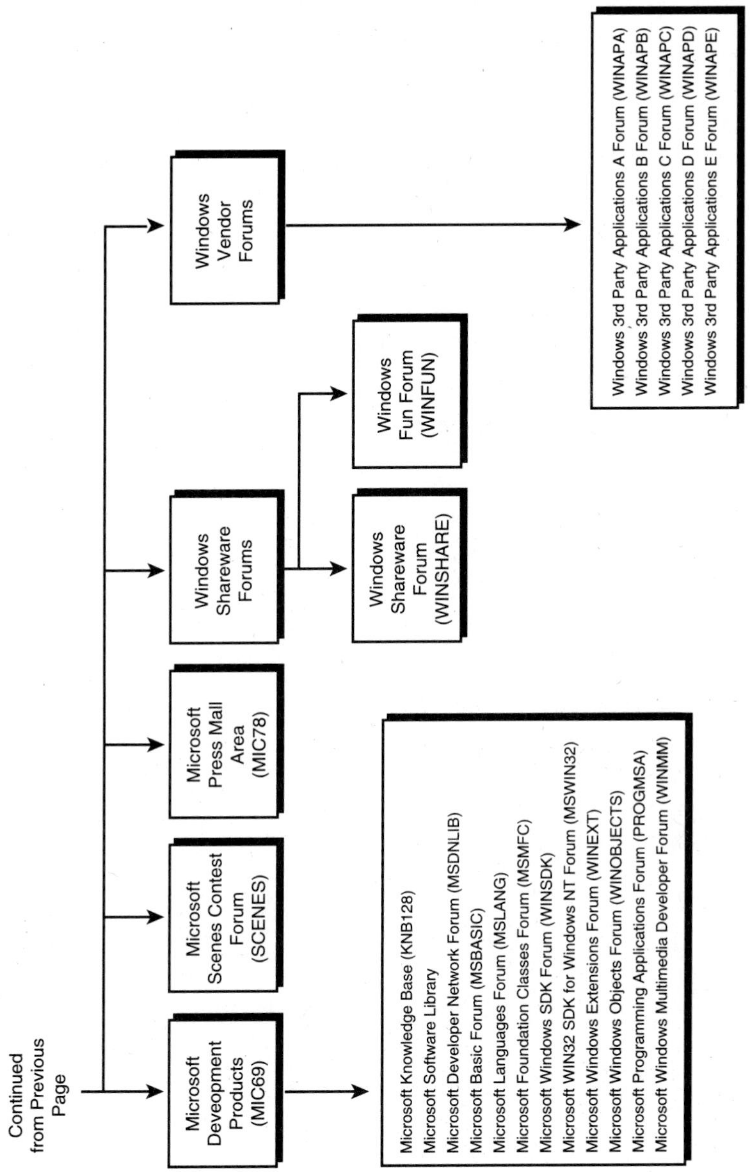

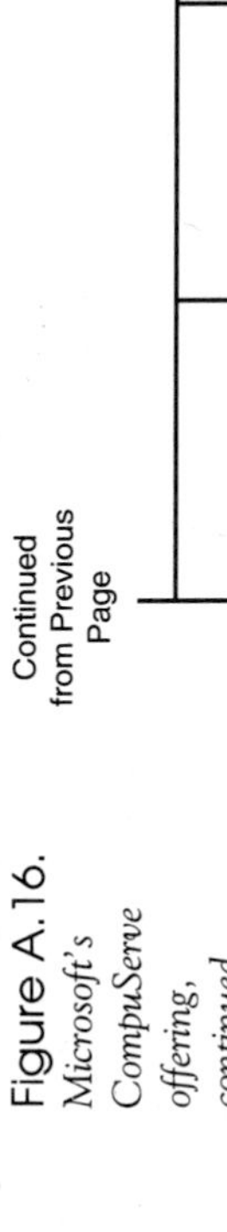

Figure A.16. *Microsoft's CompuServe offering, continued.*

Note: There's one special `GO` word that these figures don't contain. You can use `GO MSP` to get to the Microsoft Press section of the CompuServe mall. Think of the CompuServe mall as an electronic form of the one that you visit to go shopping. You'll find a wide variety of stores here in addition to Microsoft Press. You can use the Microsoft Press forum in the CompuServe mall to order books or a catalog. Using it can save you a trip to the bookstore by providing you with a complete list of the Microsoft Press books you can order. Even the best-stocked bookstore in the world might miss a selection or two out of the vast array of Microsoft Press books.

The following text describes the sections you'll find in the Microsoft US section.

Information on Microsoft

There are four Microsoft-information-related forums on CompuServe:

- The About Microsoft Support Network section tells you all about Microsoft's service support offerings. It specifically looks at what the Microsoft Support Network offers.
- Use the Microsoft Sales and Information Services selection to obtain sales and service information.
- The Authorized Training Center section provides information about Microsoft's authorized training center program. It also provides a phone number you can use to obtain further information.
- Finally, the Microsoft Address and Phone List selection provides a complete list of telephone numbers and addresses. It includes individual product service numbers as well as numbers for various Microsoft subsidiaries.

You can download any of these four items for future reference. Each one tells you about a different component of Microsoft. Unfortunately, this section doesn't provide any interactive capability. Microsoft provides these services through the plethora of forums described in the following section. Overall, this section provides you with quick references—essentially, it contains the telephone numbers you need to obtain further information.

Microsoft Knowledge Base and Microsoft Software Library

Both of these selections are covered earlier in this appendix. I'd like to provide a couple of additional paragraphs about the Microsoft Software Library, however, since it appears by itself in some areas. It provides some additional features when it appears by itself that it doesn't provide when shown as part of the Microsoft Knowledge Base. You'll see what I mean when you start using Figures A.14 through A.16 to find various areas of interest on CompuServe.

The Microsoft Software Library provides access to a wide assortment of Microsoft tested and approved software. This is differentiated from the software you normally download from forums, which Microsoft might not have tested. The Software Library uses a search engine similar to that used by the Knowledge Base. Of course, there are a few differences, due to the differences in the tasks performed by these two services.

Once you find the software you need, the Software Library gives you the opportunity to download it. There's no real difference between the download procedure for the software library and any other service on CompuServe. All you need to do is provide a filename for your computer and specify the download protocol. In most cases, your communications software will take care of the rest.

Microsoft Services

The Microsoft Services menu entry contains two submenus: Microsoft Developer Services and Microsoft TechNet Services. The Microsoft Developer Services entry provides access to all the developer-related services, such as the Microsoft Developer Network forum. A developer is someone who writes applications using any number of tools, including compilers and debuggers. This particular forum is heavily tied to the Microsoft Developer Library (formerly the Microsoft Developer Network) subscription service. This is a CD-ROM packed with information, Knowledge Base articles, books, and even some software. You can even download a special version of WinCIM in this area. This version provides special menu entries that relate to the Microsoft developer services.

Like the Developer Services area, the Microsoft TechNet Services area revolves around a CD-ROM-based subscription service. The subscription is called the Microsoft TechNet. This service is designed for people who require in-depth information on Microsoft products and how to support them. This differs from the programming language and operating system support provided by the Developer Network. The TechNet forum allows users to exchange ideas and provide feedback to Microsoft. It also provides access to TechEd information. TechEd stands for *technical education* and refers to Microsoft's education services outside the programming or operating system arena. As with the Developer Services area, you can download a special version of WinCIM for this area. This version provides special menu entries that relate to the Microsoft TechNet services.

Microsoft Desktop Applications

This area of Microsoft's CompuServe support provides access to all the user-oriented tools, such as Word, Excel, Access, and FoxPro. In fact, these four products have their own special forums. FoxPro rates two forums: one for developers and the other for users. You can usually obtain information about the other Microsoft applications by going to the Microsoft Applications forum.

Four special menu entries allow you to access the Knowledge Base, Software Library, sales, and Programming Applications forum. All four entries work just like their counterparts in other areas.

Microsoft Personal Operating Systems

Microsoft differentiates between single-user and multiuser operating systems. This area deals with single-user or personal operating systems. There are three operating systems in this category: MS-DOS, Windows, and Windows for Workgroups. The menu entries for each area are pretty self-explanatory.

Notice the special entry for the Microsoft MS-DOS 6.22 Download Area. Going to this entry allows you to download the MS-DOS 6.22 step-up software free of charge (except for connect time).

As with the other areas described in this appendix, Microsoft provides access to its Knowledge Base and Software Library in this area as well.

Microsoft Advanced Operating Systems

Microsoft set aside a special area for users of advanced operating systems. Currently only one operating system, Windows NT, falls into this category. However, you can see from the figures that a lot is going on with this one product. Notice the special areas for SNA and SQL Server. Like the other areas described in this appendix, this one also contains access to the Knowledge Base and the Software Library.

If you're a developer, you'll probably want to visit more than one of these forums. For example, if you develop Windows NT applications, you'll probably need to visit the Windows NT and Networks forums.

An application user can probably get by with just one forum. In most cases, a visit to the Windows NT forum will give you all the information you need. Unlike the developer, you work with the operating system to a greater extent in getting applications to work together properly. As a result, you'll probably want to download all the messages in this forum. Check the section titles carefully; you might find that you can eliminate one or two of them from your list. Remember, you'll probably want to visit this forum in addition to application-specific forums.

Microsoft Development Products

There's a special area in addition to the Developer Network section for application developers. The Development Products area is much more general in nature. It gives you access to all the language products that Microsoft provides. Note the special forums for Basic users and multimedia developers.

If you're a developer, you'll probably want to visit more than one of these forums. For example, if you develop Windows applications, you'll probably need to visit the Languages forum and the Windows SDK forum. Sometimes you might want to visit three or four forums. Talk about information overload! If you don't monitor your time carefully, you could easily spend all your time gathering information instead of performing useful work. Fortunately, you'll probably find that you won't need to read all the messages on the forum, just the few related to your specific areas of interest.

Microsoft Scenes Contest Forum

This is a temporary forum (just how temporary remains to be seen) that allows you to submit your photographs to the Microsoft Scenes contest. There are a few limitations and some rules that you must follow in order to enter.

Microsoft Press Mall Area

This is a special area for the computer press. You won't need to go here in most cases unless you're interested in press releases and so forth.

Windows Shareware Forums

Many people discount the value of shareware software, but Microsoft doesn't. Shareware can provide the same quality as an off-the-shelf commercial product (or better), and at a greatly reduced price. It always pays to check this area for special needs. You never know when you'll find something that a client has asked for in the past but you couldn't find.

The Windows Shareware Forums area is split into two forums: Windows Shareware Forum and Windows Fun Forum. Both forums are designed to provide a venue for you to talk with shareware authors who create Windows products. The main difference between the two forums is that one is for application products you can use for serious work and the other provides items such as screen savers that you can use for fun.

Windows Vendor Forums

This group of five forums is a place for smaller commercial product vendors to provide their services. Each vendor occupies one section of the forum. (There are 18 sections in each forum, but at least one section is private in most cases.) This includes one message and one library area. They all share the conference rooms. You might want to check each area to see whether a vendor of a product you use is present.

Windows BBSs

Some people will find the cost of using an online service such as CompuServe just a bit too high for what they get out of it. They like to frequent local BBSs and find information that way. Not only is this information free, but the cost of calling isn't too high, either.

Trying to find a Windows-specific BBS in your area won't be hard at all. The best place to start looking is your local user group. Most larger cities also have a local computer magazine or two. You'll find these free magazines in your local software stores and some of the larger technical bookstores. Near the back of such a magazine, you'll usually find a listing of all the local BBSs. Although these listings usually don't provide a lot of information, the BBS name usually implies its orientation.

If these methods of finding a local BBS fail, you can always try to call the Association of Personal Computer User Groups (APCUG) at (914) 876-6678. This number will at least help you find a user group in your area. Many of them run their own BBSs as well. Finding a BBS this way could actually double the benefit you receive, because then you'll know how to contact the user group as well.

A local BBS will have limitations that an online service won't, but I mentioned most of them in the early part of this appendix. I usually tell businesses that they'll make back the cost of using an online service with increased employee productivity and better sources of information for problem resolutions. However, the payback for a home user isn't as easy to see. You'll probably want to at least try both an online service and a BBS for a while to see which one best meets your needs.

Microsoft's Presence on the Internet

If you haven't heard much about the Internet lately, you must live on a desert island without television. I'm constantly surprised at just how much press the Internet is getting these days. In fact, many of your favorite television shows maintain a Web site. Advertisements and just about every other form of media makes use of the Internet as well.

All of this press wasn't wasted on Microsoft. They started a move to the Internet quite some time ago. Now they've just about abandoned any other form of support in favor of this media. If you really want to know what's going on with anything Microsoft, the Internet is the way to go. Microsoft's main URL on the Internet is `http://www.microsoft.com`. Obviously, that's only the tip of the iceberg, but it's a good place to start.

Getting a Good Start

It would be difficult at best to come up with a definitive hierarchy of URLs for all the sites that Microsoft supports (like the earlier sections of this appendix do for their CompuServe setup). One of the reasons that the Internet is such a good place to provide information is that it's totally freeform.

In addition, the means for changing the structure of your site resides on your own server. Online services such as CompuServe reserve this capability for themselves, which makes vendors think twice about any changes. Because Microsoft controls the format and presentation of their Web site, they can and usually do change it quite often. Figure A.17 shows how the main Microsoft page looked at the time of this writing.

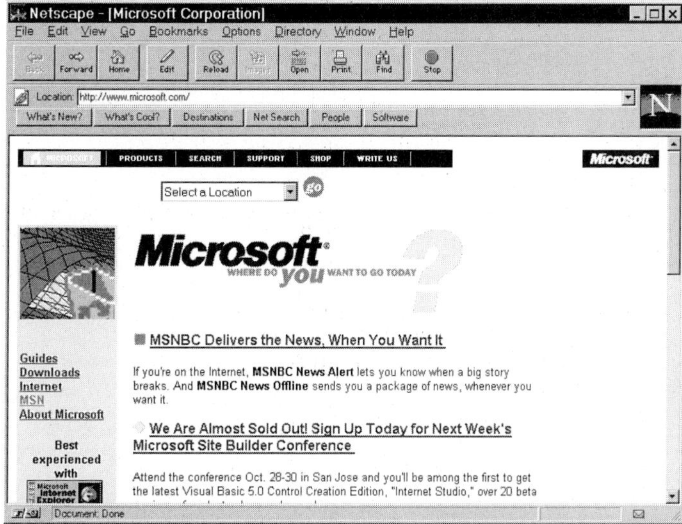

Figure A.17.
The main Microsoft Web page gives you some clues as to how to find information quickly.

The question you need to answer is how you're going to find anything without resorting to the search techniques discussed in the section "Finding What You're Looking For" in Chapter 21. Microsoft usually follows the same pattern in creating their Web pages, so coming up with a search method is pretty easy.

Look at the left side of the page and you'll see a bar. This bar usually contains a list of related topics. Figure A.17 shows five topics: Guides, Downloads, Internet, MSN, and About Microsoft. Clicking one of these links takes you to another section of the Microsoft Web site—a general area, in this case.

You'll also find a method of finding more specific information on most Microsoft Web pages. Open the drop-down list containing Select a Location, then click Go. The sites you can select on this page take you to areas that cater to other languages. Other Web pages take you to places where you can find specifics about the language you're using or other topics of interest.

Figure A.18 shows another kind of Microsoft page. In this case, the page acts more like a menu of options than anything else. Notice, however, that it follows the same format just described. On the left is a list of related topics that you can link to. The main part of the document allows you to refine your search by looking for more specific information.

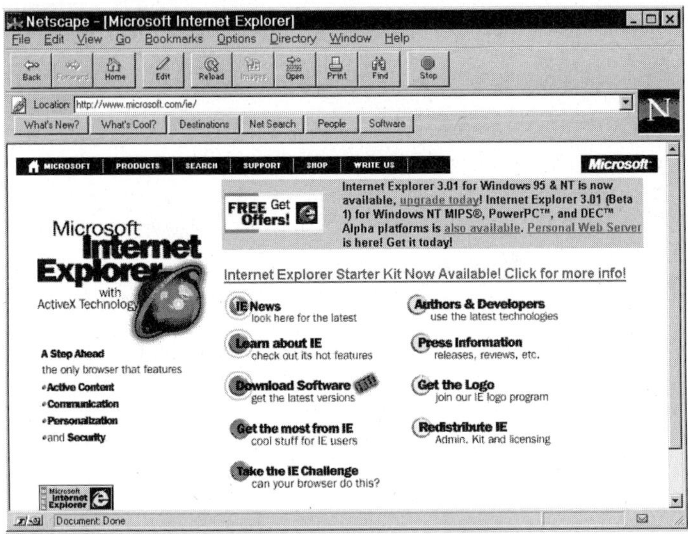

Figure A.18.
Some Microsoft Web sites are more like menus than information sources.

Finding a Newsgroup

Getting information isn't the only reason to use the Internet. A whole range of newsgroups allow you to exchange information with other people. The newsgroups also allow you to get additional information or learn how to perform a task.

Microsoft provides more than a few newsgroups; finding the right one might be a little difficult if they didn't provide some kind of menu system. Finding what you need in the way of newsgroups is a three-step process. First, go to `http://www.microsoft.com/support/news/` (see Figure A.19). As you can see, the whole purpose of this page is to select a product type.

Because this is a Windows 95 book, I selected the Windows 95 entry in the Microsoft Windows Family group, and then clicked the Go button next to the drop-down list box (see Figure A.19). Figure A.20 shows what you'll see next—a list of all the kinds of Windows 95 information that you can find out about in a newsgroup.

Once you find the kind of information that you need, click the link to the newsgroup. A news reader like the one in Figure A.21 automatically pops up. In this case, I selected the Dial-Up Networking entry for Windows 95. Notice that the subscription check box isn't marked automatically. You need to check this box if you find the information provided by the newsgroup useful and want to update your news reader automatically.

Figure A.19.
The first step in finding the right newsgroup is selecting a product type.

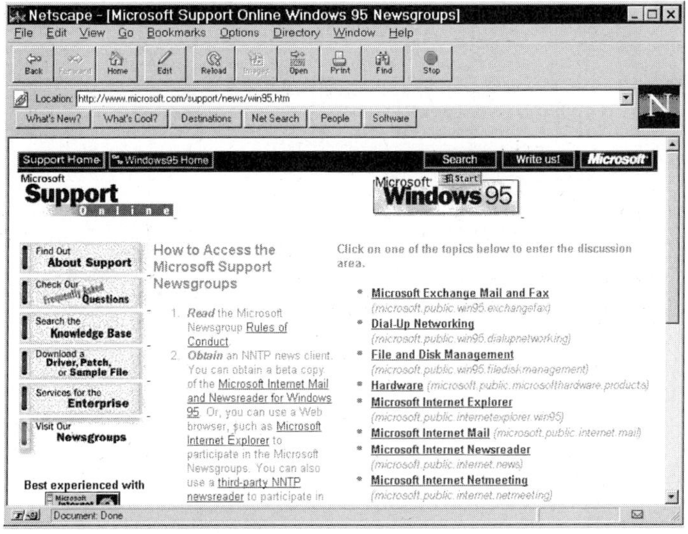

Figure A.20.
Once you select a product type, you can find out what newsgroups are available for it.

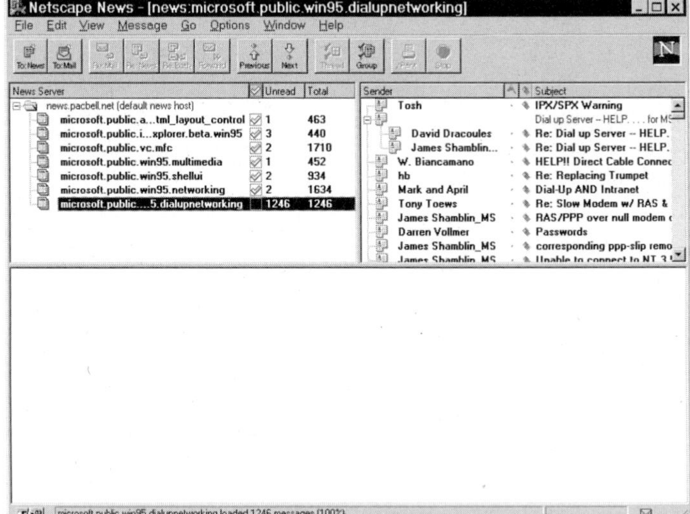

Figure A.21.
Your news reader will automatically display the newsgroup you selected, but won't subscribe to the newsgroup for you.

B

Internet Service Providers

You need to think about connections before installing the latest Internet browser on your machine. Unlike a BBS or online service such as CompuServe, Internet access requires some type of direct connection—usually through a UNIX or Windows NT server with a TCP/IP connection. If you have enough people in your company who require Internet access, you might set up your own server. Some of us have neither the time nor the inclination to make such an investment, however. In that case, you need an Internet service provider. A provider is someone who gives you access to their host to the Internet. In essence, you call the provider, who in turn provides access to the Internet.

Unfortunate as it may seem, some people are intent on making the Internet as mysterious as possible. This includes getting a connection. There are a lot of ways to get a connection, most of which are very easy. The cost and level of service you'll see when using a particular connection type is one of the big determining factors.

The following sections look at several types of Internet service providers. I'll tell you up front that this list is far from complete (when compiling the list, I looked for a variety of ISP types to give you an idea of what's available); more service providers are entering the market every day, and it would take an entire book to list them all. My purpose is to give you an overview of the *kinds* of connections you'll find. You can decide on a connection type and go from there. Hopefully, one of the providers listed in this appendix will meet your needs. If not, don't stop looking here. Use this appendix as a basis for finding other service providers who will meet your needs.

Phone Companies

There's a certain amount of logic to using a telephone company as your Internet service provider, especially if you already use it for other services, such as long-distance telephone services. All the major long-distance telephone companies offer some type of Internet service, and you may find that some of the smaller ones do as well. Paying one bill per month for all your communications needs certainly reduces the number of stamps you'll use.

Beyond mere convenience, there are some other practical reasons to use your telephone company as an Internet provider (if it supplies that service). Getting combined services from one place might make it easier for the vendor to provide price breaks as well. I've heard of some people who've gotten quotes as low as $19.95 per month for unlimited Internet access (this is, in fact, becoming the standard rate). This particular quote included a one-time service fee for the software required to make the connection. Check with your telephone company first, though, to see exactly how much it costs; rates and level of service vary widely. Be sure to ask about any fees that you'll encounter if you have a limited service plan (like many Ameritech users). A limited service plan may require you to pay a per-call charge in addition to your normal Internet service fees. Make sure you ask about surcharges for non-customer access. For example, AT&T charges a mere $19.95 for unlimited access, but only if you're a customer. The cost for someone who's not a customer is $24.95, as of this writing. Every telephone company has other surcharges as well. For example, you'll pay a surcharge for 800-

number access. That surcharge could be worthwhile, though, if you don't have a local telephone number to use and want to avoid inordinate long-distance charges. Here's the current set of telephone numbers for the three major telephone companies in the United States:

- **AT&T:** (800) 967-5363
- **MCI:** (800) 550-0927
- **Sprint:** (800) 359-3900

Don't discount the regional Bell operating companies (RBOCs) when it comes to Internet service, either. Pacific Bell (among others) has been making headlines in the trade presses recently because of the types of service they offer. They actually offer a lower $14.95 starting rate with a cap of $19.95. In other words, if you don't use up a certain number of hours of online time, Pacific Bell gives you a break on the cost. This price break beats anything you'll get from the long-distance companies. In addition, RBOCs normally provide better service to small towns than the long-distance carriers do. Give your local telephone company a call to see what services it provides, if any. Some companies offer only business-related services; others cater to both home and business. As with the long-distance companies, services and rates will vary.

Tip: If you don't want to spend a lot of time on the phone trying to switch from one ISP to another, you can always look for their site online. For example:

AT&T	`http://www.att.com/worldnet/`
MCI	`http://www.mci.com/`
Sprint	`http://www.sprint.com/fornet/`

Local telephone companies have sites online as well. For example, Pacific Bell maintains their site at `http://dialup.pacbell.net/`. Contact your local telephone company for details. (Look at those brochures that come with your monthly bill; many telephone companies are providing a lot of information on how to get connected.)

There are a few problems you should consider when using an RBOC instead of a long-distance carrier like MCI. The most fundamental of these problems is travel. If you want to use the same account in both Los Angeles and New York, you may be out of luck when using an RBOC such as Pacific Bell (unless you want to pay some pretty hefty long-distance charges). Long-distance carriers don't suffer from this problem—they normally provide 800 numbers for all major cities within the same country. In addition, most of the long-distance carriers provide better transmission equipment, meaning that you get a higher-quality Internet connection. (Pacific Bell happens to be an exception to this rule.)

Online Services

Using an online service provider such as CompuServe or America Online is another way to grab an Internet connection. This is probably the easiest and fastest route to go if you're already a member of the online service. In many cases, the software for accessing the Internet is provided as part of the online service provider's software. For example, WinCIM (the software offered by CompuServe) includes a Spry Mosaic browser as part of the package. Accessing the Internet is as easy as starting your communications software. (By the time you read this, CompuServe may be shipping Microsoft's Internet Explorer as an Internet browser in place of Spry Mosaic.)

I've found a few problems with this approach, though, and you need to be aware of them. One of the biggest problems when dealing with online services is a lack of bandwidth. Bandwidth determines how smooth your Internet access appears and how fast you can grab information. I've found that most of the online services don't provide enough bandwidth to make long-term Internet access feasible. It takes me almost twice the amount of time to download a file from an FTP site using CompuServe as it does with a dedicated Internet account from AT&T, for example. Even though many of the online services, most notably America Online, have started updating their equipment to handle the additional load, the update will take time, and you definitely won't see the effects immediately.

You may also hear the loud ticking of a meter if you use the Internet through an online service. CompuServe currently provides 10 hours of free Internet access as part of your monthly fee. After that, you get charged an hourly rate for continued access. If you're a light Internet user, 10 hours per month may be more than sufficient. For others, 10 hours is probably enough for a week—or even less, in some cases. (CompuServe and other online service providers, such as America Online, have recently started offering enhanced plans that provide unlimited Internet access, but you'll probably need to sign up for these plans separately. Don't assume that you'll get the benefit of these new plans automatically. In addition, you may need to change your online service plan if you don't use the online service provider for your ISP. For example, the fees for America Online doubled when they began to offer unlimited Internet access as their default service. Users actually have to request to switch to a limited service plan if they use a separate ISP for Internet access.)

Do all these limitations mean that online services provide inherently less value than a dedicated connection? Not really. You have to consider that at least part of your Internet access needs will be taken care of by the service through other methods. I can send as many mail messages as I want to someone on the Internet from CompuServe without charge, for example. And some of the services you'll find on the Internet are repeated on the online service. Borland maintains forums on both CompuServe and the Internet, for example. I've found more than a few vendors that follow the same plan. The bottom line when accessing the Internet from an online service is that you may have to pay for the convenience of using it—in both time and money.

Tip: I've listed the common online services here, but don't stop here if your needs aren't met. In addition to standard online services, many BBSs now offer Internet access for a nominal monthly fee. You'll find that they provide top-notch connections, but the connection might not be available all the time because most BBSs have limited connections. One of the advantages of using a BBS is that "small-town feel" to the service you'll get. In addition, you'll be supporting a small business in your community. Obviously, you'll have to spend some time researching a BBS before you choose one. Make sure that they have the kinds of connections you need and that the owner is solvent enough to stick around for a while.

The following list gives you the names and addresses of some of the more common online services:

America Online
America Online, Inc.
8619 Westwood Center Drive
Vienna, VA 22182
Voice: (800) 827-6364, (703) 448-8700
Internet e-mail: `fulfill2@aol.com`
Web site: `http://www.aol.com`

CompuServe
CompuServe
500 Arlington Centre Boulevard
P.O. Box 20961
Columbus, OH 43220
Voice: (800) 848-8990
Internet e-mail: `70006,101@compuserve.com`
Web site: `http://www.compuserve.com`

Microsoft Network
Microsoft Corporation
One Microsoft Way
Redmond, WA 98052-6399
Voice: (206) 882-8080
Sales: (800) 426-9400
Fax: (206) 936-7329
BBS: (206) 936-6735
Web site: `http://www.microsoft.com`

Prodigy
Prodigy Services Company
445 Hamilton Way
White Plains, NY 10601
Voice: (800) 776-3449, (914) 448-8000
Web site: `http://www.prodigy.com`

Are Online Services a Dying Breed?

Some people may question the viability of online services for the future. I have to agree. Recent events seem to point to the Internet as the major place to exchange information in the future. For example, some users have started to complain that the connection delays and other online service equipment-related problems that they're experiencing are on the rise. Other users have noticed the lower level of participation on some online forums as the number of users frequenting them decreases.

Users aren't the only ones to notice this trend. Many vendors are making changes in the way that they do business to emphasize the trend in Internet usage. It's a matter of simple statistics that are showing these vendors that online services are no longer as profitable as they once were. In addition, the Internet is proving to be more convenient for companies that need to maintain both public and private access.

A few of the changes that online services are experiencing are more profound than others. The biggest change that CompuServe users noticed recently was that Microsoft completely abandoned their forums on that service. The only place you'll find a Microsoft presence now is on the Internet. Novell wasn't very far behind Microsoft in this case—you need to go to the Internet to find Novell as well. The Microsoft connection from Microsoft isn't completely dead, however. Groups like WUGNET (see Appendix A) have taken up the slack. This group now maintains many of the forums that you could formerly find from Microsoft. The big difference is that the help you'll receive is from other users alone, rather than a Microsoft representative.

Does this mean that online services are passé and that they'll die a slow death in the void of cyberspace? Not by a long shot. Online services will simply evolve the kinds of products they offer and the way in which they offer them. You'll probably find that online services will fill niche roles in the future and offer specialized attention to people who need it.

Public Service Access

These Internet service providers fall into a special group. They're normally attached to a university or a public service organization. In most cases, you have to pay a nominal monthly fee; in other cases, access is free. The majority of these connections use low-speed modems and other old technology components, so you shouldn't expect very good performance from them. (On the other hand, some of the supercomputing centers provide state-of-the-art connections.) In addition, some of these lines aren't available 24 hours a day or 7 days a week. A few of these sites are set aside for educational or scientific use; you might have to work a bit harder to get a connection in the first place. Check with the provider for details on pricing and limitations.

The following list provides some ideas on where to look for public access to the Internet:

BARRNet
Service area: Northern and central California
Specialties: Business, education, and government
Voice: (415) 723-7003
Internet e-mail: `info@barrnet.net`
FTP site: `FTP://ftp.barrnet.net`

CERFnet
Service area: California and international
Specialties: Business and education
Voice: (800) 876-2373, (619) 455-3900
Internet e-mail: `help@cerf.net`
FTP site: `FTP://nic.cerf.net`

CICNet
Service area: Minnesota, Wisconsin, Iowa, Indiana, Illinois
Specialties: Education
Voice: (313) 998-6104
Internet e-mail: `info@cic.net`

CONCERT Network
Service area: North Carolina
Specialties: Business and education
Voice: (919) 248-1999
Internet e-mail: `info@concert.net`
FTP site: `FTP://ftp.concert.net`

Global Enterprise Services, Inc.
Service area: U.S. and international
Specialties: Business, education, and government
Voice: (800) 358-4437
Internet e-mail: `market@jvnc.net`

MichNet/Merit
Service area: Michigan
Specialties: Education, research, and community organizations
Voice: (313) 764-9430
Internet e-mail: `info@merit.edu`
FTP site: `FTP://nic.merit.edu`

MOREnet
The Missouri Research and Education Network
Service area: Missouri
Specialties: Business, education, government, and research
Voice: (314) 882-2000
Internet e-mail: `bill@more.net`

MRNet
Service area: Minnesota
Specialties: Business and education
Voice: (612) 342-2570
Internet e-mail: `info@mr.net`
FTP site: `FTP://ftp.mr.net`
Gopher site: `GOPHER://gopher.mr.net`

Msen
Service area: Michigan, Ohio, Indiana, Illinois
Specialties: Business and education
Voice: (313) 998-4562
Internet e-mail: `info@msen.com`
FTP site: `FTP://ftp.msen.com:/pub/vendor/msen`

NEARnet
Service area: Maine, Vermont, New Hampshire, Connecticut, Rhode Island, Massachusetts, and New York
Specialties: Business, education, and research
Voice: (617) 873-8730
Internet e-mail: `nearnet-join@nic.near.net`
FTP site: `FTP://ftp.near.net`

NevadaNet
Service area: Nevada
Specialties: Education
Voice: (702) 895-4580
Internet e-mail: `mitch@nevada.edu`

NYSERNet
Service area: New York
Specialties: Education and research
Voice: (315) 453-2912
Internet e-mail: `info@nysernet.org`
Gopher site: `GOPHER://telnet.nysernet.org`

Note: If you use the NYSERNet Gopher site, it asks for a login name. Use the generic name of `nysernet` (all lowercase).

PREPnet
Service area: Pennsylvania
Specialties: Education
Voice: (412) 268-7870
Internet e-mail: `nic@prep.net`
FTP site: `FTP://nic.prep.net`

SDSCnet
Service area: California
Specialties: Education and research
Voice: (619) 534-8328
Internet e-mail: `tep@sdsc.edu`

UANet
Service area: Arizona
Specialties: Education
Voice: (602) 621-6666
Internet e-mail: `rapagnani@arizona.edu`

WEdNet
Washington Education Network
Service area: Washington (state)
Specialties: Education
Voice: (206)775-8471 ext. 4500
Internet e-mail: `jhanson@wsipc.wednet.edu`

Westnet
Service area: Arizona, Colorado, Idaho, and New Mexico
Specialties: Education
Voice: (303) 491-7260
Internet e-mail: `pburns@westnet.net`
FTP site: `FTP://westnet.net`

WiscNet
Service area: Wisconsin
Specialties: Business, education, government, and research
Voice: (608) 262-5888
Internet e-mail: `wn-info@nic.wiscnet.net`
FTP site: `FTP://nic.wiscnet.net`

WVNET
Service area: West Virginia
Specialties: Education
Voice: (304) 293-5192
Internet e-mail: `cc011041@wvnvms.wvnet.edu`

Other Types of Service Providers

Some service providers just don't fit neatly into a category. You'll find that the vast majority of these providers have the most modern equipment available because that's the only way they can compete with the big companies. Expect to pay a monthly payment for basic service in addition to an hourly rate for special services, in some cases. Obviously, getting first-class quality service means that you'll have to pay for it somewhere along the way.

The following list provides some of the other vendors you can try when looking for an Internet service provider:

AlterNet TCP/IP Network Service
UUNET Technologies, Inc.
Voice: (800) 488-6383, (703) 206-5600
Internet e-mail: `alternet-info@uunet.uu.net`
FTP site: `ftp://ftp.uu.net`

ANS CO+RE Systems, Inc.
Voice: (800) 456-8267, (313) 663-7610
Internet e-mail: `info@ans.net`
FTP site: `ftp://ftp.ans.net`

CENTnet

Service area: Eastern Massachusetts (unless you're willing to pay the long-distance bill). They provide 19.2Kb or 56Kb dedicated leased lines or dial-up SLIP.

The Cambridge Entrepreneurial Network
Voice: (617) 354-5800
Internet e-mail: `love@ora.com`

MIDnet

Service area: Arkansas, Iowa, Kansas, Missouri, Nebraska, Oklahoma, and South Dakota
MIDnet Information Center
Voice: (402) 472-7600
Internet e-mail: `nic@westie.mid.net`
FTP site: `FTP://westie.mid.net`

MV.COM

Service area: New Hampshire
MV Communications, Inc.
P. O. Box 4963
Manchester, NH 03108-4963
Voice: (603)429-2223
Internet e-mail: `mv-admin@mv.mv.com`
Auto-reply e-mail: `info@mv.mv.com`
FTP site: `FTP://ftp.mv.com:/pub/mv`

NETCOM

NETCOM On-Line Communication Services, Inc.
3031 Tisch Way
San Jose, CA 95128
Voice: (408) 983-5950
Fax: (408) 983-1537
Internet e-mail: `info@netcom.com`
Web site: `http://www.netcom.com`

OARnet

Service area: Ohio and surrounding areas
2455 North Star Road
Columbus, OH
Voice: (614) 292-8100
Internet e-mail: `demetris@oar.net`
FTP site: `FTP://oar.net`
Gopher site: `GOPHER://gopher.oar.net`

PSINet
Voice: (800) 827-7482, (703) 620-6651
Internet e-mail: `info@psi.com`
FTP site: `FTP://ftp.psi.com.cd~uuc`

SURAnet
Voice: (301) 982-4600
Internet e-mail: `marketing@sura.net`
FTP site: `FTP://ftp.sura.net`

Tip: If you didn't find the ISP you need in this appendix, there are a few other things you can do to find one. Obviously, you can talk with other users to see which ISP they're using. Besides finding out how happy they are with the service the ISP provides, be sure to ask questions about features that you're specifically interested in. However, you'll find that your friends probably won't have all of the answers when it comes to getting on the Internet. Fortunately, the Internet provides another solution. The List (`http://thelist.iworld.com/`) is one of the sites you can visit to find an ISP. The feature I like about this particular site is that they review the various ISPs and provide more than just a quick overview of the ISP-provided services. For example, you'll find pricing information for most of the ISPs here, along with some idea of the type of clientele they serve. Be sure to verify any pricing information with the ISP, though, because pricing plans are changing on a continual basis.

C

Glossary

Tip: Although this glossary contains all the acronyms you'll see in this book, it doesn't contain acronyms you'll see in other places. If you don't see an acronym you need here, check out the Internet site at `http://www.hill.com/acrolist.html`. It contains more computer-related acronyms than the average person will ever see.

American Standard Code for Information Interchange See *ASCII*.

API (application programming interface) A method of defining a standard set of function calls and other interface elements. It usually defines the interface between a high-level language and the lower-level elements used by a device driver or operating system. The ultimate goal is to provide some type of service to an application that requires access to the operating system or device feature set.

application independence A method of writing applications so that they don't depend on the specific features of an operating system or hardware interface. It normally requires the use of a high-level language and an API. The programmer also needs to write the application in such a way as to avoid specific hardware or operating system references. All user and device interface elements must use the generic functions provided by the API.

application programming interface See *API*.

ASCII (American Standard Code for Information Interchange) A standard method of equating the numeric representations available in a computer to human-readable form. For example, the number 32 represents a space. There are 128 characters (7 bits) in the standard ASCII code. The extended ASCII code uses 8 bits for 256 characters. Display adapters from the same machine type usually use the same upper 128 characters. Printers might reserve these upper 128 characters for nonstandard characters. For example, many Epson printers use them for the italic representations of the lower 128 characters.

B-step processor An older 80386 processor type that incorporated elements that are incompatible with Windows 95. The normal reason for using this processor type was to provide additional system functionality or improved speed characteristics.

Bi-directional support Defines a printer's capability to transfer information both ways on a printer cable. Input usually contains data or printer control codes. Output usually contains printer status information or error codes.

binary value Refers to a base 2 data representation in the Windows Registry. Normally used to hold status flags or other information that lends itself to a binary format.

.BMP files Windows standard bitmap graphics data format. This is a raster graphic data format that doesn't include any form of compression. OS/2 can also use this data format to hold graphics of various types.

cascading style sheets See *CSS*.

CDFS (compact disc file system) The portion of the file subsystem specifically designed to interact with compact disc drives. It also provides the user interface elements required to tune this part of the subsystem. The CDFS takes the place of an FSD for CD-ROM drives.

class ID See *CLSID*.

client The recipient of data, services, or resources from a file or other server. This term can refer to a workstation or an application. The server can be another PC or an application.

CLSID (class ID) A method of assigning a unique identifier to each object in the Registry. Also refers to various high-level language constructs.

CMOS (complementary metal oxide semiconductor) Normally refers to a construction method for low-power, battery-backed memory. When used in the context of a PC, this term usually refers to the memory used to store system configuration information and the real-time clock status. The configuration information normally includes the amount of system memory, the type and size of floppy drives, the hard drive parameters, and the video display type. Some vendors include other configuration information as part of this chip as well.

compact disc file system See *CDFS*.

complementary metal oxide semiconductor See *CMOS*.

compound document An OLE document that contains two or more embedded or linked documents. For example, a word processing document could contain graphics and spreadsheets in their original format.

Compressed Serial Line Interface Protocol See *CSLIP*.

container Part of the object-oriented terminology that has become part of OLE. A container is a drive, file, or other resource used to hold objects. The container is normally referenced as an object itself.

CSLIP (Compressed Serial Line Interface Protocol) An IETF-approved method for transferring data by using a serial port. This particular data transmission method uses compression to improve performance.

CSS (cascading style sheets) A method for defining a standard Web page template. This may include headings, standard icons, backgrounds, and other features that would tend to give each page at a particular Web site the same appearance. The reason for using CSS includes speed of creating a Web site (it takes less time if you don't have to create an overall design for each page) and consistency. Changing the overall appearance of a Web site also becomes as easy as changing the style sheet instead of each page alone.

DAT (digital audio tape) drive A tape drive that uses a cassette to store data. The cassette and the drive use the same technology as the audio version of the DAT drive. However, the internal circuitry of the drive formats the tape for use with a computer system. The vendor must also design the interface circuitry with computer needs in mind. DAT tapes allow you to store large amounts of information in a relatively small amount of space. Typical drive capacities range from 1.2GB to 8GB.

data-centric The method used by modern operating systems to view the user interface from a data perspective rather than from the perspective of the applications used to create the data. Using this view allows users to worry more about manipulating the data on their machines than about the applications required to perform a specific task.

DDE (dynamic data exchange) The ability to cut data from one application and paste it into another application. For example, you could cut a graphic image created with a paint program and paste it into a word processing document. Once pasted, the data doesn't reflect changes made to it by the originating application. DDE also provides a method of communicating with an application that supports DDE and requesting data. For example, you could use an Excel macro to call Microsoft Word and request the contents of a document file. Some applications also use DDE to implement file-association strategies. For example, Microsoft Word uses DDE in place of command-line switches to gain added flexibility when a user needs to open or print a file.

device-independent bitmap See *DIB*.

DIB (device-independent bitmap) A method of representing graphic information that doesn't reflect a particular device's requirements. This has the advantage of allowing the same graphic to appear on any device in precisely the same way, despite differences in resolution or other factors that normally change the graphic's appearance.

digital audio tape drive See *DAT*.

direct memory access See *DMA*.

disk defragmenter An application used to reorder the data on a long-term storage device such as a hard disk or floppy disk drive. Reordering the data so that it appears in sequential order—file by file—reduces the time required to access and read the data. Sequential order allows you to read an entire file without moving the disk head at all, in some cases, and only a little in others. This reduction in access time normally improves overall system throughput and therefore enhances system efficiency.

.DLL (dynamic link library) A special form of application code loaded into memory by request. It isn't executable by itself. A .DLL does contain one or more discrete routines that an application can use to provide specific features. For example, a .DLL could provide a common set of file dialog boxes used to access information on the hard drive. More than one application can use the functions provided by a .DLL, reducing overall memory requirements when more than one application is running.

DMA (direct memory access) A memory-addressing technique in which the processor doesn't perform the actual data transfer. This method of memory access is faster than any other technique.

DOS protected-mode interface See *DPMI*.

DPMI (DOS protected-mode interface) A method of accessing extended memory from a DOS application, using the Windows extended-memory manager.

drag and drop A technique used in object-oriented operating systems to access data without actually opening the file by using conventional methods. For example, this system allows the user to pick up a document file, drag it to the printer icon, and drop it. The printer then prints the document, using the default printer settings.

dual-ported video RAM See *VRAM*.

Dvorak layout An alternative method of laying out the keyboard so that stress is reduced and typing speed is increased. It's different from the more familiar QWERTY layout used by most keyboards and typewriters.

dynamic data exchange See *DDE*.

dynamic link library See *.DLL*.

EIA (Electronics Industry Association) The standards body responsible for creating many hardware-related PC standards. For example, the EIA was responsible for the serial port interface used on most PCs. The EIA also participates in other standards efforts.

Electronics Industry Association See *EIA*.

embedded systems A combination of processor, operating system, and device-specific applications used in concert with a special-purpose device. For example, the control used to set the time and temperature on a microwave oven is an embedded system. Another form of embedded system is the computer that controls engine efficiency in a car.

EMF (enhanced metafile) Used as an alternative storage format by some graphics applications. This is a vector graphic format, so it provides a certain level of device independence and other features that a vector graphic normally provides.

EMM (expanded memory manager) A device driver such as EMM386.EXE that provides expanded memory services on 80386 and above machines. (Special drivers work with 80286 and a few 8088/8086 machines.) An application accesses expanded memory by using a page frame or other memory-mapping techniques from within the conventional or upper memory area (0 to 124KB). The EMM usually emulates expanded memory by using extended memory managed by an extended-memory manager (XMM) such as HIMEM.SYS. An application must change the processor's mode to protected mode in order to use XMS. Some products, such as 386MAX.SYS and QEMM.SYS, provide both EMM and XMM services in one driver.

EMS (expanded memory specification) Several versions of this specification are in current use. The most popular version is 3.2, even though a newer 4.0 specification is available. This specification defines one method of extending the amount of memory that a processor can address from the conventional memory area. It uses an area outside of system memory to store information. An EMM provides a window view into this larger data area. The old 3.2 specification requires a 64KB window in the UMB. The newer 4.0 specification can create this window anywhere in conventional or UMB memory.

enhanced metafile See *EMF*.

expanded memory manager See *EMM*.

expanded memory specification See *EMS*.

FAT (file allocation table) The method of formatting a hard disk drive used by DOS and other operating systems. This technique is one of the oldest formatting methods available.

file allocation table disk format See *FAT*.

file system driver See *FSD*.

file transfer protocol See *FTP*.

floptical A specialized form of floppy disk drive that relies on optical media to extend its data storage capacity. The most common size floptical currently in use stores 20MB of data. One of the things that differentiates a floptical from other optical media drives is that a floptical can normally read standard floppy disks as well.

FSD (file system driver) A file subsystem component responsible for defining the interface between Windows and long-term storage. The FSD also defines features such as long filenames and what types of interaction the device supports. For example, the CD-ROM FSD wouldn't support file writes unless you provided a device that could perform that sort of task.

FTP (file transfer protocol) One of several standard data-transfer protocols originated by the IETF. This protocol is designed for efficient file transfer.

GDI (graphics device interface) One of the main Windows root components. It controls the way that graphic elements are presented on-screen. Every application must use the API provided by this component to draw or perform other graphics-related tasks.

GDT (global descriptor table) A memory construct that contains the information required to control all the extended memory in an 80386 or above processor. The GDT normally passes control of smaller memory segments to the LDTs used by an individual application.

general protection fault See *GPF*.

global descriptor table See *GDT*.

global positioning satellite See *GPS*.

GPF (general protection fault) A processor or memory error that occurs when an application makes a request that the system can't honor. This type of error results in some type of severe action on the part of the operating system. Normally, the operating system terminates the offending application.

GPS (global positioning satellite) A special satellite that sends positioning data to a location on Earth. Using satellite tracking allows for precise position updates to a device such as a PC. The PC must include special software that allows it to display the positioning data on a map overlay.

graphical user interface See *GUI*.

graphics device interface See *GDI*.

GUI (graphical user interface) A system of icons and graphic images that replaces the character-mode menu system used by many machines. The GUI can ride on top of another operating system (such as DOS or UNIX) or reside as part of the operating system itself (such as Windows or OS/2). Advantages of a GUI are ease of use and high-resolution graphics. Disadvantages are higher workstation hardware requirements and lower performance over a similar system using a character-mode interface.

hand-held PC See *HPC*.

high memory area See *HMA*.

high-performance file system See *HPFS*.

HMA (high memory area) The 64KB area of memory beyond the 1MB boundary that the processor can access in real mode on an 80286 or above processor.

HPC (hand-held PC) A special small-footprint-size PC designed to replace small notebooks or calendars. Many HPCs run a very limited version of the Windows operating system. Most don't offer features like handwriting analysis that plagued earlier versions of the pocket-sized PC.

HPFS (high-performance file system) The method of formatting a hard disk drive used by OS/2. Although it provides significant speed advantages over other formatting techniques, only the OS/2 operating system and applications designed to work with that operating system can access a drive formatted using this technique.

HTML (Hypertext Markup Language) A special language that relies on a series of tag words to define character and paragraph formatting. In some cases, HTML has been extended to provide graphic information as well as access to ActiveX controls and Java applets. In essence, HTML defines all the characteristics of a Web page.

HTTP (Hypertext Transfer Protocol) The IETF-supported protocol used to transfer an HTML-formatted document from a Web server to the client browser.

hub A device used to connect two or more nodes on a network. A hub normally provides other features such as automatic detection of connection loss.

Hypertext Markup Language See *HTML*.

Hypertext Transfer Protocol See *HTTP*.

ICM (image color matcher) A special component of the graphics subsystem that allows Windows to match the colors produced by one device with those available on another device. The result is that the output of both devices doesn't show the normal variations in color that Windows applications currently produce.

icon A symbol used to graphically represent the purpose and/or function of an application or file. For example, a text file might appear as a sheet of paper with the filename below the icon. Applications designed for the environment or operating system usually appear with a special icon depicting the vendor's or product's logo. Icons normally are part of a GUI environment or operating system such as Windows or OS/2.

IFS (installable file system) manager The API component of the file subsystem. It provides a consistent interface that applications can use to access a variety of devices, local and remote. This component also provides a standard interface that device drivers can use to provide services such as file opening and drive status.

image color matcher See *ICM*.

IMA (International Multimedia Association) A standards body responsible for defining multimedia standards on the Internet. One of the more important efforts of this standards body is the adaptive delta pulse code modulation (ADPCM) standard, which is used for the serial wave driver in Windows 95.

.INF file A special form of device or application configuration file. It contains all the parameters that Windows requires to install or configure the device or application. For example, an application .INF file might contain the location of data files and the interdependencies of .DLLs. Both application and device .INF files contain the Registry and .INI file entries required to make Windows recognize the application or device.

Infrared Data Association See *IrDA*.

International Multimedia Association See *IMA*.

installable file system helper A special real-mode component of the IFS manager used to allow access of Windows drive functions by DOS applications. It uses the same DOS interface as before, but all processing is performed by the protected-mode manager.

installable file system manager See *IFS manager*.

Internet service provider See *ISP*.

interrupt request See *IRQ*.

IrDA (Infrared Data Association) The standards association responsible for creating infrared data port standards. These ports are normally used to create a connection between a laptop and a device or network. Devices include printers, PCs, modems, and mice.

IRQ (interrupt request) The set of special address lines that connect a peripheral to the processor. Think of an IRQ as an office telephone with multiple incoming lines. Every time a device calls, its entry lights up on the front of the phone. The processor selects the desired line and picks up the receiver to find out what the device wants. Everything works fine as long as there's one line for each device that needs to call the processor. If more than one device tried to call in on the same line, the processor wouldn't know who was at the other end. This is the source of IRQ conflicts that you hear about from various sources. Older PC-class machines provided 8 interrupt lines. The newer AT-class machines provide 16. However, only 15 of those are usable, because 1 line is used for internal purposes.

ISP (Internet service provider) A vendor that provides one or more Internet-related services through a dial-up, ISDN, or other outside connection. Normal services include e-mail, newsgroup access, and full Internet Web site access.

LAN (local area network) A combination of hardware and software used to connect a group of PCs to each other and/or to a minicomputer or mainframe computer. There are two main networking models in use: peer-to-peer and client-server. The peer-to-peer model doesn't require a dedicated server. In addition, all the workstations in the group can share resources. The client-server model uses a central server for resource sharing, but some special methods are provided for using local resources in a limited fashion.

LDT (local descriptor table) A memory construct that controls access to the memory used by a single application or a group of applications that share the same memory. The LDT is subservient to the GDT that manages system memory overall.

list box A windowing construct that contains a list of items. Normally, the user selects one or more of these items in order to respond to an application or operating system query.

local area network See *LAN*.

local descriptor table See *LDT*.

macro One of several methods for performing automated tasks on a computer. Macros normally include a simple programming language that's executed by an interpreter within an application. In some cases, the application will automatically record a macro, based on user keystrokes. The user can later modify this file as needed to complete a task.

management information file See *MIF*.

MAPI (messaging API) The set of functions and other resources that Windows provides to communications programs. It allows the application to access a variety of communications channels using a single set of calls and without regard to media. This is the component of Windows 95 that allows Microsoft Exchange to process information from e-mail and online services by using the same interface.

MCA (microchannel architecture) A specialized bus introduced by IBM. It's faster than the old ISA bus and gives the operating system information about the peripheral devices connected to the bus. It also provides the means for devices to become self-configuring.

messaging API See *MAPI*.

microchannel architecture See MCA.

MIF (management information file) A vendor-supplied file that contains all the particulars about a piece of equipment. When the System Management Server on a Windows NT server looks at a workstation and finds this file, it adds its contents to a SQL database that you can open with any number of products.

miniport driver A specialized Windows component that provides access to a resource, normally a peripheral device of some type. It's also used to access pseudo-devices and network resources.

MMX (multimedia extension) processor The latest edition of the Intel family of processors includes multimedia-specific commands within the chip. Instead of issuing multiple commands to perform a multimedia-related task, one command will do. This version of the chip should boost overall system performance. It should also allow vendors to produce less expensive PCs by using less-complex parts in construction.

Motion Picture Experts Group See *MPEG*.

MPEG (Motion Picture Experts Group) A standards group that provides file formats and other specifications in regard to full-motion video and other types of graphic displays.

multimedia extension processor See *MMX processor*.

multiple-boot configuration A method of creating a configurable environment that was first introduced with DOS 5.0. The user simply selects the operating environment from a list of environments presented prior to the boot sequence. This technique provides an additional layer of flexibility and allows the user to optimize the operating environment to perform specific tasks.

multitasking The ability of some processor and environment/system combinations to perform more than one task at a time. The applications appear to run simultaneously. For example, you can download messages from an online service, print from a word processor, and recalculate a spreadsheet, all at the same time. Each application receives a slice of time before the processor moves to the next application. Because the time slices are fairly small, it appears to the user that these actions are occurring simultaneously.

multithreading The capability of an application to perform more than one task at once. For example, a word processing application could print in the background while you type in the foreground. Using multithreading techniques allows an application to make maximum use of processor cycles. In most cases, it does this by processing data in the background while the foreground task waits for user input.

national language support See *NLS*.

nested objects Two or more objects that are coupled in some fashion. The objects normally appear within the confines of a container object. Object nesting allows multiple objects to define the properties of a higher-level object. It also allows the user to associate different types of objects with each other.

network interface card See *NIC*.

network provider See *NP*.

NIC (network interface card) The device responsible for allowing a workstation to communicate with the file server and other workstations. It provides the physical means of creating the connection. The card plugs into an expansion slot in the computer. A cable that attaches to the back of the card completes the communication path.

NLS (national language support) A method of reconfiguring the keyboard and other system components to support more than one language through the use of code pages. Each code page defines a different language configuration. Unfortunately, this technique doesn't change the language used for display purposes. In other words, NLS won't cause your English-language version of Windows to suddenly display prompts and other text in German.

NP (network provider) The software responsible for performing all the network protocol-specific functions that an application requires. It makes or breaks connections, returns network status information, and provides a consistent interface for the multiple provider router (MPR) to use. An application never calls the NP; only the MPR performs this function.

NTFS (Windows NT file system) The method of formatting a hard disk drive used by Windows NT. Although it provides significant speed advantages over other formatting techniques, only the Windows NT operating system and applications designed to work with that operating system can access a drive formatted using this technique.

object conversion A method of changing the format and properties of an object created by one application to the format and properties used by another. Conversion moves the data from one application to another, usually without a loss in formatting, but always without a loss of content.

object linking and embedding See *OLE*.

ODBC (open database connectivity) A Microsoft-supported standard method for accessing databases. In most cases, this involves three steps: installing an appropriate driver, adding a source to the ODBC applet in the Control Panel, and using SQL statements to access the database.

OEM (original equipment manufacturer) One term used to identify hardware vendors that produce some type of PC hardware. For example, a vendor that designs and builds display adapters is considered an OEM. An OEM is normally responsible for writing drivers and other software required to use the hardware it sells. In some cases, a vendor that puts PCs together using off-the-shelf parts is also considered an OEM, but only with regard to higher-level software such as an operating system. For example, someone who sells turnkey systems that have all the software installed and configured would be considered an OEM.

OLE (object linking and embedding) The process of packaging a filename and any required parameters into an object and then pasting this object into a file created by another application. For example, you could place a graphic object within a word processing document or spreadsheet. When you look at the object, it appears as if you simply pasted the data from the originating application into the current application (similar to DDE). When linked, the data provided by the object automatically changes as you change the data in the original object. When embedded, the data doesn't change unless you specifically edit it; but the data still retains its original format, and you still use the original application to edit the data. Often you can start the originating application and automatically load the required data by double-clicking the object. The newer OLE 2 specification allows for in-place data editing as well as editing in a separate application window.

open database connectivity See *ODBC*.

original equipment manufacturer See *OEM*.

packet internet groper See *PING*.

password caching A method of saving the passwords for resources that a user might need to access. The user still needs to enter the main password required to access Windows, but Windows remembers the passwords required to access other resources, such as a network or an online service that directly supports the Windows password-caching capability.

PCMCIA (Personal Computer Memory Card International Association) A standards group responsible for the creation of credit-card-sized devices originally used in laptop PCs. A PCMCIA card could contain devices such as a modem or network card. Some of the more esoteric uses for this card include solid-state hard drives and added system memory.

.PCX file A raster graphic data format originally used by ZSoft Paintbrush. This format has gone through many nonstandard transitions and occasionally presents problems when accessed by applications other than the original. It provides for various levels of color and includes data compression.

PD (port driver) Performs the task of communicating with the device through an adapter. It's the last stage before a message leaves Windows and the first stage when a message arrives from the device. The PD is usually adapter-specific. For example, you would have one VxD for each hard drive and one PD for each hard drive adapter.

PDA (personal digital assistant) A very small PC normally used for personal tasks such as taking notes and maintaining an itinerary during business trips. PDAs normally rely on special operating systems and lack any standard application support.

Personal Computer Memory Card International Association See *PCMCIA*.

personal digital assistant See *PDA*.

PIF (program information file) A special configuration file that Windows and OS/2 use to define the environment for a DOS application. The PIF usually includes various memory settings along with the application's command path and working directory.

PING (packet internet groper) A special utility program used to determine whether a TCP/IP connection exists between a workstation and a server. This utility is normally used in conjunction with the Internet, but it can be used to test any TCP/IP connection.

plug and play The combination of BIOS, operating system, and peripheral device components that provides a self-configuring environment. This self-configuring feature allows the operating system to avoid potential hardware conflicts by polling the peripheral devices, assessing their requirements, and determining and implementing optimal settings for each device.

port driver See *PD*.

POST (power-on self test) The set of diagnostic and configuration routines that the BIOS runs during system initialization. For example, the memory counter you see during the boot sequence is part of this process.

power-on self test See *POST*.

program information file See *PIF*.

protected mode The processor mode in which the processor can access all of extended memory. This mode also provides a better level of application error detection than real mode as part of the processing cycle.

protected-mode mapper A special application that converts real-mode device driver calls into those used by a protected-mode counterpart. It enables you to use your DOS drivers under Windows. Without the support of this VxD, Windows couldn't support legacy devices that lack Windows-specific drivers.

quoting The practice of including all or part of an original message within a response. Quoting allows the viewer to see what the original question was without looking up the original message.

real mode A Windows operating mode that supports the capabilities of the 8088/8086 processor. This essentially limits you to loading one application within the confines of conventional memory. Windows versions after 3.0 don't support this mode. You must use these versions with workstations containing an 80286 or higher processor.

.REG file A special file used by the Windows Registry to hold a text version of the keys and values that the Registry contains. Some applications provide .REG files that you can use to incorporate their file associations and OLE capabilities into Windows.

`Registry` **key** This is a Registry heading. It provides the structure required to hold configuration values and other information required by both Windows and the applications it runs.

Registry value Each value provides some type of Windows configuration information. There are three types of Registry values: string, DWORD, and binary. Of the three, the only human-readable form is string.

remote access The ability to use a remote resource as you would a local resource. In some cases, this also means downloading the remote resource to use as a local resource.

remote procedure call See *RPC*.

RPC (remote procedure call) The capacity to use code or data on a remote machine as if it were local. This is an advanced capability that will eventually pave the way for decentralized applications.

SCSI manager Windows NT introduced something called the miniport driver. With Windows 95, you can use the Windows NT miniport binaries. However, before you can actually do this, Windows 95 must translate its commands to a format that the miniport driver will understand. The SCSI manager performs this service.

SCSIzer This is a file subsystem component that deals with the SCSI command language. Think of the command language as the method that the computer uses to tell a SCSI device to perform a task. The command language isn't the data the SCSI device handles; rather, it's the act that the SCSI device will perform. There's one SCSIzer for each SCSI device.

serial line interface protocol See *SLIP*.

server An application or workstation that provides services, resources, or data to a client application or workstation. The client usually makes requests in the form of OLE, DDE, or other command formats.

shell extension A special application that gives some type of added value to the operating system interface. In most cases, the application must register itself with the Registry before the operating system will recognize it.

simple network architecture See *SNA*.

simple network management protocol See *SNMP*.

SLIP (serial line interface protocol) An IETF-approved method for transferring data by using a serial port. One of the problems with this method is that it doesn't compress the data and therefore suffers from poor performance. CSLIP is a newer form of this protocol that provides improved performance.

SNA (simple network architecture) A standard IBM mainframe networking protocol. A PC user would normally use this protocol to access the mainframe, using a dial-up connection.

SNMP (simple network management protocol) A network protocol (originally designed for the Internet) to manage devices from different vendors.

system resource Data, peripheral devices, or other system components used to create, delete, or manipulate documents and produce output.

system VM (virtual machine) The component of the Windows operating system tasked to create virtual machines and manage DOS applications.

TAPI (Telephony API) An interface used by applications to interface with various types of communication equipment. This currently includes both modems and fax devices.

task-switching The capacity of an operating system to support more than one application or thread of execution at a time. The foreground application or task is the only one that executes. All other threads of execution are suspended in the background. Contrast this with multitasking, in which all threads—background and foreground—execute.

Transaction Control Protocol/Internet Protocol See *TCP/IP*.

TCP/IP (Transaction Control Protocol/Internet Protocol) A standard communications-line protocol developed by the United States Department of Defense. Think of a protocol as a type of language used by two devices. The TCP/IP protocol allows the two devices to talk with each other. In most cases the two devices are computers, but they don't have to be. The most common use for TCP/IP is a LAN or the Internet.

Telephony API See *TAPI*.

Telephony service provider See *TSP*.

terminate-and-stay-resident program See *TSR*.

thunk The programming interface that translates 32-bit data and system calls to their 16-bit counterparts. The opposite translation takes place, going from a 16-bit application to its 32-bit counterpart.

TrueType A special form of vector font originally provided with Windows but used with other operating systems as well. This vector font provides hinting and other features that give it a smoother appearance on-screen.

TSD (type-specific driver) Part of the file subsystem, this layer deals with logical device types rather than specific devices. For example, one TSD handles all the hard drives on your system, and another TSD handles all the floppy drives. A third TSD would handle all network drives.

TSP (Telephony service provider) A special Windows 95 driver that handles program requests such as dialing and answering the phone line. It's normally associated with voice modems.

TSR (terminate-and-stay-resident) program An application that loads itself into memory and stays there after you execute it. The program usually returns you directly to the DOS prompt after loading. Pressing a hot-key combination activates the application, allowing you to use the application. In most cases, TSRs provide some type of utility, print spooling, or other short-term function.

type-specific driver See *TSD*.

UAE (unrecoverable application error) A processor or memory error that occurs when an application makes a request that the system can't honor. The operating system normally doesn't detect an error of this type. The result is that the system freezes or becomes unstable to the point of being unusable. See also *GPF*.

UART (universal asynchronous receiver transmission) The chip that allows a serial port to communicate with the outside world. Serial-type devices such as internal modems also rely on this chip for communications purposes. Newer versions of this chip include special features such as a buffer that stores incoming and outgoing characters until the CPU can process them.

UMB (upper memory block) The area of memory between 640KB and the 1MB boundary. IBM originally set aside this area of memory for device ROMs and special device memory areas. Use of various memory managers allows you to load applications and device drivers in this area.

universal asynchronous receiver transmission See *UART*.

universal serial bus See *USB*.

unrecoverable application error See *UAE*.

upper memory block See *UMB*.

USB (universal serial bus) A form of serial bus that allows multiple external devices to share a single port. This technique reduces the number of interrupts and port addresses required to service the needs of devices such as mice and modems.

VBA (Visual Basic for Applications) A true subset of the Visual Basic language. This form of Visual Basic is normally used within applications in place of a standard macro language. Normally you can't create stand-alone applications using this language in its native environment; however, you could move a VBA program to Visual Basic and compile it there.

VCPI (virtual control program interface) A method of accessing extended memory from a DOS application by using a third-party XMM. See also *DPMI*.

VDD (virtual display driver) Windows 3.x used this module as its sole source of communications with the display adapter. Windows 95 provides it for compatibility purposes and for DOS applications. It translates application requests into graphics commands and draws the result in video memory.

vector font A type of font that uses mathematical expressions instead of a bitmap to define its characteristics.

vector table The place in lower memory where ROM and DOS store pointers to operating-system-specific routines. Most of these routines allow an application to access a device or perform some specific task, such as opening a file.

VESA (Video Electronics Standards Association) A standards group responsible for creating display adapter and monitor specifications. This group has also worked on other standards, such as the VL bus used in some PCs.

VFAT (virtual file allocation table) An enhanced method of disk formatting based on the FAT system. It allows for additional functionality, such as long filenames.

Video Electronics Standards Association See *VESA*.

virtual anything driver See *VxD*.

virtual control program interface See *VCPI*.

virtual display driver See *VDD*.

virtual file allocation table See *VFAT*.

virtual memory management See *VMM*.

Visual Basic for Applications See *VBA*.

VMM (virtual memory management) The device driver responsible for managing extended (and in some cases expanded) memory. VMMs first appeared in the DOS environment. In the Windows 95 environment, this device driver is also responsible for managing the swap file on disk.

volume tracking driver See *VTD*.

VRAM (dual-ported video RAM) A special form of memory that allows simultaneous reads and writes. It provides a serial read interface and a parallel write interface. The advantage of using VRAM is that it's much faster and doesn't require as much detection code on the part of the application or device driver.

VTD (volume tracking driver) This file subsystem component handles any removable devices attached to your system.

VxD (virtual anything driver) A special form of .DLL that provides low-level system support.

Windows NT file system See *NTFS*.

wizard A specialized application that reduces the complexity of using or configuring your system. For example, the Printer Wizard makes it easier to install a new printer.

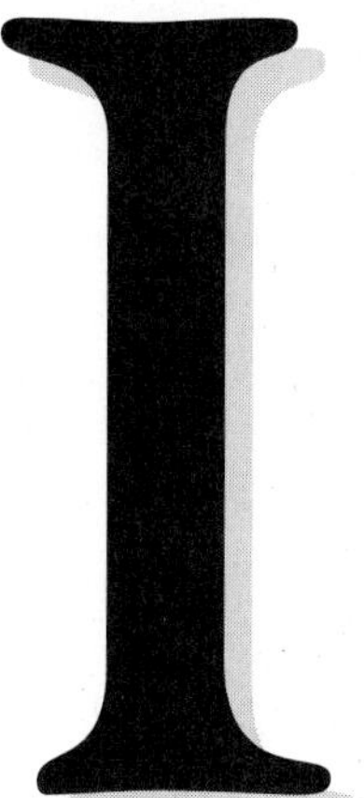

Index

SYMBOLS

A

B

C

D

F

I

J-K

L

M

N

P

Q-R

T

W

X-Y-Z

Support:

If you need assistance with the information in this book, please access the Knowledge Base on our Web site at **http://www.mcp.com**. Our most Frequently Asked Questions are answered there. If you do not find the answer to your questions on our Web site, contact Macmillan Technical Support **(317) 581-3833** or e-mail us at **support@mcp.com**.